T0182977

Lecture Notes in Computer Science 13531

More information about this series at https://link.springer.com/bookseries/558

Elias Pimenidis · Plamen Angelov ·
Chrisina Jayne · Antonios Papaleonidas ·
Mehmet Aydin (Eds.)

Artificial Neural Networks and Machine Learning – ICANN 2022

31st International Conference on Artificial Neural Networks
Bristol, UK, September 6–9, 2022
Proceedings, Part III

 Springer

Editors
Elias Pimenidis ⓘ
University of the West of England
Bristol, UK

Plamen Angelov ⓘ
Lancaster University
Lancaster, UK

Chrisina Jayne ⓘ
Digital Innovation
Teeside University
Middlesbrough, UK

Antonios Papaleonidas ⓘ
Democritus University of Thrace
Xanthi, Greece

Mehmet Aydin ⓘ
The University of the West of England
Bristol, UK

ISSN 0302-9743   ISSN 1611-3349 (electronic)
Lecture Notes in Computer Science
ISBN 978-3-031-15933-6   ISBN 978-3-031-15934-3 (eBook)
https://doi.org/10.1007/978-3-031-15934-3

This Springer imprint is published by the registered company Springer Nature Switzerland AG
The registered company address is: Gewerbestrasse 11, 6330 Cham, Switzerland

Preface

The International Conference on Artificial Neural Networks has entered this year its fourth decade. After two years of disturbance the conference has returned in a hybrid mode with delegates attending on site and remotely via an immersive online space. In 2022 the 31st ICANN was organized under the auspices of the European Neural Networks Society (ENNS) and hosted by the University of the West of England, in Bristol, United Kingdom.

The event attracted a large number and wide range of new and established researchers from five continents and 27 countries in total. The delegates came from Australia, Belgium, Brazil, Canada, China, Czech Republic, Egypt, Finland, France, Germany, Greece, India, Israel, Italy, Japan, Mexico, Morocco, New Zealand, Norway, Portugal, Slovakia, Spain, Sweden, Switzerland, Turkey, UK, and USA.

The research themes explored all innovative pathways in the wider area of Neural Networks and Machine Learning. There were 561 papers submitted. These were reviewed by at least two reviewers with the average number of reviews being 3 per paper. The quality of the submitted work was very high and the program committee chairs had the challenge and delight to be able to select 259 papers in total to be presented orally at the conference. These papers are included in the four volumes of these proceedings. Out of the selected papers, 255 were regular papers, with an additional four submissions accepted for presentation as extended abstracts. These, despite their short length, represent future concepts that promise very high quality research outputs, and the program committee agreed to offer the authors the opportunity to share their ideas with the delegates of the conference.

The papers included in these four volumes of the Lecture Notes in Computer Science series addressed a variety of topics, representing a wide breadth of research, not just in the area of Artificial Neural Networks but in related AI topics themes too: Deep Learning, Neural Network Theory, Neural Network Models, Recurrent Networks, Reinforcement Learning, Natural Language Processing, Generative Models, Graphical Models, Supervised Learning, Image Processing, CNN, Evolutionary Neural Networks, Unsupervised NN, Relational Learning, Image Processing, Recommender Systems, and Features Based Learning.

The conference delegates benefited from the inspiring keynote speeches by four distinguished invited speakers, details of which are given below.

Agnieszka Wykowska leads the unit Social Cognition in Human-Robot Interaction at the Italian Institute of Technology, Genoa, Italy. Her background is cognitive neuroscience with a Ph.D. in psychology from Ludwig Maximilian University Munich. In 2016 she was awarded an ERC Starting grant for InStance: Intentional Stance for Social Attunement, which addresses the question of attribution of intentionality to robots. She is Editor-in-Chief of the International Journal of Social Robotics. She is the President of the European Society for Cognitive and Affective Neuroscience (ESCAN). She is a delegate to the European Research Area (ERA) Forum, and a member of ELLIS (European Lab for Learning and Intelligent Systems). Her research bridges psychology, cognitive neuroscience, robotics and healthcare. Among other work her team develops robot-assisted training protocols to help children diagnosed with autism-spectrum disorder improve social skills.

Věra Kůrková is a senior scientist in the Institute of Computer Science of the Czech Academy of Sciences. She received a Ph.D. in mathematics from Charles University, Prague, and a Dr. Sc. in theoretical computer science from the Czech Academy of Sciences, from which she received the Bolzano Medal for her contribution to mathematical sciences. Her main interests are the mathematical theory of neurocomputing and machine learning. She has served as president of the European Neural Network Society (ENNS), and she is a member of the editorial boards of the journals Neural Networks, Neural Processing Letters, and Applied and Computational Harmonic Analysis. She has been involved in the organization of many conferences, among them ICANN 2008 and 2001.

The Anh Han is a professor of Computer Science and head of the Centre for Digital Innovation, Teesside University. His research covers several topics in AI and interdisciplinary research, including evolutionary game theory, behavioural and cognitive modelling, agent-based simulations, knowledge representation and reasoning, and AI safety. He has published over 100 peer-reviewed articles in top-tier conferences (AAAI, IJCAI, AAMAS) and journals. He regularly serves in the program committees of top-tier AI conferences, and he is on the editorial boards of several journals (Adaptive Behavior, PLOS One, Frontiers in AI and Robotics, Entropy). He has been awarded prestigious research fellowships and grants from the Future of Life Institute, the Leverhulme Trust Foundation, and FWO Belgium.

Lyndon Smith is a professor in the Centre for Machine Vision, University of the West of England, Bristol. He has over 28 years of research experience in the field of Computer Simulation and Machine Vision, with particular emphasis on 3D analysis of complex surface textures and object morphologies. A strong area of ongoing research is the development of deep learning for vision-based solutions for complex problems, the automation of which had been previously considered intractable. This is leading to strong industrial impact in a number of sectors.

September 2022

Plamen Angelov
Mehmet Aydin
Chrisina Jayne
Elias Pimenidis

Organization

General Chairs

Elias Pimenidis   University of the West of England, UK
Angelo Cangelosi   University of Manchester, UK

Organizing Committee Chairs

Tim Brailsford   University of the West of England, UK
Larry Bull   University of the West of England, UK

Honorary Chairs

Stefan Wermter (ENNS President)   University of Hamburg, Germany
Igor Farkaš   FMPI, Comenius University in Bratislava, Slovakia

Program Committee Chairs

Plamen Angelov   Lancaster University, UK
Mehmet Aydin   University of the West of England, UK
Chrisina Jayne   Teesside University, UK
Elias Pimenidis   University of the West of England, UK

Communication Chairs

Paolo Masulli   ENNS, Technical University of Denmark
Kristína Malinovská   FMPI, Comenius University in Bratislava, Slovakia
Antonios Papaleonidas   Democritus University of Thrace, Greece

Steering Committee

Jérémie Cabessa   Université Versailles Saint-Quentin-en-Yvelines, France
Włodzisław Duch   Nicolaus Copernicus University, Torun, Poland
Igor Farkaš   Comenius University, Bratislava, Slovakia
Matthias Kerzel   Universität Hamburg, Germany
Věra Kůrková   Czech Academy of Sciences, Prague, Czechia

Alessandra Lintas	Université de Lausanne, Switzerland
Paolo Masulli	iMotions A/S, Copenhagen, Denmark
Alessio Micheli	University of Pisa, Italy
Erkki Oja	Aalto University, Finland
Sebastian Otte	Universität Tübingen, Germany
Jaakko Peltonen	Tampere University, Finland
Antonio J. Pons	Universitat Politècnica de Catalunya, Barcelona, Spain
Igor V. Tetko	Helmholtz Zentrum München, Germany
Alessandro E. P. Villa	Université de Lausanne, Switzerland
Roseli Wedemann	Universidade do Estado do Rio de Janeiro, Brazil
Stefan Wermter	Universität Hamburg, Germany

Local Organizing Committee

Nathan Duran	University of the West of England, UK
Haixia Liu	University of the West of England, UK
Zaheer Khan	University of the West of England, UK
Antonios Papaleonidas	Democritus University of Thrace, Greece
Nikolaos Polatidis	Brighton University, UK
Antisthenis Tsompanas	University of the West of England, UK

Hybrid Facilitation and Moderation Committee

Anastasios Panagiotis Psathas	Democritus University of Thrace, Greece
Dimitris Boudas	Democritus University of Thrace, Greece
Ioanna-Maria Erentzi	Democritus University of Thrace, Greece
Ioannis Skopelitis	Democritus University of Thrace, Greece
Lambros Kazelis	Democritus University of Thrace, Greece
Leandros Tsatsaronis	Democritus University of Thrace, Greece
Nikiforos Mpotzoris	Democritus University of Thrace, Greece
Nikos Zervis	Democritus University of Thrace, Greece
Odysseas Tsonos	Hellenic Open University, Greece
Panagiotis Restos	Democritus University of Thrace, Greece
Tassos Giannakopoulos	Democritus University of Thrace, Greece
Vasilis Kokkinos	Democritus University of Thrace, Greece

Program Committee

Abdelhamid Bouchachia	Bournemouth University, UK
Abdur Rakib	University of the West of England, UK
Abraham Yosipof	College of Law and Business, Israel
Akihiro Inokuchi	Kwansei Gakuin University, Japan

Alaa Zain — Hosei University, Japan
Albert Bifet — LTCI, Telecom ParisTech, France
Alejandro Cabana — Universidad Autónoma de Madrid, Spain
Alexander Claman — University of Miami, USA
Alexander Gepperth — ENSTA ParisTech, France
Alexander Ilin — Aalto University, Finland
Alexander Kovalenko — Czech Technical University in Prague, Czechia
Alexander Krawczyk — HAW Fulda, Germany
Ali Zoljodi — MDU, Sweden
Aluizio Araújo — Universidade Federal de Pernambuco, Brazil
Amit Kumar Kundu — University of Maryland, College Park, USA
An Xu — Donghua University, China
Anastasios Panagiotis Psathas — Democritus University of Thrace, Greece
André Artelt — Bielefeld University, Germany
Andre de Carvalho — University of São Paulo, Brazil
Andrea Castellani — Bielefeld University - CITEC, Germany
Andrea Galassi — University of Bologna, Italy
Angelo Cangelosi — University of Manchester, UK
Anmol Biswas — Indian Institute of Technology, Mumbai, India
Anna Jenul — Norwegian University of Life Sciences, Norway
Annie DeForge — Bentley University, USA
Anselm Haselhoff — Hochschule Ruhr West, Germany
Antisthenis Tsompanas — University of the West of England, UK
Antonio García-Díaz — Université libre de Bruxelles (ULB), Belgium
Antonio Pons — Universitat Politècnica de Catalunya, Spain
Antonios Papaleonidas — Democritus University of Thrace, Greece
Argyris Kalogeratos — CMLA, ENS Cachan, France
Asada — Osaka University, Japan
Asei Akanuma — Goldsmiths College, University of London, UK
Atsushi Koike — Tohoku University, Japan
Baris Serhan — University of Manchester, UK
Barkha Javed — University of the West of England, UK
Benedikt Bagus — Hochschule Fulda, Germany
Benyuan Liu — University of Massachusetts, Lowell, USA
Bernhard Pfahringer — University of Waikato, New Zealand
Bi Yan-Qing — National University of Defense Technology, China
Binyi Wu — TU Dresden, Germany
Binyu Zhao — Harbin Institute of Technology, China
Bo Mei — Texas Christian University, USA
Boyu Diao — ict, China
Cao Hongye — Northwestern Polytechnical University, China

Carsten Marr	German Research Center for Environmental Health, Germany
Chao Ma	Hong Kong Polytechnic University, Hong Kong, China
Cheng Feng	Fujitsu R&D Center, China
Ching-Chia Kao	Academia Sinica, Taiwan
Chrisina Jayne	Teesside University, UK
Christian Bauckhage	Fraunhofer IAIS, Sankt Augustin, Germany
Christian Oliva	Universidad Autónoma de Madrid, Spain
Christoph Linse	Universität zu Lübeck, Germany
Chuan Lu	Aberystwyth University, UK
Chuang Yu	University of Manchester, UK
Chunhong Cao	Xiangtan University, China
Chun-Shien Lu	Academia Sinica, Taiwan
Claudio Bellei	Elliptic, UK
Claudio Gallicchio	University of Pisa, Italy
Claudio Giorgio Giancaterino	Catholic University of Milan, Italy
Connor Gäde	University of Hamburg, Germany
Constantine Dovrolis	Georgia Institute of Technology, USA
Cornelius Weber	University of Hamburg, Germany
Coşku Can Horuz	University of Tübingen, Germany
Cui Wang	Macao Polytechnic University, China
Dan Fisher	University of North Carolina, Wilmington, USA
Daniel Kluvanec	Durham University, UK
David Dembinsky	German Research Center for Artificial Intelligence, Germany
David Martínez	DataSpartan Ltd., UK
Dayananda Herurkar	DFKI, Germany
Denise Gorse	University College London, UK
Dennis Becker	Lüneburg University, Germany
Dimitrios Bountas	Democritus University of Thrace, Greece
Dimitrios Michail	Harokopio University of Athens, Greece
Diyuan Lu	Frankfurt Institute for Advanced Studies, Germany
D. J. McMoran	University of North Carolina, Wilmington, USA
Domenico Tortorella	University of Pisa, Italy
Dominique Mercier	German Research Center for Artificial Intelligence, Germany
Doron Nevo	Bar-Ilan University, Israel
Douglas Nyabuga	Donghua University, China
Efe Bozkir	University of Tübingen, Germany
Eisuke Ito	Ritsumeikan University, Japan

Elias Pimenidis	University of the West of England, UK
Fabian Hinder	Bielefeld University, Germany
Fanglin Chen	Harbin Institute of Technology, Shenzhen, China
Fares Abawi	University of Hamburg, Germany
Federico Tavella	University of Manchester, UK
Feixiang Zhou	University of Leicester, UK
Feng Wei	York University, Canada
Florence Dupin de Saint-Cyr	IRIT, Université Paul Sabatier, France
Francesco Semeraro	University of Manchester, UK
Francois Blayo	Neoinstinct, Switzerland
Frank Gyan Okyere	Rothamsted Research, UK
Frederic Alexandre	Inria, France
Gang Yang	Renmin University, China
Giannis Nikolentzos	Athens University of Economics and Business, Greece
Gonzalo Martínez-Muñoz	Universidad Autónoma de Madrid, Spain
Grégory Bourguin	LISIC/ULCO, France
Guillermo Martín-Sánchez	Graduate Training Center of Neuroscience, Germany
Gulustan Dogan	University of North Carolina, Wilmington, USA
Habib Khan	Islamia College Peshawar, Pakistan
Hafez Farazi	University of Bonn, Germany
Haixia Liu	University of the West of England, UK
Haizhou Du	Shanghai University of Electric Power, China
Hang Gao	Institute of Software, Chinese Academy of Sciences, China
Haopeng Chen	Shanghai Jiao Tong University, China
Hazrat Ali	Hamad Bin Khalifa University, Qatar
Heitor Gomes	University of Waikato, New Zealand
Hideaki Yamamoto	Tohoku University, Japan
Hina Afridi	NTNU, Norway
Hiroyoshi Ito	University of Tsukuba, Japan
Hisham Ihshaish	University of the West of England, UK
Hong Qing Yu	University of Bedfordshire, UK
Hongchao Gao	South China University of Technology, China
Honggang Zhang	University of Massachusetts, Boston, USA
Hugo Eduardo Camacho Cruz	Universidad Autónoma de Tamaulipas, Mexico
Hugues Bersini	Université libre de Bruxelles, Belgium
Huifang Ma	Northwest Normal University, China
Huiyu Zhou	University of Leicester, UK
Hy Dang	Texas Christian University, USA
Igor Farkaš	Comenius University in Bratislava, Slovakia

Ioannis Pierros	Aristotle University of Thessaloniki, Greece
Iveta Bečková	Comenius University in Bratislava, Slovakia
Jae Hee Lee	University of Hamburg, Germany
James J. Q. Yu	Southern University of Science and Technology, Hong Kong, China
James Msonda	Aberystwyth University, UK
Jan Faigl	Czech Technical University in Prague, Czechia
Jan Feber	Czech Technical University in Prague, Czechia
Jan Kalina	Czech Academy of Sciences, Czechia
Jérémie Cabessa	University Paris 2, France
Jia Cai	Guangdong University of Finance & Economics, China
Jiajun Liu	CSIRO, Australia
Jianhua Xu	Nanjing Normal University, China
Jian-Wei Liu	China University of Petroleum, Beijing, China
Jianyong Chen	Shenzhen University, Shenzhen, China
Jichao Bi	Zhejiang University, China
Jie Shao	University of Science and Technology, Chengdu, China
Jim Smith	University of the West of England, UK
Jing Yang	Hefei University of Technology, China
Jingyi Yuan	Arizona State University, USA
Jingyun Jia	Florida Institute of Technology, USA
Johannes Brinkrolf	CITEC Centre of Excellence, Germany
Jonathan Jakob	Bielefeld University, Germany
Jonathan Lawry	University of Bristol, UK
Jonathan Mojoo	Hiroshima University, Japan
Jordi Cosp-Vilella	Universitat Politècnica de Catalunya, Spain
Jordi Madrenas	Universitat Politècnica de Catalunya, Spain
Joseph Jaja	University of Maryland, USA
Juan Liu	Wuhan University, China
K. L. Eddie Law	Macao Polytechnic University, Macao, China
Kamran Soomro	University of the West of England, UK
Katsiaryna Haitsiukevich	Aalto University, Finland
Kenneth Co	Imperial College London, UK
Koji Kyoda	RIKEN Center for Biosystems Dynamics Research, Japan
Koloud Alkhamaiseh	Western Michigan University, USA
Kostadin Cvejoski	Fraunhofer IAIS, Sankt Augustin, Germany
Kostantinos Demertzis	Democritus University of Thrace, Greece
Kristian Hovde Liland	Norwegian University of Life Sciences, Norway
Kuntal Ghosh	Indian Statistical Institute, India

Larry Bull	University of the West of England, UK
Lei Luo	Kansas State University, USA
Leiping Jie	Hong Kong Baptist University, Hong Kong, China
Lian Yahong	Dalian University of Technology, China
Liang Ge	Chongqing University, China
Liang Zhao	Dalian University of Technology, China
Liang Zhao	University of São Paulo, Brazil
Lingfei Dai	ICT - CAS, China
Linlin Shen	Shenzhen University, China
Lu Wang	Macao Polytechnic University, Macao
Luca Oneto	University of Genoa, Italy
Luca Raggioli	University of Manchester, UK
Luís A. Alexandre	UBI and NOVA LINCS, Portugal
Luis Lago	Universidad Autónoma de Madrid, Spain
Lun-Ing Zhang	China University of Petroleum, Beijing, China
Magda Friedjungová	Czech Technical University in Prague, Czechia
Manon Dampfhoffer	Université Grenoble Alpes, France
Marc Wenninger	Technische Hochschule Rosenheim, Germany
Marcello Trovati	Edge Hill University, UK
Marco Perez Hernandez	University of the West of England, UK
Maria Papadaki	University of Derby, UK
Marika Kaden	HS Mittweida, Germany
Markus Kollmann	Heinrich Heine Universität, Germany
Marta Romeo	University of Manchester, UK
Martin Butz	University of Tübingen, Germany
Martin Ferianc	University College London, UK
Masanari Kimura	ZOZO Research, Japan
Masoud Daneshtalab	Mälardalen University, Sweden
Matthew Evanusa	University of Maryland, USA
Matthias Karlbauer	University of Tübingen, Germany
Matthias Kerzel	University of Hamburg, Germany
Mattias Dahl	Blekinge Institute of Technology, Sweden
Md Delwar Hossain	Nara Institute of Science and Technology, Japan
Mehmet Emin Aydin	University of the West of England, UK
Mihaela Oprea	University Petroleum-Gas of Ploiesti, Romania
Mohammad Loni	MDU, Sweden
Moritz Wolter	University of Bonn, Germany
Mu Hua	University of Lincoln, UK
Muhammad Usama Javaid	Eura Nova, Belgium
Nashwa El-Bendary	Arab Academy for Science, Technology & Maritime Transport, Egypt
Nathan Duran	University of the West of England, UK

Wenxin Yu	Southwest University of Science and Technology, China
Xi Cheng	Nanjing University of Science and Technology, China
Xia Feng	Civil Aviation University, China
Xian Zhong	Wuhan University of Technology, China
Xiang Zhang	National University of Defense Technology, China
Xiaoqing Liu	Kyushu University, Japan
Xiumei Li	Hangzhou Normal University, China
Xizhan Gao	University of Jinan, China
Xuan Yang	Shenzhen University, China
Yan Chen	Chinese Academy of Sciences, China
Yangguang Cui	East China Normal University, China
Yapeng Gao	University of Tübingen, Germany
Yaxi Chen	Wuhan University, China
Yiannis Aloimonos	University of Maryland, USA
Yihao Luo	Huazhong University of Science and Technology, China
Yipeng Yu	Tencent, China
Yuan Li	Academy of Military Science, China
Yuanyuan Chen	Sichuan University, China
Yuchen Zheng	Shihezi University, China
Yuchun Fang	Shanghai University, China
Yue Gao	Beijing University of Posts and Telecommunications, China
Yuji Kawai	Osaka University, Japan
Zhaoxiang Zang	China Three Gorges University, China
Zhaoyun Ding	National University of Defense Technology, China
Zhengfeng Yang	East China Normal University, Shanghai, China
Zhenjie Yao	CMCC, China
Zhiping Lai	Fudan University, China
Zhiqiang Zhang	Hosei University, Japan
Zhixin Li	Guangxi Normal University, China
Zhongnan Zhang	Xiamen University, China

Contents- Part III

Adaptive Channel Encoding Transformer for Point Cloud Analysis

Guoquan Xu[1]($\boxtimes$) (iD), Hezhi Cao[2] (iD), Yifan Zhang[1], Yanxin Ma[1], Jianwei Wan[1], and Ke Xu[1]

[1] National University of Defense Technology, Changsha, Hunan, China
{xuguoquan19,zhangyifan16c,mayanxin,xuke}@nudt.edu.cn
[2] University of Science and Technology of China, Hefei, Anhui, China
caohezhi21@mail.ustc.edu.cn

Abstract. Transformer plays an increasingly important role in various computer vision areas and has made remarkable achievements in point cloud analysis. Since existing methods mainly focus on point-wise transformer, an adaptive channel-wise Transformer is proposed in this paper. Specifically, a channel encoding Transformer called Transformer Channel Encoder (TCE) is designed to encode the coordinate channel. It can encode coordinate channels by capturing the potential relationship between coordinates and features. The encoded channel can extract features with stronger representation ability. Compared with simply assigning attention weight to each channel, our method aims to encode the channel adaptively. Moreover, our method can be extended to other frameworks to improve their preformance. Our network adopts the neighborhood search method of feature similarity semantic receptive fields to improve the performance. Extensive experiments show that our method is superior to state-of-the-art point cloud classification and segmentation methods on three benchmark datasets.

Keywords: Transformer · Point cloud analysis · Adaptive channel encoding

1 Introduction

3D point cloud is widely used in many fields because it contains geometric information and can be simply represented. However, point clouds are point sets embedded in irregular 3D space, unlike images which are arranged on regular pixel grids. This makes direct processing of point clouds challenging. In order to meet this challenge, many methods have been proposed and can be roughly divided into three categories: voxel-based method, projection-based method and point-based method.

Voxel-based method [1, 2] attempts to voxelize the 3D space so that the point cloud is distributed in an artificial regularized space. However, voxelization will lead to massive computation, and there is no point cloud distribution in many voxel grids, resulting in a waste of memory.

Projection-based method [3, 4] maps 3D point clouds into 2D space so that 2D convolution can be implemented. This will cause the point cloud data to lose its biggest

E. Pimenidis et al. (Eds.): ICANN 2022, LNCS 13531, pp. 1–13, 2022.
https://doi.org/10.1007/978-3-031-15934-3_1

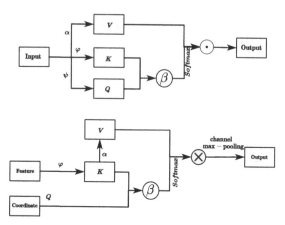

Fig. 1. The diagrams of point-wise transformer (top) and our channel-wise transformer (bottom). ψ, φ and α are feature transformations which implemented with MLPs or linear projections. β indicates a relation function (e.g., subtraction) and produces an attention matrix. $\odot$ means matrix multiplication and $\otimes$ means element-wise multiplication.

advantage: structure information. At the same time, it will also bring a large amount of calculation.

PointNet [5] proposes a point-wise method which employs MLPs to extract features point by point, and finally uses global pooling to obtain global features. However, this method ignores the structure information in the process. Therefore, PointNet++ [6] which explores the local information aggregation method is proposed as an improvement work. Inspired by them, the follow-up works [7–11] which design convolution-like operations on point clouds to exploit spatial correlations is mainly this kind of method.

Transformer has achieved excellent performance in various fields because of its powerful representation ability. It is especially suitable for point cloud processing, because the self-attention operator as the core of transformer network is essentially a set operator: it is invariant to permutation and cardinality of the input. The main operation of transformer is shown in Fig. 1 (top). The key is to learn an attention matrix through a relational function β. There are some point-wise transformer-based works in the field of point cloud for now [12, 13].

Motivation. Inspired by these point-wise works, a channel-wise transformer is proposed in this paper. Encoding the channel before feature extraction can improve the ability of feature representation. Generally, features are obtained from coordinates, so features can help encode coordinate channels. Specifically, a channel encoding mechanism called TCE is designed as shown in Fig. 1 (bottom). It can be seen that a channel attention matrix is obtained by learning the potential relationship between coordinate channels and feature channels, and then the feature channels are weighted. Subsequently, the coordinate channels are screened by a max-pooling in the direction of the channel to retain the most important channels. Finally, the features with channel filtering will be input into the standard graph convolution [7] network to deal with the tasks of classification and segmentation. In addition, in order to better capture neighborhood information, feature similarity among points is used to replace fixed spatial location. The k points with the greatest similarity are selected as neighbors.

The main contributions of this paper include the following:

- A channel encoding mechanism called TCE is proposed. The contribution of channels can be determined by it which can learn the potential relationship between feature channels and coordinate channels.
- The designed TCE can be simply transplanted to other networks to enhance its performance.
- Extensive experiments over multiple domains and datasets are carried out and the experiment parameters and network structure are introduced in detail. The results show that our method achieves the state-of- the-art performance.

2   Related Work

2.1   Point-Based Method

Permutation-invariant operators implemented by point-wise MLPs and pooling layers are proposed in PointNet [5] to aggregate features. PointNet++ [6] establishes a hierarchical spatial structure which can increase sensitivity to the local geometric layout. This is a further improvement of PointNet. DGCNN [7] designs EdgeConv which can learn the point relationship as the edge of the graph in the high-dimensional feature space to capture similar local information. Moreover, DGCNN proposes to re-search the nearest neighbors of the central points on each layer in the feature space every time, so as to build the dynamic graph. RS-CNN [8] is committed to learn high-level geometric priors from low-level geometric information in 3D space. PAConv [9] further designs an adaptive convolution on spatial points. A dynamic convolution algorithm which can adaptively learn the weight coefficients from the point position is designed. AdaptConv [10] generates adaptive kernels according to their dynamically learned features. Our method also learns a dynamic attention matrix from the channel relationships between features and coordinates. Unlike the popular attention methods, our method achieves adaptability rather than simply assigning weights.

2.2   Transformer-Based Method

Transformer has achieved great success in natural language processing and image processing. Inspired by attention mechanism, SE block [14] is proposed for spatial encoding. A residual attention method [15] is proposed for image classification. Because it also has excellent applicability to point cloud processing, some works introduce it into the field of point cloud. PCT [12] uses the inherent order invariance of Transformer to avoid defining the order of point cloud data, and carries out feature learning through attention mechanism. Point Transformer [13] designs a Point Transformer layer with strong representation ability for point cloud processing. This layer is invariant to permutation and cardinality, so it is naturally suitable for point cloud tasks. They are point-wise methods and achieve great results. In contrast, a channel-wise transformer comes up in this paper. The popular transformer has been improved to meet the needs of operation on the channel.

3   Method

In this section, the design of TCE is introduced in detail in Sect. 3.1. Then the difference between our method and point-wise transformer is discussed. Finally, our network structure on different point cloud processing tasks is shown in Sect. 3.2.

3.1   Tce

Suppose $X = \{x_i | i = 1, 2, ..., N\} \in \mathbb{R}^{N \times 3}$ represents a point cloud with corresponding features $F = \{f_i | i = 1, 2, ...N\} \in \mathbb{R}^{N \times C}$. Here, N is the number of points and C is the number of channels. $\mathcal{N}(x_i)$ means the neighbor set of x_i. The process of TCE is shown in Fig. 2. Following the terminology in PCT [12], let Q, K and V be the *query, key* and *value* matrices respectively. They are defined as:

$$Q = (x_i, x_j - x_i), \tag{1}$$

$$K = MLP(f_i, f_j - f_i), \tag{2}$$

$$V = combine(MLP_1(K), ..., MLP_C(K)). \tag{3}$$

Unlike the popular transformer, Q is obtained directly from coordinate without any linear transformation. This is because removing this part of the linear transformation has little effect on the results and can reduce the computation cost. K is derived from feature, not from coordinate. This is because the channel attention matrix needs to be learned from the channel relationship between feature and coordinate. Since only the coordinates are used as the original input of the network, K in the first layer is also derived from coordinates, and takes the output features of the first layer as the input in the second layer. The relationship is the contribution of each channel of coordinate to each channel of feature. This process can be expressed as:

$$A = Q \otimes K^T, \tag{4}$$

where A indicates the channel attention matrix and $\otimes$ means element-wise multiplication rather than matrix dot-product. Equation (4) represents the contribution of each channel of coordinate to each channel of feature. For example, the first column of A is the contribution of each channel of coordinate to the first channel of feature. Hence, the *Softmax* operation is done in columns:

$$\tilde{A}_{i,j} = softmax(A_{i,j}) = \frac{\exp(A_{i,j})}{\sum_C \exp(A_{C,j})} \tag{5}$$

$\tilde{A}$ is the final channel attention matrix. V is generated by K and it can produce a response matrix B with $\tilde{A}$:

$$B = \tilde{A} \otimes V \tag{6}$$

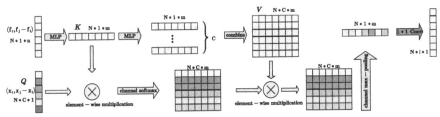

Fig. 2. The flow chart of TCE. The coordinates and features are set as the query and key matrices respectively. The attention matrix is obtained by the corresponding relationship between coordinates and feature channel by channel because all features come from coordinates. The value matrix is obtained by mapping the key matrix. Because they are all based on key matrix, there is a response relationship between the value matrix and attention matrix. Element-wise multiplication is used to capture this response relationship. Then, max-pooling in the channel direction is used to filter out the strongest response as the encoded channel. Finally, a 1*1 convolution is used to extract the features of the encoded channel as the input of the next layer.

Equation (6) indicates that an excitation (V) is applied to the attention matrix ($\tilde{A}$) to obtain the corresponding response. The elements in B represent the strength of the corresponding response. Its significance is to use feature channels to test the contribution learned from feature channels and coordinate channels. The greater the contribution, the stronger the response. Channel with the strongest response of each column is preserved as the new coordinate channels:

$$\tilde{B}_j = \max_{i \in C} B_{i,j} \tag{7}$$

Here, $\max_{i \in C}()$ indicates max-pooling in the channel direction. $\tilde{B}$ is the encoded new coordinate channel and each of its channels has the greatest contribution to feature. Then a 1*1 convolution is applied to extract feature as the input to the next layer:

$$f_i' = \mathcal{A}\left(Conv\left(\tilde{B}_j\right), \forall x_j \in \mathcal{N}(x_i)\right), \tag{8}$$

where $Conv$ means 1*1 convolution and $\mathcal{A}$ means the aggregate function. In particular, since our method is to encode the channel, the position coding is omitted.

Our method is very different from the point-wise transformer. Our channel attention matrix is obtained through the relationship between coordinate and feature, not the coordinate itself. Coordinate is input and feature is target and the channel attention matrix essentially captures the relationship between input channels and target channels. V is generated by K and is essentially a test matrix which checks the channel attention matrix.

3.2 Network Architecture

Our main idea is to use TCE for channel encoding, and then send the encoded channels to graph convolution neural network for feature extraction. Thus, the network architecture can be mainly divided into two parts: channel encoding layer and feature extraction layer. As shown in Fig. 3, the channel encoding has two layers which is a unified design in classification and segmentation networks. In the feature extraction layers, standard graph convolution [7] is adopted. This is to verify the performance improvement brought by embedding our method into other networks. There are two feature extraction layers in the classification network and three in the segmentation network. Through the dual feature similarity method, the receptive field is expanded and the dynamic graph is built.

In the classification network, pooling and interpolation are not designed. The output of the second channel encoding layer and the two feature extraction layers is concatenated. Feature similarity is used to select neighborhood rather than k-nearest neighbors (KNN) or ball query. Specifically, the feature distance is calculated instead of the coordinate distance, and the nearest k points are selected as neighbors.

Different from the classification network, the segmentation network adopts pooling and interpolation. The farthest point sampling algorithm (FPS) is used to down sample the point cloud, and a rough map is established on the sampling points according to the feature similarity.

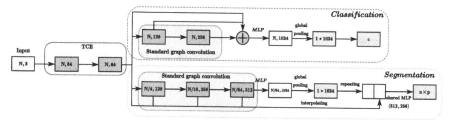

Fig. 3. Classification and segmentation network structure. Our network consists of two channel coding layers with TCE. This is the general part of classification and segmentation. Standard graph convolution Standard graph convolution is implemented for feature extraction. It is worth mentioning that the classification network has no down sampling.

4   Experiments

In order to verify the performance of our network and the effectiveness of TCE, sufficient comparative experiments are carried out on ModelNet40 [16], ShapeNet [17] and ScanObjectNN [18]. After that, a series of ablation experiments and robustness experiments are designed to verify our method.

4.1   Classification on ModelNet40

ModelNet40 [16] contains 12,311 3D models, of which 9,843 models are used for training, and the remaining 2,468 models are used as test models. Like other papers, each model is uniformly sampled 1024 points and normalized to a unit sphere. In addition, all points are enhanced by random anisotropic scaling in the range of [-0.66, 1.5] and translation in the range of [-0.2, 0.2]. The main parameter settings are as follows: the rate of dropout is set to 50% in the last two fully-connected (FC) layers; batch normalization and LeakyReLU are applied on all layers; the SGD optimizer with momentum set to 0.9 is adopted; The initial learning rate is donated to 0.1 and is dropped to 0.001 by cosine annealing.

Table 1 reports the results of the most advanced methods and our methods in order of results. For a clear comparison, the input data type and the number of points corresponding to each method are shown. Our method achieves the best performance with only 1k points as input.

Table 1. Classification accuracy (%) on ModelNet40.

Method	Input	Accuracy
3D-GCN [19]	1k points	92.1
PCNN [20]	1k points	92.3
SpiderCNN [21]	5k points + normal	92.4
PointConv [22]	1k points + normal	92.5
PointCNN [11]	1k points	92.5
PointASNL [23]	1k points	92.9
DGCNN [7]	1k points	92.9
Grid-GCN [24]	1k points	93.1
PCT [12]	1k points	93.2
AdaptConv [10]	1k points	93.4
Our method	**1k points**	**93.4**

4.2   Part Segmentation on ShapeNet

ShapeNet [17] is employed to test the performance of our segmentation network. The dataset contains 16,881 shapes in 16 categories and a total of 50 parts for annotation. Each object is marked with 2–6 labels. The dataset provided by PointNet++ [6] is put in use as a benchmark and its experimental setting is followed as well. Each object has 2k points as the input, which is different from classification task.

The quantitative comparisons with the state-of-the-art methods are shown in Table 2. All methods are measured by the class mean IoU (mIoU) and instance mean IoU. To facilitate comparison, the results of instance mIoU are adopted to sort. It can be seen that our method has achieved satisfactory results on both class mIoU and instance mIoU.

Our segmentation results are displayed in Fig. 4 (second row). In order to more intuitively reflect the advantages of our results, the ground truth (first row) and the difference between ours and the ground truth (third row) are displayed together. The red points indicate the wrong prediction, and the blue points indicate the correct prediction. You can see that the proportion of red points is very small in most models. There are more red points in the motorbike than other models because it is the most complex model.

Table 2. Shape part segmentation results (%) on ShapeNet.

Method	Class mIoU	Instance mIoU
PointNet [5]	80.4	83.7
PCNN [20]	81.8	85.1
PointNet++ [6]	81.9	85.1
3D-GCN [19]	82.1	85.1
DGCNN [7]	82.3	85.2
SpiderCNN [21]	81.7	85.3
SPLATNet [25]	83.7	85.4
PointConv [22]	82.8	85.7
Our method	**83.4**	**86.0**

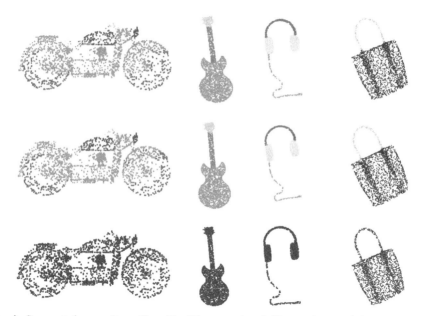

Fig. 4. Segmentation results on ShapeNet. The ground truth (first row), our results (second row) and their difference (third row) are shown at the same time. The red points in the third row mean the wrong points.

4.3 Classification on ScanObjectNN

Since the above two experiments are carried out on the idealized datasets, ScanObjectNN [18] is adopted to further evaluate the performance of our method. This dataset is obtained by scanning the real indoor scenes. The Hardest is a subset of ScanObjectNN. The subset contains the real targets which are processed by translating, rotating (around the gravity axis), and scaling the ground truth bounding box. This makes the dataset closer to the complex situation of the real-world.

The results are summarized in Table 3, and our method transcends all other methods. Compared with the most advanced method BGA-PN++ [18], our method is improved by 1.4%. The result of SpiderCNN [21] decreased by 18.7% when the dataset is changed from ModelNet40 to the Hardest. AdaptConv [10] achieves 93.4% on ModelNet40, but decreases to 78.9% on the Hardest. Our method still performs well on the real-world dataset, which proves that our method has higher practical value.

Table 3. Classification accuracy (%) on ScanObjectNN.

Method	Hardest
PointNet [5]	68.2
SpiderCNN [21]	73.7
PointNet++ [6]	77.9
RS-CNN [8]	78.0
DGCNN [7]	78.1
PointCNN [11]	78.5
AdaptConv [10]	78.9
BGA-DGCNN [18]	79.7
BGA-PN++ [18]	80.2
Our method	**81.6**

4.4 Ablation Studies

In this subsection, a series of experiments are designed to prove the effectiveness of our design.

First of all, our core design TCE is replaced by Channel-wise Attention [26], Point-wise Attention [27] respectively. This is to prove that TCE is different from them and more effective. Besides, TCE is also replaced by standard graph convolution (Graph-Conv) in order to eliminate the influence of standard graph convolution on the experiment. Only the channel encoding part is replaced, and the network structure and parameter settings remain unchanged. This set of experiments is carried out on ShapeNet [17] and the results are shown in Table 4. By comparison, TCE performs better than other methods.

The design of TCE has a pooling operation in the channel direction as mentioned in Sect. 3.1. Table 5 compares the effects of different pooling methods on the results of classification. Max-pooling is obviously better than the other two methods because it plays a screening role and retains the most influential channels.

Table 4. The comparison results (%) on ShapeNet.

Ablations	Class mIoU	Instance mIoU
GraphConv	81.9	85.3
Point-wise attention	78.1	83.3
Channel-wise attention	77.9	83.0
TCE	**83.4**	**86.0**

Table 5. The comparison results (%) on ModelNet40.

Ablations	Accuracy
Mean-pooling	92.7
Sum-pooling	92.5
Max-pooling	**93.4**

4.5 Robustness Experiments

In this subsection, the robustness of our method to sparse points on ModelNet40 [16] is further evaluated. Similarly, GraphConv and Channel-wise Attention [26] are used for comparison. All networks have 1024 points as the input during training, and 1024, 512, 256 and 128 points are used as the inputs for testing respectively. Figure 5 shows that our method outperforms the other two methods.

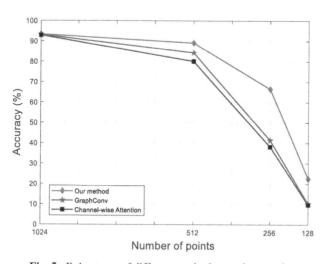

Fig. 5. Robustness of different methods to point sparsity.

In order to compare the complexity of our method with the previous method, Table 6 lists some relevant results. From the table, it can be seen that our method achieves the best performance of 93.4% overall accuracy and the model size is relatively small. The latter half of our model adopts the module of DGCNN. It can be seen that our method has only 0.06M more parameters than it, but the performance is improved by 0.5%.

Table 6. The number of parameters and overall accuracy of different methods

Method	#parameters	Accuracy (%)
PointNet [6]	3.5M	89.2
PointNet++ [7]	1.48M	90.7
DGCNN [8]	1.81M	92.9
KPConv [20]	14.3M	92.9
PCT [12]	2.88M	93.2
Our method	1.87M	93.4

5   Conclusion

In this paper, a channel-wise convolution called TCE is designed based on Transformer. It is different from the popular Transformer with self-attention mechanism. TCE encodes the coordinate channels by adaptively learning the relationships between feature channels and coordinate channels, and expands the coordinate channels. More expressive features can be extracted with the encoded channels. In addition, a dynamic graph construction method is designed to expand the receptive field. Sufficient experiments on three datasets, especially on the real-world dataset, prove that our method achieves the state of the arts.

References

1. Maturana, D., Scherer, S.: Voxnet: a 3d convolutional neural network for real-time object recognition. In: Proceedings of the IEEE/RSJ International Conference on Intelligent Robots and Systems, pp. 922–928, IEEE, Hamburg, Germany (2015)
2. Feng, Y., Zhang, Z., Zhao, X., Ji, R., Gao, Y.: Gvcnn: group-view convolutional neural networks for 3d shape recognition. In: Proceedings of the IEEE Conference on Computer Vision and Pattern Recognition, pp. 264–272, IEEE, Salt Lake City, UT, USA (2018)
3. Han, Z., et al.: Seqviews2seqlabels: learning 3d global features via aggregating sequential views by rnn with attention. IEEE Trans. Image Processing **28**(2), 658–672 (2019)
4. Gadelha, M., Wang, R., Maji, S.: Multiresolution tree networks for 3d point cloud processing. In: Proceedings of the European Conference on Computer Vision, pp. 105–122, Springer, Munich, Germany (2018) https://doi.org/10.1007/978-3-030-01234-2_7
5. Qi, C.R., Su, H., Mo, K., Guibas, L.J.: Pointnet: deep learning on point sets for 3d classification and segmentation. In: Proceedings of the IEEE Conference on Computer Vision and Pattern Recognition, pp. 652–660, IEEE, Honolulu, HI, USA (2017)

6. Qi, C.R., Su, H., Guibas, L.J.: Pointnet++: deep hierarchical feature learning on point sets in a metric space. In: Advances in Neural Information Processing Systems, pp. 5099–5180, ACM, Long Beach California USA (2017)

7. Wang, Y., Sun, Y., Liu, Z., Sarma, S.E., Bronstein, M., Solomon, M.: Dynamic graph cnn for learning on point clouds. ACM Trans. Graphics **38**(5), 146:1–146:12 (2019)

8. Liu, Y., Fan, B., Xiang, S., Pan, C.: Relation-shape convolutional neural network for point cloud analysis. In: Proceedings of the IEEE Conference on Computer Vision and Pattern Recognition, pp. 1–10, IEEE, Long Beach, USA (2019)

9. Xu, M., Ding, R., Zhao, H., Qi, X.: Paconv: position adaptive convolution with dynamic kernel assembling on point clouds. In: Proceedings of the IEEE Conference on Computer Vision and Pattern Recognition, pp. 9621–9630, IEEE, Nashville, TN, USA (2021)

10. Zhou, H., Feng, Y., Fang, M., Wei, M., Qin, J., Lu, T.: Adaptive graph convolution for point cloud analysis. In: Proceedings of the IEEE International Conference on Computer Vision, IEEE, Montreal, Canada (2021)

11. Li, Y., Bu, R., Sun, M., Chen, B.: Pointcnn: convolution on x-transformed points. In: Advances in Neural Information Processing Systems, pp. 828–838, ACM, (2018)

12. Guo, M., Cai, J., Liu, Z., Mu, T., Martin, R., Hu, S.: Pct: point cloud transformer. Comput. Visual Media **7**, 187–199 (2021)

13. Zhao, H., Jiang, L., Jia, J., Torr, P., Koltun, V.: Point transformer. In: Proceedings of the IEEE Conference on Computer Vision and Pattern Recognition, pp. 134826–134840, IEEE, Nashville, TN, USA (2021)

14. Hu, J., Shen, L., Albanie, S., Sun, G., Wu, E.: Squeeze-and-excitation networks. IEEE Trans. Pattern Anal. Mach. Intell. **42**(8), 2011–2023 (2020)

15. Wang, F., et al.: Residual attention network for image classification. In: Proceedings of the IEEE Conference on Computer Vision and Pattern Recognition, pp. 6450–6458, IEEE, Honolulu, HI, USA (2017)

16. Wu, Z., et al.: 3d shapenets: a deep representation for volumetric shapes. In: Proceedings of the IEEE Conference on Computer Vision and Pattern Recognition, pp. 1912–1920, IEEE, Boston, MA, USA (2015)

17. Yi, L., et al.: A scalable active framework for region annotation in 3d shape collections. ACM Trans. Graphics **35**(6), 1–12 (2016)

18. Uy, A., Pham, H., Hua, S., Nguyen, T., Yeung, K.: Revisiting point cloud classification: a new benchmark dataset and classification model on real-world data. In: Proceedings of the IEEE International Conference on Computer Vision, pp. 1588–1597, IEEE, Seoul, Korea (South) (2019)

19. Lin, Z., Huang, S., Wang, Y.: Convolution in the cloud: learning deformable kernels in 3d graph convolution networks for point cloud analysis. In: Proceedings of the IEEE Conference on Computer Vision and Pattern Recognition, pp. 1797–1806, IEEE, Seattle, WA, USA (2020)

20. Atzmon, M., Maron, H., Lipman, Y.: Point convolutional neural networks by extension operators. ACM Trans. Graphics **4**(71), 1–14 (2018)

21. Xu, Y., Fan, T., Xu, M., Zeng, L., Qiao, Y.: Spidercnn: deep learning on point sets with parameterized convolutional filters. In: Proceedings of the European Conference on Computer Vision, pp. 90–105, Springer, Munich, Germany (2018) https://doi.org/10.1007/978-3-030-01237-3_6

22. Wu, W., Qi, Z., Li, F.: Pointconv: deep convolutional networks on 3d point clouds. In: Proceedings of the IEEE Conference on Computer Vision and Pattern Recognition, pp. 9621–9630, IEEE, Long Beach, USA (2019)

23. Yan, X., Zheng, C., Li, Z., Wang, S., Cui, S.: Pointasnl: robust point clouds processing using nonlocal neural networks with adaptive sampling. In: Proceedings of the IEEE Conference on Computer Vision and Pattern Recognition, pp. 5588–5597, IEEE, Seattle, WA, USA (2020)

24. Xu, Q., Sun, X., Wu, C., Wang, P., Neumann, U.: Grid-gcn for fast and scalable point cloud learning. In: Proceedings of the IEEE Conference on Computer Vision and Pattern Recognition, IEEE, Seattle, WA, USA (2020)

25. Su, H., et al.: Splatnet: sparse lattice networks for point cloud processing. In: Proceedings of the IEEE Conference on Computer Vision and Pattern Recognition, pp. 2530–2539, IEEE, Salt Lake City, UT, USA (2018)

26. Wang, L., Huang, Y., Hou, Y., Zhang, S., Shan, J.: Graph attention convolution for point cloud semantic segmentation. In: Proceedings of the IEEE Conference on Computer Vision and Pattern Recognition, pp. 10296–10305, IEEE, Long Beach, USA (2019)

27. Verma, N., Boyer, E., Verbeek, J.: FeaStnet: feature-steered graph convolutions for 3d shape analysis. In: Proceedings of the IEEE Conference on Computer Vision and Pattern Recognition, pp. 2598–2606, IEEE, Salt Lake City, UT, USA (2018)

ARB U-Net: An Improved Neural Network for Suprapatellar Bursa Effusion Ultrasound Image Segmentation

Zhengyu Wang[1], Qi Yang[1], Han Liu[1], Le Mao[1], Haijiang Zhu[1(✉)], and Xiaoyu Gao[2]

[1] College of Information and Technology, Beijing University of Chemical Technology, Beijing 100029, China
zhuhj@mail.buct.edu.cn

[2] Department of Function Test, First Teaching Hospital of Tianjin University of Tradition Chinese Medicine, Tianjin 300193, China

Abstract. The research on making accurate segmentation of images in ultrasound inspecting is a challenging in the medical image segmentation domain. It is tough to obtain a satisfactory segmentation of U-Net networks in deep learning. The difficulties are contributed to low contrast between detected targets and surrounding tissues, the large differences between target edges and shapes, and so forth. Based on batch-free normalization (BFN) and a residual attention block, a class of Attention Res BFN U-Net (ARB U-Net) network with a deep encoder and a shallow decoder is proposed, and the depth and the performance of the network is improved. With utilizing Dice loss and BCE loss are utilized as segmentation loss and classification loss respectively, a kind of Dice-BCE loss function is constructed on the basis of multi-task weighting strategy. 450 ultrasound images were used as the training set and another 50 images were used as the test set. The average segmentation accuracy of the test data set reached 97.1%, which is about 3% better than that of the traditional U-Net and its common variants. The experimental results show that the proposed network can significantly improve the accuracy and precision of ultrasound image segmentation of suprapatellar bursa.

Keywords: Attention Res BFN U-Net · Res Attention Gate · Dice-BCE loss function · Basicblock

1 Introduction

Synovitis is a common clinical condition, the main symptom of which is fluid in the knee joint. The knee joint is composed of the medial and lateral condyles of the femur, the medial and lateral condyles of the tibia, and the patella. It is the largest joint in the human body with the most complex structure and more opportunities for injury. Therefore, it has more opportunities for injury and infection. Numerous studies have shown that timely and proper treatment can reduce or reverse suprapatellar bursal disease in the knee. However, if the condition is not treated promptly and effectively, the condition may further progress to synovial osteochondromatosis, dendritic lipoma, plica synovialis syndrome, and eventually lead to vascular and hemorrhagic lesions and complications. Therefore, it is of great significance to accurately diagnose suprapatellar bursal disease in the knee.

In recent years, in the field of ultrasound imaging technology, hardware and imaging algorithms have been greatly developed, and the quality of medical ultrasound images has also been greatly improved. This not only makes it possible to extract high-throughput imagingomics features from ultrasound images, but also promotes the development and application of imagingomics in ultrasound disease diagnosis. At present, there are relatively few radiomics studies on ultrasound data. Qiao et al. [1] and Zhang et al. [2] extracted high-throughput radiomics features from two-dimensional ultrasound images for the identification of breast tumors with significant results. Using single-focus ultrasound images of papillary thyroid cancer, Shichong Zhou et al. [3] uncovered fourteen highly pointing ultrasound features with 73% accuracy in predicting lymph node metastasis. Jiawei Li et al. [4] studied ultrasound imaging of invasive breast cancer and discussed the predictive value of radiomics features for hormone receptor expression. With the continuous development of ultrasound imaging and data mining techniques, the research value of ultrasound radiomics has become increasingly prominent. However, there is no ultrasound radiomics research on the evaluation of suprapatellar bursal effusion in the knee.

To improve the accuracy of noninvasive assessment of suprapatellar bursae in the knee by researchers, this paper performs fully automated image segmentation of suprapatellar bursae in the knee by means of deep learning combined with imaging histology. This paper proposes a variant of this method, ARB U-Net, based on BFN, residual attention block, consisting of a deep encoder and a shallow decoder. In terms of loss function, to ensure optimal segmentation and classification effects, this paper proposes a Dice-BCE loss function based on multi-task uncertainty processing, which can dynamically penalize task items with large uncertainty and thus weight the important tasks. Experimental results show that ARB U-Net outperforms U-Net and its common variant networks [5–8].

2   ARB U-Net Network Structure

Based on the original U-Net architecture [9] and the attention gate [10] module, this paper improves the phenomenon that the eigenvalues of pixel points are reduced after the multi-layer stacking of the attention gate module, and adds the residual block [11] to the attention module. Moreover, this paper deals with the problem that the BN estimates are accumulated, and proposes a variant of this method, ARB U-Net, based on BFN and residual attention block (see Fig. 1).

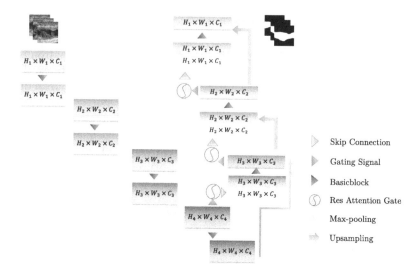

Fig. 1. The proposed ARB U-Net network structure diagram. The encoder is down-sampled by the basicblock residual module, and the decoder uses the R-AGs module for feature selection followed by jump connection. The schematic diagrams of basicblock and R-AGs are shown in Fig. 2 and Fig. 3, respectively.

2.1 Encoder

The encoder proposed in this paper is shown below. The encoder consists of a basicblock residual block and a max-pooling layer, where the basicblock residual block consists of a 1×1 two-dimensional convolution layer and two 3×3 convolution layers as well as a normalization layer and a nonlinear activation layer. Since the number of input and output channels of the basicblock residual block is required to be equal, this paper introduce a 1×1 convolution layer to adjust the number of channels. Specifically, to solve the problem of gradient disappearance and gradient explosion during the training process, this paper use BFN [12] as the normalization layer instead of BatchNorm (BN). Compared with the traditional BN as the normalization layer, we consider that the estimates are accumulated due to the stacking effect of BN in the network, which has a negative impact on the test performance, so we add BFN as the improved BN to the residual module in this paper. In addition, this paper uses Leaky ReLU instead of sigmoid as the nonlinear activation layer [13]. Since for deep networks, when the sigmoid function is backpropagated, the gradient is prone to disappear, and the exponential calculation of the sigmoid function is more computationally intensive, which greatly reduces the computational efficiency of the network.

Compared with the traditional twice convolution, once downsampling coding operation, this paper proposes an improved basicblock residual module. This is because the risk of overfitting during training the network in the field of image segmentation, where the dataset of medical image segmentation is small, and thus we construct constant mapping to effectively suppress the appearance of overfitting.

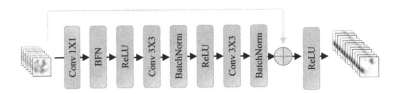

Fig. 2. Schematic diagram of the improved basicblock module. The normalization layer is chosen to replace the conventional BN with BFN.

2.2 Decoder

The decoder structure as a whole is the opposite of the encoder structure, where the decoder consists of an Res Attention Gates (R-AGs) module, one upsampling and a concat layer. Specifically, we choose to introduce an attention mechanism (R-AGs module) to automatically focus on the target region before the fusion of features at each resolution of the encoded and decoded maps to highlight the salient features of the target region without adding an additional deep supervision module, avoiding the problem that the model requires a large number of parameters. In addition, R-AGs improve the model sensitivity and accuracy of dense label prediction by suppressing feature activation in irrelevant regions, realigning the output features of encoder and decoder. The module generates a gating signal that is used to suppress the background feature responses that are not relevant to the target cumulus region, avoiding segmentation of false positive results.

Among them, the R-AGs module is an improved version of the traditional AGs module with feature enhancement.

Specifically, since g comes from the upper layer of x^l, and thus the number of channels of g is $\frac{1}{2}$ of x^l. Firstly, the feature map g in the same layer of encoding layer and the feature map x^l in the same layer of decoding layer are subjected to 1×1 convolution [14] operation to obtain $W_g^T g, W_x^T x^l$. The purpose of this step is that the number of channels and size of feature map g and feature map x_l are adjusted to be the same, so that the two feature maps achieve point-by-point summation.

In order to increase the depth of the network, a Leaky ReLU layer and a linear layer with 1×1 convolution are added after the point-by-point summation of the feature map g and the feature map x^l. Considering that 1×1 convolution operations are performed on g and x^l respectively, adding the Leaky ReLU layer after 1×1 convolution can substantially improve the nonlinear characteristics of

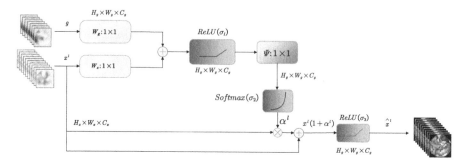

Fig. 3. Schematic diagram of the R-AGs module. Where g is the gating signal, x^l is the input feature, α is the residual attention coefficient, and $\hat{x}^l$ is the feature matrix of the output image.

the network and increase the depth of the network. The attention matrix after feature addition is as follows.

$$q_{att}^l = \psi^T \sigma_1 \left(W_x^T x^l + W_g^T g + b_g \right) + b_\psi \tag{1}$$

Since the ultrasound image of the suprapatellar bursa of the knee has some noise interference in the effusion part of the lesion area, once the triple classification problem of normal tissue, effusion and lesion area is considered, it cannot be directly used in this problem if the sigmoid function is chosen. Instead, if the softmax function is chosen, it can be directly applied to the multi-classification problem. Therefore, the softmax function [15] rather than the sigmoid function is chosen for further discussion in this paper. For the suprapatellar bursa knee fluid segmentation problem, the output attention weight matrix α^l is as follows.

$$\alpha^l = \frac{1}{1 + e^{-\left[\psi^T \sigma_1 \left(W_x^T x^l + W_g^T g + b_g \right) + b_\psi \right]}} \tag{2}$$

The calculated attention coefficient ($\alpha \in (0, 1]$) is Element-wise (element-by-element dot product), because the output normalized to between 0 and 1 and then dot product with the trunk branch will make the output response of the feature map weaker. If this structure is superimposed in multiple layers, the value at each point of the final output characteristic graph will become very small. So after adding 1 to α, the phenomenon of lowering the feature value of each point after multi-layer superposition can be effectively avoided, and the final output feature image will be.

$$\hat{x}^l = \sigma_3 x^l \left(1 + \alpha^l \right) \tag{3}$$

The essence of attention coefficient is a weight matrix, and the value of each element in this matrix is obtained by target learning, which finally achieves the suppression of noise in irrelevant regions and highlights the weight of target regions.

2.3   Loss Function

In the segmentation process of suprapatellar bursa fluid in the knee, the loss function has two contributions, one is segmentation loss and the other is classification loss. In this paper, Dice loss [16] is used as segmentation loss and BCE loss [17] as classification loss, respectively.

$$
\begin{cases}
L_{BCE} = -\left[x_{\text{label}} \ln x_{pt} + (1 - x_{\text{label}}) \ln (1 - x_{pt})\right] \\
L_{\text{Dice}} = 1 - \frac{2|x_{\text{label}} \cap x_{pt}| + 1}{|x_{\text{label}}| \cap |x_{pt}| + 1}
\end{cases}
\tag{4}
$$

Considering the simple approach of defining a hybrid loss function by linear summation for each subtask, the robustness of this hybrid loss function will be poor if the individual tasks are sensitive to the weight parameters. Thus this paper adopts the multi-task likelihoods [18] loss function weighting formula. The loss function dynamically penalizes task terms with large uncertainty, enabling weighting for important tasks. The Dice-BCE loss function is defined as follows.

$$
\begin{aligned}
L_{Dice-BCE} = {} & \frac{1}{2\sigma_1^2} \left\{ -\left[x_{label} \ln x_{pt} + (1 - x_{label}) \ln (1 - x_{pt})\right]\right\} \\
& + \frac{1}{2\sigma_2^2} \left(1 - \frac{2\,|x_{label} \cap x_{pt}| + 1}{|x_{label}| \cap |x_{pt}| + 1}\right) + \ln \sigma_1 \sigma_2
\end{aligned}
\tag{5}
$$

where x_{label} is the label value, x_{pt} is the predicted value, σ_1, σ_2 are the weight relationship factors of the loss functions of the two regression tasks, and $\ln \sigma_1 \sigma_2$ is the regular term of the weight relationship factors σ_1, σ_2.

Since $\ln \sigma_1 \sigma_2$ and $\frac{1}{2\sigma_1^2}, \frac{1}{2\sigma_2^2}$ terms are square logarithms, and the regular term has limited effect on the loss function. We consider changing $\ln \sigma_1 \sigma_2$ to $2\ln \sigma_1 \sigma_2$, so that $2\ln \sigma_1 = s_1$ and $2\ln \sigma_2 = s_2$. So the loss function after the change of simplification is given as follows.

$$
\begin{aligned}
L_{Dice-BCE} = {} & \frac{1}{2e^{s_1}} \left\{ -\left[x_{label} ln x_{pt} + (1 - x_{label}) ln (1 - x_{pt})\right]\right\} + \\
& \frac{1}{2e^{s_2}} \left(1 - \frac{2\,|x_{label} \cap x_{pt}| + 1}{|x_{label}| \cap |x_{pt}| + 1}\right) + s_1 + s_2
\end{aligned}
\tag{6}
$$

The idea of this Dice-BCE loss function is that the uncertainty is measured by σ_1, σ_2. It can be considered that tasks with high uncertainty are noisy and difficult to learn, and the model subsequently weakens the weight of this type of task, thus making the training of the multi-task model smoother and more efficient.

3   Result

3.1   Experimental Environment and Dataset Annotation

The experimental data used in this paper is obtained from a hospital in Tianjin. 450 ultrasound images of the suprapatellar bursa of the knee are selected as the sample training set and 50 images as the test set. The web environment for this article is Python 3.6, Pytorch framework, CPU AMD Ryzen 7 3700X, GPU NVIDIA GeForce RTX 3060 Ti.

Firstly, the image is pre-processed for the frame by frame cropped image, the peripheral irrelevant area of the image is cropped, the effective area of the middle ultrasound image is retained. Moreover, some of the ultrasound image images that are not scanned to the target area are deleted. The remaining image images are reshape, and the image size is all changed to 512×512. Then, the region of suprapatellar bursa accumulation in the ultrasound image is annotated to obtain the mask image with the largest range of the accumulation area, followed by image binarization, setting the target region to 1 and other regions to 0. Afterwards, a series of suprapatellar bursa images are obtained that can be used as training samples. We set the initial learning rate to 0.001, epoch to 200, and batch size to 8. Finally, use Adam optimizer to read the data set into the network for training.

3.2   Evaluation Index

In this paper, the performance of the proposed ARB U-Net network is evaluated using three measures: Dice Coefficient [19], Sensitivity and Hausdorff Distance [20].

Dice Coefficient:

$$Dice = \frac{2\,|x_{label} \bigcap x_{pt}|}{|x_{label}|\bigcap|x_{pt}|} \tag{7}$$

Sensitivity:

$$Sensitivity = \frac{x_{label} \bigcap x_{pt}}{x_{pt}} \tag{8}$$

Harsdorf Distance:

$$d_H = \max\left\{ \max_{x_{pt}\in pt}\left\{ \min_{x_{label}\in label}\left\{ d\,(x_{pt}, x_{label})\right\}\right\}, \max_{x_{label}\in label}\left\{ \min_{x_{pt}\in pt}\left\{ d\,(x_{pt}, x_{label})\right\}\right\}\right\} \tag{9}$$

where x_{label} is the manually labelled image and x_{pt} is the predicted image for the network.

3.3   Quantitative and Qualitative Analysis

We visualised the predicted results to facilitate qualitative analysis by setting the epoch to 5, 10, 20, 50 and 200 respectively and observing the changes in the predicted images(see Fig. 4).

Fig. 4. Changes in predicted images and performance metrics of ARB U-Net networks as epoch increases.

It can be seen that as the epoch increases, the attention of the network is more focused on the part of the suprapatellar bursa fluid in the knee. When the epoch was small, the network was less able to differentiate between the diseased tissue inside the effusion and the normal tissue outside the effusion. As the number of training sessions increased, the differentiation between the diseased tissue and the normal tissue outside the effusion gradually increased, enhancing the network's ability to judge the noise. When the epoch reached 200, the predicted image of the network was very close to the label, and the network learned to focus on the effusion, diseased tissue and normal tissue.

To validate the performance of the ARB U-Net network proposed in this paper, the performance of the network was verified against the U-Net network and several variants of the U-Net network (Fig. 5 and Table 1).

Raw image   Ground truth   U-Net   Large U-Net   Res U-Net   Attention U-Net ARB U-Net

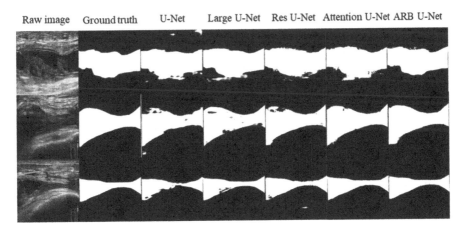

Fig. 5. Comparison of predicted and labeled images from different networks.

Table 1. Quantitative experiments of the proposed segmentation network.

Method	Dice Coefficient	Sensitivity	Hausdorff Distance (mm)
U-Net [9]	0.924	0.971	18.61
Large U-Net [21]	0.951	0.990	4.813
Res U-Net [11]	0.944	0.982	9.590
Attention U-Net [10]	0.923	0.992	14.73
ARB U-Net	0.971	0.994	1.600

Based on the predicted images of the segmentation results, it can be seen that the Large U-Net network uses 5×5 convolution kernels for convolution operation, which increases the amount of operations to nearly three times of the original operations. It is also more capable of edge recognition and has less smooth edge noise. But there is interference from diseased tissues inside the segmented cumulus (it is difficult to distinguish diseased tissues from normal tissues). Therefore, there is more noise for the result segmented inside the effusion. The Res U-Net is weaker than the other networks in terms of both edge recognition and internal noise. The Attention U-Net is inadequate in recognizing the edges of ultrasound images. In summary, it can be seen that the ARB U-Net network proposed in this paper outperforms the other networks in both edge recognition and internal noise reduction.

4   Conclusion

This paper develops a deep learning network to apply to ultrasound image segmentation of suprapatellar capsular effusion in the knee, which is a variant of the BFN, residual attention block-based U-Net network with $L_{Dice-BCE}$ as the loss function to improve the performance of this network. The experimental results show that the proposed model achieves 97.1% accuracy and 99.4% sensitivity in the data set of this paper, while the Harsdorf distance is only 1.6 mm. This work will help physicians to make better clinical diagnosis and treatment planning.

Acknowledgements. This work was supported in part by the National Natural Science Foundation of China under grant No. 61672084.

References

1. Qiao, M., Hu, Y., Guo, Y., et al.: Breast tumor classification based on a computerized breast imaging reporting and data system feature system. J. Ultrasound Med. **37**(2), 403–415 (2018)
2. Zhang, Q., Xiao, Y., Suo, J., et al.: Sonoelastomics for breast tumor classification: a radiomics approach with clustering-based feature selection on sonoelastography. Ultrasound Med. Biol. **43**(5), 1058–1069 (2017)

3. Zhou, S., Liu, T., Zhou, J., et al.: Preliminary study on the application of imaging histology in thyroid cancer. Oncol. Imaging **26**(2), 102–105 (2017)
4. Jiawei, L., Zhaoting, S., Yi, G., et al.: Exploratory study on the predictive value of ultrasound imaging histomics for hormone receptor expression in invasive breast cancer. Oncol. Imaging **26**(2), 128–135 (2017)
5. An, T., Guy, C., Szeverenyi, N.M., et al.: Ultrasound elastography and MR elastography for assessing liver fibrosis: Part 2, diagnostic performance, confounders, and future directions. Am. J. Roentgenol. **205**(1), 33–40 (2015)
6. Castera, L., Vergniol, J., Foucher, J., et al.: Prospective comparison of transient elastography, Fibrotest, APRI, and liver biopsy for the assessment of fibrosis in chronic hepatitis C. Gastroenterology **128**(2), 343–350 (2005)
7. Colli, A., Fraquelli, M., Andreoletti, M., et al.: Severe liver fibrosis or cirrhosis: accuracy of US for detection-analysis of 300 cases. Radiology **227**(1), 89–94 (2003)
8. Aube, C., Oberti, F., Korali, N., et al.: Ultrasonographic diagnosis of hepatic fibrosis or cirrhosis. J. Hepatol. **30**(3), 472–478 (1999)
9. Ronneberger, O., Fischer, P., Brox, T.: U-Net: convolutional networks for biomedical image segmentation. In: Navab, N., Hornegger, J., Wells, W.M., Frangi, A.F. (eds.) MICCAI 2015. LNCS, vol. 9351, pp. 234–241. Springer, Cham (2015). https://doi.org/10.1007/978-3-319-24574-4_28
10. Bi, R., Ji, C., Yang, Z., et al.: Residual based attention-UNet combing DAC and RMP modules for automatic liver tumor segmentation in CT. Math. Biosci. Eng. **19**(5), 4703–4718 (2022)
11. He, K., Zhang, X., Ren, S., Sun, J., et al.: Deep residual learning for image recognition. In: CVPR (2016)
12. Huang, L., Zhou, Y., Wang, T., et al.: Delving into the estimation shift of batch normalization in a network. In: CVPR (2022)
13. Kiliçarslan, S., Celik, M.: RSigELU: a nonlinear activation function for deep neural networks. Expert Syst. Appl. **174**, 114805 (2021)
14. Song, Z., Ma, Y., Tan, F., et al.: Hybrid dilated and recursive recurrent convolution network for time-domain speech enhancement. Appl. Sci. **12**(7), 3461 (2022)
15. Tu, R.C., Mao, X.L., Guo, J.N., Wei, W.: Partial-softmax loss based deep hashing. In: Proceedings of the Web Conference 2021, pp. 2869–2878 (2021)
16. Prencipe, B., Altini, N., Cascarano, G.D., et al.: Focal dice loss-based V-Net for liver segments classification. Appl. Sci. **12**(7), 3247 (2022)
17. Trinh, M.-N., Nguyen, N.-T., Tran, T.-T., Pham, V.-T.: A deep learning-based approach with image-driven active contour loss for medical image segmentation. In: Saraswat, M., Roy, S., Chowdhury, C., Gandomi, A.H. (eds.) Proceedings of International Conference on Data Science and Applications. LNNS, vol. 288, pp. 1–12. Springer, Singapore (2022). https://doi.org/10.1007/978-981-16-5120-5_1
18. Wang, S., Zhu, Y., Lee, S., et al.: Global-local attention network with multi-task uncertainty loss for abnormal lymph node detection in MR images. Med. Image Anal. **77**, 102345 (2022)
19. Soomro, T.A., Afifi, A.J., Gao, J., et al.: Strided U-Net model: retinal vessels segmentation using dice loss. In: Digital Image Computing: Techniques and Applications 2018, pp. 1–8. IEEE (2018)
20. Wu, W., Zhang, X., Qiao, D., et al.: A faulty feeder selection method based on improved Hausdorff Distance Algorithm for neutral non-effectively grounded system. Electric Power Systems Research **203**, 107648 (2022)
21. Zhang, Z., Chen, G., Wang, X., et al.: Fore-Net: efficient inlier estimation network for large-scale indoor scenario. ISPRS J. Photogramm. Remote. Sens. **184**, 165–176 (2022)

BPGG: Bidirectional Prototype Generation and Guidance Network for Few-Shot Anomaly Localization

Junhang Zhang, Zisong Zhuang, Junjie Xu, Tianlong Ma$^{(\boxtimes)}$, and Liang He

East China Normal University, Shanghai, China
{51215901038,51215901056,10195102509}@stu.ecnu.edu.cn,
{tlma,lhe}@cs.ecnu.edu.cn

Abstract. Few-shot anomaly localization task is pixel-level detection of unseen images with only a tiny amount of anomaly training samples. Bound by reality, most conventional training data are defect-free, and models are difficult to accommodate various anomaly types. To this end, we propose a bidirectional prototype generation and guidance network (BPGG), which implements non-parametric metric learning with the help of prototypes. We first trade the position of the support set and query set to construct the adaptive reverse branch. The bidirectional branch structure forces the support set and query set to align with each other and build a consistent metric space. For leveraging the benefits of regular data, we also insert the normal images into the support set and balance the proportion of normal and defective samples. Our experimental study on the MVTec anomaly detection dataset demonstrates that our proposed algorithm outperforms current few-shot SOTA methods, comparable to other unsupervised and self-supervised algorithms. Besides, our BPGG Network is general to detect various types of real-world defects and perform stable detection. The rational utilization of data and innovative architecture in our study provide a novel breakthrough for the task of anomaly location.

Keywords: Anomaly localization · Few-shot learning · Prototype learning

1 Introduction

Anomaly localization detects pixel-wise image regions that deviate from seen non-defective samples. In recent years, anomaly detection has gained widespread traction due to industrial inspection [1,2], video surveillance [15], and medical image analysis [22] applications. The first challenge for anomaly detection is that the anomaly samples are difficult or even impossible to obtain because of the limitations of actual conditions. The high annotation cost has hindered the

---

J. Zhang and Z. Zhuang—Contributed equally.

E. Pimenidis et al. (Eds.): ICANN 2022, LNCS 13531, pp. 24–36, 2022.
https://doi.org/10.1007/978-3-031-15934-3_3

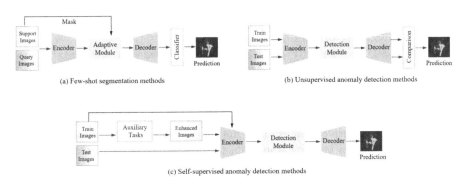

Fig. 1. Illustration of general (a) few-shot segmentation method, (b) unsupervised anomaly detection method and (c) self-supervised anomaly detection method.

general applicability of anomaly detection. For this reason, existing models are required to detect unknown anomaly patterns under the condition that only defect-free data is provided in training sets. Another non-negligible issue is the high intra-class variance, which renders models' generalization and adaptability capabilities valuable.

The majority of existing anomaly localization methods are conducted under unsupervised and self-supervised settings, as shown in Fig. 1. Unsupervised one-class classification pipelines often follow the "reconstructing given samples-checking generated exceptions" paradigm. However, the condition that there is no access to abnormal samples makes it difficult to detect each pixel precisely without instance guidance. Self-supervising models learn high-quality representations by solving different agency tasks [11]. A broad range of studies has designed a variety of complex data enhancement schemes, while the model performance has not met their expectations. We discover that the few-shot setting can effectively alleviate the anomaly localization issue in this scenario.

Few-shot learning is presented to deal with the problem of sample shortage, and it empowers models in the mining and identifying ability by training with only a small amount of data. A wide range of existing studies has proved the considerable generalization and adaptability of few-shot learning. The mainstream ideas adopt meta-learning [6,23] and metric learning [24,25] to eliminate the need to label an extensive training data set. Meta-learning with episodic training strategies [23] enables the model to adapt to a novel class represented by a support set consisting of as few as a single image. Prototype learning in the few-shot scenario, such as [24], takes advantage of the knowledge learned by the model to condense sample features into one or several vectors called prototypes.

Few-shot segmentation pipeline often contains an encoder, a decoder, and a classifier, shown as Fig. 1(a). The encoder conducts the representation of each pixel from input images, the decoder guided by prototypes calculates the likelihood of similarity, and finally the classifier gives the prediction results. Few-shot segmentation and anomaly localization are essentially counted as pixel-level classification tasks. Besides, similar to few-shot segmentation, anomaly localization also faces the context of data acquisition difficulties and requires the ability to adapt to a wide range of intra-class defect differences.

Nevertheless, we can only transfer the idea of few-shot segmentation to anomaly localization due to the two tasks being inconsistent in several details. Multiple defect-free samples are provided in standard anomaly datasets while they can not be routinely utilized for supervised few-shot learning. We present the branch of normal prototype generation and guidance to take full advantage of the non-defective images. This means can alleviate the incompleteness of specific information in a few abnormal samples and provide a more prosperous reference for the pixels of the normal area in testing images. Furthermore, due to the subtlety and diversity of defects, it is tough to develop the ability to quickly pixel-recognize novel classes. To tackle this issue, we append a bidirectional prototype generation and guidance method. We enforce constraints between the original and adaptive prototypes to guarantee that the model will not be tendentious in learning prototypes because of the small sample size.

We make the following contributions in this paper: (1) We propose the bidirectional prototype generation and guidance network (BPGG), a metric-based bidirectional framework for few-shot anomaly localization; (2) We exploit an adaptive reverse branch that aims to fuse the information of both support and query samples so that the query samples can fit prototypes more evenly; (3) For making the most of the normal samples in the existing anomaly localization dataset, we present the prototype guidance branch of normal images. To the best of our knowledge, we are the first to introduce normal samples into a few-shot for anomaly localization; (4) We conduct extensive experiments with two well-known backbones (VGG and ResNet) and achieve state-of-the-art performance on the MVTec AD dataset [1], a real-world industrial visual inspection benchmark.

2   Related Work

2.1   Anomaly Localization

Anomaly localization is a pixel-level form of anomaly detection that addresses abnormal regions' localization in unseen images. Most of the recent unsupervised systems are trained only on anomaly-free images and aim to widen the reconstruction gap between regular and defective samples. These reconstruct methods can be bifurcated into AE-based [3,17] and GAN-based [20,29]. However, some subtle anomalies that are intrinsically different from normal samples are hard to detect, which means these anomalies are often well reconstructed and make the detection less accurate. Some other approaches take advantage of pre-trained models [18,21], which have the generalization ability to transfer knowledge learned from extensive datasets to unsupervised tasks.

All these above methods focus on obtaining high-quality feature representations from normal samples, while recent self-supervised models learn from normal samples that perform auxiliary tasks [9,28]. These auxiliary tasks aim at simulating defects that override real situations. Geometric transformations and geometric augmentations [7,10] are the most familiar modes. However, methods relying on geometric auxiliary perform poorly on defect detection benchmarks due to the relatively shape-constrained generation manner. To evade the issues above, we customize a few-shot anomaly localization setting for this task.

2.2 Few-Shot Learning

Few-shot Learning aims to empower models the mining and identifying ability by training with only a small amount of data. The essential peculiarity of the few-shot setting is that the categories in the train and test set are not intersecting. Models develop strong generalization capabilities through training data and quickly adapt to unseen classes. The majority of existing methods commonly concentrate on two branches: i) Meta-learning: In meta-learning-based methods, the data set is broken down into multiple meta-tasks. The models learn effective weights from small support sets and adapt to new classifications quickly with specific optimization functions [6,26]. ii) Metric learning: The metrics-based methods map the information to a hyperplane space and measure the similarity between samples by specific distance rules [24,25]. Primarily, the utilization of the prototype provides a valuable reference for measurement and leads to a significant improvement in the model performance.

2.3 Few-Shot Segmentation

Few-shot segmentation is a particular case of semantic segmentation in few-shot scenarios, and it focuses on the pixel-level classification of unseen categories with several support samples. OSLSM [23], which attached a conditioning branch for one-shot learning in testing classes, firstly proposed the concept of few-shot segmentation. Dong *et al.* [5] introduced metric learning by measuring the similarity between prototypes and pixels in the query image. Since then, the prototype has been widely used in few-shot segmentation. SG-One [30] presented mask average pooling to obtain object-related prototypes. PMM [27] leveraged the EM algorithm to generate multiple prototypes incorporating spatial semantics from limited support images. However, prototypes have the same relevance in this model. To address this problem, ASGNet [12] utilized the similarity between each prototype and the query feature to select the most relevant prototype.

3 Method

3.1 Problem Definition

Unlike general semantic segmentation, the essential peculiarity of the few-shot setting is that the categories in the training set and testing set are disjoint. It means that the detection model is supposed to perform anomaly localization over novel images from the testing classes totally unseen in the training procedure. Concretely, let $D_{train} = \{(S_i, Q_i)\}, i \in \{1, \cdots, N_{train}\}$ be the training set and

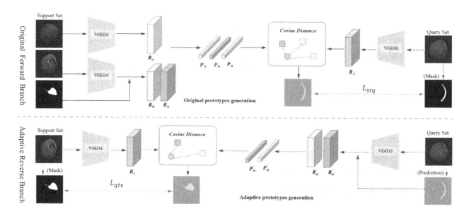

Fig. 2. The overall architecture of the proposed BPGG Network.

$D_{test} = \{(S_j, Q_j)\}, j \in \{1, \cdots, N_{test}\}$ be the testing set, where S and Q denote the support and query, N represents the number of episodes. D_{train} and D_{test} is conducted from non-overlapping classes C_{seen} and C_{unseen} ($C_{seen} \cap C_{unseen} = \emptyset$), respectively. We follow the most frequently used N-way K-shot setting [23] which align training and testing with the episodic paradigm, and for each episode, $S/Q = \left\{ \left(I_{S/Q}^i, M_{S/Q}^i \right) \right\}, i \in \{1, \cdots, K_{S/Q}\}$ are image-binary mask pairs. Here I indicates the image, M refers to the ground truth and K is the sample size. We train our anomaly localization model on the tasks sampled from D_{train} in the training stage and evaluate it on D_{test} in the testing stage. We further discuss the experimental details of the K = 1 case in Sect. 4.

3.2 Method Overview

Previously, due to the difficulty of meeting the training conditions in natural scenes, defect samples are hardly treated as general training sets, and most of the existing training data adopt the form of defect-free. Therefore, to make the best use of the small amount of available anomaly data, we introduce a bidirectional model for few-shot anomaly localization tasks. As illustrated in Fig. 2, our proposed BPGG Network transfers the core idea of prototype learning and metric learning in few-shot segmentation. We first extract the prototypes from the provided samples and classify each pixel by measuring the distance between the representation and the prototypes, as detailed in Sect. 3.3. Based on the prototype learning routine, our bidirectional detection model consists of the original forward branch and adaptive reverse branch which are introduced in Sects. 3.4 and 3.5 respectively. In this section, we elaborate on our proposed model and training strategy in more detail step by step.

3.3 Prototype Generation and Guidance

Prototype Generation. We adopt a weight-shared VGG16 network as the backbone to extract feature information from images of both the support set and query set, which provides a consistent embedding space by learning end-to-end. Then, feature maps in each channel are spatially partitioned into the abnormal features and other features according to the masks. Here we only consider the general defect and the other part. The normal sample and prototype will be explained in Sect. 3.4. Considering that a good many defective images contain only one single object, the information of these images is relatively monotonous and each part of the image is closely related, we calculate the global pixel information as prototypes.

Suppose that R_* and P_* mean the representation and prototype of the particular class, where $* \in \{a, o\}$. In this way, R_a, R_o denote the representation maps of anomaly regions and other regions, and correspondingly P_a, P_o represent the defect and defect-removed prototypes, which are yielded as:

$$P_* = \frac{1}{N_{R_*}} \sum r_*^{x,y} \, \mathbb{C} \left[(x, y) \in M_* \,\&\, r_* \in R_* \right] \tag{1}$$

where N is the total number of pixels in the current R_* region according to the mask M_*, and $\mathbb{C}$ is a two-valued judgement function, when the coordinate (x, y) locates in the M_*, and the r_* belongs to R_* output 1, otherwise 0. Our global pixel method of prototype generation decides to introduce a mask after capturing feature maps through the neural network, which can preserve the characteristics of specific defect information while merging global information. Besides, compared with the strategy of utilizing the mask to segment the original images, our method takes full advantage of the comparative features between the abnormal region and other regions.

Prototype Guidance. Metric learning abstracts the similarity between elements into their distance in the metric space. Most existing methods frequently adopt complex convolutional networks as classifiers but ignore the sample simplicity in a few-shot setting. Fussy convolution and pooling operation can aggravate the over-fitting, especially in the one-shot scene. Therefore, we are inspired by the idea of non-parameter metric learning and introduce the cosine distance $D_*^{x,y}$ between prototypes and pixel-level features as follows:

$$D_i^{x,y}(P_i, r^{x,y}) = \mu \frac{P_i \cdot r^{x,y}}{\|P_i\| \cdot \|r^{x,y}\|} \, , \, i \in \{a, o\} \tag{2}$$

where $r^{x,y}$ denotes the feature of the pixel located at spatial coordinates of (x, y); μ is an empirical expansion coefficient with the value of 30. The final segmentation prediction $G^{x,y}$ is denoted as:

$$G^{x,y} = \underset{i \in \{a,o\}}{\mathrm{argmax}} \left(\frac{exp[-D_i^{x,y}(P_i, r^{x,y})]}{\sum_{i \in \{a,o\}} exp[-D_i^{x,y}(P_i, r^{x,y})]} \right) \tag{3}$$

After harvesting the predictions, the prototype generator is optimized end-to-end through the feedforward cross-entropy loss.

We have completed the basic encoding-decoding routine by means of prototype generation and guidance so far. According to the characteristics of the anomaly localization task, we propose the bidirectional detection framework and append the normal prototype into the support set, which is explained below.

3.4   Original Forward Branch

In reality, the occurrence of defect samples is sporadic, which brings inevitable difficulties to data collection. Therefore, most of the samples in the training set are defect-free, while scarce defect data is used primarily for testing. By this premise, we continue the few-shot anomaly localization setting, take several samples from the testing set and regard them as training samples. We also take normal samples from the original training set of each category to make the most of the defect-free data in the existing anomaly localization dataset. On this basis, we insert the prototype line of normal samples in the original forward branch, as shown in Fig. 2. To maintain the balance between normal and defective samples, we also adopt a one-shot setting with a normal sample. The randomly selected normal sample is regarded as a separate category and participates in the prototype generation and guidance in the original forward branch. As for prototype generation, we take the pixel-level feature average value of the entire image as the typical prototype P_n:

$$P_n = \frac{\sum_{(x,y)\in I_n} r_*^{x,y}}{N_{I_n}} \qquad (4)$$

where N is the total number of pixels in the normal image I_n.

Similar to the method described in Sect. 3.3, we compute the cosine distance by Eq. (2) and adjust segmentation prediction $G^{x,y}$ as follows:

$$G^{x,y} = \operatorname*{argmax}_{i\in\{n,a,o\}} \left(\frac{exp[-\omega_i D_i^{x,y}(P_i, r^{x,y})]}{\sum_{i\in\{n,a,o\}} exp[-\omega_i D_i^{x,y}(P_i, r^{x,y})]} \right) \qquad (5)$$

We attach different confidence coefficients to each prototype through the hyperparameter ω: 0.5 to ω_n and 1 to others. The "Support-to-Query" loss L_{stq} of this branch is defined as:

$$L_{stq} = CE_{Loss}(G_q^{x,y}, M_q^{x,y}) \qquad (6)$$

where $CE_{Loss}(\cdot)$ is the standard cross-entropy loss. With the normal prototype, providing more comprehensive regular information for metric learning alleviates the problem of confusing the defect-free pixels in the non-background region.

3.5   Adaptive Reverse Branch

Due to the monotonous semantic information in the few-shot setting, the general learning routine can not efficiently generalize the model to accommodate novel anomaly categories. Besides, the metric space built by the prototypes of the support set can be biased and not lend itself well to query images. Therefore, we present the adaptive reverse branch to encourage the model to learn consistent embedding prototypes for the support and query set. Our adaptive reverse branch switches the position of the support set and query set. The predictions $G_q^{x,y}$ produced by original forward branches play the role of query masks. With the guidance of $G_q^{x,y}$, the features R_a', R_o' are extracted through the shared VGG and the prototypes P_a', P_o' are calculated according to Eq. (1). The other cross-entropy loss L_{qts} and the whole loss $\mathcal{L}$ are as follows:

$$L_{qts} = CE_{Loss}(G_s^{x,y}, M_s^{x,y}) \, , \tag{7}$$

$$\mathcal{L} = L_{stq} + \alpha L_{qts} \tag{8}$$

where $\alpha = 1$ is an equilibrium number to control variable optimization. Specifically, as an innovative training strategy, the adaptive reverse branch only works in the course of training. During testing, the route ends when the original forward branch is complete.

4   Experiments

4.1   Experiment Setup

Dataset and Metrics. We choose *MVTecAD* [1], a widely used dataset for benchmarking anomaly detection, to evaluate our model performance. *MVTecAD* is an industrial inspection dataset consisting of images from 15 different types of objects. There are 3.6k images of anomaly-free objects in the training set, and 1.7k images in the testing set including 1.2k defective images and 467 images without defects. For the sake of data balance, we fetch 1725 images from the testing set in our work. Similar to previous works, the area under the receiver operating characteristic curve (AUROC) is utilized. Besides, for a more rounded evaluation, we also introduce the foreground-background IoU (FB-IoU) to reflect the accuracy of the anomaly prediction in a global view.

Implementation Details. We adopt VGG16, ResNet18 and ResNet50 as the backbone network. We only retain the first five convolutional layers of VGG16 as the encoder. In order to keep the output size of the feature extractor consistent with the original input size, we enlarge the input image to double and set the stride of the 4th pooling layer to 1. ResNet is adjusted in the same way. The base network is initialized by the pre-trained weights on ILSVRC [19], and then trained end-to-end by SGD with the momentum of 0.9 and 30000 iterations. We set the initial learning rate to 0.001 and reduced it by 0.1 every 10,000 iterations. The weight decay is 0.0005 and the batch size is 1. We exploit data augmentation during training. Input images are transformed with a random scale and then resized to 417×417 as training samples. We make the aspect ratio of cropped

Table 1. AUROC in % among different pixel-level anomaly localization methods on MVTecAD dataset [1]. * represents the omission of some letters.

Method	Group-1			Group-2			Group-3			Group-4			Group-5			Mean
	Bo*	Cab*	Cap*	Car*	Gr*	Ha*	Le*	Me*	Pi*	Sc*	Ti*	To*	Tr*	Wo*	Zi*	
AE_{SSIM} [8]	93	82	94	87	94	97	78	89	91	96	59	92	90	73	88	87
AE_{l2} [8]	86	86	88	59	90	95	75	86	85	96	51	93	86	73	77	82
AnoGAN [22]	86	78	84	54	58	87	64	76	87	80	50	90	80	62	78	74
CNN-FD [16]	78	79	84	72	59	72	87	82	68	87	93	77	66	91	76	78
VEVAE [14]	92	91	92	74	96	98	93	91	93	95	65	99	92	84	87	89
SMAI [13]	88	92	86	93	92	97	80	62	86	85	97	96	96	92	90	89
GDR [4]	74	93	93	92	91	96	84	65	92	92	98	99	95	91	87	89
P-Net [31]	57	91	89	84	79	98	98	97	99	82	97	99	100	70	90	89
MKD [21]	96	82	96	96	92	95	98	86	90	96	83	96	76	85	94	90.7
PMM [27]	90	86	94	99	79	88	99	94	94	97	88	93	78	96	96	91.5
ASGNet [12]	85	51	93	89	97	88	86	98	90	95	87	78	91	94	91	87.5
Ours	94	92	93	98	97	96	99	93	90	96	94	92	83	95	95	**94.0**

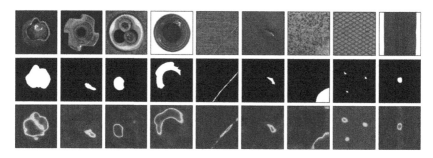

Fig. 3. Illustration of anomaly localization performance on sample classes (arranged vertically by image, ground truth and prediction map).

regions obey U(3/4, 4/3), and the target area ratio obeys U(0.5, 1.0). Following the cross-validation strategy, we split 15 types of objects into five groups, with each group containing three types of objects. As for the one-shot setting, we ensure that there is a normal sample and a defective sample randomly selected in the support set.

4.2 Qualitative Results

We report the comparison results of our method performance on anomaly localization using MVTecAD [1]. Since we are the first to propose the supervised few-shot anomaly localization setup, we can only compare our model with the existing defect detection methods and few-shot segmentation methods. The comparison results are shown in Table 1. Our method is superior to other existing methods in the mean of AUROC. It indicates that only a few additional anomaly samples can significantly improve the defect recognition ability of the model, such

Table 2. Ablation results of normal prototype and bidirectional branches on different backbones.

Method	Prototype$_{normal}$	Bi-branches	AUROC	FB-IoU
ResNet18	✓		91.04(↓ 2.93)	93.01(↓ 2.21)
		✓	91.07(↓ 2.90)	93.53(↓ 1.69)
	✓	✓	90.96(↓ 3.01)	93.11(↓ 2.11)
ResNet50	✓		92.23(↓ 1.74)	91.71(↓ 3.51)
		✓	92.75(↓ 1.22)	92.08(↓ 3.14)
	✓	✓	92.63(↓ 1.34)	92.70(↓ 2.52)
VGG16	✓		93.03(↓ 0.94)	94.51(↓ 0.71)
		✓	93.22(↓ 0.75)	94.89(↓ 0.33)
	✓	✓	93.97(↓ 0.00)	95.22(↓ 0.00)

as the one-shot in this experiment. Due to the difference in the training settings, our work requires less sample size and no additional tasks, the evaluation is not limited to accuracy but is more concerned with adaptability and stability to different(novel) samples. To further demonstrate the effectiveness of the proposed model, we also visualize the anomaly localization map as shown in Fig. 3. It can be observed that the prediction result is very close to the ground truth, and even minor defects can be accurately detected.

4.3   Ablation Study

Backbone. We compare the results on *MVTecAD* with different backbones in Table 2. It can be seen that VGG16 shows better performance than ResNet18 and ResNet50, which suggests that the increased depth of the model can benefit our proposed framework.

Bidirectional Branches. Based on the prototype learning routine, our bidirectional detection model consists of the original forward branch and adaptive reverse branch. To verify the efficacy of the proposed bidirectional branches, we compare the results with $\alpha = 0$ and 1. As shown in Table 2, the adaptive reverse branch brings greater generalization capacity, enabling the proposed model to mine precise feature representations in the consistent embedding space. With the assistance of a bidirectional structure, the model's performance is improved on the detection task.

Normal Prototype. Without normal samples, the model can be affected by the boundary of objects and misidentify the defect-free regions. We remove the normal image input to validate this conjecture in practice. Table 2 displays the experimental results, which illustrates that the introduction of normal prototypes does significantly enhance the validation of defect-free pixels in metric learning.

We engage that normal prototypes can provide contrast for defective images, alleviate the incompleteness of specific information in a few abnormal samples and provide a more prosperous reference for the pixels of the normal area in testing images, and finally reduce the probability of normal pixels being identified as defective pixels by the model.

5   Conclusions

In this paper, we propose a bidirectional prototype generation and guidance network (BPGG) for the task of anomaly localization. Aiming at alleviating the problem of data deficiency and defect diversity, we continue with the few-shot setting. Our model training framework follows the kernel of non-parametric metric learning and consists of two branches. In the original forward branch, we enhanced the influence of non-defect semantic information by introducing a normal sample into the support set. To force the model to fit the unseen images, we add the adaptive reverse branch by interchanging the role of support and query set. We achieve superior results in various experiments and reveal the potential of a few-shot setting for anomaly detection. We expect that more researchers will continue to explore anomaly detection methods under the few-shot settings and present anomaly detection datasets that are more suitable for few-shot learning in the future.

Acknowledgement. This research is funded by the Science and Technology Commission of Shanghai Municipality (20511101205), The computation is performed in ECNU Multifunctional Platform for Innovation (001).

References

1. Bergmann, P., Fauser, M., Sattlegger, D., Steger, C.: MVTec AD-a comprehensive real-world dataset for unsupervised anomaly detection. In: CVPR, pp. 9592–9600 (2019)
2. Bergmann, P., Fauser, M., Sattlegger, D., Steger, C.: Uninformed students: student-teacher anomaly detection with discriminative latent embeddings. In: CVPR, pp. 4183–4192 (2020)
3. Collin, A.S., De Vleeschouwer, C.: Improved anomaly detection by training an autoencoder with skip connections on images corrupted with stain-shaped noise. In: ICPR, pp. 7915–7922. IEEE (2021)
4. Dehaene, D., Frigo, O., Combrexelle, S., Eline, P.: Iterative energy-based projection on a normal data manifold for anomaly localization. In: ICLR (2019)
5. Dong, N., Xing, E.P.: Few-shot semantic segmentation with prototype learning. In: BMVC, vol. 3 (2018)
6. Finn, C., Abbeel, P., Levine, S.: Model-agnostic meta-learning for fast adaptation of deep networks. In: ICML, pp. 1126–1135. PMLR (2017)
7. Golan, I., El-Yaniv, R.: Deep anomaly detection using geometric transformations. In: NIPS, vol. 31 (2018)
8. Hadsell, R., Chopra, S., LeCun, Y.: Dimensionality reduction by learning an invariant mapping. In: CVPR, vol. 2, pp. 1735–1742. IEEE (2006)

9. He, K., Fan, H., Wu, Y., Xie, S., Girshick, R.: Momentum contrast for unsupervised visual representation learning. In: CVPR, pp. 9729–9738 (2020)
10. Hendrycks, D., Mazeika, M., Kadavath, S., Song, D.: Using self-supervised learning can improve model robustness and uncertainty. In: NIPS, vol. 32 (2019)
11. Li, C.L., Sohn, K., Yoon, J., Pfister, T.: CutPaste: self-supervised learning for anomaly detection and localization. In: CVPR, pp. 9664–9674 (2021)
12. Li, G., Jampani, V., Sevilla-Lara, L., Sun, D., Kim, J., Kim, J.: Adaptive prototype learning and allocation for few-shot segmentation. In: CVPR, pp. 8334–8343 (2021)
13. Li, Z., et al.: SuperPixel masking and inpainting for self-supervised anomaly detection. In: BMVC (2020)
14. Liu, W., et al.: Towards visually explaining variational autoencoders. In: CVPR, pp. 8642–8651 (2020)
15. Liu, Y., Li, C.L., Póczos, B.: Classifier two sample test for video anomaly detections. In: BMVC, p. 71 (2018)
16. Napoletano, P., Piccoli, F., Schettini, R.: Anomaly detection in nanofibrous materials by CNN-based self-similarity. Sensors **18**(1), 209 (2018)
17. Park, H., Noh, J., Ham, B.: Learning memory-guided normality for anomaly detection. In: CVPR, pp. 14372–14381 (2020)
18. Reiss, T., Cohen, N., Bergman, L., Hoshen, Y.: PANDA: adapting pretrained features for anomaly detection and segmentation. In: CVPR, pp. 2806–2814 (2021)
19. Russakovsky, O., et al.: ImageNet large scale visual recognition challenge. IJCV **115**(3), 211–252 (2015)
20. Sabokrou, M., Khalooei, M., Fathy, M., Adeli, E.: Adversarially learned one-class classifier for novelty detection. In: CVPR, pp. 3379–3388 (2018)
21. Salehi, M., Sadjadi, N., Baselizadeh, S., Rohban, M.H., Rabiee, H.R.: Multiresolution knowledge distillation for anomaly detection. In: CVPR, pp. 14902–14912 (2021)
22. Schlegl, T., Seeböck, P., Waldstein, S.M., Schmidt-Erfurth, U., Langs, G.: Unsupervised anomaly detection with generative adversarial networks to guide marker discovery. In: Niethammer, M., et al. (eds.) IPMI 2017. LNCS, vol. 10265, pp. 146–157. Springer, Cham (2017). https://doi.org/10.1007/978-3-319-59050-9_12
23. Shaban, A., Bansal, S., Liu, Z., Essa, I., Boots, B.: One-shot learning for semantic segmentation. In: BMVC (2017)
24. Snell, J., Swersky, K., Zemel, R.: Prototypical networks for few-shot learning. In: NIPS, vol. 30 (2017)
25. Vinyals, O., Blundell, C., Lillicrap, T., Wierstra, D., et al.: Matching networks for one shot learning. NIPS **29**, 3630–3638 (2016)
26. Wang, Y.-X., Hebert, M.: Learning to learn: model regression networks for easy small sample learning. In: Leibe, B., Matas, J., Sebe, N., Welling, M. (eds.) ECCV 2016. LNCS, vol. 9910, pp. 616–634. Springer, Cham (2016). https://doi.org/10.1007/978-3-319-46466-4_37
27. Yang, B., Liu, C., Li, B., Jiao, J., Ye, Q.: Prototype mixture models for few-shot semantic segmentation. In: Vedaldi, A., Bischof, H., Brox, T., Frahm, J.-M. (eds.) ECCV 2020. LNCS, vol. 12353, pp. 763–778. Springer, Cham (2020). https://doi.org/10.1007/978-3-030-58598-3_45
28. Ye, M., Zhang, X., Yuen, P.C., Chang, S.F.: Unsupervised embedding learning via invariant and spreading instance feature. In: CVPR, pp. 6210–6219 (2019)
29. Zaheer, M.Z., Lee, J.H., Astrid, M., Lee, S.I.: Old is gold: redefining the adversarially learned one-class classifier training paradigm. In: CVPR, pp. 14183–14193 (2020)

30. Zhang, X., Wei, Y., Yang, Y., Huang, T.S.: SG-One: similarity guidance network for one-shot semantic segmentation. TCYB **50**(9), 3855–3865 (2020)
31. Zhou, K., et al.: Encoding structure-texture relation with P-Net for anomaly detection in retinal images. In: Vedaldi, A., Bischof, H., Brox, T., Frahm, J.-M. (eds.) ECCV 2020. LNCS, vol. 12365, pp. 360–377. Springer, Cham (2020). https://doi.org/10.1007/978-3-030-58565-5_22

CoPrGAN: Image-to-Image Translation via Content Preservation

Xiaoming Yu[✉] and Gan Zhou

National Computer System Engineering Research Institute of China, Beijing, China
xyuforart@gmail.com

Abstract. Image-to-image translation is an interesting and challenging application. At present, it has developed from single-domain to multi-domain and many other aspects. But losing content structure is still an inevitable problem, which is manifested in the details of the objects or the global features of the images. We propose a new framework named CoPrGAN to alleviate the lack of content. CoPrGAN focuses on the expressive ability of content and style in different dimensions. In this way, the model uses multiple dynamic paths between the content encoder and the decoder to transform domains while preserving content structure. The content structure we are concerned with is not just posture and location, but also birthmarks, hair color, environment, etc. Experiments are arranged in animal face change that focus on local details and seasonal change that focus on global information. Both the comparative experiments with state-of-the-art and the ablation experiments demonstrate the superiority of CoPrGAN.

Keywords: GAN · Image-to-Image translation · Dynamic paths

1 Introduction

Image-to-image (I2I) translation has shown great capabilities. It can change the image style in various scenarios, such as oil painting [2], day and night transitions [1], and seasons transitions [35]. In addition to simple scenarios, it can also complete tasks with complex semantics, realizing the exchange of arbitrary faces [5] and the transformation of animal faces [9].

I2I translation usually translates style in the form of latent code or reference image. The latent code is a mapping of image style in the target domain, and the reference image is an image in the target domain. Researchers prefer to perform image translation in both forms at the same time [9,34]. There has been a lot of excellent works on I2I translation. But there are still limitations in content preservation of source domain images. For example, in animal face transformation, most works [9,14] only focus on the changes in the domain, ignoring the hair distribution, body contour, facial features and even the hair color in the source domain animals. In scene style transfer, most works [15,34] focus on style rendering, while ignoring the outlines and positions of different

E. Pimenidis et al. (Eds.): ICANN 2022, LNCS 13531, pp. 37–49, 2022.
https://doi.org/10.1007/978-3-031-15934-3_4

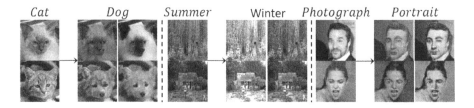

Fig. 1. The generation results of CoPrGAN, including three tasks of Cat→Dog, Summer→Winter, and Photograph→Portrait.

objects in the scene. The preservation of content structure and the fusion of style are two different aspects. Whether we focus more on content structure or more on style is a problem worth considering.

To address the above problem, we propose CoPrGAN, which achieves I2I translation while keeping content information unchanged. Based on the skip connections of the content feature maps, the network dynamically selects branches in each skip connection path, so that the network adaptively maintains the content or fuses style. To achieve end-to-end training of the network and autonomous agency of branch selection, each content feature map before skip path is adaptively converted to branch selection code. Due to the dynamic path module, CoPrGAN generates great results, as shown in Fig. 1. The left side of the arrow represents the source domain images, and the right side of the arrow represents the target domain images. The images maintain the structure specific to the content itself, only the features representing the domain are transformed. The main contributions are as follows:

- We propose a new I2I translation framework, CoPrGAN.
- We use dynamic paths to make the network adaptively preserve content or integrate style.
- Experiments show that, compared with the baselines, CoPrGAN retains the image content and completes the domain translation in the optimal form.

2   Related Work

Image-to-Image Translation. The framework of I2I translation is mainly based on GANs. Initially, researchers focus on supervised image translation [15,31], where the dataset is paired images. Faced with the difficulty of paired image collection, I2I translation develops to the unsupervised stage [35], which includes one-to-one mapping [4,10] and multi-model-based mapping [14,21,26]. Single-domain image translation needs to increase the number of networks in multi-domain conversion scenarios, which will bring deployment difficulties. Driven by the problem, researchers began to use a single model to implement multi-domain image translation [8,24]. [32] use labels to guide the generator to generate images. [9] proposes a multi-branch encoder to map images from different domains to different style space.

Disentanglement. Images are disentangled into content and style to enable I2I translation. MUNIT [14] and DRIT [21] propose that source and target domains share content space and have independent style space. In order to preserve the content structure, images of different domains in DSMAP [3] correspond to independent content space and style space. DMIT [34] implements multi-domain image translation by adding domain vectors based on the shared content space and style space. With the unique structure of U-Net, [1] achieves high-resolution translation. Domain-dependent and domain-independent disentangling in style code helps image generation [33]. This disentanglement also occurs in the few-shot domain [25]. In addition to being disentangled into content and style, [27] uses a domain encoder to extract the domain code, and the interpolation of the domain code helps it complete continuous image translation. For better disentangling, [11] encodes images into relevant and irrelevant attributes.

Dynamic Networks. The structure of the dynamic network is not fixed, and different network structure will be adaptively selected according to different data. [30] uses dynamic paths to improve the accuracy of classification tasks. [29] extends it to realize multi-domain image translation. [22] implements image editing with multiple dynamic paths processing attribute code. There are also works proposing dynamic convolution networks [6] and dynamic filter networks [18] to demonstrate the efficient performance of dynamic structure. [17] fuses content and style with adaptive convolution for multi-domain image translation.

3   Approach

Given source domain images, CoPrGAN can transform the images to the target domain while maximally preserving the content structure. We describe the proposed method in detail. Section 3.1 is an overview of the model. Section 3.2 is the selection of dynamic paths. Section 3.3 includes the loss function and training strategy.

3.1   Model Overview

The overall architecture of CoPrGAN is shown in Fig. 2. Same as MUNIT [14], the source domain images and the target domain images share the content space and have differences in the style space. Thus, we reconstruct the target domain images. On the left is the reconstructed part. The target domain image Y obtains the content code C and the style code S through the content encoder E_c and the style encoder E_s, respectively, where C is multiple content feature maps. C and S are mixed in decoder Dec to generate a reconstructed image. L_{rec} is the reconstruction loss, and L_{KL} is the KL distance between the style code and the prior distribution code. On the right is the translation process. The source domain image X is converted to content code by the content encoder. In order to preserve the content structure of source domain image, style code $p(s)$ is sampled from a standard Gaussian distribution $\mathcal{N}(0, I)$, rather than using a

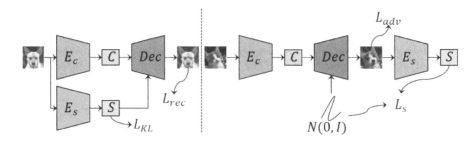

Fig. 2. Overview of the model. On the left is the reconstruction process of the target domain images. On the right is the translation process from the source domain to the target domain.

reference image to guide the generation. The generated image is passed through the style encoder to obtain the reconstructed style code. L_{adv} is the adversarial loss. L_s is the reconstruction loss for style code. It is worth noting that the style encoder is only used for the reconstruction of the target domain image and the reconstruction of the style code. During translation, no style encoder is involved. We omit discriminator D in Fig. 2. It chooses the multi-scale discriminator in [34] and we remove the embedding of domain code. Discriminating the authenticity of images from multiple scales helps the generator to grasp more domain information, increasing the quality of the generated images and the stability of training [31].

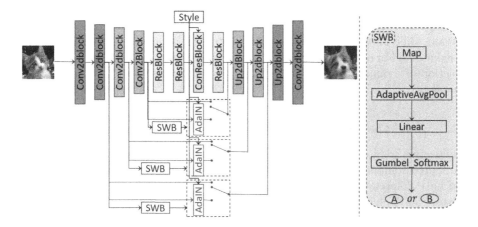

Fig. 3. The selection of dynamic paths. On the left is the dynamic connection paths between the content encoder and the decoder. On the right is the switch block (SWB) for selecting path branches.

3.2 Dynamic Paths

The purpose of CoPrGAN is to preserve the content of the source domain images without affecting the domain transformation. It mainly uses dynamic paths to retain content and integrate style. The structure of the dynamic paths is shown in Fig. 3. The entire network includes three dynamic paths. In the path selection, the content feature map adopts a direct skip connection in the first branch. Another branch uses AdaIN [13] to incorporate style code into feature map. At the end of the skip, the feature map is connected with the decoder in the form of element-wise addition. We don't set dynamic path in the main part of the network. Because skip connection cannot guarantee that at least one branch fits into the style code and the feature map of the main path has richer semantic information. We choose AdaIN to incorporate style code in the main body of the network. In the end, we get four forward paths.

The choice of each dynamic path should not be fixed. Different images have different levels of difficulty in expressing content and style. The model should autonomously choose different branches based on different images. Thus, the dynamic branch is determined by skipping feature maps. The feature map is firstly encoded by SWB to obtain a 1×2 code, and the code represents two branches respectively. The SWB structure is on the right in Fig. 3. The feature map is encoded by AdaptiveAvgPool. Next, a multi-layer Linear transform code dimension. We need an end-to-end network that chooses branches probabilistically. Softmax can make the code reflect the meaning of probability. For branch selection, the intuitive method is to use argmax to decide the branch. But argmax cannot calculate the gradient, and the network cannot be updated. Gumbel_Softmax is available in [16]. We use the trick of Straight-Through Gumbel_Softmax to get discrete values to select branch. The output A (first branch) or B (second branch) in the SWB is determined by Gumbel_Softmax.

Each skip connection contains two branches. If the network is directly trained, there will be extreme states, the network only passes through the first branch or the second branch, which makes the dynamic paths invalid. Inspired by [30], we set a penalty on the branch selection ratio, introducing an additional loss. The loss function is detailed in Sect. 3.3. Taking the second branch as the criterion, the target probability of the network passing through the second branch is t. We expect that different images can adapt to their own branches, the t can affect the generated results. The numerical choice of t is discussed in the ablation study.

3.3 Training Strategy

Figure 2 includes several losses for model training. Among them are adversarial loss, image reconstruction loss, style reconstruction loss and style KL loss.

Adversarial Loss. Adversarial loss can help model transform domains. The form of LSGAN [28] is used to compute the adversarial loss.

$$L_{adv}^{D} = \|D(Y) - 1\|_2 + \|D(G(E_c(X), p(s))) - 0\|_2 \tag{1}$$

$$L^G_{adv} = \|D(G(E_c(X), p(s))) - 1\|_2 \tag{2}$$

Image Reconstruction Loss. In CoPrGAN, the source and target domains share the content space but not the style space. Therefore, we compute the reconstruction loss for the target domain images. L1 norm is used to calculate the difference between target domain image and reconstructed image.

$$L_{rec} = \|G(E_c(Y), E_s(Y)) - Y\|_1 \tag{3}$$

Style Reconstruction Loss. The calculation of the style reconstruction loss is partly the style code sampled from the prior distribution, and the other part is the style code of the generated image. L1 norm is used to compute the loss for both code.

$$L_s = \|E_s(G(E_c(X), p(s))) - p(s)\|_1 \tag{4}$$

KL Loss. When VAE [20] is used as a style encoder [34], we expect the output of the encoder to gradually approach the prior Gaussian distribution.

$$L_{KL} = KL(E_s(Y)\|p(s)) \tag{5}$$

Additional Loss. The second branch of the skip connection requires fusing style. In the three paths z, all are opened with probability t.

$$L_{add} = \sum_{i=1}^{3}(z_i - t)^2 \tag{6}$$

Total Loss. We can get the loss functions of the generator and discriminator.

$$L_D = L^D_{adv} \tag{7}$$

$$L_G = L^G_{adv} + \lambda_{rec}L_{rec} + \lambda_s L_s + \lambda_{KL}L_{KL} + \lambda_{add}L_{add} \tag{8}$$

Training Strategy. In all translation tasks, the learning rate is kept at 0.0001 and the batch size is 4. The weight of the loss function is set to $\lambda_{rec} = 10$, $\lambda_s = 1$, $\lambda_{KL} = 0.01$, $\lambda_{add} = 2$. In full model, the values of t are 0.5 and 0.6. We choose Adam as the optimizer with parameters set to (0.5, 0.999). Image size remains 256×256. Experiments are trained in NVIDIA RTX 3080 GPU.

4   Experiments

In this section, we demonstrate the content-preserving capability of CoPrGAN. Experiments are conducted in animal image translation and landscape image translation. First, we introduce the datasets and baselines. Then, the generated results of CoPrGAN and baselines are evaluated both visually and numerically. Next, ablation experiments are performed to verify the effectiveness of dynamic paths. Some discussion follows.

4.1   Datasets

Cat→Dog. We choose the animal dataset provided in StarGAN v2 [9]. The dataset includes three categories: cats, dogs, and wild animals. The cat and dog images are extracted for training CoPrGAN.

Summer→Winter. Landscape image translation selects summer2winter-yosemite. This public dataset is provided by CycleGAN [35].

4.2   Baselines

We choose four I2I translation models as baselines. MUNIT [14] disentangles images into content and style. The source domain images and the target domain images share the content space and have independent style space. DSMAP [3] maps shared content space into domain-specific to hold content. GDWCT [7] is a combination of WCT [23] and image translation. U-GAT-IT [19] implements unsupervised image translation using an attention module and a functional instance normalization layer AdaLIN.

4.3   Quality Comparison

Visual Evaluation. Figure 4 shows the generated results of CoPrGAN and baselines. In animal face translation, the images generated by MUNIT and GDWCT have obvious artifacts. The animal face preservation of DSMAP is better, but the backgrounds of the images are changed. On the contrary, the animal faces generated by U-GAT-IT are not clear enough, but the preservation of the backgrounds is improved. The animal faces and environments generated by CoPrGAN are most similar to the original images. In landscape image translation, both the generated images of MUNIT and DSMAP have artifacts, and the content of the original image remains unclear. The content of GDWCT and U-GAT-IT is well preserved, but the global feature conversion is not enough. CoPrGAN captures winter features and remains content structure.

Numerical Evaluation. Domain-invariant perceptual distance (DIPD) [14,25] is used to evaluate the structural similarity between the generated images and the input images, the lower the value, the more similar the structure. Frechet inception distance (FID) [12] is often used to evaluate the quality of the generated

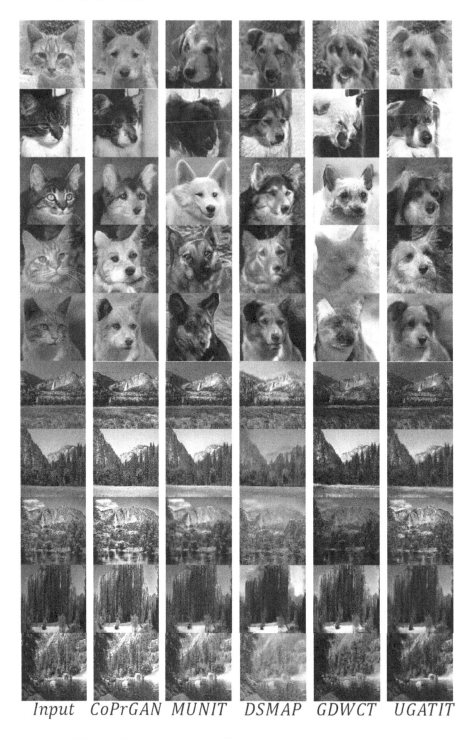

Input   CoPrGAN   MUNIT   DSMAP   GDWCT   UGATIT

Fig. 4. The comparisons of Cat→Dog and Summer→Winter.

Table 1. The results of DIPD and FID.

Tasks	Cat→Dog		Summer→Winter	
	DIPD↓	FID↓	DIPD↓	FID↓
MUNIT [14]	1.922	85.9	1.790	91.7
DSMAP [3]	1.900	98.9	1.737	95.9
GDWCT [7]	1.710	143.0	1.387	94.2
U-GAT-IT-light [19]	1.904	111.6	1.777	76.2
w/o AdaIN	1.539	96.9	0.800	71.9
w/o skip	1.672	96.3	1.051	66.0
w/o AS	1.662	86.7	1.446	79.7
$t = 0.4$	1.612	91.5	0.813	67.9
$t = 0.5$	**1.565**	**89.5**	0.887	64.6
$t = 0.6$	1.612	98.3	**0.957**	**60.3**

images. We take the generated images and the target domain images as input, and calculates the distribution similarity of the two types, that is, the smaller the value, the higher the quality. For multi-output models, we take the first 100 images of the test set as input, and randomly output 10 images from each input. For single-output models, we use all test set images. Table 1 contains the results of DIPD and FID. In Cat→Dog, The DIPD of CoPrGAN reaches the lowest, with a minimum difference of 0.145 from baselines. MUNIT achieves the lowest FID, but compared with CoPrGAN, DIPD differed by the largest 0.357, while FID differed by 3.6. 0.357 is more than 2 times of 0.145. We want maximum retention of content, so trade FID (3.6) for DIPD. In Summer→Winter, both DIPD and FID of CoPrGAN reach the minimum compared with baselines.

4.4   Ablation Study

To verify the effectiveness of the dynamic paths, we ablate them. Each dynamic path consists of two branches, one focusing on content and the other focusing on style. Therefore, we set up three group experiments: w/o AdaIN (retaining the direct addition branch of the content), w/o skip (retaining the AdaIN branch), w/o AS (removing the two branches).

The choice of t affects the direction of the path, too large or too small can make the model enter extreme states. We choose intermediate values 0.4, 0.5, 0.6 for experiments. The cases of w/o AdaIN and w/o skip are equivalent to experiments in extreme states of $t = 0$, $t = 1$.

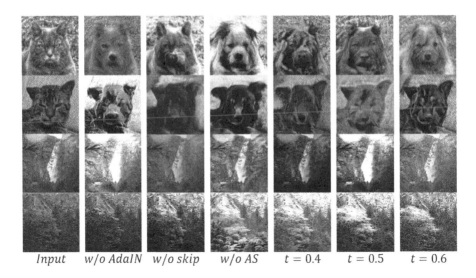

| Input | w/o AdaIN | w/o skip | w/o AS | t = 0.4 | t = 0.5 | t = 0.6 |

Fig. 5. The results of ablation study.

Input   *Output*   *Input*   *Output*

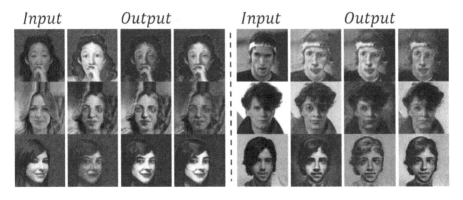

Fig. 6. Additional experiment. The dataset named portrait is provided by DRIT [21].

Figure 5 shows the results of the ablation experiments. The content and style represented by the two branches are different, and the probability of their passing can affect the quality of the images. Through t, a balance between style and content can be found to improve the generation effect. Table 1 also contains the results of the ablation experiments. w/o AdaIN uses content skip connections to achieve the lowest DIPD but higher FID values. Neither w/o skip nor w/o AS hold content well. In the experiments of t, we choose the values of t corresponding to the minimum value of FID as the generative model.

4.5 Discussions

I2I translation is also widely used in face scenarios. Face image translation requires high semantic information, which is usually accompanied by changes in the shape of objects. These changes are similar to animal face transformation. We add an additional experiment, Photograph→Portrait. Figure 6 is the generated results. From a subjective point of view, CoPrGAN can convert photographs into vivid portraits.

Through multiple sets of experiments, the content retention of CoPrGAN has been verified. Figures 1 and 6 show the generation results under random style in different tasks. There are only minor differences between each set of generated images, but this is the result of maximizing the preservation of content structure and does not represent a breakdown. The model relies on strong content constraints to still change features that only represent the domain, such as a dog's nose and eyes, snow in winter, and paint colors in portraits, so the model is successful.

5   Conclusion

This paper proposes a model for I2I translation that solves the problem of losing content. The skip connections between the content encoder and the decoder are in the form of dynamic paths. In each dynamic path, the content feature map passes through the SWB to determine the direction of conveying information, whether to convey content or style. Compared to baselines, the model generates high-quality images that preserve poses, birthmarks, hair color, etc., and are translated from the source domain to the target domain. In the future, we will continue to explore the disentanglement of content and style, increase user control over the process, and create more beneficial applications.

Acknowledgements. We thank the reviewers for their constructive comments. And we thank predecessors in the field of I2I translation for their inspiring works.

References

1. Anokhin, I., et al.: High-resolution daytime translation without domain labels. In: CVPR, pp. 7488–7497 (2020)
2. Barzilay, N., Shalev, T.B., Giryes, R.: Miss GAN: a multi-illustrator style generative adversarial network for image to illustration translation. Pattern Recogn. Lett. **151**, 140–147 (2021)
3. Chang, H.-Y., Wang, Z., Chuang, Y.-Y.: Domain-specific mappings for generative adversarial style transfer. In: Vedaldi, A., Bischof, H., Brox, T., Frahm, J.-M. (eds.) ECCV 2020. LNCS, vol. 12353, pp. 573–589. Springer, Cham (2020). https://doi.org/10.1007/978-3-030-58598-3_34
4. Chen, J., Liu, G., Chen, X.: AnimeGAN: a novel lightweight GAN for photo animation. In: Li, K., Li, W., Wang, H., Liu, Y. (eds.) ISICA 2019. CCIS, vol. 1205, pp. 242–256. Springer, Singapore (2020). https://doi.org/10.1007/978-981-15-5577-0_18

5. Chen, R., Chen, X., Ni, B., Ge, Y.: SimSwap: an efficient framework for high fidelity face swapping. In: ACM MM, pp. 2003–2011 (2020)
6. Chen, Y., Dai, X., Liu, M., Chen, D., Yuan, L., Liu, Z.: Dynamic convolution: attention over convolution kernels. In: CVPR, pp. 11030–11039 (2020)
7. Cho, W., Choi, S., Park, D.K., Shin, I., Choo, J.: Image-to-image translation via group-wise deep whitening-and-coloring transformation. In: CVPR, pp. 10639–10647 (2019)
8. Choi, Y., Choi, M., Kim, M., Ha, J.W., Kim, S., Choo, J.: StarGAN: unified generative adversarial networks for multi-domain image-to-image translation. In: CVPR, pp. 8789–8797 (2018)
9. Choi, Y., Uh, Y., Yoo, J., Ha, J.W.: StarGAN V2: diverse image synthesis for multiple domains. In: CVPR, pp. 8188–8197 (2020)
10. Dong, H., Neekhara, P., Wu, C., Guo, Y.: Unsupervised image-to-image translation with generative adversarial networks. arXiv preprint arXiv:1701.02676 (2017)
11. Gabbay, A., Hoshen, Y.: Scaling-up disentanglement for image translation. In: ICCV, pp. 6783–6792 (2021)
12. Heusel, M., Ramsauer, H., Unterthiner, T., Nessler, B., Hochreiter, S.: GANs trained by a two time-scale update rule converge to a local nash equilibrium. In: NeurIPS, vol. 30 (2017)
13. Huang, X., Belongie, S.: Arbitrary style transfer in real-time with adaptive instance normalization. In: ICCV, pp. 1501–1510 (2017)
14. Huang, X., Liu, M.Y., Belongie, S., Kautz, J.: Multimodal unsupervised image-to-image translation. In: ECCV, pp. 172–189 (2018)
15. Isola, P., Zhu, J.Y., Zhou, T., Efros, A.A.: Image-to-image translation with conditional adversarial networks. In: CVPR, pp. 1125–1134 (2017)
16. Jang, E., Gu, S., Poole, B.: Categorical reparameterization with Gumbel-Softmax. arXiv preprint arXiv:1611.01144 (2016)
17. Jeong, S., Lee, J., Sohn, K.: Multi-domain unsupervised image-to-image translation with appearance adaptive convolution. In: ICASSP, pp. 1750–1754. IEEE (2022)
18. Jia, X., De Brabandere, B., Tuytelaars, T., Gool, L.V.: Dynamic filter networks. In: NeurIPS, vol. 29 (2016)
19. Kim, J., Kim, M., Kang, H., Lee, K.H.: U-GAT-IT: unsupervised generative attentional networks with adaptive layer-instance normalization for image-to-image translation. In: ICLR (2020)
20. Kingma, D.P., Welling, M.: Auto-encoding variational Bayes (2014)
21. Lee, H.Y., Tseng, H.Y., Huang, J.B., Singh, M., Yang, M.H.: Diverse image-to-image translation via disentangled representations. In: ECCV, pp. 35–51 (2018)
22. Li, B., et al.: DyStyle: dynamic neural network for multi-attribute-conditioned style editing. arXiv preprint arXiv:2109.10737 (2021)
23. Li, Y., Fang, C., Yang, J., Wang, Z., Lu, X., Yang, M.H.: Universal style transfer via feature transforms. In: NeurIPS, vol. 30 (2017)
24. Liu, A.H., Liu, Y.C., Yeh, Y.Y., Wang, Y.C.F.: A unified feature disentangler for multi-domain image translation and manipulation. In: NeurIPS, vol. 31 (2018)
25. Liu, M.Y., et al.: Few-shot unsupervised image-to-image translation. In: ICCV, pp. 10551–10560 (2019)
26. Mao, Q., Lee, H.Y., Tseng, H.Y., Ma, S., Yang, M.H.: Mode seeking generative adversarial networks for diverse image synthesis. In: CVPR, pp. 1429–1437 (2019)
27. Mao, Q., Tseng, H.Y., Lee, H.Y., Huang, J.B., Ma, S., Yang, M.H.: Continuous and diverse image-to-image translation via signed attribute vectors. In: IJCV, pp. 1–33 (2022)

28. Mao, X., Li, Q., Xie, H., Lau, R.Y., Wang, Z., Paul Smolley, S.: Least squares generative adversarial networks. In: ICCV, pp. 2794–2802 (2017)
29. Nguyen, T.P., Lathuiliére, S., Ricci, E.: Multi-domain image-to-image translation with adaptive inference graph. In: ICPR, pp. 5368–5375. IEEE (2021)
30. Veit, A., Belongie, S.: Convolutional networks with adaptive inference graphs. In: ECCV, pp. 3–18 (2018)
31. Wang, T.C., Liu, M.Y., Zhu, J.Y., Tao, A., Kautz, J., Catanzaro, B.: High-resolution image synthesis and semantic manipulation with conditional GANs. In: CVPR, pp. 8798–8807 (2018)
32. Wu, P.W., Lin, Y.J., Chang, C.H., Chang, E.Y., Liao, S.W.: RelGAN: multi-domain image-to-image translation via relative attributes. In: ICCV, pp. 5914–5922 (2019)
33. Yang, G., Fei, N., Ding, M., Liu, G., Lu, Z., Xiang, T.: L2M-GAN: learning to manipulate latent space semantics for facial attribute editing. In: CVPR, pp. 2951–2960 (2021)
34. Yu, X., Chen, Y., Liu, S., Li, T., Li, G.: Multi-mapping image-to-image translation via learning disentanglement. In: NeurIPS, vol. 32 (2019)
35. Zhu, J.Y., Park, T., Isola, P., Efros, A.A.: Unpaired image-to-image translation using cycle-consistent adversarial networks. In: ICCV, pp. 2223–2232 (2017)

Cross Domain Evaluation of Text Detection Models

Adamu Ali-Gombe[1], Eyad Elyan[1], Carlos Moreno-García[1],
and Chrisina Jayne[2(✉)]

[1] Robert Gordon University, Aberdeen, UK
[2] Teesside University, Middlesbrough, UK
`c.jayne@tees.ac.uk`

Abstract. Text detection is a very common task across a wide range of domains, such as document image analysis, remote identity verification, amongst others. It is also considered an integral component of any text recognition system, where the performance of recognition tasks largely depends on the accuracy of the detection of text components. Various text detection models have been developed in the past decade. However, localizing text characters is still considered as one of the most challenging computer vision tasks within the text recognition task. Typical challenges include illumination, font types and sizes, languages, and many others. Furthermore, detection models are often evaluated using specific datasets without much work on cross-datasets and domain evaluation. In this paper, we present an experimental framework to evaluate the generalization capability of state-of-the-art text detection models across different application domains. Extensive experiments were carried using different established methods: EAST, CRAFT, Tessaract and Ensembles applied to various publicly available datasets. The generalisation performance of the models was evaluated and compared using precision, recall and F1-score. This paper opens a future direction in investigating ensemble models for text detection to improve generalisation.

Keywords: Text detection · Efficient and Accurate Scene Text Detector · Character Aware Region Awareness for Text Detection · Tesseract · Ensembles

1 Introduction

Text detection separates text from non-text objects in a given image or video while recognition classifies and identifies text from images. An example is extracting labels, and annotations from engineering diagrams [8]. Text recognition is common across a wide range of applications. Examples include surveillance, number plate recognition, information retrieval, and others [16]. Similar to other computer vision tasks, text detection and recognition have seen significant progress in recent years due to the latest development in Deep Learning [4]. Traditional text recognition methods consist of localising individual characters, building a features space, and use specific machine learning algorithms for the classification tasks (recognition) [16]. In the deep learning era, it is common to see an end-to-end framework for text recognition, or simply splitting it into detection and recognition components [15].

Despite the significant achievement in text detection and recognition in recent years [12,24,25], localising and recognising text in specific domains still a very challenging task. For example, consider the Processing and Instrumentation Diagram (P&ID) which is commonly used in the Oil and Gas industry (Fig. 2). Such diagrams contain various types of graphic elements (symbols, lines, other shapes), and text which in most cases overlap with other elements and thus makes the text detection task more challenging [8]. This scenario shows that the complexity of text detection/recognition can also be found in many other domains, including document verification, medical images, and others.

A relatively recent review paper [18] shows that, despite the significant progress in deep learning, and in particular applied to the computer vision domain, traditional text detection and recognition methods are still widely used in such complex scenarios. Nonetheless, they are largely ineffective as they are incapable of dealing with the aforementioned issues (i.e. shape overlap).

The typical approach in deep learning is to use a Convolution Neural Network (CNN) to detect and localise text [13]. For recognition, a Recurrent Neural Network (RNN) is commonly employed [12] to read words and sequences from image features. Other end-to-end systems combine both CNN and RNN to localise and recognise text from images [26]. Deep learning approaches have become more popular recently because learned features are more invariant to text recognition challenges. However, some challenges like text perspective are better handle with dedicated modules such as the rectification network in [26]. This can add to the complexity/scalability of the model in a typical application domain. The availability of public datasets and text detection challenges have elevated the performance of text recognition models. These datasets have provided text detection task in three main scenarios; text detection from a scanned document, focused text detection and text detection in the wild. Samples and tasks in these datasets are carefully curated and may not necessarily reflect the real-world domain.

In this paper, we evaluate the performance of state-of-the-art text detection models. We analysed how these models generalise on similar tasks in different datasets. We focused on the text detection task and we consider the text detection models: Efficient and Accurate Scene Text Detector (EAST) [33], Character Aware Region Awareness for Text Detection (CRAFT) [2], and Tesseract. We evaluate these models on ICDAR2013 [10], ICDAR2015 [9], MIDV-500 [1] datasets and P&ID diagrams. We also created an ensemble of the outputs from various models to address text detection challenges in P&ID.

The rest of the paper is organised as follows. In Sect. 2, related text recognition literature is reviewed and discussed. Section 3 presents the methods used in this work. Section 4 discusses in details the experimental set-up and the datasets used. Findings are discussed in Sect. 5. Finally, we conclude and suggest future directions in Sect. 6.

2 Related Work

Traditional Optical Character Recognition (OCR) systems rely on features engineering to isolate a character. These are good at localising text from a scanned document and focused texts. However, they require pre-processing steps such as binarisation and de-blurring to de-noise images in most cases. Pre-processing steps could be domain-dependent and adds an extra step in the detection pipe. For instance, Strokelets [32] are a multiscale representation of different structural characteristics of characters ranging from arcs and corners to the character itself. Again, a region-based detector like Features pooling [11], combines pixelwise low-level features by using a region-based pooling scheme. This was found to perform better than Histogram of Gradients (HOG) features in terms of both speed and accuracy. However, Curved text, perspective text and text detection in the wild are challenging for traditional OCR system. Thus, there is a renewed interest in modern deep learning approaches.

Deep learning based models are preferred over traditional approaches because they address text detection challenges better [8,16]. These approaches could be categorised based on different characteristics such as prediction pipeline (single shot/text proposal networks), model type (discriminative/generative model), the task (document, perspective text and text in the wild) or bounding box post-processing technique (bounding box regression and binarisation methods). Loosely, we use the detection pattern to categorise deep learning approaches: character-based, word-based, line-based or a text segmentation-based approach.

2.1 Character-Based Detectors

Character-based methods rely on character features and shape in the detection pipeline to isolate, fine-tune or build the final text. Shi *et al.* [23] proposed Segment Linking (SegLink) approach to detecting oriented texts. Segments are parts of a word or text line while a link connects two adjacent segments belonging to the same word. Both were predicted using a VGG-16 backbone with convolutional predictors. A depth-first search was used to find connected segments from a word. SegLink is efficient in terms of speed and in detecting oriented texts. However, spaces between texts are not uniform, and SegLink fails in detecting text with large character spacing.

Similarly, Character Region Awareness Text Detector (CRAFT) [2] is a deep model that performs text detection using character-level detection with character affinity. CRAFT was designed to handle curved and long texts which are challenging cases for rigid word box predictors. CRAFT uses weak supervision to estimate character-level ground truths which are lacking in-text detection datasets. Affinity and region scores are used to guide the model during training. Craft out-performed state-of-the-art model on ICDAR2013, ICDAR2015, ICDAR2017 and MSRA-TD500 datasets.

2.2   Word-Based Detectors

Words are irregular in the wild with obvious challenges such as scale, perspective and curved sequences [26]. Irregular texts detection was addressed by Attention Scene Text Recognizer with Flexible Rectification (ASTER) using a rectification network. The rectification step uses Spatial Transformer Networks (STN) [7] to transforms curved texts into regular horizontal text image before a recognition model is applied. An interesting aspect of this is that rectification does not require human annotation or character level detection. Experiments were conducted on ICDAR datasets [9,10], CUTE80 [22], SVT-Perspective [20], Street View Text (SVT) [29] and IIIT5k-Words (IIIT5k) [17] and SynthText [5], and results reported show superior performances over existing techniques.

Using a fully convolutional network and NMS, Efficient and Accurate Scene Text Detector (EAST) [33] achieved state-of-the-art performance on ICDAR2015 dataset. EAST uses a novel loss function and does not require text region proposal, word partitioning or other intermediate steps. The Fully Convolutional Network (FCN) outputs text score maps and geometry from multiple channels which are passed to Non-Maximum Suppression (NMS) for post-processing. The model was designed to use rotated boxes or quadrangles for detection and a separate loss was used for each case. Results showed that EAST performed well in challenging scenarios such as irregular illumination, low resolution, orientation and perspective distortion.

2.3   Line-Based Detectors

Line-based detectors combine a sequence of text detection into text lines or directly localise text line as objects. Cascade Convolutional Text Network (CCTN) [6] detect whole text region and text line from a coarse low-resolution image to fine-grain as regions are enlarged. Interestingly, this approach does not rely on any post-processing. Rectangular convolutions with in-network fusion is employed to handle multi-shape and multi-scale text lines. The model consists of a coarse network that outputs per pixel heat map that indicates the location and probability of the text region. And a fine network that outputs two heats map representing a finer text line and text area. Experiments showed that CCTN has a high discriminative ability to distinguish text and no text line in multiple text variations while surpassing best results on ICDAR datasets.

Connectionist Text Proposal Networks (CTPN) [28] is an extension of Region Proposal Networks (RPN) [21] in text detection. Text line proposals are generated from convolution maps obtained from a VGG-16 network. Then a vertical anchor mechanism is used to predict text, non-text score and y-axis location of each proposal. An in-network recurrence layer is used to improve text context (using RNN with LSTM) to refine location in the vertical direction. Then side refinement is used to estimate offsets of each proposal in a horizontal direction. This essentially connects sequential text proposals. CTPN was effective on multi-lingual and multi-scale (i.e. small scale text) problems and are quite fast at about 0.14s per image (GPU time). CTPN out-performed other existing detection methods on ICDAR, SWT and MULTILINGUAL [19] datasets.

2.4 Segmentation-Based Detectors

While other approaches rely on word/text/line proposals and eliminate false detection in post processes, segmentation methods approach detection in a holistic manner [31]. For instance, Liao *et al.* used a lightweight segmentation network with a novel Differentiable Binarisation (DB) module [14] to detect text from images. DB adaptively predict threshold values at different pixels to isolate text from background. The DB+segmentation set-up is trainable end-to-end, lightweight and consequently a very fast detector. At inference, bounding boxes are generated from binary and probability maps. Extensive experiments showed that DB is robust and effective in detecting curved and multi-lingual texts. Subsequently, DB became the choice detector in text recognition system such as PP-OCR [3] for its computational efficiency.

Yao *et al.* in [31] approached text detection as a semantic segmentation task. Using a single CNN, the authors detected texts from pixel-wise prediction maps and build a graph that predicts character properties such as scale, location, orientation and others. The framework predicts text regions, individual characters and the relationships between them at run time. Experiments were conducted on COCO-Text, ICDAR2013, ICDAR2015 and MSRA-TD500 dataset. The results show that the model out-performed existing methods and was invariant to text orientation, font, scale and local distractors.

All these models excel in many different ways but are limited in certain context. For instance, contextual information is lost in selecting correct text boxes in proposals and also text bounding boxes have a much larger aspect ratio than objects. A common limitation of all segmentation approaches is that they fail to detect correctly text that is enclosed in another text.

3 Models

3.1 EAST

The EAST model utilised in this experiment uses a ResNet50 stem rather than PVANet2x. Although the same U-shape is maintained with the model divided into feature extraction branch, a feature merging branch and the output branch. The network outputs a score map (confidence) for pixel locations and a set of geometry representing the predicted text boxes. Again, the output geometry is based on a rotated box only. Outputs regions are further post-processed by binarising each region followed by a locality aware NMS to obtain the best possible text location. The loss function is a sum of the score map loss and the geometry loss, $L = L_s + \lambda_g L_g$ where λ_g is a hyper-parameter. Score map is evaluated using class-balanced cross entropy [30] as shown in Eq. 1. The geometry loss is the sum of IOU using Axis-Aligned Bounding Box (AABB), and the rotation angle loss, $L = L_{AABB} + L_\theta$. This is shown in Eq. 2.

$$L_s = balanced\text{-}xent(\hat{Y}, Y^*)$$
$$= -\beta Y^* \log \hat{Y} - (1 - \beta)(1 - Y^*) \log(1 - \hat{Y})$$

$$(1)$$

$$L_{AABB} = -\log IoU(\hat{R}, R^*)$$
$$L_\theta = 1 - \cos(\theta, \hat{\theta^*})$$

(2)

where $\hat{Y}$ is the predicted score map, Y^* is the ground truth, β is a balancing factor, $\hat{R}$ is the predicted AABB geometry, R^* is the ground truth, $\hat{\theta}$ is the predicted rotation angle and θ^* is the corresponding ground truth. See [33] for details on the loss functions.

3.2 CRAFT

CRAFT model is similar to EAST in terms of architecture. Both use the same U-Net structure however, CRAFT relied on a VGG-16 backbone. Again, CRAFT is built for character level detection. The final output of the model is a region score and an affinity score. The region score predicts the centre of a character while the affinity score is the centre probability of space between adjacent characters. As most text detection datasets use word-level annotations, character level annotations are generated using weak supervision. CRAFT uses connected component labelling to generate word boxes by finding the rotation angle. The loss function is shown in Eq. 3.

$$L = \sum_p S_c(p) \cdot (||S_r(p) - S_r^*(p)||_2^2 + ||S_a(p) - S_a^*(p)||_2^2$$

(3)

where $S_c(p)$ is the pixel-wise confidence, S_r and S_a are the predicted region score and affinity score, S_r^* and S_a^* are the pseudo-ground truth region score and affinity score. For more details, the reader is referred to [2].

3.3 Tesseract

Tesseract is an open-source OCR engine developed by Hewlett Packard and now maintained by Google. Tesseract-4 was used in our experiment which is extended with a deep learning engine. In particular, Tesseract-4 uses LSTM based recogniser to predict text which is better than the traditional pipeline in 3.0. Images are processed by sliding window over the image. Each window is fed to the LSTM engine in a sequence [27]. Tesseract still requires ideal images for improved performances.

3.4 Outputs Ensemble

Our final model is an ensemble that combines outputs from the models described above. The aim is to boost performance by merging the outputs of participating models. Different permutations of the models were considered, and a total of ten ensembles were created. Multiple detections and overlap conflicts were resolved through post-processing using three criteria. The first case coalesces the results based on a reference model. The reference model is the first model in the ensemble name. Outputs from the reference model and non overlapping boxes from the other model(s) are chosen as output candidates. Thus, overlapping boxes from other models are eliminated using a threshold value. The second scheme eliminates overlaps by selecting the box from the models with the highest confidence. And the third criterion averages overlapping boxes from all models in the ensembles. Results from all these three scenarios are reported and compared.

4   Experiment

4.1   Datasets

Four datasets were considered in this experiment, namely ICDAR2013 [10], ICDAR2015 [9], MIDV-500 [1] and P&ID [18] datasets.

ICADAR2013, which is a focused scene text localisation dataset, consist of 229 samples in train set and 233 samples in test set. Samples contain random images of text in sign post and written text from different scenes and backgrounds. Generally, text are focused in the image center.

ICDAR2015, which contains an incidental scene text localisation dataset, consist of 1500 samples with 1000 images for training and 500 samples for testing. Samples are challenging with cluttered scene and texts of different shape, size and orientation.

Meanwhile, MIDV-500 dataset consist of 15000 card samples from 50 countries from around the world. Card samples were generated from a single card from each country by taking a picture of the card in different view angle, cluttered environment, lightening condition and camera. Each sample creates a more challenging task for card detection, face localisation and text field OCR.

Finally, the P&ID dataset consists of engineering drawings cluttered with text and symbols. Thus P&IDs have text with varying fonts, font sizes and different orientations. The images are large (approximately 5239 by 7417) with uniform white background. The texts here are symbol names and standard acronyms which are mostly alpha-numeric. The models were evaluated on 155 P&ID drawings with 39538 ground-truth boxes in total.

4.2   Experimental Set-Up

For the first experiment, we conducted a text localisation test using EAST. We used a pre-trained model from[1] (which we refer to as EAST-1). We also trained another EAST model from scratch on ICDAR2015 dataset only using the same protocol (also referred to as EAST-2.). A pre-trained CRAFT model[2] and Tesseract[3] were also evaluated on these datasets.

---

[1] https://github.com/argman/EAST.
[2] https://github.com/clovaai/CRAFT-pytorch.
[3] https://github.com/madmaze/pytesseract.

Our second set of experiments consisted of text localisation on MIDV-500. This was more challenging because ground truths are not available for all card samples text fields. However, the base card from which the samples were generated contains text annotation of the data fields. The dataset also provided a card annotation box (only) for all samples. To work around this, we used the provide card quadruple box to crop the card images from the samples. Then we applied perspective transform on the cropped card to neutralise any orientation change. Finally, cards are resized to the size of the base card in the categories. Then, ground truth from the base card is overlaid on the card crop serving as a pseudo ground truth. The number of text fields across the card type differs between 2–11. For evaluation, we discard partially occluded card but allowed for irregularly illuminated cards. In total, 12000 card samples were used to evaluate the models. A point to note is that no model was trained on this dataset. We used models trained from our initial detection experiments described earlier. Again, we ignored picture annotations, signature annotations and text detected by models that are not part of the annotated fields. In this case, false-negative detections were considered as missed field boxes and false positives are detections that are below the IOU threshold (0.5).

The third set of experiments were carried out on text detection in P&IDs with the ensembles. Again, no model was trained on this dataset hence, all images were used for evaluation. In these experiments, detected bounding boxes from the legend sections were discarded as no ground truth was available for comparison and the IOU threshold was kept at 0.4.

5   Results and Discussion

Tables 1 and 2 shows the quantitative performances of the methods described in Sect. 3 on different datasets. We employed precision, recall and the f1-score to compare these performances. For ICDAR2013 and ICDAR2015, the official evaluation script from[4] was used. MIDV-500 and P&ID required us to write a separate evaluation script to meet the experimental requirements. Figures 2 and 1 shows sample detections from models.

Table 1. Text detection results. The highest value for the selected metrics in each dataset is highlighted in bold

	ICDAR 2013				ICDAR 2015				MIDV-500				P&ID			
	East-1	East-2	CRAFT	Tesseract	East-1	East-2	CRAFT	Tesseract	East-1	East-2	CRAFT	Tesseract	East-1	East-2	CRAFT	Tesseract
Precision	0.88	0.80	**0.90**	0.41	0.84	0.84	**0.85**	0.05	0.49	**0.59**	0.35	0.32	**0.52**	0.50	0.45	0.13
Recall	**0.93**	0.76	0.92	0.27	0.77	0.77	**0.79**	0.04	**0.51**	0.41	0.50	0.15	**0.46**	0.34	0.12	0.20
F1-score	0.90	0.78	**0.91**	0.33	0.81	0.80	**0.82**	0.04	**0.50**	0.49	0.34	0.21	**0.49**	0.40	0.18	0.15

EAST-1 and EAST-2 performances are identical on ICDAR2015. However, EAST-1 showed better recall on ICDAR2013 which is no surprise given that

---

[4] https://rrc.cvc.uab.es/?ch=14.

(a) EAST-1   (b) CRAFT

Fig. 1. Sample detection from models.

the model was trained on a combined dataset conformed of ICDAR2013 and ICDAR2015. Again, ICDAR2013 contains focused text images and a smaller test set hence, performance from EAST-1 was high. On the other hand, this was not the case for EAST-2 where the performance dropped slightly. The results from EAST-2 on ICDAR2013 indicated the true performance of the model across a different dataset. The CRAFT and EAST models also performed well on ICDAR2015 with CRAFT obtaining slightly better precision, recall and f1-score among all models.

Tesseract performance was poor, particularly on ICDAR2015. The experiments highlighted the limitations of Tesseract in scene detection while the poor results on focused text detection indicated its reliance on traditional approaches to isolate text from background. The tesseract detector also had a lot of false detection and missed texts. Tesseract struggles because it relies on preprocessing and in most cases, there is no clear text-background separation in samples.

More interesting to this research are the results from MIDV-500 and P&ID datasets which shows across domain performance. The results indicated a considerable drop in performance across models. In particular, on MIDV-500, apart from missing on complete word detection, some fields were detected halfway or a single field may be detected with two separate bounding boxes. The effect of text orientation is not significant here as cards were transformed to a natural horizontal position before detection but some text boxes appeared with a skewed orientation such as in Fig. ?? (EAST-1). While the polygon points returned by EAST help with curved texts, these conditions could contribute to bounding box shape distortion. These conditions can push IoU down and may have reduced the number of positive boxes detected. Furthermore, different text languages on cards have also contributed to low performance. For instance, the Chinese ID card is written in the Chinese alphabet which is drastically different from the mostly English training examples.

Similarly, models performances dropped significantly on P&ID. This can be attributed to the challenging nature of the domain. Apart from text orientation, size and fonts, the resolution of diagrams in relation to the text size negatively affected performance. Figure 2a shows a sample detection from EAST-1 which

Table 2. Text detection results on P&ID from outputs ensemble.

Models	Coalesce			Confidence			Average		
	Precision	Recall	F1-score	Precision	Recall	F1-score	Precision	Recall	F1-score
EAST-1 + EAST-2	0.50	0.53	0.51	**0.52**	0.62	0.57	0.52	0.45	0.48
EAST-1 + CRAFT	0.51	0.6	0.55	**0.52**	0.62	0.56	0.52	0.45	0.48
EAST-1 + Tesseract	**0.52**	0.6	0.56	0.51	0.62	0.56	0.52	0.45	0.48
EAST-1 + EAST-2 + CRAFT	0.49	0.67	0.57	0.52	0.77	0.62	0.52	0.45	0.48
EAST-1 + EAST-2 + Tesseract	0.5	0.67	0.57	0.51	0.77	0.61	0.52	0.45	0.48
EAST-1 + EAST-2 + CRAFT +Tesseract	0.49	**0.79**	**0.61**	0.51	**0.87**	**0.64**	0.52	0.45	0.48
EAST-2 + CRAFT	0.49	0.48	0.48	0.49	0.5	0.5	0.5	0.34	0.4
EAST-2 + Tesseract	0.5	0.47	0.48	0.48	0.5	0.49	0.49	0.34	0.4
EAST-2 + CRAFT + Tesseract	0.49	0.62	0.54	0.48	0.67	56	0.49	0.34	0.4
CRAFT + Tesseract	0.45	0.19	0.27	0.45	0.21	0.28	0.46	0.12	0.19

was by far the best model on P&ID. In comparison, majority of the text within symbols were missed by Tesseract. Moreover, there were diagrams that Tesseract missed all none horizontal texts.

With ensemble outputs, there is a noticeable performance improvement. Overall, the best results from the P&ID are obtained when confidence is used as the voting criterion. That said, in terms of individual performances, no ensemble setup out-performed its peers in all three metrics. For instance, the best recall was obtained when all four models are combined based on confidence however, this was at the expense of a slight dip in precision.

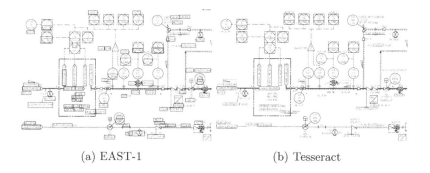

(a) EAST-1   (b) Tesseract

Fig. 2. Sample detection from cross-section of a P&ID.

6   Conclusion

In this paper, we analysed the performances of state-of-the-art text detection algorithms. Experiments were conducted to compare models trained on public datasets with varying text detection scenarios. Furthermore, the performances of these models were evaluated across the datasets using different metrics. The results indicated that despite the models trained on challenging scene text detection tasks, the performance dropped significantly when tested on text field detection on identity documents, and P&ID (Processing and Instrumentation Diagrams) with varying text fonts and background conditions. Hence, this highlighted some of the limitations of established text detection models in generalising to different text detection scenarios and domains. Future direction for this work is to investigate ensemble learning in the text detection across domains.

References

1. Arlazarov, V.V., Bulatov, K.B., Chernov, T.S., Arlazarov, V.L.: MIDV-500: a dataset for identity document analysis and recognition on mobile devices in video stream (2019)
2. Baek, Y., Lee, B., Han, D., Yun, S., Lee, H.: Character region awareness for text detection. In: Proceedings of the IEEE Conference on Computer Vision and Pattern Recognition (2019)
3. Du, Y., et al.: PP-OCR: a practical ultra lightweight OCR system. arXiv preprint arXiv:2009.09941 (2020)
4. Goodfellow, I., Bengio, Y., Courville, A.: Deep Learning. MIT, Cambridge (2016)
5. Gupta, A., Vedaldi, A., Zisserman, A.: Synthetic data for text localisation in natural images. In: IEEE Conference on Computer Vision and Pattern Recognition (2016)
6. He, T., Huang, W., Qiao, Y., Yao, J.: Accurate text localization in natural image with cascaded convolutional text network. arXiv preprint arXiv:1603.09423 (2016)
7. Jaderberg, M., Simonyan, K., Zisserman, A., et al.: Spatial transformer networks. In: Advances in Neural Information Processing Systems (2015)
8. Jamieson, L., Moreno-Garcia, C.F., Elyan, E.: Deep learning for text detection and recognition in complex engineering diagrams. In: 2020 International Joint Conference on Neural Networks (IJCNN), pp. 1–7 (2020)
9. Karatzas, D., et al.: ICDAR 2015 competition on robust reading. In: 2015 13th International Conference on Document Analysis and Recognition (ICDAR). IEEE (2015)
10. Karatzas, D., et al.: ICDAR 2013 robust reading competition. In: 2013 12th International Conference on Document Analysis and Recognition. IEEE (2013)
11. Lee, C.-Y., Bhardwaj, A., Di, W., Jagadeesh, V., Piramuthu, R.: Region-based discriminative feature pooling for scene text recognition. In: Proceedings of the IEEE Conference on Computer Vision and Pattern Recognition (2014)
12. Lee, C.-Y., Osindero, S.: Recursive recurrent nets with attention modeling for OCR in the wild. In: Proceedings of the IEEE Conference on CVPR (2016)
13. Liao, M., Shi, B., Bai, X.: Textboxes++: a single-shot oriented scene text detector. IEEE Trans. Image Process. (2018)
14. Liao, M., Wan, Z., Yao, C., Chen, K., Bai, X.: Real-time scene text detection with differentiable binarization. In: Proceedings of the AAAI Conference on Artificial Intelligence, pp. 11474–11481 (2020)
15. Liu, X., Meng, G., Pan, C.: Scene text detection and recognition with advances in deep learning: a survey. Int. J. Doc. Anal. Recogn. (IJDAR) **22**, 143–162 (2019)
16. Long, S., He, X., Yao, C.: Scene text detection and recognition: the deep learning era. Int. J. Comput. Vis. **129**, 161–184 (2020)
17. Mishra, A., Alahari, K., Jawahar, C.V.: Top-down and bottom-up cues for scene text recognition. In: 2012 IEEE Conference on Computer Vision and Pattern Recognition. IEEE (2012)

18. Moreno-García, C., Elyan, E., Jayne, C.: New trends on digitisation of complex engineering drawings. Neural Comput. Appl. **31**, 1695–1712 (2018)
19. Pan, Y.-F., Hou, X., Liu, C.-L.: A hybrid approach to detect and localize texts in natural scene. IEEE Trans. Image Process. **20**(3), 800–813 (2010)
20. Phan, T.Q., Shivakumara, P., Tian, S., Tan, C.L.: Recognizing text with perspective distortion in natural scenes. In: Proceedings of the IEEE International Conference on Computer Vision (2013)
21. Ren, S., He, K., Girshick, R., Sun, J.: Faster R-CNN: towards real-time object detection with region proposal networks. arXiv preprint arXiv:1506.01497 (2015)
22. Risnumawan, A., Shivakumara, P., Chan, C.S., Tan, C.L.: A robust arbitrary text detection system for natural scene images. Expert Syst. Appl. **41**, 8027–8048 (2014)
23. Shi, B., Bai, X., Belongie, S.: Detecting oriented text in natural images by linking segments. In: Proceedings of the IEEE Conference on Computer Vision and Pattern Recognition (2017)
24. Shi, B., Bai, X., Yao, C.: An end-to-end trainable neural network for image-based sequence recognition and its application to scene text recognition. IEEE Trans. Pattern Anal. Mach. Intell. **39**, 2298–2304 (2016)
25. Shi, B., Wang, X., Lyu, P., Yao, C., Bai, X.: Robust scene text recognition with automatic rectification. In: Proceedings of the IEEE Conference on Computer Vision and Pattern Recognition (2016)
26. Shi, B., Yang, M., Wang, X., Lyu, P., Yao, C., Bai, X.: Aster: an attentional scene text recognizer with flexible rectification. IEEE Trans. Pattern Anal. Mach. Intell. **41**(9), 2035–2048 (2018)
27. Smith, R.: Tesseract OCR modernizationefforts.pdf (2016). https://github.com/tesseract-ocr/docs/blob/master/das_tutorial2016/6ModernizationEfforts.pdf
28. Tian, Z., Huang, W., He, T., He, P., Qiao, Yu.: Detecting text in natural image with connectionist text proposal network. In: Leibe, B., Matas, J., Sebe, N., Welling, M. (eds.) ECCV 2016. LNCS, vol. 9912, pp. 56–72. Springer, Cham (2016). https://doi.org/10.1007/978-3-319-46484-8_4
29. Wang, K., Babenko, B., Belongie, S.: End-to-end scene text recognition. In: 2011 International Conference on Computer Vision. IEEE (2011)
30. Xie, S., Tu, Z.: Holistically-nested edge detection. In: Proceedings of the IEEE International Conference on Computer Vision (2015)
31. Yao, C., Bai, X., Sang, N., Zhou, X., Zhou, S., Cao, Z.: Scene text detection via holistic, multi-channel prediction. arXiv preprint arXiv:1606.09002 (2016)
32. Yao, C., Bai, X., Shi, B., Liu, W.: Strokelets: a learned multi-scale representation for scene text recognition. In: Proceedings of the IEEE Conference on Computer Vision and Pattern Recognition (2014)
33. Zhou, X., et al.: East: an efficient and accurate scene text detector. In: Proceedings of the IEEE conference on Computer Vision and Pattern Recognition (2017)

Cross-Domain Learning
for Reference-Based Sketch Colorization
with Structural and Colorific Strategy

Haowei Zhong[1], Xianzhi Tu[2], Hailong Liu[1], Yulu Fu[1], and Jinrong Cui[1(✉)]

[1] College of Mathematics and Informatics, South China Agricultural University,
Guangzhou, China
tweety1028@163.com
[2] Animation Department, College of Arts, South China Agricultural University,
Guangzhou, China

Abstract. This paper aims to tackle the colorization task of sketch image given an already-colored reference image. Sketch colorization is a thorny task for computer vision since neither grayscale values nor semantic information exists in sketch images. To address this, We propose to jointly train the domain alignment network with a simple adversarial strategy, that we term the structural and colorific conditions, to learn the semantical correspondence between information-scarce sketch and the given instructive reference. Specifically, the inputs from distinct domains will be aligned to an embedding space where the semantical correspondence is established, then, the generator will reconstruct the sketch image according to the established correspondence. We demonstrate the effectiveness of our proposed method in sketch colorization tasks via quantitative and qualitative evaluation against existing approaches in terms of image quality as well as style relevance.

Keywords: Image translation · Sketch colorization · Multimedia content creation

1 Introduction

Sketch colorization is a challenging subset of image translation and synthesis. Nowadays, conditional image translation and synthesis gain giant success in color image translation (such as a real photograph to style specific painting). In the community of computer vision, image translation is studied as a generalized problem of texture synthesis in style transfer, which is to abstract and transfer the texture information from source target [8,13,16,19]. However, we argue such methods may fail to handle a more challenging mapping like intricate sketches to

This work supported by the Opening Project of Guangdong Province Key Laboratory of Computational Science at the Sun Yat-Sen. University.2021011, and Guangdong Provincial Department of Education, China: No.PROJ007143460458860544,2019.

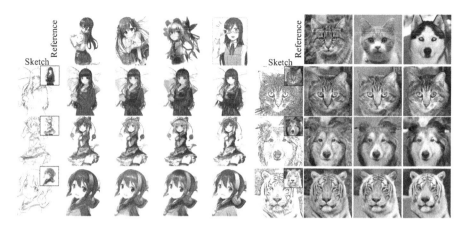

Fig. 1. Qualitative results of our method on the partial dataset. Each row has the same semantic content while each column has the same reference style, and the groundtruth is at the top right of sketch images.

colored images for the reason that neither grayscale values nor semantic information exist in sketch images. Consequently, the Sketch form of conditional image synthesis is our concern, Specifically, it converts a grayscale sketch to a color image by giving a referential image (Fig. 1).

Generally, two types of methods of sketch colorization tasks have been explored: stroke-based (e.g., brush strokes, hints, scribbles) approach and reference-based approach. In the former case, it come up with the intuitive idea of colorizing sketch images with condition information given by users, such as user hints [24], scribbles [6,26], color palette [29], or textual tags [9]. Although all these methods show us impressive results in terms of sketch colorization, they still suffer the requirement of unambiguous color information and precise spatial user inputs for every step.

To surmount such problems, a more convenient approach, utilizing a colored image as a reference input, has been introduced. The goal of reference-based learning is to learn a mapping between source and reference, which leads to a critical issue that how to incorporate the visual correspondence between them. Early methods [1,21,30] focus on utilizing the low-level features to compose colorization. Recent study [11,15,25] usually compose mapping from semantic mask extracting from encoder (pre-train or not) network to reference-related results. These composition methods however tend to be sensitive to specific domains, thereby most are not suitable for a sketch with only complex grayscale composition. Also, the style latent code only marries the global context style, regardless of spatially relevant information and partial local style.

Consequently, to address these issues, our focus of reference-based sketch colorization is mainly on two issues: Firstly, how to model and extract local and non-local style from an image? Secondly, how to reconstruct the grayscale sketch with desired style information extracted from reference while preserving the sketch composition? For the first issue, we proposed a cross-domain alignment module that transforms the inputs from distinct domains to shared embedded space, where solid feature alignment can be established at. Then a set of spatially-variant de-normalization blocks [15] similar to [27] are applied in decoder part to preserve the local and non-local style from the target domain with the output feature of cross-domain alignment module. For the second issue, A specific adversarial framework for sketch colorization tasks, dual multiscale discriminators with the capability of distinguishing sketch composition and reference coloration respectively, has been introduced in this paper to facilitate and guide the reconstruction of stylized output. Our methods outperform the previous methods in terms of quality and vividness in sketch colorization tasks. The pivotal contribution of this paper can be summarized as follows:

- A cross-domain alignment module is proposed for imposing the distinct domain to a shared embedded space for progressively aligning, and outputting the warped image in a coarse-to-fine manner.
- With the cross-domain alignment, we proposed a specific adversarial strategy for reference-based sketch colorization task to facilitate the imaging quality.

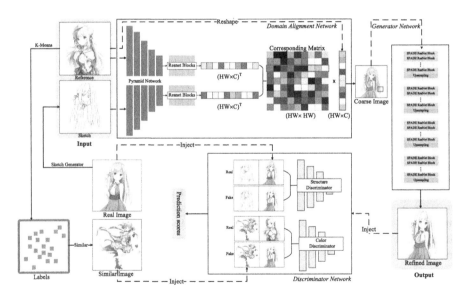

Fig. 2. The illustration of the proposed framework. It contains three parts: Domain Alignment Network, Coarse-to-fine generator, and discriminator with color and structure strategy. Given the sketch input $x_a \in D_s$ and the reference input $x_r \in D_r$, the Domain Alignment Network adapts them into a common domain D_c, where the corresponding can be established by the calculated corresponding matrix. Then the generator refine the coarse images from the previous stage and output the refined images.

2   Related Work

2.1   Conditional Sketch Colorization

Sketch colorization can be codified as the problem of mapping from one grayscale scene contour to corresponding colored images. [2,8] try to handle the sketch colorization problem by directly learning a mapping from handcrafted sketch to realistic photograph using condition GAN (cGAN) [8]. Ci [4] improved the colorization quality by introducing an independent local feature network in cGAN. PaintsTorch [6] is based on Ci's model, introducing a double generator to improve visual fidelity. Style2Paints [26] can generate visually pleasing colorization results by splitting line art images into different parts and colorizing them respectively. However, they suffer the requirement of unambiguous color information and precise spatial user inputs for every step, and they are also unable to translate image-specific style in sketch colorization tasks.

2.2   Reference-Based Colorization

It is an intuitive way to control the style of colorization by a given image. Here, we deem two main categories according to input forms: Grayscale colorization [22,23,25] and Sketch colorization [11,18,28]. The former is easier than the latter for the reason that sketch images only have black-and-white values and contain more noise than gray images. The latter use sketch as semantic features and reference as style guidance to synthesize images. However, all these methods require to constitute style consistency image pairs, which mean the limitations of a specific domain.

3   Proposed Method

3.1   Domain Alignment Network

We aim to learn the dense correspondence from edge information to colored information at a spatial scale. To tackle this, we proposed a cross-domain correspondence module to learn the mapping of edge and color information, which we term the domain alignment network.

Domain Alignment. To be specific, we let $x_s \in \mathbb{R}^{\times H \times W \times 1}, x_r \in \mathbb{R}^{\times H \times W \times 3}$, x_s denotes the sketch input, where subscript s refers to the sketch domain, x_r denotes the reference input, where subscript r refers to the reference domain, H, W denote the height and width respectively. Also, we construct y_r and y_s as paired training samples, which y_r represents the sample that is semantically similar to x_s but have different domain in r and y_s represents the sample that is semantically similar to x_r but domain in s.

As shown in Fig. 2, we adapt the input images to a common domain D_c where the representation is able to represent the semantics for both input domains (sketch domain D_s and reference domain D_r). Firstly, x_s and x_r are fed into the feature pyramid network [12] which is responsible for extracting the multi-scale semantic features. The extracted feature maps are further to mapping to D_c by a set of ResNet Blocks and reshaping, denoted by $\hat{x}_s \in \mathbb{R}^{HW \times C}$ and $\hat{x}_r \in \mathbb{R}^{HW \times C}$ (H, W are feature maps size). Therefore, the feature alignment process can be expressed as follows:

$$\hat{x}_s = \mathcal{E}_{s->c}(x_s, \theta_{\mathcal{E}}) \tag{1}$$

$$\hat{x}_r = \mathcal{E}_{r->c}(x_r, \theta_{\mathcal{E}}) \tag{2}$$

where θ denotes the learnable parameter. In practice, domain alignment is crucial for correspondence, because only when x_s and x_r stay in the same domain D_c can they further match some similarity measures.

With the extracted feature representation, we align the correspondence of feature $\hat{x}_s$ and $\hat{x}_r$ by calculating the pairwise similarity

Correspondence with Shared Domain. We establish the correspondence of $\hat{x}_s$ and $\hat{x}_r$ with the correspondence layer proposed by [25]. Formally, we compote a cosine corresponding matrix $\mathcal{M}$ of which each element is a pairwise correlation at position u and v.

$$\mathcal{M}(u,v) = \frac{(\hat{x}_s(u) - \mu_s)^{\mathrm{T}} \cdot (\hat{x}_r(v) - \mu_r)}{\|\hat{x}_s(u) - \mu_s\|_2 \cdot \|\hat{x}_r(v) - \mu_r\|_2} \tag{3}$$

where μ_s, μ_r denote the mean feature vectors respectively, and $\mathcal{M}(u,v) \in \mathbb{R}^{HW \times HW}$ represents the advanced semantic features corresponding similarity between input x_s and input x_r.

3.2 Coarse-to-Fine Generator

Now the main issue is how to get the coarse image from mapping μ without conditional supervised samples. Our idea is to jointly train the domain alignment network and apply efficient unsupervised generation, which preserves structural and semantic features as much as possible. The model may find that only by generating the correct semantic correspondence can high-quality images be generated. We hence proposed to calculate the weighted sum of reshaped reference vector to estimate the semantic corresponding relation in input sketch, then we get warped coarse result $coarse \in \mathbb{R}^{HW \times C}$. Specifically, we mapping the most correlated pixels between reference x_r at position v and sketch x_s at position u, and the $coarse(u)$ can be denoted as:

$$coarse(u) = \sum_{v}^{HW} softmax(\alpha \mathcal{M}(u,v) \cdot x_r(v)) \tag{4}$$

where α is a hyperparameter at 10 by default.

Under the guidance $coarse_{r->s}$, we apply SPADE [15] in our generator to retain semantic information as much as possible and project the spatially variant reference style to different activation locations. As opposed to [15], a well-designed strategy is introduced into the spatially-variant denormalization for high-fidelity style transfer from reference, which we term structural and colorific strategy. In this way, we get a reasonable result while preserving style from reference and structure information from a sketch given the joint training mode using structural and colorific strategy.

3.3 Structural and Colorific Strategy

Thanks to the joint train with structural and colorific strategy, can we get reasonable and aesthetic coloring results. Next, we will describe the structural and colorific strategy in detail.

Structural Condition. Structural conditions are a brief overview and representation of objects. We use a series of binary black-and-white images to represent them, which is also the sketch we are using. Specifically, we apply xDoG [20] to generate the simulated sketch in the training stage, and it can constitute our structural conditions.

Colorific Condition. Colorific Condition indicates whether images match or not, and it is the key to generating reasonable color. We compute the 3D Lab color histogram ($8 \times 8 \times 8$) of each RGB image similar to [18], and then measure their similarity by K-means clustering to merge the reference image if their colors are close to each other. As Fig. 2 shown, our model will get an image with a color similar to the reference input as our color condition input.

Paired Structural and Colorific Discriminators. As Fig. 2 illustrated, we apply paired discriminators with the structural condition and colorific condition to jointly train the generator part. Concretely, the structural discriminator is responsible for determining whether the resulting structure is reasonable and aesthetically pleasing, and we carefully designed pairs of positive and negative samples to force it to be sensitive only to the resulting structure. The colorific discriminator is responsible for determining whether the resulting colors are reasonable. We make positive and negative samples of pictures with different structures but similar colors, which forces the color discriminator to be more sensitive to changes in color patterns.

3.4 Loss for Reference-Based Sketch Colorization

Loss for Reference Translation. Firstly, the output should be consistent with the semantics of x_s and yield to the given x_r in style. We thereby penalize the perceptual loss to minimize the semantic discrepancy.

$$\mathcal{L}_{perc} = \|\phi_l(G(x_s, x_r)) - \phi(y_r)\|_1 \tag{5}$$

where the ϕ_l denotes the $relu5\_2$ layer in the pre-trained VGG network. Meanwhile, we employ the *contextual* loss same as [27] to make the generated images adopt the style from the semantically corresponding from x_r.

$$\mathcal{L}_{context} = \sum_l \omega_l \left[-log(\frac{1}{n_l} \sum_i \max_j A^l(\phi_i^l(G(x_s, x_r), \phi_j^l(x_r)))) \right] \qquad (6)$$

where i and j index the feature map of layer ϕ^l which controls n_l features and ω_l restrains relative importance of different layers.

Loss for Pseudo Reference Pairs. We construct reference training pairs by using paired data $\{x_s, y_r\}$, which y_r is a semantically aligned colored sample with different domains. Then a series of data enhancements, such as flipping and perturbation, are applied to y_s to get $\hat{y}_r$, In this way, we get the pseudo reference pairs and intend to utilize them to pull the distance in the common domain.

$$\mathcal{L}_{pseudo} = \sum_l^L \|\phi_l(\hat{y}_r) - \phi_l(G(x_s, x_r))\|_1 \qquad (7)$$

where ϕ_l denotes the active layer l in the pre-trained VGG-19 network

Loss for Domain Alignment. The target of domain alignment is to make sure the embedding features x_s and x_r are projected into a common space. In order to achieve this goal, we use the paired training data to optimize it.

$$\mathcal{L}_{align} = \|\mathcal{E}_{s->c}(x_s) - \mathcal{E}_{r->c}(y_r)\|_1 \qquad (8)$$

Loss for Adversarial Framework. We train a dual discriminator [5] with the structural and colorific conditions to discriminate the translation images and the groundtruth sample of the domain s and r.

$$\begin{aligned} \mathcal{L}_{adv} = \ &\mathbb{E}[log D_s(I_{gt}, x_s) + log D_r(I_{similar}, x_r)] \\ &+ \mathbb{E}[log(1 - D_s(G(x_s, x_r), x_s)) \\ &+ log(1 - D_r(G(x_s, x_r), x_r))] \end{aligned} \qquad (9)$$

where I_{gt}, $I_{similar}$ are the groundtruth of conditions x_s and x_r respectively.

4   Experiments

4.1   Implementation

We use Adam [10] solver for optimization with $\beta_1 = 0$, $\beta_2 = 0.9$. The learning rates are set to 1e−4 and 4e−4 for generator and discriminator respectively following TTUR [7] strategy.

| Sketch | Reference | Pix2Pix (2017) | CycleGAN (2017) | SPADE (2019) | Sun et.al(2019) | CoCosNet (2020) | Ground truth | Ours |

Fig. 3. Qualitative comparison of colorized results with baselines trained on anime dataset. Note that the goal of the task does not reconstruct the ground truth image, all results are generated from the unseen dataset with sketch input and reference image under random selection within the validation set.

4.2 Datasets

Anime-Sketch-Colorization-Pair. We train our model on animation sketch using Anime-sketch-colorization-pair in Kaggle. it contains 14,224 training samples and 3,545 test samples with paired handcrafted sketch images and colored images.

CelebA-HQ. CelebA-HQ [14] contains high quality human face images. We apply canny edge detector on its mask images to obtain the sketch images.

Animal Face. We use Animal Face dataset [3] which contains 16,130 high-quality images at 512×512 resolution and three domains of classes, Cat, Dog, and Wild Animal. Our model performs well in all categories on this dataset.

4.3 Qualitative Comparison

Baseline. We select different state-of-the-art image translation methods for visual comparison: (1) Pix2Pix [8], an advanced image-to-image translation method. (2) CycleGAN [31], a leading unsupervised image translation method. (3) SPADE [15], a recent image translation method which supports style injection of reference images. (4) Sun et al. [18], a recent reference-based sketch colorization method whose results have been achieved on icon dataset. (5) CocosNet [27], an exemplar-based translation method that also utilizes the shared embedded space learned for domain alignment. The qualitative comparison results are shown in the Fig. 3 (Fig. 5).

Table 1. Model performance on metric of FID. sc means structural condition and cc means colorific condition, and DAN means the Domain Alignment Network

Methods	Animal face			Comics	Human
	Cat	Dog	Wild	Anime-pair	CelebA-HQ
SPADE	41.23	36.21	49.32	57.44	32.32
CycleGAN	80.92	90.54	101.24	99.98	87.95
Sun et al.	55.21	54.12	59.69	68.65	48.26
Cocos Net	32.33	34.21	28.86	27.96	20.64
Ours (w/o *cc*)	28.19	27.35	29.99	32.21	28.32
Ours (w/o *sc*)	30.20	26.65	33.65	32.06	32.14
Ours (w/o DAN)	46.28	46.21	49.69	47.62	41.21
Ours (*full*)	**22.26**	**24.62**	**25.67**	**22.11**	**20.61**

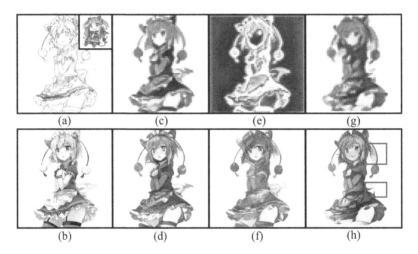

Fig. 4. (a) sketch and reference (upper right); (b) ground truth; (c) coarse image; (d) output; (e) coarse image (w/o colorific condition); (f) output (w/o colorific condition); (g) coarse image (w/o structural condition); (h) output (w/o structural condition)

Fig. 5. Qualitative results on celebA-HQ dataset

4.4   Ablation Study

Ablation studies were performed in terms of structural and color conditions. The visualization results are shown in Fig. 4. Here we would like to emphasize two key factors, as shown in Fig. 4(c) and (f), which are more likely to cause style conversion failures and mismatches when the coloring condition is the default. Similarly, as shown in Fig. 4(h), it is easy to encounter loss of detail and diffusion problems. We also quantitatively measured the effect of different conditions in Table 1, both showing that the two conditional discriminators we added are effective. Also, we performed ablation experiments on the domain alignment module and found that the domain alignment network effectively contributed to the coloring results, which is perhaps why our results are superior to those of Sun et al.

4.5   User Research

We conduct a user study to evaluate the subjective quality. We randomly selected three pictures in different models, a total of 18 for comparison. Two tasks are designed to allow users to rate in terms of the image quality and the style relevance following the Mean Opinion Score [17] (MOS) rule. The illustrated result is shown in Fig. 6, which demonstrates our method outperforms others in image quality and style relevance.

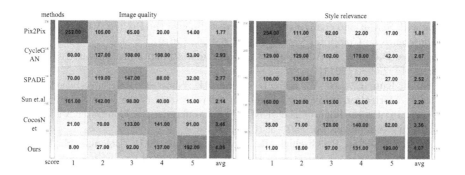

Fig. 6. User research with 5 baselines among 152 users. The values in the block represent frequency and weighted average respectively

5   Conclusion

In this paper, we have presented an available cross-domain framework for sketch colorization according to the given reference image. We get good coloring results by applying the effective strategy, that we term the structural and colorific condition, on the conditional generative network to facilitate the establishment of correspondence between distinct domains. The evaluation results demonstrate that our method achieves preferable performance than previous leading methods, which shows the significant potentials in the practice of content creation and other fields.

References

1. Bugeau, A., Ta, V.T., Papadakis, N.: Variational exemplar-based image colorization. IEEE Trans. Image Process. **23**(1), 298–307 (2013)
2. Chen, W., Hays, J.: SketchyGAN: towards diverse and realistic sketch to image synthesis. In: Proceedings of the IEEE Conference on Computer Vision and Pattern Recognition, pp. 9416–9425 (2018)
3. Choi, Y., Uh, Y., Yoo, J., Ha, J.W.: StarGAN v2: diverse image synthesis for multiple domains. In: Proceedings of the IEEE Conference on Computer Vision and Pattern Recognition (2020)
4. Ci, Y., Ma, X., Wang, Z., Li, H., Luo, Z.: User-guided deep anime line art colorization with conditional adversarial networks. In: Proceedings of the 26th ACM International Conference on Multimedia, pp. 1536–1544 (2018)
5. Goodfellow, I., et al.: Generative adversarial nets. In: Advances in Neural Information Processing Systems 27 (2014)
6. Hati, Y., Jouet, G., Rousseaux, F., Duhart, C.: PaintsTorch: a user-guided anime line art colorization tool with double generator conditional adversarial network. In: European Conference on Visual Media Production, pp. 1–10 (2019)
7. Heusel, M., Ramsauer, H., Unterthiner, T., Nessler, B., Hochreiter, S.: GANs trained by a two time-scale update rule converge to a local Nash equilibrium. In: Advances in Neural Information Processing Systems 30 (2017)
8. Isola, P., Zhu, J.Y., Zhou, T., Efros, A.A.: Image-to-image translation with conditional adversarial networks. In: Proceedings of the IEEE Conference on Computer Vision and Pattern Recognition, pp. 1125–1134 (2017)
9. Kim, H., Jhoo, H.Y., Park, E., Yoo, S.: Tag2Pix: line art colorization using text tag with SECat and changing loss. In: Proceedings of the IEEE/CVF International Conference on Computer Vision, pp. 9056–9065 (2019)
10. Kingma, D.P., Ba, J.: Adam: a method for stochastic optimization. arXiv preprint arXiv:1412.6980 (2014)
11. Lee, J., Kim, E., Lee, Y., Kim, D., Chang, J., Choo, J.: Reference-based sketch image colorization using augmented-self reference and dense semantic correspondence. In: Proceedings of the IEEE/CVF Conference on Computer Vision and Pattern Recognition, pp. 5801–5810 (2020)
12. Lin, T.Y., Dollár, P., Girshick, R., He, K., Hariharan, B., Belongie, S.: Feature pyramid networks for object detection. In: Proceedings of the IEEE Conference on Computer Vision and Pattern Recognition, pp. 2117–2125 (2017)
13. Liu, M.Y., Breuel, T., Kautz, J.: Unsupervised image-to-image translation networks. In: Advances in Neural Information Processing Systems, pp. 700–708 (2017)
14. Liu, Z., Luo, P., Wang, X., Tang, X.: Deep learning face attributes in the wild. In: Proceedings of the IEEE International Conference on Computer Vision, pp. 3730–3738 (2015)
15. Park, T., Liu, M.Y., Wang, T.C., Zhu, J.Y.: Semantic image synthesis with spatially-adaptive normalization. In: Proceedings of the IEEE/CVF Conference on Computer Vision and Pattern Recognition, pp. 2337–2346 (2019)
16. Richardson, E., et al.: Encoding in style: a styleGAN encoder for image-to-image translation. In: Proceedings of the IEEE/CVF Conference on Computer Vision and Pattern Recognition, pp. 2287–2296 (2021)
17. Streijl, R.C., Winkler, S., Hands, D.S.: Mean opinion score (MOS) revisited: methods and applications, limitations and alternatives. Multimedia Syst. **22**(2), 213–227 (2016)

18. Sun, T.H., Lai, C.H., Wong, S.K., Wang, Y.S.: Adversarial colorization of icons based on contour and color conditions. In: Proceedings of the 27th ACM International Conference on Multimedia, pp. 683–691 (2019)
19. Wang, T.C., Liu, M.Y., Zhu, J.Y., Tao, A., Kautz, J., Catanzaro, B.: High-resolution image synthesis and semantic manipulation with conditional GANs. In: Proceedings of the IEEE Conference on Computer Vision and Pattern Recognition, pp. 8798–8807 (2018)
20. Winnemöller, H., Kyprianidis, J.E., Olsen, S.C.: XDoG: an extended difference-of-gaussians compendium including advanced image stylization. Comput. Graph. **36**(6), 740–753 (2012)
21. Winnemöller, H., Olsen, S.C., Gooch, B.: Real-time video abstraction. ACM Trans. Graph. (TOG) **25**(3), 1221–1226 (2006)
22. Xu, Z., Wang, T., Fang, F., Sheng, Y., Zhang, G.: Stylization-based architecture for fast deep exemplar colorization. In: Proceedings of the IEEE/CVF Conference on Computer Vision and Pattern Recognition, pp. 9363–9372 (2020)
23. Yin, W., Lu, P., Zhao, Z., Peng, X.: Yes, "attention is all you need", for exemplar based colorization. In: Proceedings of the 29th ACM International Conference on Multimedia, pp. 2243–2251 (2021)
24. Yuan, M., Simo-Serra, E.: Line art colorization with concatenated spatial attention. In: Proceedings of the IEEE/CVF Conference on Computer Vision and Pattern Recognition, pp. 3946–3950 (2021)
25. Zhang, B., et al.: Deep exemplar-based video colorization. In: Proceedings of the IEEE/CVF Conference on Computer Vision and Pattern Recognition, pp. 8052–8061 (2019)
26. Zhang, L., Li, C., Simo-Serra, E., Ji, Y., Wong, T.T., Liu, C.: User-guided line art flat filling with split filling mechanism. In: Proceedings of the IEEE/CVF Conference on Computer Vision and Pattern Recognition, pp. 9889–9898 (2021)
27. Zhang, P., Zhang, B., Chen, D., Yuan, L., Wen, F.: Cross-domain correspondence learning for exemplar-based image translation. In: Proceedings of the IEEE/CVF Conference on Computer Vision and Pattern Recognition, pp. 5143–5153 (2020)
28. Zhang, Q., Wang, B., Wen, W., Li, H., Liu, J.: Line art correlation matching feature transfer network for automatic animation colorization. In: Proceedings of the IEEE/CVF Winter Conference on Applications of Computer Vision, pp. 3872–3881 (2021)
29. Zhang, R., et al.: Real-time user-guided image colorization with learned deep priors. arXiv preprint arXiv:1705.02999 (2017)
30. Zhao, M., Zhu, S.C.: Portrait painting using active templates. In: Proceedings of the ACM SIGGRAPH/Eurographics Symposium on Non-photorealistic Animation and Rendering, pp. 117–124 (2011)
31. Zhu, J.Y., Park, T., Isola, P., Efros, A.A.: Unpaired image-to-image translation using cycle-consistent adversarial networks. In: Proceedings of the IEEE International Conference on Computer Vision, pp. 2223–2232 (2017)

Data Augmented Dual-Attention Interactive Image Classification Network

Qiangxi Zhu and Zhixin Li[✉]

Guangxi Key Lab of Multi-source Information Mining and Security, Guangxi Normal University, Guilin 541004, China
lizx@gxnu.edu.cn

Abstract. Fine-grained classification requires identifying images that belong to multiple subcategories within the same category. There are only subtle differences between highly similar images. Most existing methods only use baseline networks or a single attention module to extract features from images to discriminate similar images, which will limit the model to finding fine-grained regions hidden in images. This article proposes an effective method to solve this problem. The first is a novel layered training method that enhances the feature extraction capability of baseline models. The second step is to find multiple attention regions based on the features extracted by the baseline model. Here, the improved Long Short-Term Memory (LSTM) and Multi-Head Attention can be used to focus on the key areas of the image, which is conducive to the discovery of fine-grained features. In the third step, the attention features extracted based on the dual network are spatially mapped using a multi-layer perceptron (MLP). Then, the interaction dot product of the corresponding channels is performed on the attention features and the mapping features to guide the classification. Finally, to achieve good performance, we test several standard benchmark datasets, CUB-200-2011, FGVC Aircraft, and Stanford Cars.

Keywords: Data augmentation · Hierarchical training · Denoising autoencoder and Dual attention mechanism · Interactive attention

1 Introduction

Fine-grained visual classification aims to identify specific classes of objects, often subclasses of the same general class. Similar objects are usually only slightly different and difficult to distinguish. This is a more challenging problem than traditional classification due to the inherent subtle intra-class object variation between sub-categories. With the rapid development of neural networks such as baseline networks VGG [1] and ResNet [2], the feature extraction ability of neural networks for images has been significantly improved. Deep learning is also increasingly applied to fine-grained classification. But relying only on baseline networks to learn fine-grained features is not enough. Because the discriminative features of fine-grained images mainly only exist in subtle local regions. In reality, as described in Fig. 1, it is difficult to distinguish between the common kingfisher and the great spotted kingfisher; they are very similar in size. However, the ear feathers of the common kingfisher are orange-yellow, and the ear feathers of the great spotted kingfisher are blue. At the same time, the difference between male and female birds of the same species is that the beak is black, while the lower beak of the female is red. It can be seen that subtle differences tend to be concentrated in local areas of objects. So far, the most efficient solutions rely on neural networks to localize local regions of an image and then learn fine-grained feature maps from the local regions.

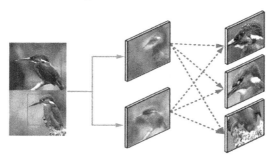

Fig. 1. Most of the previous methods only used baseline models to extract features or did not pay enough attention to feature regions. We use baseline networks for data enhancement and then use dual attention and multilayer perceptron interactive modeling to capture features and amplify details.

Therefore, this paper proposes a new framework with a hierarchical structure, including three main contributions. (1) Data enhancement based on residual network, combined with multi-level convolution, trains each layer separately to enrich global feature information. (2) Input the features based on data augmentation into the dual attention network, extract global key feature regions through dual attention, and filter out some unimportant edge information. (3) The features extracted based on dual attention are spatially mapped and clustered through a multilayer perceptron. Then, the feature extracted by double attention and the feature of MultiLayer Perceptron (MLP) clustering are multiplied element by element, and the attention area is expanded to obtain the discriminative feature.

2   Related Work

In recent years, fine-grained image classification has been widely used in academia and industry. Fine-grained classification based on deep learning has experienced rapid development from strong supervision to weak supervision. While this strong supervision performs well, this strongly supervised approach [3, 4] requires a lot of labor to mark annotation boxes, local region locations, and other additional manual annotation information, and the acquisition of annotation information is costly. This is impractical in fine-grained image recognition.

Consequently, recent research on fine-grained images has shifted from a strongly supervised domain to a weakly supervised domain that relies only on labels, with simple operation and high performance [5–13].

2.1 Method Based on Strong Supervision

The so-called strong-supervised fine-grained image classification model refers to that in order to obtain better classification performance during model training, in addition to image category labels, additional manual labeling information is used, such as object labeling boxes and location labeling points. For example, the Pose Normalized CNN [4] network first uses algorithms such as Selective Search to generate Object Proposals for objects or parts of objects that may appear in fine-grained images. Then with the help of Object Bounding Box and Part Annotation in fine-grained images, three detection models can be trained: one for fine-grained object-level detection, one for object head detection, and one for torso part detection. The obtained target region are then used as input to train a CNN separately. CNN can learn the features of each part of the object. Finally, the feature fusion of the three fully connected layers is used as the feature representation of the whole fine-grained image. It can be seen that the cost of obtaining partial annotations is unusually high.

2.2 Method Based on Weak Supervision

This subsection divides the most relevant studies of weak supervision into the following categories: attention-based fine-grained classification methods and fine-grained classification methods for multi-scale networks.

Multiscale Subnetworks Method: There are also some models that cooperate with multi-scale sub-networks for fine-grained classification, mainly to locate the key local regions of the image, enlarge the local feature maps, and improve the robustness of the feature regions. Among them, the MMAL-Net [14] model uses multiple sub-networks to locate key image regions to find discriminative features. First, the overall features of the object are learned through CNN to obtain feature maps. The original image is then cropped according to the bounding box information of the feature maps and input to the following CNN network to get a finer-scale target image. Finally, according to the feature maps of the target image, several local regions with the least redundancy are obtained and input to the CNN again for training. This can guide the classification of images based on networks of different sizes.

Attention Network Method: Some people also use channel attention to dig fine-grained features of images, For example, the B-CNN [8] network uses the attention generated by bilinear channel interactions for end-to-end training to guide classification. The bilinear network generates features of 1×512 at each image location, and then performs an outer product operation on the features extracted by the two networks. This will result in high data costs and require relatively large hardware. In order to reduce its computational complexity, Compact Bilinear Pooling [10] tends to use fewer feature dimensions. At the same time, the HBP [9] model further proposes a hierarchical bilinear pooling structure, which includes more convolutional layer features by cascading multiple cross-layer bilinear pooling modules. However, these models only use attention generated by simple interactions of bilinear networks. Not conducive to finding local regions with discriminative features between images.

In summary, our model is different from the above B-CNN [8]; we mainly propose the powerful learning ability based on LSTM recurrent attention and multi-head attention to focus on the target region of the image. It can better focus on the target area's detailed information based on the attention mechanism's learning ability while suppressing the useless information. In addition, we also propose the global feature extraction problem of improving weak baseline networks, mainly by performing data augmentation on the baseline networks. When the features extracted by the baseline network are richer, attention can find more target regions. Finally, for the MMAL-Net [14] model, the difference is that we use the feature map obtained by MLP spatial mapping and the attention mechanism to obtain features for element-wise channel multiplication. Target regions in the image can be zoomed in to find more discriminative features.

3   Method

As shown in Fig. 2, We use data-enhanced dual-attention interaction method to perform fine-grained classification with an image and its corresponding label. Based on the enhanced baseline network to enrich global features, the dual-attention mechanism finds more local attention points, and the processing of interactive channels Discover more discriminative features to guide classification.

3.1   Data Augmentation

The ResNet network is improved based on VGG [1], which greatly improves the network performance by increasing the network depth. Residual networks are structured such that stacked layers are called blocks. For each block, a residual module is used to connect, which can easily deepen the depth of the network. Adding a residual block to its internal network and using jump connections can better solve the problem of exploding or dissipating gradients. The performance of the network will not be degraded.

Based on the ResNet50 baseline network, we fuse the channel features from the lower block layers of the convolutional network to the higher block layers one by one. The features of each layer are the fusion of the previous features of this layer, and the whole process is equivalent to enriching the global features. At the same time, the training is also carried out in layers. As the number of layers increases, different weights are assigned because the features at the bottom will contain larger receptive fields, while the features at the top will contain more

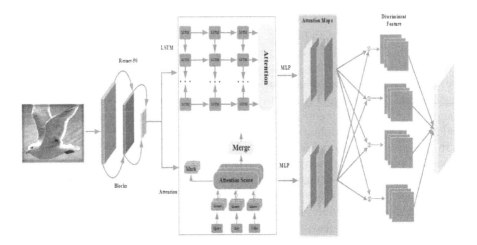

Fig. 2. Based on the data-enhanced dual attention interactive fine-grained classification network, the dual attention area adds distinguishable features. The interactive module expands the local attention area and highlights the distinguishing features to guide the final classification.

semantic image features. The training process from low-level to high-level can force the layer-by-layer convolutions of the ResNet network to learn finer-grained features. Based on the baseline network extractor, it is divided into three layers; each layer outputs $F_i \in R^{H \times W \times C}$, where H, W, and C are the feature maps of the i-th layer of convolution, respectively height, width, dimensions. Where $i = \{1, 2, 3\}$. Our goal is to impose a classification loss on the extraction of feature maps at different intermediate stages of the baseline network.

$$S_{concat} = concat[F_2, F_3 \oplus F_2, F_4 \oplus F_3 \oplus F_2] \tag{1}$$

3.2   Dual Attention Network

Since the attention mechanism can often use limited attention resources to obtain high-value information from a large amount of information quickly and ignore other irrelevant information, so here, we use an attention mechanism to discover key feature regions with discriminative power in an image. After the hierarchical training of the ResNet network, rich global feature maps are obtained. Then the attention features are extracted using the improved LSTM and the multi-head attention dual-attention network. Among them, LSTM loop attention can find the patch of the image and gradually loop the small patch of the image for finer clustering. As described in the RA-CNN [15] paper, LSTM can also be viewed as a multi-scale attention framework; the most significant advantage of a multi-scale network is that it can gradually focus on key regions during training. In this loop, we can find fine-grained features that are imperceptible. The specific formula is as follows. For the features extracted by the data augmentation network ResNet,

$G_i \in R^{w \times h \times c}$ is obtained, G_i goes through LSTM in turn, and the output feature is represented as $[\phi(G_i^1), ..., (G_i^T)]$. i represents the channel number, T is the time step, ϕ is the LSTM function, and W^t is the parameter to be trained. $F_{Attention}$ is the key feature area of the image obtained by attention, where A_i represents the output of the LSTM attention layer, and W_l represents the feature map obtained by the data augmentation network.

$$A_i = \sum_{t=1}^{T} \alpha^t \phi(G_i^t) \tag{2}$$

$$\alpha^t = \frac{\exp(W^t * \phi(G_i^t))}{\sum_{i=1}^{T} \exp(W^t * \phi(G_i^t))} \tag{3}$$

$$F_{Attention} = W_l * A_i \tag{4}$$

Similarly, multi-head attention uses multiple independent attentions to compute key feature regions of an image. This article uses vector headers Q, K, and V for linear layer mapping, mutual point multiplication, and regularization. First, Q, K, and V are linearly transformed, and each attention mechanism function is only responsible for one subspace in the final output sequence, that is, which is independent of each other. The specific operation in this network is to reduce the original Q, K, and V from the original high-dimensionality to a lower dimension (since eight headers are used). Second, through the linear transformation between them, the original multi-dimensional features are stitched together to obtain more important features. Among them, K and V are in one-to-one correspondence and measure the similarity between Q and K, and the accepted similarity measure is scaled and standardized. Finally, the weight of the calculated similarity measure function is weighted by the softmax function with V. When calculating the similarity between Q and V, the final multi-head attention value is obtained using the dot product. Based on the data augmentation module to obtain the global feature map F^i, we accept three identical features as the attention input $(F_Q^i, F_K^i, F_V^i) = (F^i, F^i, F^i)$. Where F^i represents the ith feature map of F. The specific formula is as follows:

$$F'_{Attention} = F^i + soft\max(\frac{F_Q^i (F_K^i)^T}{\sqrt{d_K}})F_V^i \tag{5}$$

3.3   Channel Interaction and Local Feature Fusion

Based on the features extracted by the dual attention network, more discriminative features can be discovered through the interaction of channels. In deep learning, MLP is also known as Artificial Neural Network (ANN). It can have multiple hidden layers in addition to the input and output layers. The simplest MLP contains only one hidden layer, a three-layer structure. The layers of a multilayer perceptron are fully connected.

Firstly, the features extracted by the dual attention mechanism undergo spatial mapping and channel dimensionality reduction through MLP. The spatial mapping of the multilayer perceptron is equivalent to a feature filtering mechanism, which can filter out some noisy features. This operation through the multilayer perceptron is equivalent to generating two finer-grained feature maps. Then, the two attention feature maps extracted by dual attention and the feature map generated by MLP are multiplied element by element, which can enlarge the image's key local areas and help find more discriminative features. We end up with four distinct local regions corresponding to different parts of the image-such as the bird's head, torso, tail, and paws. Feature fusion methods for different parts of an image have irreplaceable importance in fine-grained classification. A suitable feature fusion method can better describe the overall characteristics of the image. Therefore, based on fusing the four local features, the overall training is carried out to better obtain the global discriminative features. The specific formula is as follows, where f_m represents the multilayer perceptron function, and $\otimes$ represents channel multiplication. In addition, $F_{Attention}$ and $F'_{Attention}$ are the feature maps obtained by dual Attention, respectively.

$$A_1 = f_m(F_{Attention}), A_2 = f_m(F'_{Attention}) \tag{6}$$

$$w_k = A_1 \otimes F'_{Attention}, (k = 1, 2), w_k = A_2 \otimes F_{Attention}, (k = 3, 4) \tag{7}$$

$$W = Concat(w_1, w_2, w_3, w_4) \tag{8}$$

4   Experimental Results and Analysis

Experimental analysis and performance demonstrations are performed here, comparing our model approach with other newer approaches. Then the ablation experiments are analyzed for each module in the model framework. The comparison highlights the innovation and performance advantages of our models.

4.1   Datasets and Implementation Details

This step mainly details the dataset used in the experiments. The data set CUB-200–2011 [16] has 11788 bird images, including 200 bird subcategories and the training data set. There are 5994 images, and the test set has 5794 images. Each image provides image tag information, the bounding box of the bird in the image, the key part information of the bird, and the attribute information of the bird. The FGVC Aircraft [17] dataset contains images of 10,200 aircraft, 102 of which are different aircraft, each with 100 images. The data set of Stanford Cars [18] contains 16,185 photos of 196 types of vehicles; among them, the training set is 8144, and the test set is 8041.

We perform all experiments on a GTX 3090 GPU using PyTorch version 1.6. Our experiments are mainly based on the hierarchical training of residual networks to extract global features. Each of these layers is trained individually. In addition, the whole model is roughly divided into three different training parts: data augmentation part, dual attention part, and channel interaction fine-grained part. Different weights are assigned to each training part. During training, images were resized to 448×448, and a stochastic gradient descent (SGD) optimizer was used. At the same time, when training the neural network, fine-tune the learning rate of each loss and convolution module. Initially, our overall learning rate was 0.002, and the corresponding learning rate decreased by 0.1 after every 50 epochs. For all the above models, we use 0.0005 weight decay and 0.9 momenta to train up to 300 epochs with a batch size of 16.

4.2 Experimental Results on Three Fine-Grained Data Sets

As shown in Table 1, we conduct performance comparison experiments on three different datasets. Good performance is an important indicator of model quality, and most of the papers compared are relatively recent. Discovered from the CUB-200-2011 dataset in the table, compared to the typical model RA-CNN [15] and DCL [19] performance increases by 4.1%, 1.6%. The RA-CNN [15] model uses a multi-scale network to locate regions of interest in an image and crop and zoom in on local feature regions of the image, which can refine the content of local features. Likewise, we also zoom in on local feature regions to find more discriminative feature maps. We perform channel-wise element-wise dot product interactions based on features obtained from MLP spatial mapping and features obtained through dual attention. The discriminative features expanded in this way can be better used to guide fine-grained image classification, and our method also does not impose an excessive model burden due to multiple networks. The DCL [19] model extracts its features by randomly partitioning the image and reconstructing the image, training it using an adversarial network. According to the authors, the main purpose of scrambling an image is to let the neural network find more hidden fine-grained feature maps without relying on global constraints. In general, scrambled images bring in too much noise. Later fine-grained features are also difficult to extract, which is not conducive to practical applications. We propose a data augmentation method to obtain rich global feature maps by using hierarchical training of residual networks. In summary, our model can extract more global features and dig deep into fine-grained local feature regions and finally find fine-grained discriminative regions. Experiments with this model are performed only on the traditional cross-entropy loss model.

4.3 Data Augmentation and Dual Attention Visualization

Our model is further visualized in Fig. 3. First, we randomly select bird pictures from the CUB-200-2011 dataset. Feed the image into the model and use Grad-CAM [26] to visualize it accordingly. A visual comparison of each layer of the original baseline network and the baseline data augmentation network is then performed. As can be seen from a in Fig. 3, the receptive field of the hierarchical training data augmentation module with channel stacking is larger than the original feature receptive field and contains more information. Furthermore, we also show the visualization of feature maps in the corresponding dual attention section. As shown in b in Fig. 3, based on the features obtained by the residual

Table 1. The method of our model is compared with the method of the newer paper on the three data sets of CUB-200-2011, Stanford Motors, and FGVC aircraft.

Method	Backbone	Input size	CUB (%)	FGVC (%)	Stanford (%)
RA-CNN [15]	VGG-19	448 × 448	85.3	92.5	–
MA-CNN [20]	VGG-19	448 × 448	86.5	89.9	92.8
BilinearCNN [8]	VGG-16	448 × 448	84.1	84.1	91.3
HBP [9]	VGG-19	448 × 448	87.1	90.3	93.7
NTSNet [21]	ResNet50	448 × 448	87.5	91.4	93.9
MAMC [22]	ResNet50	448 × 448	86.2	91.2	94.1
Cross-X [6]	ResNet50	448 × 448	87.7	92.6	94.5
DCL [19]	ResNet50	448 × 448	87.8	93.0	94.5
S3N [23]	ResNet50	448 × 448	88.5	92.8	94.7
MC-Loss [7]	ResNet50	448 × 448	87.3	92.6	93.7
IU-Module [24]	ResNet50	448 × 448	87.6	92.3	94.1
SMA-Net [5]	VGG-19	448 × 448	87.7	–	94.3
iSQRT-COV [25]	ResNet50	448 × 448	88.9	91.7	94.3
Attentive cutout [11]	ResNet50	448 × 448	86.6	92.4	94.0
Ours	ResNet50	448 × 448	89.4	93.1	94.9

network, we use the dual attention network to find local key regions with discriminative ability in the image; it can be seen that the discriminative feature regions of images without attention are not easily detected. Instead, our dual attention can effectively focus on key regions of the image. As expected, our model successfully captured features of birds with distinguishing parts, such as heads, claws, and tails.

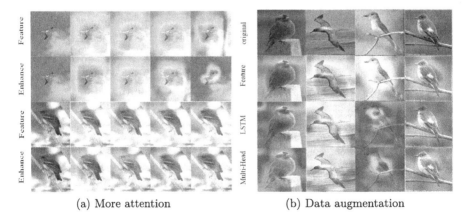

(a) More attention   (b) Data augmentation

Fig. 3. Hierarchical visualization of the baseline data augmentation module and visualization of the dual attention module.

4.4 Ablation Experiments

Here an ablation study of our model is performed to understand each part of our model better. Reasonable ablation experiments can better demonstrate the role of each module in the model. This experiment uses the classic ResNet50 baseline network as our backbone network and performs all ablation experiments on the CUB-200-2011 dataset, and other datasets have the same experimental results.

Table 2. Analyze and compare the role of each sub-module under the general framework of the model.

B-Stream	D-Attention	L-Stream	Accuracy (%)
	$\checkmark$	$\checkmark$	87.3
$\checkmark$		$\checkmark$	88.1
$\checkmark$	$\checkmark$		88.8
$\checkmark$	$\checkmark$	$\checkmark$	89.4

The ablation experiments in Table 2 are mainly to compare and analyze the various components of the model. The baseline extraction module of ResNet50 is B-Stream, which mainly performs hierarchical training on the residual network to obtain rich global features. The dual attention module is D-Attention, which utilizes Multi-Head Attention and LSTM recurrent attention to locate global features and quickly discover discriminative regions in images. Finally, L-Stream is based on control vectors for local feature channel interactions. Equivalent to an extension of fine-grained discriminative features. Through experiments, the influence of each module on the overall performance of the model is highlighted.

Table 3. Comparative analysis of their respective internal parameters about the channel interaction module and the data enhancement module.

Interactive parameters	Accuracy (%)	Training parameters	Accuracy (%)
$K = 16$	88.9	$G = (1, 1, 1, 1)$	88.6
$K = 32$	89.4	$G = (1, 2, 3, 4)$	89.0
$K = 64$	89.4	$G = (1, 1, 1, 2)$	89.4

The first half of the experiment in Table 3 mainly compare and analyze the parameter K of the channel interaction between the feature map extracted by the dual attention network and the feature map generated by the MLP module. The parameters in the interaction module will affect the discriminative features of the model's extended images, and a good discriminative feature is a key to distinguishing similar objects. The experimental structure shows that as the parameter K increases, its performance gradually improves. When $K = 32$, the model's performance has reached the best of level. As K increases, the contribution to performance remains the same.

The second half of the same table compares the effect of G parameters on global feature extraction. This parameter is equivalent to setting a threshold for each layer of the data enhancement module and assigning a certain weight to facilitate better training. In this way, the bottom network can be forced to find more global receptive fields, while the top network can learn more global semantic features while discovering more image features. Different weight training promotes different layers to recognize the global features of the image better.

5   Conclusions

This paper proposes a data-augmented dual-attention interaction network, which can gradually search for key points of an image and find its discriminative regions through a powerful attention mechanism and interaction between channels. In addition, it can be embedded in other models as a plug-and-play unit. The method in this paper is obtained by ingenious improvement of existing modules. Therefore, as mentioned above, this network is a practical and efficient method for fine-grained classification. For future work, it would be interesting to add other external knowledge to the network for testing, such as the recently proposed combination of data-augmented network properties.

Acknowledgments. This work is supported by National Natural Science Foundation of China (Nos. 61966004, 61866004), Guangxi Natural Science Foundation (No. 2019GXNSFDA245018), Guangxi "Bagui Scholar" Teams for Innovation and Research Project, Guangxi Talent Highland Project of Big Data Intelligence and Application, and Guangxi Collaborative Innovation Center of Multi-source Information Integration and Intelligent Processing.

References

1. Simonyan, K., Zisserman, A.: Very deep convolutional networks for large-scale image recognition. arXiv preprint arXiv:1409.1556 (2014)
2. He, K., Zhang, X., Ren, S., Sun, J.: Deep residual learning for image recognition. In: Proceedings of the IEEE Conference on Computer Vision and Pattern Recognition, pp. 770–778 (2016)
3. Zhang, N., Donahue, J., Girshick, R., Darrell, T.: Part-based R-CNNs for fine-grained category detection. In: Fleet, D., Pajdla, T., Schiele, B., Tuytelaars, T. (eds.) ECCV 2014. LNCS, vol. 8689, pp. 834–849. Springer, Cham (2014). https://doi.org/10.1007/978-3-319-10590-1_54
4. Branson, S., Van Horn, G., Belongie, S., Perona, P.: Bird species categorization using pose normalized deep convolutional nets. arXiv preprint arXiv:1406.2952 (2014)
5. Liu, C., Huang, L., Wei, Z., Zhang, W.: Subtler mixed attention network on fine-grained image classification. Appl. Intell. **51**(11), 7903–7916 (2021). https://doi.org/10.1007/s10489-021-02280-y

6. Luo, W., et al.: Cross-X learning for fine-grained visual categorization. In: Proceedings of the IEEE/CVF International Conference on Computer Vision, pp. 8242–8251 (2019)

7. Chang, D., et al.: The devil is in the channels: mutual-channel loss for fine-grained image classification. IEEE Trans. Image Process. **29**, 4683–4695 (2020)

8. Lin, T.-Y., Chowdhury, A.R., Maji, S.: Bilinear CNN models for fine-grained visual recognition. In: Proceedings of the IEEE International Conference on Computer Vision, pp. 1449–1457 (2015)

9. Yu, C., Zhao, X., Zheng, Q., Zhang, P., You, X.: Hierarchical bilinear pooling for fine-grained visual recognition. In: Ferrari, V., Hebert, M., Sminchisescu, C., Weiss, Y. (eds.) Computer Vision – ECCV 2018. ECCV 2018. Lecture Notes in Computer Science, vol. 11220. Springer, Cham (2018). https://doi.org/10.1007/978-3-030-01270-0_35

10. Wang, H., Wang, Q., Gao, M., Li, P., Zuo, W.: Multi-scale location-aware kernel representation for object detection. In: Proceedings of the IEEE Conference on Computer Vision and Pattern Recognition, pp. 1248–1257 (2018)

11. Guo, C., Lin, Y., Xu, M., et al.: Inverse transformation sampling-based attentive cutout for fine-grained visual recognition. Vis. Comput., 1–12 (2022). https://doi.org/10.1007/s00371-022-02481-7

12. Li, Z., Lin, L., Zhang, C., Ma, H., Zhao, W., Shi, Z.: A semi-supervised learning approach based on adaptive weighted fusion for automatic image annotation. ACM Trans. Multimed. Comput. Commun. Appl. **17**(1), 1–23 (2021)

13. Zhou, T., Li, Z., Zhang, C., Ma, H.: Classify multi-label images via improved CNN model with adversarial network. Multimedia Tools Appl. **79**(9), 6871–6890 (2020)

14. Zhang, F., Li, M., Zhai, G., Liu, Y.: Multi-branch and multi-scale attention learning for fine-grained visual categorization. arXiv preprint arXiv:2003.09150 (2020)

15. Fu, J., Zheng, H., Mei, T.: Look closer to see better: recurrent attention convolutional neural network for fine-grained image recognition. In: Proceedings of the IEEE Conference on Computer Vision and Pattern Recognition, pp. 4438–4446 (2017)

16. Wah, C., Branson, S., Welinder, P., Perona, P., Belongie, S.: The caltech-UCSD birds-200-2011 dataset. Technical report 2010–001, California Institute of Technology (2011)

17. Maji, S., Rahtu, E., Kannala, J., Blaschko, M., Vedaldi, A.: Fine-grained visual classification of aircraft. arXiv preprint arXiv:1306.5151 (2013)

18. Liu, M., Yu, C., Ling, H., Lei, J.: Hierarchical joint CNN-based models for fine-grained cars recognition. In: Sun, X., Liu, A., Chao, H.-C., Bertino, E. (eds.) ICCCS 2016. LNCS, vol. 10040, pp. 337–347. Springer, Cham (2016). https://doi.org/10.1007/978-3-319-48674-1_30

19. Chen, Y., Bai, Y., Zhang, W., Mei, T.: Destruction and construction learning for fine-grained image recognition. In: Proceedings of the IEEE/CVF Conference on Computer Vision and Pattern Recognition, pp. 5157–5166 (2019)

20. Song, K., Yang, H., Yin, Z.: Multi-scale attention deep neural network for fast accurate object detection. IEEE Trans. Circ. Syst. Video Technol. **29**(10), 2972–2985 (2018)

21. Yang, Z., Luo, T., Wang, D., Hu, Z., Gao, J., Wang, L.: Learning to navigate for fine-grained classification. In: Ferrari, V., Hebert, M., Sminchisescu, C., Weiss, Y. (eds.) Computer Vision – ECCV 2018. LNCS, vol. 11218, pp. 438–454. Springer, Cham (2018). https://doi.org/10.1007/978-3-030-01264-9_26

22. Sun, M., Yuan, Y., Zhou, F., Ding, E.: Multi-attention multi-class constraint for fine-grained image recognition. In: Ferrari, V., Hebert, M., Sminchisescu, C., Weiss, Y. (eds.) ECCV 2018. LNCS, vol. 11220, pp. 834–850. Springer, Cham (2018). https://doi.org/10.1007/978-3-030-01270-0_49
23. Ding, Y., Zhou, Y., Zhu, Y., Ye, Q., Jiao, J.: Selective sparse sampling for fine-grained image recognition. In: Proceedings of the IEEE/CVF International Conference on Computer Vision, pp. 6599–6608 (2019)
24. Zheng, Y., Chang, D., Xie, J., Ma, Z.: IU-module: intersection and union module for fine-grained visual classification. In Proceedings of the IEEE International Conference on Multimedia and Expo, pp. 1–6. IEEE (2020)
25. Li, X., Yang, C., Chen, S.-L., Zhu, C., Yin, X.-C.: Semantic bilinear pooling for fine-grained recognition. In: Proceedings of the 2020 25th International Conference on Pattern Recognition, pp. 3660–3666. IEEE (2021)
26. Zhou, B., Khosla, A., Lapedriza, A., Oliva, A., Torralba, A.: Learning deep features for discriminative localization. In: Proceedings of the IEEE Conference on Computer Vision and Pattern Recognition, pp. 2921–2929 (2016)

Deep Dictionary Pair Learning for SAR Image Classification

Kang Wei, Jiwen Dong, Wei Hu, Sijie Niu, Hui Zhao, and Xizhan Gao[✉]

Shandong Provincial Key Laboratory of Network based Intelligent Computing,
School of Information Science and Engineering, University of Jinan,
Jinan 250022, China
`ise_gaoxz@ujn.edu.cn`

Abstract. Projective dictionary pair learning (DPL) provides an effective solution to the image classification problem by jointly learning two dictionaries, i.e., the synthesis dictionary and the analysis dictionary, for the purpose of image representation and discrimination. However, the DPL algorithm focuses only on dictionary learning, ignores the importance of feature learning. Therefore, we propose a new deep dictionary pair learning (DDPL) network that combines feature learning and dictionary learning in an end-to-end architecture. Specifically, the DPL approach is embedded in a deep convolutional neural network (DCNN) by introducing two dictionary learning layers. In other words, the DCNN is used to learn high-quality and appropriate image features, while the DPL uses the learned deep features for dictionary learning and guides the update of the deep network. Finally, our network architecture is trained by a backpropagation algorithm that minimizes the standard deep dictionary pair learning loss function, which is simpler than the traditional alternating direction method of multipliers (ADMM) optimization algorithm. Experimental results on three SAR image classification datasets show that our approach significantly outperforms some state-of-the-art SAR classification methods in terms of classification accuracy.

Keywords: SAR image classification · Projective dictionary pair learning · Neural networks · Deep learning

1 Introduction

Synthetic aperture radar (SAR) utilizes the synthesis aperture principle, pulse compression techniques, and signal processing methods to provide a large amount of land cover information in all weather and all-time conditions, and has an important position in imaging radar. In terms of applications, SAR plays an important role in the fields of geology, agriculture, and oceanography, and has a wide range of application potential that is beginning to receive the attention of many research scholars. In particular, image classification is one of the most fundamental applications of SAR images [23], i.e., identifying the label of each SAR images, which has far-reaching research value.

E. Pimenidis et al. (Eds.): ICANN 2022, LNCS 13531, pp. 87–100, 2022.
https://doi.org/10.1007/978-3-031-15934-3_8

Nowadays many attempts have been made in the field of SAR image classification using deep convolutional neural networks, and a large number of SAR image classification methods based on deep learning have emerged [4,17,25]. Chen et al. proposed A-ConvNets containing only sparse connections and not fully connected layers [1], and Yu proposed a SAR image targeting method based on FCNN and improved convolutional self-encoder (ICAE) [22]. Later, Guo proposed a multi-feature fusion decision convolutional neural network framework (MFFD-CNN) with better stability [9]. Zhao et al. proposed a new fusion framework that achieves higher classification accuracy, stronger noise robustness, and superior classification performance for targets of the same class of subjects and different subclasses [24].

Sparse representation or dictionary learning is originally proposed in the field of signal processing, which aims to use as few atoms as possible in an overcomplete dictionary to represent a set of signals. In view of the strong representation ability of dictionary learning, many scholars have started to introduce it to the field of image classification and have achieved good results [7,21]. In particular, Gu et al. proposed a projective dictionary pair learning (DPL) algorithm, which jointly learned a synthesis dictionary and an analytic dictionary for image representation and discrimination purposes, it can greatly reduce the time complexity of training and testing, and achieved competitive accuracy in image classification tasks [8]. After that, in view of its powerful classification ability, DPL and its variants are introduced to the SAR image classification tasks. For example, the MDPL-SAE method [3] combines projective dictionary pair learning (MDPL) and sparse self-encoder (SAE) for PolSAR image classification, while semicoupled projective DPL method with SAE (SAE-SDPL) [2] inherits advantages from SAE, DPL, and semicoupled dictionary learning (SCDL), and have obtained excellent results in PolSAR image classification.

Although the DPL-based method has achieved some success in SAR image classification. However, the DPL algorithm ignores the importance of image feature learning, and the features extracted by using the existing DCNN directly do not match with the dictionary learning, thus leading to limited improvement of classification results (this can be proved in Sect. 4.3). In addition, the traditional DPL algorithm uses ADMM to optimize the DPL model, and the optimization process is relatively complicated. Inspired by this, this paper integrates deep feature learning with dictionary learning and proposes an end-to-end network - deep dictionary pair learning network. This network aims to learn deep features and discriminative dictionaries simultaneously. More specifically, the DDPL network introduces two dictionary learning layers on top of the DCNN model to learn synthesis dictionaries and analysis dictionaries, while using a backpropagation algorithm to optimize this network.

The main contributions of this paper are:

- A deep dictionary pair learning network is proposed which combines DCNN and DPL in an end-to-end architecture. In this network, DCNN is used to learn discriminative features applicable to dictionary learning, while DPL is used to learn the discriminative dictionary and back-guide DCNN's update.

- The simple but effective backpropagation algorithm is used to optimize the proposed network, which is easier to understand than the traditional ADMM algorithm. Experimental results show that our method significantly outperforms some advanced SAR classification methods in terms of classification accuracy.

2 Related Work

2.1 Discriminative Dictionary Learning

Discriminative dictionary learning reconstructs the samples as sparsely as possible by learning a synthesis dictionary while training a discriminative term representation to distinguish between various types of samples [5,13]. The general model can be formulated as follows.

$$\min_{D,A} \|X - DA\|_F^2 + \alpha\|A\|_1 + \varphi(D, A) \tag{1}$$

where X denotes the input sample, α is a scalar, D denotes the synthesis dictionary, A denotes the coding coefficient on sample X through the synthesis dictionary D, $\|X - DA\|_F^2$ denotes the reconstruction term of the sample, $\|A\|_1$ will make the coding coefficient A more sparse, and the model ensures that the sample can be reconstructed as much as possible with sufficient sparsity and with certain discriminatory properties.

On this basis, dictionary learning algorithms were introduced for application in the field of SAR image classification [10,16]. Chen et al. proposed a PolSAR image classification method based on multilayer projective dictionary pair learning (MDPL) and sparse self-encoder (SAE), in which MDPL was first used for feature extraction and SAE was later used to obtain the nonlinear relationship between vectors [3], which achieved good results in three PolSAR image tests, but the quality of features extracted by using MDPL needs to be improved. Meanwhile, Chen [2] et al. proposed a new semi-coupled projective DPL method (SAE-SDPL) for PolSAR image classification. This method can obtain classification results efficiently and accurately while providing a new method for matching different features.

2.2 Deep Convolutional Neural Network

CNN is a machine learning model proposed by LeCun [14,15] and consists of multiple convolutional layers and pooling layers, which are topped by a fully-connected layer. In recent years, the development of computing power and the availability of a large number of labeled datasets have driven the progress and development of deep convolutional neural networks. DCNNs have gradually become the preferred structure in most image recognition and classification detection tasks [18]. In recent work, self-attention mechanisms have been continuously introduced to computer vision tasks, especially image classification tasks [12]. Wang pioneered the introduction of self-attention into computer vision and proposed a novel nonlocal network, where the network captures long-term dependencies through nonlocal operations, and nonlocal blocks can be combined with any existing architecture with great success in video understanding and target detection [20].

In particular, in the field of SAR image classification, Chen et al. proposed A-ConvNets [1] that contained only sparse connections without using fully connected layers, reducing the number of free parameters and achieving an average accuracy of 99% for 10 classes of targets on the MSTAR dataset, but the generalization of the tested model needed to be improved. Later, Guo proposed a multi-feature fusion decision convolutional neural network framework (MFFD-CNN), which used two downsampling methods in the pooling layer and chose to perform the fusion operation by concatenating or adding features that do merge the convolutional and pooling layers, and this structure not only can over the average accurate recognition rate of 1.2% higher than FCNN but also had better stability [9].

3   Proposed Method

3.1   Projective Dictionary Pair Learning

The l_1 paradigm of discriminative dictionary learning will take a lot of time. Meanwhile, the projective dictionary pair learning algorithm with two joint learning dictionaries i.e. synthesis dictionary and analysis dictionary can be better discriminative than the former. This method not only reduces the time complexity of the training and testing phases significantly but also achieves very competitive accuracy rates in various vision tasks [6,8]. The specific model can be formulated as follows:

$$\min_{P,D} \sum_{k=1}^{K} \|X_k - D_k P_k X_k\|_F^2 + \|P_k \overline{X_k}\|_F^2 \quad s.t. \|d_i^k\|_2^2 \le 1 \tag{2}$$

where X_k denotes the features of kth class, D_k denotes the synthesis dictionary of kth class, P_k denotes the analysis dictionary of kth class, and $\overline{X_k}$ denotes the complementary matrix of kth class, i.e., $\overline{X_k} = [X_1, ..., X_{k-1}, X_{k+1}, ..., X_K]$, where there are K classes and d_i denotes the ith atom of the synthesis dictionary D_k. $\|X_k - D_k P_k X_k\|_F^2$ denotes the coding coefficients of the sample with k^{th} generated after $P_k X_k$ and reconstructs the sample by D_k synthesis dictionary. $\|P_k \overline{X_k}\|_F^2$ denotes the discriminant term of the sample, i.e., $P_k X_i \approx 0 (k \ne i)$.

3.2   Dictionary Learning Layers

The goal of this paper is to construct a deep end-to-end network to simultaneously perform feature learning and dictionary learning, such that the latent features are well-suited to dictionary learning, and the latent dictionary has powerful discrimination ability. To this end, two new dictionary learning layers are introduced in this subsection.

Specifically, consider the dictionary learning term in Eq. (1): $\|X - DA\|_F^2$, which equals to $\sum_{i=1}^{m} \|x_i - D\alpha_i\|_2^2$. It means that the dictionary D is used to encode x_i, or decode the coding vector α_i, i.e., use D to project α_i, such that the input sample is as similar as the decoding vector as possible. Hence, for $D\alpha_i$, we can use a linear layer without bias and activation to represent it.

Similarly, consider the dictionary pair learning term in Eq. (2): $\|X_k - D_k P_k X_k\|_F^2$, which equals to $\sum_{i=1}^{N} \|x_i^k - D_k P_k x_i^k\|_2^2$, where x_i^k denotes the ith sample belongs to k^{th} class. This term consists of two parts: $P_k x_i^k$ and $D_k \alpha_i^k$, where $\alpha_i^k = P_k x_i^k$. For $D_k \alpha_i^k$, according to the above analysis, it can be represented by a linear layer. For $P_k x_i^k$, it can be seen as a linear projection of the sample x_i^k, which can naturally be represented using a linear layer without bias and activation.

To summarize, for dictionary pair learning term, two consecutive dictionary learning layers (which are both linear layers) can be used to model it, i.e., we first encode the input as a low-dimensional vector using the encoding dictionary learning layer, and then decode the low-dimensional vector as a reconstruction vector using the decoding dictionary learning layer. The weights of these two dictionary learning layers correspond to the analysis dictionary P and the synthesis dictionary D in Eq. (3), respectively. Therefore, our dictionary learning layers essentially let us directly learn the discriminative dictionaries via the network. Moreover, the constraint $\|d_i^k\|_2^2 \leq 1$ simply translates to adding a regular term to the weights of the decoding dictionary learning layer.

Finally, as shown in Fig. 1, we assume that there are K classes of images, and each class of images X_k has N samples, i.e. $X = [X_1, \ldots, X_K]$, $X_k = [x_1^k, \ldots, x_N^k]$. Let Θ denotes the parameters of the DCNN, and let $Z_k = [z_1^k, \ldots, z_N^k]$ denotes the input of the dictionary learning layer, i.e., the depth features of the kth class of training samples, denote the parameters of decoding dictionary learning layer as D_k and the parameters of encoding dictionary learning layers P_k. Our loss function can be formulated as:

$$L = \frac{\lambda_2}{2} \sum_{i=1}^{N} \|z_i^k - D_k P_k z_i^k\|_2^2 + \frac{\lambda_1}{2} \sum_{i=1}^{N} \|P_k \overline{z_i^k}\|_2^2 + \frac{\lambda_3}{2} \sum_{i=0}^{m} (\|d_i^k\|_2^2 - 1)^2 \quad (3)$$

In Eq. (3), the first term can be called the data-fitting term, which is used to minimize the reconstruction error between the kth class samples. The second term can be called the discriminant term, which is used to minimize the coding vector of other class samples by using the analysis dictionary of the kth class.

Using this loss function, we can solve Θ and dictionaries D_k, P_k jointly by using the Backpropagation algorithm.

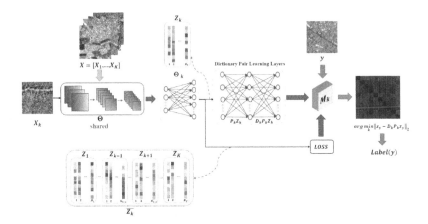

Fig. 1. Deep dictionary pair learning overall network architecture.

3.3 Network Architecture

The overall architecture of the deep dictionary pair learning network is shown in Fig. 1, and we have specifically divided the network architecture into three parts: The basic network part Θ, the class-specific network part Θ_k and the dictionary learning part (D_k, P_k).

For basic network part, the ResNet50-NonLocal network is used. Specifically, for ResNet50 we truncate at Conv4_x and introduce four embedded Gaussian blocks (i.e., Non-local Blocks) based on the self-attention mechanism. Non-local Block and an AdaptiveAvgPool for further feature extraction, and then trained with SoftMax+CrossEntropy to generate a DCNN model Θ of the K classes image set. This part is learned on all training samples with the aim of learning the common features of all class samples.

For the class-specific network part, the FC layer is used, and it relies the class label. Specifically, during training, all samples of the kth class are used in a single batch, with the aim of learning class-specific features, i.e., learning the unique features of each class.

The dictionary learning part is constructed by using two fully connected linearly layers without bias and non-linear activations. Specifically, the first dictionary learning layer is called "analysis dictionary learning layer", whose parameters correspond to the analysis dictionary P, and the number of input neurons is the dimension p of the output z of the class-specific network, the number of output neurons is m, i.e., the number of atoms in the dictionary, and usually $p \gg m$. The second dictionary learning layer is called "synthesis dictionary learning layer", whose parameters correspond to the synthesis dictionary D, and the number of input neurons in this layer is m and the number of output neurons is p.

3.4   Training and Inference

Our detailed training and inference detail are shown in Fig. 2. In the training process, the basic network part is first pre-trained on ImageNet and then fine-tuned using all K classes training data with cross-entropy loss to learn the common features of all class samples. After that, the class-specific network part and the dictionary learning part are jointly trained on each class with the proposed deep dictionary pair learning loss function in Eq. (3) to learn the unique discriminative dictionaries of each class. Note that, our three parts can also be trained in an end-to-end fashion, i.e., fine-tuning our whole network on each class, however, this behavior will consume a lot of memory and increase the computing cost.

In the Inference process, we generate the f_y by inputting the test sample y into the Θ. z_y is generated by the class-specific network, and is fed into the dictionary learning model $M = [M_1, ..., M_K]$, where $M_i = (P_i, D_i)$, to discriminate and reconstruct it. Thus our classification process can be expressed as Eq. (4):

$$Label(y) = arg \min_{k} \|z_y - D_k P_k z_y\|_2 \tag{4}$$

For y, the sparse coding generated by P_k will be discriminative, if y comes from k^{th} class, then the reconstruction error will be small after the synthesis dictionary; if y does not come from k^{th} class, the reconstruction error will be large. To verify this, Fig. 3 shows the block diagonal structure and the general process of classification that we generated in the classification stage of land cover dataset.

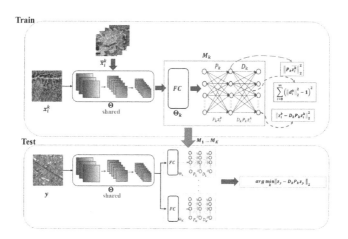

Fig. 2. Training and testing detail.

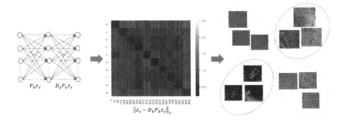

Fig. 3. Classification effect on land cover dataset.

4   Experiments

4.1   DataSet

To evaluate the classification performance of our method, we used three SAR image sets to verify our classification accuracy. The three SAR datasets include: Land cover datasets, FUSAR-Ship [11], and TenGeoP-SARwv dataset [19]. Example images of the three datasets are shown in Fig. 4.

The Land cover dataset consists of SAR image pairs from the Sentinel-1 satellite provided by the Technical University of Munich. We searched the original dataset provided by TUM for images taken in autumn and selected images that could belong to four categories: wasteland, grassland, agricultural land, and urban areas. Each class has 2800 images for training and 1200 images for testing.

The FUSAR-Ship dataset consists of high-resolution GF-3 SAR datasets constructed by running the program on 126 GF-3 scenes covering a variety of marine, land, coastal, river, and island scenes. It includes more than 5000 ship chips with AIS information and contains 15 major ship categories divided into 98 subcategories covering a variety of marine, land, coastal, river, and island scenes. The 15 classes of images in the dataset are Cargo, DiveVessel, Dredger, Fishing, High-SpeedCraft, LawEnforce, Other Passenger, PortTender, Reserved, SAR, Tanker, Tug, Unspecified, and WingInGrnd.

The TenGeoP-SARwv dataset was manually selected from the 2016 Sentinel-1A WV acquisition. A subset of more than 37,000 SAR images was tagged to correspond to ten geophysical phenomena, which cover the entire open ocean and include both oceanic and meteorological features. The dataset is the first one that deals with different oceanic or atmospheric phenomena on the open ocean. The 10 classes of the dataset are Pure Ocean Waves, Wind Streaks, Micro Convective Cells, Rain Cells, Biological Slicks, Sea Ice, Iceberg, Low Wind Area, Atmospheric Front, Oceanic Front.

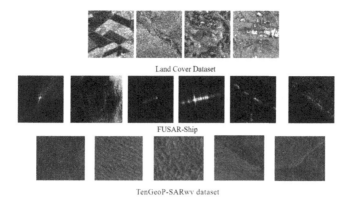

Land Cover Dataset

FUSAR-Ship

TenGeoP-SARwv dataset

Fig. 4. Example images from Land Cover & FUSAR-Ship & TenGeoP-SARwv datasets.

4.2 Setting

The division of our three image sets is uniformly divided into training and test sets according to 7 : 3, the optimizer is uniformly used Adam, the learning rate is $5e - 5$, the output dimension of the class-specific network part is set to 4096, the atom number of reconstructed samples is uniformly set to 50, and all experiments are performed on NVIDIA Tesla T4 GPUs.

For the Land cover Dataset, we make $\lambda_1 = 5e - 3$, $\lambda_2 = 1e - 2$, and $\lambda_3 = 5e - 4$. For the FUSAR-Ship dataset, we let $\lambda_1 = 8e - 3$, $\lambda_2 = 1e - 2$, $\lambda_3 = 5e - 4$. Each class has 2–1479 images for training and 1–635 images for testing. For the TenGeoP-SARwv dataset, we let $\lambda_1 = 8e - 3$, $\lambda_2 = 1e - 2$, $\lambda_3 = 5e - 4$, and 839–3430 are used for training and 360–1470 images are used for testing.

4.3 Results

We used SVM, DCNN + DPL, and some state-of-the-art SAR image classification methods: ResNet50, A-ConvNets, MFFD-CNN, and CNN-CIS-Fusion as our comparison methods. The overall accuracies of the three datasets are shown in Table 1. The results in the table are implemented by us. From this table, we observe that our method achieves significant results in the land cover, ship, and ocean-atmosphere domain datasets respectively, proving that the DDPL model has good generalization ability.

For Land cover datasets, our DDPL method achieves a 99.83% correct rate, reducing the error rate to 0.17%. It can also be seen that the ResNet50-NonLocal used for our extracted features exceeds ResNet50 by 1.56%, and DDPL exceeds ResNet50-NonLocal by 1.94% correct rate and also exceeds the most relevant method (DCNN+DPL) by 27.53%. For FUSAR-Ship, our DDPL method achieves a 72.68% correct rate, reducing the error rate to 27.2%. It can also be seen that the ResNet50-NonLocal used for our extracted features exceeds ResNet50 by 0.82%, and DDPL exceeds ResNet50-NonLocal by 1.02% correct rate and also exceeds the most relevant method (DCNN+DPL) by 30.18%. For TenGeoP-SARwv, our DDPL method achieves a 99.95% correct rate, reducing the error rate to 0.05%. It can also be seen that the ResNet50-NonLocal used for our extracted features exceeds ResNet50 by 1.45%, and DDPL exceeds ResNet50-NonLocal by 1.92% correct, and also exceeds the most relevant method (DCNN+DPL) by 17.95%, and this improvement is very significant. Also, DDPL substantially exceeds the algorithms proposed in the field of SAR image classification (A-ConvNets, MFFD-CNN, CNN-CIS-Fusion).

Table 1. Results on the Land cover datasets & FUSAR-Ship & TenGeoP-SARwv.

Results	Land cover datasets	FUSAR-Ship	TenGeoP-SARwv
ResNet50	96.33%	70.84%	96.58%
ResNet50-NonLocal	97.89%	71.66%	98.03%
DCNN+DPL	72.3%	42.5%	82.0%
SVM	61.8%	51.42%	56.69%
A-ConvNets	94.94%	11.76%	6.67%
MFFD-CNN	84.10%	55.53%	89.79%
CNN-CIS-Fusion	93.0%	65.21%	95.39%
DDPL (ours)	**99.83%**	**72.68%**	**99.95%**

The above experimental results for the three datasets firstly demonstrate that the feature extraction network we used has a very strong feature extraction capability. At the same time, the experiments show that even if we use DCNN+DPL for classification, the results are still not satisfactory, so the direct use of DCNN to extract features does not match with dictionary learning, where the main reason is that the two do not do joint learning, which is consistent with our earlier part of theoretical analysis. At the same time, the DPL algorithm ignores the importance of image feature learning and needs DCNN's extraction of effective features as support. Therefore, our proposed DDPL that adds a dictionary pair learning layer and uses a backpropagation algorithm to guide the network parameter update for joint learning achieves good results compared to DCNN+DPL, DPL, and using only DCNN for classification tasks. Also, our proposed DDPL model outperforms more mature deep learning method frameworks not only in the traditional machine learning domain but also in the SAR image classification domain.

5   Discussion

5.1   Ablation Study

We will perform a removal operation on the class-specific network part, using the best parameters of our upper part for each data set and keeping the rest of the parameters unchanged. And compare with the network that retains the class-specific network part, where FC denotes the class-specific network part, the experimental results are shown in Table 2.

We will also keep the dictionary pair learning layer and the parameters of each network unchanged, and conduct experiments to compare the effectiveness of the deep dictionary pair network and the traditional projective dictionary pair learning method by introducing ResNet50 and the feature extraction network we used. The experimental results are shown in Table 3.

Table 2. Results on the Land cover datasets & FUSAR-Ship & TenGeoP-SARwv.

Ablation	Land cover datasets	TenGeoP-SARwv	FUSAR-Ship
FC	99.83%	99.95%	72.68%
NO FC	63.52%	65.95%	41.43%

Table 3. Experimental results of feature extraction network comparison.

Ablation	ResNet50+DPL	Ours DCNN+DPL	ResNet50-DDPL	Ours DDPL
Land cover datasets	59.17%	**72.3%**	97.75%	**99.83%**

Table 4. Results on the Land cover datasets & FUSAR-Ship & TenGeoP-SARwv.

Parameter	Land cover datasets	TenGeoP-SARwv	FUSAR-Ship
512	99.50%	99.86%	67.68%
1024	99.79%	99.88%	69.58%
2048	99.81%	99.94%	70.27%
3072	99.79%	99.94%	71.98%
4096	99.83%	99.95%	72.68%

The results of the ablation experiments for the class-specific network part show that the use of the class-specific network part can learn class-specific features effectively, and this also means that the joint learning of class-specific network and the dictionary learning can improve the discrimination ability of the network. Also in our ablation experiments using different DCNNs for extracting features, we show that introducing a self-attentive mechanism can help us to extract features that are beneficial for the classification task and also demonstrate that our deep dictionary pair learning layer can be embedded in any network that can extract high-quality image features.

5.2   Parameter Comparison Study

In this section we will transform the output dimension of the class-specific network part, the dimensions are set to 512, 1024, 2048, 3072, 4096, and use the best parameters for each data set and keep them constant, respectively, to compare the effect than low-dimensional linear transformation and high-dimensional linear transformation. The experimental results are shown in Table 4.

By comparing experimental results for the class-specific network part parameters, it is shown that the use of the high dimension allows atoms to choose more freely more suitable features for sample discriminative and reconstruction work, so it is more competitive in terms of accuracy.

6   Conclusion

In this paper, we propose a new deep dictionary pair learning (DDPL) network that combines feature learning and dictionary learning in an end-to-end architecture. By introducing two dictionary learning layers, the DPL method is embedded in a deep convolutional neural network in which the DCNN is used to learn high-quality and suitable image features, while the DPL uses the learned deep features for dictionary learning and guides the update of the deep network. Finally, our network architecture is trained by a backpropagation algorithm that minimizes the standard deep dictionary pair learning loss function. The experimental results on three SAR datasets demonstrate the importance of high-quality features for dictionary pair learning and joint learning of DCNN and dictionary learning. Moreover, our proposed DDPL model outperforms not only the traditional machine learning domain in SAR image classification, but also more mature deep learning method frameworks. At the same time, the dictionary pair learning layer can be perfectly embedded into the mainstream DCNN framework as a plug-in.

Acknowledgements. The work was supported by the National Natural Science Foundation of China under Grant No. 62101213, 62103165, the Shandong Provincial Natural Science Foundation under Grant No. ZR2020QF107, ZR2020MF137, China Postdoctoral Science Foundation under Grant No. 2017M612178, the Shandong Provincial Key Research, and Development Project under Grant No. 2017CXGC0810.

References

1. Chen, S., Wang, H., Xu, F., Jin, Y.Q.: Target classification using the deep convolutional networks for SAR images. IEEE Trans. Geosci. Remote Sens. **54**(8), 4806–4817 (2016)
2. Chen, Y., et al.: A novel semicoupled projective dictionary pair learning method for polSAR image classification. IEEE Trans. Geosci. Remote Sens. **57**(4), 2407–2418 (2018)
3. Chen, Y., Jiao, L., Li, Y., Zhao, J.: Multilayer projective dictionary pair learning and sparse autoencoder for polSAR image classification. IEEE Trans. Geosci. Remote Sens. **55**(12), 6683–6694 (2017)

4. Cheng, D., Yang, X., Wang, J., Yang, X., Dong, Z.: Dense-connected global covariance network with edge sample constraint for SAR image classification. Remote Sens. Lett. **12**(6), 553–562 (2021)
5. Deng, C., Tang, X., Yan, J., Liu, W., Gao, X.: Discriminative dictionary learning with common label alignment for cross-modal retrieval. IEEE Trans. Multimedia **18**(2), 208–218 (2015)
6. Deng, D., Li, X.: Face recognition based on improved projection dictionary pair learning algorithm. In: 2017 4th International Conference on Systems and Informatics (ICSAI), pp. 1394–1399. IEEE (2017)
7. Feng, Z., Yang, M., Zhang, L., Liu, Y., Zhang, D.: Joint discriminative dimensionality reduction and dictionary learning for face recognition. Pattern Recogn. **46**(8), 2134–2143 (2013)
8. Gu, S., Zhang, L., Zuo, W., Feng, X.: Projective dictionary pair learning for pattern classification. In: Advances in Neural Information Processing Systems 27 (2014)
9. Guo, L.: Sar image classification based on multi-feature fusion decision convolutional neural network. IET Image Proc. **16**(1), 1–10 (2022)
10. Hou, B., Ren, B., Ju, G., Li, H., Jiao, L., Zhao, J.: SAR image classification via hierarchical sparse representation and multisize patch features. IEEE Geosci. Remote Sens. Lett. **13**(1), 33–37 (2015)
11. Hou, X., Ao, W., Song, Q., Lai, J., Wang, H., Xu, F.: FUSAR-ship: building a high-resolution SAR-AIS matchup dataset of Gaofen-3 for ship detection and recognition. Sci. Chin. Inf. Sci. **63**(4), 1–19 (2020)
12. Huang, Z., Wang, X., Huang, L., Huang, C., Wei, Y., Liu, W.: CCNet: criss-cross attention for semantic segmentation. In: Proceedings of the IEEE/CVF International Conference on Computer Vision, pp. 603–612 (2019)
13. Jiang, Z., Lin, Z., Davis, L.S.: Label consistent K-SVD: learning a discriminative dictionary for recognition. IEEE Trans. Pattern Anal. Mach. Intell. **35**(11), 2651–2664 (2013)
14. LeCun, Y., Bengio, Y., Hinton, G.: Deep learning. Nature **521**(7553), 436–444 (2015)
15. LeCun, Y., Bottou, L., Bengio, Y., Haffner, P.: Gradient-based learning applied to document recognition. Proc. IEEE **86**(11), 2278–2324 (1998)
16. Li, M., Guo, Y., Li, M., Luo, G., Kong, X.: Coupled dictionary learning for target recognition in SAR images. IEEE Geosci. Remote Sens. Lett. **14**(6), 791–795 (2017)
17. Maggiori, E., Tarabalka, Y., Charpiat, G., Alliez, P.: Convolutional neural networks for large-scale remote-sensing image classification. IEEE Trans. Geosci. Remote Sens. **55**(2), 645–657 (2016)
18. Rawat, W., Wang, Z.: Deep convolutional neural networks for image classification a comprehensive review. Neural Comput. **29**(9), 2352–2449 (2017)
19. Wang, C., et al.: A labelled ocean SAR imagery dataset of ten geophysical phenomena from Sentinel-1 wave mode. Geosci. Data J. **6**(2), 105–115 (2019)
20. Wang, X., Girshick, R., Gupta, A., He, K.: Non-local neural networks. In: Proceedings of the IEEE Conference on Computer Vision and Pattern Recognition, pp. 7794–7803 (2018)
21. Wright, J., Ma, Y., Mairal, J., Sapiro, G., Huang, T.S., Yan, S.: Sparse representation for computer vision and pattern recognition. Proc. IEEE **98**(6), 1031–1044 (2010)
22. Yu, L., Wang, Y., Xie, X., Lin, Y., Hong, W.: SAR ATR based on FCNN and ICAE. J. Radars **7**(5), 622–631 (2018)

23. Zhang, A., Yang, X., Jia, L., Ai, J., Dong, Z.: Sar image classification using adaptive neighborhood-based convolutional neural network. Eur. J. Remote Sens. **52**(1), 178–193 (2019)
24. Zhao, J., Yang, J., Yuan, Z., Lin, Q.: A novel fusion framework without pooling for noisy SAR image classification. In: 2020 IEEE International Conference on Systems, Man, and Cybernetics (SMC), pp. 3531–3536. IEEE (2020)
25. Zhou, Y., Wang, H., Xu, F., Jin, Y.Q.: Polarimetric SAR image classification using deep convolutional neural networks. IEEE Geosci. Remote Sens. Lett. **13**(12), 1935–1939 (2016)

Deepfake Video Detection Exploiting Binocular Synchronization

Wenjie Wang, Zhongyuan Wang$^{(\boxtimes)}$, Guangcheng Wang, and Qin Zou

National Engineering Research Center for Multimedia Software,
School of Computer Science, Wuhan University, Wuhan, China
edgarwang@whu.edu.cn,
wzy_hope@163.com

Abstract. How to accurately figure out Deepfake face video has recently been a popular research topic. The normal genuine faces exhibit binocular synchronization phenomenon of eye movements, either blinking or saccade. Instead, Deepfake faces may not be able to maintain this consistency of binocular movements provided that Deepfake videos are generated frame by frame without coordinating adjacent frames. In view of this, we propose a binocular-synchronization-based authenticity method for Deepfake videos. In particular, our methods combine convolutional latent representations with bidirectional recurrent structures. The latent representations for both binocular blinking and movement are extracted and fed into a recurrent framework to leverage the inconsistency between adjacent frames. Experimental results demonstrate the effectiveness of the developed features and the promising performance of our method in detecting forgery videos.

Keywords: Face Deepfake · Video forgery · Binocular synchronization · Eye patterns

1 Introduction

Face forgery has recently obtained substantial success. Due to the significant progress of generative models such as Variational Autoencoders (VAE), and Generative Adversarial Network (GAN) [9], various manipulation methods have been proposed. Face manipulation methods rely on deep neural networks and public video footage to synthesize someone else's face onto pre-existing videos frame by frame, rendering them unrecognizable to human eyes. Although some benign Deepfake videos exist, they remain a minority. So far, these forgery techniques have been broadly abused for malicious purposes, causing severe security and legal issues such as political propaganda, celebrity pornography [25] and infringement of personal portrait rights. Therefore, it is of paramount importance to develop effective strategies for detecting face forgery.

A common Deepfake approach involves transplanting key facial features while keeping the background and less important features unaltered, like facial expressions or poses. Nevertheless, these spontaneous and unconscious physiological

© The Author(s), under exclusive license to Springer Nature Switzerland AG 2022
E. Pimenidis et al. (Eds.): ICANN 2022, LNCS 13531, pp. 101–112, 2022.
https://doi.org/10.1007/978-3-031-15934-3_9

activities, such as breathing, blinking, eye movements, etc., are often overlooked in the process of synthesizing fake videos. Thereby, the general method most followed is to unveil the inconsistency of human physiological signals that are not well presented in the synthesized video.

Researches have been conducted on how to capture such inconsistency. Li et al. [18] proposed a Long-term Recurrent Convolutional Network (LRCN) method to describe eye blinking for detecting Deepfake faces due to the fact of the lack of eye blinking in synthesized face videos. This method is based on the observation that fake video faces blink less frequently. However, as the forgery becomes more realistic, it is not reliable to use blinking frequency alone as the criteria for discrimination. DeepVision [12] exploited eye the blinking pattern in terms of the period, repeated number, as well as elapsed eyeblink time and compared it with the eye blink database to verify the anomaly. The limitation of this method is that blinking is correlated with a bundle of mental facts, which can invalidate the verification. Li et al. [16] defined four features that could characterize eye movement differences. However, eye movements in some datasets are slight and vague thus they are hard to precisely capture.

In this paper, we make an essential observation that the temporal inconsistency of the eye region has remained distinct throughout the evolution of Deepfakes. We divide a general eye pattern into the eye movement period and blink period. Theoretically, left and right eyes blink nearly synchronously on a genuine face in the state of eye blink. Similarly, eye-gaze movements are spontaneous and consistent during the state of eye-opening [24]. A genuine person's left and right eyes rarely move in opposite directions simultaneously. These phenomena occur naturally in humans, but in the feature replacement scenarios of Deepfake generation, the separate transplantation of two eyes has no restrictions on coordination. Therefore, a forged video would contain inconsistency in the eye region between adjacent frames, whereas those of a pristine video must be consistent across all frames. By capturing these temporal inconsistencies, we can detect forgery videos.

Specifically, we explore the potential of binocular synchronization in the authentication of Deepfake face videos, including vertical motion synchronization and horizontal motion synchronization. The former refers to whether the blinking of the left and right eyes are synchronized, and the latter refers to whether the saccades of the left and right eyes keep the same. First, we utilize a pre-trained LRCN method to capture the temporal regularities and phenomenological patterns in the process of eye blinking. Eye gaze vectors are also extracted as the representation of eye movement. Both features are extracted separately as left eye and right eye. Then, these features are fed into a two-level Bi-directional Long Short-Term Memory (Bi-LSTM) module to learn a latent representation capable of discriminating between facial manipulations and pristine faces. Extensive experiments demonstrate that our method achieves state-of-the-art performance on different existing datasets, including FaceForensics++ [23] and Celeb-V2 [28].

The major contributions of this paper are summarized as follows:

- We explore the inconsistency of binocular movement patterns of Deepfake faces. In particular, we propose to use the phenomenon of binocular synchronization and design a bidirectional recurrent structure to identify Deepfake face videos, including blinking synchronization in the up and down directions and saccade synchronization in the left and right directions.

- We adopt an enhanced LRCN method and gaze vector estimation method for extracting eye blinking and movement features, respectively. A two-level Bi-LSTM is adopted to learn a latent representation for classification.

2   Related Work

In this section, we briefly overview the work in the field of face Deepfake generation and detection as well.

Deepfake Generation. Effective synthesized video and image generation techniques are developed and can be split into two general types: face swaps and face re-enactment. In the former, a target face is stitched into a source head. This manipulation output usually required a post-process to blend the edges of the overlay so that it matches the original source's face outline. FaceSwap[1] and Deepfakes[2] provide branches of fundamental face swap methods.

The latter, face re-enactment is used to produce target facial movement guiding by source video and make the target appear to act and speak like the source. Face2Face [27] and Neural Textures [26] are face re-enactment methods that transplant the facial expressions of a source object to a target while keeping the facial feature and identity of the target.

More recent Deepfake methods adopt GANs. ProGan [13] proposes a novel idea that grows both the generator and discriminator progressively, from coarse to fine, to generate a high-resolution face image. StyleGan [14] adopts a style-based design that can automatically separate the high-level attributes and stochastic variations in generated images. StarGAN [5] addresses two major challenges in image-to-image translation; translating an image of one domain to diverse images of a target domain, and supporting multiple target domains.

Deepfake Detection. In the wake of these forgery methods, defenders are also evolving on improving detection accuracy and generalization, forming an enduring arms race. Recurrent neural networks [10] and various types of 3D ConvNets [20] are utilized to detect the forgery artifacts across the video frames. However, several localization methods are introduced through either multi-task learning [21] or attention-based [7] mechanisms. To improve the generalization ability, DSP-FWA [19] and Face X-ray [15] also make their data generation pipeline and the latter focuses on predicting the blending boundaries in fake video frames. [3] uses paired images across different compression levels to improve the capacity of handling compressed facial forgery. Defakehop [4] utilizes the successive subspace learning principle to extract features automatically from various parts of face images.

---

[1] FaceSwap: https://github.com/MarekKowalski/FaceSwap.
[2] Deepfakes: https://github.com/deepfakes/faceswap.

Binocular Consistency Learning. The proliferation of deepfake methods enabled realistic face creation and manipulation. However, all of these approaches still lack consistency on biometric signals such as blink and gaze. Several methods take binocular inconsistency feature as the detection criteria. Li *et al.* [18] proposes an LRCN structure to capture blink patterns and judge the forgery videos by the existence of blink. DeepVision [12] exploits the blinking pattern in terms of the period, repeated number, as well as elapsed eye-blink time and compared it with the eye blink database to verify the anomaly. Li *et al.* [16] defines four features about the binoculus movements which are fed to Support Vector Machine (SVM) for classification. Demir *et al.* [8] compile several prominent eye and gaze features into signatures and formulate geometric, visual, metric, temporal and spectral variations. This method generalizes this formulation to deepfake detection.

3   Proposed Method

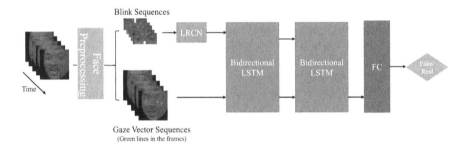

Fig. 1. The overall architecture of the proposed method. Dual feature inputs are passed into a two-level Bi-LSTM model to make a prediction.

Given an input video, our goal is to detect if the identity or expression of the subject is replaced with that of another object. Observing that the temporal inconsistency of the eye region has remained distinct throughout the evolution of Deepfakes, we proposed a framework to explore the potential of binocular synchronization, as shown in Fig. 1

3.1   Preprocessing

The face preprocessing module locates face areas in each frame of the video and extracts the corresponding eye region. First, 68 facial landmarks are detected by OpenFace2 [2] on each frame of the video. Due to the head movement and orientation change, subtle distortions are introduced between adjacent frames. These frame-to-frame inconsistencies are corrected via a linear smoothing filter.

From the aligned face, 12 of 68 landmarks outline the iconic profile of the eye region. Two rectangular boxes covering eye regions are generated. Specifically, the rectangles are generated by first calculating the bounding box of two separate eye's landmarks, then enlarging the bounding box by (1.25,1.75) in the horizontal and vertical directions which ensure that the eye region should be included in the rectangle. These bounding boxes are resampled to 32×32 pixels and normalized to zero mean and unit variance.

3.2   Architecture

Blink and Gaze Pattern Extraction. We follow the idea of Li *et al.* [18] by introducing deep learning into blink detection. They employed the LRCN model, which can be roughly defined as a combination of CNN and RNN. The CNN unit plays a role of a feature extractor and the RNN unit takes charge of sequence learning. As human eye blink is periodic, cyclic and binocularly synchronized, the strong temporal consistency exhibiting in binocular blinking patterns agrees with the characteristic of LRCN model well.

We propose an enhanced LRCN model (see Fig. 2) to extract the blinking feature more precisely. The input of the LRCN model is the n frames of the video, $f_1, f_2, \cdots, f_n$. The LRCN model is composed of two parts, namely, feature extraction and sequence learning. Specifically, feature extraction converts the input eye region into discriminative features. Resnet50 [11] plays the role of a CNN backbone. The output from the feature extraction is fed into sequence learning, in which we replace the Long Short-Term Memory (LSTM) with Gate Recurrent Unit (GRU) as an RNN unit to adapt to the short-term blink behavior. A GRU unit is composed of a reset gate and an update gate. Update gate controls what parts of hidden state are updated or preserved. Reset gate controls what parts of previous hidden state are used to compute new features. Due to the design of input gate, output gate and forget gate, LSTM can deal with long sequences and is very suitable for classifying time series data. Though similar to LSTM, GRU is computationally cheaper. A typical blink only lasts for 2 to 3 frames, which only accounts for about 15% of a video sequence. Since the structure of LSTM is more complicated than GRU, LSTM requires more data for training. This makes GRU more suitable for blink detection than LSTM.

In the proposed framework, LRCN plays the role of feature extractor. The output of each RNN unit is passed to a fully connected layer. The output of the proposed model is the dynamic blink state prediction of the given frame, which denotes the probability of eye state in the range of [0:1], with 0 representing eye closing and 1 denoting eye opening. We use the binary cross-entropy loss to supervise the blink prediction, and more formally,

$$Loss = \frac{1}{N} \sum BCE(s_i, \widetilde{s}_i), \tag{1}$$

where $\widehat{s}_i$ is the prediction and s_i is the ground truth.

In addition to eye blinking, eye pattern mostly presents as the state of regular eyeball movements. Unlike real eyes, fake eyes, without limitation during gener-

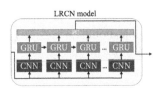

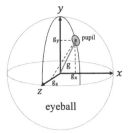

Fig. 2. Illustration of the LRCN module.   **Fig. 3.** Illustration of the gaze vector.

ation, do not necessarily show the binocular coordination relationship. Following this observation, we estimate the gaze vector (see Fig. 3) pointing from the eyeball center to the pupil by Openface2 [2]. After finishing training LRCN model, all the layers except the state prediction layer are frozen so that a 2048-dim eye blink feature vector incorporating the gaze vector is fed into the Bi-LSTM model as dual inputs.

Bidirectional LSTM Module. The binocular features from above are passed into a first Bi-LSTM layer. The outputs of the first Bi-LSTM layer are passed to a second Bi-LSTM layer to produce secondary feature abstraction. Bidirectional LSTM is a variant of LSTM which consists of a forward layer on the original input sequence and a backward layer on the reversed sequence. Conceptually, the Bi-LSTM outperforms the traditional LSTM because the forward and backward networks combine both forward and backward context information of the input sequence. This design allows Bi-LSTM to discover additional patterns that cannot be found by LSTM with only one recurrent layer. Under our circumstances, as the prediction depends on both the above and behind states, the utilization of Bi-LSTM helps to comprehend the eye pattern we proposed better.

The feature vector from the last LSTM unit of this second bidirectional layer is passed into a fully-connected layer and finally to a classification layer. Dropout is added to the fully-connected layer for regularization. Faces from real videos are hypothesized to have their own embedding distribution, while different types of generated fake videos can either be clustered or in separate distributions. To discriminate the real video distribution from that of the forgery ones, we select the KL divergence loss as the loss function used in classification. The KL-Divergence learning metric is defined as:

$$L_{KL} = \sum_{i=1}^{n} y_i \log(\frac{y_i}{\widehat{y_i}}),\tag{2}$$

where $\widehat{y_i}$ is the prediction and y_i is the ground truth.

4   Experiment and Analysis

4.1   Datasets

FaceForensics++. [23] (FF++) contains 1,000 original videos collected from YouTube and corresponding manipulated videos by four different types of deepfake videos, namely, Face2Face [27], FaceSwap, Deepfakes and NeuralTextures [26]. To better simulate real-world scenarios and challenge the generalization of proposed model, these videos are also compressed using the H.264 codec to two compressions, i.e. C23 (slightly-compressed version, HQ) and C40 (heavily-compressed version, LQ). All these videos contain full frontal faces with out any occlusions.

Celeb-DF (v2). [28] consists of high-quality forged celebrity videos using advanced synthesis process to handle issues such as color inconsistency and low-frequency smoothing. It contains 590 real face videos and 5639 forgery videos. Celeb-DF (v2) has more diverse and challenging data, which is beneficial to verify the generalization of the proposed method.

4.2   Implementation Details

We employ Openface2 [2] to detect and landmark faces. Openface2 also helps calculate the gaze vector. The cropped eye region are resized to $32 \times 32 \times 3$ to meet the network input. We use a pre-trained ResNet50 as CNN backbone for LRCN. The initial learning rate is 10^{-5} and decays 0.9 every 1000 iterations. The training process is terminated at 100 epochs. After finishing training LRCN model, all the layers except the state prediction layer are frozen so that a 2048-dim eye blink feature vector incorporating the gaze vector is fed into the Bi-LSTM model as dual inputs.

We trained our bidirectional recurrent model and the baseline models on the combination of the full FaceForensics++ and Celeb-DF v2 datasets. For the training, validation, and test splits, we used the instructions provided along with the datasets. As Celeb-DF v2 does not offer any validation split, we randomly chose 50 real and 134 fake videos from the training data to create a validation split. The test sets for both datasets are left unaltered. We set the learning rate to 10^{-4}. The optimizer is Adam. A dropout of 0.5 is added to the fully-connected layer. Based upon hyperparameter tuning results, we set the sequence length to 12 frames.

4.3   Feature Effectiveness

To prove the effectiveness of the blink and gaze feature, Dynamic Time Warping (DTW) distance and Pearson correlation coefficient are adopted to measure the correlation between two vectors of left and right eyes. We define S_{blink} and $S_{movement}$ as the correlation of blink and eye movement respectively. For an N-frame video, S_{blink} and $S_{movement}$ can be calculated as follows:

$$S_{blink} = DTW(B_l, B_r) \qquad (3)$$

$$DTW(B_l, B_r) = \min \sqrt{\sum d(B_l, B_r)^2}, \qquad (4)$$

Let vectors $g_i = (g_x^i, g_y^i, g_z^i)$ and $g_{i-1} = (g_x^{i-1}, g_y^{i-1}, g_z^{i-1})$ denote the feature vectors of two successive frames, we define the rotation angle between the ith frame and the $(i-1)th$ frame as θ_i.

$$S_{movement} = corr(G_l, G_r), \qquad (5)$$

$$corr(\ ,\ ) = \frac{\sum_{N-1}^{i=0}(\theta_l^i - \overline{\theta_l})(\theta_r^i - \overline{\theta_r})}{\sqrt{\sum_{N-1}^{i=0}(\theta_l^i - \overline{\theta_l})^2}\sqrt{\sum_{N-1}^{i=0}(\theta_r^i - \overline{\theta_r})^2}}, \qquad (6)$$

$$\theta_i = \arccos(\frac{g_i \cdot g_{i-1}}{\|g_i\| \cdot \|g_{i-1}\|}), \qquad (7)$$

where B_l, B_r is the output of LRCN as well as the result of blink state prediction and G_l, G_r refers to gaze vector.

To verify the effectiveness, we randomly select 30 genuine videos and 30 manipulated videos from FaceForensics++ for validation. Figure 4 and Fig. 5 respectively show the comparison between real and fake videos with respect to S_{blink} and $S_{movement}$. Since $S_{movement}$ represents Pearson correlation, the larger the value, the more consistent it is. Instead, because S_{blink} represents DTW distance, the smaller the value, the more consistent it is.

As seen, in the case of S_{blink}, the statistical distribution shows that the fake group is greater than the real group, which indicates that the fake eyes blink less synchronized than the real eyes. It can also be seen that the distribution of "Real" $S_{movement}$ is greater than "Fake" one. This shows that real eyes are indeed more coordinated than fake eyes. This experiment confirms that the binocular synchronization of eye movements (up and down and left and right) can indeed distinguish the authenticity of Deepfake faces.

4.4 In-Dataset Evaluation

In-dataset evaluation focus on specialization but not generalization. To compare against the existing work, especially eye-based methods, we consider two most popular yet challenging datasets, which are FF++ and Celeb-DF v2. Given a dataset, we trained our model on both real and fake data from train split, and evaluate performance on the corresponding test set.

The results of in-dataset evaluation are shown in Table 1. The lack of eye blink database in DeepVision [12] and classification criteria in Li et al. [18] make it difficult to compare the eye-based methods we mentioned above. Most recent methods perform well on in-dataset evaluation. Compared with the state-of-the-art methods, our approach is on par with S-MIL-T and outperforms other methods on both two datasets. We improve the XceptionNet baseline from 97.03% to 99.52% in FF and 89.55% to 90.51% in Celeb-DF on average.

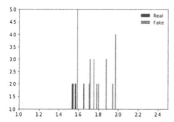 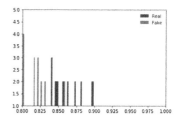

Fig. 4. Distribution of S_{blink}, where the abscissa and ordinate respectively denote the S_{blink} value and the number of samples.

Fig. 5. Distribution of $S_{movement}$, where the abscissa and ordinate respectively denote the $S_{movement}$ value and the number of samples.

Table 1. In-dataset evaluation results in terms of video-level AUC on FF++ & Celeb-DF v2. Note that some comparison results are from [29]

Method	FF++ (RAW)					Celeb-DF v2
	DF	F2F	FS	NT	Overall	
MesoNet [1]	89.52	84.44	83.56	75.74	70.74	54.8
ConvLSTM [10]	88.72	85.71	92.91	90.61	87.84	78.17
EyeMovement [16]	91.8	–	–	–	–	63.5
CapsuleForensics [22]	96.88	97.40	96.00	97.22	95.54	–
XceptionNet [6]	96.13	98.14	99.21	99.89	97.03	89.55
S-MIL-T [17]	99.84	99.34	**99.61**	98.85	99.41	**98.84**
Ours	**99.76**	**99.83**	99.53	**99.12**	**99.56**	93.51

4.5 Cross-Dataset Evaluation

The cross-dataset evaluation is a widely-used approach to demonstrate the generalization ability. It shows the accuracy of the defense method without prior knowledge. We choose FF++ as train set and Celeb-DF as test set. Our method achieves convincing results in terms of AUC. From the results in Table 2, it is evident that incorporating the blink and eye movement input into the model significantly improves the forgery detection accuracy across domains.

Table 2. Cross-dataset evaluation results in terms of video-level AUC.

Method	Train set	Test set
		Celeb-DF v2
DSP-FWA [19]	FF++	69.30
XceptionNet	FF++	73.04
EyeMovement	FF++	68.80
Ours	FF++	**86.35**

Table 3. AUC(%) performance comparison of different components.

LRCN		Eye movement	FaceForensics++	
GRU	LSTM		HQ	Raw
✓			75.59	80.21
	✓	✓	77.30	83.50
	✓	✓	83.65	87.71
✓		✓	**92.85**	**99.56**

4.6 Ablation Study

To inspect the effectiveness of each component in the feature extractor, we conduct a quantitative evaluation of the framework and its variants, as shown in Table 3. We first test the single effect of the LRCN module and eye movement module. Compared with single LRCN or eye movement, the proposed model achieves better performance at both Raw and HQ levels. The combination of two modules significantly improves the performance of detection and demonstrates the robustness to different compression levels. We further replace the GRU module with LSTM module. These results indicate that, regarding different RNN units, GRU is more helpful to learn the blinking pattern.

4.7 Limitations

Although our results are encouraging, our approaches still have limitations, which raise opportunities for future work. As the competition between counterfeiters and detectors continues, the inconsistencies on which developed detection methods rely can be improved. In the future, face synthesis methods with binocular consistency constraints may generate videos that satisfy the synchronization requirement, which cannot be detected in our hypothesis. More subtle features are needed to exploit so that this type of face forgery can be handled.

5 Conclusion

This paper investigates the feasibility of forgery detection based on eye movement patterns. A novel framework is developed to reveal binocular synchronization. We propose an enhanced LRCN model to improve the extraction of blink patterns. The latent representations for both binocular blinking and movement are extracted and fed into a recurrent framework to leverage the inconsistency between adjacent frames. Experiments on public datasets demonstrate the effectiveness and robustness of the proposed method.

Acknowledgements. This research is funded in part by the National Key Research and Development Program of China (2021YFF0602102), National Natural Science Foundation of China (U1903214, 62171324, 62071339), Hubei Province Key R&D Project (2020BAB018), and Natural Science Foundation of Hubei Province (2021CFB464).

References

1. Afchar, D., Nozick, V., Yamagishi, J., Echizen, I.: MesoNet: a compact facial video forgery detection network. In: 2018 IEEE International Workshop on Information Forensics and Security (WIFS), pp. 1–7 (2018). https://doi.org/10.1109/WIFS.2018.8630761
2. Baltrusaitis, T., Zadeh, A., Lim, Y.C., Morency, L.P.: OpenFace 2.0: facial behavior analysis toolkit. In: 2018 13th IEEE International Conference on Automatic Face Gesture Recognition, FG 2018, pp. 59–66 (2018). https://doi.org/10.1109/FG.2018.00019
3. Cao, S., Zou, Q., Mao, X., Ye, D., Wang, Z.: Metric learning for anti-compression facial forgery detection. In: Proceedings of the 29th ACM International Conference on Multimedia, pp. 1929–1937 (2021)
4. Chen, H.S., Rouhsedaghat, M., Ghani, H., Hu, S., You, S., Kuo, C.C.J.: DefakeHop: a light-weight high-performance DeepFake detector. In: 2021 IEEE International Conference on Multimedia and Expo (ICME), pp. 1–6. IEEE (2021)
5. Choi, Y., Choi, M., Kim, M., Ha, J.W., Kim, S., Choo, J.: StarGAN: unified generative adversarial networks for multi-domain image-to-image translation. In: Proceedings of the IEEE Conference on Computer Vision and Pattern Recognition, pp. 8789–8797 (2018)
6. Chollet, F.: Xception: deep learning with depthwise separable convolutions. In: Proceedings of the IEEE/CVF Conference on Computer Vision and Pattern Recognition, pp. 1251–1258 (2017)
7. Dang, H., Liu, F., Stehouwer, J., Liu, X., Jain, A.K.: On the detection of digital face manipulation. In: Proceedings of the IEEE/CVF Conference on Computer Vision and Pattern Recognition, pp. 5781–5790 (2020)
8. Demir, I., Ciftci, U.A.: Where do deep fakes look? Synthetic face detection via gaze tracking. In: ACM Symposium on Eye Tracking Research and Applications, pp. 1–11 (2021)
9. Goodfellow, I.J., et al.: Generative adversarial nets. In: Proceedings of the 27th International Conference on Neural Information Processing Systems - Volume 2, NIPS 2014, vol. 2, pp. 2672–2680 (2014)
10. Güera, D., Delp, E.J.: Deepfake video detection using recurrent neural networks. In: 2018 15th IEEE International Conference on Advanced Video and Signal Based Surveillance (AVSS), pp. 1–6 (2018). https://doi.org/10.1109/AVSS.2018.8639163
11. He, K., Zhang, X., Ren, S., Sun, J.: Deep residual learning for image recognition. In: Proceedings of the IEEE Conference on Computer Vision and Pattern Recognition, pp. 770–778 (2016)
12. Jung, T., Kim, S., Kim, K.: DeepVision: deepfakes detection using human eye blinking pattern. IEEE Access **8**, 83144–83154 (2020). https://doi.org/10.1109/ACCESS.2020.2988660
13. Karras, T., Aila, T., Laine, S., Lehtinen, J.: Progressive growing of GANs for improved quality, stability, and variation. arXiv preprint arXiv:1710.10196 (2017)
14. Karras, T., Laine, S., Aila, T.: A style-based generator architecture for generative adversarial networks. In: Proceedings of the IEEE/CVF Conference on Computer Vision and Pattern Recognition, pp. 4396–4405 (2019). https://doi.org/10.1109/CVPR.2019.00453
15. Li, L., et al.: Face X-ray for more general face forgery detection. In: Proceedings of the IEEE/CVF Conference on Computer Vision and Pattern Recognition, pp. 5001–5010 (2020)

16. Li, M., Liu, B., Hu, Y., Wang, Y.: Exposing deepfake videos by tracking eye movements. In: 2020 25th International Conference on Pattern Recognition (ICPR), pp. 5184–5189 (2021). https://doi.org/10.1109/ICPR48806.2021.9413139

17. Li, X., et al.: Sharp multiple instance learning for deepfake video detection. In: Proceedings of the 28th ACM International Conference on Multimedia, pp. 1864–1872 (2020)

18. Li, Y., Chang, M.C., Lyu, S.: In Ictu Oculi: exposing AI created fake videos by detecting eye blinking. In: 2018 IEEE International Workshop on Information Forensics and Security (WIFS), pp. 1–7 (2018). https://doi.org/10.1109/WIFS.2018.8630787

19. Li, Y., Lyu, S.: Exposing deepfake videos by detecting face warping artifacts. In: Proceedings of the IEEE/CVF Conference on Computer Vision and Pattern Recognition (CVPR) Workshops, June 2019

20. de Lima, O., Franklin, S., Basu, S., Karwoski, B., George, A.: Deepfake detection using spatiotemporal convolutional networks. arXiv preprint arXiv:2006.14749 (2020)

21. Nguyen, H.H., Fang, F., Yamagishi, J., Echizen, I.: Multi-task learning for detecting and segmenting manipulated facial images and videos. arXiv preprint arXiv:1906.06876 (2019)

22. Nguyen, H.H., Yamagishi, J., Echizen, I.: Capsule-forensics: using capsule networks to detect forged images and videos. In: 2019 IEEE International Conference on Acoustics, Speech and Signal Processing (ICASSP), ICASSP 2019, pp. 2307–2311. IEEE (2019)

23. Rössler, A., Cozzolino, D., Verdoliva, L., Riess, C., Thies, J., Niessner, M.: Face-Forensics++: learning to detect manipulated facial images. In: Proceedings of the IEEE International Conference on Computer Vision, pp. 1–11 (2019). https://doi.org/10.1109/ICCV.2019.00009

24. Schor, C.M., Tyler, C.W.: Spatio-temporal properties of Panum's fusional area. Vis. Res. **21**(5), 683–692 (1981)

25. Spivak, R.: "deepfakes": the newest way to commit one of the oldest crimes. Georgetown Law Technol. Rev. **3**(2), 339–401 (2019)

26. Thies, J., Zollhöfer, M., Nießner, M.: Deferred neural rendering: image synthesis using neural textures. ACM Trans. Graph. (TOG) **38**(4), 1–12 (2019)

27. Thies, J., Zollhöfer, M., Stamminger, M., Theobalt, C., Nießner, M.: Face2Face: real-time face capture and reenactment of RGB videos. In: Proceedings of the IEEE/CVF Conference on Computer Vision and Pattern Recognition, pp. 2387–2395 (2016). https://doi.org/10.1109/CVPR.2016.262

28. Li, Y., Yang, X., P.S.H.Q., Lyu, S.: Celeb-DF: a large-scale challenging dataset for deepfake forensics. In: IEEE Conference on Computer Vision and Patten Recognition (CVPR) (2020)

29. Zhao, T., Xu, X., Xu, M., Ding, H., Xiong, Y., Xia, W.: Learning self-consistency for deepfake detection. In: Proceedings of the IEEE/CVF International Conference on Computer Vision, pp. 15023–15033 (2021)

Dep-ViT: Uncertainty Suppression Model Based on Facial Expression Recognition in Depression Patients

Jiayu Ye[1], Gang Fu[1], Yang Liu[2], Guanwei Cheng[3], and Qingxiang Wang[1(✉)]

[1] School of Computer Science and Technology, Qilu University of Technology (Shandong Academy of Sciences), Jinan, China
`wangqx@qlu.edu.cn`
[2] Institute of Acumox and Tuina, Shandong University of Traditional Chinese Medicine, Jinan, China
[3] School of Data Engineering, Nanchang University, Nanchang, China

Abstract. Clinical investigations have demonstrated that depression patients' facial expression mimicry and cognitive capacities are substantially weakened, therefore their facial expressions have great uncertainty. Great uncertainty and limited data of depression patients make facial expression recognition (FER) based on depression patients a difficult endeavor. In this paper, we proposed Depression Vision Transformer (Dep-ViT) to solve the above problems. Firstly, we invited 164 subjects to participate in the Voluntary Facial Expression Mimicry (VFEM) experiment. VFEM contains seven expressions, including neutrality, anger, Disgust, Fear, happiness, sadness and surprise. We employed Person correlation analysis to characterize the action units (AUs) in VFEM at the same time. Secondly, to limit the uncertainty, each small sample in Dep-ViT had a block composed of Squeeze-Excitation (SE) and the self attention layer for the local attention information and sample importance. The sample label that received the least attention will be re-labeled using the Rank Regularization. Thirdly, in addition to the label of the VFEM itself, we manually labeled each expression image of the VFEM again, and used the manual label to assist the model training. The results showed that Dep-ViT obtains excellent results, with an accuracy of 0.417 in the VFEM.

Keywords: Dep-ViT · FER · SE · Manual label · VFEM

1 Introduction

One of the most direct and natural methods to communicate emotional states between people is through facial expressions. Based on cross-cultural studies, Ekman and Friesen [6] postulated six primary facial expressions: anger, disgust, fear, happiness, sadness, and surprise. The core classification of FER is made up of these expressions.

Supported by Qilu University of Technology (Shandong Academy of Sciences).

Depression patients have problems in their ability to recognize emotions, according to research [13]. Wexler et al. [16] found that depression patients were slow to respond to both positive and negative emotional stimuli. Depression patients were less responsive to cheerful smiles, but there was no discernible difference in sad expressions, according to Zwick et al. [19]. Differences in facial expressions in patients with depression provide the possibility for fer.

FER had gotten a lot of attention in recent years because it helps computers understand human behavior and emotions by automatically recognizing facial expressions. Researchers collected a large amount of facial expression data to construct new models for facial expression recognition. FER had three steps: face detection, feature extraction and classifier design. In the slabele of face detection, MTCNN [17] and Dlib [1] were common methods, which can recognize and locate faces in complex environments. FER feature extraction methods usually include geometric features and high dimensional features. Geometric features include Local Binary Patterns (LBP) [14] and Non-negative Matrix Factorization (NMF) [18]. High-dimensional features are often derived from deep learning models. Such as Kahou et al. [10] used deep Convolutional Neural Networks (CNN) to extract features. Classifier design includes machine learning methods such as Support Vector Machine (SVM) [14]. However, FER based on depressed patients is uncommon due to privacy concerns and high time and labor expenditures. Gaebel et al. [7] analyzed the facial expressions of depressed patients through manual scoring, while there were only 21 depressed subjects.

The following issues arise when recognizing facial expressions in depressed patients. First, the sample size of the data set is small. Second, the uncertainty of labels. In light of the aforementioned issues, we proposed the following solutions and contributions.

* Large number of subjects participated in the VFEM experiment. For the time being, we have not found a larger data set in the related depression VFEM experiment. Simultaneously, we examined the features of AUs in VFEM using Person correlation analysis. And it was discovered that the AUs of the case group tended to be negative, meanwhile the AUs of the control group tended to be positive.
* For the first time, we applied ViT [4] to the depression-related FER task. At the same time, we added blocks composed of SE [9] and self-attention layer. SE can fill in the gaps in local knowledge that ViT lacks, and the weight of the attention layer determines the credibility of each sample label.
* We proposed an attention ranking method that combines Ranking Regularization [15] and KL divergent (Kullback-Leibler). Initial labels with low confidence will be permuted using Rank Regularization.
* We manually labeled the expression pictures of VFEM. We inserted manual labels and set thresholds to suppress uncertain labels to a certain extent throughout the training.

2   VFEM

Expression collection and expression scoring make up the entirety of the VFEM. Expression collection refers to the collection of pictures of subjects' facial expressions. Expression scoring refers to the manual rating of subjects' facial expressions.

Why did we decide on VFEM? To acquire facial expression data, researchers typically use Spontaneous Facial Expression Mimicry (SFEM). They observed the unconscious facial expressions of depressed patients and labeled them based on their judgment. Subjective SFEM labelling can lead to misinterpretations of participants' expressions. The usage of VFEM is a better alternative for collecting with depression-related data.

2.1   Expression Collection

The VFEM subjects were all Chinese, native speakers, and ranged in age from 18 to 65. Before participating in the VFEM, each subject was asked to fill out an assessment plan containing general information and demographic information, including health history, age, sex, education status and employment status. Subjects in the case group all met the Diagnostic and Statistical Manual of Mental Disorders (DSM-IV) screening rules, Subjects in the control group were required to have a HAMD score of less than 8, be demographically comparable to subjects in the case group, and had no history of mental illness.

To avoid influence from external factors, we set up a green screen behind the participants, and only the relevant staff are allowed to enter. A total of 1148 facial expression images were collected, with 82 case group (43 women, 39 men) and 82 control group (43 women, 39 men). Then, we used Opencv to locate and extracted faces from facial expression images.

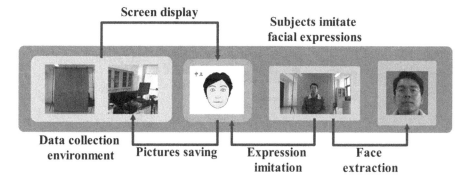

Fig. 1. The experimental process of VFEM. The subject in the picture is the control group N059. We have obtained his consent before the article is delivered.

Our work had been approved by the Ethics Committee of China Clinical Trial Registration and was carried out in strict accordance with the ethical code of the World Medical Association (Declaration of Helsinki). The above process is shown in Fig. 1.

2.2   Emoticon Scoring

To assess VFEM face expressions, we selected nine healthy raters from area graduate schools who had no history of mental illness (5 men, 4 women). Face-expression photos were jumbled and kept in a software where raters provided an emotional label to each image. The expression scoring is divided into a warm-up stage and a marking stage. In the warm-up stage, 15% of the collected images will be randomly selected for practice. The picture is divided into four parts during the marking step, with 15 min of break between each component to reduce weariness.

The staff will collect each rater's scoring results after the emoticon scoring is concluded. The scorer chose the most labels as manual labels in the scoring results. It's worth mentioning that this label was chosen by more than half of the raters. The original label will be utilized if the scoring result cannot determine the label.

2.3   Facial Feature Extraction and Analysis

After finishing face detection, we used the OpenFace [2] to extract AUs. An example is shown in Fig. 2. There are two types of AUs features, where the suffix r indicates the strength of the AU, and the value ranges from 0 to 5. For example, AU10_c indicates the strength of AU10. The suffix c indicates whether the AU exists, the presence is 1, and the absence is 0.

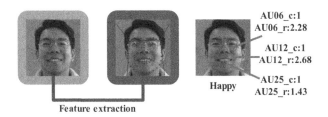

Fig. 2. AUs feature extraction.

To examine the association between AUs and labels, we employed Pearson correlation coefficients. The Pearson correlation coefficient can be used to measure the similarity between vectors. Its value range is -1 to 1. [-1,0] means negative correlation and [0,1] means positive correlation. We used the absolute value of the correlation coefficient because just the correlation is considered.

The results are shown in Table 1. According to clinically relevant studies [5], We found that AUs in control subjects were more strongly associated with positive expressions, such as happy, surprise. While the AUs of the control subjects were more strongly associated with negative expressions, such as sadness.

Table 1. The degree of correlation between AUs and labels measured by Pearson correlation coefficients, we took the top 5.

Case group	Relevance	Control group	Relevance
AU10_c	0.254	AU25_c	0.266
AU20_r	0.203	AU26_c	0.198
AU26_c	0.197	AU25_r	0.194
AU01_c	0.196	AU12_c	0.180
AU04_c	0.168	AU10_c	0.166

3 Dep-ViT

Dep-ViT has the following 4 parts. The first is encoder, the second is a block composed of SE and self-attention layer, the third is Rank Regularization and Relabeling, and the fourth is a loss function based on manual labeling.

Before introducing the method, we briefly explain the meaning of each label. **Initial label** refers to the original label of VFEM, that is, the expression label imitated by the subjects. **Manual label** refers to the label that 9 healthy raters annotate the image in emoticon scoring. **Relabel** refers to the labels transformed by Dep-ViT during training. **Model label** refers to the label predicted by the model.

3.1 Encoder

In the encoder part, we referred to the encoder of ViT. During data input, the 2D image will be divided into patches of equal height and width $\mathbf{x} \in \mathbb{R}^{H \times W \times C}$. Then serialize to $\mathbf{x}_p \in \mathbb{R}^{N \times (P^2 \cdot C)}$. Where H, W are the height and width before cutting, N is the number of patches, C is the number of channels, and P^2 is the size of patches. Since the downstream task is a classification task, the trainable marker [cls] is added to the model. The information of Patches, 1D position embeddings and trainable markers [cls] form the input of the encoder.

The core of encoder is Multi-Head Attention (MHA) composed of N self-attention. Self-attention is to use Q (query), K and V (key-value pairs) to calculate the positional relationship in a single sequence and obtain the sequence representation. The expression of self-attention is as follows.

$$\text{Attention} \left(Q, K, V\right) = \text{softmax} \left(\frac{QK^T}{\sqrt{d_k}}\right) V \tag{1}$$

If W^0, W_i^Q, W_i^K, W_i^V is the weight matrix, MHA has the following expression.

$$\text{MHA}(Q, K, V) = \text{Concat}\,(\text{head}_0, \ldots, \text{ head }_z)\,W^O$$
$$\text{head }_i = \text{Attention}\left(QW_i^Q, KW_i^K, VW_i^V\right) \tag{2}$$

3.2   SE and Self-attention Layer

SE can effectively improve the performance of CNN. The squeeze part is set to reduce the dimensionality of the convolutional layer. The structure of ViT and CNN is different, we only need to use the excitation part here. The Excitation part consists of two fully-connected (FC) layers. Assuming that the output of the encoder is cls, the first fully connected layer compresses the features to d_{cls}/r channels, and then uses the ReLu function to activate, where r is the channel compression ratio. The second fully connected layer restores the feature to d_{cls} channels and activates it with the Sigmoid function. SE can learn more local attention relations to optimize Dep-ViT. The formula is shown below.

$$\text{Excitaion(cls)} = \text{Sigmoid}\left(FC_1\left(\text{ReLU}\left(FC_2(\text{cls})\right)\right)\right) \tag{3}$$

$$SE(\text{cls}) = \text{cls} \odot \text{Excitaion(cls)} \tag{4}$$

where FC_1 and FC_2 represent the first and second full connection layers. $\odot$ means pointwise multiplication. Then SE is again represented by flatten as a one-dimensional vector for self-attention calculation. The purpose of self-attention is to find the importance weight of each feature and append the importance weight to the output. The self-attention process consists of a fully connected layer and Simoid function. Among them, α_i is the importance information of the i-th sample, and $w_a^\top$ is the transposition of the importance weight.

$$\alpha_i = \text{Sigmod}\left(w_a^\top SE_i\right) \tag{5}$$

3.3   Rank Regularization Based on KL Divergence and Relabeling

The role of Rank Regularization is to regularize the attention weights. Instead of sorting the attention weights in descending order directly, we used the KL divergence to process the attention weights. The normal attention distribution probability should be satisfied with a uniform distribution. Attention weights that are far from uniform distribution should be taken seriously. Therefore, we constructed new attention weights $\overline{\alpha_i}$. First, α_i represents the output of the Self-attention Layer, which is the original attention distribution, and $\frac{1}{M}\sum_{i=0}^M \alpha_i$ represents a uniform distribution. By KL divergence, we can get $\overline{\alpha_i} = \ln\sum_{i=0}^M e^{\alpha^i} - \frac{1}{M}\sum_{i=0}^M \alpha^i \leq \ln\left(M \cdot \max_{i=0}\left\{\alpha^i\right\} - \frac{1}{M}\alpha^i\right)$. After removing the constant term, the new attention weight can be defined as:

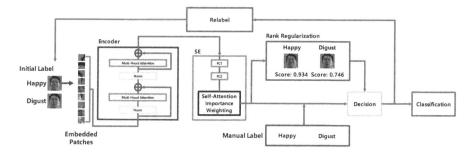

Fig. 3. Dep-ViT model structure.

$$\overline{\alpha_i} = \max_M \{\alpha_i\} - \frac{1}{M} \sum_{i=0}^{M} \alpha_i \tag{6}$$

Then $\overline{\alpha_i}$ is divided into high importance group and low importance group. The average attention weight of the high importance group needs to be higher than the low importance group, otherwise the regularization loss will be set to 0, which is defined as follows:

$$\text{Loss}_{RR} = \max \begin{cases} 0 \\ \delta_1 - (\alpha_H - \alpha_L) \end{cases} \tag{7}$$

$$\alpha_H = \frac{1}{M} \sum_{i=0}^{M} \overline{\alpha_i}, \alpha_L = \frac{1}{N-M} \sum_{i=M}^{N} \overline{\alpha_i} \tag{8}$$

Among them, δ_1 is a fixed or learnable hyperparameter, and M, N-M represent the number of samples in the high-importance group and the low-importance group, respectively. Uncertain samples are usually in the low importance group. These samples are output in the form of maximum probability. If the maximum probability is greater than the probability of a given label, they will be set as a new label. In Dep-ViT, uncertain labels will be repaired by reweighting and relabeling.

3.4 Loss Function Based on Manual Labeling

Dep-ViT creates a new loss function in order to leverage manual labeling to aid model training. CrossEntropyLoss is calculated according to the original label and manual label, and Loss_{RR} is added in the training process at the same time. The definition of Loss is as follows.

$$\text{Loss} = \frac{1}{N} \sum_i - \sum_{c=1}^{M} y_{ic} \log\left(p_{ic}\right) + \gamma \frac{1}{N} \sum_j - \sum_{c=1}^{M} y_{jc} \log\left(p_{jc}\right) + \text{Loss}_{RR} \tag{9}$$

where M is the number of categories. y_{ic}, y_{jc} represent indicator variables, if the predicted value and the category of the sample i are the same, it is 1, otherwise it is 0. p_{ic}, p_{jc} represent the predicted probability that the observed sample i and j belong to c. γ is the trade-off ratio. The complete model structure is shown in Fig 3.

4 Experiment and Result Analysis

4.1 Parameter Settings

The VFEM training and test sets are divided into 8:2 groups, with the number of case and control groups being equal. GPU is V100 cluster. All image sizes are set to 224, batch size is set to 32, learning rate is set to 0.008, dropout is set to 0.5, and epoch is set to 800. Label modification is completed for every 100 epoches, and SGD is selected as the optimizer. The pre-training model is VITB_16, and the best value of γ is 0.4. The evaluation indicators of the experiment are mainly F1 score and Accuracy. The most popular evaluation index is accuracy, which is defined as the proportion of correct samples in all samples. F1 score is determined by Precision and Recall.

Table 2. Acc represents Accuracy. Ang, Dis, Fea, Hap, Neu, Sad and Sur represent the F1 score of anger, disgust, fear, happiness, Neutrality, sadness and surprise respectively.

Model	Acc	Ang	Dis	Fea	Hap	Neu	Sad	Sur
Deep-Emotion [12]	0.308	0.280	**0.337**	0.226	0.307	0.333	0.043	0.461
ResNet_18 [8]	0.382	0.229	0.162	0.204	0.434	**0.493**	0.371	0.582
SCN [15]	0.387	0.290	0.327	0.208	0.407	0.447	0.475	0.466
ViT [4]	0.395	0.225	0.125	0.200	**0.483**	0.467	0.535	0.529
Dep-ViT	**0.417**	**0.352**	0.307	**0.473**	0.455	0.489	**0.571**	**0.607**

4.2 Experimental Results

In the VFEM, Dep-ViT is compared with several excellent models, and the results are shown in Table 2. Dep-ViT had the highest accuracy of 0.417, as well as the highest F1 Score, out of four expressions: anger, fear, sadness, and surprise. It's worth noting that the F1 score is the indicator for all seven expressions. There are large differences in the performance of VFEM in different models. Deep-Emotion [12] cannot correctly identify sadness, and Dep-ViT generally obtains a better recognition rate in each expression, especially in anger and fear, far exceeding other models. Overall, the recognition rate of surprise is the most significant, with the highest recognition rate reaching 0.609, while the recognition rates of anger and disgust are generally poor, with the highest F1 Score of 0.352 and 0.337, respectively.

Why is the experimental result of VFEM inferior to the general FER dataset? First, some datasets include professional actors as subjects, such as KDEF [11] and AFEW [3]. They have the ability to produce more pronounced expression modifications. VFEM is for depressed patients. Second, VFEM differs from other datasets in that respondents were instructed to emulate naturally rather than consciously.

4.3   Ablation Experiment

We conducted four ablation experiments in this section. First, We further analyzed ViT and Dep-ViT, and the case group and control group of the test set are separately entered into the model. Second, we analyzed the influence of different modules in Dep-ViT on the experimental results. Third, we established a confusion matrix to analyze the experimental results of Dep-ViT. Fourth, we analyzed the variation of the four labels across instances.

Table 3. of the performance of ViT and Dep-ViT between the case group and the control group.

Model	Acc	Ang	Dis	Fea	Hap	Neu	Sad	Sur
ViT(Case)	0.373	0.133	0.122	0.181	0.432	0.476	0.466	0.357
ViT(Control)	0.434	0.400	0.166	0.250	0.510	0.468	0.521	0.666
Dep-ViT(Case)	0.382	0.214	0.325	0.154	0.400	0.385	0.485	0.444
Dep-ViT(Control)	0.434	0.279	0.372	0.276	0.552	0.500	0.519	0.652

The results of the first ablation experiment are shown in Table 3. We can get the following conclusions. First, in the two models, the results of the control group are significantly better than those of the case group, and the facial expressions of the control group are easier to recognize. Second, the F1 score of the control group in surprise is much higher than that of the case group. This proves that the case group is relatively insensitive to surprise. Third, We found that the results here are relevant to the analysis of AUs. Among the negative expressions, the index differences between the case and control subjects were smaller than those of the positive expressions, especially sadness and disgust.

Table 4. Effects of different modules on Dep-ViT.

ViT	SE	Relabel	Manual label	Accuracy
✓				0.395
✓	✓			0.400
✓	✓	✓		0.408
✓	✓	✓	✓	0.417

This experimental result proves to a certain extent that the expressions of the subjects in the case group tend to be negative.

The results of the second part are shown in Table 4, we can find that different modules play different roles. After adding SE, the accuracy of the model improved by 0.005. By relabeling, the accuracy improves by 0.008. During training, adding Manual Label to the loss function improved the accuracy most significantly, reaching 0.009. The overall accuracy of Dep-ViT is higher than that of ViT.

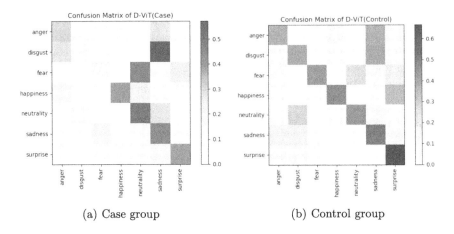

(a) Case group   (b) Control group

Fig. 4. Confusion matrix based on Dep-ViT.

The results of the third part are shown in Fig. 4. In the case group, we found that anger and digust were easily misidentified as sadness, and fear was easily identified as neutrality. In the control group, anger and digust were also easily misidentified as sadness, but overall, the control subjects were significantly better at identifying them than the case subjects.

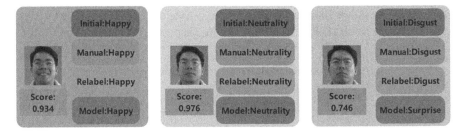

Fig. 5. The difference between the initial label, manual label, relabel, and model label.

The results of the fourth part are shown in Fig. 5. Relabels are used as an auxiliary repair function in manual labeling. However, not all manual labels and relabels can be used for repairs. As shown in disgust, although the manual label and relabel are consistent, the model label of the Dep-ViT predicts it as surprise.

5   Limitation

Our work has a number of limitations. First, the case group in VFEM are patients with a high degree of depression and need to be hospitalized. Their condition will be more complex than that of persons suffering from depression in general. Second, some expressions, such as disgust, have a low recognition rate.

6   Conclusion

We proposed Dep-ViT to solve the facial expression recognition problem of patients with depression. Dep-ViT effectively increased the accuracy of facial expression identification in depressed individuals while also addressing the issue of uncertainty. The core of Dep-ViT has four parts, the block composed of Encoder, SE and self-attention layer, Rank Regularization improved by KL divergence and Relabeling, and loss function based on manual labels. Encoder completes the feature extraction. The block composed of SE and the self-attention layer is used to focus on local attention information and distinguish the importance of samples. KL divergence-improved Rank Regularization and Relabeling do attention optimization, grouping, and sorting. The loss function of the manual label plays a role of assisting in repairing the label. The design idea of Dep-ViT can be used not only for depression patients, but also for facial expression recognition related to other mental illnesses.

Acknowledgment. This work was supported by the Shandong Provincial Natural Science Foundation, China (Grant No: ZR2021MF079, ZR2020MF039). the National Natural Science Foundation of China (Grant No: 81573829). The Key Research and Development Program of Shandong Province (Grant No.2020CXGC010901).

References

1. Amos, B., Ludwiczuk, B., Satyanarayanan, M., et al.: Openface: a general-purpose face recognition library with mobile applications. CMU Sch. Comput. Sci. **6**(2) (2016)
2. Baltrusaitis, T., Robinson, P., Morency, L.P.: Openface: an open source facial behavior analysis toolkit. In: IEEE Winter Conference on Applications of Computer Vision (2016)
3. Dhall, A., Goecke, R., Lucey, S., Gedeon, T.: Collecting large, richly annotated facial-expression databases from movies. IEEE Multimedia **19**(03), 34–41 (2012)
4. Dosovitskiy, A., et al.: An image is worth 16×16 words: Transformers for image recognition at scale. arXiv preprint arXiv:2010.11929 (2020)

5. Du, S., Tao, Y., Martinez, A.M.: Compound facial expressions of emotion. Proc. Natl. Acad. Sci. USA **111**(15), E1454 (2014)
6. Ekman, P., Friesen, W.V.: Constants across cultures in the face and emotion. J. Pers. Soc. Psychol. **17**(2), 124 (1971)
7. Gaebel, W., Wölwer, W.: Facial expression and emotional face recognition in schizophrenia and depression. Eur. Arch. Psychiatry Clin. Neurosci. **242**(1), 46–52 (1992)
8. He, K., Zhang, X., Ren, S., Sun, J.: Deep residual learning for image recognition. In: Proceedings of the IEEE Conference on Computer Vision and Pattern Recognition, pp. 770–778 (2016)
9. Hu, J., Shen, L., Sun, G.: Squeeze-and-excitation networks. In: Proceedings of the IEEE Conference on Computer Vision and Pattern Recognition, pp. 7132–7141 (2018)
10. Kahou, S.E., et al.: Combining modality specific deep neural networks for emotion recognition in video. In: Proceedings of the 15th ACM on International Conference on Multimodal Interaction, pp. 543–550 (2013)
11. Lundqvist, D., Flykt, A., Öhman, A.: Karolinska directed emotional faces. Cogn. Emot. **22**(6), 1094–1118 (1998)
12. Minaee, S., Minaei, M., Abdolrashidi, A.: Deep-emotion: facial expression recognition using attentional convolutional network. Sensors **21**(9), 3046 (2021)
13. Schaefer, K.L., Baumann, J., Rich, B.A., Luckenbaugh, D.A., Zarate, C.A., Jr.: Perception of facial emotion in adults with bipolar or unipolar depression and controls. J. Psychiatr. Res. **44**(16), 1229–1235 (2010)
14. Shan, C., Gong, S., McOwan, P.W.: Facial expression recognition based on local binary patterns: a comprehensive study. Image Vis. Comput. **27**(6), 803–816 (2009)
15. Wang, K., Peng, X., Yang, J., Lu, S., Qiao, Y.: Suppressing uncertainties for large-scale facial expression recognition. In: Proceedings of the IEEE/CVF Conference on Computer Vision and Pattern Recognition, pp. 6897–6906 (2020)
16. Wexler, B.E., Levenson, L., Warrenburg, S., Price, L.H.: Decreased perceptual sensitivity to emotion-evoking stimuli in depression. Psychiatry Res. **51**(2), 127–138 (1994)
17. Zhang, K., Zhang, Z., Li, Z., Qiao, Y.: Joint face detection and alignment using multitask cascaded convolutional networks. IEEE Signal Process. Lett. **23**(10), 1499–1503 (2016)
18. Zhi, R., Flierl, M., Ruan, Q., Kleijn, W.B.: Graph-preserving sparse nonnegative matrix factorization with application to facial expression recognition. IEEE Trans. Syst. Man Cybern. Part B (Cybern.) **41**(1), 38–52 (2010)
19. Zwick, J.C., Wolkenstein, L.: Facial emotion recognition, theory of mind and the role of facial mimicry in depression. J. Affect. Disord. **210**, 90–99 (2017)

Ensemble of One-Class Classifiers Based on Multi-level Hidden Representations Abstracted from Convolutional Autoencoder for Anomaly Detection

Xin-tan Wang and Jian-wei Liu(⊠)

Department of Automation, College of Information Science and Engineering,
China University of Petroleum, Beijing, China
liujw@cup.edu.cn

Abstract. Image anomaly detection has recently emerged a large number of methods, which are widely used in industry, medicine and other fields. In this paper, we propose a novel image anomaly detection method, named Ensemble of One-Class Classifiers based on multi-level hidden representations abstracted from convolutional autoencoder (EOCCA), which is a two-stage method. Specifically, in the training process of the model, first, we train the convolutional autoencoder with the goal of minimizing the reconstruction error, thereby extracting the features from different layers of the encoder. Second, we train multiple one-class support vector machines based on the multi-level hidden representations abstracted from convolutional autoencoder. During inference, we ensemble all trained one-class classifiers for anomaly detection. Experimental results on several image anomaly detection benchmark datasets demonstrate that our proposed method is on par or outperforms current state-of-the-art image anomaly detection methods.

Keywords: Image anomaly detection · Ensemble learning · One-class support vector machine · Convolutional autoencoder

1 Introduction

Anomaly detection 1 is a task to detect whether the sample deviates from the mode of the normal sample. Anomaly detection has a wide range of applications areas, such as disease detection in the medical field [2], defective product detection in the industrial field [3], and fraud detection in the financial industry [4]. This paper focuses on image anomaly detection, which is a research hotspot in recent years.

X. Wang and J. Liu—This work was supported by the Science Foundation of China. University of Petroleum, Beijing (No.2462020YXZZ023).

E. Pimenidis et al. (Eds.): ICANN 2022, LNCS 13531, pp. 125–136, 2022.
https://doi.org/10.1007/978-3-031-15934-3_11

In reality, abnormal image samples are very rare, the cost of labeling is also very expensive. Therefore, in the typical image anomaly detection method, only normal samples are used to construct the image anomaly detection model. When the input image sample deviates from the mode of the training data set, it is regarded as an abnormal sample.

One-Class Support Vector Machines (OCSVMs) [5] is a typical and effective method for image anomaly detection. However, the performance of this method is limited by the representation of the input data. A good data representation can greatly improve its performance.

Therefore, in order to obtain high-quality data representation and thus improve the detection performance of one-class classifiers, a number of hybrid anomaly detection methods have emerged. It first uses representation learning methods to extract features from normal examples, which are then used to train OCSVMs.

We found that in existing hybrid anomaly detection methods, only the final features obtained by the representation learning method are used when training a one-class classifier, and multi-level features are not utilized. For example, when training a one-class classifier, Andrews et al. [6], Cao et al. [7] and Iglesias et al. [8] only utilized the bottleneck features of the autoencoder, Gupta et al. [9] only use the feature of the AlexNet penultimate layer. However, different levels of features have different abstract level semantic information, which is especially important for image anomaly detection.

Therefore, we propose a novel image anomaly detection method, named Ensemble of One-Class Classifiers based on multi-level hidden representations abstracted from Autoencoder (EOCCA). One of the most remarkable features of our EOCCA method is to train the base classifier by using the semantic features of different abstract levels on normal images extracted by convolutional autoencoder, which effectively grasp the different abstract level semantic information underlying in normal images and improves the detection performance.

In the EOCCA method, we use One-Class Support Vector Machines (OCSVMs) as the base classifier. Our EOCCA is a two-stage approach. In the training process of the EOCCA model, firstly, we use the normal sample set to train the convolutional autoencoder with the goal of minimizing the reconstruction error, so as to extract the features from different layers in the convolutional encoder. Secondly, we train OCSVMs according to the features of each layer of the convolutional encoder. During inference, we ensemble all trained OCSVMs for anomaly detection.

Experimental results on image anomaly detection benchmark datasets (MNIST, Fashion-MNIST, and MVTec AD) demonstrate that our proposed EOCCA method is on par or outperforms current state-of-the-art image anomaly detection methods.

In summary, the main contributions of our work are as follows.

Firstly, the proposed EOCCA is an ensemble learning method. EOCCA trains multiple base classifiers (OCSVMs) based on the extracted image semantic features at different levels, which effectively improves the performance of image anomaly detection.

Secondly, the proposed EOCCA is an ensemble learning method. EOCCA trains multiple base classifiers (OCSVMs) based on the extracted image semantic features at different levels, which effectively improves the performance of image anomaly detection.

2 Related Work

2.1 OCSVMs

One-Class Support Vector Machines (OCSVMs) [5], proposed by Scholkopf et al. in 2001, is a classic anomaly detection algorithm. It uses kernel functions (such as Gaussian kernel, polynomial kernel, etc.) to implicitly map sample data to Reproducing Kernel Hilbert Space (RKHS). The goal of one-class support vector machines is to learn a hyperplane in Reproducing Kernel Hilbert Space (RKHS) that separates the mapped normal sample data from the origin and maximizes the distance from the origin to the hyperplane. A sample is considered an anomaly if its features are in the half-space containing the origin. The performance of this method is limited by the quality of the input data representation.

2.2 Hybrid Approach

The hybrid approach is a two-stage anomaly detection method. In the first stage, the features of the samples are extracted using representation learning. In the second stage, based on the extracted features, a classical one-class classifier is trained. For example, Andrews et al. [6] first used a single-layer feedforward neural network-type autoencoder to extract representations of normal class examples, and then used it to train one-class support vector machines (OCSVMs); Cao et al. [7] first uses autoencoder and variational autoencoder with regularizers to extract high-quality normal sample features, and then uses them to train a class of classifiers (eg, KDE, OCSVM); Iglesias et al. [8] first used the convolutional autoencoder to extract the representation of the training samples, then used it to train one-class support vector machines, and finally fused the reconstruction error and the classification output of one-class support vector machines as the final identification result; Gupta et al. [9] used AlexNet pre-trained on the ImageNet dataset to extract the features of normal samples, and then used its train one-class support vector machines (OCSVMs), etc.

The current hybrid methods only use the final features obtained by the representation learning method, and do not extract different levels of semantic features, which is a great deficiency of the existing hybrid methods.

3 Ensemble of One-Class Classifiers

In this section, we will describe in detail our proposed image anomaly detection method, EOCCA. As illustrated in Fig. 1, EOCCA composes of a two-stage procedures. In the first stage, we resort to convolutional autoencoder to extract image semantic features with different levels; in the second stage, we establish multiple base classifiers (OCSVMs) based on extracting image semantic features with different abstract semantic levels. Finally, we fuse the scores of samples on all base classifiers (OCSVM) as the final abnormal decision results.

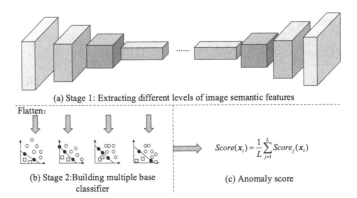

(a) Stage 1: Extracting different levels of image semantic features

Flatten:

(b) Stage 2:Building multiple base classifier

(c) Anomaly score

$$Score(\boldsymbol{x}_i) = \frac{1}{L}\sum_{j=1}^{L} Score_j(\boldsymbol{x}_i)$$

Fig. 1. The structure of our proposed EOOCA.

3.1 Extracting Different Levels of Image Semantic Features

In existing hybrid methods, only the bottleneck features extracted by convolutional autoencoder are used to facilitate the abnormal discrimination. However, in convolutional neural networks, the feature mappings by different layers of convolution operations have different levels of semantic information, which is very important for image anomaly detection. The feature mappings by the shallow convolution has a small receptive field, which contains the local features of the image; the feature mappings by the deep convolution has a large receptive field, which contains the more abstract global semantic features underlying in the image.

Therefore, as shown in Fig. 1(a), we use convolutional autoencoder to identify image semantic features at different levels. Assume that the encoder of autoencoder is a convolutional neural network with L layers. The structure of the decoder is symmetrical with the structure of the encoder.

Given a training set $D_{train} = \{\boldsymbol{x}_1, \boldsymbol{x}_2, ..., \boldsymbol{x}_n\}$ with n normal image examples. The loss function of convolutional autoencoder is reconstruction loss, as shown in Eq. (1).

$$L_{\text{Restruction}} = \frac{1}{m}\sum_{i=1}^{m} \left\| x_i - \widehat{x}_i \right\|^2 \tag{1}$$

where x_i represents the image samples in the training set (normal image set), $\widehat{x}_i$ denotes the reconstructed image samples, and m denotes the number of samples in a min-batch.

When training convolutional autoencoder, we use the method of early stopping to prevent overfitting. After the convolutional autoencoder is trained, we feed the samples to the encoder to extract image semantic features $\{f_1(\boldsymbol{x}_i), f_2(\boldsymbol{x}_i), ..., f_L(\boldsymbol{x}_i)\}$ from the L convolutional layers. $\{f_1(\boldsymbol{x}_i), f_2(\boldsymbol{x}_i), ..., f_L(\boldsymbol{x}_i)\}$ contains the semantic features of the image from local to global, which is very beneficial for image anomaly detection.

3.2 Building Multiple Base Classifiers with Extracted Features

Based on the different levels of image semantic features extracted in the previous stage, we train multiple base classifiers.

We choose the classical one-class support vector machine as the base classifier. The process of training the j-th base classifier (one-class support vector machine) based on the j-th layer image semantic features is as follows.

First, we choose the RBF kernel function to implicitly map the extracted j-th layer image semantic features to the Reproducing Kernel Hilbert Space (RKHS), as follows,

$$k(f_j(x_i), f_j(x_{i'})) = < \phi(f_j(x_i)), \phi(f_j(x_{i'})) > \tag{2}$$

where k indicates the RBF kernel function, and $\phi(f_j(x_i))$ expresses the feature vector of the j-th layer image semantic feature of sample i in the Reproducing Kernel Hilbert Space (RKHS). The j-th layer image semantic features of the training set are expressed as $\{\phi(f_j(x_1)), \phi(f_j(x_2)), ..., \phi(f_j(x_n))\}$ in the Reproducing Kernel Hilbert Space (RKHS).

Next, in the Reproducing Kernel Hilbert Space (RKHS), in order to find a hyperplane as shown in Eq. (3),

$$w_j \cdot \phi(f_j(x)) - b_j = 0 \tag{3}$$

whose normal vector is w_j and intercept is b_j, separating the feature set from the origin, and for maximizing the distance between the hyperplane and the origin, we solve the following quadratic optimization problem,

$$\min_{w_j, b_j, \xi} \frac{1}{2} \|w_j\|^2 + \frac{1}{vn} \sum_{i=1}^{n} \xi_{j,i} - b_j \tag{4}$$

$$s.t. w_j \cdot \phi(f_j(x_i)) \geq b_j - \xi_{j,i}, \xi_{j,i} \geq 0, i \in 1, 2, \dots n$$

where the slack variable $\xi_{j,i}$ makes the margin to be soft, and the hyperparameter $v \in (0, 1]$ controls the balance between the margin and the slack variable.

We introduce the Lagrangian multiplier $\alpha_{j,i}, \lambda_{j,i} \geq 0$, and obtain the Lagrangian function as depicted in Eq. (4),

$$L(w_j, \xi_j, b_j, \alpha_j, \lambda_j) = \frac{1}{2} \|w_j\|^2 + \frac{1}{vn} \sum_{i=1}^{n} \xi_{j,i} - b_j$$

$$- \sum_{i=1}^{n} \alpha_{j,i}(w_j \cdot \phi(f_j(x_i)) - b_j + \xi_{j,i}) \tag{5}$$

$$- \sum_{i=1}^{n} \lambda_{j,i} \xi_{j,i}$$

Then, let the partial derivatives of $L(w_j, \xi_j, b_j, \alpha_j, \lambda_j)$ with respect to w_j, ξ_j, b_j be zero, we have,

$$w_j = \sum_{i=1}^{n} \alpha_{j,i} \phi(f_j(x_i)) \tag{6}$$

$$\alpha_{j,i} = \frac{1}{vn} - \lambda_{j,i} \leq \frac{1}{vn} \tag{7}$$

$$\sum_{i=1}^{n} \alpha_{j,i} = 1 \tag{8}$$

Substituting Eq. (6)-(8) into Eq. (5), the corresponding dual problem of Eq. (4) is obtained as,

$$\min_{\alpha} \frac{1}{2} \sum_{i,i'=1}^{n} \alpha_{j,i}\alpha_{j,i'} k(f_j(x_i), f_j(x_{i'}))$$

$$s.t. 0 \leq \alpha_{j,i} \leq \frac{1}{vn}, \sum_{i=1}^{n} \alpha_{j,i} = 1 \tag{9}$$

The optimal solution α_j^* is obtained by solving Eq. (9), and then w_j^* is obtained by Eq. (6). Through the Karush-Kuhn-Tucker condition, we know that when $0 < \alpha_{j,i} < \frac{1}{vn}$, the feature $\phi(f_j(x_i))$ falls on the hyperplane, then $f_j(x_i)$ can be used to obtain b_j^*,

$$b_j^* = w \cdot \phi(f_j(x_i)) = \sum_{i'=1}^{n} \alpha_{j,i'} k(f_j(x_{i'}), f_j(x_i)) \tag{10}$$

Therefore, through the above solution process, we can obtain the optimal hyperplane satisfying Eq. (4). The training process of other base classifiers is similar to the training process of the j-th base classifier.

3.3 Classifier Fusion for Image Anomaly Evaluation

After training the L base classifiers, we perform anomaly evaluation on the image samples in the test set. We first send the image samples in the test set to the trained convolutional autoencoder, and extract image semantic features at different levels based on the encoder. Then, image anomaly detection is performed based on the trained multiple base classifiers.

The anomaly score of the image sample x_i on the j-th base classifier is,

$$Score_j(x_i) = -\frac{w_j^* \cdot \phi(f_j(x_i)) + b_j^*}{\left\| w_j^* \right\|} \tag{11}$$

As shown in Eq. (11), we take the distance between the feature of the sample and the hyperplane in the Reproducing Kernel Hilbert Space (RKHS) as the anomaly score. At the same time, we preset that if the feature of the sample is in the half space containing the origin, the anomaly score is positive; otherwise, the anomaly score is negative.

We fuse the evaluation results of image sample x_i in all base classifiers to get the final anomaly score,

$$Score(x_i) = \frac{1}{L} \sum_{j=1}^{L} Score_j(x_i)$$

$$= \frac{1}{L} \sum_{j=1}^{L} -\frac{w_j^* \cdot \phi(f_j(x_i)) + b_j^*}{\left\| w_j^* \right\|} \qquad (12)$$

4 Experiments

4.1 Datasets and Setup

In this subsection, we briefly introduce the image anomaly detection dataset and related setup of dataset used in the experiments.

MVTec AD: The MVTec AD dataset contains common image sample categories in industrial production. It is a dataset specially used for image anomaly detection. The MVTec AD dataset contains 5 texture images and 10 object images. Each category of the MVTec AD dataset has a corresponding training set and test set, in which the training set contains only normal examples of the class, and the test set contains normal examples and abnormal examples. The training set contains 3629 image samples. The test set contains 1725 image samples. In the experiment, we scale the pixel of all image samples on the original training set and test set to 256 × 256, and then we crop the image with a 32 × 32 sliding window, and its step size is 4, so as to obtain patches corresponding to each image. On the MVTec AD dataset, we have 15 image anomaly detection tasks, and the score of the test image sample is,

$$Score(x) = \max\{ Score(patch_j) | j = 1, 2, \ldots, N \} \qquad (13)$$

where N represents the total number of patches corresponding to image sample x.

MNIST: The MNIST dataset contains 10 classes of handwritten digits from digit 0 to digit 9. The training set contains 60,000 image samples, of which each class has about 6,000 image samples. The test set has 10,000 image samples, of which each class contains 1,000 image samples. The resolution of the images on the MNIST dataset is 28 × 28. We take one class of handwritten digits as the normal class and the other classes of handwritten digits as the abnormal class. In our experiments, we use the original training and testing splits. However, unlike image classification tasks, we only use image examples in the training set that are considered normal classes to train the model. Therefore, we have a total of 10 image anomaly detection tasks on the MNIST dataset. On the MNIST dataset, the score of the test image sample is shown in Eq. (12).

Fashion-MNIST: The Fashion-MNIST dataset contains 10 categories of clothing examples. The training set contains 60,000 image samples, of which each class contains 6,000 image samples. The test set contains 10,000 image samples, of which each class contains 1,000 image samples. The resolution of the images on the Fashion-MNIST dataset is 28 × 28. The anomaly detection task on the Fashion-MNIST dataset is configured in the same way as the MNIST dataset. Like the MNIST dataset, we also have a total of 10 image anomaly detection tasks on the Fashion-MNIST dataset. On the Fashion-MNIST dataset, the score of the test image sample is shown in Eq. (12).

4.2   Baseline Methods

In order to verify the performance of our proposed EOCCA method, we compare it with some state-of-the-art image anomaly detection methods.

Shallow methods: One-Class Support Vector Machines (OCSVMs) [5] is a classic image anomaly detection method. For a detailed introduction of OCSVM, see the previous related work. In the Kernel Density Estimation (KDE) [10], the probability distribution of the normal category image samples is estimated first, and then the image anomaly detection is performed according to the established probability distribution model of the normal category image samples.

Methods of image reconstruction: AE [11], AnoGAN [12], GANomaly [13], Puzzle-AE [14] are abnormal detection methods based on image reconstruction. The core idea of this method is that the reconstruction error of normal image is small and that of abnormal image is large. This kind of method uses normal image training reconfiguration network to learn the pattern of normal image. Among them, in AnoGAN [12], GANomaly [13], Puzzle-AE [14], the reconstruction quality of normal image is effectively improved through the adversarial training of discriminator and autoencoders.

Hybrid methods: In DAGMM [15], the hidden representation of normal image is extracted by autoencoder, and then the probability distribution of normal image is learned by Gaussian mixture model.

Methods of building classification surface: In ONE-CLASS DEEP SVDD [16], the normal image samples are used to pre-train the autoencoder, and then the encoder is fine tuned in the feature space to minimize the distance between the feature point and the center point. This method takes the distance from the feature point to the center point as the anomaly score. In GeoTrans [17], the original image is processed by geometric transformation, so as to divide the normal image of a single category into multiple subcategories. Then, the classifier is trained with the normal image data set divided into several subclasses to predict the geometric transformation mode used. After geometric transformation of abnormal samples, the classifier cannot determine its geometric transformation mode.

4.3   Model Configuration

When extracting different levels of image semantic features, we use a LeNet-type convolutional neural structure as an encoder, where each convolutional module consists of a convolutional layer followed by leaky ReLU activation function and max-pooling layer. The structure of the decoder is symmetrical with that of the encoder, where each deconvolution module consists of a deconvolution layer followed by leaky ReLU activation function and interpolating layer.

On the MNIST and Fashion-MNSIT datasets, the pixels of the images are all 28×28, and the channels of the images are all 1. Therefore, we use the same structure of convolutional autoencoder on the MNIST and Fashion-MNSIT datasets to extract image semantic features at different levels.

When training convolutional autoencoders with normal class images, we use the Adam optimizer to optimize the model parameter with learning rate η set to 10^{-3}. At the same time, in order to prevent over fitting, we use early stopping. We set the size of the encoder to 128.

We take One-Class Support Vector Machines (OCSVMs) as the base classifier. At the same time, we choose the Gaussian kernel as the kernel function, in which we use the grid search method to select the scale parameter γ of the Gaussian kernel from $\{2^{-9}, 2^{-8}, \ldots, 2^2\}$ on a small holdout set. In the experiments, we set the hyperparameter v to 0.1.

4.4 Performance Evaluation Metric

In the image anomaly detection task, a widely used performance evaluation metric is the area under the receiver operating curve (AUC). We use AUC to evaluate the performance of our model and compare it to the baseline methods.

4.5 Results and Analysis

Table 1. Average AUCs in % over 10 runs on MVTec AD dataset.

Class	GeoTrans[*]	LSA[†]	GANomaly[*]	AnoGAN[†]	Puzzle-AE	Our Method
Carpet	43.7	74.0	69.9	49.0	65.7	**75.2**
Grid	61.9	54.0	70.8	51.0	75.4	**79.3**
Leather	84.1	70.0	84.2	52.0	72.9	**85.1**
Tile	41.7	70.0	79.4	51.0	65.5	**83.9**
Wood	61.1	75.0	83.4	68.0	**89.5**	85.3
Bottle	74.4	86.0	89.2	69.0	94.2	**95.3**
Cable	78.3	61.0	75.7	53.0	**87.9**	86.1
Capsule	67.0	71.0	73.2	58.0	67.0	**81.6**
Hazelnut	35.9	80.0	78.5	50.0	**91.2**	88.4
MetalNut	81.3	67.0	70.0	50.0	66.3	**89.5**
Pill	63.0	**85.0**	74.3	62.0	71.6	84.1
Screw	50.0	75.0	74.6	35.0	57.9	**76.9**
Toothbrush	97.2	89.0	65.3	57.0	97.8	**98.3**
Transistor	86.9	50.0	79.2	67.0	86.0	**88.6**
Zipper	82.0	**88.0**	74.5	59.0	75.7	84.9

Our experimental results on the MVTec AD dataset, Fashion-MNIST dataset, and MNIST dataset are presented in Table 1, Table 2, and Table 3, respectively. On the MVTec

Table 2. Average AUCs in % over 10 runs on MNIST dataset.

Class	OCSVM*	KDE*	AE†	DAGMM†	AnoGAN†	DEEP SVDD*	Our Method
0	96.7	97.1	98.8	50.0	96.6	98.0	**99.0**
1	99.1	98.9	99.3	76.6	99.2	**99.6**	**99.6**
2	79.3	79.0	**91.7**	32.6	85.0	**91.7**	87.8
3	85.9	86.2	88.5	31.9	88.7	91.9	**92.1**
4	94.2	87.9	86.2	36.8	89.4	94.9	**96.1**
5	72.8	73.8	85.8	49.0	88.3	88.5	**92.3**
6	95.1	87.6	95.4	51.5	94.7	98.3	**98.8**
7	91.8	91.4	94.0	50.0	93.5	94.6	**96.1**
8	88.6	79.2	82.3	46.7	84.9	**93.9**	**93.9**
9	92.5	88.2	96.5	81.3	92.4	96.5	**97.0**

Table 3. Average AUCs in % over 10 runs on Fashion-MNIST dataset.

Class	OCSVM*	KDE*	AE†	DAGMM†	AnoGAN†	DEEP SVDD*	Our Method
0	90.6	88.3	71.6	51.9	89.0	79.1	**92.7**
1	97.5	94.3	96.9	34.0	97.1	94.0	**99.2**
2	88.1	87.7	72.9	26.9	86.5	83.0	**91.4**
3	91.3	88.4	78.5	57.0	91.2	82.9	**93.7**
4	88.5	86.3	82.9	50.4	87.6	87.0	**91.8**
5	87.6	85.9	**93.1**	70.5	89.6	80.3	92.6
6	81.4	74.7	66.7	48.3	74.3	74.9	**85.2**
7	98.4	96.1	95.4	83.5	97.2	94.2	**98.7**
8	86.0	84.6	70.0	55.1	81.9	79.1	**88.3**
9	97.7	94.2	80.7	34.0	89.9	93.2	**98.8**

AD dataset, our method outperforms the baseline method on 10 image anomaly detection tasks, while achieving above average results on the remaining 5 image anomaly detection tasks. On the MNIST dataset, our method outperforms the baseline method on 7 image anomaly detection tasks, while slightly lowering the highest AUC on the remaining 3 image anomaly detection tasks. On the Fashion-MNIST dataset, our method outperforms the baseline method on 9 image anomaly detection tasks, while slightly lowering the highest AUC on the remaining one image anomaly detection tasks. In conclusion, the experimental results on 3 image anomaly detection benchmark datasets demonstrate the superiority of our proposed method.

5 Conclusion and Future Work

We propose an image anomaly detection method called Ensemble of One-Class Classifiers based on multi-level hidden representations abstracted from Autoencoder (EOCCA), which is a two-stage hybrid method and also an ensemble learning method. First, we train a convolutional autoencoder with the goal of minimizing the reconstruction error, thereby extracting image semantic features at different levels, which contain image semantic information from local to global and are very beneficial for image anomaly detection. Second, we train a base classifier (OCSVM) based on image semantic features at different levels. In the inference stage, we integrate the results of all base classifiers as the final image anomaly evaluation result. Experimental results on image anomaly detection benchmark datasets demonstrate that our proposed method achieves superior image anomaly detection results.

In the future, based on our proposed two-stage and ensemble image anomaly detection framework, we will try more shallow methods as base classifiers, such as KDE, IF, etc. to develop the effect of our framework.

References

1. Pang, G., Shen, C., Cao, L., Hengel, A.V.D.: Deep learning for anomaly detection: a review. ACM Comput. Surv. **54**, 1–38 (2021)
2. Fernando, T., et al.: Neural memory plasticity for medical anomaly detection. Neural Netw. **127**, 67–81 (2020)
3. Bergmann, P., Fauser, M., Sattlegger, D., Steger, C.: MVTec AD--A comprehensive real-world dataset for unsupervised anomaly detection. In: Proceedings of the IEEE/CVF Conference on Computer Vision and Pattern Recognition, pp. 9592–9600 (2019)
4. Asha, R.B., Suresh Kumar, K.R.: Credit card fraud detection using artificial neural network. Global Transitions Proceedings, vol. 2, pp. 35–41 (2021)
5. Schölkopf, B., Platt, J.C., Shawe-Taylor, J., Smola, A.J., Williamson, R.C.: Estimating the support of a high-dimensional distribution. Neural Comput. **13**, 1443–1471 (2001)
6. Andrews, J.T., Morton, E.J., Griffin, L.D.: Detecting anomalous data using auto-encoders. Int. J. Machine Learning Comput. **6**, 21 (2016)
7. Cao, V.L., Nicolau, M., McDermott, J.: Learning neural representations for network anomaly detection. IEEE Trans. Cybernetics **49**, 3074–3087 (2019)
8. Tellaeche Iglesias, A., Campos Anaya, M.Á., Pajares Martinsanz, G., Pastor-López, I.: On Combining Convolutional Autoencoders and Support Vector Machines for Fault Detection in Industrial Textures. Sensors **21**, 3339 (2021)
9. Gupta, K., Bhavsar, A., Sao, A.K.: Detecting mitotic cells in HEp-2 images as anomalies via one class classifier. Comput. Biol. Med. **111**, 103328 (2019)
10. Svensén, M., Bishop, C.M.: Pattern recognition and machine learning. Springer, Berlin/Heidelberg, Germany (2007). https://doi.org/10.1007/978-0-387-45528-0
11. Mei, S., Yang, H., Yin, Z.: An unsupervised-learning-based approach for automated defect inspection on textured surfaces. IEEE Trans. Instrum. Meas. **67**, 1266–1277 (2018)
12. Schlegl, T., Seebück, P., Waldstein, S.M., Schmidt-Erfurth, U., Langs, G.: Unsupervised anomaly detection with generative adversarial networks to guide marker discovery. In: International Conference on Information Processing in Medical Imaging, pp. 146–157 (2017)
13. Akcay, S., Atapour-Abarghouei, A., Breckon, T.P.: Ganomaly: Semi-supervised anomaly detection via adversarial training. In: Asian conference on computer vision, pp. 622–637 (2018)

14. Salehi, M., Eftekhar, A., Sadjadi, N., Rohban, M.H., Rabiee, H.R.: Puzzle-AE: Novelty Detection in Images through Solving Puzzles. ArXiv, vol. abs/2008.12959 (2020)
15. Zong, B., Song, Q., Min, M.R., Cheng, W., Lumezanu, C., Cho, D., Chen, H.: Deep autoencoding gaussian mixture model for unsupervised anomaly detection. In: International Conference on Learning Representations (2018)
16. Ruff, L., et al.: Deep one-class classification. In: International Conference on Machine Learning, pp. 4393–4402 (2018)
17. Golan, I., El-Yaniv, R.: Deep anomaly detection using geometric transformations. In: Proceedings of the 32nd International Conference on Neural Information Processing Systems, pp. 9781–9791 (2018)

Images Structure Reconstruction from fMRI by Unsupervised Learning Based on VAE

Zhiwei Zhao, Haodong Jing, Jianji Wang, Weihua Wu, and Yongqiang Ma[✉]

Institute of Artificial Intelligence and Robotics, Xi'an Jiaotong University,
Xi'an, China
{zhaozw,jinghd}@stu.xjtu.edu.cn, musayq@xjtu.edu.cn

Abstract. How to reconstruct the stimulus images from fMRI signals is an important problem in the field of neuroscience. Limited by the complexity and the acquisition accuracy of brain signals, it is still very difficult to completely reconstruct the realistic images from fMRI signals by the artificial intelligence related technology. In the experiments related to brain signals stimulated by real images, we found that: as subjects, when stimulated by continuous realistic images, they are more sensitive to the high-frequency information in the stimulus images, such as image contour, color upheaval area, etc., The human vision and cerebral cortex seem to respond more strongly to these. Based on this discovery, we propose a method that pays more attention to the image structure to reconstruct images from fMRI signals. In order to fully decode the voxels in fMRI signals and solve the problem of insufficient amount of fMRI data, we use a back-to-back model based on Variational Auto-Encoder, which can decode more voxels in fMRI recordings into meaningful image features and introduce more unlabeled data to improve the overall performance of the model. Experiments demonstrate that our method performers better than other mainstream methods.

Keywords: fMRI · Image structure · Image reconstruction · Variational auto-encoder

1 Introduction

fMRI (functional magnetic resonance imaging) signals measure the changes of hemodynamics caused by neuronal activity [1]. And fMRI signals can reveal the relationship between visual stimulus and visual cortical activities [2]. Reconstructing images from fMRI signals went through a process from simple to complex. The initial reconstruction is to decode the fMRI by linear relationship [3] between fMRI recordings and the original stimulus images. limited by the limitation of linear relationship, the performance of image reconstruction is not satisfactory, because the relationship between fMRI signals and stimulus images is more than a simple linear relationship, especially when the stimulus is a natural image rather than a simple gray image; The rapid development of biologically inspired artificial intelligence [4] provides a new idea for image reconstruction. The related work of Kyoto University [5] pushed the reconstruction from fMRI signals to a peak. They used deep neural network to simulate the brain's encoding process of visual information and achieved good results. Since then, with the maturity and large-scale application of deep learning related methods, The methods of using Bayesian correlation model [6–8] and convolutional neural network [5,9,10] to build encoder-decoder model to reconstruct images from fMRI signals were also proposed, espically Generative adversarial networks[6,11–13]. These methods succeeded in finding the complex relationship between fMRI signals and original stimulus images and achieve good reconstruction results. In addition, Siyu Yu et al. [14] had also achieved some success in decoding fMRI signals by looking for the relationship between voxels in fMRI. Beliy et al. [15] proposed an unsupervised learning method using encoder and decoder back-to-back connection, which had achieved amazing performance in the case of only a small amount of labeled fMRI data.

Limited by the amount of fMRI data, it is difficult to fully train the model [15] and more unlabeled data need to be introduced. Additional, these methods mentioned above also have the problems of insufficient voxel decoding in fMRI data, this usually leads to the loss of image features after reconstruction. And The objective function used in the image reconstruction model does not conform to the human visual system [16]. These problems may lead to poor performance of reconstruction.

In the process of collecting relevant fMRI recordings, we found that the subjects have a deeper impression of the high-frequency information of the stimulus images, and the sensitivity of human vision to image edges and contours is higher than that of human vision to smooth areas and texture areas [17,18]. Some existing studies have also shown that human visual cortex are more sensitive to the deviation between visible light [16,19], so fMRI signals may store more high-frequency information about the original stimulus images, and the structural features of the image can be used as the target features in the process of reconstruction from fMRI signals. Besides, according to the relationship between voxels intensities in fMRI signals and visual stimulus, for the same subject, the same voxels will theoretically show the same intensities to the same visual stimulus [5], so the specific intensities of the same voxels can decode specific image features, Then the VAE [20] model can be used to generalize this: according to the image features corresponding to the known voxel intensity, infer the image features corresponding to the unknown voxel intensity nearby. Therefore, we propose a back to back connection framework based on VAE to make voxels decoding more sufficient. The contributions of our work are summarized as follows:

(1) We propose a method to infer the image features corresponding to the unknown voxel intensity according to the image features corresponding to the known voxel intensity for image reconstruction from fMRI signals.

(2) Based on relevant experiments and previous studies, we propose to take the reconstructed image structure as the focus of image reconstruction from

fMRI signals, which is more in line with the characteristics of human vision and can achieve better results.

(3) We propose a back-to-back connection model based on VAE, it can fully decode voxels in fMRI data recordings while overcoming the shortage of samples.

2   Method

2.1   Basic Model and Loss Function

Variational Auto-encoder(VAE). The encoder of the VAE is to learn the potential feature distribution of the images. The output of the encoder includes two parts: mean and variance, which constitute the potential feature distribution. In this way, the encoder constructs a feature space, all feature points have practical meaning in the feature space, and the decoder extracts samples from the feature distribution by sampling for decoding. In order to simplify the training, the standard Gaussian distribution is usually regarded as the prior distribution of potential feature. The training process can be regarded as optimizing the parameters of encoder and decoder by minimizing the reconstruction loss and the KL divergence between potential feature distribution and Gaussian distribution.

Let E_ϕ denotes the encoder of VAE, D_φ denotes the decoder of VAE, ϕ and φ denotes the parameters of the encoder and decoder to be optimized. And let z denotes latent variables and x denotes the input images. $p(z)$ denotes the prior distribution of z, and it is usually set to Gaussian distribution $N(u, \sigma)$. $q(z|x)$ denotes the posterior distribution of z and $p(x|z)$ denotes the likelihood of x given z under the decoder can be computed as follows:

$$q(z|x) = E_\phi(x) = N(u_z, \sigma_z) \tag{1}$$

$$p(x|z) = D_\varphi(z) \tag{2}$$

The loss of VAE is minus the sum of the expected log likelihood (the reconstruction error) and a prior regularization term:

$$loss = -\mathrm{E}_{q(z|x)}[\log \frac{p(x|z)p(z)}{q(z|x)}] = -\mathrm{E}_{q(z|x)}[\log p(x|z)] + D_{KL}(q(z|x)||p(z)) \tag{3}$$

D_{KL} is the Kullback-Leibler divergence. The first item in loss can be regarded as reconstruction loss, and the another item is the error between the a prior and a posterior distributions of z. The KL divergence part in the VAE loss can be considered to enhance the generation function of VAE, Optimizing the reconstruction loss is to enhance the reconstruction function of VAE. As a result of this, different weights can be given to the two parts of the loss function of VAE, so that VAE can no longer give equal attention to image generation and reconstruction, and can dynamically enhance the image generation function or image reconstruction function of VAE, just like [21], the loss function can be expressed as:

$$loss = -\mathrm{E}_{q(z|x)}[\log p(x|z)] + \beta * D_{KL}(q(z|x)||p(z)) \tag{4}$$

When $\beta = 1$, it is the ordinary VAE, if $\beta > 1$, the image generation function of VAE will be enhanced, or the reconstruction function.

Structural Similarity (SSIM). SSIM [22] is used to evaluate the similarity between images, Just like MSE and PSNR, SSIM can also be used as the objective function of the model as an image quality evaluation index[23]. SSIM measures the similarity of images from the perspective of neuroscience that human beings pay more attention to the structural similarity of the two images rather than calculating the difference between the two images pixel by pixel, which has the same meaning as our hypothetical "fMRI is sensitive to the color deviation of the images".

SSIM measures the structural similarity of the images from three levels, namely luminance l, contrast c and structure s. And it is used to evaluate the structural similarity between gray images,If the images to be compared are three channels, the average value of the three channels needs to be calculated. Let $x = \{x_i | i = 1, 2, 3, 4, ..., N\}$ and $y = \{y_j | j = 1, 2, 3, 4, ..., N\}$ respectively denote two gray-scale images with the same size, where N is the number of image pixels. And u_x denote the mean of x, u_y denote the mean of y. σ_x and σ_y denotes the variance x of and y respectively, σ_{xy} denotes the covariance of x and y. We can express the luminance, contrast and structure with mean, variance and covariance:

$$l(x, y) = \frac{2u_x u_y + C_1}{u_x^2 + u_y^2 + C_1} \tag{5}$$

$$c(x, y) = \frac{2\sigma_x \sigma_y + C_2}{\sigma_x^2 + \sigma_y^2 + C_2} \tag{6}$$

$$s(x, y) = \frac{\sigma_{xy} + C_3}{\sigma_x \sigma_y + C_3} \tag{7}$$

C_1, C_2, C_3 are constants to prevent inaccurate results due to too small mean and variance. Especially $C_1 = (K_1 L)^2$ and $0 < K_1 << 1$. Normally $K_1 = 0.01$. L is the gray level of the image, when the pixel of image is 8-bit, $L = 255$, $C_2 = (K_2 L)^2$, K_2 is same to K_2, and it is usually taken as 0.03. $C_3 = C_2/2$. SSIM can be obtained by combining luminance l, contrast c and structure s:

$$SSIM_{(x,y)} = l_{(x,y)} c_{(x,y)} s_{(x,y)} = \frac{(2u_x u_y + C_1)(2\sigma_{xy} + C_2)}{(u_x^2 + u_y^2 + C_1)(\sigma_x^2 + \sigma_y^2 + C_2)} \tag{8}$$

According to SSIM calculation formula, $0 <= SSIM_{(x,y)} <= 1$. When calculating the similarity of two images, an $n * n$ window is usually used and the window is slid pixel by pixel to calculated SSIM of each window. Finally, the average value of SSIM in windows is taken as the SSIM value of the whole image.

2.2   Overview of the Proposed Framework

We proposed a model of Encoder-Decoder-Encoder based on VAE, each part of the model can be trained separately with different training data. in which the input images are encoded by the encoder, and the output fMRI recordings individual voxels obey a specific distribution to simulate the processing process of human brain for visual stimulus. The decoder is responsible for decoding the fMRI recordings into the original stimulus images, The dual encoder and decoder form a back-to-back VAE structure, which can carry out unsupervised training [15], allowing the introduction of more unlabeled data to train the model. The framework of our proposed method is shown in Fig. 1.

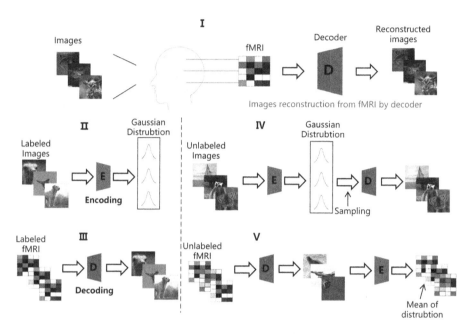

Fig. 1. The method of us. (I)The task is to train a decoder to decode fMRI recordings into images. (II)The encoder is used to simulate the process that the brain converts images into fMRI recordings, but in our method, the images are converted into Gaussian distribution. (III)The decoder restores fMRI recordings to stimulus images. (IV)(V)In order to further train the decoder, the unsupervised training of Encoder-Decoder and Decoder-Encoder is needed. In the training process, the distribution of encoder output needs to be sampled in a special way as the input of decoder in (IV). And the output of training only considers the mean part of the encoder(V). It should be noted in IV and V that the parameters of the encoder are fixed.

Encoder. We learn the structure of encoder from [15]. Firstly, using the pre-trained Alexnet network to extract the image features. After features normalization, going through 3×3 revolution with 32 channels, relu activation with stripe 2, and batch normalization for 3 times, Finally, two independent full connection layers are used to output the mean and variance of fMRI recordings distribution respectively.

We understand the mean and variance of the fully connected output from the perspective of AE: the mean of the output of the fully connected layer is used as the potential features, and the output variance is used as the generated noise to interfere with the reconstruction performance of VAE model, but it can also enhance the generation performance of the model. The mean and variance together constitute the distribution of potential features. Due to the lack of prior distribution information of potential features, the prior of potential feature distribution is set as the standard Gaussian distribution. But In our experiment, we found that the values of fMRI signals are relatively concentrated, and the difference between voxels intensities shall not exceed 1, so if the variance 1 in the standard Gaussian distribution is used, it will cause too much noise and cannot converge. So Gaussian distribution is $N(0, 0.2)$ selected as the prior distribution.

Let y denotes fMRI signals and x denotes the labels of fMRI data. In our experiment, fMRI data with image labels are used as training samples, and the images corresponding to fMRI data are input into the encoder. Then the error between the mean u output of the encoder and y is taken as the loss function of the reconstruction term, and the KL divergence between the distribution composed of mean u, variance σ and Gaussian distribution $N(0, 0.2)$ is taken as the loss function of the generation term. So the loss function can be expressed by:

$$loss_{Encoder} = loss(y, u) - \beta * D_{KL}[(N(u, \sigma)||N(0, 0.2)]$$ (9)

$$loss_{(y,u)} = ||y - u||_2$$ (10)

Significantly, the former term of the loss function enables the encoder to simulate the process of human vision transforming images into fMRI recordings, and the latter term enables the encoder to generate an fMRI recordings space conforming to Gaussian distribution. Different from the traditional VAE, the reconstruction process only simulates the brain to generate fMRI signals, so there is no need to limit the variance in the reconstruction process.

Decoder. We implemented the decoder model provided by [15]. Firstly, a full connection layer is used to map fMRI recordings into 64 feature maps with spatial resolution 14×14, and then three same convolution blocks are used to process the feature maps. Each convolution block first performs convolution operation, uses 3 * 3 convolution core, and then performs up sampling and normalization with relu activation function. The final output is a three channel image, so finally, it needs to use a 3 * 3 convolution and sigmoid function to limit the three channel output value to the range of 0–1.

When training the decoder, the input are the fMRI data sampled from the potential feature space and the real fMRI recordings collected, and the output are images for additional training or real stimulus images. The training loss of the decoder is only the image reconstruction error. The human visual system is more sensitive to the high-frequency information of the images, we only consider taking structural similarity as the loss of image reconstruction. But taking structural similarity as the objective function can only reconstruct the high-frequency information of the images, so additional we choose feature-extractor ψ to reconstruct the colors of the images. In order to reduce the noise of the images and smooth the images pixels, we also use total variation (TV) regulation. Let $D_\varphi(y)$ denotes images reconstructed by decoder. The loss function of the decoder can be expressed as:

$$loss_{Decoder} = \alpha * loss_{structure}[D_\varphi(y), x] + \beta * loss_{color}[D_\varphi(y), x] + TV[D_\varphi(y)] \tag{11}$$

$$loss_{structure} = SSIM[D_\varphi(y), x] \tag{12}$$

$$loss_{color} = ||\psi(D_\varphi(y)) - \psi(x)||_1 \tag{13}$$

The function of decoder is to decode fMRI signals into corresponding images.

Implementation Details. In the experiment, the training of the whole model includes four parts: First we trained the encoder. In order to avoid the impact of additional images on the encoder in the training process, it is necessary to pre train the encoder. 1200 labeled fMRI data training data are selected, the stimulus is reshaped to 112 * 112 pixels. Considering the rotation of subjects' eyeballs in the process of collecting fMRI recordings, the stimulus is randomly offset as the input of the encoder to improve the performance of the encoder. During training, $\beta = 0.2$, with an initial learning rate of 0.1, with a predefined learning rate scheduler. The encoder is trained 80 times in total. Next we trained the decoder. The labeled fMRI data are used to train the decoder and set parameters $\alpha = 2$ and $\beta = 0.16$.

However, only relying on 1200 labeled fMRI data can not fully train the decoder, and additional unlabeled images are needed to train the Encoder-Decoder structure and unlabeled fMRI data to train the Decoder-Encoder structure. So then we used additional 50000 natural images with 3-channel for training. The parameters of the encoder need to be fixed during training, and the objective function of the decoder consists of only the reconstruction loss between the generated images $D_\varphi[E_\phi(x)]$ and the ground truth images x. The objective function of the Encoder-Decoder is the same as that of training decoder. In the training process, the encoder generates the mean and variance to form a Gaussian distribution $N(u, \sigma)$, which needs to be sampled from the distribution as the input of the decoder. it is not advisable to sample directly in Gaussian distribution for training, it can be replaced by sampling from standard Gaussian distribution $N(0, 1)$ by reparameterization trick. Let $z_{N(u,\sigma)}$ denotes the sample taken from $N(u, \sigma)$ and $z_{N(0,1)}$ denotes the sample taken from $N(0, 1)$:

$$z_{N(u,\sigma)} = u + \sigma * z_{N(0,1)} \tag{14}$$

Finally we trained the Decoder-Encoder. The input of the decoder are unlabeled fMRI data, let y denotes that, and the output images are used as the input of the encoder. The output of the encoder is a distribution composed of mean u and variance σ. the objective function of the Decoder-Encoder is the same as the loss of reconstruction in Encoder.

The whole training process is similar to [15], the specific process is shown in Fig. 2. After the training, take out the decoder part separately and take the test fMRI data as the input. In theory, the corresponding images should be output.

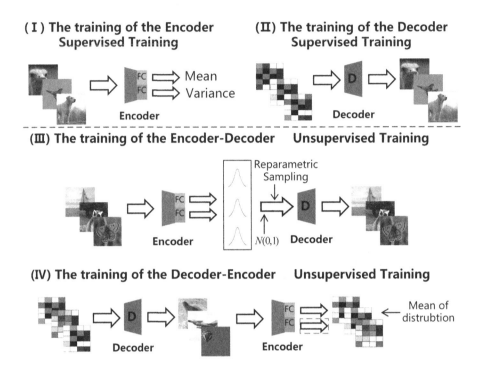

Fig. 2. The training of the whole model. (I)The training of the encoder: The output layer of the encoder includes two independent full connection layers, output a Gaussian distribution of voxels intensity composed of mean and variance. (II)The training of the decoder:Training the decoder with labeled fMRI. (III)The training of Encoder-Decoder: Similar to the training standard VAE model, training decoder with the trained encoder. (IV)The training of Decoder-Encoder: The output of encoder is a distribution, and the loss cannot be calculated, so only the mean part of the distribution output by the encoder is selected.

3 Experimental Results

3.1 Datasets and Evalution

Experimental Data. We conducted experiments on the fMRI data set [5] published by Kyoto University. The fMRI data set published by Kyoto University includes the fMRI recordings of 5 subjects. The stimulus source is from public data set ImageNet [24]. A total of 1000 training images and 50 test images are from 200 categories, of which 50 test images belong to different categories. The cerebral visual cortex can be divided into low-level visual cortex and high-level visual cortex. The low-level visual cortex includes V1, V2, V3 and V4, and the high-level visual cortex includes LOC, PPA and FFA. All fMRI recordings are divided into voxels according to the collected cerebral visual cortex. In this experiment, we selected about 4500 voxels from the visual cortex. We need additional images with 3 channels for unsupervised training. Therefore, we also use the additional images from ImageNet, which contains 5000 unlabeled natural images, and the additional natural images used for training are different from the stimulus images previously used for fMRI recordings acquisition.

Performance Evaluation. In order to evaluate the performance of our method, we evaluate the reconstructed images with visual comparison subjectively and quantitative comparison objectively. For quantitative comparison, pairwise similarity comparison analysis was used to measure the reconstructed images' quality [9]. We use one reconstructed image to compare with the ground-truth image and a randomly selected test image to test if its correlation with the ground truth image is higher. We use structural similarity as the evaluation index which is more in line with the characteristics of human vision. Besides, we also used PSNR [25] as evaluation index in ablation experiment to prove the usefulness of our proposed loss function and model.

3.2 Comparison of Images Reconstruction Performance with Others

We compared our experimental results with advanced approaches [10,11,15] in the field. For [15], we also ran the code published with the paper. In order to make the comparison result more convincing, we compare it from the perspective of Visual comparison and Quantitative comparison. As for Visual comparison, we compare our reconstructed images with the results published in the papers above. In addition, SSIM were also used to objectively evaluate the quality of the reconstructed images. In the experiment, we conducted three experiments to eliminate the randomness of the experimental results, and used the average value of the three experiments as the results to be compared. Same to[11], We tested the fMRI of three subjects. From the visual effect of the reconstructed images in Fig. 3 (I), the reconstructed image pixels are relatively smooth without significant noise, that is the characteristic of VAE model. The reconstruction images has no obvious meaningless pixels and the contours are clearer, thanks to the use of structural loss function in the training process of the model according to the characteristics of human vision. As the result above shows from Fig. 3 (II), in the comparison of structural similarity with [10,11,15], our method performs slightly better than [15](66.4% vs 64.3% on average), [11](66.4% vs 65.3% on average) and [10](66.4% vs 62.9% on average).

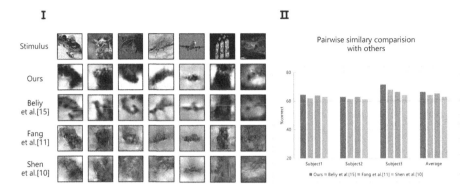

Fig. 3. Our reconstruction performance comparison with others. (I)Visual comparison of reconstructed images. (II)Quality comparison of reconstructed images.

3.3   Ablation Experiment

Effectiveness of VAE. In order to evaluate the effectiveness of our model, we use the AE model and our VAE model to reconstruct the images from fMRI respectively with the ordinary loss function. The comparison results are shown in Fig. 4. The images reconstructed by AE model have many unexplained pixels and are not smooth due to the model will decode some unrecognized data into pixels with no practical significance. The VAE model will reasonably infer the pixels in the images corresponding to the undetermined data according to the image pixels corresponding to the determined data. So the reconstructed images looks smoother and contains more feature information in Fig. 4(I). And the model of VAE performs better than AE(65.2% vs 64.3% on average) in Fig. 4(II).

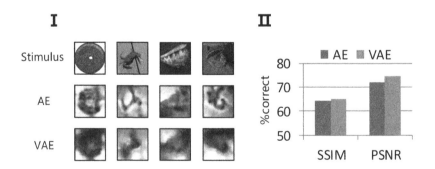

Fig. 4. Performance comparison of models: (I)Visual comparison of reconstructed images from different models. (II)Quality comparison of reconstructed images from different models.

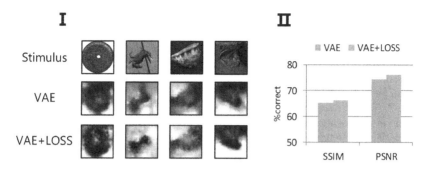

Fig. 5. Performance comparison of loss function: (I)Visual comparison of reconstructed images with different loss function. (II)Quality comparison of reconstructed images with different loss function.

Effectiveness of the Loss of Structural Similarity. To evaluate the effectiveness of structural loss function, we use different loss functions in our model for evaluation. As can be seen from Fig. 5(I), the images reconstructed with the loss of structural similarity has clearer contour and boundary. This is because the loss is more in line with human visual characteristics, which is consistent with the studies that fMRI recordings are more sensitive to light deviation and human eyes are more sensitive to image high-frequency information. Besides, the loss of SSIM performs better than the loss in [15](66.4% vs 65.2% on average) in Fig. 5(II).

4   Conclusion

According to the theory that the brain shows similar fMRI signals to similar visual stimulus, we propose a framework of back-to-back connection based on VAE, which can fully decode the voxels in fMRI data; Besides, according to the phenomenon that the human visual system is more sensitive to the high-frequency information of the images, we propose to reconstruct the structure of the stimulus images as the main goal of the whole model. Experiments show that our proposed method can achieve good results and significantly enhance the performance of image reconstruction from fMRI signals. The improvement of the performance is great help to human beings to better understand the working mechanism of the brain. And it can promote the research in neuroscience, brain computer interface and other related fields.

References

1. Engel, S.A., Rumelhart, D.E., et al.: fmri of human visual cortex. Nature 369, 525 (1994)
2. Yoshida, T., et al.: Natural images are reliably represented by sparse and variable populations of neurons in visual cortex. Nat. Commun. **11**(1), 1–19 (2020)

3. Miyawaki, Y., et al.: Visual image reconstruction from human brain activity using a combination of multiscale local image decoders. Neuron **60**(5), 915–929 (2008)
4. Zheng, N.n., Liu, Z.y, et al.: Hybrid-augmented intelligence: collaboration and cognition. Front. Inf. Technol. Elect. Eng. **18**(2), 153–179 (2017)
5. Horikawa, T., Kamitani, Y.: Generic decoding of seen and imagined objects using hierarchical visual features. Nat. Commun. **8**(1), 1–15 (2017)
6. Ren, Z., et al.: Reconstructing seen image from brain activity by visually-guided cognitive representation and adversarial learning. Neuroimage **228**, 117602 (2021)
7. Naselaris, T., Prenger, R.J., et al.: Bayesian reconstruction of natural images from human brain activity. Neuron **63**(6), 902–915 (2009)
8. VanRullen, R., Reddy, L.: Reconstructing faces from fmri patterns using deep generative neural networks. Commun. Bio. **2**(1), 1–10 (2019)
9. Shen, G., Dwivedi, K., et al.: End-to-end deep image reconstruction from human brain activity. Front. Comput. Neurosci. **13**, 21 (2019)
10. Shen, G., Horikawa, T., et al.: Deep image reconstruction from human brain activity. PLoS Comput. Biol. **15**(1), e1006633 (2019)
11. Fang, T., Qi, Y., Pan, G.: Reconstructing perceptive images from brain activity by shape-semantic gan. Adv. Neural. Inf. Process. Syst. **33**, 13038–13048 (2020)
12. St-Yves, G., Naselaris, T.: Generative adversarial networks conditioned on brain activity reconstruct seen images. In: 2018 IEEE International Conference on Systems, Man, and Cybernetics (SMC), pp. 1054–1061. IEEE(2018)
13. Seeliger, K., Güçlü, U., et al.: Generative adversarial networks for reconstructing natural images from brain activity. Neuroimage **181**, 775–785 (2018)
14. Yu, S., Zheng, N., et al.: A novel brain decoding method: a correlation network framework for revealing brain connections. IEEE Trans. Cogn. Dev. Syst. **11**(1), 95–106 (2018)
15. Beliy, R., Gaziv, G., et al.: From voxels to pixels and back: self-supervision in natural-image reconstruction from fmri. In: Advances in Neural Information Processing Systems, vol. 32 (2019)
16. Nonaka, S., Majima, K., et al.: Brain hierarchy score: which deep neural networks are hierarchically brain-like? Iscience **24**(9), 103013 (2021)
17. Hammill, H.B., Holladay, T.M.: The effects of certain approximations in image quality evaluation from edge traces. Opt. Eng. **8**(6), 223–228 (1970)
18. Ni, Z., Ma, L., et al.: Esim: Edge similarity for screen content image quality assessment. IEEE Trans. Image Process. **26**(10), 4818–4831 (2017)
19. Birman, D., Gardner, J.L.: A flexible readout mechanism of human sensory representations. Nat. Commun. **10**(1), 1–13 (2019)
20. Kingma, D.P., Welling, M.: Auto-encoding variational bayes. arXiv preprint arXiv:1312.6114 (2013)
21. Chen, R.T., Li, X., et al.: Isolating sources of disentanglement in variational autoencoders. In: Advances in Neural Information Processing Systems, vol. 31 (2018)
22. Wang, Z., Bovik, A.C., et al.: Image quality assessment: from error visibility to structural similarity. IEEE Trans. Image Process. **13**(4), 600–612 (2004)
23. Zhao, H., Gallo, O., et al.: Loss functions for image restoration with neural networks. IEEE Trans. Comput. Imaging **3**(1), 47–57 (2016)
24. Deng, J., et al.: Imagenet: a large-scale hierarchical image database. In: 2009 IEEE Conference on Computer Vision and Pattern Recognition, pp. 248–255. IEEE (2009)
25. Bjontegaard, G.: Calculation of average psnr differences between rd-curves.VCEG-M33 (2001)

Inter-subtask Consistent Representation Learning for Visual Commonsense Reasoning

Kexin Liu, Shaojuan Wu, Xiaowang Zhang$^{(\boxtimes)}$, and Song Wang

College of Intelligence and Computing, Tianjin University, Tianjin, China
{kexinliu2020,shaojuanwu,xiaowangzhang}@tju.edu.cn, songwang@cec.sc.edu

Abstract. Given an image and a related question, Visual Commonsense Reasoning (VCR) requires to select the correct answer (question answering subtask) and the rationale (answer justification subtask). The commonsense semantic hidden between subtasks is essential for complex reasoning for VCR. Most of the previous studies of VCR focus on the leaning of cross-modal semantics and optimize the two subtasks independently, ignoring the hidden semantic correlations between answers and rationales. In this paper, we propose an Inter-subtask Consistent Representation Learning (ICRL) framework to learn the hidden commonsense semantics. Specifically, we design a joint learning framework to establish the connection between the two subtasks. Furthermore, we propose a multi-level contrastive learning network to ensure the semantic consistency of subtasks in the feature space. Experiments on the VCR dataset demonstrate that the proposed ICRL brings significant performance gain over the state-of-the-arts.

Keywords: VCR · Joint learning · Contrastive learning

1 Introduction

Given an image, the goal of VCR [23] is to answer a relevant question, and then provide a rationale justifying the answer. As show in Fig. 1, for **question answering subtask** ($Q \rightarrow A$), the model requires to answer a challenging question "*Why is [person1] holding a flower*" according to the given image correctly. Then the **answer justification subtask** ($QA \rightarrow R$) performs high-order understanding to explain why the answer "*[person1] is in the garden working*" is true. VCR is designed to perform complex cognitive-level reasoning, not just cognitive-level perception. A major challenge of VCR is to perform complex reasoning by learning hidden commonsense rather than surface clues. Inter-subtask consistency [22] is crucial for the learning of such hidden commonsense for VCR. For example, as shown in Fig. 1, the prediction results of the two subtasks are different aspects of one hidden commonsense "*People usually wear apron and hold a basket to work in the garden*". Hence inconsistency in the predictions implies contradiction (i.e., at least one of the predictions is wrong).

E. Pimenidis et al. (Eds.): ICANN 2022, LNCS 13531, pp. 149–161, 2022.
https://doi.org/10.1007/978-3-031-15934-3_13

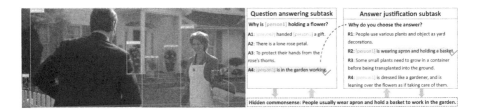

Fig. 1. An example of the VCR task. VCR requires the model to answer a question about an image while giving a rationale to justify the answer. Question answering and answer justification usually require a hidden commonsense.

Existing methods for the VCR can be broadly divided into two types: 1) utilize attention mechanisms to achieve semantic alignment across modalities for visual contents and linguistic expression understanding [19,21,23]. Such methods are often difficult to perform complex reasoning due to their inability to learn commonsense. 2) Introduce commonsense from external knowledge bases or out-of-domain datasets into models to help reasoning [5,15,17,18]. Despite achieving impressive results, these kind of methods usually suffer from the high cost of manual annotation of knowledge bases and are difficult to be implemented efficiently on hardware devices. All of the above methods perform reasoning and prediction on each individual subtask, ignoring the inter-subtask consistency of VCR and thus make it difficult for effective reasoning.

Inspired by the above discussion, we propose an Inter-subtask Consistent Representation Learning (ICRL) framework to learn hidden commonsense semantics for complex reasoning of VCR. Specifically, we design a joint learning framework based on pseudo-siamese network [3], which trains two subtasks in one model to achieve an interaction between two subtasks. Moreover, inspired by the achievements of contrastive learning [7] in representation learning, we propose a multi-level contrastive learning network, which contains answer-rationale contrastive learning (Answer-rationale CL) and visual-textual contrastive learning (Visual-textual CL) to learn consistent representations. Specifically, Answer-rationale CL pulls together correct answer and correct rationale representations while pushing apart mismatched response representations to ensure the semantic consistency of answers and rationales in the feature space. The Visual-textual CL pulls together visual and correct response representations while pushing apart visual and wrong responses representations to achieve cross-modal semantic alignment. In this way, we can learn latent inter-subtask hidden commonsense semantics to help the reason for both VCR subtasks.

The major contributions of this work are summarized as follows:

- We present a novel joint learning framework, which can jointly optimize question answering subtask and answer justification subtask of VCR to achieve interaction between answers and rationales.
- We propose to utilize multi-level contrastive learning (i.e., Answer-rationale CL and Visual-textual CL) for cross-modal semantic and inter-subtask consistent representation learning to improve the reasoning ability of VCR model.

- We conduct extensive experiments on the VCR dataset with comprehensive analysis and the results demonstrate that our model achieves a significant improvement in performance compared to state-of-the-arts.

2   Related Work

This section reviews the related work on VCR, Siamese Network, and Contrastive Learning.

2.1   Visual Commonsense Reasoning

The objective of VCR is to answer commonsense visual questions, and provide rationales justifying its answers. In order to give the correct answer and rationale, the VCR model requires not only a comprehensive understanding of visual scenes and language expressions, but also commonsense knowledge about how the world works. Some work has been proposed to address the challenges of VCR[13,19,21,23,24]. Rowan et al. [23] proposed an attention-based benchmark model R2C to obtain contextualized representations by performing an attention mechanism on visual and textual representations. It is worth noting that in the benchmark of Rowan et al. [23], the two subtasks of question answering and answer justification use the same model structure but are trained separately thus have no direct influence on each other. Later methods also followed this approach to handle the two subtasks. Weijiang et al. [21] constructed question-answer heterogeneous graph and vision-answer heterogeneous graph to achieve semantic alignment among vision, questions and answers. Zhang et al. [24] proposed multi-level counterfactual contrastive learning framework(MCC) for VCR to learn inter-modal and intra-modal representations. In order to combine commonsense knowledge to solve VCR task, some works introduce external knowledge into the model to help reasoning [12,15,18]. Dandan et al. [15] extracted knowledge from knowledge graph to learn knowledge combined representations. Zhang et al. [18] proposed to transfer external knowledge into visual content through transfer learning. Different from all of these methods, our proposed ICRL jointly optimize question answering subtask and answer justification subtask, and learn commonsense knowledge from the interaction of answers and rationales for VCR.

2.2   Siamese Network

Siamese network is a kind of neural structure containing two or more identical structures (e.g., answers encoder and rationales encoder in Fig. 2) to make multi-class prediction or entity comparison [3]. Siamese network is implemented by sharing the parameters of the neural networks. The applications of Siamese network include signature, object tracking, image matching and others. In this work, we adopt siamese network to achieve interaction and information sharing between question answering subtask and answer justification subtask for VCR.

2.3   Contrastive Learning

Contrastive Learning (CL) [7] is a commonly used self-supervised learning method. Typical contrastive learning works learn representations by a contrastive loss which pushes apart dissimilar samples while pulling together similar samples. Formally, given input sample q, contrastive learning methods sample similar samples to produce positive pairs (q, q^+) and dissimilar samples to produce negative pairs (q, q^-). Common contrastive loss function has the general form:

$$L = -\log \frac{\exp(q \cdot q^+)}{\exp(q \cdot q^+) + \sum_{q^-} \exp(q \cdot q^-)} \tag{1}$$

where $q \cdot q^+$ is the dot product between two vectors. Recently, CL has been introduced to various fields such as visual representation learning, visual question answering and image captioning with great success. In this paper, we introduce CL into a multi-subtask joint learning framework to learn cross-modal relationships through Visual-textual CL, and learn the relationships between answers and rationales through Answer-rationale CL to gain hidden commonsense semantic for VCR.

3   Proposed Approach

In VCR task, the dataset S can be formalized as a collection of n quadruples $\{V_i, Q_i, A_i, R_i\}_{i=1}^n$, where $V_i \in V$ is an image, $Q_i \in Q$ is a question about image V_i, $A_i \in A$ is the set of four candidate answers to question Q_i, and $R_i \in R$ is the set of four candidate rationales. Current works optimize two functions for question answering subtask and answer justification subtask respectively: (1) $f_{q2a} : V \times Q \to \mathbb{R}^{|A_i|}$ to produce correct answer and (2) $f_{qa2r} : V \times Q \times \tilde{A} \to \mathbb{R}^{|R_i|}$ to produce correct rationale, where $\tilde{A}$ is the correct answer set. Different from these works, we jointly train two subtasks with one model to produce correct answer and correct rationale simultaneously through learning the correlation between subtasks. Formally, we define the VCR task as follows:

$$\tilde{a}_i = \underset{a_{i,j} \in \mathcal{A}_i}{argmax} P(a_{i,j}|V_i, Q_i; \theta, \theta_a) \tag{2}$$

$$\tilde{r}_i = \underset{r_{i,k} \in \mathcal{R}_i}{argmax} P(r_{i,k}|V_i, Q_i; \theta, \theta_r) \tag{3}$$

where θ denotes the shared learnable parameters to both subtasks, and θ_a and θ_r are their respective parameters. Given image V_i and question Q_i, the model predicts the answer $\tilde{a}_i \in \mathcal{A}_i$ and the rationale $\tilde{r}_i \in \mathcal{R}_i$ simultaneously via jointly maximizing the two probabilities in Eq. (2) and Eq. (3).

We propose a Inter-subtask Consistent Representation Learning (ICRL) framework to jointly predict the answers and rationales for VCR. The architecture of ICRL is shown in Fig. 2 consisting of three parts: 1) Feature Extraction, 2) Multi-level Contrastive Learning, and 3) Classification.

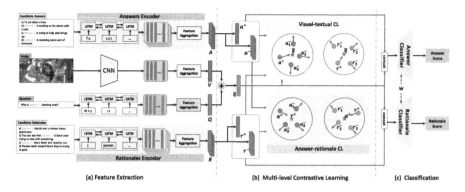

(a) Feature Extraction   (b) Multi-level Contrastive Learning   (c) Classification

Fig. 2. The overall architecture of ICRL, which contains feature extraction module, multi-level contrastive learning module (visual-textual CL and answer-rationale CL), and classification module.

3.1 Joint Learning Framework

We design a joint learning framework to lay two subtasks in the same model structure to jointly optimize the model and obtain the prediction results of the two subtasks simultaneously. In the joint learning framework, the two streams of question answering and answer justification interact by sharing partial representations and parameters, as shown in Fig. 2.

In the feature extraction part, our model shares the representations of images and questions between subtasks. Furthermore, the textual encoders for candidate answers and candidate rationales share parameters. We then build a contrastive learning structure between answers and rationales for interaction between the two subtasks, which are described in more detail below. Moreover, the framework shares the parameters of the answer classifier and the rationale classifier for joint prediction in the classification module.

It should be pointed out that, unlike prior works which take the correct answer as an input for the answer justification subtask, the answer justification stream in our joint learning framework is not explicitly fed with correct answer, but obtain answer information from the interaction with question answering stream. In this way, there is a mutually reinforcing effect between answer prediction and rationale prediction.

3.2 Feature Extraction

In the feature extraction stage, we extract visual features for image and textual features for question, candidate answers and candidate rationales.

Given image I, we first obtain n visual region features $\{v_i\}_{i=1}^n$ from a pretrained Faster R-CNN [14] with ResNet-101 [8] backbone. Thereafter, the visual feature is fused with its position feature p_i to get new visual region feature $\hat{v}_i \in \mathbb{R}^d$ as follows:

$$\hat{v}_i = \sigma(W_{vp}((W_v v_i + b_v)||(W_p p_i + b_p)) + b_{vp}) \tag{4}$$

where W_v, W_p and W_{vp} are weights, b_v, b_p and b_{vp} are biases, $\sigma(\cdot)$ denotes the activation function, and $(\cdot||\cdot)$ denotes the concatenation operation. Following [24], we then obtain a integrated image representation $V \in \mathbb{R}^d$ through a visual feature aggregation module:

$$V = \sum_{i=1}^{n} \alpha_i \hat{v}_i, \quad \alpha_i = \frac{\exp\left(\sigma\left(W_v' \hat{v}_i + b_v'\right)\right)}{\sum_{j=1}^{n} \exp\left(\sigma\left(W_v' \hat{v}_j + b_v'\right)\right)} \tag{5}$$

where W_v' is the weight, b_v' is the bias, $\sigma(\cdot)$ represents the activation function and $\alpha = [\alpha_1, \alpha_2, ..., \alpha_n] \in \mathbb{R}^n$ are the learned weights.

As for the textual modality, we adopt pre-trained BERT [6] to obtain context-enhanced embeddings from the given text, which are then fed into bidirectional LSTM to produce textual features $\{q_i\}_{i=1}^{l_q}$, $\{a_i\}_{i=1}^{l_a}$ and $\{r_i\}_{i=1}^{l_r}$, where $q_i \in \mathbb{R}^d$, $a_i \in \mathbb{R}^d$ and $r_i \in \mathbb{R}^d$ correspond to the i-th token in the question, each candidate answer and each candidate rationale respectively, and l_q, l_a and l_r denote sequence length. Note that the parameters of bidirectional LSTM for candidate answers and candidate rationales are all shared. Afterwards we use textual feature aggregation module to generate global textual representations $Q \in \mathbb{R}^d$, $A_k \in \mathbb{R}^d$, $R_k \in \mathbb{R}^d$ for each sentence through similar steps as in Eq. (5), where $k \in \{1, 2, 3, 4\}$ denotes four candidates.

3.3 Multi-level Contrastive Learning

The Multi-level Contrastive Learning network shown in Fig. 2 consists of two modules: Answer-rationale CL and Visual-textual CL.

Answer-Rationale CL. The Answer-rationale CL is designed to achieve semantic alignment between answers and rationales thus learn consistent representations for subtasks. First, we project answers and rationales into a common logical space and get their respective representations $\tilde{A} \in \mathbb{R}^{4 \times d'}$ and $\tilde{R} \in \mathbb{R}^{4 \times d'}$:

$$\tilde{A} = \{\tilde{A}_k\}_{k=1}^{4}, \quad \tilde{A}_k = \sigma(W_{la} A_k + b_{la}) \tag{6}$$

$$\tilde{R} = \{\tilde{R}_k\}_{k=1}^{4}, \quad \tilde{R}_k = \sigma(W_{lr} R_k + b_{lr}) \tag{7}$$

where $\tilde{A}_k \in \mathbb{R}^{d'}$ and $\tilde{R}_k \in \mathbb{R}^{d'}$ denotes the k-th candidate answer and rationale representation in the common logic space respectively, $W_{la} \in \mathbb{R}^{d' \times d}$ and $W_{lr} \in \mathbb{R}^{d' \times d}$ are two linear projection matrices, b_{la} and b_{kr} are biases, and $\sigma(\cdot)$ represents the activation function. We then separate out the correct answer $a^+ \in \mathbb{R}^{d'}$ and wrong answers $\{a_k^-\}_{k=1}^{3} \in \mathbb{R}^{3 \times d'}$ from $\tilde{A}$. Similarly, the correct rationale $r^+ \in \mathbb{R}^{d'}$ and wrong rationales $\{r_k^-\}_{k=1}^{3} \in \mathbb{R}^{3 \times d'}$ are separated from $\tilde{R}$. In the logical feature space, the representations of correct answer and correct rationale should be close, while the presentations of the correct answer and the wrong rationales, and the presentations of the correct rationale and the wrong answers should be much farther. Therefore, we treat a^+ as an anchor, (a^+, r^+) as the positive pair and take $\{(a^+, r_1^-), (a^+, r_2^-), (a^+, r_3^-)\}$ as three negative pairs for contrastive learning. The contrastive loss is defined as follows:

$$L_{a2r} = -log \frac{\exp\left(s\left(a^+, r^+\right)/\tau\right)}{\exp\left(s\left(a^+, r^+\right)/\tau\right) + \sum\limits_{k=1}^{3} \exp\left(s\left(a^+, r_k^-\right)/\tau\right)} \tag{8}$$

where $s(\cdot, \cdot)$ is dot product evaluating the similarity of two vectors, and τ is a hyperparameter controlling the sensitivity of $s(\cdot, \cdot)$. Through the similar step, when treat r^+ as anchor, we can obtain another contrastive loss:

$$L_{r2a} = -log \frac{\exp\left(s\left(r^+, a^+\right)/\tau\right)}{\exp\left(s\left(r^+, a^+\right)/\tau\right) + \sum\limits_{k=1}^{3} \exp\left(s\left(r^+, a_k^-\right)/\tau\right)} \tag{9}$$

where the notations have the same meaning as in Eq. (8). Through the training, as shown in the yellow rectangle in Fig. 2, the features for matched answer-rationale pairs are directed to be close while the features for mismatched answer-rationale pairs are farther apart. Based on this, the model can ensure the semantic consistency of answers and rationales in feature space.

Visual-Textual CL. The visual-textual contrastive learning module is designed to model cross-modal relationships for VCR inspired by [24]. Specifically, we adopt element-wise adding operation followed by a linear mapping for fusing the visual representation V and question representation Q to get fused query representation $\tilde{q} \in \mathbb{R}^{d'}$. After that, similar to Answer-rationale CL, adopting $\tilde{q}$ as the anchor, correct options as positive samples and wrong options as negative samples, the contrastive losses of Visual-textual CL are formulated as follows:

$$L_{v2a} = -log \frac{\exp\left(s\left(\tilde{q}, a^+\right)/\tau\right)}{\exp\left(s\left(\tilde{q}, a^+\right)/\tau\right) + \sum\limits_{k=1}^{3} \exp\left(s\left(\tilde{q}, a_k^-\right)/\tau\right)} \tag{10}$$

$$L_{v2r} = -log \frac{\exp\left(s\left(\tilde{q}, r^+\right)/\tau\right)}{\exp\left(s\left(\tilde{q}, r^+\right)/\tau\right) + \sum\limits_{k=1}^{3} \exp\left(s\left(\tilde{q}, r_k^-\right)/\tau\right)} \tag{11}$$

where $s(\cdot, \cdot)$ and τ are as in Eq. (8). As shown in the green rectangle in Fig. 2, by minimizing these losses, the representation $\tilde{q}$ and the ground-truth responses representations are trained to be near in feature space, while the features with different semantics are trained to be farther. Therefore, Visual-textual CL helps the model achieve cross-modal semantic alignment.

3.4 Classification and Loss

We construct classifiers in the classification module to predict answers and rationales. For the question answering stream, we first use a concatenation operation to fuse the representations of the query $\tilde{q}$ and the candidate answer A_k. We then feed the fused representation into a 1-layer MLP classifier and use a typical cross-entropy loss for classification to get answer prediction loss L_a. The answer justification stream is handled in the same way to get rationale prediction loss L_r. The final loss is defined as follows:

$$L = L_a + L_r + \lambda_1(L_{a2r} + L_{r2a}) + \lambda_2(L_{v2a} + L_{v2r}) \tag{12}$$

where λ_1 and λ_2 are the trade-off parameters. Jointly training the classification losses and the contrastive losses, our model can learn inter-subtask consistent representations enabling efficient reasoning for VCR. During test, given an image, a question, four candidate answers and four candidate rationales, we feed them into the trained ICRL network to get the prediction probabilities of answers and rationales and select the best answer and the best rationale as the final results.

4   Experiments

In the present section, we first present the VCR dataset [23] and the implementation details of the proposed method. We then compare the experimental results of ICRL with the state-of-the-arts. Finally, we perform ablation studies to explore the effectiveness of every module in ICRL.

4.1   Datasets and Implementation Details

We carry out experiments on VCR dataset [23] containing 290 K multiple-choice questions for both answers and rationales. Each image in the VCR dataset corresponds to several questions. Most of these questions are related to complex life scenarios and require commonsense-related reasoning to get answers. There are around 213 k questions in the training set, 27 k in the validation set and 1 5k in the test set of VCR. As mentioned above, we jointly train two subtasks (i.e., $Q \rightarrow A$ and $QA \rightarrow R$) in the same framework sharing the visual representations, question representations, and the parameters of the textual encoders. The prediction result of $Q \rightarrow AR$ is correct only if both $Q \rightarrow A$ and $QA \rightarrow R$ predict correctly. The activation functions in Eq. (4) is ReLU function. Equation (6) and Eq. (7) use LeakyReLU activation functions. The temperature τ in Eq. (8), Eq. (9), Eq. (10) and Eq. (11) is set 0.2, 0.2, 0.1 and 0.1, respectively. In Eq. (12), λ_1 is 0.1 and λ_2 is 0.7. We set the batch size to 96 and train the model for 25 epochs. The Adam optimizer [11] with 0.00005 weight decay and 0.9 beta are used to optimize our model. The initial learning rate is set to 0.0001, and multiplied by 0.2 when the validation accuracy does not increase. Pytorch is used to implement the proposed method and all ablated versions. We evaluate the model using accuracy as metric.

Table 1. Performance comparison between ICRL and the state-of-the-art baselines on VCR. **Best** results are highlighted in each column. (Since the test accuracies of VC-RCNN and CL-VCR are not reported in their work, and the test accuracy of VCR dataset can only be obtained by uploading the prediction results to the VCR leaderboard, we only show their validation accuracies.)

| | Method | $Q \rightarrow A$ | | $QA \rightarrow R$ | | $Q \rightarrow AR$ | |
		Val	Test	Val	Test	Val	Test
Text-only	BERT	53.8	53.9	64.1	64.5	34.8	35.0
	BERT (response only)	27.6	27.7	26.3	26.2	7.6	7.3
	ESIM + ELMO	45.8	45.9	55.0	55.1	25.3	25.6
	LSTM + ELMO	28.1	28.3	28.7	28.5	8.3	8.4
VQA	RevisitedVQA	39.4	40.5	34.0	33.7	13.5	13.8
	BottomUpTopDown	42.8	44.1	25.1	25.1	10.7	11.0
	MLB	45.5	46.2	36.1	36.8	17.0	17.2
	MUTAN	44.4	45.5	32.0	32.2	14.6	14.6
VCR	R2C(2019)	63.8	65.1	67.2	67.3	43.1	44.0
	HGL(2019)	69.4	70.1	70.6	70.8	49.1	49.8
	CCN(2019)	67.4	68.5	70.6	70.5	47.7	48.4
	TAB-VCR(2019)	69.9	70.4	72.2	**71.7**	50.6	50.5
	CKRM(2020)	66.2	66.9	68.5	68.5	45.6	45.9
	VC-RCNN(2020)	67.4	–	69.5	–	–	–
	CL-VCR(2021)	69.9	–	70.6	–	–	–
	ICRL(Ours)	**71.0**	**70.7**	**72.7**	71.6	**51.9**	**50.9**

4.2 Performance Comparison

We compare the performance of ICRL with the following three types of methods to evaluate the effectiveness of the proposed model:

1) Text-only baselines in [23], including BERT [6], BERT (response only), ESIM+ELMo [4] and LSTM+ELMo. By comparing with this kind of methods, we can validate the effect of our model on visual content in representation learning.
2) VQA-based baselines, including Bottom-up and Top-down attention (BottomUpTopDown) [1], RevisitedVQA [9], Multimodal Low-rank Bilinear Attention (MLB) [10], and Multimodal Tucker Fusion (MUTAN) [2]. By comparing with such methods, we can verify the complex reasoning ability of our model.
3) Methods specially designed for the VCR, including R2C [23], CCN [19], TAB-VCR [13], CKRM [18], HGL [21], VC-RCNN [16] and CL-VCR [20]. The ability of our model to perform complex reasoning can be verified by comparison with these methods.

As with previous VCR-specific works, we do not compare ICRL with models pre-training on large external corpora such as UNITER [5] and SGEITL [17] since our approach does not rely on out-of-domain datasets. The results are shown in Table 1.

Our proposed approach obtains best performance compared with state-of-the-art methods on both validation set and test set of VCR dataset. On validation set, our approach gains accuracy of 71.0%, 72.7% and 51.9% for $Q \rightarrow A$, $QA \rightarrow R$ and $Q \rightarrow AR$ subtasks, respectively. Specifically, compared with the text-only methods, our approach obtains an improvement of 17.1% to 44.3% on the $Q \rightarrow AR$ subtask, which suggests the importance of visual content on the VCR task. Our model improves 34.9% to 41.2% on $Q \rightarrow AR$ over the VQA methods. This reflects the lack of inference ability of VQA methods for VCR task. Compared with VCR specific methods, our approach still achieves the best, which is 1.1% higher on $Q \rightarrow A$, 0.5% higher on $QA \rightarrow R$ and 1.3% higher on $Q \rightarrow AR$ than the second. Moreover, although R2C, HGL, CCN, and CKRM utilize sophisticated attention mechanisms, our proposed method still outperforms them. This is probably because our method can achieve not only cross-modal alignment but also learn inter-subtask consistent representations, which helps the model extract more reasonable and discriminative features for VCR.

4.3   Ablation Studies

To explore the effect of each module in our model, we conduct different ablation model.

- **Base.** The *Base* version handles the two subtasks of question answering and answer justification independently like previous works. The *Base (correct answer)* model takes the right answer as an input to the answer justification subtask. Because our model does not explicitly take the correct answer as an input for answer justification, we design the *base (predict answer)* version which takes predicted answer rather than the right answer as an input for fair comparison.
- **Base + Joint L.** *Base + Joint L* means joint learning of two subtasks based on the *Base* network. Note that the *Base + Joint L* architecture does not explicitly taken the correct answer or predicted answer as input.
- **Base + Joint L + Visual-textual CL.** This variant adds Answer-rationale CL into *Base + Joint L*, which can perform contrastive learning between image representation and option representations.
- **Base + Joint L + Answer-rationale CL.** These variant adds Answer-rationale CL into *Base + Joint L*, which can perform contrastive learning between answer representations and rationale representations.

Table 2. Ablation analysis of our proposed model over validation split. Base: only one subtask loss; Joint L: both subtasks losses; Visual-textual CL: visual-textual contrastive learning loss; Answer-rationale CL: answer-rationale contrastive learning loss.

Method	$Q \to A$	$QA \to R$	$Q \to AR$
Base (correct answer)	69.11	72.01	50.07
Base (predict answer)	69.11	70.75	49.12
Base + Joint L	69.42	71.52	49.69
Base + Joint L + Visual-textual CL	70.65	72.40	51.27
Base + Joint L + Answer-rationale CL	69.71	71.41	49.99
ICRL	**71.04**	**72.70**	**51.86**

The results of ablation analysis of $Q \to A$, $QA \to R$ and $Q \to AR$ subtasks on VCR validation set are shown in Table 2. From the table, we conclude the following:

1) Compared with *Base (predict answer)*, *Base (correct answer)* has a slightly better effect on $QA \to R$ subtask, which reflects that the correct answer has an important positive effect on rationale prediction.
2) *Base + Joint L* has improved performance compared to *Base (predict answer)*. This implies a mutually reinforcing influence between the two subtasks, validating the effectiveness of joint learning for VCR.
3) The comparison between *Base + Joint L + Visual-textual CL* and *Base + Joint L* shows that visual-textual contrastive learning can help model learn discriminative representations by learning cross-modal semantics.
4) Compared with *Base + Joint L*, *Base + Joint L + Answer-rationale CL* also improves the effect, which verifies that Answer-rationale CL helps the model obtain better prediction results by learning inter-subtask consistent representations.
5) As compared to *Base + Joint L*, the performance of our overall model is significantly improved, which further validates the effectiveness of multi-level contrastive learning module.

5   Conclusion

In this paper, we proposed a novel inter-subtask consistent representation learning framework to learn inter-subtask hidden commonsense semantics for VCR. Specifically, the proposed multi-level contrastive learning module learned consistent representations by achieving cross-modal and inter-subtask semantic alignment, so as to help the model carry out effective reasoning for VCR. Extensive experiments on VCR dataset demonstrated the effectiveness of proposed approach. We plan to generalize our approach to more general inter-task learning in the future.

References

1. Anderson, P., et al.: Bottom-up and top-down attention for image captioning and visual question answering. In: CVPR, pp. 6077–6086 (2018)
2. Ben-Younes, H., Cadene, R., Cord, M., Thome, N.: Mutan: multimodal tucker fusion for visual question answering. In: ICCV, pp. 2612–2620 (2017)
3. Bromley, J., et al.: Signature verification using a "siamese" time delay neural network. IJPRAI **7**(04), 669–688 (1993)
4. Chen, Q., Zhu, X., Ling, Z., Wei, S., Jiang, H., Inkpen, D.: Enhanced lstm for natural language inference. In: ACL, pp. 1657–1668 (2017)
5. Chen, Y.-C., et al.: UNITER: UNiversal image-TExt representation learning. In: Vedaldi, A., Bischof, H., Brox, T., Frahm, J.-M. (eds.) ECCV 2020. LNCS, vol. 12375, pp. 104–120. Springer, Cham (2020). https://doi.org/10.1007/978-3-030-58577-8_7
6. Devlin, J., Chang, M.W., Lee, K., Toutanova, K.: Bert: Pre-training of deep bidirectional transformers for language understanding. In: NAACL, pp. 4171–4186 (2018)
7. Hadsell, R., Chopra, S., LeCun, Y.: Dimensionality reduction by learning an invariant mapping. In: CVPR, vol. 2, pp. 1735–1742 (2006)
8. He, K., Zhang, X., Ren, S., Sun, J.: Deep residual learning for image recognition. In: CVPR, pp. 770–778 (2016)
9. Jabri, A., Joulin, A., van der Maaten, L.: Revisiting visual question answering baselines. In: Leibe, B., Matas, J., Sebe, N., Welling, M. (eds.) ECCV 2016. LNCS, vol. 9912, pp. 727–739. Springer, Cham (2016). https://doi.org/10.1007/978-3-319-46484-8_44
10. Kim, J.H., On, K.W., Lim, W., Kim, J., Ha, J.W., Zhang, B.T.: Hadamard product for low-rank bilinear pooling. In: ICLR (2017)
11. Kingma, D.P., Ba, J.: Adam: A method for stochastic optimization. In: ICLR (2015)
12. Lee, J., Kim, I.: Vision-language-knowledge co-embedding for visual commonsense reasoning. Sensors **21**(9), 2911 (2021)
13. Lin, J., Jain, U., Schwing, A.: Tab-vcr: tags and attributes based vcr baselines. In: NIPS, pp. 15589–15602 (2019)
14. Ren, S., He, K., Girshick, R., Sun, J.: Faster r-cnn: towards real-time object detection with region proposal networks. TPAMI **39**(6), 1137–1149 (2016)
15. Song, D., Ma, S., Sun, Z., Yang, S., Liao, L.: Kvl-bert: knowledge enhanced visual-and-linguistic bert for visual commonsense reasoning. Knowl.-Based Syst. **230**, 107408 (2021)
16. Wang, T., Huang, J., Zhang, H., Sun, Q.: Visual commonsense r-cnn. In: CVPR, pp. 10760–10770 (2020)
17. Wang, Z., et al.: Sgeitl: scene graph enhanced image-text learning for visual commonsense reasoning. arXiv (2021)
18. Wen, Z., Peng, Y.: Multi-level knowledge injecting for visual commonsense reasoning. TCSVT **31**(3), 1042–1054 (2020)
19. Wu, A., Zhu, L., Han, Y., Yang, Y.: Connective cognition network for directional visual commonsense reasoning. In: NIPS, pp. 5669–5679 (2019)
20. Ye, K., Kovashka, A.: A case study of the shortcut effects in visual commonsense reasoning. In: AAAI, pp. 3181–3189 (2021)
21. Yu, W., Zhou, J., Yu, W., Liang, X., Xiao, N.: Heterogeneous graph learning for visual commonsense reasoning. In: NIPS, pp. 2765–2775 (2019)

22. Zamir, A.R., et al.: Robust learning through cross-task consistency. In: CVPR, pp. 11197–11206 (2020)
23. Zellers, R., Bisk, Y., Farhadi, A., Choi, Y.: From recognition to cognition: visual commonsense reasoning. In: CVPR, pp. 6720–6731 (2019)
24. Zhang, X., Zhang, F., Xu, C.: Multi-level counterfactual contrast for visual commonsense reasoning. In: MM, pp. 1793–1802 (2021)

InvisibiliTee: Angle-Agnostic Cloaking from Person-Tracking Systems with a Tee

Yaxian Li[1,2], Bingqing Zhang[1,2], Guoping Zhao[1,2], Mingyu Zhang[1,2], Jiajun Liu[4(✉)], Ziwei Wang[4], and Jirong Wen[1,2,3]

[1] School of Information, Renmin University of China, Beijing, China
[2] Beijing Key Laboratory of Big Data Management and Analysis Methods, Beijing, China
[3] Gaoling School of Artificial Intelligence, Renmin University of China, Beijing, China
[4] Data 61, CSIRO, Pullenvale, Australia
Jiajun.liu@csiro.au

Abstract. After a survey for person-tracking system-induced privacy concerns, we propose a black-box adversarial attack method on state-of-the-art human detection models called **InvisibiliTee**. The method learns printable adversarial patterns for T-shirts that cloak wearers in the physical world in front of person-tracking systems. We design an angle-agnostic learning scheme which utilizes segmentation of the fashion dataset and a geometric warping process so the adversarial patterns generated are effective in fooling person detectors from all camera angles and for unseen black-box detection models. Empirical results in both digital and physical environments show that with the **InvisibiliTee** on, person-tracking systems' ability to detect the wearer drops significantly (Code is available at https://github.com/invisibilitee/invisibilitee).

Keywords: Object detection · Human tracking · Adversarial attack

1 Introduction

Person-tracking systems are widely deployed in metropolitan areas across the world for various purposes. According to the latest Comparitech report,[1] approximately 770 million cameras have already been used globally, which include many smart cameras enabled with person-tracking systems. While making contributions to public safety, these network-enabled systems suffer from software/hardware vulnerabilities and are often prone to cyber-attacks,[2] raising serious concerns about privacy breaches. Thus, average citizens are now facing even stronger privacy risks. For instance, after hacking into camera-based person-tracking systems, it is not only possible but even unchallenging to precisely recover a person's daily routine.

---

[1] https://www.comparitech.com/vpn-privacy/the-worlds-most-surveilled-cities/.
[2] https://www.scmp.com/news/china/article/1727145/chinese-surveillance-camera-supplier-confirms-hacking-loophole.

© The Author(s), under exclusive license to Springer Nature Switzerland AG 2022
E. Pimenidis et al. (Eds.): ICANN 2022, LNCS 13531, pp. 162–175, 2022.
https://doi.org/10.1007/978-3-031-15934-3_14

Fig. 1. An adversarial pattern and its physical attack results with a person wearing corresponding "InvisibiliTee".

To learn how this issue is perceived by the general public, we conducted a small-scale questionnaire-based survey. Among the 20 participants, all are concerned with the person-tracking systems' potential breach of privacy and 90% responded that they feel the need to leverage latest technology to protect personal privacy, as a counter-balance to the evolving person-tracking technology. This interesting study inspires our research for the "InvisibiliTee", a tee that cloaks wearer in front of the tracking system. As illustrated in Fig. 1, people can successfully fool the person detection system with the "InvisibiliTee" on. Before diving into the technical details of the "InvisibiliTee", we first show how the survey is conducted and what we could conclude from the results.

1.1 User Study

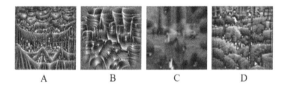

Fig. 2. Adversarial patterns in the questionnaire.

As shown in Table 1, there are 4 questions in the questionnaire. It involves the urgency of privacy issues, the acceptance of technical means and adversarial patterns. The 20 participants surveyed are college students aged between 22 to 30, with higher education background and living experience in metropolis. They are also the target demographic group that InvisibiliTee tries to help - younger generations with stronger awareness of privacy risks and open mindset towards early technology adoption. Among the 20 people surveyed, all are worried about the camera's invasion of personal privacy, of which 55% are concerned and 35% are extremely concerned. 90% say they feel the need to leverage technical approaches to protect personal privacy and over a half show the willingness to wear an "InvisibiliTee". There are 7 people who think the patterns of "InvisibiliTee" not fashionable enough to wear. But others do consider these patterns acceptable, among which pattern C in Fig. 2 is most popular, chosen by 10 people.

Table 1. Questions in the user study questionnaire.

ID	Question	Choices
1	Are you worried that cameras in public places will infringe on personal privacy?	A. Don't mind at all B. Somewhat concerned C. Concerned D. Extremely concerned
2	Do you think there is a need to use technical means to protect personal privacy?	A.Yes B. No
3	If there is an "InvisibiliTee" to protect personal privacy, are you willing to wear it?	A. Yes B. No C. Depends
4	The following pictures in Fig. 2 are different "InvisibiliTee" patterns. Please select the patterns that are acceptable. (multiple choices)	A. Pattern A B. Pattern B C. Pattern C D. Pattern D E. Unacceptable

Motivated by a strong need for privacy protection in the current world where person-tracking systems are often abused, an angle-agnostic black-box adversarial attack method, namely **InvisibiliTee**, is proposed in this paper. Its advantages are summarized as follows: 1, **Cross-model genenralizability.** The learned attack patterns achieve competitive black-box attack results on unseen detection models. 2, **Cross-scene/subject genenralizability.** The same learned adversarial pattern can be used by applied on unseen wearers in unseen scenes without re-training. 3, **Angle-agnostic.** In the digital world, adversarial patterns can be applied on images taken from different angles. In the physical world, we use fabric with fully printed adversarial pattern to tailor a T-shirt, achieving angle-agnostic "invisible" effect and qualitative analysis shows effectiveness of attack to some extent.

2   Literature Review

In person tracking system, a critical step is to utilize object detection algorithms to generate bounding box to crop the images with persons. Fast R-CNN [8] introduced a RoIPooling operation to accelerate detection speed while maintaining detection performance. He et al. proposed Faster R-CNN [20], utilizing Regional Proposal Network to generate proposals instead of time-consuming selective search [23]. R-FCN [4] comes up with position-sensitive RoIPooling for further improving efficiency. Single-stage frameworks, such as YOLO [5,18,19] and SSD [6,14,15], directly classify and regress bounding boxes.

Although detectors are getting better performances, recent studies have proven that the deep object detection models are vulnerable to attacks from adversarial examples [9,21]. Adversarial attack methods can be divided into two categories, which are **white-box** attack and **black-box** attack. In white-box attack, the attacker can interact with the machine learning system in the process of generating adversarial attack data, obtaining the gradient during the training process. While in black-box attack, attackers do not know the algorithms nor parameters of the target model. But attackers can still observe the output through any input. Several attempts have been made on attacking Re-ID systems via black-box methods [24,30]. Although existing works demonstrate the feasibility of performing black-box attacks on classification and Re-ID vision systems, the research on person detection system has not yet been sufficiently investigated.

Liu et al. [16] propose DPATCH, which is a universal black-box adversarial attack method. It borrows the idea of adversarial patch [1] that simultaneously attacks bounding boxes regression and classification. Later, Lee et al. [13] consider a normalized steepest ascent approach, PGD [17], to update loss function. Thys et al. [22] try to attack the object with high level of intra-class variety such as person. Recently, Wu et al. [26] design an "invisibility cloak" that decreases the scores of a series of object detector. However, to the best of our knowledge, only a few works [26] focused on designing a pattern on a T-shirt which can attack detectors without direction restrictions. We propose "InvisibiliTee", which is an angle-agnostic adversarial attack method.

3   Method

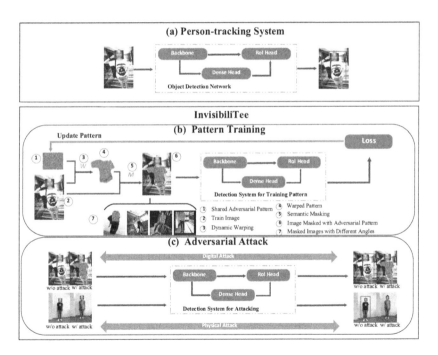

Fig. 3. An overview of normal object detection networks in persons-tracking systems (a) and the framework of InvisibiliTee (b)(c). (a) is a normal detection pipeline. (b) illustrates the process of adversarial pattern training, including dynamic warping, semantic masking and pattern training. (c) describes the process of adversarial attack in both digital and physical scenario.

3.1 Overview

As illustrated in Fig. 3(b), the InvisbiliTee's network contains two parts: the attack head and object detection system. Attack head is designed to generate the shared adversarial pattern which consists of three steps. 1, **Dynamic Warping.** According to the clothing key points annotation, the angle and position of the pattern are adjusted dynamically through warping. 2, **Semantic Masking.** We obtain the clothing polygon mask from annotation and attach the pattern onto the original image to generate the attack picture. 3, **Pattern Training.** Adversarial pattern consists of color pixels, which are directly derived from learnable neural network parameters. During training, only the parameters of adversarial pattern are updated, while the pre-trained detection model remains fixed. A set of adversarial attacking losses and geometric constraint losses are proposed to update pattern parameters.

The second part of the network is object detection system. According to the different processing stages, single-stage framework YOLO [5,18,19] and two-stage framework Faster R-CNN [20] are implemented. Note that following the practice of previous research [16], the adversarial pattern here is a group of network parameters. So it can be optimized during model training. It is randomly initialized and updated iteratively. The learned adversarial pattern is tested on other unseen models following black-box attack protocols to evaluate the attacking performance, as shown in Fig. 3(c).

3.2 Attack and Geometric Constraint Loss Functions

Attack Loss. Attack Losses are optimized to fool the detectors into making wrong decisions. When training with YOLO architecture, $Loss_{attk}$ consists of three training losses.

$$Loss_{attk} = \theta_{11} Loss_{cla} + \theta_{12} Loss_{coord} + \theta_{13} Loss_{wh}. \tag{1}$$

When training with Faster R-CNN architecture, $Loss_{attk}$ consists of two training losses.

$$Loss_{attk} = \theta_{21} Loss_{cla} + \theta_{22} Loss_{bbox}. \tag{2}$$

Classification cross-entropy attack loss is expressed as

$$Loss_{cla} = \sum_{i=0}^{C-1} y_i \log(\hat{y}_i) \tag{3}$$

where y_i stands for the ground truth category label, $\hat{y}_i$ indicates the probability that current sample belongs to the i-th category and C is the number of categories. Bounding box coordinate cross-entropy attack loss is defined as

$$Loss_{coord} = \sum_{i=1}^{2} x_i \log(\hat{x}_i) \tag{4}$$

where x_i stands for the ground truth bounding box coordinate $x_i = (x_i^1, x_i^2)$, $\hat{x}_i$ indicates the predicted one. Bounding box width-height mean squared error attack loss is presented as

$$Loss_{wh} = e^{-\frac{1}{2}\left((w-\hat{w})^2 + (h-\hat{h})^2\right)} \tag{5}$$

where w and h stand for the width and height of the bounding box respectively. Bounding box L1 attack loss is presented as

$$Loss_{bbox} = e^{-|\hat{t}_i - t_i|} \tag{6}$$

$\hat{t}_i$ is a vector representing the 4 parameterized coordinates of the predicted bounding box, and t_i is that of the ground-truth box.

Geometric Constraint Loss. To learn a more continuous as well as printable adversarial pattern, we introduce total variation loss and non-printability score to constrain the pattern in the training process.

Total Variation (TV) loss encourages spatial smoothness in the generated image. The TV loss is defined as follows,

$$L_{tv}(P) = \sum_{i,j} \sqrt{\left(a_{i,j} - a_{i+1,j}\right)^2 + \left(a_{i,j} - a_{i,j+1}\right)^2} \tag{7}$$

where P is the adversarial pattern, $a_{i,j}$ stands for the pixel value in the pattern of position (i,j). $L_{tv}(P)$ minimizes the distance between neighboring pixels. Thus it can make the pattern more natural and smooth.

Non-printability score [22] reflects how difficult it is to print the pattern, and the lower the value, the less distorted it will be printed. It is defined as:

$$L_{print}(P) = \sum_{a_{(i,j)} \in P} \min_{c_{print} \in C} \left| a_{(i,j)} - c_{print} \right|. \tag{8}$$

where c_{print} stands for the pre-defined printable colors. $L_{print}(P)$ minimizes the distance between pattern pixels and printable pixels.

The Joint Constraint Loss $Loss_{cons}$ can be represented by the equation below:

$$Loss_{cons} = \alpha_1 L_{tv}(P) + \alpha_2 L_{print}(P) \tag{9}$$

where α_1 and α_2 are hyper-parameters.

Overall Loss Function. The final loss L of our attack model can be expressed as:

$$L = Loss_{attk} + Loss_{cons} \tag{10}$$

3.3   Geometric Warp and Masking

As shown in Fig. 4, we apply geometric warp to the pattern according to the T-shirt key points before attack via a polygonal mask. In Fig. 4, brown lines stand for information supervision while blue lines stand for transformation. Geometric warp operation is also known as perspective transformation, widely used to project the image to a new viewing plane, and its general transformation formula is:

$$\begin{bmatrix} x' & y' & w' \end{bmatrix} = \begin{bmatrix} u & v & w \end{bmatrix} \cdot T \tag{11}$$

(u, v) are the original image pixel coordinates, $(x = x'/w', y = y'/w')$ are the transformed image pixel coordinates. T is the perspective transformation matrix. Given corresponding four pairs of pixel coordinates before/after perspective transformation, the perspective transformation matrix T can be obtained. We warp the pattern image to fit the input image, so the original 4 pairs of coordinates are the 4 corners of the pattern.

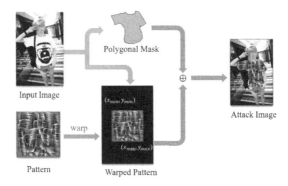

Fig. 4. The process of geometric warp and masking.

After geometric warping, we use the polygonal mask M formed by the T-shirt key points to attach the pattern onto the image, replacing the original T-shirt outward appearance.

$$I_{attk} = (1 - Mask) \odot I_{ori} + M \odot P \tag{12}$$

4   Attacks in the Digital World

4.1   Dataset and Experiment Setup

The Deep Fashion2 dataset [7] is a comprehensive fashion dataset containing pictures of people wearing various types of clothing with annotations of clothing key points(Table 2). Each image has around 15–30 key points to outline the clothes, which is shown in Fig. 6. We leverage the open sourced object detection project MMDetection [3] and pre-trained models to implement our experiments. YOLOv3 [5] and Faster R-CNN [20] are chosen as the training detection model. The adversarial pattern is trained on the modified Deep Fashion2 dataset with Adam optimizer with initial learning rate $1e^{-3}$. The hyper-parameters $\theta_{11} \sim \theta_{13}$, α_1 and α_2 are 5, 1, 1, 100, 100 respectively in YOLOv3. And $\theta_{21}, \theta_{22}, \alpha_1$ and α_2 are 500, 10, 18, 100 in Faster R-CNN, balancing the loss terms into the same scale. Figure 5 shows the changing of total loss during training.

Table 2. Dataset information after reconstruction.

Split	No human	Frontal viewpoint	Size/back viewpoint	Total
Train	6,664	56,121	8,860	64,981
Val	1,027	9,855	1,674	11,529

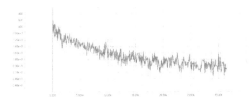

Fig. 5. Train loss with YOLO architecture.

Fig. 6. Key point annotations in one image

4.2   Experimental Results

We train on a specific object detection model and then transfer the trained pattern to attack other unseen models.

Table 3. The black-box (digital) attack results on SOTA detectors with an adversarial pattern trained on YOLOv3 [5] and Faster-RCNN [20]. The patterns used are shown in Fig. 2 A and B respectively.

Target model	AP@IoU = 0.50:0.95			AP@0.50			AP@0.75		
	Without attack	Faster R-CNN pattern attack	YOLO pattern attack	Without attack	Faster R-CNN pattern attack	YOLO pattern attack	Without attack	Faster R-CNN pattern attack	YOLO pattern attack
YOLOv3 [5]	0.254	0.204	0.003	0.601	0.512	0.022	0.178	0.131	0.000
SSD [15]	0.256	0.184	0.187	0.598	0.532	0.558	0.133	0.100	0.102
RetinaNet [14]	0.216	0.000	0.000	0.607	0.000	0.000	0.120	0.000	0.000
Faster-RCNN [20]	0.213	0.001	0.177	0.564	0.007	0.512	0.128	0.000	0.090
Faster-RCNN+softnms	0.217	0.041	0.087	0.573	0.164	0.270	0.131	0.009	0.042
Mask R-CNN [10]	0.210	0.047	0.071	0.573	0.197	0.256	0.117	0.010	0.026
Cascade Mask R-CNN [2]	0.221	0.063	0.089	0.599	0.232	0.291	0.124	0.019	0.041
Cascade R-CNN [2]	0.23	0.038	0.061	0.607	0.159	0.216	0.132	0.010	0.031
Dynamic R-CNN [28]	0.227	0.053	0.078	0.600	0.202	0.264	0.133	0.015	0.035
CornerNet [12]	0.222	0.153	0.084	0.541	0.438	0.249	0.157	0.084	0.044
RepPoints [27]	0.369	0.046	0.067	0.567	0.190	0.252	0.397	0.011	0.023
FreeAnchor [29]	0.218	0.000	0.078	0.598	0.000	0.265	0.121	0.000	0.038
SABL [25]	0.265	0.058	0.076	0.657	0.210	0.249	0.175	0.020	0.040
PAA [11]	0.243	0.075	0.089	0.607	0.237	0.276	0.178	0.036	0.045

Black-Box Attacks. Table 3 shows the black-box attack performance on several different SOTA detection models, where AP stands for Average Precision, the most commonly used evaluation metric for target detection. Our attack model is able to significantly reduce AP at different IoU ratios. The $AP@IoU = 0.50 : 0.95$ corresponds to average mAP calculated over a range of IoU thresholds, from 0.50 to 0.95 with the uniform step size 0.05. As shown in column 2 and 3, the $AP@IoU = 0.50 : 0.95$ is reduced from about 0.25 to about 0.08. In column 5, it can be seen that even under the most relaxed threshold condition ($IoU > 0.5$ means that it was a hit), our method reduces the evaluation to less than half in most models. When the IoU threshold is set to 0.75, it can be considered that the detector is close to completely invalid after attack.

Effect of Different Pattern Resolution. Figure 7 shows several adversarial patterns with different resolutions. (a) are patterns in size 200×200 while (b) are

Table 4. Black-box experiment results of different pattern resolutions trained on Faster-RCNN. "w/o attack" means no attack is performed. P 200, p 100, p 50 stand for adversarial pattern resolution of 200×200, 100×100 and 50×50 pixels, respectively.

Target model		CornerNet	Cascade R-CNN	Mask R-CNN	Faster R-CNN	Faster-RCNN + softnms	Cascade Mask R-CNN	YOLOv3
AP@0.50	w/o attack	0.541	0.607	0.573	0.564	0.573	0.599	0.601
	p 200	0.438	0.159	0.197	0.007	0.164	0.232	0.512
	p 100	0.437	0.150	0.165	0.126	0.136	0.208	0.529
	p 50	0.443	0.185	0.211	0.174	0.188	0.289	0.524

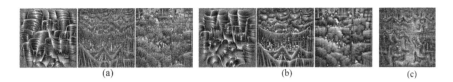

(a)   (b)   (c)

Fig. 7. Adversarial patterns trained with different resolution in pixels. (a) and (b) are random initialized while (c) is initialized by a texture.

corresponding patterns in size 100×100. The first pattern on left is trained on Faster-RCNN and the last two are trained on YOLOv3. Figure 8 shows several adversarial patterns initialized by different textures. We use downsampling in training to study the effect of image resolution. These corresponding patterns with different resolutions are firstly random initialized in size 400×400 with the same random seed and then they are downsampled to different resolutions before dynamic warping. As Table 4 indicates, high-resolution adversarial pattern performs slightly better in most cases, but the advantage is not obvious. It is believed that a relatively lower resolution can be better considering a limited scale of training set.

4.3 Case Studies of Digital Attacks

Figure 9 shows the digital attack results when we use the adversarial pattern trained on YOLOv3 [5] to attack the target model CornerNet [12]. Only bounding boxes with a confidence score over 0.5 are shown. As Fig. 9 indicates, successful attack results can be roughly divided into following three types, which are namely detection failure, bounding box miss and category error. Most cases belong to the first type, which are (a) 1, (a) 3–8 and (c) 1–5. (a) 2 and (c) 6 provide a miss-leading or incomplete bounding box. In (c) 7, the target model recognizes it as a cake instead of a person. There are also some failure cases as (c) 8. However, wearing a "InvisibiliTee" still manages to make the confidence score drop from 0.86 to 0.64.

5   Attacks in the Physical World

We print the adversarial pattern on fabric and tailor it into an "InvisibiliTee" to evaluate attack effects in physical world.

Figure 10 shows a typical scene in real life when a pedestrian walked from a outdoor parking lot into a building. Note that the mosaics are added for anonymity only and do not have any impact in the experiments. When he wears an "InvisibiliTee", detectors fail to identify the person. But at the same time it is able to recognize other objects or even people.

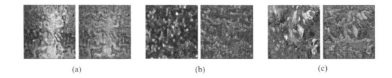

Fig. 8. Adversarial patterns initialized by different textures. In each group, the left one is the texture and the right one is the corresponding adversarial pattern.

Fig. 9. Digital attack results. "w/ attack" and "w/o attack" stand for with attack and without attack respectively.

Fig. 10. Adversarial attack in real world. In (a), the pedestrian wears an "InvisibiliTee" while (b) not.

5.1   Additional Discussion

There are perceived security concerns for developing technologies to cloak from person-tracking systems, for potential malicious uses. Although this is a valid concern to some degree, we argue that the risk is manageable for the following reasons: 1, The adversarial patterns are generated in a way that makes them easily differentiable from daily clothing, almost making a public statement that the wearer does not intend to be detected by person-tracking systems. They can be extremely noticeable and therefore discouraging for malicious parties to wear. 2, In critical areas where additional security is required, the InvisibiliTee model could be used in adversarial training to improve robustness against such attacks.

6   Conclusion

This paper presented a black-box attack method, **InvisibiliTee**, to perform digital and physical adversarial attacks on the human detection models for individual privacy preservation. An angle-agnostic scheme trained by the attack and geometric constraint losses was proposed to generate adversarial patterns. Both digital and physical attacking experiments were conducted on a group of state-of-the-art human detection systems, demonstrating the effectiveness of the learned adversarial patterns. The results have shown that the **InvisibiliTee** can significantly reduce the average precision of person detection systems especially in the digital attacks. In addition, 3D adversarial attack is an emerging research. Therefore, it is challenging to extent **InvisibiliTee** to a 3D model.

References

1. Brown, B.T., Mané, D., Roy, A., Abadi, M., Gilmer, J.: Adversarial patch. CoRR (2017)
2. Cai, Z., Vasconcelos, N.: Cascade R-CNN: high quality object detection and instance segmentation. TPAMI, 1 (2019). https://doi.org/10.1109/tpami.2019.2956516
3. Chen, K., et al.: MMDetection: open MMLab detection toolbox and benchmark. arXiv preprint arXiv:1906.07155 (2019)
4. Dai, J., Li, Y., He, K., Sun, J.: R-FCN: object detection via region-based fully convolutional networks. In: NeurIPS, pp. 379–387 (2016)
5. Farhadi, A., Redmon, J.: YOLOv3: an incremental improvement. In: CVPR, pp. 1804–2767. Springer, Heidelberg (2018). https://doi.org/10.48550/arXiv.1804.02767
6. Fu, C.Y., Liu, W., Ranga, A., Tyagi, A., Berg, C.A.: DSSD: deconvolutional single shot detector. In: CVPR (2017)
7. Ge, Y., Zhang, R., Wu, L., Wang, X., Tang, X., Luo, P.: A versatile benchmark for detection, pose estimation, segmentation and re-identification of clothing images. In: CVPR (2019)

8. Girshick, R.: Fast R-CNN. In: CVPR, pp. 1440–1448 (2015)
9. Goodfellow, J.I., Shlens, J., Szegedy, C.: Explaining and harnessing adversarial examples. In: ICLR (2014)
10. He, K., Gkioxari, G., Dollár, P., Girshick, R.: Mask R-CNN. In: CVPR, pp. 2961–2969 (2017)
11. Kim, K., Lee, H.S.: Probabilistic anchor assignment with IoU prediction for object detection. In: Vedaldi, A., Bischof, H., Brox, T., Frahm, J.-M. (eds.) ECCV 2020. LNCS, vol. 12370, pp. 355–371. Springer, Cham (2020). https://doi.org/10.1007/978-3-030-58595-2_22
12. Law, H., Deng, J.: CornerNet: detecting objects as paired keypoints. In: Ferrari, V., Hebert, M., Sminchisescu, C., Weiss, Y. (eds.) Computer Vision – ECCV 2018. LNCS, vol. 11218, pp. 765–781. Springer, Cham (2018). https://doi.org/10.1007/978-3-030-01264-9_45
13. Lee, M., Kolter, Z.: On physical adversarial patches for object detection. CoRR (2019)
14. Lin, T.Y., Goyal, P., Girshick, B.R., He, K., Dollár, P.: Focal loss for dense object detection. In: ICCV, pp. 318–327 (2017)
15. Liu, W., et al.: SSD: single shot MultiBox detector. In: Leibe, B., Matas, J., Sebe, N., Welling, M. (eds.) ECCV 2016. LNCS, vol. 9905, pp. 21–37. Springer, Cham (2016). https://doi.org/10.1007/978-3-319-46448-0_2
16. Liu, X., Yang, H., Liu, Z., Song, L., Chen, Y., Li, H.: DPatch - an adversarial patch attack on object detectors. In: SafeAI@AAAI (2019)
17. Madry, A., Makelov, A., Schmidt, L., Tsipras, D., Vladu, A.: Towards deep learning models resistant to adversarial attacks. In: ICLR (2018)
18. Redmon, J., Divvala, K.S., Girshick, B.R., Farhadi, A.: You only look once: unified, real-time object detection. In: CVPR (2016)
19. Redmon, J., Farhadi, A.: YOLO9000: better, faster, stronger. In: CVPR (2017)
20. Ren, S., He, K., Girshick, R., Sun, J.: Faster R-CNN: towards real-time object detection with region proposal networks. TPAMI **39**(6), 1137–1149 (2016)
21. Szegedy, C., et al.: Intriguing properties of neural networks. In: ICLR (2014)
22. Thys, S., Van Ranst, W., Goedemé, T.: Fooling automated surveillance cameras: adversarial patches to attack person detection. In: CVPR (2019)
23. Uijlings, J.R., Van De Sande, K.E., Gevers, T., Smeulders, A.W.: Selective search for object recognition. IJCV **104**(2), 154–171 (2013). https://doi.org/10.1007/s11263-013-0620-5
24. Wang, H., Wang, G., Li, Y., Zhang, D., Lin, L.: Transferable, controllable, and inconspicuous adversarial attacks on person re-identification with deep misranking. In: CVPR, June 2020
25. Wang, J., et al.: Side-aware boundary localization for more precise object detection. In: Vedaldi, A., Bischof, H., Brox, T., Frahm, J.-M. (eds.) ECCV 2020. LNCS, vol. 12349, pp. 403–419. Springer, Cham (2020). https://doi.org/10.1007/978-3-030-58548-8_24
26. Wu, Z., Lim, S.-N., Davis, L.S., Goldstein, T.: Making an invisibility cloak: real world adversarial attacks on object detectors. In: Vedaldi, A., Bischof, H., Brox, T., Frahm, J.-M. (eds.) ECCV 2020. LNCS, vol. 12349, pp. 1–17. Springer, Cham (2020). https://doi.org/10.1007/978-3-030-58548-8_1
27. Yang, Z., Liu, S., Hu, H., Wang, L., Lin, S.: RepPoints: point set representation for object detection. In: ICCV, October 2019
28. Zhang, H., Chang, H., Ma, B., Wang, N., Chen, X.: Dynamic R-CNN: towards high quality object detection via dynamic training. In: Vedaldi, A., Bischof, H., Brox,

T., Frahm, J.-M. (eds.) ECCV 2020. LNCS, vol. 12360, pp. 260–275. Springer, Cham (2020). https://doi.org/10.1007/978-3-030-58555-6_16

29. Zhang, X., Wan, F., Liu, C., Ji, R., Ye, Q.: FreeAnchor: learning to match anchors for visual object detection. In: NeurIPS (2019)

30. Zheng, Y., Lu, Y., Velipasalar, S.: An effective adversarial attack on person re-identification in video surveillance via dispersion reduction. IEEE Access **8**, 183891–183902 (2020)

Makeup Transfer Based on Generative Adversarial Network for Large Angle Spatial Misalignment

Cairun Wang, Weiling Cai[✉], and Zhiwei Li

Nanjing Normal University, Nanjing 210097, China
caiwl@njnu.edu.cn

Abstract. The makeup transfer task aims to transfer makeup styles from a reference makeup image to another non-makeup image. Previous methods achieved great progress with the same face angle, but failed to achieve good results when transferring between images with large spatial misalignment of face angles. In this paper, We propose a method for facial makeup transfer for large-angle spatial misalignment which based on generative adversarial networks. It first utilizes the Neural Head Reconstruction Module to process the reference image to obtain a new reference image. The new reference image maintains the original makeup style but has the same face angle as the source image, and it still has high definition and realism. Thus, the subsequent makeup transfer will be much easier. In addition, in order to ensure the authenticity and clarity of local details as much as possible, we also introduce the concept of local perception to transfer the makeup while keeping the color of the original character's eyeballs, ears and neck unchanged. Besides, we can also realize controllable and partial makeup transfer. Experimental results show that our method achieves the state-of-the-art compared to existing methods.

Keywords: Makeup transfer · Spatial misalignment · Neural head reconstruction

1 Introduction

In the long history of thousands of years, human beings are often fascinated by beautiful faces. Especially for women, looking attractive is a key part of this. Among various beauty techniques, makeup is the most mainstream method, and the accompanying makeup products include eye shadow, lipstick, blush, etc.

Due to the popularity of beauty makeup, makeup testing has become an important application in retail and entertainment. Among all makeup testing methods, facial makeup transfer is the most effective and convenient one. The makeup transfer task is to transfer the makeup style from one reference face to another. This task is not as easy as it seems. It not only needs to extract makeup component information from the reference face picture, but also analyze the facial features. The structure thus correctly transfers makeup information to the unpaired face. There are many factors that need to be considered, including head posture, brightness, facial expression, posture, and occlusion.

The makeup transfer tasks we mentioned, which mainly aims to transfer makeup styles from a reference makeup image to another non-makeup image. It can be widely used in major beauty and makeup applications. Most of the existing makeup transfer methods are based on Generative Adversarial Networks [1]. They usually adopt the framework of CycleGAN [2] and use facial landmarks as a basis for the following processing.

However, the existing methods [2, 4, 5, 7, 8] have some drawbacks. First of all, they are only suitable for frontal images with neutral expression, because they are specially designed modules to process the misalignment of the image and the frontal image. When the angle misalignment of the transferred face image is large, the transfer effect will often be poor. Secondly, the existing methods will cause local smudges and teeth staining of lipstick, resulting in rough local details of the generated face image. Finally, when the images have large-angle spatial misalignment, they usually generate a lot of computational consumption, which greatly increases the time to train the model.

In this paper, we overcome the makeup transferred barriers and poor local detail caused by large-angle spatial misalignment. On the one hand, our method improves the traditional makeup loss, adds Neural Head Reenactment module[3], adjusts the face angle of the original reference image to be consistent with the source image, and maximizes the effect of histogram matching. On the other hand, the introduced local perceptual loss can better preserve the local detail information of the image, which makes the generated image appear realistic and vivid. We make the following contributions in this paper:

- We propose a large-angle face makeup transfer method, which effectively solves the problem of poor transfer effect when the face angle difference is too large.
- Our method introduces local perception loss, and transfers makeup while keeping the colors of the original characters' eyeballs, ears, and background unchanged.
- Compared with the existing methods, our method achieves state-of-the-art in terms of facial local details and large angle transfer.

2 Related Work

2.1 Facial Makeup Transfer

Makeup transfer has been extensively studied in recent years. BeautyGAN[4] first proposed a GAN framework for simultaneous makeup transfer and removal, and it also has dual inputs and outputs. They also introduce a makeup loss that matches the color histograms of different parts of the face for instance-level makeup transfer. Beauty-Glow [5] proposed a similar idea and decomposed cosmetic and non-cosmetic components on the Glow framework. PairedCycleGAN [6] introduced an asymmetric function to accomplish the task of makeup transfer/removal and a variant of the cycle consistency loss to support makeup transfer using specific makeup images. LADN [7] utilized multiple overlapping local discriminators and asymmetric loss functions to ensure consistency of local details. Although the above methods can perform makeup transfer to a certain extent, they do not specifically consider the problem of spatial misalignment between source and reference images. PSGAN [8] proposed the first attempt to explicitly solve the spatial misalignment problem by introducing an attention mechanism [9]. They build the pixel-wise correspondences and achieve partial makeup transfer by leveraging the face parsing masks and facial landmarks. However, when transferring at a large angle, its effect is not good, and even smudges may occur.

2.2 Style Transfer

The main task of style transfer is to combine the content and style of different images, and it has been widely explored [13, 14, 19, 20]. [10] proposed a method to generate reconstructed images by reducing the reconstruction loss of content and style. [11] proposed that image representations can be obtained using CNNs, and that it can separate and recombine them to synthesize images. [12] found that instance normalization plays a significant role in achieving fast style transfer in style transfer networks. Although their method can only transfer a fixed set of styles, it cannot transfer arbitrary new styles. However, existing style transfer methods usually transfer style from one domain to another and they lack the understanding of local features and controllability. Therefore, they are not suitable for facial makeup transfer applications.

3   Related Work

3.1   Formulation

Let X and Y be the non-makeup image domain and the makeup image domain. Then, we utilize $\{x_n\}_{1,...,N}, x_n \in X$ and $\{y_m\}_{1,...,M}, y_m \in Y$ to denote the examples of two domains respectively. Given a non-makeup image and a makeup image, we can learn mapping functions $\bar{x} = G(x, y)$ and $\bar{y} = G(y, x)$, where the transferred image has the makeup style of and the face identity of x. Note that there is no paired data for training.

3.2   Framework

As shown in Fig. 1, we propose an adversarial generative network makeup transfer method combined with image face angle reconstruction. Inspired by previous methods, our model adopts encoder-bottleneck-decoder structure. Encoder extracts the features and makeup style of the reference image. The parts that need to be extracted include the eyes, skin and lips. In the network, the extracted features adjusted by the attention mechanism will be consistent with the source image, and finally combined with the source image through the decoder to generate a new makeup image. The detailed process of our method is as follows. First, we input the makeup image y_{ref} and non-makeup image x_{source} into the generator G, through the encoder we can get two makeup matrices α and β, but since the makeup image and the non-makeup image may have large difference in expressions, poses, and face angles, the extracted makeup matrix cannot be directly used for makeup transfer. We use the Attentive Makeup Morphing module proposed in [8] to obtain new makeup matrices α' and β', so as to substitute into the generator G to obtain the transferred images y_{ref}^{new}, x_{source}^{new}. The generated images are fed into the same G to build the reconstruction images y_{ref}^{rec}, x_{source}^{rec}.

In the actual scene of the image makeup transfer task, when the images have large spatial misalignment, the retouched regions between images are misaligned and they vary greatly in size, position, and perspective distortion. It seriously affects the histogram matching results, reducing the effectiveness of this histogram loss. To overcome this problem, we introduce Neural Head Reenactment module, as shown in Fig. 2. We input the source image and the reference image into the model, and utilize the identity encoder to obtain the identity information of the reference image and the pose encoder to obtain the pose information of the original image. Then, integrate them into a new identity code and generate a new reference image through a layer-by-layer network. The new reference image maintains the original makeup style but has the same face angle and pose as the source image, and the new reference image still has high definition and realism. This ensures that we can get as much useful information as possible when training, thereby improving the image transfer performance of our model as a whole.

Compared to the PSGAN model, our method is more strict on the local details of the transfer. In order to utilize the limited inter-image information to improve the image transfer performance as much as possible, our method increases the local makeup perception loss on the original basis, which makes the transferred images more realistic and clear.

3.3   Neural Head Reenactment Module

Since the source image and the reference image may have different face angles and expressions, the makeup information of the face cannot be completely extracted during the makeup transfer task. By utilizing the NHR module, two face images with large differences in complex poses can be converted into images with the same facial pose and expression, which greatly reduces the difficulty of the problem.

The Neural Head Reenactment system [3] is driven by the latent pose representation, which can change the pose and facial expression information of the original image according to the input image pose. As shown in Fig. 2, we input the each image I_k into the identity encoder, and we will get a di-dimensional vector $x_k = F(I_k)$, which we call the identity encoding of I_k. Identity embeddings mainly contain pose-independent information about people, such as lighting, clothing, etc. If gives K frames, we will average over $X_1,..,X_K$ to get a single identity vector $\bar{x}$. For pose source image I_{k+1}, it will go through a random pose augmentation transformation A. We call A pose augmentation because it is applied to pose source and can be seen as a form of data augmentation, and it is important for pose-identity disentanglement to keep person's pose intact. Then, $A(I_{k+1})$ will be passed into pose encoder G, which is a network of much lower capacity. The pose encoder will eventually generate a dp-dimensional pose embedding $y_{k+1} = G(A(I_{k+1}))$ that is independent of person identity information.

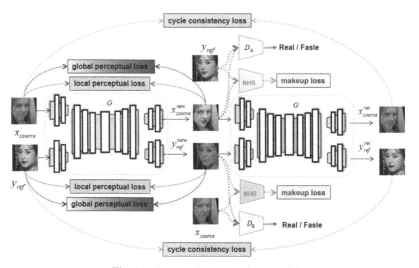

Fig. 1. The overall system of our model.

The previously obtained pose and identity embeddings are passed to a generator network, which tries to reconstruct the image I_{k+1} as accurately as possible. Unlike [15] which uses stickman images to send pose information, we rely on the AdaIN [16] mechanism to pass pose and identity embeddings into the generator. In the generator, we also need the help of some loss functions to get the desired results. Firstly, the dice coefficient loss [17] is introduced to match Segmentation maps. Secondly, we use the same combination of losses in [15] to match the head images with background blacked out. Also, $I^G \odot S^G$ and $I_{k+1} \odot S_{k+1}$ will be passed to the discriminator to calculate the adversarial loss that ensure the generated images are realistic, the discriminator feature matching loss. Finally, we can get a new image I_k, which maintains the original identity information but has a new pose. Thus, the makeup transfer task becomes a simple transfer of the same angle pose.

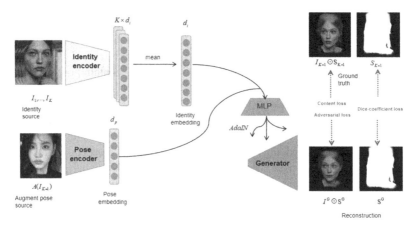

Fig. 2. Structure of the Neural Head Reenactment Module.

3.4 Full Objective

Adversarial Loss. The adversarial loss is introduced to allow the generator to produce a more realistic face image. In this paper, We use two discriminators Dx and Dy to discriminate whether the x of the source image domain and the y of the reference image domain are real or fake. Therefore, the definition of the adversarial loss of the generator L_G^{adv} and the discriminator L_G^{adv} are as follows

$$
\begin{aligned}
L_D^{adv} = &-E_{x\sim X}[\log D_X(x)] - E_{y\sim Y}[\log D_Y(y)] \\
&-E_{x\sim X, y\sim Y}[\log(1 - D_X(G(x, y)))] \\
&-E_{x\sim X, y\sim Y}[\log(1 - D_Y(G(y, x)))]
\end{aligned}
\tag{1}
$$

$$
\begin{aligned}
L_G^{adv} = &-E_{x\sim X, y\sim Y}[\log(D_X(G(x, y)))] \\
&-E_{x\sim X, y\sim Y}[\log(D_Y(G(y, x)))]
\end{aligned}
$$

Global Perceptual Loss. When transferring the makeup, the transferred image needs to retain personal identity, rather than directly measuring pixel-level differences. We adopt the VGG-16 pre-trained model on ImageNet to compare the activations of the source facial image and the generated facial image in the hidden layer. we introduce global perceptual loss L_{global}^{per} to calculate the difference used by L2-norm. L_{global}^{per} defines as

$$
\begin{aligned}
L_{global}^{per} = &E_{x\sim X, y\sim Y}[||F_l(G(x, y)) - F_l(x)||_2] \\
&+E_{x\sim X, y\sim Y}[||F_l(G(y, x)) - F_l(y)||_2]
\end{aligned}
\tag{2}
$$

where $F_l(.)$ denotes the features of the l-th layer of the VGG-16 model.

Local Perceptual Loss. When transferring makeup, we not only need the global perception loss, but also need to keep the color of the parts that do not need to be transferred, such as the neck, eyeballs, and ears. Local perceptual loss L_{local}^{per} defines as

$$
\begin{aligned}
L_{local}^{per} = &\sum_{i=1}^{l} [||F_l(G(x, y) \odot M_{x,i}) - F_l(x \odot M_{x,i})||_2] \\
&+ \sum_{i=1}^{l} [||F_l(G(y, x) \odot M_{y,i}) - F_l(y \odot M_{y,i})||_2]
\end{aligned}
\tag{3}
$$

Cycle Consistency Loss. Since makeup images and non-makeup images are not paired, we train the model in a cyclic way. Here, we introduce cycle consistency loss, which is defi-ned as L_G^{cyc}.

$$
\begin{aligned}
L_G^{cyc} = &E_{x\sim X, y\sim Y}[||G(G(x, y), x) - x||_2] \\
&+E_{x\sim X, y\sim Y}[||G(G(y, x), y) - y||_2]
\end{aligned}
\tag{4}
$$

Makeup Loss. The makeup loss was first proposed in [3], which is mainly to match the color distribution of the reference and transfer images. In Existing methods, the makeup regions are not well aligned, and they vary greatly in size, position and deformation.

It seriously affects the histogram matching results and reduces the effectiveness of the histogram loss. In order to solve this problem, we align the reference image and the source image before the histogram matching. The generated image will have te same facial expression and facial posture as the source image, but it will still keep the identity information and makeup of the reference image. Histogram matching(HM) consists of local matching of 3 different face regions: skin, lips and eyes. Furthermore, the three transferred parts are integrated into the pseudo ground truth.

$$L_G^{makeup} = E_{x \sim X, y \sim Y}[||G(x, y) - HM(x, NHR(x, y))||_2] \tag{5}$$

Total Loss. The total loss of the whole network is defined as L_{total}

$$L_{total} = \lambda_D L_D^{adv} + \lambda_G L_G^{adv} + \lambda_g L_{global}^{per} + \lambda_l L_{local}^{per}$$
$$+ \lambda_{cyc} L_G^{cyc} + \lambda_{makeup} L_G^{makeup} \tag{6}$$

where λ_D, λ_G, λ_g, λ_l, λ_{cyc}, λ_{makeup} are the weights of the corresponding loss function above.

4   Experiments

4.1   Implementation Details

We train our model on the MT-Dataset which contains 3834 female images and test it on the MT-Dataset and the Makeup-Wild Dataset. Makeup-Wild Dataset was proposed by PSGAN. There are many large-angle face pictures in the data set, which can facilitate the large-angle transfer test.

In our experiments, we resize the images to 256×256. We extract features from the Relu41 layer of VGG16 to compute local perceptual loss and global perceptual loss. We use the Adam optimizer to train the generator and two discriminators and set the learning rate 0.0002.The batch size is set to 1.

4.2   Comparisons

To test the effect of our model on the results, we conducted comparative experiments. In Fig. 3, we show a comparison of the transfer results of each method when the angle between the reference image and the source image is the same and there is a large spatial misalignment, respectively. We compare our method with four state-of-the-art makeup transfer methods: BeautyGAN [4], LADN [7] and PSGAN [8], SCGAN [18].

In the first row of Fig. 3, We show qualitative comparisons with four methods when there is no spatial misalignment between the reference and source images. For Beauty-GAN, it performs well when there is no spatial misalignment problem. After the transfer of LADN, there will be blurring and unnatural in the transferred images. PSGAN can also generate visually acceptable results but locally suffers from color bleeding problem, which affects the aesthetic feeling of the results. Meanwhile, PSGAN cannot correctly transfer the tonal information of the face in the source image, resulting in a chromatic aberration between the lip color of the source image and the generated image. SCGAN and our method perform best without spatial misalignment, the generated images are more realistic and natural compared to other methods.

To test the effect of pose and angle spatial misalignment, we compare our method with four makeup transfer models which shows in the last three lines of Fig. 3. When spatial misalignment occurs, BeautyGAN and LADN fail to have a good result. For BeautyGAN, it is not able to properly transfer the color of the skin. LADN still has a lot of facial smudges, and the generated images are unnatural and realistic. Compared with the previous two methods, PSGAN performs slightly better, but there will still be unnatural shadows on the face. SCGAN also has some flaws, there are still black spots and color inconsistencies in local details. Comparing with other methods, our method can generate the most natural results.

| Source | Reference | BeautyGAN | LADN | PSGAN | SCGAN | Ours |

Fig. 3. Qualitative comparisons with existing models.

4.3 Ablation Studies

Neural Head Reenactment Module. In our method, Neural Head Reenactment(NHR) module is used to generate a new reference image with the same face angle as the source image. In the previous methods, the area alignment of the face is computationally expensive and the alignment is not good. They vary widely in size, position, and perspective distortion. It seriously affects the histogram matching results and reduces the effectiveness of the histogram loss. Our method can fully utilize the effect of histogram matching, so that the generated image has the same face color as the reference image and looks more vivid and realistic. For Fig. 4,we can see that the face makeup of the image looks unnatural and the color of the lips is uneven without NRF. Experiments show that the NFR module can perform makeup transfer between images between large angles and achieve good results.

Local Perceptual Loss. In addition to the existing conventional losses, we introduce a local perceptual loss to maintain the consistency of facial features and facial details between source and generated images. We can observe from Fig. 4 that the color of the lipstick is inconsistent with the reference image without local perceptual loss. And there will be a little smudge effect on the face. Furthermore, the images with local perceptual loss are very sharp with more local details.

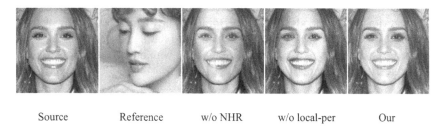

Source   Reference   w/o NHR   w/o local-per   Our

Fig. 4. Ablation study of Neural Head Reenactment(NHR) and local perceptual loss.

4.4 Controllable Makeup Transfer

Since we use style codes w to represent the makeup style of the image. It makes it easy to control shadows by manipulating the style code. We extract the style-codes from the reference image and the source image. Then we apply a linear interpolation to control the shade. (coefficient $\alpha \in [0, 1]$)

$$w = (1 - \alpha)w_{ref} + \alpha w_{source} \qquad (7)$$

Our method also Supports fusing the styles from multiple reference images with linear interpolation.

$$w = \alpha w_{ref1} + (1-\alpha)w_{ref2} \qquad (8)$$

Figure 5 shows the results for two reference images with different contributions.

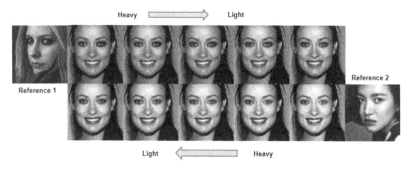

Fig. 5. Makeup transfer with two reference images by linear interpolating two style-codes.

4.5 Partial Makeup Transfer

Figure 6 shows the results of partially mixing makeup transfer from two references. The image in the third column is a recombination of the lip makeup of Reference 1 and the rest of the makeup of Reference 2. Experiments show that the resulting images are realistic and natural.

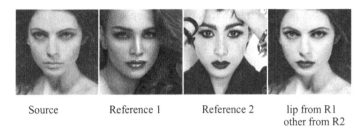

Source   Reference 1   Reference 2   lip from R1
                                                          other from R2

Fig. 6. Given a source image (column 1), transfer lipstick from reference 1 and other makeup from reference 2 to generate a transferred image (column 4).

4.6 Makeup Remove

Since our model learns the transfer between the two domains in a recursive manner, we can achieve removal by exchanging source and reference images. That is, the non-makeup image x is used as the reference image, and the makeup image y is used as the source image. Figure 7 shows the makeup removal results.

Source   Removed

Fig. 7. Refer to a non-makeup image (column 2), remove the makeup from source image.

5 Conclusion

In this paper, we introduce a Neural Head Reenactment Module and local perceptual loss to overcome the challenge of spatial misalignment in makeup transfer. Unlike previous methods, which rely on cumbersome and ambiguous dense correspondence between source image and reference image, we propose a new solution to ease the transfer difficulty. The proposed model exhibits a great degree of flexibility and controllability, which supports controllable makeup transfer, partial makeup transfer and large-angle spatial misalignment transfer. Since our model generates a new reference image according to the angle of the source image, it is not affected by spatial misalignment. Therefore, our method can perfectly accomplish the task of makeup transfer.

References

1. Goodfellow, I.J., Pouget-Abadie, J., Mirza, M., Xu, B., Warde-Farley, D., Ozair, S., Courville, A.C., Bengio, Y.: Generative adversarial nets. In: NeurIPS (2014)
2. Zhu, J.-Y., Park, T., Isola, P., Efros, A.A.: Unpaired image-to-image translation using cycleconsistent adversarial networks. In: ICCV (2017)
3. Burkov, E., Pasechnik, I., Grigorev, A., et al.: Neural Head Reenactment with Latent Pose Descriptors. IEEE (2020)
4. Zhu, W., Lin, L.: Beautygan: Instance-Level Facialmakeup Transfer with Deep Generative Adversarial Network. In: ACM MM (2018)
5. Chen, H.-J., Hui, K.-M., Wang, S.-Y., Tsao, L.-W., Shuai, H.-H., Cheng, W.-H.: Beautyglow: Ondemand makeup transfer framework with reversible generative network. In: CVPR pp. 10042–10050 (2019)
6. Chang, H., Lu, J., Yu, F., Finkelstein, A.: Pairedcyclegan: Asymmetric style transfer for applying and removing makeup. In: CVPR (2018)
7. Gu, Q., Wang, G., Chiu, M.T., Tai, Y.-W., Tang, C.-K.: Ladn: Local adversarial disentangling network for facial makeup and de-makeup. In: ICCV (2019)
8. Jiang, W., et al.: Psgan: Pose and expression robust spatial-aware gan for customizable makeup transfer. In: CVPR, pp. 5194–5202 (2020)
9. Vaswani, A., et al.: Attention is all you need. In: NeurIPS (2017)
10. Gatys, L.A., Ecker, A.S., Bethge, M.: A neural algorithm of artistic style. arXiv preprint arXiv:1508.06576 (2015)
11. Johnson, J., Alahi, A., Fei-Fei, L.: Perceptual losses for real-time style transfer and super-resolution. In: Leibe, B., Matas, J., Sebe, N., Welling, M. (eds.) ECCV 2016. LNCS, vol. 9906, pp. 694–711. Springer, Cham (2016). https://doi.org/10.1007/978-3-319-46475-6_43
12. Dumoulin, V., Shlens, J., Kudlur, M.: A learned representation for artistic style. ArXiv, abs/1610.07629, 2016. 2
13. Gatys, L.A., Ecker, A.S., Bethge, M.: Image style transfer using convolutional neural networks. In: CVPR (2016)
14. Luan, F., Paris, S., Shechtman, E., Bala, K.: Deep photo style transfer. In: CVPR (2017)
15. Zakharov, E., Shysheya, A., Burkov, E., Lempitsky, V.: Few-shot adversarial learning of realistic neural talking head models. In: Proc. ICCV (2019)
16. Huang, X., Belongie, S.: Arbitrary style transfer in realtime with adaptive instance normalization. In: Proc. ICCV (2017)
17. Milletari, F., Navab, N., Ahmadi, S.-A.: V-net: Fully convolutional neural networks for volumetric medical image segmentation. pp. 565–571 (2016)

18. Deng, H., Han, C., Cai, H., Han, G., He, S.: Spatially-invariant style-codes controlled makeup transfer. In: CVPR, pp. 6549–6557 (2021)
19. Zhao, M., Zhu, S.-C.: Portrait painting using active templates. In: Proceedings of the ACM SIGGRAPH/Eurographics Symposium on Non-Photorealistic Animation and Rendering, pp. 117–124 (2011)
20. Park, T., Liu, M.-Y., Wang, T.-C., Zhu, J.-Y.: Semantic image synthesis with spatially-adaptive normalization. In: CVPR (2019)

Making Images Resilient to Adversarial Example Attacks

Shixin Tian[(✉)], Ying Cai, Forrest Bao, and Ramakrishna Oruganti

Iowa State University, Ames, IA, USA
{stian,yingcai,fsb,ramak}@iastate.edu

Abstract. Adversarial example attacks twist an image to cause image classifiers to output a wrong prediction, yet the perturbation is too subtle to be perceived by a human. Existing research has focused on improving the accuracy of image classifiers as a defense. In this paper, we consider the problem of thwarting adversarial example attacks from a different aspect. Instead of developing better image classifiers, our idea is to make images themselves more resilient to the attacks. Specifically, we propose to convert an image into an *adversary-proof example* to have three properties: 1) The modification is barely noticeable to human eyes; 2) The new image will receive same predictions from image classifiers; and 3) It is much harder for one to compute an adversarial example from the new image than from the original one. We present two solutions to compute adversary-proof examples, and evaluate their performance with two datasets, MNIST and CIFAR10. Our results show that the concept of adversary-proof example can indeed serve effectively as the first line of defense against adversarial example attacks.

1 Introduction

Deep Neural Networks (DNNs) have been shown vulnerable to *adversarial examples* [5,15] which are manipulated inputs with subtle perturbations to make model predictions wrong. Since its introduction [15], various sophisticated attack algorithms were developed to generate adversarial examples [1,3,13,16].

The existence of adversarial examples presents a significant threat to the DNNs-based applications, especially mission-critical ones such as self-driving. Such attacks have received great attention from both academia and industry, and a good number of defense techniques have been developed [8,12,17–19]. Despite their differences, all existing approaches aim at making models more robust against adversarial example attacks.

However, we argue that there are two lines of defence against adversarial attack. Defending against adversarial examples, the focus of existing effort, is the second line. The first line is to prevent an example from being adversarially changed, at least easily. Moving the defence from the second line to the first line can be more cost-effective and ultimate in many critical cases. For example, in auto-driving systems, the correct recognition of traffic signs is important. The entire traffic system is safe only when all cars are protected against adversarial traffic signs. As long as one single car is fooled, the effort on improving adversarial robustness for all other cars is in vain. Hence, instead of

E. Pimenidis et al. (Eds.): ICANN 2022, LNCS 13531, pp. 188–199, 2022.
https://doi.org/10.1007/978-3-031-15934-3_16

the uncoordinated effort to make all cars more adversary-proof, it is more cost-effective and ultimate to build traffic signs that cannot be adversarially attacked.

Based on the motivation above, in this paper, we approach adversarial example attacks from an unexplored perspective. Instead of making models more adversary robustness, we make examples more resilient to adversarial attacks. While adversarial attack can be in many modalities, we limit our study in image-related cases. Specifically, we propose adding perturbations to an image such that the perturbations are non-distinguishable by both human eyes and image classifiers (i.e., the predictions unchanged) but are significantly more difficult to generate adversarial images from. We refer the resulting image as an *adversary-proof example*, alluding to the process that forges it to withstand the adversarial example attacks. We summarize the main contributions of this paper as follows:

- To our knowledge, the notion of adversary-proof example is new. Our research complements existing work by creating the first line of defense, i.e., making images themselves more resilient to the attacks.
- To address the challenges of computing adversary-proof examples, we develop two approaches, namely *R(everse)-PGD* which serves as a baseline approach and the *ZigZag* approach which formalizes the problem as robust optimization.
- We evaluate the proposed techniques extensively on three datasets: MNIST, CIFAR10 and ImageNet. The results show that the concept of adversary-proof example indeed works. It is significantly harder to compute an adversarial example out of an adversary-proof example than that from a normal image.

2 Adversary-Proof Examples

Our idea of protecting an image x is to add a perturbation δ to generate a new image x' that has these properties:

1. x' appears to be the same as x from human vision.
2. x' is classified the same as x by models.
3. It is harder for one to compute an adversarial example from x' than from x which will be classified differently.

We refer to x' as an adversary-proof example of x, alluding to the fact that it is generated to withstand adversarial example attacks.

2.1 Baseline: R-PGD

The basic idea of adversarial example attacks is to move an image toward (or across) the decision boundaries of a model. An intuitive counter strategy is to reverse this procedure by moving the image away from the decision boundaries. In other words, we can modify an image in the opposite direction as adversarial example attacks in order to find adversary-proof examples. Formally, we want to add a small perturbation δ to minimize the loss value $Loss(\mathcal{C}(x + \delta))$ in Eq. 1:

$$\underset{||\delta||<\epsilon}{\arg\min} \underset{(x,y)\in\mathcal{X}}{\mathrm{E}} Loss(\mathcal{C}(x+\delta)), y) \qquad (1)$$

where ϵ is the upper bound of the norm of the perturbation added and $\mathcal{X}$ is the set of the inputs we need to protect. In our implementation, we use the infinity norm as the distance measurement, i.e., $||\delta||_\infty < \epsilon$.

We propose a baseline approach called *Reverse-PGD* (short as R-PGD), modified from the existing PGD algorithm [6], to generate adversary-proof examples. A more formal description of R-PGD is given in Algorithm 1. In each iteration of the original PGD, the gradient signs are added up to the inputs to maximize the loss. In contrast, our approach takes away these gradient signs from the inputs to minimize the loss in Eq. 2.

$$x^{t+1} = x^t - \alpha \cdot \mathrm{sign}(\nabla_x Loss(\mathcal{C}(x^t), y)) \qquad (2)$$

Algorithm 1: The R-PGD Approach

Input: Image x, label y, ϵ, k, α, model $\mathcal{C}$
Output: Adversary-proof example x'
1 Initialize variables : $i = 0$, $x' = x$;
2 **while** $i < k$ **do**
3 $\quad$ $x' = x' - \alpha \cdot \mathrm{sign}(\nabla_{x'} Loss(\mathcal{C}(x'), y))$;
4 $\quad$ $x' = \mathrm{Clip}(x', x - \epsilon, x + \epsilon)$;
5 $\quad$ $x' = \mathrm{Clip}(x', 0, 1)$;
6 $\quad$ $i = i + 1$;
7 Return x';

Our algorithm is very efficient because it only estimates gradients for a limited number of rounds (i.e., k). The produced new image x' is in the l_∞ ball of normal ϵ around x, i.e., $||x' - x||_\infty \le \epsilon$.

2.2 Advanced: ZigZag

Here we present a more advanced version of our approach. Recall that adversarial example attacks try to maximize the empirical risk over adversarial examples (Eq. ??). Given an image x, we add a perturbation δ to generate a new image x' in order to minimize the maximization of the loss over the adversarial examples targeting x'. This is to minimize the risk over the adversarial examples generated based on x', which can be formalized in Eq. 3:

$$\underset{||\delta||<\epsilon}{\arg\min} \underset{(x,y)\in\mathcal{X}}{\mathrm{E}} [\underset{||\Delta||<\epsilon'}{\max} Loss(\mathcal{C}(x+\delta+\Delta)), y)] \qquad (3)$$

where ϵ is the upper bound of the norm of the perturbation we want to add, ϵ' denotes the upper bound of the norm of the perturbation added by the adversary, and $\mathcal{X}$ is the set of the inputs we need to protect.

Equation 3 defines a robust optimization problem. To solve this problem, we propose an iterative two-stage algorithm referred to as *ZigZag*. It has a number of iterative steps, each of which has two stages.

In the first stage, we treat δ as a constant and maximize the maximization problem by modifying Δ. We use adversarial example attack algorithms to solve the inner maximization problem. Consider an adversary that uses an efficient function Gen($\cdot$) to generate adversarial examples. Given an image x, the adversarial perturbation could be generated by executing the function, i.e., $\Delta = \text{Gen}(x)$. Thus, to solve the inner maximization problem, we only need to compute $\text{Gen}(x + \delta)$.

In the second stage, we treat Δ as a constant and solve the outer minimization problem by adjusting δ. To achieve this goal, we compute the signs of the input gradient of the loss $Loss(\mathcal{C}(x_{adv}), y)$ and change δ along the reverse direction by a small step α.

The iteration stops when it exceeds a maximum number of steps or when Gen could not generate successful adversarial perturbations. A more formal description of ZigZag is given in Algorithm 2.

Algorithm 2: The ZigZag Approach

Input: Image x, label y, ϵ, k, α, model $\mathcal{C}$, adversarial example generator Gen
Output: Adversary-proof example x'
1 Initialize variables : $i = 0$, $x' = x$;
2 **while** $i < k$ **do**
3   Generate adversarial example $\Delta = \text{Gen}(x')$;
4   **if** $\arg\max_i \mathcal{C}(x' + \Delta) == y$ **then**
5          $\lfloor$ Break the loop;
6      $x' = x' - \alpha \cdot \text{sign}(\nabla_{x'} Loss(\mathcal{C}(x' + \Delta), y))$;
7      $x' = \text{Clip}(x', x - \epsilon, x + \epsilon)$;
8      $x' = \text{Clip}(x', 0, 1)$;
9      $i = i + 1$;
10 Return x';

The produced new image x' by this algorithm is in the l_∞ ball of normal ϵ around x. This is the same as in Algorithm 1. However, generating adversarial examples can be time consuming, so this approach may not be as efficient as the previous one. We will discuss more in Sect. 3.

3   Empirical Study

In this section, we evaluate the effectiveness of the adversary-proof examples generated using the proposed approaches against various attaches. We first give the general settings of our experiments and then present and analyze the empirical results.

3.1 Experiment Settings

We train convolutional neural networks (CNN) on MNIS and residual neural networks (ResNet) on CIFAR10. The structures of these two models are given in Fig. 1. CNN and ResNet are trained on 50 epochs of the training data. Data augmentation is used for training ResNet. For ImageNet, we use the pre-trained model, Inception V3 for evaluation.

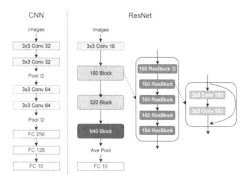

Fig. 1. Model Structures. The CNN model is used for MNIST and the ResNet model is used for CIFAR10.

We use three representative algorithms to perform adversarial example attacks, namely FGSM, PGD and CW. Note that we use untargeted attacks, i.e., the adversaries try to make the models give wrong and random predictions. Hence, a low prediction accuracy means a high success rate of the adversarial example attack.

Given a model $\mathcal{C}(\cdot)$ and a set of input images X to protect, we generate the corresponding adversary-proof examples X'. Then we apply the attack algorithms to generate the adversarial examples from X' based on the model. Finally, we use $\mathcal{C}(\cdot)$ to classify the adversarial examples and record the accuracy. A higher prediction accuracy means a better defense.

3.2 R-PGD Against FGSM

Figure 2 shows the effectiveness of R-PGD against FGSM. On each the datasets, the prediction accuracy on the adversarial examples targeting the adversary-proof images generated by R-PGD is higher than that targeting the original images (the green lines). This means that the adversary has a smaller probability to find successful adversarial examples on the adversary-proof images.

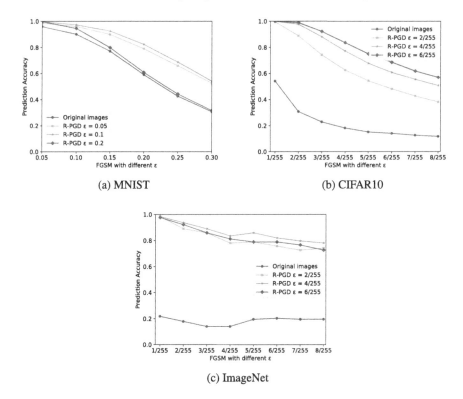

(a) MNIST

(b) CIFAR10

(c) ImageNet

Fig. 2. R-PGD against FGSM. The success rate of FGSM on adversary-proof images is lower than on the images without protection. (Color figure online)

Observed on both original images and adversary-proof images, the prediction accuracy drops when ϵ of FGSM increases. The reason is quite straightforward. The ϵ of FGSM represents the capability of the adversary. A larger ϵ gives the adversary a higher chance of finding successful adversarial examples.

Likewise, the ϵ of R-PGD represents its capability of protecting the inputs. We may expect a larger ϵ to result in a better protection. However this is not always true and we can find a counter-example on MNIST (purple line in Fig. 2(a)) where increasing ϵ does not improve the effectiveness of R-PGD against FGSM attacks. The essential idea of R-PGD is to decrease the prediction loss by modifying the images in advance. However since the prediction loss converges to zero quite fast, increasing ϵ cannot lower the prediction loss further.

Table 1. R-PGD Against PGD

Accuracy On MNIST		Accuracy On CIFAR10		Accuracy On ImageNet	
Clean data	0	Clean data	0	Clean data	0
PGD $\epsilon = 0.1$	0.384	PGD $\epsilon = 2/255$	0.566	PGD $\epsilon = 2/255$	0.093
PGD $\epsilon = 0.2$	0.007	PGD $\epsilon = 4/255$	0.056	PGD $\epsilon = 4/255$	0.046
PGD $\epsilon = 0.3$	0.003	PGD $\epsilon = 6/255$	0	PGD $\epsilon = 6/255$	0

3.3 R-PGD Against PGD

Table 1 shows the effectiveness of R-PGD against PGD. We compute the prediction accuracy on the adversarial examples targeting the adversary-proof examples generated by R-PGD with $\epsilon = 0.3$ on MNIST, $\epsilon = 8/255$ on CIFAR10 and ImageNet. The results are presented in Table 1 which shows that PGD can make prediction accuracy very low with a larger ϵ.

As a baseline approach, R-PGD is not effective in protecting images against PGD attacks. The attack success rate of PGD is almost 100% for all the generated adversary-proof examples with $\epsilon = 0.3$. It fails because a low prediction loss does not guarantee a small probability to find adversarial examples. What we really want is to push the input images further from the decision boundaries so that it becomes difficult for the adversary to find successful adversarial examples. However, a small prediction loss does not necessarily mean being further away from the decision boundaries. PGD, which is stronger than FGSM, can attack the adversary-proof examples generated by R-PGD easily.

3.4 ZigZag Against FGSM

The effectiveness of the optimization-based approach, ZigZag (Algorithm 2), in defending against FGSM is shown in Fig. 3. The prediction accuracy on the adversarial examples targeting the adversary-proof examples (especially those generated by ZigZag with a larger ϵ), on all the datasets, are higher than that targeting the original images. This shows ZigZag's effectiveness in protecting the images against FGSM. Comparing Fig. 2 with Fig. 3, we see that ZigZag usually has a higher prediction accuracy than R-PGD under the same ϵ. This means that ZigZag is more effective than R-PGD in defending against FGSM.

Our study further shows that defenses with a larger ϵ usually outperform those with a smaller ϵ. A larger ϵ means that the defense algorithm can search in a larger space for a 'safe' spot of the input. Enlarging ϵ gives ZigZag a chance to generate an adversary-proof example that is more resilient to the attacks.

3.5 ZigZag Against PGD

The effectiveness of the ZigZag approach (Algorithm 2) against PGD is showed in Fig. 4. By comparing the results of ZigZag against FGSM (Fig. 3) and PGD (Fig. 4), we

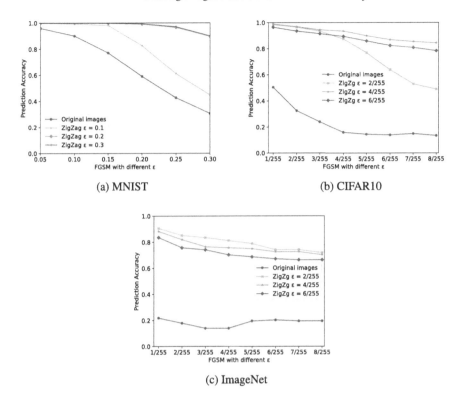

(a) MNIST

(b) CIFAR10

(c) ImageNet

Fig. 3. Evaluation of the effectiveness of the ZigZag approach against FGSM. The prediction accuracies on the adversarial examples targeting the protected images are very high which means that ZigZag is effective in defending against FGSM.

can find that PGD is much stronger than FGSM in its attacking capability as PGD has a lower prediction accuracy (almost zero). When the prediction accuracy on the original data drops to zero, it means that PGD can almost always find successful adversarial examples.

Meanwhile, the prediction accuracy on the adversary-proof images is much higher than that on the original images. The adversarial examples generated from the original images are so deceitful that they can hardly be classified correctly. On CIFAR10, prediction accuracy drops to near zero with PGD attack at $\epsilon = \frac{2}{255}$. However, the prediction accuracy on the adversary-proof images is almost 0.9. This means that the adversary has a chance of only 10% to generate successful adversary examples out of adversary-proof images. This study proves that the proposed ZigZag is very effective.

We also observe that the accuracy decreases as ϵ of the attack algorithm increases. This phenomenon is expected since a larger ϵ means a stronger capability to attack the inputs.

In addition, on all three datasets, we can see the optimization-based approach could not defend against attacks with a large ϵ. The main reason is that in Algorithm 2, the

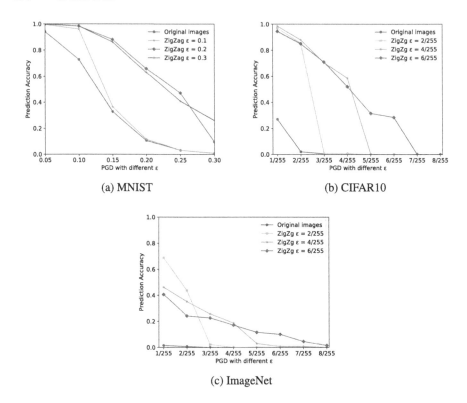

(a) MNIST

(b) CIFAR10

(c) ImageNet

Fig. 4. The effectiveness of the ZigZag approach against PGD. The success rate of PGD on the adversary-proof images is lower than that on the original images.

adversarial example generator Gen uses PGD with the same ϵ as ZigZag does. Hence, it may not be able to capture the patterns of the adversarial examples with a large ϵ.

3.6 ZigZag Against CW

Now we evaluate the performance of ZigZag in defense of the CW attack, the state of the art attacking algorithm [2].

We use CW-l_2 attack minimizes the Euclidean distance between the adversarial examples and the original images. Unlike FGSM and PGD, CW-l_2 does not guarantee the distances are constrained within an upper bound. To generate successful adversarial examples, the CW attack could search a larger space by allowing larger distortions. In our evaluation, CW-l_2 does show its excellence in attacking the inputs by achieving a prediction accuracy of zero on the adversarial examples it generated. Hence, in the following evaluations, we just evaluate the distortions of the adversarial examples generated by CW attack. Distortion represents how much effort CW attack algorithm has spent on finding successful adversarial examples. A larger distortion means that it is harder for CW to find adversarial examples. In other words, there is a higher probability for human to find out the images is not original.

In our evaluation, we use l_2-norm, i.e., $||x'_{adv} - x||_2$ to measure the distortion. As shown in Table 2, we test the CW attack on the adversary-proof examples generated by ZigZag with different ϵ. It can be observed that the distortions on the adversary-proof images are higher than that on the original images. With low confidence (confidence=0) of CW attack, the distortion on adversary proof examples ($\epsilon = 0.3$) is 65% higher than the distortion on original data; with high confidence (confidence = 30), the distortion on adversary proof examples is 34% higher.

Table 2. Distortion of Adversarial Examples by CW on Adversary-proof Images by ZigZag

Confidence	Clean data	$\epsilon = 0.1$	$\epsilon = 0.2$	$\epsilon = 0.3$
0	1.41	1.72	2.09	2.33
10	1.78	2.07	2.49	2.67
20	2.14	2.43	2.91	2.99
30	2.51	2.80	3.25	3.37

3.7 Transferability Evaluation

In this section, we evaluate the transferability of adversary-proof examples. Once adversary-proof examples are generated based on a given model $\mathcal{C}(\cdot)$, the adversary would attack these images based on an alternative model $\mathcal{C}'(\cdot)$ who behaves similarly to $\mathcal{C}(\cdot)$.

We first generate the adversary-proof images X' using our defense algorithms given the model $\mathcal{C}(\cdot)$ to evaluate and a set of input images X to protect. Then we reveal X' to the adversary who will generate the adversarial examples X'_{adv} based on $\mathcal{C}'(\cdot)$. In our evaluation, $\mathcal{C}(\cdot)'$ and $\mathcal{C}(\cdot)$ have similar structures but different numbers of neurons. Finally, we evaluate the prediction accuracy of $\mathcal{C}'(\cdot)$ on X'_{adv}. As an example, we only evaluate ZigZag against PGD and FGSM on CIFAR10. The results are shown in Fig. 5.

We can observe that ZigZag is still effective, i.e., the prediction success rates of adversarial examples generated on adversary proof examples are higher than that on original images. When testing ZigZag against FGSM ($\epsilon = \frac{6}{255}$ for instance, while the success rate of original images drops to 20%, the success rate of adversary proof examples (ZigZag with $\epsilon = \frac{4}{255}$) remains more than 70%.

Adversary-proof examples show transferability among models which they have never seen before. On both datasets, the prediction accuracy on the adversarial examples generated on adversary-proof examples are higher than that generated on original images.

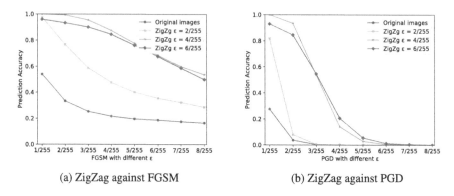

(a) ZigZag against FGSM   (b) ZigZag against PGD

Fig. 5. Evaluation of the transferability of the ZigZag on CIFAR10. Adversary-proof examples show more resilience to FGSM and PGD attacks than original images.

4 Related Work

Many defense mechanisms have been proposed to thwart adversarial example attacks. One strategy is to modify the structures of the neural networks [10, 11] or add auxiliaries [7, 9, 19]. There are also works aimed at building more robust models by employing new and sophisticated training processes [8, 15, 17, 18]. For example, the adversarial training adds adversarial examples into the training set for the models to withstand the attacks. This strategy has been shown to be effective in practice. A different trend of research has been established which provides provable robustness against adversarial examples [4, 12, 14]. These works develop models which are provably robust to adversarial perturbations on the training set.

In summary, all existing techniques were developed to improve the robustness of models. This is different than our research which is to protect the input to the models.

5 Concluding Remarks

Enhancing the robustness of DNNs is clearly crucial in thwarting the attacks. This alone, however, is not sufficient. Our safety in this society relies not just on law enforcement agencies, but also other measurements such as self defenses. In light of this, we propose the idea of making images more resilient to attacks as the first line of defense. Specifically, we want to convert an image into an adversary-proof example, which appears to be the same as the original one but becomes much harder for one to twist it further into an adversarial example. For its implementation, we have developed two algorithms, *R-PGD* and *ZigZag*, and evaluated their effectiveness in defense. Our extensive results show that computing an adversarial example out of an adversary-proof example is indeed much more difficult than out of a normal image.

References

1. Baluja, S., Fischer, I.: Adversarial transformation networks: learning to generate adversarial examples. arXiv preprint arXiv:1703.09387 (2017)
2. Carlini, N., Wagner, D.: Adversarial examples are not easily detected: bypassing ten detection methods. In: Proceedings of the 10th ACM Workshop on Artificial Intelligence and Security, pp. 3–14. ACM (2017)
3. Carlini, N., Wagner, D.: Towards evaluating the robustness of neural networks. In: IEEE Symposium on Security and Privacy, pp. 39–57. IEEE (2017)
4. Cohen, J.M., Rosenfeld, E., Kolter, J.Z.: Certified adversarial robustness via randomized smoothing. arXiv preprint arXiv:1902.02918 (2019)
5. Goodfellow, I.J., Shlens, J., Szegedy, C.: Explaining and harnessing adversarial examples. In: International Conference on Learning Representations (ICLR) (2015)
6. Kurakin, A., Goodfellow, I., Bengio, S.: Adversarial machine learning at scale. arXiv preprint arXiv:1611.01236 (2016)
7. Liao, F., Liang, M., Dong, Y., Pang, T., Hu, X., Zhu, J.: Defense against adversarial attacks using high-level representation guided denoiser. In: Proceedings of the IEEE Conference on Computer Vision and Pattern Recognition, pp. 1778–1787 (2018)
8. Madry, A., Makelov, A., Schmidt, L., Tsipras, D., Vladu, A.: Towards deep learning models resistant to adversarial attacks. In: International Conference on Learning Representations (2018)
9. Meng, D., Chen, H.: MagNet: a two-pronged defense against adversarial examples. In: Proceedings of the 2017 ACM SIGSAC Conference on Computer and Communications Security, pp. 135–147. ACM (2017)
10. Nayebi, A., Ganguli, S.: Biologically inspired protection of deep networks from adversarial attacks. arXiv preprint arXiv:1703.09202 (2017)
11. Papernot, N., McDaniel, P., Wu, X., Jha, S., Swami, A.: Distillation as a defense to adversarial perturbations against deep neural networks. In: 2016 IEEE Symposium on Security and Privacy (SP), pp. 582–597. IEEE (2016)
12. Phan, N., Jin, R., Thai, M.T., Hu, H., Dou, D.: Preserving differential privacy in adversarial learning with provable robustness. arXiv preprint arXiv:1903.09822 (2019)
13. Qiu, H., Xiao, C., Yang, L., Yan, X., Lee, H., Li, B.: SemanticAdv: generating adversarial examples via attribute-conditioned image editing. In: Vedaldi, A., Bischof, H., Brox, T., Frahm, J.-M. (eds.) ECCV 2020. LNCS, vol. 12359, pp. 19–37. Springer, Cham (2020). https://doi.org/10.1007/978-3-030-58568-6_2
14. Raghunathan, A., Steinhardt, J., Liang, P.: Certified defenses against adversarial examples. arXiv preprint arXiv:1801.09344 (2018)
15. Szegedy, C., et al.: Intriguing properties of neural networks. In: International Conference on Learning Representations (2014)
16. Tramer, F., Carlini, N., Brendel, W., Madry, A.: On adaptive attacks to adversarial example defenses. arXiv preprint arXiv:2002.08347 (2020)
17. Tramèr, F., Kurakin, A., Papernot, N., Boneh, D., McDaniel, P.: Ensemble adversarial training: attacks and defenses. arXiv preprint arXiv:1705.07204 (2017)
18. Wong, E., Rice, L., Kolter, J.Z.: Fast is better than free: revisiting adversarial training. arXiv preprint arXiv:2001.03994 (2020)
19. Zhang, S., Gao, H., Rao, Q.: Defense against adversarial attacks by reconstructing images. IEEE Trans. Image Process. **30**, 6117–6129 (2021)

Multi-Class Lane Semantic Segmentation of Expressway Dataset Based on Aerial View

Yongnian Fan[1,2] , Zhiguang Wang[1,2](✉), Cheng Chen[1,2] , Xue Zhang[1,2], and Qiang Lu[1,2]

[1] Beijing Key Laboratory of Petroleum Data Mining,
China University of Petroleum, Beijing, China
`cwangzg@cup.edu.cn`
[2] Department of Computer Science and Technology,
China University of Petroleum, Beijing, China

Abstract. Multi-Class Lane Semantic Segmentation (MCLSS) is a hot topic in the computer vision research, which is of great significance for detecting violations of vehicles on expressway. At present, there is a lack of public dataset for semantic division of complete road areas. This paper completes the collection, cleaning, analysis, classification and labeling of expressway data on aerial view and proposes a semantic segmentation model "Deeplab-ERFC" (DeepLab with Erosion Loss and a Fully-Connected Conditional Random Field). This model extends DeepLabv3+ by adding a Erosion Loss (ER Loss) that can improve boundary prediction performance using corrosion operation to estimate Hausdorff Distance (HD) and a Fully-Connected Conditional Random Field (Fully-Connected CRF) that will reduce the generation of cavities through two gaussian kernel functions considering the color intensity and position relationship between pixels. Based on mean Intersection over Union (mIoU), our proposed Deeplab-ERFC achieves the best semantic segmentation performance on our Expressway Dataset, reaching 83.9% mIoU in the test set.

Keywords: Lane Semantic Segmentation · Boundary loss · Conditional Random Fields

1 Introduction

Semantic segmentation is a core and difficult high-level task in computer vision [1], which aims to detect and classify objects, and predict the pixel-level results. As Deep Convolutional Neural Networks (DCNNs) gradually shows excellent ability in extracting features, they have been applied in advanced visual tasks including semantic segmentation [2–8], and obtained better results than traditional manual

This work is supported by National Natural Science Foundation of China (No. 61972414), National Key R&D Program of China (No. 2019YFC0312003) and Beijing Natural Science Foundation (No. 4202066).

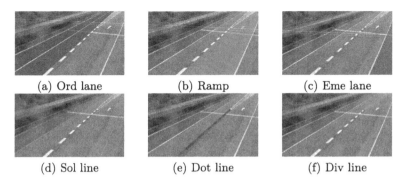

(a) Ord lane   (b) Ramp   (c) Eme lane

(d) Sol line   (e) Dot line   (f) Div line

Fig. 1. Six classification annotation examples of this dataset. (a) Ord lane (Ordinary lane), the general driving areas of vehicles; (b) Ramp, which changes the driving direction of vehicles, generally involves the merging and separation of lanes; (c) Eme lane (Emergency lane), the area where special vehicles are allowed to drive or stop; (d) Sol line (Solid line), which not allows vehicles to change lanes between their separated lanes; (e) Dot line (dotted line), which allows vehicles to change lanes between their separated lanes; (f) Div line (Division line), which reminds the driver of the change in the number of lanes and prohibit driving in the area.

features in public datasets [9,10]. In the lane detection task, most lane detection datasets [11–13] provide the data collected from the vehicle perspective, which can not provide the information of distant road. Under these limitations, lane detection methods [14–16] usually divide lanes by predicting lane boundaries, which overcomes the problem of lack of road information, but this will lead to further neglect of road information. Compared with the vehicle perspective, the aerial view can provide farther and wider road information. However, collecting the aerial view data requires certain hardware equipment conditions, which is more difficult than collecting data from the camera in the car.

To provide the complete road semantic information and reduce the hardware requirements, we work with a third-party organization to collect the road data by overhead camera. Thanks to the rotation and zoom functions of cameras, the data we collected can provide information of different perspectives and visual fields of the same road section, which can enrich the diversity of scenes. Expressway images can usually be divided into two categories according to the scene: long straights, which has no lane merging and separation on the road; Ramp intersection, which has merging and separation of ramps. By analyzing the road information of these two scenarios, we divide the roads into six categories, as shown in Fig. 1.

Since the process of judging traffic violations often depends on accurate and complete lanes, we use two methods to improve the accuracy of the boundary prediction: One is to use Erosion Loss (ER Loss) [17], which can strengthens the model's learning of the boundary. The other is to post-process the prediction of the model by Fully-Connected Conditional Random Fields (Fully-Connected

CRFs) [18], which can more accurately show the detailed boundary information and fill the internal cavity.

2   Related Work

2.1   Lane Detection Datasets

In the field of lane detection, there have been some vehicle view datasets [11–13] that are usually used in automatic driving tasks. Tusimple [11] is a dataset containing 6498 images of American highway roads, which are taken under different weather conditions. Pan et al. [13] proposed a more complex dataset with larger traffic flow, which collected 133235 images. Unlike those two datasets, ELAS [12] labeled not only the road boundary, but also the road and road center to meet the requirements of some challenging tasks. Although ELAS [12] adds annotation methods, due to the limitation of vehicle perspective, these datasets generally can not provide complete details of edge roads and opposite lanes.

2.2   Semantic Segmentation Models Based on DCNNs

With the development of deep learning architecture [19,20], those models [2–4] combined with DCNNs have achieved excellent performance in semantic segmentation tasks. After the full convolution network architecture is proposed, an ordinary DCNN can be transformed into a full convolution neural network to effectively utilize DCNNs' ability of extracting high-level semantic information, such as U-Net [4,5], FPN [6] and DeepLab [7,8]. To extract multi-scale features and obtain the context information of images, those models usually includes two main processes: encoder and decoder. The multi-layer convolution, like ResNet [20], is often used as encoder to extract deep features. After the multi-layer convolution operation, the size of the feature image will gradually be reduced and cannot adapt to the size of the original image. To solve this problem, the decoder restores the size of the feature map through a certain number of upsampling. The process can improve the classification accuracy of detailed pixels.

2.3   Hausdorff Distance Loss

Hausdorff Distance (HD) [21] refers to calculating the maximum value of the nearest distance from all points in one set to another set, but it is not easy to optimize because of its non-convexity. To solve the problem, Karimi et al. [17] proposed three variables based on HD that combine measurement use cases (Distance Transforms, Erosion, Circular/Spherical Kernels) and ensure that the loss function is easy to handle. In the Distance Transforms of an image, the value of each pixel is equal to its distance from the target of interest in the image. This distance can accurately represent HD, but it has a large amount of calculation and will cause computational redundancy. To calculate HD more efficiently, Erosion Loss makes a fast approximate estimation of HD through corrosion operation, which is easier to train and will meet the demand for the accuracy of loss function in model training.

Table 1. Proportion of different road sections and road scenes in the original data.

	Long straights	Ramp intersection	Total
Urban road	5.29%	6.38%	11.67%
Expressway	29.46%	58.87%	88.33%
Total	34.75%	65.25%	

2.4   Conditional Random Fields

Conditional Random Fields (CRFs) [22] are frameworks for segmenting and labeling sequence data. Hanna [23] Proposed a method to improve the training performance of CRFs by using numerical optimization technology, which greatly enhances the practicability of CRFs in labeled sequence data. In terms of semantic segmentation, koltun et al. [18] realized efficient inference using Fully-Connected CRFs, and then DeepLabv1 [7] used Fully-Connected CRFs as post-processing of prediction results to improve the sharpness of prediction boundary.

3   Multi-class Lane Semantic Segmentation

3.1   Expressway Dataset Based on Aerial View

Data Acquisition. This paper collects 6075 road images by using overhead cameras in several different sections. Figure 2 shows some of the original data we collected. The images can be divided into urban sections (a, b) and high-speed sections (c-l) according to the road sections, and can also be divided into long straight lanes (b, e-h) and ramp intersection (a, c, d, i, j) according to the road scenes. The proportion of road sections and road scenes of all original data is shown in Table 1. At the same time, the original data we collected can also be divided into three parts according to the field of view: small field of view, as shown in the Fig. 2 (c, d); unidirectional field of view, as shown in the Fig. 2 (a); two way vision, as shown in the Fig. 2 (e, f, i, j).

Data Cleaning. According to the analysis of various scenarios of the original data, Fig. 2 shows five situations that we need to clean. The conditions to be screened are: *Urban scene.* The roads and traffic conditions in the urban scene are overly complex; *Small visual fields.* Images with small visual fields can not effectively provide the spatial relationship between lanes and obtain semantic information; *Recurring images.* The repeated appearance of the same image will bring redundancy to the data and affect the scene balance; *The same road section and perspective.* To prevent redundancy caused by images of the same road section and perspective, we limit the number of those images to no more than 5; *Fuzzy images.* Fuzzy images can not provide clear lane boundaries, which will seriously affect the learning of boundary prediction.

After data cleaning, our dataset contains a total of 1510 images. We divide the data into two sets for training and testing, in which the training set contains

Fig. 2. Raw data display. There are five situations in the original data that need to be cleaned. Among them, (a, b) represents the urban scene, (c, d) represents the small field of view scene, (e–h) represents the repeated images, (i, j) represents the images of the same road section and angle of view, (k, l) represents the fuzzy images. According to our cleaning method, those filtered images are marked by a red rectangle separately.

Table 2. The proportion of pictures of the two scene types in total pictures.

Scene type	Training set	Test set
Long straights	26.25%	26.67%
Ramp intersection	73.75%	73.33%

1370 pictures and the test set contains 140 pictures. When splitting, we ensure that the pictures in the test set and the pictures in the training set are not in the same perspective of the same road section, and provide corresponding labels for the training set and the test set. According to the road scene, as shown in Table 2, the proportion of long straights and ramp intersection in training set and test set is both about 3:7, which ensures the consistency of sample proportion and shows that the dataset contains abundant complex scenes.

Data Annotations. Semantic segmentation under occlusion often requires additional conditions, such as spatio-temporal semantic information provided by continuous frames [24]. Considering that the camera on the highway cannot provide continuous stream, we need to take the part obscured by the vehicle as the background. On the other hand, to achieve the requirements of strict differentiation of different lanes, our annotations need to separate different lanes through a complete lane boundary. So we need to label complete dotted lines. Figure 3 shows the two different annotation methods of occlusion, and the difference between our dataset and the other common datasets in dotted line annotation.

Fig. 3. Different annotation methods for occluded scenes and dotted lines. The first from the left is the method including occlusion; The second is the way to label only visible roads; The third indicates that only the solid part of the dotted line is labeled; The last indicates that the complete dotted line is labeled.

Table 3. The proportion of area and instances of each category annotation. The instance area of each class can be expressed by the ratio of area to the number of instances. According to IoU of each class as shown in Table 5, it can be found that there is a negative correlation between the ratio and the prediction results.

Annotation categories	Proportion of area	Proportion of instance
Ord lane	50.83%	28.28%
Ramp	20.01%	7.33%
Eme lane	15.44%	13.32%
Dot line	2.18%	15.68%
Sol line	3.54%	29.35%
Div line	8.00%	6.04%

According to the annotation method proposed by us, Fig. 1 shows in detail the six classification annotation we have completed on our Expressway Dataset. As shown in Table 3, on the basis of labeling, we analyze the area proportion and instance label proportion of six categories in the dataset, which provides a data basis for the Eq. 3 we proposed to set category training weight.

3.2 DeepLab-ERFC

On our Expressway Dataset, some semantic segmentation models [5,6,8,25,26] can achieve certain results, but the prediction effect of the boundary is poor and will produce certain holes. In order to further improve the segmentation effect, as shown in the Fig. 4, we added the Erosion Loss (ER Loss) [17] to strengthen the boundary learning of the model, and added a Full-Connected CRF [18] to effectively remove internal holes.

ER Loss. We define the prediction segmentation matrix as p and the real partition matrix as g. The corrosion operation is to utilize the structural element with calculation radius r completely corroding the intersection of p and g, and the number of calculation is expressed as $ER((p - g)^2, r)$. Then, ER Loss is defined as a form of relaxed loss function:

$$Loss_{ER}(p, g) = \frac{1}{|G|} \sum_{G} \sum_{r=1}^{R} (ER((p - g)^2, r)r^{\alpha}) \tag{1}$$

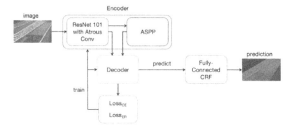

Fig. 4. DeepLab-ERFC uses atrous convolutionary layers to extract features of different sizes, and adds a simple decoder integrating semantic features and low-level features.

In Eq. 1, the parameter g represents the ground truth; The parameter α determines the correction degree of large segmentation errors, which default setting is 2.0.

In training, we retained the Cross-Enterprise Loss (CE Loss). Therefore, the final definition of the loss function is:

$$Loss = \frac{1}{|C|} \sum_{c=1}^{C} (w_c(1 - w_{ER}) \times Loss_{CE}(p, g)) \ + \ w_{ER} \times Loss_{ER}(p, g) \quad (2)$$

In Eq. 2, w_{ER} represents the weight of ER Loss in calculating the loss function; w_c represents the weight of CE Loss for different categories. w_c is defined as:

$$w_c = W_{max} - \frac{W_{max} - 1}{A_{max} - A_{min}}(A_c - A_{min}) \quad (3)$$

In Eq. 3, A_{max} represents the largest area in the average marked area of each category; A_{min} represents the smallest area in the average marked area of each category; A_c represents the average marked area of category c; W_{max} represents the maximum value of the value range of the weight. By using the Eq. 3, we limit the value range of categories' weights to $[1, W_{max}]$.

Fully-Connected CRFs. In modern DCNNs architecture, local-range CRFs can obtain more boundary details to smooth the target boundary, but still lose some fine structures. In this paper, we use a more effective method to recover the details of the target boundary: Fully-Connected CRFs [18]. The energy function defined by the model:

$$E(x) = \sum_{i} (\varphi_i(x_i) \ + \ \sum_{j,j \neq i} \varphi_{ij}(x_i, x_j)) \quad (4)$$

In Eq. 4, x represents all pixels in the label. $\varphi_i(x_i)$ is defined as $-log P(x_i)$, where $P(x_i)$ is the classification probability of pixel i. $\varphi_{ij}(x_i, x_j)$ is defined as $\sum_{c=1}^{K}(w_c \times k_c(f_i, f_j))$, where K represents the number of categories, w_c represents the weight set for Gaussian kernel function, and f_i represents the feature extracted at pixel i. Gaussian kernel function k_c comprehensively considers the position relationship and color intensity, which is defined as:

$$k_c = w_1 exp(-\frac{||p_i - p_j||^2}{2\mu_\alpha^2} - \frac{||I_i - I_j||^2}{2\mu_\beta^2}) + w_2 exp(-\frac{||p_i - p_j||^2}{2\mu_\gamma^2}) \qquad (5)$$

In Eq. 5, p is the pixel position, I is the intensity of RGB color and the domain of Gaussian kernel is respectively adjusted by μ_α, μ_β and μ_γ.

3.3   Update Strategy

During the calculation of the Fully-Connected CRF [18], we need to deal with the semantic segmentation predicted by DeepLab-ERFC. As shown in Fig. 5 (b), there is some road information inside the Dot line and Div line, which will cannot be updated as parts of lanes. Thus, we propose a update strategy: First, only the Ord lane, Eme lane and Ramp will be calculated by Fully-Connected CRF. Then, only the background part of the prediction is updated. Figure 5 (c) shows the results processed by our update strategy. It can be seen that the prediction results of the three lane categories can not only ensure that the road parts in the dotted line and diversion line are not affected, but also reduce the holes in them.

Fig. 5. The first from the left represents the prediction results before the Full-Connected CRF processing; The second represents the prediction results of Full-Connected CRF processing directly for all categories; The last represents the prediction results processed according to the update strategy we proposed.

4   Experiment

We train the model with Stochastic gradient descent (SGD) optimizer. The momentum and weight decay of SGD are set to 0.9 and 10^{-4} respectively, while the learning rate of backbone is 0.001 and that of classifier is 0.01. In Eq. 2, w_{ER} set to 0.5 and settings of w_c are shown in Table 4.

4.1   Comparison Experiment

We compare different loss functions and their combinations evaluated by mean Intersection over Union (mIoU), as shown in Table 5. The results show that CE

Table 4. The weight of each category corresponding to CE Loss. All weights are calculated by Eq. 3, where W_{max} is set to 3.3.

	Background	Ord lane	Eme lane	Ramp	Sol line	Dot line	Div line
Weight	1.000	1.000	2.138	2.610	3.191	3.300	2.822

Loss + ER Loss achieves the best prediction result, which is 83.6% mIoU, and its training time in each iteration is about 2.56 s less than CE Loss + DT Loss. According to the update strategy we proposed, the Full-Connected CRF is added to all loss function combinations respectively and improve each combination's prediction about 0.4% mIoU.

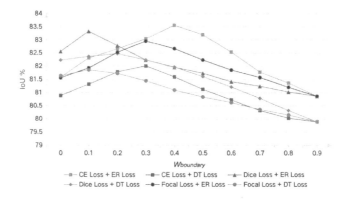

Fig. 6. Comparison of different $W_{boundary}$ of six loss combinations. Where $W_{boundary}$ means the weight of ER Loss or DT Loss, and the weight of the other three losses is $1 - W_{boundary}$.

For the weights of different loss combinations, we conducted a comparative experiment with the weight ratio of boundary loss from 0 to 1 and the step size of 0.1, and the specific results are shown in the Fig. 6. The results show that the traditional loss function combined with the boundary loss function can significantly improve the effect, and CE Loss + ER Loss obtains the best result under the $W_{boundary}$ setting of 0.4.

4.2 Evaluation on Expressway Dataset

We trained five other semantic segmentation models [5,6,8,25,26] on our Expressway Dataset, and evaluated those models on our test set, IoU of each category and mIoU are shown in Table 6. The results show that our DeepLab-ERFC achieves the best results in multiple categories, reaching 83.9% mIoU. Especially in the two categories of Sol line and Dot line, the model can increase IoU to more than 70%.

Table 5. IoU of each class, mIoU and training efficiency of the three loss functions. We also added a Full-Connected CRF to each model after training to compare the improvement effect, where ✓ indicates the addition of the Full-Connected CRF.

Loss function	Fully-Connected CRF	Background	Ord lane	Eme lane	Ramp	Sol line	Dot line	Div line	mIoU	Training efficiency(s/it)
CE Loss		92.8	90.3	82.0	87.7	67.6	58.8	84.8	80.6	4.31
CE Loss	✓	93.5	90.7	83.2	88.1	67.6	58.8	84.8	81.0	
DT Loss		92.6	89.4	80.6	87.7	69.6	60.8	83.9	80.7	7.98
DT Loss	✓	93.1	90.2	81.9	88.5	69.6	60.8	83.9	81.1	
CE Loss + DT Loss		92.7	90.2	82.9	89.0	70.7	64.2	84.4	82.0	8.84
CE Loss + DT Loss	✓	93.3	90.7	84.8	89.8	70.7	64.2	84.4	82.3	
ER Loss		92.8	90.4	82.0	87.7	68.0	58.9	84.7	80.6	5.68
ER Loss	✓	**93.5**	91.0	83.4	88.3	68.0	58.9	84.7	81.1	
CE Loss + ER Loss		92.9	90.7	83.9	89.2	72.1	70.7	85.4	83.6	6.28
CE Loss + ER Loss	✓	93.4	**91.2**	**84.8**	**90.0**	**72.1**	**70.7**	**85.4**	**83.9**	

Table 6. IoU of each class and mIoU of the six semantic segmentation models.

Model	Background	Ord lane	Eme lane	Ramp	Sol line	Dot line	Div line	mIoU
FPN [6]	93.6	86.1	86.0	86.7	64.3	64.2	82.8	80.5
DeepLabv3+ [8]	94.6	88.1	85.0	87.2	64.3	63.7	83.7	80.9
Unet++ [5]	**97.7**	86.6	82.3	80.1	66.7	67.7	83.4	80.6
PAN [25]	91.7	89.3	**85.7**	87.7	63.1	61.6	83.1	80.3
MAnet [26]	93.8	86.1	83.7	89.5	65.9	65.4	83.4	81.1
DeepLab-ERFC (ours)	93.4	**91.2**	84.8	**90.0**	**72.1**	**70.7**	**85.4**	**83.9**

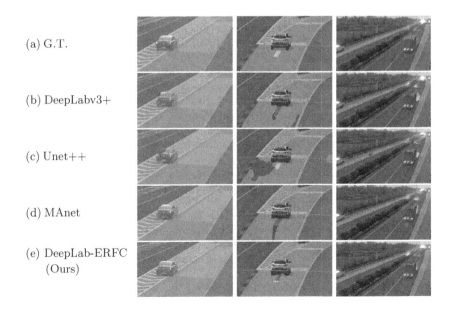

(a) G.T.

(b) DeepLabv3+

(c) Unet++

(d) MAnet

(e) DeepLab-ERFC (Ours)

Fig. 7. Comparison of DeepLabv3+, Unet++, MAnet and DeepLab-ERFC.

Figure 7 contains the prediction results of some test samples on our test set. From the results, we can see: In the left column, our model can predict the vehicle boundary more accurately; In the middle column, our model can better inhibit the generation of cavities; In the right column, our model can provide more accurate prediction for lanes with smaller scale in the distance.

5 Conclusion

In this paper, we complete the collection, cleaning, semantic analysis, category classification and annotation of the Expressway Dataset based on Aerial View. Then, we propose DeepLab-ERFC which added ER Loss and a Fully-Connected CRF. According to the actual results of the Full-Connected CRF processing, we also propose an update strategy to ensure that the connectivity of Dot line and Div line is not destroyed. It is evaluated with other five models [5,6,8,25,26] on our test set and the results show that DeepLab-ERFC could effectively improve the accuracy of boundary prediction and reduce the holes in the prediction results. In the future, we plan to complete the instance segmentation task based on the Expressway Dataset, or try to apply the annotation method in this paper to public vehicle perspective datasets.

References

1. Zhao, B., Feng, J., Wu, X., Yan, S.: A survey on deep learning-based fine-grained object classification and semantic segmentation. Int. J. Autom. Comput. **14**(2), 119–135 (2017). https://doi.org/10.1007/s11633-017-1053-3
2. Ferianc, M., Manocha, D., Fan, H., Rodrigues, M.: ComBiNet: compact convolutional Bayesian neural network for image segmentation. In: Farkaš, I., Masulli, P., Otte, S., Wermter, S. (eds.) ICANN 2021. LNCS, vol. 12893, pp. 483–494. Springer, Cham (2021). https://doi.org/10.1007/978-3-030-86365-4_39
3. Wang, J., MacKenzie, J.D., Ramachandran, R., Chen, D.Z.: A deep learning approach for semantic segmentation in histology tissue images. In: Ourselin, S., Joskowicz, L., Sabuncu, M.R., Unal, G., Wells, W. (eds.) MICCAI 2016. LNCS, vol. 9901, pp. 176–184. Springer, Cham (2016). https://doi.org/10.1007/978-3-319-46723-8_21
4. Weng, W., Zhu, X.: INet: convolutional networks for biomedical image segmentation. IEEE Access **9**, 16591–16603 (2021)
5. Zhou, Z., Siddiquee, M., Tajbakhsh, N., Liang, J.: UNet++: redesigning skip connections to exploit multiscale features in image segmentation. IEEE Trans. Med. Imaging **39**(6), 1856–1867 (2020)
6. Lin, T.Y., Dollar, P., Girshick, R., He, K., Hariharan, B., Belongie, S.: Feature pyramid networks for object detection. IEEE Computer Society (2017)
7. Chen, L.C., Papandreou, G., Kokkinos, I., Murphy, K., Yuille, A.L.: Semantic image segmentation with deep convolutional nets and fully connected CRFs. Comput. Sci. **6**, 357–361 (2014)
8. Chen, L.-C., Zhu, Y., Papandreou, G., Schroff, F., Adam, H.: Encoder-decoder with atrous separable convolution for semantic image segmentation. In: Ferrari, V., Hebert, M., Sminchisescu, C., Weiss, Y. (eds.) ECCV 2018. LNCS, vol. 11211, pp. 833–851. Springer, Cham (2018). https://doi.org/10.1007/978-3-030-01234-2_49

9. Lin, T.Y., et al.: Microsoft COCO: common objects in context. In: Fleet, D., Pajdla, T., Schiele, B., Tuytelaars, T. (eds.) ECCV 2014. LNCS, vol. 8693, pp. 740–755. Springer, Cham (2014). https://doi.org/10.1007/978-3-319-10602-1_48

10. Cordts, M., Omran, M., Ramos, S., Rehfeld, T., Schiele, B.: The cityscapes dataset for semantic urban scene understanding. In: IEEE (2016)

11. The tuSimple lane challenge. http://benchmark.tusimple.ai/

12. Berriel, R.F., Aguiar, E.D., Souza, A.D., Oliveira-Santos, T.: Ego-Lane Analysis System (ELAS): dataset and algorithms. arXiv:1806.05984 (2017)

13. Pan, X., Shi, J., Luo, P., Wang, X., Tang, X.: Spatial as deep: spatial CNN for traffic scene understanding. arXiv:1712.06080 (2017)

14. Liang, D., Guo, Y.-C., Zhang, S.-K., Mu, T.-J., Huang, X.: Lane detection: a survey with new results. J. Comput. Sci. Technol. **35**(3), 493–505 (2020). https://doi.org/10.1007/s11390-020-0476-4

15. Fan, R., Dahnoun, N.: Real-time stereo vision-based lane detection system. Meas. Sci. Technol. **29**(7), 074005 (2018)

16. Lee, S., et al.: VPGNet: vanishing point guided network for lane and road marking detection and recognition. In: IEEE (2017)

17. Karimi, D., Salcudean, S.E.: Reducing the Hausdorff distance in medical image segmentation with convolutional neural networks. IEEE Trans. Med. Imaging **39**(2), 499–513 (2020)

18. Krhenbühl, P., Koltun, V.: Efficient inference in fully connected CRFs with Gaussian edge potentials. In: NIPS (2011)

19. Machado, P., Cosma, G., McGinnity, T.M.: NatCSNN: a convolutional spiking neural network for recognition of objects extracted from natural images. In: Tetko, I.V., Kurková, V., Karpov, P., Theis, F. (eds.) ICANN 2019. LNCS, vol. 11727, pp. 351–362. Springer, Cham (2019). https://doi.org/10.1007/978-3-030-30487-4_28

20. He, K., Zhang, X., Ren, S.: Deep residual learning for image recognition. In: IEEE (2016)

21. Taha, A.A., Hanbury, A.: Metrics for evaluating 3D medical image segmentation: analysis, selection, and tool. BMC Med. Imaging **15**(29), 1–28 (2015)

22. Lafferty, J.: Conditional random fields: probabilistic models for segmenting and labeling sequence data. In: ICML (2001)

23. Wallach, H.: Efficient training of conditional random fields (2002)

24. Ding, M., Wang, Z., Zhou, B., Shi, J., Lu, Z., Luo, P.: Every frame counts: joint learning of video segmentation and optical flow. In: Proceedings of the AAAI Conference on Artificial Intelligence, vol. 34, no. 7, pp. 10713–10720 (2020)

25. Li, H., Xiong, P., An, J., Wang, L.: Pyramid attention network for semantic segmentation. arXiv:1805.10180 (2018)

26. Fan, T., Wang, G., Li, Y., Wang, H.: MA-Net: a multi-scale attention network for liver and tumor segmentation. IEEE Access **8**, 179656–179665 (2020)

Mutil-level Local Alignment and Semantic Matching Network for Image-Text Retrieval

Zhukai Jiang and Zhichao Lian[✉]

Nanjing University of Science and Technology, Nanjing, China
lzcts@163.com

Abstract. Image-text retrieval is a challenging task in the field of vision and language. The existing methods mainly compute the similarity of image-text pairs by the alignment between image regions and text words. Although these methods based on fine-grained local features achieve good results, these methods only explore the correspondence between salient objects and ignore the deep semantic information expressed by the whole image and text. Thus, we propose a novel multi-level local alignment and semantic matching network (MLASM) that introduces a multi-level semantic matching module after local alignment. This module supplies our model with more sufficient semantic information to understand the complex correlations between images and texts. Experiment results on two benchmark datasets Flickr30K and MS-COCO show that our MLASM achieves state-of-the-art performance.

Keywords: Local region-word alignment · Visual-semantic embedding · Multi-level features · Image-text retrieval

1 Introduction

In the past few decades, with the explosion of multimodal data on social networks, cross-modal information processing has become increasingly important. In all modal of data, images and texts occupy dominant positions, thus the understanding of vision-and-language has attracted extensive attention from researchers. Thanks to the rapid development of deep learning technology, many vision-and-language tasks have achieved remarkable results, such as image caption [2], text-to-image synthesis [20], visual question answering [1] and image-text retrieval [5]. In this paper, we focus on the task of image-text retrieval, which refers to measuring the visual-semantic similarity between image-text pairs.

Existing image-text retrieval methods focus on learning a deep neural network to explore the potential relevance between image-text pairs. A common idea is to mapping images and texts into a joint representation space to obtain the global representation of image-text pairs, and calculating image-text similarity in this space. Based on some excellent deep feature extraction networks

E. Pimenidis et al. (Eds.): ICANN 2022, LNCS 13531, pp. 212–224, 2022.
https://doi.org/10.1007/978-3-031-15934-3_18

Fig. 1. For image-text pairs A and B with similar scenes, only adopting the alignment of local salient objects and ignoring semantic information of entire image or text will cause false matches.

(VGGt [17], ResNet [6], GRU [4]), this method has achieved some achievements [5,23]. With the development of research, people focus on the more fine-grained local region-word alignment method. In fact, the text corresponding to an image is often the description of some regions in the image. Therefore, the methods [3,11,22] based on local region-word alignment achieve good results. However, the local alignment method still has some disadvantages. Taking two image-text pairs with similar scenes shown in Fig. 1 as an example, only local alignment will cause the wrong matching. Text B contains more similar salient objects, "man", "table" and "pizza", so text B and image A will get higher local alignment similarity. However, the core semantics of image A is taking pictures and we can see that the background of the image A is a restaurant, thus text A should be the more matching text. Intuitively, we should consider not only the alignment of significant objects but also the matching of overall semantics when doing retrieval.

To solve this problem, we propose a **M**ulti-level **L**ocal **A**lignment and **S**emantic **M**atching Network (**MLASM**) for image-text retrieval. Our method builds on classic local region-word alignment method SCAN [11] and adds a multi-level semantic matching module. Multi-level is for image data, because image local features are fine-grained representations of salient regions of the image. These local features do not contain the background information in the original image that is helpful to understand the image content and lack a certain integrity. Therefore, we need the global features of the entire image for sufficient semantic understanding. Our main contribution is to propose a mutil-level semantic matching module that achieves accurate semantic matching at the global level. Although there have been some attempts [8,12,21] to provide additional global semantic information for the network based on local alignment, these methods have ignored the role of vision-semantic embedding. Without complex transformation, the images and texts can be embedded into the potential representation space by using the embedding layer, and the extraction ability of neural network itself can be used to obtain excellent semantic matching results. We conduct sufficient experiments on two benchmark datasets MS-COCO [14] and Flicker30K [15], experiment results show that our MLASM achieves state-of-the-art performance. Code for the implementation is at: https://github.com/xiaohu306/MLASM.

2 Related Work

Existing image-text retrieval methods can be roughly divided into three categories: (1) global visual-semantic embedding aiming to mapping images and texts into a latent embedding space, (2) local region-word alignment aiming to explore the correspondence between image regions and text words, (3) hybrid methods aiming to match at both local and global levels.

Global Visual-Semantic Embedding. VSE++ [5] proposed the triplet loss based on hard negatives, which greatly improved the model performance. DSCMR [23] minimized discrimination loss in label space and common representation space, and eliminated cross-modal differences in multimedia data in common representation space using a weight sharing strategy. DSRAN [19] utilized the graph attention module to capture both the object-level semantic relations and global-regional semantic relations. Although these methods have achieved some early success, coarse-grained global embedding lacks fine-grained interaction and understanding between image-text pairs.

Local Region-Word Alignment. SCAN [11] proposed a stacked cross attention mechanism which aligns each regions with all words and aligns each words with all regions, and aggregated the local similarities into the overall similarity of the images and texts. IMRAM [3] utilized an iterative matching method to capture the deeper correspondences between regions and words on the basis of SCAN. CAAN [22] simultaneously utilized global inter-modal alignments and intra-modal correlations to discover latent semantic relations.

Hybrid Methods. In order to fully explore the complex correspondence between image-text pairs, there have been some studies [7,8,12,18,21] to do image-text matching at both local and global levels. Specifically, BSSAN [7] added the word to regions attention and the object to word attention in each path to compute attention-based attention. VSRN [12] performed global semantic reasoning on region features with relationship information, which can select the discriminative information and filter out unimportant one to obtain the final representation for the whole image. SHAN [8] utilized progressive alignment strategy to perform local-to-local, global-to-local and global-to-global alignments, which provides enough semantic information for model to understand complex correspondence between image-text pairs.

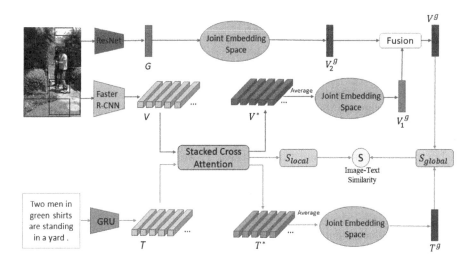

Fig. 2. The framework of our proposed MLASM.

3   Method

Figure 2 is our proposed network framework, given an image-text pair, our MLASM first use the extracted local features for local region-word alignment and obtain the local alignment score. After that, the global representation of the image-text pair is obtained through three embedding layers to calculate the global semantic matching score. The addition of local alignment score and global semantic matching score is our final similarity. We will introduce the details of our proposed MLASM from the following four parts.

3.1   Generic Representation Extraction

Image Representation. For each input image, we follow DSRAN [19] to extract K region-level features $F = \{f_1, f_2, .., f_K\}, f_i \in \mathbb{R}^{2048}$, with the Faster R-CNN [16] model pretrained on Visual Genomes [10] dataset. Then we add a full-connect layer to transform them into D-dimensional vectors and further normalize them as local region representations $V = \{v_1, v_2, .., v_K\}, v_i \in \mathbb{R}^d$.

Besides, we follow vse++ [5] to extract image global feature $G_0 \in \mathbb{R}^{4096}$ with the pretrained ResNet152 model. Then we add a full-connect layer to transform it into D-dimensional vector $G \in \mathbb{R}^D$.

Text Representation. For each input text, we follow DSRAN [19] to split it into L words with tokenization technique. For the j-th word in the text, we represent it with a one-hot vector showing the index of the word in the vocabulary, then leverage a pre-trained word embedding model Glove to embed the word into a 300-dimensional vector x_j. Next, we employ a bidirectional GRU to enhance the word-level features. Finally, we can obtain the normalized word-level features $T = \{t_1, t_2, .., t_L\}, t_i \in \mathbb{R}^D$.

3.2   Local Region-Word Alignment

The Stacked Cross Attention [11] method is the first method to match the image-text pairs with the attention mechanism, which has been proven effective since it accurately measures the interaction between image regions and sentence words. In our method, we follow this attention module for region-word alignment.

For region features V and word features T, we first compute the similarity for each pairwise region and word as:

$$s_{ij} = v_i^T t_j, i \in [1, K], j \in [1, L]. \tag{1}$$

Here, s_{ij} represents the similarity of i-th region and the j-th word. For Image-Text Stack Cross Attention, each region feature is used as a query to assign weights over the L words. We first normalize the similarity matrix as:

$$\bar{s}_{ij} = \frac{[s_{ij}]_+}{\sqrt{\sum_{i=1}^{K}[s_{ij}]_+^2}}, \tag{2}$$

where $[x]_+ \equiv max(x, 0)$.Then we compute the weighted combination of all the words to get the region-attended text representations $T^* = \{t_1^*, t_2^*, ..., t_k^*\}$ for each region, i.e.

$$t_i^* = \sum_{j=1}^{L} \alpha_{ij} t_j, \quad \alpha_{ij} = \frac{exp(\lambda_1 \bar{s}_{ij})}{\sum_{j=1}^{L} exp(\lambda_1 \bar{s}_{ij})}, \tag{3}$$

where λ_1 is the temperature parameter of the softmax function.

Likewise, for Text-Image Stack Cross Attention, each word feature is used as a query to assign weights over the K regions. We normalize the similarity matrix as:

$$\tilde{s}_{ij} = \frac{[s_{ij}]_+}{\sqrt{\sum_{j=1}^{L}[s_{ij}]_+^2}}, \tag{4}$$

then we compute the weighted combination of all the regions to get the word-attended image representations $V^* = \{v_1^*, v_2^*, ..., v_L^*\}$ for each region, i.e.

$$v_j^* = \sum_{i=1}^{K} \beta_{ij} v_i, \quad \beta_{ij} = \frac{exp(\lambda_2 \tilde{s}_{ij})}{\sum_{i=1}^{K} exp(\lambda_2 \tilde{s}_{ij})}, \tag{5}$$

where λ_2 is the temperature parameter of the softmax function.

For image I and text T, we define local Image-Text matching scores and local Text-Image matching scores as:

$$S_{I2T}(I, T) = \frac{\sum_{i=1}^{K} R(v_i, t_i^*)}{K},$$

$$S_{T2I}(I, T) = \frac{\sum_{j=1}^{L} R(t_j, v_j^*)}{L}, \tag{6}$$

where $R(x, y)$ computes the cosine similarity of two vectors as:

$$R(x, y) = \frac{x^T y}{\|x\| \|y\|}. \tag{7}$$

Finally, the region-word alignment score between image I and text T is defined as follows:

$$S_{local}(I, T) = \mu_1 * S_{I2T}(I, T) + (1 - \mu_1) * S_{T2I}(I, T). \tag{8}$$

3.3 Multi-level Semantic Matching

In this part, we utilize the local features enhanced by stack cross-modal attention and the feature of the entire image for visual-semantic embedding. Then we utilize the global representation of image and text for semantic matching to obtain the global matching score.

Specifically, for the region-attended text representations T^*, we compute its average vector as $\overline{T}^* = \frac{\sum_{i=1}^{K} t_i^*}{K}$. Then let the average vector input into the joint embedding space defined by linear projection to get the final text global representation T^g:

$$T^g = W_t^T \overline{T}^*, \ W_t \in \mathbb{R}^{D \times D}, \tag{9}$$

where W_t is a learnable embedding matrix.

For the image part, we compute the average vector of word-attended image representations as $\overline{V}^* = \frac{\sum_{j=1}^{L} v_j^*}{L}$ and let it into the joint embedding space:

$$V_1^g = W_v^T \overline{V}^*, W_v \in \mathbb{R}^{D \times D}. \tag{10}$$

where W_v is a learnable embedding matrix. The V_1^g we get is the global feature aggregated from several salient region features, which lacks the image background information and some unimportant but useful information to understand the image. Thus, we also let the feature of entire image G into the joint embedding space:

$$V_2^g = W_g^T G, W_g \in \mathbb{R}^{D \times D}, \tag{11}$$

where W_g is a learnable embedding matrix.

Finally, we use an adaptive gated fusion layer to get the final image global representation V^g:

$$\begin{aligned} V^g &= (1 - t) * V_1^g + t * V_2^g, \\ t &= \sigma(W \, cat(V_1^g, V_2^g) + b), \end{aligned} \tag{12}$$

where W and b are the fully-connected layer parameters, σ is the sigmoid function, $cat()$ denotes concatenation operation.

The global matching score between image I and text T is also defined by cosine similarity:

$$S_{global}(I, T) = R(V^g, T^g). \tag{13}$$

3.4   Loss Function

According to the local and global matching score obtained earlier, the final matching score between image I and text T can be defined as follows:

$$S(I,T) = \mu_2 * S_{local}(I,T) + (1 - \mu_2) * S_{global}(I,T).\tag{14}$$

Then, we adopt a hinge-based triplet ranking loss with emphasis on hard negatives [5]. The loss function is defined as:

$$L = [m + S(I,\widehat{T}) - S(I,T)]_+ + [m + S(\widehat{I},T) - S(I,T)]_+,\tag{15}$$

where $[x]_+ \equiv max(x,0)$, m is a margin parameter, $\widehat{T} = argmax_{t \neq T}S(I,t)$ and $\widehat{I} = argmax_{i \neq I}S(i,T)$ stand for hardest negatives in a mini-batch.

4   Experiments

4.1   Dataset and Evaluation Metric

We evaluate our model on the MS-COCO and Flickr30K datasets. MS-COCO contains 123,287 images, and each image is annotated with five text descriptions. We follow VSE++ [5] to split the dataset into 5000 images for validation, 5000 images for testing and the rest 113287 images for training. Results on MS-COCO are reported by averaging over 5 folds of 1K test images. Flickr30K contains 31,000 images, and each image is annotated with five text descriptions. We follow VSE++ [5] to split the dataset into 1000 images for validation, 1000 images for testing and the rest 29,000 images for training.

For image-text retrieval, we measure the performance by Recall at K (R@K) defined as the proportion of queries whose ground-truth is ranked within the top K. We follow DSRAN [19] to adopt R@1, R@5, R@10 and Rsum as our evaluation metrics.

4.2   Implementation Details

To validate the effectiveness of the proposed MLASM, we experiment with three of its variants: (1) MLASM-1 only use V_1^g as the final image global representation; (2) MLASM-2 only use V_2^g as the final image global representation; (3) MLASM-Full uses the fused V^g as the image global representation.

In all datasets, we set the dimension of joint embedding space D to 1024, the number of regions K to 36, max epoch to 20 and the margin m to 0.2. Parameter λ_1 is set to 4 and λ_2 is set to 9.

For the Flickr30K dataset, the learning rate is set to $2e-4$ at first and declines by ten times every 10 epochs. For MLASM-1, MLASM-2 and MLASM-Full, we set μ_1 to 0.5 and μ_2 to 0.5, 0.5, 0.6 respectively. For the MS-COCO dataset, the learning rate is set to $5e-4$ at first and declines by ten times every 10 epochs. For MLASM-1, MLASM-2 and MLASM-Full, we set μ_1 to 0.3, 0.3, 0.5 respectively and μ_2 to 0.6, 0.5, 0.8 respectively. All the experiments are performed on one NVIDIA 3090 GPU with the batch size setting to 128.

Table 1. Results on Flickr30k

Method	Image-to-Text			Text-to-Image			Rsum
	R@1	R@5	R@10	R@1	R@5	R@10	
VSE++ [5]	52.9	80.5	87.2	39.6	70.1	79.5	409.8
DSRAN [19]	74.9	94.5	97.0	58.6	85.8	91.3	502.1
SCAN [11]	67.4	90.3	95.8	48.6	77.7	85.2	465.0
CAAN [22]	70.1	91.6	97.2	52.8	79.0	87.9	478.6
IMRAM [3]	74.1	93.0	96.6	53.9	79.4	87.2	484.2
VSRN [12]	71.3	90.6	96.0	54.7	81.8	88.2	482.6
SHAN [8]	74.6	92.5	96.9	55.3	81.3	88.4	490.0
MLASM-1	**94.7**	99.4	99.7	55.6	75.3	81.9	506.7
MLASM-2	76.2	94.4	97.6	59.8	**86.2**	**92.3**	506.5
MLASM-Full	94.6	**99.5**	**99.8**	**63.5**	83.4	88.9	**529.6**

Table 2. Results on MS-COCO 1K

Method	Image-to-Text			Text-to-Image			Rsum
	R@1	R@5	R@10	R@1	R@5	R@10	
VSE++ [5]	64.6	90.0	95.7	52.0	84.3	92.0	478.6
DSRAN [19]	78.0	95.6	98.5	64.2	90.4	95.8	522.5
SCAN [11]	72.7	94.8	98.4	58.8	88.4	94.8	507.9
CAAN [22]	75.5	95.4	98.5	61.3	89.7	95.2	515.6
IMRAM [3]	76.7	95.6	98.5	61.7	89.1	95.0	516.6
VSRN [12]	76.2	94.8	98.2	62.8	89.7	95.1	516.8
SHAN [8]	76.8	96.3	98.7	62.6	89.6	95.8	519.8
MLASM-1	**93.4**	**99.3**	**99.8**	60.7	82.0	88.0	523.2
MLASM-2	76.6	95.5	98.3	63.9	92.0	96.5	522.8
MLASM-Full	82.2	97.7	99.4	**66.3**	**92.7**	**96.9**	**535.2**

4.3   Comparison with State-of-the-Art Methods

We compare our MLASM model with current state-of-the-art methods in the two benchmark datasets. As mentioned before, these compared methods can be divided into three groups (we don't compare with some pre-training methods, such as [9,13]). (1) Global Visual-Semantic Embedding Methods: VSE++ [5], DSRAN [19];(2)Local Region-Word Alignment Methods: SCAN [11], CAAN [22], IMRAM [3]; (3) Hybrid Methods: SHAN [8], VSRN [12].

Table 1 and Table 2 are the experimental results on Flickr30k dataset and MS-COCO dataset respectively, and the highest performance of each metric is made bold. We can see that our method achieves the best results on both datasets. Compared to the current best method DSRAN [19], our MLASM-

Table 3. Results of ablation studies on Flickr30K

Index	Ablation model				Image-to-text			Text-to-image			Rsum
	Loc	Glo	Glo emb	Glove	R@1	R@5	R@10	R@1	R@5	R@10	
①	✓				63.7	88.4	94.4	45.7	75.2	82.6	450.0
②	✓			✓	70.0	92.0	95.6	50.4	78.9	86.3	473.2
③	✓	✓		✓	76.8	94.9	97.9	48.5	73.9	82.6	474.6
④	✓		✓		90.1	98.2	99.2	60.0	80.2	86.0	513.7
⑤	✓		✓	✓	**94.6**	**99.5**	**99.8**	**63.5**	**83.4**	**88.9**	**529.6**

Table 4. Results of ablation studies on MS-COCO 1K

Index	Ablation model				Image-to-text			Text-to-image			Rsum
	Loc	Glo	Glo emb	Glove	R@1	R@5	R@10	R@1	R@5	R@10	
①	✓				66.1	91.9	97.3	53.2	84.6	92.6	485.7
②	✓			✓	67.6	92.6	97.5	53.7	85.4	93.2	490.0
③	✓	✓		✓	68.6	92.7	97.7	53.5	85.6	93.3	491.4
④	✓		✓		81.1	97.2	99.2	66.2	92.3	96.8	532.8
⑤	✓		✓	✓	**82.2**	**97.7**	**99.4**	**66.3**	**92.7**	**96.9**	**535.2**

Full model obtains 27.5% improvement(Rsum) on Flick30K dataset and 12.7% improvement(Rsum) on MS-COCO dataset. In addition, our MLASM-1 model can achieve a very significant improvement in image-to-text retrieval. The reason may be that the text itself is composed of several words. Local alignment can remove word information unrelated to the image content, so the text local features can better correspond to the images.

We use these features for global semantic embedding, which further expands the difference between texts belonging to different images. Different from text, artificially dividing the image into several regions will lose some semantic information expressed by the entire image, so MLASM-1 have little improvement in text-to-image retrieval. The experimental results also prove that our MLASM-Full model can obtain good improvement in image-text bidirectional retrieval.

4.4 Ablation Study and Analysis

In this section, we conduct ablation studies on both two datasets to validate the effectiveness of our proposed method. We design various ablation models, the experimental results are shown in Table 3 and Table 4. Some symbols in the table are explained as follows: 1) "Loc" denotes using local region-word alignment; 2) "Glo" means to directly use aligned local features for global semantic matching; 3) "Glo emb" means to first perform visual-semantic embedding with aligned local features and then perform semantic matching. 4) "Glove" denotes using the pre-trained word embedding Glove model. Model ⑤ ("Loc"+"Glo emb"+"Glove") is our MLASM-Full, and we denote model ② ("Loc"+"Glove") as MLASM-base.

Query	MLASM-base	MLASM-Full
Flickr30K	1. Many men in suits waiting, one man is on his cellphone. 2. A man in light colored clothing photographs a group of men wearing dark suits and hats standing around a woman dressed in a strapless gown . 3. A photographer takes a picture of a group of one girl in a pink dress and 10 boys in suits and hats .	1. A bride in a light pink dress poses for a picture with male relatives and is being photographed by a man in a cream shirt with white pants . 2. A photographer takes a picture of a group of one girl in a pink dress and 10 boys in suits and hats . 3. A man in light colored clothing photographs a group of men wearing dark suits and hats standing around a woman dressed in a strapless gown .
A gray colored dog walks in wet sand at a beach .		
MS-COCO	1. Mythical character with white horse standing on grooved surface. 2. Three different horse figurines are placed beside each other. 3. Three plastic horse figurines standing next to each other on a shelf.	1. Horse figurines next to walk on a table 2. Three different horse figurines are placed beside each other. 3. Three plastic horse figurines standing next to each other on a shelf.
An elephant in a zoo stands in front of the crowd.		

Fig. 3. Comparison of retrieval examples obtained by two models: MLASM-base and MLASM-Full. We have selected an instance of image-to-text and text-to-image retrieval for MS-COCO dataset and Flickr30K dataset respectively. We give the top-three ranking texts for every image query and top-four ranking images for every text query, and the ground-truth texts and images are marked as red. (Color figure online)

Observing the experimental results, we can find that semantic matching directly on the aligned local features does not bring significant improvement. After visual-semantic embedding, the network can learn the overall semantics expressed by local salient objects, which brings significant improvement to the base model ②. We can also see that the pre-trained word embedding model has improved significantly on Flickr30k dataset, and the improvement is small on the COCO dataset with a larger amount of data. Furthermore, our MLASM-Full achieves state-of-the-art performance with or without pre-trained word embedding model.

4.5 Visualization of Retrieval Results

In this section, we present several typical visual results of retrieved sentences and images by the two models: MLASM-base and MLASM-Full in Fig. 3.

Taking the image-to-text retrieval in Flick30K dataset as an example, MLASM-base wrongly gives the text "Many men in suits waiting, one man is on his cellphone." the highest matching score. Because MLASM-base only uses local region-word alignment, the query image and this text do have the same salient objects "men", "suits", "man" and "cellphone". In fact, the most important message expressed in this image is to take a picture of the bride. Our MLASM-Full is not disturbed by this similar text after adding the global visual-semantic embedding module, and successfully selects the correct text. Then, taking the text-to-image retrieval in MS-COCO dataset as an example, we can find that although MLASM-base ranks the ground-truth text in the third place, the top-four images all contain the important information "elephant" of the query text. Our MLASM-Full successfully matches the ground-truth text, but there are two images in the top-four that look less relevant. The possible reason is that the semantic information in the query text is complicated. When the model pays attention to the global information of "in a zoo" and "stands in front of the crowd", thus the important object "elephant" is ignored. In general, these examples demonstrate the effectiveness of our method.

5 Conclusion

In this paper, we propose a novel multi-level local alignment and semantic matching network (MLASM) to explore the complex correspondence between image-text pairs. Our MLASM can not only find the corresponding relevance of local salient objects in image-text pairs, but also achieves precise global semantic matching. We validate our models on two benchmarks Flickr30K and MS-COCO datasets. Experiment results on all datasets show that our MLASM achieves state-of-the-art performance.

Acknowledgement. This work is supported by the National Key R&D Program of China (2021YFF0602104-2).

References

1. Agrawal, A., et al.: VQA: visual question answering. Int. J. Comput. Vis. **123**, 4–31 (2015)
2. Anderson, P., et al.: Bottom-up and top-down attention for image captioning and visual question answering. In: 2018 IEEE/CVF Conference on Computer Vision and Pattern Recognition, pp. 6077–6086 (2018)
3. Chen, H., Ding, G., Liu, X., Lin, Z., Liu, J., Han, J.: IMRAM: iterative matching with recurrent attention memory for cross-modal image-text retrieval. In: 2020 IEEE/CVF Conference on Computer Vision and Pattern Recognition (CVPR), pp. 12652–12660 (2020)

4. Cho, K., et al.: Learning phrase representations using RNN encoder-decoder for statistical machine translation (2014)
5. Faghri, F., Fleet, D.J., Kiros, J.R., Fidler, S.: VSE++: improving visual-semantic embeddings with hard negatives (2018)
6. He, K., Zhang, X., Ren, S., Sun, J.: Deep residual learning for image recognition. In: 2016 IEEE Conference on Computer Vision and Pattern Recognition (CVPR), pp. 770–778 (2016)
7. Huang, F., Zhang, X., Zhao, Z., Li, Z.: Bi-directional spatial-semantic attention networks for image-text matching. IEEE Trans. Image Process. **28**(4), 2008–2020 (2019)
8. Ji, Z., Chen, K., Wang, H.: Step-wise hierarchical alignment network for image-text matching. ArXiv arXiv:2106.06509 (2021)
9. Kim, W., Son, B., Kim, I.: ViLT: vision-and-language transformer without convolution or region supervision, vol. 139, pp. 5583–5594 (2021)
10. Krishna, R., et al.: Visual genome: connecting language and vision using crowd-sourced dense image annotations. Int. J. Comput. Vis. **123**(1), 32–73 (2017). https://doi.org/10.1007/s11263-016-0981-7
11. Lee, K.H., Chen, X., Hua, G., Hu, H., He, X.: Stacked cross attention for image-text matching. ArXiv arXiv:1803.08024 (2018)
12. Li, K., Zhang, Y., Li, K., Li, Y., Fu, Y.R.: Visual semantic reasoning for image-text matching. In: 2019 IEEE/CVF International Conference on Computer Vision (ICCV), pp. 4653–4661 (2019)
13. Li, X., et al.: Oscar: object-semantics aligned pre-training for vision-language tasks. In: Vedaldi, A., Bischof, H., Brox, T., Frahm, J.-M. (eds.) ECCV 2020. LNCS, vol. 12375, pp. 121–137. Springer, Cham (2020). https://doi.org/10.1007/978-3-030-58577-8_8
14. Lin, T.Y., et al.: Microsoft COCO: common objects in context. In: Fleet, D., Pajdla, T., Schiele, B., Tuytelaars, T. (eds.) ECCV 2014. LNCS, vol. 8693, pp. 740–755. Springer, Cham (2014). https://doi.org/10.1007/978-3-319-10602-1_48
15. Plummer, B.A., Wang, L., Cervantes, C.M., Caicedo, J.C., Hockenmaier, J., Lazebnik, S.: Flickr30k entities: collecting region-to-phrase correspondences for richer image-to-sentence models. In: 2015 IEEE International Conference on Computer Vision (ICCV), pp. 2641–2649 (2015)
16. Ren, S., He, K., Girshick, R.B., Sun, J.: Faster R-CNN: towards real-time object detection with region proposal networks. IEEE Trans. Pattern Anal. Mach. Intell. **39**, 1137–1149 (2015)
17. Simonyan, K., Zisserman, A.: Very deep convolutional networks for large-scale image recognition (2015)
18. Wang, S., Chen, Y., Zhuo, J., Huang, Q., Tian, Q.: Joint global and co-attentive representation learning for image-sentence retrieval. In: Proceedings of the 26th ACM International Conference on Multimedia (2018)
19. Wen, K., Gu, X., Cheng, Q.: Learning dual semantic relations with graph attention for image-text matching. IEEE Trans. Circ. Syst. Video Technol. **31**, 2866–2879 (2021)
20. Xu, T., et al.: AttnGAN: fine-grained text to image generation with attentional generative adversarial networks. In: 2018 IEEE/CVF Conference on Computer Vision and Pattern Recognition, pp. 1316–1324 (2018)
21. Xu, X., Wang, T., Yang, Y., Zuo, L., Shen, F., Shen, H.T.: Cross-modal attention with semantic consistence for image-text matching. IEEE Trans. Neural Netw. Learn. Syst. **31**(12), 5412–5425 (2020)

22. Zhang, Q., Lei, Z., Zhang, Z., Li, S.: Context-aware attention network for image-text retrieval. In: 2020 IEEE/CVF Conference on Computer Vision and Pattern Recognition (CVPR), pp. 3533–3542 (2020)
23. Zhen, L., Hu, P., Wang, X., Peng, D.: Deep supervised cross-modal retrieval. In: 2019 IEEE/CVF Conference on Computer Vision and Pattern Recognition (CVPR), pp. 10386–10395 (2019)

NAS4FBP: Facial Beauty Prediction Based on Neural Architecture Search

Pingjian Zhang[1,2(✉)] and Yuankai Liu[2]

[1] Nanchang Jiaotong Institute, Nanchang, China
[2] South China University of Technology, Guangzhou, China
pjzhang@scut.edu.cn

Abstract. Facial Beauty Prediction (FBP) is an important task in image processing, which simulates human perception of facial beauty. In related studies, most methods are based on canonical convolutional backbones. However, can the canonical backbones perform best in FBP? To tackle this problem, we propose a NAS4FBP framework, which adopts a multi-task neural architecture search strategy to auto determine the backbone structure. In our multi-task learning scheme, we propose HBLoss to better reveal the nature of facial aesthetic hierarchy. In addition, we introduce a new pre-processing method to enhance the data diversity and propose a non-local spatial attention module, to further improve the model performance. Our model achieves 0.9387 PC on the SCUT-FBP5500 benchmark dataset, surpassing other related models and reaching a new state-of-the-art.

Keywords: Facial beauty prediction · Neural architecture search · Multi-task learning

1 Introduction

Facial attractiveness plays an important role in our daily lives. For example, people usually share photos of themselves or their idols on social networking platforms. In addition, facial attractiveness has a significant impact on social acceptance, employment and interpersonal relationships [24]. Some studies have even found that humans tend to choose more attractive faces as early as infancy [22]. Therefore, this leads to a precious topic in image recognition - facial beauty prediction [10].

Facial beauty prediction attracts researchers from different fields such as computer science and medicine, and promotes the development of automatic face beautification [15], automatic face enhancement [19] and beauty-based face retrieval [5].

In early studies, researchers tried to design rule-based features (e.g., average, symmetry, facial geometry, and golden ratio). However, manually designed features and rules lack standardization and effectiveness. With the rapid development of deep learning, the research on facial beauty prediction has entered a new era.

E. Pimenidis et al. (Eds.): ICANN 2022, LNCS 13531, pp. 225–236, 2022.
https://doi.org/10.1007/978-3-031-15934-3_19

Most FBP-related methods are based on several classical networks. However, these classical networks are inadequate for the perception of facial attractiveness, because they are not specifically designed for facial beauty prediction. We know that redesigning an efficient backbone is challenging and laborious, but fortunately, the Neural Architecture Search (NAS) technology can auto select the most suitable structure from various candidate operations in the search space. Currently, the NAS-based networks even perform better than hand-designed networks. Therefore, it is necessary and meaningful to employ "Neural Architecture Search" to get an efficient network specially designed for facial beauty prediction.

To our knowledge, we are the first to apply NAS to facial beauty prediction. In this paper, we propose a NAS4FBP framework, in which we refer to P-Darts [7] and further customize the searching process and measurement criteria to search for an FBP backbone. We also propose a Hierarchical Beauty Loss (HBLoss) and a data pre-processing method to improve the network. In addition, we propose a non-local spatial attention module (NSAM), which utilizes self-attention to help the model fuse long-range features. In model training, we first pre-train the FBP backbone on an external dataset to learn more general facial features. Then, we fine-tune the NAS4FBP Net on the target benchmark dataset with our multi-task learning schema. The experimental results show that our method achieves excellent accuracy.

2   Related Work

2.1   Facial Beauty Prediction Based on Deep Learning

In recent years, empowering machines to judge facial beauty has become an emerging research topic in AI [17]. Because of the traditional machine learning algorithms lack depth and robustness, deep learning methods become the protagonist.

Liang et al. [16] considered FBP as a single-label regression problem and proposed SCUT-FBP5500 dataset as the benchmark. Xu et al. [27] proposed CRNet that rounds the float facial score to the nearest integer to do classification in parallel to assist the main regression task. Fan et al. [8] formulated FBP to be a label distribution learning problem rather than single-label supervised learning. Chen et al. [6] introduced an adaptive label distribution learning method to predict face attractiveness. Lin et al. [17] proposed R^3CNN to integrate the relative ranking of faces in terms of aesthetics to improve performance. 2M BeautyNet [1], a Multi-input Multi-task beauty network, employed a automatic learning strategy of loss weights to improve the performance. Gao et al. [11] combined FBP with multi-task learning and encoded the features of geometric facial landmarks. Further, Xu et al. proposed that HMTNet [26] also adopted multi-task learning, but they were the first to consider gender and race classification as one of the auxiliary tasks.

To address the challenge of annotation scarcity in FBP, Shi et al. [23] employed segmentation tools to generate masks of several facial components (including two eyes, two eyebrows, nose, mouth, facial skin, hair, and background.). In addition, they proposed "co-attention" to focus on those facial components and the feature channels. However, their method still needs to process the test-set images in order to get those masks of facial components, which is slightly unfair. Vahdati et al. [25] pre-trained their model on the MS-Celeb-1M [12] and VGGFace2 [4] datasets successively, to get lots of general facial features. Similarly, we also have the idea of transfer learning, but we only use the VGGFace2 [4] for pre-training. Interestingly, although we use less extra data, our method performs better.

2.2 Neural Architecture Search

According to different optimization strategies, NAS can be divided into three types: Reinforcement Learning (RL), Evolutionary Algorithm (EA), and Gradient Descent (GD).

RL algorithms consider NAS as a decision about architecture sequence, which cares about long-term returns. In 2017, Zoph B et al. [30] proposed to represent the architecture of neural networks by variable sequences. In later work, they further proposed NASNet [31], which only needs to learn two network units (called "Normal Cell" and "Reduction Cell"). To reduce GPU resources during training, Google proposed ENAS [20], which improves efficiency by forcing subnet weights to be shared, and their approach shortened training time by over 1000 times. As a zeroth-order optimization algorithm, EA has the advantages of saving gradient calculation and no back propagation, and it is possible to obtain global optimal results. EA's search space is more free, but large search space also brings some inefficient. The representative works based on EA include AmoebaNet [21], CARS [29] and so on.

Different from the previous two methods where the search space is discrete, the GD-based method mixes the candidate operations with *softmax*, so that the search space becomes continuous and the loss function becomes differentiable. Darts [18] alternately optimizes architecture parameters α and weight parameters ω by gradient descent strategy. However, with the increase of training iterations, the performance of Dart may collapse due to too much "skip connection". To solve this problem, Darts+ [14] proposed some early stop strategies. Another problem in Darts is the performance gap between the searching process and the evaluation process, because they used 8 cells in the search process and 20 cells in the evaluation. Therefore, P-Darts [7] divided the search process into three stages, using 5, 11, and 17 cells successively to reduce the gap. SGAS [13] find out that architectures with high accuracy on validation set may not perform well in evaluation, thus, they design some criteria for decision in advance and use greedy strategies to select and prune candidate operations. Other GD-based representative works include PC-Darts [28], ProxylessNAS [2], etc. The advantages of GD-based methods are that they are differentiable and efficient, however, it is still a greedy algorithm and is easy to fall into a local minimum.

In our reproduction experiments, P-Darts [7] has the highest accuracy and the most stable performance, so we choose it for subsequent experiments.

3   Method

In this section, we will introduce our contributions corresponding to the Fig. 1, which can be summarized as:

1. *Align-Crop.* In this part, we propose Align-Crop, a new data pre-processing method, to enhance data diversity.
2. *Backbone.* In this part, we use the NAS4FBP framework to auto-search an FBP backbone.
3. *NSAM.* In this part, we propose a non-local spatial attention module to better perceive the global aesthetic feeling of a face image.
4. *Multi-task Head.* In this part, we will introduce our multi-task learning scheme and HBLoss for hierarchical beauty.

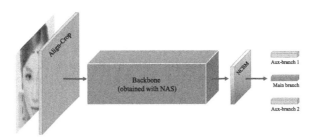

Fig. 1. NAS4FBP framework.

3.1   Align-Crop

Data pre-processing is often used to augment data diversity, which makes limited data more valuable. However, facial beauty is an abstract sense, and a minor change may bring a big difference in aesthetic. Therefore, it is not ideal to apply ordinary data pre-processing methods directly in FBP, as shown in Fig. 2.

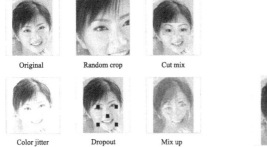

Fig. 2. Improper pre-processing. Ordinary data prep-processing methods seriously affect the facial beauty.

Fig. 3. Align-Crop. We first detect the face region, then align the face horizontally and crop it.

We think that the horizontally aligned faces make it easier for humans, also for machines, to evaluate facial attractiveness. We also think the beauty score strongly depends on the region of face, and weakly depends on the background. Therefore, we propose Align-Crop pre-processing, as shown in Fig. 3. In addition, we do not change the annotations, including beauty score, gender, and race, and we mix the original and pre-processed images for training, which doubles the training data.

In summary, our pre-processing method can augment the facial images from the perspectives of rotation, scale, and region of interest.

3.2 NAS for an FBP Backbone

In this section, we will introduce how NAS4FBP framework automatically searches for an FBP backbone.

Exploring the Number of Cells. In Darts [18] series, they stacked 20 cells to get the final network. However, a network with too high complexity will not only take up a lot of gpu memory but also easily lead to over-fitting. Therefore, we employ the cell genotype of the P-Darts [7] paper to find the suitable number of cells in facial beauty prediction.

Our experiments show that networks with too many cells have poor performance, and when the number of cells is 7, the PC reaches the maximum, and both the mean absolute error and root mean squared error reach the minimum. So we think 7 cells are the most suitable for FBP task. We show the relevant experimental results in Table 3.

Searching for an FBP Backbone. We adopt a progressive search strategy similar to P-Darts [7], but with differences as shown in Table 1.

Table 1. Differences from the P-Darts [7] **algorithms**

	Search	Evaluation	Proxy	Care about
P-Darts [7]	5,7,11 Cells	20 Cells	✓	Class of images
NAS4FBP	7 Cells	7 Cells	✗	Beauty score and hierarchy, race and gender

The 1st difference is that we stack 7 cells in both the search and evaluation phases. Compared with P-Darts [7] that stacks a different number of cells, our strategy can reduce the performance gap between the two phases. The 2nd difference is that we directly conduct NAS experiments on the target dataset with no proxy tasks, which further reduces the performance gap. The 3rd difference is that we transform the NAS's task from a single classification to multiple tasks, aiming to search for an FBP architecture with multiple perspectives.

Finally, we get NAS4FBP Net as shown in Fig. 4, and its normal cell and reduction cell are shown in Fig. 5 and Fig. 6. The normal cell is used for feature extraction, and the reduction cell is used for down-sampling. Interestingly, the cell searched by our framework is better than that of P-Darts [7] in FBP as shown in Table 4, which shows that the NAS4FBP framework is very effective, and also reflects our contribution to FBP based on NAS.

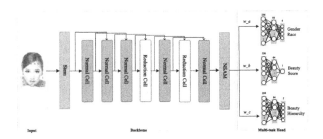

Fig. 4. NAS4FBP Net. We get the genotype of "Cell" through Neural Architecture Search. The "Multi-task Head" corresponds to our multi-task learning scheme.

Fig. 5. Normal cell   **Fig. 6.** Reduction cell

3.3   Non-local Spatial Attention Module

Global spatial information is important for image regression or classification. However, in ordinary spatial attention method, the kernel size of convolution limits the region of interest, leading to local features. Although adding more convolutional layers can broaden the interest window, it still can't receive information outside of the current convolution.

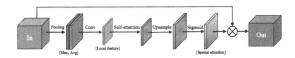

Fig. 7. Non-local Spatial Attention Module.

Therefore, we propose NSAM as shown in Fig. 7, which incorporates the self-attention mechanism to capture long-range features that contribute to a global view of the model. In addition, we put NSAM after the last convolution layer, so the calculation is very minimal.

3.4   Multi-task Learning Scheme with HBLoss

As shown in Fig. 1, our multi-task head has 3 branches.

The Branch of Beauty Score. This branch is our primary task, which aims to predict the facial attractiveness score. We use MSELoss as the loss function, which is expressed as:

$$MSELoss = \frac{1}{N}\sum_{i=1}^{N}(y_i - x_i)^2 \tag{1}$$

where y_i denotes the ground-truth beauty score of the i-th face image, x_i represents the score predicted by the model.

The Branch of Gender and Race. Gender and race are considered for the first time in HMTNet [26], but the binary classification task is too easy for model learning. Therefore, we put gender and race in the same branch. In addition, in the human mechanism of aesthetic perception, only when both the gender and race are the same, the scoring standard is more consistent. In this branch, we use CELoss as the criterion, which is expressed as:

$$CELoss = -\frac{1}{N}\sum_{i=1}^{N}y_i log(p_i) \tag{2}$$

where y_i denotes ground truth, p_i denotes the predicted probability of the i-th category after passing through the softmax layer, and N means the batch size.

The Branch of Beauty Hierarchy. The CELoss is good at those classification tasks with independent classes. However, there is an orderly relationship between different beauty hierarchies. Therefore, we propose the HBLoss, which is expressed as:

$$HBLoss = \rho \sum_{i=1}^{C} P_i \cdot |y - i| \tag{3}$$

where ρ is a scaling parameter, C is the total number of classes, y means the ground truth, and P_i is the predicted probability for the i-th class.

Table 2. CEloss vs. HBLoss

Case	Prediction	CELoss	HBLoss
Case 1	$[0.3_\times, 0, 0, 0.4_\checkmark, 0.3_\times]$	0.9	1.2
Case 2	$[0, 0, 0.3_\times, 0.4_\checkmark, 0.3_\times]$	0.9	**0.7**

"$\checkmark$" means correct probability and "$\times$" means wrong probability

As shown in Table 2, the CELoss cannot distinguish case 1 from case 2 because it only cares about the probability of being correct, so it gives the same loss value. However, our HBLoss thinks case 2 is less wrong than case 1, because the predicted probability of case 2 is closer to the ground truth, so HBLoss gives case 2 a lower loss value. Therefore, HBLoss can better guide the model to analyze the beauty hierarchy, and the experimental results also show that HBLoss has a better effect than CELoss.

4 Experimental Results

4.1 Experimental Setup

Dataset. We conduct experiments on SCUT-FBP5500 [16] benchmark dataset, which provides 5.5k facial images of different genders and races (Asian and Caucasian). There are 60 labelers who give each face image an integer score from 1 to 5. The ground-truth label of each image is the average score given by the raters.

Metrics. We adopt the widely used metrics to evaluate the performance of our model, which are Pearson Coefficient (PC), Mean Absolute Error (MAE), and Root Mean Squared Error (RMSE). The three metrics are formulated as:

$$PC = \frac{\sum_{i=1}^{n}(x_i - \bar{x})(y_i - \bar{y})}{[\sum_{i=1}^{n}(x_i - \bar{x})^2 \sum_{i=1}^{n}(y_i - \bar{y})^2]^{\frac{1}{2}}} \tag{4}$$

$$MAE = \frac{1}{n}\sum_{i=1}^{n}|y_i - x_i| \tag{5}$$

$$RMSE = \sqrt{\frac{1}{n}\sum_{i=1}^{n}(y_i - x_i)^2} \tag{6}$$

where y_i and x_i denote the ground-truth label and predicted score of the i-th image, and $\bar{x}$ and $\bar{y}$ denote the average of all ground-truth labels and predicted scores, respectively.

Implementation Details. We use PyTorch for code programming. In the phase of searching the backbone, we use 80% images in the SCUT-FBP5500 [16] dataset for training weight parameters ω, and 20% images for optimizing architecture parameters α. The initial learning rates (lr) of weight optimizer and architecture optimizer are 0.025 and 6E-4, respectively. The batch size of search phase is 6. After getting a good FBP backbone, we pre-train it on an external dataset, and than fine-tune our NAS4FBP Net on the target dataset. We use cosine annealing scheduler to adjust the lr, and the epochs of fine-tuning is 90, the input size is 224*224, the batch size is 6, the initial lr is 0.005, the minimum lr is 1e-5.

4.2   Experiments of Applying NAS to FBP

As shown in Table 3, the networks of 13-Cell and 20-Cell have poor performance, and the 7-Cell network achieves the highest PC and the smallest MAS and RMSE. So we think 7 cells are the most suitable for FBP scenario.

Table 3. Network performance of different complexity

Complexity	MAE	RMSE	PC
20-Cell	0.4233	0.5565	0.7407
13-Cell	0.2621	0.3506	0.858
9-Cell	0.2556	0.3386	0.8667
8-Cell	0.2528	0.3354	0.8723
7-Cell	**0.2489**	**0.3327**	**0.8754**
6-Cell	0.2553	0.3451	0.8614

The train-set is 60% and the test-set is 40%

As shown in Table 4, the NAS4FBP framework outperforms P-Darts by almost 1% on average, indicating that the architecture selected by our framework works better in FBP than P-Darts.

Table 4. Performance comparison with P-Darts in FBP

Cell genotype	1	2	3	4	5	Avg PC
P-Darts	0.8908	0.8945	0.8855	0.9024	0.9012	0.8949
NAS4FBP (Ours)	**0.9022**	**0.9003**	**0.9017**	**0.9113**	**0.9058**	**0.9043**

Table 5. Performance comparisons on the SCUT-FBP5500 dataset.

Model	Pre-training	MAE	RMSE	PC
AlexNet (baseline1)	ImageNet	0.2651	0.3481	0.8634
ResNet-18 (baseline2)	ImageNet	0.2419	0.3166	0.8900
ResNeXt-50 (baseline3)	ImageNet	0.2291	0.3017	0.8997
2M BeautyNet [9]	ImageNet	–	–	0.8996
Cao at al. [3]	ImageNet	0.2287	0.3014	0.9003
R^3CNN [17]	ImageNet	0.2120	0.2800	0.9142
Chen at al. [6]	ImageNet	0.2000	0.2690	0.9200
Shi at al. [23]	ImageNet	0.2020	0.2660	0.9260
Vahdati at al. [25]	MS-Celeb-1M & VGGFace2	0.1833	0.2424	0.9372
NAS4FBP Net (Ours)	ImageNet	0.1939	0.2579	0.9275
NAS4FBP Net (Ours)	VGGFace2	**0.1797**	**0.2380**	**0.9387**

4.3 Comparison with the Related State-of-the-Art Models

Satisfactorily, with the same or less pre-training data, our model outperforms other related models, reaching the new state-of-the-art. As shown in Table 5, our model surpasses all relevant models when pre-trained with ImageNet. When pre-trained with VGGFace2, a smaller dataset than MS-Celeb-1M, our model achieves better results than [25]. Further, our network has only 1.55 MB of parameters and 5.5 MB of file size, which is smaller than many hand-designed networks, meaning that our network is not only accurate but also light.

4.4 Ablation and Analysis

Table 6. Ablation of NAS4FBP Net

Pre-training	Align-Crop	HBLoss	NSAM	Avg PC
None				0.9043
None	✓			0.9076
ImageNet	✓			0.9236
ImageNet	✓	✓		0.9261
ImageNet	✓	✓	✓	0.9275
VGGFace2	✓			0.9356
VGGFace2	✓	✓		0.9379
VGGFace2	✓	✓	✓	**0.9387**

As shown in Table 6, our network can reach 0.9043 PC without pre-training, showing that the backbone searched through our NAS4FBP framework is very efficient. When we add pre-processed images into the train-set, the Avg PC improves by 0.33%, showing that our Align-Crop pre-processing effectively augments the training data through multiple perspectives.

We supplement ImageNet pre-training and VGGFace2 pre-training in the experiments in line 3 and 6, respectively. The experiments in line 4 and 7 in Table 6 show that HBLoss can better guide the classification of beauty hierarchy than CELoss, thus improving the model performance. The experiments in lines 5 and 8 in Table 6 show that our NSAM further improves the NAS4FBP Net by providing non-local spatial attention.

5 Conclusion

As far as we know, we are the first to apply NAS in facial beauty prediction. In this paper, we a NAS4FBP framework based on a multi-task NAS strategy, which can auto-generate a efficient and light backbone for FBP. We also propose Align-Crop pre-processing to augment the data diversity and HBLoss to better measure the facial aesthetic hierarchy. In addition, we propose NSAM incorporating self-attention to provide global attention, which further improves model performance.

We mainly conduct experiments on the SCUT-FBP5500 [16] benchmark dataset, and our network reaches 0.9387 PC, achieving a new state-of-the-art.

In this work, we pay little attention to candidate operations in NAS's search space, and just use some simple constructs. Other choices outside our current search space may also contribute to our framework, such as irregular convolutions, the number of cells, group convolution. Therefore, how to design and full use the search space is worth exploring and will be the direction of our future work.

References

1. 2M BeautyNet. Facial Beauty Prediction Based on Multi-Task Transfer Learning. IEEE Access **8**, 20245–20256 (2020)
2. Cai, H., Zhu, L., Han, S.: ProxylessNAS: Direct Neural Architecture Search on Target Task and Hardware". arXiv preprint arXiv:1812.00332 (2019)
3. Cao, K., et al.: Deep learning for facial beauty prediction. Inf. **11**, 391 (2020)
4. Cao, Q., et al.: VGGFace2: a dataset for recognising faces across pose and age. In: 2018 13th IEEE International Conference on Automatic Face & Gesture Recognition (FG 2018), pp. 67–74 (2018)
5. Chen, F., Xiao, X., Zhang, D.: Data-driven facial beauty analysis: prediction, retrieval and manipulation. IEEE Trans. Affect. Comput. **9**, 205–216 (2018)
6. Chen, L., Deng, W.: Facial attractiveness prediction by deep adaptive label distribution learning. In: CCBR (2019)
7. Chen, X., et al.: Progressive DARTS: Bridging the Optimization Gap for NAS in the Wild. arXiv preprint arXiv:1912.10952 (2021)
8. Fan, Y., et al.: Label distribution-based facial attractiveness computation by deep residual learning. IEEE Trans. Multim. **20**, 2196–2208 (2018)
9. Gan, J., et al.: 2M BeautyNet: facial beauty prediction based on multi-task transfer learning. IEEE Access **8**, 20245–20256 (2020)
10. Gan, J., et al.: Deep self-taught learning for facial beauty prediction. Neurocomputing **144**, 295–303 (2014)
11. Gao, L., et al.: Automatic facial attractiveness prediction by deep multi-task learning. In: 2018 24th International Conference on Pattern Recognition (ICPR), pp. 3592–3597 (2018)
12. Guo, Y., et al.: MS-Celeb-1M: a dataset and benchmark for large-scale face recognition. In: ECCV (2016)
13. Li, G., et al.: SGAS: sequential greedy architecture search. In: 2020 IEEE/CVF Conference on Computer Vision and Pattern Recognition (CVPR), pp. 1617–1627 (2020)
14. Liang, H., et al.: DARTS+: Improved Differentiable Architecture Search with Early Stopping". arXiv preprint arXiv:1909.06035 (2019)
15. Liang, L., Jin, L., Li, X.: Facial skin beautification using adaptive region-aware masks. IEEE Trans. Cybern. **44**, 2600–2612 (2014)
16. Liang, L., et al.: SCUT-FBP5500: a diverse benchmark dataset for multi-paradigm facial beauty prediction. In: 2018 24th International Conference on Pattern Recognition (ICPR), pp. 1598–1603 (2018)
17. Lin, L., Liang, L., Jin, L.: Regression guided by relative ranking using convolutional neural network (R3CNN) for facial beauty prediction. In: IEEE Transactions on Affective Computing, p. 1 (2019)

18. Liu, H., Simonyan, K., Yang, Y.: DARTS: Differentiable Architecture Search. arXiv preprint arXiv:1806.09055 (2019)
19. Ou, X., et al.: Beauty eMakeup: a deep makeup transfer system. In: Proceedings of the 24th ACM international conference on Multimedia (2016)
20. Pham, H., et al.: Efficient neural architecture search via parameter sharing. In: ICML (2018)
21. Real, E., et al.: Regularized evolution for image classifier architecture search. In: AAAI (2019)
22. Rubenstein, A., Kalakanis, L., Langlois, J.: Infant preferences for attractive faces: a cognitive explanation. Develop. Psychol. **35**(3), 848–55 (1999)
23. Shi, S., et al.: Improving facial attractiveness prediction via coattention learning. In: ICASSP 2019–2019 IEEE International Conference on Acoustics, Speech and Signal Processing (ICASSP), pp. 4045–4049 (2019)
24. Thornhill, R., Gangestad, S.: Facial attractiveness. Trends Cognit. Sci. **3**, 452–460 (1999)
25. Vahdati, E., Suen, C.: Facial beauty prediction using transfer and multi-task learning techniques. In: ICPRAI (2020)
26. Xu, L., Fan, H., Xiang, J.: Hierarchical multi-task network for race, gender and facial attractiveness recognition. In: 2019 IEEE International Conference on Image Processing (ICIP), pp. 3861–3865 (2019)
27. Xu, L., Xiang, J., Yuan, X.: CRNet: classification and regression neural network for facial beauty prediction. In: PCM (2018)
28. Xu, Y., et al.: PC-DARTS: partial channel connections for memory-efficient architecture search. In: ICLR (2020)
29. Yang, Z., et al.: CARS: continuous evolution for efficient neural architecture search. In: 2020 IEEE/CVF Conference on Computer Vision and Pattern Recognition (CVPR), pp. 1826–1835 (2020)
30. Zoph, B., Le, Q.V.: Neural architecture search with reinforcement learning. In: arXiv preprint arXiv:1611.01578 (2017)
31. Zoph, B., et al.: Learning transferable architectures for scalable image recognition. In: 2018 IEEE/CVF Conference on Computer Vision and Pattern Recognition, pp. 8697–8710 (2018)

Object Detector with Recursive Feature Pyramid and Key Content-Only Attention

Yuchao Lu[ID], Tao Zhang[(✉)][ID], Jiali Jin[ID], and Li Zhang[ID]

School of Artificial Intelligence and Computer Science, Jiangnan University,
Wuxi 214122, China
taozhang@jiangnan.edu.cn
http://ai.jiangnan.edu.cn/

Abstract. To detect objects, human visual perception focuses on the key content of interest and then transmits high-level semantic information through feedback connections, selectively enhancing and suppressing neuronal activation. Inspired by the human visual system, our detector incorporates the recursive feature pyramid in the backbone to integrate the feedback information of the FPN into the backbone network so that the features of the secondary training of the backbone network can be better adapted to the detection task. Furthermore, we propose a key content-only attention mechanism to seek the balance between accuracy and efficiency, which adopts the attention configuration of the key content-only term with deformable convolution to achieve the best accuracy and efficiency trade-off. Both of these can improve our baseline AP by > 4%, and combining them further enhances the performance of our detector. On COCO test dev, our detector achieves 45.1% box AP with ResNet-50.

Keywords: Recursive feature pyramid · Key content-only attention · Deformable convolution

1 Introduction

Object detection is one of the most critical and challenging tasks, and it aims to locate the target of interest from a given image or video and perform target classification. As a cornerstone of image understanding and computer vision, object detection is widely beneficial to the fields of autonomous driving, intelligent security, and human-computer interaction, etc.

For object detection, since objects in an image may have varying scales, it is much desired to obtain multi-scale feature maps that have fused high-level and low-level features with sufficient spatial resolution at every distinct scale. This motivated Feature Pyramid Networks (FPN [21]) and its improved versions, such as BiFPN proposed in EfficientDet [26] and Path Aggregation Network (PANet [23]), etc. The limitation of existing methods related to feature pyramid networks is that the highest-level features at the top of the pyramid must propagate

E. Pimenidis et al. (Eds.): ICANN 2022, LNCS 13531, pp. 237–248, 2022.
https://doi.org/10.1007/978-3-031-15934-3_20

through multiple intermediate scales and interact with the features at these scales before reaching the features at the bottom. During such propagation and interaction, essential feature information may be lost or weakened. In addition, another limitation is that the backbone only passes through FPN once and cannot fully utilize its features to adjust network parameters.

In this paper, we propose Recursive Feature Pyramid (RFP) to overcome the above limitations. We incorporate Atrus Spatial Pyramid Pooling (ASPP) [6,7] into FPN to enhance the interaction between different scales. The function of recursion is to make the error return information of target detection more direct feedback and adjust the parameters of the backbone network to speed up training and improve performance. In addition, we added the key content-only attention module to the backbone, which can improve the accuracy of detection tasks with hardly any additional computation.

We are inspired by the idea of looking and thinking twice; the mechanism of looking and thinking twice has been widely used in computer vision and achieved outstanding performance [2,3,25]. Following this idea, our proposed RFP builds on top of the FPN by incorporating extra feedback connections from the FPN layers into the bottom-up backbone layers. The recursive structure enables our object detector to look at the images twice. This operation integrates the feedback information of the FPN into the backbone network so that the features of the secondary training of the backbone network can be better adapted to the detection task. We obtain a backbone for our object detector by expanding the recursive structure into a sequential implementation, which looks like a repeating stack of models. We propose a novel strategy to achieve an effective fusion of features included with proposed the ASPP-enriched FPN. Our proposed RFP implements a sequential design of looking and thinking twice, where the bottom-up backbone and FPN are run twice to enhance the input features of the detection head and obtain better detection performance.

Human visual perception selectively enhances and suppresses neuron activation bypassing high-level semantic information through feedback connections [1,12,20]. Attention mechanisms enable a neural network to focus more on relevant elements of the input than on irrelevant parts. They were first studied in natural language processing (NLP), where certain key elements (e.g., source words in the input sentence) are prioritized in the process of computing the output for a given query element (e.g., a target word in the output sentence) according to the query. Later, self-attention modules were presented for modelling intra-sentence relations [4,13,16,18,19], where both the key and query are from the same elements. The success of attention modeling has led to its adoption in object detection, where the query and key are visual elements such as image pixels or regions of interest. When determining the attention weights assigned to a key for a given query, only a few input attributes are usually considered. One is the content of the query, and another is the content of the key; the third is the relative position of the query and key.

Based on these input properties, there are four possible attention factors: (1) the query and key content, (2)the query content and relative position, (3) the key content only, and (4) the relative position only. In the latest version of Transformer attention [10], attention weights are expressed as a sum of four terms (E1, E2, E3, E4), one for each of these attention factors. We proposed key content-only attention, which exclusively uses the key content-only term(E3), which captures saliency information and can effectively improve the performance with little additional overhead.

Combining the proposed RFP and Key content-only Attention results in our detector. On COCO test-dev, we validate the performance of our proposed method. We achieve 45.1% box AP for object detection with ResNet-50[53] as the backbone significantly improves Cascade R-CNN by 4.8% box AP.

2   Related Works

Multi-scale Features. Previously, SSD [24] directly used multiple feature maps extracted from the backbone, while FPN incorporates a top-down path to sequentially fused features at different scales. Shu Liu et al. add another bottom-up path on top of FPN to pass the location information of the bottom layer to the upper layer [23]. NAS-FPN [8] and Auto-FPN [28] use neural architecture search [29] to find the optimal FPN structure. EfficientDet proposes BiFPN, which repeats an effective block in the FPN so that the size of the FPN can be flexibly controlled. Unlike them, our proposed Recursive Feature Pyramid enriches the representation power of FPN by repeating the bottom-up backbone. Additionally, we incorporate the ASPP into FPN to enrich features.

In this paper, we aim to enhance FPN to generate increasingly powerful representations. Compared to the work mentioned above, the unique characteristic of our Recursive Feature Pyramid network is that the features of the first FPN output are recursively passed through the ASPP module and then input to the backbone network again. In addition, we designed an additional fusion module to calculate the weighted sum of the features of FPN and RFP to constitute an updated feature for calculating the final output feature of RFP.

Attention Mechanisms. Two kinds of attention are commonly used in convolutional neural networks: spatial attention and channel attention and mixed attention. Jie Hu et al. designed a Squeeze-and-Excitation module to assign weights to each channel [16]; this increases the sensitivity of the model to channel features. Xiang Li et al. starts from the perspective of receptive field adaptation to generate feature maps of different scales through convolution kernels of different sizes [20]. Then the information from different scales is aggregated to generate global selection weights. Finally, the feature maps of different scales are re-aggregated by global selection weights. It is well known that deformable convolution can exploit query content & relative position effectively and efficiently in image recognition tasks. We propose the key content attention module, which combines the deformable convolution and key content-only terms, delivering the best precision-efficiency trade-off.

3   RecursiveFeaturePyramid

RecursiveFeaturePyramid. First, let's look at feature fusion in FPN. Let B_i represent the i-th layer convolution operation on the backbone, and x_i is the feature after its convolution operation, F_i represents x_i after FPN, $\{f_i \mid i = 1, ..., S\}$ represents the result of F_i after pooling, where S is the number of the stages. For example, $S = 3$ in Fig. 1a. $\forall i = 1, ..., S$, the f_i is defined by

$$f_i = F_i(f_{i+1}, x_i), x_i = B_i(x_{i-1}) \tag{1}$$

Object detectors using FPN depend on f_i for detection computation.

Our proposed RFP adds feedback connections to FPN as in Fig. 1b. Let R_i represent the feature transformations before connecting them back to the backbone. Then, the output feature $\{f_i \mid i = 1, ..., S\}$ of RFP is defined by

$$f_i = F_i(f_{i+1}, x_i), x_i = B_i(x_{i-1}, R_i(f_i)) \tag{2}$$

which makes RFP a recursive operation. We unroll it to a sequential network, as shown in Fig. 1c. In our implementation, RFP fixed recursion once and F_i and R_i are shared across different steps.

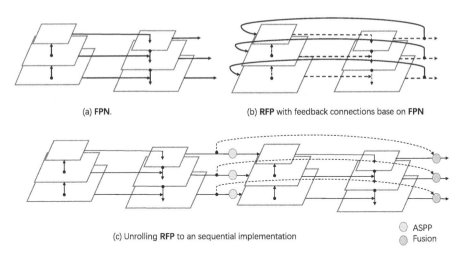

(a) **FPN**.   (b) **RFP** with feedback connections base on **FPN**

(c) Unrolling **RFP** to an sequential implementation

○ ASPP
● Fusion

Fig. 1. The architecture of the Recursive Feature Pyramid (RFP). (a) The architecture of Feature Pyramid Networks (FPN). (b) Recursive Feature Pyramid (RFP) incorporates feedback connections into FPN. (c) Recursive Feature Pyramid (RFP) unrolled to a sequential network.

We make changes to the ResNet [14] backbone B to allow it to take both x and $R(f)$ as its input. ResNet has four stages, each of which is composed of several similar blocks. We only make changes to the first block of each stage, as shown in Fig. 2. This block computes a 3-layer feature and adds it to the feature computed by a shortcut. To use the feature $R(f)$, we add a convolutional layer with a kernel size of 1×1. The weight of this layer is initialized with 0 to prevent it from having any effect when we load the pre-trained weights.

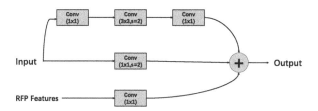

Fig. 2. Recursive Feature Pyramid (RFP) adds transformed features to the first block of each stage of ResNet.

ASPP as the Connecting Module. We use ASPP to implement the connecting module **R**, which transforms f_i in the first cycle to the RFP feature used in Fig. 3. In this module, there are four parallel branches taken f_i from different stages in the backbone as inputs, then concatenate together the outputs along the channel dimension to form the final output of **R**. On the transformation of features, their three branches use a convolutional layer, followed by a ReLU layer, and their number of output channels is 1/4 of the number of input channels. The convolutional layers in those three branches are of the following configurations: kernel size = [1, 3, 3], atrous rate =[1, 3, 6], padding = [0, 3, 6]. The last branch uses a global average pooling layer to compress the feature, followed by a 1×1 convolutional layer and a ReLU layer to transform the compressed feature to 1/4-size of the input feature channels. Finally, resized and concatenated with the features from the other three parallel branches.

Fusion Module. As shown in Fig. 4., our RFP additionally uses a fusion module to combine outputs of FPN and RFP. The fusion procedure is similar to the update process in recurrent neural networks [15]. The fusion module uses the feature of RFP to compute an attention map by a convolutional layer followed by a Sigmoid operation. The resulting attention map is used to compute the weighted sum of features of FPN and RFP to form updated features. This updated feature will be used in the feature calculation of RFP.

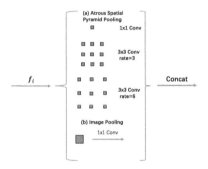

Fig. 3. Specific configuration structure for the connection module R, which used Atrous Spatial Pyramid Pooling (ASPP).

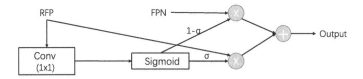

Fig. 4. The fusion module used in RFP σ is the output of Sigmoid, which is used to fuse features from different steps.

4   Key Content-Only Attention

Generalized Attention Formulation. We develop a generalized attention formulation capable of representing various modular designs. We then show how the main attention mechanism can be represented in this formulation. Given a query element and a set of key elements, where the query and key are visual elements, the outputs of multiple attention functions (heads) are linearly aggregated with learnable weights, enabling the model to focus on key content from different presentation subspaces and locations. Let q index a query element with content Z_q, and k index a key element with content X_k. Then the multi-head attention feature Y_q is computed as

$$y_q = \sum_{m=1}^{M} W_m \left[\sum_{k \in \Omega_q} A_m\left(q, k, z_q, x_k\right) \odot W_m' x_k \right] \tag{3}$$

where m indexes the attention head, Ω_q specifies the supporting key region for the query, $A_m\left(q, k, z_q, x_k\right)$ denotes the attention weights in the m-th attention head, and W_m and W_m' are learnable weights. Usually, the attention weights are normalized within Ω_q, as $\sum_{k \in \Omega_q} A_m\left(q, k, z_q, x_k\right) = 1$.

Transformer Attention. In the instantiation of the Transformer attention module [10], the attention weight of each query-key pair is computed as the sum of four terms $(\varepsilon_1, \varepsilon_2, \varepsilon_3, \varepsilon_4)$ based on different attention factors. Let q index a query element with content z_q, and k index a key element with content x_k. Then transformer attention is represented as

$$A_m^{Trans}(q, k, z_q, x_k) \propto exp(\sum_{j=1}^{4} \varepsilon_j) \tag{4}$$

normalized by $\sum_{k \in \Omega q} A_m^{Trans}(q, k, z_q, x_k) = 1$ *where* Ωq specifies the supporting key region for the query, which spans the key elements (e.g., the whole input sentence).

The ε_1 and ε_2 terms are sensitive to the query content. The ε_1 term measures the compatibility of the query and key content, which enables the network to focus more on the keys compatible with the query in terms of content. For the ε_2 term, it is based on the query content and relative position, which allows the network to adaptively determine where to assign high attention weight according to the query content. The ε_3 and ε_4 terms are irrelevant to the query content. The ε_3 term refers only to key content, and the ε_4 term refers only to relative position.

Deformable Convolution. Deformable convolution can be deemed as special instantiations of spatial attention mechanisms, where subsets of the attention factors are involved. Similar to the ε_2 term, deformable convolution is based on query content and relative position. But the deformable convolution only samples a sparse set of key elements for each query, and its complexity is linear with the number of query elements. Therefore, the calculation speed of deformable convolution is much faster than that of ε_2 in image recognition.

In deformable convolution [9,17], learnable offsets are added to adjust the key elements' sampling positions to capture spatial transformations. The learnable offsets are predicted based on the query content and are thus dynamic to the input. The key and the query elements are from the same set. It can also be incorporated into the generalized attention formulation as a special instantiation of self-attention, where the attention weight is

$$A_m^{deform}(q, k, x_q) = G(k, q + p_m + \omega_m^\top x_q) \tag{5}$$

Key Content-Only Attention. We seek to disentangle the effects of different attention factors among the four items $(\varepsilon_1, \varepsilon_2, \varepsilon_3, \varepsilon_4)$. We have introduced manual switches in the Transformer attention module that allows us to activate/deactivate particular terms manually. It is expressed as

$$\hat{A}_m^{Trans}(q, k, z_q, x_k) \propto exp(\sum_{j=1}^{4} \beta_j^{Trans} \varepsilon_j) \tag{6}$$

where $\left\{\beta_j^{Trans}\right\}$ takes values in $\{0,1\}$ to control the activation of corresponding terms, and $\hat{A}_m^{Trans}(q,k,z_q,x_k) = 1$ is normalized by $\sum_{k \in \Omega_q} \hat{A}_m^{Trans}(q,k,z_q,x_k) = 1$.

In self-attention, the only key content term captures salient information, which can effectively improve performance with little additional overhead. We design the self-attention mechanism in Fig. 5. The Transformer attention module is incorporated by applying it to the 3×3 convolution output in the residual block. To insert the pre-trained model without breaking the initial behaviour, the Transformer attention module includes a residual connection whose output is multiplied by a learnable scalar initialized to zero, as shown in [27]. We replace the 3×3 regular convolutions in the residual block with deformable convolutions. The resulting architecture is called "Attended Residual Block", shown in Fig. 5. We applied the attended residual blocks to the last two stages (conv4 and conv5 stages) of ResNet-50. In Transformer attention, the relative position encoding is of the same dimension as the content feature embedding, specifically 256-d and 512-d in the conv4 and conv5 stages, respectively.

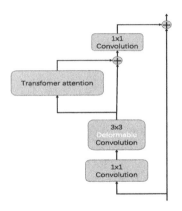

Fig. 5. Illustration of Key content-only attention module configurations for self-attention.

5   Experiments

5.1   Experimental Details

Experiments are implemented based on the open source mmdetection [5] code base and conducted on the COCO dataset [22]. It consists of 115k images for training (train-2017) and 5k images for validation (val-2017). There are also 20k images in test-dev that have no disclosed labels. We train models on train-2017 and report ablation studies and final results on test-dev. All reported results follow standard COCO-style Average Precision (AP) metrics.

Our baseline model is Cascade R-CNN, and ImageNet [11] pre-trained ResNet-50 is utilized as the backbone. FPS is measured on a single NVIDIA RTX 2080Ti graphics card. In our experiments, the networks are trained on 2 GPUs with 2 images per GPU for 12 epochs, and the learning rate is initialized to 10^{-4}. All other hyper-parameters follow the settings in mmdetection if not specifically noted.

5.2 Ablation Studies

In all ablation studies, the input image scale used for training and testing the model is 1333 × 800 pixels. Larger input sizes tend to bring improvements(see [26]). We evaluated the contribution of the Recursive Feature Pyramid and Key content-only Attention to our detector in Table 1. which use Cascade R-CNN with ResNet-50 and FPN as its baseline. To analyze the importance of each proposed method, we report the overall ablation studies in Table 1. We gradually add Recursive Feature Pyramid and Key content-only Attention to our baseline. Experiments for ablation studies are implemented with the same precomputed proposals for fair comparisons.

Table 1. Ablation study results on COCO val2017 with the ResNet-50 as backbone. The models are trained for 12 epochs. CR represents Cascade R-CNN, RFP represents Recursive Feature Pyramid and KA represents Key content-only Attention, respectively.

CR	RFP	KA	AP	AP_{50}	AP_{75}	AP_S	AP_M	AP_L	FPS
✓			40.3	58.6	44.0	22.5	43.8	52.9	**14.7**
✓		✓	44.7	63.8	48.6	26.2	48.4	59.1	14.6
✓	✓		44.8	63.3	48.7	26.1	**48.7**	58.3	9.4
✓	✓	✓	**45.1**	**64.0**	**49.0**	**26.9**	48.6	**59.8**	9.2

From the comparison of Fig. 6., we notice that RFP, similar to the human visual perception that selectively enhances or suppresses neuron activations, can find occluded objects more efficiently, for which the nearby context information is more critical. In comparison, Key content-only Attention pay more attention to the key content to help us reduce the occurrence of missed inspections.

5.3 Main Results

We compare our model with the state-of-the-art object detection approaches on the COCO test-dev the bounding box detection results are shown in Tabel 2. For fair comparisons with corresponding models, we report our re-implemented results, which are generally similar to what were reported in papers. The FPS results were all performed on the same machine with a single RTX 2080Ti GPU.

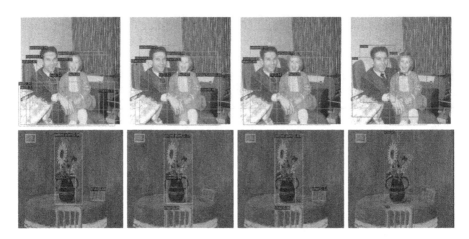

Fig. 6. From left to right: visualization of the detection results by 'Cascade R-CNN + RFP', 'Cascade R-CNN + Key content-only Attention', 'Cascade R-CNN + RFP + Key content-only Attention' and the ground truth.

Through the Recursive Feature Pyramid, which can better fuse multi-scale features, our detector achieves 44.8 box AP with ResNet-50 [14], which is 4.5 points higher AP than our baseline. Then we add Key content-only Attention to the baseline Cascade R-CNN which can effectively improve the performance with little additional overhead. Our detector achieves 44.7% box AP with no loss in detection speed. Combining them results in our detector, which achieves 45.1% box AP at 9.2 FPS.

Table 2. Accuracy and speed comparison with State-of-the-art detectors on COCO test-dev for bounding box object detection. FPS is measured on the same machine with a single RTX 2080Ti GPU.

Mothod	Backbone	AP	AP_{50}	AP_{75}	AP_S	AP_M	AP_L	FPS
RetinaNet	ResNet-50	36.5	55.4	39.1	20.4	40.3	48.1	16.6
Cascade R-CNN	ResNet-50	40.3	58.6	44.0	22.5	43.8	52.9	14.7
FCOS + DCN [9]	ResNet-50	42.3	61.2	45.5	24.5	45.9	55.8	1.7
NAS-FPN	ResNet-50	40.5	58.4	43.1	19.9	46.5	56.3	**26.6**
ATSS	ResNet-50	39.5	57.6	42.8	23.6	42.9	50.3	19.2
YOLOv3 + ASFF	DarkNet-53	43.8	63.9	48.9	26.6	46.9	53.4	24
Libra-RCNN	ResNet-50	38.3	59.5	41.9	22.1	42.0	48.5	18.2
Double-Heads	ResNet-50	40.0	59.4	43.5	22.9	43.6	52.8	8.7
Ours	ResNet-50	**45.1**	**64.0**	**49.0**	**26.9**	**48.6**	**59.8**	9.2

6   Conclusion

In this paper, we proposed a novel detector that combined the Recursive Feature Pyramid and Key content-only Attention. Recursive Feature Pyramid implements thinking twice at the feature extraction phase, where the outputs of FPN are brought back to each stage of the bottom-up backbone through feedback connections. Key content-only Attention can effectively improve the performance with little additional overhead. Both can be applied in other detectors to improve the feature extraction ability and obtain better detection results.

References

1. Beck, D.M., Kastner, S.: Top-down and bottom-up mechanisms in biasing competition in the human brain. Vis. Res. **49**(10), 1154–1165 (2009)
2. Cai, Z., Vasconcelos, N.: Cascade r-cnn: delving into high quality object detection. In: Proceedings of the IEEE Conference on Computer Vision and Pattern Recognition, pp. 6154–6162 (2018)
3. Cao, C., et al.: Look and think twice: capturing top-down visual attention with feedback convolutional neural networks. In: Proceedings of the IEEE International Conference on Computer Vision, pp. 2956–2964 (2015)
4. Cao, J., Cholakkal, H., Anwer, R.M., Khan, F.S., Pang, Y., Shao, L.: D2det: towards high quality object detection and instance segmentation. In: Proceedings of the IEEE/CVF Conference on Computer Vision and Pattern Recognition, pp. 11485–11494 (2020)
5. Chen, K., et al.: Mmdetection: open MMLAB detection toolbox and benchmark. arXiv preprint arXiv:1906.07155 (2019)
6. Chen, L.C., Papandreou, G., Schroff, F., Adam, H.: Rethinking atrous convolution for semantic image segmentation. arXiv preprint arXiv:1706.05587 (2017)
7. Chen, L.C., Zhu, Y., Papandreou, G., Schroff, F., Adam, H.: Encoder-decoder with atrous separable convolution for semantic image segmentation. In: Proceedings of the European Conference on Computer Vision (ECCV), pp. 801–818 (2018)
8. Chiasi, G., Lin, T.Y., Le, Q.V.N.: Learning scalable feature pyramid architecture for object detection. In: Proceedings of the IEEE Computer Vision and Pattern Recognition, pp. 7029–7038
9. Dai, J., et al.: Deformable convolutional networks. In: Proceedings of the IEEE International Conference on Computer Vision, pp. 764–773 (2017)
10. Dai, Z., Yang, Z., Yang, Y., Carbonell, J., Le, Q.V., Salakhutdinov, R.: Transformer-xl: attentive language models beyond a fixed-length context. arXiv preprint arXiv:1901.02860 (2019)
11. Deng, J., Dong, W., Socher, R., Li, L.J., Li, K., Fei-Fei, L.: Imagenet: a large-scale hierarchical image database. In: 2009 IEEE Conference on Computer Vision and Pattern Recognition, pp. 248–255. IEEE (2009)
12. Desimone, R.: Visual attention mediated by biased competition in extrastriate visual cortex. Philos. Trans. Roy. Soc. Lond. Ser. B: Biol. Sci. **353**(1373), 1245–1255 (1998)
13. He, K., Gkioxari, G., Dollár, P., Girshick, R.: Mask r-cnn. In: Proceedings of the IEEE International Conference on Computer Vision, pp. 2961–2969 (2017)

14. He, K., Zhang, X., Ren, S., Sun, J.: Deep residual learning for image recognition. In: Proceedings of the IEEE Conference on Computer Vision and Pattern Recognition, pp. 770–778 (2016)
15. Hochreiter, S., Schmidhuber, J.: Long short-term memory. Neural Comput. **9**(8), 1735–1780 (1997)
16. Hu, J., Shen, L., Sun, G.: Squeeze-and-excitation networks. In: Proceedings of the IEEE Conference on Computer Vision and Pattern Recognition, pp. 7132–7141 (2018)
17. Jain, S., Wallace, B.C.: Attention is not explanation. arXiv preprint arXiv:1902.10186 (2019)
18. Jiang, C., Xu, H., Zhang, W., Liang, X., Li, Z.: Sp-nas: serial-to-parallel backbone search for object detection. In: Proceedings of the IEEE/CVF Conference on Computer Vision and Pattern Recognition, pp. 11863–11872 (2020)
19. Li, J., Raventos, A., Bhargava, A., Tagawa, T., Gaidon, A.: Learning to fuse things and stuff. arXiv preprint arXiv:1812.01192 (2018)
20. Li, X., Wang, W., Hu, X., Yang, J.: Selective kernel networks. In: Proceedings of the IEEE/CVF Conference on Computer Vision and Pattern Recognition, pp. 510–519 (2019)
21. Lin, T.Y., Dollár, P., Girshick, R., He, K., Hariharan, B., Belongie, S.: Feature pyramid networks for object detection. In: Proceedings of the IEEE Conference on Computer Vision and Pattern Recognition, pp. 2117–2125 (2017)
22. Lin, T.-Y., et al.: Microsoft COCO: common objects in context. In: Fleet, D., Pajdla, T., Schiele, B., Tuytelaars, T. (eds.) ECCV 2014. LNCS, vol. 8693, pp. 740–755. Springer, Cham (2014). https://doi.org/10.1007/978-3-319-10602-1_48
23. Liu, S., Qi, L., Qin, H., Shi, J., Jia, J.: Path aggregation network for instance segmentation. In: Proceedings of the IEEE Conference on Computer Vision and Pattern Recognition, pp. 8759–8768 (2018)
24. Liu, W., et al.: SSD: single shot multiBox detector. In: Leibe, B., Matas, J., Sebe, N., Welling, M. (eds.) ECCV 2016. LNCS, vol. 9905, pp. 21–37. Springer, Cham (2016). https://doi.org/10.1007/978-3-319-46448-0_2
25. Ren, S., He, K., Girshick, R., Sun, J.: Faster r-cnn: towards real-time object detection with region proposal networks. Adv. Neural Inf. Process. Syst. **28** (2015)
26. Tan, M., Pang, R., Le, Q.V.: Efficientdet: scalable and efficient object detection. In: Proceedings of the IEEE/CVF Conference on Computer Vision and Pattern Recognition, pp. 10781–10790 (2020)
27. Wang, X., Girshick, R., Gupta, A., He, K.: Non-local neural networks. In: Proceedings of the IEEE Conference on Computer Vision and Pattern Recognition, pp. 7794–7803 (2018)
28. Xu, H., Yao, L., Zhang, W., Liang, X., Li, Z.: Auto-fpn: automatic network architecture adaptation for object detection beyond classification. In: Proceedings of the IEEE/CVF International Conference on Computer Vision, pp. 6649–6658 (2019)
29. Zoph, B., Le, Q.V.: Neural architecture search with reinforcement learning. arXiv preprint arXiv:1611.01578 (2016)

O-LGMD: An Opponent Colour LGMD-Based Model for Collision Detection with Thermal Images at Night

Yicheng Zhang[1,3], Jiannan Zhao[2], Mu Hua[3], Hao Luan[4], Mei Liu[1], Fang Lei[1,3], Heriberto Cuayahuitl[3], and Shigang Yue[3(✉)]

[1] Guangdong University of Petrochemical Technology (GDUPT), Maoming, China
{zhangyicheng,liumei}@gdupt.edu.cn
[2] Guangxi University, Nanning 530004, China
[3] University of Lincoln (UoL), Brayford Pool, Lincoln LN6 7ST, UK
{YiZhang,MHua,FLei,HCuayahuitl,SYue}@lincoln.ac.uk
[4] Tianjin University of Technology, Tianjin 300072, China

Abstract. It is an enormous challenge for intelligent robots or vehicles to detect and avoid collisions at night because of poor lighting conditions. Thermal cameras capture night scenes with temperature maps, often showing different pseudo-colour modes to enhance the visual effects for the human eyes. Since the features of approaching objects could have been well enhanced in the pseudo-colour outputs of a thermal camera, it is likely that colour cues could help the Lobula Giant Motion Detector (LGMD) to pick up the collision cues effectively. However, there is no investigation published on this aspect and it is not clear whether LGMD-like neural networks can take pseudo-colour information as input for collision detection in extreme dim conditions. In this study, we investigate a few thermal pseudo-colour modes and propose to extract colour cues with a triple-channel LGMD-based neural network to directly process the pseudo-colour images. The proposed model consists of three sub-networks—each dealing with one specific opponent colour channel, i.e. black-white, red-green, or yellow-blue. A collision alarm is triggered if any channel's output exceeds its threshold for a few successive frames. Our experiments demonstrate that the proposed bio-inspired collision detection system works well in quickly detecting colliding objects in direct collision course in extremely low lighting conditions. The proposed method showed its potential to be part of sensor systems for future robots or vehicles driving at night or in other extreme lighting conditions—to help avoiding fatal collisions.

Keywords: Collision detection · LGMD · Opponent colour

Supported by the GDUPT-UoL joint research lab, which is also named Computational Intelligence Laboratory (CIL) at the University of Lincoln.

E. Pimenidis et al. (Eds.): ICANN 2022, LNCS 13531, pp. 249–260, 2022.
https://doi.org/10.1007/978-3-031-15934-3_21

1   Introduction

Vision-based collision detection solutions need to adaptive to their environments in order to enhance the intelligence of robots and autonomous vehicles. In case of poor visibility, such as in low lighting or in adverse weather, applying thermal cameras is a potentially useful complement to optical cameras for collision detection tasks. Typically, thermal cameras provide users with several pseudo-colour schemes. The question "how to make better use of these pseudo-colour images for collision detection tasks?" is still open and worth exploring.

Mimicking the Lobula Giant Motion Detector (LGMD) in the locust visual system, the LGMD-based imminent collision detection methods are simple, robust, and energy-saving [16]. As an algorithm fit for impending obstacle detection in dynamic environments [28], it has been used in many scenarios, such as unmanned aerial vehicles(UAVs) [23,31], robots [13,27], ground vehicles [6,29], among others. However and as shown in Fig. 1, most approaches convert colour images into grayscale ones in the presynaptic part of the neural networks. Thus, only the luminance information is preserved in the postsynaptic network, and the colour cues are lost during processing.

Spectral selectivity is independent of intensity as a cue for decision making in vision tasks [18]. Except for those without colour vision, chromatic information plays an important role in the behaviours of animals like foraging, mating, and avoiding predators [25]. Results in [17] show that under natural lighting conditions, dogs rely more on colour cues than brightness to distinguish things. This suggests that preserving colour information in the collision detection neural network is a sensible thing to do.

Although much detail about how the brain processes colour information remains to be learned, the two major colour vision theories—Young-Helmholtz trichromatic theory and Hering opponent-process theory [19]—are used to explain different levels of the nervous system. The Helmholtz theory can describe the colour selectivity of three types of cone photoreceptors in the retina that are sensitive to different wavelengths of light [11]. The Hering theory postulates three independent opponent-colour pairs as the basis for colour perception [12]. This better explains the synaptic connectivity and functional pathways in the retina [3]. Consequently and from a biological perspective, the circuits that connect bipolar cells, amacrine cells, and ganglion cells transform the trichromatic signals into opponent-pairs information [21].

Inspired by the knowledge of colour vision of primates [4,9], we proposed an opponent colour LGMD-based model (named O-LGMD) as illustrated in Fig. 2. This model can be divided into two main parts. The *first part* of the network mimics the mechanism from the retina to the lateral geniculate nucleus (LGN) in an old-world monkey's brain, which transforms RGB images into the opponent colour data. The *second part* is responsible for detecting imminent collisions, which consists of three parallel LGMD networks inspired by the lobula of locusts.

The main contributions of this work are summarized as follows: (1) we verified the fact that the LGMD-based model still works in collision detection, when taking the pseudo-colour thermal images as input. (2) by combining the

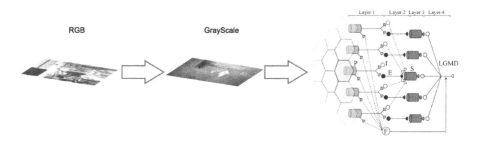

Fig. 1. Pipeline in the classic Lobula Giant Motion Detector (LGMD) model, where colour images are grayscaled and then fed into a four-layer LGMD neural network. (Color figure online)

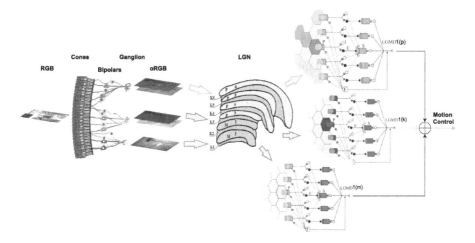

Fig. 2. The proposed triple-channel opponent-colour LGMD model. Similarly to the three pathways relayed by the Magnocellular, Parvocellular, and Koniocellular layers in the primate's lateral geniculate nucleus, we decompose the colour image into three sets of opponent colour data (black-white, red-green, and blue-yellow) then send them to their corresponding LGMD1 for detection (Color figure online)

mammalian colour perception with the locust motion detector, we established a triple-channel O-LGMD model for collision detection using pseudo-colour thermal images as input. (3) we explore the effect of different pseudo colour modes on the results of collision detection using LGMD-based models.

2   Related Work

2.1   Colour Models

A colour model is a mathematical representation of colours, see Ibraheem et al. [15] for a review of the most common colour models and their characteristics and application areas. Some recent studies have used multiple colour models to complement each other, for example, Dong et al. [5] introduce an RLCM method that uses both red-green-blue (RGB) and International Commission on Illumination (CIE) L*a*b models to enhance underwater images. New colour models have also been proposed in specific application areas. Yan et al. present a quantum colour model based on the original hue-saturation-lightness (HSL) model (named QHSL) in [26]. Bratkova et al. [1] establish a practical opponent colour model (oRGB) to obtain a true red-green opponent channel. Due to their low computational cost, colour-based methods are widely adopted to recognise objects known to have relatively fixed colours, such as flames [10], fruits [24], etc. Colour models are also applied to other computer vision tasks, e.g. image segmentation, object tracking, etc. But to the best of our knowledge, very few motion perception approaches make the use of colour cues.

2.2   LGMD-Based Collision Detection Model

In 1996, Rind and Bramwell introduced a practical LGMD1 computational model [22]. This 4-layer feed-forward neural network with lateral inhibition was proved to be sensitive to fast-approaching objects. Soon after, Yue and Rind further improved the above model into a 5-layer one [28]. With an extra group excitation and decay processing layer, the new LGMD1 model is more robust and adaptive to dynamic backgrounds in robotic experiments. Then, Fu and Yue set up an LGMD2 model with ON/OFF channels after the photoreceptor layer [8]. Although the LGMD2 model is only selective for lighting change from bright to dark, it mended up some drawbacks of LGMD1, such as better resisting the disturbance of the ambient illumination.

More recently, LGMD-based methods have demonstrated a diverse development trend and improved models for specific problems have emerged. For UAV applications, Zhao et al. proposed a distributed presynaptic connection-based LGMD1 model (D-LGMD1) [31] using spatial and temporal filters in lateral inhibition, which is suitable for scenarios when the camera is moving at high speed. Lei et al. demonstrated an enhanced LGMD1 model with ON/OFF dual channels [20]. By judging the combination results from both pathways, this model effectively inhibits the responses to translation motions.

On the other hand, the proven LGMD models have become part of newly proposed synthetic vision systems. For example, Zhang et al. proposed a neural network integrating LGMD and direction-selective network(DSN) for collision prediction [30]. By applying different detection neurons to different regions of the visual field, the fusion model is more practical for ground driving scenarios. Hu and Fu recently established a visual motion cues discrimination neural network (ViMDNN), which includes four motion detection neurons: LGMD1, LGMD2 and two DSNs [7,14]. In their model, vision cues are extracted with different presynaptic neurons and synthesized in the postsynaptic part with lateral inhibition.

3   Proposed Method

As shown in Fig. 2, the O-LGMD model comprises two major functions. One is the opponent colour transformer which transforms the data from the RGB colour space to the oRGB space. The other is the LGMD-based collision detector which consists of three parallel and independent LGMD1 neural networks. Each LGMD1 neuron is responsible for detecting one opponent-colour channel.

3.1   The oRGB Transformation

As stated above, the opponent process occurs from the retina to the LGN pathway within the primate visual system. To mimic the mechanism of the opponent pathway optic nervous system, we simply convert RGB images into the oRGB data using the method introduced in [1].

The opponent colour transformation includes two steps. The **first step** is a linear transformation form the non-linear $R'G'B'$ values to an intermediate space which is denoted as $L'C_1'C_2'$ [1].

$$\begin{bmatrix} L' \\ C_1' \\ C_2' \end{bmatrix} = \begin{bmatrix} 0.2990 & 0.5870 & 0.1140 \\ 0.5000 & 0.5000 & -1.0000 \\ 0.8660 & -0.8660 & 0.0000 \end{bmatrix} \begin{bmatrix} R' \\ G' \\ B' \end{bmatrix} \tag{1}$$

To orthogonalise the axis of both opponent colour pairs, the **second step** of the transformation is a non-uniform rotation around the luma axis L' as

$$\theta_o = \begin{cases} (3/2)\theta & \text{if } \theta < \pi/3 \\ \pi/2 + (3/4)(\theta - \pi/3) & \text{if } \pi \geq \theta \geq \pi/3, \end{cases} \tag{2}$$

where $\theta = atan(C_2', C_1')$ is the original angle in the $L'C'C'$ linear chroma plane, and θ_o is the final angle after rotation. Then the new coordinates in oRGB space can be calculated according to

$$\begin{bmatrix} C_{yb}' \\ C_{rg}' \end{bmatrix} = \begin{bmatrix} \cos(\theta_0 - \theta) & -\sin(\theta_0 - \theta) \\ \sin(\theta_0 - \theta) & \cos(\theta_0 - \theta) \end{bmatrix} \begin{bmatrix} C_1' \\ C_2' \end{bmatrix} \tag{3}$$

By extending the positive half-plane and compressing the negative half-plane of the x-axis, we obtain a colour gamut with Hering-style opponent axes.

3.2   The LGMD-Based Neural Network

As mentioned above, there are several LGMD-based models available. The LGMD2 neuron is only sensitive to changes from light to dark, it is true that most of the time the objects are darker than their back ground in well light optical data, but the situation is quite different in the thermal pictures, where objects are often brighter. D-LGMD1 may be another good option, but LGMD1 model runs faster because of its relative simple structure. Therefore, we chose the LGMD1 computational model to perceive the looming motion in each channel

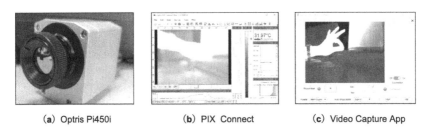

(a) Optris Pi450i   (b) PIX Connect   (c) Video Capture App

Fig. 3. Experiment environment: (a) the camera we used is an Optris Pi450i LWIR camera with specifications: frame 80 Hz, resolution 382 × 288, FOV 53 × 38, NETD 34mK; (b) the manufacturer-provided camera data acquisition software PIX Connect; (c) the MATLAB APP we developed for recording mp4/avi format clips, which is based on EVOCORTEX SDK. [https://github.com/zhangyicheng79/ThermalRecorder]

of the opponent colour space. All the formulas and the parameters we used are exactly the same as that in Yue and Rind's paper [27]. Note that the proposed O-LGMD model has three independent LGMD1 neural networks, an OR logical operation is adopted to synthesis these three outputs in the final step.

4   Experiments and Discussion

We carried out two kinds of experiments to verify the effectiveness of the O-LGMD model. One used synthetic clips to test the colour recognition ability of the proposed model. Afterwards, pseudo-colour videos of real-world collision scenes were employed to further validate whether the colour cues help to improve the LGMD1 model in looming objects detection, especially in dim environments.

4.1   Experimental Setup

This study was motivated by the use of thermal cameras as a potential alternative in low lighting or extreme weather conditions when optical cameras fail to identify collisions. Therefore, the Optris Pi450i long-wave infrared (LWIR) camera (see Fig. 3a) has been selected as the main data acquisition device and all data were collected in a lighting environment below 2 lx. The PIX Connect (Fig. 3b) applicaiton provided by the manufacturer is very powerful and friendly. However, it can only output videos in ravi format, which is inconvenient for other programs to access. Thus, we developed another video-capture program (Fig. 3c) based on the Evocortex SDK, which is able to save clips in either mp4 or avi format. All our programs are developed in MATLAB(R2021b) and are running on a desktop PC with one 3.4 GHz quad core CPU and 32 GB RAM.

4.2   Colour Discrimination Test

It is certain that when colour images are converted into grayscale ones, they will lose a lot of information as the colour space is reduced from 3 dimensions to 1

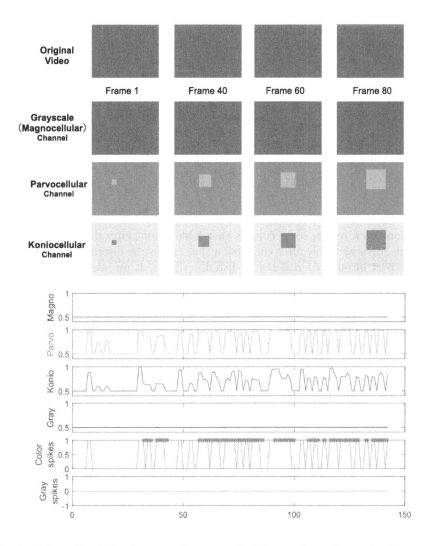

Fig. 4. Colour discrimination experiment result. The top row shows the frames in the synthetic video, the front block's RGB colour is set to (103,129,13), the background colour is (240,59,13). The second row includes the frames in the grayscale channel, as can be seen, both previous colours have exactly the same illumination after being grayscaled—which means that the object cannot be seen using grayscale images. The third and the fourth rows are the frame data in two opponent colour channels. The upper three plots (Magno, Parvo, Konio) are the membrane potentials in the O-LGMD's opponent channels, and the fourth plot (Gray) is the membrane potentials in the grayscale channel. The second to last plot (Color Spikes) are the spikes given by the O-LGMD model, and the bottom plot (Gray Spikes) with no spikes is the output of the LGMD1 model. It can be seen that whilst the LGMD1 shows no response to the colour object, the proposed O-LGMD responds to the object with spikes. (Color figure online)

Table 1. Colour Pairs used in our experiments. Each pair contains two colours that are clearly different in chromatic vision, but they are not applicable to be recognised after conversion to grayscale data. Such colour pairs are easily derived from the RGB and grayscale conversion formulas of Rec.ITU-R BT.601-7.

No.	The foreground colour (r, g, b values)	The background colour (r, g, b values)
1	240, 59, 13	103, 129, 13
2	240, 59, 134	103, 129, 134
3	23, 25, 250	23, 231, 210
4	136, 240, 3	136, 40, 42

dimension. As a result, some colours that look significantly different may have the same grayscale value after conversion that cannot be discriminated at all. In the first part of our experiments, as listed in Table 1, we selected some colour pairs that satisfy the above conditions to generate videos. Each synthetic video includes two colour squares, the foreground rectangle gradually expands from small to large, which simulates the scene where a distant object is approached to the camera. Then we take these clips as input to the neural networks and observe the membrane potential and collision warning spikes that they output.

One of these results is displayed in Fig. 4, as expected, it is impossible to distinguish the foreground and background in the grayscale/Magnocellular channel. Instead, the Parvocellular channel and the Koniocellular channel are sensitive to the colour differences. Based on the above experiments and compared against the traditional LGMD pipeline, the triple-channel O-LGMD model has a better colour discrimination ability. This capability may be useful for motion detection through pseudo-colour images output by thermal cameras.

4.3 Pseudo-colour Thermal Clips Test

To further verify the effect of the O-LGMD model in real scenes, we use 396 pseudo colour clips as input to the neural network. These data can be roughly divided into 3 categories: (1) Objects approaching the camera (32 scenes × 6 colour schemes); (2) Camera moving around (21 scenes × 6 colour schemes); (3) Pedestrian scenes (13 scenes × 6 colour schemes).

Figure 5 contains some experimental scenarios and results. It can be seen from Fig. 5(h) and Fig. 5(i) that benefit from the existence of the Magnocellular channel, the O-LGMD model has the same detection sensitivity as the LGMD1 model when dealing with monochrome data, the collision alarms are given out at the exact same frame in the image sequence. Figure 5(g) reveals that the O-LGMD is a bit more sensitive than the LGMD1 model in the monoblue palette. We believe this is because according to the color-to-grayscale conversion formula of Rec.ITU-R BT.601-7 [2], the data loss in the blue channel is bigger.

Despite the O-LGMD being sensitive to colours, it does not always prevail when dealing with colour images. Although Fig. 5(c), (e) and (f) indicate that

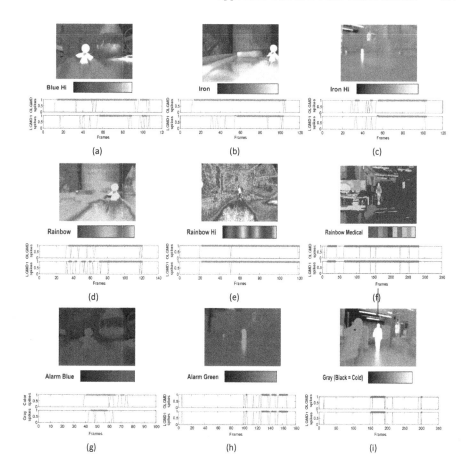

Fig. 5. Collision detection results comparing O-LGMD and LGMD1 in different pseudo colour palettes. The upper images are sample frames in a special pseudo-colour palette that is supported by Optris Pi cameras. The text on the left of the ribbon in the middle of each group is the name of the palette used in the test. The bottom half of each set shows the outputs of two LGMD-based models. In scenes (a), (b), (d), (e) and (g), the camera is fixed on the table and a ball rolls from a distance along a specific track in direction to the camera lens. In (c) and (h), a hot target is placed on the ground, and an electric car carrying the camera approached the target. In (f) and (i), a pedestrian and the camera car moved towards each other. The O-LGMD responds to the colliding objects a number of frames early in many of the test scenes, and the Blue Hi and Iron are the best performed pseudo colour palettes. (Color figure online)

O-LGMD has some advantages in the IronHi, RainbowHi, and Rainbow Medical palettes, the benefits of applying O-LGMD in Rainbow mode (Fig. 5(d)) are not obvious in most situations. Nonetheless and most of the time in our experiments, the O-LGMD outperforms the LGMD1 in the BlueHi and Iron palettes—as shown in Fig. 5(a), (b). Our experimental results generally show

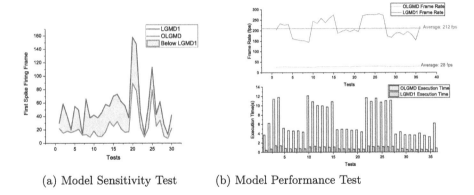

(a) Model Sensitivity Test   (b) Model Performance Test

Fig. 6. Comparison of the O-LGMD and the LGMD1 results taking images in the BlueHi pseudo colour scheme as input. (a) The horizontal axis is the experimental/test number, and the curves represent the frame number when the model first fires a spike. (b) The upper diagram indicates the frame rate of the two models, the numbers to the right of the curve are their average frame rates. The bar chart shows the execution time of the two neural networks.

that when a pseudo-colour palette contains too many colours, the O-LGMD model will be scattered. Therefore, the O-LGMD model is especially suitable for collision detection tasks with the pseudo-colour schemes consisting of 2 or 3 colours, such as BlueHi and Iron.

Figure 6(a) compares the first frame when a collision warning signal is given out between the LGMD1 and O-LGMD models in the BlueHi pseudo colour scheme. In a limited number of 30 tests, only 2 times LGMD1 and O-LGMD spiked almost simultaneously. The two have the greatest gap of nearly 70 frames in the 21st experiment shown in the picture. This result indicates that the O-LGMD model can identify approaching objects earlier in the same image sequences, which means the O-LGMD is more sensitive than the LGMD1. Figure 6(b) demonstrates the running speed of the two models, the above curves shows the the LGMD1 model has an average running frame rate of 7.5 times more than that of the O-LGMD model. The bar chart shows the collision detection execution time of the two models. It is easy to see from the figure that the detection time of O-LGMD is longer than that of the LGMD1 for the same detection task due to the need for colour channel separation and calculation of three LGMD neurons.

4.4 Discussion

By expanding the parallel number of neurons, we introduced an LGMD-based collision detection neural network O-LMGD above that can make better use of colour cues. Especially when there are different colours with equal grayscale values, it can identify targets clearly when an LGMD1 model cannot. However, as more information is processed, the model requires more execution time and computing resources. Since the collision is often a vital safety issue in many application scenarios, it is worth spending more resources to make sure imminent collisions can be detected despite of additional resource costs.

5 Conclusion

This paper proposes an O-LGMD neural network with three opponent colour processing pathways for collision detection at night time from thermal images. Similarly to the structure of the lateral geniculate nucleus in the primate thalamus, the proposed network has one channel for the luminance signal and two for the chromatic information. Experimental results indicate that the O-LGMD network utilises the advantages of opponent colour processing methods well to effectively distinguish colours that are ambiguous in grayscale images. Our study also demonstrates that the model can help to improve the sensitivity of collision recognition in specific infrared pseudo-colour palettes such as Blue Hi and IRON.

Acknowledgement. This research was supported by the EU HORIZON 2020 project ULTRACEPT (778062) and the National Natural Science Foundation of China project (62073091).

References

1. Bratkova, M., Boulos, S., Shirley, P.: oRGB: a practical opponent color space for computer graphics. IEEE Comput. Graph. Appl. **29**(1) (2008)
2. BT, R.I.R., et al.: Studio encoding parameters of digital television for standard 4:3 and wide-screen 16:9 aspect ratios. International Radio Consultative Committee International Telecommunication Union, Switzerland, CCIR Rep. (2011)
3. Buchsbaum, G., Gottschalk, A.: Trichromacy, opponent colours coding and optimum colour information transmission in the retina. Proc. Roy. Soc. Lond. Ser. B Biol. Sci. **220**(1218) (1983)
4. Dacey, D.M.: Parallel pathways for spectral coding in primate retina. Annu. Rev. Neurosci. **23**(1) (2000)
5. Dong, L., Zhang, W., Xu, W.: Underwater image enhancement via integrated RGB and LAB color models. Signal Process. Image Commun. (2022)
6. Fu, Q., et al.: A visual neural network for robust collision perception in vehicle driving scenarios. In: MacIntyre, J., Maglogiannis, I., Iliadis, L., Pimenidis, E. (eds.) AIAI 2019. IAICT, vol. 559, pp. 67–79. Springer, Cham (2019). https://doi.org/10.1007/978-3-030-19823-7_5
7. Fu, Q., Hu, C., Liu, P., Yue, S.: Synthetic neural vision system design for motion pattern recognition in dynamic robot scenes. arXiv preprint arXiv:1904.07180 (2019)
8. Fu, Q., Yue, S.: Modelling LGMD2 visual neuron system. In: International Workshop on Machine Learning for Signal Processing (MLSP). IEEE (2015)
9. Grünert, U., Martin, P.R.: Cell types and cell circuits in human and non-human primate retina. Prog. Retinal Eye Res. **78** (2020)
10. Hashemzadeh, M., Zademehdi, A.: Fire detection for video surveillance applications using ICA K-medoids-based color model and efficient spatio-temporal visual features. Exp. Syst. Appl. **130** (2019)

11. Helmholtz, H.V.: The Young-Helmholtz theory of color vision, 1860 (1948)
12. Hering, E.: Outlines of a theory of the light sense (1964)
13. Hu, C., Arvin, F., Xiong, C., Yue, S.: Bio-inspired embedded vision system for autonomous micro-robots: the LGMD case. IEEE Trans. Cognit. Develop. Syst. **9**(3) (2016)
14. Hu, C., Xiong, C., Peng, J., Yue, S.: Coping with multiple visual motion cues under extremely constrained computation power of micro autonomous robots. IEEE Access **8** (2020)
15. Ibraheem, N.A., Hasan, M.M., Khan, R.Z., Mishra, P.K.: Understanding color models: a review. ARPN J. Sci. Technol. **2**(3) (2012)
16. Jayachandran, D., et al.: A low-power biomimetic collision detector based on an in-memory molybdenum disulfide photodetector. Nat. Electron. **3**(10) (2020)
17. Kasparson, A.A., Badridze, J., Maximov, V.V.: Colour cues proved to be more informative for dogs than brightness. Proc. Roy. Soc. B Biol. Sci. **280**(1766) (2013)
18. van der Kooi, C.J., Stavenga, D.G., Arikawa, K., Belušič, G., Kelber, A.: Evolution of insect color vision: from spectral sensitivity to visual ecology. Annu. Rev. Entomol.**66** (2021)
19. Lakowski, R.: Theory and practice of colour vision testing: a review part 1. Occupat. Environ. Med. **26**(3) (1969)
20. Lei, F., Peng, Z., Liu, M., Peng, J., Cutsuridis, V., Yue, S.: A robust visual system for looming cue detection against translating motion. IEEE Trans. Neural Netw. Learn. Syst. (2022)
21. Lyapidevskii, V.: Experimental verification of the opponent theory of human color vision. Biophysics **51**(2) (2006)
22. Rind, F.C., Bramwell, D.: Neural network based on the input organization of an identified neuron signaling impending collision. J. Neurophysiol. **75**(3) (1996)
23. Salt, L., Indiveri, G., Sandamirskaya, Y.: Obstacle avoidance with LGMD neuron: towards a neuromorphic UAV implementation. In: 2017 IEEE International Symposium on Circuits and Systems (ISCAS). IEEE (2017)
24. Smith, A.C., Buchanan-Smith, H.M., Surridge, A.K., Osorio, D., Mundy, N.I.: The effect of colour vision status on the detection and selection of fruits by tamarins (saguinus spp.). J. Exp. Biol. **206**(18) (2003)
25. Song, B.M., Lee, C.H.: Toward a mechanistic understanding of color vision in insects. Front. Neural Circuits **12** (2018)
26. Yan, F., Li, N., Hirota, K.: QHSL: A quantum hue, saturation, and lightness color model. Inf. Sci. **577** (2021)
27. Yue, S., Rind, F.C.: A collision detection system for a mobile robot inspired by the locust visual system. In: Proceedings of the 2005 IEEE International Conference on Robotics and Automation. IEEE (2005)
28. Yue, S., Rind, F.C.: Collision detection in complex dynamic scenes using an LGMD-based visual neural network with feature enhancement. IEEE Trans. Neural Netw. **17**(3) (2006)
29. Yue, S., Rind, F.C., Keil, M.S., Cuadri, J., Stafford, R.: A bio-inspired visual collision detection mechanism for cars: optimisation of a model of a locust neuron to a novel environment. Neurocomputing **69**, 13–15 (2006)
30. Zhang, G., Zhang, C., Yue, S.: LGMD and DSNs neural networks integration for collision predication. In: International Joint Conference on Neural Networks (IJCNN). IEEE (2016)
31. Zhao, J., Wang, H., Bellotto, N., Hu, C., Peng, J., Yue, S.: Enhancing LGMD's looming selectivity for UAV with spatial-temporal distributed presynaptic connections. IEEE Trans. Neural Netw. Learn. Syst. (2021)

Semantic Diversity Image Translation Based on Deep Feature Difference and Attention Mechanism

Le Xu, Weiling Cai(✉), Zhiwei Li, and Cairun Wang

Nanjing Normal University, Nanjing 210097, China
caiwl@njnu.edu.cn

Abstract. To improve the semantic diversity and visual authenticity of image translation, in this paper we propose Generative Adversarial Networks based on deep feature difference and attention mechanism. In our model, we employ a pre-trained image classification network to extract different level features of the generated images and then calculate the perceptual similarity based on these features. Such perceptual similarities are introduced into the adversarial learning to control the differences in high-level semantic features. Furthermore, in order to ensure the quality of the translated image, the residual network structure with the attention mechanism is utilized in our model. According to the importance of each feature channel, the different attention is strengthened on the useful features. In addition, we not only employ the discriminator on the generated images to discriminate whether the images are real or fake, but also make a discrimination on the reconstructed images. The main contributions of this paper are as follows: (1) Previous studies on the diversity of image translation mainly focus on the low-level features of the image, such as hair color and skin color. Our method focuses on semantic differences through deep features, with the aim of improving the semantic diversity of images in the styles. (2) Our model adopts the channel-attention mechanism and reconstructed-image discriminator, which not only highlight the feature details of the generated image, but also ensure the translated images as real as possible. The results on Celeba-HQ dataset verify the superiority of our model on both visual quality and semantic diversity.

Keywords: Image-to-image translation · Deep feature difference · Semantic diversity

1 Introduction

Image-to-image translation aims to learn a mapping between different visual domains. Early works [1–4] learn a deterministic mapping between two domains by Generative Adversarial Networks (GAN) with the cycle consistency. This gives rise to an issue: How to generate the images with different styles.

E. Pimenidis et al. (Eds.): ICANN 2022, LNCS 13531, pp. 261–272, 2022.
https://doi.org/10.1007/978-3-031-15934-3_22

Most of the existing methods [5–9] attempted to control the diversity of generated images in a random way. For example, the classic method StyleGAN [8] introduced a non-linear mapping function that embedded an input latent code into a style space to better represent the factors of variation. DRIT [9] and MUNIT [10] attempted to embed images in two spaces to capture cross-domain shared information of invariant domain content space and domain-specific attribute space. However, the above methods do not control the latent vectors, and thus the translator does not have enough guidance information to make the training model reach the ideal state, as a result, the mode collapse or the poor generation results often occur in the training phrase.

Recently, some researchers have made a series of attempts to control the diversity of generated images, however such image diversity seems not to be reflected in the semantic level. For example, the references [5, 6] proposed the mode-seeking based methods to control the distance rate between generated images and latent vectors. Although these methods [5, 6] can generate a variety of results, the diversity is mainly reflected on low-level features such as background color, hair color and skin color. It is worth noting that diversity based on distance metrics is obviously different from human perception [11]. The underlying reason is that the pixel-based distance ignores the structural information of images, and only focuses on the low-level semantic features. An ideal image translation model should consider not only the differences of low-level features, but also the high-level features, such as the hair styles, the makeup styles, etc.

To address the semantic diversity, we propose Generative Adversarial Networks for image translation based on deep feature difference and attention mechanism (DFattGAN). DFattGAN employs the pre-trained deep feature network to extract the deep features and calculates the style difference between the generated images. By introducing the style difference to the adversarial learning, our model can generate the images with different styles on the high-level semantic features. To further improve the authenticity of image translation, we input both the generated image and reconstructed image into discriminator D to ensure that the outputs of generator G are real. In addition, we adopt the attention mechanism in the down-sampling stage of the generator to obtain the importance of each channel. This mechanism can make our model focus on the image parts that need to be changed in style, and thus enhancing the visual quality of image details. We conduct the extensive experiments on the dataset Celeba_HQ. Both qualitative and quantitative results show that DFattGAN has better results in visual quality and style diversity than baseline [6, 9, 10]. The contributions of this paper are as follows:

- We propose a novel image translation method called DFattGAN for generating images with semantic diversity. This method can control the diversity of image styles from the perspective of deep feature differences.
- DFattGAN utilizes channel attention mechanism and multiple discriminators in image translation. Our model not only highlights the details of the generated image, but also ensures the generated image as realistic as possible.
- Experiments show that DFattGAN achieves state-of-the-art performance on two scenarios: one is the scene in which the latent variable guides the style for generated image; the other is the scene in which the reference image guides the image style.

2 Related Work

Image-to-Image Translation. Image translation has attracted increasing attentions since its widely practical application, such as colorization, super resolution, semantic synthesis and domain adaption. Pix2pix [12] is the first unified framework for image translation based on conditional GANs. Recent studies have attempted to learn image translation without supervision. Some works enforce the translation to preserve certain properties of the source domain data, such as pixel values, pixel gradients, semantic features, class labels, or pairwise sample distances. Another popular approach is to take advantage of cycle consistency loss [1–3]. The main idea is that by translating the input image to the target domain and then back to the source domain, the output results should be similar to the source images. MUNIT [10] assumes that the image representation can be decomposed into domain invariant content code and style code. Beside improving the visual quality, the semantic diversity is another important goal for image translation. Some methods attempt to generate multiple outputs with the same input and encourage them to be different. BicycleGAN [13] proposes a framework that can model continuous and multi-modal distributions. To generate images with diversity, recent methods reinforce the connection between stochastic noise and the generated image by marginal matching, latent regression [10], and diversity regularization [5].

Generative Adversarial Networks. Generative adversarial networks [4] have gained remarkable results. After training, the generator is able to produce outputs which are similar to the real samples. GANs also have shown impressive results in many computer vision tasks such as image synthesis, colorization and super-resolution. Recently, LSGAN [14] changed the objective function of GAN from the cross-entropy loss to the least square loss, WGAN-GP [15] proposed the gradient penalty and used Wasserstein distance instead of JS divergence, and SNGAN [16] proposed the spectral normalization for the parameter matrix W of neural network. MSGAN [5] solves the problem of training instability caused by mode collapse by designing a special loss function. These methods improve the image quality and the training stability of GANs.

3 Our Model

In this section, we propose Generative Adversarial Networks (DFattGAN) based on Deep Feature Diversity and Attention mechanism to improve semantic diversity and visual authenticity of generated images.

3.1 Framework

Our model DFattGAN trains a generator G that can produce the semantic diverse images corresponding to the specific domain for the input images x. To generate semantic diverse images, our model can learn the domain-specific style vectors for each domain in two different ways. As shown in Fig. 1, there are two ways to yield a style vector for style embedding. In Fig. 1(a), given a latent vector z and a domain y, our mapping network module M can generate a domain-specific style vector $\tilde{s} = M_y(x)$.

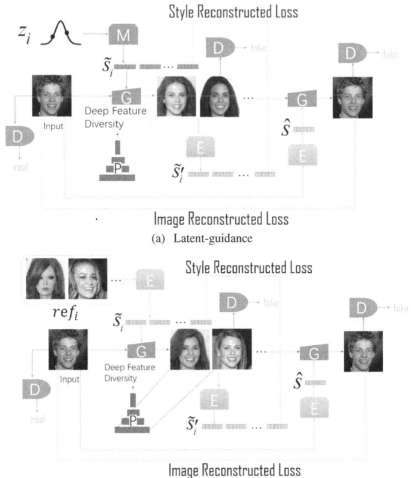

Fig. 1. Our model consists of five modules. The style mapping network M transforms latent vector into style vector. The style encoder E transforms reference image into style vector. The deep feature network P extracts the deep features of the generated images, and calculates the deep feature difference between the generated images. The inputs of generator G are source image and style vector, and the outputs are images corresponding to the different style vectors. The discriminator D discriminates whether the image is real or fake.

In Fig. 1(b), given a reference image x and its corresponding domain y, our style encoding module E can generate a style vector $\tilde{s} = E_y(x)$. Similar to M, the style encoding module E can generate different style vectors for different reference images. According to Fig. 1, our model at first obtains a style vector s through mapping module M or style encoding module E, and then convert the input image x into the output domain y according to the given style vector s.

In our model, the discriminator D is a multi-task discriminator, which consists of the multiple output branches. The discriminator D is used to discriminate whether the image x is a real or fake image of its domain y. In order to ensure the reality of the images, the traditional generative adversarial network [4] performs the reality discrimination on generated images through discriminators to distinguish whether images belong to real distribution or generated distribution. We require that both the generated image and the reconstructed image should be close to the reality, so the authenticity discrimination for both is carried out in the training phrase, so as to further improve the visual authenticity of the image generated by the generator.

3.2 Deep Feature Diversity

To further improve the images diversity, the traditional methods [5, 6] force the generator G to explore the image space and find meaningful style features to generate diverse images by maximizing L2 distance between $G(x, s_1)$ and $G(x, s_2)$. As shown in Fig. 2, the traditional methods for computing diversity generally consider the distance between the pixels of the generated images, and thus fail to consider the local and global relationship of the images, resulting in the loss of a lot of semantic information. While it is easy for humans to quickly judge the degree of difference between two images, the underlying process is thought to be quite complex. The widely used distance ratio, L1 distance and so on are very simple functions, which cannot explain human perception well. Recent works [11] have verified the effectiveness of using deep features to measure differences between images. As an example given by Fig. 2, the deep features perform better than previously widely used methods in simulating perceived differences.

Therefore, our model adopts the pre-trained AlexNet [17] as the deep feature extraction network P. Specifically, the deep features of image are at first extracted, and then the L1 distance between the deep features is computed to measure the image differences. By maximizing the deep difference between $G(x, s1)$ and $G(x, s2)$, the generator G in our model can explore the high-level semantic space and thus generate images with semantic diversity.

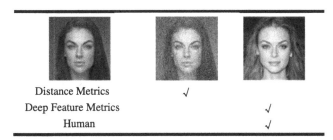

Distance Metrics	$\checkmark$	
Deep Feature Metrics		$\checkmark$
Human		$\checkmark$

Fig. 2. Determine which image is more different from the left given image. The mark '$\checkmark$' indicates the corresponding image is more different from the left given image. The traditional metrics (L2, PSNR, SSIM, etc.) disagree with human judgments. The deep networks can provide an embedding which agrees surprisingly well with humans.

3.3 Attention Mechanism

For better image translation effect, we use the channel-based attention mechanism to help the model focus on the features of the input image that need stylistic changes. In fact, we introduce Squeeze-and- Excite Network [18] into the residual block at the down-sampling stage. As shown in Fig. 3, it can generate weights for each feature channel according to the correlation between feature channels. The output for the Squeeze and congestion operations can be viewed as the importance of each feature, and then be weighted to the previous feature. This completes the re-calibration of the original feature on the channel dimension. We then take the down-sampling result with attention and the style vector s as the up-sampling input, and finally make the generated result of generator G focus on reflecting the part of style transformation we need, which improves the accuracy of the image translation result and reduces the interference of the secondary information in the image to the generated result.

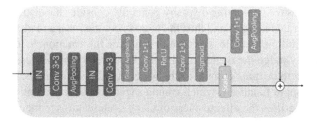

Fig. 3. The residual block structure with channel attention.

3.4 Objective Function

Adversarial Loss. In the training process, we adopt two ways to generate the style vector $\tilde{s}$: one is to generate style vector $\tilde{s}$ for a specific domain by randomly sampling latent vector $z \in Z$ and the target domain $\tilde{y} \in y$. The other is to generate style $\tilde{s}$ by randomly selecting a reference image x. On this basis, the input image x and style code $\tilde{s}$ are taken as the input of generator G, and the antagonistic loss is constructed to learn to generate image $G(x, \tilde{s})$. The objective function can be written in the following form:

$$L_{adv} = E_{x,y}\left[\log\left(D_y(x)\right)\right] + E_{x,\tilde{y},z}\left[\log\left(1 - D_{\tilde{y}}\left(G\left(x, \tilde{s}\right)\right)\right)\right]$$

$$+E_{x,\tilde{y},y,z}\left[\log\left(1 - D_{\tilde{y}}(G(G(x, \tilde{s}), \hat{s}))\right)\right] \tag{1}$$

where $\hat{s}$ is the style vector. The output of D represents whether the image is real in the corresponding domain y. The generator G expects that the generated image $G(x, \tilde{s})$ guided by the style vector $\tilde{s}$ is difficult to be distinguished by the discriminator D. In addition, generator G is expected to generate reconstructed images that are indistinguishable from discriminator.

Reconstruction Loss. We adopt the loss of image reconstruction to ensure that the essential features of the input image are not lost; Meanwhile, we adopt the style reconstruction to ensure that the style vector can be effectively utilized during image generation.

$$L_{recon} = E_{x,\tilde{y},z}[\| \ \tilde{s} \ -E_{\tilde{y}}\Big(G\Big(x,\tilde{s}\Big)\Big)\|_1]$$

$$+E_{x,y,\tilde{y},z}[\||x - G(G\Big(x,\tilde{s}\Big),\hat{s})\|_1]] \tag{2}$$

where $\hat{s} = E_y(x)$ is the style vector of the corresponding domain y of the input image x. The generator G can retain the essential features of the input image while changing the input image style through image reconstruction loss learning.

Diversity Loss. In order to allow generator G to generate images with different styles, we propose to constrain generator G with the diversity loss of deep feature difference.

$$L_{ds} = E_{x,\tilde{y},z_1,z_2}\Big[Perc\Big(G\Big(x,\tilde{s_1}\Big),G\Big(x,\tilde{s_2}\Big)\Big)\Big] \tag{3}$$

Style vector $\tilde{s}_1$ and $\tilde{s}_2$ are generated from random hidden variables z_1 and z_2 by sampling through mapping network module M, and similarly can be generated from two random reference images by style encoding module E. By maximizing the loss of diversity between generated images, the generator G can explore the image space and discover rich stylistic features, thus generating more diverse images. It is worth mentioning that the traditional distance rate-based methods often fail to capture the high-level semantic features of images, and the diversity of images are embodied only at the pixel level. Our diversity loss is based on the perceptual similarity of image deep features, paying more attention to the differences in advanced features between images and encouraging generators to generate images with more diverse semantic features.

Full Loss. Our complete objective function can be summarized as follows:

$$\min_{G,M,E} \max_{D} L_{adv} + \lambda_{recon}L_{recon} - \lambda_{ds}L_{ds} \tag{4}$$

where λ_{ds} and λ_{recon} represent the weight of diversity loss and reconstruction loss. By using this objective function, our model can generate more visually real images with more diverse styles while maintaining the original features of the images.

4   Experiment

4.1   Experiment Setting

We adopt MUNIT, DRIT, and Starganv2 as our baseline. All comparison methods are trained using the implementation provided by the authors. We evaluate our model on Celeba-HQ dataset which has two domains: male and female. We use FID and LPIPS to evaluate the visual quality and diversity of the generated images.

4.2 Experiment Result

In this section, we divide the experimental results into two parts, the generation of latent-guidance and the generation of reference-guidance.

Latent-guidance. As shown in Fig. 4, each method can generate different images through the latent variables. According to these experimental results, it is not difficult to find that

Fig. 4. Latent-guidance image synthesis results on Celeba_HQ. The first column is the source images, and the rest columns are images generated by our model, DRIT, MUNIT and StarGANv2, respectively.

MUNIT and DRIT methods have limited visual quality and diversity, and cannot produce significant changes to the source image. Our method has better visual quality and image diversity than the contrast method. It is worth mentioning that our approach encourages the model to retain the basic information of the source image while generating images with a greater variety of styles, such as more hair styles and makeup.

Table 1. Latent-guidance results

Quantitative Comparison	Celeba_HQ	
	FID	LPIPS
DRIT	52.1	0.178
MUNIT	31.4	0.263
StarGANv2	20.6	0.425
Ours	**18.6**	**0.455**

Table 1 gives FID and LPIPS of image translation results under the guidance of hidden variables for our method and comparison methods. For dataset Celeba_HQ, our method achieves the FID index of 18.6, indicating that our method is superior to the baseline in image quality. At the same time, our method has the highest LPIPS, which means that the output results of our model under the guidance of latent variables are the most diverse. The underlying reason is that DRIT and MUNIT make few major changes to the source image, resulting in a lower LPIPS score.

Reference-guidance. In Fig. 5, each method can generate different images from the reference image. Compared with the baseline, the outputs of our method are more similar to the reference image in terms of makeup shade, hair color and animal species, which indicates that our method can better reflect the style of the reference image.

Table 2 show FID and LPIPS of image translation results under the guidance of reference image for our method and baselines. Our method obtains FID of 23.1, indicating that our method has good visual quality. The highest LPIPS also means that our method generates the most diverse results under the guidance of reference images.

4.3 Ablation Study

To explore the influence of each part of our method, we perform three ablation experiments under different settings.

Input   Reference   MUNIT   DRIT   StarGANv2   Ours

Fig. 5. Reference-guidance image synthesis results on celeba HQ. The first column and the second column are source images and reference images, while the rest are images generated by our proposed model, DRIT, MUNIT and StarGANv2.

Table 2. Reference-guidance results

Quantitative Comparison	Celeba_HQ	
	FID	LPIPS
DRIT	53.3	0.311
MUNIT	107.1	0.176
StarGANv2	24.6	0.385
Ours	**23.1**	**0.412**

The visual performances and evaluation indicators of the ablation experiment are given in Fig. 6 and Table 3. Firstly, we remove the residual network structure with channel attention mechanism in the generator, and the results show that removing it will cause insufficient image quality and feature detail in the generated results. Secondly, we remove the deep feature diversity loss. As expected, we observe that the diversity among the output images is greatly reduced after removing it, which also proves that the deep feature diversity loss is of great significance for the diversity of the output results. Finally, we show the complete model architecture including channel attention mechanism and deep feature diversity loss. From the visualization and evaluation indicators, it is not difficult to find that the model achieves the best performance.

Fig. 6. Visualization of model ablation. The First column is the input images, the second column is the result of eliminating the attention mechanism and the diversity loss of deep features, the third column is the result of eliminating the attention mechanism alone, the fourth column is the result of eliminating the diversity loss alone, the fifth column is the result of the complete model.

Table 3. Ablation results

Quantitative Comparison	FID	LPIPS
None	21.6	0.355
w/o channel attention	20.1	0.421
w/o perceptual loss	18.7	0.363
Full	**18.6**	**0.455**

5 Conclusion

We proposed a semantic style diversity image translation method (DFattGAN)based on deep feature difference and attention mechanism. By controlling the difference of deep features between images, the generator can explore the image space and find more meaningful style features to generate diverse images and realize the image translation with semantic diversity. Compared with various distance measures, deep feature differences are more consistent with human perception and the generated results are more satisfying to the semantic diversity of human vision. In addition, we introduced a channel attention mechanism into the model to make the model focus on some features of the image that we need to transform the style. A large number of experiments on different data sets show that our proposed image-to-image translation method has strong performance, remarkable effect and reliability.

References

1. Zhu, J.Y., Park, T., Isola, P., Efros, A.A.: Unpaired image-to-image translation using cycle-consistent adversarial networks. ICCV (2017)
2. Yi, Z., Zhang, H., Tan, P., Gong, M.: Dualgan: Unsupervised dual learning for image-to-image translation. ICCV (2017)
3. Kim, T., Cha, M., Kim, H., Lee, et al.: Learning to discover cross-domain relations with generative adversarial networks. ICML (2017)
4. Goodfellow, I.J., Pouget-Abadie, J., Mirza, M., et al.: Generative adversarial networks. NIPS (2014)
5. Mao, Q., Lee, H.Y., Tseng, H.Y., Ma, S., Yang, M.H.: Mode seeking generative adversarial networks for diverse image synthesis. CVPR (2019)
6. Choi, Y., Uh, Y., Yoo, J., Ha, J.W.: Stargan v2: Diverse image synthesis for multiple domains. CVPR (2020)
7. Li, X., Zhang, S., Hu, J., Cao, L., Hong, X., Mao, X., Ji, R.: Image-to-image Translation via Hierarchical Style Disentanglement. arXiv preprint : 2103.01456 (2021)
8. Karras, T., Laine, S., Aila, T.: A style-based generator architecture for generative adversarial networks. CVPR (2019)
9. Lee, H.-Y., Tseng, H.-Y., Huang, J.-B., Singh, M., Yang, M.-H.: Diverse image-to-image translation via disentangled representations. In: Ferrari, V., Hebert, M., Sminchisescu, C., Weiss, Y. (eds.) ECCV 2018. LNCS, vol. 11205, pp. 36–52. Springer, Cham (2018). https://doi.org/10.1007/978-3-030-01246-5_3
10. Huang, X., Liu, M.-Y., Belongie, S., Kautz, J.: Multimodal unsupervised image-to-image translation. In: Ferrari, V., Hebert, M., Sminchisescu, C., Weiss, Y. (eds.) ECCV 2018. LNCS, vol. 11207, pp. 179–196. Springer, Cham (2018). https://doi.org/10.1007/978-3-030-01219-9_11
11. Hao, X., et al.: Real-time semantic segmentation with weighted factorized-deepwise convolution. Image Vis. Comput. 114, 104269 (2021)
12. Isola, P., Zhu, J.Y., Zhou, T., Efros, A.A.: Image-to-image translation with conditional adversarial networks. CVPR (2017)
13. Zhu, J.Y., Zhang, R., Pathak, D., et al.: Toward multimodal image-to-image translation. NIPS (2017)
14. Mao, X., Li, Q., Xie, H., Raymond Y.L., Wang, Z., Stephen, P.S.: Least squares generative adversarial networks. ICCV (2017)
15. Ishaan, G., Faruk, A., Martin, A., Vincent, et al.: Improved training of wasserstein gans. NIPS (2017)
16. Takeru, M., Toshiki, K., Masanori, K., Yuichi, Y.: Spectral normalization for generative adversarial networks. ICLR (2018)
17. Krizhevsky, A., Sutskever, I., Hinton, G.E.: Imagenet classification with deep convolutional neural networks. NIPS (2012)
18. Hu, J., Shen, L., Sun, G.: Squeeze-and-excitation networks. CVPR (2018)

Spatial Foreground Bigraph Matching for Generalizable Person Re-identification

Jiaxin Zhang$^{(\boxtimes)}$ and Wei Yang

School of Computer Science and Technology, University of Science and Technology of China,
Hefei, China
jiayou@mail.ustc.edu.cn, qubit@ustc.edu.cn

Abstract. Most existing Domain Generalization person re-identification (DG ReID) methods often evaluate similarity using global features. However, the spatial information will be lost after global pooling, which leads to a lack of interpretability and decreased generalization ability. In this paper, to address these issues, we propose a novel interpretable and generalizable ReID framework, named *Spatial Foreground Bigraph Match* (SFBM), which is plug-and-play and no training is required. Our SFBM consists of two sub-parts, namely Contextual Foreground Region Extraction (CFE) and Feature Bigraph Module (FBM). The former extracts the foreground in the query's feature map and uses it to filter out the background noise in the matching relationship. The latter then establishes a matching relationship between each local feature in the feature map of query and gallery. Particularly, we present a judicious definition of the distance from query to gallery based on SFBM to enhance the robustness of existing models when the target domain has an occlusion. Extensive experimental results on three subtasks of DG ReID show that our method is model-agnostic and enables to improve the performance of various methods without re-training the models.

Keywords: Domain generalization · Person re-identification · Spatial feature

1 Introduction

Person re-identification (ReID) is an important task that aims at recognizing a specific person across images from non-overlapped cameras under various viewpoints and locations. Although state-of-the-art supervised models [4,11,22] can still achieve results that are close to our human eyes on many datasets [16,19,21], the performance often drops significantly in unseen datasets. Why do domain biases have such a big impact on ReID models? To find out the answer to this question, recently, most researchers have paid attention to the feature extracted by the backbone network and proposed some high-performance methods [1,7,18]. Although these methods can perform better than the baseline, there is still much space for improvement. As shown in Fig. 1(a), we train OSNet with Makert1501 as the source domain, and the model still makes low-level mistakes when the target domain is DukeMTMC-reID. This is because many previous works neglect the spatial information in the feature map. Specifically, after the feature maps of the query and the gallery are extracted by the backbone network, the existing methods will generally compress the feature maps to the global features through

E. Pimenidis et al. (Eds.): ICANN 2022, LNCS 13531, pp. 273–285, 2022.
https://doi.org/10.1007/978-3-031-15934-3_23

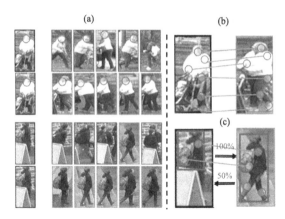

Fig. 1. Illustration of unsuccessful generalization scenarios and our motivation. (a) Each plot contains the top-5 similar gallery images given a query. Two examples are shown above, where red and green denote incorrect and correct matches, respectively. For each example, the first row is the result obtained by OSNet, and the second row below is the result after using our SFBM. (b) We view the local features between the query and gallery as a complete bigrapgh, and apply matching strategies. (c) By overcoming the harsh situations in the occlusion target domain, we propose an asymmetrical definition of distance. (Color figure online)

global pooling, and then calculate the cosine distance or Euclidean distance of these two features. However, there are many background noises in global features, and the local features between the query and the gallery are not aligned with each other. Thus, we propose that these issues may cause the generalization of the model to deteriorate, and that using spatial information is crucial when calculating distances. Meanwhile, using spatial information can make DG ReID methods more interpretable, and it makes it easier for us to analyze and improve the methods.

In this paper, to deal with the above issues, we put forward an interpretable ReID framework, namely *Spatial Foreground Bigraph Match* (SFBM), which is plug-and-play and only works during the testing phase. Our SFBM consists of two sub-parts, i.e., *Contextual Foreground Region Extraction* (CFE) and *Feature Bigraph Module* (FBM). The former adopts the local self-attention and differentiable binarization [9] operation to encode a feature map into a foreground map where the value of the foreground part is close to 1 and the value of the background part is close to 0. As shown in the second example of Fig. 1(a), hard negative galleries have the same background as the query. The foreground map obtained by CFE can effectively remove background noises in the query. The latter utilizes matching strategies to align features in the feature map of the query and the gallery, as shown in Fig. 1(b). After matching, each feature in the query only need to compute distance with the matched feature in the gallery. As the shown in first example of Fig. 1(a), the alignment is indispensable for improving the model's generalization capability in a complex environment. In particular, we propose a judicious definition of the distance from the query to the gallery. As shown in Fig. 1(c), our new distance is asymmetrical. Specifically, the foreground of the query only includes the upper body, which can obviously match the upper body of the gallery. Therefore, the similarity score from the query to the gallery is 100%. However, the similarity score from the gallery to the query can only be 50%.

Finally, we test our framework on three subtasks of DG ReID: 1) single domain test; 2) multi-domain test; 3) occlusion domain test; The first two tasks are divided as usual by the number of source domains. Besides, since testing in the target domain whose images have occlusion is more challenging, the third task is in this scenario. Moreover, when the model is tested on a seen domain, our distance can be easily combined with the cosine distance between global features to further improve performance.

Our main contributions can be summarized as follows:

- We provide a different perspective to analyze the reasons for the significant performance degradation in DG ReID.
- We propose an interpretable and generalizable ReID framework called SFBM, which is plug-and-play to tackle the problem of exiting methods by exploiting the spatial information. Besides, a novel definition of the distance from query to gallery is proposed based on our framework.
- We conduct extensive experiments on three subtasks of DG ReID and normal ReID tasks. The results demonstrate that our framework is model-agnostic and enables to improve the performance of off-the-shelf backbone networks without re-training the models.

2 Related Work

2.1 Generalizable Person Re-identification

Domain generalizable person re-identification (DG ReID) aims to learn a robust model for obtaining good performance on an arbitrary target domain. In order to learn domain-invariant features, various DG ReID methods add normalization modules [6, 15] to the backbone network or increase the source domain diversity. Recently, meta-learning has been applied to DG ReID. The meta-learning based methods [1, 2, 18] split the source domains into meta-train and meta-test to simulate the domain biases, so as to improve the model generalization. However, these methods are dedicated to improving the domain generalization capability of the features extracted by the backbone network. As far as we know, these methods ignore how to better use features for distance calculation. [10] utilized the QAconv to align local features that share the same idea as our FBM, but did not consider the background noise between feature pairs. Besides, QAconv applied a BN-FC-BN block to get the final similarity score that is supervised by the focal loss.

2.2 Partial Person Re-identification

As to partial person ReID, existing studies have been developed from two perspectives: 1) training the backbone network to adapt to arbitrary input size; 2) locating shared regions between the partial image and the reference one [14]. There are also few methods [5] that try to solve both of them in a unified framework. Overall, the above methods require either additional supervision or multi-stage training. In addition, it is usually

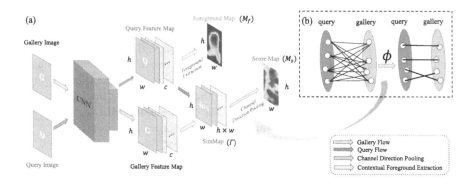

Fig. 2. Overall flowchart. (a) Our Generalizable and Interpretable Person Re-Identification Framework can work with most of the pre-trained ReID models. The gray arrows and blue arrows indicate the flow of gallery features and query features, respectively. The yellow arrow and green arrow indicate local self-attention operation and channel selected pool operation, respectively. (b) According to the matching strategy selected, we can get a function ϕ to pool a complete bipartite graph to a sparse graph. In the same way, ϕ indicates how to pool Γ from the channel direction. (Color figure online)

difficult to combine one of these methods with other ReID methods. Unlike the above methods, our SFBM is a framework for DG ReID mainly. We test it in the occlusion target domain since this scenario is more challenging for existing DG ReID methods. Furthermore, our SFBM is a plug-and-play method that can be applied to off-the-shelf backbone networks without re-training the networks.

3   The Proposed Approach

The framework of our SFBM is shown in Fig. 2. In the field of Person Re-Identification, we use $F \in \mathbb{R}^{c \times h \times w}$ to represent the feature map extracted from images by the backbone network generally, where c is the number of output channels, and h and w are the height and width of the feature map, respectively. In the traditional framework, when we calculate the similarity between a query image (Query) and a gallery image (Gallery), we first aggregate their feature maps F_q and F_g separately into global features $G_q, G_g \in \mathbb{R}^c$ by a global average pooling (GAP) operation. And then the cosine similarity between G_q and G_g can be formulated as:

$$cos \langle G_q, G_g \rangle = \frac{G_q^T G_g}{||G_q||_2 \times ||G_g||_2} \tag{1}$$

where $|| \cdot ||_2$ computes the L2 norm of a vector. We denote Query and Gallery's global features of size c by G_q and G_g, respectively. In addition, the cosine distance between G_q and G_g is denoted as D_{cos}, and $D_{cos} = 1 - cos \langle G_q, G_g \rangle$.

However, there are many background noises in G_q. In addition, if we let $f_{qi}, f_{gj} \in \mathbb{R}^{c \times 1 \times 1}$ denote the i-th feature of F_q and the j-th feature of F_g, respectively. $G_q^T G_g$ can produce n^2 terms that look like $f_{qi}^T f_{gj}$, leading to the problem of mismatching. In the rest of Sect. 3. we first propose a foreground region extraction method to remove the background noises in Sect. 3.1. second, our alignment strategy is introduced in Sect. 3.2 which can enhance model's generalization capability in the complex environment. Finally, we present how to use them together in distance calculation in Sect. 3.3.

3.1 Contextual Foreground Region Extraction

Local Self-Attention. For each local feature f_{qi} in the feature map of Query, we calculate the inner product with all the features in a $k \times k$ square centered on itself to get $k \times k$ attention values for each feature, and then average those $k \times k$ values to get the final attention value a_i for f_{qi}. Consequently, the attention map $A_q \in \mathbb{R}^{h \times w}$ of Query can be obtained, where a_i is the i-th value of A_q. Specifically, the kernel size is a hyperparameter that controls how much contextual information is used for each local feature.

Binarization. The original activation map A_q focuses on local features such as head, shoulder, backpack, etc., and the background information has not been completely removed. To enlarge the foreground area and completely remove the background information, we let:

$$A_q = \frac{A_q - min(A_q)}{max(A_q) - min(A_q)} \tag{2}$$

$$M_f = DB(A_q) = \frac{1}{1 + \exp(-k(A_q - t))} \tag{3}$$

where $k > 0$, and t is the threshold. The min-max normalization in Eq. (2) ensures all elements in A_q to have values in the range $[0, 1]$, which can facilitate subsequent binarization. The purpose of the binarization operation in Eq. (3) can ensure that the foreground area is larger, and the weight of the irrelevant background area is set to 0. The introduction of the DB function [9] is to ensure that the whole process is differentiable. The result obtained by Eq. (3) is the foreground map that is denoted as $M_f \in \mathbb{R}^{h \times w}$.

3.2 Feature Bigraph Module and Part-Part Match Strategy

In this subsection we give our Feature Bigraph Module (FBM) and our opinion on how local features should be matched. Consider such a complete bipartite graph $G = (S \cup T, E)$, $S = \{f_{qi} \mid i = 1, 2, ..., n\}$ is composed of local features in Query, $T = \{f_{gi} \mid i = 1, 2, ..., n\}$ is composed of local features in Gallery, $|S| = |T| = h \times w = n$, and $|E| = n^2$. For each $v \in S$, $w \in T$, $e_{vw} \in E$ is an edge between v and w, and the weight $C(v, w) \in \mathbb{R}$ of e_{vw} satisfies the following formula:

$$C(v, w) = cos \langle v, w \rangle \tag{4}$$

As shown in Fig. 2(b), the blue region represents the set of all local features in a query image, and the orange region stands for the set of all local features in a gallery image.

One-to-One Matching. Hungarian algorithm [12] is a classical algorithm commonly used in bipartite graph matching, and has been widely used in many fields of computer vision, such as object tracking, object detection and so on. Here we first attempt to apply it to local feature matching of pedestrians. We set the goal of the Hungarian algorithm to find an injection ϕ that satisfies the following objective function:

$$\arg\max_{\phi} \sum_{v \in S} C(v, \phi(v)) \tag{5}$$

where ϕ is a one-to-one function. The high time complexity is a disadvantage of the Hungarian algorithm. The computational cost of completing such a matching between S and T is $O(N^3)$ [3].

N-to-N Matching. An important reason for the high time complexity of the one-to-one matching algorithm is to ensure that every element in T is connected by an edge. Note that different gallery images can be compared in retrieval since a query image is used as the medium, and thus the features of Query are more important than those of Gallery in retrieval. Therefore, we just need to make sure that all elements in S are connected by edges. The matching algorithm of N-to-N is designed according to this point.

When we first see the two images, we focus on the most similar parts of them. By mimicking this process, we come up with an N-to-N matching strategy: all features in S match only the most similar features in T, respectively. For all $v \in S$, the N-to-N strategy ϕ satisfies the following equation:

$$\phi(v) = \arg\max_{w \in T} C(v, w), \quad v \in S \tag{6}$$

At this point, the time complexity of the algorithm is down to a maximum of $O(N^2)$.

3.3 Final Distance Definition

Till now we have calculated the cosine similarity between each local feature between S and T, which can form $\Gamma \in \mathbb{R}^{n \times h \times w}$, whose spatial dimensions denotes each local feature in S and the channel dimension denote its similarity to all features in T. Here we introduce $M_s \in \mathbb{R}^{h \times w}$, which is made up of $cos \langle v, \phi(v) \rangle$ in the spatial dimension. One can view M_s as pooled in the channel direction of Γ.

Query-Gallery Distance. The query-gallery distance D_{q2g} can be defined by the following formula:

$$D_{q2g} = 1 - \frac{Sum(M_s \cdot M_f)}{Sum(M_f)} \tag{7}$$

where Sum denotes the sum of all the elements in the matrix, and $\cdot$ denotes the dot product of two matrices. Specifically, $Sum(M_f)$ represents the foreground area of Query, and $Sum(M_s \cdot M_f)$ represents the matching degree between the foreground of Query and the Gallery. In order to remove background noises, M_f is used as a mask to multiply M_s.

Algorithm 1. Overall Algorithm

Input: The sorted sequence of galleries $RowList$, the query image's feature map F_q and the set of gallery images' feature maps F_m^g.

Parameter: K, Match strategy

Output: $RowList$

  1: Initialize an empty list: Sim;
  2: $InitList \leftarrow$ Top K terms of $RowList$;
  3: Calculate M_f of F_q according to Eq. (2–3);
  4: **for** each $idx \in InitList$ **do**
  5:    Calculate Γ between F_q and F_{idx}^g;
  6:    Obtain ϕ by Eq. (5) or Eq. (6);
  7:    Pooling Γ by ϕ to get M_s;
  8:    Calculate D_{final} by Eq. (7–8);
  9:    $Sim[idx] \leftarrow D_{final}$;
10: **end for**
11: Reorder the top K items of $RowList$ according to Sim;
12: **return** $RowList$

Final Distance. When the model has been trained in the target domain (either supervised or unsupervised), the model will fit $cos \langle G_q, G_g \rangle$ to make it meaningful. At this time, the final distance D_{final} is obtained by weighting D_{q2g} and $cos \langle G_q, G_g \rangle$, and α is 0.5 by default. When the model is tested on an unseen domain, $\alpha = 0$. Hence, the final distance is:

$$D_{final} = (1 - \alpha)D_{q2g} + \alpha(1 - cos \langle G_q, G_g \rangle) \tag{8}$$

Overall Algorithm. First, we sort gallery samples according to the $cos \langle G_q, G_i^g \rangle$ from high to low to get $RowList$. In order to shorten the evaluation time, we take K gallery samples [17] with the highest scores for the calculation of D_{final}. Then, M_f can be calculated according to Eqs. (2–3). By computing Γ, we can get the function ϕ with respect to the selected matching strategy and Γ. After using ϕ to pool Γ to M_s, D_{q2g} and D_{final} can be calculated by Eq. (7–8). Finally, we can reorder the selected k samples according to D_{final} from low to high. The overall methodological flow of SFBM is summarized in Algorithm 1.

4 Experiments

4.1 Experimental Settings

Datasets. To evaluate the generalization capability of our method, we employ the single domain test, the multi-domain test, the occlusion domain test and the normal ReID test. In the following experiments, we evaluate our proposed method on nine person ReID datasets: Market-1501 [19], DukeMTMC-reID [21], MSMT17 [16], CUHK03 [8], Occluded-REID [23], Partial-REID [20], P-DukeMTMC-reID [23], P-ETHZ [23] and Partial-iLIDS [20]. Regarding the abbreviations, MS is MSMT17; M is Market1501; D is DukeMTMC-reID; and C is CUHK03.The large-scale DG ReID benchmark means that three of these four datasets (M, MS, D, C) are selected as the training set, and the remaining one is used as the test set, and MS+M+D→C demotes that MSMT17, Market1501 and DukeMTMC-reID constitute the training set. Com(MS) demotes that we combine training set and test set of MSMT17 as the source dataset. The statistics of these nine datasets are shown in Table 1.

Table 1. Statistics of person ReID datasets.

Dataset	#ID	#image	Dataset	#ID	#image
M	1,501	32,668	Occluded-REID	200	2,000
MS	4,101	126,441	Partial-REID	60	900
D	1,404	36,441	P-DukeMTMC-reID	1,299	24,143
C	1,467	14,097	P-ETHZ	85	3,897
–	–	–	Partial-iLIDS	119	238

Implementation Details. In all the experiments below, we resize the person image size to 256×128. For each query, K is set to 100 during test. The parameters k and t in the DB function are set to 50 and the mean of A_q's all elements, respectively. We empirically set the kernel size of the local self-attention operation to 3. N-to-N matching strategy is used by default. The experimental details of different tasks are introduced one by one in Sect. 4.2.

Evaluation Metrics. In this paper, we follow the typical evaluation metrics for Re-ID as mean Average Precision (mAP) and Cumulative Matching Characteristic (CMC) at Rank-k.

4.2   Results

Single Domain Subtask and Multi-domain Subtask. OSNet-IBN, OSNet-AIN and OSNet [22] in Table 2 are trained as described in [22]. SNR is trained for 160 epochs with the setting in [7]. Besides, we train Res50-IBN [13] for 90 epochs (batch size is 256) and perform random cropping and random flipping for data augmentation. We use the warmup strategy in the first ten epochs and the learning rate is initialized as 3.5×10^{-4} and divided by 10 at the 30th, 50th and 70th epochs, respectively. As shown in Table 2, SFBM can be well combined with these methods. On several tasks, SFBM has improved Rank-1 accuracy by more than 5%, even up to 9.8%.

Occlusion Domain Task. The models in this experiment are all trained on the training split of Market-1501, and the training method is the same as the previous subsection.

Table 2. Comparison with different distances on three benchmarks. The first column describes the subtask type. The best results are highlighted in bold. D_{cos} means the traditional cosine distance between global features of Query and Gallery and we use D_{cos} as the baseline.

Single domain	Methods	Distance	Com(MS)→M			Com(MS)→D			Com(M)→D			Com(D)→M		
			mAP	Rank-1	Rank-5	mAP	Rank-1	Rank-5	mAP	Rank-1	Rank-5	mAP	Rank-1	Rank-5
	OSNet-IBN	D_{cos}	39.8	66.7	81.9	48.8	68.1	81.1	33.0	54.1	68.4	30.5	61.1	76.8
		D_{final}	**44.1**	**73.8**	**86.6**	**50.9**	**70.3**	**83.3**	**38.3**	**60.3**	**74.2**	**35.9**	**69.4**	**82.5**
	OSNet-AIN	D_{cos}	43.3	70.1	84.1	52.7	71.1	83.3	34.9	55.2	69.1	32.8	62.2	78.3
		D_{final}	**47.0**	**76.9**	**88.3**	**53.6**	**72.8**	**84.2**	**40.1**	**62.3**	**74.4**	**38.8**	**73.0**	**85.4**
	Res50-IBN	D_{cos}	46.2	73.9	86.3	55.3	71.8	84.3	36.8	54.5	68.3	33.2	62.2	76.6
		D_{final}	**48.1**	**77.6**	**88.9**	**56.8**	**74.4**	**85.9**	**40.7**	**60.1**	**73.1**	**37.7**	**68.7**	**81.3**
	SNR	D_{cos}	38.3	66.7	81.9	45.8	64.5	78.0	33.0	54.8	69.5	34.5	65.9	81.0
		D_{final}	**41.8**	**73.1**	**86.2**	**48.0**	**68.6**	**80.7**	**37.5**	**60.9**	**73.7**	**39.2**	**72.4**	**85.4**

Multi domain	Methods	Distance	MS+D+C→M			MS+M+C→D			M+C+D→MS			D+MS+M→C		
			mAP	Rank-1	Rank-5	mAP	Rank-1	Rank-5	mAP	Rank-1	Rank-5	mAP	Rank-1	Rank-5
	OSNet-IBN	D_{cos}	44.9	73.0	86.4	45.7	64.6	77.9	16.2	39.8	53.4	25.4	25.7	43.5
		D_{final}	**48.1**	**78.8**	**89.4**	**48.9**	**69.1**	**81.4**	**19.1**	**48.9**	**61.0**	**26.9**	**26.8**	**45.1**
	OSNet-AIN	D_{cos}	45.8	73.3	86.5	47.2	65.6	79.2	16.2	40.2	53.3	27.1	27.4	46.1
		D_{final}	**48.7**	**78.6**	**90.4**	**50.3**	**68.9**	**82.5**	**18.8**	**48.7**	**60.4**	**28.7**	**28.8**	**48.1**
	OSNet	D_{cos}	44.2	72.5	86.0	47.0	67.2	80.1	12.6	33.2	46.0	23.3	23.9	41.1
		D_{final}	**48.2**	**79.4**	**89.5**	**51.1**	**70.5**	**81.6**	**15.1**	**41.7**	**53.4**	**25.3**	**25.0**	**43.9**

Occlusion domain	Methods	Distance	P-DukeMTMC-reID		Occluded-REID		Partial-REID		P-ETHZ		Partial-iLIDS	
			mAP	Rank-1	mAP	Rank-1	mAP	Rank-1	mAP	Rank-1	mAP	Rank-1
	Res50-IBN	D_{cos}	24.5	40.1	56.5	62.4	59.6	62.7	34.9	40.5	65.6	55.4
		D_{final}	**28.4**	**47.4**	**63.5**	**70.8**	**60.6**	**66.3**	**35.6**	**42.1**	**70.5**	**63.9**
	OSNet	D_{cos}	21.0	34.4	36.5	40.2	49.0	50.3	28.7	33.9	58.7	46.2
		D_{final}	**25.3**	**44.6**	**48.3**	**56.4**	**52.9**	50.7	**32.4**	**41.9**	**66.7**	**58.8**

We use occluded person images as the query set and full-body person images as the gallery set. As shown in Table 2, compared with the other two datasets (Partial-REID, P-ETHZ), our method obviously performs better on Occluded-REID, P-DukeMTMC-reID and Partial-iLIDS. Especially on the Occluded-REID dataset, SFBM brings a 16.2% increase in Rank-1 accuracy and an 11.8% increase in mAP. This is because the data in these three datasets mainly have occlusion and illumination variance, whereas the other two datasets have considerable scale variance. In general, our method can greatly improve the generalization of the model even if images in the target domain have occlusion.

Normal ReID Task. OSNet is trained as described in [22] and the training method of Res50-IBN [13] is the same as before. As shown in Table 3, since the model has been fully trained on the target domain, at this time, the traditional way of retrieval has been able to obtain a high accuracy. In addition, only using D_{q2g} to retrieve can achieve comparable accuracy. If the two distances D_{q2g} and D_{cos} can be added together in a simple way, the accuracy can be further improved.

Table 3. Comparison with the distances in ReID problem. The best results are highlighted with bold and underscored ones indicate the second best.

Methods	Distance	DukeMTMC-reID		Market-1501	
		mAP	Rank-1	mAP	Rank-1
Res50-IBN	D_{cos}	<u>78.9</u>	88.7	<u>86.7</u>	<u>94.7</u>
	D_{q2g}	78.0	<u>89.3</u>	85.7	94.5
	D_{final}	**79.7**	**89.7**	**87.4**	**95.0**
OSNet	D_{cos}	<u>72.7</u>	<u>87.0</u>	<u>83.6</u>	94.2
	D_{q2g}	72.0	86.7	82.9	<u>94.8</u>
	D_{final}	**74.5**	**88.6**	**85.4**	**95.3**

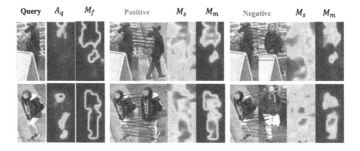

Fig. 3. Visualization of intermediate variables in MS+M+C-→D. Here the backbone network is OSNet. We mark the edges with a weight of more than 0.7 in red and bold. $M_m = M_f \cdot M_s$. The samples in the first row are q_1, pos_1, neg_1 from left to right, respectively. Similarly, the next row are q_2, pos_2, neg_2. (Color figure online)

4.3   Ablation Study and Visualization

We perform comprehensive ablation experiments to show the effectiveness of our Interpretable and Generalizable Person Re-Identification Framework, as well as detailed components through the performance on the large scale DG ReID benchmark. We use the case where OSNet does not use our contextual foreground extraction as the baseline. As shown in Fig. 3 and Table 4, if the foreground is not extracted, background noises in M_s will seriously interfere with the accuracy of the matching strategy, which will greatly reduce the overall performance of the algorithm. M_m is the result of M_s masked by M_f.

Influence of Hyperparameters. Similar to the binarization of gray histograms, if we use 0.05 or 0.1 as the threshold, this strategy is called static threshold. If our threshold changes with the input, then this strategy is dynamic threshold. As shown in Table 4, we give three static thresholds and one dynamic threshold (mean). The dynamic threshold strategy is more robust in Table 4. As shown in Table 4, when the kernel size is reduced to 1×1, the contextual information that can be used in the calculation process will be less. Therefore, the performance is generally worse than when the kernel size is 3×3.

Table 4. Ablation study of our model. In the baseline, it is assumed that all the features in the feature map are foreground, that is to say, all the elements of the M_f are 1. no_DB denotes that $M_f = A_q$. The best results are highlighted with bold. We use One-to-One matching strategy in mean*.

Threshold	Kernel size	MS+D+C→M		MS+M+C→D	
		mAP	Rank-1	mAP	Rank-1
Baseline	–	36.4	59.0	31.7	38.7
0.05	1×1	46.3	75.4	47.5	64.3
	3×3	**46.5**	**75.6**	**47.7**	**64.9**
0.1	1×1	47.9	78.4	50.8	**69.8**
	3×3	**48.2**	**78.7**	**50.9**	69.7
0.2	1×1	45.3	75.7	49.3	69.5
	3×3	**47.3**	**78.4**	**50.9**	**70.6**
mean	1×1	48.1	79.0	50.8	69.9
	3×3	**48.2**	**79.4**	**51.1**	**70.5**
mean*	1×1	46.3	77.7	49.2	68.6
	3×3	**46.5**	**77.8**	**49.5**	**68.9**
no_DB	1×1	46.8	77.7	50.4	69.6
	3×3	**47.0**	**78.3**	**50.7**	**70.1**

The performance of One-to-One matching strategy is weaker than the N-to-N matching strategy on Table 4. We think it may be because that the Hungarian algorithm can cause mismatches when it takes care of the global optimum in Eq. (5).

Interpretability. All the variables in Fig. 3 are represented by heat maps. D_{cos} and D_{final} from q_1 to pos_1 are 0.29 and 0.3. D_{cos} and D_{final} from q_1 to neg_1 are 0.26 and 0.48. In the traditional ReID framework, neg_1 is even closer to q_1. As shown in M_s, this is because the background between q_1 and neg_1 is very similar. It is worth noting that D_{final} from pos_1 to q_1 is 0.38 because of the occlusion. In addition, D_{final} from q_2 to neg_2 is 0.5. This is because that their pants are very similar while the upper bodies are different. However, D_{cos} from q_2 to neg_2 is 0.36.

5   Conclusion

In this paper, we focused on Domain Generalization person re-identification (DG ReID) and proposed an interpretable and generalizable ReID framework, called SFBM, which jointly considers the foreground extraction (CFE) and the feature alignment (FBM). Furthermore, we put forward a novel distance definition based on SFBM. Extensive experiments on three subtasks of DG ReID demonstrate that SFBM can be applied to off-the-shelf backbone networks as a plug-and-play method. In order to protect privacy, we mask the face in our research.

Acknowledgments. This work was supported by the National Natural Science Foundation of China (No. 62172385).

References

1. Choi, S., Kim, T., Jeong, M., Park, H., Kim, C.: Meta batch-instance normalization for generalizable person re-identification. In: CVPR, pp. 3425–3435 (2021)
2. Dai, Y., Li, X., Liu, J., Tong, Z., Duan, L.Y.: Generalizable person re-identification with relevance-aware mixture of experts. In: CVPR, pp. 16145–16154 (2021)
3. Edmonds, J., Karp, R.M.: Theoretical improvements in algorithmic efficiency for network flow problems. JACM **19**(2), 248–264 (1972)
4. He, S., Luo, H., Wang, P., Wang, F., Li, H., Jiang, W.: Transreid: transformer-based object re-identification. arXiv preprint arXiv:2102.04378 (2021)
5. He, T., Shen, X., Huang, J., Chen, Z., Hua, X.S.: Partial person re-identification with part-part correspondence learning. In: CVPR, pp. 9105–9115 (2021)
6. Ioffe, S., Szegedy, C.: Batch normalization: Accelerating deep network training by reducing internal covariate shift. In: ICML, pp. 448–456. PMLR (2015)
7. Jin, X., Lan, C., Zeng, W., Chen, Z., Zhang, L.: Style normalization and restitution for generalizable person re-identification. In: CVPR, pp. 3143–3152 (2020)
8. Li, W., Zhao, R., Xiao, T., Wang, X.: Deepreid: deep filter pairing neural network for person re-identification. In: CVPR, pp. 152–159 (2014)
9. Liao, M., Wan, Z., Yao, C., Chen, K., Bai, X.: Real-time scene text detection with differentiable binarization. In: AAAI, vol. 34, pp. 11474–11481 (2020)
10. Liao, S., Shao, L.: Interpretable and generalizable person re-identification with query-adaptive convolution and temporal lifting. In: Vedaldi, A., Bischof, H., Brox, T., Frahm, J.-M. (eds.) ECCV 2020. LNCS, vol. 12356, pp. 456–474. Springer, Cham (2020). https://doi.org/10.1007/978-3-030-58621-8_27
11. Liu, C., Chang, X., Shen, Y.D.: Unity style transfer for person re-identification. In: Proceedings of the IEEE/CVF Conference on Computer Vision and Pattern Recognition, pp. 6887–6896 (2020)
12. Munkres, J.: Algorithms for the assignment and transportation problems. J. Soc. Indust. Appl. Math. **5**(1), 32–38 (1957)
13. Pan, X., Luo, P., Shi, J., Tang, X.: Two at once: enhancing learning and generalization capacities via ibn-net. In: ECCV, pp. 464–479 (2018)
14. Suh, Y., Wang, J., Tang, S., Mei, T., Lee, K.M.: Part-aligned bilinear representations for person re-identification. In: ECCV, pp. 402–419 (2018)
15. Ulyanov, D., Vedaldi, A., Lempitsky, V.: Instance normalization: the missing ingredient for fast stylization. arXiv preprint arXiv:1607.08022 (2016)
16. Wei, L., Zhang, S., Gao, W., Tian, Q.: Person transfer gan to bridge domain gap for person re-identification. In: CVPR, pp. 79–88 (2018)
17. Zhao, W., Rao, Y., Wang, Z., Lu, J., Zhou, J.: Towards interpretable deep metric learning with structural matching. In: CVPR, pp. 9887–9896 (2021)
18. Zhao, Y., Zhong, Z., Yang, F., Luo, Z., Lin, Y., Li, S., Sebe, N.: Learning to generalize unseen domains via memory-based multi-source meta-learning for person re-identification. In: CVPR, pp. 6277–6286 (2021)
19. Zheng, L., Shen, L., Tian, L., Wang, S., Wang, J., Tian, Q.: Scalable person re-identification: a benchmark. In: ICCV, pp. 1116–1124 (2015)
20. Zheng, W.S., Li, X., Xiang, T., Liao, S., Lai, J., Gong, S.: Partial person re-identification. In: ICCV, pp. 4678–4686 (2015)

21. Zheng, Z., Zheng, L., Yang, Y.: Unlabeled samples generated by gan improve the person re-identification baseline in vitro. In: ICCV, pp. 3754–3762 (2017)
22. Zhou, K., Yang, Y., Cavallaro, A., Xiang, T.: Learning generalisable omni-scale representations for person re-identification. IEEE Trans. Pattern Anal. Mach. Intell. (2021)
23. Zhuo, J., Chen, Z., Lai, J., Wang, G.: Occluded person re-identification. In: ICME, pp. 1–6. IEEE (2018)

TSN-CA: A Two-Stage Network with Channel Attention for Low-Light Image Enhancement

Xinxu Wei, Xianshi Zhang, and Yongjie Li[✉]

MOE Key Lab for Neuroinformation, School of Life Sciences and Technology,
University of Electronic Science and Technology of China, Chengdu, China
xinxu.wei@std.uestc.edu.cn, {zhangxianshi,liyj}@uestc.edu.cn

Abstract. Low-light image enhancement is a challenging low-level computer vision task because after enhancing the brightness of the image, amplified noise, color distortion, detail loss, blurred edges, shadow blocks and halo artifacts occur. In this paper, we propose a Two-Stage Network with Channel Attention (denoted as TSN-CA) to enhance the brightness of the low-light image and restore the enhanced images from various kinds of degradation. In the first stage, the brightness of the low-light image is enhanced in HSV space using a U-Net based enhancement network, which uses the information of H and S channels to help recover the details in V channel. In the second stage, Channel Attention (CA) mechanism is integrated into the skip connection of a U-Net in order to restore the brightness-enhanced image from several kinds of degradation in RGB space, especially the halo and shadow blocks. Extensive experiments performance demonstrate that our method achieves excellent effect on brightness enhancement as well as denoising, detail preservation and halo artifact elimination.

Keywords: Low-light image enhancement · Image denoising · Attention mechanism · Artifacts elimination

1 Introduction

Images captured in low-light conditions suffer from poor visibility, low contrast, and severe noise. After enhancing the brightness, noise hidden in the darkness will be amplified [3,4,21,24], and color distortion [24], shadow blocks [25], and halo artifacts [32] will appear, which negatively affect high-level computer vision tasks. When noise is removed from a noise-polluted image, details are smoothed along with the noise [13,25], resulting in blurred edges. We propose a method to simultaneously and effectively enhance brightness, remove noise, correct color distortion, preserve details, restore blurred edges, and eliminate halo and shadow artifacts.

As shown in Fig. 1, when a noise-free image captured in normal-light conditions is decoupled into hue (H), saturation (S), and value (V) channels, the V channel has normal brightness and contains many high-frequency details without noise, and the H and S channels have little noise and degradation. However, when a low-light image captured from the real world is decoupled into these channels, the V channel suffers from low brightness and invisible noise, details are hidden in the darkness, and the H and S channels suffer from severe noise and other types of degradation. Many methods[3,4,7,24,25,32] directly and effectively enhance the brightness of a low-light image in the red, green, blue (RGB) space, but suffer from problems such as noise amplification [4,24], color distortion [3,24,32], detail loss [10,13], shadow blocks [10,25], and halo artifacts [32]. Compared with enhancement in RGB space, enhancing brightness in HSV space has many benefits and advantages. The reasons for and advantages of enhancing brightness in HSV space and restoring the enhanced but degraded image in RGB space are explained in the Motivation and Analysis section.

Previous HSV-based enhancement methods[28,33] enhance the brightness of the V channel and then convert the enhanced image from HSV space back to RGB space, without considering noise and other degradation in the H and S channels. Natural images captured from the real world via imaging equipment have much noise and degradation; hence, it is not sufficient to consider only the contrast of the V channel. Previous HSV-based methods [28,33] have also not considered the noise in the V channel and the useful features in the H and S channels that facilitate enhancement and restoration.

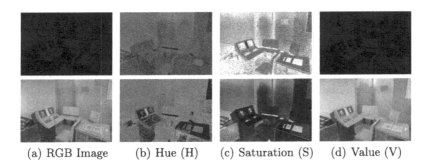

(a) RGB Image   (b) Hue (H)   (c) Saturation (S)   (d) Value (V)

Fig. 1. Visual comparison of H, S, and V channels decoupled from low-light image and normal-light ground truth. First and second rows are H, S, V channels of low-light image and corresponding normal-light ground truth, respectively. There is severe noise in the H and S channels, which is decoupled from the low-light image.

To overcome the inherent deficiencies of previous HSV-based enhancement methods, we propose a two-stage network with channel attention (TSN-CA) to enhance the brightness of the V channel of a low-light image in HSV space and restore enhanced but degraded images suffering from various kinds of degradation in RGB space. Our work is inspired by previous methods [28,33], but our pipeline enhances and restores a low-light image in two stages.

We highlight the contributions of this paper:

- A two-stage network is proposed to enhance the brightness of a low-light image in HSV space and restore the enhanced but degraded image from RGB space;
- A channel attention mechanism is introduced to U-Net to suppress noise and eliminate shadow blocks and halo artifacts.

Extensive experiments were conducted to qualitatively and quantitatively compare the performance of our method to the state of the art.

2   Related Work

2.1   Traditional Methods

The fusion-based MF [2] enhances illumination. LIME [4] uses a structure prior to estimate a structure-aware illumination map, and enhances it. CRM [27] uses the response characteristics of cameras for enhancement. JED [13] is a joint low-light enhancement and denoising strategy. LECARM [14] deals with color and illumination using a camera response model.

2.2   Deep Learning-Based Methods

GLADNet [21] estimates global illumination and achieves a good enhancement effect in terms of detail preservation. MBLLEN [10] fuses the enhanced results generated by multiple subnets. RetinexNet [24] decomposes a low-light image into reflectance and illumination, denoises the reflectance, and increases the brightness. EnlightenGan (EnGan) [7] is an unsupervised generative adversarial network (GAN). KinD [32] decomposes low-light images into noisy reflectance and smooth illumination, and uses a deep U-Net to recover reflectance and a convolutional neural network (CNN) to enhance the brightness. RDGAN [19] combines retinex decomposition with a GAN. Zero-DCE [3] estimates the optimal brightness curve of the input image by a lightweight network. KinD++ [31] uses an MSIA module to deal with color distortion and noise. DA-DRN [25] uses a degradation-aware deep retinex network to directly restore degraded reflectance, and preserves detail information during decomposition by leveraging the dependency between reflectance and the illumination map.

3   Motivation and Analysis

We compare enhancement methods based on RGB and HSV space, discuss the advantages of HSV space, and explain why we enhance the brightness in HSV space and restore degraded images in RGB space.

Many methods [4,7,24,25,32] enhance image brightness in RGB space with good results. However, they have shortcomings, mainly from the aspects of color distortion, noise amplification, detail loss, shadow blocks and halo artifacts.

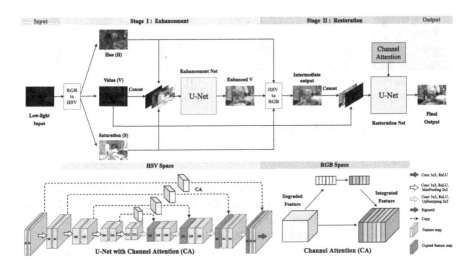

Fig. 2. Network architecture of TSN-CA.

Our model enhances the brightness of the V channel and restores the enhanced but degraded images in RGB space, which can effectively overcome the above three shortcomings, based on the following analysis.

The H, S, and V channels are independent. The V channel affects brightness but not color and saturation. In contrast, increasing the brightness of an RGB image may easily result in color distortion.

To enhance an image by a CNN amplifies noise hidden in darkness [25]. When an image is decomposed into H, S, and V channels, the noise is distributed in these three channels. When we increase the brightness of the V channel via CNN, the noise distributed in H and S is unaffected, and is not amplified. In contrast, if the brightness of an RGB image is enhanced through CNN, while the brightness can be enhanced, the noise hidden in darkness is amplified, resulting in a low SNR of the enhanced image.

Noise removal and detail preservation have always been difficult to balance in image enhancement. After the brightness of an RGB image is enhanced, details hidden in darkness emerge, along with noise. Some denoising methods may remove details, and noise may remain if we try to preserve details. From observation, we see that most details are hidden in the darkness of the V channel. H and S also contain some details, textures, edges, and other high-frequency information, which help to recover details and structure from darkness while enhancing the V channel. When restoring enhanced but degraded images in RGB space, the V channel can provide rich details.

4   Methodology

As shown in Fig. 2, we develop TSN-CA for low-light image enhancement and restoration after enhancement [28].

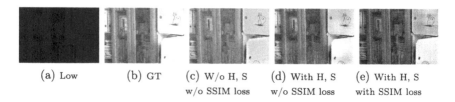

(a) Low   (b) GT   (c) W/o H, S   (d) With H, S   (e) With H, S
                       w/o SSIM loss   w/o SSIM loss   with SSIM loss

Fig. 3. Visual comparison of output of stage I and ablation study of loss functions in stage I.

In stage I, we convert low-light images from RGB space to HSV space and separate the H, S, and V channels from the HSV image. Following DA-DRN [25], we train a deep U-Net to learn the mapping of normal/low-light images. Plain CNN without an up-and-down sampling structure may amplify noise. The V channel differs from an illumination map, which, according to retinex theory [8], is smooth enough to have no high-frequency noise. However, after the image is converted to HSV and the three channels are separated out, the noise is distributed in the H, S, and V channels. Yue et al. [28] focused on enhancing the brightness and contrast of the V channel, but ignored noise in the three channels and other degradation in the H and S channels. We train a deep U-Net to directly learn the mapping of normal/low-light image pairs of the V channel, which can enhance brightness, suppress noise, and restore detail information of the V channel with the help of the H and S channels.

Although H and S decoupled from low-light contain much noise and differ greatly from their counterparts decoupled from normal-light ground truth, they contain relatively complete details and texture information, which are helpful in the restoration of details in the V channel. Therefore, we concatenate H and S with the V channel as a three-channel input tensor of the enhancement network in stage I, whose output is the corresponding single-channel brightness-enhanced V with enhanced brightness and restored details.

The total enhancement loss in stage I is

$$L_{total}^{I} = \|V_{output} - V_{high}\|_1 + \|\nabla(V_{output}) - \nabla(V_{high})\|_1$$
$$+ \frac{1}{CHW}\|F(V_{output}) - F(V_{high})\|_2^2, \tag{1}$$

where V_{output} and V_{high} denote the V channel generated by our enhancement network and decoupled from normal-light ground truth; ∇ denotes the gradients in the horizontal and vertical directions; F is the 31st feature map obtained by the VGG16 [17] network pretrained on the ImageNet database; and C, H, and W are the number of channels, height, and width, respectively, of the input image.

As shown in Fig. 2, after stage I, we combine the enhanced V channel with the original degraded H and S channels and convert them back to the RGB space, so as to obtain intermediate enhanced results. However, although the brightness is enhanced, there is serious noise in the images, and the detail information is drowned in severe noise and other degradation, which blurs the image edges.

Due to underfitting after directly estimating the V channel, we convert the three channels from HSV space back to RGB space, and shadow blocks and halo artifacts appear. It is essential to restore these images.

As shown in Fig. 2, we use U-Net to restore the enhanced but degraded images [32]. The total restoration loss in stage II is

$$L_{total}^{II} = \|I_{low} - I_{high}\|_2^2 - SSIM(I_{low}, I_{high})$$
$$+ \|\nabla(I_{output}) - \nabla(I_{high})\|_2^2, \tag{2}$$

where I_{low} and I_{high} are respectively the degraded and ground-truth normal-light outputs of stage I; SSIM is SSIM loss; and ∇ denotes the gradients in the horizontal and vertical directions.

Although this can achieve good denoising and restoration effects, the PSNR and SSIM indices of the restored images are still not very high, which means that some noise still exists in the restored results, and there is still unreasonable in the structure and details. Furthermore, as shown in Fig. 4, there are obvious shadow blocks and halo artifacts in the restored results after stage II. Because before restoration, in the results obtained through stage I, details, textures, structure and other useful information are covered by severe noise, and all useful features are hidden under the degraded useless features. This severe degradation causes difficulty in the training of network learning and the restoration of useful features such as details, structure, and corrected color information, with the result that degradation still exists in the generated restoration results after stage II. In addition, some shadow blocks and halo artifacts appear in the enhanced results after stage I because the estimation of the V channel is inaccurate, and these are amplified after stage II. All of these problems result in poor final restoration results in terms of quantitative metrics and visual effects. To solve these problems, we introduce the channel attention mechanism to the skip connection of the U-Net restoration network in stage II.

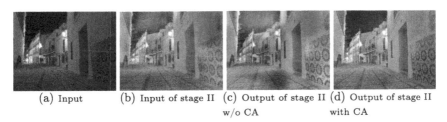

(a) Input   (b) Input of stage II   (c) Output of stage II (d) Output of stage II
                                              w/o CA   with CA

Fig. 4. Ablation study of output in different stages and function of channel attention module. The channel attention (CA) can eliminate shadow blocks and halo artifacts very effectively.

4.1   Channel Attention for Image Restoration

We embed the squeeze-and-excitation (SE) channel attention module in the skip connection of U-Net to remove noise, restore details, and eliminate shadow blocks and halo artifacts [6,34].

We hypothesize that severe residual noise, shadow blocks, and halo artifacts appear in the generated restoration results because the skip connections of U-Net pass degraded features directly to the upsampling stage by concatenating upsampled features with degraded downsampled features. Hence, the key to removing these effects lies in the skip connections of U-Net, and this problem can be solved by adding a module to filter the passed degraded features, as they are directly transmitted from the downsampling stage to the upsampling stage via the skip connection of U-Net.

As shown in Fig. 2, the channel attention (SE) modules are embedded in the U-Net skip connections by integrating the downsampled image features in the channel dimension before passing them to the unsampling stage. The channel attention mechanism is similar to the ventral "what" pathway in the human brain [18]. Because human attention resources are limited, the brain and visual system usually pay more attention to useful things. The channel attention mechanism

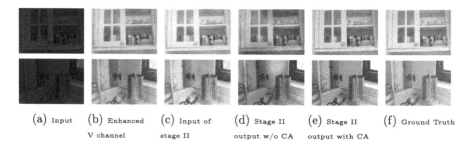

(a) Input   (b) Enhanced   (c) Input of   (d) Stage II   (e) Stage II   (f) Ground Truth
            V channel   stage II   output w/o CA   output with CA

Fig. 5. Visual comparison of output of different stages and ablation study of channel attention (CA). Obvious halo artifacts appear in (d).

Table 1. Quantitative comparison of several metrics between our method and other state-of-the-art methods on **LOL REAL-WORLD** dataset. Mean, Median and Avg represent the mean and median values of the Angular Error and the average value of them, respectively. "↑" indicates the higher the better, "↓" indicates the lower the better. Red: the best, Blue: the second best.

Methods	PSNR↑	SSIM↑	VIF↑	LPIPS↓	FSIM↑	UQI↑	SRER↑	RMSE↓	SAM↑	Mean↓	Median↓	DeltaE↓
Input	7.7733	0.1914	0.2407	0.4173	0.7190	0.0622	47.5772	0.0264	76.5801	3.8061	3.9728	76.5837
LIME [4]	16.7586	0.4449	0.4500	0.4183	0.8549	0.8805	52.1989	0.0094	86.9102	3.2096	4.0825	21.1816
NPE [20]	16.9697	0.4839	0.3943	0.4156	0.8964	0.8943	52.2944	0.0093	87.0226	3.5588	4.2505	22.6374
JED [13]	13.6857	0.6509	0.3985	0.3549	0.8812	0.7143	50.5667	0.0146	87.3038	3.4064	3.8651	33.8342
CRM [27]	17.2032	0.6229	0.4114	0.3748	0.9456	0.8441	52.4903	0.0099	87.0542	3.4396	3.6790	23.7405
MBLLEN [10]	17.8583	0.7247	0.4911	0.3672	0.9262	0.8261	52.7664	0.0086	86.1212	3.2716	4.4620	21.5774
RetinexNet [24]	16.7740	0.4249	0.2370	0.4670	0.8642	0.9110	52.2075	0.0094	88.2461	3.7501	4.4975	21.3550
GLAD [21]	19.7182	0.6820	0.4091	0.3994	0.9329	0.9204	53.7990	0.0070	88.2170	3.3110	3.8021	16.0393
RDGAN [19]	15.9363	0.6357	0.3620	0.3985	0.9276	0.8296	51.7681	0.0114	87.4576	4.3899	5.3027	26.3796
Zero-DCE [3]	14.8671	0.5623	0.3849	0.3852	0.9276	0.7205	51.2269	0.0126	85.9968	4.1051	4.6860	31.4451
EnGan [7]	17.4828	0.6515	0.4234	0.3903	0.9226	0.8499	52.5934	0.0095	87.7195	4.5296	5.2536	21.9113
KinD [32]	20.3792	0.8056	0.5137	0.2711	0.9397	0.9250	54.1233	0.0066	87.5607	2.2947	2.6376	13.9618
KinD++ [31]	21.8037	0.8253	0.4954	0.2592	0.9275	0.9620	54.8074	0.0053	87.7490	2.2537	2.6731	11.0270
DA-DRN[25]	20.7282	0.7939	0.4327	0.3126	0.9458	0.9378	54.1478	0.0061	88.2747	2.1638	2.3149	12.9350
TSN-CA w/o CA	21.4727	0.8375	0.5460	0.2592	0.9572	0.9315	54.6206	0.0056	88.1231	2.4883	3.0704	13.1755
TSN-CA	22.4301	0.8452	0.5624	0.2433	0.9631	0.9338	55.1780	0.0043	88.1604	2.2462	2.5946	12.4946

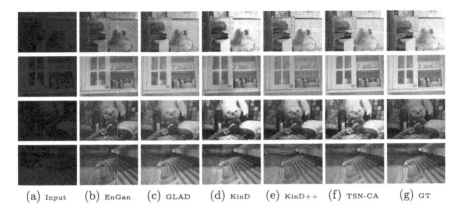

(a) Input   (b) EnGan   (c) GLAD   (d) KinD   (e) KinD++   (f) TSN-CA   (g) GT

Fig. 6. Visual comparison with state-of-the-art methods on LOL real-world dataset. GT means ground truth.

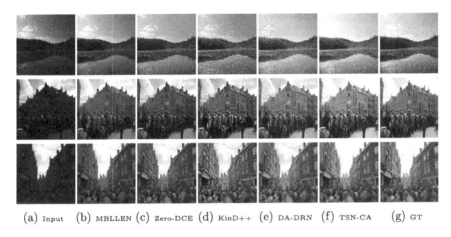

(a) Input   (b) MBLLEN   (c) Zero-DCE   (d) KinD++   (e) DA-DRN   (f) TSN-CA   (g) GT

Fig. 7. Visual comparison with state-of-the-art methods on LOL synthetic dataset. GT means ground truth.

(a) Input   (b) NPE   (c) GLAD   (d) RetinexNet   (e) KinD   (f) KinD++   (g) TSN-CA

Fig. 8. Visual comparison with state-of-the-art methods on several datasets without ground truth. TSN-CA was trained on the LOL real-world dataset.

Table 2. Quantitative comparison of several metrics between our method and other state-of-the-art methods on **LOL SYNTHETIC** dataset.

Methods	PSNR↑	SSIM↑	VIF↑	LPIPS↓	FSIM↑	UQI↑	SRER↑	RMSE↓	SAM↑	Mean↓	Median↓	DeltaE↓
Input	10.2533	0.4193	0.4248	0.2871	0.7802	0.3502	48.9243	0.0112	77.5350	3.2315	3.1539	51.9337
LIME [4]	17.0682	0.7606	0.6311	0.2040	0.8617	0.8804	52.3908	0.0092	85.8743	3.2096	4.0825	21.1816
NPE [20]	14.6603	0.7724	0.5708	0.1866	0.9036	0.7921	51.1505	0.0123	85.1261	2.4371	2.6856	23.4608
JED [13]	15.0805	0.7145	0.4397	0.2562	0.8815	0.7990	51.3495	0.0118	84.7191	3.4064	3.8651	33.8342
CRM [27]	14.9942	0.7689	0.6011	0.1831	0.9115	0.7850	51.3881	0.0122	85.5286	3.9513	4.5929	23.9757
MBLLEN [10]	14.2620	0.6552	0.4726	0.2903	0.9039	0.7013	50.9951	0.0132	84.1075	2.5991	3.1658	27.5349
RetinexNet [24]	17.2025	0.7639	0.3512	0.2467	0.8639	0.8888	52.4594	0.0095	88.1026	1.7625	2.7897	18.2853
GLAD [21]	16.2292	0.8007	0.6005	0.1888	0.9378	0.8406	52.1234	0.0105	86.2192	3.6618	3.8868	19.4709
RDGAN [19]	18.2270	0.8368	0.6006	0.1706	0.9415	0.8971	53.1087	0.0084	87.1588	3.1857	3.4799	16.6347
Zero-DCE [3]	16.5206	0.8173	0.5809	0.1772	0.9256	0.8150	52.2576	0.0102	85.2074	4.0482	3.6468	21.8502
EnGan [7]	15.2653	0.7516	0.5390	0.1754	0.8947	0.7953	51.4678	0.0117	85.9107	3.0516	3.8443	22.0353
KinD [32]	16.2156	0.8173	0.5825	0.1457	0.9306	0.8257	51.9733	0.0102	85.5904	1.7839	3.1954	18.7326
KinD++ [31]	16.4247	0.7845	0.4949	0.2618	0.8864	0.8639	52.1112	0.0097	85.8265	3.4677	4.6003	19.4102
DA-DRN[25]	20.5360	0.8388	0.4627	0.1691	0.9549	0.9359	54.1278	0.0063	87.2474	1.5082	1.7007	12.3788
TSN-CA w/o CA	22.1771	0.9094	0.6632	0.1093	0.9715	0.9418	54.9230	0.0056	86.9985	1.4571	2.1176	10.6888
TSN-CA	22.3467	0.9208	0.7195	0.0767	0.9801	0.9481	55.1215	0.0056	87.2226	1.3551	1.6288	9.5615

Table 3. Quantitative comparison in terms of **NIQE** Metric between our method and state-of-the-art methods on **LIME, DICM, MEF, and NPE** datasets.

Methods	LIME	DICM	MEF	NPE
Input	4.3577	3.8608	5.1884	3.6784
LIME [4]	4.1549	3.0005	4.4466	3.7715
NPE [20]	3.9048	2.8448	4.2556	3.3997
JED [13]	4.1456	3.5704	4.7250	3.5947
CRM [27]	3.8546	2.9908	4.0080	3.4867
EFF [26]	3.8596	2.9142	4.0533	3.4317
MBLLEN [10]	4.5138	3.6654	4.6901	3.9788
RetinexNet [24]	4.5978	4.5779	5.1747	4.5472
GLAD [21]	4.1282	3.1147	3.6897	3.5311
RDGAN [19]	4.1186	3.0737	3.6314	3.5836
Zero-DCE [3]	3.7690	2.8348	4.0240	3.5862
EnGan [7]	3.6574	2.9172	3.5373	3.5623
KinD [32]	4.7632	3.5651	4.7514	3.8605
KinD++ [31]	3.7362	2.9573	3.7818	3.3596
DA-DRN [25]	4.9852	3.7964	4.3252	4.1270
TSN-CA w/o CA	3.6749	2.7985	3.5462	3.2560
TSN-CA	3.5947	2.7106	3.5233	3.2234

can simulate this selective attention mechanism. It can integrate image features in channel dimensions by assigning more weight to useful features, such as color, detail, and texture, allowing the network to better learn them, and assigning little or no weight to less important or useless features, such as noise, distorted color, shadow blocks, and halo artifacts.

5   Experiments

5.1   Implementation

We trained and evaluated the model on the LOL [24] real-world and synthetic training datasets, and tested it on the LIME [4], DICM [9], MEF [11], and NPE [20] datasets.

5.2   Ablation Study

From Fig. 3, we notice that if the image of the V channel is directly used as the input to train the enhancement network, the noise in the brightness-enhanced output is removed, but the high-frequency details are lost, resulting in blurred edges. SSIM loss can effectively help a network to recover and reconstruct high-frequency details, but it allows noise to be retained, and introduces large shadow blocks and halo artifacts. So, instead of using SSIM loss, we fused the V, H, and S channels to recover the detail and structure information.

In Fig. 4 and Fig. 5, we notice that color over-saturation emerges in the enhanced image because the V channel is only responsible for brightness and the color is determined by the H and S channels, which are decoupled directly from the input low-light images, resulting in a high degree of degradation. After restoration of images suffering from over-saturation and severe noise, the noise can be removed, and the details and structrue restored. However, distinct halo and shadow blocks appear. Integrating the channel attention module in the skip connection of U-Net solves these problems.

5.3   Quantitative Comparison

We adopted PSNR, SSIM [23], VIF [16], LPIPS [30], FSIM [29], UQI [22], signal-to-reconstruction error ratio (SRER), root-MSE (RMSE), and spectral angle mapper (SAM) [1] as metrics to evaluate the quality of enhanced images. Following DA-DRN [25], we used angular error [5] and DeltaE [15] as indicators of color distortion. We tested our model on LOL real-world and synthetic datasets and four commonly used datasets without ground truth: LIME [4], DICM [9], MEF [11], and NPE [20]. We used NIQE [12] as a non-reference metric. As shown in Tables 1 and 2, our method achieves good effects and outperforms many state-of-the-art methods in terms of several indicators. Our results are far better in terms of PSNR and SSIM, which indicates that noise is removed well and details are well preserved. In terms of the index of color distortion, our results are similar to those of DA-DRN [25] and KinD++ [31], which are designed to deal with color distortion. Since our method is enhanced in HSV space, it does not cause too much color distortion in enhanced images. As shown in Table 3, our method surpasses all others on the NIQE index.

5.4   Qualitative Comparison

As shown in Figs. 6, 7, and 8, with other enhancement methods, there is still much noise and severe color distortion, as well as unpleasant shadow blocks and halo artifacts. In contrast, our method achieves a good noise-removal effect and color distortion correction. Also, by combining the channel attention (CA) mechanism with the skip connection of U-Net and embedding the SE Module in the skip connection, shadow blocks and halo artifacts can be well eliminated with minimal added computation cost because channel attention can selectively enhance important features and suppress less important ones.

Conclusion

We proposed a two-stage network for low-light image enhancement and restoration. In stage I, we transformed a low-light image from RGB space to HSV space, trained the network to enhance the brightness of the V channel, and leveraged the information of H and S to help the V channel to reconstruct the details and structure during enhancement. In stage II, we combined the brightness-enhanced and detail-preserved V channel with the original degraded H and S channels and converted them from HSV space back to RGB space. We trained a U-Net to restore the enhanced but degraded images. We introduced the channel attention mechanism to help the restoration network remove noise, restore details, and eliminate shadow blocks and halo artifacts. In the future, we plan to deal with the problem of undersaturation for some images (as shown in Fig. 6) by better balancing the color preseveration and noise removal.

References

1. De Carvalho, O.A., Meneses, P.R.: Spectral correlation mapper (scm): an improvement on the spectral angle mapper (sam). In: Summaries of the 9th JPL Airborne Earth Science Workshop, JPL Publication 00–18, vol. 9. JPL publication Pasadena, CA (2000)
2. Fu, X., Zeng, D., Huang, Y., Liao, Y., Ding, X., Paisley, J.: A fusion-based enhancing method for weakly illuminated images. Signal Process. **129**, 82–96 (2016)
3. Guo, C., et al.: Zero-reference deep curve estimation for low-light image enhancement. In: Proceedings of the IEEE/CVF Conference on Computer Vision and Pattern Recognition, pp. 1780–1789 (2020)
4. Guo, X., Li, Y., Ling, H.: Lime: low-light image enhancement via illumination map estimation. IEEE Trans. Image Process. **26**(2), 982–993 (2016)
5. Hordley, S.D., Finlayson, G.D.: Re-evaluating colour constancy algorithms. In: Proceedings of the 17th International Conference on Pattern Recognition, ICPR 2004, vol. 1, pp. 76–79. IEEE (2004)
6. Hu, J., Shen, L., Sun, G.: Squeeze-and-excitation networks. In: Proceedings of the IEEE Conference on Computer Vision and Pattern Recognition, pp. 7132–7141 (2018)
7. Jiang, Y., et al.: Enlightengan: deep light enhancement without paired supervision. IEEE Trans. Image Process. **30**, 2340–2349 (2021)

8. Land, E.H.: The retinex theory of color vision. Sci. Am. **237**(6), 108–129 (1977)
9. Lee, C., Lee, C., Kim, C.S.: Contrast enhancement based on layered difference representation of 2d histograms. IEEE Trans. Image Process. **22**(12), 5372–5384 (2013)
10. Lv, F., Lu, F., Wu, J., Lim, C.: Mbllen: Low-light image/video enhancement using cnns. In: BMVC, p. 220 (2018)
11. Ma, K., Zeng, K., Wang, Z.: Perceptual quality assessment for multi-exposure image fusion. IEEE Trans. Image Process. **24**(11), 3345–3356 (2015)
12. Mittal, A., Soundararajan, R., Bovik, A.C.: Making a "completely blind" image quality analyzer. IEEE Signal Process. Lett. **20**(3), 209–212 (2012)
13. Ren, X., Li, M., Cheng, W.H., Liu, J.: Joint enhancement and denoising method via sequential decomposition. In: 2018 IEEE International Symposium on Circuits and Systems (ISCAS), pp. 1–5. IEEE (2018)
14. Ren, Y., Ying, Z., Li, T.H., Li, G.: Lecarm: low-light image enhancement using the camera response model. IEEE Trans. Circuits Syst. Video Technol. **29**(4), 968–981 (2018)
15. Sharma, G., Wu, W., Dalal, E.N.: The ciede2000 color-difference formula: Implementation notes, supplementary test data, and mathematical observations. Color Res. Appli. **30**(1), 21–30 (2005)
16. Sheikh, H.R., Bovik, A.C.: Image information and visual quality. IEEE Trans. Image Process. **15**(2), 430–444 (2006)
17. Simonyan, K., Zisserman, A.: Very deep convolutional networks for large-scale image recognition. arXiv preprint arXiv:1409.1556 (2014)
18. Ungerleider, L.G., Haxby, J.V.: 'what'and 'where'in the human brain. Curr. Opin. Neurobiol. **4**(2), 157–165 (1994)
19. Wang, J., Tan, W., Niu, X., Yan, B.: Rdgan: retinex decomposition based adversarial learning for low-light enhancement. In: 2019 IEEE International Conference on Multimedia and Expo (ICME), pp. 1186–1191. IEEE (2019)
20. Wang, S., Zheng, J., Hu, H.M., Li, B.: Naturalness preserved enhancement algorithm for non-uniform illumination images. IEEE Trans. Image Process. **22**(9), 3538–3548 (2013)
21. Wang, W., Wei, C., Yang, W., Liu, J.: Gladnet: low-light enhancement network with global awareness. In: 2018 13th IEEE International Conference on Automatic Face & Gesture Recognition (FG 2018), pp. 751–755. IEEE (2018)
22. Wang, Z., Bovik, A.C.: A universal image quality index. IEEE Signal Process. Lett. **9**(3), 81–84 (2002)
23. Wang, Z., Bovik, A.C., Sheikh, H.R., Simoncelli, E.P.: Image quality assessment: from error visibility to structural similarity. IEEE Trans. Image Process. **13**(4), 600–612 (2004)
24. Wei, C., Wang, W., Yang, W., Liu, J.: Deep retinex decomposition for low-light enhancement. arXiv preprint arXiv:1808.04560 (2018)
25. Wei, X., et al.: Da-drn: Degradation-aware deep retinex network for low-light image enhancement. arXiv preprint arXiv:2110.01809 (2021)
26. Ying, Z., Li, G., Ren, Y., Wang, R., Wang, W.: A new image contrast enhancement algorithm using exposure fusion drameawork. In: Felsberg, M., Heyden, A., Krüger, N. (eds.) CAIP 2017. LNCS, vol. 10425, pp. 36–46. Springer, Cham (2017). https://doi.org/10.1007/978-3-319-64698-5_4
27. Ying, Z., Li, G., Ren, Y., Wang, R., Wang, W.: A new low-light image enhancement algorithm using camera response model. In: Proceedings of the IEEE International Conference on Computer Vision Workshops, pp. 3015–3022 (2017)

28. Yue, H., Yang, J., Sun, X., Wu, F., Hou, C.: Contrast enhancement based on intrinsic image decomposition. IEEE Trans. Image Process. **26**(8), 3981–3994 (2017)
29. Zhang, L., Zhang, L., Mou, X., Zhang, D.: Fsim: A feature similarity index for image quality assessment. IEEE Trans. Image Process. **20**(8), 2378–2386 (2011)
30. Zhang, R., Isola, P., Efros, A.A., Shechtman, E., Wang, O.: The unreasonable effectiveness of deep features as a perceptual metric. In: Proceedings of the IEEE Conference on Computer Vision and Pattern Recognition, pp. 586–595 (2018)
31. Zhang, Y., Guo, X., Ma, J., Liu, W., Zhang, J.: Beyond brightening low-light images. Int. J. Comput. Vision **129**(4), 1013–1037 (2021)
32. Zhang, Y., Zhang, J., Guo, X.: Kindling the darkness: a practical low-light image enhancer. In: Proceedings of the 27th ACM International Conference on Multimedia, pp. 1632–1640 (2019)
33. Zhang, Y., Di, X., Zhang, B., Ji, R., Wang, C.: Better than reference in low light image enhancement: Conditional re-enhancement networks. arXiv preprint arXiv:2008.11434 (2020)
34. Zhao, M., Zhong, S., Fu, X., Tang, B., Pecht, M.: Deep residual shrinkage networks for fault diagnosis. IEEE Trans. Industr. Inf. **16**(7), 4681–4690 (2019)

Two-Stream Interactive Memory Network for Video Facial Expression Recognition

Lingyu Chen[1], Yong Ouyang[1(✉)], Ranyi Xu[2], Sisi Sun[3], and Yawen Zeng[4(✉)]

[1] Hubei University of Technology, Wuhan 430068, China
oyywuhan@163.com
[2] Hunan University, Changsha 410012, China
[3] Minzu University of China, Beijing 100081, China
[4] Tencent Inc., Shenzhen 518000, China
yawen_zeng@163.com

Abstract. The task of video facial expression recognition is widely applied in human-computer, psychology interaction and other fields. Existing methods are generally based on LSTM or CNN, but these frameworks are under-developed for the following two reasons. 1) Some own small memory capacity, and their memory storage encoded by hidden states cannot precisely remember past changes; 2) Others only focus on the local appearance of faces. Therefore, how to exploit longer dynamic facial changes and refine local information in video is a non-trivial work.

To solve the above problems, a two-stream interactive memory network based on channel/spatial attention(TM-CSA) is proposed in this paper. Specifically, a channel attention module attempts to extract more distinctive features among different channels, and a spatial attention module encodes the pixel-level context of the entire image. In this way, a interactive memory module of TM-CSA mines the interaction and correlation within and between images. Correspondingly, the TM-CSA has ability to remember enough past facts and reduce information redundancy. The experimental results tested on the three public datasets, JAFFE, CK+ and ImaSeDS show our TM-CSA has better performance.

Keywords: Video facial expression recognition · Channel/spatial attention · Bi-directional long short-term memory

1 Introduction

The task of video facial expression recognition is a promising sensing technology, and plays an important role in human interaction and other fields [1,2]. However, due to various facial appearances and different habits of expressing emotions, it is urgent in this task to make the most of expression information when coping with the expression features of different individuals.

Especially in a video, the process of facial change is complex, fluctuating and longer. A realistic example is shown in Fig. 1, where (a) is a static single image and (b) is a short-term frames, whose changes are minor. However, when the

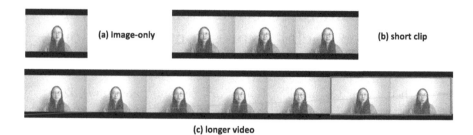

Fig. 1. Examples of image-only, short clip and longer video. (Color figure online)

time lasts longer, as shown in (c), more changes will appear (e.g. the red box). In fact, the expression recognition task should be required to deal with long videos, such as the expressions of guests in exhibition scenes and restaurant scenes are longer, continuous and procedural. Therefore, how to capture and identify facial expression changes in long videos is worth researching and applying.

Traditional facial expression recognition methods [3,4] generally extract handcraft features, such as LBP and geometric features. However, these traditional and shallow handcraft extraction algorithms lack effective features information, which are not enough to mine deep semantics of images and consume lots of computational resources. Benefiting from the merit of deep learning, CNN [5,6] and RNN [7] are applied to capture the dynamic changes of expression. Further, LSTM [8,9] gradually replaces RNN to deal with related issues. However, these frameworks are under-developed for the following two reasons. 1) LSTM-based methods suffer from small memory capacity, and memory storage encoded by hidden states cannot accurately remember past changes; 2) CNN-based solutions only focus on the local appearance of faces and ignore large-scale pixel-level context. **Therefore, how to capture longer dynamic facial changes and refine local information in video is a non-trivial work.**

To solve the above issues, we contribute a two-stream interactive memory network based on channel/spatial attention (abbrebiated as TM-CSA). As shown in Fig. 2, the external storage component of the first memory sub-network with channel attention (CAMN) is adopted to store channel attention maps, and another memory module employed spatial attention (SAMN) is designed for spatial maps. Among them, the spatial attention encodes the dependencies in the entire feature, which map to determine the position of the person's eyes, lips, and other organs. Meanwhile, the channel attention handles the relationship between any two channels. The main contributions of our work are summarized as follows:

a) To the best of our knowledge, this is the first work that introduces a two-stream interactive memory network for video facial expression recognition. It captures longer dynamic facial changes and refine local information in video.

b) We contribute a TM-CSA framework, which combines channel attention with spatial attention to extract features and explore the correlation between the

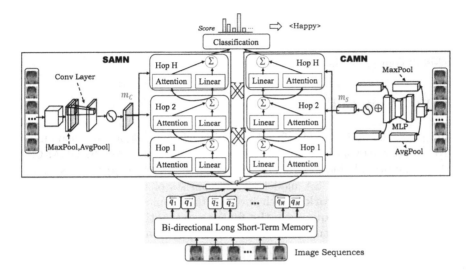

Fig. 2. Overview of Our TM-CSA framework.

two. Therefore, TM-CSA extracts high-level semantics in different channels and encodes the pixel-level context of the entire image.

c) Extensive experiments on the three public databases, JAFFE [17], CK+ [18] and ImaSeDS [19] are performed to validate the effectiveness of TM-CSA.

2 Related Work

2.1 Memory Network

The memory network was proposed by Weston [10] as a general framework for the task of prediction, of which main idea was to use a long-term storage component that can be read, written, or jointly learned for inference. MemNet [11] was composed of multiple computational layers with shared parameters. When inferring a certain emotional polarity, the article can analyze the importance of every word in the context. MIMN [12] learned not only the interactive influences between cross-modal data but also the self-influence in mono-modal data. In this work, we introduce a two-stream interactive memory network to store factual information and mine a variety of correlations in the expression data.

2.2 Attention Mechanism

Sun et al. [13] extracted facial local features by the stack of convolutional layers and embedded attention model to automatically determine the area of interest. SENet [14] modeled the interdependence between channels to recalibrate feature response at the channel level. CBAM [15] replaced the explicit calculation of 3D attention maps by learning channel and spatial-wise attention, and in this process, the amount of calculation and overhead of parameter became less. Meanwhile, we combine the channel attention with spatial attention to extract high-level semantics closer to the category in different channels, and encodes the pixel-level context of the entire image.

3 Our Proposed Framework

In this paper, we design a video facial recognition framework, a two-stream interactive memory network based on channel/spatial attention (TM-CSA). TM-CSA analyses the overall emotional tendency of characters when expressions change over a while. The TM-CSA model mainly consists of two modules: (1) **Feature extraction network,** which involves three units: **the hidden states extraction of facial sequences, the feature extraction based on channel attention and the feature extractor with spatial attention,** respectively. The aim of this network is to extract the depth information in the expression images and eliminate redundant information as much as possible. (2) **Two-stream interactive memory network,** which focuses on mining the correlations between contextual features, so as to better predict the expression category.

3.1 Feature Extraction Network

To promote the performance of video facial expression recognition, we advocate to firstly utilize the multi-task convolutional neural network (MTCNN) to pre-process (face detection, face alignment, etc.) images in sequences, and then input them into VGG16 to capture expression features.

   In the following, we briefly describe the three feature extractors adopted in this paper. Notably, since the feature extraction steps are roughly the same for the extractors with channel attention and spatial attention, we will broadly describe the process of extracting features in the two parts together.

BiLSTM as Feature Extractor. The hidden states extraction of Image Sequences. The expression changes help to explore structural relationships, which can be employed as prior knowledge to predict the overall emotional tendency. Specifically, our TM-CSA implements a bidirectional long and short-term memory network (BiLSTM) to model the expression change process. At each time step, the model acquires the hidden state q_j of the j-th image by merging the forward result $\vec{q_j} \in \mathbb{R}^D$ and backward result $\overleftarrow{q_j} \in \mathbb{R}^D$ which are obtained by BiLSTM. Then we take the average of all hidden vectors of the sequence as the final feature vector $q^v \in \mathbb{R}^{2 \times D}$ in Eq. (1), where $2 \times D$ is the dimension information.

$$q^V = \frac{1}{N} \sum_j q_j, q_j = [\vec{q_j}, \overleftarrow{q_j}] \tag{1}$$

Attention Feature Extractors. There exists two local feature extractors that connect the channel or spatial attention unit. Afterwards, we simultaneously distribute feature maps into the corresponding external storage component.

Feature extraction based on channel attention. Making use of the attention mechanism by channels can be seen as the process of selecting semantic attributes. Through average and max pooling operations, our model aggregates the feature information and generates two descriptors $V_{avg}^{k,l(c)}$ and $V_{max}^{k,l(c)}$, then generates channel attention maps $m_k^C \in \mathbb{R}^{C \times 1 \times 1}$ by Multi-Layer Perceptor (MLP) in Eq. (2):

$$
\begin{aligned}
m_k^C &= Sigmoid(MLP(AvgPool(V_k^l)) + MLP(MaxPool(V_k^l))) \\
&= Sigmoid(W_1(W_0(V_{avg}^{k,l(c)})) + W_1(W_0(V_{max}^{k,l(c)})))
\end{aligned}
\tag{2}
$$

Feature extraction based on spatial attention. Due to the dynamic changes in the expression sequences, the global and local feature distribution has a certain regularity. To encode effectively, we model a wide range of context by convolution feature extractor based on spatial attention. It does not consider each region of the image equally but tries to pay more attention to the semantically related regions. The merger operation taken along the channel axis has proved effective to highlight the information area [16]. The model generates spatial attention maps $m_i^S \in \mathbb{R}^{H \times W}$ along the channel axis in Eq. (3), which encode for the emphasized or suppressed position.

$$
\begin{aligned}
m_i^S &= Sigmoid(CNN^{7 \times 7}([AvgPool(V_i^l); MaxPool(V_i^l)])) \\
&= Sigmoid(CNN^{7 \times 7}([V_{avg}^{i,l(s)}; V_{max}^{i,l(s)}]))
\end{aligned}
\tag{3}
$$

3.2   Two-Stream Interactive Memory Network

In this section, we first describe how channel and spatial attention maps are utilized in either layer of the two sub-networks separately, and then show how TM-CSA combines the two streams of **CAMN** and **SAMN** for interactive recurrent processing to refine the local information in video.

Two Memory Sub-networks with Channel/Spatial Attention Maps. Each sub-network consists of multiple computational layers (hops), and each layer (hop) contains an attention layer. **The first memory sub-network CAMN** provides high-level semantic attributes to convey emotion, combing hidden states that represent the temporal structure relationship of sequence with channel attention maps, to enhance the robustness of our model. We fuse the channel attention maps m_k^C with hidden states q^V and get the average output feature $V_C^{(1)}$ based on the self-attention in Eq. (4).

$$
v_C^{(1)} = Att(m_k^C, q^V)
\tag{4}
$$

e^V is obtained through a linear transformation of input q^V at the linear layer contained in the first computational layer. Then we synthesize the output of the first computational layer of the CAMN $vec_C^{(1)}$:

$$
vec_C^{(1)} = Linear(v_C^{(1)}, e^V)
\tag{5}
$$

The other second memory sub-network SAMN leverages a spatial attention to extract features of specific areas in images beneficial to classification. To make up for the shortcomings of structural information of sequences in spatial features, the memory storage component m_S and hidden state vector q^V are seen as input. Then we infer the output of the first computational layer in the SAMN is $vec_S^{(1)}$.

Combination of Recurrent Two-Stream Interactive Memory Network. TM-CSA stacks multiple computational layers (hops), which can learn the deep abstract representation of data. As to the t-th layer of the CAMN, it will use external storage component m_C and output $vec_C^{(t-1)}$ of the (t-1)-th layer as the input, and output feature representation of the (t-1)-th attention layer v_C^t:

$$v_C^t = Att(m_C, vec_C^{(t-1)}), t \in [2, H] \tag{6}$$

To mine the interactive influence and correlation of two attention maps for prediction, we average the output $vec_C^{(t-1)}$ and $vec_S^{(t-1)}$ of the corresponding computational layer in the SAMN as the input of the t-th linear layer. Therefore, we conclude that integrated output $vec_C^{(t)}$ of the t-th layer (hop t) in the CAMN, which H represents the number of computational layers:

$$v_L^t = Linear(\frac{vec_C^{(t-1)} + vec_S^{(t-1)}}{2}), t \in [2, H] \tag{7}$$

$$vec_C^{(t)} = tanh(W_C^{(t)}(v_C^{(t)} + v_L^{(t)})), t \in [2, H] \tag{8}$$

The recurrent situation is the same when the t-th computational layer is executed on the SAMN. After the expression information is processed circularly by the computational layer in H rounds, the output of the last layer in the sub-networks is the final high-level semantic information $vec_C^{(H)}$ and image feature $vec_s^{(H)}$. The model merges them to predict the expression classification of character in this period time.

4   Experiment

To verify the robustness and effectiveness of TM-CSA, this paper conducts experiments under the public datasets JAFFE [17], CK+ [18] and ImaSeDS [19]. Our model has been fully verified through comparing the superior results of the various advanced methods, and it has shown excellent performance in some real scenes. In addition, Accuracy and Recall will be used to evaluate the proposed model. Among them, Recall refers to the proportion of correctly judged positive examples in the total positive examples, and recall@3 means the fact that, when the expression category corresponding to the model prediction probability ranked in the top three in descending order, there exists the same class as the facial label, and it is recorded as a correct determination.

Fig. 3. An example of ImaSeDS [19], which corresponds to a defined label: Surprise.

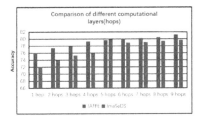

Fig. 4. Comparison of different computational layers. We set different numbers of computational layers to determine its impact for the interactive memory network.

4.1 Datasets

This paper mainly uses three expression datasets: JAFFE [17], CK+ [18] and ImaSeDS [19]. Unlike the other two, ImaSeDS [19] collects 6 kinds from multiple people except 'disgust' and has 20520 images. Each expressional label corresponds to a 10-frame image sequence, as Fig. 3 shows.

4.2 Comparison of Different Computational Layers (Hops)

The experiment in this section primarily achieves model training and testing on JAFFE [17] and ImaSeDS [19]. We compare the recognition rates of different computational layers in the memory network. Experiments from one computational layer (1 hop) to nine computational layers (9 hops) and the results are shown in Fig. 4.

It can be observed from the Fig. 4 that using more computational layers generally improves the performance of model, especially when the number of computational layers is less than six. When the model contains 5 or 9 computation layers, it can reach peak performance. In both datasets, TM-CSA achieves high accuracy. However, it is found that the higher the number of calculation layers, the greater the time complexity of the model. Therefore, it is more appropriate to select the number of computational layers as five to six.

4.3 Performance Analysis of TM-CSA

TM-CSA needs to be compared with state-of-the-art methods to prove its practicality and generalization. The empirical results are listed based on MLHaar [20], LRandF [21], AMSCNN [22], SRNN [23] and other algorithms in Table 1. Note that the ImaSeDS [19] is used, and the number of calculation layers of the

Table 1. Comparison of TM-CSA with popular methods on ImaSeDS [19].

State-of-the-art methods	Recall@1	Recall@2	Recall@3
MLHaar [20]	0.438	0.532	0.609
LRandF [21]	0.443	0.581	0.613
AMSCNN [22]	0.611	0.669	0.697
SRNN [23]	0.648	0.685	0.708
3DGRU [24]	0.498	0.615	0.670
AAM-LSTM [25]	0.653	0.716	0.753
TM-CSA (Ours-5 Hops)	0.694	0.755	**0.799**

TM-CSA is selected as 5. Adam optimization algorithm is applied to train the model by minimizing cross-entropy loss, and Dropout is implemented to avoid over-fitting.

From Table 1, the performance of the methods based on deep learning out-perform universally better than those based on traditional methods. It can be inferred that the local features extracted by convolution are more effective for the model than traditional manual features, which proves the importance of feature extraction to the model. Among the three recurrent models including SRNN [23], 3DGRU [24] and AAM-LSTM [25], Recall@3 evaluation indicator of our model is 9.1% higher than SRNN [23] and 4.6% higher than ANN-LSTM [25], because the existence of external storage components of the memory network not only solves the problem about gradient vanishing that RNN encounters, but also deals with the small memory capacity. At the same time, the interactive influence between the channel and spatial attention feature maps mines more correlations of data. Compared with AMSCNN [22], TM-CSA is about 10% higher, indicating that the features extracted by channel and spatial attention are more expressive and representative.

Table 2. Comparison of TM-CSA with methods on JAFFE [17].

State-of-the-art methods	Accuracy
LBP+TOP [26]	0.809
HOG [27]	0.714
Kernel collaboration [28]	0.688
Gabor Filter [29]	0.809
CF+CT [30]	0.770
IACNN [31]	0.750
AMSCNN [22]	0.752
SRNN [23]	0.789
AAM-LSTM [25]	0.816
TM-CSA (Ours-5 Hops)	**0.825**

The results of the algorithm are shown in Table 2 by using JAFFE [17] for model training. The accuracy is consistent with Table 1: The evaluation indicator of TM-CSA is the highest, reaching 82.5%, which is 0.9% higher than the LSTM-based algorithm and 3.6% higher than the SRNN [23]. Simultaneously, deep learning models show a more striking success than traditional methods.

Table 3. Comparison of TM-CSA with popular methods on CK+ [18].

State-of-the-art methods	Accuracy
3D SIFT [32]	0.813
LBP+TOP [26]	0.889
TMS [33]	0.918
IT-RBM [34]	0.871
ASModel [35]	0.894
MicroExpNet [36]	0.907
Fan et al. [37]	0.837
Eskil et al. [38]	0.768
TM-CSA (Ours-5 Hops)	**0.941**

To qualitatively demonstrate the effectiveness of our approach, we also conduct experiments on CK+ [18]. Empirical results are in Table 3. Consistent with previous results, TM-CSA obtains the best performance with 5 hops. Overall speaking, traditional methods consume more hours and computation source of the machine. However, deep models promote the accuracy of the recognition task efficiently, except TM-CSA of 10 hops.

4.4   Model Component Analysis

To verify TM-CSA benefits from all components, we have some ablation experiments with ImaSeDS [19]. The results are reported in the Table 4 in the form of Recall@3. TM-CSA firstly removes CAMN and SAMN module respectively, to certify the importance of channel or spatial attention. And then the proposed network deals without the whole attention module or memory network. From Table 4, superior consequences show that CAMN extracts more distinctive features among different channels, and SAMN encodes the pixel-level context of the entire image. At the same time, the structure of memory network mines the interaction and correlation within and between images. In the end, TM-CSA analyses expression data directly, that is, we carry out the experiment without processing by BiLSTM. Integrated TM-CSA seems to have a extremely better results than other ablation models.

4.5 Visualization of Attention Map

In the CAMN/SAMN with attention maps, the former focuses on encoding the context at the pixel level, while the latter tries to extract more discriminative channel information between different channels. This section uses the response feature map to calculate the visualization result of fusing the heat map on the original image. Figure 5 shows the attention map of CAMN/SAMN. We know that both channel attention and spatial attention are beneficial to reduce interference factors and background information, so that the TM-CSA model can effectively calculate the target area. Specifically, #1 and #2 mappings are selected from multiple channels in the two types of attention maps.

Table 4. The results of TM-CSA without specific components on ImaSeDS database.

Models	Recall@3			
	1 Hop	5 Hops	10 Hops	0 Hop
w/o CAMN	0.752	0.777	0.772	–
w/o SAMN	0.689	0.772	0.743	–
w/o Attention Module	0.662	0.684	0.587	–
w/o memory network	–	–	–	0.592
w/o BiLSTM	–	–	–	0.694
TM-CSA (Ours)	0.719	**0.799**	0.795	–

Fig. 5. Visualization of the attention map.

5 Conclusion

This paper proposes a two-stream interactive memory network, TM-CSA, which combines the channel and spatial attention. The advantage of this framework is that: 1) The TM-CSA provides external storage components to cope with problems which are related to the establishment of a long-term dependency relationship and a small capacity to store information. 2) The attention modules extract high-level semantic attributes in different channels and encode context at the pixel level to find local features that need to be focused on. 3) Moreover, TM-CSA can learn interactive influences between various features of data.

The experimental results of the JAFFE [17] and ImaSeDS [19] show that the TM-CSA has better recognition performance and robustness.

However, the external storage component of TM-CSA may not be sufficient for more sophisticated video facial expression recognition, which only resolves around spatial and channel attention. Thus, in the future, we plan to establish a Transformer-based model to mine the relationships between global and local features for better classification results.

Acknowledgements. This paper is supported by National College Student Innovation and Entrepreneurship Training Program (S202010500049).

References

1. An, F., Liu, Z.: Facial expression recognition algorithm based on parameter adaptive initialization of cnn and lstm. The Visual Computer (2019)
2. Chen, L., Ouyang, y., Zeng, Y., Li, Y.: Dynamic facial expression recognition model based on bilstm-attention. In: ICCSE (2020)
3. Cugu, I., Sener, E., Akbas, E.: Microexpnet: An extremely small and fast model for expression recognition from face images. In: IPTA (2019)
4. Deng, L., Wang, Q., Yuan, D.: Dynamic facial expression recognition based on deep learning. In: 14th International Conference on Computer Science & Education, ICCSE 2019, Toronto, ON, Canada, 19–21 August 2019, pp. 32–37. IEEE (2019)
5. Ekman, P., Friesen, W.V.: A new pan-cultural facial expression of emotion. Motiv. Emot. **10**(2), 159–168 (1986)
6. Eskil, M.T., Benli, K.S.: Facial expression recognition based on anatomy. Comput. Vis. Image Underst. **119**, 1–14 (2014). https://doi.org/10.1016/j.cviu.2013.11.002
7. Benitez-Quiroz, C.F., Srinivasan, R., Martinez, A.M.: Discriminant functional learning of color features for the recognition of facial action units and their intensities. IEEE Trans. Pattern Anal. Mach. Intell. **41**, 2835–2845 (2018)
8. Fan, X.: Tjahjadi, Tardi: a spatial-temporal framework based on histogram of gradients and optical flow for facial expression recognition in video sequences. Pattern Recogn. J. Pattern Recogn. Soc. **48**(11), 3407–3416 (2015)
9. Goyani, M., Patel, N.: Template matching and machine learning-based robust facial expression recognition system using multi-level haar wavelet. Int. J. Comput. Appli. **42**, 1–12 (2017)
10. Hu, M., Wang, H., Wang, X., Yang, J., Wang, R.: Video facial emotion recognition based on local enhanced motion history image and CNN-CTSLSTM networks. J. Vis. Commun. Image Represent. **59**, 176–185 (2019)
11. Jain, S., Hu, C., Aggarwal, J.K.: Facial expression recognition with temporal modeling of shapes. In: ICCV (2011)
12. Jie, H., Li, S., Gang, S., Albanie, S.: Squeeze-and-excitation networks. IEEE Trans. Pattern Anal. Mach. Intell. 42, PP(99) (2017)
13. Lei, J., Liu, Z., Zou, Z., Li, T., Xu, J., Feng, Z., Liang, R.: Facial expression recognition by expression-specific representation swapping (2021)
14. Li, T.S., Kuo, P., Tsai, T., Luan, P.: CNN and LSTM based facial expression analysis model for a humanoid robot. IEEE Access **7**, 93998–94011 (2019)
15. Li, Z., Wu, S., Xiao, G.: Facial expression recognition by multi-scale cnn with regularized center loss. In: ICPR (2018)

16. Liu, C., Hirota, K., Ma, J., Jia, Z., Dai, Y.: Facial expression recognition using hybrid features of pixel and geometry. IEEE Access PP(99), 1–1 (2021)
17. Lucey, P., Cohn, J.F., Kanade, T., Saragih, J., Matthews, I.: The extended cohn-kanade dataset (ck+): A complete dataset for action unit and emotion-specified expression. In: CVPR Workshops (2010)
18. Lyons, M.J., Kamachi, M., Gyoba, J.: Coding facial expressions with gabor wavelets (ivc special issue) (2020)
19. Meng, Z., Ping, L., Jie, C., Han, S., Yan, T.: Identity-aware convolutional neural network for facial expression recognition. In: IEEE International Conference on Automatic Face and Gesture Recognition (2017)
20. Miyoshi, R., Nagata, N., Hashimoto, M.: Facial-expression recognition from video using enhanced convolutional lstm. In: 2019 Digital Image Computing: Techniques and Applications (DICTA) (2019)
21. Munasinghe, M.I.N.P.: Facial expression recognition using facial landmarks and random forest classifier. In: 17th IEEE/ACIS International Conference on Computer and Information Science, ICIS 2018, Singapore, 6–8 June 2018, pp. 423–427. IEEE Computer Society (2018)
22. Nigam, S., Singh, R., Misra, A.K.: Efficient facial expression recognition using histogram of oriented gradients in wavelet domain. Multimedia Tools Appli. **77**(21), 28725–28747 (2018). https://doi.org/10.1007/s11042-018-6040-3
23. Scovanner, P., Ali, S., Shah, M.: A 3-dimensional sift descriptor and its application to action recognition. In: MM, pp. 357–360 (2007)
24. Sun, W., Zhao, H., Jin, Z.: A visual attention based roi detection method for facial expression recognition. Neurocomputing **296**, 12–22 (2018)
25. Sun, X., Xia, P., Ren, F.: Multi-attention based deep neural network with hybrid features for dynamic sequential facial expression recognition. Neurocomputing **444**, 378–389 (2020)
26. Sun, Z., Hu, Z.P., Chiong, R., Wang, M., He, W.: Combining the kernel collaboration representation and deep subspace learning for facial expression recognition. J. Circuits Syst. Comput. **27**(8), 1850121.1-1850121.16 (2018)
27. Tang, D., Qin, B., Liu, T.: Aspect level sentiment classification with deep memory network (2016)
28. Wang, S., Zheng, Z., Yin, S., Yang, J., Ji, Q.: A novel dynamic model capturing spatial and temporal patterns for facial expression analysis. IEEE Trans. Pattern Anal. Mach. Intell. **42**, 2082–2095 (2019)
29. Wang, Y., Hui, Y., Stevens, B., Liu, H.: Dynamic facial expression recognition using local patch and lbp-top. In: International Conference on Human System Interactions (2015)
30. Weston, J., Chopra, S., Bordes, A.: Memory networks. Eprint Arxiv (2014)
31. Woo, S., Park, J., Lee, J.-Y., Kweon, I.S.: CBAM: Convolutional block attention module. In: Ferrari, V., Hebert, M., Sminchisescu, C., Weiss, Y. (eds.) ECCV 2018. LNCS, vol. 11211, pp. 3–19. Springer, Cham (2018). https://doi.org/10.1007/978-3-030-01234-2_1
32. Xu, N., Mao, W., Chen, G.: Multi-interactive memory network for aspect based multimodal sentiment analysis. In: AAAI (2019)
33. Yu, J., Bhanu, B.: Evolutionary feature synthesis for facial expression recognition. Pattern Recognit. Lett. **27**(11), 1289–1298 (2006)
34. Zagoruyko, S., Komodakis, N.: Paying more attention to attention: Improving the performance of convolutional neural networks via attention transfer (2016)

35. Zeng, Y., Cao, D., Lu, S., Zhang, H., Xu, J., Zheng, Q.: Moment is important: language-based video moment retrieval via adversarial learning. ACM Trans. Multim. Comput. Commun. Appl. **18**, 56:1–56:21 (2022)
36. Zeng, Y., Cao, D., Wei, X., Liu, M., Zhao, Z., Qin, Z.: Multi-modal relational graph for cross-modal video moment retrieval. In: CVPR, pp. 2215–2224. IEEE (2021)
37. Zhao, G., Pietikainen, M.: Dynamic texture recognition using local binary patterns with an application to facial expressions. IEEE Trans. Pattern Anal. Mach. Intell. **29**, 915–928 (2007)
38. Zhi, R., Wan, M.: Dynamic facial expression feature learning based on sparse rnn. In: ITAIC (2019)

Utilize Spatial Prior in Ground Truth: Spatial-Enhanced Loss for Semantic Segmentation

Yu Zhang[1], Fagui Liu[1,2](✉), and Quan Tang[1]

[1] South China University of Technology, Guangzhou 510006, China
{csemoszy,csquantang}@mail.scut.edu.cn, fgliu@scut.edu.cn
[2] Peng Cheng Laboratory, Shenzhen 518055, China

Abstract. Most supervised semantic segmentation methods to date choose cross-entropy loss (CE) as the default choice. Standard CE treats all pixels in the image indiscriminately, which lacks consideration of context differences between pixels, leading to the model being overwhelmed by numerous homogeneous pixels in large-scale objects. It ignores an essential spatial prior that can be deduced from Ground Truth-the segmentation edges, which can be practical to distinguish the excessive homogeneous pixels. Therefore, we propose a novel loss function termed Spatial-enhanced Loss (SL), in which the image is spatially separated into the edge region and the body region with the assistance of the edge derived from Ground Truth. Experiments evidence that SL has impressive superiority over Focal Loss, standard cross-entropy loss, class-balanced cross-entropy loss and Dice Loss. We achieve substantial improvements on multiple models without using any tricks, up to 1.60% mIoU.

Keywords: Spatial-enhanced loss · Edge-body separation · Weighted cross-entropy · Semantic segmentation

1 Introduction

Semantic segmentation, classifying all pixels in an image to obtain the segmentation map, is a fundamental task that has been widely studied in computer vision. It lays a solid foundation for many application scenarios, e.g. autonomous driving, medical diagnosis and remote sensing. Since Fully Convolutional Network (FCN) [18] replaces fully connected layers with convolution layers in traditional classification networks, thereby migrating the classification networks to the segmentation task, Deep convolutional neural networks have been widely studied for semantic segmentation. Dilated convolution [21] is applied to increase the receptive field. Parsenet [17] applies global average pooling to perceive global clues. DeepLab [4–7] and PSPNet [23] propose ASPP and PPM respectively to perform multi-scale feature aggregation. DANet [11] utilizes channel-wise and spatial-wise attention mechanisms to improve feature discrimination.

E. Pimenidis et al. (Eds.): ICANN 2022, LNCS 13531, pp. 312–321, 2022.
https://doi.org/10.1007/978-3-031-15934-3_26

Fig. 1. Left: ground truth, **Middle**: prediction, **Right**: distribution of misclassified pixels (black). (Color figure online)

Most of the works pursue innovations in network architectures and focus on effectively incorporating contextual cues, but these works are still carried out using standard cross-entropy loss (CE). However, in complex multi-class semantic segmentation scenarios, data imbalance is still a major obstacle [3], which is hard to address only by modifying network structures. The standard CE accumulates all pixels in the image indiscriminately, making the model dominated by large-scale objects [2,14]. The fact is usually ignored that the standard CE lacks the ability to modeling the context differences between pixels.

Some previous works advocate balancing CE based on class frequencies [2, 14,22]. The class-balanced cross-entropy loss shows improvements in some few-class scenes, but the improvement is often limited in complex multi-class scenes. Most current works still apply standard CE as the default choice in multi-class scenarios.

Apart from the class imbalance problem, classification difficulty varies dramatically with different positions in the image [15,16]. The hard-easy imbalance can also harm the training. Contexts exhibit minor changes in the object's body region where samples are excessive, which bias the model towards them. While the hard pixels, clustering in the edge region, are often insufficient and their contexts are more diverse, making them more challenging. As shown in Fig. 1, most misclassified pixels are concentrated near the edges. Focal Loss [16] adds a dynamic scaling factor based on confidence to up-weights hard pixels, down-weight easy pixels, which help the model to dynamically perceive the context difference in the loss layer.

Unlike many works focused on pursuing feature enhancement, we start from another perspective and perform loss enhancement in the spatial dimension. The edge prior, derived from GT, is utilized to explicitly separate the image into the edge and body region. We further propose a novel loss function termed Spatial-enhanced Loss, which is enhanced spatially with the separated regions.

The main contributions of this paper are:

- This paper proposes a novel semantic segmentation loss termed Spatial-enhanced Loss, where the loss is enhanced spatially with the separated edge and body regions.
- We provide a novel region separation method where a circular-filled convolution kernel is applied to object edges so that all pixels within a specified distance from edges can be sampled, thus dividing an image into two regions of edge and body.

– Results on Cityscapes and PASCAL VOC 2012 datasets evidence the efficacy of Spatial-enhanced loss. Our method achieves substantial performance
improvements and enhances the robustness of training.

2   Related Work

2.1   Focus on Hard Pixels

Pixels of classes in most real-world multi-class semantic segmentation scenes
exhibit a long tail distribution [3], in which few large-scale classes occupy most
of the positions in the image. This data imbalance problem weakens the model's
discrimination, making the model fit large-scale classes more preferentially.

Li et al. [15] divides the image into three sets of easy, moderate, and hard
according to the prediction confidence, making predictions on pixels of different
difficulty intervals with features after different stages. It boosts the accuracy and
speed of segmentation. Pixel-level weights in Focal Loss [16] are also generated
based on the prediction confidence, adaptively reducing weights of easy pixels
and increasing weights of hard pixels, making the network more focused on hard
pixels.

2.2   Class Imbalance

In some few-class application scenarios, the number of foreground and background pixels of images is extremely unbalanced, such as medical images [20],
aerial images, and satellite remote sensing images [2,14]. In these scenarios, standard cross-entropy loss usually does not work well. Class Balancing methods are
often applied to improve the model's fit to small-scale foreground objects. The
commonly adopted method is weighting based on the inverse class frequency or
hyper-parameters set by cross-validation. However, as classes increase, the image
composition becomes more complicated in which the effectiveness of Class Balancing cross-entropy loss is often limited. Thus, most studies still adopt cross-
entropy loss by default.

2.3   Dice Loss

Unlike the widely used cross-entropy loss, Dice loss [19] is a set based loss. It is
calculated by directly optimizing the Dice coefficient, which is commonly used
to measure the similarity of two sets (ground truth and predict mask).

3   Method

3.1   Separation of the Body and Edge Region

We set a threshold distance d to separate the two regions. The process of separating edge and body regions is shown in Fig. 2. Suppose ground truth is $G \in R^{h \times w}$.

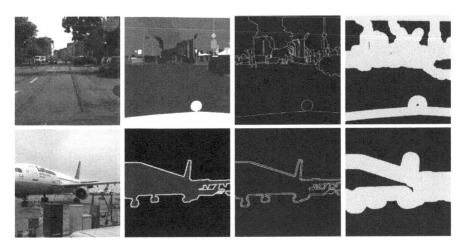

Fig. 2. Process of separating edge and body. example from Cityscapes validation set. **First column**: input images. **Second column**: ground truth. **Third column**: object edges. **Fourth column**: separated edge region (yellow) and body region (purple) (d = 30). **Best viewed in color.** (Color figure online)

We first obtain semantic object edges $E \in R^{h \times w}$ from G. For e_i in E if e_i is located at the junction of two objects, then $e_i = 1$, otherwise $e_i = 0$. Next, all pixels whose distance to edges is within range of d in G are taken as edge region $G_{edge,d}$. The remaining pixels are taken as body region $G_{body,d}$.

Specifically, we use a circular-filled convolution kernel $kernel_d \in R^{(2d+1) \times (2d+1)}$ with radius d. $kernel_d$ is shown in Fig. 3, where positions within the range of d from the center point are 1, and the rest are 0. The convolution operation is applied to E with $kernel_d$ to obtain E', denoted in the fourth column of Fig. 2. In the calculated E', all pixel positions whose distance to edges is within the range of d are non-zero values, regarded as the edge region. Other pixel positions whose distance to edges is outside the range of d are all 0, regarded as the body region.

3.2 Rescale Based on Regions

Based on the threshold distance d, we divide an image into two regions: edge and body. We set a dynamic weight based on the ratio of valid pixels in the corresponding region. As shown in Eq. 1, we first calculate the proportion of valid pixels in the corresponding region.

$$t_{region} = \frac{c_{region}}{c_{image}} \tag{1}$$

In Eq. 1, c_{region} is the valid pixel counts in the corresponding region. c_{image} is the overall pixel counts in the image sample.

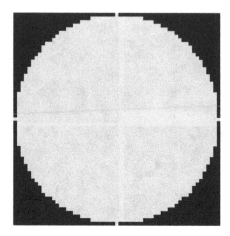

Fig. 3. Circular-filled convolution kernel. **Yellow region** (Color figure online): 1. **Purple region**: 0.

As shown in Eq. 2, we further apply an independent hyper-parameter weight λ_{region} to pixels in each region. p_i is the predicted probability for the labeled class at pixel i. n is the number of pixels in the image.

$$\mathcal{L}_{SL} = -\frac{1}{n} \sum_{i=1}^{n} \frac{\lambda_{region}}{t_{region}} log(p_i) \tag{2}$$

4   Experiments

4.1   Implement Details

Stochastic gradient descent (SGD) is adopted in experiments. We employ ImageNet [9] pre-trained ResNet-50 [13] as the backbone and use dilated convolution in last two stages. Momentum and weight decay are set to 0.9 and 1e−4, respectively. Following prior works [6,23], we use poly strategy $lr = baselr \times (1 - \frac{iter}{total\_iter})^{power}$ to adjust the learning rate where $power = 0.9$. The learning rate is initialized to 0.001 for backbone layers and 0.01 for others. Note that the learning rate is initialized to 0.01 for all layers of DANet.

Cityscapes Dataset. Cityscapes dataset [8] is one of the widely studied datasets in semantic segmentation. We validate our method on 5000 fine-annotated images, with a size of 2048 × 1024, including 2975 training images, 500 validation images, and 1525 test images. During training, images are randomly cropped to 768 × 768. We set the batch size to 8 and train 150 epochs for FCN, 200 epochs for DeepLabv3 and 240 epochs for DANet.

Table 1. Results of different threshold distance.

Dataset	Treshold distance	mIoU	mIoU gain
Cityscapes	CE	72.16%	–
	10	72.88%	+ 0.72%
	20	73.00%	+ 0.84%
	30	**73.21%**	**+ 1.05%**
	40	73.00%	+ 0.84%
	50	72.72%	+ 0.56%
VOC 2012	CE	70.30%	–
	10	**71.16%**	**+ 0.86%**
	20	70.70%	+ 0.40%
	30	72.63%	+ 0.33%

PASCAL VOC 2012 Dataset. In order to verify the superiority of our Spatial-enhanced Loss, we also carry out experiments on PASCAL VOC 2012 dataset [10]. Note that we train networks with the augmented VOC dataset [12] with a crop size of 480 × 480 and a batch size of 16 in experiments. The epochs are set to 70, 100, 120 respectively for FCN, DeepLabv3 and DANet.

4.2 Analysis of Threshold Distance d

We first fix the hyper-parameter weights of two regions, set $\lambda_{edge} = \lambda_{body}$. Next, we adjust the threshold distance d for experiments with FCN and strive to find an appropriate and robust threshold value. Due to the different image styles, we find that setting a smaller λ_{region} can often achieve better results in the VOC dataset. Thus, λ_{edge} and λ_{body} are both set to 1.0 in the Cityscapes dataset and 0.5 in the VOC dataset.

Because edge regions have fewer pixels, it would generate higher weights in edge regions, i.e. $t_{edge} < t_{body}$. Table 1 shows the experimental results. Compared with the standard cross-entropy loss, Spatial-enhanced Loss achieves a significant improvement of 1.05% mIoU. Due to the different image styles in the VOC dataset, we find that setting a smaller λ_{region} can often achieve better results. In the Cityscapes and VOC datasets, the best results are obtained when d is 30 and 10, respectively, so we fix these values in subsequent experiments.

4.3 Analysis of Region Weights

In Spatial-enhanced Loss, the dynamic weights are composed of two parts: t_{region} and λ_{region}. We try multiple combinations of λ_{edge} and λ_{body} for validation. The experimental results are listed in Table 2. Experiments show that setting smaller weights in body regions often results in better performance. In order to balance these two regions, we set the weight of the edge region to be bigger than that of the body region, which achieves a significant improvement of 1.42% mIoU (λ_{edge} = 1.0, λ_{body} = 0.5) in Cityscapes dataset and 1.22% mIoU (λ_{edge} = 0.5, λ_{body} = 0.2) in PASCAL VOC 2012 dataset.

Table 2. Results of different region weights.

Dataset	Region weights	mIoU	mIoU gain
Cityscapes	CE	72.16%	–
	$\lambda_{edge} : 1.0, \lambda_{body} : 0.3$	72.83%	+ 0.67%
	$\lambda_{edge} : 1.0, \lambda_{body} : 0.5$	**73.58%**	**+ 1.42%**
	$\lambda_{edge} : 1.0, \lambda_{body} : 0.7$	73.30%	+ 1.14%
	$\lambda_{edge} : 1.0, \lambda_{body} : 1.0$	73.21%	+ 1.05%
	$\lambda_{edge} : 0.7, \lambda_{body} : 1.0$	72.79%	+ 0.63%
	$\lambda_{edge} : 0.5, \lambda_{body} : 1.0$	72.12%	− 0.04%
VOC 2012	CE	70.30%	–
	$\lambda_{edge} : 0.5, \lambda_{body} : 0.1$	71.42%	+ 1.12%
	$\lambda_{edge} : 0.5, \lambda_{body} : 0.2$	**71.52%**	**+ 1.22%**
	$\lambda_{edge} : 0.5, \lambda_{body} : 0.3$	71.33%	+ 1.03%
	$\lambda_{edge} : 0.5, \lambda_{body} : 0.5$	71.16%	+ 0.86%

Table 3. Results on different models and datasets.

Dataset	Model	CE	FL	Dice	WCE_M	WCE	SL
Cityscapes	FCN	72.16%	71.94%	62.24%	67.80%	72.87%	**73.58%**
	DeepLabv3	77.24%	77.24%	–	–	77.72%	**78.30%**
	DANet	77.49%	77.20%	–	–	77.57%	**78.08%**
VOC 2012	FCN	70.30%	70.21%	65.60%	70.23%	70.75%	**71.52%**
	DeepLabv3	77.44%	77.15%	–	–	77.74%	**78.46%**
	DANet	77.19%	76.64%	–	–	77.82%	**78.79%**

4.4   Comparison with Other Methods

To verify the effectiveness of Spatial-enhanced Loss, we further carry out experiments with other representative models: DeepLabv3 [6] and DANet [11] and losses: Focal Loss (FL) [16], class-based weighted cross-entropy loss and Dice loss [19]. Among them, we verify two class-based weighting methods: median frequency balancing (WCE_M) [1,2,14] and the method in OCNet (WCE) [22]. One thing to note is that since the results of Dice loss and weighted cross-entropy with median frequency balancing are significantly lower than other methods, we only conduct experiments on FCN. As shown in Table 3, FL does not perform well in multi-class semantic segmentation scenarios. The Class Balancing method (WCE) is more effective, but the improvement is limited. The proposed method also shows a considerable performance improvement, which evidences the effectiveness.

IoU over Classes. In order to further explore the effectiveness of Spatial-enhanced Loss for small-scale classes, we verify the IoU over each class of

Table 4. IoU (%) over classes on Cityscapes validation set. CE represents cross-entropy loss. FL represents Focal Loss. Dice represents Dice loss. WCE represents class-based weighted cross-entropy loss from OCNet. SL represents Spatial-enhanced Loss.

Loss	Road	Sidewalk	Building	Wall	Fence	Pole	Traffic light	Traffic sign	Vegetation	Terrain	Sky	Person	Rider	Car	Truck	Bus	Train	Motorcycle	Bicycle	mIoU
CE	97.31	80.86	90.85	42.8	54.32	59.1	69.02	76.89	91.83	60.92	93.94	80.16	58.62	93.73	53.2	74.43	55.08	61.32	76.65	72.16
FL	97.3	80.3	91.06	41.11	54.53	58.77	69.3	76.74	91.75	60.6	93.66	80.11	57.55	93.63	52.86	75.68	54.23	60.77	76.84	71.94
Dice	95.33	78.65	89.79	42.49	51.41	60.73	71.73	78.64	91.49	60.25	93.94	80.86	60.67	92.01	0.0	0.0	0.0	57.71	77.28	62.24
WCE	97.37	81.1	91.17	44.16	54.86	60.37	70.1	77.9	91.9	60.69	93.8	80.36	59.66	93.73	54.09	76.06	57.57	62.34	77.25	72.87
SL	97.28	81.11	91.0	44.59	55.28	62.79	72.05	79.27	92.07	61.02	94.13	81.92	61.29	93.98	52.68	77.33	57.09	64.8	78.27	73.58

Table 5. IoU (%) over classes in the edge regions.

Loss	Road	Sidewalk	Building	Wall	Fence	Pole	Traffic light	Traffic sign	Vegetation	Terrain	Sky	Person	Rider	Car	Truck	Bus	Train	Motorcycle	Bicycle	mIoU
CE	91.58	76.8	84.22	39.88	48.71	59.5	68.68	75.76	85.96	55.56	91.01	78.78	58.48	89.03	48.82	68.31	45.78	59.16	73.83	68.41
WCE	91.97	77.37	84.86	40.71	49.28	61.3	69.65	76.62	86.05	55.58	90.95	79.04	59.52	89.3	51.11	68.99	48.48	59.4	74.47	69.19
SL	92.02	78.12	84.95	40.27	50.93	63.68	71.7	78.47	86.46	56.39	91.45	80.56	61.2	89.72	51.12	72.31	51.59	62.86	75.74	70.50

Spatial-enhanced Loss (SL), cross-entropy (CE) loss, Focal Loss (FL), class-based weighted cross-entropy (WCE) loss from OCNet and Dice loss with FCN on the Cityscapes validation set. As shown in Table 4, we can get the following conclusions: results of CE and FL are similar, and the performance of FL is slightly worse than CE. WCE and SL can effectively improve the model's fitting of small-scale classes in multi-class semantic segmentation scenarios, and SL achieve better results in most classes. The result of Dice loss in multi-class semantic segmentation scenarios is obviously inferior to the method based on cross-entropy. Another point worth noting is that the model in Dice loss does not fit some few-sample classes at all, and its IoU for the truck, bus, and train classes is 0.

IoU Improvements over Edge Regions. Furthermore, we count the IoU in the separated edge regions over each class with FCN on the Cityscapes validation set. As shown in Table 5, SL is ahead of CE and WCE in almost all classes in edge regions, which evidences that SL effectively improves the discrimination of hard pixels in edge regions.

5   Conclusion

This paper proposes a novel semantic segmentation loss termed Spatial-enhanced Loss based on the edge and body regions. We perform experimental validations on the Cityscapes dataset and PASCAL VOC 2012 dataset with representative models. Results show that the proposed Spatial-enhanced Loss can effectively improve training robustness, and better results can be achieved with existing models.

Acknowledgements. This work was supported in part by the Guangdong Major Project of Basic and Applied Basic Research under Grant 2019B030302002, in part by the Science and Technology Major Project of Guangzhou under Grant 202007030006, in part by the Industrial Development Fund Project of Guangzhou under Project x2jsD8183470, in part by the Engineering and Technology Research Center of Guangdong Province for Logistics Supply Chain and Internet of Things under Grant GDDST [2016] 176, in part by the Hi-Tech Industrialization Entrepreneurial Team Project of Foshan Hi-Tech Zone under Grant FSHT[2020]88.

References

1. Badrinarayanan, V., Kendall, A., Cipolla, R.: Segnet: a deep convolutional encoder-decoder architecture for image segmentation. IEEE Trans. Pattern Anal. Mach. Intell. **39**(12), 2481–2495 (2017)
2. Bischke, B., Helber, P., Borth, D., Dengel, A.: Segmentation of imbalanced classes in satellite imagery using adaptive uncertainty weighted class loss. In: IGARSS 2018–2018 IEEE International Geoscience and Remote Sensing Symposium, pp. 6191–6194. IEEE (2018)
3. Bulo, S.R., Neuhold, G., Kontschieder, P.: Loss max-pooling for semantic image segmentation. In: 2017 IEEE Conference on Computer Vision and Pattern Recognition (CVPR), pp. 7082–7091. IEEE (2017)
4. Chen, L.C., Papandreou, G., Kokkinos, I., Murphy, K., Yuille, A.L.: Semantic image segmentation with deep convolutional nets and fully connected CRFS. arXiv preprint arXiv:1412.7062 (2014)
5. Chen, L.C., Papandreou, G., Kokkinos, I., Murphy, K., Yuille, A.L.: Deeplab: semantic image segmentation with deep convolutional nets, atrous convolution, and fully connected CRFS. IEEE Trans. Pattern Anal. Mach. Intell. **40**(4), 834–848 (2017)
6. Chen, L.C., Papandreou, G., Schroff, F., Adam, H.: Rethinking atrous convolution for semantic image segmentation. arXiv preprint arXiv:1706.05587 (2017)
7. Chen, L.C., Zhu, Y., Papandreou, G., Schroff, F., Adam, H.: Encoder-decoder with atrous separable convolution for semantic image segmentation. In: Proceedings of the European Conference on Computer Vision (ECCV), pp. 801–818 (2018)
8. Cordts, M., et al.: The cityscapes dataset for semantic urban scene understanding. In: Proceedings of the IEEE Conference on Computer Vision and Pattern Recognition, pp. 3213–3223 (2016)
9. Deng, J., Dong, W., Socher, R., Li, L.J., Li, K., Fei-Fei, L.: Imagenet: a large-scale hierarchical image database. In: 2009 IEEE Conference on Computer Vision and Pattern Recognition, pp. 248–255. IEEE (2009)
10. Everingham, M., Eslami, S.A., Van Gool, L., Williams, C.K., Winn, J., Zisserman, A.: The pascal visual object classes challenge: a retrospective. Int. J. Comput. Vis. **111**(1), 98–136 (2015)
11. Fu, J., et al.: Dual attention network for scene segmentation. In: Proceedings of the IEEE Conference on Computer Vision and Pattern Recognition, pp. 3146–3154 (2019)
12. Hariharan, B., Arbeláez, P., Bourdev, L., Maji, S., Malik, J.: Semantic contours from inverse detectors. In: 2011 International Conference on Computer Vision, pp. 991–998. IEEE (2011)

13. He, K., Zhang, X., Ren, S., Sun, J.: Deep residual learning for image recognition. In: Proceedings of the IEEE Conference on Computer Vision and Pattern Recognition, pp. 770–778 (2016)
14. Kampffmeyer, M., Salberg, A.B., Jenssen, R.: Semantic segmentation of small objects and modeling of uncertainty in urban remote sensing images using deep convolutional neural networks. In: Proceedings of the IEEE Conference on Computer Vision and Pattern Recognition Workshops, pp. 1–9 (2016)
15. Li, X., Liu, Z., Luo, P., Change Loy, C., Tang, X.: Not all pixels are equal: difficulty-aware semantic segmentation via deep layer cascade. In: Proceedings of the IEEE Conference on Computer Vision and Pattern Recognition, pp. 3193–3202 (2017)
16. Lin, T.Y., Goyal, P., Girshick, R., He, K., Dollár, P.: Focal loss for dense object detection. In: Proceedings of the IEEE International Conference on Computer Vision, pp. 2980–2988 (2017)
17. Liu, W., Rabinovich, A., Berg, A.C.: Parsenet: looking wider to see better. arXiv preprint arXiv:1506.04579 (2015)
18. Long, J., Shelhamer, E., Darrell, T.: Fully convolutional networks for semantic segmentation. In: Proceedings of the IEEE Conference on Computer Vision and Pattern Recognition, pp. 3431–3440 (2015)
19. Milletari, F., Navab, N., Ahmadi, S.A.: V-net: fully convolutional neural networks for volumetric medical image segmentation. In: 2016 Fourth International Conference on 3D Vision (3DV), pp. 565–571. IEEE (2016)
20. Rezaei, M., Yang, H., Meinel, C.: Recurrent generative adversarial network for learning imbalanced medical image semantic segmentation. Multim. Tools Appl. 15329–15348 (2019). https://doi.org/10.1007/s11042-019-7305-1
21. Yu, F., Koltun, V.: Multi-scale context aggregation by dilated convolutions. arXiv preprint arXiv:1511.07122 (2015)
22. Yuan, Y., Huang, L., Guo, J., Zhang, C., Chen, X., Wang, J.: Ocnet: object context network for scene parsing. arXiv preprint arXiv:1809.00916 (2018)
23. Zhao, H., Shi, J., Qi, X., Wang, X., Jia, J.: Pyramid scene parsing network. In: Proceedings of the IEEE Conference on Computer Vision and Pattern Recognition, pp. 2881–2890 (2017)

Weighted Pooling from Salient Regions for Place Recognition

Yaojun Ou, Xiaofeng Zhang$^{(\boxtimes)}$, Zhe Chen, and Mei Wang

School of Information Science and Technology, Nantong University,
Nantong 226019, China
`zxf@ntu.edu.cn`

Abstract. We address the visual place recognition problem by identifying salient regions in images. The core problem of visual place recognition is how to generate robust image representations by reducing the interference caused by viewpoint changes, appearance changes, and dynamic object occlusions. We propose a novel method of weighted pooling from salient regions, which highlights more discriminative regions that positively contribute to the similarity measure while suppressing task-irrelevant local region features. Detailed experiments have been conducted on benchmark datasets with different appearances and viewpoint variations to verify the effectiveness of our proposed method. The results show that our proposed method outperforms the state-of-the-art. Finally, we visualize the learned weight mask to gain insight into the discriminative regions learned by the network.

Keywords: Place recognition · Salient regions · Weighted pooling · Multi-scale extraction

1 Introduction

Visual place recognition (VPR) has been an active research field in computer vision, due to its wide-ranging applications including mobile robots for long-term autonomous navigation [1,2] and geo-localization [3,4].

Visual place recognition can be regarded as a large-scale image retrieval task. According to the query image, the most similar image is retrieved from the database. However, in outdoor scenes, visual place recognition becomes very difficult due to the occlusion of dynamic objects, different viewpoints and illumination and seasonal changes. Even in the same place, there will be completely different appearances. Therefore, how to create a robust image representation has always been challenging.

Over the past few decades, researchers have made various attempts on the representation of images. Methods based on descriptors aggregation such as Fisher Vector (FV) [5] and Vector of Locally Aggregated Descriptors (VLAD) [6], etc., have shown acceptable performance. However, not all visual cues are task-relevant because the images contain some repetitive or confusing features.

E. Pimenidis et al. (Eds.): ICANN 2022, LNCS 13531, pp. 322–333, 2022.
https://doi.org/10.1007/978-3-031-15934-3_27

Directly aggregating all visual cues into the image representation leads to a decrease in the accuracy of the task.

To distinguish task-related visual cues, the image attention mechanism was introduced. Recent image attention mechanisms can be divided into two types, data-driven methods and rule-based methods. Rule-based methods rely too much on prior knowledge and tend to ignore factors other than human's cognition. The data-driven methods are trained in a large amount of data and detect discriminative regions, usually represented by rectangular boxes. Yet salient objects such as buildings, road signs, etc. may be in any shape. Therefore, those methods that only detect salient visual cues with bounding boxes are flawed. To better notice task-related visual cues, it is necessary to build an weight mask that automatically adapts to the shape of saliency regions, so that more robust image representations can be obtained in dynamic environment.

Based on this motivation, this paper proposes an image representation method based on weighted pooling from salient regions. After the high-dimensional features extracted from CNN, the local descriptor of the image is obtained by region pooling. Then, the previously extracted local descriptors are weighted by the weight mask proposed in this paper to obtain a compact global descriptor. The proposed method is designed to be trained in an end-to-end manner, and utilizes the triplet loss [7] to subtract the work of labeling images, which is beneficial to spend all the time on training. The contributions of this paper mainly include: (1) A novel salient region detection method is proposed as a weighted representation of image local descriptors. Unlike general box-based saliency detection, the proposed method can extract saliency regions of arbitrary shape. (2) This paper performs region pooling on feature maps, combined with a weighting method for saliency regions, and shows how to build an end-to-end way to train the proposed method. (3) In this paper, three CNN architectures VGG16 [8], ResNet101 [9], SE-ResNet [10] were respectively integrated into the proposed method for comparative experiments. The existing state-of-the-art methods are compared, and the accuracy results are better than all methods.

2   Related Work

Earlier, approaches tended to extract hand-crafted descriptors from images and fuse them into a fixed-length global image representation. Clustering-based approaches such as BoW [11] aggregate features into visual words to obtain a codebook, then assign features to the nearest visual words, and finally obtain a fixed-length histogram as an image representation. VLAD [6] is encoded by computing the residual between each local descriptor and the cluster center. Fisher Vector (FV) [5] aggregates local descriptors by using alternative Fisher kernels.

As CNNs become more and more popular in various application domains, hand-crafted descriptors are gradually replaced by deep convolutional features. NetVLAD [12] makes VLAD a trainable end-to-end approach, Mohedano et al. [13] uses CNN convolutional features to replace handcrafted features to build a bag of words structure. Sünderhauf et al. [14] compared and analyzed the robustness of the features output by different layers in the convolutional neural network under the interference of viewpoint changes and scene changes through a large number of experiments. Xu et al. [15] analyzed the variance of each channel of the activation value of the convolutional neural network, it is found that the feature map of the channel with the larger variance contains richer spatial texture information.

Obviously, using all the features extracted by CNN will cause a dimensional disaster, and researchers have begun to selectively encode some more distinguishable regions, reducing the dimensionality of features while maintaining accuracy. R-MAC [16] extends the integral image to handle max-pooling on convolutional layer activations to encode multiple image regions. On this basis, Kim et al. Chen et al. [17,18] arranges the mean size of the region activation values in the feature map extracted by CNN, detects more prominent regions of the image, and has good robustness to viewpoint changes and appearance changes.

Another effective method is the image attention mechanism [19], this type of method perceives the importance of various positions in the image. Different from regional coding, the image attention mechanism is generally pixel-level and can perceive task-related objects of different shapes. APANet [20] proposes an attention mechanism-based pyramid pooling to encode multi-scale buildings containing geographic information, and adds attention blocks to highlight regions with high recognition. The PCA-whitened strategy avoids the dimensional disaster. Peng et al. [21] suppresses task-irrelevant local features, and uses a semantically enhanced local weighting scheme to refine local features. And a parameter normalization method is proposed to adjust the contribution of feature clustering to image descriptors.

3   Method

In this section, we detail the proposed region encoding method and the process of generating weighted masks. We innovatively combine the two modules and design them into an end-to-end model. Combined with the Triple Loss function, the entire training can be performed under weak supervision.

3.1   Feature Extraction

The first step of the method is to extract features from the input image through a pre-trained CNN model. The experiments in [14] show that the convolutional layers usually embeds rich spatial information, so the feature map output by the convolutional layer can be regarded as the feature descriptor extracted by the convolution kernels in the images. Therefore, after inputting the image into the CNN model, the feature map of dimension $W \times H \times C$ was output before the full connection operation, where W and H are the width and height of the feature map respectively, and C is the number of channels of the feature map. We treat this feature map as a set of image descriptors. As shown in the Eq. (1), where C is the dimension of each feature descriptor, and there

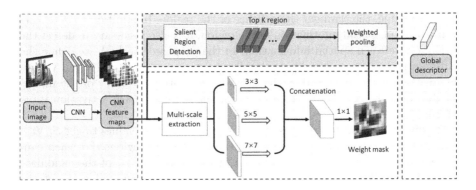

Fig. 1. The overall flow chart of the proposed method

are $W \times H$ features in total. Each descriptor represents the receptive field of a region in the input image (Fig. 1).

$$F = \{f_i \in \mathbb{R}^C \mid i \in \{1, ..., W \times H\}\} \tag{1}$$

3.2   Salient Regions Detection

For the set of image local descriptors F generated by the previous step, the CNN model extracts the corresponding descriptors for each uniform region of the image. However, local descriptor cannot represent a representative building or object in the image, it may be part of a landmark or some non-representative spatial information. Therefore, it is necessary to detect representative saliency regions from local descriptors.

The descriptor set F contains the receptive field of the image under a single-scale rigid grid. In the process of descriptor extraction, the convolution kernel only extracts the image on average. This process does not consider whether the object information is completely extracted in the local descriptor. For example, the factor that can identify a place is usually a landmark in the place, which may even account for 50% of the size of an image, and the shape and location are uncertain. Dividing multiple scales of spatial grids in the image and extracting features under different receptive fields, these methods based on multi-scale pooling [16,18] also have the same shortcomings. Therefore, in order to accurately detect regions of saliency spatial information, we propose a maximum mean region search method, and the search scope is all channels on the feature map.

The activation value in the feature map can be regarded as the detection score obtained by the image after the convolution operation. Therefore, the non-zero value in the feature map represents meaningful semantic information in the receptive field. Moreover, when the activation value is larger, the visual cues of the region are more salient, usually corresponding to some semantically meaningful regions [18]. From this observation, we assume that the larger the activation value, the stronger the salience of the region. In addition to detecting the intensity of spatial information in the region, it is also necessary to detect the correlation between spatial information. In the proposed method, we define the candidate region as an 8-connected region between non-zero activation values. This method not only considers the spatial information intensity of the image, but also links the receptive field regions corresponding to each activation value to form a salient region.

We divide 8 connected regions with non-zero activation values to get $S_i, \forall i \in \{1, ..., M\}$ where M represents the number of candidate regions. For each candidate region S_i , we calculate the mean of the activation A_i of the candidate regions S_i, and keep the N regions with the largest average value to get the salient region K

$$A_i = \frac{1}{|S_i|} \sum_j a_j^i, \forall a_j^i \in S_i \tag{2}$$

$$K_j = \{S_i \mid A_i > t, i \in \{1, ..., M\}, j \in \{1, ..., N\}\} \tag{3}$$

Equation (2) calculate the mean activation of all candidate regions, the salient region set K was determined by the saliency threshold t in Eq. (3), but this is not enough to form a global descriptor, in the next section we will explain how to use the salient region Local descriptor weighted fusion. This work will be done by a weight mask.

3.3   Feature Fusion by Weight Mask

In the previous steps, we have obtained the salient region set K. Note that by analyzing connected regions with non-zero activation values, task-irrelevant informations may still embedded into the features, such as pedestrians and vehicles and other dynamic objects on the street. In a visual sense, these informations are salient enough to attract attention, but they are not helpful for place recognition, and even reduce the accuracy. Therefore, we propose weighted pooling with the weight mask based on the set of salient regions K obtained in the previous steps, which helps suppress task-independent features and strengthen task-relevant features.

The weight mask layer is composed of three convolution kernels of different sizes and one convolution kernel fused across channels following the feature map output by the CNN model. Using convolution kernels of different sizes can generate different visual receptive fields, which helps to detect and extract spatial information and edges of multiple scales. After multi-scale extraction, the activations of the feature map are connected in the channel dimension, and then a cross-channel convolution kernel is used to fuse the multi-scale features into the weights. The cross-channel convolution kernels can learn fusion parameters between channels. Equation (4) describes the generation of the weight mask m:

$$m_i = w_p \cdot a_i^p + c \, (i = 1, ..., W \times H) \tag{4}$$

where w_p is the fusion factor of the p-th channel of the activation map, and c is the bias value, which are all learned through the training process. a_i^p is the i-th value on the p-th channel in the activations of the feature map. After obtaining the weight mask m, we can perform weighted fusion of the local features of the salient region to obtain the global feature F_g:

$$F_g = \sum_i^N \sum_j^R m_j \cdot a_j, \forall a_j \in K_i \tag{5}$$

3.4   D. Learning with Triple Loss

The triplet loss function [7] is often used in place recognition tasks [3,20]. For the query image I_q, the matching image I_r^+ and the non-matching image I_r^- are selected to form an image triplet, and the parameters are determined by the triplet loss function. Through the learning of the parameters of the triple loss function, the query image becomes closer to the positive reference image I_r^+ in the representation of the feature space, and the distance from the negative reference image I_r^- becomes farther. During the training process, the query image I_t, the negative sample image I_r^- and the positive sample image I_r^+ will be fed into the network as a triplet, and the loss L is calculated:

$$L = \max\left(0, \left\|F_g\left(I_t\right) - F_g\left(I_t^+\right)\right\|_2 - \left\|F_g\left(I_t\right) - F_g\left(I_t^-\right)\right\|_2 + \delta\right) \tag{6}$$

where $F_g\left(\cdot\right)$ is the operation for computing the global descriptor of image I. After minimizing the triplet loss, our designed end-to-end network learns which parts of the feature space need to be suppressed and which parts need to be highlighted.

4   Experiment

4.1   Datasets and Evaluation Methodology

During training, we used the Tokyo TM [12] benchmark dataset and the Pittsburgh 250k [23] benchmark dataset, which were downloaded from Google Street View's image database, where each set of images contained the same location, but with different shooting times and Different years, each with different angles and GPS tags. Since the images in the Google Street View database are panoramic images, some images will appear completely different even in the same location due to the large change in angle. Therefore, it is necessary to divide the pictures with large angle changes and define the difference between them to different locations, which is more conducive to the training and learning of the network. We use these labels and angles to divide the image into groups, and each group representing a location.

Three benchmark datasets are used to test the performance results of the proposed method. These datasets contain a large number of images of scene changes and viewpoint changes, and they are often used to verify the effectiveness of place recognition algorithms. Table 1 lists the information of these benchmark datasets.

Table 1. Description of the three benchmark datasets.

Dataset/Sub-dataset	Ref./Query images	Condition changes	Viewpoint changes
Tokyo24/7	75984/1125	Severe	Moderate
Gardens-Point	200/200	Severe	Severe
Pittsburgh 250k	254064/24000	Severe	Severe

We follow the standard place recognition evaluation procedure [12] to evaluate our proposed method. If at least one of the retrieved top N database images is within a distance value of $d = 25$ meters from the ground truth, it is considered that the correct image is queried, which is a successful query. Plot the percentage of correct queries (Recall) against different values of N to compare with other state-of-the-art methods.

4.2   Implementation Details

We build networks on pre-trained VGG16 [8], ResNet101 [9], and SE-ResNet [10] respectively, and according to existing research [3] shows that fine-tuning the pre-trained network can spend less resources and time to obtain better performance. We crop at their last convolutional layers and discard fully connected layers. All training images are resized to 416×416 before being input to the network, and after being processed by the cropped network, a feature map of $13 \times 13 \times D$ is output, where D is different in different network outputs. The network uses the adaptive moment estimation algorithm (Adam) for backpropagation with a learning rate of 10^{-3} and an interval of 0.1 for the triplet loss. According to the local features extracted by different networks, and finally fused into global features according to weight masks Graphs are used for comparative analysis.

In our comparative experiments, several state-of-the-art methods were selected for performance comparison, including Chen et al. [18] proposed Region-VLAD method based on VGG-16, R-MAC [16] method based on multiple regional max pooling, NetVLAD [12] method that applies trainable VLAD pooling to the final convolutional feature map. We use the PCA whitening method to unify the dimensions of the global descriptors of all methods for fair comparison.

4.3   Experimental Results

To demonstrate the progress of our proposed method for image representation, we compare the proposed method results with Region-VLAD [17]. Our salient region detection part is similar to the Region-VLAD architecture, in addition, with the addition of our proposed weight mask, weighted fusion of region features. Figure 2 depicts the accuracy curves of our method and Region-VLAD based on VGG16, ResNet and SE-ResNet for different top result numbers. It can be seen that the accuracy is improved after adding the weight mask, and our SE-ResNet-based method performs the best among several methods, with a gap of 16% compared to the Region-VLAD method.

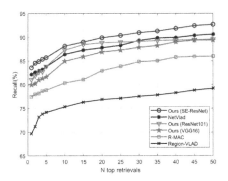

Fig. 2. Comparison of recalls with the state-of-the-arts methods. (Color figure online)

Figure 2 compares the recall curves obtained by our proposed method based on different network extraction features. The compared networks include SE-ResNet, ResNet101 and VGG16, of which SE-ResNet (red) has the best performance, because the network mechanism itself has a channel attention mechanism. After training and learning through our training set, it can extract the ratio of More robust features of other networks. The performance of VGG16 (green) and ResNet101 (pink) is slightly worse than SE-ResNet. When the value of N is small, the recall value of ResNet101 is higher than that of VGG16.

Table 2. Recall curves of our proposed method and other methods on Gardens-Point dataset.

Method	Top-1	Top-5	Top-10	Top-15
Ours (SE-ResNet)	**83.6**	**85.1**	**86.4**	**90.6**
Ours (ResNet101)	82.1	83.2	85.9	88.1
NetVLAD	81.3	82.1	86.2	89.8
Ours (VGG16)	80.2	82.4	84.8	86.1
R-MAC	77.4	78.6	80.3	83.3
Region-VLAD	70.2	71.5	75.8	79.8

As can be seen in Table 2, our method based on SE-ResNet can achieve better recall than other methods, therefore, in the following experiments, we only use SE-ResNet for comparative experiments.

Figure 3(a) shows the recall curves of these methods for different N values on the Tokyo 24/7 dataset. It is obvious that our method can achieve better performance than other methods. We believe that the large changes in light and appearance of images in the Tokyo 24/7 dataset lead to a decrease in the clustering effect, so the positive samples queried by the clustering-based NetVLAD method are ranked lower. Even so, the performance of NetVLAD is state-of-the-art, and our proposed method outperforms it by 1.3% in the case of $N = 1$.

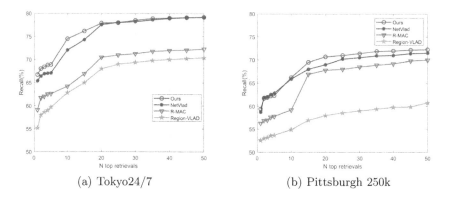

(a) Tokyo24/7   (b) Pittsburgh 250k

Fig. 3. Comparison of recalls with the state-of-the-arts methods. (Color figure online)

The other two region-based methods, RMAC and Region-VLAD, perform worse. Since only regions are used as image representations, this method has certain disadvantages. It cannot focus on representing more important regions, so that the task-independent factors are also used, resulting in a decrease in accuracy (Table 3).

Figure 3(b) is the recall curve obtained from the comparative test on the Pittsburgh 250k test dataset. It can be seen from the Fig. 3(b) that when the N value is lower than 15, our proposed method (red) and NetVLAD (blue), the performance of our proposed method is almost the same, and the recall rate obtained by our proposed method is larger when the value of N becomes larger. In addition, the recall of R-MAC (pink) increases greatly in the interval of N value from 10 to 15, but our proposed method still outperforms the method based on region pooling, which shows that in our model Benefits.

Table 3. Comparison of ORB descriptors and LDB descriptors.

Dataset		Ours	NetVLAD	RMAC	RegionVLAD
Tokyo 24/7	top-1	**66.7**	65.4	59.1	55.2
	top-5	**68.9**	67.1	62.6	59.7
	top-10	**74.5**	72.7	64.2	62.8
Pitts250k test	top-1	**59.4**	58.7	56.3	52.6
	top-5	62.3	**62.8**	57.8	53.7
	top-10	**66.2**	65.9	59.2	54.9

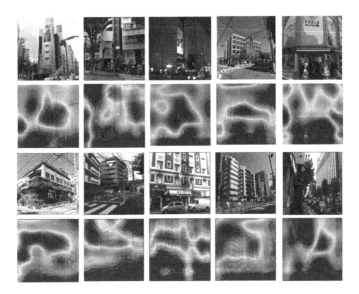

Fig. 4. Illustration of the weight mask learned by our proposed network. As can be seen from the figure, the static building parts are highlighted (red), while dynamic objects and confounding factors such as the sky or pedestrians, cars, etc. are suppressed (blue). (Color figure online)

To more intuitively observe the effect of our proposed weight mask on the outdoor scenes, we select eight representative image examples in the dataset, and these weight masks are trained by our proposed training pipeline. As shown in Fig. 4, the weight mask indicates the most concerned regions (the red part) of our proposed method, which are the most salient regions in the image space and can be represented by it as a scene. It can be seen from the Fig. 4 that the weight mask successfully filters out the ambiguity factors that reduce the accuracy of the task.

5 Conclusion

In this paper, we propose an end-to-end method using weighted pooling from salient region to overcome challenges in place recognition tasks. First, after extracting the CNN features, several salient regions are detected according to the activation value of the feature map. Then, the multi-scale convolution kernels are used to extract contextual features and obtain a weight mask. According to the obtained weight mask, the salient regions are weighted fusing to form a global descriptor. To the best of our knowledge, this is the first time that the weighted mask-to-region pooling method is used for place recognition, and it has better accuracy than previous work. Evaluations of the state-of-the-art on several benchmark datasets show that our method can suppress task- irrelevant local region features, while at the same time, it can also highlight discriminative regions. In future work, we fuse high-level semantic information into our training pipeline to further improve the performance of the method.

Acknowledgement. This work is supported by the grant of National Natural Science Foundation of China (No. 62002179), Natural Science Foundation of Jiangsu Province (BK20191445), Natural Science Key Foundation of Jiangsu Education Department (21KJA510004) and Nantong Social Livelihood Science and Technology Project (MS12020078).

References

1. Chalmers, E., Contreras, E.B., Robertson, B., Luczak, A., Gruber, A.: Learning to predict consequences as a method of knowledge transfer in reinforcement learning. IEEE Trans. Neural Netw. Learn. Syst. **29**(6), 2259–2270. https://doi.org/10.1109/TNNLS.2017.2690910
2. McManus, C., Churchill, W., Maddern, W., Stewart, A.D., Newman, P.: Shady dealings: robust, long-term visual localisation using illumination invariance. In: 2014 IEEE International Conference on Robotics and Automation (ICRA), pp. 901–906. IEEE (2014). https://doi.org/10.1109/ICRA.2014.6906961
3. Kim, H.J., Dunn, E., Frahm, J.M.: Learned contextual feature reweighting for image geo-localization. In: 2017 IEEE Conference on Computer Vision and Pattern Recognition (CVPR), pp. 3251–3260. IEEE (2017). https://doi.org/10.1109/CVPR.2017.346
4. Zhang, X., Wang, L., Su, Y.: Visual place recognition: a survey from deep learning perspective. Pattern Recogn. **113**, 107760 (2021). https://doi.org/10.1016/j.patcog.2020.107760
5. Perronnin, F., Liu, Y., Sánchez, J., Poirier, H.: Large-scale image retrieval with compressed fisher vectors. In: 2010 IEEE Computer Society Conference on Computer Vision and Pattern Recognition, pp. 3384–3391. IEEE (2010). https://doi.org/10.1109/CVPR.2010.5540009
6. Jégou, H., Perronnin, F., Douze, M., Sánchez, J., Pérez, P., Schmid, C.: Aggregating local image descriptors into compact codes. IEEE Trans. Pattern Anal. Mach. Intell. **34**(9), 1704–1716 (2011). https://doi.org/10.1109/TPAMI.2011.235
7. Gordo, A., Almazan, J., Revaud, J., Larlus, D.: End-to-end learning of deep visual representations for image retrieval. Int. J. Comput. Vis. **124**(2), 237–254 (2017). https://doi.org/10.1109/TPAMI.2008.128
8. Simonyan, K., Zisserman, A.: Very deep convolutional networks for large-scale image recognition. arXiv preprint arXiv:1409.1556 (2014)
9. He, K., Zhang, X., Ren, S., Sun, J.: Deep residual learning for image recognition. In: Proceedings of the IEEE Conference on Computer Vision and Pattern Recognition, pp. 770–778 (2016). https://doi.org/10.1109/CVPR.2016.90
10. Hu, J., Shen, L., Sun, G.: Squeeze-and-excitation networks. In: Proceedings of the IEEE Conference on Computer Vision and Pattern Recognition, pp. 7132–7141 (2018). https://doi.org/10.48550/arXiv.1709.01507
11. Sivic, J., Zisserman, A.: Video google: a text retrieval approach to object matching in videos. In: IEEE International Conference on Computer Vision, vol. 3, pp. 1470–1470. IEEE Computer Society (2003). https://doi.org/10.1109/ICCV.2003.1238663

12. Arandjelovic, R., Gronat, P., Torii, A., Pajdla, T., Sivic, J.: NetVLAD: CNN architecture for weakly supervised place recognition. In: Proceedings of the IEEE Conference on Computer Vision and Pattern Recognition, pp. 5297–5307 (2016). https://doi.org/10.1109/TPAMI.2017.2711011

13. Mohedano, E., McGuinness, K., O'Connor, N.E., Salvador, A., Marques, F., Giró-i-Nieto, X.: Bags of local convolutional features for scalable instance search. In: Proceedings of the 2016 ACM on International Conference on Multimedia Retrieval, pp. 327–331 (2016). https://doi.org/10.1145/2911996.2912061

14. Sünderhauf, N., Shirazi, S., Dayoub, F., Upcroft, B., Milford, M.: On the performance of convnet features for place recognition. In: 2015 IEEE/RSJ International Conference on Intelligent Robots and Systems (IROS), pp. 4297–4304. IEEE (2015). https://doi.org/10.1109/IROS.2015.7353986

15. Yu, J., Zhu, C., Zhang, J., Huang, Q., Tao, D.: Spatial pyramid-enhanced NetVLAD with weighted triplet loss for place recognition. IEEE Trans. Neural Netw. Learn. Syst. 31(2), 661–674 (2019). https://doi.org/10.1109/TNNLS.2019.2908982

16. Tolias, G., Sicre, R., Jégou, H.: Particular object retrieval with integral max-pooling of CNN activations. arXiv preprint arXiv:1511.05879 (2015)

17. Khaliq, A., Ehsan, S., Chen, Z., Milford, M., McDonald-Maier, K.: A holistic visual place recognition approach using lightweight cnns for significant viewpoint and appearance changes. IEEE Trans. Robot. 36(2), 561–569 (2019). https://doi.org/10.1109/TRO.2019.2956352

18. Chen, Z., Maffra, F., Sa, I., Chli, M.: Only look once, mining distinctive landmarks from convnet for visual place recognition. In: 2017 IEEE/RSJ International Conference on Intelligent Robots and Systems (IROS), pp. 9–16. IEEE (2017). https://doi.org/10.1109/IROS.2017.8202131

19. Peng, G., Yue, Y., Zhang, J., Wu, Z., Tang, X., Wang, D.: Semantic reinforced attention learning for visual place recognition. In: 2021 IEEE International Conference on Robotics and Automation (ICRA), pp. 13415–13422. IEEE (2021). https://doi.org/10.1109/ICRA48506.2021.9561812

20. Zhu, Y., Wang, J., Xie, L., Zheng, L.: Attention-based pyramid aggregation network for visual place recognition. In: Proceedings of the 26th ACM International Conference on Multimedia, pp. 99–107 (2018). https://doi.org/10.1145/3240508.3240525

21. Peng, G., Zhang, J., Li, H., Wang, D.: Attentional pyramid pooling of salient visual residuals for place recognition. In: Proceedings of the IEEE/CVF International Conference on Computer Vision, pp. 885–894 (2021). https://doi.org/10.1109/ICCV48922.2021.00092

22. Torii, A., Arandjelovic, R., Sivic, J., Okutomi, M., Pajdla, T.: 24/7 place recognition by view synthesis. In: Proceedings of the IEEE Conference on Computer Vision and Pattern Recognition, pp. 1808–1817 (2015). https://doi.org/10.1109/TPAMI.2017.2667665

23. Torii, A., Sivic, J., Pajdla, T., Okutomi, M.: Visual place recognition with repetitive structures. In: Proceedings of the IEEE Conference on Computer Vision and Pattern Recognition, pp. 883–890 (2013). https://doi.org/10.1109/TPAMI.2015.2409868

Efficient LSTM Training with Eligibility Traces

Michael Hoyer[1] , Shahram Eivazi[2] , and Sebastian Otte[1(✉)]

[1] Neuro-Cognitive Modeling, University of Tübingen, Sand 14,
72076 Tübingen, Germany
m-hoyer@gmx.de, sebastian.otte@uni-tuebingen.de
[2] Autonomous Systems Lab, University of Tübingen, Sand 14,
72076 Tübingen, Germany
shahram.eivazi@uni-tuebingen.de

Abstract. Training recurrent neural networks is predominantly achieved via backpropagation through time (BPTT). However, this algorithm is not an optimal solution from both a biological and computational perspective. A more efficient and biologically plausible alternative for BPTT is e-prop. We investigate the applicability of e-prop to long short-term memorys (LSTMs), for both supervised and reinforcement learning (RL) tasks. We show that e-prop is a suitable optimization algorithm for LSTMs by comparing it to BPTT on two benchmarks for supervised learning. This proves that e-prop can achieve learning even for problems with long sequences of several hundred timesteps. We introduce extensions that improve the performance of e-prop, which can partially be applied to other network architectures. With the help of these extensions we show that, under certain conditions, e-prop can outperform BPTT for one of the two benchmarks for supervised learning. Finally, we deliver a proof of concept for the integration of e-prop to RL in the domain of deep recurrent Q-learning.

Keywords: LSTMs · Recurrent neural networks · E-prop · Reinforcement learning

1 Introduction

During the last decades, artificial neural networks (ANNs) have constantly pushed the boundaries of artificial intelligence further and further [12]. While doing so, ANNs have diverged quite far in both architecture and ways of learning from their original source of inspiration: the human brain.

The long short-term memory (LSTM) [8], for example, was not designed to model the recurrent networks of our brains, but specifically to learn long-term dependencies. The gold standard for training recurrent neural networks (RNNs) like LSTMs is backpropagation through time (BPTT) [14]. This method propagates errors backwards through the network and time to calculate error gradients with respect to specific weights. To do so, the whole network has to be unrolled before the error can be propagated backwards. This unrolling process

E. Pimenidis et al. (Eds.): ICANN 2022, LNCS 13531, pp. 334–346, 2022.
https://doi.org/10.1007/978-3-031-15934-3_28

is not only memory intensive, it makes effective online learning difficult and impractical. The longer a sequence is, the larger this problem becomes. BPTT views the optimization of networks purely from a mathematical perspective. There is no biological foundation BPTT is based on. In fact, we do not know how the connections between neurons in the brain are optimized. What we do know is that error backpropagation is most likely not the method used in the brain [5]. The optimization of the highly recurrent networks of our brains must therefore be done differently. This raises hopes that such methods can be applied to train RNNs more efficiently.

One biologically inspired method here is e-prop [2,3]. This method works by refactoring the equation of BPTT so that gradients can be computed as a combination of eligibility traces, computed forward in time, and online learning signals, estimating the loss [2,3]. This alleviates the needs for error backpropagation and unrolling of networks which makes this algorithm far more efficient than BPTT. E-prop was originally designed for spiking neural networks but can also be applied to LSTMs.

We apply e-prop to LSTMs and introduce possible extensions to increase it's performance and stability. To evaluate the algorithm and the extensions, we compare the performance for supervised learning tasks with BPTT. Furthermore we deliver a proof of concept that e-prop can be integrated into recurrent Q-learning and compare this approach to a BPTT based one. Considering real world problems are often a partially observable Markov decision process (POMDP). One possible solution for dealing with POMDPs is to incorporate RNNs into deep Q-learning [6]. However, the same drawbacks as in supervised learning persist, which is a problem since RL tasks can take several hundred timesteps to be solved.

2   E-Prop

E-prop calculates gradients in forward manner and hence is far more efficient than BPTT. This is achieved by refactoring the gradient computation from BPTT,

$$\frac{dE}{dw_{jk}} = \sum_t \frac{dE}{dz_k^t} \left[\frac{dz_k^t}{dw_{jk}} \right]_{\text{local}}. \tag{1}$$

The local gradient in this equation is not an approximation, it collects the maximal amount of information about $\frac{dE}{dw_{jk}}$ that can be computed in forward manner. For e-prop it is defined as the eligibility trace

$$e_{jk}^t \overset{\text{def}}{=} \left[\frac{dz_k^t}{dw_{jk}} \right]_{\text{local}}. \tag{2}$$

The other part of Eq. 1, $\frac{dE}{dz_k^t}$, is replaced by an approximation of the loss gradient, the online learning signal l_k^t. The computation of gradients with e-prop is therefore a combination of learning signals and eligibility traces

$$\frac{dE}{dw_{jk}} = \sum_j e_{jk}^t l_k^t. \tag{3}$$

Eligibility Traces for LSTMs. When applying e-prop to LSTMs, there are several aspects that need to be considered. Firstly, following [3], we use the cell state of the LSTM c_k^t as hidden state for e-prop. Secondly, since LSTMs have individual weight matrices for the individual gates for both input and recurrent connections, individual eligibility traces need to be computed. We introduce $A \in \{i, f, \tilde{c}\}$ for input gate, forget gate and cell state candidate and $B \in \{\text{in}, \text{rec}\}$ for the connection type to specify an eligibility trace. A specific eligibility trace $e_{jk}^{(A,B),t}$ is then given by

$$e_{jk}^{(A,B),t} = \epsilon_{jk}^{(A,B),t} \frac{\partial z_k^t}{\partial c_k^t}, \tag{4}$$

where $\epsilon_{jk}^{(A,B),t}$ denotes a specific eligibility value of timestep t. The derivative in this equation is independent from the gate and calculated by

$$\frac{\partial z_k^t}{\partial c_k^t} = \frac{\partial}{\partial c_k^t} \left(o_k^t \tanh(c_k^t) \right) = o_k^t \tanh'(c_k^t). \tag{5}$$

The computation of an eligibility value $\epsilon_{jk}^{(A,B),t}$ is described by

$$\epsilon_{jk}^{(A,B),t} = \epsilon_{jk}^{(A,B),t-1} \frac{\partial c_k^t}{\partial c_k^{t-1}} + \frac{\partial c_k^t}{\partial w_{jk}^{(A,B)}}, \tag{6}$$

where $\frac{\partial c_k^t}{\partial c_k^{t-1}}$ resembles the internal dynamics of the network, which can be modeled by the forget gate f_k^t for LSTMs [2,3]. The crucial part for the computation of an eligibility value is $\frac{\partial c_k^t}{\partial w_{jk}^{(A,B)}}$. This derivative depends on the specific weights of a gate and therefore has to be calculated individually for input and recurrent weights as well as the bias of the gates.

As an example, we derive the eligibility trace for the input weights of the input gate. The crucial derivative is described by

$$\frac{\partial c_k^t}{\partial w_{jk}^{(i,\text{in})}} = \tilde{c}_k^t i_k^t (1 - i_k^t) x_j^t, \tag{7}$$

which leads to the complete expression of the eligibility trace $e_{jk}^{(i,\text{in}),t}$ being

$$e_{jk}^{(i,\text{in}),t} = \Big(\underbrace{\epsilon_{jk}^{(i,\text{in}),t-1} f_k^t + \tilde{c}_k^t \sigma'\big(net_k^{(i),t}\big)x_j^t}_{\underbrace{\phantom{\epsilon_{jk}^{(i,\text{in}),t-1} f_k^t + \tilde{c}_k^t \sigma'(net_k^{(i),t})x_j^t}}_{\epsilon_{jk}^{(i,\text{in}),t}} \frac{\partial c_k^t}{\partial w_{jk}^{(i,\text{in})}}}\Big) \underbrace{o_t^j \tanh'(c_k^t)}_{\frac{\partial z_k^t}{\partial c_k^t}}. \tag{8}$$

The output gate contributes only to the hidden state h_k^t of an LSTM. Since we defined c_k^t as the hidden variable for e-prop, we do not need to calculate eligibility traces to compute gradients for the output gates. Instead, we can use the same factorization of the error gradient as in BPTT. The gradient of the error with respect to $w_{jk}^{(o,\text{in})}$ is therefore expressed as

$$\frac{dE}{dw_{jk}^{(o,\text{in})}} = \sum_t \frac{dE}{dz_k^t} \frac{\partial dz_k^t}{\partial w_{jk}^{(o,\text{in})}} = \sum_t \frac{dE}{dz_k^t} \tanh'(c_k^t) o_k^t (1 - o_k^t) x_j^t. \qquad (9)$$

Learning Signals. According to [2,3] a learning signal at timestep t is given by

$$l_k^t = \sum_n m_{kn}(y_n^t - y_n^{*,t}), \qquad (10)$$

where y_n^t is the current output of the network for the neuron n and $y_n^{*,t}$ is the target. The value m_{kn} is determined by a feedback matrix M. We consider two versions of e-prop to define M. For random e-prop, a random matrix, initialized in the same way as the network's weights, is used. For symmetric e-prop, the transpose of the weights to the output layer is chosen $M = W^\top$. This can be straightforwardly applied to LSTMs. Note that the output layer is updated via plain backpropagation since it is not involved in any recurrent computations.

Depending on the problem, there are two options how learning signals can be used – either at all timesteps or only at the final timestep. Therefore, gradients can be computed either by accumulating the combination of eligibility traces and learning signals over time, as described in Eq. 3, or by using only the combination of the final eligibility trace and the final learning signal

$$\frac{dE}{dw_{jk}^{(A,B)}} = e_{jk}^{(A,B),T} l_k^T. \qquad (11)$$

2.1   Extensions to LSTM Based E-Prop

Initialization of the Forget Gate Bias. The idea of initializing the forget gate bias with higher values was already discussed at the introduction of forget gates [4] and later work proved this can boost training significantly [9]. Doing so is a change to the architecture and can also be applied when training LSTMs with BPTT. However, e-prop will profit differently from this due to the special role of the forget gate on which e-prop highly depends. As seen in Eq. 6, the influence of previous eligibility values on current ones depends exclusively on the forget gate. We can make use of this by initializing the bias of this gate with a higher value, which increases the influence of the previous eligibility value on the current one in e-prop during the initial training phase.

Trace Echo. Using only the final eligibility trace and learning signal can be problematic for longer sequences or sequences where most of the information lies in the first timesteps since the eligibility trace could fade over time. To tackle this specific problem, we introduce the trace echo.

The trace echo is a modulated signal of all eligibility traces during a sequence accumulated over time decoupled from the (supervised) learning signal. It resembles the overall influence of the networks weights on the output of the postsynaptic neuron given presynaptic activity over the whole sequence. The trace echo term can thus be seen as an additional unsupervised learning component, loose implementing a form of Hebbian-learning [7].

In order to apply the trace echo, we add a weighted sum of all eligibility traces over time to the gradient computation:

$$\frac{dE}{dw_{jk}} = e_{jk}^T l_k^T + \lambda \underbrace{\sum_{t=0}^{T} e_{jk}^t}_{\text{trace echo}}. \tag{12}$$

Of course, the trace echo is neither limited to learning with only the final timestep nor to LSTM based e-prop.

Trace Scaling. During experiments with DRQN, we discovered that in the beginning of training, the computation of eligibility values can be highly unstable. This can lead to suboptimal weight changes which make further learning impossible. To address this problem, we introduce trace scaling.

Trace scaling heavily scales down the eligibility traces, and therefore their influence on weight updates, by introducing a factor μ to their computation,

$$e_{jk}^{(A,B),t} = \mu_B \epsilon_{jk}^{(A,B),t} \frac{\partial z_k^t}{\partial c_k^t}. \tag{13}$$

Trace scaling also shifts the focus for weight updates more towards the output layer since the updates for this layer are not computed via e-prop. This can be advantageous when there is an imbalance in the updates of the two layers. Learning with trace scaling will be slower for the recurrent layer and the output layer can learn to adapt to the recurrent layer, rather than simply counterbalancing the output of the recurrent layer. It should be noted that optimizers with adaptive learning rates can prevent this. Trace scaling is neither limited to LSTM based e-prop nor to DRQN.

2.2   E-Prop in the Context of Reinforcement Learning

DRQN [6] is an approach, able to deal with POMDP, that uses LSTMs to estimate Q-values. LSTMs are able to learn to internally store relevant information about previous timesteps, which can then be used in addition to current observations to choose the best possible action. Training is done with BPTT on sequences of experiences. These sequences are sampled at a fixed and rather short length from the episodes an agent performs on an environment. This is done for two reasons. Firstly, we need to store the experience-sequences for later replay and shorter sequences take up less space. Secondly, and even more importantly, it is impractical to use long sequences when training with BPTT. Because e-prop can work forward in time, the network no longer has to be unrolled, putting e-prop into an advantageous position for RL. For this work we use DRQN with the inclusion of actions to the network input [15]. To our knowledge, the integration of e-prop to recurrent Q-learning is novel. Integrating e-prop to DRQN is therefore only supposed to be a proof of concept for this approach.

3   Experiments and Results

3.1   Classification of Handwritten Digits

Image classification tasks like MNIST are typically learned feedforward with convolutional neural networks, but can also be learned sequentially. For sequential MNIST (sMNIST) the images are transformed into a sequence of single pixels going from the upper left corner to the bottom right one. This results in a sequence with a length of 784 pixels. Learning MNIST in sequential manner provides one with a quite difficult temporal credit assignment problem on long sequences, where information is sparse. Permuting the order of the pixels by a fixed permutation [11] yields a harder version of sMNIST, where the information is still sparse but not clustered like before.

We established a BPTT baseline with an architecture of 128 LSTM units and one output layer with a softmax activation function based on [1] for both tasks. In contrast to [1], we found that a lower learning rate of 0.0005 for RMSProp [13] and no gradient clipping yields better results for BPTT.

sMNIST Results. E-prop worked best with a learning rate of 0.001. We performed five training runs with both symmetric and random e-prop, where a label was presented at the final timestep only. Furthermore we performed runs with a higher initialized forget gate bias, the trace echo extension and a combination of both. The forget bias was initialized as the other weights, before increasing it by 1.8. For the trace echo $\lambda = \frac{1}{\text{sequence length}} 10^{-4}$ was used. The final results are given in Table 1.

During the first 100 epochs, the extensions had a negative impact on random e-prop, training was unstable and multiple runs broke during training. Symmetric e-prop was improved considerably during the first epochs. However, this improvement is not persistent and the final results after 350 epochs are comparable to the plain version. The influence of the extensions during the first 120 epochs of training is visualized in Fig. 1.

Permuted sMNIST Results. BPTT reached a mean accuracy of 91.55% on the test set after 350 epochs over five runs. The saturation of training was reached earlier then previously. Plain symmetric e-prop reached a mean accuracy of 84.83%. An effect of combining trace echo and higher forget gate bias initialization is less pronounced than previously. Extended e-prop archives a final mean accuracy of 85.36 %. The results are depicted in Fig. 2.

Table 1. Results for sMNIST. Given is the mean accuracy of five runs on the test set after 350 epochs.

Algorithm	Plain	Forget gate bias	Trace echo	Combined
Random e-prop	88.77%	58.30%	65.99%	70.69%
Symmetric e-prop	92.76%	93.49%	91.37%	92.49%
BPTT	98.92%	–	–	–

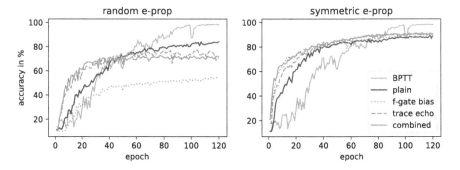

Fig. 1. Comparison of e-prop extensions and BPTT on sMNIST. Depicted is the mean accuracy of five runs on the test set for both random e-prop (left) and symmetric e-prop (right) for the first 120 epochs of training. A BPTT baseline is given for both.

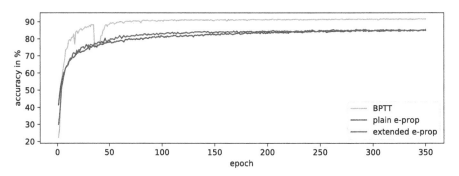

Fig. 2. BPTT vs. symmetric e-prop on permuted sMNIST. Given is the mean accuracy on the test set during training. BPTT performs better than symmetric e-prop. Performance of e-prop can be improved by trace echo and higher forget gate bias for the beginning of training.

3.2 Solving Another Temporal Credit Assignment Problem

TCA Task. To further investigate temporal credit assignment (TCA) we introduce another task, where sequences consists of four different channels. The first two channels produce random values between zero and one during the whole sequence. The third one indicates, with a probability of 0.5, whether the information of the first two channels is valuable (one) or not (zero). After 15 timesteps, the channel remains zero for a certain delay. The last channel produces zeros until the last timestep, where it switches to one. A possible sequence could be:

$$
\begin{array}{rl}
\textbf{left:} & \begin{bmatrix} 0.42 \; 0.49 \; 0.35 \; 0.76 \; 0.69 \; 0.19 \; 0.99 \; \ldots \; 0.85 \; 0.23 \; 0.42 \\ 0.75 \; 0.67 \; 0.86 \; 0.57 \; 0.37 \; 0.92 \; 0.55 \; \ldots \; 0.47 \; 0.28 \; 0.40 \\ 0 \quad\; 1 \quad\; 0 \quad\; 1 \quad\; 1 \quad\; 0 \quad\; 0 \quad\; \ldots \quad 0 \quad\; 0 \quad\; 0 \\ 0 \quad\; 0 \quad\; 0 \quad\; 0 \quad\; 0 \quad\; 0 \quad\; 0 \quad\; \ldots \quad 0 \quad\; 0 \quad\; 1 \end{bmatrix} \\
\textbf{right:} & \\
\textbf{cue:} & \\
\textbf{done:} &
\end{array}
$$

A network has to compare the value of the first two channels whenever the third is active. The side with the higher value wins. In the end, a decision, which side has won more often, has to be made. The network, therefore, has to learn when it should listen, to compare two numbers, to count the number of wins for each side, to determine a winning side, and to store this information over time.

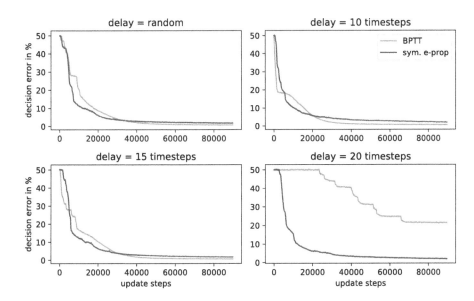

Fig. 3. Training of BPTT and extended symmetric e-prop on the TCA task, mean of 10 runs. Shown is the running mean over 250 update steps of the decision error of a batch during training. E-prop was able to learn the task independently from the delay condition. BPTT failed to master the task in the condition with the largest delay and is outperformed by e-prop.

New batches of data were generated for all update steps. This ensures that networks learn to generalize. A test or validation set is, therefore, not needed, the running mean of the training error is sufficient for an analysis.

Results. A network with 32 LSTM cells, followed by an output layer, was used. The hyper-parameters of the e-prop extensions were chosen as previously. 90,000 updates on batches with a size of 64 were performed with a delay of 10, 15, 20 and a random value between 10 and 20 timesteps. We performed 10 different runs for a extended version of symmetric e-prop with higher initialized forget gate bias and trace echo, and for BPTT.

RMSProp worked best for e-prop and Adam [10] for BPTT except for the 20 timestep delay condition, where RMSProp worked better. Extended e-prop was trained with a learning rate of 0.01. Training with an increased learning rate failed for both plain e-prop and BPTT. Figure 3 shows the training of BPTT and extended e-prop for all conditions, the final results are given in Table 2.

To ensure that the extended e-prop version did not perform better due to the initialization of the forget gate bias alone, we performed 10 additional runs with 50,000 updates on the conditions with a delay of 10 and 20 timesteps. The results are depicted in Fig. 4 as well as the results of plain e-prop for these conditions. It should be noted that reliable training with plain e-prop was only possible in the condition with a delay of 10 timesteps. The final results are given in Table 3.

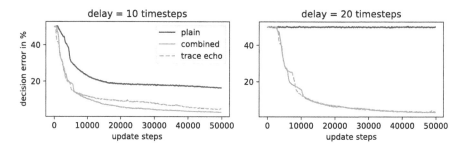

Fig. 4. Training of e-prop versions on the TCA task, mean of 10 runs. Shown is the running mean over 250 update steps of the decision error of a batch during training. The trace echo boosts training considerably

4   Solving Easy RL Environments with DRQN

4.1   Environment

CartPole-v0 was chosen as an environment because it is fairly easy to learn and, therefore, suited for a proof of concept. A network with 32 LSTM units and an output layer was used with Adam (lr=0.0003). For the e-prop based version, a high value for $\epsilon_{\text{Adam}} = 0.1$ proved to be essential to solve the environment. For trace scaling we used $\mu_{\text{in}} = 10^{-4}$ and $\mu_{\text{rec,bias}} = 10^{-8}$. To fill the replay buffer, 200 episodes of random actions were performed at the beginning of training.

Inspired by flickering Atari games [6], we present a partially observable version of CartPole-v0, by zeroing out the observations with a probability of 0.2.

CartPole Results. Solving the environment with e-prop based DRQN was made possible by trace scaling. However in a direct comparison with BPTT, e-prop proved to be inferior. BPTT based e-prop was able to solve the environment significantly faster for all runs we performed. Training is depicted in Fig. 5.

Partially Observable CartPole Results. Training takes considerably longer, showing the increased difficulty of the environment. Training with BPTT starts comparable to standard CartPole until a mean return of around 150 is reached. All five runs with BPTT solved the environment. Only one out of five e-prop runs was successful, the others show learning, and achieved mean returns of over 150 but failed to solve the environment. The results can be observed in Fig. 6. Runs without trace scaling failed again.

Table 2. Results for the TCA task after 90,000 update steps. Given is the decision error for BPTT and e-prop with trace echo and a higher initialized forget gate bias.

Delay	Extended e-prop	BPTT
Random	1.79%	0.72%
10	2.03%	0.62%
15	1.79%	0.64%
20	2.02%	21.37%

Table 3. Results for the TCA task after 50,000 updates. Given is the decision error for BPTT and the different e-prop variations used for the easiest and hardest delay condition.

		e-prop		
Delay	BPTT	Plain	Trace echo	Combined
10	0.94%	16.35%	4.82%	3.0%
20	31.19%	50.10%	3.32%	3.07%

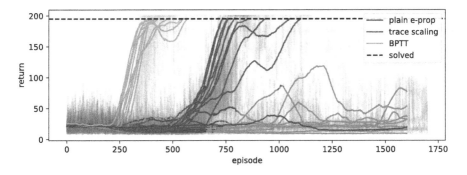

Fig. 5. Training of CartPole-v0 with BPTT and e-prop. Shown are 10 training runs for BPTT, e-prop with trace scaling and plain e-prop. The running mean of the returns over the last 100 episodes is highlighted. BPTT learns to solve the environment significantly faster than e-prop. Training with plain e-prop was not achieved.

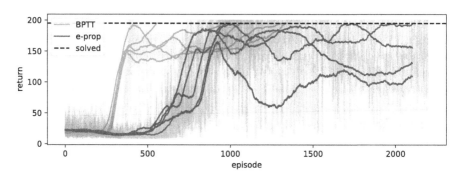

Fig. 6. Training of a partially observable CartPole-v0 with BPTT and e-prop. Shown are the returns of five training runs smoothed over the last 100 episodes for BPTT and e-prop with trace scaling.

5   Discussion

sMNIST. Our results prove that the forward computation of eligibility traces is stable for sequences of several hundred timesteps, and that the final eligibility trace is sufficient for the computation of weight updates. Both random and symmetric e-prop were able to learn the sequential MNIST task but ultimately achieved lower accuracies than BPTT. Random e-prop turned out to be inferior to symmetric e-prop, which is no surprise since symmetric e-prop works with better learning signals, computed with the true backward connections.

We showed that our extensions can improve training with symmetric e-prop. A combination of trace echo and a higher initialized forget gate bias stabilized training during the initial training phase considerably. Both of these extensions on their own boosted training during the initial phase as well. Significantly improved results were not achieved with our extensions after full training.

Compared to BPTT, the results for e-prop are not satisfactory. The initial training phases of both random and symmetric e-prop look considerably smoother than the training of BPTT. However, BPTT reaches a significantly higher accuracy than e-prop.

TCA. The trace echo in combination with a biased forget gate allowed symmetric e-prop to learn the TCA task. The performance of e-prop was drastically increased by the extensions. Learning TCA with plain e-prop was not possible for most conditions.

Extended e-prop outperforms BPTT by far in the hardest condition and performs comparable in the others. By replicating these results with only the trace echo, we show that this success is due to the trace echo and not due to the changed initialization of the forget gate bias alone, which could boost BPTT in theory as well.

The discovery that the trace echo can improve e-prop in such a drastic manner is a major contribution. With the trace echo extension, we introduce an unsupervised learning signal that resembles a sort of Hebbian learning to e-prop, which differs from the type of learning performed by plain e-prop and BPTT.

DRQN. Trace scaling proved to be indispensable for achieving any learning with e-prop based DRQN. Even though it allowed reliable training with e-prop based DRQN, the performance is not comparable to BPTT based DRQN, which solved the environment considerably faster. This is partially due to higher values of ϵ_{Adam} for e-prop runs, however, without a smaller ϵ_{Adam}, the environment was not solved. Learning with e-prop based DRQN was also achieved for our partially observable version of CartPole-v0. But, unlike BPTT, e-prop based DRQN was not able to solve this environment reliably.

The main problem that e-prop has to face in DRQN is that the targets for the LSTM are only estimates based on the ever-increasing experience of an agent. The better an agent gets, the higher the accumulated returns and targets become. The result of these ever-increasing targets is, in contrast to supervised learning, that the loss can indeed rise during training when the agent is performing better. The fact that this estimation of Q-values diverges and is unstable is one of the main problems of DQN approaches. Using a less stable optimization algorithm like e-prop increases this problem and is most likely the cause for our problems with the CartPole environments. Future works with e-prop based DRQN should include already known DQN extensions.

6   Conclusion

In this work, we covered the application of e-prop to LSTMs. Our results show that symmetric e-prop is a highly capable algorithm for the optimization of LSTMs. The introduced extensions were able to further improve symmetric e-prop. The trace echo extension proved to be particularly valuable. It includes an unsupervised learning signal based on past eligibility traces and clearly alleviates some of the limitations of e-prop. We showed that under certain conditions, symmetric e-prop with the trace echo can outperform BPTT. Furthermore, we delivered a proof of concept for the application of e-prop to recurrent Q-Learning.

References

1. Arjovsky, M., Shah, A., Bengio, Y.: Unitary evolution recurrent neural networks. In: International Conference on Machine Learning, pp. 1120–1128. PMLR (2016)
2. Bellec, G., Scherr, F., Hajek, E., Salaj, D., Legenstein, R., Maass, W.: Biologically inspired alternatives to backpropagation through time for learning in recurrent neural nets. arXiv preprint arXiv:1901.09049 (2019)
3. Bellec, G., et al.: A solution to the learning dilemma for recurrent networks of spiking neurons. Nat. Commun. **11**(1), 1–15 (2020)
4. Gers, F.A., Schmidhuber, J., Cummins, F.: Learning to forget: Continual prediction with LSTM. Neural Comput. **12**(10), 2451–2471 (2000)

5. Grossberg, S.: Competitive learning: from interactive activation to adaptive resonance. Cognit. Sci. **11**(1), 23–63 (1987)
6. Hausknecht, M., Stone, P.: Deep recurrent q-learning for partially observable MDPS. arXiv preprint arXiv:1507.06527 (2015)
7. Hebb, D.: The organization of behavior. Emphnew York (1949)
8. Hochreiter, S., Schmidhuber, J.: Long short-term memory. Neural Comput. **9**(8), 1735–1780 (1997)
9. Jozefowicz, R., Zaremba, W., Sutskever, I.: An empirical exploration of recurrent network architectures. In: International Conference on Machine Learning, pp. 2342–2350. PMLR (2015)
10. Kingma, D.P., Ba, J.: Adam: a method for stochastic optimization. arXiv preprint arXiv:1412.6980 (2014)
11. Le, Q.V., Jaitly, N., Hinton, G.E.: A simple way to initialize recurrent networks of rectified linear units. arXiv preprint arXiv:1504.00941 (2015)
12. LeCun, Y., Bengio, Y., Hinton, G.: Deep learning. Nature **521**(7553), 436–444 (2015)
13. Tieleman, T., Hinton, G.: Lecture 6.5-rmsprop, coursera: Neural Networks for Machine Learning. University of Toronto, Technical Report (2012)
14. Werbos, P.J.: Backpropagation through time: what it does and how to do it. Proc. IEEE **78**(10), 1550–1560 (1990)
15. Zhu, P., Li, X., Poupart, P., Miao, G.: On improving deep reinforcement learning for pomdps. arXiv preprint arXiv:1704.07978 (2017)

Improving Stylized Image Captioning with Better Use of Transformer

Yutong Tan[1,2], Zheng Lin[1,2], Huan Liu[1(✉)], and Fan Zuo[3]

[1] Institute of Information Engineering, Chinese Academy of Sciences, Beijing, China
{tanyutong,linzheng,liuhuan}@iie.ac.cn
[2] School of Cyber Security, University of Chinese Academy of Sciences, Beijing, China
[3] State Grid Zhenjiang Power Supply Company, Beijing, China

Abstract. Stylized Image Captioning aims to generate more human-like captions that can preserve the semantics of the image and have various style characteristics. Most existing methods adopt a framework consisting of CNN for encoding and RNN for decoding and develop the decoder to get better results. Compared with the attention in RNN which only models inter-modal interactions (i.e., object-to-word), attention mechanisms in Transformer can't only characterize inter-modal interactions but also intra-modal interactions (i.e., word-to-word and object-to-object). However, even Transformer Encoder is adopted to help capture internal relationships of image regions, it's still hard for decoders to stylize captions. To this end, we attempt to reconstruct transformer to achieve the goals of stylization and content preservation in two ways. Moreover, to better preserve image content, we adopt a Multi-Task Learning framework that generates factual and stylized captions of the same image. In this way, our models can generate stylized captions having style and also maintaining strong relevance with images. Experiments on two benchmark datasets indicate that our models outperform the state-of-the-art systems on average.

Keywords: Stylized image captioning · Attention mechanism · Multimodal · Transformer

1 Introduction

Recently, Image Captioning has achieved high-level results due to the rapid development of technology, such as encoder-decoder framework based on large image-caption dataset. In this way, the generated captions turn out to be more factual, denoted as factual captions, which describe the image from an objective perspective. However, human-like captions can describe images from different perspectives which are various and vivid. Take Fig. 1 as an example, a positive caption describes the building as *beautiful* while a negative caption describes the building as *ugly*. There is no doubt that such stylized captions have stronger expressibility and more human-like than factual captions.

© The Author(s), under exclusive license to Springer Nature Switzerland AG 2022
E. Pimenidis et al. (Eds.): ICANN 2022, LNCS 13531, pp. 347–358, 2022.
https://doi.org/10.1007/978-3-031-15934-3_29

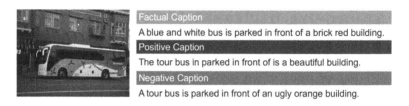

Fig. 1. Examples of factual and stylized image captions.

Stylized Image Captioning is generating a stylized caption of the given image, which has two requirements: 1) contains various style characteristics; 2) contains the accurate image content. To stylize captions, most existing methods of Stylized Image Captioning [4,7,13–15,21] adopt an encoder-decoder framework like Standard Image Captioning [19]: extract the deep-level feature of the image using a CNN as an encoder, and generate stylized captions based on the image features through a decoder. Mathews [13] and Gan [7] design different structures of the decoder to capture stylized domain knowledge. However, they take the image features as the input at the initial step of decoders, which leads to the loss of visual information through long distance. The lack of effects of visual information on words makes it hard to preserve the content of the given image. To describe the image accurately, [14,15] adopt attention mechanism to feed visual information to the decoder at every time step like previous works of Image Captioning [11,20]. However, the attention in RNN only models inter-modal interactions (i.e., object-to-word) while attention mechanisms in Transformer [17] can't only characterize inter-model interactions but also intra-modal interactions (i.e., word-to-word and object-to-object). But it's still hard for it to stylize captions because even Transformer Encoder is adopted, it mainly helps capture internal relationships of image regions to preserve image content.

To alleviate the above problems, we propose two novel models based on Transformer structure to reconcile the need for stylization and content preservation. After extracting the spatial image features by CNN, instead of attending the image features to the decoder directly, the first proposed model computes fused context vectors to guide stylized caption generation via Fused Attention with the image features and the generated words. Close interaction with information from two modality helps make full use of small-scaled stylized caption datasets to generate stylized captions. The second proposed model adopts the gate mechanism [11] to Transformer to decide when to rely on linguistic information to generate stylized words and when to rely on visual information to preserve the image content. Besides, we adopt a Multi-Task Learning framework [12] to use not only stylized caption datasets during fine-tuning [15], but also factual caption datasets. Because factual captions have the complete semantic meaning of the image, Multi-Task Learning can help preserve the image content. Given the same image, different decoders generate factual caption and stylized caption respectively at the same time. Thus, different decoders can capture factual and stylized domain knowledge respectively along with semantics of images.

Our contributions are concluded as follows: 1) To resolve two daunting problems (image relevance and stylization) in Stylized Captioning, we propose a framework based on Transformer and Multi-Task Learning. 2) Within the framework, we design two transformer-refined models. The first model can stylize captions by fusing images and text for the decoder. The second model can decide the weights of the image features and the generated words. They can both help generate stylized captions. 3) Experiments on two benchmark datasets indicate that our models outperform the state-of-the-art systems in all evaluation on average.

2 Related Work

Recently, increasing efforts have been devoted to Stylized Image Captioning. Most supervised works use small-scaled stylized caption/large-scaled factual caption datasets for fine-tuning/pre-training.

Most existing works [4,7,13,21] build an encoder-decoder framework. [13] builts an encoder-decoder framework, which consists of two parallel CNN+RNNs to generate factual word and specialize in words with sentiment separately. [21] introduces Direct Injection and Injection by Sentiment Flow these two approaches. The former concatenates the sentiment label with word embedding as the input of RNN, and the latter adds a Sentiment Cell to LSTM to decide whether to use the sentiment information. But they need extra word-level annotations of sentiment while it's hard to get word-level labeled dataset. [7] replaces RNN with Factored LSTM which can learn style-specific word matrix set and share other parameters between different styles. [4] uses Style-factual LSTM which can learn two groups of matrices generating the factual caption and adding specific style information and four gates to control the proportions of those matrices respectively. They apply visual features only in the initial time step of the decoder, which may lead to the loss of visual information through long distance. Thus, the generated stylized captions may lose relevance with image content. To this end, spatial image features are attended to make captions more relative [14], which applies two complementary sentiment information including high-level and word-level but it needs word-level sentiment supervisions. [15] employs an attention mechanism to attend fine-grained image regions and uses a discriminator to distinguish whether the caption is real or fake. However, it's hard for models to stylize captions but to generate more factual captions due to the large margin of different dataset size. So it is the major challenge for this task to generate captions with style and also related to the image.

3 Methodology

Given an image I, our goal is to generate a stylized caption $Y = \{y_1, y_2, ..., y_n\}$ to describe the image with a specific style, such as positive and negative. Here, n is the length of the caption.

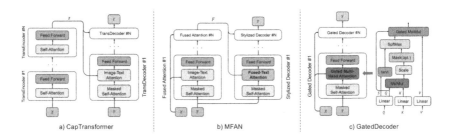

Fig. 2. Illustration of three Transformer-based models. (a) CapTransformer (b) MFAN (take Stylized Decoder as an example) (c) GatedDecoder. Here X is the image features extracted from CNN, T is generated words.

3.1 Base Model: CapTransformer

The CapTransformer consists of an encoder $Enc(X; \theta_E)$ which maps image features X encoded by CNN to a sequence of continuous representations z and a decoder $Dec(z; \theta_D)$ which predicts the conditional probability for the output sentence Y in an auto-regressive way. As it's shown in Fig. 2, the construction of CapTransformer is the same with the original Transformer model [17].

3.2 Multi-step Fused Attention Network

The first proposed model Multi-step Fused Attention Network (MFAN) adopts a Multi-Task Learning framework (see Fig. 3) which consists of a shared Fused Attention module and two different decoders. Given the spatial image features X, at every time step t, Fused Attention fuses the image features X and generated stylized words $y_{1:t-1}$ to a fused context vector F_t. It also takes generated factual words $\hat{y}_{1:t-1}$ as inputs to generate a fused context vector $\hat{F}_t$ for factual caption generation. Based on the fused context vector, Factual Decoder produces factual outputs probabilities while Stylized Decoder produces stylized outputs probabilities.

$$p(F_t|y_{1:t-1}, X) = f_{FA}(y_{1:t-1}, X) \tag{1}$$

$$p(\hat{F}_t|y_{1:t-1}, X) = f_{FA}(\hat{y}_{1:t-1}, X) \tag{2}$$

$$p(y_t|y_{1:t-1}, F_t) = g_{Style}(y_{1:t-1}, F_t) \tag{3}$$

$$p(\hat{y}_t|\hat{y}_{1:t-1}, \hat{F}_t) = g_{Factual}(\hat{y}_{1:t-1}, \hat{F}_t) \tag{4}$$

where f_{FA} is the computation unit in the Fused Attention, g_{Style} and $g_{Factual}$ are the computation unit in the Stylized/Factual Decoder, respectively.

Fused Attention. It is composed of a stack of $N = 6$ layers $(A_{FA}^1, ..., A_{FA}^N)$. Each layer has three sub-layers which are Self Attention, Multi-Head Attention, and Feed Forward network (see Fig. 2). To generates fused context vectors for the decoder to generate captions, at every time step t, Fused Attention takes

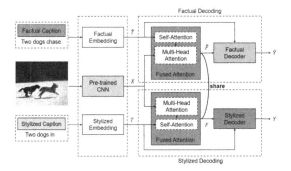

Fig. 3. The proposed Multi-step Fused Attention Network with Multi-task Learning.

the inputs from both the image features X and previous word $T_{1:t-1}$, including factual and stylized captions. The attended image features C_t^n is computed by A_{FA}^n based on the previous outputs C_t^{n-1},

$$C_t^n = A_{FA}^n(X, C_t^{n-1}) \tag{5}$$

where the caption representations $T_{1:t-1}$ is denoted as C_t^0, the fused context vector F_t is the outputs C_t^N from the last layer A_{FA}^N.

Factual/Stylized Decoder. The construction of Factual Decoder and Stylized Decoder is the same, which are both composed of a stack of $N = 6$ identical layers $(A_{dec}^1, ..., A_{dec}^N)$ with three sub-layers which are Self Attention, Multi-Head Attention and Feed Forward network (see Fig. 2). Here takes Stylized Decoder as an example. At every time step t, Stylized Decoder takes the fused context vector F_t and the ground stylized caption representation $T_{1:t-1}$ as inputs. The attended word features Y_t^n is computed by A_{dec}^n,

$$Y_t^n = A_{dec}^n(F_t, Y_t^{n-1}) \tag{6}$$

where the caption representation $T_{1:t-1}$ is denoted as Y_t^0. The probability of next word y_t is computed based on the outputs Y_t^N from the last layer A_{dec}^N.

3.3 Gated Decoder Model

The second proposed model Gated Decoder Model (GatedDecoder) for Stylized Image Captioning also adopts the same Multi-Task Learning framework with MFAN which consists of two different decoders: Factual Decoder and Gated Decoder. Given the spatial image features X, at every time step t, Factual Decoder takes generated factual words $\hat{y}_{1:t-1}$ as input to produce factual outputs probabilities while Gated Decoder takes generated stylized words $y_{1:t-1}$ as input to produce stylized outputs probabilities.

$$p(y_t|y_{1:t-1}, X) = f_{Gated}(y_{1:t-1}, X) \tag{7}$$

$$p(\hat{y}_t|\hat{y}_{1:t-1}, X) = g_{Factual}(\hat{y}_{1:t-1}, X) \tag{8}$$

where $\boldsymbol{f}_{Gated}$ and $\boldsymbol{g}_{Factual}$ are the computation unit in the Gated Decoder and the Factual Decoder, respectively.

The construction of the Factual Decoder is the same with Decoders in Cap-Transformer while for the Gated Decoder, we adopt the gate mechanism to Multi-Head Attention inspired by [11]. The Gated Decoder is composed of a stack of $N = 6$ identical layers $(A_{Gated}^1, ..., A_{Gated}^N)$. Each layer has three sub-layers which are Self Attention, Gated Multi-Head Attention, and Feed Forward network (see Fig. 2).

Gated Multi-head Attention. It decides the weights of the image features and generated words, which helps the decoder to know when to rely on linguistic information to contain stylized characteristics and when to rely on visual information to preserve the image content. Similar to Multi-Head Attention, it has H attention heads which perform the attention function in parallel. Attention heads project the generated words as $\boldsymbol{Q}$, the image features as $\boldsymbol{K}$ and $\boldsymbol{V}$ with different projections to $\boldsymbol{Q}^h$, $\boldsymbol{K}^h$, $\boldsymbol{V}^h$. We design a linguistic vector $\boldsymbol{S}^h$ projected from $\boldsymbol{Q}$ contains linguistic information from the generated words.

$$\boldsymbol{Q}^h, \boldsymbol{K}^h, \boldsymbol{V}^h, \boldsymbol{S}^h = \boldsymbol{Q}\boldsymbol{W}_h^Q, \boldsymbol{K}\boldsymbol{W}_h^K, \boldsymbol{V}\boldsymbol{W}_h^V, \boldsymbol{Q}\boldsymbol{W}_h^S \tag{9}$$

To compute the attended features $\hat{\boldsymbol{O}}^h$ of the hth attention head on query $\boldsymbol{Q}^h$, key $\boldsymbol{K}^h$, value $\boldsymbol{V}^h$ and the linguistic vector $\boldsymbol{S}^h$, the transformer model adopt a Scaled Dot-Product Attention with a gate mechanism,

$$\hat{\boldsymbol{O}}^h = g^h \boldsymbol{Q}^h + (1 - g^h)Att(\boldsymbol{Q}^h, \boldsymbol{K}^h)\boldsymbol{V}^h \tag{10}$$

$$\hat{\boldsymbol{\alpha}} = softmax([\frac{\boldsymbol{Q}^h \boldsymbol{K}^{hT}}{\sqrt{d_h}}; tanh(\boldsymbol{S}^h)]) \tag{11}$$

where $[;]$ indicates concatenation and $\sqrt{d_h}$ is scaling factor. We interpret the last element of this vector to be the gate value: $g^h = \hat{\boldsymbol{\alpha}}[n+1]$.

At every time step t, Gated Decoder takes the inputs from both the image features $\boldsymbol{X}$ and the stylized caption representations $\boldsymbol{T}_{1:t-1}$. The attended word features Y_t^n is computed by A_{Gated}^n,

$$Y_t^n = A_{Gated}^n(\boldsymbol{X}, Y_t^{n-1}) \tag{12}$$

where the caption representations $\boldsymbol{T}_{1:t-1}$ is denoted as Y^0. The probability of next word y_t is computed based on the outputs Y_t^N from the last layer A_{Gated}^N.

3.4 Overall Learning Strategy

Similar to [4,7,13,15], we adopt a two-stage learning strategy to train two models, which is sequentially trained by two independent stages.

In the first stage, we train models only using the paired images and ground truth factual captions. Two decoders are both trained to generate factual captions and the parameters of two models are updated via MLE loss.

$$\mathcal{L} = -\sum_{t=1}^n p(\hat{y}_t|\boldsymbol{X}, \hat{\boldsymbol{y}}_{1:t-1}) - \sum_{t=1}^n p(y_t|\boldsymbol{X}, \boldsymbol{y}_{1:t-1}) \tag{13}$$

where y and $\hat{y}$ generated from Stylized Decoder/Gated Decoder and Factual Decoder respectively are both factual captions.

In the second stage, we fine-tune two models using paired images and ground truth factual captions and stylized captions. Given an Image I along with the ground truth factual caption $\hat{y}$ and stylized caption y, the loss of the entire model consists of two parts: factual caption word probability and stylized caption word probability. Their weight is controlled by hyper-parameter λ,

$$\mathcal{L} = -\lambda \sum_{t=1}^{n} log(p(\hat{y}_t|\boldsymbol{X}, \hat{\boldsymbol{y}}_{1:t-1})) - (1-\lambda) \sum_{t=1}^{n} log(p(y_t|\boldsymbol{X}, \boldsymbol{y}_{1:t-1})) \qquad (14)$$

where y generated from Stylized Decoder is stylized caption and $\hat{y}$ generated from Factual Decoder is factual caption.

4   Experiments

4.1   Dataset

We evaluate experiments on two publicly available stylized image caption datasets **SentiCap** [13] and **FlickrStyle** [7]. **SentiCap** contains images that are labeled by positive and/or negative sentiment captions. The POS and NEG subsets contain 998/673 and 997/503 images for training/testing, respectively. Each image in **FlickrStyle** is labeled with 5/1/1 factual/humorous/romantic captions. The same with [4], we randomly select 6000/1000 samples for training/testing. Besides, we use corresponding factual image-caption datasets **COCO** [5] and **Flickr30K** [22].

4.2   Implementation Details

In our experiments, we extract the 2048-dimension image features by the last pooling layer of ResNet152 [8] pre-trained using the ImageNet [6] dataset. For the captions, we replace the words which appear less than five times with UNK and crop the length of sentences to 16. The number of hidden units in the attention layer and the size of the input word embedding is 512. We use the same Adam optimizer [9] in Transformer [17] with *warmup_steps* value set as 20000. The initial learning rate is 5e-4 for both pre-training and fine-tuning and it decays every 3 epochs at a rate of 0.8. The λ value in Eq 14 is set as 0.4, 0.3 for MFAN on SentiCap and FlickrStyle and 0.6, 0.4 for GatedDecoder on SentiCap and FlickrStyle after testing.

4.3   Results

To evaluate the performance of the proposed models in generating stylized image captions, we compare them with these baseline approaches: Models built based on **Neural Image Caption (NIC)** [19] and feed image features at the initial

Table 1. Average performance comparisons on the test splits of Pos and Neg styles.

Model	B-1	B-2	B-3	B-4	M	R	C	S
NIC	48.55	29.25	18.30	11.50	16.60	36.95	55.00	–
SentiCap	49.55	30.15	18.90	11.95	16.80	37.20	58.10	–
SF-LSTM + Adap	50.40	30.90	19.60	12.70	16.40	38.00	59.85	–
Direct Injection	51.70	32.10	20.50	13.10	17.15	39.10	64.75	–
Sentiment Flow	51.05	32.20	20.65	13.55	16.95	39.00	65.45	–
ATTEND-GAN	56.55	33.85	20.80	13.05	17.90	44.45	63.20	15.75
SENTI-ATTEND	**58.10**	34.80	21.40	13.70	18.95	**45.40**	70.25	17.05
Adaptive	52.39	32.92	21.19	13.63	17.78	39.82	66.23	17.67
Top-Down	53.30	33.75	21.88	14.27	18.48	40.38	73.48	18.38
CapTransformer	56.28	36.95	24.62	16.16	19.69	42.47	82.46	20.58
MFAN (Ours)	57.14	**38.14**	**26.21**	**18.03**	**20.24**	44.09	**88.28**	**20.99**
GatedDecoder (Ours)	55.09	36.15	24.51	16.74	19.49	42.68	82.45	19.96

Table 2. Average performance comparisons on the test splits of Humorous and Romantic styles.

Model	B-1	B-2	B-3	B-4	M	R	C	S
NIC	26.65	13.60	7.65	4.45	10.80	24.60	36.00	–
StyleNet	24.75	11.70	6.30	3.70	9.70	22.75	27.30	–
SF-LSTM + Adap	27.60	14.50	8.35	4.95	11.10	25.40	38.50	–
Adaptive	28.23	15.28	8.71	5.07	11.93	26.57	43.21	15.31
Top-Down	29.84	17.50	10.96	7.06	13.12	29.29	58.77	18.04
CapTransformer	30.61	18.45	11.82	7.69	13.88	30.17	66.37	19.93
MFAN (Ours)	30.96	18.52	11.81	7.72	13.97	30.41	66.41	20.20
GatedDecoder (Ours)	**31.22**	**18.91**	**12.23**	**8.17**	**14.21**	**30.83**	**69.27**	**20.39**

step of decoder: **SentiCap** [13]; Models are built with attention mechanism: **SENTI-ATTEND** [14]; **ATTEND-GAN** [15]. We also consider some representative attention-based works for image captioning: **Adaptive** [11]; **Top-Down** [2] and Transformer-based model **CapTransformer**. To make a fair comparison, all baseline models are trained using both the factual dataset for pre-training and the stylized dataset for fine-tuning. It's noteworthy that some baselines are designed just for generating specific stylized captions.

The same with previous work [4,7,13,15], we adopt the following metrics to evaluate each system. We count the BLEU [16], METEOR [3], ROUGE-L [10], CIDEr [18] , SPICE [1] between the generated captions and the ground truth stylized captions[1]. B-n, M, R, C, S are short for BLEU-n, METEOR, ROUGE-L, CIDEr, SPICE, respectively. Table 1 and Table 2 show results of different models on SentiCap and FlickrStyle. It is observed that the performance of attention-based models is much better even some models aren't designed for Stylized Image

---

[1] These scores are computed using `coco-caption`.

Table 3. Human evaluation comparisons on the test splits of Humorous and Romantic styles.

Model	Humorous		Romantic		Average	
	Relevancy	Style	Relevancy	Style	Relevancy	Style
Top-Down	1.63	1.01	1.71	0.81	1.67	0.91
CapTransformer	1.83	0.91	1.95	0.91	1.89	0.91
MFAN	1.73	0.91	1.94	**1.03**	1.84	**0.97**
GatedDecoder	**1.81**	**1.03**	**1.99**	0.83	**1.90**	0.93

Captioning. Moreover, those Transformer-based models can get better results, which indicates that it's significant to focus on the internal relationship. The fact that our models outperform other Transformer-based models shows the effectiveness of two proposed models.

Image Captioning with Sentiments. Table 1 shows evaluation results of different models. From the results, we can observe that MFAN achieves the best performance by almost all measures except BLEU-1. More specifically, our model MFAN outperforms the-state-of-art model SENTI-ATTEND by over 4 BLEU-4 points and 18 CIDEr points averaged on positive and negative captions. Compared with it, MFAN feeds text-guided fused context vectors to the decoder to generate stylized captions, which means previously generated text can impact the attention weights of different image regions to pay more attention to relevant and detailed ones. Although GatedDecoder can't outperform MFAN, it still has a competitive result. The reason why GatedDecoder can't get better scores than MFAN on SentiCap dataset may be that the stylized characteristics are mainly presented by stylized adjective words and the main core of the sentences in SentiCap dataset is the image content but not stylized words, which limits the capability of stylized word generation for GatedDecoder.

Image Captioning with Styles. Table 2 shows evaluation results of different models based on ground truth captions with different styles. From the results, we can see that GatedDecoder achieves the best performance by all measures and MFAN also has competitive performance. More specifically, our model GatedDecoder significantly outperforms the-state-of-art model SF-LSTM + Adap by over 7 CIDEr points averaged on humorous and romantic captions. The reason why MFAN can't get better scores than GatedDecoder on FlickrStyle dataset may be that the stylized sentences in FlickrStyle dataset consist of many imaginary stylized words which don't show in the input features while MFAN concerns more about how to adjust the attention weights on image regions to better stylize captions.

5   Human Evaluation

Futhermore, we perform human evaluation on the generated captions in terms of relevancy and style appropriateness. We randomly selected 50 images from the

testing set and generate stylized captions for each image, resulting totally 50 ×
4 image-caption pairs to be evaluated for four models. We asked 3 volunteers to
rate the captions. The volunteers were asked to rank the generated captions in
terms of their relevancy, and style appropriateness. Relevancy was rated from 0
(unrelated) to 3 (very related). Style appropriateness means whether a caption
appropriately owns the desired styles, rated from 0 (bad) to 3 (perfect). The
scores on FlickrStyle dataset are shown in Table 3. As we can see, the two models
we proposed have achieved good results on the whole (Table 4).

Table 4. Average ablation study results on two datasets.

	SentiCap				FlickrStyle			
	B-1	B-4	C	S	B-1	B-4	C	S
MFAN	**57.13**	**18.03**	**88.28**	**20.99**	30.96	7.72	66.41	20.20
MFAN w/o MTL	56.68	17.53	85.77	20.83	30.81	7.48	63.73	19.44
MFAN w/o FA	55.50	15.54	83.26	20.01	30.53	7.45	62.28	18.74
GatedDecoder	55.09	16.74	82.45	19.96	**31.22**	**8.17**	**69.27**	**20.39**
GatedDecoder w/o MTL	55.26	16.49	82.84	19.93	30.87	7.70	65.92	19.78
GatedDecoder w/o GMHA	55.50	15.54	83.26	20.01	30.53	7.45	62.28	18.74
FA + GatedDecoder + MTL	56.51	17.31	86.25	20.89	30.91	7.76	66.95	20.29

5.1   Ablation Study

In this section, we give a deep analysis of the key components of our models. We
compare MFAN with models which ablate Fused Attention(FA) and Multi-Task
Learning(MTL) and GatedDecoder with models which ablate Gated Multi-Head
Attention(GMHA) and MTL. It's noteworthy that the construction of MFAN
w/o FA and GatedDecoder w/o GMAH are the same which feeds the image
features into Transformer decoders directly, which only consists of 6 layers. To
evaluate the effect of Multi-Task Learning, we only use stylized caption datasets
for fine-tuning. We also consider the united model denoted as FA + Gated-
Decoder + MTL. Table 1 and Table 2 show ablation study results, we can see
that FA proves to be critical to improving overall performance as it takes generated words into consideration to interact with image features. The results on
FlickrStyle also indicate that GMHA contributes to the overall performance,
especially for the BLEU results as it helps generate more stylized words under
the guidance of generated words. Moreover, it's proved that MTL helps preserve
the image content for two models. However, even though FA and GMHA both
are effective, they can't promote each other to achieve the best results on two
datasets. Actually, both FA and GMHA affect the weights through the generated words. When they are united, the generated words have too much influence,
which may limit word generation according to the image information. After all,
stylized words still account for a small number in sentences, so the united model
can't achieve the best results on two datasets instead.

Fig. 4. Stylized Captions generated by our approach and baseline [17].

5.2 Case Study

In this section, we present four randomly sampled generation examples of MFAN, GatedDecoder and a representative baseline system and analyze the strengths and weaknesses of them. Figure 4 shows the example outputs of different styles. We can observe that: (1) MFAN can generate captions with style characteristics based on fused context vectors, like *ugly* train in the first image. GatedDecoder can generate stylized words *catch a ball* based on linguistic information. Besides, Multi-Task Learning helps to better keep image content to describe the train like *an ugly orange train*. (2) The baseline system tends to sacrifice the image relevance, for example the description of the train in the second image. (3) Both MFAN and GatedDecoder generate captions with different styles that perfectly reach two requirements ((image relevance and stylization).

6   Conclusion

In this paper, we propose two refined models based on transformer structure. The first proposed model Multi-step Fused Attention Network fuses image features and previously generated words via Fused Attention. It encourages the encoder to pay more attention to regions that will facilitate the stylization. The second proposed model Gated Decoder decides when to rely on the linguistic or visual information through Gated Multi-Head Attention. It helps the decoder make automatic decisions during stylized words generation. To allow two models to preserve factual information and stylize captions in a balanced way, Multi-Task Learning is adopted to generate factual and stylized captions on the same image. Experiments on two public datasets demonstrate that our models outperform the state-of-the-art models for stylized image captioning on average.

References

1. Anderson, P., Fernando, B., Johnson, M., Gould, S.: Spice: semantic propositional image caption evaluation. In: ECCV, pp. 382–398 (2016)

2. Anderson, P., He, X., Buehler, C., Teney, D., Johnson, M., Gould, S., Zhang, L.: Bottom-up and top-down attention for image captioning and visual question answering. In: CVPR, pp. 6077–6086 (2018)

3. Banerjee, S., Lavie, A.: Meteor: an automatic metric for MT evaluation with improved correlation with human judgments. In: IEEvaluation@ACL (2005)

4. Chen, T., et al.: "Factual" or "emotional": stylized image captioning with adaptive learning and attention. In: ECCV, pp. 519–535 (2018)

5. Chen, X., et al.: Microsoft coco captions: Data collection and evaluation server. arXiv preprint arXiv:1504.00325 (2015)

6. Deng, J., Dong, W., Socher, R., Li, L.J., Li, K., Fei-Fei, L.: Imagenet: a large-scale hierarchical image database. In: CVPR, pp. 248–255 (2009)

7. Gan, C., Gan, Z., He, X., Gao, J., Deng, L.: Stylenet: generating attractive visual captions with styles. In: CVPR, pp. 3137–3146 (2017)

8. He, K., Zhang, X., Ren, S., Sun, J.: Deep residual learning for image recognition. In: CVPR, pp. 770–778 (2016)

9. Kingma, D.P., Ba, J.: Adam: a method for stochastic optimization. arXiv preprint arXiv:1412.6980 (2014)

10. Lin, C.Y.: Rouge: a package for automatic evaluation of summaries. In: Text Summarization Branches Out, pp. 74–81 (2004)

11. Lu, J., Xiong, C., Parikh, D., Socher, R.: Knowing when to look: adaptive attention via a visual sentinel for image captioning. In: CVPR, pp. 375–383 (2017)

12. Luong, M.T., Le, Q.V., Sutskever, I., Vinyals, O., Kaiser, L.: Multi-task sequence to sequence learning. arXiv preprint arXiv:1511.06114 (2015)

13. Mathews, A.P., Xie, L., He, X.: Senticap: generating image descriptions with sentiments. In: AAAI (2016)

14. Nezami, O.M., Dras, M., Wan, S., Paris, C.: Senti-attend: image captioning using sentiment and attention. arXiv preprint arXiv:1811.09789 (2018)

15. Nezami, O.M., Dras, M., Wan, S., Paris, C., Hamey, L.: Towards generating stylized image captions via adversarial training. In: PRICAI, pp. 270–284 (2019)

16. Papineni, K., Roukos, S., Ward, T., Zhu, W.J.: Bleu: a method for automatic evaluation of machine translation. In: ACL, pp. 311–318 (2002)

17. Vaswani, A., et al.: Attention is all you need. In: NIPS (2017)

18. Vedantam, R., Zitnick, C.L., Parikh, D.: Cider: consensus-based image description evaluation. In: CVPR, pp. 4566–4575 (2014)

19. Vinyals, O., Toshev, A., Bengio, S., Erhan, D.: Show and tell: a neural image caption generator. In: CVPR, pp. 3156–3164 (2015)

20. Xu, K., et al.: Show, attend and tell: Neural image caption generation with visual attention. In: ICML, pp. 2048–2057 (2015)

21. You, Q., Jin, H., Luo, J.: Image captioning at will: a versatile scheme for effectively injecting sentiments into image descriptions. arXiv preprint arXiv:1801.10121 (2018)

22. Young, P., Lai, A., Hodosh, M., Hockenmaier, J.: From image descriptions to visual denotations: new similarity metrics for semantic inference over event descriptions. TACL **2**, 67–78 (2014)

Investigating Current-Based and Gating Approaches for Accurate and Energy-Efficient Spiking Recurrent Neural Networks

Manon Dampfhoffer[1,2]([✉]) [ID], Thomas Mesquida[2] [ID], Alexandre Valentian[2] [ID], and Lorena Anghel[1] [ID]

[1] University of Grenoble Alpes, CEA, CNRS, Grenoble INP, INAC-Spintec, 38000 Grenoble, France
`manon.dampfhoffer@cea.fr`
[2] University of Grenoble Alpes, CEA, List, 38000 Grenoble, France

Abstract. Spiking Neural Networks (SNNs) with spike-based computations and communications may be more energy-efficient than Artificial Neural Networks (ANNs) for embedded applications. However, SNNs have mostly been applied to image processing, although audio applications may better fit their temporal dynamics. We evaluate the accuracy and energy-efficiency of Leaky Integrate-and-Fire (LIF) models on spiking audio datasets compared to ANNs. We demonstrate that, for processing temporal sequences, the Current-based LIF (Cuba-LIF) outperforms the LIF. Moreover, gated recurrent networks have demonstrated superior accuracy than simple recurrent networks for such tasks. Therefore, we introduce SpikGRU, a gated version of the Cuba-LIF. SpikGRU achieves higher accuracy than other recurrent SNNs on the most difficult task studied in this work. The Cuba-LIF and SpikGRU reach state-of-the-art accuracy, only <1.1% below the accuracy of the best ANNs, while showing up to a 49x reduction in the number of operations compared to ANNs, due to the high spike sparsity.

Keywords: SNN · RNN · GRU · Speech recognition

1 Introduction

Artificial Neural Networks (ANNs) have shown impressive results in a wide range of applications such as speech recognition or object detection. However, their energy consumption limits their use in embedded applications. Spiking Neural Networks (SNNs) are a promising research direction targeting the reduction of energy consumption in specialized neuromorphic hardware. SNN computations and communications closely mimick biological neural networks. Spiking neurons communicate with pulses (spikes) instead of continuous-valued activations. They accumulate input spikes in their membrane potential and fire an output spike when the potential reaches a threshold. Similar to biological neural networks,

E. Pimenidis et al. (Eds.): ICANN 2022, LNCS 13531, pp. 359–370, 2022.
https://doi.org/10.1007/978-3-031-15934-3_30

SNNs have an inherent temporal dynamics. They integrate spikes over time and the network inference is performed over several algorithmic timesteps. Therefore, SNNs computations are based on accumulate (AC) instead of multiply-and-accumulate (MAC) operations, which consume more energy [10]. Moreover, SNN computations can be handled in an event-based manner in neuromorphic hardware [7], allowing to exploit their natural spike sparsity.

SNNs have been mostly benchmarked on static vision tasks, such as image classification. However, the inference on static data must be decomposed over several timesteps in order to match the SNN temporal dynamics. Moreover, there is a trade-off between the SNN accuracy and latency (the number of timesteps used to decompose the SNN inference) [8]. On the other hand, SNNs have been less considered for audio applications, although their inherent temporal dynamics may better fit temporal rather than static data. Indeed, the data are already sequential, which means that the latency is not increased compared to a processing by a standard ANN. Moreover, spiking neurons have a self recurrence due to the spike accumulation in the membrane potential over time which may help learning temporal dependencies. Besides, bio-inspired dynamic sensors, such as artificial cochleas [2], are a relevant application for SNNs as they produce data already in the form of spikes. This spiking data can be fed into the SNNs without pre-processing in order to benefit from the high sparsity and high temporal resolution of these sensors [13]. Recently, spiking audio datasets based on a neurophysiology-inspired processing, outputting data in a similar format than dynamic audio sensors, have been proposed to benchmark SNNs [6,16].

SNNs for deep learning applications are based on variants of the Leaky Integrate-and-Fire (LIF) model [1]. For instance, in the Current-based LIF (Cuba-LIF) model, spikes are integrated into a current variable prior to the membrane potential. Moreover, artificial neuron models can be used with recurrent topologies to improve the accuracy on sequential data. In addition, gated recurrent networks, such as the Long Short-Term Memory (LSTM) [9] and the Gated Recurrent Unit (GRU) [5] models, have been proposed to improve the performance of simple Recurrent Neural Networks (RNNs).

In this paper, we investigate the performance of LIF and Cuba-LIF models with recurrent topologies on three spiking audio datasets from a Dynamic Audio Sensor (DASDIGITS [2]) or from a neurophysiology-inspired pre-processing (SHD and SSC [6]), for digits and single words classification. Moreover, we introduce the Spiking Gated Recurrent Unit (SpikGRU), which is an extension of the Cuba-LIF with a gate. Finally, we compare the accuracy and energy-efficiency of the LIF, Cuba-LIF, SpikGRU and ANN models (RNN and GRU). The main contributions of this paper are summarized as follows:

- We show that, for processing temporal sequences, the Cuba-LIF outperforms the LIF model by showing higher accuracy for a similar energy-efficiency.
- We propose SpikGRU, a novel spiking gated recurrent model achieving higher accuracy than other spiking models on the most difficult task (SSC).
- We demonstrate state-of-the-art accuracy compared to previous works using SNNs on the SHD and SSC datasets, bridging the gap with ANN accuracy, while showing up to a 49x improvement in energy compared to the GRU.

2   Related Work

2.1   Leaky Integrate-and-Fire and Current-Based Models

The LIF model is commonly used in SNNs for deep learning applications. The LIF model with a recurrent network topology can be described as:

$$v_t^l = \beta \odot v_{t-1}^l + W_v s_t^{l-1} + U_v s_{t-1}^l + b_v - v_{th} s_{t-1}^l \tag{1}$$

$$s_t^l = H[v_t^l - v_{th}] \tag{2}$$

v_t^l and s_t^l are vectors corresponding respectively to the membrane potential and output spikes of neurons from layer l at time t. $\odot$ denotes element-wise multiplication. Spike firing happens when the membrane potential is superior to the threshold v_{th}, which corresponds to the Heaviside step function H. After each spike, v_{th} is substracted from the membrane potential of spiking neurons. The parameters of the models are W_v and U_v, the weight matrices of feed-forward and recurrent connections (resp.), and b_v, the bias vector. The time constant β corresponds to an exponential decay of v over time.

Neuron models with more temporal dynamics than the simple LIF model can achieve superior accuracy for processing temporal data. For instance, recent works [3,22,23] show the superiority of the Adaptive LIF (Adapt-LIF) over the LIF model for speech recognition. Adapt-LIF uses an adaptive threshold with temporal dynamics (the threshold is increased after each spike fired and decays exponentially with time). In addition, heterogeneous time constant parameters learned per neuron (as opposed to fixed for a layer) can improve the learning on temporal data, allowing the neurons to specialize at different time scales [17]. The Cuba-LIF model is another variant of the LIF introducing an input current i, which integrates the incoming spikes before transmitting them to v with a time constant α and parameters W_i, U_i and b_i. v_t^l is thus defined as a linear combination of its previous state v_{t-1}^l and input i_t^l. Note that in our work, α and β time constants of LIF and Cuba-LIF models are defined as vectors (different constants per neuron) of trainable parameters as in [17]. We use the following definition of the Cuba-LIF model, similar to [17]:

$$i_t^l = \alpha \odot i_{t-1}^l + W_i s_t^{l-1} + U_i s_{t-1}^l + b_i \tag{3}$$

$$v_t^l = \beta \odot v_{t-1}^l + (1 - \beta) \odot i_t^l - v_{th} s_{t-1}^l \tag{4}$$

$$s_t^l = H[v_t^l - v_{th}] \tag{5}$$

2.2   Gated Recurrent Networks

RNNs learn temporal dependencies by reusing the information from previous timesteps due to the recurrent connections. However, their training can be unstable due to vanishing and exploding gradient problems, which can prevent the learning of long-term dependencies [4]. Gated RNNs, such as LSTM and GRU, can mitigate these problems. Indeed, the gating mechanism allows to better control the flow of information over the timesteps and can create temporal shortcuts which prevent gradient vanishing. Some gated SNNs inspired by the LSTM model have been proposed [14,18,20]. In [20], a LSTM is converted to a spiking version using piece-wise linear counterparts for the activation functions. A spiking LSTM model that can be directly trained with backpropagation through time is proposed in [14]. A hybrid analog and spiking LSTM is demonstrated in [18]. This hybrid network benefits from event-based spike accumulation, but at the expense of decomposing each LSTM timestep into 128 SNN timesteps. However, the LSTM model is computationally expensive due to the use of three gates per unit, which highly increases the number of synaptic operations per layer compared to a simple RNN. The GRU and its variants demonstrate that it is possible to achieve similar accuracy with fewer gates per unit [5,19].

3   SpikGRU: A Spiking Gated Recurrent Unit

We investigate the benefits of gated units in recurrent SNNs by proposing a new model: SpikGRU (Spiking Gated Recurrent Unit). It is inspired by the current-based approach of the Cuba-LIF and the gated approach of the Light-GRU [19], a light version of the GRU model with a single gate. Indeed, SpikGRU can be seen as an extension of the Cuba-LIF model with an additional gate, z, instead of the parameter β. z is computed using the incoming spikes and another set of parameters, W_z, U_z and b_z, and is processed with a sigmoid activation function. The purpose of z is to determine the best combination of the previous state v_{t-1}^l and the input current (or candidate state) i_t^l used in the computation of v_t^l, similar to the update gate in the Light-GRU. We define SpikGRU as:

$$i_t^l = \alpha \odot i_{t-1}^l + W_i s_t^{l-1} + U_i s_{t-1}^l + b_i \tag{6}$$

$$z_t^l = \sigma(W_z s_t^{l-1} + U_z s_{t-1}^l + b_z) \tag{7}$$

$$v_t^l = z_t^l \odot v_{t-1}^l + (1 - z_t^l) \odot i_t^l - v_{th} s_{t-1}^l \tag{8}$$

$$s_t^l = H[v_t^l - v_{th}] \tag{9}$$

Figure 1 illustrates the comparison between the LIF, Cuba-LIF and SpikGRU models. Unlike other spiking versions of gated networks [14,20] we did not use spikes to transmit information between the variables (i, z, v) but instead we transmit directly the value of the variable, which is continuous (represented as a floating point value in our simulations). This is similar to the idea of the Cuba-LIF where v takes i as input, introducing element-wise multiplications instead of only additions. This increases the accuracy (as there is no discretization of the information) at the expense of only a small increase in energy consumption. Indeed, these operations occur only at the neuron level and not at each synapse, the number of synapses being proportional to the square of the number of neurons in a fully connected topology. Moreover, contrary to LSTM networks, we use a single gate instead of three, which limits the computational cost of the model.

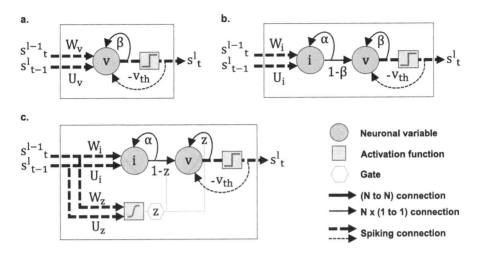

Fig. 1. Recurrent SNN models described in equations (1–9), considering a layer with input and output size N and omitting biases for clarity. a. LIF. b. Cuba-LIF. c. Proposed SpikGRU.

4 Experiments

4.1 Methods

Datasets and Pre-processing. We used three spiking datasets with a classification task to benchmark our SNN models with different degrees of task complexity. DASDIGITS [2] corresponds to the recording from a Dynamic Audio Sensor (64 channels) of the TIDIGITS audio dataset. DASDIGITS consists of 11 classes corresponding to the english digits "one" to "nine" plus "oh" and "zero", spoken by 111 (resp. 109) individuals for training (resp. testing) samples. The single digit version of the dataset contains 2,464 training and 2,486 testing samples. We used the dataset from the CochleaAMS1b sensor and a constant time bin pre-processing 200 Hz. We cut the samples after 1.25 s (almost no spikes are emitted from the sensor after that time) to obtain samples of length 250 timesteps. Therefore, at each timestep, the spike count (number of spikes produced during the time bin) from each channel is fed to both SNN and ANN models in order to compare them with the same data pre-processing. SHD and SSC [6] are created with an audio-to-spiking conversion procedure inspired by neurophysiology using 700 channels. SHD is a spiking version of the Heidelberg Digits audio dataset consisting in 20 classes of spoken digits in English and German from 12 speakers. It contains 8,156 training and 2,264 testing samples. The test set contains samples from 2 individuals that are not used in the training set plus 5% of samples from other speakers. SSC is a more difficult task based on the Google Speech Command dataset. It contains 35 classes corresponding to 35 english words (digits, single word commands and auxiliary words).

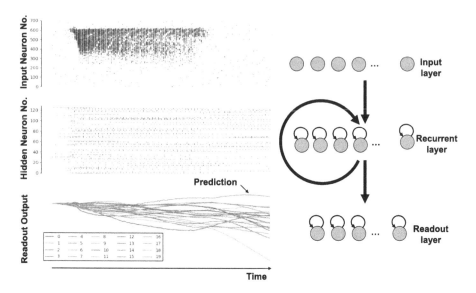

Fig. 2. Sample from the SHD dataset and response from a SNN with 1 recurrent layer.

In this dataset, samples from 1864 individuals are randomly split between training (75,466), validation (9,981) and test (20,382) sets. SHD and SSC samples have 1s duration and spikes are binned 250 Hz. The obtained spike count is also fed directly to the models at each of the 250 timesteps.

Training Procedure. We use network topologies with 1 or 2 recurrent layers of 128 units and a readout layer (fully-connected to the last recurrent layer), as shown in Fig. 2. The readout layer consists of neurons integrating inputs with a self-recurrence, similar to LIF neurons, without the spiking and resetting mechanisms. We use this readout layer for all models as it increases the accuracy compared to a standard fully connected layer, except for the GRU. For the training with DASDIGITS and SHD, we set 20% and 10% (resp.) of the training set as validation set. To avoid overfitting on the SHD and SSC datasets, we introduce noise in the input samples during training using spike jitter across channels, as in [6,17]. We use the max-over-time loss described in [6], which is the cross-entropy loss applied on the maximum value of the neurons of the readout layer over all timesteps. All models are trained with backpropagation through time using Adam [11] optimizer with a learning rate 0.001 for 200 epochs and a batch size 128 (512 for SSC). The standard RNN model leads to unstable training and low accuracy on these tasks. We mitigated theses problems by initializing the recurrent weight matrices with the identity matrix scaled by a factor (0.5) and using the Rectified Linear Unit (ReLU) activation function as proposed in [12]. For the SNNs, weights and biases are initialized from a uniform distribution $U(-k^{-1/2}, k^{-1/2})$, with k being the input size of the layer. The time constants

α and β are learnable parameters per neuron and initialized at 0.9. During training, they are clipped between 0 and 1 to avoid unstable behaviors. The spiking threshold v_{th} is set to 1. The input currents i and membrane potentials v are clipped during training as we observe it improves the accuracy. As the spiking activation function is not differentiable, we define a surrogate gradient using a piece-wise linear triangular function [15].

4.2 Results and Discussion

Table 1 shows the average accuracy of the SNN and ANN models on the three datasets with the 1×128 and 2×128 topologies. We compare our results with previous works on recurrent SNNs on these datasets (except for DASDIGITS for which we are not aware of other works using similar settings). For all three tasks, the GRU achieves the best accuracy, except with the 2-layer topology for SSC and SHD where it is similar to the RNN and Cuba-LIF, respectively. However, these tasks may be too easy for the GRU. Indeed, the accuracy is not significantly increased from the 1-layer to the 2-layer topology for DASDIGITS and SHD compared to spiking models. Moreover, for the SSC task, the GRU shows a high level of overfitting, which is not entirely solved by the addition of spike jitter accross input channels. We observe that the RNN trained with the special settings described in the previous section has similar accuracy than the GRU on the DASDIGITS and SSC tasks. However, this RNN does not reach a satisfactory average accuracy on the SHD task, partly due to an unstable training, as shown by the large confidence interval. It is interesting to note that spiking RNNs (LIF and Cuba-LIF) do not present such training instability. This may be due to the self recurrence of spiking neurons that is weighted by a time constant with value close to (but lower than) 1, which may help preventing gradient vanishing.

Comparing SNN models, we observe that the accuracy of the LIF is below the Cuba-LIF on all tasks, up to a 8.4% difference on the SSC task with the 1-layer topology. The 2-layer Cuba-LIF yields 85.5% accuracy on DASDIGITS, which is <1% below the accuracy of the 1-layer and 2-layer GRU. On SHD, the 2-layer Cuba-LIF achieves 87.8% accuracy, which is superior to the accuracy of the 1-layer and 2-layer GRU (86.8% and 87.3% resp.). For the more difficult SSC task, SpikGRU outperforms other spiking models for both topologies. Indeed, SpikGRU achieves 74.7% (resp. 77.0%) accuracy with 1-layer (resp. 2-layer) topology, which is only 0.8% (resp. 1.1%) below the best ANN accuracy. Moreover, all our spiking models show higher accuracy on the SHD task than the Adapt-LIF in [22], for the same topology and number of timesteps. However, they use strictly binary inputs, meaning that if there is more than one spike in the time bin it is considered as 1. On the other hand, we directly used the spike count. Indeed, the average input sparsity measured on the testset is only increased from 4.6% to 4.7% (resp. 4.7% to 4.8%) spikes per neuron per timestep on SHD (resp. SSC) for a pre-processing 250 Hz. Therefore, the additional energy consumption is small while the model accuracy is increased as no spikes are lost. Note that, on SHD and SSC, for a pre-processing with high frequency (such as

Table 1. Testing accuracy (%) of the spiking (LIF, Cuba-LIF, SpikGRU) and non-spiking (RNN, GRU) models on the DASDIGITS, SHD and SSC datasets, shown with the 95% confidence interval. The best accuracy for each topology for spiking and non-spiking models is highlighted. Results from related works are also indicated.

	DASDIGITS	SHD	SSC
1 × 128 network			
GRU	**85.9** ± 1.4	**86.8** ± 1.2	**75.5** ± 0.2
RNN	85.8 ± 1.4	74.9 ± 3.1	75.3 ± 0.7
LIF	78.3 ± 1.9	80.6 ± 2.0	63.1 ± 0.8
Cuba-LIF	81.1 ± 1.1	**83.7** ± 1.3	71.5 ± 0.4
SpikGRU	**81.8** ± 1.1	**83.7** ± 1.5	**74.7**± 0.4
Adapt-LIF * [22]	–	79.4	–
Cuba-LIF† [6]	–	71.4	50.9
Cuba-LIF† [17]	–	82.7	60.1
2 × 128 network			
GRU	**86.2** ± 1.3	**87.3** ± 0.9	77.9 ± 0.3
RNN	84.9 ± 1.4	75.0 ± 7.3	**78.1** ± 0.3
LIF	82.7 ± 0.8	85.8 ± 1.7	70.3 ± 1.3
Cuba-LIF	**85.5** ± 0.9	**87.8** ± 1.1	75.7 ± 0.2
SpikGRU	83.3 ± 1.7	86.4 ± 1.8	**77.0** ± 0.4
Adapt-LIF * [22]	–	84.4	–
Adapt-LIF [23]	–	87.8	74.2‡

* Binary inputs. † 2000 Hz pre-processing. ‡ 2 × 400 network.

2000 Hz Hz), spike count and binary inputs are equivalent as there is never more than one spike per time bin. Our Cuba-LIF also achieves better accuracy than the Cuba-LIF from [6,17] on both the SHD and SSC datasets for the same topology. However, in [6,17], the pre-processing is set at 2000 Hz Hz which results in 2000 timesteps. The higher the number of timesteps, the higher the precision of the inputs, but also the higher the difficulty of the task. Indeed, it increases the sequence length, making it harder for recurrent units to retain relevant information. The lower accuracy of the Cuba-LIF in [6] can be explained by the fact that they use fixed time constants per layer [17]. The best results among the previous works with SNNs on SHD and SSC datasets are demonstrated in [23], also using 250 Hz pre-processing. For the same topology their Adapt-LIF network shows the same accuracy (87.8%) as our Cuba-LIF on SHD. However, in the SSC task, even with a larger topology (2 × 400), the accuracy of their Adapt-LIF (74.2%) is lower than the accuracy of our 2-layer Cuba-LIF (75.7%) and SpikGRU (77.0%).

5   Energy-Efficiency

In this section, we compare the energy-efficiency of the previously presented models based on the total effective number of MAC and AC operations. We did not translate the MAC and AC operations into their respective energy consumption because most of the energy consumption of neural networks in specialized architectures comes from memory accesses associated with arithmetic operations rather than from the arithmetic operations themselves [10]. However, memory accesses cannot be predicted only based on the number of arithmetic operations, as they also depends on data reuse and sparsity exploitation, which are highly architecture-dependent [21]. Therefore, in the interests of comparing the different neuron models, we have ignored the energy associated with memory accesses, and have used the number of MAC and AC operations as a figure of merit for energy efficiency.

Spiking models exhibit a high sparsity. On the given tasks, our spiking models produce on average between 0.06 and 0.21 spikes per neuron per timestep for processing one sample. The 2-layer Cuba-LIF yields 0.06 spikes per neuron per timestep on DASDIGITS and SSC, which means that a neuron produces on average only 15 spikes during the 250 timesteps (or 1 spike every 17 timesteps). Similarly, the 2-layer SpikGRU achieves 0.09 spikes per neuron per timestep on SSC. Therefore, the number of operations per sample is highly reduced compared to an ANN where operations are performed at each timestep. Table 2 indicates the number of MAC and AC operations per timestep of one layer of the ANN and SNN models to process a sample. We observe that in ANN models (GRU and RNN) there are mainly MAC operations (except for the bias of neurons), while in SNN there are mainly AC operations (and some element-wise multiplications). In SNN models, the number of AC is weighted by the activity rate (spikes per neuron per timestep) of the SNN layers, which decreases (resp. increases) the number of operations if it is inferior (resp. superior) to 1, compared to an ANN. Note that the Cuba-LIF has similar number of operations than the LIF. Indeed, the input current variable represents only additional MACs at the neuron level, which is negligible compared to the operations in the feedforward and recurrent synaptic connections. On the other hand, the SpikGRU model increases significantly the number of operations compared to LIF and Cuba-LIF due to the additional feedforward and recurrent synaptic connections.

Figure 3 shows the accuracy vs. total effective number of operations (MAC + AC) per timestep of SNN and ANN models on the three datasets. The number of operations in the 2-layer Cuba-LIF is decreased by 16x compared to the 1-layer GRU while the models have similar accuracy on DASDIGITS. On SHD, the 2-layer Cuba-LIF even slightly outperforms the 1-layer and 2-layer GRU while reducing by 37x and 49x (resp.) the number of operations. On SSC, the number of operations in the 2-layer SpikGRU is reduced by 8x (resp. 24x) while the model yields an accuracy only ≈1% below the accuracy of the 2-layer RNN (resp. GRU). Compared to the Cuba-LIF on SSC, the SpikGRU model shows better accuracy but at the expense of 2x the number of operations. Our models are compared with the Adapt-LIF from [23] using the number of MAC and AC operations provided in their paper. Our most accurate 2-layer spiking models are more energy-efficient than the Adapt-LIF. Indeed, the number of operations per timestep is 8.6k (Cuba-LIF) vs. 11.5k for the SHD task, and 17.6k (SpikGRU) vs. 28.5k for SSC.

Table 2. Number of MAC and AC operations per timestep per sample for one layer of the ANN and SNN models. m and n are respectively input and output size of the layer. For SNN models, a_{in} and a_{out} are respectively input and output activity rate (spikes per neuron per timestep) of the layer.

Model	Nb MAC	Nb AC
GRU	$3mn + 3n^2 + 3n$	$3n$
RNN	$mn + n^2$	n
LIF	n	$mn * a_{in} + (n^2 + n) * a_{out} + n$
Cuba-LIF	$3n$	$mn * a_{in} + (n^2 + n) * a_{out} + n$
SpikGRU	$3n$	$2mn * a_{in} + (2n^2 + n) * a_{out} + 2n$

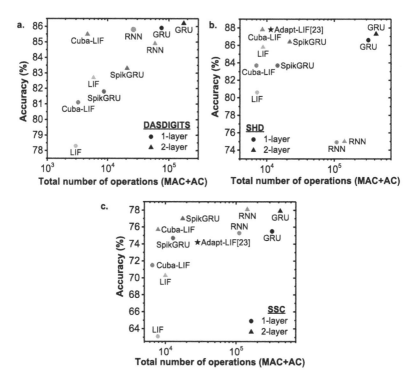

Fig. 3. Accuracy vs. total number of operations (MAC + AC) per timestep for processing one sample from the (a) DASDIGITS, (b) SHD and (c) SSC datasets.

6   Conclusion and Perspectives

Our experiments on the DASDIGITS, SHD and SSC datasets demonstrate the ability of recurrent SNNs to perform classification on sequential data with high energy-efficiency. The number of operations in the Cuba-LIF and proposed Spik-GRU models is reduced by up to 49x and 24x (resp.) compared to the GRU, for almost the same accuracy (<1.1% below). Moreover, we demonstrate that the Cuba-LIF model outperforms the LIF model, as it achieves better accuracy for approximately the same number of operations. In addition, the Cuba-LIF may also outperform the Adapt-LIF model for these tasks. Indeed, the Cuba-LIF achieved better accuracy than the Adapt-LIF from previous works, for a similar model complexity. Moreover, our proposed SpikGRU model shows a high potential to outperform non-gated recurrent SNNs on more difficult tasks, at the expense of an increased number of operations. However, this must be further investigated. Indeed, we studied tasks with different degrees of difficulty, due to the input size and number of classes, but we must also evaluate its ability to retain longer-term dependencies than the Cuba-LIF using tasks with different temporal sequence length. Besides, our results show that the number of operations in SNNs is highly dependent on their spiking activity. However, in our work, we did not specifically tune the spiking activity of the SNN models. Therefore, methods to boost sparsity in SNNs will result in further energy savings.

Acknowledgements. This work has been partially supported by MIAI @ Grenoble Alpes, (ANR-19-P3IA-0003).

References

1. Abbott, L.: Lapicque's introduction of the integrate-and-fire model neuron (1907). Brain Res. Bullet. **50**(5), 303–304 (1999). https://doi.org/10.1016/S0361-9230(99)00161-6
2. Anumula, J., Neil, D., Delbruck, T., Liu, S.C.: Feature representations for neuromorphic audio spike streams. Front. Neurosci. **12** (2018). https://doi.org/10.3389/fnins.2018.00023
3. Bellec, G., Salaj, D., Subramoney, A., Legenstein, R.A., Maass, W.: Long short-term memory and learning-to-learn in networks of spiking neurons. In: Advances in Neural Information Processing Systems: NeurIPS, pp. 795–805 (2018)
4. Bengio, Y., Simard, P., Frasconi, P.: Learning long-term dependencies with gradient descent is difficult. IEEE Trans. Neural Netw. **5**(2), 157–166 (1994). https://doi.org/10.1109/72.279181
5. Cho, K., et al.: Learning phrase representations using RNN encoder-decoder for statistical machine translation. In: Proceedings of the 2014 Conference on Empirical Methods in Natural Language Processing (EMNLP), pp. 1724–1734. Association for Computational Linguistics, Doha (2014). https://doi.org/10.3115/v1/D14-1179
6. Cramer, B., Stradmann, Y., Schemmel, J., Zenke, F.: The Heidelberg spiking data sets for the systematic evaluation of spiking neural networks. IEEE Trans. Neural Netw. Learn. Syst. 1–14 (2020). https://doi.org/10.1109/TNNLS.2020.3044364
7. Davies, M., et al.: Loihi: a neuromorphic manycore processor with on-chip learning. IEEE Micro **38**(1), 82–99 (2018). https://doi.org/10.1109/MM.2018.112130359
8. Han, B., Srinivasan, G., Roy, K.: RMP-SNN: residual membrane potential neuron for enabling deeper high-accuracy and low-latency spiking neural network. In: 2020 IEEE/CVF Conference on Computer Vision and Pattern Recognition (CVPR), pp. 13555–13564 (2020). https://doi.org/10.1109/CVPR42600.2020.01357

9. Hochreiter, S., Schmidhuber, J.: Long short-term memory. Neural Comput. **9**(8), 1735–1780 (1997). https://doi.org/10.1162/neco.1997.9.8.1735

10. Horowitz, M.: Computing's energy problem (and what we can do about it). In: 2014 IEEE International Solid-State Circuits Conference Digest of Technical Papers (ISSCC), pp. 10–14 (2014). https://doi.org/10.1109/ISSCC.2014.6757323

11. Kingma, D.P., Ba, J.: Adam: a method for stochastic optimization. arXiv preprint arxiv:1412.6980 (2014)

12. Le, Q.V., Jaitly, N., Hinton, G.E.: A simple way to initialize recurrent networks of rectified linear units. arXiv preprint arXiv:1504.00941 (2015)

13. Lichtsteiner, P., Posch, C., Delbruck, T.: A 128× 128 120 db 15 μs latency asynchronous temporal contrast vision sensor. IEEE J. Solid-State Circuits **43**(2), 566–576 (2008). https://doi.org/10.1109/JSSC.2007.914337

14. Lotfi Rezaabad, A., Vishwanath, S.: Long short-term memory spiking networks and their applications. In: International Conference on Neuromorphic Systems 2020, pp. 1–9. ACM (2020). https://doi.org/10.1145/3407197.3407211

15. Neftci, E., Mostafa, H., Zenke, F.: Surrogate gradient learning in spiking neural networks: bringing the power of gradient-based optimization to spiking neural networks. IEEE Signal Process. Magaz. **36**, 51–63 (2019). https://doi.org/10.1109/MSP.2019.2931595

16. Pan, Z., Chua, Y., Wu, J., Zhang, M., Li, H., Ambikairajah, E.: An efficient and perceptually motivated auditory neural encoding and decoding algorithm for spiking neural networks. Front. Neurosci. **13** (2020). https://doi.org/10.3389/fnins.2019.01420

17. Perez-Nieves, N., Leung, V.C.H., Dragotti, P.L., Goodman, D.F.M.: Neural heterogeneity promotes robust learning. Nature Commun. **12**(1), 5791 (2021). https://doi.org/10.1038/s41467-021-26022-3

18. Ponghiran, W., Roy, K.: Hybrid analog-spiking long short-term memory for energy efficient computing on edge devices. In: 2021 Design, Automation & Test in Europe Conference & Exhibition (DATE), pp. 581–586 (2021). https://doi.org/10.23919/DATE51398.2021.9473953

19. Ravanelli, M., Brakel, P., Omologo, M., Bengio, Y.: Light gated recurrent units for speech recognition. IEEE Trans. Emerg. Topics Comput. Intell. **2**(2), 92–102 (2018). https://doi.org/10.1109/TETCI.2017.2762739

20. Shrestha, A., et al.: A spike-based long short-term memory on a neurosynaptic processor. In: 2017 IEEE/ACM International Conference on Computer-Aided Design (ICCAD), pp. 631–637 (2017). https://doi.org/10.1109/ICCAD.2017.8203836

21. Sze, V., Chen, Y.H., Yang, T.J., Emer, J.S.: Efficient processing of deep neural networks: a tutorial and survey. Proc. IEEE **105**(12), 2295–2329 (2017). https://doi.org/10.1109/JPROC.2017.2761740

22. Yin, B., Corradi, F., Bohté, S.M.: Effective and efficient computation with multiple-timescale spiking recurrent neural networks. In: International Conference on Neuromorphic Systems 2020, pp. 1–8. ACM (2020). https://doi.org/10.1145/3407197.3407225

23. Yin, B., Corradi, F., Bohté, S.M.: Accurate and efficient time-domain classification with adaptive spiking recurrent neural networks. Nat. Mach. Intell. **3**(10), 905–913 (2021). https://doi.org/10.1038/s42256-021-00397-w

Research on USV Path Planning Method Based on Improved Option-Critical Algorithm

Jian Gao, Dawei Zhao[✉], and Xiaogong Lin

College of Intelligent Systems Science and Engineering, Harbin Engineering University,
Harbin 150001, China
daweizhao@hrbeu.edu.cn

Abstract. In hierarchical reinforcement learning, time abstraction is the key to enhance the learning ability and planning ability of agents. Option-Critic provides a framework for defining action plans with time abstraction ability. In the past ten years, autonomous learning time abstraction has been widely studied by scholars. The algorithm has the advantages of flexibility and efficiency, and has achieved good results in the classic four room navigation task and yadali game. However, option-critic still has the disadvantage of converging to a single action. At the same time, there is a big gap between the four room navigation task environment and the water surface environment during Unmanned Surface Vehicle (USV) navigation. In order to apply the option-critic framework to the path planning task of USV, this paper improves it, and changes the neural network of the feature extractor into a recurrent neural network. The network input is the action state sequence of unmanned craft, in order to extract as many environmental state features as possible. Through simulation experiments, the feasibility and effectiveness of the algorithm to realize route planning are tested in a more complex unknown map environment.

Keywords: Path planning · Reinforcement learning · Option-critic · Recurrent neural network

1 Introduction

Path planning capability is a core function of autonomous surface unmanned vehicle, which refers to the process of USV moving from the current position to the target position without collision [1]. Traditional algorithms usually need high-precision sensors to provide environmental information or artificially design rules through expert experience [2], which is difficult to apply to USV path planning tasks in complex and unknown environments [3]. Different from the traditional algorithm, the reinforcement learning method not only avoids the dependence on the environment map and expert experience, but also has strong adaptive ability [4] by learning the action strategy interactively with the environment [5].

In recent years, deep reinforcement learning has made great progress. We can use the powerful function fitting ability of deep learning to learn the complex mapping relationship between environmental state and control action, so as to obtain better strategies

© The Author(s), under exclusive license to Springer Nature Switzerland AG 2022
E. Pimenidis et al. (Eds.): ICANN 2022, LNCS 13531, pp. 371–381, 2022.
https://doi.org/10.1007/978-3-031-15934-3_31

However, for the complex unknown environment and the increase of map size, the existing reinforcement learning algorithms still can not well achieve the task of path planning. Therefore, the application of hierarchical reinforcement learning in path planning has become a research hotspot in this field [6]. The main idea of hierarchical reinforcement learning is to decompose the task to be solved into multiple subtasks, and then solve the whole task by solving the subtasks respectively. Its representative methods include Option [7] proposed by Sutton, HAM [8] proposed by Parr and MAXQ [9] proposed by Dieterich. Among the above three methods, the option framework proposed by Sutton can not only reduce the complexity of state representation and improve the training speed, but also realize experience migration by reusing the abstract action strategy option [10] and improve the generalization ability of the algorithm.

The algorithm based on option framework is good at solving tasks with large state scale, while the actor critic algorithm based on policy gradient has the advantage of direct learning strategy. The option critic (OC) combining them was proposed by Bacon et al. [11] in 2016. It is not so much a reinforcement learning algorithm as a framework. It is based on the option framework and combined with the policy gradient to realize the time abstraction of actions. Only by specifying the number of options, you can learn the corresponding intra option policy with a framework similar to actor critic. In order to solve the problem that option may degenerate into basic action in the later stage of end-to-end learning of OC, Harb et al. Proposed the improved framework A2OC [12] of OC in 2017, and formed a parallel algorithm similar to A3C based on this framework.

This paper proposes an improved option critic algorithm. The input of the network is not a single state, but a sequence (macro action) with a certain length composed of state, action and reward. Because the neural network considers the environmental interaction history in a certain period of time, it considers the previous series of action states as a state, which is helpful for the neural network to recognize the pattern of continuous action sequence (macro action). Therefore, improving actor network and critical network under option critic framework will consider macro actions rather than isolated single actions. We can see from the simulation experiment that the improved option critic algorithm has obvious advantages over the option critic algorithm based on fully connected network, with small average steps, high average reward, high success rate, shorter and smoother planned path. This shows that the algorithm can reach the target faster, and can achieve better results when the training times are less. The improved network has achieved the expected goal.

2   Materials and Methods

2.1   Option-Critic Algorithm

First, briefly introduce the option critic algorithm. OC assumes that all States can select all options: $\forall s \in S, \forall \omega \in \Omega : s \in I_\omega$ where $I_\omega \subseteq S$ is the initial state set of options. In addition, OC does not learn explicit high-level strategies, but only focuses on learning the termination conditions of low-level strategies and options. The following is a further description of the option critic framework and the concept of option:

1) Option Critic Framework

At present, the focus of option based hierarchical reinforcement learning is to search task sub goals, and then learn how to achieve these sub goals. However, the cost of learning strategies related to sub goals in data use and training time will also be very huge. For this reason, the option critic method is proposed, which blurs the boundary between different option problems in machine learning option. According to the strategy gradient theorem [13], people can also draw new conclusions. It is this result that the neural network can gradually learn the underlying strategy and termination function, and implement the strategy at the same time. In discrete or continuous state and action space, this method can work naturally with linear or nonlinear function approximators.

2) Option

Option and strategy gradient method are the core of the algorithm: the underlying strategy and the gradient theorem of termination function. Different from other methods, option critic only needs to specify the number of options required, without sub goals and additional rewards. This is an end-to-end method of learning option, which can be efficiently extended to a wider field. To put it bluntly, option is the underlying strategy. The high-level strategy makes decisions and selects an option: $\omega \in \Omega$, which contains two parts: 1 Action strategy of option: $\pi_\omega(a|s)$, 2 Termination function of option: $\beta_\omega(s) \to \{0, 1\}$.

When the termination function returns 0, the next action will be determined by the current option; When the termination function returns 1, the policy executed by the option ends temporarily and the control of the action is returned to the high-level policy. We use the action strategy and termination function of each option to represent the neural network (function approximator) with parameters, i.e. $\pi_{\omega,\theta}(a|s)$ And $\beta_{\omega,\upsilon}(s)$. Only these options are not enough to form a complete strategy. We also need high-level strategies to choose between these options. $\pi_\Omega(\omega|s)$ Indicates the probability of selecting optio ω in state S. With these concepts, the goal of the algorithm is to learn options end-to-end, instead of manually dividing the underlying strategies like expert learning. The structure of the option critic framework is shown in Fig. 1.

As shown in Fig. 2, a deep neural network is used to approximate the state action value function and represent the underlying strategy and termination function. The calculation adopts the first three convolution layers proposed by mnih et al. [14] in 2013, which are the same as the network: the first level uses 32 8*8, a convolution filter with a step size of 4; The second level uses 64 4*4 high pass filter with step size of 2; The third layer uses sixty-four 3*3 high pass filter with step size of 1. Then, the output of the third layer is input into the dense shared layer composed of 512 neurons. Finally, the underlying strategy is expressed as the linear softmax of the fourth layer to output the action output probability distribution based on the current state. The termination function uses the sigmoid function, and each option has an output neuron. The empirical playback mechanism is used to train the critic network and update the network parameters online. In order to ensure a certain exploration ability, the green strategy is used as the high-level output strategy [15].

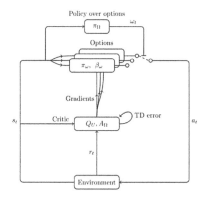

Fig. 1. Option critic framework structure

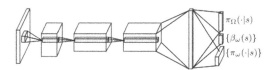

Fig. 2. Network structure of option critic framework

2.2 Option-Critc Framework Based on RNN

The improvement of the option critic framework is mainly the feature extraction of the environment state. We will use RNN to replace the fully connected network. At the same time, this paper focuses on the learning of the underlying strategy and terminal value function. Too many options are not conducive to training, and will interfere with the judgment of the high-level strategy. Therefore, the number of options is set to 4 for simulation. Now we have the basic structure of the option critic framework. On this basis, we can define various value functions to construct the option based semi Markov theoretical framework.

On this basis, we can define various value functions to construct the option based semi Markov theoretical framework. It is similar to the ordinary Markov decision process, except that the state s is changed to option. Sutton gave the Behrman equation under the option framework in his paper [16] in 1999, which is highly unified with the Behrman equation in general MDP in mathematical form. This shows that option based MDP becomes a semi Markov decision process (SMDP), which has the corresponding optimal value function in Eq. (1) and Eq. (4). MDP learning and planning algorithms have corresponding algorithms in this case. The existence of option provides the possibility of learning a variety of different options in parallel: This is the underlying strategy. As for the high-level strategy, it is more reflected by switching different options through the termination function. The definitions of three core concepts under the option framework are given below. The cumulative reward expectation generated by selecting option in status s is defined as:

$$Q_\Omega(s, \omega) = \sum_a \pi_{\omega,\theta}(a|s) Q_U(s, \omega, a) \tag{1}$$

When option ω is selected in status s, the cumulative reward expectation generated by taking action a is defined as:

$$Q_U(s, \omega, a) = r(s, a) + \gamma \sum_{s'} P(s'|s, a) U(\omega, s') \qquad (2)$$

When option ω is selected, the cumulative reward expectation generated by reaching status s' is defined as:

$$U(\omega, s') = (1 - \beta_{\omega,\upsilon}(s')) Q_\Omega(s', \omega) + \beta_{\omega,\upsilon}(s') V_\Omega(s') \qquad (3)$$

$V_\Omega : S \to \mathbb{R}$ in Eq. (3) represents the value function of state s, and has:

$$V_\Omega(s') = \sum_{\omega'} \pi_\Omega(\omega'|s') Q_\Omega(s', \omega') \qquad (4)$$

Two important formulas can be obtained from the above equation.
   Intra option policy gradient formula:

$$\frac{\partial Q_\Omega(s_0, \omega_0)}{\partial \theta} = \sum_{s,\omega} \mu_\Omega(s, \omega, s_0, \omega_0) \sum_{a} \frac{\partial \pi_{\omega,\theta}(a|s)}{\partial \theta} Q_U(s, \omega, a) \qquad (5)$$

Termination gradient formula:

$$\frac{\partial U(\omega_0, s_1)}{\partial \upsilon} = -\sum_{s',\omega} \mu_\Omega(s', \omega|s_1, \omega_0) \frac{\partial \beta_{\omega,\vartheta}(s')}{\partial \upsilon} A_\Omega(s', \omega) \qquad (6)$$

With the above formula, then we can design the algorithm of surface unmanned boat path planning based on improved option critical framework.

3   Algorithm

3.1   Environment and Reward Design

Environment setting: we set the simulation environment as a 320*320 map, and the obstacle distribution of the map will be more complex, so as to test the effectiveness of the option. The main obstacles encountered during USV navigation are reefs, shoals, sunken ships, fishing reefs, etc. in the construction of the environment, larger obstacles can be designed based on the actual situation. Here we will add some complex obstacles that may make the network fall into local minima. The goal of unmanned craft is to find the best path to reach the target point. The state of the unmanned boat is defined as a triple (x, y, α), where x and y are the real-time coordinates of the unmanned boat in the simulation map, and α is the yaw angle between the unmanned boat and the target point. If the initial coordinate of the unmanned boat is (x_0, y_0), the actual heading angle is initialized to $\theta = \arctan(x_0, y_0)$. If the current coordinate is (x, y) and the target coordinate is (p, q), the calculation formula of the expected heading is β:

$$\beta = \arctan(x - p, y - q) - \arctan(x, y) \tag{7}$$

The actual heading angle θ of the unmanned boat changes with each action. If the corresponding direction angle of action a is a_θ, the update formula of θ is:

$$\theta_{new} = \theta_{old} + a_\theta \tag{8}$$

Yaw angle α is defined as:

$$\alpha = \beta - \theta \tag{9}$$

Steering angle $\Delta\theta$ is defined as:

$$\Delta\theta = \theta_{new} - \theta_{old} \tag{10}$$

Design of reward function: Although option is added, option training and updating parameters as the underlying strategy are not different from conventional actor critical. However, for different options, the Q value is not estimated by the same network, but an additional dimension with the number of options is added to the Q network to estimate the decision actions made by different options separately. In order to reduce the adverse impact of sparse reward, we further optimize the reward for unmanned boats. The interactive reward rules between unmanned boats and the environment are set as follows:

1. When the unmanned boat reaches the final target, reward + 100.
2. If the unmanned boat encounters obstacles or boundaries, reward - 2.
3. The distance between the unmanned boat and the target decreases (increases), and the reward is + 1 (- 1).
4. The smaller the yaw angle of the unmanned boat, the greater the reward. This is to encourage the unmanned boat to reduce the number of turns.
5. The smaller the steering angle of the unmanned boat, the greater the reward.

This is to encourage the unmanned boat to reduce the steering angle.

In order to meet the requirements of 4 and 5, we will take the cosine value of the corresponding angle as the reward.

When using the memory playback mechanism, we sum the rewards of the state sequence with a length of 8 as the reward of this macro action. Such a reward setting can allow the critic network to evaluate the quality of macro actions and enhance the network's ability to judge the quality of various action sequences.

3.2 Algorithm

The specific implementation steps of the surface unmanned boat path planning algorithm based on the improved option critical framework are as follows:

1. Initialize option critical network parameter θ, υ, training cycle counter count.
2. Initialize start state $s \leftarrow s_0$ and input sequence input.
3. Select an option ω according to the greedy policy.
4. Select action a according to the underlying strategy $\pi_{\omega,\theta}(a|s)$ and execute the action to obtain environmental feedback: next state s', immediate reward r, end signal done, collision signal collision.
5. Judge whether done is true. If yes, end the training and jump to 2.
6. Estimate the cumulative reward expectation generated by action a when option ω is selected in State s:

$$\delta \leftarrow r - Q_U(s, \omega, a) \tag{11}$$

$$\delta \leftarrow \delta + \gamma\left(1 - \beta_{\omega,\vartheta}(s')\right)Q_\Omega(s', \omega) + \gamma\beta_{\omega,\vartheta}(s') \max_{\overline{\omega}} Q_\Omega(s', \overline{\omega}) \tag{12}$$

$$Q_U(s, \omega, a) \leftarrow Q_U(s, \omega, a) + \alpha_\delta \delta \tag{13}$$

7. Use the $Q_U(s, \omega, a)$ calculated in the previous step to update the network parameters:

$$\theta \leftarrow \theta + \alpha_\theta \frac{\partial \log \pi_{\omega,\theta}(a|s)}{\partial \theta} Q_U(s, \omega, a) \tag{14}$$

$$\upsilon \leftarrow \upsilon - \alpha_\upsilon \frac{\partial \beta_{\omega,\upsilon}(s')}{\partial \upsilon}\left(Q_\Omega(s', \omega) - V_\Omega(s')\right) \tag{15}$$

8. Judge whether the output of the termination function is true. If so, select a new option ω' according to the greedy policy $\pi_\Omega(s')$.
9. The agent synchronizes the network value and target network parameters every 20 steps.
10. Judge whether collision is true. If yes, return to the previous state and jump to 3.
11. Judge whether the count reaches the maximum value, end the training or jump to 2.

4 Simulation Experiment

We will conduct simulation experiments on two different maps. Each map will be trained 2000 times, and the upper limit of each training is set as 500 steps. If more than 500 steps have not reached the final goal, it will be regarded as failure. The comparison indicators include average steps, average reward and success rate. The control group is the option critical algorithm constructed by fully connected neural network. The parameter settings of the simulation experiment are shown in Table 1 below:

Table 1. Simulation experiment parameter setting

Parameter	Value
Maximum Single Iteration Steps	500
Maximum Number of Iterations	2000
Initial Exploration Rate ε_0	0.9
Lower Limit of Exploration Rate ε_{min}	0.05
Decreasing Exploration Rate η	0.0005
Number of Options	4
$\pi_{\omega,\theta}(a\|s)$ Learning Rate α_θ	0.001
$\beta_{\omega,\upsilon}(s)$ Learning Rate α_υ	0.001
$Q_U(s,\omega,a)$ Learning Rate α_δ	0.001

The simulation environment is shown in Figure 3 and Figure 4 below. As before, the black rectangular block of the environment represents the obstacle, the red triangle represents the starting point, and the green Pentagram represents the target point. Train 2000 times and give the path planning trajectories of the two algorithms. The red trajectories represent the improved option critic algorithm and the blue trajectories represent the option critical algorithm.Figure 3 shows the final path trajectory of the two algorithms. The trajectory planned by the improved OC algorithm is more gentle, with a trajectory length of 2275.96 m. The trajectory planned by the option critical algorithm has more turns, with a trajectory length of 2308.51 m.Figure 4 shows that the trajectory length planned by the improved OC algorithm is 2172.55 m, and the trajectory planned by the option critical algorithm has more turns, and the trajectory length is 2184.02 m. Comparing the two simulation experiments, it can be seen that the improved OC algorithm is only slightly smaller than the option critical algorithm in path length, and has little

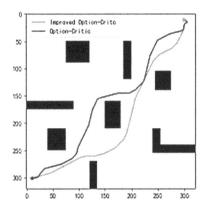

Fig. 3. Simulation Experiment 1

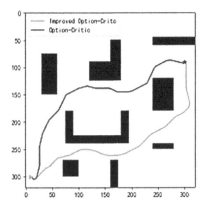

Fig. 4. Simulation Experiment 2

improvement in this index except that the trajectory is slightly gentle. Figures 5, 6, 7, 8, 9, 10 show the comparison index data of the two simulation experiments:

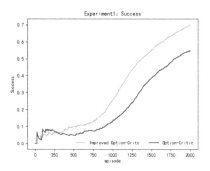

Fig. 5. Simulation Experiment 1 Success

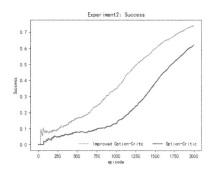

Fig. 6. Simulation Experiment 2 Success

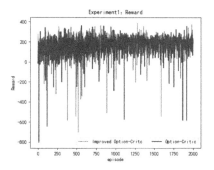

Fig. 7. Simulation Experiment 1 Reward

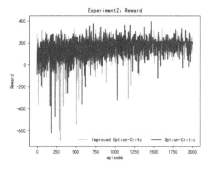

Fig. 8. Simulation Experiment 2 Reward

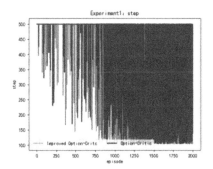

Fig. 9. Simulation Experiment 1 Step

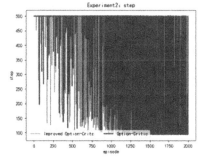

Fig. 10. Simulation Experiment 2 Step

Table 2 and Table 3 list the statistical data of the two simulation experiments:

Table 2. Simulation experiment 1

Simulation experiment 1	Improved option-critic algorithm	Option-critic algorithm
Average reward	176.03	159.84
Average step	368.38	399.81
Success	70.04	54.69
Path length	2275.96 m	2308.51 m
Turns	3	12

Table 3. Simulation experiment 2

Simulation experiment 2	Improved option-critic algorithm	Option-critic algorithm
Average reward	158.73	147.92
Average step	349.98	368.64
Success	74.01	62.04
Path length	2272.55 m	2184.02 m
Turns	4	11

5 Conclusion

It can be seen from the simulation data that the average reward of the improved OC algorithm is higher than that of the option critical algorithm; The average number of steps is small; The number of turns is less, the path is smoother, and the length of the path is closer; In simulation experiment 1, the success rate of the improved OC algorithm surpassed the option critical algorithm from act 500; In simulation experiment 2, the success rate of the improved OC algorithm surpassed the option critical algorithm from act 100; The success rate has obvious advantages. Compared with simulation experiment 2, the obstacles near the target point are more likely to block the route of the unmanned boat in simulation experiment 1, so the number of test failures is higher.

This paper proposes a path planning method based on improved option critical framework. The simulation experiment is carried out by using two maps with relatively complex obstacle distribution. Because the cyclic neural network is used as the state feature extractor of the whole network framework, different from the usual option critical network, the input of the network is a sequence composed of state, action and reward. The improved option critical algorithm uses cyclic neural network to obtain the historical information of environmental state, and improves the selection ability of high-level decision network for option. We can see from the simulation experiment that this algorithm has better effect than the option critical algorithm based on fully connected neural network, with smoother path, small average steps, high average reward and high success rate. This shows that the improved network can better the path planning task, and the network performance is improved.

References

1. Jiang, H.G., Wang, H., Yau, W.Y., et al.: A brief survey: deep reinforcement learning in mobile robot navigation. In: Proceedings of the IEEE Conference on Industrial Electronics and Applications. Kristiansand: IEEE, pp. 592–597 (2020)
2. Quan, H., Li, Y.S., Zhang, Y.: A novel mobile robot navigation method based on deep reinforcement learning. Int. J. Advanced Robotic Syst. **17**(3), 1729881420921672 (2020)
3. Sun, H.H., Hu, C.H., Zhang, J.G.: Mobile robot motion planning Deep reinforcement learning method. Control and decision making, **36**(6), 1281–1292 (2021)
4. Xiao, X.S., Liu, B., Warnell, G., et al.: Motion Control for Mobile Robot Navigation Using Machine Learning: A Survey. arXiv: 2011.13112 (2020)
5. Fan, T., Long, P., Liu, W., et al.: Distributed multi-robot collision avoidance via deep reinforcement learning for navigation in complex scenarios. Int. J. Robotics Res. **39**(7), 856–892 (2020)
6. Zhou, W.J., Yu, Y.: Summarize of hierarchical reinforcement learning. CAAI Trans. Intelligent Syst. **12**(5), 590–594 (2017)
7. Sutton, R.S., Precup, D., Singh, S.: Between MDPs and semi-MDPs: a framework for temporal abstraction in reinforcement learning. Artif. Intell. **112**(1), 181–211 (1999)
8. Parr, R., Russell, S.: Reinforcement learning with hierarchies of machines. Adv. Neural Inf. Process. Syst. 1043–1049 (1998)
9. Dietterich, T.G.: The MAXQ method for hierarchical reinforcement learning. In: Proceedings of the 15th International Conference on Machine Learning. Morgan Kaufmann, San Francisco, pp. 118–126 (1998)
10. Konidaris, G., Barto, A.G.: Building portable options: skill transfer in reinforcement learning. In: Proceedings of 20th International Joint Conference on Artificial Intelligence, USA: IJCAI, pp. 895–900 (2007)
11. Bacon, P.L., Harb, J., Precup, D.: The Option-Critic Architecture (2016)
12. Harb, J., Bacon, P.L., Klissarov, M., et al.: When Waiting is not an Option : Learning Options with a Deliberation Cost (2017)
13. Sutton, R.S., McAllester, D.A., Singh, S.P., Mansour, Y.: Policy gradient methods for reinforcement learning with function approximation. In NIPS **12**, 1057–1063 (2000)
14. Mnih, V., et al.: Playing Atari with Deep Reinforcement Learning. CoRR abs/1312.5602 (2013)
15. Mnih, V., et al.: Asynchronous methods for deep reinforcement learning. In: ICML (2016)
16. Sutton, R.S., Precup, D., Singh, S.: Between MDPs and semi-MDPs: a framework for temporal abstraction in reinforcement learning – ScienceDirect. Artificial Intell. **112**(1–2), 181–211 (1999)

Bi-level Optimization Method for Automatic Reward Shaping of Reinforcement Learning

Ludi Wang, Zhaolei Wang$^{(\boxtimes)}$, and Qinghai Gong

Beijing Aerospace Automatic Control Institute, Beijing 100854, China
`beiliwzl123@163.com`

Abstract. The key to lowering the threshold of the application of reinforcement learning is the simplicity and convenience of reward function design. At present, reinforcement learning with good performance mostly adopts complex rewards of artificial trial and error, or adopts supervised learning to track the artificial trajectory, but these methods increase the workload. Assuming that the basic mathematical elements (operators, operands) can be used to automatically accomplish the combinatorial search process, it is possible to search for a compact, concise and informative reward model. Starting from this idea, this paper explores the reward function of reinforcement learning, which can find the optimal or suboptimal solution that can meet the multi-optimization index through operator search without clear prior knowledge. Based on AutoML-zero, the automatic search method of operator-level reward function based on evolutionary search is realized, and the reward function algorithm which can satisfy the constraint conditions is found to be equal to or better than human design.

Keywords: Credit assignment · Reward shaping · AutoML-zero · Evolutionary search

1 Introduction

Research in numerous domains is now focusing on deep reinforcement learning (DRL), which has recently demonstrated tremendous capabilities, and various value-based and policy-based algorithms have constantly appeared in recent years. Despite this, reinforcement learning (RL) hasn't been used as much as deep learning in imaging. For control problems with multiple optimization indicators, it is difficult to find a reasonable mathematical formula to describe the reward only through manual experience, which raises the threshold for the application of RL. The root cause of this is the rapidly changing control environment, which makes it difficult to set the reward function.

The reward design is a significant aspect in the RL training process. Literature [1] demonstrates through trials that training DDPG directly with sparse rewards has an effect comparable to that of a random method, whereas extrinsic reward shaping considerably

---

This work is supported by the National Natural Science Foundation of China under Grant U21B2028.

improves the training effect. Reasonable reward shaping is critical because the shape and amount of information contained in the shaping have an effect on the agent's exploration process and hence on the convergence process. However, reward shaping is not something that can be accomplished immediately and requires careful consideration. Even before the advent of DRL, an abundance of research was conducted on effective reward shaping. Wu Enda proved that shaping with potential function is of convergence consistency with the original problem [2]. Literature [4] proposed a more complex reward function for enhancing the robustness and learning efficiency of robotic arm trajectory planning in an unknown environment, by incorporating Coulomb's law to model the relationship between the robotic arm and obstacles and target points, which requires incorporating a great deal of prior knowledge.

However, the rewards of manual trial and error frequently suffer from the following four issues: To begin, unreasonable design result in "shaping bug." Manual designed rewards may change the original problem. The optimal strategy after shaping is no longer the optimal solution to the original problem. Literature [2] details numerous instances of "shaping bugs." Second, the architecture predisposes the training to local optimality, and some rewards provide insufficient guidance to the agents, causing them to converge on the laziest local optimal solution. Third, the form of reward shaping has a significant impact on the training process, and certain forms of reward shaping will lengthen the training period. Literature [3] contrasts the shape of a smooth and differentiable reward function to the shape of a non-differentiable reward function at both ends, concluding that the former will enable agent to learn a more precise and time-optimal strategy. Fourth, the amount of knowledge contained in the reward has an effect on the agent's exploration process. Reward settings with less a priori information demand a higher sampling efficiency for exploration, which add to the time complexity.

Based on the numerous difficulties associated with manual shaping incentives, it is critical to investigate an automated and simple way for reward shaping that minimizes the need for manual experience. Literature [5] developed a way for modeling immediate rewards (reward modeler) in order to accurately capture the trainer's intention and so obtain the required action. On the other hand, inverse reinforcement learning (IRL) in literature [6, 7] aims to inversely learn the reward from the MDP trajectory given by human experts (assumed to be optimal). However, some scholars argue that it is preferable to bypass the process of building the reward function and directly imitate the expert trajectory, which is referred to in the literature as the Imitation Learning (IL) such as GAIL [8]. GAIL use the generator in the GAN as the actor and the discriminator as the Critic to separate expert behavior from agent's behavior. As a reward, the generator uses the likelihood of the discriminator's output to finally create a policy that is as near to the expert policy as possible. It is an imitation under strong constraints, and to introduce some exploration, Literature [9] employs a generative adversarial approach to combine reinforcement and imitation learning in a weakly constrained manner, incorporating expert knowledge as prior knowledge, in order to train an unbiased model that is robust to suboptimal trajectories or noisy situations.

External reward shaping has never found an all-encompassing solution, thus researchers have concentrated on the agent's internal drive. Curiosity algorithm was initially proposed in 2017 literature [10]. It essentially improves the exploration and sampling efficiency of the agent, but does not give guidance to the agent according to the task distribution itself, so this does not mean that it has the same impact as direct external reward shaping. Reference [11] researches multi-agent's adaptive confrontation training process in game. For external reward shaping, it establishes a look-up table for 13 indicators of this game, and uses evolutionary search to find out their proportions for combination to form a simple reward. This shaping is obviously not universal. Recently, reference [12] tries to make single agent adaptively learn the task distribution based on meta-learning to learn an external reward shaping without introducing any expert experience. The prior knowledge of the task is learned from a set of similar tasks and continuously revised when the task model is unknown in advance. But it can be noticed that this training is offline and time-consuming.

Until now, it is difficult to motivate RL to achieve a good performance without human experience or expertise in the task. This paper designs a method of shaping rewards automatically according to the environment and gives reasonable mathematical expressions based on AutoML-zero. An evaluation standard is given to judge the convergence of the typical "goal-reaching" RL task in the field of motion control. Search method and search space were designed, and a variety of approaches to improve efficiency were designed, and finally achieved good results. As a result, the conclusion and future perspective are provided.

2 Algorithm Design

2.1 The Theoretical Basis and Problem Description of Reward Shaping

Any control problem which can be solved by RL can be abstracted as a Markov chain $M = (S, A, T, \gamma, r)$, where $S \in R^n$ describes the n-dimensional state space of the reinforcement learning problem, A describes the actions that the agent can take, and T is the transition probability from (s, a) to s', γ is the discount factor of the future expected cumulative return, r is the immediate reward of the current step, which is a function of s, a, s'. The purpose of reward shaping is to increase information which can be fed back to the agent at each step. It modifies the original reward function as $r'(s, a, s') = r(s, a, s') + f(s, a, s')$ (the original reward is mostly sparse in the natural environment) which changes the original problem $M = (S, A, \{P_{sa}\}, \gamma, r)$ to another $M' = (S, A, \{P_{sa}\}, \gamma, r')$.

The key to shaping is to make the optimal strategy under the new problem still applicable to the original problem to some extent, which requires careful design of f. Current shaping methods are usually based on the potential function $\Phi(s)$ of the current state, which can be proved that the obtained solution is policy invariant. But this is under the assumption that shaping with the potential function $f(s, a, s') = \gamma \Phi(s') - \Phi(s)$ is optimal. But in practice, although this shaping method has good mathematical properties, it cannot guarantee the maximum integration of state and action information so that DRL can converge the fastest and best. Therefore this paper abdicate the method of approximating $\Phi(s)$ but taking s,a,s' as input, and directly searching the part of $f(s, a, s')$ to explore more possibilities. f represents a mapping relationship, which can be characterized by complex or short mathematical formulas, and can be regarded as the tight immediate reward with guiding significance.

In this paper, bi-level optimization is used to find the optimal shaping f of the optimal policy under the original problem. The cumulative return of RL at each state is expressed as $R'_t = \sum_{i=t}^{T} \gamma^{(i-t)} r'_i(s_i, a_i, s'_i)$. In the inner loop, the training objective of RL is to maximize the cumulative shaped reward expectation while fixing the mapping f:

$$J = \mathrm{E}_{s,s' \sim \rho^\pi, r' \sim (\Xi, f), a \sim \pi^\theta} [R'_1] \tag{1}$$

where ρ^π represents the state-visiting distribution under policy π which is converged to according to the shaped reward, Ξ represents the environment, f represents the fixed mapping, and π^θ represents the parameterized policy (neural network), so the optimization goal of an inner-loop agent is:

$$J_{inner}(\pi_\theta | \omega \sim \Omega, f) = \mathrm{E}_{s,s' \sim \rho^\pi, r \sim \Xi, a \sim \pi^\theta} \sum_{t=0}^{T} [r(s, a, s') + f(s, a, s')] \tag{2}$$

where ω represents the hyperparameter and seed setting in RL (same for all agents).

The purpose of the outer loop is to find a reward-shaping mapping f that allows the agent to converge as less time-consuming as possible and maximize the cumulative return expectation under the original reward:

$$f = \arg\max_f \mathrm{E}_{r_i \sim E} \sum_{i=0}^{T} r_i \tag{3}$$

or other global goal:

$$f = \arg\max_f g(trans(s_1, a_1, r_1, s_2) : trans(s_T, a_T, r_T, s_{T+1})) \tag{4}$$

where $trans$ represents the state transitions at a certain time step, and g represents the mapping from all transitions in this episode to the global goal. Therefore, its optimization objective is:

$$J_{outer}(f | \pi^{\theta'}, \omega \sim \Omega) = \mathrm{E}_{s,s' \sim \rho^\pi, r \sim \Xi, a \sim \pi^{\theta'}} \sum_{t=0}^{T} r(s, a, s'), \theta' = \arg\max_\theta J_{inner}(\pi^\theta | \omega \sim \Omega) \tag{5}$$

where θ' represents the parameters of the trained policy of the last few episodes. The final bi-level optimization objective is as follows:

$$\max_f \mathrm{E}_{s,s' \sim \rho^\pi, r \sim \Xi, a \sim \pi^{\theta'}} \sum_{t=0}^{T} r(s, a, s')$$

$$s.t. f \in F$$

$$\theta' = \arg\max_\theta \mathrm{E}_{s,s' \sim \rho^\pi, r \sim \Xi, a \sim \pi^\theta} \sum_{t=0}^{T} [r(s, a, s') + f(s, a, s')]$$

$$s.t. \theta \in \Theta, \tag{6}$$

It can be seen that there is no explicit functional relationship between the mapping f and the cumulative return under the original reward. But there is an indirect dependency between them. f affects the final cumulative return by affecting the next-step strategy θ'.

2.2 Algorithm Design Based on AutoML_zero

In the absence of expert experience, this paper draws on the method of the mathematical elements' combination and searching in AutoML-zero to design the reward shaping of RL, so that the agent can explore the environment generation by generation in order to continuously extract the task characteristics or distributions. As a result, the shaping form is steadily optimized with the accumulation of RL agents' experience. Thereby, the optimal solution of reward shaping is approached.

This paper does not use the approach of neural network approximation, but directly applies mathematical formulas to represent rewards, because this can fully integrate the information of s, a, s' in a short formula, thereby enriching the expression of the mapping f. The reward function in RL is often concise and without loops, which indicates that search for such a simple formula won't be too time-consuming and is highly achievable. The entire mapping f can be represented as a directed acyclic graph (DAG) as follows (Fig. 1):

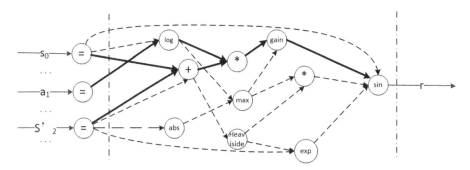

Fig. 1. Schematic diagram of reward shaping DAG algorithm

The dotted line in the figure represents all possible paths that can be connected from the starting point to the end point, and the solid line represents the final searched path.

Search Method. The complete search framework is established mathematically by a bi-layer optimization model with an inner and an outer loop. The outer loop keeps aknowledge base F of reward shaping formulas, and then uses an evolutionary learning method to perform genetic and mutation searches on the shaping algorithms contained within the knowledge base. At each iterative step, K shaping methods are selected from the knowledge base and are verified by RL procedure in the inner loop. The inner loop is composed of a huge population of RL agents that are responsible for evaluating the various shaping algorithms. Originally, the performance of each algorithm should be evaluated after the RL training is converged i.e. the final strategy θ' is approached and fixed. However, the goal of this paper is not only to find the optimal shaping that is consistent with the original problem, but also to require that the shaping leads the RL process to converge as quickly as possible. Therefore, the total number of episodes in one training process and the maximum training steps in one episode are restricted. After the RL agents in the inner loop submit their results to the outer loop, the outer loop will evaluate them. Finally, the shaping algorithms that possess the highest score will be mutated and slightly changed, and then added to the knowledge base for further evaluation and evolution.

The shaping-algorithms to be searched are divided into two modules, namely *Setup* and *Calculate*, with *Setup* accomplishing hyperparameter setup and *Calculate* providing the output of the mapping f at each time step, namely r′.

Original AutoML-0's search is random and not constrained by searching rules, which often leads to bad logic and interpretability of the searched algorithm. Some algorithm may even fail to use the three inputs s, a, $s′$ or doesn't give a result of r′. To improve the framework's usability and efficiency, this paper improves the shaping algorithm's initialization rules and mutation rules: 1) later sub-formulas' input can only come from the previous formulas' output (scalar or vector), and the first sub-formula's input can only come from the given state, action, and next state s, a, $s′$; 2) the last sub-formula is bound to output at r′ but not at other variables.

Search Space. In order to overcome the defect that AutoML_zero's search space is too large and the computation consumption is too high, this paper simplifies the search space and adapt it to cope with the task. RL task's state as input is often composed of different units, which have different specific physical meanings, such as position, velocity, angle, etc. In order to include the useful information for modeling and ignore the useless information, it's necessary to group the unit's elements according to their physical meanings together to operate the unit as a whole. In conclusion, new mathematical operators need to be designed.

In this paper, a rich operator library is designed to combine the information of different operands as sufficiently as possible, so as to express simple or complex mapping functions with fewer operations. Therefore, in addition to the common operators in basic mathematics, the operation of randomly setting the input vector to 0 by unit is added. Assuming that the input vector is n-dimensional, it can be divided into γ units according to the physical meaning, the number of elements in the unit is I, and the elements in the unit can only take 0 or 1 at the same time, then each unit obeys the Bernoulli distribution with probability p,

$$\Pr(unit_i = \underbrace{[1, 1, ..., 1]}_{I_i}) = p \quad \Pr(unit_i = \underbrace{[0, 0, ..., 0]}_{I_i}) = 1 - p$$

$$o = [unit_1, unit_2, ..., unit_\gamma]^n \circ vector^n \tag{7}$$

The coefficient's relative magnitudes of each component in the reward function is more important, so this paper adds three gain(γ) operators, and it can be expressed as:

$$gain(\gamma) = \gamma \bullet scalar, \gamma \in \{0.01, 0.1, 10\} \tag{8}$$

In this way, the coefficients are endowed once the multiplication operation is given, which speeds up the search efficiency.

3 Improvement of Search Efficiency

Because the compositions of the search space are mathematical operands and operators, the solution can be very sparse, the search of which consumes much time and computational power. In addition to the simplification of the search space and strategy, this paper also use other methods to improve the search efficiency to solve the problem in an all-around way.

Equivalence Test. In order to prevent repeatedly acquiring functionally duplicated algorithms even though they have different forms, an extra program which perceives the change of the algorithm's output at each time step is added. The first few episodes' immediate rewards, which are the outputs of the algorithm at each time step are encoded and stored. If the single-step rewards in the first few episodes of the current algorithm are exactly the same as the stored single-step rewards of one of the previous algorithms, the current algorithm is then considered to be a duplicate one, which is functionally equivalent to the previous algorithm and discarded. Or the algorithm itself has the same reward output at all time steps, it is considered an invalid algorithm and discarded.

Double-Layer Parallel Search. Because of the time complexity of discrete search, this paper designs hierarchical parallelism, which improves the computational efficiency by distributing the evaluation part in the outer loop and the RL part of the inner loop to different computing cores.

Validity Test. The framework always keeps top-n shaping algorithms with the best performing scores. And the algorithms which are currently being trained are compared with the top-n best performance algorithms once in a while. Once the performance verification inequality holds, the training process of this current algorithm is then pruned by giving it an ultra-low score like -10000 (so that it won't evolve next time) to save training resources. At the same time, the kept top-n algorithms are updated from time to time by better performing algorithms. The details are described in Sect. 4.1.

The final algorithm is as follows:

```
Algorithm train
      Input: one or a group of homologous task distribution p(T)
      Input: Various hyperparameters such as learning rate α
      Output: reward shaping mapping f
      Initialize the general knowledge base F, the first-level
workers for Evaluation and their sub knowledge base F'
      Set up a random seed;
      Each first-level worker:
      For evolutionary_iteration = 1, 2, 3, ⋯10000:
            Sampling a batch algorithms from F';
            Build up second-level RL workers for each algorithm;
```

```
            For each RL worker.
                5 epochs of training with different random seeds
                Compare the performance with top-n algorithms at
    end of each epoch. Prune it or update the top-n library.
                Evaluate the final performances of 5 epochs, and
    send it back to the relative first-level worker.
            End for
            Evaluate and compare the score of each RL submission
            Select the algorithm with the best performance for
    inheritance and mutation, and add it to F'
            Remove the oldest algorithm from F'
            If evolutionary_iteration satisfies the number of
    commits:
                Submit part of the best algorithms in F' to F in
    the central node.
                Replace half of F' with algorithms sampled with
    probability p from F
            End if
        End for
    Extract the top n algorithms from the knowledge base F for
    final testing and model bias verification to confirm their gen-
    eralization performance
```

4 Experiments

4.1 Experimental Setup

In order to verify the effect of the search architecture, the task scenario cannot be too simple, otherwise the problem can be solved easily by manual design. Therefore, this paper designs a special task, which takes the trajectory planning and guidance process of the aircraft as the learning object. The purpose of RL controller is to design a path and guide the aircraft to successfully reach the goal point without a given standard trajectory. The RL controller acts like a guidance system and needs to give accurate instructions online in real time to meet the requirement of speed, position accuracy and attitude error range when reaching the goal point. So that's a typical 'goal-reaching' problem with extreme sparse immediate reward.

The RL input is a six-dimensional state: position x_t, y_t, z_t, velocity v_{x_t}, v_{y_t}, v_{z_t}. The action space adopts thrust P, pitch angle φ and yaw Ψ angle. So the state space is 6-dimensional $S \subset \mathbb{R}^6$, the action space is 3-dimensional $A \subset \mathbb{R}^3$, and the actions are zero-padded to match the states' dimensions.

The search architecture and aircraft model are implemented in Python and tensorflow. This paper adopts DDPG as the basic framework of inner-loop RL agent, in order to better handle the RL task with high-dimensional continuous state and action space. And the actor and critic networks are also designed simple to accelerate training. Because the rewards which perform well on simple networks will perform better on complex and more effective networks.

For the goal-reaching RL problem, the goal state is crucial to evaluate the quality of training. The evaluation standard can be based on how far it is from the goal state when reaching the maximum episode time. In order to avoid that the RL which did not converge is only near a good result by chance, the evaluation index should comprehensively consider the mean and standard deviation of the errors in the last few episodes.

$$f = \arg\min_f \mathrm{E}_{episode}(\tilde{g}(trans1:T) - \mathrm{goal})^2 + \sigma_{episode}(\tilde{g}(trans1:T) - \mathrm{goal})^2,$$

where $\tilde{g}$ represents the mapping from the state transition to a certain global optimization index. To simplify the problem, this paper formulates an evaluation standard based on the difference between the end state and the goal state:

$$score = -(\underset{episode=N-10:N}{\mathrm{E}} \max|s_{done} - s_{t\,arg\,et}| + \underset{episode=N-10:N}{\sigma} \max|s_{done} - s_{t\,arg\,et}|)$$

$$(9)$$

where $\max|.|$ is in representation of the largest difference of all the differences between the 2 vectors' all corresponding elements, a kind of distance between 2 states.

As stated in Sect. 3, an early stop and pruning is made when compared with the top-n algorithms and the performance verification inequality (10) holds:

$$mean_{algorithm}(distance_{last\_episodes}) - std_{algorithm}(distance_{last\_episodes})$$
$$\geq mean_{top\_n\_algorithm}(distance_{last\_episodes}) + 2std_{top\_n\_algorithm} + \arg\max_l(std_{l \in N})$$

$$(10)$$

where $distance_{last\_episodes}$ means the distance from the end state to the goal state of the last few episodes, N means the set of the top-n algorithms, and l means one of the top-n algorithms. As can be seen, if the smallest distance of the current algorithm is still larger than the biggest of top-n, the algorithm is then considered performing badly. And not only the deviation between different episodes, but also the deviation between the top-n algorithms is taken into consideration.

In favor of simple and interpretable expressions, but at the same time keeping a large option range of operations, the *Setup* module of the algorithm is limited to maximum 5 operations, and the *Calculate* module is limited to 10 operations.

This paper distributes two-level workers on 72 cores of a high-functional CPU, which is implemented through process programming. Each out-loop worker processes a knowledge base with a population size of 1000. Each worker exchanges algorithms with the central knowledge base once after ten evolutionary iterations.

4.2   Analysis of Results

After just a few hours of searching, this article has found a series of algorithms that perform well on this task, including algorithms that are similar to and surpass human designs. This paper finds that the best shaping mappings are very compact.

Some of the algorithms found are shown in the following figure (Fig. 2):

```
Algorithm1:
al: score5.332971319543526
setup:
v2=[-0.06463651 -0.77783223 0.22624957 0.93382334 0.20984597 0.32576995
  -1.00973647 0.19575462 0.99489049] gaussian(0.3143484160072982 4, 0.7970048880633219)
s3=1.7085706078227116 gaussian(-0.5142142402776209, 0.8863456342121653)
v9=[0.    0.    0.    0.    0.99561990.    0.    0.    0.  ] v9(4) = 0.9956199002547215
s6=-0.3242572884039 3275 uniform(0.14905087137614115, -0.49080063360487514)
v5=[0.    0.    0.    0.    0.    0.    0.    0.85295999 0.  ] v5(7) = 0.8529599933102208
calculate:
v3(i) = |v2(i)| for all i vector abs
v6 = 1.0 / v0
v5 = v6-v1
s8 = v3 .* v1
v7 = maximum(v2, v2)
v2 = v3 * v2
v2(i) = |v7(i)| for all i  abs
s8 = 1/s8
v5(i) = (1)1.0 if v5(i)>0.0 (2)0.0 if v5(i)<=0.0  for all i
s0=std(v5)
```

```
Algorithm2:
al: score8.324
setup:
s6=-0.0265193528259 24658 uniform(-0.781, 0.049)
s6 = -0.262
s1=0.6807027714606229 gaussian(0.784, 0.776)
v2=[0.    0.    0.   -0.96547017 0.    0.    0.    0.    0.  ] v2(3) = -0.965
v4=[ 0.61410946 -0.30753851 0.48485271 0.05295281 -0.15294789 0.11646941
  -0.46753046 0.36332059 -0.40922401] uniform(-0.497, 0.633)
calculate:
s1 = min(s6, s6)
v6 = 1.0 / v0
s7=std(v6)
s0 = sin(s6)
s4=norm(v1)
v2(i) = (1)1.0 if v0(i)>0.0 (2)0.0 if v0(i)<=0.0  for all i
v3 = 1.0 / v0
v2 = v0 * s1
v6(i) = |v6(i)| for all i
s0 = ln(s7)
```

Fig. 2. Code example during the search process

The curve of the search process is as follows (Fig. 3):

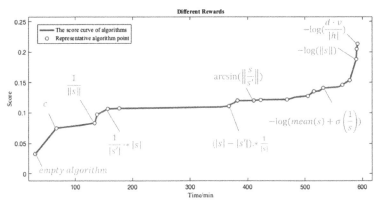

Fig. 3. The evolutionary search experiment process of reinforcement learning's reward function shaping

This graph selects the typical time when a better algorithm first appeared in the search process. In the figure, c represents a random constant, d represents distance, v represents speed, and h represents height. The ordinate score is the reciprocal of the original error. It is worth noting that while these algorithms are found, there are still a large number of invalid algorithms in progress. As can be seen from the figure, the search tends to find the more concise form, and it takes a long time in the early stage. There are several points worth noting: 1) The first three effective algorithms are close to the form designed by humans; 2) The first significant algorithm with a greater improvement is the *arcsin* form, presumably because it plays a normalizing role; 3) The other is that after the logarithm form appears, the score has risen sharply, proving that the log form is very suitable for the goal-reaching problem; 4) In the last form, the shaping learns to classify by the units with physical meaning in the state and perform well.

To use the found-out form $-\log(norm(s))$ and the simple form $-abs(s)$ which are easy to be designed by humans as the reward shaping respectively, a comparison experiment was carried out to compare how they influent the RL agent to explore. And the results are as follows (Fig. 4):

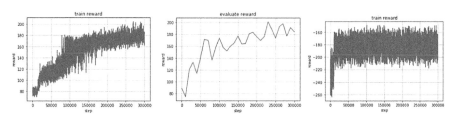

Fig. 4. Comparison of the effect of the shaping form found in this paper and the simple shaping form designed by hand

Among them, the left 1 and 2 are the results of the shaping form found in this article. They are the changes of the maximum cumulative return during the training and verification respectively; and the left 3 is the change of the maximum cumulative return during training of the manual designed reward. As can be seen from the figure, the artificial reward form gives mostly negative rewards, as the training goes on, the negative reward cumulates gradually, i.e., the agent will be punished as soon as it starts to act, which makes it difficult to perform exploring. While the searched form gives a small amount of negative reward when the agent is far from the landing point, but the positive reward increases exponentially when the agent is getting closer to the landing point, which is a good guidance to the agent. So the maximum cumulative return continues to rise even after 30,000 steps.

5   Conclusion

This paper designs a method of adaptively designing reward shaping according to the task, and finds the best representation form of reward shaping by searching the DAG graph composed of the basic elements of mathematics. Experiments show that this method is suitable for challenging reward shaping tasks. It is possible to search for shapes that are comparable or even better than human designers. The bi-level optimization method still has a large room for improvement, and the outer-loop discrete search can be further differentiated continuously, so that dual optimization can be used to further accelerate the calculation process and save computing power and computing resources. Multi-tasks can also be added to the outer loop to train an external reward shape suitable for a class of homogeneous tasks, so as to avoid the inconvenience of having to spend a lot of energy to try out new reward shapes in the manual design process if the task is only slightly changed.

References

1. Yang, R., Yan, J., Li, X.: Survey of sparse reward algorithms in reinforcement learning—theory and experiment. CAAI Trans. Intell. Syst. **15**(05), 888–899 (2020)

2. Ng, A.Y.: Shaping and policy search in reinforcement learning. Ph.D. thesis, University of California, Berkeley (2003)
3. Sutton, R.S., Barto, A.G.: Reinforcement Learning in Feedback Control—Challenges and Benchmarks from Technical Process Control. MIT Press, Cambridge (1998)
4. Li, Y., Shao, Z., Zhao, Z., et al.: Design of reward function in deep reinforcement learning for trajectory planning. Comput. Eng. Appl. **56**(2), 226–232 (2020)
5. Knox, W., Stone, P.: Framing reinforcement learning from human reward: reward positivity, temporal discounting, episodicity, and performance. Artif. Intell. **225**(C), 24–50 (2015)
6. Abbeel, P., Ng, A.Y.: Apprenticeship learning via inverse reinforcement learning. In: Proceedings of the 21st International Conference on Machine Learning, Banff, pp. 1–8 (2004)
7. Ziebart, B.D., Maas, A.L., Bagnell, J.A., et al.: Maximum entropy inverse reinforcement learning. In: Proceedings of the 23rd AAAI Conference on Artificial Intelligence, Illinois, pp. 1433–1438 (2008)
8. Ho, J., Ermon, S.: Generative adversarial imitation learning. In: Proceedings of the 30th Conference and Workshop on Neural Information Processing Systems, Barcelona, pp. 4565–4573 (2016)
9. Wu, Y., Mozifian, M., Shkurti, F.: Shaping rewards for reinforcement learning with imperfect demonstrations using generative models. In: The 2021 International Conference on Robotics and Automation, Xi'an, pp. 6628–6634 (2021)
10. Pathak, D., Agrawal, P., Efros, A.A., et al.: Curiosity-driven exploration by self-supervised prediction. In: Proceedings of the 2017 IEEE Conference on Computer Vision and Pattern Recognition Workshops, Hawaii, pp. 488–489 (2017)
11. Jaderberg, M., Czarnecki, W.M., Dunning, I., et al.: Human level performance in first-person multiplayer games with population-based deep reinforcement learning. arXiv (2018)
12. Zou, H., Ren, T., Dong, Y., et al.: Learning task-distribution reward shaping with meta-learning. In: The 35th AAAI Conference on Artificial Intelligence, New York (2021)

Category-Guided Localization Network for Visual Sound Source Separation

Huasen Wang[(⊠)], Lingling Gao, Qianchao Tan, and Chenxu Zhao

School of Computer Science and Engineering, University of Electronic Science
and Technology of China, Chengdu, China
hausen.w@foxmail.com
https://gr.uestc.edu.cn/

Abstract. Learning audiovisual correspondence plays an important role
in understanding outside world. The object of this work is to clearly separate the audio corresponding to the given visual object from mixed audio,
i.e., visually guided sound source separation. However, accurately obtaining and matching reference features in visual and audio modalities, which
is crucial in separation tasks, still remains a tough challenge. In this
paper, we propose a novel three-modality audio-visual separation framework, Category-Guided Localization Network (CGLN), to address this
problem. The proposed category-guided approach can cover the sound
object more precisely than others to obtain better separation. Object and
motion features are used as guiding signals to realize sound source separation in an end-to-end manner Extensive experiments are performed on
two publicly-available datasets, MUSIC and AudioSet. Our method has
achieved the goal of modality matching and alignment, and the results
could outperform other state-of-the-art approaches.

Keywords: Audio-visual · Sound separation · Sound localization

1 Introduction

It is natural for a human to perceive the outside world through looking and lis-
tening. Considering appearance and its acoustics characteristic jointly can often
bring a more comprehensive understanding of natural objects. Sound contains
rich information and most of them in nature are mixed. As humans, we have the
remarkable ability to distinguish different sounds. However, it is a huge challenge
for machine learning, as their ability declines rapidly when the number of sounds
increases. In this paper, our task is to clearly separate the audio corresponding
to the given visual object from mixed audio.

Traditional sound source separation methods [1–3,16] try to recover original signals relying on audio information only. Recently, deep neural network
algorithms [4,6,9,14,20,21,23] made impressive achievements on visual sound
separation. Gao *et al.* [6] chooses to use object detection results, obtained by
a finetuned Faster R-CNN [12], to guide sound source separation. Zhao *et al.*
[20] and Gan *et al.* [4] adopt motion cues and hand movements extracted in the

E. Pimenidis et al. (Eds.): ICANN 2022, LNCS 13531, pp. 394–404, 2022.
https://doi.org/10.1007/978-3-031-15934-3_33

videos as guidance. However, It's observed that object detection quality seriously affects the separation performance, and cross-modality feature matching remain a tough task. Since features of different modalities share completely different distributions, it is difficult to separate mixed audio with the guidance of visual modality data.

Facing these challenges, we propose a novel three-modality audio-visual separation framework CGLN, which combines the image and video with audio to get effective object and motion features as guiding information. We propose a Category-Guided Audio source Localization (CGAL) module to obtain the corresponding object in the visual modality in a complex background. Furthermore, we design a Background Remove and Fusion (BRF) module to guide the modality matching of audio and object. Finally, the proposed framework is performed on MUSIC and AudioSet, and achieves competitive results.

Our contributions can be summarized as follows: i) a novel three-modality audio-visual separation framework is proposed to take both object and motion features as guiding information, ii) the proposed category-guided approach can cover the sound object more precisely than others to obtain better separation, and iii) our framework achieves competitive results on MUSIC and AudioSet.

2   Method

2.1   Overview

This task aims to clearly separate the audio corresponding to the given video from the mixed audio. And the training procedure follows the commonly used "Mix-and-Separate" way, firstly proposed by [21].

Given a video, (V_k, I_k, S_k) represents the sequence of frames, one frame extracted in the middle, and audio signal, respectively. We mix N audio signals from N randomly selected video clips to form the audio mixture $S_{mix} = \sum_{k=1}^{N} S_k$. Our framework is trained to take (V_k, I_k, S_{mix}) as input and output the predicted audio $\hat{S}_k$. To be noted, the framework is trained under the supervision of S_k before mixing. The framework of our proposed CGLN is illustrated as Fig. 1. Concretely, the framework consists of three branches: an audio branch, an image-attention branch and a video-attention branch. The image-attention branch and the video-attention branch obtain object features and motion features as instructional information. The audio branch uses Short-Time Fourier Transform (STFT) to convert waveform S_{mix} to spectrogram and adopts down-convolution of U-Net [13] to get audio features f_A. In the end, we adopt up-convolution of U-Net to predict the mask of mixed spectrogram to separate clean spectrogram and rebuild audio S_k by Inverse Short-Time Fourier Transform (ISTFT).

2.2   Image-Attention Branch

The Image-attention branch aims to obtain appropriate object features as the guidance of audio separation. The original image I_k is one frame extracted in the middle of the video. We adopt a pretrained ResNet-18 [8] network to extract

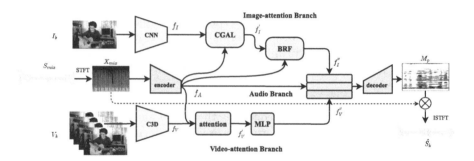

Fig. 1. The architecture of our proposed CGLN. The Image-attention branch extracts object features with the help of its CGAL and BRF module. The Video-attention branch extracts motion features. The audio branch predict mask on spectrograms to rebuild the clean sound with the guidance of object and motion features.

image features f_I. As mentioned before, the features of different modalities share entirely different distributions. It is challenging for us to obtain the corresponding object in the visual modality with a complex background. To solve this problem, we propose a Category-Guided Audio source Localization (CGAL) module to extract object features from the background. Moreover, we design a Background Remove and Fusion (BRF) module to match audio and object features, as illustrated in Fig. 2(a).

Category-Guided Audio Source Localization. We aim to realize audio source localization with the guidance of global features of audio. Inspired by [18], We use max-pooling and average-pooling simultaneously to aggregate spatial information. It has been proved that exploiting these features together improves the representation power of networks rather than using each independently. Then the max-pooled features and the average-pooled features are propagated to fully-connected layer and normalization layer. Finally, the aggregated global audio features f_{Ag} can be got by element-wise summation.

Cosine similarity function $h \in \mathbb{R}^{h \times w}$ is used to compute the audio-image correspondence between global audio features f_{Ag} and normalized image features f_I, using f_{Ag} as a probe vector. Then we obtain the object features by simply multiplying similarity h and f_I. The process can be summarized as Eqs. 1, 2 and 3.

$$f_{Ag} = \omega(AvgPool(f_A)) + \omega(MaxPool(f_A)) \tag{1}$$

$$h_{u,v} = \frac{\langle f_{Ag}, f_{I_{u,v}} \rangle}{\|f_{Ag}\| \|f_{I_{u,v}}\|}, uv \in [h] \times [w] \tag{2}$$

$$f_I' = h \times f_I \tag{3}$$

where $\omega(\cdot)$ denotes full-connected layer and $\langle \cdot \rangle$ denotes multiplication in element wise. The heatmap h indicates how strongly each area located in image responses to audio, in short, h locates the sound source.

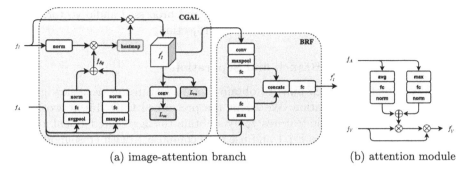

Fig. 2. Architecture of (a) image-attention branch and (b) attention module in video-attention branch. The CGAL module distinguishes the object with category guidance. The BRF module removes background and fuses features.

Sadly, according to the experimental results, it is still hard to automatically locate the corresponding area in image in an end-to-end manner. To solve this problem, we use category labels to supervise the localization of sound sources. The study of Class Activation Mapping (CAM) [22] proves that classification is a powerful tool to highlight the object in the image. Thus a cross-entropy loss(L_{ce}) is applied on f_I' to help locating the object area.

Additionally, the issue of CAM is that only the most discriminative regions are activated, misleading by the local extremely high response. Therefore, we adopt the restricted activation loss function (L_{ra}) mentioned in [10] to drive the heatmap to cover the object extent. Observing that the deviation values within background area are distributed much evenly, we can roughly distinguish the object area from the background by standard deviation. the losses are defined as:

$$M_{bg} = \mathbb{I}(Var(softmax(f_I')) < \tau_l)$$
$$M_{obj} = \mathbb{I}(Var(softmax(f_I')) > \tau_h)$$

(4)

$$L_{ra} = \frac{1}{hw} \sum_{u,v} (f_I' * M_{bg} + f_I' * (1 - M_{obj}))|_{u,v}$$

(5)

where $\mathbb{I}(\cdot)$ is the indicator function, and $Var(\cdot)$ is the standard deviation of each position on f_I' in the channel dimension. M_{bg} and M_{obj} are background mask and object mask, respectively. τ_l and τ_h denote threshold hyperparameters for M_{bg} and M_{obj}.

Background Remove and Fusion. The BRF module aims to remove background features and guide the correct matching of audio and object features. As we have highlighted the sound source in the CGAL module, a simple way to remove background features is max-pooling. Specifically, features f_I' are successively forwarded by a convolution layer, a max-pooling layer and a linear projection layer. We concate the image vector and processed audio vector, and obtain the object features f_I'' using a linear projection.

2.3 Video-Attention Branch and Separation

The video-attention branch aims to obtain motion features as necessary guiding signal of sound separation. We adopt the pretrained C3D [15] network as backbone to extract motion features f_V. We obtain the aggregated global audio features in the same way as Eq. 1 and use it to compute f_V' with cross-modality attention weighted, as illustrated in Fig. 2(b). Then f_V' is forwarded to a Multi-Layer Perceptron (MLP) to get motion features f_V''.

We replicate f_A'' and f_V'' to the same size as f_A in spatial dimension and concatenate three of them in channel dimension. Then up-convolution of U-Net is performed on the concatenated feature map to generate a predicted spectrogram mask M_p. In the meantime, the ground-truth ratio mask, M_g can be calculated by Eq. 6:

$$M_g = X_k / X_{mix} \tag{6}$$

where X_k denotes the spectrogram obtained by STFT on waveform S_k, and X_{mix} denotes the spectrogram obtained by STFT on waveform S_{mix}. We train the framework by minimizing the mask-consistency loss L_{mc}:

$$L_{mc} = ||M_g - M_p||_1 \tag{7}$$

And the total loss is calculated as:

$$L = L_{mc} + \alpha L_{ce} + \beta L_{ra} \tag{8}$$

where α, β denotes hyperparameters for loss L_{ce} and L_{ra}.

Table 1. Separation performance comparisons on MUSIC. Our framework outperforms other state-of-the-art approaches.

Method	2-mix		3-mix	
	SDR	SIR	SDR	SIR
NMF [17]	2.78	6.70	2.1	2.08
Deep separation [1]	4.75	7.00	–	–
MIML [5]	4.25	6.23	1.76	3.32
Sound of pixels [21]	7.52	13.01	3.65	8.77
Co-separation [6]	7.38	13.7	3.94	8.93
Sound of motion [20]	8.31	14.82	4.87	9.48
Music gesture [4]	10.12	15.81	5.41	11.47
Ours	**11.03**	**15.96**	**6.23**	**11.83**

3 Experiment

3.1 Datasets

To evaluate the effectiveness of our algorithm, we train our network on two main datasets, MUSIC and AudioSet [7], to compare with other algorithms.

MUSIC [21]. The MIT MUSIC dataset is a musical instrument video dataset, containing 11 instrument categories. It contains 685 videos, 536 solo videos and 149 duet, collected for training audio-visual source separation models. The dataset is available on YouTube. Note that we obtain 511 solo videos, for some videos are not available at present. To evaluate sound source separation results fairly, we construct the same training and test set as [6] do.

AudioSet [7]. AudioSet is a large-scale audio-visual dataset consisting of mainly 10-second video clips. Following [5,6], we filter the dataset to extract video clips of 15 musical instruments for training and evaluation purposes.

3.2 Implementation Details

The proposed framework is implemented in PyTorch. For audio processing, following [6], we sample the waveform at 11 kHz. STFT is employed to produce a 512×256 spectrogram and re-sample it on a log-frequency scale to obtain a 256×256 magnitude spectrogram. We adopt U-Net as the encoder and decoder structure. For image processing, only the middle frame of the raw video is used. We resize it to 224×224 and send it to pretrained ResNet-18. For video processing, we evenly sample 16 frames from the raw video and resize them to tensor of $16 \times 224 \times 224$. The pretrained C3D is adopted to extract motion features.

As for the training stage, the Adam optimizer is adopted, and the learning rate decay is set to 0.1 for every 10^4 batches, with the start learning rate 1×10^{-4}. The MLP is a structure with two fully connected layers with a ReLU activation function. The hyperparameters α, β are set to 0.5, 0.1, respectively. And τ_l, τ_h are set to 0.3, 0.5, respectively.

Table 2. The 2-mix separation performance on AudioSet

Method	SDR	SIR
NMF-MFCC	0.25	4.19
Sound of Pixels [21]	1.66	3.58
MIML [5]	1.83	–
Co-Separation [6]	4.26	7.07
Ours	**4.47**	**7.51**

Table 3. Evaluation on loss functions. We list the 2-mix and 3-mix separation results on MUSIC with/without corresponding losses.

L_{mc}	L_{ce}	L_{ra}	2-mix		3-mix	
			SDR	SIR	SDR	SIR
w	w/o	w/o	7.28	11.82	3.51	8.14
w	w	w/o	9.89	14.75	5.74	9.07
w	w/o	w	9.27	13.87	5.16	8.82
w	w	w	**11.03**	**15.96**	**6.23**	**11.83**

Table 4. Evaluation on hyperparameters. We list the separation results under the different values of four parameters on MUSIC.

α	β	τ_h	τ_l	2-mix		3-mix	
				SDR	SIR	SDR	SIR
0.5	0.1	0.5	0.3	**11.03**	**15.96**	**6.23**	**11.83**
0.5	0.3	0.5	0.3	10.42	14.68	5.78	10.21
0.5	0.5	0.5	0.3	10.09	13.96	5.82	8.71
1.0	0.1	0.5	0.3	10.77	15.04	5.82	9.74
0.5	0.1	0.5	0.2	10.74	14.79	5.17	9.06
0.5	0.1	0.6	0.2	10.48	14.53	5.02	8.96
0.5	0.1	0.6	0.3	10.52	14.56	5.26	9.15

4   Results and Discussion

4.1   Separation Results

Following [6,19–21,24], there are three separation metrics including Signal-to-Distortion Ratio (SDR), Signal-to-Interference Ratio (SIR) and Signal-to-Artifact Ratio (SAR). SDR and SIR capture separation accuracy. Note that SAR only captures the absence of artifacts which can be high even if separation is poor [6]. SAR has been abandoned in [4], we mainly use SDR and SIR as evaluation, calculated by open-source *mir_eval* library [11].

Table 1 provides the comparison results compared with state-of-the-art methods on MUSIC. We perform 2-mix separation experiment using two single-source samples to compose a mixture and 3-mix separation experiment using three single-source samples. It could be seen that our method performs better than all the baselines on both SDR and SIR. The proposed framework has a significant improvement in SDR and a slight improvement in SIR. Especially the SDR in 2-mix experiment is raised by nearly one point compared with current state-of-the-art approach.

We also perform the 2-mix separation experiment on AudioSet, and the results are shown in Table 2. In case that samples in AudioSet contain more noise, the results are poorer than MUSIC. But the proposed framework still outperforms related baselines (4.47(ours) vs 4.26 and 7.51(ours) vs 7.07).

Fig. 3. Visualization of the localization maps. It's observed that the proposed framework tends to cover the object (instruments) extent and overcomes the local extremely high response problem.

4.2 Ablation Study

Evaluation on Loss Functions. We set three losses for network training in our proposed approach, L_{mc}, L_{ce}, L_{ra}. Among them, the mask-consistency loss L_{mc} is used to reconstruct the separated spectrogram. The cross-entropy loss L_{ce} is used to help locating the object area. The restricted activation loss L_{ra} is used to drive the heatmap to cover the object extent. Since L_{cm} is the fundamental loss we used in our work, we mainly evaluate the other two losses. As illustrated in Table 3, we list the 2-mix and 3-mix separation results on MUSIC. Note that "w,w/o" means the model is trained with/without corresponding losses. As shown in the table, when we abandon L_{ce} or L_{ra} in the training, the separation results would have a significant decline. It drops a lot especially when we abandon L_{ce}. This experiment demonstrates the effectiveness of each loss.

Evaluation on Hyperparameters. There are four hyperparameters used in our proposed approach, α, β, τ_h and τ_l. The hyperparameters α, β are used as the weights of losses α and β. And τ_l, τ_h denote threshold hyperparameters for M_{bg} and M_{obj}. We list the separation results under the different values of these parameters, as illustrated in Table 4. 2-mix and 3-mix separation experiments are performed on MUSIC dataset. As shown in the table, we find it performs better when the L_{ra} has a lower weight. We obtain best result with the weight of "0.5, 0.1, 0.5, 0.3".

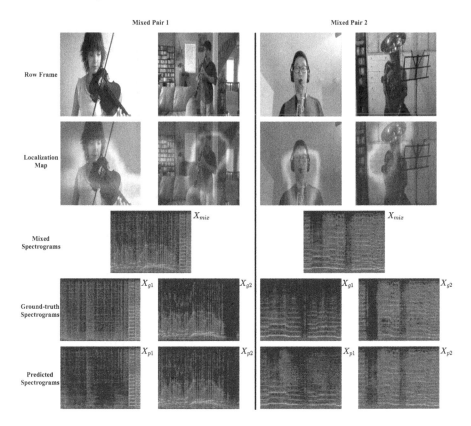

Fig. 4. Visualization of the localization maps and spectrograms for 2-mix separation experiments on MUSIC. The predicted spectrogram is highly consistent with ground-truth one.

4.3 Qualitatively Analysis

In order to intuitively display the experiment results, we visualize some convincing intermediate results. Figure 3 visualizes the results of sound source localization. It's observed that the proposed framework tends to cover the object (instruments) extent and overcomes the local extremely high response problem. It proves that the our CGAL module could obtain the corresponding object in the visual modality with a complex background. Accurate object localization ensures accurate cross-modality matching.

To directly show the separation results, Fig. 4 visualizes the localization maps and spectrograms for 2-mix separation experiments on MUSIC. The first line shows the raw frames we extracted from one mixed pair. While second line shows the localization map. We also provide relevant spectrograms. X_{g1} and X_{g2} denotes the ground-truth single-source spectrograms to be mixed. X_{mix} denote the mixed spectrograms. X_{p1} and X_{p2} denote the predicted spectrograms. Visually, we observe that the predicted spectrograms are very similar to the ground-truth ones.

5   Conclusion

We propose a novel three-modality audio-visual separation framework CGLN. To solve the problem of modality matching and aligning, we propose a novel three-modality audio-visual separation framework. The CGAL module is designed to locate corresponding object more precisely by category guiding, and BRF is adopted to fulfil modality matching. The experiments on two datasets prove the effectiveness and superiority of our work.

References

1. Chandna, P., Miron, M., Janer, J., Gómez, E.: Monoaural audio source separation using deep convolutional neural networks. In: Tichavský, P., Babaie-Zadeh, M., Michel, O.J.J., Thirion-Moreau, N. (eds.) LVA/ICA 2017. LNCS, vol. 10169, pp. 258–266. Springer, Cham (2017). https://doi.org/10.1007/978-3-319-53547-0_25
2. Cichocki, A., Zdunek, R., Phan, A.H., Amari, S.I.: Nonnegative Matrix and Tensor Factorizations: Applications to Exploratory Multi-way Data Analysis and Blind Source Separation. Wiley, New York (2009)
3. FitzGerald, D., Cranitch, M., Coyle, E.: Non-negative tensor factorisation for sound source separation. In: IEE Conference Publication, vol. 511, p. 8. Institution of Electrical Engineers, London 1999 (2005)
4. Gan, C., Huang, D., Zhao, H., Tenenbaum, J.B., Torralba, A.: Music gesture for visual sound separation. In: 2020 IEEE/CVF Conference on Computer Vision and Pattern Recognition (CVPR), pp. 10478–10487 (2020)
5. Gao, R., Feris, R., Grauman, K.: Learning to separate object sounds by watching unlabeled video. In: Ferrari, V., Hebert, M., Sminchisescu, C., Weiss, Y. (eds.) ECCV 2018. LNCS, vol. 11207, pp. 36–54. Springer, Cham (2018). https://doi.org/10.1007/978-3-030-01219-9_3
6. Gao, R., Grauman, K.: Co-separating sounds of visual objects. In: 2019 IEEE/CVF International Conference on Computer Vision (ICCV), pp. 3879–3888 (2019)
7. Gemmeke, J.F., et al.: Audio set: an ontology and human-labeled dataset for audio events. In: 2017 IEEE International Conference on Acoustics, Speech and Signal Processing (ICASSP), pp. 776–780 (2017)
8. He, K., Zhang, X., Ren, S., Sun, J.: Deep residual learning for image recognition. In: 2016 IEEE Conference on Computer Vision and Pattern Recognition (CVPR), pp. 770–778 (2016)
9. Lee, J., Chung, S.W., Kim, S., Kang, H.G., Sohn, K.: Looking into your speech: learning cross-modal affinity for audio-visual speech separation. In: Proceedings of the IEEE/CVF Conference on Computer Vision and Pattern Recognition, pp. 1336–1345 (2021)
10. Pan, X., et al.: Unveiling the potential of structure preserving for weakly supervised object localization. In: Proceedings of the IEEE/CVF Conference on Computer Vision and Pattern Recognition, pp. 11642–11651 (2021)
11. Raffel, C., et al.: Mir_eval: a transparent implementation of common MIR metrics. In: ISMIR, pp. 367–372 (2014)
12. Ren, S., He, K., Girshick, R., Sun, J.: Faster R-CNN: towards real-time object detection with region proposal networks. In: Advances in Neural Information Processing Systems, vol. 28 (2015)

13. Ronneberger, O., Fischer, P., Brox, T.: U-Net: convolutional networks for biomedical image segmentation. In: International Conference on Medical Image Computing and Computer-Assisted Intervention, pp. 234–241 (2015)
14. Tian, Y., Hu, D., Xu, C.: Cyclic co-learning of sounding object visual grounding and sound separation. In: Proceedings of the IEEE/CVF Conference on Computer Vision and Pattern Recognition, pp. 2745–2754 (2021)
15. Tran, D., Bourdev, L., Fergus, R., Torresani, L., Paluri, M.: Learning spatiotemporal features with 3D convolutional networks. In: 2015 IEEE International Conference on Computer Vision (ICCV), pp. 4489–4497 (2015). https://doi.org/10.1109/ICCV.2015.510
16. Vincent, E., Bertin, N., Gribonval, R., Bimbot, F.: From blind to guided audio source separation: how models and side information can improve the separation of sound. IEEE Signal Process. Mag. **31**(3), 107–115 (2014)
17. Virtanen, T.: Monaural sound source separation by nonnegative matrix factorization with temporal continuity and sparseness criteria. IEEE Trans. Audio Speech Lang. Process. **15**, 1066–1074 (2007)
18. Woo, S., Park, J., Lee, J.Y., Kweon, I.S.: CBAM: convolutional block attention module. In: Proceedings of the European Conference on Computer Vision (ECCV), pp. 3–19 (2018)
19. Xu, X., Dai, B., Lin, D.: Recursive visual sound separation using minus-plus net. In: 2019 IEEE/CVF International Conference on Computer Vision (ICCV), pp. 882–891 (2019)
20. Zhao, H., Gan, C., Ma, W.C., Torralba, A.: The sound of motions. In: 2019 IEEE/CVF International Conference on Computer Vision (ICCV), pp. 1735–1744 (2019). https://doi.org/10.1109/ICCV.2019.00182
21. Zhao, H., Gan, C., Rouditchenko, A., Vondrick, C., McDermott, J., Torralba, A.: The sound of pixels. In: The European Conference on Computer Vision (ECCV), September 2018
22. Zhou, B., Khosla, A., Lapedriza, A., Oliva, A., Torralba, A.: Learning deep features for discriminative localization. In: 2016 IEEE Conference on Computer Vision and Pattern Recognition (CVPR), pp. 2921–2929 (2016)
23. Zhou, H., Xu, X., Lin, D., Wang, X., Liu, Z.: Sep-stereo: visually guided stereophonic audio generation by associating source separation. In: Vedaldi, A., Bischof, H., Brox, T., Frahm, J.-M. (eds.) ECCV 2020. LNCS, vol. 12357, pp. 52–69. Springer, Cham (2020). https://doi.org/10.1007/978-3-030-58610-2_4
24. Zhu, L., Rahtu, E.: Visually guided sound source separation using cascaded opponent filter network. In: Ishikawa, H., Liu, C.-L., Pajdla, T., Shi, J. (eds.) ACCV 2020. LNCS, vol. 12627, pp. 409–426. Springer, Cham (2021). https://doi.org/10.1007/978-3-030-69544-6_25

Gaussian Mixture Model-Based Registration Network for Point Clouds with Partial Overlap

Xiang Li[1], Jianwen Sun[2], Chung-Ming Own[1(✉)], and Wenyuan Tao[1]

[1] Tianjin University, Tianjin, China
chungming.own@tju.edu.cn
[2] Tianjin University of Technology, Tianjin, China

Abstract. Mainstream methods of point cloud registration can be divided into two categories: strict point-level correspondence, which is commonly used but incompatible with real-world data; and statistical calculations, which compensate for the shortcomings of point-level methods but are inflexible, mainly when applied to scenes containing partial overlap. This paper proposes a novel registration network (poGMM-Net), the first statistical registration method to successfully align two partially overlapping point clouds. Specifically, our model modifies the registration problem to involve the minimization of Kullback-Leibler divergence in Gaussian mixture models (GMMs), focusing on overlapping regions. In poGMM-Net, the GMMs are associated with points in the point clouds by the learned potential correspondence matrix. The fitting of nonoverlapping points and outliers is avoided by fusing learned secondary feature sets. Application of models to ModelNet40 datasets demonstrated that poGMM-Net achieves state-of-the-art performance under various registration conditions, outperforming both point-level-based and statistical methods.

Keywords: Point cloud registration · Registration network · Gaussian mixture model

1 Introduction

Three-dimensional (3D) point cloud registration technology is critical in numerous emerging fields, including 3D graphics [12], robotics [8], and autonomous driving [16]. The essential concept underlying point cloud registration is achieving pose alignment between the source and target point clouds by finding the best rigid transformation. Multiple studies have investigated point cloud registration; however, existing point cloud registration methods are limited by numerous factors, such as poor transformation initialization, noisy points, partially overlapping point cloud pairs, and outliers.

The iterative closest point (ICP) algorithm [4] is the classical registration method, which assumes that there is a one-to-one correspondence between the two point clouds. Consequently, ICP requires excellent initialization support and

E. Pimenidis et al. (Eds.): ICANN 2022, LNCS 13531, pp. 405–416, 2022.
https://doi.org/10.1007/978-3-031-15934-3_34

is sensitive to noisy or outlier points. Deep closest point (DCP) [21], an extension of ICP based on deep learning techniques. DCP also assumes perfect correspondences between the two point clouds and ignores the characteristics of real-world data; moreover, it cannot handle common problems such as sensor errors or scan noise. For handling real-world data, studies [13,15,25] have represented point clouds by using statistical distributions and not relying on strict point correspondence. The representative method DeepGMR [25] maps the points in the point cloud to the latent Gaussian mixture model (GMM). DeepGMR accommodates more noise and reduces registration time. Unfortunately, this method is inflexible and cannot handle point clouds with partial overlapping.

To overcome the aforementioned limitations, this paper proposes a novel registration network called the poGMM-Net. Compounded with the advantages of statistical approaches, poGMM-Net adds a moderating mechanism to the Gaussian mixture model(GMM). Our poGMM-Net is insensitive to initialization, noise, and outliers and is suitable for partially visible point cloud registration. To the best of our knowledge, poGMM-Net is the first statistical-based registration method that can solve the issue of partial overlapping.

The main contributions of this paper are as follows:

- We design the first statistical-based registration network that can align partially overlapping point clouds.
- We employ a DGCNN variant with added cross-attention layers to learn the features of points without requiring any additional geometric information from manual annotation or learning.
- We propose a joint SegNet and ClaNet module to learn the potential correspondence between the points and the GMMs and instruct GMMs to focus on overlapping regions.
- Experimental results from ModelNet40 datasets reveal that our poGMM-Net achieves SOTA under various registration conditions.

2 Related Works

Point-Level Methods. Point-to-point-based registration methods usually calculate differences between points or pairs of points, which obtain the rigid transformation between two point clouds by performing point-level matching. The most classical approach is ICP [4], which alternates between computing point-to-point correspondence and minimizing the corresponding distances. Some similar ICP deformations [6,19,20] are also susceptible to noise and initialization. DCP [21] uses deep learning techniques to optimize the classical ICP and introduces an attention mechanism, which reduces sensitivity to initialization but cannot overcome the effects of outliers. Subsequently, studies [10,22,24] have explored solutions for aligning partially overlapping point clouds. RPM-Net [24] estimates soft correspondences by using hybrid features, and RGM [10] constructs graph structures from points in the point cloud with surrounding points. These methods rely on an idealized point-to-point correspondence, which is not guaranteed in practical applications. PointNetLK [2,3] and FGR [26], which are based on feature-level global registration, and Predator [14], which considers point clouds as voxels, are essentially similar to point-level methods. Specifically, the point-level registration method does not work well in practical applications when conditions involve poor initialization, sensor data loss, or noise interference.

Statistical Methods. Because statistical-based methods require a large amount of statistical knowledge, they are slightly less sophisticated than approaches based on direct point-level processing. NDT [5], an early method for statistical registration, introduced normal distribution transformation to the point cloud registration. Later, GMMReg [15] used Gaussian mixture models (GMMs) [18] to fit two point clouds. Unfortunately, distribution-based methods are susceptible to changes in perspective and quantitative divisions. HGMR [9] uses an iterative approach to optimize the statistical distributions of and correspondence between point clouds. However, HGMR [9] has only local convergence [1]. Similarly, PointGMM [13] constructs a hierarchical GMM tree by using an encoder-decoder network. DeepGMR [25], which replaced the conventional iterative expectation-maximization algorithm [7,11] iteration process with a learning-based approach [17], is the most advanced statistical technique but has poor performance when applied to partially overlapping point clouds. Statistical registration does not rely on point-to-point correspondence, is more consistent with real-world data, and involves faster computation. However, most statistical registration methods are not sufficiently flexible in solving the outliers, and none can handle partially overlapping point clouds. Our approach is statistical-based and has the accompanying advantages. However, instead of directly using the single GMM approach, we added a GMM adjustment mechanism to achieve more robust registration results.

Problem Formulation. We aim to find the optimal transformation T^* between a given pair of point clouds $P = \{p_i \in R^3 \mid i = 1, \cdots, M\}$ and $Q = \{q_j \in R^3 \mid j = 1, \cdots, N\}$, called the source and target point clouds, respectively, by using deep learning techniques. T consists of two components: rotation $R \in SO(3)$ and translation $t \in R^3$ and help us align P to Q. In most studies, the optimal T^* is found by minimizing the distance between the transformed source point cloud $T(P)$ and the target point cloud Q. Instead of directly employing the point-level solution, we use GMMs to fit these two point clouds and obtain individual potential Gaussian distribution representations as P_{GMM} and Q_{GMM}. According to [25], the solution can be transformed to minimize the KL divergence of the two potential Gaussian mixture distributions:

$$T^* = \underset{T}{argmin} \; KL(T(\hat{\Theta}) \mid \Theta) \tag{1}$$

where $\hat{\Theta}$ and Θ denote the parameters of P_{GMM} and Q_{GMM}, respectively. Moreover, $T(\hat{\Theta})$ represents the transformed Gaussian mixture model parameters of the source point cloud.

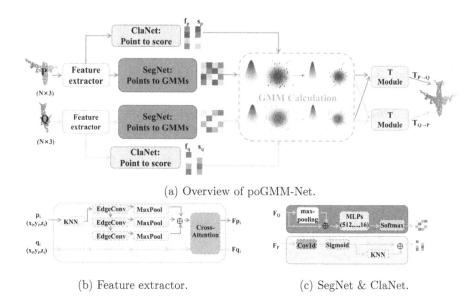

(a) Overview of poGMM-Net.

(b) Feature extractor.   (c) SegNet & ClaNet.

Fig. 1. Overall structure and partial details of poGMM-Net, where ⊕ indicates concatenation.

3 IT2GMM-Net

Figure 1 presents the structure and some details of po2GMM-Net. This novel statistical-based registration network, designed to align partially overlapping point clouds, comprises four modules: the feature extractor, SegNet & ClaNet, GMM calculation, and T calculation. First, for the input pair of point clouds, we extract the features of each point by using a shared feature extractor. Then, through SegNet, we can learn the corresponding potential distribution between points and GMMs, and from ClaNet, obtain the possibilities of whether the points are located in overlapping regions. The GMM calculation module fuses the corresponding distributions with probabilistic features to adjust and calculate the GMMs parameters. Finally, by minimizing the KL divergence between GMMs, the T calculation module can output the transformation T between the two point clouds.

3.1 Feature Extractor

To better learn the mapping of the source point cloud P and the target point cloud Q to GMMs parameters, we first extract the features of the points. Specifically, the input point cloud coordinates are passed through the simplified DGCNN, consisting of a graph feature extractor, a multilayer perceptron, and a max-pooling layer to obtain the initial features. The 3D point coordinates can be converted into high-dimensional point features $R^3 \rightarrow R^d$. For a point $p_i(x_i, y_i, z_i)$ in P, we can obtain the feature representation $F_{p_i}^1$ in the initial stage:

$$F_{p_i}^1 = f_\theta^1 \{(p_i, p_k) \mid \forall k \in K_i\} \tag{2}$$

where f_θ^1 is the simplified DGCNN, θ represents the parameters, p_k represents a point in the k-nearest neighbors of point p_i, and $F_{p_i}^1$ represents the learned initial features; $F_{q_i}^1$ is obtained similarly for $F_{p_i}^1$.

To learn more robust features, information about the points in the corresponding point clouds is linked and supplemented by the cross-attention layer. In our cross-attention layer, the keys $k_j \in R^d$ in the corresponding point clouds are queried by using $r_i \in R^d$ to obtain the weighted update values $v_j \in R^d$:

$$r_i = \omega_k F_{p_i}^1 , \quad k_j = \omega_r F_{q_j}^1 , \quad v_j = \omega_v F_{q_j}^1 \tag{3}$$

where ω_k, ω_r and ω_v are updatable matrices with different weights. We can obtain information from the corresponding point clouds by updating the features:

$$F_{p_i} = F_{p_i}^1 + f_\theta^2(r_i, \sum softmax(r_i^T k_j / \sqrt{d}) v_j) \tag{4}$$

where $softmax(r_i^T k_j / \sqrt{d})$ denotes the attention weight and f_θ^2 denotes the cross-attention layer function. The features are more robust because they contain the information itself and the corresponding point cloud. This method yields point features as $F_P, F_Q \in R^d$.

3.2 SegNet and ClaNet Module

SegNet and ClaNet are simultaneous branches of segmentation and classification modules, respectively. SegNet learns the potential correspondence distribution between points and GMMs. The purpose of ClaNet is to learn the secondary feature sets $[f_P, s_P]$ or $[f_Q, s_Q]$ for the points contained in GMMs for fine-tuning.

SegNet applies max pooling to the features F_P and F_Q from the feature extractor to obtain the global features and concatenate them with the point features. The correspondence between points and GMMs is learned by limiting the probability sum of the points from all Gaussian models to one. Assuming that the features of the input N points are mapped to G Gaussian models, we can obtain a matrix D with dimensions $N \times G$:

$$D_{P \to P_{GMM}} = Seg_\phi(cat[F_P, maxpool(F_P)]) \tag{5}$$

where Seg_ϕ denotes SegNet and $D_{P \to P_{GMM}}$ denotes the correspondence between point cloud P and GMM P_{GMM}; $D_{Q \to Q_{GMM}}$ is defined similarly for Q. Figure 2 shows the potential correspondence matrix obtained by processing the Model-Net40 [23]. Significant color values indicate a strong correspondence between the points and the Gaussian model. We only give the correspondence between some points and the Gaussian model considering the display space.

ClaNet, by contrast, processes the output from the feature extractor to obtain the probability of points that lie in the overlapping region; these are the first overlap features f_P, f_Q. Considering the influence of outlier points, we also retain

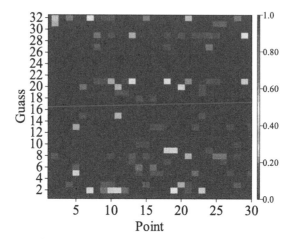

Fig. 2. Potential correspondence matrix of ModelNet40. The correspondence between 30 points and 32 Gaussian models is shown in the matrix.

the second overlap features s_P, s_Q, which indicate the probability of neighboring points located in the overlapping region:

$$f_{p_i} = Softmax(F_{p_i}) \tag{6}$$

$$s_{p_i} = \sum_{k=1}^{K} w_{ik} f_{p_k} \tag{7}$$

where f_{p_i} and s_{p_i} denote the overlap features of point p_i, respectively, and w_{ik} is the distance weight of point p_k to p_i. Accordingly, secondary feature sets $[f, s]$ are used to lead the subsequent adjustment of the GMM, Enabling the GMM to better fit the positions of the points located in the overlapping region.

3.3   GMM and T Calculation Module

Assuming the source point cloud is P as an example, we can adjust the potential correspondence matrix $D_{p \rightarrow P_{GMM}}$ by overlap feature sets $[f, s]$. Accordingly, the weights π, means μ, and covariances Σ of the Gaussian model P_{GMM} can be obtained through the GMM calculation module. Referring to [25], but our model does not require a strict overlap between two point clouds. The triplet parameters of the source and target GMMs are defined as $\hat{\Theta}(\hat{\pi}, \hat{\mu}, \hat{\Sigma})$ and $\Theta(\pi, \mu, \Sigma)$. In our study, finding the optimal transformation T^* is converted into a problem involving the minimization of the KL divergence of two potential distributions $T(\hat{\Theta})$ and Θ. Equation (1) is equivalent to solving for the maximum log-likelihood function of the transformed source point cloud under the target distribution:

$$T^* = \underset{T}{argmax} \sum_{i=1}^{N} \ln \sum_{g=1}^{G} \pi_g N(T(\hat{p}_i) \mid \mu_g, \Sigma_g) \tag{8}$$

where $N()$ represents the Gaussian function. Further simplify, the alignment is performed by using the centroids of each distribution to reduce the computational effort from Mahalanobis distances to weighted Euclidean distances. Here,

$$T^* = \underset{T}{argmin} \sum_{g=1}^{G} \frac{\hat{\pi}_g}{\sigma_g^2} \| T(\hat{\mu}_g) - \pi_g \|^2 \tag{9}$$

where σ_g denotes the centroid of the Gaussian g. Finally, using our weighted singular value decomposition solver, the optimal transformation T^* is obtained.

3.4   Loss

poGMM-Net is an end-to-end neural network with two losses in the training phase. The fundamental transformation $\overline{T}$ is used as supervised information.

Transformation Loss. For a given pair of point clouds P and Q, two bidirectional transformation matrices T_P^Q and T_Q^P are generated through our proposed network. With the transformation $\overline{T}$, the transformation loss L_T is

$$L_T = \| T_P^Q \ \overline{T}^{-1} - I \|^2 + \| T_Q^P \ \overline{T} - I \|^2 \tag{10}$$

where I denotes a unit matrix of the same size as $\overline{T}$.

Classification Loss. The ClaNet module performs a binary classification task. The label that denotes a point lying in the overlapping region can be determined by exploring the correspondence between the source and target point clouds. Thus, the true labels can be obtained by the transformation $\overline{T}$. Subsequently, the classification loss L_C can be computed by the binary cross-entropy:

$$L_{C_P} = \frac{1}{|P|} \sum_{i=1}^{P} \overline{c}_{p_i} \ \log(f_{p_i}) + (1 - \overline{c}_{p_i}) \log(1 - f_{p_i}) \tag{11}$$

where L_{C_P} denotes the binary loss of the point cloud P and c_{p_i} denotes the true label of p_i. The final classification loss is the sum of the losses of the two inputs.

4   Experiments

In this section, we apply poGMM-Net to the synthetic dataset generated from ModelNet40 [23]. Our poGMM-Net is implemented via PyTorch, experimenting with an NVIDIA GeForce RTX 3090 graphics processing unit. We compared with those of STOA statistical and point-level registration methods, including DeepGMR [25], ICP [4], DCP [21], PointNetLK [2], and RGM [10].

4.1   ModelNet40

Dataset. ModelNet40 consists of 12 311 artificial CAD models from 40 categories. We employed 5112 samples for training, 1202 samples for validation, and 1266 samples for testing, following [24]. From ModelNet40 we generated three experimental cases. For all cases, we used only 20 categories for training and the remaining 20 categories for testing.

Clean Data. We randomly sampled 1024 points in the ModelNet40 dataset as the source point cloud and generated the target point cloud after applying the transformation $\overline{T}$. The two point clouds have strict one-to-one correspondences.

Noisy Data. Noise sampled from $N(0, 0.01)$ is added for each axis based on the clean data. These pairs were no longer in strict correspondence.

Partially Overlapping Data. Following [24], we projected each point cloud onto a unit sphere, only retain 70% of the points by moving the plane in one direction after splitting by an arbitrary plane.

Metrics. To evaluate the network performance from multiple perspectives, six evaluation metrics were employed. Following [24], the relative error over rotation R and translation t were used as R_{MIE} and t_{MIE}, and the root mean squared errors R_{RMSE} and t_{RMSE} from [21]. Furthermore, the modified Chamfer distance CCD from [10] and the *Recall* from DeepGMR [25] were used (Table 2).

Table 1. Results for ModelNet40 (clean data).

Contation	Method	R_{MIE}	t_{MIE}	R_{RMSE}	t_{RMSE}	CCD	*Recall*
Clean	ICP [4]	6.4277	0.0539	5.4659	0.0415	0.0311	82.2%
	DCP-V2 [21]	4.1618	0.0392	4.1502	0.0331	0.0187	85.9%
	PointNetLK [2]	2.8994	0.0315	2.6547	0.0029	0.0031	87.4%
	RGM [10]	5.0622	0.0342	4.7031	0.0325	0.0436	**100%**
	DeepGMR [25]	**0.0400**	0.0977	**0.2337**	**0.0011**	0.0022	**100%**
	Ours	4.0410	**0.0286**	3.6407	0.0245	**0.0016**	**100%**
Noisy	ICP [4]	7.0066	0.0618	9.8949	0.0537	0.0536	80.3%
	DCP-V2 [21]	9.2043	0.0688	11.7568	0.0495	0.0696	83.5%
	PointNetLK [2]	3.3681	0.0296	4.8314	0.0318	0.0558	84.1%
	RGM [10]	**1.8863**	0.0179	3.4401	0.0282	0.0503	99.4%
	DeepGMR [25]	29.0212	0.1648	39.7681	0.1542	0.1048	71.5%
	Ours	2.4331	**0.0103**	**3.1257**	**0.0138**	**0.0044**	**99.7%**
Partially	ICP [4]	27.9849	0.2912	29.9706	0.3152	0.1514	32.6%
	DCP-V2 [21]	14.4384	0.1839	16.0068	0.1698	0.1202	41.7%
	PointNetLK [2]	31.5868	0.3242	24.4165	0.2755	0.1349	34.9%
	RGM [10]	6.2160	0.0661	10.1995	0.1067	0.0396	91.4%
	DeepGMR [25]	89.5320	0.5334	78.3870	0.3616	0.1849	11.6%
	Ours	**5.7302**	**0.0581**	**5.1447**	**0.0599**	**0.0246**	**94.9%**

Results. As presented in Table 1, existing some advanced networks have excellent capabilities in processing clean data, and our network also achieved the 100% recall rate. When applied to the noisy data and partially overlapping data, our poGMM-Net outperformed all other methods. Figure 3 presents a visualization of the application of poGMM-Net on ModelNet40, and the Table 4 presents the results for the last 20 categories in the partially overlapping data. Figure 4 gives comparisons of our IT2GMM-Net with these methods for different test scenarios. Specifically, in any case, the recall of our method is the highest.

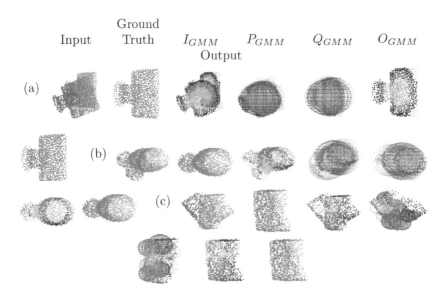

Fig. 3. Qualitative registration examples for ModelNet40: (a) clean data, (b) noisy data, (c) partially overlapping.

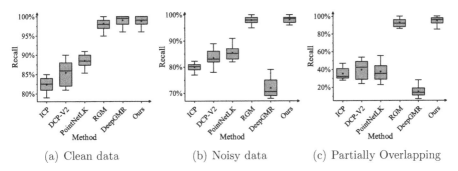

Fig. 4. Recall of different methods on ModelNet40.

Table 2. Ablation experiments (partially overlapping data).

Method	R_{MIE}	t_{MIE}	R_{RMSE}	t_{RMSE}	CCD	$Recall$
poGMM-v1	8.2107	0.1522	6.0817	0.0964	0.0714	83.1%
poGMM-v2	21.9330	0.2569	10.9687	0.1258	0.1872	38.3%
poGMM	**5.7302**	**0.0581**	**5.1447**	**0.0599**	**0.0246**	**94.9%**

Table 3. Time (in milliseconds) required to test a pair of clean point clouds.

Points	ICP [4]	DCP-V2 [21]	PointNetLK [2]	RGM [10]	DeepGMR [25]	Ours
717	177	62	195	179	**13**	**27**
1024	189	83	201	187	**14**	**29**

Table 4. Experimental results on the last 20 categories of ModelNet40.

Category	R_{MIE}	t_{MIE}	R_{RMSE}	t_{RMSE}	CCD	$Recall$
Airplane	1.1608	0.0158	0.0365	2.9033	0.0223	100%
Laptop	1.2160	0.025	0.0578	2.8531	0.0257	100%
Mantel	1.4201	0.0211	0.0488	3.3938	0.0295	98.0%
Monitor	4.1319	0.0278	0.0642	4.7025	0.0266	91.0%
Night_stand	1.1318	0.0171	0.0395	2.7538	0.0336	100%
Person	3.1900	0.0273	0.063	5.0897	0.0148	95.0%
Piano	2.0425	0.0256	0.0591	4.9728	0.0297	97.0%
Plant	5.6634	0.0777	0.1087	8.7098	0.0447	86.0%
Radio	1.4851	0.0199	0.0459	3.435	0.0292	100%
Range_hood	1.4520	0.0187	0.0432	3.5286	0.0311	99.0%
Sink	3.4306	0.0218	0.0504	3.2856	0.0293	90.0%
Sofa	1.4910	0.0193	0.0446	3.5089	0.0277	99.0%
Stairs	3.5112	0.037	0.0854	5.6376	0.0201	90.0%
Stool	3.4413	0.0226	0.0523	6.906	0.0194	100%
Table	2.2623	0.0202	0.0468	3.0312	0.0261	90.0%
Tent	1.9220	0.0243	0.0562	4.3739	0.0328	100%
Toilet	1.7121	0.0209	0.0482	4.0495	0.0306	99.0%
Tv_stand	1.3929	0.0205	0.0473	3.2734	0.0287	99.0%
Vase	5.6815	0.0485	0.0657	7.5552	0.0354	87.0%
Wardrobe	5.8335	0.0551	0.0549	6.8341	0.0282	88.0%
Xbox	1.2408	0.017	0.0393	2.9652	0.0274	100%

4.2   Ablation Experiments and Computational Efficiency

Variants. To further analyze the performance of our network, we modified the network by removing the cross-attention part of the feature extractor notated as poGMM-v1 and replacing SegNet&ClaNet with a single split-to network notated as poGMM-v2, respectively. Table 4 shows the importance of using DGCNN with cross-attention and joint SegNet&ClaNet modules, which contributes significantly to the improvement of registration performance.

Computational Efficiency. Table 3 presents the test processing times of each compared method for different points. Our time spent is second only to Deep-GMR [25], but our registration performance exceeds that of all methods.

5   Conclusion

We propose poGMM-Net, the first statistical-based registration method that aligns partially overlapping point clouds. We use SegNet and ClaNet modules to learn the potential corresponding distributions of points to GMMs and the overlapping feature sets of points located in GMMs, respectively. poGMM-Net is insensitive to initialization or noise and can handle the most challenging task of aligning point clouds with partial overlap. Moreover, our network has acceptable computational efficiency. In the future, we aim to enhance the network to accommodate larger point clouds.

References

1. Anzai, Y.: Pattern Recognition and Machine Learning. Elsevier, Amsterdam (2012)
2. Aoki, Y., Goforth, H., Arun Srivatsan, R., Lucey, S.: PointNetLK: robust & efficient point cloud registration using PointNet. In: The IEEE Conference on Computer Vision and Pattern Recognition (CVPR), June 2019
3. Baker, S., Matthews, I.: Lucas-Kanade 20 years on: a unifying framework. Int. J. Comput. Vision 56(3), 221–255 (2004)
4. Besl, P.J., McKay, N.D.: Method for registration of 3-D shapes. In: Sensor Fusion IV: Control Paradigms and Data Structures, vol. 1611, pp. 586–606. International Society for Optics and Photonics (1992)
5. Biber, P., Straßer, W.: The normal distributions transform: a new approach to laser scan matching. In: Proceedings 2003 IEEE/RSJ International Conference on Intelligent Robots and Systems (IROS 2003) (Cat. No. 03CH37453), vol. 3, pp. 2743–2748. IEEE (2003)
6. Chetverikov, D., Stepanov, D., Krsek, P.: Robust Euclidean alignment of 3D point sets: the trimmed iterative closest point algorithm. Image Vis. Comput. 23(3), 299–309 (2005)
7. Dempster, A.P., Laird, N.M., Rubin, D.B.: Maximum likelihood from incomplete data via the EM algorithm. J. Roy. Stat. Soc.: Ser. B (Methodol.) 39(1), 1–22 (1977)
8. Dhawale, A., Shankar, K.S., Michael, N.: Fast Monte-Carlo localization on aerial vehicles using approximate continuous belief representations. In: Proceedings of the IEEE Conference on Computer Vision and Pattern Recognition, pp. 5851–5859 (2018)
9. Eckart, B., Kim, K., Kautz, J.: HGMR: hierarchical gaussian mixtures for adaptive 3D registration. In: Proceedings of the European Conference on Computer Vision (ECCV), pp. 705–721 (2018)

10. Fu, K., Liu, S., Luo, X., Wang, M.: Robust point cloud registration framework based on deep graph matching. In: Proceedings of the IEEE/CVF Conference on Computer Vision and Pattern Recognition, pp. 8893–8902 (2021)

11. Granger, S., Pennec, X.: Multi-scale EM-ICP: a fast and robust approach for surface registration. In: Heyden, A., Sparr, G., Nielsen, M., Johansen, P. (eds.) ECCV 2002. LNCS, vol. 2353, pp. 418–432. Springer, Heidelberg (2002). https://doi.org/10.1007/3-540-47979-1_28

12. Handa, A., Whelan, T., McDonald, J., Davison, A.J.: A benchmark for RGB-D visual odometry, 3D reconstruction and slam. In: 2014 IEEE International Conference on Robotics and Automation (ICRA), pp. 1524–1531. IEEE (2014)

13. Hertz, A., Hanocka, R., Giryes, R., Cohen-Or, D.: PointGMM: a neural GMM network for point clouds. In: Proceedings of the IEEE/CVF Conference on Computer Vision and Pattern Recognition, pp. 12054–12063 (2020)

14. Huang, S., Gojcic, Z., Usvyatsov, M., Wieser, A., Schindler, K.: Predator: registration of 3D point clouds with low overlap. In: Proceedings of the IEEE/CVF Conference on Computer Vision and Pattern Recognition, pp. 4267–4276 (2021)

15. Jian, B., Vemuri, B.C.: Robust point set registration using gaussian mixture models. IEEE Trans. Pattern Anal. Mach. Intell. **33**(8), 1633–1645 (2010)

16. Pomerleau, F., Colas, F., Siegwart, R.: A review of point cloud registration algorithms for mobile robotics. Found. Trends Robot. **4**(1), 1–104 (2015)

17. Qi, C.R., Su, H., Mo, K., Guibas, L.J.: PointNet: deep learning on point sets for 3D classification and segmentation. In: Proceedings of the IEEE Conference on Computer Vision and Pattern Recognition, pp. 652–660 (2017)

18. Reynolds, D.A.: Gaussian mixture models. Encyclopedia Biometrics **741**, 659–663 (2009)

19. Rusinkiewicz, S.: A symmetric objective function for ICP. ACM Trans. Graph. (TOG) **38**(4), 1–7 (2019)

20. Segal, A., Haehnel, D., Thrun, S.: Generalized-ICP. In: Robotics: Science and Systems, , Seattle, WA, vol. 2, p. 435 (2009)

21. Wang, Y., Solomon, J.M.: Deep closest point: learning representations for point cloud registration. In: The IEEE International Conference on Computer Vision (ICCV), October 2019

22. Wang, Y., Solomon, J.M.: PRNet: self-supervised learning for partial-to-partial registration. arXiv preprint arXiv:1910.12240 (2019)

23. Wu, Z., et al.: 3D ShapeNets: a deep representation for volumetric shapes. In: Proceedings of the IEEE Conference on Computer Vision and Pattern Recognition, pp. 1912–1920 (2015)

24. Yew, Z.J., Lee, G.H.: RPM-Net: robust point matching using learned features. In: Conference on Computer Vision and Pattern Recognition (CVPR) (2020)

25. Yuan, W., Eckart, B., Kim, K., Jampani, V., Fox, D., Kautz, J.: DeepGMR: learning latent Gaussian mixture models for registration. In: Vedaldi, A., Bischof, H., Brox, T., Frahm, J.-M. (eds.) ECCV 2020. LNCS, vol. 12350, pp. 733–750. Springer, Cham (2020). https://doi.org/10.1007/978-3-030-58558-7_43

26. Zhou, Q.-Y., Park, J., Koltun, V.: Fast global registration. In: Leibe, B., Matas, J., Sebe, N., Welling, M. (eds.) ECCV 2016. LNCS, vol. 9906, pp. 766–782. Springer, Cham (2016). https://doi.org/10.1007/978-3-319-46475-6_47

More Diverse Training, Better Compositionality! Evidence from Multimodal Language Learning

Caspar Volquardsen[✉], Jae Hee Lee, Cornelius Weber, and Stefan Wermter

Knowledge Technology, Department of Informatics, University of Hamburg,
Hamburg, Germany
{caspar.volquardsen,jae.hee.lee,cornelius.weber,
stefan.wermter}@uni-hamburg.de
www.knowledge-technology.info

Abstract. Artificial neural networks still fall short of human-level generalization and require a very large number of training examples to succeed. Model architectures that further improve generalization capabilities are therefore still an open research question. We created a multimodal dataset from simulation for measuring the compositional generalization of neural networks in multimodal language learning. The dataset consists of sequences showing a robot arm interacting with objects on a table in a simple 3D environment, with the goal of describing the interaction. Compositional object features, multiple actions, and distracting objects pose challenges to the model. We show that an LSTM-encoder-decoder architecture jointly trained together with a vision-encoder surpasses previous performance and handles multiple visible objects. Visualization of important input dimensions shows that a model that is trained with multiple objects, but not a model trained on just one object, has learnt to ignore irrelevant objects. Furthermore we show that additional modalities in the input improve the overall performance. We conclude that the underlying training data has a significant influence on the model's capability to generalize compositionally.

Keywords: Compositional generalization · Computer vision · Multimodality · Sequence-to-sequence · Robotics

1 Introduction

Artificial neural networks made great advances in the last decade and are state of the art for natural language processing and computer vision tasks [13]. Neural networks learn to approximate functions in high dimensional space from a set of samples from the target function. The goal is to generalize outside of the known training examples. But neural networks still fall short of human-level generalization and need a lot of training data to approximate their target

The authors acknowledge support from the German Research Foundation DFG under project CML (TRR 169) and from the BMWK under project SiDiMo.

E. Pimenidis et al. (Eds.): ICANN 2022, LNCS 13531, pp. 417–428, 2022.
https://doi.org/10.1007/978-3-031-15934-3_35

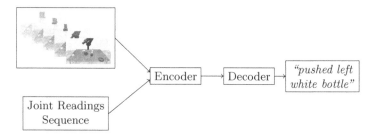

Fig. 1. The task of the model. It is tested on novel action-color-object combinations that are not part of the training data.

function well [11]. Compositionality in language learning describes the ability to understand and produce novel combinations from known components [15]. For example, a neural model should be able to generate a novel word combination on demand, such as "red banana", if it visually perceives such an object for the first time. Recent work showed that neural networks struggle to combine known elements in a new way, even in simple cases [1,3,6,7,10,14,16]. These limitations can be attributed to the binding problem that describes the inability of neural networks to bind information that is distributed throughout the network and form symbol-like entities [3]. Using models that can better generalize compositionally reduces the amount of data required to handle new scenarios. It is therefore an open research question what aspects benefit neural networks' capabilities to generalize outside of the learned data distribution. We show that our neural network architecture is able to generalize compositionally, but the capabilities to do so are strongly impacted by the underlying data distribution. The model maps input video sequences, enriched with sensor data sequences, to short descriptive sentences. Figure 1 gives a brief overview of our problem setting. We created the dataset in a way, that we systematically leave out word combinations to check if our model generalizes to these new combinations.

2   Related Work

Compositional generalization is part of different fields in artificial intelligence research. Different benchmarks and customized architectures have been presented with the goal of understanding limitations and pushing the abilities of current systems.

The SCAN dataset is designed to test compositional generalization on a sequence-to-sequence task [10]. Natural language descriptions are mapped to a sequence of navigation commands. The authors used different recurrent neural network (RNN) architectures to learn the mapping of the input description to the command sequence output. They found that RNNs showed good generalization capabilities in testing when commands were arbitrarily split between train and test set, but they failed in cases that required compositionality. They also show that the generalization problem is related to the problem that RNNs learn embeddings for new verbs which are different to the representation of known verbs. Loula et al. [14] confirm these findings when they investigated other kinds of compositionality on the SCAN dataset, which envoled combining highly familiar words in new ways to create novel meaning.

The grounded SCAN dataset (gSCAN) extends the SCAN dataset by another modality [16]. The task is again to produce an output sequence of commands, but in addition to the description of the action, a two dimensional grid world with an agent and different objects is part of the input. In contrast to reinforcement tasks only the initial world state is part of the input and the complete command sequence has to be generated from that. The objects placed in the world have different sizes, shapes and colors and the input sentence describes what actions the agent should perform. The task descriptions contain relative terms like "small", where the model needs to understand the underlying concept. The authors use two encoders for the different modalities in the input, a bidirectional LSTM for the language encoding and a convolutional neural network for the image of the world state. A decoder LSTM attends to the inputs and produces the output sequence. Ruis et al. [16] report that their model failed on most compositional generalization tests.

Eisermann et al. [1] investigated the effect of the data distribution on the ability of a recurrent neural network-based architecture to generalize and do compositional generalization. For this, they created a multimodal dataset to systematically measure the ability of a model to do compositional generalization. The dataset contained sequences showing interactions of a robotic arm with various objects on a table and a descriptive sentence as label. Their results showed some significant factors of the dataset for the model to generalize well. They showed that more diverse training data with more overlap of attributes improved the generalization performance significantly. Leaving away additional sensory data and only relying on vision data led to worse results not only of the generalization performance but also of the training performance. A noticeable problem of the model was the introduction of a distractor object on the table, which means a second object which is not part of the action and thus not part of the label sentence. In this setting even the accuracy on the training data was poor and significantly worse than with one visible object. This implies that the underlying model architecture was not able to process the visual input in a sufficient way, because it could not separate the features of the two objects, as is evident in the binding problem. This limitation was the motivation for our work, with the goal to overcome this problem and further improve the compositional generalization with a different model architecture.

The EMIL dataset is a quite similar dataset, which consists of recordings of real interactions of a humanoid robot [5]. The robot interacts with objects on a table in front of him in a child-like manner, performing actions which an external teacher describes. The recordings contain image data from the robot's two cameras, auditory data recorded by the robot's microphones and additionally sensorimotor data describing the different joints of the robot. This dataset is comparably small with 240 sequences. Heinrich et al. [6] use different continuous

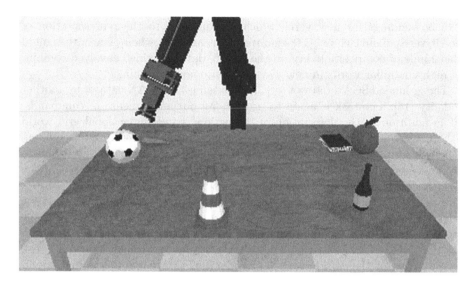

Fig. 2. Example frame with six visible objects. After putting down the banana it is partially occluded.

time RNN-based architectures which take multimodal sensory input and map it to language. They report that all models struggle on generalization tasks. They also find that their models tend to rely on a single modality when the training dataset is smaller, but with a larger training set, the model benefits from the additional modalities.

3   Multimodal Dataset

Based on the work of Eisermann et al. [1] we created a dataset and expanded it to more complex scenes. It consists of sequences of varying length that show video data capturing a robot arm behind a table, which interacts with objects on the table and corresponding sensory data. See Fig. 2 for an example frame of a sequence. There are between one and six objects on the table depending on experimental condition. The camera capturing the scene is placed in front of the table looking down on it towards the robot arm, also capturing white background and some space to the left and to the right of the table. A scene captures one of four different actions, which the robot arm performs with exactly one object. In addition to the video data, for each frame, the corresponding joint angles of the robot arm are part of the data. The dataset was generated using the robot simulation software CoppeliaSim (www.coppeliarobotics.com). The sequences consist on average of 20 frames, where each frame is the combination of a 224×398 8bit RGB pixel image and six 32bit floating point numbers representing the sensor readings of the six joint positions of the robot arm. Each sequence has a corresponding descriptive sentence of three words, describing the interaction of the

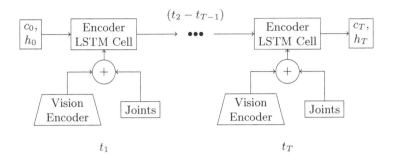

Fig. 3. Encoder architecture

robot arm. The four different actions are *"pushed right"*, *"pushed left"*, *"picked up"* and *"put down"*. For the action *"push left"* the robot arm moves to the object, places the gripper (front end of the robot arm) to the right of the object, and pushes the object to the left. If the object lays near the left end of the table the object can get pushed off the table which is also partly captured by the camera. *"pushed right"* happens vice versa. The action *"picked up"* captures the robot arm moving to the object placing the gripper on the object, gripping it and moving it up. In the air the capturing of the action *"put down"* begins where the robot arm moves the object in the air to a random location over the table and lays it down. When multiple objects are visible simultaneously on the table the collision of the objects with each other and the gripper are all simulated. It can therefore happen that the path that the gripper pushes an object collides with another object leading to multiple objects being moved. In these cases it is necessary to consider the relative positioning of the objects towards the gripper and the entire sequence to describe it correctly. Another challenging scenario of multiple objects is occlusion, or partial occlusion of objects in parts of the sequence. In this case the model needs to recognize the object in parts where it is visible and compose this information. These difficulties happen at a higher frequency with increasing number of visible objects.

4   Model

The task of our model is to find the correct description given the input sequence. We use an LSTM encoder-decoder architecture similar to the architecture Sutskever et al. used for language translation [19], because it can naturally deal with sequences of varying length. One LSTM is used to encode the input sequence one time step after another into a fixed size vector. This vector is used as the hidden state input to the decoder LSTM which produces the output sentence token by token. Figure 3 illustrates our encoder architecture. At each time step t_i the input to the encoder is the image data and the joint positions. Similar to Eisermann et al. [1] we use a convolutional neural network as vision encoder to preprocess the high dimensional image data and encode it to a lower dimensional

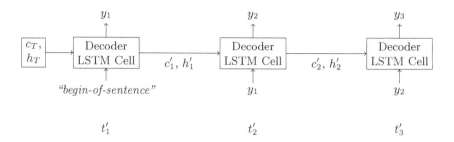

Fig. 4. Decoder architecture

feature vector [2,9,12,13]. We modified a ResNet18 network to fit to our image dimensions, since it 224×224 pixel images of the ImageNet challenge [4,17].After the convolutional layers of the ResNet we use a fully connected layer which outputs a vector of dimension d_{image}. The encoded image vector concatenated with the 6-dimensional vector of the joint positions is the input to the encoder LSTM at each time step. At time t_0 the initial cell state and hidden state vectors are zero vectors and the resulting cell state and hidden state after t_i gets passed to the next time step t_{i+1}. After all inputs at time step t_T the resulting cell and hidden state c_T and h_T contain the encoded information of the input sequence and form the input to the decoder (Fig. 4).

The decoder takes the cell state and hidden state vectors from the encoder and gets a *"begin-of-sequence"*-token as input for the first output generation. Each token is a 19-dimensional vector, where we use one-hot encoding of all possible words which are 4 actions, 6 colors and 9 objects. The begin-of-sequence vector is an zero vector. The tokens get generated through a linear transformation applied on the LSTM output of dimension d_{hidden} which maps to the output dimension 19. A softmax function transforms the output to a probability distribution over the 19 dimensions. After the first output at t'_1 the generated output y_1 is the input to the decoder at t'_2. The same is applied to t'_3. Note that we do not require an *"end-of-sequence"*-token for the decoder to stop [19]. Since all output sentences have the same length of three tokens we simply take the first three outputs. This change could however be made if varying output lengths were required.

5   Training Setup

For our experiments we created several different training and validation datasets in a systematic way. We altered four parameters for the dataset composition and generated the datasets accordingly. We trained our model the same way on all datasets and evaluated the model on a constant test set and a compositional generalization test set. For comparability of our results we took the same action-color-object combinations for the constant test sets as Eisermann et al. [1] and organized the training and validation datasets in a similar way. The constant test set contains the four different combinations *"pushed right white football"*, *"pushed right yellow banana"*, *"pushed left brown bottle"* and *"pushed left red ring"*. All these action-color-object combinations were part of every training and validation set and only varied in the randomised positions on the table of the objects and robot arm. The compositional generalization test set on the other hand contained only action-color-object combinations which were excluded from the training and validation datasets. The scenes contained are *"pushed left white football"*, *"pushed left yellow banana"*, *"pushed right brown bottle"* and *"pushed right red ring"*, which are the opposite pushing directions than in the constant test set. The training and validation datasets were generated according to the following parameters:

V1, V2, V6: The given number denotes the number of simultaneously visible objects. This affects also the constant test and compositional generalization test set, where as many objects are visible as in the corresponding training and validation set.

C1, C6: The number of different colors each object can randomly appear in. **C1** means that each object always appears in the same color. The six possible colors are *red, green, blue, white, brown,* and *yellow.*

O4, O9: The number of object types that can show up in a scene. **O4** shows the same objects as in the constant test set, which are a*football, banana, bottle,* and *ring.* **O9** shows additional five object types, which are not part of the test sets.

X, ¬X: This parameter controls whether the colors of the objects in the test sets are exclusive to them. Exclusive meaning that no other object appears in the same color as the objects in the test set. For example, only the banana would appear in yellow in the training and validation set if the colors were exclusive.

J, ¬J: Specifies whether the positions of the robot arm joints are part of the input sequence. If not, the model needs to generate a descriptive sentence solely relying on the visual input.

Each training set contained 5000 samples and the validation set 2500. We trained the model on each dataset for 20 epochs and evaluated the model after each epoch on the validation dataset. Here we calculated the word-wise accuracy on the validation dataset and saved the model parameter corresponding to the epoch with the highest accuracy, as a kind of early stopping procedure [2]. Word-wise accuracy means the percentage of correctly generated words in the output sentence. At each epoch we trained the model in mini-batches of size 16 with the Adam optimizer [8]. We calculated the loss for each output using the cross-entropy loss function and back-propagate through time, also jointly updating the parameter of the vision encoder. At the start of training we initialised the weights of the ResNet18 convolutional layers with weights pretrained on the ImageNet dataset to speed up the learning process [17]. For our experiments we used a hidden dimension for c_i and h_i of $d_{hidden} = 512$ and the dimension for the encoded images of $d_{image} = 256$. We found these dimensions to perform the best in a prior hyperparameter search.[1]

---

[1] The source code for the model and the data generation can be found at this link: https://github.com/Casparvolquardsen/Compositional-Generalization-in-Multimodal-Language-Learning.

Table 1. Sentence-wise accuracy of our model for the different training datasets in percent. The abbreviation "Comp. Gen." stands for the compositional generalization test set.

		4 Objects (**O4**)		9 Objects (**O9**)	
		Exclusive colors (**X**)		Color overlap (¬**X**)	
		1 Color (**C1**)	6 Colors (**C6**)	1 Color (**C1**)	6 Colors (**C6**)
		*With joint readings (**J**)*			
1 Visible object (**V1**)	Training	93.3	99.5	99.9	99.9
	Constant test	99.9	100.0	99.9	100.0
	Comp. Gen.	**1.25**	**56.7**	**64.4**	**99.4**
2 Visible object (**V2**)	Training	99.1	99.8	99.0	99.2
	Constant test	97.3	98.8	96.7	92.6
	Comp. Gen.	**7.0**	**44.6**	**38.6**	**87.6**
6 Visible object (**V6**)	Training	100.0	99.7	99.8	99.2
	Constant test	98.6	96.5	95.35	87.0
	Comp. Gen.	**7.2**	**48.1**	**42.4**	**76.5**
		*Without joint readings (¬**J**)*			
1 Visible object (**V1**)	Training	96.7	99.6	99.9	100.0
	Constant test	100.0	99.9	99.9	100.0
	Comp. Gen.	**0.0**	**54.0**	**35.1**	**99.5**
2 Visible object (**V2**)	Training	98.9	99.6	99.0	99.4
	Constant test	98.6	98.8	94.3	88.5
	Comp. Gen.	**5.5**	**40.1**	**33.9**	**78.4**
6 Visible object (**V6**)	Training	99.9	99.8	99.9	99.4
	Constant test	97.4	96.5	95.1	80.6
	Comp. Gen.	**7.9**	**42.0**	**34.0**	**68.6**
Num. different sentences		12	44	32	212
Samples per sentence		416	113	156	23

6 Results

Table 1 shows the results of our experiments. We report the sentence-wise accuracy which is the percentage of label sentences which were generated completely correct. This metric is more informative than the word-wise accuracy regarding the compositional generalization capabilities, because the sentences in the compositional generalization set differ only in one word to sentences contained in the training set and so a word-wise accuracy would be misleadingly high when the model does not generalize compositionally. We summarize our findings as follows:

Distractor Objects can be Handled: Compared to the model of Eisermann et al. [1] our model achieved better training and constant test accuracy for every dataset. On the datasets with joint readings our model achieved on average 43.5%

better constant test results [1]. Our model especially overcame the problem of significant worse performance with two visible objects pointed out by Eisermann et al. [1]. Our average constant test performance with two visible objects and joint readings was 96.4% compared to 56.1% [1]. We therefore tested our model also on the more complex scenarios with six visible objects and found only a minor drop in performance with still better test results than the previous model on simpler datasets [1].

Successful Compositional Generalization: We achieve over 99% compositional generalization test accuracy for the V1-C6-O9 dataset. Given here one visible object (V1) and the largest diversity in colors (C6) and object types (O9), the compositional generalization performance comes close to the training and constant test performance (see rightmost column in Table 1). Our model also surpasses the compositional generalization capabilities of Eisermann et al. [1] in nearly all cases, the only exception being the V1-C6-O4-X-J data set, which is challenging in its small number of object types and exclusive colors.

More Diverse Training Set Increases Compositional Generalization: We find that both showing each object in more different colors (C1 to C6) and increasing the number of different objects that are shown (O4 to O9) benefit the models' capability to generalize compositionally, confirming the findings of Eisermann et al. [1]. For only one visible object (V1) we achieve the highest compositional generalization capabilities with an accuracy of over 99%. For multiple visible objects on the C6-O9 datasets the compositional generalization accuracies are still between 68.6% and 87.6%. A more detailed analysis of the results shows that the datasets V1-C1-O4-X with the lowest sentence-wise compositional generalization performance, have a much higher word-wise accuracy of 66.6%, where in most cases the model correctly named color and object, but not the correct action.

More Diverse Training Set Decreases Constant Test Accuracy: The highest constant test accuracies are achieved in the least diverse datasets (C1-O4) where the training set only contains sequences of 12 different sentences, where four of them are inside the constant test set. We found the worst constant test accuracies for the most diverse datasets (C6-O9) where 212 different sentences were part of the training set. Because we use the same number of training samples for each experiment, the number of samples per word combination is lower in these cases and therefore also the number of samples of the sentences contained in the constant test set (see in the bottom two rows of the Table 1).

Removing a Sensory Modality Decreases Overall Performance: We find that leaving away the joint readings as input to the model decreased the overall performance slightly. In these cases the model had to rely solely on the vision input with no additional modality. The joint readings in theory are able on their own to specify which action was performed by the robot arm. We found that leaving the joint readings away decreases the constant test accuracy on average by only 1% and the compositional generalization accuracy by 13%. Therefore

(a) Original input image.
Label: *"pushed left brown bottle"*

(b) Model trained on one visible object.
Predicted: *"pushed right yellow banana"*

(c) Model trained on two visible objects.
Predicted: *"pushed left brown bottle"*

(d) Model trained on six visible objects.
Predicted: *"pushed left brown bottle"*

Fig. 5. An example frame input of the constant test set with six visible objects. (b), (c), and (d) show input feature importance from the attribution method integrated gradients for models trained on different datasets, given input (a). The model used for (b) fails to focus and predicts a wrong sentence.

we confirm the finding of Eisermann et al. [1], but show a lower influence on the performance of our model.

Models Trained on One Visible Object Fail on Multiple Objects: Evaluating the models also on the constant test sets with a different number of visible objects as in the training set shows that models which were trained on V2 or V6 training datasets also generalize well to samples with 1–6 visible objects. On the other hand, models which were trained on the V1 datasets generalize poorly to more visible objects and achieve a sentence-wise accuracy of below 55% in all cases when tested on constant test sets with 2–6 visible objects. We further analysed the functioning of the models using the integrated gradients attribution method [18]. Integrated Gradients is an axiomatic model interpretability algorithm that assigns an importance score to each input feature by approximating the integral of gradients of the model's output with respect to the inputs. We find that models trained on multiple visible objects form their color and object output mostly based on the input pixels near the robot arm gripper and do not consider the rest of the image. Contrarily models trained on only one visible object also consider input pixels at distractor objects for their prediction leading to wrong predictions. Figure 5 shows an example frame and the corresponding visualization of the integrated gradients method for three different models.

7   Discussion

Our model achieves over 99% compositional generalization performance in the best condition, compared to 65.62% of the model by Eisermann et al. [1]. We hypothesize that our encoder-decoder design forces the model to encode the information contained in the sequence in an organized way which benefits compositional generalization. Especially the increasing performance with more diverse training sets supports this hypothesis, because the relatively small hidden vector is less able to store the information for each word combination separately, but needs a common way of encoding the information. Another cause for improvement could be our ResNet vision encoder. Both our higher encoding dimension and the fact that we train it jointly with the rest of the network, including the convolutional kernels, may contribute to the improved performance.

The compositional generalization test set does not contain any unseen color-object combinations. For example, while *"pushed left yellow banana"* is unseen, the yellow banana was part of the training set together with other actions. Future research could extend the dataset to also investigate to what degree models are able to decompose the shape and color attributes of the objects.

Our results show that the model does not separate the features action type, color or object automatically, but only with sufficient variability in the training data. The lacking compositional generalization for the least diverse datasets indicates that input features are not separated compositionally in those cases, so the naming of the action is not only based on the motion of the robot arm, but influenced by the shape and color of the object. Such a phenomenon was also found in other experiments [1,10,14,16] and indicates a need for neural network architectures that use object-centric encoding [3]. It remains for future research to find generic architectures that further improve compositional generalization.

8   Conclusion

In summary, we created a dataset to investigate compositional generalization in multimodal sequences of a 3D environment. We showed a model, which can handle complex scenes with multiple visible objects, and is able to generalize compositionally with sufficient training data. An analysis with the integrated gradients method shows, that a model trained with only one visible object fails to focus if multiple objects are shown. In contrast, a model trained on two or six visible objects generalizes to arbitrary numbers of objects. We found remaining limitations of the model to systematically generalize compositionally, when trained on less diverse data, which confirms previous findings [1,10,14,16], while additional input modalities improve the model's generalization capabilities. The results provide guidance for model architecture design and training data selection that promise good generalization to unseen data.

428 C. Volquardsen et al.

References

1. Eisermann, A., Lee, J.H., Weber, C., Wermter, S.: Generalization in multimodal language learning from simulation. In: Proceedings of the International Joint Conference on Neural Networks (IJCNN 2021)(2021)
2. Goodfellow, I., Bengio, Y., Courville, A.: Deep Learning. MIT Press, Adaptive Computation and Machine Learning (2016)
3. Greff, K., van Steenkiste, S., Schmidhuber, J.: On the binding problem in artificial neural networks. arXiv:2012.05208 (2020)
4. He, K., Zhang, X., Ren, S., Sun, J.: Deep residual learning for image recognition. arXiv:1512.03385 (2015)
5. Heinrich, S., Kerzel, M., Strahl, E., Wermter, S.: Embodied multi-modal interaction in language learning: the EMIL data collection. In: Proceedings of the ICDL-EpiRob Workshop on Active Vision, Attention, and Learning (ICDL-Epirob 2018 AVAL). Tokyo, Japan (2018)
6. Heinrich, S., et al.: Crossmodal language grounding in an embodied neurocognitive model. Front. Neurorobotics **14** (2020)
7. Keysers, D., et al.: Measuring compositional generalization: a comprehensive method on realistic data. arXiv:1912.09713 (2019)
8. Kingma, D.P., Ba, J.: Adam: A method for stochastic optimization. arXiv:1412.6980 (2017)
9. Krizhevsky, A., Sutskever, I., Hinton, G.E.: ImageNet classification with deep convolutional neural networks. In: Pereira, F., Burges, C.J.C., Bottou, L., Weinberger, K.Q. (eds.) Advances in Neural Information Processing Systems. vol. 25, Curran Associates, Inc. (2012)
10. Lake, B.M., Baroni, M.: Generalization without systematicity: on the compositional skills of sequence-to-sequence recurrent networks. arXiv:1711.00350 (2017)
11. Lake, B.M., Ullman, T.D., Tenenbaum, J.B., Gershman, S.J.: Building machines that learn and think like people. arXiv:1604.00289 (2016)
12. LeCun, Y.: Generalization and network design strategies. Technical Report CRG-TR-89-4, University of Toronto (1989)
13. LeCun, Y., Bengio, Y., Hinton, G.: Deep learning. Nature 521, 436–44 (2015)
14. Loula, J., Baroni, M., Lake, B.M.: Rearranging the familiar: testing compositional generalization in recurrent networks. arXiv:1807.07545 (2018)
15. Montague, R.: Universal Grammar, vol. 36. Blackwell Publishing Ltd. (1970)
16. Ruis, L., Andreas, J., Baroni, M., Bouchacourt, D., Lake, B.M.: A benchmark for systematic generalization in grounded language understanding. arXiv:2003.05161 (2020)
17. Russakovsky, O.: ImageNet large scale visual recognition challenge. arXiv:1409.0575 (2014)
18. Sundararajan, M., Taly, A., Yan, Q.: Axiomatic attribution for deep networks. In: International Conference on Machine Learning, pp. 3319–3328, PMLR (2017)
19. Sutskever, I., Vinyals, O., Le, Q.V.: Sequence to sequence learning with neural networks. arXiv:1409.3215 (2014)

MT-TCCT: Multi-task Learning for Multimodal Emotion Recognition

Yandan Wang⬤, Zhongtang Chen$^{(\boxtimes)}$, Shuang Chen, and Yu Zhu

Shenyang Jianzhu University, Shenyang 110000, Liaoning, China
chen630609@163.com

Abstract. Multimodal emotion recognition is an emerging research field, which aims to capture affective information from multimodal data, such as natural language, facial expression, and voice intonation. However, most existing methods focus more on modality-common information, and the modality-specific features are neglected. How to learn the two kinds of modal features effectively is a challenging problem. In this paper, we introduce unimodal sub-tasks and present a multi-task framework to provide subspaces to learn modality-private and modality-shared features respectively. These represen-tations provide a holistic view for emotion recognition. Besides, modal fragment-absence is also a challenging problem, as text modality has been proven to have more affective features, a text-centered feature reconstruction module employing cross-modal attention mechanism is designed to adapt semantics from one modality to another. To evaluate the performance of the proposed model, the experiments are conducted on CH-SIMS and CMU-MOSI datasets. The results validate the efficiency and generalization of the multi-task training-based framework.

Keywords: Multi-task learning network · Cross-modal attention · Multimodal emotion recognition

1 Introduction

With the rapid growth of social media platforms such as YouTube, Instagram, and TikTok, people now tend to express their opinions on a topic through these public platforms. The video consists of vision and audio, and the text is usually transcript in subtitles. The sentiment embedded in these valuable data has provided researchers with a new research direction (i.e., emotion recognition), which aims to capture and analyze human emotions through the information of various modalities.

Previous studies have achieved promising results on unimodal emotion recognition (UniER), such as text emotion recognition [1], image emotion recognition [2], and audio emotion recognition [3], but ignore the complementary affective information in multimodal data. How to fuse these various kinds of data is the core problem of multimodal emotion recognition (MER). There has been

E. Pimenidis et al. (Eds.): ICANN 2022, LNCS 13531, pp. 429–442, 2022.
https://doi.org/10.1007/978-3-031-15934-3_36

a surge of work proposed to integrate the data from different sources. Li and Chen [4] propose to use Convolutional Neural Networks (CNNs) to capture consecutive multimodal fusion, and use Long Short-Term Memory network (LSTM) to project the concatenated fusion. To learn the multimodal contextual information in real-time, Huan et al. [5] designed an attention fusion network, which can calculate the distribution of attention at each moment of multiple modalities.

As most multimodal emotion recognition models put more attention on the multimodal fused feature, the intra-modal information is ignored. To tackle this issue, some promising algorithms have been proposed. For example, Wu et al. [6] explore shared and private semantics via text-to-vision and text-to-audio models and capture the features with higher prediction losses as modality-private information. Han et al. [7] designed a model that hierarchically maximizes the Mutual Information(MI) in unimodal input pairs to keep modality-invariant contents.

Motivated by the human behaviors that handle multiple tasks simultaneously, the multi-task learning (MTL) algorithm has attracted increasing attention from the community recently, for it enables the model to extract features from related tasks simultaneously. The MTL algorithm is first proposed in the field of Computer Vision [8], and a series of researchers have demonstrated that MTL performs better than single-task frameworks [9].

Inspired by the information-sharing mechanism of multi-task learning, which can maintain the task-invariant content, we design a multi-task setup architecture to divide the multimodal emotion recognition problem into sub-tasks. As shown in Fig. 1, the unimodal emotion recognition modules are exploited to learn the task-private features. The interaction between unimodal and multimodal task denotes that the inter-dependence between them will en-hance the accuracy of unimodal emotion recognition.

The model can jointly learn representations in three unimodal tasks (i.e., text emotion recognition, vision emotion recognition, and audio emotion recognition) and multimodal emotion recognition, by which the more emotionally inclined textual, visual, and acoustic representations can be learned, thereby improving the effect of modal fusion.

To this end, we design Multi-Task learning Text-Centered Cross Transformer (MT-TCCT) for multimodal emotion recognition in this paper. We firstly design a reconstruction module to learn the multimodal shared features, which employs a cross-modal attention mechanism to latently adapt the semantic information from one modality to another. This can make up for the loss caused by the missing part of modalities. For unimodal sub-tasks, the unimodal-private features will be extracted and concatenated with their corresponding shared feature to get a whole view of modalities, which enhances the performance of unimodal emotion recognition. Besides, inspired by the efficient correlation capturing and modeling ability of Transformer model, we apply a single backbone Transformer to learn the joint features of modality-shared and modality-private features to compute the correlations among all modalities. The main contributions of this work are as follows:

- We leverage the inter-dependence of sub-tasks (i.e., textual, visual, acoustic, and multimodal emotion recognition), and employ modality-private and modality-shared representations to improve each other's performance.
- To emphasize the dominant role of text, we design a reconstruct mod-ule to model the visual and acoustic modal features based on text represen-tation. The cross-modal attention mechanism is employed to enrich the vis-ual and acoustic features by textual information.
- We conduct comprehensive experiments on CMU-MOSI, where our proposed model gains superior and comparable results. To validate the generalization of MT-TCCT, we experiment on the Chinese dataset SIMS additionally, which illustrates the efficiency of our model further.

2 Related Work

Since the combination of discriminative emotion features of the text, vision and audio will provide richer semantic information, multimodal emotion recognition is playing an increasingly important role in emotion recognition, and how to extract the interactions among modalities has become the core challenge in MER.

According to the fusion stage, previous methods can be divided into two types: early fusion and late fusion. Early fusion methods usually exploit sophisticated attention mechanisms for multimodal fusion. Memory Fusion Network (MFN) [10] integrates view-specific interactions and cross-view interactions across different modalities and timesteps. The late fusion method performs an inter-modal fusion process on the intra-modal representation. Liu et al. [11] employ a low-rank cross-modal fusion approach to reduce computational complex-ity. Motivated by the machine translation framework, Tsai et al. [12] propose cross-modal Transformers (MULT), which adopt directional pairwise cross-modal attention to learn the feature interactions between modalities and adapt streams from one modality to another. Rahman et al. [13] propose a method for fine-tuning the pre-trained Transformer efficiently for multimodal emotion recognition.

Previous work on MER recognized that the text modality involves more affective information than both visual and acoustic modality, which should be a dominant role while fusing with other modal representations. Mai et al. [14] designed a gating mechanism to enhance the text representation across corresponding visual and acoustic features. Wang et al. [15] proposed a recurrent attended variation embedding network, which dynamically shifted word representations based on the nonverbal modal features.

As most of the methods put more attention on the multimodal shared features, the modality-private feature is neglected. To discriminate modality-invariant and -specific representations, Hazarika et al. [10] propose two subspaces for each modality, which are used to learn the common and characteristic features respectively. Inspired by cotraining framework, multi-task learning will enable the model to learn shared features of related works and maintain the task-private feature simultaneously. Zhang et al. [16] apply joint learning

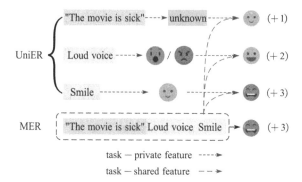

Fig. 1. Interaction of unimodal and multimodal emotion recognition tasks. If the speaker says "The movie is sick" in loud voice with a smile face, it will be recognized as happy, while it can be difficult to recognize only by language. A smiling face along can be recognized as weakly positive, and if the utterance is said in loud voice, it is difficult to determine it de-notes whether anger or surprise. The +1, +2, and +3 represent the intensity of emotion.

of interaction, relationship prediction, and multimodal feature fusion for video understanding. Zhang et al. [17] introduce unimodal sub-tasks and dynamically adjust the weights of the results of multimodal emotion recognition tasks. In addition, some important features may be easier for the model to learn on specific tasks, while on other tasks, the learning of the model may be hindered by the complex interaction or the interference of other features. To this end, we introduce unimodal sub-tasks to learn the modality-private feature, and model the inter-dependence between unimodal tasks and multimodal tasks.

3   Approach

In this section, we describe the MT-TCCT framework for multimodal emotion recognition. The architecture of the model is shown in Fig. 2. Each video is segmented into several continuous utterances, which consists of three input sequences from text(l), vision(v) and audio(a) modalities. These are represented as $X_l \in \mathbb{R}^{N_l \times d_l}$, $X_v \in \mathbb{R}^{N_v \times d_v}$, and $X_a \in \mathbb{R}^{N_a \times d_a}$ respectively. Here, N_m and d_m denotes the length and dimension of modality m.

For all tasks, we first encode low-level features in the feature learning module, and then pass the embedding through different parts of all tasks respectively. In the following subsections, we explain each of the novel components of our network in detail.

3.1   Modality Feature Learning

Textual Features. Traditionally, language modality features are GloVe [18] embeddings for each token in the utterance. Following recent works, pre-trained

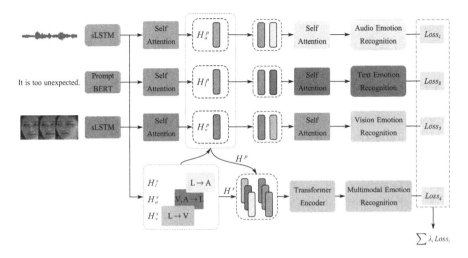

Fig. 2. The overall architecture of MT-TCCT. It consists of self-attention blocks for acoustic (A), textual (L) and visual (V) feature extraction, a text-centered reconstruction for modality-shared feature extraction, four prediction modules. H^p, H^s indicate private and shared features respectively. The yellow boxes represent all kinds of loss functions from different tasks. (Color figure online)

BERT based on prompt strategy [19] is efficient on text emotion recognition tasks. To obtain the accurate features of the language, we encode the raw text in the prompt template by Prompt-BERT instead of traditional embedding to encode the textual input into H_l.

$$H_l = \mathrm{BERT}(X_l; \theta_{bert}) \tag{1}$$

Visual and Acoustic Features. For acoustic embeddings, the pitch energy, normalized amplitude quotient, Mel-frequency cepstral coefficients, peak slope, and energy slope are calculated. And the visual features include facial action units, facial landmarks, eye gaze, head pose, and orientation. Following the previous work [20,21], we exploit a single directional LSTM to learn utterance-level contextual features and long-term dependencies, which maps the utterance sequence $X_{m\in\{v,a\}} \in \mathbb{R}^{BN \times L_m \times d_m}$ to a fixed-size vector $H_{m\in\{v,a\}} \in \mathbb{R}^{BN \times d_h}$. Here, BN and L_m denote batch size and length of input respectively. The last hidden state representations are used as the whole sequence vectors.

$$H_a = \mathrm{sLSTM}_m(X_m; \theta_m) \tag{2}$$

3.2 Emotion Recognition

Unimodal Representation Learning. For unimodal task, self-attention mechanism is applied to project the unimodal features into the task-private subspace. For self-attention, we set $Q = K = V = H_m \in \mathbb{R}^{BN \times d_m}$.

$$H_m^p = \text{Self} - \text{Attention}(H_m) \tag{3}$$

where m denotes a single modality and p represents the private feature.

Text Centered Feature Reconstruction. As the text sequence involves more sentimental information compared with the other modalities, we design the text-centered reconstruction framework that transforms the textual information into visual and acoustic features H_m^p, $m \in v, a$.

The text-centered modal fusion module includes three encoders, which stacks several cross-modal attention blocks, and each of them consists of N layers. We define the Queries as $Q_m = X_m W_{Q_m}$, Keys as $K_m = X_m W_{K_m}$, and Values as $V_m = X_m W_{V_m}$, where $W_{Q_m} \in \mathbb{R}^{d_m \times d_k}$, $W_{K_m} \in \mathbb{R}^{d_m \times d_k}$, $W_{V_m} \in \mathbb{R}^{d_m \times d_k}$ are trainable matrices.

$$H_{i \in \{v,a\}}^s = \mathbf{CM}(H_i, H_l)$$
$$= \text{softmax}(\frac{Q_i K_l^T}{\sqrt{d_k}})V_l \tag{4}$$

$$H_{l,j \in \{v,a\}}^s = \mathbf{CM}(H_l, H_j)$$
$$= \text{softmax}(\frac{Q_l K_j^T}{\sqrt{d_k}})V_j \tag{5}$$

In this process, nonverbal features are reconstructed based on text feature, and text feature is fused with nonverbal information as well.

Multimodal Post Fusion. Modeling multimodal features involves capturing correspondences and integrating them from multiple heterogeneous sources of data. For post cross-modal fusion, we stack the shared and private features into a matrix as the input of the cross-modal Transformer, which enables the model comprehensively learn the modal features and the modal representations can be aware of each other.

$$H_f = \text{MultiHead}([H_l^s, H_l^p, H_v^s, H_v^p, H_a^s, H_a^p]) \tag{6}$$

3.3 Prediction Layer

Unimodal Emotion Recognition. As unimodal emotions are highly reliant on multimodal contextual representations, we concatenate the unimodal private and shared features, and then apply attention to whole view to reveal the contributing features.

$$F_m = \text{Self} - \text{Attention}([H_m^s; H_m^p]) \tag{7}$$

Finally, the task predictions are generated by a softmax classifier to obtain the final label:

$$\hat{y}_m = W_{so}(\text{ReLU}(W_f F_m + b_f)) + b_{so} \tag{8}$$

where W_f, W_{so}, b_f and b_{so} are learnable parameters of the classified layer.

Multimodal Emotion Recognition. For multimodal emotion recognition, we take the output of the Transformer and stack a joint vector, which is used for multimodal emotion prediction.

$$F_{fusion} = \text{ReLU}(W_f^T[\hat{H}_l^s \oplus \hat{H}_l^p \oplus \hat{H}_v^s \oplus \hat{H}_v^p \oplus \hat{H}_a^s \oplus \hat{H}_a^p] + b_f) \qquad (9)$$

Finally, the task prediction $\hat{y}_f$ is generated by a linear classifier.

3.4 Optimization Objectives

We adopt L1Loss and Cross-Entropy Loss as the basic objective of regression and classification tasks respectively. Given the prediction of all tasks, the combined multi-objective loss function forces the model to minimize the loss between prediction and true distribution for all tasks:

$$\mathcal{L}_{total} = \sum_{k=1}^{N} \lambda_j \mathcal{L}_t(\hat{y}_j, y_j) + \alpha \sum \mathcal{L}_{sim} + \beta \sum \mathcal{L}_{diff} \qquad (10)$$

where $tin \in$ {classification, regression}, and λ_j is the weight for task j. In this paper, we set λ_j to $1/N$ for all N tasks to make a balance. Besides, α and β are weights denoting the contribution of each loss objective for achieving the task-shared and -private subspace properties.

CMD Metric [22]. Central Moment Discrepancy (CMD) is proposed as a distance function on probability distributions.

$$CMD_K(X, Y) = \frac{1}{|b - a|} ||\mathbf{E}(X) - \mathbf{E}(Y)||_2$$
$$+ \sum_{k=2}^{K} \frac{1}{|b - a|^k} ||C_k(X) - C_k(Y)||_2 \qquad (11)$$

where $\mathbf{E}(X)$ and $\mathbf{E}(Y)$ are the empirical expectation vectors of sample X and Y. $[a, b]$ denotes the interval of probability distribution, and $C_k(X) = \mathbf{E}\left((x - \mathbf{E}(X))^k\right)$ is the vector of all k^{th} order sample central moments of the coordinates of X. For the private features, we minimize the CMD loss between each pair of modalities to reduce the discrepancy of them.

$$\mathcal{L}_{sims}^{m_1, m_2} = \text{CMD}_K(H_{m1}^p, H_{m2}^p) \qquad (12)$$

where $(m1, m2) \in \{(l, v), (l, a), (v, a)\}$.

Besides, we adopt difference loss to ensure the difference between task-shared features H_m^s and task-private features H_m^p.

$$\mathcal{L}_{diff}^m = -\text{CMD}_K(H_m^s, H_m^p) \qquad (13)$$

where $m \in \{l, v, a\}$.

4   Experiments

In this section, we briefly describe the experimental setup, and experimentally show that this proposed approach improves the performance of the Transformer-based MER model over traditional frameworks.

4.1   Datasets

To comprehensively evaluate the performance of the proposed model, the experiments are conducted on the popular emotion recognition dataset CMU-MOSI [23]. To verify the model performance, we also conduct experiments on the Chinese dataset CH-SIMS [20].

CMU-MOSI. The CMU-MOSI dataset is a standard English dataset, which is popularly used in MER. It consists 2 199 video clips which are manually annotated according to emotion intensity with a continuous score between $[-3, +3]$, where -3 and $+3$ denote strongly negative and strongly positive respectively. For UniER task evaluation, we experiment with the compared models on the unimodal data of CMU-MOSI.

CH-SIMS. The CH-SIMS is a Chinese dataset consisting of 2 281 short video clips collected from different movies and various TV shows. Each sample is annotated with a sentiment score between $[-1, +1]$, where -1 and $+1$ denote strongly negative and strongly positive respectively.

4.2   Evaluation Metrics

Following previous works, we report the experimental results in two forms: classification and regression. For classification, we report a weighted F1 score (F1) for 2-class and 3-class. The results of 2-class and 3-class are segmented by marker -/-. For regression, we report the mean absolute error (MAE), and correlation (Corr) as our evaluation metrics. Except for MAE, higher values denote better performance for all metrics.

4.3   Basic Settings

The multimodal features exploited in our experiments are described as follows. For text modality, we utilize prompt-BERT to map the raw text into 768-dimensional vectors. For the SIMS dataset, acoustic embeddings by Librosa [24] is used as the input of the sLSTM layer. For the MOSI dataset, visual and acoustic features are extracted by FACET [25] and COVAREP [26]. We show our model configurations in Table 1.

Table 1. Model configurations.

Param	Settings
Activations	ReLU
Optimizer	Adam (lr = 2e−5)
Loss	Cross-Entropy Loss for classification
	L1 loss for regression
α	0.3
β	0.8
d	0.4
Dropout	16

Table 2. UniER experimental results on MOSI unimodal data of classification. We present the overall performance of accuracy. The best results are in **bold**.

Models	Text	Vision	Audio
BERT	73.2	–	–
Visual-CNN	–	55.8	–
LSTM	–	–	56.3
MT-TCCT	**82.9**	**64.9**	**57.6**

4.4   Baselines

We compare the MER performance of MT-TCCT with the following baselines: EF-LSTM, MFN, Self-MM [9], MISA [10], LMF [11], MULT [12], TFN [21], Graph-MFN [27]. For the UniER task, we compare the proposed model with Visual-CNN for vision emotion recognition and BERT for text emotion recognition, and LSTM for audio emotion recognition.

5   Results and Analysis

5.1   Quantitative Results

Unimodal Emotion Recognition. The experimental results of unimodal emotion recognition are shown in Table 2. Compared with other UniER models, our model achieves the best performance. In single-task learning, back-propagation of gradients tends to get stuck in local minima, which are different in multi-task learning, so training with related tasks and interacting with each other will avoid the hidden layer getting into the local minima. Furthermore, the latent correlations among the different features complement each other by sharing information and can improve each other's performance.

Multimodal Emotion Recognition. We compare our model with several baselines, and the experimental results of MOSI and SIMS are shown in Table 3.

Table 3. Experimental results on MOSI and SIMS. We present the overall performance of Accuracy and F1 for classification, Corr, and MAE for regression. The best results are in **bold**.

Dataset	MOSI				SIMS			
Model	Acc	F1	Corr	MAE	Acc	F1	Corr	MAE
EF-LSTM	77.8/75.3	77.7/73.4	67.3	93.1	69.3/54.2	56.8/38.1	2.14	59.3
TFN	74.6/72.89	74.8/71.4	67.3	94.3	76.1/66.0	76.0/60.5	58.6	44.4
LMF	77.4/75.2	77.5/73.5	68.5	94.8	77.0/68.0	77.6/64.2	54.9	44.2
Graph-MFN	76.2/74.4	76.4/73.0	64.9	98.1	77.0/66.9	76.9/62.6	57.8	44.2
MFN	79.3/76.5	79.0/74.5	65.2	95.3	77.3/65.2	77.4/62.3	56.1	45.5
MULT	80.1/77.9	80.2/76.2	66.7	88.5	75.9/66.7	76.4/64.8	57.9	44.0
MISA	82.8/79.7	82.5/77.7	76.1	78.3	77.9/64.7	75.6/57.5	–	–
SELF-MM	–	–	79.0	72.9	–	–	61.3	39.9
CT	76.5/74.3	76.7/72.8	–	–	77.4/67.4	77.3/64.2	–	–
TCCT	82.1/79.8	82.2/77.1	79.1	71.6	79.4/68.9	79.7/65.6	63.2	39.6
MT-TCCT	**83.1/80.4**	**82.4/81.8**	**79.3**	**70.0**	**83.5/73.6**	**82.6/72.4**	**67.5**	**39.1**

Compared with the model of the intricate fusion mechanisms, such as TFN and LFN, our model outperforms them on both Chinese and English datasets.

Our model outperforms the other baselines as well. The performance improvement is mainly achieved by the MTL algorithm and cross-modal Transformer fusion process, which indicates the cross-modal framework enables the model to exploit useful clues for interactions between different modalities. And the gain of MT-TCCT is also attributed to the MTL mechanism that takes advantage of the inter-dependence of all tasks.

5.2   Ablation Study

Role of Text-Guided Transformation. As shown in Table 4, we conduct an ablation experiment for text-guided modal feature transformation. We observe that the performance of the model consisting unimodal transformation module is improved compared with that unimodal feature learning, which denotes the transformation module can adapt streams from one modality to another, and enrich the semantic information by each other.

Compared with unimodal transformation, multimodal transformation learns the inter-dependence among three modalities, which leads to the best experimental results. Besides, the results show that the better result can be obtained when face and context are used as inputs. As shown in experimental results, face encoding network and context encoding network enable the model to focus on the emotional regions compared with the original images.

Role of Cross-Modal Transformer Fusion. To verify the effectiveness of the cross-modal Transformer, we conduct the ablation experiments. As shown

Table 4. Ablation study on reconstruction based on MOSI. T, A, V denote text, audio, vision modality respectively.

Modality		Acc	F1	Corr	MAE
Unimodal learning	A	64.1	68.9	31.4	76.6
	V	65.2	71.0	33.4	75.8
	T	76.3	78.2	64.5	65.4
Unimodal reconstruction	L → A	77.2	78.7	65.9	73.5
	L → V	78.4	77.9	66.1	72.7
	V, A → L	80.1	80.4	67.0	70.5
Multimodal reconstruction	MT-TCCT	83.1	82.4	79.3	70.0

Table 5. Ablation study of cross-modal Transformer on MOSI and SIMS. "-CT" refers to the cross-modal Transformer fusion strategy. The best results are in **bold**.

Dataset	MOSI				SIMS			
Model	Acc	F1	Corr	MAE	Acc	F1	Corr	MAE
TFN	74.6	74.8	67.3	94.3	76.1	76.0	58.6	44.4
TFN-CT	79.0	79.0	68.0	92.5	78.5	78.6	59.7	44.0
Self-MM	–	–	73.0	79.0	–	–	39.9	61.3
Self-MM-CT	–	–	73.2	78.4	–	–	58.4	41.7
MT-TCCT	**83.1**	**82.4**	**79.3**	**70.0**	**83.5**	**82.6**	**67.5**	**39.1**

in Table 5, we take TFN and Self-MM for example, and replaced the post-fusion method with a cross-modal Transformer. The performance of TFN-CT and Self-MM-CT both achieve better performance compared with the original model, which indicates the model with cross-modal Transformers is more efficient. This is because the CT module enables the model to learn cross-modal contextualized representations compared with the general concatenate fusion.

Role of MTL. We conduct ablation experiments to verify the contribution of the multi-task learning framework and report the unimodality-experimental results of both single-task (STL) and multi-task learning framework in Table 6. Firstly, we train the unimodal task with the multimodal task jointly, the classification accu-racy of audio, video, and text surpasses the model without joint training by 10%, 6.9%, and 6.7% respectively, and the jointly training model also gets the best results on the other metrics. For multimodal emotion recognition, the proposed model outperforms the model without MTL by 1% and 1.2% on accuracy and F1 score. Additionally, we can see that multimodal emotion recognition provides better performance than unimodal, which indicates the multimodal representation contains the task-complementary features. Secondly, it is evident that the multi-task learning framework successfully leverages the

Table 6. Ablation study of MTL on MOSI.

Task	Acc	F1	Corr	MAE
T	76.2	77.2	50.1	92.1
V	58.0	58.2	18.9	92.7
A	47.6	46.4	15.2	93.6
M	82.1	81.2	79.1	71.6
M, T	82.9	78.6	68.3	90.3
M, A	57.6	56.7	40.1	91.3
M, V	64.9	75.7	45.2	91.4
M, T, A, V	**83.1**	**82.4**	**79.3**	**70.0**

inter-dependence of all unimodal tasks in improving overall performance compared with single-task learning.

The experimental results also demonstrate that the text modality involves more affective information, and proves the feasibility of the text-centered feature reconstruction further. This could be for the prompt-BERT is a pre-trained model with better expressive power compared with acoustic and visual features extractors, and the specific template makes the textual representations more targeted for emotion recognition.

6   Conclusion

In this paper, we propose a multi-task learning framework MT-TCCT aiming to leverage the inter-dependence between unimodal and multimodal emotion recognition tasks. Our proposed approach adopts cross-attention to enable the model to capture text dominated feature and learn the modality-shared information. In addition, we exploit a modality-unified Transformer to capture the correlation among all modalities, which enhances the performance of MER efficiently. We also demonstrate the generalized ability of MT-TCCT by experiments conducted on Chinese and English datasets, and the experimental results of the proposed model are superior to existing methods. As one of the future works, more challenging scenarios, such as modality-absence, and noisy datasets, will be tested on the proposed method.

Acknowledgements. This work is supported by the Natural Science Foundation of Liaoning Province (No. 20180550060).

References

1. Abdi, A., Shamsuddin, S.M., Hasan, S., Piran, J.: Deep learning-based sentiment classification of evaluative text based on multi-feature fusion. Inf. Process. Manag. **56**, 1245–1259 (2019)

2. Truong, Q.-T., Lauw, H.W.: Visual sentiment analysis for review images with item-oriented and user-oriented CNN. In: Proceedings of the 25th ACM International Conference on Multimedia, pp. 1274–1282. Association for Computing Machinery, New York (2017). https://doi.org/10.1145/3123266.3123374

3. Guo, L., Wang, L., Dang, J., Chng, E.S., Nakagawa, S.: Learning affective representations based on magnitude and dynamic relative phase information for speech emotion recognition. Speech Commun. **136**, 118–127 (2022). https://doi.org/10.1016/j.specom.2021.11.005

4. Li, X., Chen, M.: Multimodal sentiment analysis with multi-perspective fusion network focusing on sense attentive language. In: Sun, M., Li, S., Zhang, Y., Liu, Y., He, S., Rao, G. (eds.) CCL 2020. LNCS (LNAI), vol. 12522, pp. 359–373. Springer, Cham (2020). https://doi.org/10.1007/978-3-030-63031-7_26

5. Huan, R.-H., Shu, J., Bao, S.-L., Liang, R.-H., Chen, P., Chi, K.-K.: Video multimodal emotion recognition based on Bi-GRU and attention fusion. Multimedia Tools Appl. **80**(6), 8213–8240 (2020). https://doi.org/10.1007/s11042-020-10030-4

6. Wu, Y., Lin, Z., Zhao, Y., Qin, B., Zhu, L.-N.: A text-centered shared-private framework via cross-modal prediction for multimodal sentiment analysis. In: Findings of the Association for Computational Linguistics: ACL-IJCNLP 2021, pp. 4730–4738 (2021)

7. Han, W., Chen, H., Poria, S.: Improving multimodal fusion with hierarchical mutual information maximization for multimodal sentiment analysis. In: Proceedings of the 2021 Conference on Empirical Methods in Natural Language Processing, Online and Punta Cana, Dominican Republic, pp. 9180–9192. Association for Computational Linguistics (2021)

8. Zhang, Z., Luo, P., Loy, C.C., Tang, X.: Facial landmark detection by deep multi-task learning. In: Fleet, D., Pajdla, T., Schiele, B., Tuytelaars, T. (eds.) ECCV 2014. LNCS, vol. 8694, pp. 94–108. Springer, Cham (2014). https://doi.org/10.1007/978-3-319-10599-4_7

9. Yu, W., Xu, H., Yuan, Z., Wu, J.: Learning modality-specific representations with self-supervised multi-task learning for multimodal sentiment analysis. In: Proceedings of the AAAI Conference on Artificial Intelligence, pp. 10790–10797 (2021)

10. Hazarika, D., Zimmermann, R., Poria, S.: MISA: modality-invariant and -Specific representations for multimodal sentiment analysis. In: Proceedings of the 28th ACM International Conference on Multimedia, pp. 1122–1131. Association for Computing Machinery, New York (2020)

11. Liu, Z., Shen, Y., Lakshminarasimhan, V.B., Liang, P.P., Zadeh, A., Morency, L.-P.: Efficient low-rank multimodal fusion with modality-specific factors. In: ACL (2018)

12. Tsai, Y.-H.H., Bai, S., Liang, P.P., Kolter, J.Z., Morency, L.-P., Salakhutdinov, R.: Multimodal transformer for unaligned multimodal language sequences. In: Proceedings of the 57th Annual Meeting of the Association for Computational Linguistics, pp. 6558–6569 (2019)

13. Rahman, W., et al.: Integrating multimodal information in large pretrained transformers. In: Proceedings of the 58th Annual Meeting of the Association for Computational Linguistics, p. 2359. NIH Public Access (2020)

14. Mai, S., Xing, S., Hu, H.: Analyzing multimodal sentiment via acoustic- and visual-LSTM with channel-aware temporal convolution network. IEEE/ACM Trans. Audio Speech Lang. Process. **29**, 1424–1437 (2021)

15. Wang, Y., Shen, Y., Liu, Z., Liang, P.P., Zadeh, A., Morency, L.-P.: Words can shift: dynamically adjusting word representations using nonverbal behaviors. In: Proceedings of the AAAI Conference on Artificial Intelligence, vol. 33, no. 1, pp. 7216–7223 (2019)

16. Zhang, B., Yu, F., Gao, Y., Ren, T., Wu, G.: Joint learning for relationship and inter-action analysis in video with multimodal feature fusion. In: Proceedings of the 29th ACM International Conference on Multimedia, pp. 4848–4852. Association for Computing Machinery, New York (2021)

17. Zhang, Q., Shi, L., Liu, P., Zhu, Z., Xu, L.: ICDN: integrating consistency and difference networks by transformer for multimodal sentiment analysis. Appl. Intell. (2022). https://doi.org/10.1007/s10489-022-03343-4

18. Pennington, J., Socher, R., Manning, C.: GloVe: global vectors for word representation. In: Proceedings of the 2014 Conference on Empirical Methods in Natural Language Processing (EMNLP), Do-ha, Qatar, pp. 1532–1543. Association for Computational Linguistics (2014). https://doi.org/10.3115/v1/D14-1162

19. Liu, P., Yuan, W., Fu, J., Jiang, Z., Hayashi, H., Neubig, G.: Pre-train, prompt, and predict: a systematic survey of prompting methods in natural language processing. arXiv preprint arXiv:2107.13586 (2021)

20. Yu, W., et al.: CH-SIMS: a Chinese multimodal sentiment analysis dataset with fine-grained annotation of modality. In: Proceedings of the 58th Annual Meeting of the Association for Computational Linguistics, pp. 3718–3727 (2020)

21. Zadeh, A., Chen, M., Poria, S., Cambria, E., Morency, L.-P.: Tensor fusion network for multimodal sentiment analysis. In: Proceedings of the 2017 Conference on Empirical Methods in Natural Language Processing, Copenhagen, Denmark, pp. 1103–1114. Association for Computational Linguistics (2017). https://doi.org/10.18653/v1/D17-1115

22. Zellinger, W., Grubinger, T., Lughofer, E., Natschläger, T., Saminger-Platz, S.: Central Moment Discrepancy (CMD) for domain-invariant representation learning. arXiv:1702.08811 [cs, stat] (2019)

23. Zadeh, A., Zellers, R., Pincus, E., Morency, L.-P.: MOSI: multimodal corpus of sentiment intensity and subjectivity analysis in online opinion videos. arXiv preprint arXiv:1606.06259 (2016)

24. McFee, B., et al.: Librosa: audio and music signal analysis in python. In: Proceedings of the 14th Python in Science Conference, pp. 18–25 (2015)

25. Rosenberg, P.E.E.L., Smith, M.B., et al.: What the Face Reveals: Basic and Applied Studies of Spontaneous Expression Using the Facial Action Coding System (FACS). Oxford University Press, USA (1997)

26. Degottex, G., Kane, J., Drugman, T., Raitio, T., Scherer, S.: COVAREP-a collaborative voice analysis repository for speech technologies. In: 2014 IEEE International Conference on Acoustics, Speech and Signal Processing (ICASSP), pp. 960–964 (2014)

27. Bagher Zadeh, A., Liang, P.P., Poria, S., Cambria, E., Morency, L.-P.: Multimodal language analysis in the wild: CMU-MOSEI dataset and interpretable dynamic fusion graph. In: Proceedings of the 56th Annual Meeting of the Association for Computational Linguistics (Volume 1: Long Papers), Melbourne, Australia, pp. 2236–2246. Association for Computational Linguistics (2018). https://doi.org/10.18653/v1/P18-1208

NeoSLAM: Neural Object SLAM for Loop Closure and Navigation

Younès Raoui[1(✉)], Cornelius Weber[2], and Stefan Wermter[2]

[1] LIMIARF Team, Department of Physics, Faculty of Sciences, Mohammed V University in Rabat, 4 Avenue Ibn Battouta, BP 1014 Rabat, Morocco
y.raoui@um5r.ac.ma
[2] Knowledge Technology, Department of Informatics, University of Hamburg, Hamburg, Germany
{cornelius.weber,stefan.wermter}@uni-hamburg.de
https://www.knowledge-technology.info

Abstract. Simultaneous Localization and Mapping (SLAM) with fixed landmark objects creates topological maps by extracting semantic information from the environment. In this paper, we propose a new method for mapping, Neural Object SLAM (NeoSLAM), which uses objects seen in stereo images to learn associations between the pose of the robot and the observed landmark objects. We perform mapping with a biologically inspired approach based on creating patterns memorizing places in a network of grid cells and head direction cells. Our model is inspired by the object vector cells discovered recently by neuroscientists exploring the navigation of mammals. We model the firing field of these cells with a feed-forward neural network and create keyframes of objects with their 3D pose in a world-centered frame of reference. We train a Hebbian network connecting keyframe templates to the grid cells to memorize familiar places. We use the NeuroSLAM algorithm to train the grid cells and the head direction cells with the 4 Degree of Freedom (DoF) poses of the robot. Then, we detect loops in the trajectory by matching objects in the keyframes. Finally, we create an object experience map and correct the cumulative error if we detect loop closure candidates. Thus, our system performs object-based place recognition with a brain-inspired approach and produces 2D/3D object topological maps.

Keywords: SLAM · Autonomous robotic · Loop closure detection · Fixed landmark objects · Object vector cells · Object experience map · NeuroSLAM

1 Introduction

Robot Simultaneous Localization and Mapping (SLAM) creates a topological or metric map of the environment and simultaneously computes the robot's position within the map. New techniques exploit recent advances in neuroscience for making updated algorithms for robotic navigation. They map the environment

E. Pimenidis et al. (Eds.): ICANN 2022, LNCS 13531, pp. 443–455, 2022.
https://doi.org/10.1007/978-3-031-15934-3_37

with Continuous Attractor Networks [15], with Slow Feature Analysis [16] or with Long Short Term Memory (LSTM) [3]. Indeed, they are inspired by the models of navigation of mammals using place cells, grid cells, and head direction cells. The place cells create a map of places, the grid cells compute the pose in the world frame, and the head direction cells are responsible for learning a model that predicts the angle of the head. In the current methods of brain-inspired navigation, several artificial neural network models are applied, such as Growing When Required Networks GWR [16], or deep learning methods such as autoencoders [9]. Teams of researchers learn how to compute the robot's pose with a dynamic neural field or a deep reinforcement network and predict the direction of the head of the robot with a Continuous Attractor Network (CAN) [3]. We create a brain-inspired topological map of places connected with edges representing the distance between them. We look for loop closure candidates by detecting familiar places to correct the pose of the graph's nodes. Recent SLAM techniques use visual objects like cars, trees, bicycles (outdoor scenes), chairs, desks, or laptops (indoor scenes) to represent maps.

Although these works revealed the importance of neural models in navigation, it is not clear how to use neural models for mapping with visual objects. New cells, named object vector cells, were discovered to be responsible for coding the objects in the entorhinal cortex in mouse cognition [8]. These object vector cells encode the vector between the mouse and the object. These cells spike when a mouse is near an object where the firing field has an elliptical shape. The current models train a neural network of grid cells and place cells with the appearance of images. Still, they do not train with objects, so they do not show a sensitivity to the high-level understanding of a given scene. Even so, the complexity of training only with visual landmarks is high, especially in large-scale environments.

This paper develops a new navigation system named NeoSLAM (Neural Object SLAM). We model the object vector cells using a feed-forward network to predict the firing rate from the direction and the distance from the object to the robot. Then we train a three dimensional CAN to model the grid cells. We detect loop closure candidates using the cluster spectrum correspondence method to match objects between two places [5]. We apply a Hebbian rule to learn a model that predicts the familiarity of a place, and we create an object experience map to avoid the problem of multiple representations of the environment and the hash collisions. Thus, we propose a new architecture of SLAM and we found that the translational error of the mapping is reduced when we relax the object experience map after detecting a loop. The score of matching keyframes is maximal when a familiar place is seen. We start with presenting the module-based architecture of our system NeoSLAM; then give the results, and discuss the implications.

2   Related Works

In many works, SLAM considers objects as visual landmarks because they have semantic labels. They improve the data association with techniques such as particle filters [4] which maximizes the likelihood of the estimation of the map with the semantic labels of the observed objects. Also, they construct topological maps with methods of image segmentation based on Convolutional Neural Networks [1] or with algorithms of object detection with geometrical primitives [5]. Loop closure with objects was developed in many algorithms, e.g. [4,5], because it reduces the error of the pose and promotes stability in the CAN. Also, new methods for the visual control of autonomous systems for short or end-to-end driving have been developed with variational neural networks or continuous-time neural networks [11].

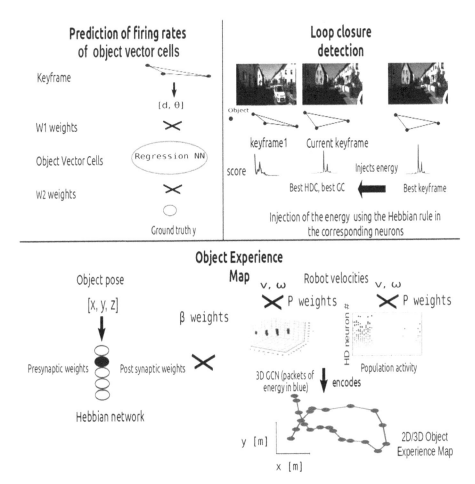

Fig. 1. The Object Vector Cells (ovc) model that learns their activity by training a regression neural network: inputs are the distance and the direction from the robot to the object of the keyframe, the output is the normalized sum of the firing rate of the active ovc (top left). The loop closure scheme based on the computation of the optimal score of matching objects [5] (top right). The model of NeoSLAM that trains a GCN and HDC for the path integration with the velocity inputs. It trains a Hebbian network for simulating the associative memory of places (bottom)

Several works in modern robotics have implemented the model of grid cells and place cells by creating an associative memory of places with the Growing-When-Required networks [16]. In addition, grid cells have been modeled with LSTM for path integration or goal-oriented navigation implemented with deep reinforcement learning [3]. This shows us that neural networks can be used in robot navigation and place recognition. Furthermore, in bio-inspired navigation, the RatSLAM and NeuroSLAM are neural systems that create an associative memory for navigation through a 2D/3D CAN to obtain patterns of the robot pose and to make associations with the perceived images via Hebbian rules. They also creates a 2D/3D experience map to visualize the internal activity of the 2D/3D CAN [2,12,15]. Finally, as discovered in [8], the cells named object vector cells in the entorhinal cortex are responsible for mammals' navigation with objects using a vector representation of the pose of the objects necessary for spatial memory. This gives us the opportunity to make a neural model of object mapping for robots.

3   Description of the NeoSLAM System

The NeoSLAM system (see Fig. 3a) is initialized with the starting pose state of the robot and the objects (see Fig. 2a) detected with the Yolo software. A feed-forward neural network for the regression model named Object Vector Cells Network (OVCN) was developed to model the object vector fields of the object vector cells. We use the predicted responses of the OVCN to learn neural associations between the objects and the robot's pose when a familiar place is perceived. Then, we create keyframes, which are assembled to make an object experience map from the patterns of the 3D CAN, and correct the map using the robot's pose.

We create our system following the steps described below, from initializing the frame with objects and the robot pose to correcting the map:

1. We detect objects and describe them with ORB features; then, we create the frames at each step using the robot's pose, quaternion, and translational and angular velocities.
2. We create the keyframes that contain the current object's vertex and all object vertices within a threshold distance.
3. We train a regression feed-forward neural network to model the firing rate response of the object vector cells.
4. We train grid cells and head direction cells using the NeuroSLAM technique [15].
5. We detect loop closure candidates by matching the keyframes of objects [10]; we make an object experience map with the created keyframes, then we correct the map using the relaxation algorithm of the graph of the chosen keyframes.

3.1 Object Detection and Description for Scene Understanding with Appearance

The frame is created by computing the 3D pose of the robot, the quaternion of the orientation, and the translational and rotational velocities. Objects are detected from each new frame with Yolo [13], which provides the bounding boxes, the labels, and the 3D poses of the objects in the camera and the absolute frames. The depth of the objects is computed by matching and triangulating the ORB feature points from stereo images provided in Kitti datasets with the calibration parameters. We extract the objects with Yolo in the stereo images, match them, then compute the 3D pose in the robot coordinate frame – we compute the 3D pose in the world frame using the odometry data, which is affected by drifts. Then, we represent an object with the pixel coordinates of the upper left and the lower right corners, the label, the identifier, and the current left image.

3.2 Keyframe Detection and Loop Closure Detection

We first create the keyframe composed from the current object and all objects within a distance $e^{max} = 1.5$ m away.

The distance between two objects is given as:

$$e_{ij} = (||cv_j - cv_i||, \Sigma_{2x2}) \tag{1}$$

where i, j are the indices of the two objects. cv_i and cv_j are the 3D coordinates of their centers in the absolute frame. Σ_{2x2} is the covariance error on the distance between two objects (we set it as the identity matrix).

Keyframes Matching

Given G that represents the set of all detected objects, and the current keyframe's objects G_1, we define $\{G_2\} = G \setminus G_1$ to not compare a keyframe to itself. G_1 is composed of objects represented with pairs of objects $(i, j)_k$ for $k = 1...n$. $\{G_2\}$ is composed of objects $(i', j')_k$ for $k = 1...m$. (n and m are the numbers of objects in the two datasets). We perform a one-to-many mapping from G_1 to $\{G_2\}$ [10].

We calculate the affinity M with the following method:

$$H^r_{iji'j'} = e^{max} - ||e_{ij} - e_{i'j'}|| \tag{2}$$

$$H^l_{iji'j'} = \begin{cases} 1 & \text{if } label_i \text{ matches } label_j \text{ and } label_{i'} \text{ matches } label_{j'} \\ 0 & \text{otherwise} \end{cases} \tag{3}$$

and

$$M_{iji'j'} = \begin{cases} H^r_{iji'j'} \cdot H^l_{iji'j'} & \text{if } i \text{ matches } j \text{ and } i' \text{ matches } j' \\ 0 & \text{otherwise} \end{cases} \tag{4}$$

We measure the similarity between two objects by comparing the images where they appear using the Root Mean Square Deviation (RMSE = 80).

The best matching X^* is given by finding the optimal solution of this equation. X is the assignment matrix from G_1 to G_2:

$$X^* = argmax \ X^T M X \tag{5}$$

3.3 Training the Grid Cell (GCN) and the Head Direction Cell Networks (HDN)

We train the GCN and HDC to create a memory of the poses of the robot that move to stable states in the attractor neural network. In the NeuroSLAM, we initialize the GCN and HDC with a first pattern, then compute the next pattern by doing path integration based on velocities computed with visual odometry. We calculate the similarity between patterns by computing the distance between the poses encoded in the cells (x, y, z, and θ) directions [15].

The weights of the GCN are given as follows:

$$\epsilon_{u,v,w}^{gc} = \frac{1}{\delta_x\sqrt{2\pi}} \cdot e^{\frac{-u^2}{2\delta_x^2}} \cdot \frac{1}{\delta_y\sqrt{2\pi}} \cdot e^{\frac{-v^2}{2\delta_y^2}} \cdot \frac{1}{\delta_z\sqrt{2\pi}} \cdot e^{\frac{-w^2}{2\delta_z^2}} \tag{6}$$

where (u, v, w) represents the estimated distance between two robot poses in the absolute space, and δ_x, δ_y and δ_z are constants of variance for the 3D spatial distribution.

For modeling the HDC, we create a 1D continuous attractor network using the yaw Euler angle and 36 neurons to represent a single pattern of this angle.

3.4 Modeling the Firing Fields of the Object Vector Cells

Overview of the Object Vector Cells. Object vector cells are mapping neurons located in the medial entorhinal cortex in mammal brains [8]. They are responsible for the navigation of mice, and react to objects of different sizes and types. They fire when the mouse is at a certain distance from particular confined objects [8]. The authors suggest that object vector cells intermingle with the GCN and HDN; their function can be replicated using a feed-forward network and a Hebbian network. We represent the vector information with the distance and the direction to the object (see Fig. 2b). Figure 2c shows a firing map of object vector cells 2 and 9.

Ground Truth of Firing Field of the Object Vector Cells. Let $d(x, y)$ be the distance between the robot pose and an object pose and let ϕ be the direction between the object and the robot in a world-centered reference frame. We suppose for simplicity that each object activates only one object vector cell. The experiments were performed on a mouse in [8]. The firing rate of the OVCN is modeled with an elliptical field which suggests that the firing rate will decrease from its defined maximum, relative to the preferred vector between the mouse in a cage and the object.

$$f(d) = a \cdot \exp[-d^T A d] + b \tag{7}$$

We set $a = 1.2$ Hz and $b = 0$. A is a diagonal matrix and R is a rotation matrix:

$$A = R^T A R \tag{8}$$

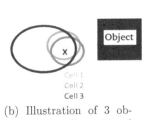

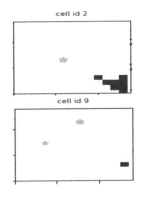

(a) Detection of object "car" with Yolo (Kitti dataset) (the car represents the rat in NeoSLAM)

(b) Illustration of 3 object vector cells activated when the agent (rat x) is near an object

(c) The object vector firing field of two cells (blue), and objects (red stars)

Fig. 2. Illustration of object detection and object vector cells (Color figure online)

where

$$R = \begin{bmatrix} cos(\phi) & sin(\phi) \\ -sin(\phi) & cos(\phi) \end{bmatrix} \tag{9}$$

and

$$A = \begin{bmatrix} \frac{1}{2 \cdot \sigma^2} & 0 \\ 0 & \frac{1}{2 \cdot \sigma^2} \end{bmatrix} \tag{10}$$

The Model. We propose to train an Object Vector Cell Network with a feed-forward neural network for regression (OVCN). We consider the values of the model in [8] as the ground truth (see Eq. 7). The learning rate is 0.001, and the number of epochs is 10 (20 keyframes in each epoch). The inputs of the model are the distance and the direction of the object from the robot, and the output is computed using N hidden neurons. We update the OVCN with the back-propagation of the error in the neural network.

We have:

$$X_t = [d_t, \phi_t] \tag{11}$$

X_t is the observation at time t, and the ground truth of the firing rate of the activated object vector cells is computed with the function f (see Eq. 7):

$$y_t = f(X_t)$$

The output of the network is:

$$O_t = g(W \cdot X_t + b) \tag{12}$$

where g is an exponential linear unit; W are the weights of the OVCN. O_t is the predicted value of the firing response of the OVCN.

We compute the loss of the training using L2 norm as loss function:

$$\mathcal{L}(y_t, O_t) = \frac{1}{2}(y_t - O_t)^2 \tag{13}$$

3.5 Learning Associations Between Keyframe Templates and GCN

We create a single-layer neural network where inputs are the keyframes objects and the outputs are the neural excitation computed with the OVCN. Associations between the current pattern of the OVCN and GCN are learned using the Hebb rule between the pre-synaptic neurons of the keyframes, which fire simultaneously with the postsynaptic one of the GCN. The weight β between the two neurons is learned (see Fig. 1):

$$\beta_{k,x,y,z,\theta}^{t+1} = max(\tau O_t^k \cdot P_{x,y,z,\theta}, \beta_{k,x,y,z,\theta}^t) \tag{14}$$

where $P_{x,y,z,\theta}$ is the neural activity of the grid cell of coordinates (x, y, z), and its corresponding head direction cell firing at the angle θ. O_i^k is the activity of the template of keyframe k. It is given as $O_t^k = \frac{1}{N}\sum_{i=1}^N O_{ti}^k$, where N is the number of objects in the current keyframe.

3.6 Object Experience Map Creation

The next step of our work is to create an experience map to overcome the problems of multiple scene representations and hash collisions. For this purpose, an Object experience map is built, inspired by the NeuroSLAM algorithm. We initialize the map with the first pose of the robot given with the following state:

$$Xr_t = \begin{bmatrix} x_t & y_t & z_t & q_t & v_t & \omega_t \end{bmatrix} \tag{15}$$

where x_t, y_t, z_t is the robot pose in the absolute frame. q_t is the quaternion of the orientation. v_t and ω_t are the translational and rotational velocities.
We represent an experience with the following vector:

$$exp_t = \begin{bmatrix} P_t^{gc}, P_t^{hdc}, Xr_t, KF_t \end{bmatrix} \tag{16}$$

where P_t^{gc} and P_t^{hdc} are the poses of the current active pose cell and the current active head direction cell of the highest energy. KF_t is the index of the current active keyframe template. We compute the similarity score:

$$S_t = \mu^{gc}|P_i^{gc} - P_t^{gc}| + \mu^{hdc}|P_i^{hdc} - P_t^{hdc}| \tag{17}$$

i is the index of the previous experiences, KF_t is equal to the index of the familiar keyframe if the score of matching is higher than a threshold; else, it is equal to zero. Also, another criterion for creating a new experience, proposed in NeuroSLAM, is that the similarity score S_t is higher than S_{max} for all the previous experiences. Concerning links, if we create a new experience, we link it to the last one by setting the euclidean distance value as a cost; if we find a similar experience, we relate it to the current one.

Processing Loop Closure Candidates and Map Relaxation. We calculate the distance between the pose of the candidate keyframe in the grid cell network and the head direction cell network, and the current keyframe. If this distance is higher than a threshold (near seven bins in the GCN), we discard it. Otherwise, we excite the grid cell connected to the keyframe cell.

We correct the map by updating the poses of the current experience (t) and the connected experience $(t + 1)$. We apply the following update equation where c_f is the factor of the correction [15]. Having $Xr_t = [x_t, y_t, z_t]$, the pose of the experience, and the pitch angle θ_t:

$$Xr_t = Xr_t + (Xr_{t+1} - l) \cdot c_f \tag{18}$$

where l represents the displacement from the experience t to the experience $t+1$.

4   Discussion and Results

We used the Yolo software to experiment with object detection from extracted frames [13]. We use the scheme in the Fig. 1. We use viso2ros for the visual odometry [7]. We test our system with sequence 5 of the Kitti odometry dataset under ROS Noetic distribution [6] because it contains several loops and the ground truth data.

4.1   Training the OVCN

We can model the object vector fields with an OVCN that predicts the firing fields when a keyframe is created or recognized. We find that the loss of the training of the OVCN decreases with the number of iterations (see Fig. 4a). We could improve the model of object vector cells with a single layer Hopfield neural network HNN, which stores the pose of the objects, their size, color, and labels. This network will converge to a stable state in the neural field that memorizes places with their furniture (objects). Its inputs are the object features, and the weights are initialized with random values.

4.2   Loop Closure Detection

We create the frames, detect the objects, and triangulate 7 ORB keypoints of these objects in the right and the left image to compute the depth (baseline = 0.53 m) [14]. Our method of matching gives good results, as shown in Fig. 4d. We find three candidate hypotheses of loop closures having a score higher than 1. Using the memory patterns in the GCN and HDN, we select the most accurate candidate identified by the highest score. Moreover, we improve the time complexity of the algorithms of G_2 creation by using a dynamic programming method. We matched in Fig. 4c the initial keyframe to the stored keyframes, and we found that the loop closure is detected at the key position 200.

4.3   Object Experience Map Creation and Update

Figs. 3d and 3b show in 2D and 3D, respectively, results for mapping using NeoSLAM compared to noisy data and ground truth. We apply a Gaussian noise to the ground truth between 0 and $1\,\mathrm{m/s}$ for the translational velocity, 0 and $0.5\,\mathrm{rad/s}$ for the angular velocity to obtain the predicted experience map. We find that the updated experience map is more accurate, as is proved by the calculation of the Euclidean distance in Fig. 4b. Figure 3c shows the different labels of objects that compose the keyframes created during the navigation (car, bicycle, person, and truck).

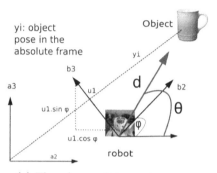

(a) The scheme of the environment

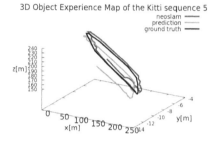

(b) The ground truth, predicted and corrected Object experience map in 3D

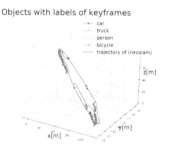

(c) The trajectory with labels of the objects of the keyframes

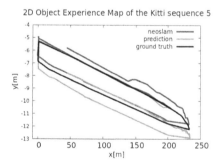

(d) The ground truth, predicted and corrected Object experience map in 2D

Fig. 3. Results of the mapping with NeoSLAM

We showed that extracted objects from images could play a role in the navigation of robots, better than processing only images with their intensities. We remark that two parameters affect the precision of the correction: the distance between objects i and j, d_{ij} and the distance from the robot to the object i r_i. We notice that if d_{ij} is close to $10\,\mathrm{m}$ and r_i is close to $1\,\mathrm{m}$, the correction is

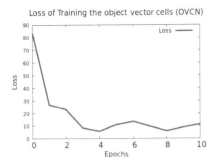

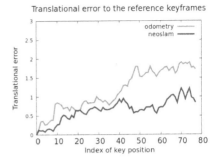

(a) The loss of training of the OVCN

(b) The translational error

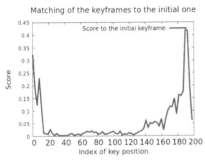

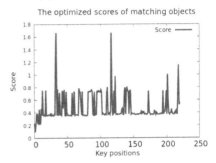

(c) Matching keyframe 1, the loop closure is at the key position 190

(d) 3 candidates for loop closure (score>1), the correct candidate at key position 225

Fig. 4. Results of the OVCN modeling and the loop closure detection with NeoSLAM

more accurate. Moreover, the correction accuracy is improved when we increase the dimension of the grid cells or the number of iterations for experience map correction or the correction rate.

5   Conclusion

This paper presents a new method of creating Object experience maps with visual objects. We propose to model the firing rate of the object vector cells with a OVCN neural network. Loop closures are detected by matching keyframes with their objects. We train a 3D CAN to create an associative memory of localization and mapping. A Hebbian neural network creates associations between the objects and the robot's pose. Our loop closure method enables robust creation of an object experience map of the robot. We find that the accuracy of the correction depends on the distance between objects and the depth of the objects, which is not the case for other methods of brain-inspired SLAM, that do not use single objects for anchoring. Thus, our system performs object-based place recognition with a brain-inspired approach. We propose in the future to model the object vector fields with a deep learning method such as LSTM in a dynamic environment. Next, we suggest interpreting visual objects in terms of their ORB visual words by learning a visual dictionary during the loop closure detection. However, NeoSLAM doesn't consider dynamic objects which is the case in many robotic scenarios. Also, the time of computation in the loop closure detection still considerable even if we do dynamic programming. NeoSLAM could have several applications, such as exploring in depth the functions of the object vector cells to understand them better or doing SLAM in an indoor environment where the semantic information is important.

References

1. Ambruş, R., Bore, N., Folkesson, J., Jensfelt, P.: Meta-rooms: building and maintaining long term spatial models in a dynamic world. In: 2014 IEEE/RSJ International Conference on Intelligent Robots and Systems, pp. 1854–1861 (2014). https://doi.org/10.1109/IROS.2014.6942806
2. Ball, D., Heath, S., Wiles, J., Wyeth, G., Corke, P., Milford, M.: OpenRatSLAM: an open source brain-based SLAM system. Auton. Robot. **34**, 149–176 (2013)
3. Banino, A., Barry, C.: Vector-based navigation using grid-like representations in artificial agents. Nature **557**, 429–433 (2018)
4. Doherty, K., Baxter, D., Schneeweiss, E., Leonard, J.: Probabilistic data association via mixture models for robust semantic SLAM. In: 2020 IEEE International Conference on Robotics and Automation (ICRA), pp. 1098–1104 (2020)
5. Finman, R., Paull, L., Leonard, J.: Toward object-based place recognition in dense RGB-D maps (2015)
6. Fritsch, J., Kuehnl, T., Geiger, A.: A new performance measure and evaluation benchmark for road detection algorithms. In: International Conference on Intelligent Transportation Systems (ITSC) (2013)
7. Geiger, A., Ziegler, J., Stiller, C.: StereoScan: dense 3D reconstruction in real-time. In: Intelligent Vehicles Symposium (IV) (2011)
8. Høydal, Ø.A., Skytøen, E., Andersson, S., Moser, M.B., Moser, E.: Object-vector coding in the medial entorhinal cortex. Nature **568**, 1–8 (2019). https://doi.org/10.1038/s41586-019-1077-7
9. Kiggundu, A., Weber, C., Wermter, S.: A compressing auto-encoder as a developmental model of grid cells. In: Human Brain Project HBP Student Conference, Austria, pp. 35–37 (2017)
10. Leordeanu, M., Hebert, M.: A spectral technique for correspondence problems using pairwise constraints. In: Tenth IEEE International Conference on Computer Vision (ICCV 2005), vol. 2, 1482–1489 (2005)
11. Liu, Z., Amini, A., Zhu, S., Karaman, S., Han, S., Rus, D.: Efficient and robust lidar-based end-to-end navigation. In: 2021 IEEE International Conference on Robotics and Automation (ICRA), pp. 13247–13254 (2021)
12. Müller, S., Weber, C., Wermter, S.: RatSLAM on humanoids - a bio-inspired SLAM model adapted to a humanoid robot. In: Wermter, S., et al. (eds.) ICANN 2014. LNCS, vol. 8681, pp. 789–796. Springer, Cham (2014). https://doi.org/10.1007/978-3-319-11179-7_99
13. Redmon, J., Farhadi, A.: YOLOv3: an incremental improvement. ArXiv arXiv:1804.02767 (2018)

14. Rublee, E., Rabaud, V., Konolige, K., Bradski, G.R.: ORB: an efficient alternative to SIFT or SURF. In: 2011 International Conference on Computer Vision, pp. 2564–2571 (2011)
15. Yu, F., Shang, J., Hu, Y., Milford, M.: NeuroSLAM: a brain-inspired SLAM system for 3d environments. Biol. Cybern. **113**(5–6), 515–545 (2019). https://doi.org/10.1007/s00422-019-00806-9, https://eprints.qut.edu.au/198104/
16. Zhou, X., Weber, C., Wermter, S.: A self-organizing method for robot navigation based on learned place and head-direction cells. In: 2018 International Joint Conference on Neural Networks (IJCNN), pp. 1–8 (2018)

Trajectory-Based Mobile Game Bots Detection with Gaussian Mixture Model

Yueyang Su[1,2], Di Yao[1(✉)], Jingwei Li[3], Baoli Wang[1,2], Jingping Bi[1(✉)], Shiwei Zhao[4], Runze Wu[4], Jianrong Tao[4], and Hao Deng[4]

[1] Institute of Computing Technology, Chinese Academy of Sciences, Beijing, China
{suyueyang19b,yaodi,wangbaoli,bjp}@ict.ac.cn
[2] University of Chinese Academy of Sciences, Beijing, China
[3] Department of Computer Science and Engineering, University of Buffalo, SUNY, New York, USA
jli379@buffalo.edu
[4] NetEase Fuxi AI Lab, Beijing, China
{zhaoshiwei,wurunze1,hztaojianrong,denghao02}@corp.netease.com

Abstract. Recent developments in mobile games have heightened the need for mobile game bots detection, while related researches are scarce. Compared with PC games, detecting game bots in mobile games is more challenging in the following aspects: (I) Privacy. User information in mobile games is more sensitive than on PC. It is unacceptable to employ the program logs or locations to detect the bots. (II) User operations in mobile games are complex. To achieve the same goal, the operations may be completed by multiple fingers and can be various in different users. (III) The labeled data samples are few. The bots in mobile games change frequently, leading that the labeled samples for recent bots could be extremely rare. Unfortunately, these problems have not been well-solved in recent literatures. Thus, in this paper, we propose a reconstruction-based model, namely MUTIL-VIEW GMTVAE, which utilizes the finger touch records collected by screen sensors to infer the potential cheating players in a semi-supervised way. MUTIL-VIEW GMTVAE models the complex operation records in a latent space with a VAE-enhanced GMM which learns more general representations for records reconstruction. Extensive experiments on two NetEase games show that MUTIL-VIEW GMTVAE achieves better performance than the baselines and is general to detect bots in different mobile games.

Keywords: Bots detection · Transformer · Gaussian mixture model · Trajectory

1 Introduction

Recently, the widely equipped smart devices have led to a fast growing of mobile games. With success of mobile games, game bots have become a major concern

This work has been supported by the National Natural Science Foundation of China under Grant No.: 62077044, 61702470, 62002343.

which severely destroy the stable mobile game environment. It can not only lead to a degradation of gaming experience for players but also bring in serious financial losses for game publishers [18]. Although the importance of mobile game bots detection, there have little researches aiming to solve it. Existing game bots detection methods are mostly designed for PC games [1,12]. These works can be categorized into two groups, *i.e.*, the rule-based methods [19] and learning-based methods [6,16]. Rule-based methods maintain blacklists to identify the suspicious processes as game bots. While learning-based models [6,16,18] are designed to study the social behavior, network traffic and profiles of players with machine learning models(*e.g.*, neural networks and SVM) for abnormal players detection. Nevertheless, different from PC games, these diverse data are always inaccessible because of the data privacy of mobile devices. And in most cases, only screen sensor data which records the players' finger operations is available. Moreover, the operations in mobile games are mostly completed with mutil-finger touches, leading to complex operation patterns and make it difficult to study. Due to the characteristics of the screen sensor data, most methods in the above two groups are limited and poor in detection accuracy.

Detecting mobile game bots is not trivial, it has following three challenges. (I) The Privacy. Due to the privacy policies of mobile devices, it is unacceptable to access the process logs or locations for detection. The screen sensor data, collected by the sensors under screens, might be the only available data in most cases [8]. (II) The Complexity. Most mobile games are operated with multiple fingers to release skills. Thus, the records are mostly parallel double-trajectories with a large amount of time overlaps. Moreover, for the same goal, the operations generated by different players (or even the same player at different times) can be various. The complexity of the finger touch records make them challenging to model. (III) Label scarcity. The labeled game bot samples are not usually available for mobile games. Firstly, it is time-consuming and labor-intensive to label the game bot samples manually. Secondly, the novel game bots are constantly emerging in mobile games. The labeled samples of novel game bots are hardly to obtain.

To solve these challenges, we propose a *M*util-view *G*aussian *M*ixture *T*rajec-tory *V*ariational *Auto-E*ncoder for mobile game bots detection, named MUTIL-VIEW GMTVAE. In general, MUTIL-VIEW GMTVAE is a reconstruction-based model. For the privacy problem, MUTIL-VIEW GMTVAE only takes the finger touch records as input. To model the complex operation patterns, we use Gaussian mixture distribution to build the latent space in which each Gaussian distribution is adopted to describe a potential operation pattern. Then we introduce a finger touch records reconstruction module to generate the reconstructed records in a sequential generation scheme. Finally, with the assumption that real players' finger touch records can be reconstructed better than the mobile game bots', the samples with higher reconstruction losses are detected as game bots. Moreover, for the unstable reconstruction of MUTIL-VIEW GMTVAE, we introduce a stability constraint based on gradients variation for model optimization. Especially, MUTIL-VIEW GMTVAE can be trained with only normal records in a semi-supervised way and is effective to detect with few labeled bot samples.

Overall, the main contributions are summarized as follows: (I) To the best of our knowledge, this is the first work to detect mobile game bots with finger touch records in a semi-supervised way. (II) We propose a reconstruction-based model named MUTIL-VIEW GMTVAE which is capable of modeling complex operation patterns and detecting game bots. Besides, a stability constraint based on gradients variation is introduced to improve the performance. (III) Extensive experiments on two real Netease games show that MUTIL-VIEW GMTVAE not only achieve state-of-the-art performance but also general for different games.

2   Related Work

The past decade has seen a rapid development of online games and has attracted a lot of interests in game bots detection. There has been a proliferation of studies [10,17] on this topic while most of them are proposed for PC games. Rule-based methods, such as anti-cheating systems [19], are implemented with dynamically maintainable blacklists of bots processes and identify the suspicious programs as game bots. However, these methods are easy to be attacked (e.g., modifying the registry) and are poor in the environment with novel bots emerging. Recent trends in machine learning have led to a proliferation of studies that focus on learning-based bots detection methods. The existing methods focus on diverse heterogeneous data [6,16] and detect bots from different perspectives. Thawonmas [18] analyzed the game log records for database rollback and proposed a two-stage game bots detection method. Kim [7] focused on the window event sequences of game players and achieved a great performance. The above mentioned methods are all artificial features-based which is sensitive to features selection and poor in generalization. Some researchers [4,9] proposed self-similarity methods with the hypothesis that game bots would repeat highly similar action sequences. For example, Lee [11] encoded the frequency of action events into vectors and measured the self-similarity by the cosine distance with unit vectors. These self-similarity methods are in urgent need of operation action data and are limited in the game categories.

There are also some other models for PC game bots detection, but very little attention has been paid to mobile games. Considering the privacy protection of mobile and generality among mobile games, we focus on the finger touch records collected from mobile screen sensors and attempt to propose a novel mobile game bots detection model.

3   Preliminary

3.1   Problem Definition

In this section, we summarize the notations and define the mobile game bots detection problem.

The finger touch records collected by the screen sensors are operation events sequences. And a specific one with M operation events can be denoted as $E = [(T_1, e_1), \cdots, (T_M, e_M)]$, in which each tuple represents an event and is composed of a trajectory and corresponding event type. Note that the operation events are the basic operation units of the games including tap, swipe, and etc.. The trajectory in the ith event is denoted as $T_i = (p_1, p_2, \cdots, p_{N_i})$, where N_i is the length of the trajectory. Each coordinate $p_j = (x_j, y_j, t_j)$ is also a tuple, in which x_j and y_j are the pixel coordinates and t_j is the timestamp.

The goal of mobile game bots detection is to separate the finger touch records which are unlikely to be generated by a real player from the sensor data. In this paper, we aim to detect bots in a semi-supervised way.

Definition 1. (Mobile game bots detection) Formally, given the normal samples dataset $\mathcal{E}_{train} = \{E_1, E_2, \cdots, E_j, \cdots, E_n\}$, in which E_i is the ith finger touch record with label $y_i = 0$. Our task is to detect the bot samples in an unlabeled dataset $\mathcal{E}_{infer} = \{E_1, E_2, \cdots, E_m\}$ with the knowledge in $\mathcal{E}_{train}$.

4   Methodology

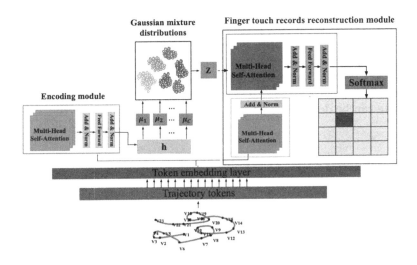

Fig. 1. The model architecture of MUTIL-VIEW GMTVAE.

In this section, we discuss our framework in detail. As shown in Fig. 1, the MUTIL-VIEW GMTVAE is introduced to detect game bots based on variational auto-encoder in a semi-supervised way and involves three main components. (I) Encoding module: uses the Transformer encoder to extract the spatio-temporal information between coordinates and learn the latent representations of the records. (II) Modeling latent trajectory with Gaussian mixture distribution: constructs the latent space with Gaussian mixture distribution to model the complex patterns of finger touch records and samples a general representation for reconstruction. (III) Finger touch records reconstruction module: reconstructs with transformer decoder in a sequential generation schema.

Specifically, our MUTIL-VIEW GMTVAE is optimized with an extra constraint based on gradients variation for model stability. Next, we specify the details of these components respectively.

4.1 Preprocess

Given a finger touch record $E_i = [(T_1, e_1), \cdots, (T_i, e_i), \cdots, (T_{M_i}, e_{M_i})]$, in which M_i is the amount of the operation events. Assuming that the length of the trajectory in the jth event (T_j, e_j) is N_j, then $T_j = (p_1, p_2, \cdots, p_{N_j})$.

Within each event, the coordinates in trajectory are captured to determine the event type. In MUTIL-VIEW GMTVAE, we consider the event type as an attribute of coordinates. Then the record is converted to a sequence of coordinates, $i.e.$, $E_i = [(p_1, p_2, \cdots, p_k, \cdots, p_{N_1}), \cdots, (p_1, p_2, \cdots, p_{N_{M_i}})] = (p_1, p_2, \cdots, p_k, \cdots, p_{L_i})$, in which $L_i = N_1 + N_2 + \cdots + N_{M_i}$ is the length of sequence and $p_k = (x_k, y_k, t_k, e_k)$ is a tuple. Specially the elements in the tuple represent the x coordinate, y coordinate, recording time and events type respectively, and the e_k is the type of the event that p_k belongs to. We first introduce the method of the data preprocessing.

Coordinate Information. Since different samples are collected from different devices, the absolute position is usually irrelevant to the analysis of game bots. To solve this problem, we map the screen to a specified grids space. Then the position information can be expressed as a sequence of grid tokens, and the coordinate can be denoted as follows:

$$p_k = (r_k, t_k, e_k), r_i \in \mathfrak{R} \qquad (1)$$

where r_k is the grid token of the kth coordinate, $\mathfrak{R}$ is the grids space. Then, we introduce an embedding matrix to embed the discrete token r_k in a vector R_k.

Time Information. In bots detection, the time gaps between coordinates contain more meaningful information compared to the absolute time. Therefore, in MUTIL-VIEW GMTVAE, we use time gaps as temporal features.

$$f_k^t = t_k - t_{k-1}; f_1^t = 0 \qquad (2)$$

Then we use a min-max normalization method to convert the time information as follows:
$$f_{max}^t = max(f_1^t, \cdots, f_L^t); f_{min}^t = min(f_1^t, \cdots, f_L^t)$$
$$f_k^t = \frac{f_k^t - f_{min}^t}{f_{max}^t - f_{min}^t} \qquad (3)$$

Event Type. We construct a randomly initialized d-dimensional vector for each event type. In other words, if there are O types of event, the embedding matrix can be denoted as $\boldsymbol{E} \in d \times O$. For a tuple $p_k = (r_k, t_k, e_k)$, the representation of event e_k is formulated as follows:

$$e_k = \text{Embedding}(e_k, \boldsymbol{E}) \tag{4}$$

We integrate the above-mentioned features by concatenating them into $\boldsymbol{f}_k$ and take it as the input of encoder.

$$\boldsymbol{f}_k = \text{concat}(R_k, f_k^t, e_k) \tag{5}$$

4.2 Multi-view GM-TVAE

As shown in Fig. 1, the MUTIL-VIEW GMTVAE contains the following components.

Encoding Module: After the data preprocessing, we adopt Transformer encoder to learn the trajectory representation in latent space. Formally, let L denotes the length of the coordinates sequence, then the Transformer encoder takes $\boldsymbol{f}_{1\cdots L}$ as input and generate the representation $\boldsymbol{v}$ with the following formulas:

$$\boldsymbol{v} = E_{Transformer}(\boldsymbol{f}_{1\cdots L}, \phi_e) \tag{6}$$

Next, we learn a conditional probability distribution $q_\phi(\boldsymbol{z}|T)$ on the trajectory representation $\boldsymbol{v}$, in which $\boldsymbol{z}$ is a variable in the latent space of current trajectory. Then a more general latent variable $\boldsymbol{z}_T$ can be drawn from the posterior distribution.

$$\boldsymbol{\mu}_T = g_1(\boldsymbol{v}, \phi_\mu)$$
$$\boldsymbol{\sigma}_T = g_2(\boldsymbol{v}, \phi_\sigma) \tag{7}$$
$$\boldsymbol{z}_T \sim q_\phi(\boldsymbol{z}|T) = \mathcal{N}(\boldsymbol{\mu}_T, \boldsymbol{\sigma}_T^2 I)$$

where $\boldsymbol{\mu}_T \in \mathbb{R}^d$, $\boldsymbol{\sigma}_T \in \mathbb{R}^d$ are the mean and standard deviation, and $g(\cdot)$ is a fully connected layer to be learned, I is an identity matrix.

Modeling Latent Trajectory with Gaussian Mixture Distribution: To model the diverse patterns of players' operations, the Gaussian mixture distribution is introduced as the prior distribution which consists of a multinomial distribution and several Gaussian distributions. Each Gaussian distribution describes a potential pattern. And the multinomial distribution is the probability that trajectories belong to each pattern. Supposed that there are C operation pattern types, the multinomial distribution can be expressed as:

$$p_\psi(c) = Cat(\boldsymbol{\pi}) \tag{8}$$

where $\boldsymbol{\pi} \in \mathbb{R}^C$, and $\Sigma_{i=1}^C \pi_i = 1$. The Gaussian distribution of a certain type c can be expressed as:

$$p_\psi(\boldsymbol{z}|c) = \mathcal{N}(\boldsymbol{\mu}_c, \boldsymbol{\sigma}_c^2 I) \tag{9}$$

where $\boldsymbol{\mu}_c \in \mathbb{R}^d$, $\boldsymbol{\sigma}_c \in \mathbb{R}^d$ are the mean and standard deviation of the Gaussian distribution. Then the latent space can be expressed as:

$$p_\psi(\boldsymbol{z}) = p_\psi(\boldsymbol{z}|c)p_\psi(c) \tag{10}$$

In particular, we consider the trajectories of a particular pattern c as those close to μ_c, then the posterior probability $q_\phi(c|T)$ can be denoted as:

$$q_\phi(c|T) = softmax(\frac{\boldsymbol{z}_T - \boldsymbol{\mu}_c}{\Sigma_{i=1}^C \boldsymbol{z}_T - \boldsymbol{\mu}_i}) \tag{11}$$

With the consideration of latent pattern type c, the joint distribution function can be expressed as:

$$q_\phi(\boldsymbol{z}, c|T) = q_\phi(\boldsymbol{z}|T)q_\phi(c|T) \tag{12}$$

Finger Touch Records Reconstruction Module: Considering the time dependency among coordinates, we introduce a sequential generation schema to reconstruct the trajectory with the latent representation $\boldsymbol{z}_T$ of a specific record. To achieve this, the Transformer decoder is introduced which takes the latent variable $\boldsymbol{z}_T$ and the previously coordinates as input, the operation is formulated as follows:

$$\boldsymbol{g}_i = D_{Transformer}(\boldsymbol{z}_T, \boldsymbol{g}_{i-1}, \theta_d) \tag{13}$$

Then the reconstructed coordinate p_i' can be generated by a reconstruction layer, the operation is formulated as follows:

$$p_i' \sim p_\theta(p|p_{<i}, \boldsymbol{z}) = softmax(g_3(\boldsymbol{g}_i, \theta_g)) \tag{14}$$

where $i = 1, 2, \cdots, L$ and $g_3(\cdot)$ is a learnable non-liner function. Specifically, g_3 converts $\boldsymbol{g}_i$ into a $|\mathfrak{R}|$-dimensional vector, which equals to the total number of grids. Then the softmax fuction is applied to convert the vector into probability.

Loss Function: The target of the MUTIL-VIEW GMTVAE is to detect game bots with reconstruction error. And the objective is to maxmize the marginal log-likelihood of reconstruction. Same as the general vae [5], the loss can be optimized with the evidence lower bound and can be denoted as follows:

$$logp_\theta(T) \geq \mathcal{L}_{ELBO} = \mathbb{E}_{q_\phi(c,z|T)}[log\frac{p_{\theta,\psi}(c,\boldsymbol{z})p_\theta(T|\boldsymbol{z})}{q_\phi(\boldsymbol{z},c|T)}]$$
$$= \mathbb{E}_{q_\phi(c,z|T)}[logp_\theta(T|\boldsymbol{z})] - KL[q_\phi(c,\boldsymbol{z}|T)\|p_{\theta,\psi}(c,\boldsymbol{z})] \tag{15}$$

Model Stability Constraint Based on Gradients Variation: Traditional VAE suffers from unstable training [2] and the reconstruction performance varies greatly between different samples. For finger touch records, the complexity of data makes it worse. In order to improve the model stability, we introduce a constraint based on gradients variation. The gradients provide direction information for a model to adjust parameters, which can be intuitively considered as an optimization mode of a model. Therefore, we introduce a novel loss based on gradients variation to constrain the model to optimize in a similar way.

Specifically, given a finger touch record E_i, the loss calculated with the Eq. 15 can be denoted as $\mathcal{L}^i_{ELBO}$. All the parameters to be learned in MUTIL-VIEW GMTVAE are denoted as $\gamma = \{\phi, \psi, \theta\}$. And the gradients can be extracted as follows:

$$grad_i = \frac{\partial(\mathcal{L}^i_{ELBO})}{\partial(\gamma)} \tag{16}$$

Then we introduce the gradients variation as an extra loss which can be formulated as follows:

$$\mathcal{L}_{grad} = \nabla grad_i = Similarity(grad_i, \frac{1}{i-1}(\Sigma^{i-1}_{w=1}grad_w)) \tag{17}$$

where $Similarity(\cdot)$ is the cosine metric. Then the final loss can be expressed as:

$$\mathcal{L} = \mathcal{L}_{ELBO} + \mathcal{L}_{grad} \tag{18}$$

5   Experiment

5.1   Experimental Settings

We first introduce the datasets, evaluation metrics and compared baselines of our experiments. Then we evaluate MUTIL-VIEW GMTVAE against other state-of-the-art methods.

Datasets. We focus on two mobile game datasets from NetEase Inc, named Battle and Rookie. And collect screen sensor data from April 21 to April 27, 2021 at a frequency of 400 ms a coordinate. The bot samples in the datasets are labeled by the experts in Netease product teams, which are either positive (bots) or negative (normal). In order to select records with a reasonable length, we further drop the records less than 20. In training, we adopt only normal samples(100000 samples in each game) for model optimization, And a dataset containing bot samples is selected for testing(30000 normal samples and 7440 bots samples in Battle; 30000 normal samples and 6008 bots samples in Rookie).

Evaluation Metrics. We adopt Precision, Recall, and F1-score as metrics to evaluate the performance of MUTIL-VIEW GMTVAE.

Compared Methods. We compare MUTIL-VIEW GMTVAE with the following baselines. (I) **Angle distribution-based method(ADM)** [6]: This is a rule-based method for PC game bots detection which focuses on the differences in angle distribution of mouse movement between robots and players. (II) **TRAOD** [13]: This is a two-stage detection method, named partition-and-detect framework. (III) **DBOTD** [14]: This is a density-based method for trajectory anomaly detection. (IV) **Traj2vec** [3]: This is a semi-supervised representation learning method of trajectory. To detect bot samples, we classify the learned representations with a clustering algorithm. (V) **EncDec-AD(ED-AD)** [15]: This is a LSTM-based encoder-decoder model for sequence data anomaly detection which classifies with a predefined reconstruction error. (VI) **CVAE** [20]: A LSTM-based CVAE model which has a great performance in sequence data reconstruction. And we adopt the same classification strategy as **ED-AD**.

Ablations of Mutil-view GMTVAE. (I) **TAE**: A degenerate model of GM-TVAE with no Gaussian distribution. (II) **TVAE**$_{one}$: A degenerate model of GM-TVAE, with only a single Gaussian distribution as the prior distribution of the latent space. (III) **GM-TVAE**: A degenerate model of MUTIL-VIEW GMTVAE, which is optimized without the model stability constraint.

5.2   Experimental Results

The results of the comparison experiments for MUTIL-VIEW GMTVAE are shown in Table 1. This table is quite revealing in several ways. First, our proposed MUTIL-VIEW GMTVAE outperforms the baseline methods in all metrics on both Battle and Rookie, which proves the superiority of our model in mobile game bots detection. Second, among the baselines, CVAE achieves the best performance but is still worse than our model. We attribute this result to the poor effectiveness of the model for handling records with complex patterns because of the single latent space and the ineffective encoder. Third, the ADM which is popular in PC game bots detection fails on both Battle and Rookie. This result may be explained by the fact that the traditional pre-selected feature methods are unable to describe the complex patterns of finger touch records. And the statistical features of known bots in pre-training are not suitable for emerging bots types and may lead to error detection.

Table 1. Performance comparison results w.r.t. Precision, Recall and F1-score

		ADM	TRAOD	DBOTD	Traj2vec	ED-AD	CVAE	Ours
Battle	Recall	0.3795	0.6218	0.5927	0.7305	0.7359	0.8146	**0.9248**
	Precision	0.5320	0.3556	0.4138	0.6021	0.5186	0.6512	**0.7683**
	F1-score	0.4430	0.4525	0.4874	0.6601	0.6084	0.7238	**0.8393**
Rookie	Recall	0.3651	0.4962	0.579	0.6995	0.7627	0.7936	**0.9025**
	Precision	0.4983	0.2795	0.2651	0.5735	0.2995	0.6759	**0.7196**
	F1-score	0.4214	0.3576	0.3637	0.6303	0.4301	0.73	**0.801**

Table 2. Performance comparison results w.r.t. Precision, Recall and F1-score in ablation study

	Battle			Rookie		
	Recall	Precision	F1-score	Recall	Precision	F1-score
TAE	0.7285	0.6172	0.6682	0.7163	0.5708	0.6353
TVAE$_{one}$	0.8237	0.6958	0.7544	0.8029	0.6597	0.7243
GM-TVAE	**0.8925**	**0.7539**	**0.8274**	**0.8542**	**0.703**	**0.7713**

5.3   Ablation Study

We conduct an ablation study to validate the effectiveness of the main components of MUTIL-VIEW GMTVAE.

Contribution of Gaussian Mixture Distribution. To verify the superiority of the Gaussian mixture distribution in modeling the latent space of finger touch records, we compare the performance of TAE, $TVAE_{one}$ and GM-TVAE. As shown in Table 2, GM-TVAE shows significant improvement in all metrics, especially on Battle, with about 7%, 16% improvement compared with TVAE and TAE in F1-score. We attribute this to the excellent performance of Gaussian mixture distribution to model the diverse latent space of the complex operation patterns.

Contribution of Model Stability Constraint. We also analysis the reconstruction loss of GM-TVAE and MUTIL-VIEW GMTVAE in normal samples. GM-TVAE shows a large fluctuation while our model is more stable on both Battle and Rookie. Moreover, we take the results on Battle as an example and illustrate them in Fig. 2. As shown in the figures, the reconstruction loss of GM-TVAE reaches a maximum of about 0.01784 and a minimum of about 0.00153. However, the reconstruction loss of our model fluctuates between 0.00298 and 0.01465 which has a smaller range.

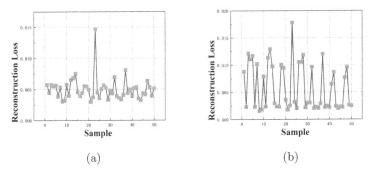

(a)   (b)

Fig. 2. (a) The reconstruction loss of normal samples using MUTIL-VIEW GMTVAE; (b) The reconstruction loss of normal samples using GM-TVAE.

5.4   Hyper-parameter Studies

In this subsection, we evaluate the influence of the key parameter in MUTIL-VIEW GMTVAE, , the number of Gaussian distribution components C. Specifically, we analyze the changing of the performance on two datasets as C varies from 1 to 15. A closer inspection of Fig. 3(c) shows that C has a significant effect on the model's performance. When the value is taken as 1, the model degrades to $TVAE_{one}$ and perform worst in F1-score on both Battle and Rookie. MUTIL-VIEW GMTVAE achieves the best performance when $C = 5$ on both Battle and

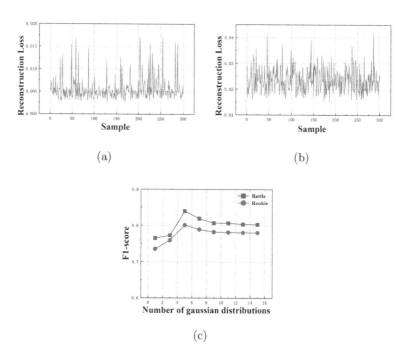

Fig. 3. (a) The reconstruction loss of normal samples; (b) The reconstruction loss of bot samples; (c) The F1-score of different number of Gaussian distributions.

Rookie which means that $C = 5$ is more suitable to model the latent space with 5 operation event types.

To further quantify the reconstruction performance, we present the reconstruction losses of some selected samples in Fig. 3(a) and Fig. 3(b). It is clear that the reconstruction losses of normal and bot samples are in different ranges with a few overlaps, which means that the reconstruction loss is effective in identifying bots.

6   Conclusion

In this paper, we study the problem of mobile game bots detection in a semi-supervised way. Considering the privacy of mobile data, we focus on finger touch records and propose a reconstruction-based model for mobile game bots detection. To model the complex operation patterns, we adopt the Transformer encoder to learn the semantic-rich representation and build a latent space with Gaussian mixture distribution. To reconstruct the records, we introduce a finger touch records reconstruction module based on Transformer decoder to generate coordinates in a sequential generation schema. Moreover, a novel loss based on gradients variation is introduced to constrain the model optimization and alleviate the model instability caused by the operation complexity. Our MUTIL-VIEW

GMTVAE is trained with only normal samples and is effective for the label scarcity of bots samples. Comprehensive experiments demonstrate that the proposed model significantly outperforms all compared baselines and is general for different mobile games.

References

1. Chung, Y., Park, C.Y., Kim, N.R., et al.: Game bot detection approach based on behavior analysis and consideration of various play styles. Etri J. **35**(6), 1058–1067 (2013)
2. Dehaene, D., Brossard, R.: Re-parameterizing vaes for stability. CoRR
3. Di, Y., Chao, Z., Zhu, Z., Huang, J., Bi, J.: Trajectory clustering via deep representation learning. In: 2017 International Joint Conference on Neural Networks (2017)
4. Lee, E.-J., et al.: A study on game bot detection using self-similarity in mmorpgs. J. Korea Inst. Inf. Sec. Crypto. **26**(1), 93–107 (2016)
5. Jiang, Z., Zheng, Y., Tan, H., Tang, B., Zhou, H.: Variational deep embedding: an unsupervised and generative approach to clustering (2016)
6. Kesteren, M.V., Langevoort, J., Grootjen, F.: A step in the right direction: Bot-detection in mmorpgs using movement analysis (2009)
7. Kim, H. ., et al.: Detection of auto programs for mmorpgs. In: AI 2005: Advances in Artificial Intelligence, 18th Australian Joint Conference on Artificial Intelligence (2005)
8. Kreuter, F., Haas, G.S., et al.: Collecting survey and smartphone sensor data with an app: opportunities and challenges around privacy and informed consent. Soc. Sci. Comput. Rev. **38**(5) (2018)
9. Kwon, H., Kim, H.K., et al.: Self-similarity based bot detection system in mmorpg. In: The 3rd International Conference on Internet (2011)
10. Kwon, H., Woo, K., Kim, H.C., Kim, C.K., Kim, H.K.: Surgical strike: a novel approach to minimize collateral damage to game bot detection. In: 2013 12th Annual Workshop on Network and Systems Support for Games (NetGames) (2013)
11. Lee, E., Woo, J., Kim, H., Kim, A.: You are a game bot!: uncovering game bots in mmorpgs via self-similarity in the wild. In: Network & Distributed System Security Symposium (2016)
12. Lee, E., Woo, J., et al.: No silk road for online gamers!: Using social network analysis to unveil black markets in online games
13. Lee, J.G., Han, J., et al.: Trajectory outlier detection: a partition-and-detect framework. In: IEEE International Conference on Data Engineering (2008)
14. Lv, Z., Xu, J., Zhao, P., Liu, G., Lei, Z., Zhou, X.: Outlier trajectory detection: A trajectory analytics based approach (2017)
15. Malhotra, P., Ramakrishnan, A., et al.: Lstm-based encoder-decoder for multi-sensor anomaly detection. CoRR, abs/1607.00148 (2016)
16. Seo, D.M., Woo, J.Y., et al.: Detecting gold-farmers' group in mmorpg by analyzing connection pattern. J. Korea Inst. Inf. Sec. Crypt. **22**(3), 585–600 (2012)
17. Thawonmas, R., Kurashige, M., Chen, K.T.: Detection of landmarks for clustering of online-game players. Int. J. Virtual Reality **6**(3), 11–16 (2007)
18. Thawonmas, R., Kashifuji,Y., Chen,K.T.: Detection of mmorpg bots based on behavior analysis. In: Proceedings of the International Conference on Advances in Computer Entertainment Technology (2008)

19. Tian, Y., Chen, E., et al.: Swords and shields - a study of mobile game hacks and existing defenses. In: Conference on Computer Security Applications (2016)
20. Wang, T., Wan, X.: T-cvae: Transformer-based conditioned variational autoencoder for story completion. In: Twenty-Eighth International Joint Conference on Artificial Intelligence IJCAI 2019 (2019)

Unsupervised Domain Adaptation Using Temporal Association for Segmentation and Its Application to *C. elegans* Time-Lapse Images

Hiroaki Nozaki$^{(\boxtimes)}$ (iD) and Yukako Tohsato (iD)

Ritsumeikan University, Shiga, Japan
is0423ki@ed.ritsumei.ac.jp, yukako@fc.ritsumei.ac.jp

Abstract. With the widespread use of live-cell imaging technologies for observing the dynamics of live cells under a microscope, there is a need for semantic image segmentation to quantitatively detect structural changes of the targeting objects in the various resulting time-lapse images. Although supervised learning of convolutional neural networks such as U-Net is one way to achieve segmentation, pixel-level labeling for images is a time-consuming task and requires domain knowledge. Unsupervised domain adaptation (UDA) methods have been proposed to transfer the learning knowledge gained from labeled datasets (i.e., the source domain) to unlabeled datasets (i.e., the target domain). However, to date, there has been no reported application of a UDA method to consider the temporal association of features with the aim of using semantic segmentation for time-lapse microscopy images. This paper proposes a new UDA method that considers the class-specific feature distribution in both the source and target domains as well as the temporal association of features. We also present manually created annotations of true nuclear regions for two kinds of open time-lapse image datasets of *Caenorhabditis elegans* early embryos. Using the annotated datasets, we demonstrate that the accuracy of the proposed method is more than 7% higher than that of other UDA methods with static images and videos as inputs. The code and annotations are available at https://github.com/tohsato-lab/T-MCD.

Keywords: Domain adaptation · Video semantic segmentation · Biological benchmark datasets · *Caenorhabditis elegans*

1 Introduction

In the field of life science, live-cell imaging, microscopy technologies that allow imaging of cells and tissues in their living state, is widely used to observe temporal dynamics in the internal structure and biochemical processes of living organisms. Semantic segmentation, which is the process of classifying every pixel in an image into a semantic class, is important to quantitatively evaluate the resulting time-lapse images. The segmentation can be achieved by supervised learning of the labeled images with a convolutional neural network (CNN) such as U-Net [1]. To obtain microscopy images and the corresponding label data, bioimaging databases can be used [2].

However, even if labeled images are available for an observation target and supervised learning can be achieved, the segmentation accuracy of the learned model will decrease for newly obtained images under different conditions because there are differences in the distribution of labeled data from one domain (called the source domain) and unlabeled data from another domain (called the target domain). In the case of small-scale imaging with the same observation target under different conditions (e.g., lenses), the labeling task becomes an efficiency problem.

To improve labeling efficiency, unsupervised domain adaptation (UDA), which transfers knowledge from the source domain to the target domain, has been proposed. UDA improves the segmentation accuracy for the target domain by reducing domain gaps in the feature distribution of the middle layer or the probability distribution of the output class from the network. Many UDA methods for semantic segmentation have introduced adversarial learning [3–6]. Among them, Saito et al. [6] proposed calculating the discrepancy loss, or maximum classifier discrepancy (MCD), between the output probability distributions obtained from two classifiers. However, to date, no UDA method has been applied to consider the temporal association of features with the aim of using semantic segmentation for time-lapse images obtained by live-cell imaging.

This paper presents a novel UDA method for semantic segmentation called temporal-associated MCD (T-MCD) that performs domain adaptation by the discrepancy between two classifiers in a co-detection CNN [7] that developed as a CNN for tracking cells from input time-lapse images. The method is applied to semantic segmentation of the nuclear region for time-lapse images of *Caenorhabditis elegans* (*C. elegans*) early embryos, one of the major model organisms in life sciences. We confirmed that the segmentation accuracy of the proposed method is higher than that of previous methods, which are UDAs using static images and optical flows obtained from videos. Our main contributions are as follows:

- We propose a novel and simple UDA learning method for time-lapse images that achieves MCD while accounting for temporal consistency.
- We manually create labeling data of the true nuclear regions for two kinds of open time-lapse differential interference contrast microscopy images of *C. elegans* embryos and release it as a new benchmark.
- We demonstrate the effectiveness of our method in the segmentation of time-lapse images using the annotated datasets.

2 Related Work

UDA for semantic segmentation can be classified into image-based UDA, which uses static images as inputs, and video-based UDA, which uses temporal dynamics from time-lapse images as inputs [8].

Many of the previous methods are image-based UDAs and introduce adversarial learning to reduce domain gaps in the image-based UDA [3–6]. MCD [6] was devised based on the premise of using the network architecture consisting of one generator that extracts features from one-input datum and two classifiers that decode the extracted features. Adversarial learning considering the class distribution is realized by using the discrepancy loss of the two classifiers. In UDA for semantic segmentation using real data (Cityscapes [9]) and synthetic data (GTA5 [10]) from in-vehicle cameras as benchmarks, MCD using DRN-d-105 (DRN for short) [11] as the network architecture showed higher accuracy than previous methods such as DANN. There is also an extension to MCD that introduces Kullback-Leibler divergence, which calculates the degree of divergence between the output probability distributions of two classifiers to apply to universal domain adaptation; this extension assumes practical conditions such as incorrect labeling and different numbers of classes across domains [12]. However, there is no report of an extension to MCD that considers temporal information.

Recently, the use of temporal information in time-lapse images has been tried, and several video-based UDA methods have been proposed. One such approach is the style transformation approach proposed for use in medical videos [13]. However, because that proposed method does not directly attempt domain adaptation, it is not included in this study. As a benchmark for video-based UDA for semantic segmentation, it would be possible to use Cityscapes-VPS [14], which are newly added time-lapse annotation data to Cityscapes. For such datasets, methods using optical flow information extracted from time-lapse images [8, 15, 16] were proposed in 2021. In this study, we selected DA-VSN [15] from the existing group of video-based UDA methods to perform domain adaptation for cell images.

On the other hand, U-Net [1] was developed for biomedical image segmentation and has an architecture consisting of an encoder, a decoder, and a skip connection between the encoder and the corresponding decoder. U-Net has performed well in segmentation for relatively small-scale image datasets, and various extensions have been attempted [7, 17]. In 2020, Nishimura et al. proposed co-detection CNN [7] as a method for weakly supervised tracking of time-lapse cell images. They extended U-Net to a structure that simultaneously inputs two images at time points t and $t + 1$ and outputs information at two corresponding time points. Haq et al. proposed CellSegUDA [17] as an image-based UDA for semantic segmentation in cell images. The entire network consists of a U-Net for semantic segmentation, an additional domain discriminator for adversarial learning, and a decoder to generate the original image from the segmentation result. Using the network, they succeeded in detecting the nuclear regions with high accuracy. We therefore selected CellSegUDA as the image-based UDA and U-Net extension.

3 Proposed Method

3.1 Problem Definition in Video-Based UDA

In this UDA, our aim was to segment regions for an unlabeled time-lapse image $x^T = \{x_1^T, x_2^T, ..., x_t^T ...\}$ $(x^T \in \mathbf{X}^T)$ in the target domain using knowledge of a time-lapse image $x^S = \{x_1^S, x_2^S, ..., x_t^S ...\}$ $(x^S \in \mathbf{X}^S)$ labeled with the true class $y^S = \{y_1^S, y_2^S, ..., y_t^S ...\}$ $(y^S \in \mathbf{Y}^S)$ at the pixel level in the source domain. Let X_t^S, Y_t^S denote the set of images and the corresponding label information collected from the source domain as a mini-batch starting at time point t, respectively. Similarly, X_t^T denotes the set of images collected from the target domain as a mini-batch starting at time point t.

3.2   Overall Idea and Network

The network used for training is divided into one encoder module and two segmentation modules (Fig. 1). Let E be the encoder module, and S_1 and S_2 be the segmentation modules. The entire network is distinguished by the combination of an encoder module and two segmentation modules, $N_1 = S_1 \circ E$ and $N_2 = S_2 \circ E$, respectively. The encoding module consists of two encoding components that share the same weights and one fusion component. The encoder module extracts features from input images at two time points. After concatenating the two features extracted from the encoder components, we obtain the association from the two time points in the fusion component. The two segmentation modules output the class probabilities for the pixels at each time point. As in U-Net, feature maps of the same size between the encoder module and segmentation modules are concatenated with skip connections. The proposed method realizes adversarial learning between the encoder module and the segmentation modules to improve the classification accuracy for the target data (see Sect. 3.3 for details).

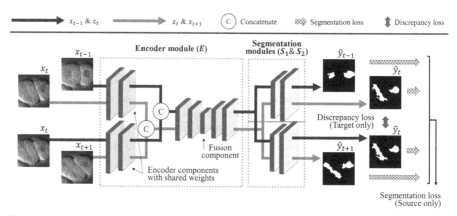

Fig. 1. Overview of the proposed method. x is the image, $\hat{y}$ is the class output probability obtained from the network, and $t-1, t$, and $t+1$ are the time points. Domain adaptation is done in a two-input, two-output network consisting of one encoder module (E) and two segmentation modules (S_1 & S_2). Segmentation losses are calculated in the source domain, and discrepancy losses are calculated from the output corresponding to the image at a common time point t in the target domain.

3.3   Training Steps

Given the network as described in Sect. 3.2, we propose three training steps. Step 1 is supervised learning of the network in the source domain, whereas Steps 2 and 3 are adversarial learning in the source and target domains. Given time-lapse images, Steps 2 and 3 are expected to suppress false feature extraction in two ways and consequently to improve the segmentation accuracy for the target domain (Fig. 2). The first way is the mapping of features obtained from images to the feature space. While MCD [6] maps time-lapse images with temporal continuity into the feature space independently, the proposed method simultaneously inputs images at time points $t-1, t$, and $t+1$, allowing us to try to map features into the feature space while considering the time series (Fig. 2a). The second way is feature extraction. The proposed method learns two decision boundaries obtained in the source domain by extracting features at time point t from two types of features obtained from the input images at time points $t-1, t$, and $t+1$ in the target domain (Fig. 2b). The three steps use repeated learning by mini-batches. Each step is described below.

Step 1: To obtain the features and decision boundaries required for classification from the source domain, we train the entire network consisting of the encoder module and segmentation modules simultaneously. Given images x_{t-1}^S, x_t^S, and x_t^S, x_{t+1}^S at continuous time points, the parameters of the network are updated to minimize segmentation loss $\mathcal{L}_{seg}$ by mini-batch for the inputs using the objective function as follows:

$$
\min_{E, S_1, S_2} \frac{\mathcal{L}_{seg}\left(N_1\left(X_{t-1}^S, X_t^S\right), Y_{t-1}^S\right) + \mathcal{L}_{seg}\left(N_2\left(X_{t-1}^S, X_t^S\right), Y_t^S\right)}{+ \mathcal{L}_{seg}\left(N_1\left(X_t^S, X_{t+1}^S\right), Y_t^S\right) + \mathcal{L}_{seg}\left(N_2\left(X_t^S, X_{t+1}^S\right), Y_{t+1}^S\right),} \tag{1}
$$

where $\mathcal{L}_{seg}$ is defined by the cross-entropy [6] as follows:

$$
\mathcal{L}_{seg}\left(\hat{Y}_t, Y_t\right) = -\mathbb{E}_{(\hat{y}_t, y_t) \sim (\hat{Y}_t, Y_t)} \sum_{k=1}^{K} \mathbb{1}_{[k=y_t]} \log \hat{y}_{t,k}, \tag{2}
$$

where y_t is the true label at time point t and $\hat{y}_{t,k}$ is the output probability at time point t for class k obtained from the network.

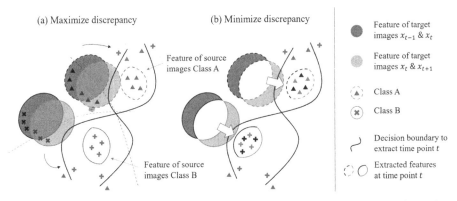

Fig. 2. Adversarial learning steps that (a) map the two features from the images at time points $t-1$ and t, and t and $t+1$ to the feature space and detect the target domains that are not mapped correctly by maximizing the discrepancy loss, and (b) extract features of time point t that are common at the pre-trained decision boundary by minimizing the discrepancy loss, and thereby guiding them to the correct locations.

Step 2: We fix the parameters of the encoder module and train the parameters of segmentation modules to minimize segmentation loss $\mathcal{L}_{seg}$ in the source domain and to maximize discrepancy loss $\mathcal{L}_{disc}$ in the target domain obtained from the two networks using the objective function as follows:

$$\min_{S_1,S_2} \begin{array}{l} \mathcal{L}_{seg}\left(N_1\left(X_t^{\mathbb{S}}, X_{t+1}^{\mathbb{S}}\right), Y_t^{\mathbb{S}}\right) + \mathcal{L}_{seg}\left(N_2\left(X_{t-1}^{\mathbb{S}}, X_t^{\mathbb{S}}\right), Y_t^{\mathbb{S}}\right) \\ -\mathcal{L}_{disc}\left(N_1\left(X_t^{\mathbb{T}}, X_{t+1}^{\mathbb{T}}\right), N_2\left(X_{t-1}^{\mathbb{T}}, X_t^{\mathbb{T}}\right)\right), \end{array} \tag{3}$$

where $\mathcal{L}_{disc}$ is defined by L1-distance [6] as follows:

$$\mathcal{L}_{disc}\left(\widehat{Y}_t^1, \widehat{Y}_t^2\right) = \mathbb{E}_{(\hat{y}_t^1, \hat{y}_t^2) \sim (\widehat{Y}_t^1, \widehat{Y}_t^2)} \frac{1}{K} \sum_{k=1}^{K} \left| \hat{y}_{t,k}^1 - \hat{y}_{t,k}^2 \right|, \tag{4}$$

where $\hat{y}_{t,k}^1$ and $\hat{y}_{t,k}^2$ are the output probabilities for class k at the same time point t obtained from the two networks N_1 and N_2, respectively.

Step 3: We fix the parameters of the segmentation modules and train the parameters of the encoder module to minimize discrepancy loss using the objective function as follows:

$$\min_{E} \mathcal{L}_{disc}\left(N_1\left(X_t^{\mathbb{T}}, X_{t+1}^{\mathbb{T}}\right), N_2\left(X_{t-1}^{\mathbb{T}}, X_t^{\mathbb{T}}\right)\right). \tag{5}$$

This step is repeated n times for the same mini-batch. The number is a hyperparameter, and we set $n = 3$ in all the experiments. Note that the main idea of UDA comes from MCD [6]; the main differences are in Eqs. (1), (3), and (5).

4 Experiments

We prepared two different datasets by adding true labels to time-lapse images of the same biological object obtained with the same type of microscope. Using the datasets, we performed two different experiments for the same time periods in the source and target domains. First, we assumed semantic segmentation when images were captured at the same interval in the source and target domains; we then verified the accuracy of the UDA. Next, we examined the change in the accuracy of the UDA when time-lapse images were captured at different intervals in both domains.

4.1 Datasets

To evaluate the proposed method, we used two datasets, dbScreen[1] (**D**) [18] and from WDDD[2] (**W**) [19] (Worm Developmental Dynamics Database); each dataset contained time-lapse images of nuclear division from the one-cell stage in a different *C. elegans* wild-type embryo (Fig. 3). In the time-lapse images, the rough-textured area is a cell, and the smooth textured area inside the cell is the nucleus and mitotic spindles after the breakdown of the nuclear envelope. In this study, these areas are collectively regarded as the nucleus or nuclear regions.

---

[1] http://worm-srv1.mpi-cbg.de/dbScreen/movies/wildtype.mov.
[2] http://so.qbic.riken.jp/wddd/cdd/.

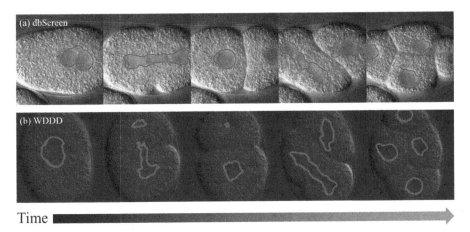

Fig. 3. The contours of the nuclear regions are extracted from the manually created true data and overlaid on the corresponding input images of (a) dbScreen and (b) WDDD in blue. The rough textured region in the image is the cell, and the smooth textured region in the images is the nucleus; the nuclear division dynamics from the one-cell to the four-cell stages are recorded. (Color figure online)

These time-lapse images were obtained by differential interference contrast (DIC) microscope, but under different imaging conditions, such as time interval and period, presence of a Z-stack, image resolution, image file formats, and orientation of the recorded embryos. In dbScreen, two-dimensional (2D) images (8-bit, 768×512 pixels grayscale, resolution not available) in compressed formats were recorded at 5-s intervals using a 100×1.25 N.A. objective lens; there are only time-lapse images of the wild-type embryo taken during the creation of a large imaging dataset of various *C. elegans* embryos (see [18] for details). In WDDD, three-dimensional (3D) images (16-bit, 600×600 pixels grayscale, 0.105 μm/pixel) in uncompressed formats were created by stacking 66 focal planes (0.5-μm intervals); they were recorded at 40-s intervals using a 100×1.40 N.A. objective lens (see [19] for details).

In this study, we aimed to segment nuclear regions from targeted images from the one- to four- cell stages and created the true label by visually determining the nuclear regions from the target image and manually tracing the outline (Fig. 3). We generated 433 true labels corresponding to all images from dbScreen. Because WDDD has a lower temporal resolution than dbScreen, there are only 42 time-lapse images for each Z-axis in the target time period. Therefore, we extracted the 31st, 33rd, and 35th Z-slice images and created the true labels for the extracted images (a total of 126 true labels).

The two datasets were considered to have approximately equal image resolution visually. As the preprocessing steps to prepare the images for inputs to the network, the original images were unified into 8-bit grayscale images, resized to 384×256 pixels for dbScreen and 384×384 pixels for WDDD, and cropped to 256×256 pixels based on the center of both images due to the limitations of the graphics processing unit (GPU) memory size. The preprocessed images and the corresponding true labels were used as training data for training the model, validation data for selecting the model, and test data for evaluating the accuracy of the model's predictions. In WDDD, each data point was assigned to each Z-axis, whereas in dbScreen, there is only one piece of Z-axis information, so each data point was assigned without a time overlap.

4.2 Experimental Conditions

For the previous models for supervised learning, we focused on DRN [9], the architecture with the highest accuracy in experiments of semantic segmentation in MCD [6]; U-Net [1]; and co-detection CNN [7]. The models trained in the source domain as "source only" and models trained in the target domain as "target only" were used to confirm the difficulty of domain adaptation and segmentation, respectively, in the target domain. The structure of up convolution in the U-Net was unified with the structure used in the co-detection CNN (i.e., the structure used in our method).

In addition to CellSegUDA [17] and MCD with DRN architecture [6] as the previous image-based UDA methods, we also compared MCD with the U-Net and co-detection CNN architectures that we created. For the segmentation and decoder networks in CellSegUDA, we adopted the structure of U-Net, which is the basis of co-detection CNN. The rest of the experimental conditions followed those of Zhang et al. [16], the discriminator was based on DCGAN [20], and the hyperparameters were $\lambda_{adv} = 0.001$ and $\lambda_{rec} = 0.01$. In MCD with DRN architecture, the branching point in the network was determined at the same position as in Saito et al. [6]. In MCD with U-Net architecture, the branching point in the network was determined before the last up-convolution layer of the U-Net, based on the results of verifying the relationship between the branching point and the accuracy of domain adaptation. The branching point in MCD with co-detection CNN architecture was set at the same position as for the proposed method.

We also compared the proposed method and DA-VSN [15], a video-based UDA method. In this comparison, the segmentation network was the pre-trained ACCEL [21], and the hyperparameters were set at $\lambda_{sa} = 1$, $\lambda_{wd} = 1$, and $\lambda_u = 0.001$.

To confirm the effect of the proposed methods in learning continuous temporal information, we compared segmentation accuracy under three different data input methods: (1) the original data input method, in which the image sets X_{t-1}, X_t, and X_{t+1} are inputted so that temporal association can be considered ("constant"); (2) the case that does not consider the time series, in which the image sets X_t, X_t, and X_t are inputted to check the change accuracy due to different network structures ("same"); and (3) the case that only considers positions of target regions without temporal continuity ("random"). In the latter case, for an image at time point t, we continued to randomly select images x_a and x_b at two time points, ignoring the time direction. The resulting images sets X_a, X_t, and X_b were inputted.

We used Adam (learning rate = 0.001, weight decay = 0.0005) as the optimization function. The batch size was set to one for DA-VSN and five for the others. We trained the models until the loss values converged, and then we evaluated the model with the best accuracy. In MCD, the result of adding the two outputs obtained from one input image of the validation data (or test data) was used for evaluation, whereas the proposed method used the result of simultaneously adding two of the four outputs obtained from four input images. The evaluation metrics are the mean and standard deviation of the time averages of the Intersection over Union (IoU) for the nuclear regions in five trials.

The experiments used an Intel Core i7-9700k CPU and an NVIDIA GeForce RTX 2080 Ti GPU with 11 GB of memory.

4.3 The Case with the Same Time Intervals in the Domains

In this experiment, we set up the same condition for image time intervals in the source and target domains. In both dbScreen and WDDD, we prepared 42 images of training data, validation data, and test data, respectively, with a 40-s interval and without overlapping. Table 1 shows the segmentation accuracy for the test data when adapting from dbScreen to WDDD and from WDDD to dbScreen for the proposed and previous methods. Figure 4 shows examples of semantic segmentation.

Table 1. Segmentation accuracy (%) for both dbScreen (D) and WDDD (W) using images at 40-s intervals. Mean ± standard deviation values are shown for five trials of the time averages of IoU for the nuclear regions in the test data. The best values are highlighted in bold.

Method	Main architecture	D → W	W → D
Source only	DRN [9]	19.1 ± 10.6	24.7 ± 9.2
	U-Net [1]	15.0 ± 6.3	21.0 ± 11.4
	co-detection CNN [7]	14.2 ± 12.0	15.0 ± 4.8
DA-VSN [15]	ACCEL [21]	15.1 ± 2.0	27.2 ± 2.2
CellSegUDA [17]	U-Net	37.9 ± 7.9	36.2 ± 5.9
MCD [6]	DRN [6]	27.3 ± 24.1	54.1 ± 11.4
	U-Net	59.8 ± 8.7	70.9 ± 3.0
	co-detection CNN	68.5 ± 2.5	66.5 ± 5.3
T-MCD (ours)	co-detection CNN (same)	61.3 ± 9.9	74.8 ± 1.8
	co-detection CNN (random)	70.6 ± 2.0	78.1 ± 0.2
	co-detection CNN (constant)	**75.7 ± 1.3**	**79.1 ± 0.6**
Target only	DRN	77.2 ± 1.4	83.4 ± 0.4
	U-Net	78.3 ± 0.8	84.3 ± 0.2
	co-detection CNN	78.8 ± 1.4	84.8 ± 0.3

The segmentation accuracies of the three types of source-only models were less than 25% of IoU for the target domain in both adaptive conditions. MCD with U-Net architecture and MCD with co-detection CNN architecture showed better segmentation accuracy (<71% IoU) than DA-VSN, CellSegUDA, and MCD with DRN architecture. Under conditions such as our datasets (see Sect. 4.2 for details), where the target region of segmentation is inside a dynamically fluctuating object (i.e., cell), the flow vectors cannot be generated and used properly. Consequently, it is difficult to maximize the performance of DA-VSN.

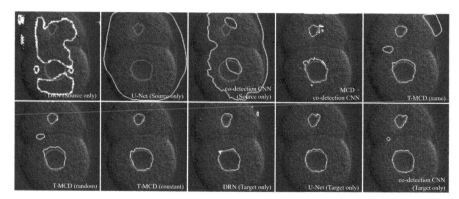

Fig. 4. Example of visualization of segmentation results for source-only models and models with > 60% IoU in Table 1 when adapting from dbScreen to WDDD. Contours of the nuclear regions are extracted from the manually created true data and segmentation results and are overlaid on the corresponding input images in blue and red, respectively. (Color figure online)

The proposed methods (same, random, and constant) achieved higher accuracies than all the previous methods. However, the difference in accuracy between the proposed method (same) and MCD with U-Net or co-detection CNN as architecture can be explained by a calculation error introduced when floating-point numbers vary depending on the position of the gradient addition during backpropagation. In particular, the proposed method (constant) achieved an accuracy more than 7% higher than the IoU value of the previous UDA methods, such as the MCD with U-Net or co-detection CNN architecture; it also significantly outperformed the segmentation accuracy of the other proposed methods (same and random) ($p \leq 0.01$ by Welch's two-tailed t-test). As shown in Fig. 4, the proposed methods (same and random) falsely detected the cellular region as the nuclear region, but the proposed (constant) method, which utilizes temporal association, was effective in suppressing such false positives.

The target-only models of supervised learning of the WDDD and dbScreen images show that segmentation of the WDDD images is more difficult than that of the dbScreen images. This may be because the nuclei are present in the focal plane in the 2D images in dbScreen, whereas nuclei are not present or are only partially present in the focal plane in the 3D images in WDDD.

Furthermore, the differences in segmentation accuracies between the source-only models and the target-only models indicate a large domain gap between datasets. Image contrast differs significantly between dbScreen and WDDD due to differences in imaging conditions, such as the type of objective lens used (see Sect. 4.1 for details). If the image contrast is the main cause of the domain gap, the gap may be reduced by data augmentation techniques. We therefore confirmed the segmentation accuracies for target domain images with U-Net models trained on source domain images to which we applied at least one of two types of simple data augmentation techniques: gamma correction for gamma values between 0.0 and 2.0 ("Contrast"); rotation of images with 90 degree increments ("Rotation"). The best IoU values were obtained when applying both Contrast and Rotation; the values were only 52.4 ± 24.7 for WDDD and 57.5 ± 15.4 for dbScreen, respectively (other results not shown). These results revealed factors other than contrast and rotation in the domain gaps, and that the proposed UDA method can reduce domain gaps that are difficult to resolve with simple data augmentation.

4.4   The Case with Different Time Intervals Between the Domains

In this experiment, we set up the different conditions for image time intervals in the source and target domains. Specifically, we fixed WDDD as target data at the same 40-s interval images ($n = 42$) as in the previous experiment and prepared three conditions for dbScreen as source data: 20-s interval images ($n = 84$), 10-s interval images ($n = 167$), and 5-s interval images ($n = 334$). Table 2 shows the changes in the segmentation accuracies for the test data when adapting from dbScreen to WDDD. Note that adaptation from WDDD to dbScreen was not performed because test data could not be prepared with 2D time-lapse images from dbScreen. In Table 2, MCD with co-detection CNN architecture (MCD + co-detection CNN) and T-MCD (random) improved accuracies as the time interval decreased, possibly because of the increase in the amount of training data. On the other hand, T-MCD (constant) was less accurate under some conditions because the temporal associations of features learned on the source data do not work well on the target data, whereas there is no such effect in T-MCD (random). These results show that the proposed T-MCD (constant) method should be used under conditions where the time interval is approximately the same across domains.

Table 2. Segmentation accuracy (%) for target data (WDDD) when varying time intervals for source data (dbScreen). Mean $\pm$ standard deviation values are shown for five trials of the time averages of IoU for the nuclear regions in the test data. The best values are highlighted in bold.

	20-s interval	10-s interval	5-s interval
MCD + co-detection CNN	65.4 ± 4.0	67.9 ± 4.6	70.3 ± 2.2
T-MCD (random)	72.9 ± 1.4	**72.3 ± 3.5**	**74.4 ± 0.6**
T-MCD (constant)	**74.5 ± 0.9**	69.5 ± 2.6	73.2 ± 0.8

5   Conclusion

In this study, we proposed a new UDA framework that considers the temporal association of features and the distribution of each class of domains, which is simpler than the previous optical flow-based UDA methods. As a new benchmark of UDA, we created and released annotation data for two kinds of open time-lapse microscopic images of *C. elegans*. Using the annotated data, we confirmed that the proposed method shows better segmentation accuracy than the state-of-the-art previous UDA methods. We hope that our benchmark will contribute to the further development of new UDA methods, and our proposed method will be effective for domain adaptation in the segmentation of time-lapse microscopy images not only for *C. elegans* but for other model organisms.

We think that ambiguity in the boundary between nuclear regions and the others makes learning difficult. Therefore, future works include improvement of the proposed method such as adding a noisy universal domain adaptation approach [12] and application of the method to other biological data.

Acknowledgments. This work was partially supported by JSPS KAKENHI Grant Numbers JP19K12226 and JP21K19281.

References

1. Ronneberger, O., Fischer, P., Brox, T.: U-Net: convolutional networks for biomedical image segmentation. In: Navab, N., Hornegger, J., Wells, W.M., Frangi, A.F. (eds.) MICCAI 2015. LNCS, vol. 9351, pp. 234–241. Springer, Cham (2015). https://doi.org/10.1007/978-3-319-24574-4_28
2. Swedlow, J.R., et al.: A global view of standards for open image data formats and repositories. Nat. Methods **18**, 1440–1446 (2021). https://doi.org/10.1038/s41592-021-01113-7
3. Ganin, Y., et al.: Domain-adversarial training of neural networks. JMLR **17**(1), 1–35 (2016). https://doi.org/10.48550/arXiv.1505.07818
4. Tzeng, E., Hoffman, J., Saenko, K., Darrellm, T.: Adversarial discriminative domain adaptation. In: IEEE CVPR, pp. 7167–7176 (2017). https://doi.org/10.1109/cvpr.2017.316
5. Hoffman, J., et al.: CyCADA: cycle-consistent adversarial domain adaptation. In: PMLR, pp. 1989–1998 (2018)
6. Saito, K., Watanabe, K., Ushiku, Y., Harada, T.: Maximum classifier discrepancy for unsupervised domain adaptation. In: IEEE CVPR, pp. 3723–3732 (2018). https://doi.org/10.1109/cvpr.2018.00392
7. Nishimura, K., Hayashida, J., Wang, C., Ker, D.F.E., Bise, R.: Weakly-supervised cell tracking via backward-and-forward propagation. In: Vedaldi, A., Bischof, H., Brox, T., Frahm, J.-M. (eds.) ECCV 2020. LNCS, vol. 12357, pp. 104–121. Springer, Cham (2020). https://doi.org/10.1007/978-3-030-58610-2_7
8. Shin, I., Park, K., Woo, S., Kweon, I.S.: Unsupervised domain adaptation for video semantic segmentation. In: IEEE CVPR (2020)
9. Cordts, M., et al.: The cityscapes dataset for semantic urban scene understanding. In: IEEE CVPR, pp. 3213–3223 (2016). https://doi.org/10.1109/cvpr.2016.350
10. Richter, S.R., Vineet, V., Roth, S., Koltun, V.: Playing for data: ground truth from computer games. In: Leibe, B., Matas, J., Sebe, N., Welling, M. (eds.) ECCV 2016. LNCS, vol. 9906, pp. 102–118. Springer, Cham (2016). https://doi.org/10.1007/978-3-319-46475-6_7
11. Yu, F., Koltun, V., Funkhouser, T.: Dilated residual networks. In: IEEE CVPR, pp. 472–480 (2017). https://doi.org/10.1109/cvpr.2017.75
12. Yu, Q., Hashimoto, A., Ushiku, Y.: Divergence optimization for noisy universal domain adaptation. In: IEEE CVPR, pp. 2515–2524 (2021). https://doi.org/10.1109/cvpr46437.2021.00254
13. Chen, J., Li, Y., Ma, K., Zheng, Y.: Generative adversarial networks for video-to-video domain adaptation. In: AAAI, vol. 34, no. 04, pp. 3462–3469 (2020). https://doi.org/10.1609/aaai.v34i04.5750
14. Kim, D., Woo, S., Lee, J.-Y., Kweon, I.S.: Video panoptic segmentation. In: IEEE CVPR, pp. 9859–9868 (2020). https://doi.org/10.1109/cvpr42600.2020.00988
15. Guan, D., Huang, J., Xiao, A., Lu, S.: Domain adaptive video segmentation via temporal consistency regularization. In: IEEE ICCV, pp. 8053–8064 (2021). https://doi.org/10.1109/iccv48922.2021.00795

16. Zhang, J., Wang, Z., Zhang, S., Wei, G.: DAVOS: semi-supervised video object segmentation via adversarial domain adaptation. In: IEEE CVPR (2021)
17. Haq, M.M., Huang, J.: Adversarial domain adaptation for cell segmentation. In: PMLR, pp. 277–287 (2020)
18. Gönczy, P., et al.: Functional genomic analysis of cell division in *C. elegans* using RNAi of genes on chromosome III. Nature, 408: 331–336 (2000). https://doi.org/10.1038/35042526
19. Kyoda, K., et al.: WDDD: worm developmental dynamics database. Nucleic Acids Res. **41**, D732–D737 (2013). https://doi.org/10.1093/nar/gks1107
20. Radford, A., Metz, L., Chintala, S.: Unsupervised representation learning with deep convolutional generative adversarial networks. In: IEEE CVPR (2015)
21. Jain, S., Wang, X., Gonzalez, J.: Accel: a corrective fusion network for efficient semantic segmentation on video. In: IEEE CVPR, pp. 8866–8875 (2019). https://doi.org/10.1109/cvpr.2019.00907

Unsupervised Multi-view Multi-person 3D Pose Estimation Using Reprojection Error

Diógenes Wallis de França Silva[1]([⊠]), João Paulo Silva do Monte Lima[1,2] [ID],
David Macêdo[3] [ID], Cleber Zanchettin[3] [ID], Diego Gabriel Francis Thomas[4] [ID],
Hideaki Uchiyama[5] [ID], and Veronica Teichrieb[1] [ID]

[1] Voxar Labs, Centro de Informática, Universidade Federal de Pernambuco,
Recife, PE, Brazil
{dwfs2,jpsml,vt}@cin.ufpe.br
[2] Visual Computing Lab, Departamento de Computação, Universidade Federal Rural
de Pernambuco, Recife, PE, Brazil
joao.mlima@ufrpe.br
[3] Centro de Informática, Universidade Federal de Pernambuco, Recife, PE, Brazil
{dlm,cz}@cin.ufpe.br
[4] Faculty of Information Science and Electrical Engineering, Kyushu University,
Fukuoka, Japan
thomas@ait.kyushu-u.ac.jp
[5] Graduate School of Science and Technology, Nara Institute of Science
and Technology, Nara, Japan
hideaki.uchiyama@is.naist.jp

Abstract. This work addresses multi-view multi-person 3D pose estimation in synchronized and calibrated camera views. Recent approaches estimate neural network weights in a supervised way; they rely on ground truth annotated datasets to compute the loss function and optimize the weights in the network. However, manually labeling ground truth datasets is labor-intensive, expensive, and prone to errors. Consequently, it is preferable not to rely heavily on labeled datasets. This work proposes an unsupervised approach to estimating 3D human poses requiring only an off-the-shelf 2D pose estimation method and the intrinsic and extrinsic camera parameters. Our approach uses reprojection error as a loss function instead of comparing the predicted 3D pose with the ground truth. First, we estimate the 3D pose of each person using the plane sweep stereo approach, in which the depth of each 2D joint related to each person is estimated in a selected target view. The estimated 3D pose is then projected onto each of the other views using camera parameters. Finally, the 2D reprojection error in the image plane is computed by comparing it with the estimated 2D pose corresponding to the same person. The 2D poses that correspond to the same person are identified using virtual depth planes, where each 3D pose is projected onto the reference view and compared to find the nearest 2D pose. Our proposed method learns to estimate 3D pose in an end-to-end unsupervised manner and does not require any manual parameter tuning, yet we achieved results close to state-of-the-art supervised methods on a public dataset. Our

E. Pimenidis et al. (Eds.): ICANN 2022, LNCS 13531, pp. 482–494, 2022.
https://doi.org/10.1007/978-3-031-15934-3_40

method achieves only 5.8% points below the fully supervised state-of-the-art method and only 5.1% points below the best geometric approach in the Campus dataset.

Keywords: 3D human pose estimation · Unsupervised learning · Deep learning · Reprojection error

1   Introduction

The 3D human pose estimation (3DHPE) estimates the 3D location of each joint of the body's skeleton from one or multiple images. 3DHPE has many applications in video surveillance, human-computer interaction, or augmented reality. Consequently, it has attracted much research in the last decades in computer vision. Originally, the 3D human pose was obtained with the help of 3D sensors such as RGB-D cameras or motion captors, which required expensive equipment and expertise. With the recent progresses in machine learning techniques, new possibilities have emerged, such as estimating reliable 3D pose from only few RGB images [10,15,19]. However, challenges remain to deal with multiple persons in the scene because of the many occlusions and difficulty to match the same person across different views.

Recently, several methods have been proposed to tackle the problem of multi-view multi-person 3D pose estimation [4,8]. These methods follow a three-step approach: (1) 2D poses in each view of each person in the scene are estimated; (2) 2D poses that correspond to the same person are matched across the different views; (3) the 3D pose of each person is obtained using triangulation or 3D pictorial structure (3DPS) techniques. The essential part of these three steps is obtaining reliable correspondences across the views. MVPose [5], for example, uses a hybrid matching algorithm that combines appearance and geometry, and with the matched 2D poses, they estimate the 3D pose using a 3DPS model with a reduced state-space. However, all these methods rely on ground truth 3D annotations on the training dataset, limiting their generalization ability. Our approach is unsupervised, and 3D annotations are not necessary to perform the training of the neural network.

The plane-sweep-based approach, as proposed by Lin et al. [12] is an alternative to the standard triangulation for 3D pose estimation. The key idea is to define a target view and estimate the depth of the persons' joints in this target view based on information from the other views using back-projection. Then, by back projecting the 2D poses from the target view in successive 3D poses located in different depth planes, each 3D pose is projected onto each reference view, generating a score matrix that encodes relative information from all the views. This score matrix is then fed to a neural network that outputs the estimated 3D pose. The advantage of such an approach is that the 3D pose estimation network can be trained end-to-end. However, the method proposed in [12] is supervised, so it also requires ground truth 3D annotations for training.

Proposed Solution Overview

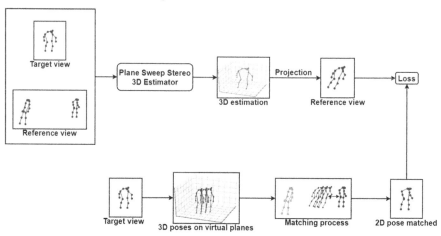

Fig. 1. Considering the multiple views available, as in [12], we define a target view, and all the others are determined as reference views. Our overview solution image has two views: the target view and only one reference view. Our approach follows two sequential steps: the first is to estimate the 3D pose using [12], go along with the projection of this 3D pose onto the reference view. The second is to utilize back-projection to make the matching process, so we establish the 2D pose compared with the 2D projection obtained from 3D estimation. Comparing these poses, we have a reprojection error loss.

We propose to extend the plane-sweep-based approach of [12] with a new geometric loss that does not require ground truth 3D annotation. This strategy allows the training of a multi-person multi-view 3D pose estimator in an unsupervised manner. The key to our method is a 2D reprojection loss that compares for each person the projection of the estimated 3D pose in each input view with the corresponding 2D pose estimated from the input images. In addition, we employ Adabelief as an optimizer instead of Adam, and we evaluate the use of a regularization term when computing the loss.

1. An end-to-end unsupervised method in multi-view multi-person 3D pose estimation;
2. A new loss using reprojection error that compares 2D poses instead of comparing the 3D estimate with the ground truth;
3. Quantitative and qualitative evaluations comparing the proposed unsupervised approach with supervised and unsupervised geometric techniques.

2 Related Work

This section presents a brief overview of the methods that use multiple views to perform 3D pose estimation of multiple persons.

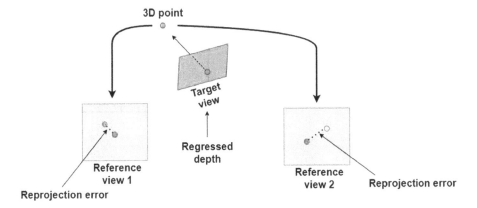

Fig. 2. Overview of the reprojection process. Once we have a point in a target view, we estimate its depth using [12] and project this point onto both the reference views. The squared Euclidean distance between the points is the reprojection error [7]. The blue and orange points represent the real position of the target point in the respective reference view. We compare the projected point (green point) with the estimated position. We are not using ground truth to verify if the 3D point is in the correct position; instead, we use the reprojection error. (Color figure online)

Some approaches use triangulation as [1,2] to create a common state space where a 3DPS is defined for each person. The 3DPS is a graph with unary and potential relations between the joints. To obtain the 3D pose, they use a loopy belief propagation algorithm. Works as [4,8] have in common a well-defined pipeline: find the 2D poses of a person in each view using a matching algorithm and build a cluster of these 2D poses. This cluster is used to estimate the 3D pose. Dong et al. [5] uses a matching algorithm that combines epipolar constraints (geometry affinity matrix) and person re-identification features (appearance affinity matrix). They use a permutation matrix that fuses the geometry and appearance matrices. To perform 3D pose estimation, they use a 3DPS model. Unlike our method, these geometric approaches are not end-to-end and commonly need manual adjustment to perform in different scenarios. Other methods, such as VoxelPose [17] deal with the cross-view challenge using an object-detection approach. Instead of searching 2D correspondences among the views, VoxelPose back-projects all the 2D poses to the same 3D space, and this 3D volumetric space is used for 3D pose estimation. VoxelPose does not need to perform cross-view matching as MVPose [5], but there are still many limitations to the 3D object detection approach, like high computational cost because of 3D CNN and low scalability of 2D pose back-projection for more significant scenes. Our method does not demand high computational cost, and it is also an end-to-end approach that does not require manually adjusting parameters to work in different scenarios.

Beyond that, state-of-the-art methods such as Huang et al. [8], VoxelPose [17], and Lin et al. [12] are fully supervised methods, so they need to use the

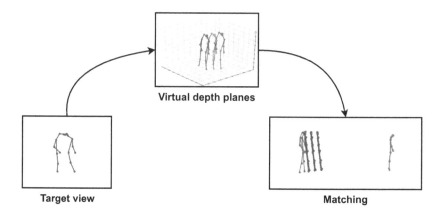

Fig. 3. The estimated 2D pose in the target view is back-projected onto successive virtual depths planes, and each 3D skeleton is projected onto the reference view. We compare the skeletons, and the nearest 2D pose in the reference view is our matched pose. This matched pose is compared with the 2D projection of the estimated 3D pose, as we discuss in Subsect. 3.1.

ground truth in the training process. Lin et al. [12] is the work by which we were inspired to obtain our regressed value. First, they define a target image where the depths of the 2D pose will be estimated. Then, they generate a score matrix that contains matching information. This matrix is the input of a neural network that outputs the depth value we use to calculate the reprojection error loss. Unlike the mentioned methods, our approach is an unsupervised way to perform 3D pose estimation, so we do not use ground truth in our training. Figure 1 presents an overview of our method. We estimate the 3D points based on Lin et al. [12], and we use the reprojection error to compute the loss, given the regressed depth obtained using [12]. The advantage of our work is that we do not need labeled data, we need calibrated cameras to make the projections, so our method can generalize well and be used in any unlabeled data. 3D annotations are costly, and not using them makes our method work in any dataset once the cameras are synchronized and we know the camera parameters.

3   UMVpose

Our proposed technique, named UMVpose (Unsupervised Multi-View Multi-Person 3D Pose Estimation), is an unsupervised method for 3D pose estimation of multiple persons using multiple views. The state of the art [12] uses the regressed depth to compute the loss against the ground truth depth. Our approach uses [12] to make the 3D inference; however, instead of comparing this 3D estimation with ground truth, we use reprojection error to compute the loss using 2D poses generated along with the training; this means we do not use ground truth anymore. We simply need camera parameters to make the projections and obtain our 3D pose estimation. Hence, we can utilize UMVpose without using any 3D pose annotation. We get the matching poses using back-projection; virtual depth planes are created, and all of them are projected onto the reference view. We get the nearest 2D pose in the reference view, and consequently, we have the skeleton correspondences between the target and reference views. Finally, we use the matched 2D pose to compare with the projected 2D pose.

As in Fig. 1, we obtain the 3D pose using the regressed depths and project it onto the reference view, so we compare it with the matching 2D pose from the reference view. We use reprojection error to compute the loss comparing the 2D pose from the reference view and the 2D pose projected from the obtained 3D pose. Therefore, we do not use ground truth anymore. Besides that, we use the Adabelief optimizer [20] instead of Adam [11]. Adabelief can be faster than Adam in convergence, and we could improve our performance. We also make experiments adding a regularizer term to our proposal.

3.1   Reprojection Error

Given a 2D pose with J joints in the target camera, we estimate the depth of each one of these joints using [12]. Once we estimated the depths, we projected the 3D points onto each of the reference images and compared them with the 2D position of that person in the respective reference view. This process is illustrated in Fig. 2.

The process of projecting a point onto an image and comparing its position with the true position of that point is called reprojection error. The goal is to quantify how well the 3D point corresponds to the projection of the point in a 2D image. Using the camera parameters, we obtain a projection matrix $\mathbf{P}$. We can project a 3D point onto a 2D point with this matrix. Now, this projection is in the same image as the true position, and we compare them by calculating the Euclidean distance between the points. The reprojection error is our loss, and we intend to minimize this value; that is, minimizing reprojection error means generating 3D points well corresponded with the true 2D points in the image.

3.2   Matching Process

Based on [12], we estimate 2D poses from all the views using an off-the-shelf method [16], and after that, we perform a back-projection for each 2D pose of the target image using virtual depth planes as shown in Fig. 3. Finally, each 3D pose in these depth planes is projected onto the reference views, and we measure the distance between this projected 3D pose and the estimated 2D poses in the reference view:

$$m = \arg \min_{r} \sum_{i=1}^{J} d(r_i, p_i), \tag{1}$$

where J is the number of joints, $d(x, y)$ is the distance between the joints x and y, $\{r\}$ is the set of the 2D poses from the reference view, p is the projected pose in reference view, and m is the nearest 2D pose in the $\{r\}$ set.

Fig. 4. Different scenes were captured by the three calibrated and synchronized cameras on the Campus Dataset. In each scene, we have the same scenario captured by different cameras. In scene 2, for example, camera 0 shows three persons, but in cameras 1 and 2, we have only two persons. In scene 3, we have two persons in camera 0, but only one in cameras 1 and 2.

3.3   Loss Function

In [12] they compute two losses, one for person position (center hip joint) and another for joints positions. With the regressed depth, they obtain the 3D hip point and joints. Then, they compare the estimates with the 3D ground truth. UMVpose uses the regressed depth to generate a 3D point (using the center hip) related to the person's position and a 3D pose with all the joints. We project the person's 3D location and the estimated 3D pose onto each reference view. Using the concept of reprojection error, we compute a loss comparing the target 3D estimate projected onto the reference view with the matched 2D pose. As in [12], we use two losses, a position loss (related to hip point) and a joint loss. Both losses are computed using MSE.

The position loss is given by

$$\mathcal{L}_{pose} = \sum_{r=0}^{R} \frac{1}{P} \sum_{i=1}^{P} (position_r(i)_{proj} - position_r(i)_{ref})^2, \qquad (2)$$

where P is the number of persons in the target view, $position_r(i)_{proj}$ is the projected pose and $position_r(i)_{ref}$ is the matched pose in the reference view, and R is the number of reference views.

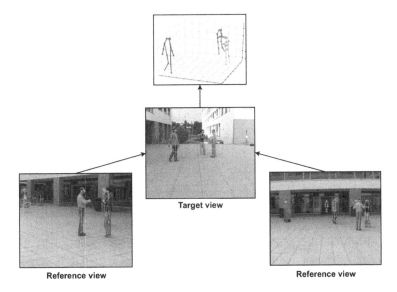

Fig. 5. 3D pose estimation using UMVpose. First, we define a target view and the reference views. Then we estimate the 3D joints using these defined views as our input. Each predicted depth is related to the 2D pose estimations from the target view, so our predictions are based on the target view skeletons.

The joint loss is obtained by

$$\mathcal{L}_{joint} = \sum_{r=0}^{R} \frac{1}{P} \sum_{i=1}^{P} \sum_{j=1}^{J} (joint_{r,j}(i)_{proj} - joint_{r,j}(i)_{ref})^2, \tag{3}$$

where P is the number of persons in the target view, $joint_{r,j}(i)_{proj}$ are the 17 joints projected onto the reference view and $joint_{r,j}(i)_{ref}$ are the joints from the matched skeleton in the reference view.

Regularizer Term. We also use a regularizer term, more precisely the Kullback-Leibler (KL) one [18], inspired by [14]. We get the keypoints positions, and we multiply each coordinate by a Gaussian distribution $\mathcal{N}(0, \sigma)$, so we apply this to projected and matched 2D poses. We apply KL divergence to these poses multiplied by λ. We also make this with the center hip point in $\mathcal{L}_{position}$. We use the parameter values $\sigma = 1$ and $\lambda = 1$, since they provide the best results in [14].

3.4 Optimizer

3D pose estimation learning methods commonly use the Adam optimizer [11]. Unfortunately, Adam takes a long time to converge, so we decided to use

Table 1. Comparison of PCP (Campus dataset) with the best methods that deal with multi-view and multi-person 3D pose estimation.

Method	Actor 1	Actor 2	Actor 3	Average
Belagiannis et al. [1]	82.0	72.4	73.7	75.8
Belagiannis et al. [3]	83.0	73.0	78.0	78.0
Belagiannis et al. [2]	93.5	75.7	84.4	84.5
Ershadi-Nasab et al. [6]	94.2	92.9	84.6	90.6
Dong et al. [5]	97.6	**93.3**	**98.0**	**96.3**
Huang et al. [8]	98.0	**94.8**	97.4	96.7
VoxelPose - Tu et al. [17]	97.6	93.8	98.8	96.7
Jiahao Lin et al. [12]	**98.4**	93.7	**99.0**	**97.0**
Ours with Adam	78.0	85.1	83.0	82.0
Ours with Adabelief	**96.9**	**87.8**	88.9	**91.2**
Ours with Adabelief and KL regularizer	93.3	86.8	**89.4**	89.8

We have two lines at the table that separate the methods in geometric methods, deep learning methods, and our methods with the respective experiments. Above the first line, we have geometric methods, and these methods need to use ground truth from training data to perform the estimation, except Dong et al. [5] that do not use any training data from the evaluated datasets, however [5] use ground truth from Human3.6M [9] dataset to obtain parameters that are used in 3DPS model to compute the inference of the 3D pose estimation. We have supervised methods between the two lines needing labeled data. Below the second line, we have the experiments with our method. Our method is unsupervised and does not need to use any labeled data. Our average performance is lower than supervised methods, but the difference from the best-supervised method is less than 6 pp. Comparing with [5] (the best geometric method), we have 5.1 pp of difference. All the results, except ours, were obtained directly from the papers. We did not reproduce the experiments from other methods.

AdaBelief [20], which has three key features: fast convergence, good generalization, and training stability. AdaBelief was faster in convergence than Adam. Therefore, we could see progress early. Furthermore, we could make the analysis faster than the Adam optimizer when we performed different tests.

4   Experimental Setup

We choose an outdoor dataset and compute the usual metrics for 3D pose estimation. We estimate the 2D pose using the off-the-shelf method HR-Net [16], that is pre-trained on the MS-COCO dataset [13]. The UMVpose method is unsupervised with a reprojection error loss. Although we compare 2D poses to get the UMVpose loss, we need to compare 3D pose estimates to get the usual metrics and verify our performance concerning other methods. This section briefly discusses the dataset and the metrics used to evaluate the results.

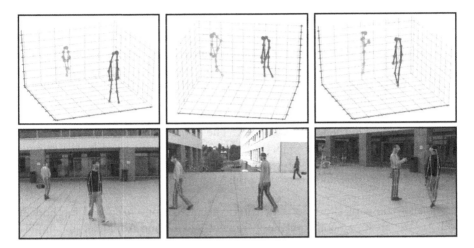

Fig. 6. Examples of 3D pose estimation using UMVpose in Campus Dataset. These examples provides a qualitative analysis of the 3D estimations, in which the green skeletons are the estimated 2D poses and the above 3D pose is related to them. (Color figure online)

4.1 Dataset

We select the Campus dataset [1] to perform our experiments because it is a famous dataset in 3D pose estimation (Fig. 4 shows some samples), and we can use it to compare our approach with state-of-the-art works. Furthermore, [12] uses this dataset, and we adapted it to obtain a new loss and make the process unsupervised, so we have a reference to check our tests.

The Campus dataset is an outdoor dataset with three persons interacting, and it was acquired using three cameras. The annotation of 3D ground-truth poses is incomplete, so following [12] we used synthesized 3D MoCap poses in order that we can be fair in our comparison. As in [5,8,17] we perform evaluation on frames 350–470, 650–750.

4.2 Metrics

As in [5,8,17], the metric we use to evaluate the accuracy of our estimated 3D pose is the Percentage of Correctly estimated Parts (PCP). Each part of the estimated 3D pose is compared with the ground truth. We compare PCP with state-of-the-art supervised methods and 3DPS methods based on projective geometry. We did not find unsupervised methods that are not based on only geometric concepts, that is, unsupervised approaches using deep learning to perform 3D pose estimation in the Campus dataset. We computed PCP for actors 1, 2, 3, and the average of these values.

5   Results and Discussions

We perform our experiments in the Campus Dataset, and we can see an example with all the views in Fig. 5 and qualitative analysis in Fig. 6. We compute only the PCP metric, and as shown in Table 1, we got a significant performance if compared with supervised methods and also geometric methods. Our method achieves 5.8 pp below of fully supervised method and 5.1 pp below the best geometric method in the Campus dataset. The advantages of our method related to supervised methods such as [8,12,17] is that we do not need to use ground truth, and related to geometric methods [1–3,5,6] is that we have an end-to-end solution that does not need to adjust parameters according to the scene manually.

We also compare the results of three variants of our proposed method in Table 1. We can see a significant improvement when using Adabelief in comparison with Adam. We also could improve the Actor3 value by 0.5 pp using a KL regularizer term, but the average is down by 1.4 pp.

Although our approach does not need to use 3D annotations, we must perform the matching process to identify the pedestrian 2D poses in each view. Our matching process is costly, considering we need to make several 3D pose projections to perform the matching process in the back-projection process. Furthermore, back-projection can associate the same 2D pose in the reference view with more than one person on the target view. To address this problem, a matching process more direct, with fewer steps, can potentially be more robust, avoiding back-projection problems. Beyond that, we can perform data augmentation, increasing the data used in our training. Using this trained model, we can fine-tune with labeled data to outperform the supervised approaches.

6   Conclusion

This work showed that reprojection error could be a way to generalize 3D pose estimation. We could change the loss using this approach and not use ground truth anymore. Once we do not need labeled data, we can use any dataset once we have the camera parameters. We could also see that when using the Adabelief optimizer, the results were close to the ones from supervised methods, so we have a powerful, fully unsupervised approach. In future work, we intend to do additional experiments with other publicly available datasets, try different regularizer terms beyond KL, such as Jensen-Shannon, and improve the matching process; in this manner, we can generalize the process even more.

References

1. Belagiannis, V., Amin, S., Andriluka, M., Schiele, B., Navab, N., Ilic, S.: 3D pictorial structures for multiple human pose estimation. In: Proceedings of the IEEE Conference on Computer Vision and Pattern Recognition, pp. 1669–1676 (2014)

2. Belagiannis, V., Amin, S., Andriluka, M., Schiele, B., Navab, N., Ilic, S.: 3D pictorial structures revisited: multiple human pose estimation. IEEE Trans. Pattern Anal. Mach. Intell. **38**(10), 1929–1942 (2015)

3. Belagiannis, V., Wang, X., Schiele, B., Fua, P., Ilic, S., Navab, N.: Multiple human pose estimation with temporally consistent 3D pictorial structures. In: Agapito, L., Bronstein, M.M., Rother, C. (eds.) ECCV 2014. LNCS, vol. 8925, pp. 742–754. Springer, Cham (2015). https://doi.org/10.1007/978-3-319-16178-5_52

4. Chen, H., Guo, P., Li, P., Lee, G.H., Chirikjian, G.: Multi-person 3D pose estimation in crowded scenes based on multi-view geometry. In: Vedaldi, A., Bischof, H., Brox, T., Frahm, J.-M. (eds.) ECCV 2020. LNCS, vol. 12348, pp. 541–557. Springer, Cham (2020). https://doi.org/10.1007/978-3-030-58580-8_32

5. Dong, J., Jiang, W., Huang, Q., Bao, H., Zhou, X.: Fast and robust multi-person 3D pose estimation from multiple views. In: Proceedings of the IEEE/CVF Conference on Computer Vision and Pattern Recognition, pp. 7792–7801 (2019)

6. Ershadi-Nasab, S., Noury, E., Kasaei, S., Sanaei, E.: Multiple human 3D pose estimation from multiview images. Multimedia Tools Appl. **77**(12), 15573–15601 (2018)

7. Hartley, R., Zisserman, A.: Multiple View Geometry in Computer Vision. Cambridge University Press, Cambridge (2003)

8. Huang, C., et al.: End-to-end dynamic matching network for multi-view multi-person 3D pose estimation. In: Vedaldi, A., Bischof, H., Brox, T., Frahm, J.-M. (eds.) ECCV 2020. LNCS, vol. 12373, pp. 477–493. Springer, Cham (2020). https://doi.org/10.1007/978-3-030-58604-1_29

9. Ionescu, C., Papava, D., Olaru, V., Sminchisescu, C.: Human3.6M: large scale datasets and predictive methods for 3D human sensing in natural environments. IEEE Trans. Pattern Anal. Mach. Intell. **36**(7), 1325–1339 (2013)

10. Iqbal, U., Molchanov, P., Kautz, J.: Weakly-supervised 3D human pose learning via multi-view images in the wild. In: Proceedings of the IEEE/CVF Conference on Computer Vision and Pattern Recognition, pp. 5243–5252 (2020)

11. Kingma, D.P., Ba, J.: Adam: a method for stochastic optimization. arXiv preprint arXiv:1412.6980 (2014)

12. Lin, J., Lee, G.H.: Multi-view multi-person 3D pose estimation with plane sweep stereo. In: Proceedings of the IEEE/CVF Conference on Computer Vision and Pattern Recognition, pp. 11886–11895 (2021)

13. Lin, T.Y., et al.: Microsoft COCO: common objects in context. In: Fleet, D., Pajdla, T., Schiele, B., Tuytelaars, T. (eds.) ECCV 2014. LNCS, vol. 8693, pp. 740–755. Springer, Cham (2014). https://doi.org/10.1007/978-3-319-10602-1_48

14. Nibali, A., He, Z., Morgan, S., Prendergast, L.: Numerical coordinate regression with convolutional neural networks. arXiv preprint arXiv:1801.07372 (2018)

15. Remelli, E., Han, S., Honari, S., Fua, P., Wang, R.: Lightweight multi-view 3D pose estimation through camera-disentangled representation. In: Proceedings of the IEEE/CVF Conference on Computer Vision and Pattern Recognition, pp. 6040–6049 (2020)

16. Sun, K., Xiao, B., Liu, D., Wang, J.: Deep high-resolution representation learning for human pose estimation. In: Proceedings of the IEEE/CVF Conference on Computer Vision and Pattern Recognition, pp. 5693–5703 (2019)

17. Tu, H., Wang, C., Zeng, W.: VoxelPose: towards multi-camera 3D human pose estimation in wild environment. In: Vedaldi, A., Bischof, H., Brox, T., Frahm, J.-M. (eds.) ECCV 2020. LNCS, vol. 12346, pp. 197–212. Springer, Cham (2020). https://doi.org/10.1007/978-3-030-58452-8_12

18. Van Erven, T., Harremos, P.: Rényi divergence and Kullback-Leibler divergence. IEEE Trans. Inf. Theory **60**(7), 3797–3820 (2014)
19. Xie, R., Wang, C., Wang, Y.: MetaFuse: a pre-trained fusion model for human pose estimation. In: Proceedings of the IEEE/CVF Conference on Computer Vision and Pattern Recognition, pp. 13686–13695 (2020)
20. Zhuang, J., et al.: AdaBelief optimizer: adapting stepsizes by the belief in observed gradients. In: Advances in Neural Information Processing Systems, vol. 33, pp. 18795–18806 (2020)

Visual Relation-Aware Unsupervised Video Captioning

Puzhao Ji[1], Meng Cao[1], and Yuexian Zou[1,2(✉)]

[1] ADSPLAB, School of ECE, Peking University, Shenzhen, China
zouyx@pku.edu.cn
[2] Peng Cheng Laboratory, Shenzhen, China

Abstract. Unsupervised video captioning aims to describe videos from unlabeled videos and sentence corpus without the reliance on human annotated video-sentence pairs. A straightforward manner is to borrow the merit from unsupervised image captioning methods, which resort to pseudo captions retrieved by visual concepts detected in image. However, directly applying this methodology to the video domain leads to sub-optimum performance since visual concepts cannot represent the major video content accurately and completely. Besides, these methods also do not consider the problem of *noise interference* caused by words unrelated to visual concept in the pseudo captions. In this paper, we propose a visual relation-aware unsupervised video captioning method which retrieves pseudo captions using visual relation. Based on these, we train the proposed visual relation-aware captioning model. Specifically, our model is designed to focus on learning from *dependable* words corresponding to the detected relation triplets. Extensive experimental results on two public benchmarks show the effectiveness and significance of our method.

Keywords: Video captioning · Visual relation · Unsupervised learning

1 Introduction

Video captioning seeks to automatically generate a sentence that describes the relation and interaction of objects in video. In applications, the video captioning model can describe the changes of people and objects around the visually impaired [1], foster and facilitate physical activities [2], automatically generate news releases for news videos [3], etc.

Most of the existing models [4–7] are trained in a supervised learning manner with human annotated video-sentence pairs (cf. Fig. 1(a)). However, manual annotation is very expensive and time-consuming due to the complex spatial and temporal dynamics of video. In addition, most of the annotations obtained by crowdsourcing are short and repetitive [8,10–13]. As a result, captioning models trained on crowdsourced annotation data have poor generalization in the wild. Therefore, it becomes increasingly important for video captioning models to get

E. Pimenidis et al. (Eds.): ICANN 2022, LNCS 13531, pp. 495–507, 2022.
https://doi.org/10.1007/978-3-031-15934-3_41

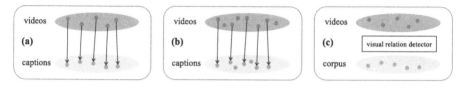

Fig. 1. Difference between visual captioning methods: (a) supervised video captioning [4], (b) semi-supervised video captioning [14,15], (c) our unsupervised video captioning.

rid of the annotated data. Recently, some semi-supervised approaches [9,14,15] have attempted to reduce reliance on annotated data. These methods use additional unlabeled video or sentences to train video captioning models. However, none of them gets rid of the dependency on human-labeled data (Fig. 1(b)). Therefore, in this paper, we address unsupervised visual captioning which only requires unlabeled data for training (Fig. 1(c)), making a more scalable solution under the large-scale easily accessible data.

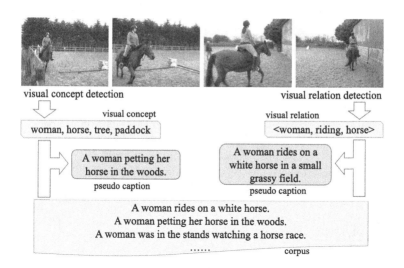

Fig. 2. The difference between the visual concept-based pseudo caption retrieve method and our method. Words in red, yellow and green indicate wrong relation between objects, noisy words and dependable words (words in visual relation triplet) respectively. (Color figure online)

It is noted that there are some works [8,10,16] are devoted to address unsupervised *image* captioning. These methods use the visual concepts detected in the images to match pseudo-labels from the corpus, and then train the decoders in the image captioning model using the pseudo-labels. However, we content that directly applies their visual concepts based methodologies to the video domain leads to inferior performance. We declare this to the following two potential reasons. **1)** The pseudo-label retrieval method based on visual concept cannot capture the action and position relation of objects in the video. These visual concepts are actually detected objects. As shown in Fig. 2, such methods do not take into account the interaction between objects and they will introduce many irrelevant and even wrong pseudo-labels. **2)** The pseudo-labels retrieved have noise at the word level. In addition to the matched visual concepts, there are still a large number of words unrelated to the video content in the pseudo captions (such as 'in the woods', 'white', 'small grassy field' in Fig. 2).

We solve the above problems through the following two aspects: **1)** Use visual relation to retrieve pseudo-labels. Actually, a video mainly describes a major action or scene. Visual relation triplet ⟨`subject`, `relation`, `object`⟩ can properly express the main action or scene in the video. The `relation` refers to interaction or positional relation between objects. The pseudo-labels obtained by our method can be consistent with the main content of the video at the sentence level. **2)** To alleviate word level noise, we proposed Visual Relation-Aware Module (VRAM). VRAM makes the model learn from dependable words by giving higher confidence scores to the words in the visual relation triplet (such as green words: 'woman', 'rides', 'horse' in Fig. 2). This reduces the impact of noise at the word level.

The contributions of this paper are three-fold: **1)** We develop a visual relation-based pseudo caption retrieve mechanism which builds a bridge between video and pseudo captions. **2)** A module is devised to alleviate noise from words that are not part of matched relation triplet in pseudo caption. **3)** Extensive results on MSVD, MSR-VTT, and multiple corpus demonstrate the effectiveness of our method. Our visualization and results also show the domain and volume of corpus have a significant impact on the quality of retrieved pseudo captions.

2 Related

2.1 Supervised Video Captioning

The early works of video captioning extract fixed content like verb, subject and object, then populate the content into predefined template [17]. Withing fixed predefined template and limited hand-crafted grammar rules, these methods are hard to generate flexible and accurate description. Benefit from the raising of deep neural networks, sequence learning based methods [4–6] which adopt encoder-decoder framework, are widely used to describe video content with flexibility. Venugopalan et al. [4] propose a stacked LSTM model and average the feature of each video frame. Yao et al. [5] introduce a soft attention mechanism to capture the feature of salient frame or region. Chen et al. [6] proposes PickNet to choose key frames to reduce redundant visual information. More recently, RecNet [18] uses a reconstructor architecture to leverages the backflow from sentence to video while generating caption. Zheng et al. [7] introduce a SAAT module to generate syntax parts in caption. To employ the POS syntactic information, Wang et al. [19] propose a POS generator and use gating block to fuse multimodal feature. However, all the above methods rely one video-sentence annotation pairs.

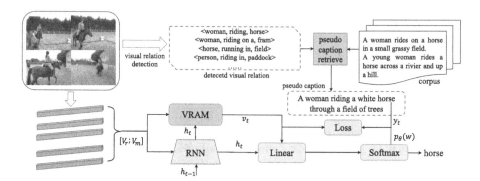

Fig. 3. The overview of our method, consisting of a pseudo caption retrieve mechanism and a visual relation-aware captioning model. Pseudo captions are matched by visual relation. The Visual Relation-Aware Module focus on dependable words that corresponding to visual relation. Words in green and red mean dependable words in relation triplet and video-irrelevant words. (Color figure online)

2.2   Unsupervised Captioning

Existing unsupervised visual captioning methods focus on image captioning, none of them are specifically designed to solve unsupervised video captioning task. Feng et al. [10] develop an architecture to align visual and textual features in common latent space to reconstruct each other, and train captioning model in adversarial manner using pseudo captions which based on visual concept. Laina et al. [8] project video and pseudo caption into a shared latent space structured by visual concepts, then decode caption from this latent space. However, these visual concept-based pseudo retrieve method fails to capture the relation between objects in video.

3   Method

An overall pipeline of proposed method is shown in Fig. 3. There are two components in our approach, a pseudo caption retrieve mechanism and visual relation-aware captioning model which consists of a language decoder and Visual Relation-Aware Module (VRAM). The captioning model learns from the results obtained by pseudo captions retrieve mechanism.

3.1   Pseudo Captions Retrieve

Compared with image which is still frame and contains limited objects, there may be environment changes and much more objects in video. In this case, visual concepts detected by the object detector are messy and cannot accurately represent the content in the video. However, the content of a video is a specific event that can be expressed as a visual relation triplet $t = \langle s, r, o \rangle$ such as $\langle$ woman, riding, horse $\rangle$. s means the subject of the relation in triplet, r is the relation, and o is the object of the relation. Similarly, the content of a sentence can also be condensed to relationships between objects.

We extract N frames from video v uniformly. For each frame, we use 2DCNN [29] and object detector [33] to get RGB feature V_r and ROI feature V_o. A pretrained visual relation detector [31] takes V_r and V_o as inputs and output the visual relation triplet t. We collect all visual relation triplet of N frames and get visual relation set $\mathcal{R}_v$ for video v. We construct a relation set $\mathcal{R}_y$ for each sentence y in corpus $\mathcal{C}$ by parsing the semantic and part-of-speech information. And the pseudo captions of this video is $\mathcal{Y} = \{y|\mathcal{R}_y \cap \mathcal{R}_v \neq \emptyset, y \in \mathcal{C}\}$. This ensures that each pseudo label has at least one identical visual relation triplet with video.

3.2   Basic Video Captioning Model

In this section, we describe the basic video captioning model directly trained by pseudo caption. Given a video, the RGB feature $V_r \in \mathbb{R}^{d_r}$ from 2DCNN and motion feature $V_m \in \mathbb{R}^{d_m}$ from 3DCNN are encoded into a single feature $V \in \mathbb{R}^{d_k}$ which is the input of basic video captioning model. The basic model directly take noisy pseudo caption $y = \{y_1, y_2, ..., y_n\}$ as the label. At time step t, the basic model generates word as follows:

$$V = \text{ReLU}(W_v[V_r; V_m]), \tag{1}$$

$$h_t = \text{RNN}(V, h_{t-1}), \tag{2}$$

$$p_\theta(w|h_t) = \text{softmax}(W_s \text{ReLU}(h_t)), \tag{3}$$

$$\hat{y}_t = \underset{w \in vocab}{\arg\max} \, p_\theta(w|h_t), \tag{4}$$

where $h_t \in \mathbb{R}^{d_h}$ is hidden state of RNN at time step t, $p(w|h_t)$ is generated word probability distribution, $W_s \in \mathbb{R}^{d_h}$ and $W_v \in \mathbb{R}^{d_k \times (d_v + d_m)}$ are learnable parameters, and the output word of basic model is $\hat{y}_t$. The parameter θ of basic model is optimized by the Cross-Entropy loss:

$$\mathcal{L}_c = -\frac{1}{n} \sum_{t=1}^{n} \log p_\theta(\hat{y}_t = y_t|h_{t-1}, V) \tag{5}$$

3.3   Visual Relation-Aware Module

This basic model works well with human annotations, but pseudo caption may contains words which are irrelevant to video or have ambiguous meaning. To alleviate the suboptimal training process by inaccurate label, we propose a Visual Relation-Aware Module (VRAM). VRAM designed to evaluate whether the hidden state of RNN at current time represents a dependable word or not. More specifically, VRAM estimate the probability that current word is part of a visual relation of input video. At time step t, a transformation matrix $W_p \in \mathbb{R}^{d_h \times d_k}$ used to project video feature to a feature space with dimension same as hidden state and get the confidence score v_t of current hidden state. The confidence score of current hidden state generated as follow:

$$v_t = \text{sigmoid}(\frac{h_t^T W_p V}{\sqrt{d_h}}) \tag{6}$$

We limit v_t between 0 and 1 using sigmoid. When a hidden state gets a high confidence score, it will play a more important role in generating words. Using VRAM, the probability distribution of the generated word is as follows:

$$p_\theta(w|h_t, V) = \text{softmax}(W_s \text{ReLU}([v_t h_t; (1 - v_t)V])) \tag{7}$$

$$\mathcal{L}_v = -\frac{1}{n} \sum_{t=1}^{n} (v_t - v_t^*)^2 \tag{8}$$

$$v_t^* = \begin{cases} 1, & y_t \in t, t \in \mathcal{R}_v \cap \mathcal{R}_y \\ 0, & otherwise \end{cases} \tag{9}$$

The VRAM optimized by relation loss $\mathcal{L}_v$ in which v_t^* is constructed from pseudo caption to train VRAM. In backpropagation, larger v_t causes the model parameters learn more from y_t in pseudo caption. Combining captioning loss $\mathcal{L}_c$ and $\mathcal{L}_v$, we get loss function of our model.

$$\mathcal{L} = \mathcal{L}_c + \mathcal{L}_v \tag{10}$$

4   Experiments

4.1   Datasets and Metrics

We take the videos in two widely used video captioning datasets: Microsoft Video Description Corpus (MSVD) [21] and Microsoft Research Video To Text (MSR-VTT) [20], and take corpus from the training split of TV show Caption (TVC) [22], Google's Conceptual Captions (GCC) [23], and VATEX [24]. VATEX and TVC are datasets of video captioning, but TVC is made to describe the tv shows, and GCC is a large image captioning dataset. We conduct experiments on them to compare the impact of corpus's domain on unsupervised video description.

Following the existing works [7], we split MSR-VTT as 6513 for training, 497 for validation, and 2,990 for testing. According to the common splits, MSVD is divided into 1200 for training, 100 for validation, and 670 for testing. The training split of TVC, GCC, and VATEX contain 182,556, 2,402,941 and 293,757 sentences respectively. Note that these descriptions do not overlap with the annotations of MSVD and MSR-VTT. We evaluate our method on the validation/test split of MSVD and MSR-VTT using widely-used metrics including BLEU@4 [25], METEOR [26], ROUGE_L [27] and CIDEr [28].

4.2   Implementation Details

For video feature extraction, we use ResNeXt [29] model and ECO [30] model which pretrained on ImageNet ILSVRC2012 dataset and Kinetics400 dataset respectively. By feeding 32 frames which sampled uniformly from video to ResNeXt and ECO, we get RGB feature of 2048 dimension and motion feature of 1536 dimension for each video.

For sentences in corpus, we remove unprintable characters, normalize punctuation, then apply part-of-speech tagging using spacy[1] to extract relation between objects. For extracted 32 frames of each video, we detect the visual relation in training split of MSVD and MSR-VTT using VDR-DSR [31], which results in 18,450 and 121,620 visual relation triplets. We use these visual relations to retrieve pseudo-labels from the corpus, taking into account the plural form of nouns and their synonyms. We adopt one layer GRU with hidden state of 512-dim as our language decoder. The word embeddings are initialized by random and embedding dimension is 512. We train our model with batch size of 32, and Adam [32] optimizer which initial learning rate is 0.001. We evaluate our model using beam search with size of 4 on test split.

4.3   Quantitative Results

We conducted extensive experiments on the MSVD dataset using three corpus. Following the common setting in unsupervised image captioning [16], the means and standard deviation of five runs results using random seed are represented. As shown in Table 1, the method "full model" is our full model, "w/o VRAM" represents GRU (without VRAM) trained by pseudo captions which retrieved by visual relations and "w/o relation" represents GRU trained by pseudo captions which retrieved by visual concepts. In "w/o relation" setting, the visual concepts are detected by FatserRCNN pretrained on OpenImage. For all three corpus, our method achieves the best results on CIDEr. It can be observed that the CIDEr's mean score of "w/o VRAM" is two times or more than the "w/o relation" on GCC and VATEX. This confirms the effectiveness of visual relation in pseudo captions matching. The results in Table 2 which is conducted on MSR-VTT using TVC corpus also support this observation. The comparison of "full model" with "w/o VRAM" demonstrates the ability of VRAM to alleviate the noise in pseudo label.

We observed that "w/o relation" achieved the best results on BLEU@4, METEOR and ROUGE_L on GCC dataset. We believe this is mainly due to there are a lot of sentences in GCC that have the same visual concepts as the video but they express completely different meanings. This resulted in the sentence generated by captioning model also have many same visual concepts as the video but have a completely different meaning with video. Concurrence-based metrics: BLEU@4, METEOR, and ROUGE_L are failed to measure their difference, while semantically based CIDEr can distinguish this situation.

---

[1] https://spacy.io.

Table 1. Performance comparison of different corpus and settings on the test split of MSVD dataset. The means and standard deviation of five runs results using random seed are represented.

Corpus	Method	BLEU@4	METEOR	ROUGE_L	CIDEr
TVC	full model	**5.3 ± 0.2**	**16.2 ± 1.1**	40.6 ± 1.7	8.8 ± 0.9
	w/o VRAM	3.6 ± 1.2	14.3 ± 1.1	39.9 ± 2.0	4.2 ± 0.8
	w/o Relation	4.2 ± 0.7	16.1 ± 0.6	40.0 ± 1.9	3.3 ± 1.8
GCC	full model	4.8 ± 0.8	14.2 ± 0.5	38.4 ± 1.8	**12.9 ± 2.0**
	w/o VRAM	1.4 ± 0.5	11.8 ± 1.1	32.5 ± 1.8	6.5 ± 2.4
	w/o relation	**5.6 ± 1.4**	**15.9 ± 0.7**	**40.7 ± 4.3**	2.8 ± 1.2
VATEX	full model	**9.6 ± 1.3**	**20.1 ± 0.9**	**42.1 ± 3.9**	**13.2 ± 0.8**
	w/o VRAM	6.7 ± 1.1	18.6 ± 0.7	39.2 ± 1.9	8.3 ± 0.9
	w/o relation	5.8 ± 1.7	16.5 ± 1.1	37.1 ± 4.9	1.3 ± 0.3

Table 2. Performance comparison on test split of MSR-VTT dataset using TVC corpus.

Method	BLEU@4	METEOR	ROUGE_L	CIDEr
full model	**8.4 ± 0.5**	**15.9 ± 0.7**	37.8 ± 1.0	**4.9 ± 0.4**
w/o VRAM	3.5 ± 1.1	15.2 ± 1.6	**42.6 ± 1.5**	2.4 ± 0.5
w/o relation	5.1 ± 1.8	12.6 ± 1.3	32.5 ± 2.8	1.1 ± 0.3

The results in Table 1 also indicate that the domain and volume of corpus have a significant impact on the quality of retrieved pseudo captions. TVC corpus is consists of captions that describe tv shows. And its content is quite different from MSVD which contains web videos of various categories. GCC is an image caption dataset, its captions tend to describe still frame. The results of GCC corpus works better than TVC on three settings in case that the two corpus do not match the domain of MSVD very well. This is because GCC has 13 times more sentences than TVC, which greatly increases the likelihood of appearance of video content related sentences. VATEX achieves the best performance in three corpus because it is also an open domain video captioning dataset.

Table 3. Ablation study on corpus which in same domain but has different volume.

Corpus	BLEU@4	METEOR	ROUGE_L	CIDEr
Oracle	27.4 ± 2.4	24.6 ± 0.7	60.4 ± 1.5	30.9 ± 2.6
MSR-VTT	13.5 ± 0.8	20.5 ± 1.2	47.5 ± 5.9	18.0 ± 1.7
VATEX	9.6 ± 1.3	20.1 ± 0.9	42.1 ± 3.9	13.2 ± 0.8
MSR-VTT+VATEX	**16.4 ± 4.7**	**21.6 ± 1.7**	**51.3 ± 7.0**	**18.5 ± 2.1**

To further investigate the effect of corpus's size, we conduct ablation experiments on MSVD with MSR-VTT, VATEX, and MSR-VTT+VATEX. It is noted that MSVD, MSR-VTT and VATEX are all open domain video captioning datasets. As shown in Table 3, the MSR-VTT+VATEX outperforms MSR-VTT and VATEX on all four metrics, which demonstrates that our method retrieves more video-related but diverse pseudo captions from a larger corpus. And following the common practice [8], we also use Oracle corpus to see if our method has the ability to retrieve better-quality pseudo captions from corpus which are more relevant to video content. The Oracle means retrieve pseudo labels from the ground truth of MSVD training set. The BLEU@4, METEOR, ROUGE_L and CIDEr of Oracle corpus both outperformed the other corpus which confirmed that correlation between corpus and videos had a great influence on the results of unsupervised video captioning. And Oracle corpus only used to show the upper limit of the ability of visual relation in pseudo label matching.

GT: {a person is forming a wad out of a mixture in a bowl, a lady take a dough from the glass bowl, a demonstration of a recipe is being shown}
Baseline: two men are playing on a large
Our: a chef is talking about a clear bowl

GT: {the man interviewed the soldier, two people are talking, the person is taking interview}
Baseline: a man is talking on a
Our: an animated jacket wearing black shirt is talking in a microphone

GT: {a man cliff dives into the water, a man does a high dive off of a cliff into the river below, a man diving in a river from a highest rock}
Baseline: the man is playing a
Our: a man is playing a rock with a tree

GT: {a person skiing down a mountain, a snowboarder is shown snowboarding down a snow covered slope}
Baseline: a man is playing a large
Our: a man is playing a helicopter skis

Fig. 4. The qualitative results between our method and visual concept based baseline. Words with red, yellow, and green backgrounds means complete irrelevant words, words that ambiguously used, and words that correctly used, respectively. (Color figure online)

4.4 Qualitative Results

Figure 4 shows four qualitative results generated by our method and visual concept-based method. In these examples, the baseline failed to capture the major content of the video, and even cannot generate correct sentence structure. Our method successfully output words such as "bowl", "talking in microphone" and "skis", but the noise in the pseudo label also cause words with unclear or wrong meanings such as "helicopter" and "animated jacket". There are also some ambiguous words generated, such as "talking about" in the upper-left example and "tree" in the bottom-left example. Limited by the detection range of visual relation detector, our method fails to recognize the object "cliff" and action "dive" in bottom-left video.

Finally, to provide more insight about retrieved pseudo labels, we visualize the t-SNE embedding of one video's pseudo captions. As shown in Fig. 5, although the pseudo captions retrieved by visual relation are closer to the human annotated labels, there is still a large gap between them. It can be inferred that pseudo caption matched by visual relation lack of details about video content.

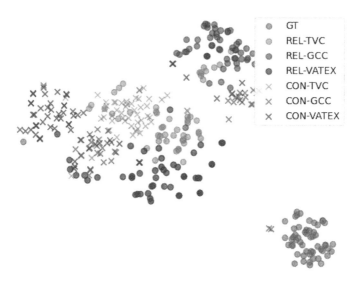

Fig. 5. t-SNE embedding of pseudo captions and ground truth. REL-X and CON-X denote pseudo captions retrieved from corpus X using visual relation and visual concept respectively. GT means human annotated captions.

5   Conclusion

In this paper, we make the first attempt to investigate unsupervised video captioning. For this purpose, we propose 1) a new visual relation-based pseudo caption retrieve method to match the major content of video. 2) Visual Relation-Aware Module(VRAM) to mitigate extra noisy caused by words irrelevant to visual relation. Our experiments show results beyond visual concepts-based method and we also show intuitive visualization of pseudo captions. In the future, we will further investigate the semantic structure of video and sentence, and design more effective pseudo label matching mechanism and module.

Acknowledgements. This paper was partially supported by NSFC (No: 62176008) and Shenzhen Science and Technology Research Program (No: GXWD202012311658 07007-20200814115301001).

References

1. Huang, Y.H., Hsieh, Y.Z.: The assisted environment information for blind based on video captioning method. In: IEEE International Conference on Consumer Electronics, pp. 1–2 (2020)
2. Amirian, S., Farahani, A., Arabnia, H.R., Rasheed, K.M., Taha, T.R.: The use of video captioning for fostering physical activity. In: International Conference on Computational Science and Computational Intelligence, pp. 611–614, (2020)
3. Whitehead, S., Ji, H., Bansal, M., Chang, S.F., Voss, C.R.: Incorporating background knowledge into video description generation. In: Proceedings of the 2018 Conference on Empirical Methods in Natural Language Processing, pp. 3992–4001 (2018)
4. Darrell, T., Venugopalan, S., Rohrbach, M., Donahue, J., Mooney, R., Saenko, K.: Sequence to sequence - video to text. In: Proceedings of the IEEE International Conference on Computer Vision, pp. 4534–4542 (2015)
5. Yao, L., et al.: Describing videos by exploiting temporal structure. In: Proceedings of the IEEE International Conference on Computer Vision, pp. 4507–4515 (2015)
6. Chen, Y., Wang, S., Zhang, W., Huang, Q.: Less is more: picking informative frames for video captioning. In: Proceedings of the 15th European Conference on Computer Vision, pp. 367–384 (2018)
7. Wang, C., Zheng, Q., Tao, D.: Syntax-aware action targeting for video captioning. In: Proceedings of the IEEE Conference on Computer Vision and Pattern Recognition, pp. 13093–13102 (2022)
8. Laina, I., Rupprecht, C., Navab, N.: Towards unsupervised image captioning with shared multimodal embeddings. In: Proceedings of the IEEE International Conference on Computer Vision, pp. 7413–7423 (2019)
9. Zhang, C., Yang, T., Weng, J., Cao, M., Wang, J., Zou, Y.: Unsupervised pretraining for temporal action localization tasks. In: Proceedings of the IEEE Conference on Computer Vision and Pattern Recognition, pp. 14031–14041 (2021)
10. Feng, Y., Ma, L., Liu, W., Luo, J.: Unsupervised image captioning. In: Proceedings of the IEEE Conference on Computer Vision and Pattern Recognition, pp. 4120–4129 (2019)
11. Zhang, C., Cao, M., Yang, D., Chen, J., Zou, Y.: CoLA: weakly-supervised temporal action localization with snippet contrastive learning. In: Proceedings of the IEEE/CVF Conference on Computer Vision and Pattern Recognition, pp. 16010–16019 (2021)
12. Cao, M., Chen, L., Shou, M.Z., Zhang, C., Zou, Y.: On pursuit of designing multimodal transformer for video grounding. In: Proceedings of Conference on Empirical Methods in Natural Language Processing, pp. 9810–9823 (2021)
13. Zhang, C., Yang, T., Weng, J., Cao, M., Wang, J., Zou, Y.: Deep motion prior for weakly-supervised temporal action localization. arXiv preprint arXiv:2108.05607 (2021)
14. Lucchi, A., Chen, W., Hofman, T.: A semi-supervised framework for image captioning. arXiv preprint arXiv:1611.05321 (2016)
15. Oh, T., Kim, D., Choi, J., Kweon, I.: Image captioning with very scarce supervised data: adversarial semisupervised learning approach. In: Proceedings of the Conference on Empirical Methods in Natural Language Processing, pp. 2012–2023 (2019)

16. Hashimoto, A., Watanabe, T., Honda, U., Ushiku, Y., Matsumoto, Y.: Removing word-level spurious alignment between images and pseudo-captions in unsupervised image captioning. In: Proceedings of the Conference of the European Chapter of the Association for Computational Linguistics, pp. 3692–3702 (2021)

17. Kojima, A., Tamura, T., Fukunaga, K.: Natural language description of human activities from video images based on concept hierarchy of actions. Int. J. Comput. Vision 50, 171–184 (2002)

18. Wang, B., Ma, L., Zhang, W., Liu, W.: Reconstruction network for video captioning. In: Proceedings of the IEEE Conference on Computer Vision and Pattern Recognition, pp. 7622–7631 (2018)

19. Wang, B., Ma, L., Zhang, W., Jiang, W., Wang, J., Liu, W.: Controllable video captioning with POS sequence guidance based on gated fusion network. In: Proceedings of the IEEE/CVF International Conference on Computer Vision, pp. 2641–2650 (2019)

20. Yao, T., Xu. J., Mei, T., Rui, Y.: MSR-VTT: a large video description dataset for bridging video and language. In: Proceedings of the IEEE Conference on Computer Vision and Pattern Recognition, pp. 5288–5296 (2016)

21. Malkarnenkar, G., et al.: Youtube2Text: recognizing and describing arbitrary activities using semantic hierarchies and zero-shot recognition. In: Proceedings of the IEEE International Conference on Computer Vision, pp. 2712–2719 (2013)

22. Bansal, M., Lei, J., Yu, L., Berg, T.L.: TVQA: localized, compositional video question answering. In: Proceedings of the Conference on Empirical Methods in Natural Language Processing, pp. 1369–1379 (2018)

23. Goodman, S., Sharma, P., Ding, N., Soricut, R.: Conceptual captions: a cleaned, hypernymed, image alt-text dataset for automatic image captioning. In: Proceedings of the 56th Annual Meeting of the Association for Computational Linguistics, pp. 2556–2565 (2018)

24. Chen, J., Li, L., Wang, Y., Wang, X.E., Wu, J., Wang, W.Y.: VATEX: a large-scale, high-quality multilingual dataset for video-and-language research. In: Proceedings of the IEEE International Conference on Computer Vision, pp. 4580–4590 (2019)

25. Ward, T., Papineni, K., Roukos, S., Zhu, W.: BLEU: a method for automatic evaluation of machine translation. In: Proceedings of the Annual Meeting of the Association for Computational Linguistics, pp. 311–318 (2002)

26. Denkowski, M.J., Lavie, A.: Meteor universal: language specific translation evaluation for any target language. In: Proceedings of the Ninth Workshop on Statistical Machine Translation, pp. 376–380 (2014)

27. Lin, C.Y.: ROUGE: a package for automatic evaluation of summaries. In: The Association for Computational Linguistics (ACL) Workshop, vol. 8 (2004)

28. Zitnick, C.L., Vedantam, R., Parikh, D.: CIDEr: consensus-based image description evaluation. In: Proceedings of the IEEE Conference on Computer Vision and Pattern Recognition, pp. 4566–4575 (2015)

29. Dollar, P., Tu, Z., Xie, S., Girshick, R.B., He, K.: Aggregated residual transformations for deep neural networks. In: Proceedings of the IEEE Conference on Computer Vision and Pattern Recognition, pp. 5987–5995 (2017)

30. Singh, K., Zolfaghari, M., Brox, T.: ECO: efficient convolutional network for online video understanding. In: Proceedings of the 15th European Conference on Computer Vision, pp. 713–730 (2018)

31. Chang, H., Liang, K., Guo, Y., Chen, X.: Visual relationship detection with deep structural ranking. In: Proceedings of the Thirty-Second Conference on Artificial Intelligence, pp. 7098–7105 (2018)

32. Kingma, D.P., Ba, J.: Adam: a method for stochastic optimization. In: 3rd International Conference on Learning Representations (2014)
33. Ren, S., He, K., Girshick, R.B., Sun, J.: Faster R-CNN: towards real-time object detection with region proposal networks. IEEE Trans. Pattern Anal. Mach. Intell. **39**, 1137–1149 (2015)

A Folded Architecture for Hardware Implementation of a Neural Structure Using Izhikevich Model

Serhat Çağdaş[1,2]([⊠]) [iD] and Neslihan Serap Şengör[2] [iD]

[1] Yalova University, 77002 Yalova, Turkey
serhat.cagdas@yalova.edu.tr
[2] Istanbul Technical University, ITU Ayazağa Campus, 34469 Maslak,
Istanbul, Turkey
{cagdas19,sengorn}@itu.edu.tr

Abstract. Neuromorphic systems are expected to equip a new paradigm in computation so that energy efficient, intelligent systems could be implemented easily. One way of fulfilling this aim is to design processes with Spiking Neural Networks (SNN). Here, we introduce an architecture to realize Izhikevich neuron model which ease the hardware implementation of large scale neural models. By using a folding method, we ensure that multiple operations of the same type are performed by one computing unit in a time multiplexed manner. In this way, we have achieved a design that uses hardware resources more efficiently, especially by saving multiplication, and allows more neurons to be implemented on the hardware. Finally, this architecture eliminates the necessity to allocate additional resources for implementing the synaptic dynamics of the neurons. Also, to present the effectiveness of the proposed architecture, a simple cerebellar granular layer structure is implemented on FPGA.

Keywords: Izhikevich · Neuromorphic circuits · FPGA · SNN · Folded architecture

1 Introduction

Unlike classical Von Neumann computers, neuromorphic circuits have distributed computing/memory units as in the brain's structure. Calculations are performed by interconnected nerve cell units rather than an arithmetic logic unit (ALU). Such hardware allows for energy efficient and/or real-time simulation of large-scale spiking neural networks [9]. Neuromorphic circuits can contain digital, analog or digital/analog mixed architectures. Majority of the digital circuits are implemented on Field Programmable Gate Arrays (FPGAs) [8,15]. FPGAs are large-scale integrated circuits composed of arrays of gates that can be programmed via hardware description languages. In terms of flexible design and

This work is supported by ITU Scientific Research Projects Office with grants MDK-2022-43588.

highly parallel computation, FPGAs are very suitable for implementing neural networks.

For the storage and processing of information in the brain, only the change of synaptic connections is not sufficient. Neurons with different electrodynamic properties may respond diversely to similar stimuli. Therefore, two regions with the same synaptic connectivity may behave differently. Spiking neuron models mimic the electro-dynamic properties of neurons at the action potential level. These models can be evaluated in terms of computational load and biological plausibility. Model selection is very important in FPGA design since they contain a limited number of logic circuit resources. Although Hodgkin-Huxley (HH) models can show many properties of cells, they cannot be used to simulate large-scale networks due to computational load. On the other hand, Integrate and fire neuron models can be implemented easily on hardware, and it is widely used in forming SNN [5] but they are inadequate at mimicing the behavior of cells such as sub-threshold oscillations and rebound spiking. One other widely used model to simulate single neuron dynamics is Izhikevich neuron model [6,11]. Izhikevich neuron model is simple but still capable of mimicing the dynamic properties of neuron behavior.

In this study a conductance based Izhikevich neuron model is implemented on hardware using a folding method. While implementing neuron models in FPGA, especially multiplication and exponential calculations cause resource problems. For simulation of large large-scale networks in FPGA, one has to consider the limited hardware resources such as registers, Look-Up Table (LUT), Digital Signal Processing (DSP) and Random Access Memory (RAM) blocks during design process. The work given in [2] performs a shared simulation of more than one neuron with a single module to attend such hardware limitations. This allows to simulate more neurons with the hardware but prevents parameters from being hard-coded and requires additional generic multipliers. On the other hand, in [12] the computational load is reduced by using piecewise linear models for the Izhikevich's differential equation nullclines. Finally, in [4] approximate results are obtained with the help of shifters and adders instead of using multipliers in the model. This is achieved with the CORDIC (coordinate rotation digital computer) algorithm. Although these two methods are quite effective and reasonable, the piecewise model needs more linear component and more multipliers to attain more precision to implement generic neuron modules as in [2]. In addition, both methods need additional hardware resource for synaptic communication.

In the architecture proposed in this work all the multiplication and adder operations belonging neural and synaptic dynamics for a single point neuron are performed in the same units by time multiplexing. A folding method which will be explained in the next section is considered to decrease resource consumption. Thus, with the proposed architecture, implementing large-scale SNN models will become possible with limited hardware sources. To show this, a simple cerebellar granular layer structure is implemented on FPGA.

One drawback of the folding method is that extra registers are allocated to keep all the output data. In this work register minimization techniques are used to overcome this disadvantage. The rest of the paper is organized as follows. In Sect. 2, conductance based Izhikvich neuron model is defined briefly. In Sect. 3, the application of folding architecture on Izhikevich neuron model is given in detail. Hardware implementation of single neuron model and SNN simulation of granular layer based on this implementation is included in Sect. 4. The hardware results are also compared to Brian2 simulation results run at a central processing unit (CPU) in Sect. 4. Finally, the pros and cons of the architecture and results are evaluated in Sect. 5.

2   Izhikevich's Spiking Neuron Model

Izhikevich neuron model is preferred here, as it is suitable to model different neural activity patterns and allocates reasonable computational resources compared to HH models [6]. The conductance based Izhikevich neuron model which will be implemented is expressed with the following equations:

$$
\begin{aligned}
C_m \dot{v} &= k(v - v_r)(v - v_t) - u + I_{syn} \\
\dot{u} &= a(b(v - vr) - u) \\
v &> v_p \Rightarrow v \longleftarrow c, u \longleftarrow u + d
\end{aligned}
\tag{1}
$$

where $v(t)$ is the membrane potential and $u(t)$ is recovery variable [6]. Biologically defined parameters C_m, v_r, v_t and v_p are membrane capacitance, resting potential, threshold potential and peak potential value respectively. Behavior of the neuron can be tuned by setting the parameters k, a, b, c and d. I_{syn} is the post-synaptic current. It consists of conductance-based excitatory and inhibitory components in this work:

$$
\begin{aligned}
I_{syn} &= g_{ex}(v - E_{ex}) - g_{inh}(v - E_{inh}) \\
\dot{g}_x &= -g_x/\tau_x + \sum (w\hat{g}_x \delta(t - t_f))
\end{aligned}
\tag{2}
$$

where E_{ex}, E_{inh} are membrane reverse potentials for excitatory and inhibitory components respectively and g_x is the membrane conductance value ??. For hardware implementation rearranged Euler method of the form is rewritten:

$$
\begin{aligned}
v_{k+1} &= v_k + C_v(v_k - v_r)(v_k - v_t) - u_k - g_{ex,k}(v_k - E_{ex}) - g_{inh,k}(v_k - E_{inh}) \\
u_{k+1} &= C_{uu}u_k + C_{uv}(v_k - v_r) \\
g_{x,k+1} &= C_{gx}g_k + W_{x,k} \\
v_k &> v_p \Rightarrow v_{k+1} \longleftarrow c, u_{k+1} \longleftarrow u + d
\end{aligned}
\tag{3}
$$

$W_{x,k}$ is the total instantaneous presynaptic input (defined as $\sum (w\hat{g}_x \delta(t - t_f))$ earlier). The part related to neural connection is not implemented in the neuron module to provide flexibility. So, the module could be easily used in neural networks with fully dedicated, shared synapse etc. architectures [1]. Thus, variables and parameters are redefined as follows:

$$u = \frac{h}{C_m}u_{old}, \qquad g_x = \frac{h}{C_m}g_{x,old}, \qquad d = \frac{h}{C_m}d_{old},$$

$$C_v = \frac{h}{C_m}k, \qquad C_{uu} = 1 - h.a, \qquad C_{uv} = h^2a\frac{b}{C_m}, \qquad C_{gx} = 1 - \frac{h}{\tau_x} \qquad (4)$$

where h is the timestep. Observing the data flow graph (DFG) given in Fig. 1 which is related to Eq. 3, 11 adders and 8 multipliers are needed for a hardware implementation of a single neuron. Considering the number of neurons in a large-scale spiking neural network and the resources that an average FPGA has, that's quite a lot for just one neuron. Especially number of multipliers used in DFG limits the number of neurons that can be fit in an FPGA. A folding architecture which will be explained in the next section is considered to decrease this resource consumption.

3   Folding Architecture for a Single Neuron

The aim of the architecture is to implement the neuron model using only one multiplier and one adder by time multiplexing. Since 11 adder operations are performed in the unfolded DFG (Fig. 1), folding factor N_{fold} is chosen as 11. Then, adder and multiplier sets are determined and written in priority order for the 11 time steps considering the input-output relations among the operations:

$$S_A = [A1, A4, A3, A11, A2, A7, A8, A10, A9, A5, A6]$$
$$S_M = [0, 0, M6, M5, M3, M4, M7, M8, M1, M2] \qquad (5)$$

These sets indicate that $A1$ operation is performed at step 0, $M6$ at step 2 and $A6$ adder is performed at step 10. In a folding architecture, throughput of an operation performed at one step should be kept until it is no longer needed. The number of delays are calculated simply between related operations (Table 1):

$$D(U \Rightarrow V) = N_{fold} - P_U + v - u \qquad (6)$$

where N_{fold} is folding factor and declared as 11 before, v and u are the time steps that the operations are performed. P_U is the pipelining stages of the functional unit (multiplier or adder) and it is set as one since each functional unit is pipelined once to be able to preserve maximum clock frequency. According to the DFG in Fig. 1, all delays are calculated using Eq. 6:

It should be noted that all the calculated delay values should be non-negative to have a realizable architecture and the condition is met in this case. Otherwise retiming methods should be applied on the DFG or another priority sets may be determined [10]. How many time steps the output of each operation X should be kept is determined by finding the $max(D(X \Rightarrow O_i))$ where O_i is the ith operation connected to X and that uses the throughput of X as input.

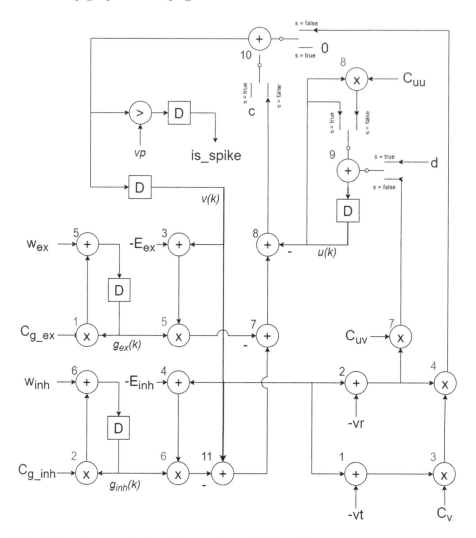

Fig. 1. Data flow graph of conductance based Izhikevich neuron model given in Eq. 3

Table 1. Delay values of the edges of the DFG in Fig. 1 according to the priority sets given in Eq. 5.

$D(A1 \Rightarrow M3) : 3$	$D(A2 \Rightarrow M4) : 0$	$D(A2 \Rightarrow M7) : 1$	$D(A3 \Rightarrow M5) : 0$	$D(A4 \Rightarrow M6) : 0$
$D(A5 \Rightarrow M1) : 9$	$D(A5 \Rightarrow M5) : 4$	$D(A6 \Rightarrow M2) : 9$	$D(A6 \Rightarrow M6) : 2$	$D(A7 \Rightarrow A8) : 0$
$D(A8 \Rightarrow A10) : 0$	$D(A9 \Rightarrow A8) : 8$	$D(A9 \Rightarrow A9) : 10$	$D(A9 \Rightarrow M8) : 9$	$D(A10 \Rightarrow A1) : 3$
$D(A10 \Rightarrow A2) : 7$	$D(A10 \Rightarrow A3) : 5$	$D(A10 \Rightarrow A4) : 4$	$D(A10 \Rightarrow A11) : 6$	$D(A11 \Rightarrow A7) : 1$
$D(M1 \Rightarrow A5) : 0$	$D(M2 \Rightarrow A6) : 0$	$D(M3 \Rightarrow M4) : 0$	$D(M4 \Rightarrow A10) : 1$	$D(M5 \Rightarrow A7) : 1$
$D(M6 \Rightarrow A11) : 0$	$D(M7 \Rightarrow A9) : 1$	$D(M8 \Rightarrow A9) : 0$		

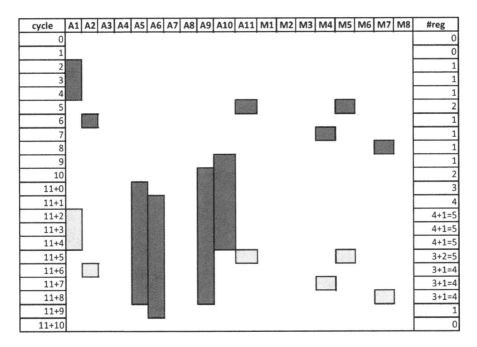

Fig. 2. Lifetime analysis for the output of each operation according to priority sets given in Eq. 5. Minimum register number needed for each step (in the right column) is determined by this analysis. The gray and yellow rectangles represent the usage of operations for calculating different samples of the model. (Color figure online)

One drawback of the folding architecture is that extra registers are allocated to keep all these output data. To overcome this disadvantage, register minimization techniques are used and one register is allocated by multiple variables at different time steps [3,7]. Hence, a lifetime analysis is necessary to determine the minimum number of registers for an accurate hardware implementation. Observing the lifetime analysis given in Fig. 2, it can be seen that at cycle indices $t = 2, 3, 4, 5$, five different output data are alive. As a result, the minimum possible number of registers needed for this architecture is concluded to be five. Using five registers and the lifetime analysis chart, a simple allocation mapping based on forward-backward register allocation algorithm [10] is produced to resolve the problem of which variable will be stored at each register at each time step. In accordance with all the design requirements, lifetime analysis and register allocation map; folded DFG is drawn using five registers, one adder and one multiplier with one stage pipelining (Fig. 3).

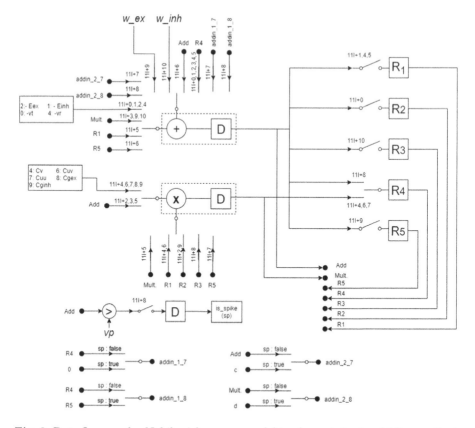

Fig. 3. Data flow graph of Izhikevich neuron model implemented using folding method.

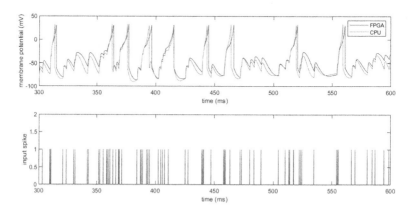

Fig. 4. Single neuron model with the same parameters is simulated on CPU and FPGA hardware based on folding architecture. Same input introduced with Poisson spike generator in both simulations.

4 FPGA Implementation and Simulation

Both DFGs for Izhikevich neuron model given in Fig. 1 and Fig. 3 are implemented using Verilog HDL targeting Xilinx's Zynq UltraScale+ ZCU104 Evaluation Board. All variables, parameters and registers are represented as 24 bits fixed point numbers, 20 of which is used as fraction. The membrane potential values are rescaled in $[-1, 1]$ interval for stability issues. DSP48 blocks are allocated for multiplication operations as they include 27×18 bits multipliers.

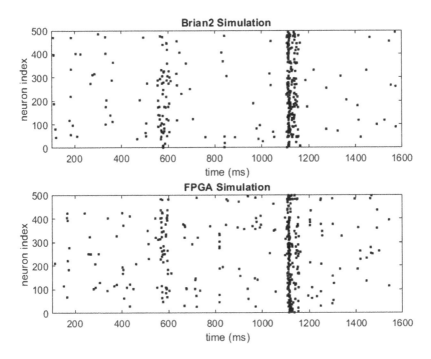

Fig. 5. A SNN consisting of 525 neurons are simulated both on CPU and FPGA. The raster plots shows the behavior of granular cell population in both simulations under similar conditions.

A single neuron model is simulated with the same parameters on FPGA and CPU to check whether the hardware run accurately or not and as given in Fig. 4 the FPGA implementation of single neuron coincides with the CPU simulation. It is seen that both simulation shows similar spiking pattern in spite of the small deviations because of floating point/fixed point difference.

For SNN simulation a simple cerebellar granular layer consisting of 500 excitatory cerebellar granule cells (Grc) and 25 inhibitory Golgi cells (Goc) are modeled as in [13]. Model parameters given in Table 3 are used with %10 random variability for all type of neurons in the SNN. The connection parameters between neural population and inputs are given in Table 4. 100 Mossy Fiber (MF)

Table 2. Hardware resource consumptions of Izhikevich neuron module implemented based on folded and unfolded architectures.

	Slice registers	Slice LUTs	DSP	Max speed (MHz)
Unfolded DFG (Fig. 1)	38	267	11	190
Folded DFG (Fig. 3)	320	145	1	376

inputs are introduced to the network with Poisson Spike Generators. Baseline spike rates of the generators are set as 3 Hz. In [550, 600] ms and [1100, 1150] ms time intervals spike rates are increased as 50 and 150 Hz respectively. Neuron modules in the network are connected in a fully dedicated architecture which provides a hardware element for each individual synapse [1]. The SNN is also simulated on CPU with the same parameters and similar MF input rates using Brian2 software which is a power a powerful simulator for SNNs [14]. Both the CPU and FPGA simulation results are given in Fig. 5.

Table 3. Neuron model parameters used in granular layer simulation.

$C(pF)$	k	a	b	c	d	$v_r(mV)$	$v_t(mV)$	$E_{inh}mV$	$\tau_{inh}ms$	$E_{ex}mV$	$\tau_{ex}ms$
1,5	7e−3	0.1	0.23	60	2.0	−70	−40	−82	10	0	0.5

Table 4. Neuron numbers, connection probabilities and synaptic strength values in the SNN.

Presynaptic cells (N)	Postsynaptic cells	Conn. prob.	Synaptic weights
MF (100)	Grc	0.01	9 nS
	Goc	0.08	2 nS
Grc (500)	Goc	0.025	0.4 nS
Goc (25)	Grc	0.1	5 nS

5   Results and Discussion

When the resource allocation of the neuron modules implemented with folded architecture and unfolded architecture are compared (Table 2), it is seen that the proposed design in this study uses only one DSP block instead of 11. However, even if register minimization techniques are exploited, the fact that the output values of the processes are kept for future steps as long as needed, leads to more consumption of slice register resources. Nevertheless, considering the decrease in the use of DSP blocks, this downside can be ignored. Moreover, the fact that more neurons can be placed on the targeted hardware, thanks to this design, reveals the advantage of the method.

When the speeds of the two implementations in the Table 2 are compared, it is seen that the folded architecture can operate at higher clock frequencies, while the output of the equation set at each time t is calculated in 11 steps because of folding factor. This makes the design disadvantageous in terms of sampling rate. However, both folded and unfolded implementations are quite fast compared to time needed for real time simulation of neural dynamics precisely where most of the time 0.1 ms time-step is sufficient. It should be noted that the positive and negative aspects mentioned above apply to the case where a multiplier and an adder are used for a neuron module. One can trade-off between DSP blocks, registers and speed using different numbers of adder/multiplier hardware.

To compare the proposed design in this study with the piecewise linear model proposed in [12] or the CORDIC Izhikevich model proposed in [4] is not completely fair. The first reason is that the simple version of the Izhikevich model is implemented in the above-mentioned alternative studies. Secondly, neuron modules are implemented with neuron specific parameters in [12] and [4] whereas in this study generic neuron models is implemented as in [2] which allows to simulate multiple neurons in one module. Furthermore, unlike this study, different hardware resources need to be allocated for synaptic conductivity dynamics in CORDIC algorithm [4] or piecewise linear model [12]. Another advantage of the method used in this study is that it can be merged with other methods. One can use CORDIC multipliers in folded architecture instead of allocating DSP blocks.

6   Conclusion

In this work a novel neuromorphic hardware is proposed based on the folding method. In order to implement this hardware, first, priority sets are determined for each unit. Second, delay values calculated for all edges in the data flow diagram according to priority sets. A lifetime analysis is performed to determine the minimum number of registers needed for the implementation. Finally, the design is completed by multiplexing registers with forward-backward minimization technique. To ensure the accuracy of the hardware, the behavior of the single neurons and the SNNs simulated both in FPGA and CPU are compared. As a case study, a simple granular layer is implemented on hardware consisting of 500 excitatory granule cells and 25 inhibitory Golgi cells.

As the neuron modules proposed in this work are capable of simulating multiple neurons in time multiplexing, it is possible to implement larger sized networks. In addition, it is seen that the proposed hardware uses DSP resources much more efficiently, sacrificing more slice registers when compared to unfolded architecture. The advantage on DSP blocks allows more neurons to work in parallel in targeted FPGA.

As a future work the proposed hardware may be analyzed in terms of energy efficiency to evaluate its preferability more, especially in realizing large-scale neural structures. In addition, as mentioned above the method can be merged with algorithms like CORDIC to be able to fit more neurons on FPGAs.

References

1. Benjamin, B.V., et al.: Neurogrid: a mixed-analog-digital multichip system for large-scale neural simulations. Proc. IEEE **102**(5), 699–716 (2014)
2. Cheung, K., Schultz, S.R., Luk, W.: A large-scale spiking neural network accelerator for FPGA systems. In: Villa, A.E.P., Duch, W., Érdi, P., Masulli, F., Palm, G. (eds.) ICANN 2012. LNCS, vol. 7552, pp. 113–120. Springer, Heidelberg (2012). https://doi.org/10.1007/978-3-642-33269-2_15
3. Ciric, V., Milentijevic, I., Vojinovic, O.: Retiming and register number minimization for adaptive fir filter architecture. In: Proceedings of a Workshop on Computational Intelligence and Information Technologies, pp. 93–96 (2003)
4. Heidarpur, M., Ahmadi, A., Ahmadi, M., Azghadi, M.R.: CORDIC-SNN: on-FPGA STDP learning with Izhikevich neurons. IEEE Trans. Circ. Syst. I Regul. Pap. **66**(7), 2651–2661 (2019)
5. Huynh, P.K., Varshika, M.L., Paul, A., Isik, M., Balaji, A., Das, A.: Implementing spiking neural networks on neuromorphic architectures: a review. arXiv preprint arXiv:2202.08897 (2022)
6. Izhikevich, E.M.: Dynamical Systems in Neuroscience. MIT Press (2007)
7. Joy, A., Vinitha, C.: Folding and register minimization transformation on DSP filter. In: 2018 5th IEEE Uttar Pradesh Section International Conference on Electrical, Electronics and Computer Engineering (UPCON), pp. 1–6. IEEE (2018)
8. Luo, J., Coapes, G., Mak, T., Yamazaki, T., Tin, C., Degenaar, P.: Real-time simulation of passage-of-time encoding in cerebellum using a scalable FPGA-based system. IEEE Trans. Biomed. Circ. Syst. **10**(3), 742–753 (2015)
9. Nawrocki, R.A., Voyles, R.M., Shaheen, S.E.: A mini review of neuromorphic architectures and implementations. IEEE Trans. Electron Devices **63**(10), 3819–3829 (2016)
10. Parhi, K.K.: VLSI Digital Signal Processing Systems: Design and Implementation. Wiley (2007)
11. Rice, K.L., Bhuiyan, M.A., Taha, T.M., Vutsinas, C.N., Smith, M.C.: FPGA implementation of Izhikevich spiking neural networks for character recognition. In: 2009 International Conference on Reconfigurable Computing and FPGAs, pp. 451–456. IEEE (2009)
12. Soleimani, H., Ahmadi, A., Bavandpour, M.: Biologically inspired spiking neurons: piecewise linear models and digital implementation. IEEE Trans. Circ. Syst. I Regul. Pap. **59**(12), 2991–3004 (2012)
13. Solinas, S., Nieus, T., D'Angelo, E.: A realistic large-scale model of the cerebellum granular layer predicts circuit spatio-temporal filtering properties. Front. Cellular Neurosci. **4**, 12 (2010)
14. Stimberg, M., Brette, R., Goodman, D.F.: Brian 2, an intuitive and efficient neural simulator. Elife **8**, e47314 (2019)
15. Yang, S., Wang, J., Zhang, N., Deng, B., Pang, Y., Azghadi, M.R.: Cerebellu-Morphic: large-scale neuromorphic model and architecture for supervised motor learning. IEEE Trans. Neural Netw. Learn. Syst. (2021)

A Spiking Neural Network Based on Neural Manifold for Augmenting Intracortical Brain-Computer Interface Data

Shengjie Zheng[1,2] , Wenyi Li[1,2], Lang Qian[3], Chenggang He[2], and Xiaojian Li[2(✉)]

[1] University of Chinese Academy of Sciences, Beijing, China
zhengshengjie20@mails.ucas.edu.cn

[2] CAS Key Laboratory of Brain Connectome and Manipulation, The Brain Cognition and Brain Disease Institute, Shenzhen Institute of Advanced Technology, Chinese Academy of Sciences, Shenzhen-Hong Kong Institute of Brain Science-Shenzhen Fundamental Research Institutions, Shenzhen, China
{sj.zheng,wy.li,xj.li}@siat.ac.cn

[3] Tsinghua Shenzhen International Graduate School, Tsinghua University, Shenzhen, China
ql20@mails.tsinghua.edu.cn

Abstract. Brain-computer interfaces (BCIs), transform neural signals in the brain into instructions to control external devices. However, obtaining sufficient training data is difficult as well as limited. With the advent of advanced machine learning methods, the capability of brain-computer interfaces has been enhanced like never before, however, these methods require a large amount of data for training and thus require data augmentation of the limited data available. Here, we use spiking neural networks (SNN) as data generators. It is touted as the next-generation neural network and is considered as one of the algorithms oriented to general artificial intelligence because it borrows the neural information processing from biological neurons. We use the SNN to generate neural spike information that is bio-interpretable and conforms to the intrinsic patterns in the original neural data. Experiments show that the model can directly synthesize new spike trains, which in turn improves the generalization ability of the BCI decoder. Both the input and output of the spiking neural model are spike information, which is a brain-inspired intelligence approach that can be better integrated with BCI in the future.

Keywords: Brain-computer interface · Spiking neural network · Brain-inspired intelligence · Data augmentation

1 Introduction

Motor control is a very important aspect of human life, and humans interact through a variety of behaviors. However, motor abilities often receive limitations such as stroke, amyotrophic lateral sclerosis (ALS), or other injuries or neurological disorders that disrupt the neural pathways connecting the brain to the rest of the body, leading to paralysis [1–3]. A motor-brain-computer interface is a system that helps patients by recording neural signals from internal areas of the brain and decoding them into control

E. Pimenidis et al. (Eds.): ICANN 2022, LNCS 13531, pp. 519–530, 2022.
https://doi.org/10.1007/978-3-031-15934-3_43

instructions, as shown in Fig. 1. Intracortical brain-computer interface systems require microelectrode arrays that can be implanted in the cerebral cortex for long periods of time to record the activity of dozens to hundreds of neurons.

In clinical trials, implantable brain-computer interface systems have not yet reached a level of performance that can widely assist patients with severe paralysis. In addition, it is unclear whether current brain-computer interface methods can be effectively used continuously for long periods of time. For example, after the brain is implanted with microelectrodes, the microelectrodes' ability to capture neural information decreases over time. This is because the electrodes cause partial damage to the brain, triggering the growth of glial scar tissue around the electrodes, blocking the electrode contacts from the neurons. At the same time, electrode contacts gradually break down in the electrolyte solution environment in the brain, reducing the electrode's electrical sensing performance. For decoding algorithms, the performance of the decoder also decreases over time. Neuroelectrodes will shift due to brain shaking, resulting in changes in the recorded information, and most decoding algorithms cannot adapt to such changes in neural information. Neuroplasticity (the learning process of neurons) leads to the reconnection of neurons as well as changes in the strength of the connections. Therefore, the neural information of the brain changes in response to the learning process. Therefore, the current BCI decoders need to be recalibrated periodically and require a large amount of neural information to obtain good performance. Also, the decoder trained based on neural information is not universal, and different subjects need to collect different neural information to train the decoder. Therefore, the training data obtained in clinical trials are very limited.

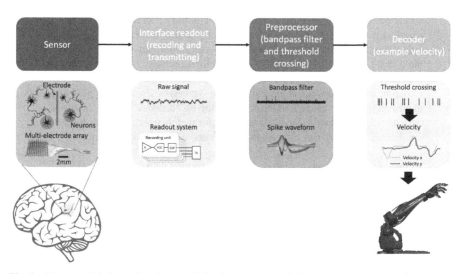

Fig. 1. The neural information is recorded using an array of electrodes, each measuring nearby neural activity. The raw neural signal is transformed into a digital signal by the signal acquisition system. The signals can be processed by band-pass filters and threshold crossing for spike detection. Finally, a decoder is used to model the neural spike signal with motor control and the control signal is sent to the prosthesis for control. Image modified from [1].

Here we will explore the data deficiency from the perspective of cortical motor neuron populations. Recent theoretical and experimental work hypothesizes that neural function is based on specific patterns of neural population activity rather than on individual neurons [4]. The neural population dynamics exist in low-dimensional neural manifolds in a high-dimensional neural space [5]. Here, we employ a bio-interpretive SNN that mimics the neural information generation as well as the communication of biological neural populations. We analyze motor cortical neural population data recorded from monkeys to derive motor-related neural population dynamics. The neural spike properties of the SNN itself allow the direct generation of biologically meaningful spike trains that match the activity of real biological neural populations. We explored the interaction between the spike train synthesizer and the BCI decoder. Our results show that based on a small amount of training data as a template, data conforming to the dynamics of neural populations are generated, thus enhancing the decoding ability of the BCI decoder.

2 Background and Related Work

2.1 Spiking Neuron

The Spiking Neuron Model simulates the membrane potential changes in biological neurons that result in action potentials (spikes). These spikes are generated by the neuronal soma and transmitted to other neurons along axons and synapses. Spiking neuronal models can be divided into various categories, the most detailed being the biophysical model based on ion channel simulation (Hodgkin-Huxley Model), which describes the change in membrane potential as a function of input current and the activation of an ion channel. In terms of mathematical calculations, a simpler one is the Leaky Integrate and fire model (LIF model), which describes the membrane potential transformation as a function of the input current and the LIF model as the basic unit of the SNN, which is expressed as follows (Eq. 1) and (Eq. 2).

$$\tau_m \frac{du_i}{dt} = -(u_i - u_{rest}) + RI_i \tag{1}$$

$$\frac{dI_i}{dt} = -\frac{I_i(t)}{\tau_s} + \sum_j W_{ij} S_j(t) \tag{2}$$

where u_i is the membrane potential of the neuron, τ_m is the membrane time constant, u_{rest} is the resting potential of the membrane, R is the membrane resistance, I_i is the input current, τ_s is the synaptic time constant, and W_{ij} is the synaptic connection strength.

When the neuronal membrane potential u_i exceeds the threshold ϑ, the neuron firing as well as resets the membrane potential to u_{rest} ($u_{rest} < \vartheta$). Incorporating the reset property, it follows that

$$\frac{du_i}{dt} == -\frac{1}{\tau_m}(u_i - u_{rest}) + RI_i + S_i(t)(u_{rest} - \vartheta) \tag{3}$$

$$S_i(t) = \sum_k \delta\left(t - t_i^k\right) \tag{4}$$

$S_i(t)$ is the spike train emitted by neuron i (represented by the sum of the Dirac delta equation, δ), and t_i^k is the spike firing time of the neuron at time k^{th} (Fig. 2).

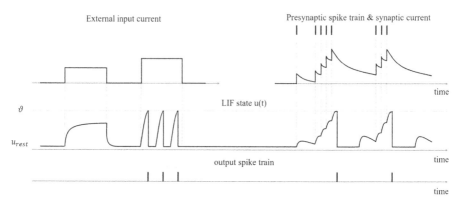

Fig. 2. The membrane potential change caused by the input current to a single LIF spiking neuron. When the membrane potential reaches a threshold, a spike is released and the membrane potential will be reset. Image modified from [6].

2.2 Neural Manifold

Recent technological developments have provided tools to detect the activity of large numbers of neurons, as well as computational statistics and modeling tools to analyze the activity of neuronal populations. The number of neurons that can be recorded simultaneously is currently about a few hundred, which is far less than the number of neurons contained in the corresponding cortex of the brain. Nevertheless, the current motor brain-computer interfaces are achieving good results. This is because in recent theories and studies it is believed that neural function is built on the activation of specific population-wide activity patterns-neural mode-rather than on the independent modulation of individual neurons [4, 7]. These neural modes define the neural manifold, which is a plane that captures most of the variance in recorded neural activity, as shown in Fig. 3.

Assuming that network connectivity constrains the possible patterns of population activity, the population dynamics will not explore the full high-dimensional neural space but will instead remain confined to a low-dimensional surface within the full space [8]. In the simplest case, the neural manifold is flat, as in the hyperplane in Fig. 3 and the plane is spanned by two neural modes u1 and u2.

Meanwhile, recent research points out that this time-dependent activation of the neural modes as their latent dynamics. In this theory, the activity of each recorded neuron expresses a weighted combination of the latent dynamics from all the neural modes. Neural modes can be estimated empirically from the recorded activity by applying dimensionality reduction techniques such as principal component analysis (PCA) to construct a low-dimensional manifold embedded in the empirical neural space spanned by the recorded neurons. Thus, this intrinsic neural manifold can exhibit to some extent the neuronal population dynamics pattern.

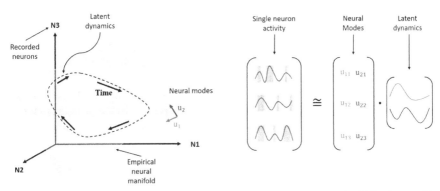

Fig. 3. The activity of recorded neurons (N1, N2 and N3) is represented within the empirical neural space, with each axis representing a recorded neuron. Recent studies suggest that neuronal activity may be a weighted combination of the latent dynamics of neural modes. Image modified from [8].

2.3 Neural Decoding

Neural decoding uses the activity recorded by the brain to predict variables in the external world. These predictions derived from decoding can be used to control devices (e.g., robotic arms) or to better understand how brain regions relate to the external world. Thus, neural decoding is a core tool for neural engineering and neural data analysis. In essence, neural decoding is a regression (or classification) problem that relates neural signals to specific variables. Decoding of neural signals has been better achieved using modern machine learning techniques.

For decoders, the aim is to understand the information contained in the neural activity or to understand how the information in the neural activity is related to external variables. Recurrent neural networks based on Simple RNN, Gated Recurrent Unit (GRU), Long Short-Term Memory Network (LSTM), and Non-recurrent Decoders such as Wiener Filter, Kalman Filter, XGBoost, Feedforward Neural Network (FNN), Naïve Bayes, Support Vector Regression (SVR) are often used [9]. For any decoder, the purpose is to predict the recorded output value based on the neural signal, as shown in Fig. 4.

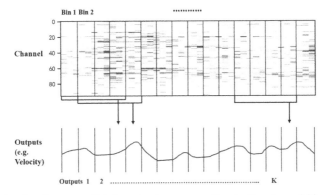

Fig. 4. Use the decoder to predict the output corresponding to the channel binned data for a specific time bin.

2.4 Related Work

In brain-computer interfaces systems, it has not been possible to explore universally applicable hidden dynamics from the neural information due to the complexity within the neural system. In recent years, there has been the use of advanced machine learning techniques to explore the interaction between spike generators and BCI decoders. For example, a data-driven generative adversarial network (GAN) based on data from multiple tasks trains the spike train generator, and the model can be used to synthesize new data quickly [10].

A recent approach, SNN_EEG [11], can generate EEG data by SNN, and the generated spike trains are converted into EEG data as templates by filters. Our approach complements this work in the following aspects. First, the SNN_EEG aims to generate EEG data, and the SNN was fitted as a regression to the EEG template. In contrast, we generate spike data, constrained in a neural population dynamics manner, to generate biologically consistent data.

3 Method

3.1 Overview Architecture

The whole data generation process is divided into four steps, as shown in Fig. 5. The first step is to process and dimensionality reduction of the neural spike data collected from the brain-computer interface of the same task trial to derive the neural population dynamics in low-dimensional neural manifold space, and the second step is to build an SNN model with the real neuron population dynamics manifold as the target function for supervised learning. In the third step, during the learning process, the spike trains generated by the SNN are subjected to principal component analysis (PCA) for dimensionality reduction, and the resulting activity laws need to be approximated by the real neuron population dynamics. In the fourth step, after the network iteration, a perturbation neuron is set in the SNN, and the perturbation neuron is responsible for generating noisy pulses, thus generating noisy and rule-based neural spike data.

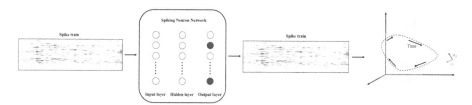

Fig. 5. The SNN generates spike trains data and the dynamics of the spiking neurons in the output layer are in the neural manifold space.

A forward SNN is used to generate the spike trains, each node is a LIF neuron model, and the network architecture consists of three layers, the input layer consists of a fixed sequence of Poisson generated spike trains with a frequency of 10 Hz as input, followed by the hidden layer and the output layer. During the training process, the spiking neurons in the output layer generate the corresponding spike trains according to the input, and each neuron in the output layer is processed with a sliding window to transform it into firing rate, followed by dimensionality reduction, so as to map the spiking neurons in the output layer into a low-dimensional neural manifold. The neural manifold activity pattern of the real neuron population in the same dimension is used as the objective function, and the mean squared difference (MSE) is used as the loss function. The training results need to satisfy that the activity pattern of the spiking neuron population in the output layer needs to approximate the activity pattern of the real neuron population.

After the iteration of the network, some neurons in the output layer of the SNN are activated, and Poisson neurons are used as the basis and set as perturbation neurons. A random spike signal based on Poisson distribution is input to the perturbation neuron, which causes the perturbation neuron to generate a noisy signal. The output layer can thus generate neural spike information data with noise and in accordance with the real biological neural population dynamics.

3.2 Surrogate Gradient Descent

The learning algorithm is based on a supervised learning algorithm that uses an algorithm called surrogate gradient descent to make the weights of the SNN to be updated [12].

$$S_i[n] \propto \Theta(u_i[n] - u_{\text{threshold}}) \tag{5}$$

$S_i[n]$ is denoted as spike trains, where $\Theta(x)$ is denoted as a Heaviside step function, due to the non-differentiable nature of the spike signal. In back propagation, the $\Theta(x)$ function is replaced by $\sigma(x)$. Then we have $S_i[n] \propto \sigma(u_i[n] - u_{\text{threshold}})$, where $\sigma(x) = 1/1 + \exp(-x)$.

3.3 Generating Spike Trains Dataset

After the network iteration is completed, some neurons in the output layer are set as perturbation neurons. A Poisson process-based spike train is input into the perturbation neuron, which causes the neuron to generate noisy spike trains.

Implemented within the program, the calculation can be simplified, and the probability that the spike is issued within the time step Δt can be considered as $r\Delta t$, where r is the firing rate and x_{rand} is a random variable with values within 0 to 1.

$$r_i \Delta t \begin{cases} >x_{\text{rand}} & \text{firing} \\ \leq x_{\text{rand}} & \text{none} \end{cases} \tag{6}$$

4 Experiments

4.1 Data Processing and Analysis

We will use a dataset from Shenoy's lab, Stanford University[1], which includes a 96-channel Utah array recording the motor cortex of a non-human primate performing a

---
[1] https://github.com/slinderman/stats320.

center-out reaching task [13], as shown in Fig. 6. The data contain spike trains recorded in each channel, as well as the cursor positions displayed on the computer screen by the monkey control, and the cursor velocities while recording 8 different trial types.

The spikes trains in the channel, as well as the position, are based on a 1ms window, by downsampling to a 25ms window. At the same time, the spike trains are converted to firing rate to improve the signal-to-noise ratio, and Gaussian smoothing is performed on the cursor position information to remove part of the noisy data.

The channel-based spike trains in the data are obtained by threshold crossing and not by spike sorting, which refers to the conversion of the acquired raw neural signal into a spike train for each neuron, based on the similarity of an action potential. In a recent study, it was shown that the neural manifold built based on the spike information of threshold crossing is similar to that of spike sorting [14]. Therefore, we choose the neural manifold built based on threshold crossing.

In the data analysis, the neural information of multiple same trials is averaged to obtain the average neural information of the same trial. Subsequently, the average neural information is dimensionalized to obtain the neural manifold corresponding to the low-dimensional neural space, as shown in Fig. 7.

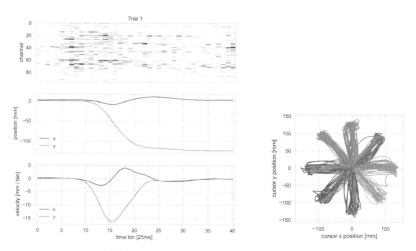

Fig. 6. BCI Data that has been processed

4.2 Experimental Setting

The SNN consists of three layers, each with 100, 400, and 100 LIF neurons, respectively, with fixed Poisson spike trains at 10 Hz as the input, followed by a hidden layer and an output layer. During the training process, the spiking neurons in the output layer generate the corresponding spike trains according to the input, and the sliding window processing is performed for each neuron of the output layer to transform it into firing rate data, followed by dimensionality reduction, thus mapping the spiking neurons in the output layer into the low-dimensional neural manifold. The neural manifold activity

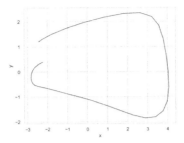

Fig. 7. The neuronal population dynamics in neural manifold for Trial 1 (Gaussian smoothing is done)

pattern of the real neuron population in the same dimension is used as the objective function, and the MSE (mean squared error) is used as the loss function. The training results need to satisfy that the activity pattern of the population of spiking neurons in the output layer needs to approximate the activity pattern of the population of real neurons.

After the network is trained, the model parameter that minimizes the loss value is selected, and for this experiment epoch 2130 is selected, and the loss value of this epoch is minimized, as shown in Fig. 8. After that, the generation of data is performed, and 1–3% of neurons in the output layer are started as perturbation neurons to generate noise information. After that, the trained SNN converts the fixed input spike trains into output spike trains. This is repeated several times to generate the spike train dataset corresponding to the brain-computer interface experiment Trial 1. In this experiment, we generated data with similar neural dynamics as the original data Trial 1, as shown in Fig. 8.

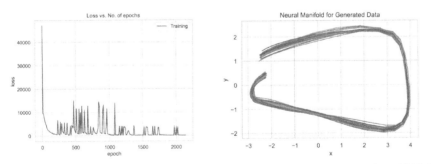

Fig. 8. The training process (Left). The neuronal population dynamics in neural manifold for generated data (Right).

After the iteration, the inputs and outputs of the model are shown in Fig. 9. The inputs to the model are always fixed and the network model training process transforms the fixed inputs into biologically meaningful spike trains. These output spike trains are sparser compared to the Poisson input.

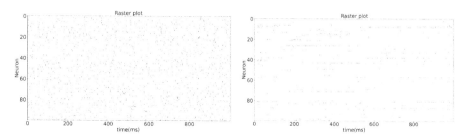

Fig. 9. Raster plot comparison, input spike trains and output spike trains for 100 neurons.

4.3 Results

We decode the generated data in combination with the original Trial1 data. Performance evaluation is performed using decoders LSTM, RNN, and FNN. Based on the original brain-computer interface experimental data combined with the generated neural spike signals, the recorded cursor movement speed values were predicted and the performance evaluation metrics were used R^2.

1. Expanded dataset based on the original dataset (96 channels) to train the decoder to derive the cursor movement x and y.
2. Expanded dataset based on part of the original dataset (10 channels) to train the decoder to derive the cursor movement x and y.
3. Meanwhile, the decoding effect of the expanding data is compared with the decoding effect of the original data set.

Table 1. Decoding results on the different datasets

Method	LSTM		RNN		FNN	
	Validate	Test	Validate	Test	Validate	Test
	x	x	x	x	x	x
	y	y	y	y	y	y
96 channels	0.790	0.900	0.651	0.666	0.735	0.874
	0.600	0.868	0.740	0.767	0.793	0.889
10 channels	0.695	0.752	0.536	0.593	0.404	0.667
	0.487	0.610	0.375	0.406	0.365	0.530
96 channels and 100 neurons	**0.887**	**0.915**	**0.749**	**0.799**	**0.789**	**0.912**
	0.870	**0.916**	**0.819**	**0.813**	**0.883**	**0.917**
10 channels and 100 neurons	**0.752**	**0.856**	**0.735**	**0.847**	**0.659**	**0.921**
	0.814	**0.830**	**0.828**	**0.818**	**0.845**	**0.849**

Comparing the results using R^2 as an evaluation metric, as shown in Table 1. In our experiments, we generated spike trains corresponding to 100 spiking neurons, and we can observe that the best results can be obtained in the complete original data combined with the generated data. In addition, even only a small amount of original data combined with the generated dataset can be obtained with good results. The results show that the network is able to generate spike trains with similar neural dynamics as the original data based on the neural manifold space as a constraint and is able to enhance the decoding ability in the corresponding decoding experiments while extending the original dataset. In our model can be suitable to be applied in clinical trials, the network model can reduce the reliance on the original data due to the limited daily data collection.

5   Conclusion

Intracortical brain-machine interfaces take neural information from the motor cortex in the cerebral cortex, and the neural information available in clinical experiments is often limited, and the decoder needs data to be retrained for fine-tuning over time. The goal of this work is to provide a method to combine an intracortical brain-computer interface with brain-inspired intelligence as a spike generator capable of generating neural population dynamics corresponding to the Trial. In the future, with the development of neuromorphic chips, SNN can be more effective with lower energy consumption and can eventually help BCI effectively.

Reference s

1. Even-Chen, N., et al.: Power-saving design opportunities for wireless intracortical brain-computer interfaces. Nat. Biomed. Eng. 4(10), 984–996 (2020)
2. Hochberg, L.R., et al.: Reach and grasp by people with tetraplegia using a neurally controlled robotic arm. Nature 485(7398), 372-U121 (2012)
3. Bouton, C.E., et al.: Restoring cortical control of functional movement in a human with quadriplegia. Nature 533(7602), 247–250 (2016)
4. Gallego, J.A., Perich, M.G., Miller, L.E., Solla, S.A.: Neural manifolds for the control of movement. Neuron 94(5), 978–984 (2017)
5. Cunningham, J.P., Yu, B.M.: Dimensionality reduction for large-scale neural recordings. Nat. Neurosci. 17(11), 1500–1509 (2014)
6. Taherkhani, A., Belatreche, A., Li, Y., Cosma, G., Maguire, L.P., McGinnity, T.M.: A review of learning in biologically plausible spiking neural networks. Neural Netw. 122, 253–272 (2020)
7. Gallego, J.A., Perich, M.G., Naufel, S.N., Ethier, C., Solla, S.A., Miller, L.E.: Cortical population activity within a preserved neural manifold underlies multiple motor behaviors. Nat. Commun. 9, 1–13 (2018)
8. Gallego, J.A., Perich, M.G., Chowdhury, R.H., Solla, S.A., Miller, L.E.: Long-term stability of cortical population dynamics underlying consistent behavior. Nat. Neurosci. 23(2), 260–270 (2020)
9. Glaser, J.I., Benjamin, A.S., Chowdhury, R.H., Perich, M.G., Miller, L.E., Kording, K.P.: Machine learning for neural decoding. eNeuro 7(4) (2020)

10. Wen, S., Yin, A., Furlanello, T., Perich, M.G., Miller, L.E., Itti, L.: Rapid adaptation of brain-computer interfaces to new neuronal ensembles or participants via generative modelling. Nat. Biomed. Eng. (2021)
11. Singanamalla, S.K.R., Lin, C.T.: Spiking neural network for augmenting electroencephalographic data for brain computer interfaces. Front Neurosci. Switz. **15**, 651762 (2021)
12. Neftci, E.O., Mostafa, H., Zenke, F.: Surrogate gradient learning in spiking neural networks: bringing the power of gradient-based optimization to spiking neural networks. IEEE Signal Process. Mag. **36**(6), 51–63 (2019)
13. Gilja, V., et al.: A high-performance neural prosthesis enabled by control algorithm design. Nat. Neurosci. **15**(12), 1752–1757 (2012)
14. Trautmann, E.M., et al.: Accurate estimation of neural population dynamics without spike sorting. Neuron **103**(2), 292–308 (2019)

An Improved Lightweight YOLOv5 Model Based on Attention Mechanism for Face Mask Detection

Sheng Xu[1($\boxtimes$)], Zhanyu Guo[2], Yuchi Liu[3], Jingwei Fan[2], and Xuxu Liu[1]

[1] Northwestern Polytechnical University, Xi'an, China
`xus@mail.nwpu.edu.cn`
[2] University of Leeds, Leeds, UK
[3] Sichuan University, Chengdu, China

Abstract. Coronavirus 2019 has brought severe challenges to social stability and public health worldwide. One effective way of curbing the epidemic is to require people to wear masks in public places and monitor their mask-wearing states by suitable automatic detectors. However, existing models struggle to simultaneously achieve the requirements of both high precision and real-time performance. To solve this problem, we propose an improved lightweight face mask detector based on YOLOv5, which can achieve an excellent balance of precision and speed. Firstly, a novel backbone ShuffleCANet that combines ShuffleNetV2 network with Coordinate Attention mechanism is proposed as the backbone. Afterward, an efficient path aggression network BiFPN is applied as the feature fusion neck. Furthermore, the localization loss is replaced with α-CIoU in model training phase to obtain higher-quality anchors. Some valuable strategies such as data augmentation, adaptive image scaling, and anchor cluster operation are also utilized. Experimental results on AIZOO face mask dataset show the superiority of the proposed model. Compared with the original YOLOv5, the proposed model increases the inference speed by 28.3% while still improving the precision by 0.58%. It achieves the best mean average precision of 95.2% compared with other seven existing models, which is 4.4% higher than the baseline.

Keywords: Face mask detection · YOLOv5 · Attention mechanism

1 Introduction

Since December 2019, the coronavirus disease 2019 (COVID-19) has spread rapidly around the world, posing a great threat to public health. To supervise mask-wearing states in public areas, most places still adopt traditional measures such as manual inspection, which wastes human resources and may cause lapses in inspection. To address the existing problems, face mask detection models based on deep learning have attracted extensive attention from researchers.

Some algorithms have achieved relatively good performance. Shylaja et al. [1] used transfer learning technique to train their face mask detection model based

© The Author(s), under exclusive license to Springer Nature Switzerland AG 2022
E. Pimenidis et al. (Eds.): ICANN 2022, LNCS 13531, pp. 531–543, 2022.
https://doi.org/10.1007/978-3-031-15934-3_44

on Faster R-CNN, which exhibited excellent identification performance on images of indoor environments and complex scenes. However, it could hardly realize real-time level detection and was difficult to be deployed. Fan et al. [2] proposed RetinaFaceMask, a one-stage face mask detector with MobileNet as backbone. It could distinguish between correct and incorrect mask-wearing states, but still did not solve the problem of precision reduction caused by the light weight.

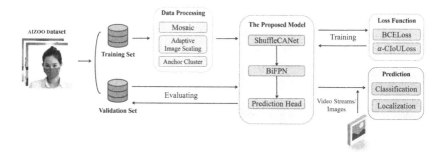

Fig. 1. The overview working pipeline of the proposed model.

In this paper, we propose a high-performance, lightweight face mask detector based on YOLOv5 [3] and attention mechanism to detect whether people wear masks. The overview working pipeline of the proposed model is shown in Fig. 1. We make some modifications to the network architecture including the proposed ShuffleCANet backbone which comprises modified ShuffleNetV2 [4] and Coordinate attention [5] mechanism, and the BiFPN [6] feature fusion neck. Moreover, we replace the localization loss with α-CIoU [7], which is more robust to lightweight models. Additionally, we also utilize several valuable methods for data processing. Generally speaking, the proposed model can achieve a balance of high accuracy and fast speed, providing an excellent solution to handle the problems associated with heavy models (difficult to deploy) and light models (struggle to achieve satisfactory performance). The main contributions of this paper are listed as follows:

1) We propose a novel backbone called ShuffleCANet with Coordinate Attention mechanism, which is lightweight but has a strong feature extraction ability. Moreover, we use BiFPN as the feature fusion neck to make full use of the features between different scales.
2) We modify the localization loss with α-CIoU to make bounding boxes regress better and obtain higher quality anchors.
3) We evaluate the proposed model on the AIZOO dataset [8]. Experimental results demonstrate that the proposed model can achieve state-of-the-art performance with real-time speed and high precision, surpassing seven other models.

The remainder of this paper is organized as follows. In Sect. 2, some related works about object detection and face mask detection are reviewed. In Sect. 3, the detailed architecture of the proposed methodology is presented. In Sect. 4, the implementation details of the proposed work are described. Finally, in Sect. 5, conclusions of the whole work are presented and future works are discussed.

2   Related Works

2.1   Object Detection

Traditional object detection algorithms are primarily based on manually designed features such as Haar [9] and Hog [10] features. However, these features have weak generalization ability and poor robustness. In recent years, deep learning based algorithms have become the mainstream research method for object detection because of their excellent performance.

Deep learning based object detection algorithms can be mainly divided into two categories: two-stage and one-stage algorithms. Two-stage algorithms first generate a group of region proposals that may contain targets, and then further classify and calibrate them. They have high precision but poor real-time performance, represented by the R-CNN [11–13] series. One-stage detectors are based on regression, which directly predict the coordinates and categories of targets in a single step. They have fast speeds but inferior precision, represented by the YOLO [3,14–17] series, RetinaNet [18], etc. Moreover, some novel anchor-free algorithms based on dense prediction have been prevalent in recent years, such as CornerNet [19] and FCOS [20]. They detect objects as paired keypoints or in a per-pixel prediction fashion instead of generating prior anchor boxes, thus avoiding the complicated computation related to anchors.

2.2   Face Mask Detection

Research on face mask detection has been prevalent since the eruption of COVID-19, because using face mask detectors to automatically monitor mask-wearing states in public places is an efficient way to help curb the epidemic.

As for two-stage detectors, Loey et al. [21] proposed a hybrid model comprising two components for face mask detection: the first for feature extraction and the second for classification, which performed well on three public face mask datasets. In [22], the authors proposed a dual-stage convolutional neural network architecture capable of detecting masked and unmasked faces. As for one-stage detectors, YOLO-based models have been extensively studied. Several methods have been applied to YOLO series to increase their performance, as noted in [23–26]. Among them, attention mechanism is widely used because it can focus on useful information and enhance the prediction ability of the model, such as convolutional block attention module (CBAM) [27] and Squeeze-and-Excitation Block (SE) [28]. Besides, the work described in [29] proposed a novel single-shot lightweight face mask detector (SL-FMDet) using MobileNet and an improved FPN with residual context attention module and Gaussian heatmap regression.

However, existing face mask detection algorithms pose some problems. On the one hand, some powerful detectors can yield extremely high precision but are too heavy and costly to be used in practice. On the other hand, some lightweight detectors are easy to deploy but struggle to achieve high-precision detection.

3 Methodology

3.1 Data Processing

The data processing methods employed in this paper include Mosaic [17], adaptive image scaling, anchor cluster and some other relevant methods. Firstly, Mosaic is applied to the original AIZOO training set, splicing four images by random scaling, and then cropping and arranging them into a single image; this increases the diversity and enriches the background of the picture. Then the adaptive image scaling operation is applied to obtain the 640 × 640 standard image for training. Moreover, in case of the large difference in size between anchors and objects, k-means algorithm is used to cluster the bounding boxes of the training set. The generated prior anchors are more suitable and efficient, which can learn more effective prior knowledge and accelerate model convergence.

3.2 Network Architecture

The network architecture of the proposed model is shown in Fig. 2. The key improvements in architecture are summarized as follows: we propose a novel backbone called ShuffleCANet based on modified ShuffleNetV2 [4] and CoordAttention [5] mechanism, which is lightweight but still achieve SOTA performance; we utilize BiFPN [6] to replace PANet as the path aggregation network for more efficient multi-scale feature fusion. To sum up, the model is lighter, faster, and more accurate, which is more efficient and practical to deploy.

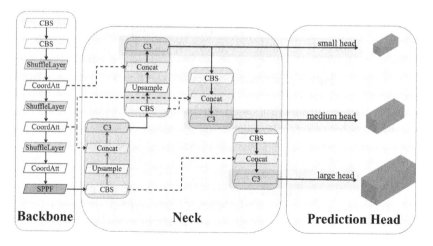

Fig. 2. The network architecture of the proposed model. a) The CBS module consists of a Conv2d layer, a BatchNorm layer, and a SILU activation. b) The detailed structure of ShuffleLayer, CoordAttention and BiFPN are illustrated in Fig. 3. c) The three prediction heads are used for small, medium, and large objects, respectively.

Modified ShuffleNetV2. ShuffleNet [30] is a highly computation-efficient CNN architecture for mobile devices with point-wise group convolution and channel shuffle operations. ShuffleNetV2 is an improved version of ShuffleNet. It introduces channel split operation and changes the element-wise addition by concatenation, followed by the channel shuffle operation to ultimately mix features.

In this paper, we use ShuffleNetV2 as the basic backbone and implement several modifications to improve its performance. Specifically, we retain the original two CBS blocks with small parameters to ensure less down-sampling loss in the initial stage and guarantee the learning ability. Moreover, in each ShuffleLayer, the kernel size of depthwise convolution is increased from 3 to 5 for a larger receptive field. The structure of ShuffleLayer in this work is shown in Fig. 3(a).

CoordAttention. CoordAttention [5] is a novel, lightweight, and efficient attention mechanism to enhance model performance, which can be easily incorporated into mobile networks to improve the accuracy with little additional computing overhead. The structure of Coordinate Attention module is shown in Fig. 3(b).

To be specific, the operation is divided into two steps: coordinate information embedding and coordinate attention generation. The first step factorizes channel attention into two 1D global pooling processes to encode each channel along the horizontal and vertical directions, respectively. The formulas are as follows:

$$Z_c^h(h) = \frac{1}{W} \sum_{0 \leq i < W} x_c(h, i), \quad Z_c^w(w) = \frac{1}{H} \sum_{0 \leq i < H} x_c(j, w) \tag{1}$$

where x_c denotes the input, $Z_c^h(h)$ and $Z_c^w(w)$ denote the output of the cth channel at height h and width w, respectively. In the second step, the produced feature maps are then concatenated and sent to a shared 1×1 convolutional transformation F_1 to obtain the intermediate feature map f as follows:

$$f = \delta \left(F_1 \left(\left[Z^h, Z^w \right] \right) \right) \tag{2}$$

where $[\cdot, \cdot]$ denotes the concatenation operation along the spatial dimension, δ is a non-linear activation function. Then f is split along the spatial dimension into two separate tensors f^h and f^w, followed by another two 1×1 convolutional functions F^h and F^w, which can be described as follows:

$$g^h = \sigma \left(F_h \left(f^h \right) \right), \quad g^w = \sigma \left(F_w \left(f^w \right) \right) \tag{3}$$

where σ denotes the Sigmoid activation function. Finally, the output y_c can be calculated as:

$$y_c(i, j) = x_c(i, j) \times g_c^h(i) \times g_c^w(j) \tag{4}$$

In this paper, we insert the CoordAttention module after each ShuffleLayer and further form the novel backbone ShuffleCANet. Benefiting from the attention mechanism, it is still lightweight but can pay more attention to the targets and enhance the feature expression ability in complex backgrounds.

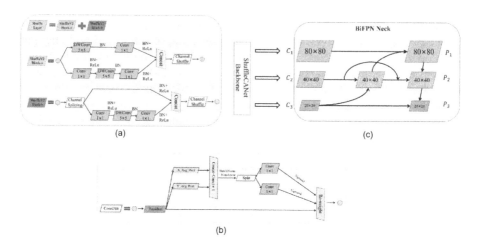

Fig. 3. a) The structure of ShuffleLayer. DWConv denotes depthwise convolution. b) The structure of CoordAttention. X_Avg_Pool and Y_Avg_Pool denote 1D horizontal global pooling and 1D vertical global pooling, respectively. c) The structure of BiFPN. $C_{1\sim3}$ and $P_{1\sim3}$ denote the input and output feature maps, respectively.

Bidirectional Feature Pyramid Network (BiFPN). In this paper, we use BiFPN [6] as the feature fusion neck with three optimizations based on the original PANet: Firstly, the nodes with only one input edge are removed because they have little contribution to the feature network; Secondly, an additional edge is added between the original input and output nodes at the same level to fuse more features; Thirdly, each bidirectional path is treated as one feature network layer, which is repeated multiple times to enable more high-level feature fusion. The BiFPN architecture can intensify the performance of the whole model by further refining and fusing output information. The structure of BiFPN in this work is shown in Fig. 3(c).

Loss Function. The total loss in this work includes three parts: confidence loss, classification loss, and localization loss. We use BCELoss for confidence loss and classification loss while α-CIoU loss for localization loss.

IoU means Intersection over Union between the predicted box (B) and ground-truth box (B^{gt}), which can be defined as:

$$IoU = \frac{B \cap B^{gt}}{B \cup B^{gt}} \tag{5}$$

CIoU is an improved version of IoU that considers overlapping area, central point distance, and aspect ratio. Thus it converges faster and is more efficient in performing bounding box regression. CIoU loss can be defined as follows:

$$L_{CIoU} = 1 - IoU + \left| \frac{\rho^2\left(b, b^{gt}\right)}{c^2} \right| + \beta v \tag{6}$$

where b and b^{gt} denote the central point of B and B^{gt}, $\rho(\cdot)$ denotes the Euclidean distance, and c is the diagonal length of the smallest enclosing box covering the two boxes. β is the trade-off parameter and v measures the consistency of the aspect ratio. v and β can be defined as follows:

$$v = \frac{4}{\pi^2}\left(\arctan\frac{\omega^{gt}}{h^{gt}} - \arctan\frac{\omega}{h}\right)^2, \quad \beta = \frac{v}{1 - IoU + v} \tag{7}$$

Based on the CIoU loss, α-CIoU [7] loss is utilized in this paper, which has a power IoU term and an additional power regularization term with a single power parameter α to improve the bounding box regression accuracy and the model robustness. The function can be defined as follows:

$$L_{\alpha-CIoU} = 1 - IoU^\alpha + \left|\frac{\rho^{2a}(b, b^{\rho t})}{c^{2a}}\right| + (\beta v)^\alpha \tag{8}$$

where α is set as 3 in this paper.

4   Experiments and Results

4.1   Dataset

The AIZOO face mask dataset is a public dataset provided by AIZOOTech [8], which combines Wider Face [31] and Masked Faces [32] datasets with three classes: face, masked face, and mask. It comprises 7959 images in total, including 6120 images for training and 1839 images for testing. The training set consists of 13,593 faces, of which approximately 78% are exposed faces, while the test set contains 3062 faces, of which about 65% are exposed faces.

4.2   Evaluation Metrics

For object detection tasks, traditional evaluation metrics include precision, recall, and mean average precision (mAP); precision (P) and recall (R) can be expressed as follows:

$$P = \frac{TP}{TP + FP}, \quad R = \frac{TP}{TP + FN} \tag{9}$$

where TP, FP, and FN denote true positive, false positive, and false negative. To calculate the mAP, the average precision (AP) of each class must be measured, which can be calculated by all-point interpolation approach to smooth the precision and recall curve. Furthermore, mAP can be computed by taking the mean of AP against each class. The formulas can be expressed as follows:

$$AP = \sum_{i=1}^{n}(R_{i+1} - R_i)\max_{\tilde{R}:\tilde{R}\geq R_{i+1}} P(\tilde{R}), \quad mAP = \frac{1}{N}\sum_{i=1}^{N}AP_i \tag{10}$$

where i is the index value, P and R denote precision and recall, respectively, N is the number of classes and AP_i is the average precision of the ith class.

In this paper, AP-Face, AP-Mask, and mAP@0.5 are used to evaluate the performance of the model, where AP-Face and AP-Mask denote APs for faces and masks, respectively. Parameter size and inference time per image are also used to evaluate the weight and speed of the model.

4.3   Implementation Details

The environment configuration of our work is based on Pytorch 1.9.0 with CUDA 11.4 and CUDNN 8.2. The models are trained on NVIDIA RTX A5000 GPU (24GB) and Xeon Gold 6139 CPU. In the training phase, we employ SGD optimizer with an initial learning rate of 1E-2 and a final learning rate of 1E-5, with the weight decay as 5E-3. Furthermore, we use three warm up epochs with a momentum of 0.8, and also apply CosineAnnealingLR method to decay the learning rate. Each experiment is trained for 200 epochs with a batch size of 16.

4.4   Ablation Study

To demonstrate the effectiveness of the proposed modifications based on YOLOv5, in this subsection we perform the ablation studies on ShuffleNetV2, CoordAttention, BiFPN and α-CIoU loss on the AIZOO dataset with YOLOv5s as a baseline. Precision, number of parameters, and inference time per image are used as evaluation metrics. The experiment results are summarized in Table 1.

Table 1. Ablation study on AIZOO dataset.

| Methods | | | Precision | Parameters | Inference time |
Backbone	Neck	Loss			per image
BottleCSP (original)	Original	CIoU	94.73	7.028 MB	1.523 ms
ShuffleNetV2	Original	CIoU	94.57	**3.274 MB**	**1.003 ms**
ShuffleNetV2	BiFPN	CIoU	94.82	3.307 MB	1.018 ms
ShuffleCANet(+CoordAttention)	BiFPN	CIoU	95.06	3.319 MB	1.095 ms
ShuffleCANet	BiFPN	α-CIoU	**95.31**	3.319 MB	1.092 ms

ShuffleNetV2. By replacing the original backbone with the modified lightweight backbone ShuffleNetV2, the size of parameters and the inference time per image are reduced by approximately 53% and 34%, respectively, while the precision is reduced by only 0.16%. The results demonstrate the superiority of ShuffleNetV2, which is lightweight but still perform well.

BiFPN. By replacing the PANet feature fusion neck with BiFPN on the basis of ShuffleNetV2 backbone, the precision is improved by 0.35%, which surpasses the original YOLOv5. Meanwhile, it keeps the parameter size almost the same. The results indicate that BiFPN neck can better fuse features for face mask detection with almost no impact on speed in this experiment.

CoordAttention. By integrating CoordAttention mechanism into ShuffleNetV2 to further form a novel backbone called ShuffleCANet, the precision increases by 0.24% with only a few extra parameters. Moreover, the model is still extremely fast and may be able to better extract features and focus on useful information.

α-CIoU. By replacing the localization loss function with α-CIoU loss in the training phase, the precision further increases by 0.25% based on ShuffleCANet and BiFPN structures. It demonstrates that α-CIoU can make bounding boxes regress better and obtain higher quality anchors with the power parameter α

4.5 Comparative Results with Other Models on AIZOO

In this subsection, we compare the performance of the proposed model on AIZOO dataset with other seven state-of-the-art models used for face mask detection. The seven models include five one-stage models, namely the baseline from AIZOO, YOLOv3 [16], RetinaFace [33], RetinaFaceMask [2], and SL-FMDet [29]; and two two-stage models, namely Faster R-CNN [13] and MSAF R-CNN [34]. The comparison results are shown in Table 2.

Table 2. The comparative results with other SOTA methods on AIZOO dataset.

Methods	AP-Face	AP-Mask	mAP
Baseline [8]	89.6	91.9	90.8
YOLOv3 [16]	92.6	93.7	93.1
RetinaFace [33]	92.8	93.1	93.0
RetinaFaceMask - MobileNet [2]	93.5	90.4	92.0
SL-FMDet [29]	93.5	94.0	93.8
Faster R-CNN - MobileNet [13]	89.9	89.7	89.8
MSAF R-CNN [34]	90.3	90.4	90.4
Proposed work	**94.2**	**96.2**	**95.2**

The comparative results demonstrate that the proposed model achieves the best performance in terms of both AP-Face, AP-Mask, and mAP. Compared with the baseline model, our model increases the three metrics by 4.6%, 4.3%, and 4.4%, respectively, which is a qualitative leap. Compared with YOLOv3 and RetinaFace, the proposed model not only achieves higher precision, but is also lighter and faster because of the light backbone. Moreover, RestinaFaceMask with MobileNet and SL-FMDet are lightweight models, but they exhibit inferior performance compared with our model. Faster R-CNN and MSAF R-CNN are two-stage models. However, their performance is not satisfactory.

We illustrate the performance of our model visually. As shown in Fig. 4, we select some representative images captured in real situations, the qualitative results of which demonstrate the robustness and effectiveness of our model.

Fig. 4. Some detection results in real-life public situations with the proposed model. Red box denotes the unmasked face, green box denotes the masked face and blue box denotes the mask. (Color figure online)

5   Conclusion

In this paper, we proposed a novel lightweight and high-performance face mask detector based on YOLOv5 with several techniques, which can achieve an excellent balance between precision and speed. To be specific, we proposed a novel backbone called ShuffleCANet that combines ShuffleNetV2 and Coordinate Attention mechanism to extract rich features and focus on useful information. After that, we used BiFPN path aggregation network for feature fusion to sufficiently merge the high-level semantic information and low-level details. Additionally, we utilized α-CIoU loss to replace the original localization loss function in model training phase to obtain higher-quality anchors. The proposed work achieved state-of-the-art performance on the public face mask dataset AIZOO. Experimental results showed that our model outperformed the seven other existing face mask detectors in terms of both AP-Face, AP-Mask, and mAP. Moreover, our model is lightweight and fast, with an inference time of only 1.092 ms per image on RTX A5000. Therefore, we believe that the proposed model can be employed in practice to help curb the spread of COVID-19 and contribute to public health.

In future work, we will handle the problem of not recognizing whether the mask is worn correctly in this work. In addition, we will focus on the detection performance of smaller faces in dense public conditions to increase its practicability.

References

1. Shylaja, H.N., Latha, H.N., Poornima, H.N., Uma, B.: Detection and localization of mask occluded faces by transfer learning using faster RCNN. SSRN Electr. J. (2021). https://doi.org/10.2139/ssrn.3835214
2. Fan, X., Jiang, M.: RetinaFaceMask: a single stage face mask detector for assisting control of the COVID-19 pandemic. In: 2021 IEEE International Conference on Systems, Man, and Cybernetics (SMC), Melbourne, Australia, pp. 832–837. IEEE (2021). https://doi.org/10.1109/SMC52423.2021.9659271
3. GitHub: YOLOv5. http://github.com/ultralytics/yolov5
4. Ma, N., Zhang, X., Zheng, H.-T., Sun, J.: ShuffleNet V2: practical guidelines for efficient CNN architecture design. In: Ferrari, V., Hebert, M., Sminchisescu, C., Weiss, Y. (eds.) Computer Vision – ECCV 2018. LNCS, vol. 11218, pp. 122–138. Springer, Cham (2018). https://doi.org/10.1007/978-3-030-01264-9_8
5. Hou, Q., Zhou, D., Feng, J.: Coordinate attention for efficient mobile network design. In: 2021 IEEE/CVF Conference on Computer Vision and Pattern Recognition Workshops (CVPRW), Nashville, TN, USA, pp. 13713–13722. IEEE (2021). https://doi.org/10.1109/CVPR46437.2021.01350
6. Tan, M., Pang, R., Le, Q.V.: EfficientDet: scalable and efficient object detection. In: 2020 IEEE/CVF Conference on Computer Vision and Pattern Recognition (CVPR), Seattle, WA, pp. 10781–10790. IEEE (2020)
7. He, J., Erfani, S., Ma, X., Bailey, J., Chi, Y., Hua, X.: Alpha-IoU: a family of power intersection over union losses for bounding box regression. arXiv:2110.13675 (2021)
8. AIZOO: Detect faces and determine whether people are wearing mask (2020). http://github.com/AIZOOTech/FaceMaskDetection
9. Lienhart, R., Maydt, J.: An extended set of Haar-like features for rapid object detection. In: Proceedings 2002 International Conference on Image Processing, Rochester, NY, USA, p. 1. IEEE (2002). https://doi.org/10.1109/ICIP.2002.1038171
10. Dalal, N., Triggs, B.: Histograms of oriented gradients for human detection. In: 2005 IEEE Computer Society Conference on Computer Vision and Pattern Recognition, CVPR 2005, San Diego, CA, USA, pp. 886–893. IEEE (2005). https://doi.org/10.1109/CVPR.2005.177
11. Girshick, R., Donahue, J., Darrell, T., Malik, J.: Rich feature hierarchies for accurate object detection and semantic segmentation. In: 2014 IEEE Conference on Computer Vision and Pattern Recognition, Columbus, OH, USA, pp. 580–587. IEEE (2014). https://doi.org/10.1109/CVPR.2014.81
12. Girshick, R.: Fast R-CNN. In: 2015 IEEE International Conference on Computer Vision (ICCV), Santiago, Chile, pp. 1440–1448. IEEE (2015). https://doi.org/10.1109/ICCV.2015.169
13. Ren, S., He, K., Girshick, R., Sun, J.: Faster R-CNN: towards real-time object detection with region proposal networks. IEEE T. Pattern Anal. **39**(6), 1137–1149 (2017). https://doi.org/10.1109/TPAMI.2016.2577031
14. Redmon, J., Divvala, S., Girshick, R., Farhadi, A.: You only look once: unified, real-time object detection. In: 2016 IEEE Conference on Computer Vision and Pattern Recognition (CVPR), Las Vegas, NV, USA, pp. 779–788. IEEE (2016). https://doi.org/10.1109/CVPR.2016.91

15. Redmon, J., Farhadi, A.: YOLO9000: better, faster, stronger. In: 2017 IEEE Conference on Computer Vision and Pattern Recognition (CVPR), Honolulu, HI, USA, pp. 6517–6525. IEEE (2017). https://doi.org/10.1109/CVPR.2017.690

16. Redmon, J., Farhadi, A.: YOLOv3: an incremental improvement. arXiv arXiv:1804.02767 (2018)

17. Bochkovskiy, A., Wang, C., Liao, H.M.: YOLOv4: optimal speed and accuracy of object detection. arXiv arXiv:2004.10934 (2020)

18. Lin, T.Y., Goyal, P., Girshick, R., He, K., Dollar, P.: Focal loss for dense object detection. IEEE T. Pattern Anal. **42**, 318–327 (2020)

19. Law, H., Deng, J.: CornerNet: detecting objects as paired keypoints. In: Ferrari, V., Hebert, M., Sminchisescu, C., Weiss, Y. (eds.) Computer Vision – ECCV 2018. LNCS, vol. 11218, pp. 765–781. Springer, Cham (2018). https://doi.org/10.1007/978-3-030-01264-9_45

20. Tian, Z., Shen, C., Chen, H., He, T.: FCOS: fully convolutional one-stage object detection. In: 2019 IEEE/CVF International Conference on Computer Vision (ICCV), Seoul, South Korea, pp. 9627–9636. IEEE (2019). https://doi.org/10.1109/ICCV.2019.00972

21. Loey, M., Manogaran, G., Taha, M.H.N., Khalifa, N.E.M.: A hybrid deep transfer learning model with machine learning methods for face mask detection in the era of the COVID-19 pandemic. Measurement **167**, 108288 (2021)

22. Chavda, A., Dsouza, J., Badgujar, S., Damani, A.: Multi-stage CNN architecture for face mask detection. In: 2021 6th International Conference for Convergence in Technology (I2CT), Maharashtra, India, pp. 1–8. IEEE (2021). https://doi.org/10.1109/I2CT51068.2021.9418207

23. Li, C., Cao, J., Zhang, X.: Robust deep learning method to detect face masks. In: Proceedings of the 2nd International Conference on Artificial Intelligence and Advanced Manufacture, Manchester, UK, pp. 74–77. Association for Computing Machinery (2020). https://doi.org/10.1145/3421766.3421768

24. Yu, J., Zhang, W.: Face mask wearing detection algorithm based on improved YOLO-v4. Sensors **21**(9), 3263 (2021). https://doi.org/10.3390/s21093263

25. Kumar, A., Kalia, A., Sharma, A., Kaushal, M.: A hybrid tiny YOLO v4-SPP module based improved face mask detection vision system. J. Ambient Intell. Humaniz. Comput., 1–14 (2021). https://doi.org/10.1007/s12652-021-03541-x

26. Zhang, S., Sun, J., Kang, J., Wang, S.: Research on recognition of faces with masks based on improved neural network. J. Healthc. Eng. **2021**, 1–8 (2021). https://doi.org/10.1155/2021/5169292

27. Woo, S., Park, J., Lee, J.-Y., Kweon, I.S.: CBAM: convolutional block attention module. In: Ferrari, V., Hebert, M., Sminchisescu, C., Weiss, Y. (eds.) ECCV 2018. LNCS, vol. 11211, pp. 3–19. Springer, Cham (2018). https://doi.org/10.1007/978-3-030-01234-2_1

28. Hu, J., Shen, L., Sun, G.: Squeeze-and-excitation networks. In: Proceedings of the IEEE Conference on Computer Vision and Pattern Recognition, pp. 7132–7141 (2018)

29. Fan, X., Jiang, M., Yan, H.: A deep learning based Light-Weight face mask detector with residual context attention and gaussian heatmap to fight against COVID-19. IEEE Access. **9**, 96964–96974 (2021). https://doi.org/10.1109/ACCESS.2021.3095191

30. Zhang, X., Zhou, X., Lin, M., Sun, J.: ShuffleNet: an extremely efficient convolutional neural network for mobile devices. In: 2018 IEEE/CVF Conference on Computer Vision and Pattern Recognition, Salt Lake City, UT, USA, pp. 6848–6856. IEEE (2018)

31. Yang, S., Luo, P., Loy, C.C., Tang, X.: WIDER FACE: A face detection benchmark. In: 2016 IEEE Conference on Computer Vision and Pattern Recognition (CVPR), pp. 5525–5533. IEEE, Las Vegas, NV, USA (2016). https://doi.org/10.1109/CVPR.2016.596

32. Ge, S., Li, J., Ye, Q., Luo, Z.: Detecting masked faces in the wild with LLE-CNNs. In: 2017 IEEE Conference on Computer Vision and Pattern Recognition (CVPR), Honolulu, HI, USA (2017). https://doi.org/10.1109/CVPR.2017.53

33. Deng, J., Guo, J., Zhou, Y., Yu, J., Kotsia, I., Zafeiriou, S.: RetinaFace: single-stage dense face localisation in the wild. arXiv arXiv:1905.00641 (2019)

34. Li, Z.C., Li, H.C., Hu, W.S., Yang, Y.J., Hua, Z.X.: Masked face detection model based on multi-scale attention-driven faster R-CNN. J. Southwest Jiaotong Univ. **56**(5), 1002–1010 (2021)

Analytical Comparison Between the Pattern Classifiers Based upon a Multilayered Perceptron and Probabilistic Neural Network in Parallel Implementation

Katsumi Takahashi, Shunpei Morita, and Tetsuya Hoya[✉]

Department of Computer Engineering, CST, Nihon University, 7-24-1, Narashino-dai, Funabashi, Chiba 274-8501, Japan
houya.tetsuya@nihon-u.ac.jp

Abstract. It is well known that, while the training mode of probabilistic neural network is quickly completed by a straightforward manner of allocating the units in a single hidden layer, its utility in the reference mode is slow in ordinary serial computing situations. In order to alleviate the slow operation, the parallel implementation is thus considered to be a desirable option. In this paper, we first quantify the overall amount of the step-wise operations required for the reference mode of a probabilistic neural network and that of a multilayered perceptron (or deep) neural network, both implemented in a parallel environment. Second, we derive the necessary condition for the reference mode of a probabilistic neural network to yield an equally fast as or faster operation than that of a deep neural network. Based upon the condition so derived, we next deduce a comparative relation between the training mode of a probabilistic neural network, where k-means clustering algorithm is applied to reduce the number of the hidden units, and that of a deep neural network operated in parallel. It is then shown that both the training and testing modes of the compact-sized network meeting these criteria can be run in a parallel environment as fast as or faster than those of a feed-forward deep neural network, while keeping a reasonably high classification performance.

Keywords: Multilayered perceptrons · Deep neural network · Probabilistic neural network · Feed-forward models · Pattern classification · Parallel computing

1 Introduction

To date, it is not too much to say that deep learning (DL) [1] based approaches have been predominant in quite a broader range of the areas relevant to artificial intelligence in both research activity and industrial application wises. In particular, deep neural networks (DNNs) [2] have played a significant role for the development of effective and efficient pattern classification methods in the last several decades.

Many of the DNN approaches are based upon a feed-forward type network, i.e. the so-called multi-layered perceptron neural network (MLP-NN) [3], where all units

© The Author(s), under exclusive license to Springer Nature Switzerland AG 2022
E. Pimenidis et al. (Eds.): ICANN 2022, LNCS 13531, pp. 544–555, 2022.
https://doi.org/10.1007/978-3-031-15934-3_45

have fully-connected interlayer connections. In an MLP-NN, the output of each unit is represented by a sigmoidal activation function. An MLP-NN with multiple hidden layers between its input and output layer is generally termed a 'deep' NN, due to the layer-by-layer basis of cumulative information encoding performed during the training mode. After the training, the encoded data are stored in the form of the varying values within the weighted interlayer connections of an MLP-NN, as well as the units' biases. Normally, these network parameters are iteratively tuned by the use of a stochastic gradient descent method, such as the well-known back-propagation (BP) [3] algorithm, given a set of the training data (i.e. each given as a pair of the input data points and target output values). The feed-forward network structure of an MLP-NN with M_0 input, M_1, M_2, ..., M_P hidden, and M_{P+1} output units can then be expressed as

$$y_j^p = f(\sum_{i=0}^{M_{p-1}} w_{ij}^{p-1} y_i^{p-1}), \quad p = 1, 2, ..., (P+1) \tag{1}$$

where $y_i^0 = 1(i = 0)/x_i(i = 1, 2, ..., M_0)$ and $y_j^{P+1}(j = 0, 1, ..., M_{P+1})$ are the input and output node values (with $y_0^p = 1$, for all p), respectively, w_{ij}^p denote the bias of the j-th hidden or output unit ($i = 0$) or the weight values between a pair of the adjacent layers ($i > 0$), respectively, and f is given by a sigmoidal activation function.

Probabilistic neural network (PNN) [4] is another feed-forward model with normally three-layers (i.e. there is only a single hidden layer between its input and output layer in a PNN) and was specifically proposed for pattern classification tasks. In contrast to an MLP-NN, the activation function of each unit in the hidden layer of a PNN is represented by a radial basis function (RBF) in terms of a Gaussian response function:

$$h(x) = \exp\left(-\frac{\|x - c\|_2^2}{\sigma^2}\right), \tag{2}$$

where $\|...\|_2$ denotes $L2$-norm, $\mathbf{x} = [x_1, x_2, ..., x_L]^T$ is the tap input vector, the vector with the same dimension as the input $\mathbf{c} = [c_1, c_2, ..., c_L]^T$ is called the centroid vector, and σ is the radius unique to all the RBFs. Although the input and hidden layers of a PNN are fully-connected, the interlayer connections in between are all fixed unity, unlike an MLP-NN, whereas the hidden and output layers are partially-connected; each output unit is connected (with, again, the connection weighted unity) *only* to the hidden layer units that belong to the same class represented by the corresponding output unit; the latter leads to an efficient implementation of a parallel computation scheme to be described later. The structure of a PNN for an N-class classification task is expressed by using a pair of (2) and the output activation computed as a normalized linear sum. of the RBFs, i.e.

$$o_k = \frac{1}{\xi} \sum_{j=1}^{m(k)} h_{u_k(j)}(x), \ \xi = \sum_{k=1}^{N} o_k \tag{3}$$

where $u_k(j)$ denote the respective labels of the RBFs, each belonging to Class k (on the assumption that there are $m(k)$ RBFs for Class k). Then, unlike the case of an MLP-NN, the training of a PNN is quite simple and generally completed only in one-pass, i.e. by allocating each training vector to c_j, with an appropriate choice of the value σ.

For either the MLP-NN or PNN case, given an input, a maximal output unit (i.e. obtained by taking a maximum using (1) for the MLP-NN and (3) for the PNN, respectively) will correspond to the final pattern classification result.

The objective of the paper is therefore to compare analytically these two neural network models implemented in parallel computing environment (cf. [5–12]).

2   Implementing an MLP-NN and PNN into Parallel Computing Environment

In the literature, a large number of the studies relevant to the parallel implementation can be found, as represented by the works [5–8] for the MLP-NN and [9–12] for the PNN. For the parallel implementation of these feed-forward network models, either an exemplar- [8, 9] or network-based [7, 10–12] partitioning, or a combination of these two strategies [5, 6] is mostly considered. Since the primary focus of the present work is to compare both the network types of MLP-NN and PNN run in a parallel environment, the network-based partitioning strategy is hereafter only taken into account.

Now, let us begin with the examination of the case where both an MLP-NN with P hidden layers and PNN model are respectively implemented into a parallel computing environment, with the same number of the input and output units i.e. $M_0 = L$ and $M_{P+1} = N$, respectively, without loss of generality, as well as the number of units in a single hidden layer of MLP-NN and that of PNN being equal to each other, i.e.

$$M_p = \sum_{k=1}^{N} m(k) = M. \tag{4}$$

Then, in order to highlight the comparison between the parallel implementation of an MLP-NN and PNN, let us hereafter assume an ideal situation where the factors pertaining to the actual parallel implementation, such as the time taken per arithmetic operation (i.e. addition, division, multiplication, or subtraction), the time for the communication cycles taken between the processing units (PUs), or the operations required to realize a nonlinear (i.e. sigmoidal/exponential) function, can be all negligible, for the comparison purpose. Also, a measurement, termed the time-step (or *step* in short), is introduced in this paper and used conveniently just to count the number of the operational steps required for the implementation in a parallel computing environment.

2.1   Feed-Forward Computation of an MLP-NN in Parallel

For an MLP-NN, the feed-forward manner of operations is performed based upon (1) in both the reference (i.e. testing) and iterative training modes. In (1), for instance, the computation for each unit in the second (i.e. the first hidden) layer y_j^1 can be performed in parallel and is decomposed into the three parts: i.e. i) a total of the $L + 1$ operations of the bias/weight value w_{ij}^0 multiplied by the element x_i, ii) the summation of all those obtained in i), and iii) application of a sigmoidal function to the result obtained from ii).

In view of the parallelism, the unit-wise multiplication operation in i) and application of the nonlinear function in iii) can be respectively performed in parallel, whereas the operation in ii) is carried out only in serial, since it requires all the values obtained in i). In sum, all the multiplication operations of $(L+1) \times M_1$ in i), across all the first M_1 hidden layer units, can be done in parallel (assuming that a total of $(L+1) \times M_1$ PUs are available) and thus take only a single step for these, whereas the summation ii) needs to be carried out serially in $L+1$ plus one more step due to iii) (i.e. regarding that the application of a sigmoidal function to the sum. Value takes a single step). Then, in total, $L+3$ steps for i) - iii) all together are required for each of the first hidden layer units (i.e. assuming that a total of M_1 parallel units are used). Table 1 shows a summary of the feed-forward operations required for the MLP-NN case. Provided that, for simplicity, an MLP-NN has a unique number of the units for all the P hidden layers, i.e. $M_1 = M_2 = \ldots = M_P = M$, the total number of steps S_MLP required for the feed-forward operations in the parallel implementation, given a single set of input data, is eventually expressed as

$$S\_MLP = L + PM + 3(P+1). \tag{5}$$

Table 1. Summary of the feed-forward operations required for an MLP-NN in parallel computing.

Operations required for	Operation per PU	Num. time-steps taken	Num. PUs operated in parallel	#ID
p-th hidden layer	$s_{ij} \leftarrow w_{ij}^{p-1} y_i^{p-1}$	1	$(M_{p-1}+1) \times M_p$	1
	$z_j \leftarrow \sum_{i=0}^{M_{p-1}} s_{ij}$	$M_{p-1}+1$	M_p	2
	$y_j^p = f(z_j)$	1	M_p	3

2.2 Feed-Forward Computation of a PNN in Parallel

For the case of a PNN, the feed-forward operations are performed on the basis of (2) and (3): computing the $L2$-norm in (2) can be performed in both parallel and serial wises; for the parallel counterpart, a subsequent operation of iv) the subtraction between the tap input vector $\mathbf{x}$ and the centroid $\mathbf{c}_j$ followed by v) a single squaring operation for each of the operations take 2 steps, using a total of $L \times M$ parallel processors. For the serial counterpart, in turn, similar to the operation ii) in the above for the MLP-NN case, the summation of the squared values obtained in iv) takes $L+2$ steps all together (i.e. L steps for the summation, one for the division by the negative squared radius value, computed prior to the parallel implementation, and another for the application of the exponential function, using a total of M parallel processors). Thus, the feed-forward operations to compute the output of each hidden layer unit correspond to iv) and v) and require $L+4$ steps.

Table 2. Summary of the feed-forward operations required for a PNN in parallel computing.

Operations required for	Operation per PU	Num. time-steps taken	Num. PUs operated in parallel	#ID
Hidden layer	$s_{ij} \leftarrow x_i - c_j(i)$	1	$L \times M$	1
	$s_{ij} \leftarrow s_{ij}^2$	1	$L \times M$	2
	$z_j \leftarrow \sum_{i=1}^{L} s_{ij}$	L	M	3
	$z_j \leftarrow \left(-\frac{1}{\sigma^2}\right) z_j$	1	M	4
	$h_j = \exp(z_j)$	1	M	5
Output layer	$z_k \leftarrow \sum_{j=1}^{M/N} h_{u_k(j)}(\boldsymbol{x})$	M/N	N	6
	$\xi \leftarrow \xi + z_k$	1	N	7
	$o_k = \frac{1}{\xi} z_k$	1	N	8

On the other hand, each output in (3) has to be, again, computed in a serial mode, owing to the summing operation of the $m(k)$ hidden units' activation (i.e. RBF) values. In a typical situation, the number of the additions required for this summation operation is, however, considered to be much less than that of the MLP-NN case; the summation is computed using *only* the values of the RBFs falling into the same class corresponding to the output unit. Now, let us assume the case where the numbers of the RBFs $m(k)$ are equal to each other across all the classes, i.e. $m(k) = M/N$. Then, the number of the steps required for computing all the output units of a PNN is calculated to be $(M/N) + 2$, by simply summing up the number of steps for all the three operations #6–#8 in Table 2. In sum, the total number of steps S_PNN in terms of the feed-forward operations required by a PNN in the parallelism is expressed as

$$\text{S\_PNN} = L + \frac{M}{N} + 6 \qquad (6)$$

2.3 Comparison of the Reference Mode Between an MLP-NN and PNN

By comparing (6) with (5), provided that the following criterion in terms of the feed-forward operations is met

$$\frac{M_{\text{PNN}}}{N} \leq PM_{\text{MLP}} + 3(P - 1), \qquad (7)$$

where MMLP corresponds to the total number of units in all the hidden layers of an MLP-NN and MPNN the number of the hidden layer units in a PNN, respectively, the reference mode of a PNN can be operated as fast as or faster than that of an MLP-NN, in a parallel environment.

Moreover, since it is considered to be valid that $MMLP >> P$ in most of the situations in practice, by dropping out the second term from (7), we eventually obtain the relation

$$M_{\text{PNN}} \leq NPM_{\text{MLP}}. \tag{8}$$

Then, the relation (8) indicates that the number of the hidden units in a PNN should be less than or equal to the total number of the units in all the hidden layers of an MLP-NN *times* the number of classes, in order to achieve a faster or equally fast reference mode of a PNN, compared to that of an MLP-NN, in a parallel computing environment. In other words, it implies that up to NP times more hidden units than those of the MLP-NN can be recruited within a PNN, while keeping the same or a faster operational speed than that of the MLP-NN.

2.4   Reduction in the Number of the RBFs in a PNN via k-Means Clustering

In the original PNN scheme [4], each of the training data is allocated to the corresponding centroid vector of an RBF, whereas the number of the hidden units in an MLP-NN can be relatively kept small. Hence, to meet the criterion (8) is still considered to be hard, dependent upon the situations.

In practice, in order to eliminate the excessive amount of computational resources due to the redundant allocation or avoid over-fitting to the training data, reduction in the number of the RBFs is normally performed, prior to the utility in the testing mode. To this aim, clustering algorithms such as k-means [13], orthogonal least squares (OLS) [14], the algorithm based upon density-based spatial clustering of applications with noise (DBSCAN) [15], or the method based upon particle swarm optimization (PSO) [16] are well-known. Among many, we consider the k-means case in this paper, as the unsupervised clustering method is relatively simple to implement but yet known to be effective. Next, we treat the reduction in the number of the RBFs by means of applying the k-means clustering algorithm as the training mode of a PNN (cf. [17]), examine the situation where it is performed in a parallel environment, and compare it with the training mode of an MLP-NN. In sum, the k-means clustering algorithm is performed according to the following steps:

Step 1) Initialize the M cluster centers $\mathbf{t}_j$ ($j = 1, 2, ..., M$).
Step 2) For each input vector $\mathbf{x}_i$ ($i = 1, 2, ..., V$), calculate the distance (typically Euclidean one; let us assume applying the $L2$-norm here) between $\mathbf{x}_i$ and each cluster center $\mathbf{t}_j$.
Step 3) For each $\mathbf{x}_i$, identify the closest center based upon the distance calculated in Step 2).
Step 4) Obtain each of the new cluster centers $\mathbf{t}_j$ as the mean of the respective closest input vectors identified in Step 3)
Step 5) If a certain criterion is met (e.g. when there is no change in $\mathbf{t}_j$), output $\mathbf{t}_j$ as the final cluster centers and then terminate. Otherwise, return to Step 2).

For the application to the reduction of the RBFs, given the training data as the input vectors, the resultant cluster centers t_j obtained in Step 5) are directly assigned to the respective centroid vectors of the RBFs in a PNN.

2.5 K-Means Clustering Algorithm Operated in a Parallel Environment

In view of the parallel implementation of the k-means clustering, it is considered that the operations required in Steps 1–4) in the above are separated from each other; the respective operations required for a single iteration in a parallel environment are summarized in Table 3. Since the k-means can be applied independently to a subset per class, the number of PUs can be reduced from V to V/N, provided that the number of training data is the same across all the N classes. In sum, the total number of steps S_KM in terms of the operations required by the k-means clustering algorithm is expressed as

$$S\_KM = L + \max(v) + M + 4 \tag{9}$$

where v denotes the total number of the closest input vectors so identified at an iteration in Step 3). Moreover, the following relation is satisfied:

$$\max(v) \leq \frac{V}{N}. \tag{10}$$

Table 3. Summary of the operations required for performing k-means clustering algorithm at a single iteration in a parallel computing environment.

Operations required for	Operation per PU	Num. time-steps taken	Num. PUs operated in parallel	#ID
Step 1)	t_{jk} (only assignment)	0	$L \times M$	1
Step 2)	$v_{ijk} \leftarrow x_{ik} - t_{jk}$	1	$L \times M \times V$	2
	$v_{ijk} \leftarrow v_{ijk}^2$	1	$L \times M \times V$	3
	$s_{ij} = \sum_{k=1}^{L} v_{ijk}$	L	$M \times V$	4
Step 3)	$q(i) = \arg\min(s_{ij})$	M	V	5
	$\varphi(q(i)) \leftarrow \{\varphi(q(i)), i\}$	1	V	6
Step 4)	$s_{jk} \leftarrow \sum_{n=1}^{v} x_{\varphi(j,n),k}$	$\leq V/N$	$L \times M$	7
	$s_{jk} = s_{jk}/v$	1	$L \times M$	8

2.6 Comparing the Training Mode of an MLP-NN with that of a Compact PNN Obtained Using the k-Means Clustering

During the training mode of an MLP-NN, the feed-forward operations shown in Table 1 are required for a single training vector at every iteration; provided that it has reached the state of a convergence at the I_{MLP}-th iteration in the training mode of an MLP-NN, using a total of V training vectors, the total number of the steps required for the feed-forward operations can be written simply as S_MLP (given by (5)) times $I_{MLP} \times V$, i.e.

$$I_{MLP} \times V \times \text{S\_MLP} = I_{MLP}V[L + PM + 3(P + 1)]. \tag{11}$$

In contrast, for the case of a PNN with reducing the number of the RBFs by means of a parallelly-implemented version of the k-means clustering, provided that the convergence criterion in Step 5) in Sect. 2.4 is met at the I_{KM}-th iteration, the total number of the steps required to obtain a set of final cluster centers can be expressed as

$$I_{KM} \times \text{S\_KM} = I_{KM}[L + \max(v) + M + 4]. \tag{12}$$

In many situations in practice, since the third term in (11) can be relatively smaller, as well as the last two terms in (12) than the other terms, it is considered that the following condition for the training mode of a PNN is eventually derived by omitting these terms from (11) and (12), respectively, and by taking the relation (10) into account, we eventually have

$$I_{KM}\Gamma_1 \le I_{MLP}V\Gamma_2,$$
$$\Gamma_1 = \max(L, \frac{V}{N}), \Gamma_2 = \max(L, PM). \tag{13}$$

Note that the relation above has been derived by only taking the feed-forward propagation of an MLP-NN, without its feed-back counterpart, into account during the training mode, whereas the training a PNN via the k-means is considered to be operated *only* in a feed-forward fashion. Moreover, the relation (13) implies that, in a parallel environment, even in the case where applying the k-means clustering algorithm in order to obtain a compact-sized PNN is considered as the training, the training mode can be completed much faster than that of an MLP-NN, provided that the RBF centroids can be obtained in a relatively small number of the iterations.

3 Empirical Justification of the Criteria (8) and (13)

Since both the criteria (8) and (13) so derived exhibit the necessary conditions on the basis only of the time-step wise operations, it is necessary to justify whether the PNN so obtained to meet these criteria can still achieve a level of the classification performance similar to that of an MLP-NN, while performing the reference mode as fast as the case of using an MLP-NN in the parallel setup; to empirically justify this, we conducted a series of the simulations using 7 publicly available datasets for pattern classification tasks, i.e. 6 obtained from the UCI machine learning repository [18] and another from the MNIST

Table 4. 7 Datasets used for the empirical justifications of the criteria (8) and (13).

Dataset	#Classes (N)	#Training	#Testing	#Features per pattern
abalone	3	2088	2089	8
isolet	26	6238	1559	617
letter-recognition	26	16000	4000	16
MNIST	10	60000	10000	784
optdigits	10	3823	1797	64
pendigits	10	7494	3498	17
wdbc	2	398	171	32

[19]. A summary of the 7 datasets used for the empirical justifications of the criteria (8) and (13) is shown in Table 4.

For the simulations, MLP-NNs with one ($P = 1$) and three ($P = 3$) hidden layers were used, respectively, and their network parameters were trained by applying Adam algorithm [20] with the parameter setting of $\alpha = 0.0001$, $\beta_1 = 0.9$, $\beta_2 = 0.999$, and $\varepsilon = 10^{-8}$, using the Scikit-learn package [21] on Python programming language. For the PNN, the unique radius σ in (2) was varied from 0.1 to 5.0, with the increment of 0.1, and the value yielded best was chosen. For the training of a PNN using the k-means clustering algorithm, since the performance varied with a random seed value given for the initial selection of the cluster centers (i.e. Step 1) in Sect. 2.4; albeit only slightly, i.e. less than 1% for most of the cases), the performance averaged over five different choices of the random value was considered. Similarly, the performance of an MLP-NN averaged over 100 different random network parameter initialization settings during the training mode was considered for the comparison. During the simulation, the performance was compared between the two models, with varying the number of the hidden layer units within both the MLP-NNs and PNN; by following the criterion (8), the number of the hidden layer units in a PNN was set as $M_{PNN} = NPM_{MLP}$, in order to see whether a performance similar to that of the MLP-NN can be achieved by a PNN. Table 5 summarizes the simulation results.

As shown in Table 5, the number of the hidden layer units in MLP-NNs/PNN was varied from an extremely small one to that around less than a half of the training data (i.e. the numbers shown in italic). It is noticeable that the classification rates with a very small number of the hidden units in the MLP-NNs were sometimes quite low, whereas those obtained using the PNN were consistently higher than those of the MLP-NNs, for all but the wdbc case. The former is considered so, due to either the numerical instability (such as slow convergence or stuck in local minima) occurred during training the MLP-NN or the failure in terms of the information encoding because of the insufficient number of the hidden units. For a relatively large number of the hidden units, it is, in contrast, observed that the overall classification performance obtained by the PNN was somewhat better, or slightly lower, if any (up to 2.2% of the performance degradation), than that of the MLP-NN, except the wdbc case with relatively small numbers of M_{PNN} (< 80) for $P = 1$. From these observations, it is said that the criterion (8) can be met, on the whole.

Table 5. Summary of the simulation results.

Dataset		Classification rates (%) with varying the number of hidden layer units M_{PNN} (=NPM_{MLP})							I_{MLP}/I_{KM} avg. (min, max)
abalone	(P = 1)	*3*	*15*	*30*	*150*	*300*			
	MLP	41.0	51.6	52.6	54.5	54.6			199 (25, 682)
	PNN	**56.4**	54.8	**58.8**	**55.6**	**55.6**			**10** (1, 40)
	(P = 3)	*9*	*45*	*90*	*450*	*900*			
	MLP	35.6	51.9	55.3	**59.2**	58.8			145 (33, 458)
	PNN	**55.3**	**56.5**	**55.4**	52.2	55.6			**9** (2, 24)
isolet	(P = 1)	*26*	*130*	*260*	*1300*	*2600*			
	MLP	18.8	82.4	91.9	**95.5**	95.7			138 (22, 779)
	PNN	**87.4**	**93.3**	**93.9**	94.3	93.8			**4** (1, 24)
	(P = 3)	*78*	*390*	*780*	*2340*	*3900*			
	MLP	8.7	76.1	89.5	**94.2**	**94.6**			105 (17, 516)
	PNN	**92.6**	**93.9**	**93.9**	93.9	93.9			**4** (1, 30)
letter-recog.	(P = 1)	*26*	*130*	*260*	*1300*	*2600*	*5200*	*7800*	
	MLP	15.6	65.0	77.9	92.9	94.8	**95.9**	**96.3**	803 (427, 1351)
	PNN	**56.2**	**72.6**	**82.7**	**93.7**	**95.0**	95.6	96.0	**6** (1, 34)
	(P = 3)	*78*	*390*	*780*	*3900*	*7800*			
	MLP	7.7	58.8	79.1	94.7	96.0			404 (24, 939)
	PNN	**65.0**	**86.9**	**92.2**	**95.4**	96.0			**7** (1, 45)
MNIST	(P = 1)	*10*	*50*	*100*	*500*	*1000*			
	MLP	26.7	81.0	91.1	**96.6**	**97.4**			127 (16, 287)
	PNN	**82.0**	**90.9**	**93.1**	95.5	96.1			**29** (1, 92)
	(P = 3)	*30*	*150*	*300*	*1500*	*3000*			
	MLP	15.4	80.4	91.8	**97.1**	**97.6**			127 (15, 410)
	PNN	**88.9**	**93.3**	**95.2**	96.3	96.7			**34** (7, 102)
optdigits	(P = 1)	*10*	*50*	*100*	*500*	*1000*	*2000*	*3000*	
	MLP	37.1	91.4	95.2	96.4	96.7	96.8	96.9	250 (112, 670)
	PNN	**89.4**	**96.0**	**97.2**	**97.9**	**98.2**	**98.2**	**98.2**	**5** (1, 23)
	(P = 3)	*30*	*150*	*300*	*1500*	*3000*			
	MLP	21.6	89.3	94.0	96.4	96.7			336 (53,1523)
	PNN	**94.1**	**97.3**	**97.5**	**98.3**	98.2			**7** (1, 47)
pendigits	(P = 1)	*10*	*50*	*100*	*500*	*1000*	*2000*	*3000*	
	MLP	41.3	92.1	**95.7**	97.2	97.3	97.4	97.4	257 (130, 567)
	PNN	**77.8**	**92.9**	95.6	97.2	**97.4**	**97.6**	**97.7**	**8** (1, 39)
	(P = 3)	*30*	*150*	*300*	*1500*	*3000*			
	MLP	21.9	90.5	95.9	97.3	97.4			351 (33, 1311)
	PNN	**90.7**	**96.5**	**96.9**	**97.5**	**97.7**			**12** (2, 65)
wdbc	(P = 1)	*2*	*10*	*20*	*80*	*140*	*200*		
	MLP	**92.6**	**96.1**	95.9	94.8	94.5	94.4		577 (396, 826)
	PNN	70.8	88.3	93.2	**96.3**	**96.6**	**96.9**		**4** (1, 13)
	(P = 3)	*6*	*30*	*60*	*180*	*300*			
	MLP	72.6	**95.0**	93.6	93.7	94.5			608 (12, 2705)
	PNN	**82.5**	94.4	**95.5**	**97.0**	**96.9**			**5** (1, 20)

On the other hand, as shown in the last column in Table 5, the number of the iterations I_{KM} for the PNN with k-means case (i.e. averaged over the five different seed value combinations) was much smaller than that of I_{MLP} for the MLP-NN, for all the cases using the 7 datasets, resulting in the empirical justification of the criterion (13).

4   Conclusion

In this paper, we have made a comparison between the pattern classifiers based upon a compact-sized PNN obtained using k-means clustering algorithm and an MLP-NN with its multiple hidden layers, by way of the analysis on the step-wise operations required for the parallel implementation. Through the analysis, the two criteria (8) and (13) have been eventually derived, for the reference mode of a PNN to be performed as fast as or faster than that of an MLP-NN, assuming an ideal situation where the processing units working in parallel, necessary to meet these criteria, are all available. Then, these criteria have been empirically shown to be valid via the simulation study using 7 publicly available real-world datasets for pattern classification tasks. In the artificial neural network community, it has long been a general consensus that the slow reference mode of PNN is a bottleneck and thus hinders its application in practice. However, the present work reveals that such drawback can be removed, once implemented in a parallel computing environment. Moreover, as seen in the simulation study, the degrees of freedom for training the PNN as in this paper (i.e. three; a random seed value for the initialization of the centers for the k-means, σ, and M_{PNN}) are less than a half of that for the MLP-NN case (seven, i.e. α, β_1, β_2, ε, M_{MLP}, P, and the initialization manner of the network parameters); a pattern classifier based upon the PNN is simpler to design. Thereby, the PNN approach even has the potential to surpass the currently dominating DL approaches in the pattern recognition domain. Future work is directed to the investigation of the cases where larger and/or more complex datasets are used and performance comparison of these two models in an actual parallel environment.

References

1. LeCun, Y., Bengio, Y., Hinton, G.: Deep learning. Nature **521**, 436–444 (2015)
2. Schmidhuber, J.: Deep learning in neural networks: an overview. Neural Netw. **61**, 85–117 (2015)
3. Rumelhart, D.E., Hinton, G.E., Williams, R.J.: Learning internal representations by error propagation. In: Rumelhart, D.E., McClelland, J.L. (eds.) Parallel Distributed Processing, vol. 1, pp. 318–362. MIT Press, Cambridge (1986)
4. Specht, D.F.: Probabilistic neural networks. Neural Netw. **3**, 109–118 (1990)
5. Azema-Barac, M.E.: A conceptual framework for implementing neural networks on massively parallel machines. In: 6th International Parallel Processing Symposium, pp. 527–530 (1992)
6. Pethick, M., Liddle, M., Werstein, P., Huang, Z., Parallelization of a backpropagation neural network on a cluster computer. In: 15th IASTED International Conference on Parallel and Distributed Computing and Systems, CA, USA, pp. 574–582. ACTA Press (2003)
7. Suresh, S., Omkar, S.N., Mani, V.: Parallel implementation of back-propagation algorithm in networks of workstations. IEEE Trans. Parallel Distrib. Syst. **16**(1), 24–34 (2005)

8. Turchenko, V., Golovko, V.: Parallel batch pattern training algorithm for deep neural network. In: International Conference on High Performance Computing & Simulation (HPCS), pp. 697–702 (2014)

9. Secretan, J., Georgiopoulos, M., Maidhof, I., Shibly, P., Hecker, J.: Methods for parallelizing the probabilistic neural network on a Beowulf cluster computer. In: IEEE International Joint Conference on Neural Network, pp. 2378–2385 (2006)

10. Bastke, S., Deml, M., Schmidt, S.: Combining statistical network data, probabilistic neural networks and the computational power of GPUs for anomaly detection in computer networks. In: 19th International Conference on Automated Planning and Scheduling, Workshop on Intelligent Security (SecArt 2009), Thessaloniki, Greece (2009)

11. Kokkinos, Y., Margaritis, K.: A parallel radial basis probabilistic neural network for scalable data mining in distributed memory machines. In: IEEE 24th International Conference on Tools with Artificial Intelligence, pp. 1094–1099 (2012)

12. Phaudphut, C., So-In, C., Phusomsai, W.: A parallel probabilistic neural network ECG recognition architecture over GPU platforms. In: 13th International Joint Conference on Computer Science and Software Engineering (JCSSE), pp. 1–7 (2016)

13. MacQueen, J.B.: Some methods for classification and analysis of multivariate observations. In: 5th Berkeley Symposium on Mathematical Statistics and Probability, pp. 281–297 (1967)

14. Chen, S., Grant, P.M., Cowan, C.F.N.: Orthogonal least squares algorithm for training multi-output radial basis function networks. In: Second International Conference on Artificial Neural Networks, pp. 336–339 (1991)

15. Bessrour, M., Elouedi, Z., Lefevre, E.: E-DBSCAN: an evidential version of the DBSCAN method. In: IEEE Symposium - Series on Computational Intelligence (SSCI-2020), pp. 3073–3080 (2020)

16. Luo, W., Zhu, W., Ni, L., Qiao, Y., Yuan, Y.: SCA2: novel efficient swarm clustering algorithm. IEEE Trans. Emerg. Top. Comput. Intell. **5**(3), 442–456 (2021)

17. Kusy, M., Kluska, J.: Assessment of prediction ability for reduced probabilistic neural network in data classification problems. Soft Comput. **21**(1), 199–212 (2016). https://doi.org/10.1007/s00500-016-2382-9

18. Dua D., Graff, G.: UCI machine learning repository, School of Information and Computer Sciences, Univ. California Irvine, Irvine, CA (2019). https://archive.ics.uci.edu/ml

19. LeCun, Y., Cortes, C., Burges, C.J.C.: The MNIST database. http://yann.lecun.com/exdb/mnist/. Accessed Jan 2022

20. Kingma, D., Lei Ba, J.: Adam: a method for stochastic optimization. In: Third International Conference on Learning Representations, San Diego, arXiv:1412.6980 (2015)

21. Pedregosa, F., et al.: Scikit-learn: machine learning in Python. J. Mach. Learn. Res. **12**, 2825–2830 (2011)

Architecture-Agnostic Time-Step Boosting: A Case Study in Short-Term Load Forecasting

Ioannis Pierros[✉][iD] and Ioannis Vlahavas[iD]

Aristotle University of Thessaloniki, 54124 Thessaloniki, Greece
{ipierros,vlahavas}@csd.auth.gr

Abstract. Time series forecasting is important for short-term operations planning and deciding the long-term growth strategy of a company. High accuracy is clearly the hardest challenge, though fast training is also important because a model can go through thousands of iterations. In this paper, we propose Time-Step Boosting, a streamlined methodology that can be applied to any type of neural network for demand forecasting, that adjusts the model's weights during training to optimize it towards the time steps that are most difficult to predict. First, we calculate the time step error and afterwards train the model anew using the errors as weights when calculating the loss during training. We apply Time-Step Boosting on short-term demand forecasting, a task that is necessary for the smooth operation of all components in the energy sector. Deviations require costly emergency actions to reset the production-demand balance and avoid damaging the substations or even overloading the electrical grid. Even though forecasting systems have advanced in recent years, they oftentimes fail to accurately predict the peaks and lows which admittedly are of utmost importance. Our methodology demonstrates considerable convergence speed and forecasting performance improvements on next-day hourly load forecasting for multiple European countries and 6 states of the U.S. with Multilayer Perceptrons, Long-Short Term Memory networks, Convolutional Neural Networks and state-of-the-art models, showcasing its applicability on more complex architectures.

Keywords: Machine learning · Time series · Forecasting · Neural networks · Energy demand · Short-term load forecasting

1 Introduction

Short-term load forecasting (STLF) is necessary for the smooth operation of all components in the energy sector, from the generation and transmission

This research was carried out as part of the project KMP6-0072250 under the framework of the Action "Investment Plans of Innovation" of the Operational Program "Central Macedonia 2014–2020", that is co-funded by the European Regional Development Fund and Greece.

of electricity to its distribution and consumption. Failure to correctly forecast the demand and especially under-forecasting it, requires emergency actions that come with a significant cost, while large differentials between forecast and demand can even lead to blackouts. On the other hand, overestimating the energy demand elicits an overproduction of electricity, which, besides the unnecessary costs of producing unused electricity, also risks overloading the electrical grid and damaging its components. Such a scenario results in load shedding and cutting off production from renewable energy sources (RES) because shutting down (or starting up) a conventional power plant is considerably time consuming.

STLF, combined with RES forecasting, are integral to European Union's envisioned fully-integrated internal energy market and the proposed goal of 40% share of RES [5]. From a company's financial perspective, accurate forecasting is essential for its effective participation in the energy markets. It helps inform the bid, avoiding harsh fines for deviations and costs for balancing the supply-demand, thus maximizing profits. This is applicable for both energy/RES energy producers and suppliers, who are under obligation of physical delivery on the next day. Furthermore, the rapidly increasing penetration of RES in the energy mix will introduce considerable fluctuations in the electricity power and frequency, making accurate forecasting of energy production from RES, a necessity.

A common forecasting scheme is the hourly prediction of the electricity demand for the next full day. A certain offset period is inadvertently inserted between the last available historical values that are used as input and the first time step that is forecasted. The offset depends on the closing time of the bidding in the energy market and the delay introduced from the time of the measurement and until the data becomes available. Traditionally, suppliers have to go to the physical location of the measurement box every couple months to get the reading, though smart meters with remote monitoring capabilities can significantly reduce the delay to a few hours or minutes. Another offset that must be considered is introduced from external information providers such as weather forecasting agencies, a common type of exogenous features that is typically used in the energy domain and significantly improves the accuracy of forecasts.

Leaving aside non-linearities and fluctuations caused by sudden changes in weather patterns, another difficult point to forecast are the peaks and dips of a daily signal. Specifically, the daily electricity demand usually includes 2 peaks, one in mid-morning when everyone is working and another one in the afternoon when people are coming back home. Accurately predicting the timing and level of these peaks, which depends on multiple factors such as working habits, weather, and holidays, usually implies an overall increased forecasting performance.

State of the art forecasting models have become quite good at properly modelling interactions between weather conditions and energy demand. Nonetheless, they still struggle at determining when the energy demand peaks and dips and at what levels. These points of change can be more important than the time intervals in-between where the energy signal gradually increases or decreases, yet they are mostly overlooked. Another critical component of training a neural network is the required time to do so. Training time requirements can add up to days or even weeks, therefore it is desirable to keep the convergence speed as high as possible.

In this paper, we propose a new methodology, coined Time-Step Boosting, that optimizes the model's weights by estimating the forecasting error for each time step in the horizon. During subsequent training it uses it as loss weights so that the model will focus on improving the time steps where it struggles the most. When training multiple variations of a neural model during hyperparameter optimization only the error weights of the first iteration are necessary. We evaluated the proposed Time-Step boosting technique using hourly electricity demand data from European countries (ENTSOE data set) and from 6 states of the U.S. (ISONE data set). Similarly, it can be applied to water demand, retail sales, traffic flow, etc., that have a set horizon. Models were trained with/without Time-Step Boosting and compared in terms of convergence speed and accuracy, showcasing that they indeed benefit from the application of the technique.

The remainder of the paper is structured as follows: Sect. 2 provides a mathematical foundation for the forecasting task and briefly reviews different forecasting schemes and the use of errors as an input to the model in recent works. Section 3 describes Time-Step boosting, how it is calculated and for which forecasting schemes it can be applied. Section 4 defines the framework for the empirical evaluations, the data sets that were used, and presents the final results that showcase improvements in convergence speed and accuracy when Time-Step Boosting is applied. Finally, Sect. 5 summarizes the derived conclusions and outlines possible future directions.

2   Related Works

The forecasting task can be formulated as a function F that takes N+1 input sequences $\mathbf{x_i}$ and calculates a single output sequence $\mathbf{y}$ ($\mathbf{x_0}$ are historical values of $\mathbf{y}$, the rest $\mathbf{x_i}$ are exogenous features). For predetermined history window W, horizon H and taking possible offsets, p_w history offset and p_h future offset into account, the forecasting task is given by:

$$\mathbf{y} \in \mathbb{R}^{H,p_h} = [y_{T+p_h+1}, y_{T+p_h+2}, \dots, y_{T+p_h+H}]$$

$$X = \mathbf{x_i} \in \mathbb{R}^{W,p_w} = [y^i_{T-p_w-W}, \dots, y^i_{T-p_w}]$$

$$\hat{\mathbf{y}}_{T+p_h|H,p_w} = F(X)$$

where $\hat{\mathbf{y}}$ denotes the values of the forecasted time steps. In this context, function F is the neural network which can commonly be a Fully Connected network (MLP), a Convolutional Neural Network (CNN) or a Long Short-Term Memory network (LSTM), though usually a combination is used.

The choice of the history window, horizon and the offsets can guide the selection process of the forecasting scheme. The two typical strategies for multi-step-ahead forecasting are the Recursive and the Multi-Input Multi-Output (MIMO) strategies [6]. In the Recursive strategy, each predicted time step is fed as input for the next time step, until the full horizon is forecasted, thus allowing for forecasts of varying lengths. However, applying a Recursive strategy can complicate the implementation details when offsets are present. On the other hand, models that follow the MIMO strategy can integrate inter-dependencies between each time step in the horizon by producing forecasts for all the time steps at once. An additional advantage is avoiding compounding errors that can arise in the Recursive strategy. Therefore, unless a varying horizon is important for the forecasting task at hand, a MIMO strategy should be considered.

A mixture of forecasting schemes and methodologies can be found in recent literature for STLF. Load data from a distribution network in Cuba were used to train autoregressive integrated moving average (ARIMA) models to forecast the load of the next day in [10]. Daily and weekly seasonalities were removed by decomposing the time series and Particle Swarm Optimization was employed to select the best performing ARIMA model for each hour of the day, creating an ensemble of ARIMA models. White noise was added in [4] to evaluate its impact on ARIMA parameter estimation and their overall robustness, concluding that it remains stable for up to 20% noise to signal ratio.

Similarly, separate MLP models were trained for each hour of the day in [3], using a multi-input scheme with the load and temperature of the past 24 h and of the same hour for the previous 4 weeks and 6 months, as well as the one hot encoding for season, weekends and holidays. Afterwards, the output of each model was concatenated to a full day and passed to a deep learning model employing residual connections with different skipping lengths. In [13], the authors considered a recursive strategy where a Radial Basis Function (RBF) network used the prediction error as feedback during the forecasting of the next step to increase the accuracy of the predictions. More recently, [2] proposed employing multi-rate input sampling of the input signal and recovering the original output sampling rate using hierarchical interpolation to forecast time series over long horizons. Stacked MLP blocks with residual connections were used for each sampling rate and it was suggested that the sampling rates either increase exponentially or match known seasonality cycles (daily, weekly, etc.).

Renowned for their performance in forecasting are Recurrent Neural Networks (RNNs) and CNNs. An in-depth overview of RNN variants (LSTM being one) and popular architectures was carried out by [1]. Following a notably extensive comparison against exponential smoothing and ARIMA, they concluded that RNNs are competitive alternatives for time series with homogeneous seasonal components. Additionally, CNNs have proved strong candidates for time series forecasting tasks as they are exceptional at extracting temporal patterns and correlations between multivariate time series. Combinations of RNNs and CNNs have also been proposed, such as [9] who used a CNN layer to extract short and long term patterns, an autoregressive component to adjust the signal's scale, and an RNN layer utilizing a Skip Connection to generate the prediction.

3   Time-Step Boosting

Neural networks forecasting electricity consumption routinely struggle with determining the timing and magnitude of peaks and dips. In the case of energy demand, this occurs around the 11 am and 5 pm peaks (shown in the next section). Even though losses such as the Mean Squared Error (MSE) negate this problem to a certain degree by enlarging the largest errors, they still struggle when forecasting slightly longer horizons because error peaks are smoothed out.

In this paper, we propose Time-Step Boosting, a technique that can be used when repeatedly training a model, for example during hyperparameter optimization, or training different models for similar data sets. As an example, European countries generally follow a similar style of living centered around an 8–9 h working schedule, therefore the error patterns are expected to be similar.

The Time-Step Boosting technique works as follows. First, a model is trained on a forecasting task with a set horizon, in this case 24 h. Next, the model is evaluated against the validation set and the forecasting error is calculated per time step. Afterwards, the model's loss is adjusted to use the time step errors as weights and multiply the loss per time step. The time step weights can be saved and used repeatedly for subsequent training of different models.

Consider N forecasts $\hat{Y}$ over a 24-h horizon validation set (offsets are omitted to avoid cluttering the equations):

$$\hat{\mathbf{y}}_{T|24} = \begin{bmatrix} \hat{y}^1_{T+1} & \cdots & \hat{y}^1_{T+24} \\ \vdots & \ddots & \vdots \\ \hat{y}^N_{T+1} & \cdots & \hat{y}^N_{T+24} \end{bmatrix},$$

then, the average error per time step can be calculated as:

$$W^t_{time-step} = \{\frac{1}{N}\sum_{i=1}^{N}(y^i_t - \hat{y}^i_t)^2, t = 1, \ldots, 24\} \tag{1}$$

Afterwards, the Time-Step error is normalized to [a,1], where $a \geq 0$ is a small value close to 0. Finally, the Time-Step errors are used as weights for the respective time step and the MSE loss during training becomes:

$$MSE = \frac{1}{H}\sum_{t=1}^{H}(y_t - \hat{y}_t)^2 * W^t_{timestep} \tag{2}$$

Time-Step Boosting is loss-agnostic, meaning that it can be applied to all commonly used losses that include some sort of function averaging over the forecasted values, regardless of architecture. Though it is suggested that parameter a is selected to be greater than 0, selecting $a = 0$ will still work by association as the model will learn to forecast the other time steps of the time series.

4   Experimental Evaluation

Time-Step Boosting was evaluated on load data from two data sets; the European Network for Transmission System Operators for Electricity (ENTSOE) and the Independent System Operator New England (ISONE) [7,11]. The ENTSOE data set is complemented with weather data from NASA's Modern-Era Retrospective Analysis for Research and Applications, Version 2 (MERRA-2) [12], which incorporates information regarding ice sheets in the North and South poles and the interactions with other physical processes in the climate system.

Forecasts are produced every day at 6 p.m. for the next full day using data of the previous 24 h. Time-Step Boosting is tested on MLP, CNN and LSTM models. For each architecture configuration the respective model is trained and evaluated. Afterwards, the average error per time step (Eq. 1) is calculated, the model's weights are reset to the initial pre-trained weights and the model is retrained using the time-step-weighted MSE loss (Eq. 2). Both models are trained on the same data set using the same training regime and for the same number of epochs. Finally, a comparison of the models' improvement over time as well as their final performance evaluation on the validation set is made.

4.1 Data Sets and Preprocessing

The ENTSOE data set includes hourly energy load data from 32 Transmission System Operators of European countries [11], who are required to publish information and data regarding the generation, load, transmission, and balancing. There are 43824 values spanning 5 years, from 2015 and until 2019, for each country. The MERRA-2 data set [12] comprises of hourly temperature, direct radiation energy and diffused radiation energy data for 19 European countries since 1980, though only the overlapping 2015–2019 period was used. The first semester of 2019 was reserved for the validation and the last for the testing.

The distribution of the electricity demand in Greece for 2015–2019 is displayed in Fig. 1, where a few hourly, daily, and monthly patterns can be discerned with ease. On an hourly level, demand peaks late in the morning around 11 am when everyone is working, dips for a few hours and quickly increases again late in the afternoon around 5 pm. The highest variance, which is harder to forecast, occurs in the early afternoon. On a monthly level the peak electricity demand coincides with the warmest and coldest months. Sudden peaks in June, July and August are primarily correlated with heatwaves. On the other hand, the daily patterns indicate comparable electricity demand regardless of the day with a minor exception for the weekend days when demand is slightly reduced.

The ISONE data set [7] is comprised of the electricity demand, dry-bulb temperature and dew-point temperature for 6 U.S. states: Maine, New Hampshire, Vermont, Connecticut, Rhode Island, and Massachusetts. All variables are at an hourly resolution. Due to its significant size, Massachusetts is further broken down to Southeast, West/Central, and Northeast. The data set ranges from 2003 to 2017 and has a total of 131496 entries, however only the last 5 years were used in the experiments to cover the same period as the ENTSOE data set.

The daily mean electricity demand in 2015 is displayed in Fig. 2, which follows similar patterns for all 6 states. The variance of the signal's amplitude between each state throughout the months can be explained by the geographical location, spatial weather conditions, the population and the general socioeconomic situation, at least to a certain degree.

An analysis was conducted to find missing values and determine the appropriate imputation approach that would preserve the periodicities and correctly

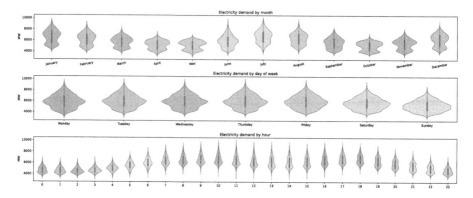

Fig. 1. Distribution of electricity demand in Greece, 2015–2019. Top: electricity demand by month. Middle: electricity demand by week. Bottom: electricity demand by hour

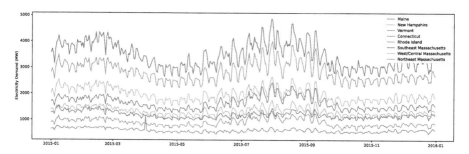

Fig. 2. Daily electricity demand for the New England region (USA) in 2015. States are annotated with different colors. Massachusetts is broken down to 3 areas.

impute peaks and dips, depending on the number of consecutive missing values. In ISONE there are only a couple missing values, therefore it is trivial to interpolate them using the adjacent hours without introducing significant noise. On the other hand, there are 44261 missing values in the ENTSOE energy data set across all countries, though Cyprus and Ukraine account for 41077 of them.

Countries that have only 1 and 2 missing values respectively, such as Germany and The Netherlands, can be filled in naively using adjacent values. Some countries like France and Greece have periods of more consecutive missing values, so imputation is done using the values of the previous/next day or week, for the same hour that is being filled in. Finally, in cases of even longer periods of consecutive missing values, for example Czech Republic which has 100 consecutive missing values in some cases, attempting to impute them would be extremely hard. In those cases, the time series is split in two parts so that the first part ends where the period of missing values starts, and the second part begins where the period of missing values ends. Further preprocessing is applied separately on each part, and they are concatenated before training.

4.2   Experiments and Results

The basic architecture design was a neural network layer that was repeated one or more times, with added Dropout layers in-between that had a small constant dropout rate of 0.1. The neural network layer was selected from an MLP, a CNN or an LSTM layer. A final Fully Connected (FC) layer with linear activation was used to produce the requested 24-h forecast. For MLPs and CNNs, hidden layers ranged between 1 to 5 layers, while the hidden units were selected from [24, 100, 300]. Architectures with CNN layers included a GlobalMaxPooling layer before the final FC layer, to reduce the dimensionality of the computed data. Furthermore, kernel size was either 2 or 3, as having a longer kernel size would be impractical due to the 24-h time step input. On the other hand, architectures with LSTM layers were limited up to 3 hidden layers and 100 hidden units, because more hidden layers or hidden units significantly increased the required training time without improving the model's performance noticeably.

A Stochastic Gradient Descent optimizer was used for calculating the gradients when training the model. The learning rate was configured between 0.1 and 0.000001, while the momentum was set either as the same value as the learning rate or at one tenth (1/10 * learning rate). The Nesterov accelerated gradient variation was chosen over the classical momentum as it often achieved a better convergence rate. Additionally, the choice of SGD over Adam, two of the most common optimizers, was made to take advantage of the greater generalization performance of the first compared to the later and the more stable training [8].

Two evaluation metrics were used in the experiments of this paper to report the results, Root Mean Squared Error (RMSE) and Mean Average Percentage Error (MAPE), both commonly used in time series forecasting tasks. The squared error in RMSE essentially highlights larger differences between forecasted and actual value and the root ensures it remains at the original scale. On the other hand, MAPE is a scale independent metric that allows for easy comparison across different data sets or time series with different scales.

The diagrams in Fig. 3 present the gradual reduction of the MSE on the validation set during training on the ENTSOE data set for the MLP, LSTM and CNN models variations. The "weighted" variation is for the model where the Time-Step Boosting technique is applied. Comparing the two evaluation curves, one can observe that the weighted model converges faster than the normal one, quickly reaching a good approximation at around 25 epochs, while the normal model had to be trained for 100 epochs (4x) for the LSTM or 250+ epochs (10x) for the MLP and the CNN until it reached a similar performance.

Generally, at the end of the training scheme the weighted model variation outperformed the other one by a small margin most of the time. However, there were cases, such as the LSTM in the middle of Fig. 3, where Time-Step Boosting helped the model escape the local minima and further improve its forecasting accuracy by up to 40%. This could be attributed to technique's capacity to focusing the model's attention on the correct source of forecasting error.

From a hyperparameter search perspective, the best RMSE and MAPE performance scores for each model type are listed in Table 1 for both the normal

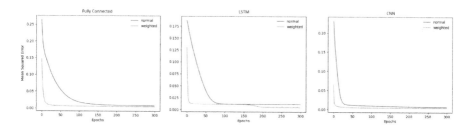

Fig. 3. Mean Squared Error evaluation during training on the validation set. FC: 5 layers, 300 units. LSTM: 5 layers, 100 units. CNN: 2 layers, 24 filters, kernel size 2.

and weighted variations. Generally, a learning rate of 0.01 was proven to be optimal for training the models, as a smaller learning rate often failed to converge. Overall, the best forecasting accuracy was achieved by a CNN model of 2 layers with 300 filters of kernel size 3. Nonetheless, satisfactory performance was also achieved with LSTM and MLP models.

Of interest to note, are the dissimilarities between normal and weighted models. MLPs and CNNs were slightly improved with the application of Time-Step Boosting, while LSTMs' accuracy almost doubled. Table 2 provides a performance report for the most accurate MLP, CNN, and LSTM models for each country. The accuracy varies between countries, though it seems that is especially true for countries with low electricity consumption on average, which results in the MAPE exploding. Overall, the application of Time-Step Boosting provided significant performance improvements.

The experiments were repeated on the ISONE data set (Table 4). The hyperparameter search space remained the same as the first study with the same arrangement of MLP, CNN and LSTM neural networks. The findings are indeed similar as before and confirm the superiority of the Time-Step Boosting technique. Cases with already low evaluation score, such as Vermont (VT), see negligible improvements, as the performance improvement is greater when the evaluation error is initially higher. Training the weighted models was also faster for most combinations.

Table 1. Combinations with highest performing models on the ENTSOE data set. Performance for weighted models is reported on the right side of the slash "/".

Layers	Units	RMSE			MAPE		
		MLP	LSTM	CNN	MLP	LSTM	CNN
2	300	463/**419**	794/**441**	469/**418**	.062/**.057**	.1098/**.059**	.0635/**.056**
1	300	466/**418**	821/**457**	465/**416**	.062/**.056**	.1125/**.062**	.0628/**.055**
2	100	492/**430**	800/**465**	471/**420**	.065/**.058**	.1095/**.062**	.0635/**.056**
5	300	493/**435**	823/**472**	466/**418**	.065/**.059**	.1133/**.063**	.0630/**.056**
2	24	539/**446**	805/**489**	542/**429**	.071/**.060**	.1083/**.066**	.0730/**.057**

Table 2. Best performing models on the ENTSOE data set. Performance for the weighted models is reported on the right side of the slash "/".

Country	RMSE			MAPE		
	MLP	LSTM	CNN	MLP	LSTM	CNN
AT	823/**678**	1096/**985**	1055/**755**	.091/**.079**	.121/**.113**	.117/**.090**
BE	778/**653**	1031/**771**	1066/**721**	.065/**.055**	.088/**.067**	.092/**.062**
CH	652/**526**	1243/**641**	890/**636**	.082/**.065**	.155/**.080**	.115/**.082**
DE	6230/**4855**	7017/**6491**	7176/**5865**	.092/**.075**	.107/**.101**	.111/**.093**
DK	362/**304**	571/**423**	483/**407**	.076/**.066**	.118/**.092**	.103/**.090**
EE	83/**71**	169/**113**	155/**80**	.070/**.062**	.150/**.101**	.136/**.072**
ES	2459/**1923**	2776/**2622**	2949/**2271**	.072/**.056**	.081/**.079**	.085/**.069**
FI	532/**480**	1650/**698**	1595/**625**	.043/**.040**	.147/**.054**	.139/**.050**
FR	4683/**3971**	10528/**4799**	10444/**4195**	.071/**.062**	.168/**.076**	.169/**.066**
GR	473/**414**	713/**572**	805/**460**	.063/**.055**	.095/**.076**	.110/**.062**
HR	166/**142**	220/**207**	224/**164**	.065/**.057**	.085/**.081**	.086/**.064**
HU	399/**345**	501/**454**	537/**388**	.065/**.058**	.084/**.077**	.086/**.065**
IT	4438/**3816**	5085/**4960**	5213/**4169**	.111/**.095**	.130/**.127**	.133/**.107**
LV	68/**58**	103/**80**	97/**70**	.064/**.058**	.099/**.081**	.096/**.071**
NL	1276/**1024**	1774/**1490**	1695/**1277**	.083/**.067**	.116/**.101**	.109/**.082**
PL	1981/**1627**	2242/**2134**	2319/**1873**	.085/**.072**	.099/**.097**	.101/**.086**
PT	537/**446**	652/**604**	678/**521**	.078/**.066**	.093/**.090**	.094/**.078**
SI	163/**138**	193/**178**	200/**158**	.094/**.087**	.114/**.109**	.118/**.096**
SK	247/**198**	335/**264**	346/**225**	.060/**.048**	.082/**.068**	.084/**.057**

Table 3. Forecasting accuracy using the model proposed by [3]. Performance for the weighted models is reported on the right side of the slash "/".

RMSE	MAPE	Units
848/**481**	.121/**.066**	300
832/**499**	.117/**.068**	100
860/**514**	.122/**.069**	10

When comparing performances between the ENTSOE and the ISONE data sets, it becomes apparent that all models that were trained on ISONE achieve worse accuracy. We consider two explanations as most probable. The first is that the dry and wet bulb temperature features are lacking, perhaps due to the size of the areas or maybe because the data collection procedure was subpar. The other possible explanation is that the direct radiation feature that was used in the previous experiments actually carries a lot of important information. Unfortunately, it is not available in the ISONE data set.

Table 4. Best performing hyperparameters on the ISONE data set. Performance for the weighted models is reported on the right side of the slash "/".

Area code	Model	RMSE	MAPE	No layers	No units
ISONE	MLP	1303/**1058**	.079/**.064**	5	300
	CNN	1818/**1649**	.117/**.104**	5	300
	LSTM	2119/**1860**	.124/**.111**	2	100
CT	MLP	327/**256**	.077/**.061**	5	300
	CNN	469/**412**	.120/**.104**	1	100
	LSTM	580/**473**	.135/**.124**	2	24
ME	MLP	145/**139**	.121/**.118**	2	300
	CNN	194/**178**	.167/**.154**	2	300
	LSTM	379/**365**	.154/**.146**	1	300
NH	MLP	137/**131**	.093/**.088**	2	300
	CNN	207/**191**	.148/**.132**	1	300
	LSTM	244/**206**	.169/**.146**	2	24
VT	MLP	67/**66**	.107/**.108**	2	300
	CNN	115/**87**	.188/**.142**	1	24
	LSTM	116/**100**	.186/**.170**	2	24
SEMA	MLP	150/**117**	.076/**.058**	5	300
	CNN	218/**197**	.114/**.103**	1	300
	LSTM	274/**214**	.140/**.114**	2	24
WCMA	MLP	302/**297**	.119/**.117**	2	300
	CNN	359/**351**	.143/**.140**	2	100
	LSTM	365/**354**	.145/**.142**	2	100

The proposed technique was further validated with the model proposed by [3]. The original configuration was used with 10 units for the layers that receive the load and temperature values and 5 units for the season and weekend encodings. Additionally, variations with 100/10 and 300/20 units were also trained because in the previous experiment it was observed that MLPs performed better with wider layers. The results shown in Table 3, indicate that increasing the number of units per layer can indeed provide a small forecasting accuracy increase. Furthermore, it is noted that the use of the Time-Step Boosting technique (reported on the right side of the slash "/" for each metric) had a significant positive impact on the models' performance.

5   Conclusions and Future Work

In this paper, we introduced Time-Step Boosting, a loss-agnostic technique for time series forecasting that can be applied to any neural network architecture. It adjusts the loss by taking into account the average loss per forecasted time step, thus focusing on the parts of the time series that are the most challenging to forecast. Experimental results showed that it significantly reduces the time needed for the model to converge and it can often help escape local minima. The technique was validated with multiple MLPs, CNNs and LSTMs of varying width and depth on energy load data of 19 European countries and 6 U.S. states, and additionally using a state-of-the-art model.

Overall, the experiments showed the Time-Step Boosting technique to be robust and offer considerable increases both in convergence speed and forecasting accuracy. Employing it during optimization or when training a single model on multiple data sets could be extremely helpful as it would greatly reduce the necessary time for exploring the hyperparameter space. It would also be interesting to see how important a fixed horizon is and to further validate the technique on different timeseries that exhibit non-uniform forecasting errors.

References

1. Benidis, K., et al.: Neural forecasting: Introduction and literature overview. arXiv (2020). https://doi.org/10.48550/arXiv.2004.10240
2. Challu, C., Olivares, K.G., Oreshkin, B.N., Garza, F., Mergenthaler, M., Dubrawski, A.: N-HiTS: Neural Hierarchical Interpolation for Time Series Forecasting (2022). https://doi.org/10.48550/arXiv.2201.12886
3. Chen, K., Chen, K., Wang, Q., He, Z., Hu, J., He, J.: Short-term load forecasting with deep residual networks. IEEE Trans. Smart Grid **10**(4), 3943–3952 (2019). https://doi.org/10.1109/TSG.2018.2844307
4. Chodakowska, E., Nazarko, J., Nazarko, L: ARIMA models in electrical load forecasting and their robustness to noise. Energies **14**(23), 7952 (2021). https://doi.org/10.3390/en14237952
5. European Commission: Questions and answers - making our energy system fit for our climate targets. (14 July 2021). https://ec.europa.eu/commission/presscorner/detail/en/qanda_21_3544. Accessed 7 Feb 2021
6. Hewamalage, H., Bergmeir, C., Bandara, K.: Recurrent neural networks for time series forecasting: current status and future directions. Int. J. Forecast. **37**(1), 388–427 (2021). https://doi.org/10.1016/j.ijforecast.2020.06.008
7. Hong, T., Xie, J., Black, J.: Global energy forecasting competition 2017: hierarchical probabilistic load forecasting. Int. J. Forecast. **35**(4), 1389–1399 (2019). https://doi.org/10.1016/j.ijforecast.2019.02.006
8. Keskar, N.S., Socher, R.: Improving Generalization Performance by Switching from Adam to SGD. arXiv (dec 2017)
9. Lai, G., Chang, W.C., Yang, Y., Liu, H.: Modeling long- and short-term temporal patterns with deep neural networks. In: The 41st International ACM SIGIR Conference on Research & Development in Information Retrieval. pp. 95–104. ACM, New York, NY, USA (2018). https://doi.org/10.1145/3209978.3210006
10. Marrero, L., Garcia-Santander, L., Carrizo, D., Ulloa, F.: An application of load forecasting based on ARIMA models and particle swarm optimization. In: 2019 11th International Symposium on Advanced Topics in Electrical Engineering (ATEE). pp. 1–6. IEEE, Bucharest, Romania (2019). https://doi.org/10.1109/ATEE.2019.8724891

11. Open Power System Data: Data Package Time series. Version 2020–10-06 (2020). 10.25832/time_series/2020-10-06
12. Open Power System Data: Data Package Weather Data. Version 2020–09-16 (2020). 10.25832/weather_data/2020-09-16
13. Zemouri, R., Patic, P.C.: Prediction error feedback for time series prediction: a way to improve the accuracy of predictions. In: Proceedings of the 4th Conference on European Computing Conference. pp. 58–62. ECC'10, World Scientific and Engineering Academy and Society (WSEAS), Stevens Point, Wisconsin, USA (2010)

ASTra: A Novel Algorithm-Level Approach to Imbalanced Classification

David Twomey[(✉)] and Denise Gorse

Department of Computer Science, University College London,
London WC1E 6BT, UK
{d.twomey,d.gorse}@cs.ucl.ac.uk

Abstract. We propose a novel output layer activation function, which we name ASTra (Asymmetric Sigmoid Transfer function), which makes the classification of minority examples, in scenarios of high imbalance, more tractable. We combine this with a loss function that helps to effectively target minority misclassification. These two methods can be used together or separately, with their combination recommended for the most severely imbalanced cases. The proposed approach is tested on datasets with IRs from 588.24 to 4000 and very few minority examples (in some datasets, as few as five). Results using neural networks with from two to 12 hidden units are demonstrated to be comparable to, or better than, equivalent results obtained in a recent study that deployed a wide range of complex, hybrid data-level ensemble classifiers.

Keywords: Classification · Class imbalance · Adaptive activation function · Asymmetric sigmoid · Confusion matrix · Geometric mean

1 Introduction

This paper addresses the challenge of handling extreme class imbalance, defined here as a situation in which negative examples, conventionally the majority, outnumber positive examples, usually the ones of most interest, by a factor of 500 or more (in other words, have an imbalance ratio (IR)$\geq$ 500). Such problems are not in fact uncommon, and arise in application areas such as fraud detection [19] and cheminformatics [5]. We make use of two methods, that tackle different, but complementary, aspects of the class imbalance problem:

- ASTra, a novel, adaptive, asymmetric output layer activation function, which makes the correct classification of minority examples easier.
- A loss function based on an approximated confusion matrix, which aggressively targets the misclassification of minority examples.

Our proposed methods have the advantage of being easy to implement and integrate into the workflow of any model that makes binary predictions normally generated by a sigmoid activation (transfer) function. In addition, the paper presents a new means of monitoring training and validation performance, especially valuable in cases of high class imbalance, that could potentially be used with any training regime, independently of the proposed methods.

E. Pimenidis et al. (Eds.): ICANN 2022, LNCS 13531, pp. 569–580, 2022.
https://doi.org/10.1007/978-3-031-15934-3_47

2   Background and Related Work

2.1   The Confusion Matrix and Its Associated Metrics

For a binary problem, in which columns refer to the prediction labels and rows to the actual labels (targets), the confusion matrix (CM) can be defined by

$$CM = \begin{pmatrix} TN & FP \\ FN & TP \end{pmatrix}, \tag{1}$$

in which TP denotes the *true positives* (correctly predicted positive examples), TN denotes the *true negatives* (correctly predicted negative examples), FN denotes the *false negatives* (positive instances predicted to be negative), and FP the *false positives* (negative instances predicted to be positive).

The most complete descriptor of classification performance that can be derived from the confusion matrix is the matrix itself. However, many summary statistics have been proposed (discussed, for example, in [13]), though some of these are of considerably more value than others for imbalanced data. For such data, where conventionally the minority class is labelled positive, false negatives are the most problematic issue: if all of the small number of positive instances are predicted wrongly, the model is effectively useless. However, the accuracy (proportion of correct predictions) may even so be deceptively very high, making accuracy the worst-choice performance statistic to quote for imbalanced data.

Conversely, the *Matthews Correlation Coefficient* (MCC) [10],

$$MCC = \frac{TP \times TN - FP \times FN}{\sqrt{(TP + FP)(TP + FN)(TN + FP)(TN + FN)}}, \tag{2}$$

is considered to be a 'gold standard' for measuring performance for imbalanced datasets [4], and hence we choose to use this measure in our results reporting.

Additionally to the MCC, we make use of the *geometric mean* (G-Mean) of the *true positive rate* (sensitivity) $TPR = TP/(TP + FN)$ and *true negative rate* (specificity) $TNR = TN/(TN + FP)$,

$$G\text{-}Mean = \sqrt{TPR \times TNR}, \tag{3}$$

both as a performance measure, for comparison with the results of [3], and to build a loss function. This *GMN loss function*, whose construction is outlined in Sect. 3.2, was proposed by us in [17], and is used in the current work due to its effectiveness in targeting false negatives, these being the most intractable element of the classification problem for datasets with a high IR.

2.2   Related Work

Methods for addressing class imbalance can be broadly grouped into three categories: data-level techniques, algorithm-level methods, and hybrid approaches [8]. *Data-level* techniques aim to reduce the level of class imbalance through some form of sampling, for example oversampling the minority or undersampling the majority class. However, oversampling can lead to overfitting, and undersampling to a loss of important information [18]. *Algorithm-level* methods, commonly implemented with a weight or cost scheme, involve modifying the underlying learner or its output in order to reduce bias toward the majority class. In cost-sensitive learning, penalties are assigned to each class through a cost matrix, though its definition often needs to be done empirically, or using expert domain knowledge [8]. *Hybrid* approaches combine data-level and algorithm-level approaches in various ways to handle the class imbalance problem. Examples include RUSBoost [16] and the recently-proposed HD-Ensemble method of [3].

An alternative algorithm-level approach, taken here, is to replace a loss function based on distance of an output from its target with one based on classification success. For imbalanced datasets, such a loss function may be able to avoid the trap of decreasing the loss by merely driving already-correct majority outputs closer and closer to their target values. The earliest work in this area, to our knowledge, dates back to 2013, when [12] proposed a loss function based on the F1 score and used this for the enhancement of document images. Two works appeared in 2017, the current authors' proposal of an approximated G-Mean [17], and a new F1 score based loss function [21]. In 2019, two further variants of the F1 score were proposed, the first [7] used to train a CNN to classify emotions in tweets, and the second [11] a proposal specifically for linear models, applied to synthetic and image data. Also in 2019, [15] used a CNN and a multi-class variant of the F1 score to perform cell segmentation. Most recently, in 2021, [1] used a CNN, trained this time with an approximated MCC, to classify skin lesions.

Notably, most of the above work used loss functions derived from the F1 score. However, this measure has been criticised for insufficiently addressing false negatives [9], and may thus not be optimal in areas such as medical diagnosis. The MCC may also, as demonstrated in 3.1, excessively emphasise false positives at the expense of false negatives. The G-Mean of Eq. (3), however, aggressively targets false negatives due to its product form, which is the reason we choose to use our approximated G-Mean loss [17] in this current work.

3   Proposed Methods

3.1   The ASTra (Asymmetric Sigmoid Transfer) Function

ASTra is an asymmetric sigmoid-type activation function, recommended for use in the final network layer only, that is designed to facilitate the classification of minority examples by allocating a larger proportion of the output range to these examples. Its form is derived from that of the Richards growth equation [14], used to model vegetation growth and the growth of young mammals and birds, and (assuming a conventional minority-1) is defined by

$$ASTra(x, b) = 1 - (1 + be^{bx})^{-\frac{1}{b}}. \tag{4}$$

The gradient of the ASTra transform is maximum at $x = 0$, which point we define as the threshold, τ, given by

$$\tau(b) = 1 - (1 + b)^{-\frac{1}{b}}.\tag{5}$$

when $b = 1$, the form of the standard sigmoid can be recovered, while for $b > 1$ lower thresholds $\tau < 0.5$ make the classification of target-1 examples, the assumed minority, easier. $y(x, b)$ and its first derivative are shown in Figs. 1(a), (b), for $\tau = 0.5, 0.25, 0.05$, noting that we have so far found 0.05 to be the lowest workable value for τ (attempts to compress all majority examples into $< 5\%$ of the output range having led to numerical instabilities).

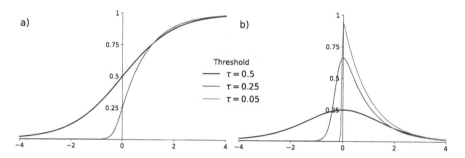

Fig. 1. (a) Activation function $ASTra(x, b)$ and (b) its first derivative, for $\tau(b) = 0.5, 0.25, 0.05$.

Adaptation of Loss Functions to Accommodate ASTra. At first sight, this looks easy: simply replace the usual sigmoid output by Eq. (4). However, it is not always so straightforward, as an examination of ASTra's effect of the computation of a binary cross-entropy (BCE) loss will show.

Consider the contribution $J_{BCE}(\hat{y}, y) = -y \log \hat{y} - (1 - y) \log(1 - \hat{y})$ of a single example, with prediction $\hat{y} = ASTra(x, b)$ and target $y \in \{0, 1\}$, to the train set loss. As is apparent in Fig. 2(a), for $b = 1$ ($\tau = 0.5$), for any input $x > 0.0$, $J_{BCE}(\hat{y}, 0) > J_{BCE}(\hat{y}, 1)$, correctly, since $\hat{y}$ will be on the 'correct side' of the threshold and so closer to target 1 than to 0, with the converse also correctly being true for inputs $x < 0.0$. However, for $b > 1$ this is not true for all values of the input x; there will be a range of x, specifically, $0 < x < (\log[(2^b - 1)/b])/b$, within which the loss contributions are wrongly ordered. Figure 2(b) shows an example of this for $\tau = 0.25$ ($b = 7.396$); within the shaded band it is the case that $J_{BCE}(\hat{y}, 0) < J_{BCE}(\hat{y}, 1)$, so outputs which are 'more right than wrong' are instead being informed that the opposite is the case.

The fundamental problem is that currently $J_{BCE}(\hat{y}, 0)$ and $J_{BCE}(\hat{y}, 0)$ cross at 0.5, not at τ, and the solution is to use within the BCE loss not $\hat{y}$ but a transform $z(\hat{y}, \tau)$, given by

$$z(\hat{y}, \tau) = \frac{\hat{y}(1 - \tau)}{\hat{y}(1 - \tau) + (1 - \hat{y})\tau},\tag{6}$$

such that $z, 1 - z$ will now cross at τ, as can be seen in Fig. 3, for $\tau = 0.5, 0.25$, and 0.05, and hence the loss contributions $J_{BCE}(z, 0)$ and $J_{BCE}(z, 1)$ will do so, also. For some loss functions, such as mean squared error, it is unnecessary to transform $\hat{y}$ in this way. However, the z-transform should be carried out for any classification loss function that implicitly pivots around a threshold of 0.5, including all loss functions, such as GMN, derived from the confusion matrix.

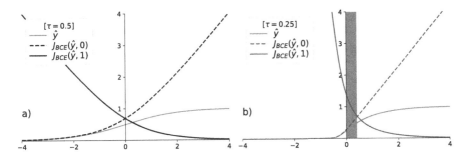

Fig. 2. Loss functions for targets 0 and 1 for (a) $\tau(b) = 0.5$ and (b) $\tau(b) = 0.25$

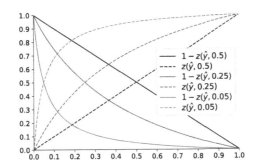

Fig. 3. z-transforms for $\tau = 0.5, 0.25, 0.05$

Learning the Threshold Value. It would in principle be possible to use a fixed value of τ and set this via hyperparameter optimisation. However, in experiments so far, it has appeared that a fixed $\tau < 0.5$ during weights-learning is non-optimal, and that it is better to begin with a somewhat larger threshold value that then decreases during the network's learning process. There is necessarily therefore a question of how τ should be decreased. While it would be possible to experiment with a schedule of decrease, for example, exponential or linear, a more attractive option is to learn the value of the underlying 'slope' parameter, b, alongside the network's weights.

For a conventional minority target of 1, the relevant values of b should be constrained to be ≥ 1(corresponding to a threshold $\tau \leq 0.5$). Given this, it is useful to express b in terms of an unconstrained underlying parameter β:

$$b = \begin{cases} 2 + \beta & \beta > 0 \\ 1 + e^{\beta} & \text{otherwise} \end{cases}. \tag{7}$$

It is preferable to begin with $b(\beta)$ in its linear range, i.e., $b \geq 2$, so that the threshold can change sufficiently quickly at the start of the learning process. We have used a value of $\tau_{init} = 0.25$ ($b = 7.396$), around halfway between the achievable threshold maximum of 0.5 and the recommended (on stability grounds) minimum of 0.05, but clearly this is a value that could be treated as a hyperparameter and optimised.

3.2   The GMN Loss Function

The construction of this loss function, first presented by us in [17], begins with an approximated confusion matrix,

$$CM_{apx} = \begin{pmatrix} TN_{apx} & FP_{apx} \\ FN_{apx} & TP_{apx} \end{pmatrix} = \begin{pmatrix} \sum_i^n (1 - \hat{y}_i)(1 - y_i) & \sum_i^n \hat{y}_i(1 - y_i) \\ \sum_i^n (1 - \hat{y}_i)y_i & \sum_i^n \hat{y}_i y_i \end{pmatrix}, \tag{8}$$

in which $\hat{y}_i$ and y_i are the predicted and target values for the ith example, and the sums are over the set of examples for which the approximated matrix is required. From CM_{apx} one can then generate the necessary approximation to the G-Mean, and our loss function

$$J_{GMN} = 1 - G\text{-}Mean_{apx} = 1 - \sqrt{\frac{\sum_i (1 - \hat{y}_i)(1 - y_i) \cdot \sum_i \hat{y}_i y_i}{m_0 \cdot m_1}}, \tag{9}$$

in which m_0, m_1 are the numbers of negative, positive examples, respectively. The necessary derivatives with respect to network outputs can then be either derived algebraically or obtained via automatic differentiation.[1]

4   Data, Experimental Process, and Performance Measurement

4.1   Data

There are not many easily available datasets with the high level of imbalance required for this work. However, a recent study [3] has looked at data with IRs ranging from 9.08 to 970.6, with data made available online [2]. It was also useful that these data were used in [3] to compare HD-Ensemble, a high-performing

---

[1] All derivatives, including those associated with the use of the ASTra transform, may be obtained from the authors on request; space precludes their inclusion here.

hybrid, data-level ensemble classifier devised by that study's authors, to seven other state-of-the-art ensemble classifiers, including RUSBoost [16]. The three most imbalanced datasets from [3], named there as *skinnonskin*, *cod-rna*, and *ijcnn1* (IR = 970.6) were downloaded from [2].[2] In addition to the original files, the two largest datasets from [2] were minority-undersampled to create more challenging problems (IRs of 3500, 4000, with one positive example in each of five folds), extracting five positive samples randomly at each run, to eliminate bias created by 'good' or 'bad' subset picks.

Table 1. Datasets used in this work. The shaded bars correspond to the original datasets of [3] and the unshaded bars to our additional minority-undersampled datasets

Dataset	IR	Abb.	n_x	m_{tot}	m_1
skinnonskin	588.24	*skin-588*	3	20034	34
above, undersampled	4000	*skin-4000*	3	20005	5
cod-rna	763.27	*cod-763*	8	19871	26
above, undersampled	3500	*cod-3500*	8	17505	5
ijcnn1	970.60	*ijcnn-971*	22	4858	5

The properties of the datasets used here are summarised in Table 1, in which n_x is the number of input features, m_{tot} the total number of examples in the dataset, and m_1 the number of minority-positive examples. It should be noted that while we followed [3] in creating stratified test folds, we used $10 \times 5CV$ testing rather than $5 \times 10CV$, using three folds for training, and one each for validation and testing, as it was unclear how tenfold stratified sampling had been done in [3] in the case of *ijcnn1*, with only five positive examples.

4.2   Details of the Experimental Process

The focus of this work is not the test problems of Table 1, per se, but a comparison of methodologies, and therefore simple choices were made for network architectures, with no attempt to optimise learning rates, etc., in order to get the best solution in each case. For each test problem, four candidates were compared: training with a binary cross-entropy loss (referred to as BCE); training with a binary cross-entropy loss and ASTra transform (BCE-ASTra); training with the GMN loss function (GMN); and training with the GMN loss function and ASTra transform (GMN-ASTra). The architecture for each test problem was a neural network with one hidden layer of Leaky ReLU neurons (negative slope coefficient of 0.3), with $n_h = ceil((n_x + n_y)/2)$, and a single ASTra output (the standard sigmoid being recoverable from this when $b = 1$). Network weights used He initialisation in the hidden layer and Glorot initialisation in the output

---

[2] Modified, where necessary, to record target-1 for the minority class and target-0 for the majority, a requirement for the application of the ASTra activation function.

layer. All models were trained using Adam, with a training rate of $\eta = 0.001$ for the network weights. η_b, the training rate associated with the slope parameter b, was set according to the adaptive rule of Eq. (10),

$$\eta_b = \begin{cases} \min(k_{mult} \cdot \eta_b, \eta_{bmax}) & \text{if } e-ratio > 1.0 \\ \max(k_{dec} \cdot \eta_b, \eta_{bmin}) & \text{if } e-ratio < 1.0 , \\ \eta_b & \text{otherwise} \end{cases} \quad (10)$$

the objective of which was to allow the threshold adjustment to proceed more quickly when the model is struggling to handle its train set class imbalance, but slow down when conditions are less taxing, as measured by the *e-ratio*,

$$e\text{-}ratio = FNR_{apx}/FPR_{apx}, \quad (11)$$

which measures the difficulty of classifying positive (minority) examples with respect to negative ones. We here chose η_{bmin} (also the starting value of η_b) to be 0.01, $\eta_{bmax} = 0.5$, $k_{mult} = 1.1$, and $k_{dec} = 0.99$. These values were not optimised, in line with our focus on comparison of training methods, rather than on outright performance.

The one form of problem-specific optimisation we performed was the extraction of the best weights (and b value, where relevant) with respect to a validation set. However, it was unfeasible to use early stopping as best validation performance could in some cases occur late, after an early setback. Therefore, we trained for a fixed 10,000 epochs, extracting a 'best-on-val' set of parameters, for whatever epoch this occurred, with respect to the chosen validation performance measure (FNR_{apx}, for the reasons discussed in the following section).

4.3   Performance Measurement

Two aspects of performance measurement need to be considered, that which is carried out during the training process, and that which is used to assess the results on the test sets. For the latter, we use the G-Mean, as it is the basis of one of our considered loss functions, and one of the two performance measures quoted in [3]. However, we do not use AUROC, as in [3], as this metric has been criticised in the case of imbalanced data [20], and we found it to distinguish very poorly between the methods of this paper. We substitute the MCC as our second measure, due to its high regard as a performance metric for imbalanced data.

Turning to in-training performance monitoring, we introduce an innovation in that we retain the explanatory value, for this purpose, of confusion matrix based metrics, but exchange the usual, counting-measure forms for ones based on the approximated matrix-i.e., we use standard formulae for G-Mean, etc., but base the calculation on the matrix elements of (4) rather than (1). Metrics derived from CM_{apx} re-introduce the 'by how much?' that counting-measure classification metrics lose. This is particularly important when monitoring validation performance, for which, in this work, we select to monitor FNR_{apx}, the approximated false negative rate, rather than MCC_{apx}, for example, as in these extreme scenarios it is test set *FNR* that largely determines classification (in terms of MCC, G-Mean) success. The other element of in-training performance monitoring relates to the train set itself, rather than to validation. We record the *e-ratio* of Eq. (11) for the train set as a way to track the difficulty a model is having with the train set class imbalance; this ratio is of interest in understanding how the methods deal with class imbalance, with a large difference being discovered between BCE loss and GMN loss training, as will be seen later.

5   Results

The results of the 10×5CV study are summarised in Table 2, below, in which averages and standard deviations (in brackets) are quoted for both G-Mean and MCC, and where BCE, GMN refer to the loss functions (J_{BCE}, J_{GMN}) used.

Table 2. Mean fold-aggregated test performance (10×5CV), with standard deviations bracketed. Cells with bold type and shading denote winners or ties, where to be deemed a winner a method needs to outperform its competitors with $p \leq 0.05$.

	Without ASTra		With ASTra	
	BCE	**GMN**	**BCE**	**GMN**
skin-588				
G-Mean	**0.892 (0.273)**	**0.966 (0.051)**	**0.981 (0.041)**	**0.946 (0.126)**
MCC	**0.892 (0.273)**	**0.966 (0.051)**	**0.976 (0.042)**	0.763 (0.273)
skin-4000				
G-Mean	**0.760 (0.436)**	**0.879 (0.331)**	**0.800 (0.408)**	**0.840 (0.374)**
MCC	0.760 (0.436)	**0.843 (0.368)**	**0.800 (0.408)**	0.688 (0.382)
cod-763				
G-Mean	0.449 (0.396)	0.768 (0.206)	**0.862 (0.208)**	**0.843 (0.206)**
MCC	0.433 (0.391)	0.419 (0.301)	**0.760 (0.229)**	0.542 (0.291)
cod-3500				
G-Mean	0.240 (0.436)	0.357 (0.486)	**0.640 (0.490)**	**0.519 (0.509)**
MCC	0.240 (0.436)	0.255 (0.397)	**0.421 (0.369)**	0.206 (0.225)
ijcnn-971				
G-Mean	0.000 (0.000)	0.120 (0.331)	**0.478 (0.508)**	**0.596 (0.497)**
MCC	-0.000 (0.001)	0.072 (0.208)	**0.162 (0.179)**	**0.179 (0.162)**

The large standard deviations, apparent also in the results of [3], are a consequence of fold-based aggregation of results in a situation where a small number of false negatives (in the case of the *skin-4000*, *cod-3500*, and *ijcnn-971* datasets, a single false negative) on an individual fold can cause its G-Mean or MCC to drop from near-unity to zero. This in turn causes some results, with a sample size of 50 (10CV), to be not statistically significantly distinguishable; e.g., in the case of the *skin-588* dataset, the G-Means of the four methods cannot be separated at $p \leq 0.05$ in spite of an apparent-win by BCE with ASTra (BCE-ASTra). Nevertheless, despite the necessity of a registering a proportion of the results as 'ties', a pattern emerges, with the problems forming a hierarchy of difficulty, at each level of which different methods will be appropriate:

– *skin-588* is an example of a problem for which no additional measures to address IR need to be taken, since vanilla BCE training can do as well (subject to the above note on statistical significance testing) as any of the more advanced methods.
– *skin-4000*, the minority-undersampled version of *skin-588*, is a more difficult problem, for which BCE training falls behind with respect to MCC. For this problem, adopting the principle that a minimal intervention is to be preferred, GMN training, without the ASTra transform, would be recommended.
– *cod-763*, *cod-3500*, and *ijcnn-971* are examples of problems that appear to clearly benefit from the ASTra transform. For the *cod* variants it is BCE-ASTra that does best with respect to both G-Mean and MCC, having fewer false positives for these problems, while for *ijcnn-971* BCE-ASTra and GMN-ASTra tie.

The above list does not include a problem for which GMN-ASTra does best. However, we would expect such problems to exist. GMN-ASTra attacks false negatives at the expense of a somewhat increased number of false positives, and if it is possible to avoid this by using BCE-ASTra, that is desirable. But it is likely there are problems that require an increase in false positives to be tolerated in order to have any chance of recognising instances of the minority class (i.e., of having G-Means and MCCs above zero), and in such cases we would expect GMN-ASTra to be preferred.

For the three datasets we have in common with [3] it is possible to draw performance comparisons with that work, though retaining our concerns about the use of AUROC for highly imbalanced data, which we found did not distinguish well between the methods. The two best-performing methods of [3], in relation to G-Mean and AUROC, were the HD-Ensemble method of [3] and RUSBoost [16]. For *skin-588*, GMN, BCE-ASTra, and GMN-ASTra all had statistically significantly indistinguishable performance from RUSBoost, with respect to both metrics. For *cod-763*, the two ASTra variants tied with RUSBoost on AUROC, but beat RUSBoost on G-Mean, while on *ijcnn-971* they achieved a better G-Mean than state-of-the-art HD-Ensemble. Given especially that we used small, single-layer neural networks, with that used for *skin-588* having only three neurons, we consider these results encouraging.

As a means of illuminating the difference between our four considered methods, Fig. 4 shows the *e-ratio* of Sect. 4.2, for the *skin-4000* (most highly imbalanced) problem. The GMN variants find handling the imbalance much easier, with *e-ratio* values up to five orders of magnitude lower; also, while ASTra is taxing in terms of *e-ratio*, this can be offset by the use of GMN.

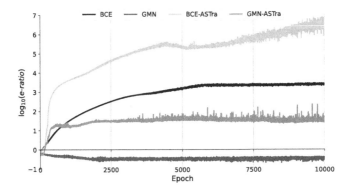

Fig. 4. Fold-averaged training behaviour for *skin-4000*, in terms of the (logged) *e-ratio* of Sect. 4.2, for each considered method.

6 Discussion

This paper has introduced a novel adaptive output layer activation function, which we have named ASTra, that can either in combination with, or separately from, our previously proposed GMN loss [17] work to facilitate the classification of minority examples for extremely high IRs. We additionally introduced a novel use of metrics based on an approximated confusion matrix for performance monitoring during training. The proposed methods were applied to the most imbalanced datasets in a recent extensive study of ensemble classifiers [3] and achieved performances comparable to those reported in [3] for RUSBoost [16], despite our restricting this initial investigation to the use of neural networks with 3–12 neurons in a single hidden layer. We emphasise, however, that for complex problems it is essential to explore the space of model architectures, since even in the case of a high IR the main difficulties may in fact lie in an insufficient model architecture. We also recommend a progressive exploration of the methods, beginning with the GMN loss alone, then advancing to the addition of the ASTra output layer activation function, as needed. We aim next to apply our methods to challenging real-world imbalanced datasets requiring deep neural network architectures. Additionally, especially given the nature of the derivatives involved in ASTra computations, we are interested in the use of sharpness-aware minimisation [6] to smooth optima and improve generalisation. Finally, we note here that it is our intention to open-source our code and to ensure its integration with popular machine learning libraries (Pytorch and Tensorflow).

References

1. Abhishek, K., Hamarneh, G.: Matthews correlation coefficient loss for deep convolutional networks: application to skin lesion segmentation (2021). https://doi.org/10.48550/arXiv.2010.13454

2. Chen, Z., Duan, J., Kang, L., Qiu, G.: HD-Ensemble datasets (2021). https://github.com/smallcube/HD-Ensemble. Accessed Apr 11 2022

3. Chen, Z., Duan, J., Kang, L., Qiu, G.: A hybrid data-level ensemble to enable learning from highly imbalanced dataset. Inf. Sci. **554**, 157–176 (2021)

4. Chicco, D., Tötsch, N., Jurman, G.: The Matthews correlation coefficient (MCC) is more reliable than balanced accuracy, bookmaker informedness, and markedness in two-class confusion matrix evaluation. BioData Min. **14**, 13 (2021)

5. Czarnecki, W., Rataj, K.: Compounds activity prediction in large imbalanced datasets with substructural relations fingerprint and EEM. In: 2015 IEEE Trust-Com/BigDataSE/ISPA, vol. 2. pp. 192–197. IEEE, New York City (2015)

6. Foret, P., Kleiner, A., Mobahi, H., Neyshabur, B.: Sharpness-aware minimization for efficiently improving generalization (2021), https://doi.org/10.48550/arXiv.2010.01412

7. Hurtado, L.F., González, J.A., Ferran, P.: Choosing the right loss function for multi-label emotion classification. J. Intell. Fuzzy Syst. **36**, 4697–4708 (2019)

8. Johnson, J.M., Khoshgoftaar, T.M.: Survey on deep learning with class imbalance. J. Big Data **6**(1), 1–54 (2019). https://doi.org/10.1186/s40537-019-0192-5

9. Maratea, A., Petrosino, A., Manzo, M.: Adjusted F-measure and kernel scaling for imbalanced data learning. Inf. Sci. **257**, 331–341 (2014)

10. Matthews, B.: Comparison of the predicted and observed secondary structure of T4 phage lysozyme. Biochim. Biophys. Acta **405**, 442–445 (1975)

11. Paradowski, M., Spytkowsk, M., Kwaśnicka, H.: A new F-score gradient-based training rule for the linear model. Pattern. Anal. Applic. **22**, 537–548 (2019)

12. Pastor-Pellicer, J., Zamora-Martínez, F., España-Boquera, S., Castro-Bleda, M.J.: F-Measure as the error function to train neural networks. In: Rojas, I., Joya, G., Gabestany, J. (eds.) IWANN 2013. LNCS, vol. 7902, pp. 376–384. Springer, Heidelberg (2013). https://doi.org/10.1007/978-3-642-38679-4_37

13. Powers, D.: Evaluation: from precision, recall and F-measure to ROC, informedness, markedness & correlation. J. Mach. Learn. Technol. **2**(1), 37–63 (2011)

14. Richards, F.: A flexible growth function for empirical use. J. Exp. Bot. **10**(29), 290–300 (1959)

15. Scherzinger, A., Hugenroth, P., Rüder, M., Bogdan, S., Jiang, X.: Multi-class cell segmentation using CNNs with F1-measure loss function. In: Brox, T., et al. (eds.) GCPR 2016, LNCS, vol. 11269, pp. 434–446. Springer, Heidelberg (2019)

16. Seiffert, C., Khoshgoftaar, T., Van Hulse, J., A., N.: RUSBoost: A hybrid approach to alleviating class imbalance. IEEE Trans. Syst., Man, Cyb. **40**(1), 185–197 (2010)

17. Twomey, D., Gorse, D.: A neural network cost function for highly class-imbalanced data sets. In: Proceedings of ESANN, pp. 207–212. i6doc.com, Bruges (2017)

18. Wang, B., Japkowicz, N.: Imbalanced data set learning with synthetic samples. In: Proceedings of IRIS Machine Learning Workshop (2004)

19. Wei, W., Li, J., Cao, L., Ou, Y., Chen, J.: Effective detection of sophisticated online banking fraud on extremely imbalanced data. World Wide Web **16**(4), 449–475 (2013)

20. Weng, C., Poon, J.: A new evaluation measure for imbalanced datasets. In: Proceedings of Seventh Australasian Data Mining Conference. pp. 27–32. Glenelg, South Australia (2008)

21. Zhang, C., Wang, G., Zhou, Y., Jiang, J.: A new approach for imbalanced data classification based on minimize loss learning. In: 2017 IEEE Second International Conference on Data Science in Cyberspace (DSC). pp. 82–87. IEEE, New York City (2017)

Attention Awareness Multiple Instance Neural Network

Jingjun Yi[✉] and Beichen Zhou

Wuhan University, Wuhan 430079, Hubei, China
2019302130106@whu.edu.cn

Abstract. Multiple instance learning is qualified for many pattern recognition tasks with weakly annotated data. The combination of artificial neural network and multiple instance learning offers an end-to-end solution and has been widely utilized. However, challenges remain in two-folds. Firstly, current MIL pooling operators are usually pre-defined and lack flexibility to mine key instances. Secondly, in current solutions, the bag-level representation can be inaccurate or inaccessible. To this end, we propose an attention awareness multiple instance neural network framework in this paper. It consists of an instance-level classifier, a trainable MIL pooling operator based on spatial attention and a bag-level classification layer. Exhaustive experiments on a series of pattern recognition tasks demonstrate that our framework outperforms many state-of-the-art MIL methods and validates the effectiveness of our proposed attention MIL pooling operators.

Keywords: MIL · Attention awareness · Neural network

1 Introduction

Multiple instance learning (MIL) was firstly developed for drug prediction [7]. In MIL, each object for classification is regarded as a bag, and each bag consists of a series of instances. [26] Bag label is used for supervision but there is no specific instance label and each instance can only be judged as either belonging or not belonging to the bag category. [6] If a bag contains at least one positive instance, then it should be categorized as positive. Otherwise, it is classified as negative. MIL mimics the real applications where we only have weakly annotated data. It was applied on a series of pattern recognition tasks such as object tracking [3] and saliency detection [15].

MIL and ANN. Artificial neural network (ANN) is effective for machine learning. While combing other solutions with MIL the whole framework is often not end-to-end [2,11,16], the combination of MIL and ANN can be trainable and it is easier to adjust to different datasets and tasks [17,24,25].

Due to the strong feature representation capability, deep learning methods have developed rapidly in the past few years. Allowing for the fact that MIL is qualified for weakly annotated data, the combination of MIL of deep neural network is drawing increasing attention in the past few years [12,19].

E. Pimenidis et al. (Eds.): ICANN 2022, LNCS 13531, pp. 581–592, 2022.
https://doi.org/10.1007/978-3-031-15934-3_48

Problem Statement. Although the combination of ANN and MIL offers a chance for end-to-end MIL solutions, however, several challenges still remain.

- *Limitation in mining key instances.*
  Although some trainable MIL frameworks have been proposed, current approaches usually use pre-defined MIL pooling operators such as mean or maximum pooling [17,22]. As is clearly pointed out in [9], non-trainable MIL operators are not effective enough to find the key instances inside a bag and they lack the flexibility to adjust to different tasks and datasets.
- *Gaps towards semantic representation.*
  Current solutions to combine ANN and MIL belong to either embedding space paradigm or instance space paradigm. Under embedding space paradigm, MIL pooling operators can not offer a direct bag-level probability distribution [1]. Under instance space paradigm, the inference of instance scores can be inaccurate because current non-trainable MIL pooling operators can be not qualified enough to mine the relation between instances and bags [9]. This weakness effects negatively on the calculation of bag scores.

Motivation and Contribution. The objective of our work is two-folds.

- *Finding an approach to effectively mine instances relevant to the bag label.*
  Bag score is calculated based on instance feature representation. As is stated above, pre-defined MIL pooling operators are not qualified enough to stress the key instances. With a solution further investigate the relation between instances and bags, bag representation capability can be enhanced.
- *Enhancing the semantic representation capability for multiple instance neural networks.* In current instance space paradigm, inaccurate instance inference leads to poor bag-level semantic representation, while in current embedding space paradigm there is no direct bag representation. Hence, the semantic representation ability remains to be improved.

Our contribution can be summarized as follows.

(1) We propose a framework to combine MIL and neural networks. It is an end-to-end solution and can further mine the relation between bags and instances. Also, this framework is under the direct supervision of bag labels. The semantic representation capability is enhanced.
(2) We propose a trainable MIL pooling operation based on spatial attention mechanism. With attention awareness, different instances are assigned with different weights so that key instances can be stressed. Also, it directly outputs a bag-level classification distribution.
(3) Our proposed attention awareness multiple instance neural network framework outperforms current MIL approaches on a series of pattern recognition tasks such as MIL classification, text classification and image classification.

2   Related Work

MIL for Aerial Image. Aerial image recognition is challenging due to the complicated object distribution and spatial arrangement in a large-scale aerial image. [5] Vatsavai et.al. proposed a Gaussian multiple instance learning (GMIL) approach to describe the complicated spatial pattern in very high resolution remote sensing images and mapped the slums. This method outperformed many pixlevel methods [14]. More recently, Bi et.al. introduced multiple instance learning into aerial scene classification [4]. The results reveal that MIL helps enhance the local semantic representation for aerial scenes.

MIL for Medical Image. MIL has been widely applied in medical image processing. Similar to [14], Kandemir et.al. also utilizes Gaussian process in MIL for medical image classification [10]. Hou et.al further investigated an approach to determine instance categories via a two-stage solution combining ANN and EM algorithms [8], but it is still not an end-to-end solution. More recently, Ilse et.al. proposed an attention based MIL pooling and offered an end-to-end solution for multiple instance neural network [9].

MIL for Document Classification. Yan et.al. proposed a sparse MIL solution to build a robust structural representation for instances and bags [20]. Zhou et.al. mined the relation inside instances for text classification [27] by considering bags as graph and using features of nodes and edges to describe the relation between instances. More recently, Wang et.al. proposed a trainable multiple instance neural network (MINet) [17].

Attention Based MIL. To further mine the key instances inside a bag and to enhance the bag representation capability, the design of trainable MIL pooling operators has recently been reported. Attention models can assign different weights to different instances and can be adopted to develop a MIL pooling operator. Thus, Ilse et.al. developed a trainable MIL pooling operator based on gated attention mechanism for medical image classification.

The major differences between our work and theirs include 1) In [9], it is under the embedding space and there is no direct bag representation, but our current work offers a direct bag probability distribution and is under the direct supervision of bag labels; 2) [9] is based on gated attention while our work is based on spatial attention; 3) We validate our solution on more backbones, more large-scale datasets and more pattern recognition tasks.

3   Preliminary

Classic MIL Formulation. A bag with label Y consists of a set of instances $X = \{x_1, x_2, \cdots, x_k\}$. Generally, each instance x_i is labeled as either a positive instance (denoted as 1) or a negative instance (denoted as 0). Hence, the label y_i of instance x_i can be represented as $y_i = \{0, 1\}$, here $i = 0, 1, \cdots, k$.

Traditionally, a bag is labeled as either a positive bag or a negative bag based on the following rule:

$$Y = \begin{cases} 0 & \text{if } \sum_{i=1}^{k} x_i = 0 \\ 1 & \text{else} \end{cases} \qquad (1)$$

Bag Probability Distribution Assumptions. Classic MIL formulation can lead to gradient vanishing problems when training a multiple instance neural network. To this end, log-likelihood function is recently utilized for optimization [9]. Here, bag label is distributed as a Bernoulli distribution with the parameter $\theta(X) \in [0, 1]$.

Decomposition of Score Function. Calculating the bag probability needs a score function $S(X)$ for the instance set X. Since MIL assumes that bag probability $\theta(X)$ must be permutation-invariant, as is stated in [23], the score function $S(X)$ is a symmetric function and can be decomposed as follows.

$$S(X) = g(\sum_{x \in X} f(X)) \qquad (2)$$

where f and g are transformations, which will be discussed later.

Functions of Decomposed Transformations. Currently, the combination of ANN and MIL is under either instance or embedding space.

For methods under instance space, here transformation g is an identity transformation and instance-level classifier f returns the score of each instance. Then, MIL pooling operator aggregates the instance scores and calculates the bag-level probability distribution $\theta(X)$.

For methods under embedding space, here transformation f transforms instances X into embedding spaces. But the feature representation after MIL pooling needs further processing to generate $\theta(X)$.

Since our attention awareness multiple instance neural network belongs to the instance space paradigm where the bag probability distribution can be directly calculated, one major task is to develop a trainable MIL pooling operator to effectively mine key instances.

4   Methodology

4.1   Network Overview

As shown in Fig. 1, our attention awareness multiple instance neural network consists of three parts, that is, an instance-level classifier, a trainable MIL pooling operator based on spatial attention, and a bag-level classification layer.

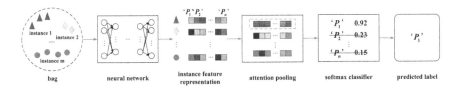

Fig. 1. Framework of our proposed attention awareness multiple instance neural network

4.2 Instance-Level Classifier

Under instance space paradigm, an instance-level classifier need to be built at first to generate the instance score or instance representation.

For two-category classification tasks, this instance representation X can be quite simple. However, for multiple category classification tasks where there are multiple bag categories, this instance representation should have a same dimension corresponding to the bag category numbers so that the instance score on each bag category can be calculated. For example, we have d bag categories and in a bag we have n instances, then this instance representation X should have a shape of $d \times n$.

4.3 Attention Based MIL Pooling

Aggregation of Instance Prediction. The key function of MIL pooling operator under instance space paradigm is to aggregate the instance predictions into a bag representation. To be specific, assume a bag contains k instances and instance i corresponds to a prediction $\{p_i\}$, where $i = 0, 1, \cdots, k$. Let p_{bag} denote the bag prediction and $O(\cdot)$ denote the aggregation function, then it can be represented as

$$p_{bag} = O(\{p_i\}). \tag{3}$$

Attention Module. To mine the key instances and to strengthen the bag representation capability, we introduce an attention model $H(\cdot)$ into MIL pooling so that different instances can be assigned to different weights. To be specific, let X denote the aforementioned instance-level feature representation, then each instance x_i will correspond to an attention weight a_i via

$$\{a_i\} = H(\{X\}). \tag{4}$$

Our attention module consists of a fully connected layer and a sigmoid activation function. Let W and b denote the weight matrix and bias matrix of the fully connected layer, and let $sigmoid$ denote the aforementioned activation operation. Then, Eq. 4 can be rewritten as

$$\{a_i\} = softmax(sigmoid(WX^T + b)), \tag{5}$$

where $softmax$ denotes the softmax operation for normalization.

In Fig. 2, our attention module is illustrated in detail.

Weighted Aggregation. Current MIL pooling operators usually utilize pre-defined operators. To be specific, the function of $O(\cdot)$ is usually to select the mean value or maximum value of $\{p_i\}$.

In contrast, our attention based MIL pooling utilizes the weighted aggregation strategy. The $O(\cdot)$ is a convex combination of all the instance probability distribution vectors to generate the bag probability, represented as

$$O(\{p_i\}) = \sum_i a_i p_i. \tag{6}$$

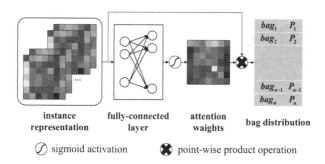

Fig. 2. Illustration of our attention based multiple instance pooling operator

Figure 2 illustrates the situation when there are multiple bag categories.

4.4 Bag-Level Classification Layer

With a bag-level probability distribution, we need to build a classification layer to form an end-to-end solution while keeping the whole network under the direct supervision of bag labels.

Here we choose the widely-used cross-entropy loss function to optimize the whole network and discuss the general situation when we have multiple bag categories. Let N denote the number of bag categories, y_c denote a bag's true label, and $\hat{y}_c$ denote the predicted bag value on category c. Then, this loss function can be represented as

$$L = -\frac{1}{N} \sum_{c=1}^{n} [y_c \log \hat{y}_c + (1 - y_c) \log(1 - \hat{y}_c)]. \tag{7}$$

5 Experiment and Analysis

To investigate the effectiveness of our attention awareness multiple instance neural network on a series of pattern recognition tasks, we conduct the experiments on five standard classic MIL datasets, two aerial image datasets, one medical image dataset and three text classification datasets and compare it with other state-of-the-art methods.

5.1   Classic MIL Datasets

Details. Many former MIL methods have been validated on five standard MIL datasets (MUSK1, MUSK2, FOX, TIGER and ELEPHANT) [17]. Compared with the former solutions where ANN is combined with MIL in a end-to-end manner [9,17], we keep backbone the same while inserting our attention module to test the performance of our solution.

Experimental Setup. The backbone we utilize is the mi-net [9,17]. The network structure is demonstrated in Table 1. Hyper-parameters such as learning rate, iteration number and weight decay all keep the same with [9,17].

Table 1. Detailed network structure for classic MIL and MIL text classification

Layer	mi-net	mi-net_A(ours)
1	fc-256 + ReLU	fc-256 + ReLU
2	dropout	dropout
3	fc-128 + ReLU	fc-128 + ReLU
4	dropout	dropout
5	fc-64 + ReLU	fc-64 + ReLU
6	dropout	dropout
7	fc-1 + sigm	mil-attention
8	mil-mean/max	fc-1

Comparison. Following the experiment protocols for standard MIL datasets, the mean accuracy and standard deviation of ten-folds cross validation are reported as the final result. The classification accuracy of our framework and other state-of-the-art MIL methods are listed in Table 2. Our solution (denoted as mi-net_A) achieves the best classification accuracy on two out of these five datasets and comparable accuracy on the rest three datasets. More importantly, our solution outperforms end-to-end solutions mi-net, MI-Net and MI-Net with gated attention MIL pooling (denoted as MI-Net_GA) on all these five datasets, indicating the effectiveness of our MIL pooling operation.

Table 2. Comparison of our framework and other state-of-the-art methods on classic MIL datasets. [1]([2]), [2]([27]), [3]([17]), [4]([9])

	MUSK1	MUSK2	FOX	TIGER	ELEPHANT
mi-SVM [1]	0.874 ± N/A	0.836 ± N/A	0.582 ±N/A	0.784 ± N/A	0.822 ± N/A
MI-SVM [1]	0.779 ± N/A	0.843 ± N/A	0.578 ±N/A	0.840 ± N/A	0.843 ± N/A
mi-graph [2]	0.889 ± 0.033	**0.903** ± 0.039	0.620 ±0.044	**0.860** ± 0.037	**0.869** ± 0.035
mi-net [3]	0.889 ± 0.039	0.858 ± 0.049	0.613 ± 0.035	0.824 ± 0.034	0.858 ± 0.037
MI-Net [3]	0.887 ± 0.041	0.859 ± 0.046	0.622 ± 0.038	0.830 ± 0.032	0.862 ± 0.034
MI-Net_GA [4]	0.900 ± 0.050	0.863 ± 0.042	0.603 ± 0.029	0.845 ± 0.018	0.857 ± 0.027
mi-net_A(Ours)	**0.900** ± 0.063	0.870 ± 0.048	**0.630** ± 0.026	0.845 ± 0.028	0.865 ± 0.024

5.2   Aerial Image Dataset

Details. Two aerial scene classification benchmarks, UCM [21] and AID [18], are utilized to test the effectiveness of our framework. UCM dataset has 21 scene categories and each category has 100 samples. AID dataset has 30 scene categories with up to 10000 samples. In our MIL solution, the backbone is from commonly-utilized CNN models for aerial scene classification. By comparing our results to the results from these models, the improvement caused by MIL approaches can be revealed. Also, gated attention based MIL pooling [9] on these backbones are tested to compare with our pooling operator.

Experimental Setup. We utilize two widely-utilized CNN models in aerial scene classification as our backbone, that is, AlexNet and VGGNet-16. The first five convolutional layers of AlexNet and the first thirteen convolutional layers of VGGNet-16 serve as our instance-level classifier. Later on, these instance representations are fed into our attention based MIL pooling, which has 64 1×1 convolutional layers and a sigmoid activation function. Finally, it is fed into a softmax classifier (demonstrated in Table 3).

Table 3. Detailed network structure for aerial image classification

Layer	Alex_A(Ours1)	VGG_A(Ours2)	AlexNet	VGGNet-16
1	conv11-96	(conv3-64) ×2	conv11-96	(conv3-64) ×2
2	maxpool	maxpool	maxpool	axpool
3	conv5-96	(conv3-128) ×2	conv5-96	(conv3-128) ×2
4	maxpool	maxpool	maxpool	maxpool
5	conv3-384	(conv3-256) ×2	conv3-384	(conv3-256) ×2
6	conv3-384	maxpool	conv3-384	maxpool
7	conv3-256	(conv3-512) ×2	conv3-384	(conv3-512) ×2
8	conv1	conv1	——	maxpool
9	mil-attention	mil-attention	(fc)×3	(fc)×3
10	softmax	softmax	softmax	softmax

The backbone in both AlexNet and VGGNet-16 utilize parameters from pre-trained AlexNet or VGG-16 model on ImageNet as the initial parameters.

The model is trained by the Adam optimizer and has a batch size of 32. The initial learning rate is set to 0.0001 and 0.00005 in AlexNet based solution and VGG-16 based solution respectively. The learning rate is divided by 10 every 30 epochs. The training process does not terminate until 90 epochs are finished. Moreover, to overcome the possible over-fitting problem, we use L_2 normalization with a parameter setting of 5×10^{-4} and the dropout rate is set to be 0.2 in all solutions.

Comparison. Following the experiment protocols in [21] and [18], the overall accuracy of ten independent runs are reported. All commonly-utilized training ratio settings (UCM 50%, UCM 80%, AID 20% and AID 50%) are all tested. Our results (denoted as Alex_A and VGG_A) are compared with the results from original AlexNet, original VGGNet-16, AlexNet with gated attention MIL pooling (denoted as Alex_GA) and VGG with gated attention MIL pooling (denoted as VGG_GA). All results are listed in Table 4.

It can be seen that our solution outperforms the backbone and the backbone with gated attention pooling operators under all four training ratio settings. Also, our solution outperforms the recently proposed multiple instance aerial scene classification solution in [4].

Table 4. Comparison of our framework and other state-of-the-art methods on aerial datasets. [1]([18]), [2]([9]), [3]([4])

	UCM50%	UCM80%	AID20%	AID50%
Alex [1]	93.98 ± 0.67	95.02 ± 0.81	86.86 ± 0.47	89.53 ± 0.31
Alex_GA [2]	96.02 ± 0.44	97.64 ± 0.64	90.60 ± 0.31	92.91 ± 0.37
Alex_A(Ours1)	**96.24 ± 0.42**	**98.22 ± 0.52**	**90.97 ± 0.14**	**93.71 ± 0.32**
VGG [1]	94.14 ± 0.69	95.21 ± 1.20	86.86 ± 0.47	89.53 ± 0.31
VGG_GA [2]	97.48 ± 0.52	98.29 ± 0.52	93.22 ± 0.23	95.98 ± 0.29
VGG_A(Ours2)	**97.92 ± 0.36**	**98.74 ± 0.48**	**93.99 ± 0.14**	**96.15 ± 0.29**
MIDCCNN [3]	94.93 ± 0.51	97.00 ± 0.49	88.26 ± 0.43	92.53 ± 0.18

5.3   Medical Image Dataset

Details. Colon cancer dataset was published for medical image recognition [13]. It consists of 100 large-scale images with 22444 nuclei. Each nuclei belongs to one of the following four categories, that is, epithelial, inflammatory, fibroblast, and miscellaneous. Bags are split from the large-scale images and each bag is a 27×27 image patch. We keep the same backbone in [9,13] for comparison.

Experimental Setup. The backbone is softmax CNN in [13]. The convolutional features are later fed into our attention based MIL pooling. The detailed network structure is listed in Table 5. Hyper-parameters such as learning rate, iteration number and weight decay all keep the same with [9,13].

Comparison. Following the experiment protocols in [13] and [9], the recall, precision and F-score of five independent runs are reported in Table 6.

It can be seen that our solution (denoted as softmaxCNN_A) outperforms all other solutions relying on pre-defined MIL pooling operators (first four rows in Table 6). Also, it outperforms the recent proposed gated attention based MIL pooling operator (denoted as softmaxCNN_GA) [9]. Results on aerial and medical datasets indicate that our MIL pooling operator is qualified in these weakly-annotated visual tasks.

Table 5. Detailed network structure for medical image classification

Layer	SoftmaxCNN	Ours
1	conv4-36	conv4-36
2	maxpool	maxpool
3	conv3-48	conv3-48
4	maxpool	maxpool
5	(fc) ×3	mil-attention
6	softmax classifier	softmax classifier

Table 6. Comparison of our framework and other state-of-the-art methods on medical dataset. [1]([9])

	Precision	Recall	F-score
instance+max [1]	0.866 ± 0.017	0.816 ± 0.031	0.839 ± 0.023
instance+min [1]	0.821 ± 0.011	0.710 ± 0.031	0.759 ± 0.017
embedding+max [1]	0.884 ± 0.014	0.753 ± 0.020	0.813 ± 0.017
embedding+min [1]	0.911 ±0.011	0.804 ± 0.027	0.853 ± 0.016
softmaxCNN_GA [1]	0.944 ± 0.016	0.851 ± 0.035	0.893 ± 0.022
softmaxCNN_A(Ours)	**0.950** ± 0.012	**0.863** ± 0.020	**0.904** ± 0.015

5.4 MIL Document Dataset

Details. We validate the performance of our MIL framework on three benchmarks for MIL text classification utilized in [17,27], that is, alt.atheism, comp.graphics and comp.windows.misc. The detailed information of these datasets are listed in [17]. Still, we keep the same backbone while inserting our attention module to test the performance of our solution.

Experimental Setup. Similar to the experiments in classic MIL datasets, the backbone we utilize is the mi-net [9,17]. Also, the attention based MIL pooling and the classification layer is the same with the experiments for classic MIL datasets (demonstrated in Table 1). Hyper-parameters such as learning rate, iteration number and weight decay all keep the same with [9,17].

Table 7. Comparison of our framework and other state-of-the-art methods on MIL text datasets. [1]([27]), [2]([17])

	alt.atheism	comp.graphic	comp.os
MI-Kernel [1]	0.602 ± 0.039	0.470 ± 0.033	0.510 ± 0.052
mi-Graph [1]	0.655 ± 0.040	0.778 ± 0.016	0.631 ± 0.015
mi-net [2]	0.758 ± N/A	0.830 ± N/A	0.658 ± N/A
MI-Net [2]	0.776 ± N/A	0.826 ± N/A	0.678 ± N/A
MI-Net_DS [2]	**0.860** ± N/A	0.822 ± N/A	0.716 ± N/A
MI-Net_RC [2]	0.858 ± N/A	0.828 ±N/A	**0.720** ± N/A
mi-net_A(Ours)	0.790 ± 0.057	**0.840** ± 0.052	0.710 ± 0.057

Comparison. Following the corresponding experiment protocols, the mean accuracy and standard deviation of ten-folds cross validation is reported as the final result. The classification accuracy of our and other state-of-the-art methods are listed in Table 7. It can be seen that our solution (denoted as mi-net_A) achieves a comparable result when advanced strategies such as deep supervision (DS) and residual connection (RC) are utilized in mi-net [17].

6   Conclusion

In this paper, we proposed an attention awareness multiple instance neural network framework. It consists of an instance-level classifier, a trainable MIL pooling operator and a bag-level classification layer. The trainable MIL pooling operator is based on spatial attention mechanism and it assigns different weights to different instances inside a bag and key instances can be stressed. Finally, the bag-level probabilities are fed into a classifier to form an end-to-end solution so that the multiple instance neural network is under the direct supervision of bag labels. Exhaustive experiments on a series of pattern recognition tasks including classic MIL problems, text classification, medical image classification and challenging aerial scene classification validate the effectiveness of our proposed framework.

References

1. Amores, J.: Multiple instance classification: review, taxonomy and comparative study. Artif. Intell. **201**(4), 81–105 (2013)
2. Andrews, S., Tsochantaridis, I., Hofmann, T.: Support vector machines for multiple-instance learning. In: Neural Information Processing Systems (2003)
3. Babenko, B., Yang, M.H., Belongie, S.: Visual tracking with online multiple instance learning. In: IEEE Conference on Computer Vision and Pattern Recognition, CVPR (2009)
4. Bi, Q., Qin, K., Li, Z.L., Zhang, H., Xu, K.: Multiple instance dense connected convolution neural network for aerial image scene classification. In: IEEE International Conference on Image Processing (2019)
5. Bi, Q., Qin, K., Zhang, H., Xia, G.S.: Local semantic enhanced convnet for aerial scene recognition. IEEE Trans. Image Process. **30**, 6498–6511 (2021)
6. Bi, Q., Zhou, B., Qin, K., Ye, Q., Xia, G.S.: All grains, one scheme (agos): Learning multi-grain instance representation for aerial scene classification. arXiv preprint arXiv:2205.03371 (2022)
7. Dietterich, T.G., Lathrop, R.H., Lozano-Pérez, T.: Solving the multiple instance problem with axis-parallel rectangles. Artif. Intell. **89**(1–2), 31–71 (1997)
8. Hou, L., Samaras, D., Kurc, T.M., Gao, Y., Davis, J.E., Saltz, J.H.: Patch-based convolutional neural network for whole slide tissue image classification. In: IEEE Conference on Computer Vision & Pattern Recognition (2016)
9. Ilse, M., Tomczak, J.M., Welling, M.: Attention-based deep multiple instance learning. In: International Conference on Machine Learning (2018)
10. Kumar, R., Melih, K.: Variational weakly-supervised gaussian processes. In: 27th British Machine Vision Conference (2019)

11. Maron, O., Ratan, A.L.: Multiple-instance learning for natural scene classification. In: Fifteenth International Conference on Machine Learning (1998)
12. Peng, T., Wang, X., Xiang, B., Liu, W.: Multiple instance detection network with online instance classifier refinement. In: IEEE Conference on Computer Vision and Pattern Recognition (2017)
13. Sirinukunwattana, K., Raza, S., Tsang, Y.W., Snead, D., Cree, I., Rajpoot, N.: Locality sensitive deep learning for detection and classification of nuclei in routine colon cancer histology images. IEEE Trans. Med. Imaging **35**(5), 1196–1206 (2016)
14. Vatsavai, R.R.: Gaussian multiple instance learning approach for mapping the slums of the world using very high resolution imagery. In: ACM SIGKDD International Conference on Knowledge Discovery & Data Mining (2013)
15. Wang, Q., Yuan, Y., Yan, P., Li, X.: Saliency detection by multiple-instance learning. IEEE Trans. Cybern. **43**(2), 660–672 (2013)
16. Wang, Q., Si, L., Zhang, D.: A discriminative data-dependent mixture-model approach for multiple instance learning in image classification. In: Fitzgibbon, A., Lazebnik, S., Perona, P., Sato, Y., Schmid, C. (eds.) ECCV 2012. LNCS, vol. 7575, pp. 660–673. Springer, Heidelberg (2012). https://doi.org/10.1007/978-3-642-33765-9_47
17. Wang, X., Yan, Y., Peng, T., Xiang, B., Liu, W.: Revisiting multiple instance neural networks. Pattern Recogn. **74**, 15–24 (2016)
18. Xia, G., et al.: Aid: A benchmark dataset for performance evaluation of aerial scene classification. IEEE Trans. Geosci.& Remote Sensing **55**(7), 3965–3981 (2017)
19. Xu, Y.Y.: Multiple-instance learning based decision neural networks for image retrieval and classification. Neurocomputing **171**(C), 826–836 (2015)
20. Yan, S., Zhu, X., Liu, G., Wu, J.: Sparse multiple instance learning as document classification. Multimedia Tools Appl. **76**(3), 4553–4570 (2016). https://doi.org/10.1007/s11042-016-3567-z
21. Yi, Y., Newsam, S.: Geographic image retrieval using local invariant features. IEEE Trans. Geosci. Remote Sens. **51**(2), 818–832 (2013)
22. Yun, W., Li, J., Metze, F.: Comparing the max and noisy-or pooling functions in multiple instance learning for weakly supervised sequence learning tasks (2018). arXiv preprint arXiv:1805.10201
23. Zaheer, M., Kottur, S., Ravanbhakhsh, S., Poczos, B., Smola, A.: Deep sets. In: Conference and Workshop on Neural Information Processing Systems (2017)
24. Zhang, M.L., Zhou, Z.H.: Improve multi-instance neural networks through feature selection. Neural Process. Lett. **19**(1), 1–10 (2004)
25. Zhang, M.L., Zhou, Z.H.: Adapting RBF neural networks to multi-instance learning. Neural Process. Lett. **23**(1), 1–26 (2006)
26. Zhou, B., Yi, J., Bi, Q.: Differential convolution feature guided deep multi-scale multiple instance learning for aerial scene classification. In: ICASSP 2021–2021 IEEE International Conference on Acoustics, Speech and Signal Processing (ICASSP), pp. 4595–4599. IEEE (2021)
27. Zhou, Z.H., Sun, Y.Y., Li, Y.F.: Multi-instance learning by treating instances as non-IID samples. In: International Conference on Machine Learning. pp. 1249–1256 (2009)

Context Reasoning Attention Network: Generating Plausible Distractors for Multi-choice Questions

Mingchao Li[1], Liuyin Wang[1], Haozhuang Liu[1], Wei Wang[1], and Hai-Tao Zheng[1,2(✉)]

[1] Shenzhen International Graduate School, Tsinghua University, Shenzhen, China
{li-mc19,ly-wang19,lhz19,w-w16}@mails.tsinghua.edu.cn,
zheng.haitao@sz.tsinghua.edu.cn
[2] Peng Cheng Laboratory, Shenzhen, China

Abstract. Distractor generation, which aims to generate the wrong option part of multi-choice questions, has been proposed to assist educators to test the examinees' reading comprehension and reasoning ability. Recently, some Seq2Seq-based models have been proposed to solve the task of automatic distractor generation. However, they did not make full use of context information to generate distractors. In order to overcome this shortcoming, we propose a context reasoning attention network for distractor generation. Experimental results show that our model outperforms state-of-the-art baselines and improves the distractive ability of the generated distractors in terms of automatic evaluation and human evaluation.

Keywords: Context reasoning · Distractor generation · Reading comprehension

1 Introduction

Reading comprehension (RC) tasks are commonly used in a variety of examinations to test the examinee's knowledge and logical reasoning ability. In an exam, reading comprehension questions often appear as multiple-choice questions (MCQs), which require examinees to understand the question and the article and identify question-related details in the article for choosing the correct answer. An example of MCQs is shown in Fig. 1. The MCQs are comprised of four components: (i) an article, the reading material; (ii) questions, related to the article; (iii) answers, the correct options to the questions; (iv) distractors, the wrong options. So the quality of MCQs is not only related to questions and answers, but also related to distractors. A good-quality distractor requires two features. First, the distractor should appear in the article and be related to the question [3]. Second, the semantics of the answer and distractors corresponding to a certain question need to be different, while the syntactic structures should

M. Li and L. Wang—Equal contribution.

© The Author(s), under exclusive license to Springer Nature Switzerland AG 2022
E. Pimenidis et al. (Eds.): ICANN 2022, LNCS 13531, pp. 593–604, 2022.
https://doi.org/10.1007/978-3-031-15934-3_49

be similar, which can confuse the examinees. In the process of building the question bank, it is very time-consuming to manually create appropriate distractors [8]. Thus, automatically generating distractors is very important.

Article:

...

One thing a good leader typically does is to communicate the big picture , so that each employee can see how the particular role he or she plays makes a contribution to the final result . Good leaders are positive and optimistic when they speak about the future . Their enthusiasm wins them plenty of supporters who help make their vision a reality . Good leaders also understand that different people are motivated by different things . For employees motivated by a need for achievement , a leader explains how the task offers an opportunity to take on a challenge with an achievable goal.

...

Words have power , including the power to make people feel whether or not they are important to the success of an organization . Good leaders believe that every team member matters and set up environments that make everyone feel important . It is no wonder they can attract the support they need to help them achieve their goals .

...

Question:

What should a good leader do for an employee who wants to succeed at work?

A. To encourage the employee to meet the challenges of his work. (Answer)

B. To promote the employee to a leadership role. (Distractor)

C. To draw a beautiful picture of the employee's future. (Distractor)

D. To let the staff know the important role the employee plays. (Distractor)

Fig. 1. A multi-choice question from the RACE dataset, consisting of an article, a question, an answer and distractors. We use the same color to mark the related content between the options and the article.

Previous neural models don't make full use of the answer and question information. Firstly, they don't explore the relationship between answers and distractors. In the real examination, the instructors tend to create distractors whose syntactic structures are the same as the answer to confuse examinees. In this way, examinees cannot guess the right option from multiple options by observing some surface features, such as the length of each option. Secondly, they don't capture the crux of the question. The different parts of the question have different effects on the generated distractors. Human experts tend to focus on the crux of the question to generate relevant distractors.

To address these issues, we propose an Context Reasoning Attention Network. Our model is based on Seq2Seq model. It contains the article encoder, the answer encoder and the distractor decoder. These two encoders encode articles and answers, separately. During the decode stage, the context reasoning attention combines the article attention and answer attention. In detail, the article encoder utilizes gated multihead self-attention to aggregate information from the whole passage. Further, the key words in the question are tagged in the article encoder.

Our contributions: 1) We propose context reasoning attention mechanism to capture the relationship between the answer and distractor, which can help generate plausible distractors 2) We add the question keyword tag to obtain the crux of the question, which makes the generated distractor related to the question. 3) Extensive experimental results show that our model outperforms all baselines and achieves high scores in BlEU-4 and ROUGE-L.

2   Problem Definition and Related Work

We use T, A and Q to represent input article, answer and question respectively, and D denotes distractor here. Automatic Distractor Generation (DG) task is to learn a model by maximizing the conditional probability $p(D|T, A, Q)$. Specifically, the input is comprised of article $T = \{w_t\}_{t=1}^{l}$, answer $A = \{a_t\}_{t=1}^{m}$ and question $Q = \{q_t\}_{t=1}^{n}$. The output is distractor $D = \{y_t\}_{t=1}^{k}$. l, m, n, k are the length of the corresponding sequence.

$$\overline{D} = \arg\max_{D} \left[\log \mathrm{P}(D|T, A, Q)\right], \tag{1}$$

The deep learning method for distractor generation are often based on Seq2Seq [16] model with attention mechanism [1]. Reference [2] uses hierarchical encoder-decoder framework and proposes a static attention mechanism. Reference [20] proposes a Co-attetion Hierarchical Network. However, these models don't make full use of the context and can not generate distractors like human do. Compare with their models, we propose two mechanism to generate plausible distractors. First, we adopt a context reasoning attention to attend the answer information. Moreover, the question crux is utilized to focus on the significant part of the question.

3   Methodology

We propose a context reasoning attention network. The overview of our model is shown in Fig. 2. The seq2seq model contains three parts: 1) The article encoder maps the article words and the question keyword tags to their word representations and uses gated multihead self-attention to aggregate information. 2) The answer encoder transfers the answer words into word representations. 3) The decoder uses context reasoning attention, which combines the answer attention and the article attention, to focus on important context information. Next, we explain our model in detail.

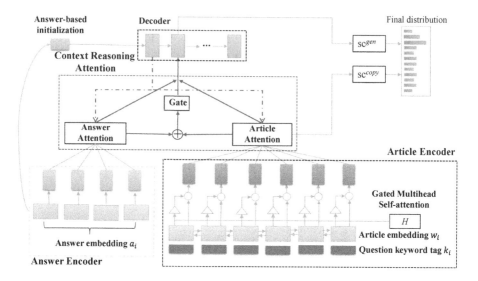

Fig. 2. End-to-end diagram for our model with context reasoning attention, gated multihead self-attention, question keyword tag, and answer-based initialization *(Better viewed in color)*.

3.1 Encoding

Word Embedding: A shared embedding lookup table is firstly used to map each word w_i in the article T into word embeddings $(\mathbf{w}_1, \mathbf{w}_2, ..., \mathbf{w}_m)$, and transform each word a_i in the answer A into word embeddings $(\mathbf{a}_1, \mathbf{a}_2, ..., \mathbf{a}_m)$, where $\mathbf{w}_i$ and $\mathbf{a}_i$ has d_w dimensions.

Question Keyword Tag: To utilize the question information efficiently, we capture the crux of the question by adding the question keyword tag to the article embedding process. The tag k_i for each word w_i in the article represents whether the word co-occurs in both the article and the question, i.e., the question keyword.

Article and Question Encoding: We adopt BiLSTM [5] to encode words in the article with the question key word tags. BiLSTM can help collect information from two directions. We concatenate the representations of forward and backward as word representations : $\mathbf{H} = \{[\overrightarrow{\mathbf{h}_t}, \overleftarrow{\mathbf{h}_t}]\}_{t=1}^{l}$.

Gated Multihead Self-attention: Unlike sentence-level passage information, the length of the article is very long. In order to aggregate the whole information from the long article and learn the word representation from context, we introduce the gated multihead self-attention mechanism, which combines the gated self-attention mechanism [19] and the multihead self-attention mechanism [17]. We get the self-attention representations of the words $\{\mathbf{s}_t\}_{t=1}^{l}$ in the article as follows:

$$\mathbf{a}_t^s = \text{softmax} \left(\mathbf{H}^T \mathbf{W}^s \mathbf{h}_t \right),$$
$$\mathbf{s}_t = \mathbf{H} \cdot \mathbf{a}_t^s, \tag{2}$$

where W^s is a trainable weight matrix, s_t is the weighted sum of all hidden states by self-attention scores for t-th word in the article.

Multihead attention is computed as follows:

$$\text{Attention}(Q, K, V) = \text{softmax} \left(\frac{QK^T}{\sqrt{d}} \right) V \tag{3}$$

$$M_i = \text{Attention} \left(QW_i^Q, KW_i^K, VW_i^V \right) \tag{4}$$

$$\text{Multihead}(Q, K, V) = \left[M^1; \ldots; M^n \right] W \tag{5}$$

where W_i^Q, W_i^K, W_i^V, W is learnable vector. d is the hidden size of input. n is the number of attention heads.

We use multihead attention to enhance the semantic representation, which computed as follows:

$$b_t = \text{Multihead}(h_t, h_t, h_t) \tag{6}$$

Then we get updated representations of words by:

$$\mathbf{f}_t = \tanh \left(\mathbf{W}^f \left[\mathbf{h}_t, \mathbf{s}_t \right] \right),$$
$$\mathbf{g}_t = \sigma \left(\mathbf{W}^g \left[\mathbf{h}_t, \mathbf{s}_t \right] \right), \tag{7}$$
$$\hat{\mathbf{h}}_t = \mathbf{g}_t \odot \mathbf{f}_t + (1 - \mathbf{g}_t) \odot \mathbf{b}_t,$$

where W^f and W^g are learnable vectors, f_t is the self-enhanced representation, g_t is the gate vector, $\hat{h}_t$ is the final representation for the word in article. σ is *sigmoid* function. $\odot$ is the element-wise multiplication.

Answer Encoding: We utilize a bidirectional LSTM to encode the word representation of answer sequence $(\mathbf{a}_1, \mathbf{a}_2, ..., \mathbf{a}_m)$ into answer representation h_t^a.

3.2 Decoding

We use one uni-directional LSTM as the decoder to generate the distractor. d_t is the hidden state of LSTM at time t, where d_0 is initialized by the last hidden state of the answer encoder. y_t represents the word generated at time t and c_t is the context vector. The decoder's lookup table is the same as the encoders'. V is the vocabulary size and W^V is a learnable vector. We compute output probabilities of each distractor word as follows:

$$\mathbf{d}_t = LSTM_{dec} \left(\mathbf{d}_{t-1}, \left[\mathbf{y}_{t-1} : \mathbf{c}_{t-1} \right] \right),$$
$$p \left(y_t \mid \{ y_{<t} \} \right) = \text{softmax} \left(\mathbf{W}^V \mathbf{d}_t \right). \tag{8}$$

Answer-Based Initialization: Rather than using the final hidden state of the article encoder, we adopt the final hidden state of the answer encoder as the initial state of the decoder. Because when human experts are designing the MCQs, they tend to first observe the question and the answer, extract distractive information from the article, and then edit answer with that information to form a related distractor.

Article and Answer Attention: Our model generates the distractor based on context reasoning attention mechanism. This mechanism contains two types of attention. We denote them as article attention mechanism and answer attention mechanism. As for the article attention, at the time t step, it takes current decoder state d_t and all hidden states of the article words to generate weight for each hidden state of article words, which is computed as follows:

$$\mathbf{o}_t = \hat{\mathbf{h}}_t \mathbf{W}^{ar} \mathbf{d_t},$$
$$\mathbf{a}_t^{\mathbf{ar}} = \text{softmax}\left(\mathbf{o}_t\right), \tag{9}$$

where W^{ar} is learnable vector. o_t is the energy value. $\mathbf{a}_t^{\mathbf{ar}}$ is the article attention distribution. Then, we use the weight to compute the context vector of the article information:

$$\mathbf{c}_t^{ar} = \hat{\mathbf{h}}_t \cdot \mathbf{a}_t^{\mathbf{ar}}. \tag{10}$$

Similarly, as for the answer attention, at the time t step, the answer context vector is computed in the same way:

$$\mathbf{r}_t = \mathbf{h}_t^{\mathbf{a}} \mathbf{W}^{an} \mathbf{d_t},$$
$$\mathbf{a}_t^{\mathbf{an}} = \text{softmax}\left(\mathbf{r}_t\right), \tag{11}$$
$$\mathbf{c}_t^{an} = \mathbf{h}_t^{\mathbf{a}} \cdot \mathbf{a}_t^{\mathbf{an}}.$$

Context Reasoning Attention Mechanism: Since the generated distractor is related to the article and the answer, we introduce a context reasoning attention mechanism. In this mechanism, we merge the article context vector and answer context vector:

$$\mathbf{g} = \sigma(\mathbf{c}_t^{\mathbf{ar}}),$$
$$\mathbf{c}_t = \mathbf{g} \circ \mathbf{c}_t^{an} + (1 - \mathbf{g}) \circ \mathbf{c}_t^{ar}, \tag{12}$$

where σ is *sigmoid* function, and $\mathbf{c}_t$ is the final context vector combined with the article context $\mathbf{c}_t^{ar}$ and answer context $\mathbf{c}_t^{an}$ under the control of gate g.

Copy Mechanism: The copy mechanism is proposed to solve the problem of Out-Of-Vocabulary words. In recent years, a lot of work [4,15,18] have been carried out based on the copy mechanism. Our model adopts copy mechanism the same as [4] to improve the quality of generated distractors.

3.3   Training Details

As for the training dataset U, each piece of data is a quadruple (T, Q, A, D), in which T, Q, A and D represent an article, a question, an answer and a distractor, respectively. The training object is to minimize the negative log-likelihood for the generated distractor conditioned on the P, Q, A:

$$\mathcal{L} = -\sum_U \log \mathrm{P}(D|P, A, Q; \Theta). \tag{13}$$

4   Experiments

4.1   Dataset and Implementation Details

Dataset. RACE dataset [6] is collected from the real English test for Chinese students, consisting of articles with different topics. The MCQs in the dataset are generated by human experts. We use the Race dataset to evaluate our model. This dataset contains near 28,000 articles and near 100,000 questions. Each MCQ in the dataset contains a variety of topics which can evaluate the examinees' ability of understanding and reasoning. Now that there exists some data inappropriate for distractor generation, we adopt the dataset processed by previous work [2].

Implementation Details. We use the GloVe word embeddings [13] as lookup table for the article encoder, the answer encoder and the distractor decoder. During training, we froze the word lookup table. The words which are not in the table are replaced by UNK symbol. The dimension of question key word tag is 2. We adapt 2 layers LSTM for the encoders and decoder. The LSTMs in encoding stage are bidirectional while the decoder LSTM is unidirectional. We set the LSTMs hidden size to 600. Dropout probability P=0.3 is applied between different layers. In the training stage, we utilize stochastic gradient descent (SGD) as the optimizer with momentum [11,14]. The batch size is 32 and the initial learning rate is set to 0.8. We train the model for 20 epochs and after 8 epochs, we halve the learning rate every 2 epochs. We use the dev dataset to evaluate the model after each epoch training and select the model with the lowest perplexity as the final model. During the inference stage, we use beam search and set the beam size to 10. The beam search stops when the model generates the EOS token or the generated sequence length is larger than the maximum length 15. We use beam search to generate three different distractors in the same way as HSA [2].

4.2   Baselines and Evaluation Metrics

We compare our model with the following baselines:
    Seq2Seq [16]: The basic sequence-to-sequence framework with attention mechanism [10]. **HRED** [7]: The model uses hierarchical encoder-decoder framework. The model first encodes the words by the hierarchical encoder, and then uses the decoder with hierarchical attention in the decoding stage. **HSA** [2]: The model is based on **HRED**. It contains a *static mechanism*, guiding the attention mechanism to focus on the content related to the question content instead of the answer content. **CHN** [20]: the model is similar with the previous one. A *co-attention* can obtain more interactive relationship between the article and question. The model also adds a similarity loss between the article and the generated distractor.
    We use the following automatic evaluation matrix metrics to evaluate our model: BLEU-1, BLEU-2, BLEU-3, BLEU-4 [12], ROUGE [9].

Table 1. Performance of all models on BLEU and ROUGE. The best performing result for each metric is highlighted in boldface.

		BLEU-1	BLEU-2	BLEU-3	BLEU-4	ROUGE-L
1st Distractor	Seq2Seq	25.28	12.43	7.12	4.51	13.58
	HERD	27.96	14.41	9.05	6.34	14.68
	HSA	28.18	14.57	9.19	6.43	14.89
	CHN	28.65	15.15	9.77	7.01	15.39
	Our Model	**34.55**	**19.41**	**12.45**	**8.54**	**29.63**
2nd Distractor	Seq2Seq	25.13	12.02	6.56	3.93	13.20
	HERD	27.85	13.39	7.89	5.22	14.48
	HSA	27.85	13.41	7.87	5.17	14.41
	CHN	27.29	13.57	8.19	5.51	14.85
	Our Model	**33.57**	**18.26**	**11.15**	**7.29**	**28.39**
3rd Distractor	Seq2Seq	25.34	11.53	5.94	3.33	13.23
	HERD	26.73	12.55	7.21	4.58	14.86
	HSA	26.93	12.62	7.25	4.59	14.72
	CHN	26.64	12.67	7.42	4.88	15.08
	Our Model	**32.41**	**17.08**	**10.16**	**6.47**	**27.46**

4.3   Main Results

We list all experiment results for our model in Table 1 and also show the results of **Seq2Seq**, **HRED**, **HAS**, **CHN** for comparison. The automatic evaluation metrics of our model outperform all other models. The experiment results show that we get high scores in BLEU-4 and ROUGE-L. These important scores are higher than the previous best score and achieves the state-of-the-art. Compared with **HAS** and **CHN**, our model use gated multihead self-attention, question keyword tag and context reasoning attention mechanism to model all parts of the MCQ. The results show the effectiveness of our model, which proves that our model makes full use of the information of the article, question and answer.

Table 2. Ablation study of our model. Here we only list results of the first distractor.

	BLEU-3	BLEU-4
Our model	**12.45**	**8.54**
-Gated multihead self-attention	11.93	8.07
-Keyword tag	11.77	7.87
-Context reasoning	11.41	6.96

4.4 Ablation Study

We ablate the model step by step, subtracting modules from our whole model each time. The Table 2 shows that as more modules are removed, the metrics are gradually decreasing. Therefore, the experiment results show that the modules we adopt are efficacious.

The minimum part of our model just contains the answer encoder to learn from the answer information. The BLEU-4 metric of such module is almost the same as the previous model. Thus, it can be proved that the previous model does not make full use of the answer information while we use it efficiently.

4.5 Human Evaluation

Table 3. Results of human evaluation.

Models	Fluency	Coherence	Distracting ability
HSA	3.72	3.10	2.79
CHN	3.85	3.24	2.83
Our model	**4.06**	**3.43**	**3.11**

In order to analyze the quality of the distractor generated by our model, we conduct the human evaluation. We randomly select 100 pieces of data from the test dataset and invite three people to evaluate distractors generated by different models. All the three people are qualified because they have CET6 level English skills and hold bachelor degree. To be specific, the human evaluation consists of three metrics: (1) **fluency**, which shows the distractor is semantic completeness and it is like human generation. (2) **coherence**, which indicates the distractor is related to the article and the question. (3) **distracting capability**, which measures the distractor's ability to confuse the examinees.

Table 3 shows the human evaluation results. We can see that our model gets the highest score. Thus, our model can generate more meaningful, frequency and plausible distractors.

4.6 Case Study

In Fig. 3, we present our case study which contains two MCQs. In each MCQ, we compare the distractor generated by our model with **HSA** and **CHN**. In the first MCQ, the article is about *Vitamin D*. The distractor generated by **HSA** is *A fat fish*, which is nearly the same meaning with *oily fish* in the article. Thus, it is semantically relevant to the article. Similarly, the distractor generated by **CHN** is *Tropical liver, cheese and egg*, which is related to the *beef liver, cheese and egg yolks* in the article. These two distractors are seemingly appropriate for the MCQ. However, in the real exam, examinees can exclude these two distractors

Article1: Vitamin D helps bones .... But many people worry about getting skin cancer and skin damage from the sun. .... Also, darker-skinned people produce less vitamin D than lighter - skinned people. The amount also decreases in older people and .... Foods high in this vitamin include oily fish and fish liver oils. .... Small amounts of vitamin D are found in beef liver, cheese and egg yolks ...
Question: Which of the following people produce the least amount of vitamin D?
Answer: Elderly darker-skinned people.
Distractors: 1. Young lighter-skinned people. 2.Elderly lighter-skinned people. 3.Young darker-skinned people.
HSA: A fat fish.
CHN: Tropical liver , cheese and egg.
Our model: Healthy - skinned people.

Article2: ...Zhao jianmin, a professor at Shanghai University, said fragmented reading was part of modern life. " The fast of life leaves many people no time to sit and read a whole book, " he said. "So making use of fragmented time to read is sure to be a trend"... "Fragmented reading is sometimes good, but don't let it take all your time, " suggested Tian Zhilng, an editor. .... He suggested people choose easy books first, then move onto more difficult ones.
Question: How does Tian Zhiling think about people should read ?
Answer: They should read both on digital devices and quality books.
Distractors: 1. They should spend more time reading on digital device. 2.They should spend days reading whole novels at a time. 3. They should read a fun way instead of a traditional way.
HSA: They don't like reading.
CHN: It can help people improve reading.
Our model: They should read more books on digital devices.

Fig. 3. Samples of distractors generated by our model and two other competitive models, HSA [2] and CHN [20]. We use colors and underlines to indicate the semantic connection between the distractor segments and article text.

very quickly. Because they will notice the question is about the people while the two distractors are not. Even they don't read the article, they can pass the two distractors. By contrast, the distractor generated by our model are both related to the article and question. In addition, it has the same pattern with answer and examinees need a reasoning process to solve the question. In the second MCQ, the article is about *reading on digital devices*. The distractor generated by our model has the same subject and object with the answer, which can confuse examinees. What' more, it is like the golden reference generated by human experts. Thus, the case study shows that our model is better than previous models.

5   Conclusions

We propose a Context Reasoning Attention Network to generate distractors for multiple choice questions. The model utilizes the context reasoning attention and question key tag, which can help make full use of context information in MCQs. The experiment results show that our model achieves the best performance and generate more meaningful, frequency and plausible distractors. Our future work lands in solving the multi-hop questions which means that the question in the MCQs need more complex reasoning.

Acknowledgment. This research is supported by National Natural Science Foundation of China (Grant No. 6201101015), Beijing Academy of Artificial Intelligence (BAAI), Natural Science Foundation of Guangdong Province (Grant No. 2021A1515012640), the Basic Research Fund of Shenzhen City (Grant No. JCYJ20210324120012033 and JCYJ20190813165003837), and Overseas Cooperation Research Fund of Tsinghua Shenzhen International Graduate School (Grant No. HW2021008).

References

1. Bahdanau, D., Cho, K., Bengio, Y.: Neural machine translation by jointly learning to align and translate. In: Bengio, Y., LeCun, Y. (eds.) 3rd International Conference on Learning Representations, ICLR 2015, San Diego, 7–9 May 2015, Conference Track Proceedings (2015). arXiv:1409.0473

2. Gao, Y., Bing, L., Li, P., King, I., Lyu, M.R.: Generating distractors for reading comprehension questions from real examinations. Proc. AAAI Conf. Artif. Intell. **33**, 6423–6430 (2019)

3. Goodrich, H.C.: Distractor efficiency in foreign language testing. In: Tesol Quarterly, pp. 69–78 (1977)

4. Gu, J., Lu, Z., Li, H., Li, V.O.K.: Incorporating copying mechanism in sequence-to-sequence learning. arXiv preprint arXiv:1603.06393 (2016)

5. Hochreiter, S., Schmidhuber, J.: Long short-term memory. Neural Comput. **9**(8), 1735–1780 (1997)

6. Lai, G., Xie, Q., Liu, H., Yang, Y., Hovy, E.: Race: large-scale reading comprehension dataset from examinations. arXiv preprint arXiv:1704.04683 (2017)

7. Li, J., Luong, M.T., Jurafsky, D.: A hierarchical neural autoencoder for paragraphs and documents. arXiv preprint arXiv:1506.01057 (2015)

8. Liang, C., Yang, X., Dave, N., Wham, D., Pursel, B., Giles, C.L.: Distractor generation for multiple choice questions using learning to rank. In: Proceedings of the Thirteenth Workshop on Innovative Use of NLP for Building Educational Applications, pp. 284–290 (2018)

9. Lin, C.Y.: Rouge: A package for automatic evaluation of summaries. In: Text Summarization Branches Out, pp. 74–81 (2004)

10. Luong, M.T., Pham, H., Manning, C.D.: Effective approaches to attention-based neural machine translation. arXiv preprint arXiv:1508.04025 (2015)

11. Nesterov, Y.: A method for unconstrained convex minimization problem with the rate of convergence o $(1/k^2)$. In: Doklady an USSR, vol. 269, pp. 543–547 (1983)

12. Papineni, K., Roukos, S., Ward, T., Zhu, W.J.: Bleu: a method for automatic evaluation of machine translation. In: Proceedings of the 40th Annual Meeting on Association for Computational Linguistics, ACL 2002, pp. 311–318. Association for Computational Linguistics, Stroudsburg (2002). https://doi.org/10.3115/1073083.1073135

13. Pennington, J., Socher, R., Manning, C.D.: Glove: global vectors for word representation. In: Empirical Methods in Natural Language Processing (EMNLP), pp. 1532–1543 (2014). https://aclanthology.org/D14-1162/

14. Qian, N.: On the momentum term in gradient descent learning algorithms. Neural Netw. **12**(1), 145–151 (1999)

15. See, A., Liu, P.J., Manning, C.D.: Get to the point: summarization with pointer-generator networks. arXiv preprint arXiv:1704.04368 (2017)

16. Sutskever, I., Vinyals, O., Le, Q.V.: Sequence to sequence learning with neural networks. In: Advances in Neural Information Processing Systems, pp. 3104–3112 (2014)
17. Vaswani, A., et al.: Attention is all you need. In: Guyon, I., et al. (eds.) Advances in Neural Information Processing Systems, vol. 30. Curran Associates, Inc. (2017). https://proceedings.neurips.cc//paper/2017/file/3f5ee243547dee91fbd053c1c4a84 5aa-Paper.pdf
18. Vinyals, O., Fortunato, M., Jaitly, N.: Pointer networks. In: Cortes, C., Lawrence, N.D., Lee, D.D., Sugiyama, M., Garnett, R. (eds.) Advances in Neural Information Processing Systems, vol. 28, pp. 2692–2700. Curran Associates, Inc. (2015). https://proceedings.neurips.cc/paper/2015/file/29921001f2f04bd3baee84a12e9809 8f-Paper.pdf
19. Zhao, Y., Ni, X., Ding, Y., Ke, Q.: Paragraph-level neural question generation with maxout pointer and gated self-attention networks. In: Proceedings of the 2018 Conference on Empirical Methods in Natural Language Processing, pp. 3901–3910. Association for Computational Linguistics, Brussels (2018). https://doi.org/10.18653/v1/D18-1424, https://aclanthology.org/D18-1424/
20. Zhou, X., Luo, S., Wu, Y.: Co-attention hierarchical network: generating coherent long distractors for reading comprehension. In: The Thirty-Fourth AAAI Conference on Artificial Intelligence, AAAI 2020, The Thirty-Second Innovative Applications of Artificial Intelligence Conference, IAAI 2020, The Tenth AAAI Symposium on Educational Advances in Artificial Intelligence, EAAI 2020, New York, 7–12 February 2020, pp. 9725–9732. AAAI Press (2020). http://aaai.org/ojs/index. php/AAAI/article/view/6522

DensEMANN + Sparsification: Experiments for Further Shrinking Already Small Automatically Generated DenseNet

Antonio García-Díaz[✉] and Hugues Bersini

IRIDIA-CoDE, Université Libre de Bruxelles (ULB), Brussels, Belgium
{Antonio.Garcia.Diaz,Hugues.Bersini}@ulb.be

Abstract. This paper presents a few experiments that we carried out using DensE-MANN (an algorithm that we are developing for automatically generating small and efficient DenseNet neural networks) and various algorithms for pruning or sparsifying neural networks at different granularity levels. The pruning algorithms that we used are based on the Lottery Ticket algorithm by Frankle and Carbin (2019), and on the Dense-Sparse-Dense (DSD) training algorithm by Han et al. (2017). Our experiments show that the pruning method based on DSD training is very efficient for reducing the parameter count of both human-designed and DensEMANN-generated neural networks while making them recover their original accuracy, and that this is especially true when sparsification is performed at the granularity level of individual convolution weights (by means of a mask that zeroes them out). Further research is nevertheless necessary to find out if (and how) this method can become an alternative to DensEMANN, or work in tandem with it, for actually shrinking already small and efficient neural networks.

Keywords: Neural network · Neural architecture search · NAS · Optimization · Self-structuring · Constructive · Growing · Pruning · Sparsification · DenseNet · EMANN · DensEMANN · Lottery ticket hypothesis · Dense-Sparse-Dense · DSD

1 Introduction

Neural architecture search (NAS) is becoming an increasingly relevant field [1–3]. Algorithms that can automatically generate or optimize neural network (NN) architectures, making them small and efficient, can be useful for quickly and easily developing quality machine learning (ML) applications for low-power or small devices [1, 2, 4]. In addition, these techniques can also help decrease the energy consumption of ML applications—and consequently, their economic cost and environmental impact [1, 5].

Among these NAS and optimization algorithms, those following a so-called "self-structuring" approach (where a NN's architecture is generated and/or modified while the network is trained on a task [1, 6]) deserve, in our opinion, greater attention by ML

A. García-Díaz—IRIDIA-CoDE (TRAIL Researcher).

© The Author(s), under exclusive license to Springer Nature Switzerland AG 2022
E. Pimenidis et al. (Eds.): ICANN 2022, LNCS 13531, pp. 605–617, 2022.
https://doi.org/10.1007/978-3-031-15934-3_50

researchers. These algorithms can not only output very small and yet very efficient NN [1, 7, 8]—they can also do so within very little time and with very little computational cost (the entire process is equivalent to training a single candidate NN) [1, 9].

In this paper, we present some experiments that we performed using DensEMANN, a NN growing algorithm that we are currently developing [1, 10], as well as various network pruning and sparsification techniques that can be executed during a NN's training process. All of these techniques can be considered as part of the "self-structuring" family. The main goal of our experiments is to evaluate and compare the performance of these techniques when used for producing optimal DenseNet [11] NN to solve simple image classification tasks, both when the growing and pruning algorithms are used separately and when they are used in tandem (i.e., when sparsification is performed on NN generated by DensEMANN). As a secondary goal, we hoped that the lessons learned from these experiments would help us improve DensEMANN and the quality of its outputted networks, both in their accuracy on target tasks and in their final size.

2 On "Self-structuring" and Related Research

We define "self-structuring" as in the works by Rami M. Mohammad et al. [6, 12], where it means algorithms that modify a NN's architecture and hyperparameters during its training process. To further classify these algorithms, we use the same categories as in [12]: "**growing**" or "**constructive**" techniques make the NN grow in size during training, and "**pruning**" or "**sparsification**" techniques make it shrink during training.

2.1 Growing and Constructive Algorithms: The Incremental Approach

The incremental approach to self-structuring consists of starting from a simple (or even minimal) NN architecture, and recursively adding new elements (layers, neurons, connections, etc.) until reaching an optimal or satisfactory result [10, 12]. Algorithms following this approach are called "constructive" [12] or "growing" [13] algorithms.

Of particular relevance for this research is **DensEMANN** [1, 10]: a growing algorithm that we are currently developing for automatically generating DenseNet [11] architectures. Based on a similar algorithm from 1994 [14], DensEMANN's latest version (v1.2, first presented in [1]) is composed of a macro-algorithm and a micro-algorithm, which act on the NN at different granularity levels. The macro-algorithm stacks up new densely-connected layers one by one until the NN's accuracy (on a validation dataset) stops improving. Meanwhile, the micro-algorithm is sometimes called to add and/or remove convolution filters in the latest layer on basis of each filter's weight values.

A notable parameter of DensEMANN v1.2 is the "layer creation strategy", which defines how the macro-algorithm generates each new layer's initial architecture. One of two different strategies may be used: update-k (where each layer's initial number of filters is the same as the previous layer's final number of filters) and same-k (where new layers are always created with the same initial number of filters, by default 12). When generating DenseNet-BC, the number of filters in bottleneck layers also depends on the layer creation strategy: it is 4 * the following convolution's initial filter count.

In [1], we showed that DensEMANN v1.2 is able to generate very compact DenseNet (less than 100.000 learnable parameters) that nevertheless perform very well (90% accuracy or more) on various simple image classification datasets (SVHN [15], CIFAR-10 [16], and Fashion-MNIST [17]).

2.2 Pruning and Sparsification Algorithms: The Decremental Approach

The decremental approach to self-structuring follows the opposite route to the incremental approach: it consists of starting from a large NN architecture, and removing elements from it until reaching an optimal or satisfactory result [10, 12]. Algorithms that follow this approach are said to "prune" [7, 12] or "sparsify" the NN [18, 19].

In this paper, we carried out experiments to test two sparsification methods, which are inspired on two notable algorithms that perform some form of pruning:

The Lottery Ticket Hypothesis. This algorithm was developed by Jonathan Frankle and Michael Carbin in 2019 [8], who used it to test the hypothesis of the same name: "A randomly-initialized dense NN contains a subnetwork that is initialized such that—when trained in isolation—it can match the test accuracy of the original network after training for at most the same number of iterations". The Lottery Ticket (LT) algorithm tries to find such "winning ticket" subnetworks through an iterative pruning strategy:

1. Randomly initialize a NN (the state of learnable parameters is θ_0).
2. For n iterative steps do:

   a. Train the network for j iterations, arriving at parameters θ_j.
   b. Prune some of the learnable parameters (a certain target percentage) by creating a mask m that sets their values to zero.
   c. Reset the remaining parameters to their values from θ_0 (the result is equivalent to applying mask m on θ_0)

3. Train the final unpruned parameters normally.

The authors of the LT algorithm obtained empirical evidence that such "winning tickets" did exist and could be found by their algorithm [8]. This evidence, as well as the results of consequent research [20], suggests that the success of "winning tickets" mainly depends on the initial signs of parameters at θ_0, and on the topology of mask m.

Dense-Sparse-Dense (DSD) Training. This is a method for training NN that was developed by Song Han, Jeff Pool, Sharan Narang et al. in 2017 [21]. It consists in training the network following a three-step process: "dense", "sparse", and "re-dense".

1. **Dense:** train the NN normally for a certain number of training epochs.
2. **Sparse:** in each layer, prune a certain target percentage of the weights, and train the network with only the remaining weights for some more epochs.
3. **Re-Dense:** restore the pruned weights (with value 0), and train the network again for a while with a reduced learning rate (LR).

Since DSD training begins and ends with the same NN architecture, it may not be considered a true NAS or network optimization algorithm. However, it remains related to the "self-structuring" family (under the definition we use) because it relies on modifying a network's architecture while it is being trained.

When using DSD training, the authors obtained improved performance for many different NN models and tasks [21]. They conjectured that one of the causes for this is that the "sparse" step helps the network escape saddle points in the solution space.

3 Methodology

For our experiments, we used the same Python implementation of DensEMANN as in [1] (available on GitHub [22]), which relies on PyTorch [23] and Fastai [24]. New functionalities for scheduled pruning were added in using the Fasterai library [25]. Inference times were measured on an MSI GT76 Titan DT laptop, with Windows 10 Pro (64-bit) OS and the following specs: Intel Core i9-10900K CPU (3.70 GHz), NVIDIA GeForce RTX 2080 Super GPU, 64.0 GB RAM (63.9 GB usable).

3.1 Tested Sparsification Methods

The two sparsification methods that we tested follow the same basic blueprint:

- The NN is trained during 900 training epochs, out of which the first 300 epochs are used for sparsification, and the last 600 for further training (with LR reduction).
- Pruning is global (i.e., all layers are not pruned equally), and may be performed at different granularities of architecture elements (e.g.: convolution filters or weights).
- A target end sparsity value must be specified. Using the same terms as [21], let this target value be s such that $0 \leq s < 1$ (it may also be expressed as a percentage), and let the NN's architecture contain N elements of the specific granularity to be pruned:

    - The elements are sorted on basis of their mean absolute weight values (MAWV), from highest to lowest.
    - The nth element is selected, where $n = N * (1 - s)$. Let its MAWV be λ.
    - All elements whose MAWV is lower than λ are "pruned" (actually a mask is applied that zeroes them out).

- The evolution of the LR value during training is similar to the one in DensEMANN [1, 10]: it starts at 0.1, becomes 0.01 at epoch 600, and then 0.001 at epoch 750.
- The weight initialization is the same as in DensEMANN. For DenseNet-BC, this often causes higher initial weights in non-bottleneck layers than in bottlenecks [1].
- The NN's final weight values are those for which it obtained the highest cross-entropy loss on the validation set after sparsification (i.e., from epoch 300 onwards).

The two methods mainly differ in how NN are sparsified during the first 300 epochs:

Method Based on the LT Algorithm. This method follows an iterative pruning approach in 3 steps: let the target end sparsity be s and the number of prunable elements in the network be N, the algorithm aims to prune $N * (s/3)$ of the original elements at epochs 75, 150 and 225 (see Fig. 1). Like in the original LT algorithm [8], after every pruning operation the remaining elements are reset to their initial configuration.

Method Based on DSD Training. Adapting DSD training into an actual pruning schedule was relatively easy: let the target end sparsity be s and the number of prunable elements be N, the "sparse" phase of DSD can be set to remove an intermediate fraction s' of the original elements such that $s < s' < 1$, and the "re-dense" phase may then restore $N * (s' - s)$ of the previously removed elements. In our case, we made s' depend on s, and set it exactly halfway between s and 1: $s' = s + (1 - s)/2$.

Also, instead of using one-shot pruning as in the original paper [21], we opted for a cosine-shaped pruning schedule as suggested in [26] (see Fig. 2). During our "sparse" step (epochs 0 to 150), the number of pruned elements evolves as in (1), and during our "re-dense" step (epochs 150 to 300), the number of restored elements evolves as in (2):

$$N_{pruned}(epoch) = N * (1 + \cos(\pi * (1 - 2 * epoch))) * s'/2 \tag{1}$$

$$N_{restored}(epoch) = N * (1 - \cos(\pi * (1 - 2 * epoch))) * (s' - s)/2 \tag{2}$$

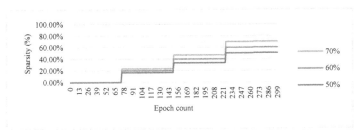

Fig. 1. Evolution of a NN's sparsity over time (in training epochs) when using the sparsification method based on the Lottery Ticket algorithm, for different target end sparsity values

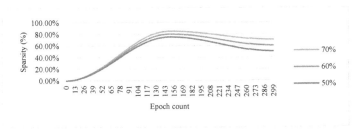

Fig. 2. Evolution of a NN's sparsity over time (in training epochs) when using the sparsification method based on Dense-Sparse-Dense training, for different target end sparsity values

3.2   Experimental Design

In our experiments, we used the same datasets as in our previous paper [1]: SVHN [15], CIFAR-10 [16], and Fashion-MNIST [17]. The training and validation sets were split as explained in [1], and for the test set we used each dataset's full set of test examples.

The experiments that we present in this paper are grouped into three rounds:

1. **In the first round**, we used the two sparsification algorithms to prune human-designed DenseNet while they were trained on SVHN [15]. The initial NN designs were based on the image classification DenseNet described in [11]: we used DenseNet-BC architectures with 3 dense blocks and 12 dense layers in each block (each dense layer consisting of a bottleneck and a standard convolution), with a growth rate (k, the number of convolution filters in each layer) of either 12 or 24.

   We ran each of the two sparsification algorithms 5 times on each of these networks, repeating the experiment at the pruning granularity levels of convolution filters and weights[1], and with target end sparsity values of 50%, 60%, and 70%[2]. We then compared the final test set accuracies obtained with these algorithms to those obtained after training the full networks 5 times for 600 or 900 epochs. To train the full networks, we used DensEMANN's weight initialization, an initial LR value of 0.1, and a schedule that divides the LR by 10 after 50% and 75% of the training epochs.

2. **In the second round**, we used the best performing sparsification method from the first round to sparsify the smallest of the two human-designed networks (3 dense blocks with 12 dense layers each, $k = 12$) while training it on SVHN. In this round, we wished to generate NN with a similar number of (non-pruned) parameters to that of DenseNet-BC generated by DensEMANN v1.2. For this reason, we chose higher target sparsity values than in the first round: 80%, 85%, 90%, and 95%.

   Again, the experiment was repeated 5 times at the granularity levels of filters and weights, and for each of the target sparsity values. The aim was to compare the validation and test set accuracies obtained with the selected sparsification algorithm to those obtained with DensEMANN v1.2 and each of its two layer creation strategies (the comparison is done against the DenseNet-BC networks that we generated in [1] for solving SVHN).

3. **Finally, in the third round** we used the same algorithm as in the second round to prune some top performing DensEMANN-generated DenseNet-BC while re-training them from random weights. We used the same top performing NN as in our previous paper [1]: out of five runs of DensEMANN v1.2, we selected the NN that obtained the lowest validation loss (cross-entropy) for each dataset.

   In this round, we used three image classification datasets: SVHN [15], CIFAR-10+[3] [16], and Fashion-MNIST [17] (the same datasets for which we generated the selected NN). We repeated the experiment 5 times on each NN, for the granularity

---

[1] We only pruned elements in convolution layers, sparing the NN's fully-connected part.

[2] As explained in Sect. 3.1, these are percentages of the number N of prunable elements of the required granularity, not of the total parameter count.

[3] CIFAR-10+ is the same as CIFAR-10, but with basic data augmentation applied on images from the training and validation sets (random crop and horizontal flip as described in [1, 11]).

levels of filters and weights, and for target sparsity values of 50%, 60%, and 70%. The goal of this experiment was to compare the test set accuracies of the networks before and after re-training and sparsifying them.

4   Results and Observations

4.1   First Round: Trying Various Sparsification Algorithms on Human-Designed DenseNet

Table 1 shows the results obtained after training the unpruned human-designed DenseNet-BC 5 times on SVHN for 600 and 900 epochs. The table contains: the total number of trainable parameters in each NN, separate parameter counts for the network's convolutional (Conv.) and fully-connected (FC) parts, the mean and standard deviation (SD) values for the accuracy (acc.) and (cross-entropy) loss on the validation and test sets, and the mean and SD values for the inference time (t) in seconds on the test set.

Table 1. Results obtained after training human-designed DenseNet-BC five (5) times on SVHN

Growth rate (k), number of training epochs		Trainable parameters			Validation set		Test set		
		Total	Conv.	FC	Acc. (%)	Loss	Acc. (%)	Loss	t (s)
$k = 12$, 600 epochs	Mean	486730	484140	2590	96.83	0.15	94.57	0.26	13.98
	SD	0	0	0	0.18	0.01	0.23	0.01	00.08
$k = 12$, 900 epochs	Mean	486730	484140	2590	96.89	0.14	94.76	0.25	13.98
	SD	0	0	0	0.19	0.01	0.07	0.01	00.07
$k = 24$, 600 epochs	Mean	1910746	1905576	5170	96.77	0.16	94.60	0.26	21.82
	SD	0	0	0	0.16	0.01	0.09	0.01	00.08
$k = 24$, 900 epochs	Mean	1910746	1905576	5170	96.94	0.13	94.60	0.26	21.74
	SD	0	0	0	0.34	0.02	0.43	0.01	00.02

A two-way analysis of variance (ANOVA) between the test set accuracies obtained by the four groups didn't show any statistically significant (stat. sign.) differences between them. We can thus assume that their performance on the test set is identical.

Table 2 shows the mean and SD for the test set accuracies and losses obtained by the same human-designed networks when, during training, they were pruned using the Dense-Sparse-Dense (DSD) and Lottery Ticket (LT) inspired algorithms.

The accuracies are noticeably higher (and the loss values are lower) for the DSD-like algorithm than for the LT-like one. As for the granularity levels, at $s = 70\%$ it seems that the DSD-like method reaches its highest accuracy values with weight-level pruning, and the LT-like method reaches its highest accuracies with filter-level pruning.

Table 2. Test set accuracies and losses obtained after running the two sparsification algorithms five (5) times on each human-designed DenseNet-BC, while training them on SVHN

Granularity level, target sparsity (s)		$k = 12$, DSD-like		$k = 12$, LT-like		$k = 24$, DSD-like		$k = 24$, LT-like	
		Acc. (%)	Loss	Acc. (%)	Loss	Acc. (%)	Loss	Acc. (%)	Loss
Filters, $s = 50\%$	Mean	94.28	0.26	92.49	0.32	94.15	0.25	93.28	0.29
	SD	0.35	0.01	0.38	0.02	0.25	0.01	0.30	0.01
Filters, $s = 60\%$	Mean	93.93	0.27	90.85	0.37	93.76	0.27	91.47	0.35
	SD	0.20	0.01	0.43	0.02	0.48	0.02	0.45	0.02
Filters, $s = 70\%$	Mean	93.08	0.30	83.98	0.54	93.47	0.27	84.73	0.53
	SD	1.09	0.03	1.81	0.06	0.21	0.01	2.46	0.07
Weights, $s = 50\%$	Mean	94.69	0.25	94.29	0.27	94.76	0.25	94.47	0.26
	SD	0.09	0.01	0.33	0.02	0.26	0.01	0.23	0.01
Weights, $s = 60\%$	Mean	94.51	0.27	93.38	0.28	94.71	0.26	93.29	0.28
	SD	0.23	0.01	0.38	0.01	0.24	0.01	0.24	0.01
Weights, $s = 70\%$	Mean	94.55	0.26	65.91	1.06	94.70	0.26	79.75	0.64
	SD	0.18	0.01	4.88	0.15	0.33	0.02	2.43	0.07

If one-way ANOVA followed by Tukey HSD tests are performed on the accuracies in Table 1 and Table 2 corresponding to the same NN, these do not show any stat. sign. differences between most of the experiments, with the exception of the two LT-like pruning experiments with s = 70% (stat. sign. differences with all other experiments, including each other), and the LT-like pruning experiment at filter level with $s = 60\%$ (stat. sign. differences with all but 3 or 4 of the other experiments).

4.2   Second Round: Further Sparsification Experiments, and Comparison with DensEMANN

Table 3 shows the results obtained after using DensEMANN v1.2 to generate DenseNet-BC trained on SVHN (the same experiment as in Table II from [1]), while Table 4 shows the results of running the DSD-like method on the human-designed NN with $k = 12$ from the previous round, for higher target sparsification values than previously.

As explained in Sect. 2.1, DensEMANN generates each new layer with a different number of filters k, relying to this aim on one of two different layer creation strategies: update-k and same-k. Since in [1] we found out that each of these two strategies has got its own benefits and drawbacks, here we will consider the results obtained with both of them.

Target sparsity values of 85% and 90% seem to produce the most similar parameter counts to those of DensEMANN networks. This is confirmed if a one-way ANOVA followed by a Tukey HSD test is performed on the total parameter counts: the only sparsity values for which the DSD-like algorithm's results do not have stat. sign. differences with

Table 3. Results obtained after running DensEMANN v1.2 five (5) times for generating DenseNet-BC trained on SVHN. The source data is the same as used in Table II from [1].

Layer creation strategy		Trainable parameters			Validation set		Test set		
		Total	Conv.	FC	Acc. (%)	Loss	Acc. (%)	Loss	t (s)
Update-k	Mean	76466.80	75314.80	1152	94.56	0.27	91.61	0.41	09.75
	SD	20682.98	20541.68	141	0.65	0.03	0.51	0.02	00.42
Same-k	Mean	65189.20	63951.20	1238	94.42	0.28	91.68	0.41	09.48
	SD	3779.18	3712.37	66.9	0.47	0.01	0.31	0.01	00.09

Table 4. Results obtained after running DSD-like sparsification five (5) times on the human-designed DenseNet-BC with 3 dense blocks, 12 layers per block, $k = 12$, while training it on SVHN

Granularity level, target sparsity (s)		Trainable parameters			Validation set		Test set		
		Total	Conv.	FC	Acc. (%)	Loss	Acc. (%)	Loss	t (s)
Filters, $s = 80\%$	Mean	97189.60	94599.60	2590	95.53	0.18	92.29	0.32	14.02
	SD	920.50	920.50	0	0.35	0.02	0.44	0.01	00.11
Filters, $s = 85\%$	Mean	81103.40	78513.40	2590	94.49	0.22	91.24	0.34	13.93
	SD	832.92	832.92	0	0.35	0.02	0.62	0.03	00.05
Filters, $s = 90\%$	Mean	63343.40	60753.40	2590	93.91	0.22	89.88	0.36	13.96
	SD	263.90	263.90	0	0.45	0.03	0.62	0.03	00.04
Filters, $s = 95\%$	Mean	47848.60	45258.60	2590	92.81	0.25	87.57	0.43	13.94
	SD	536.16	536.16	0	0.98	0.03	1.39	0.04	00.06
Weights, $s = 80\%$	Mean	111240	108650	2590	96.48	0.16	94.66	0.25	13.94
	SD	0.00	0.00	0	0.30	0.01	0.25	0.01	00.03
Weights, $s = 85\%$	Mean	87789	85199	2590	96.71	0.15	94.30	0.26	13.92
	SD	0.00	0.00	0	0.37	0.02	0.23	0.01	00.03
Weights, $s = 90\%$	Mean	64337	61747	2590	96.66	0.14	93.87	0.26	13.94
	SD	0.00	0.00	0	0.31	0.01	0.20	0.01	00.05
Weights, $s = 95\%$	Mean	40886	38296	2590	95.77	0.17	92.78	0.29	13.96
	SD	0.00	0.00	0	0.29	0.01	0.45	0.02	00.06

DensEMANN's are 85% (no differences with update-k) and 90% (no differences with both update-k and same-k), and this is true for both granularity levels.

If the same one-way ANOVA and Tukey HSD test is done on the validation or test set accuracies, the following results are obtained for $s = 85\%$ and 90%:

- Filter granularity level: for the validation set accuracy there are no stat. sign. differences with DensEMANN, for the test set accuracy there are stat. sign. differences only for $s = 90\%$. In that case the algorithm performed worse than DensEMANN (respectively under 89.9% test set accuracy vs. 91.6% to 91.7% test set accuracy).
- Weight granularity level: for both accuracies there are stat. sign. differences with DensEMANN, which the algorithm outperforms (93.9% to 94.3% test set accuracy).

It is worth noting that the pruned and unpruned versions of the human-designed NN obtained near-identical inference times (which by the way were much longer than those of the DensEMANN-generated NN). Similar observations were made during the third round (see Tables 5 and 6). This is likely because we do not actually remove any parameters, but instead apply a mask that zeroes them out. Consequently, the computations performed by our hardware remain identical regardless of "pruning".

4.3   Third Round: Applying Sparsification on DensEMANN-Generated Networks

Table 5 shows the features of the DensEMANN-generated NN that we used this round (and that we originally selected in [1]). Table 6 compares their test set accuracies, losses and inference times before and after re-training them with DSD-like sparsification.

Just like in the second round, the accuracy levels are higher if the NN is sparsified at weight level, and furthermore they seem very similar to those obtained with the original DensEMANN weights. This observation's significance is confirmed if one-way ANOVA followed by Tukey's HSD test are performed on the accuracy data in Table 6: the differences with using the original weights are always stat. sign. when the NN is pruned at filter level, and never when it is pruned at weight level.

Table 5. Features of DenseNet-BC generated by DensEMANN v1.2, manually selected out of five (5) identical runs of the algorithm as the NN with the lowest cross-entropy loss on the validation set. The source data is the same as used in Table V from [1].

Dataset	Layer creation strategy	Trainable parameters			Validation set		Test set		
		Total	Conv.	FC	Acc. (%)	Loss	Acc. (%)	Loss	t (s)
SVHN	Update-k	87264	86034	1230	95.03	0.24	92.10	0.39	10.04
	Same-k	65428	64188	1240	95.07	0.26	91.73	0.42	09.47
CIFAR-10	Update-k	80786	79576	1210	88.94	0.35	88.13	0.41	05.08
	Same-k	65566	64306	1260	89.00	0.37	88.42	0.40	04.97
Fashion-MNIST	Update-k	67974	66804	1170	94.00	0.20	93.45	0.23	04.52
	Same-k	59944	58784	1160	93.92	0.22	93.32	0.24	04.51

Table 6. Test set accuracies and losses obtained by the selected DensEMANN-generated NN, with their original weights and after re-training them five (5) times with DSD-like sparsification

Granularity level, target sparsity (s)		SVHN networks						CIFAR-10+ networks					
		Update-k			Same-k			Update-k			Same-k		
		Acc. (%)	Loss	t (s)	Acc. (%)	Loss	t (s)	Acc. (%)	Loss	t (s)	Acc. (%)	Loss	t (s)
Original weights		92.10	0.39	10.00	91.73	0.42	09.47	88.13	0.41	05.08	88.42	0.40	04.97
Filters, s = 50%	Mean	82.19	0.64	10.10	80.36	0.67	09.49	78.25	0.65	05.05	76.96	0.68	04.99
	SD	2.36	0.08	00.15	1.09	0.05	00.06	0.99	0.02	00.01	0.79	0.02	00.02
Filters, s = 60%	Mean	82.11	0.63	10.11	74.00	0.83	09.43	74.69	0.74	05.05	73.18	0.78	04.98
	SD	2.17	0.07	00.14	4.65	0.13	00.03	0.70	0.02	00.04	0.95	0.02	00.04
Filters, s = 70%	Mean	72.74	0.90	10.07	66.26	1.08	09.48	72.38	0.81	05.05	70.07	0.85	04.97
	SD	3.47	0.10	00.12	3.33	0.09	00.04	0.30	0.01	00.03	0.59	0.01	00.02
Weights, s = 50%	Mean	92.65	0.36	10.13	91.84	0.40	09.53	88.71	0.36	05.08	88.32	0.36	04.99
	SD	0.28	0.02	00.17	0.34	0.02	00.13	0.10	0.01	00.05	0.21	0.01	00.02
Weights, s = 60%	Mean	92.39	0.37	10.13	91.72	0.41	09.48	88.56	0.35	05.05	88.07	0.37	04.98
	SD	0.25	0.01	00.09	0.19	0.01	00.03	0.25	0.01	00.02	0.28	0.01	00.02
Weights, s = 70%	Mean	92.22	0.39	10.04	91.53	0.43	09.45	88.19	0.36	05.19	87.91	0.38	04.98
	SD	0.14	0.01	00.08	0.40	0.02	00.05	0.21	0.00	00.27	0.11	0.01	00.02

Granularity level, target sparsity (s)		Fashion-MNIST networks					
		Update-k			Same-k		
		Acc. (%)	Loss	t (s)	Acc. (%)	Loss	t (s)
Original weights		93.45	0.23	04.52	93.32	0.24	04.51
Filters, s = 50%	Mean	91.08	0.26	04.53	90.34	0.28	04.60
	SD	0.30	0.01	00.02	0.47	0.01	00.18
Filters, s = 60%	Mean	90.35	0.28	04.53	88.56	0.33	04.52
	SD	0.25	0.01	00.01	2.81	0.08	00.02
Filters, s = 70%	Mean	88.47	0.33	04.52	87.25	0.36	04.49
	SD	1.43	0.04	00.01	1.65	0.04	00.02
Weights, s = 50%	Mean	93.45	0.21	04.54	93.34	0.21	04.50
	SD	0.12	0.00	00.01	0.20	0.00	00.02
Weights, s = 60%	Mean	93.39	0.21	04.54	93.23	0.21	04.50
	SD	0.23	0.00	00.02	0.08	0.00	00.02
Weights, s = 70%	Mean	93.17	0.21	04.67	93.19	0.22	04.51
	SD	0.17	0.00	00.19	0.13	0.00	00.06

5 Conclusions and Future Work

In this paper, we presented two methods for sparsifying DenseNet at various granularity levels, respectively based on the Lottery Ticket (LT) algorithm [8], and on the Dense-Sparse-Dense (DSD) training method [21]. We ran experiments to evaluate these methods' ability to produce small and efficient DenseNet, and to compare one of them (the DSD-like method) with DensEMANN [1, 10], an algorithm that we are developing for the same purpose. We also evaluated the performance of this DSD-like method for optimally pruning DensEMANN-generated NN while training them from scratch.

Our results suggest that the DSD-like method is preferable over the LT-like method, as it reaches higher accuracy levels for high target sparsity values. The DSD-like method was able to very efficiently sparsify and (re-)train from scratch both human-designed and DensEMANN-generated DenseNet, especially when pruning at the granularity of individual weights. From the human-designed NN, we derived architectures that, while having similar (non-pruned) parameter counts as the DensEMANN-generated NN, performed just as well (when pruned at the granularity of convolution filters) or much better than them (when pruned at the granularity of weights). Also, when pruned with this method at the granularity of weights, the DensEMANN-generated NN could recover their original accuracies even after 70% of their weights were removed.

Future research lines could take the following directions:

- Looking for ways to truly reduce the NN model's size (here we merely used a mask), especially after weight-level pruning. Indeed, individual weights are hard to efficiently remove from convolution matrices [18]. For instance: techniques for sparse model storage, or coarser pruning patterns to apply after weight-level sparsification.
- Comparing DensEMANN and DSD-like pruning more exhaustively. It is not yet clear which of these two methods (if any) is more useful. We showed than filter-level DSD-like pruning is on par with DensEMANN regarding accuracy and parameter counts (and unlike weights, filters are easy to remove from convolution matrices [18]). Meanwhile, DensEMANN may still hold its own advantages, such as not relying on an initial seed architecture, or using less time and computation resources in early epochs (as it starts from a minimal architecture [1]).
- Training DensEMANN-generated NN from scratch with various DSD schedules.
- Using DSD-like pruning to replace DensEMANN's own pruning and recovery loop.

Acknowledgements. We thank Nathan Hubens, the creator of the Fasterai library, for his support and helpful advice. This work is part of a PhD thesis titled "Self-Optimisation of Neural Network Architectures", carried out at the IRIDIA-CoDE department (Université libre de Bruxelles, ULB). It was supported by Service Public de Wallonie Recherche under grant n° 2010235 - ARIAC by DIGITALWALLONIA4.AI, as well as by the VOCATIO foundation through a grant sponsored by McKinsey & Company.

References

1. García-Díaz, A., Bersini, H.: DensEMANN: how to automatically generate an efficient while compact DenseNet (2022, publication pending)
2. Baymurzina, D., et al.: A review of neural architecture search. Neurocomputing **474**, 82–93 (2022). https://doi.org/10.1016/j.neucom.2021.12.014
3. Elsken, T., et al.: Neural architecture search: a survey. J. Mach. Learn. Res. **20**, 1997–2017 (2019). https://doi.org/10.48550/arXiv.1808.05377
4. Ren, P., et al.: A comprehensive survey of neural architecture search. ACM Comput. Surv. **54**, 1–34 (2022). https://doi.org/10.1145/3447582
5. Wu, C., et al.: Sustainable AI: environmental implications, challenges and opportunities. arXiv (2022). https://doi.org/10.48550/arXiv.2111.00364. https://arxiv.org/abs/2111.003 64v2. Accessed 31 Mar 2022
6. Mohammad, R.M., Thabtah, F., McCluskey, L.: Predicting phishing websites based on self-structuring neural network. Neural Comput. Appl. **25**(2), 443–458 (2013). https://doi.org/10. 1007/s00521-013-1490-z
7. Liang, T., et al.: Pruning and quantization for deep neural network acceleration: a survey. Neurocomputing **461**, 370–403 (2021). https://doi.org/10.1016/j.neucom.2021.07.045

8. Frankle, J., Carbin, M.: The lottery ticket hypothesis: finding sparse, trainable neural networks. In: 7th International Conference on Learning Representations, ICLR 2019. ICLR (2019). https://doi.org/10.48550/arXiv.1803.03635

9. Elsken, T., et al.: Simple and efficient architecture search for convolutional neural networks. In: 6th International Conference on Learning Representations, ICLR 2018, Workshop Track Proceedings. ICLR (2018). https://doi.org/10.48550/arXiv.1711.04528

10. Garcia-Diaz, A., Bersini, H.: DensEMANN: building a DenseNet from scratch, layer by layer and kernel by kernel. In: 2021 International Joint Conference on Neural Networks (IJCNN). IEEE (2021). https://doi.org/10.1109/ijcnn52387.2021.9533783

11. Huang, G., et al.: Densely connected convolutional networks. In: 2017 IEEE Conference on Computer Vision and Pattern Recognition (CVPR). IEEE (2017). https://doi.org/10.1109/CVPR.2017.243

12. Mohammad, R.M., Thabtah, F., McCluskey, L.: An improved self-structuring neural network. In: Cao, H., Li, J., Wang, R. (eds.) PAKDD 2016. LNCS (LNAI), vol. 9794, pp. 35–47. Springer, Cham (2016). https://doi.org/10.1007/978-3-319-42996-0_4

13. Evci, U., et al.: GradMax: growing neural networks using gradient information. In: 10th International Conference on Learning Representations, ICLR 2022. ICLR (2022). https://doi.org/10.48550/arXiv.2201.05125

14. Salomé, T., Bersini, H.: An algorithm for self-structuring neural net classifiers. In: Proceedings of 1994 IEEE International Conference on Neural Networks (ICNN 1994). IEEE (1994). https://doi.org/10.1109/ICNN.1994.374473

15. Netzer, Y., et al.: Reading digits in natural images with unsupervised feature learning. In: NIPS Workshop on Deep Learning and Unsupervised Feature Learning 2011 (2011)

16. Krizhevsky, A: Learning multiple layers of features from tiny images. Technical report, University of Toronto (2009)

17. Xiao, H., et al.: Fashion-MNIST: a novel image dataset for benchmarking machine learning algorithms. arXiv (2017). https://doi.org/10.48550/arXiv.1708.07747. https://arxiv.org/abs/1708.07747v2. Accessed 31 Mar 2022

18. Hoefler, T., et al.: Sparsity in Deep Learning: Pruning and growth for efficient inference and training in neural networks. Journal of Machine Learning Research. 22, 241:1–241:124 (2021). https://doi.org/10.48550/arXiv.2102.00554

19. Zhou, X., et al.: Effective Sparsification of Neural Networks with Global Sparsity Constraint. In: 2021 IEEE/CVF Conference on Computer Vision and Pattern Recognition (CVPR). IEEE (2021). https://doi.org/10.1109/cvpr46437.2021.00360

20. Zhou, H., et al.: Deconstructing Lottery Tickets: Zeros, Signs, and the Supermask. In: Advances in Neural In-formation Processing Systems. 32 (2019). https://doi.org/10.48550/arXiv.1905.01067

21. Han, S., et al.: DSD: dense-sparse-dense training for deep neural networks. arXiv (2017). https://doi.org/10.48550/arXiv.1607.04381. https://arxiv.org/abs/1607.04381v2. Accessed 31 Mar 2022

22. García-Díaz, A.: DensEMANN for Pytorch + Fastai. GitHub (2021). https://github.com/AntonioGarciaDiaz/DensEMANN_PyTorch. Accessed 31 Mar 2022

23. Paszke, A., et al.: PyTorch: an imperative style, high-performance deep learning library. In: Advances in Neural Information Processing Systems 32 (2019). https://doi.org/10.48550/arXiv.1912.01703

24. Howard, J., Gugger, S.: Fastai: a layered API for deep learning. Information 11 (2020). https://doi.org/10.3390/info11020108

25. Hubens, N.: Fasterai. GitHub (2020). https://github.com/nathanhubens/fasterai. Accessed 31 Mar 2022

26. Hubens, N.: Schedules. Fasterai Read the Docs Project Page. https://nathanhubens.github.io/fasterai/schedules.html. Accessed 31 Mar 2022

Dynamic Vision Sensor Based Gesture Recognition Using Liquid State Machine

Xun Xiao, Lei Wang$^{(\boxtimes)}$, Xiaofan Chen, Lianhua Qu, Shasha Guo, Yao Wang, and Ziyang Kang

School of Computer, National University of Defence Technology, Changsha, Hunan 410071, People's Republic of China
{xiaoxun520,leiwang,guoshasah13,wangyaobsz,kangziyang14}@nudt.edu.cn

Abstract. Dynamic Vision Sensor (DVS) is a neuromorphic sensor. Compared with traditional cameras, event cameras based on DVS have the advantages of high time resolution, low power consumption, less motion blur, and low data redundancy, making DVS more suitable for computer vision tasks such as gesture recognition. However, the adaptation of traditional algorithms to computer vision tasks with DVS seems to have unsatisfying limitations. This paper implements a lightweight gesture recognition system using Liquid State Machine (LSM). LSM can use the events generated by DVS as input directly. To achieve better performance of LSM, we use a heuristic search algorithm to obtain an improved parameter configuration for LSM. Our system achieves 98.42% accuracy on the DVS128 Gesture Dataset. Our model contains remarkably 90% fewer parameters than the Inception 3D, which achieves a precision of 99.62% on the DVS128 Gesture Dataset. This work encodes and compresses the event stream into event frames by using Convolutional Neural Network (CNN) to extract features from the frame and then sending the extracted feature to reservoirs to implement the gesture recognition.

Keywords: Liquid State Machine · DVS camera · Spiking neural network · Gesture recognition

1 Introduction

In the era of artificial intelligence, gesture recognition has become an important research direction. Gesture recognition has a wide range of applications in autonomous driving, human-computer interaction [7], and other fields [20]. The gesture recognition method based on computer vision and deep learning have been developed with very high accuracy [15]. However, convolutional neural networks for video-based gesture recognition usually have excessive redundant computation, and low efficiency [16].

DVS [9] is a neuromorphic sensor that can capture motion information with high time resolution and lower power consumption. Unlike traditional RGB cameras, the DVS camera only records the pixels with changes in brightness, which

E. Pimenidis et al. (Eds.): ICANN 2022, LNCS 13531, pp. 618–629, 2022.
https://doi.org/10.1007/978-3-031-15934-3_51

are called "events." DVS only records changing pixels, which can significantly reduce redundant data.

Due to powerful learning and feature extraction capabilities, CNN has been widely used in gesture recognition system [28]. CNN-based techniques need to convert event data into video frames. Nevertheless, transforming spatially sparse event streams into frames will make the data lose the advantages of signal sparsity and time resolution [19,24]. An ideal method is to use event data as input directly. Recently, Spiking Neuron Networks (SNNs) are proposed to use events as input directly [26]. SNN has the natural ability to handle spatio-temporal events. LSM is a Recurrent Neural Network based on spiking neurons [17]. It uses events as input directly and converts events to the liquid state.

In this paper, we propose a lightweight model based on LSM for the DVS gesture recognition. We explore the structure of our LSM model using heuristic algorithms. In addition, biological learning rules are applied to our model for higher performance. Our proposed LSM contains only 343 liquid neurons. It achieves the accuracy of 98.42% on the DVS128 Gesture Dataset. Compared with the current Inception 3D model, which has the highest accuracy [5,13]. The proposed model parameters are 90% less than the former, with a minor decrease of about 1% in accuracy. Besides, we take advantage of the natural combination of LSM and DVS to solve realistic computer vision tasks. We combine the DVS camera with the proposed LSM model to realize a real-time gesture recognition system. In summary, the main contributions of this paper are as follows:

- Based on LSM, we designed an LSM model with only 343 liquid neurons for the classification of the DVS128 Gesture Dataset.
- We use classification accuracy to evaluate the performance of the LSM model. Based on the classification accuracy, we use a heuristic search algorithm to optimize model parameters to achieve higher accuracy.
- We connect the model to the DVS camera directly and build a real-time system for real-time gesture recognition and classification.

2   Background

2.1   Dynamic Vision Sensor

DVS is a neuromorphic sensor [9,18]. It uses an event-driven approach to record changing objects in the scene. When the objects in the scene cause a relative movement to the event camera, DVS will generate a series of pixel-level event outputs [4], with each event in the form of (x, y, t, p). Specifically, the x and y are the coordinate positions of the pixel. The t is the timestamp of the event, which indicates the time when the event is triggered. Moreover, the p is the polarity of the event, which represents the illumination changes of the pixel. Polarity 1 and 0 indicate an increase and decrease in brightness, respectively.

2.2 Liquid State Machine

LSM is a Recurrent Neural Network based on spiking neurons. Maass et al. [17] first proposed an LSM that uses randomly interconnected spiking neurons as a feature extractor. As shown in Fig. 1, LSM mainly consists of three parts: input layer, liquid layer, and readout layer. The core of LSM is the liquid layer, composed of spiking neurons randomly connected to each other. There are two kinds of neurons in the liquid layer: excitatory and inhibitory neurons. Spikes from excitatory neurons increase the membrane voltage of postsynaptic neurons, while spikes from inhibitory neurons lead to the opposite effect [23,29]. These two kinds of neurons are arranged in a particular proportion.

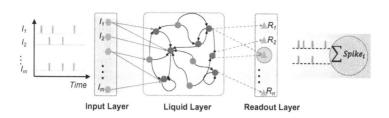

Fig. 1. The structure of LSM. A LSM mainly consists three parts, it uses spikes as input and output the liquid state of liquid layer.

2.3 STDP Learning Rule

Spike-Timing-Dependent Plasticity (STDP) learning rule is in one of the well-developed unsupervised learning rules for spiking neural networks, based on the Hebb learning rule [11,12]. STDP is a time asymmetric form of the Hebb learning rule [8]. The update of weight in STDP is related to the spiking interval between the pre-synaptic neuron and the post-synaptic neuron. Supposing that the pre-synaptic neuron emits a spike before the post-synaptic neuron, we can think that there is a relationship between pre-synaptic neurons and post-synaptic neurons. So we can strengthen the weight of the connection. Conversely, if the pre-synaptic neuron emits spikes after the post-synaptic neuron. The connection weight between neurons can be weakened. A general form of STDP is shown in Eq. (1).

$$\Delta w = \sum_{t_{pre}} \sum_{t_{post}} W(t_{pre} - t_{post}) \tag{1}$$

In the above formula, the W was defined by (2).

$$W(\Delta t) = \begin{cases} A_{pre}e^{-\Delta t/\tau_{pre}} & \Delta t > 0 \\ A_{post}e^{\Delta t/\tau_{post}} & \Delta t < 0 \end{cases} \tag{2}$$

3   Related Work

3.1   CNN for Gesture Recognition

Researchers have proposed many methods of DVS128 Gesture Dataset classification. Amir et al. [3] deployed a CNN model on the neuromorphic processing platform TrueNorth, and achieved the accuracy of 96.5% on the dataset. Nunez et al. [21] proposed a combination of a CNN and a Long Short-Term Memory (LSTM) recurrent network for temporal 3D pose recognition problems. Simone et al. [13] implement an event aggregation strategy, which converts the output of the event camera into frames that can be processed by traditional computer vision algorithms. These frames can be interpreted by the deep learning model inception 3D [5]. They call their strategy "TBR" (Temporal Binary Representation). This work has achieved state-of-the-art accuracy of 99.62% on the DVS128 Gesture Dataset. However, both 2D convolution and 3D convolution require larger models and more computation, with more energy consumption.

3.2   SNN for Gesture Recognition

In addition, George et al. [10] designed a Convolution Spiking Neural Network (CSNN) for classification based on reservoirs. An SNN with multiple convolution layers and liquid layers is used to extract Spatio-temporal information from the data stream. Using reservoirs containing 12,000 spiking neurons has achieved an accuracy of more than 95%. This work encodes and compresses the event stream into event frames by using CSNN to extract features from the frame and then sending the extracted feature to reservoirs to implement the gesture recognition.

Comparing these methods, we can find that they can all achieve very high accuracy with a limited scope of application due to their huge model size. Therefore, a more lightweight model is necessary.

4   Method

4.1   Workflow for Gesture Recognition

The overall processing flow of the algorithm is shown in Fig. 2. The work flow is mainly divided into two parts: DVS128 Gesture Dataset classification and gesture real-time recognition. In DVS128 Gesture Dataset classification, we divide the DVS data stream into samples one by one according to the label file. Each sample will be feed into the LSM in the form of a spike train, and a corresponding reservoir state will be generated in the LSM. Then we used the reservoir state for gesture classification. In real-time gesture recognition, we use the event stream captured by DVS camera to replace the event stream in the dataset.

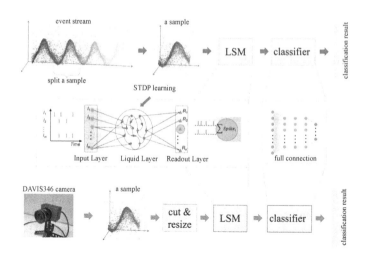

Fig. 2. Workflow of proposed method.

4.2   Preprocessing

Sample Split. The input of the LSM is a stream of consecutive events within a short duration. The data in DVS128 Gesture Dataset is saved in the form of a continuous event stream, which needs to be split into single fragments for LSM. We split the continuous gesture into sample segments according to each gesture's start and end time provided in the dataset.

Event Compression. The resolution of the DVS128 Camera is 128×128. When used as the input of LSM directly, each pixel of the camera should be corresponded to an input neuron. Therefore, a total of 16,384 input neurons are required, which is a considerable overhead. As shown in Fig. 3(a). In order to reduce the number of input neurons, we use a 2×2 max-pooling operation to map four adjacent pixels to the same input neuron. The spikes generated by these four pixels will be aggregated into a spike event. Therefore, the size of the input neuron is decreased to a quarter of the original.

The DVS camera can capture event information with a very high time resolution. However, our gesture recognition task doesn't require such high time resolution, since the dynamic information of targeted gestures is generated at a much slower rate due to human reaction time. The time resolution of the DVS128 Camera is 1μs. Sampling the event data at the scale of millisecond can effectively reduce the data amount without losing much information. As shown in Fig. 3(b), if a pixel emits multiple events, we will compress them into one. As for the polarity of events, we only use the positive events in the data, because positive and negative events only represent the two edges of moving objects.

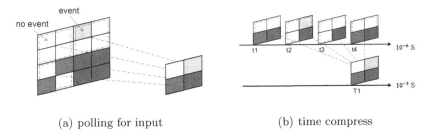

(a) polling for input   (b) time compress

Fig. 3. (a) 2×2 max pooling operation to map four adjacent pixels to the same input neuron. (b) Compression in time dimension.

4.3   LSM Structure and Parameter Search

The structure of LSM has an profounding influence on its feature extraction ability. A total of 343 liquid neurons are used in our LSM model [2]. We randomly select 20% of them as inhibitory neurons and the rest as excitatory neurons. LSM liquid neurons form a cube structure in the shape of $7 \times 7 \times 7$ [2,14]. The connections between liquid neurons follow biological rules, and the closer the neurons are to each other, the higher the connection probability is. The distance between neuron i and j is defined as shown in (3). The connection probability between neuron i and j is calculated by (4).

$$D_{i,j} = \sqrt{(x_i - x_j)^2 + (y_i - y_j)^2 + (z_i - z_j)^2} \tag{3}$$

$$P_{i,j} = C * e^{-(D_{i,j}/\lambda)} \tag{4}$$

In our LSM, we control the connection probability through the P_{input} (Probability of connection between input neurons and liquid layer neurons) and C parameter. According to the connections between different kinds of neurons, C has four values: C_{ee} between excitatory neurons and excitatory neurons, C_{ei} between excitatory neurons and inhibitory neurons, C_{ie} and C_{ii}, and so on. Different topologies can be generated by modifying the values of C and P_{input}. Different LSM structures have obviously varied effects on LSM performance. It takes a lot of time to train the LSM to achieve the best accuracy by exhaustively enumerating the combination of C and P_{input}. In order to reduce the time cost, we apply the PSO algorithm to search the parameters [22,27]. The search space is the combination of C_{ee}, C_{ei}, C_{ie}, C_{ii}, and P_{input}. From the combination of these parameters, we find a set of parameters that achieve better performance.

4.4   Real-Time Gesture Recognition System

LSM can process the events directly. The DVS camera is connected with the model to implement a real-time gesture recognition system. We use DAVIS 346 [1] event camera to record the gestures. When the camera accumulates for a sample, it will be sent to be cut and resized to fit with the LSM input array size. Since the resolution of the DAVIS 346 camera is 346 × 260, as shown in Fig. 4, we cut out the 256 × 256 area in the middle of the camera as our effective input area, and then resize it to 128 × 128.

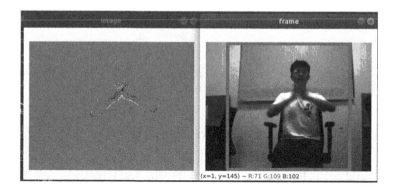

Fig. 4. Picture frame and event frame of DAVIS346 camera.

5   Experiments

5.1   Experiment Setup

The DVS128 Gesture Dataset was captured by a fixed DVS camera. Each event stream has a tag file recording the action type, the start time, and the end time of the action. According to the tag file, we split the continuous video into sample segments.

The experiment in this paper is based on the open-source SNN simulator Brian2 [25]. Brian2 is a python-based SNN simulator. Our experiments are all executed on the current updated version Brian2.4. The hardware and software configurations used in the experiment are shown in Table 1. All SNN simulation processes only involve CPU, and GPU is applied to train the proposed MLP classifier. We randomly select 80% of the samples for training and the rest for testing. We evaluate the model performance with average accuracy, recall, and F1 scores support by results from ten experiments.

5.2   Experiment Result

Accuracy. Table 2 compares our method with other work on DVS128 Gesture Dataset. We use the best configuration obtained from the experiment(sample length: 800ms, STDP itrater: 9, p_{inpute}: 0.3, p_{ee}: 1.8, p_{ei}: 0.36, p_{ie}: 1.75, p_{ii}: 0.21, Classifier: MLP), and contrasting the model size, the number of spiking neurons, and the accuracy. In comparison with the CNN-based network, the LSM model we proposed has a great reduction in parameter scale. In particular,

Table 1. The hardware and software configuration of Experimental platform.

Hardware	Software
AMD Ryzen 7 2700 Eight-Core CPU @3.2GHz	Python 3.6.12, Brian 2.4
NVIDIA GeForce RTX 2060	Keras 2.3.1, CUDA 10.0, cuDNN 7.6.5

Table 2. Results on the DVS128 Gesture Dataset.

Method	Parameters or model size	Number of spiking Neurons	Accuracy
CNN [3]	–	–	96.50%
DGCNN [6]	8.5 MB	–	98.56%
Inception 3D [13]	25M	–	**99.62%**
CSNN [10]	3.17M	12000	95%
Ours(LSM+MLP)	**1.4M**	343	98.42%

compared with the SOTA model: Inception 3D, the accuracy decrease of our model is approximately 1%, while the parameters reduction is more than 90%. Compared with the network on the basis of SNN [10], our method greatly reduces the number of spiking neurons and still improves the classification accuracy.

We conduct a series of experiments to compare the impact of model parameters on the accuracy of the DVS128 Gesture Dataset. In particular, we explor the design space in terms of the length of the sample, the number of STDP training iterations, the connection structure of the LSM, and different types of classifiers. At the same time, we use a heuristic search algorithm to find a better LSM structure by searching the parameters of LSM.

Impact of Sample Length. The more extended sample contains more information while leading to less sample amount, which will affect the model training. Therefore, it is necessary to investigate the impact of sample length on model accuracy. To split samples, we select seven different sample lengths (400 ms, 600 ms, 800 ms, 1000 ms, 1200 ms, 1400 ms, and 1600 ms).

As shown in Fig. 5, it is clear that the accuracy increases moderately before the sample length is at less than 800, after which there is a dramatic drop of accuracy with the increase of sample length. Similar trends are seen in all the five different LSM configurations. This can be well explained. When the length of a sample is too short, some gestures (such as right arm clockwise) cannot be included in a sample as a whole. As the sample duration increases, the actions contained in the sample become more complete, and the accuracy also increases. After the sample length reaches the optimal value, increasing the sample length

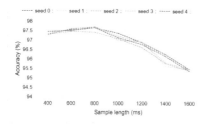
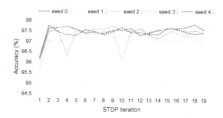

Fig. 5. The impact of sample length.   **Fig. 6.** The impact of STDP iteration.

will cause redundant information and reduce the number of available samples, leading to significant accuracy degradation instead.

Impact of STDP. In this paper, we use STDP rules to update synaptic weights, improving the network's sensitivity to specific pattern inputs. STDP can enhance the causal relationship between the liquid response and the input spike train, thus improving the performance of LSM.

Figure 6 shows the impact of different training iterations of STDP on accuracy. We find that STDP training can significantly improve the accuracy of the model. As the number of STDP training iterations increases, the accuracy of the model gradually increases and finally stabilizes. At the same time, it is concluded that only a few training iterations can achieve better results.

Liquid Parameter Search. In this paper, we use the PSO algorithm to search for LSM parameters, with the accuracy as the main metric for LSM performance. During the search, we only change the structure of the liquid layer. Figure 7 shows the accuracy changes on the DVS128 Gesture Dataset with the search iteration.

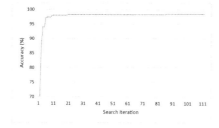
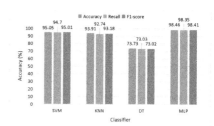

Fig. 7. The accuracy of search itera-   **Fig. 8.** Performance of different classi-
tion.   fiers on the DVS128 Gesture Dataset.

In Table 3, we select several sets of parameters in the search process and the final accuracy of the LSM model. We can find that the change of the LSM model has

Table 3. Results on the DVS128 Gesture Dataset.

P_{input}	C_{ee}	C_{ei}	C_{ie}	C_{ii}	Accuracy
0.15	1.29	1.84	0.2	1.92	69.92%
0.34	0.76	1.36	0.22	1.86	85.13%
0.39	1.26	0.66	1.80	1.73	92.61%
0.3	1.8	0.36	1.75	0.21	98.42%

a significant impact on the feature extraction ability. PSO algorithm is effective in terms of exploring a better combination of LSM parameters. In this way, LSM can better extract the Spatio-temporal features from the input spikes.

Classifier Selection. When we get the state vector of the LSM, selecting an appropriate classifier is a crucial step. We have chosen four commonly used classifiers. A good classifier should be able to achieve a high classification accuracy.

The first classifier we use is a 4-layer fully connected MLP, and the number of neurons in each layer is (1029,800,300,11). We use SGD to train our network, with learning rate, learning rate attenuation coefficient, and batch size set at 0.01, 1e−6, and 128 respectively. We also use a dropout parameter of 0.5 during training. The second classifier is SVM with RBF kernel. SVM is a supervised classifier, which can be widely used in statistical classification and regression analysis. The third classifier is DT. The classification process of decision trees is very similar to human thinking. The fourth classifier is KNN. Its core idea is to replace the category of the target sample with the category of the K samples closest to the target sample. Figure 8 shows the comparison of the classification accuracy, recall rate, and F1 score of the four classifiers.

It is found that the SVM, the KNN, and the MLP classifiers can obtain high accuracy on the dataset. It means that LSM can effectively extract the characteristic information in the input spike train. We finally choose the MLP with the highest accuracy as our classifier since it realizes the highest evaluation results.

6 Conclusion

In this paper, LSM is used to process the output Spatio-temporal data stream of DVS. Based on the fact that LSM is driven by event flow and can be fit naturally with the output of DVS, we implement an LSM-based gesture recognition system on the DVS128 Gesture Dataset. We have experimentally demonstrated that LSM can extract features from Spatio-temporal streams, which are then identified by a classifier. At the same time, it is also found that different topologies of LSM have a significant influence on its feature extraction ability. Final experimental results show that our model achieves the highest accuracy of 98.42% on the DVS128 Gesture Dataset with only 343 liquid neurons. Compared with the current state-of-the-art 3D convolution-based models, our model loses less than 1% of the accuracy but remains fewer parameters of 90%, which greatly expands the application scope of our model, especially in resource constrained scenarios such as embedded systems. For future work, we can focus on how to generate better hand-crafted reservoir structures before searching. Getting better models through more effective SNN learning methods is also worth investigating.

Acknowledgement. This work is funded by National Key R&D Program of China [grant numbers 2018YFB2202603].

References

1. Inivation Devices Secifications. https://inivation.com/wp-content/uploads/2021/08/2021-08-inivation-devices-specications.pdf. Accessed 20 Nov 2021
2. Al Zoubi, O., Awad, M., Kasabov, N.K.: Anytime multipurpose emotion recognition from EEG data using a liquid state machine based framework. Artif. Intell. Med. **86**, 1–8 (2018)
3. Amir, A., et al.: A low power, fully event-based gesture recognition system. In: Proceedings of the IEEE Conference on Computer Vision and Pattern Recognition, pp. 7243–7252 (2017)
4. Boahen, K.A.: A burst-mode word-serial address-event link-i: transmitter design. IEEE Trans. Circuits Syst. I: Regul. Pap. **51**(7), 1269–1280 (2004)
5. Carreira, J., Zisserman, A.: Quo vadis, action recognition? a new model and the kinetics dataset. In: Proceedings of the IEEE Conference on Computer Vision and Pattern Recognition, pp. 6299–6308 (2017)
6. Chen, J., Meng, J., Wang, X., Yuan, J.: Dynamic graph CNN for event-camera based gesture recognition. In: 2020 IEEE International Symposium on Circuits and Systems (ISCAS), pp. 1–5. IEEE (2020)
7. Cheng, H., Yang, L., Liu, Z.: Survey on 3d hand gesture recognition. IEEE Trans. Circuits Syst. Video Technol. **26**(9), 1659–1673 (2015)
8. Diehl, P.U., Cook, M.: Unsupervised learning of digit recognition using spike-timing-dependent plasticity. Front. Comput. Neurosci. **9**, 99 (2015)
9. Gallego, G., et al.: Event-based vision: a survey. arXiv preprint arXiv:1904.08405 (2019)
10. George, A.M., Banerjee, D., Dey, S., Mukherjee, A., Balamurali, P.: A reservoir-based convolutional spiking neural network for gesture recognition from DVS input. In: 2020 International Joint Conference on Neural Networks (IJCNN), pp. 1–9. IEEE (2020)
11. Gerstner, W., Kempter, R., Van Hemmen, J.L., Wagner, H.: A neuronal learning rule for sub-millisecond temporal coding. Nature **383**(6595), 76–78 (1996)
12. Gerstner, W., Ritz, R., Van Hemmen, J.L.: Why spikes? Hebbian learning and retrieval of time-resolved excitation patterns. Biol. Cybern. **69**(5), 503–515 (1993)
13. Innocenti, S.U., Becattini, F., Pernici, F., Del Bimbo, A.: Temporal binary representation for event-based action recognition. In: 2020 25th International Conference on Pattern Recognition (ICPR), pp. 10426–10432. IEEE (2021)
14. Kasabov, N., et al.: Evolving spatio-temporal data machines based on the neucube neuromorphic framework: design methodology and selected applications. Neural Netw. **78**, 1–14 (2016)

15. Li, J., Xu, S., Qin, X.: A hierarchical model for learning to understand head gesture videos. Pattern Recogn. **121**(1), 108256 (2021)

16. Liu, B., Cai, H., Ju, Z., Liu, H.: RGB-D sensing based human action and interaction analysis: a survey. Pattern Recogn. **94**, 1–12 (2019)

17. Maass, W., Natschläger, T., Markram, H.: Real-time computing without stable states: a new framework for neural computation based on perturbations. Neural Comput. **14**(11), 2531–2560 (2002)

18. Mahowald, M.A.: VLSI analogs of neuronal visual processing: a synthesis of form and function (1992)

19. Maqueda, A.I., Loquercio, A., Gallego, G., García, N., Scaramuzza, D.: Event-based vision meets deep learning on steering prediction for self-driving cars. In: Proceedings of the IEEE Conference on Computer Vision and Pattern Recognition, pp. 5419–5427 (2018)

20. Nama, T., Deb, S.: Teleportation of human body kinematics for a tangible humanoid robot control. In: Cognitive Computing for Human-Robot Interaction, pp. 231–251. Elsevier (2021)

21. Nunez, J.C., Cabido, R., Pantrigo, J.J., Montemayor, A.: Convolutional neural networks and long short-term memory for skeleton-based human activity and hand gesture recognition. Pattern Recogn. J. Pattern Recogn. Soc. (2018)

22. Poli, R., Kennedy, J., Blackwell, T.: Particle swarm optimization. Swarm Intell. **1**(1), 33–57 (2007)

23. Querlioz, D., Bichler, O., Dollfus, P., Gamrat, C.: Immunity to device variations in a spiking neural network with memristive nanodevices. IEEE Trans. Nanotechnol. **12**(3), 288–295 (2013)

24. Rebecq, H., Horstschaefer, T., Scaramuzza, D.: Real-time visual-inertial odometry for event cameras using keyframe-based nonlinear optimization (2017)

25. Stimberg, M., Brette, R., Goodman, D.F.: Brian 2, an intuitive and efficient neural simulator. Elife **8**, e47314 (2019)

26. Tavanaei, A., Ghodrati, M., Kheradpisheh, S.R., Masquelier, T., Maida, A.: Deep learning in spiking neural networks. Neural Netw. **111**, 47–63 (2019)

27. Wang, S., Kang, Z., Wang, L., Li, S., Qu, L.: A hardware aware liquid state machine generation framework. In: 2021 IEEE International Symposium on Circuits and Systems (ISCAS), pp. 1–5. IEEE (2021)

28. Yza, B., Lei, S., Yi, W.C., Ke, C., Jian, C., Hla, B.: Gesture recognition based on deep deformable 3d convolutional neural networks. Pattern Recogn. **107** (2020)

29. Zhang, Y., Li, P., Jin, Y., Choe, Y.: A digital liquid state machine with biologically inspired learning and its application to speech recognition. IEEE Trans. Neural Netw. Learn. Syst. **26**(11), 2635–2649 (2015)

Efficient and Accurate Text Detection Combining Differentiable Binarization with Semantic Segmentation

Yue Liu[✉], Ying Shi, Chaojun Lin, Jie Hua, and Ziqi Huang

School of Automation, Wuhan University of Technology, Wuhan, China
265442@whut.edu.cn

Abstract. Recently, segmentation-based methods have quickly become the mainstream in scene text detection, owing to their precise description of arbitrary-shape texts. However, the reduced inference speed hinders the practical application of segmentation-based methods. In this paper, we propose an efficient and accurate arbitrary-shaped text detector named ViT-Bilateral DBNet, which improves the efficiency of feature processing approach to achieve a good trade-off between accuracy and real-time performance. Specifically, we first combine Differentiable Binarization (DB) with real-time semantic segmentation BiSeNet V2 which is more suitable to process features for segmentation-based methods. Then three improvements are proposed to optimize the initial integrated network. ViT-Bilateral Network can strengthen the feature extracting capability of neural networks. Attention-driven Aggregation Layer (AAL) can adaptively fuse the details and the semantics achieved by ViT-Bilateral Network. Meanwhile, the auxiliary loss is added to make the training more sufficient. Compared with original DBNet, our method not only gains 1.17% (on IC15) and 1.34% (on CTW 1500) improvements, but also runs 1.38 times and 1.34 times faster. Notably, our detector surpasses the previous best record and maintains a high inference speed.

Keywords: Deep neural networks · Scene text detection · Semantic segmentation

1 Introduction

Scene text detection is an essential and fundamental task for many text-based applications of neural networks, such as license plate recognition, office automation and document visual question answering. The accuracy and real-time performance directly impact road safety and office efficiency. However, affected by the diversity and complexity of natural scenes, this topic still faces significant challenges [1].

Following the development of deep neural networks, current scene text detection algorithms can be divided into two categories: detection-based methods and segmentation-based methods. On basis of a generic object detector, detection-based methods directly regress the bounding boxes of the text instances. Restricted to the shape of the bounding box, these approaches cannot regress arbitrary-shaped texts teeming in

E. Pimenidis et al. (Eds.): ICANN 2022, LNCS 13531, pp. 630–642, 2022.
https://doi.org/10.1007/978-3-031-15934-3_52

natural scenes such as curve instances. In contrast, segmentation-based methods combine pixel-level prediction [2] and post-processing approaches, and thus can describe text regions of arbitrary shapes more precisely. This kind of methods obtains significantly better detection results and quickly becomes the mainstream.

However, the reduced inference speed hinders the practical application of segmentation-based methods. Two major problems cause the slow speed: the time-consuming post-processing and the inefficient feature processing approach. The first problem arises from the binarization operation which groups segmentation results to generate text instances. In order to solve the first problem, DBNet [3] proposes Differentiable Binarization (DB) to perform the operation with an approximate step function and includes it into a trainable segmentation network.

The cause of the second problem is that segmentation-based methods commonly process features by approaches designed for generic object detection tasks. For instance, DBNet applies "ResNet [4] + Feature Pyramid Networks (FPN) [5]". In ResNet, the diversified multi-scale features extracted by the deep residual network are conducive to regressing objects of various sizes, but are relatively redundant in segmentation-based methods which can perform well merely with low-level detailed features and high-level semantic features. In FPN, the promotion benefits mainly from the assignation strategy that allocates multi-scale objects to multi-scale feature layers rather than feature fusion [6]. The assignation loses efficacy when applied to segmentation-based methods that perform on a single-scale feature. The accuracy improved by FPN is unworthy of its computational cost. Compared with these approaches, segmentation algorithms are more suitable to process features for segmentation-based methods.

In order to achieve a trade-off between accuracy and inference speed, we propose an efficient and accurate scene text detector named ViT-Bilateral DBNet by improving the efficiency of feature processing. Specifically, we first combine DB with a real-time segmentation method BiSeNet V2 [7]. Then three improvements are proposed to optimize the initial integrated network, including ViT-Bilateral Network, Attention-driven Aggregation Layer and the auxiliary loss. The main contributions are as follows:

(1) Proposing to combine DB with real-time Semantic Segmentation method BiSeNet V2 to significantly raise the detection speed.
(2) Proposing an efficient feature extractor ViT-Bilateral Network by introducing the designs of Vision Transformer, notably promoting the detection accuracy.
(3) Exclusively designing an Attention-driven Aggregation Layer for ViT-Bilateral Network to fuse features.
(4) Introducing the auxiliary loss to strengthen the feature representation.

The rest of this paper is organized as follows. Section 2 reviews three groups of related work. Section 3 describes ViT-Bilateral DBNet and each component. Section 4 presents the experiments. Section 5 displays the summary and future improvements.

2   Related Work

The discussion includes scene text detection methods, real-time semantic segmentation algorithms, and Vision Transformer.

Scene Text Detection includes detection-based methods and segmentation-based methods. Detection-based methods are inspired by generic object detectors [8]. TextBoxes [9] adjusts the shape of anchors and convolution kernels to fit the aspect ratios of texts. Inspired by the anchor-free detector, EAST [10] makes pixel-level regression for multi-oriented texts. SegLink [11] predicts segment bounding boxes and their links to regress long texts. But these methods are hard to handle curve texts yet can be predicted well by Segmentation-based methods. PSENet [12] adopts ResNet and FPN to obtain segmentation features and then proposed Progressive Scale Expansion (PSE) to reconstruct text instances. PAN [13] designs Feature Pyramid Enhancement Module (FPEM) and Feature Fusion Module (FFM) to process features, and aggregate text pixels by Pixel Aggregation (PA). The post-processing procedure such as PSE is complex and time-consuming. To simplify the procedure, DBNet [3] proposes Differentiable Binarization to include the binarization operation in a trainable network.

Real-Time Semantic Segmentation requires both fast speed and high-quality prediction. ENet [14] sacrifices the last stage of the model to achieve a lightweight network and extremely high speed. ICNet [15] speeds up the segmentation model by image cascade network. DFANet [16] reuses the feature to strengthen the representation. BiSeNet [17] designs parallel detail branch and semantic branch to achieve high efficiency. Based on [17] BiSeNet V2 [7] further improves the Bilateral Network and the fusion layer, achieving the best trade-off between speed and accuracy so far.

Vision Transformer has made breakthroughs recently and has quickly become the mainstream in computer vision [18]. Swin Transformer [19] designs the hierarchical structure and shifted windows to bring in the advantages of convnets, dramatically surpassing the previous state-of-the-art. The latest work [20, 21] finds that the success of Transformer largely depends on its own ingenious structure. Therefore, ConvNeXt [21] gradually introduces the designs of Swin-T to convnets, implementing the Transformer-ify structure and achieving a similar performance as Swin Transformer.

3   ViT-Bilateral DBNet

We first briefly introduce the overall framework of the proposed ViT-Bilateral DBNet in Sect. 3.1. Next, we describe ViT-Bilateral Network in Sect. 3.2, the Attention-driven Aggregation Layer in Sect. 3.3, and the loss function in Sect. 3.4 in detail.

3.1   Overall Framework of the Integrated Network

The segmentation-based method DBNet proposes Differentiable Binarization to simplify the post-processing, but its feature processing approach is still inefficient. Segmentation algorithms are more suitable to provide features for segmentation-based methods, so we consider combining DB with BiSeNet V2 which has achieved the best trade-off between accuracy and speed by far for higher efficiency. The initial integrated network extracts features via Bilateral Network, in which the Detail Branch with high resolution encodes abundant low-level details, and the parallel Semantic Branch with a large receptive field is responsible for high-level semantics. The complementary features are fed into the Bilateral Guided Aggregation Layer (BGA) for fusion.

Furthermore, ViT-Bilateral DBNet proposes three strategies to optimize the initial integrated network. The overall framework is illustrated in Fig. 1. Firstly, we adopt ViT-Bilateral Network to strengthen the feature extracting capability of Bilateral Network. Then the details and the semantics achieved by ViT-Bilateral Network are fed into the Attention-driven Aggregation Layer (AAL) for adaptive fusion. The output layer employs the Differentiable Binarization approach. By using the aggregated feature S to predict the probability map (P) and threshold map (T), DB module sets the thresholds for binarization and calculates the approximate binary map (B) by P and T as follows:

$$B_{i,j} = \frac{1}{1 + e^{-k(P_{i,j}-T_{i,j})}} \tag{1}$$

where k is the amplifying binary map and is set as 50.

In the training period, the loss of these maps is calculated by their corresponding supervision. Meanwhile, the auxiliary loss is added to make the training more sufficient. In inference, merely the probability map is used to generate the bounding boxes.

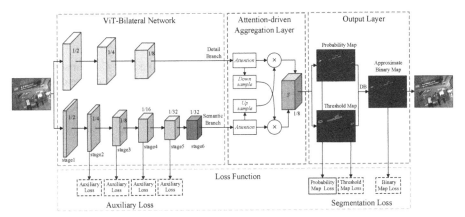

Fig. 1. Illustration of ViT-Bilateral DBNet. The orange cubes and green cubes respectively represent different stages of the Detail Branch and the Semantic Branch. AAL adaptively fuses features extracted from these two branches and obtains the feature S for segmentation.

3.2 ViT-Bilateral Network

According to the breakthrough of Vision Transformer recently, we observe that the effectiveness of BiSeNet V2 results from the Transformer-ify structure of its Semantic Branch, which is of great importance to segmentation. The comparison between Bilateral Network block and Swin-T block shown in Fig. 2(a) are as follows: (i) depthwise convolution and self-attention in Swin-T are equivalent in calculation principle, which merely mixes information over each individual channel [20]; (ii) compared with standard convolutional neural networks, Bilateral Network block achieves larger receptive field like Swin-T by stacking convolutional layers; (iii) the inverted bottleneck is correspond with the dimension change in Swin-T.

Ingenious Transformer-ify designs can provide the neural network with a global receptive field and higher feature expression ability to capture high-level semantics. Obviously, the more similar the Semantic Branch and Transformer are, the better the semantics can be extracted, and the higher the scene text detection accuracy will be. By further introducing the designs of Swin-T, we propose a more efficient text feature extractor ViT-Bilateral Network. The improvements consists of: (i) larger kernel size (7 × 7); (ii) wider network; (iii) Fewer normalization layers and activation functions.

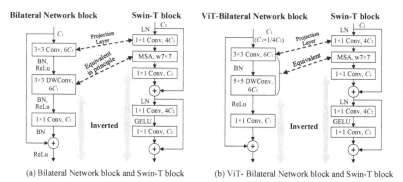

(a) Bilateral Network block and Swin-T block   (b) ViT- Bilateral Network block and Swin-T block

Fig. 2. Comparison between Bilateral Network block and Swin-T block (a). Comparison between ViT-Bilateral Network block and Swin-T block (b). 1 × 1, 3 × 3 and 5 × 5 denote convolution kernels. "DWC" denotes depthwise convolution. "MSA, w7 × 7" denotes a multi-head self-attention computed within a 7 × 7 window.

(i) **Larger kernel size.** Swin Transformer uses shifted windows to limit the computational cost of self-attention. The window size is set as 7 × 7, equivalent to a 7 × 7 conv layer in terms of the receptive field. The Bilateral Network block stacks two 3 × 3 conv layers to achieve a 5 × 5 receptive field, which is larger than vanilla convnets but still smaller than Swin-T block. So we replace the second 3 × 3 DWConv with a 5 × 5 DWConv to enlarge the receptive field to the same as Swin T's.

(ii) **Wider network.** The original channel capacity is (16, 32, 64, 128), a quarter of ResNet's (64, 128, 256, 512). Swin Transformer widens the network to (96, 192, 384, 768) compared with ResNet. The richer channel capacity can encode more affluent semantic information for the semantic branch. Therefore, we slightly expand the channel number to (24, 48, 96, 192), i.e. 1/4 of Swin Transformer.

(iii) **Fewer normalization layers and activation functions.** We are accustomed to appending a normalization layer and an activation function following each convolutional layer. This structure can improve the convergence and introduce more nonlinearity. Actually, excessively frequent normalization and nonlinear projection are detrimental to information transfer [21]. This can be proved in Transformers as well: A Transformer block with more components yet has fewer normalization and only one activation function, but always obtain better results. In view of our lightweight network, we leave single BatchNorm (BN) layers and single ReLu activation in each block.

The ultimate ViT-Bilateral Network block shown in Fig. 2(b) is almost equivalent to the Swin-T block. A convolutional layer first projects the input features. Then a DWConv mixes information over channels with the 7×7 receptive field, which is exactly equivalent to the Shifted Window based Self-Attention. The overall structure presents an inverted bottleneck and retains a BN layer and a ReLu.

3.3   Attention-driven Aggregation Layer

BiSeNet V2 designs the BGA to fuse details and semantics. Each branch merges complementary features via the guidance of the other one. But BGA cannot achieve adaptive aggregation that enables the neural network to focus on the more vital information. The attention mechanisms [22, 23] can help implement adaptively aggregating but are hard to employ because the practical effects are influenced by many factors such as the input, the type and the position of attentional mechanisms.

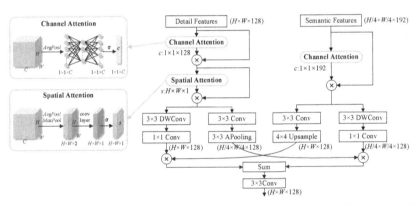

Fig. 3. Detailed design of Attention-driven Aggregation Layer. The detail features and the semantic features represent the output of corresponding branches in ViT-Bilateral Network.

We exclusively design an Attention-driven Aggregation Layer for ViT-Bilateral Network. As illustrated in Fig. 3, it determines the type and the position of attention mechanisms according to the input. It can be known from Sect. 3.1, that the detail features possess abundant channels and higher resolution. The large channel capacity can offer affluent contextual information to establish channel relations for the encoding of the channel attention. The high-resolution features provide rich spatial information to establish reasonable spatial relations for the encoding of spatial attention. So both of these two attention mechanisms are added following the Detail Branch. The channel attention weight c and the spatial attention weight s shown in Fig. 3, are defined as

$$c = \sigma(MLP(AvgPool(X))) \tag{2}$$

$$s = \sigma(conv_{7 \times 7}[AvgPool(\mathbf{X}); MaxPool(\mathbf{X})]) \tag{3}$$

where σ denotes the sigmoid function and MLP is multi-layer perceptron. The dynamic weights c and s have focused on the key position of input features. In contrast, semantic features possess more channels and low resolution. The spatial attention encoded by the low resolution is easy to mix pixels. So only the channel attention is inserted.

The guidance is obtained by a 3×3 conv and a resize operation (Average Pooling and Upsample), and then further multiplied by the complementary features of the other branch. So far adaptive aggregation is realized by the drive of attention mechanisms.

3.4 Loss Function

As shown in the yellow dotted box in Fig. 1, our loss function includes the auxiliary loss L_a in ViT-Bilateral Network and the segmentation loss L_s in the output layer.

The auxiliary loss [7] is an enhancement strategy used to strengthen the feature representation. When inserted into different stages of the Semantic Branch, it can make the training more sufficient. At every stage, we first upsample the feature and then a binary cross-entropy (BCE) loss is respectively computed. The auxiliary loss only works during training and will not influence the inference phase.

The segmentation loss L_s is the same as that in DBNet. In the training period, it can be formulated as a sum of the loss for the probability map L_p, the loss for the binary map L_b, and the loss for the threshold map L_t:

$$L_s = L_p + \alpha \times L_b + \beta \times L_t \tag{4}$$

where the equilibrium factors α and β are set as 1.0 and 10. L_s and L_b adopt BCE loss, and $L1$ distance loss is calculated for L_t. In inference, merely the approximate binary map is used to generate the bounding boxes and thus can simplify the post-processing.

4 Experiments

We first present the experimental setting. Then extensive experiments are conducted to comprehensively verify the effectiveness of our method. Finally, we compare ViT-Bilateral DBNet with many state-of-the-art scene text detection algorithms.

4.1 Datasets

SynthText [24] is a synthetic dataset containing 800K images used for pre-train.

ICDAR 2015 dataset (IC15) [25] is a regular-shaped text dataset. It has 1500 images including 1000 training pictures and 500 used for testing. These images contain lots of multi-oriented text instances which are labeled by four vertices of the quadrangle.

CTW 1500 Dataset [26] is a typical arbitrary-shaped text dataset. It also has 1000 training pictures and 500 testing pictures. CTW 1500 is centered on curve texts which are annotated by a polygon with 14 points.

4.2 Implementation details

All the models are first pre-trained on SynthText for 50K iterations. Then we respectively finetune them on IC15 and CTW 1500 for 150K iterations. The batch size was set to 4. Following [3], we use the poly learning rate strategy where the initial rate is multiplied by $(1 - iter/max\_iter)^{power}$, in which the initial learning rate is 0.007 and power is set to 0:9. We use a weight decay of 0.0001 and a momentum of 0.9.

For a fair comparison, all the models adopt the same training data augmentation following [3]. In the inference period, we keep the aspect ratio of the test images and set the short sides to 736. The inference speed is tested with a 3060 GPU.

4.3 Ablation Study

Verification on Combining DB with BiSeNet V2. Table 1 shows that "ResNet-18 + FPN" has 11.46M parameters, which is about three times larger than that of BiSeNet V2 (3.97M). The lightweight network is more favorable for deployment and practical applications. When combining DB with BiSeNet V2, i.e. replacing "ResNet + FPN" with "Bilateral Network + BGA", we can see that the integrated network runs 21.6 FPS on IC15 and 24 FPS on CTW 1500, and is 1.57 times and 1.51 times faster than DBNet. Although the segmentation network is more suitable for DBNet, the detection accuracy is inevitably decreased by 0.98% and 0.74% because BiSeNet V2 is more lightweight than "ResNet + FPN". It is well worth the significantly improved real-time performance for the slightly depressed accuracy, so the combination is obviously effective. Based on the initial integrated network, then we verify the effectiveness of each improvement.

Table 1. Verification on combining DB with BiSeNet V2. "P", "R", and "F" indicate Precision, Recall, and F-measure. "Res" and "Bila" are short for ResNet and Bilateral Network

Method	Params	ICDAR 2015				CTW 1500			
		P	R	F	FPS	P	R	F	FPS
Res-18 + FPN	11.46M	86.68	77.71	81.95	13.8	84.17	76.62	80.22	15.9
Bila + BGA	3.97M	85.98	76.50	80.97	**21.6**	84.42	75.09	79.48	**24.0**

Ablation Studies on ViT-Bilateral Network. Ablation studies of ViT-Bilateral Network are shown in Table 2. On IC15, when enlarging the kernel size, the F-measure is improved by 0.59% owing to the correspondingly larger receptive field and the richer semantics. When widening the network, 0.87% improvements are achieved. When further reducing the BN layer and the ReLu activation, the final ViT-Bilateral Network gains 1.39% improvements in terms of the F-measure because the excessively frequent normalization and nonlinear projection are really harmful to information transmission.

On CTW 1500, ViT-Bilateral Network achieves similar results. When successively adding these Transformer-ify designs, the F-feature is improved by 0.33%, 0.82% and 1.2%. The structure is beneficial to extracting semantics and then improves the text detection accuracy. The detector extracting features via ViT-Bilateral Network surpasses the original ResNet-18 model by 0.41% and 0.46%. Though the inference speed drops to 19.4FPS and 21.7FPS, it is still much faster than ResNet-18 model.

Table 2. Ablation studies on ViT-Bilateral Network

Larger kernel	Wider network	Less BN and ReLU	ICDAR 2015		CTW 1500	
			F	FPS	F	FPS
			80.97	21.6	79.48	24.0
✓			81.56	21.2	79.81	23.4
✓	✓		81.84	19.2	80.3	21.4
✓	✓	✓	**82.36**	19.4	**80.68**	21.7

Ablation Studies on Attention-driven Aggregation Layer. Ablation studies of Attention-driven Aggregation Layer are illustrated in Table 3. When we insert both the channel attention and the spatial attention following the Detail Branch, it gains 0.5% (on IC15) and 0.47% (on CTW 1500) improvements with a slight decrease in the speed. Appending the single channel attention to the Semantic Branch brings 0.72% and 0.55% improvements. The channel attention gains better results because it is conducive to the optimization of semantic features, which are more vital to segmentation. Attention-driven Aggregation Layer achieved the highest accuracy, increasing the F-measure by 0.82% and 0.72% on IC15 and CTW 1500. The FPS is merely reduced by 0.3 and 0.4.

The last two rows in Table 3 illustrate that the accuracy sharply declines when appending both of these two attention mechanisms to the Semantic Branch. This is because the spatial attention encoded by the low-resolution semantics is too abstract to represent pixel-level features. Moreover, when replacing the position of spatial attention and channel attention, similar results are obtained.

Table 3. Ablation studies on Attention-driven Aggregation Layer

Detail	Semantic	ICDAR 2015		CTW 1500	
		F	FPS	F	FPS
/	/	80.97	21.6	79.48	24.0
+both	/	81.47	21.4	79.95	23.7
/	+channel	81.69	21.5	80.03	23.9
+both	+channel	**81.79**	21.3	**80.2**	23.6
/	+both	79.95	21.4	79.17	23.7
+both	+both	80.99	21.2	79.54	23.4

Ablation Studies on the Auxiliary Loss. We attempt to add the auxiliary loss to different positions of the Semantic Branch. Stage m-n means the loss will be added to the features from stage m to stage n shown in Fig. 1. It can be seen in Fig. 4, that the enhancement strategy can obviously improve the accuracy. When inserting the auxiliary loss to stage 2–5, it gains the highest F-measure, surpassing the baseline by 0.71% and 0.32% on the IC15 dataset and the CTW 1500 dataset. In the inference period, the auxiliary loss can be discarded and the speed maintains 21.6FPS and 24FPS.

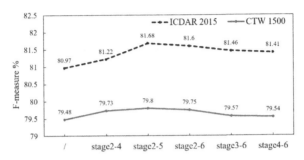

Fig. 4. The results when the auxiliary loss added to different positions of the Semantic Branch.

Overall Ablation Studies. The overall ablation studies in Table 4 show that fusing ViT-Bilateral Network and AAL causes the F-measure to raise by 1.93% and 1.76% on IC15 and CTW 1500. When further adding the auxiliary loss, the final model ViT-Bilateral DBNet is obtained, remarkably outperforming the baseline by 2.15% and 2.08%.

Compared with the original DBNet, our method not only runs 1.38 times (on IC15) and 1.34 times (on CTW 1500) faster, but also obtains 1.17% and 1.34% improvements. The features extracted by our method shown in Fig. 5(a) are clearer and of better quality. Figure 5(b–f). Compares some detection results of DBNet and ViT-Bilateral DBNet on text instances of arbitrary shapes, including multi-oriented text (a), long text lines (b–c), and curved text (d–e). Our method significantly improves the false detection (a, c and d), imprecise regression (b) and the missed detection (e) phenomenon in DBNet.

Table 4. Overall ablation studies. "ViT-Bi" is short for ViT-Bilateral Network

ViT-Bi	AAL	Auxiliary loss	ICDAR 2015				CTW 1500			
			P	R	F	FPS	P	R	F	FPS
			85.98	76.50	80.97	21.6	84.42	75.09	79.48	24.0
✓	✓		87.96	77.42	82.36	19.4	86.23	75.8	80.68	21.7
✓			88.08	78.29	82.9	19.1	85.93	77.03	81.24	21.3
✓	✓	✓	87.16	79.44	**83.12**	19.1	85.93	77.61	**81.56**	21.3

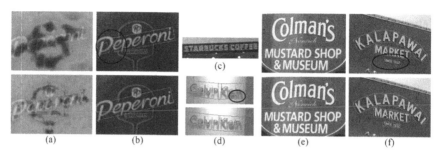

Fig. 5. Visualization results of DBNet (the first row) and ViT-Bilateral DBNet (the second row).

4.4 Comparison

We compare our method with previous state-of-the-art methods in Table 5, including detection-based methods (CTPN, EAST and SegLink) and segmentation-based methods (PSENet, PAN and DBNet). Aiming to ensure fair comparisons and the real-time performance, subsequent experiments employ ResNet-18 without deformable convolution. Among these algorithms, the overall effect of segmentation-based methods is obviously better than that of detection-based methods, especially on CTW 1500. On the IC15 dataset, PSENet achieves the highest F-measure of 83.04% with merely 9.8 FPS. PAN runs the fastest inference speed at 20.3 FPS but its F-measure is relatively low. ViT-Bilateral DBNet not only achieves the best F-measure (83.12%), surpassing PAN by 1.28%, but also maintains a high inference speed (19.1 FPS). On the CTW1500 dataset, ViT-Bilateral DBNet also outperforms all other methods in the aspect of F-measure (81.56%) and maintains a high inference speed.

Table 5. Performance comparison of the improved algorithm. * means the results from [3].

Method	ICDAR 2015				CTW 1500			
	P	R	F	FPS	P	R	F	FPS
CTPN* [7]	74.2	51.6	60.9	7.1	60.4	53.8	56.9	7.14
EAST* [9]	83.6	73.5	78.2	13.2	78.7	49.1	60.4	21.2
SegLink* [10]	73.1	76.8	75.0	–	42.3	40.0	40.8	10.7
PSENet [11]	**88.16**	78.48	83.04	9.8	**87.3**	75.16	80.78	12.3
PAN [12]	86.49	77.66	81.84	**20.3**	86.13	**76.84**	81.22	**22.8**
DBNet [3]	86.68	77.71	81.95	13.8	84.17	76.62	80.22	15.9
ViT-Bilateral DBNet	87.16	**79.44**	**83.12**	19.1	85.93	77.61	**81.56**	21.3

5   Conclusion

In this paper, we propose an efficient and accurate text detector ViT-Bilateral DBNet, which achieves a good trade-off between accuracy and real-time performance by improving the efficiency of feature processing. Extensive experimental results on ICDAR 2015 and CTW 1500 are presented to verify the effectiveness of our method. In the future, we will attempt to enlarge the model size for better performance.

Acknowledgments. The work is supported by National Natural Science Foundation of China (No. 52105528).

References

1. Long, S., He, X., Yao, C.: Scene text detection and recognition: the deep learning era. Int. J. Comput. Vis. (IJCV) **129**, 161–184 (2021). https://doi.org/10.1007/s11263-020-01369-0
2. Bonechi, S., Andreini, P., Bianchini, M., Scarselli, F.: COCO_TS dataset: pixel–level annotations based on weak supervision for scene text segmentation. In: Tetko, I.V., Kůrková, V., Karpov, P., Theis, F. (eds.) ICANN 2019. LNCS, vol. 11729, pp. 238–250. Springer, Cham (2019). https://doi.org/10.1007/978-3-030-30508-6_20
3. Liao, M., Wan, Z., Yao, C., et al.: Real-time scene text detection with differentiable binarization. In: Proceedings of the AAAI Conference on Artificial Intelligence, pp. 11474–11481 (2020)
4. He, K., Zhang, X., Ren, S., et al.: Deep residual learning for image recognition. In: Proceedings of the IEEE Conference on Computer Vision and Pattern Recognition (CVPR), pp. 770–778 (2016)
5. Lin, T.Y., Dollár, P., Girshick, R., et al.: Feature pyramid networks for object detection. In: Proceedings of the IEEE Conference on Computer Vision and Pattern Recognition (CVPR), pp. 2117–2125 (2017)
6. Chen, Q., Wang, Y., Yang, T., et al.: You only look one-level feature. In: Proceedings of the IEEE/CVF Conference on Computer Vision and Pattern Recognition (CVPR) (2021)
7. Yu, C., Gao, C., Wang, J., et al.: BiSeNet V2: bilateral network with guided aggregation for real-time semantic segmentation. Int. J. Comput. Vis. (IJCV) **129**, 3051–3068 (2021). https://doi.org/10.1007/s11263-021-01515-2
8. Tian, Z., Huang, W., He, T., He, P., Qiao, Y.: Detecting text in natural image with connectionist text proposal network. In: Leibe, B., Matas, J., Sebe, N., Welling, M. (eds.) ECCV 2016. LNCS, vol. 9912, pp. 56–72. Springer, Cham (2016). https://doi.org/10.1007/978-3-319-46484-8_4
9. Liao, M., Shi, B., Bai, X., et al.: Textboxes: a fast text detector with a single deep neural network. In: Thirty-First AAAI Conference on Artificial Intelligence (2017)
10. Zhou, X., Yao, C., Wen, H., et al.: East: an efficient and accurate scene text detector. In: Proceedings of the IEEE conference on Computer Vision and Pattern Recognition (CVPR), pp. 5551–5560 (2017)
11. Shi, B., Bai, X., Belongie, S.: Detecting oriented text in natural images by linking segments. In: Proceedings of the IEEE Conference on Computer Vision and Pattern Recognition (CVPR), pp. 2550–2558 (2017)
12. Wang, W., Xie, E., Li, X., et al.: Shape robust text detection with progressive scale expansion network. In: Proceedings of the IEEE/CVF Conference on Computer Vision and Pattern Recognition (CVPR), pp. 9336–9345 (2019)

13. Wang, W., Xie, E., Song, X., et al.: Efficient and accurate arbitrary-shaped text detection with pixel aggregation network. In: Proceedings of the IEEE/CVF International Conference on Computer Vision (CVPR), pp. 8440–8449 (2019)
14. Paszke, A., Chaurasia, A., Kim, S., et al.: ENet: a deep neural network architecture for real-time semantic segmentation. arXiv preprint arXiv:1606.02147 (2016)
15. Zhao, H., Qi, X., Shen, X., Shi, J., Jia, J.: ICNet for real-time semantic segmentation on high-resolution images. In: Ferrari, V., Hebert, M., Sminchisescu, C., Weiss, Y. (eds.) ECCV 2018. LNCS, vol. 11207, pp. 418–434. Springer, Cham (2018). https://doi.org/10.1007/978-3-030-01219-9_25
16. Li, H., Xiong, P., Fan, H., et al.: DFANet: deep feature aggregation for real-time semantic segmentation. In: Proceedings of the IEEE/CVF Conference on Computer Vision and Pattern Recognition (CVPR), pp. 9522–9531 (2019)
17. Yu, C., Wang, J., Peng, C., Gao, C., Yu, G., Sang, N.: BiSeNet: bilateral segmentation network for real-time semantic segmentation. In: Ferrari, V., Hebert, M., Sminchisescu, C., Weiss, Y. (eds.) ECCV 2018. LNCS, vol. 11217, pp. 334–349. Springer, Cham (2018). https://doi.org/10.1007/978-3-030-01261-8_20
18. Dosovitskiy, A., Beyer, L., Kolesnikov, A., et al.: An image is worth 16×16 words: transformers for image recognition at scale. arXiv preprint arXiv:2010.11929 (2020)
19. Liu, Z., Lin, Y., Cao, Y, et al.: Swin transformer: hierarchical vision transformer using shifted windows. In: Proceedings of the IEEE/CVF International Conference on Computer Vision (ECCV), pp. 10012–10022. IEEE (2021)
20. Zhou, J., Wang, P., Wang, F., et al.: ELSA: enhanced local self-attention for vision transformer. arXiv preprint arXiv:2112.12786 (2021)
21. Liu, Z., Mao, H., Wu, C.Y., et al.: A ConvNet for the 2020s. arXiv preprint arXiv:2201.03545 (2022)
22. Hu, J., Shen, L., Sun, G.: Squeeze-and-excitation networks. In: Proceedings of the IEEE Conference on Computer Vision and Pattern Recognition (CVPR), pp. 7132–7141 (2018)
23. Woo, S., Park, J., Lee, J.-Y., Kweon, I.S.: CBAM: convolutional block attention module. In: Ferrari, V., Hebert, M., Sminchisescu, C., Weiss, Y. (eds.) ECCV 2018. LNCS, vol. 11211, pp. 3–19. Springer, Cham (2018). https://doi.org/10.1007/978-3-030-01234-2_1
24. Gupta, A., Vedaldi, A., Zisserman, A.: Synthetic data for text localisation in natural images. In: Proceedings of the IEEE Conference on Computer Vision and Pattern Recognition (CVPR), pp. 2315–2324 (2016)
25. Karatzas, D., Gomez-Bigorda, L., Nicolaou, A., et al.: ICDAR 2015 competition on robust reading. In: 2015 13th International Conference on Document Analysis and Recognition (ICDAR), pp. 1156–1160 IEEE (2015)
26. Yuliang, L., Lianwen, J., Shuaitao, Z., et al.: Detecting curve text in the wild: new dataset and new solution. arXiv preprint arXiv:1712.02170 (2017)

From Open Set Recognition Towards Robust Multi-class Classification

Max Lübbering[1(✉)], Michael Gebauer[2], Rajkumar Ramamurthy[1],
Christian Bauckhage[1], and Rafet Sifa[1]

[1] Fraunhofer IAIS, Sankt Augustin, Germany
{max.lubbering,rajkumar.ramamurthy,christian.bauckhage,
rafet.sifa}@iais.fraunhofer.de
[2] TU Berlin, Berlin, Germany
michael.gebauer@iais.fraunhofer.de

Abstract. The challenges and risks of deploying deep neural networks (DNNs) in the open-world are often overlooked and potentially result in severe outcomes. With our proposed informer approach, we leverage autoencoder-based outlier detectors with their sensitivity to epistemic uncertainty by ensembling multiple detectors each learning a different one-vs-rest setting. Our results clearly show informer's superiority compared to DNN ensembles, kernel-based DNNs, and traditional multi-layer perceptrons (MLPs) in terms of robustness to outliers and dataset shift while maintaining a competitive classification performance. Finally, we show that informer can estimate the overall uncertainty within a prediction and, in contrast to any of the other baselines, break the uncertainty estimate down into aleatoric and epistemic uncertainty. This is an essential feature in many use cases, as the underlying reasons for the uncertainty are fundamentally different and can require different actions.

Keywords: Uncertainty estimation · Aleatoric uncertainty · Epistemic uncertainty · Open world recognition

1 Introduction

The tremendous progress of deep neural networks (DNNs) in recent years has led to the application of machine learning (ML) models in our daily lives, e.g., autonomous driving and medical diagnosis. However, such applications also raised severe concerns related to AI safety [1]. Firstly, these concerns can be attributed to controlled benchmark environments that often do not reflect the deployment scenarios in an open-world setting, neglecting omnipresent side-effects such as noise, dataset shift, or outlier exposure. Secondly, the empirical risk minimization (ERM) in the training process of customary DNNs solely focuses on the separation of the observed classes leading to wrong and overly confident predictions on out-of-distribution (OOD) data [7,9], as visualized in Fig. 1 for the two ensemble methods Deep Ensemble (DE) [9] and MIMO [6] and

© The Author(s), under exclusive license to Springer Nature Switzerland AG 2022
E. Pimenidis et al. (Eds.): ICANN 2022, LNCS 13531, pp. 643–655, 2022.
https://doi.org/10.1007/978-3-031-15934-3_53

a traditional MLP with Softmax output. Many incidents that can be attributed to these shortcomings have been reported in the AI Incident Database [17], stressing the importance of robust DNN methods.

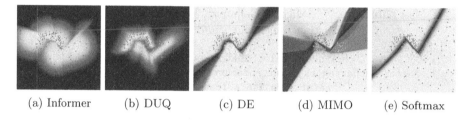

(a) Informer   (b) DUQ   (c) DE   (d) MIMO   (e) Softmax

Fig. 1. Uncertainty heatmap of our informer architecture and the baselines on the half-moon dataset. Informer and DUQ capture aleatoric and epistemic uncertainty whereas the other three ERM baselines only capture aleatoric uncertainty.

Different concepts have been proposed to formalize the transition from closed-set classification to open-world classification. Most prominently, the open set recognition (OSR) framework aims to distinguish a set of inlier classes (observed closed set) from all rest classes (partially observed classes that are contextually related to the inlier classes and unobserved OOD classes) [19]. The optimization objective is formalized as a two-fold problem of robustly rejecting OOD data while maintaining accurate classification between inliers and observed rest samples. Technically, the OSR framework jointly minimizes the empirical risk and open space risk [3,19] which has led to different DNN architectures that robustly perform this generalized one-vs-rest (OVR) classification task [2,11].

Another common approach towards robust DNNs is to leverage their subjective predictive uncertainty. Conceptually, predictive uncertainty can be divided into aleatoric and epistemic uncertainty [5,8]. Aleatoric uncertainty is referred to as the irreducible part of uncertainty which is induced by statistical uncertainty within the data. A classic example is the uncertainty of rolling fair dice that is irreducible despite an arbitrary long history of observations. Epistemic uncertainty quantifies the uncertainty induced by lack of knowledge about the best model for the given problem. Therefore, epistemic uncertainty is generally high on OOD data and can be reduced with an increase in training data. Capturing and distinguishing these two types of uncertainties is crucial in safety-critical environments such as autonomous driving. In case of high epistemic uncertainty, the system would query more data from other sensors for uncertainty reduction [8], or if more data is unavailable, apply emergency breaking as the model is operating blindly. In case of high aleatoric uncertainty, the model can make an informed decision based on risk assessment. Traditional DNNs trained with ERM are incapable of capturing epistemic uncertainty [5,8], exposing humans and other entities engaging with such a system to an unforeseeable risk.

To this end, we propose informer, a DNN architecture based on decoupling autoencoders (DAEs) from the OSR domain [11]. DAEs are trained in an adversarial fashion which minimizes/maximizes the reconstruction error for inliers/outliers by applaying gradient descent and gradient ascent, respectively. Thus, the reconstruction error becomes predictive of the inlierness of a sample. We extend this approach to multi-class classification by ensembling one DAE for each class and training them end-to-end by introducing a custom loss function jointly optimizing classification and outlier robustness performance. Further, we propose a practical uncertainty estimation module (UEM) that captures the overall uncertainty within a prediction and distinguishes aleatoric and epistemic uncertainty. Thus, this method provides interpretable uncertainty estimates; hence its name *informer*.

We benchmark our method against seven potent DNN baselines, including the two ensembles MIMO [6] and DE [9], kernel method DUQ [21] and a feed forward Softmax model on four image and text classification datasets. The key differences between these methods can be seen in Fig. 1 on the half-moon dataset. The ensemble methods and Softmax separate the inlier classes, but neglect uncertainties concerning outliers. In contrast, informer and DUQ learn a hull around the inlier classes, allowing to reject outliers. Throughout our experiments, informer expresses the highest robustness to corruptions while maintaining a competitive classification performance. Finally, we empirically show that the UEM accurately distinguishes aleatoric and epistemic uncertainty.

2   Related Work

Enabling DNN to capture and distinguish different uncertainty types is subject to an ongoing field of study with multiple methods proposed from different domains [8]. These DNN methods can be categorized into Bayesian neural networks (BNNs), ensemble methods and kernel methods. Most prominently, BNNs with their long-lasting history of uncertainty estimation [5,16], have been extended to quantify aleatoric and epistemic uncertainty [4]. However, their reliance on variational inference limits these methods to small-scale solutions.

Further, the authors of [6,9] have shown that simple, deterministic ensemble methods outperform BNNs. On the downside, these methods only provide an overall uncertainty score which mostly captures aleatoric uncertainty but lacks principled retrieval of epistemic uncertainty.

As a solution, deep learning methods based on distance-aware kernels have been proposed [10,20,21]. The work of [10] combines spectral normalization for bi-Lipschitz regularization of residual blocks with a Gaussian process output layer to increase the sensitivity for epistemic uncertainty. Similarly, DUQ [21] regularizes a two-sided Lipschitz constraint within its loss function that is more relaxed than spectral normalization [20].

Various methods on OOD robustness have been proposed based on DNN outlier detectors [11,13] and OSR methods [2], but only a few attempts leverage their sensitivity to epistemic uncertainty to improve DNN uncertainty estimation [8]. This is a gap, we would like to bridge with our contribution.

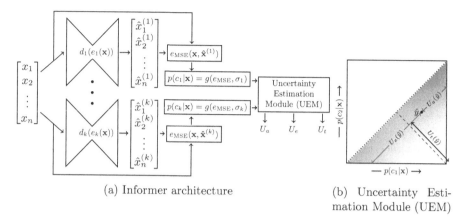

(a) Informer architecture

(b) Uncertainty Estimation Module (UEM)

Fig. 2. Informer architecture: An ensemble composed of k informer components (autoencoder $d_i(e_i(\mathbf{x}))$ for sample reconstruction, a reconstruction error module e_{MSE} for outlierness estimation, and an RBF kernel g for classification), each learning an OVR relationship for a different inlier class. UEM splits the uncertainty U_t (Manhattan distance of prediction to bottom right corner) of prediction $\hat{y}$ into a convex combination of aleatoric uncertainty U_a and epistemic uncertainty U_e. For simplicity, Fig. 2b only shows the case $p(\hat{y}_1|\mathbf{x}) > p(\hat{y}_2|\mathbf{x})$.

3 Informer

To achieve robust multi-class classification with accurate predictive aleatoric and epistemic uncertainty estimates, we propose the informer architecture based on a composition of DAEs [11,14], hereafter referred to as informer components (ICs). Given a multi-class classification problem of classes $\mathcal{C} = \{c_1, c_2, \ldots, c_k\}$, the architecture comprises k ICs each learning a different one-vs-rest (OVR) relationship for one of the classes. As shown in Fig. 2, the IC of inlier class c_i is composed of encoder e_i and decoder d_i, which reconstructs sample $\mathbf{x} \in \mathbb{R}^n$ as reconstruction $\hat{\mathbf{x}}^{(i)} \in \mathbb{R}^n$. The non-parameterized reconstruction error module e_{MSE} maps a sample/reconstruction pair onto a scalar reconstruction error value, which is subsequently mapped to probability $p(c_i|\mathbf{x})$ via the Gaussian kernel g parameterized with standard deviation σ_i. Thus, the subnetwork IC_i is given by

$$p(c_i|\mathbf{x}) = g(e_{\text{MSE}}(d_i(e_i(\mathbf{x}))), \sigma_i), \tag{1}$$

where Gaussian $g(z) = e^{-\frac{z^2}{2\sigma_i^2}}$ and the error module $e_{\text{MSE}}(\mathbf{x}, \hat{\mathbf{x}}) = \frac{1}{n}\sum_j^n (x_j - \hat{x}_j)^2$. Based on the OVR probability $p(c_i|\mathbf{x})$ of each class c_i, UEM provides estimates on the total prediction uncertainty and the aleatoric/epistemic uncertainty ratio. The informer network is defined as $\varphi(\mathbf{x}) = (p(c_1|\mathbf{x}), \ldots, p(c_k|\mathbf{x}))^T$ where $\sum_i^k p(c_i|\mathbf{x}) = 1$ is not enforced. We adapted the original DAE loss function which is optimized for the open set recognition task, such that it learns the multi-class classification problem while maintaining its robustness benefits. The derived loss function $\hat{L}$ is given by

$$\hat{L}(\mathbf{x}, y) = \sum_{i}^{k} L_R(\mathbf{x}, d_i(e_i(\mathbf{x})), \mathbb{1}(y = c_i)) + \alpha_1 L_{CE}(\varphi(\mathbf{x}), y) + \alpha_2 |\sigma|, \quad (2)$$

$$L_R(\mathbf{x}, \hat{\mathbf{x}}, y) = \begin{cases} L_{MSE}(\mathbf{x}, \hat{\mathbf{x}}), & \text{if } y \in \text{inliers} \\ -\alpha_0 L_{MSE}(\mathbf{x}, \hat{\mathbf{x}}), & \text{otherwise} \end{cases} \quad (3)$$

where $\alpha_i \in \mathbb{R}$ scale the outlier reconstruction loss, cross-entropy loss L_{CE} and the regularization of $\sigma = (\sigma_1, \ldots, \sigma_k)^T$, respectively. The loss term L_R denotes the adversarial reconstruction loss, as defined in [11] which minimizes the mean squared reconstruction loss L_{MSE} for inliers and maximizes L_{MSE} for outliers via the negation which corresponds to gradient ascent [13]. The target $y \in \mathcal{C}$ is mapped to $\{0, 1\}$ using indicator function $\mathbb{1}(y = c_i)$, reflecting the OVR relationship within a single IC. The classification cross-entropy loss L_{CE} with its primary purpose to optimize $\sigma \in \mathbb{R}^k$ across the different ICs is defined as

$$L_{CE}(\varphi(\mathbf{x}), y) = -\log(\text{softmax}_i(\varphi(\mathbf{x}))), \quad (4)$$

where target $y = c_i$ and $\text{softmax}_i(\varphi(\mathbf{x})) = \frac{e^{\varphi(\mathbf{x})_i}}{\sum_j^k e^{\varphi(\mathbf{x})_j}}$. Since $\sum_i^k \varphi_i(\mathbf{x}) = 1$ is not enforced, we apply softmax to the model output $\varphi(\mathbf{x})$ which is appropriate to the multi-class classification setting in the training data. While theoretically each IC could be trained independently, the learned decision boundaries imposed by σ can be incompatible due to calibration inaccuracies, e.g., if one IC is generally overly confident then the classification performance is harmed. This problem is alleviated by L_{CE} due to the IC interdependence within softmax. Given an informer network $\varphi(\mathbf{x}, \Theta, \sigma)$ with autoencoder weights Θ and decision boundary parameter σ and sample $\mathbf{x}$ with target $y = c_i$, the gradient w.r.t. σ_i and σ_j with $j \neq i$ computes to

$$\frac{\partial L_{CE}(\varphi(\mathbf{x}, \Theta, \sigma), y)}{\partial \sigma_i} = -\frac{\sum_l^{\{0,\ldots,k\}\setminus\{i\}} e^{\varphi_l(\mathbf{x}, \Theta, \sigma)}}{\sum_l^{\{0,\ldots,k\}} e^{\varphi_l(\mathbf{x}, \Theta, \sigma)}} \frac{\partial \varphi(\mathbf{x}, \Theta, \sigma)}{\partial \sigma_i} \quad (5)$$

$$= -(1 - p(c_i|\mathbf{x})) \frac{\partial \varphi(\mathbf{x}, \Theta, \sigma)}{\partial \sigma_i} \quad (6)$$

and

$$\frac{\partial L_{CE}(\varphi(\mathbf{x}, \Theta, \sigma), y)}{\partial \sigma_j} = \frac{e^{\varphi_j(\mathbf{x}, \Theta, \sigma)}}{\sum_l^{\{0,\ldots,k\}} e^{\varphi_l(\mathbf{x}, \Theta, \sigma)}} \frac{\partial \varphi(\mathbf{x}, \Theta, \sigma)}{\partial \sigma_j} \quad (7)$$

$$= p(c_j|\mathbf{x}) \frac{\partial \varphi(\mathbf{x}, \Theta, \sigma)}{\partial \sigma_j}, \quad (8)$$

respectively[1]. Equation (5) and Eq. (7) display two important gradient properties of L_{CE}: 1) Due to the negation in Eq. 5, σ_i and σ_j are maximized/minimized

---

[1] For space reasons, we omitted a step by step derivation.

within gradient descent, respectively. 2) The gradient scaling factors can be interpreted as probabilities $1 - p(c_i|\mathbf{x})$ and $p(c_j|\mathbf{x})$, as per the definition of the softmax function and regulate the optimization of σ_i and σ_j. Thus, L_{CE} models the interdependence of σ within the multi-class classification setting.

The loss terms L_{CE} and $|\sigma|$ jointly optimize σ, whereas L_R and L_{CE} jointly optimize autoencoder weights Θ. Importantly, even though we apply L_{CE} to all network weights, there is no information leakage between ICs at inference time since $p(c_i|\mathbf{x})$ is independent of the weights of the other ICs $p(c_j|\mathbf{x})$ $\forall i \neq j$. Hence, two ICs can predict their inlier class with maximum confidence which is interpreted as maximum aleatoric uncertainty within the overall prediction.

Given a prediction $\hat{y} = \varphi(\mathbf{x})$ for sample $\mathbf{x}$, we propose a two-step uncertainty estimation approach. Firstly, we filter the two class predictions with the highest certainty. Secondly, as shown in Fig. 2b, we derive the aleatoric and epistemic uncertainty ratios from their location on the probability plane (triangle with color gradient indicating uncertainty types). The model is aleatorically uncertain if both probabilities are high (top right triangle corner), epistemically uncertain if both probabilities are low (bottom left triangle corner), and certain if only one of the two probabilities is high (bottom right triangle corner). A prediction has maximum total uncertainty U_t if it lies on the diagonal between maximum epistemic uncertainty and maximum aleatoric uncertainty. Hence, U_t is a convex combination of aleatoric and epistemic uncertainty. Similarly, all points located on a parallel to this diagonal have equal U_t as induced by the Manhattan distance from the point of maximum certainty. Thus, omitting simple linear algebra, the uncertainty scores can be calculated from the two maximum scores $\hat{y}_1$ and $\hat{y}_2$ within prediction $\varphi(x)$ with $\hat{y}_1 > \hat{y}_2$ as follows

$$U_t(\hat{y}) = \frac{\sqrt{\frac{(1+\hat{y}_2-\hat{y}_1)^2}{2}}}{\sqrt{\frac{1}{2}}}, \quad U_a(\hat{y}) = \frac{\hat{y}_2\sqrt{2}}{\sqrt{2(1+\hat{y}_2-\hat{y}_1)}}, \quad U_e(\hat{y}) = 1 - U_a(\hat{y}). \quad (9)$$

The informer architecture has multiple advantages. While traditional DNNs generally only capture aleatoric uncertainty due to the adoption of ERM [8], the proposed informer method can capture and distinguish aleatoric and epistemic uncertainty due to weight independence between ICs at inference time and global σ optimization. This property is a crucial requirement when deploying models within the open world that is not met by the vast majority of DNN methods.

4   Evaluation Approach

As proposed by [11,15] for model evaluation within the OSR domain, the models are evaluated in three different scenarios (i.e., classification, contextual outlier exposure, and dataset shift exposure). These scenarios are represented by test splits S_c, S_o, S_d, respectively, as depicted in Table 1. We leverage the three image classification datasets FMNIST, MNIST, and EMNIST and the three text classification datasets Reuters, Newsgroups and ATIS. The models

Table 1. Three step experiment setup concerning classification (S_c), contextual outlier exposure (S_o) and dataset shift exposure (S_{d1} and S_{d2}): The two sets of inlier/rest classes within a split are denoted by the first letter of the original dataset. The training split S_t and test splits (S_c, S_o, S_d) share the same inlier classes for a given dataset. The contextual outlier split S_o and dataset shift splits S_d provide the rest classes from the same dataset and an unrelated dataset, respectively. The sets e and a refer to the classes of EMNIST and ATIS.

	FMNIST		MNIST		Reuters		Newsgroups	
Split	Inlier	Rest	Inlier	Rest	Inlier	Rest	Inlier	Rest
S_t	f_c	–	m_c	–	r_c	–	n_c	–
S_c	f_c	–	m_c	–	r_c	–	n_c	–
S_o	f_c	$f \backslash f_c$	m_c	$m \backslash m_c$	r_c	$r \backslash r_c$	n_c	$n \backslash n_c$
S_{d1}	f_c	m	m_c	f	r_c	n	n_c	r
S_{d2}	f_c	e	m_c	e	r_c	a	n_c	a

are trained on FMNIST, MNIST, Reuters, and Newsgroups with the respective inlier classes $f_c = \{t-shirt, pants, pullover, dress, sneaker\}$, $m_c = \{0, 2, 4, 6, 8\}$, $r_c =\{$acq, earn, crude, interest, money-fx$\}$ and $n_c =\{$sci.med, rec.autos, sci.space, misc.forsale, rec.sport.hockey$\}$. We add the remaining unobserved classes from the respective dataset as rest samples to split S_o for contextual outlier exposure, thereby increasing aleatoric and epistemic uncertainty. Finally, we leverage rest classes from unrelated datasets within splits S_{d1} and S_{d2} which primarily increases epistemic uncertainty in the data. As part of the preprocessing, the image samples have been z-transformed and the text samples were embedded as pooled 100-dimensional Glove embeddings [18]. The dataset preprocessing pipeline is implemented with Datastack [12].

We evaluate the closed set classification performance in terms of macro F1 score on split S_c and outlier robustness on S_o and S_d in terms of AUROC. Since we expect models to be uncertain about rest samples, this characteristic is captured by AUROC, which can be interpreted as the probability of a random rest sample being ranked higher than a random inlier sample [7,11].

We selected a MLP as a strong classification baseline and the two ensemble methods MIMO [6] and deep ensembles (DE) [9] with an improved uncertainty estimation in comparison to MLP [9]. We compare two different offline uncertainty estimation methods based on the softmax outputs, as proposed by [7], namely entropy(softmax($\hat{y}^*$)) and max(softmax($\hat{y}^*$)) of logits $\hat{y}^*$. The different variants are denoted by a leading E and M, e.g., E-MLP for entropy-based uncertainty estimation within MLP. Finally, informer is benchmarked against kernel-based DNN method DUQ [21] proposed for robust uncertainty quantization.

We applied nested CV for algorithm-level comparison. Each IC has a hidden layer sizes of $[50, 25, 12, 25, 50]$ for text classification and $[256, 128, 256]$ for image classification. For a fair comparison, all baselines can have a maximum model complexity comparable to the informer complexity. The ensemble size of MIMO

Table 2. Image classification results on the different test splits: The best performing score is highlighted in boldface for each split. Weak performances are highlighted in gray within each split when the score deviates more than 10% points from the best score. The informer architecture provides competitive classification results while being most robust to outliers/datasetshift.

| | FMNIST | | | | MNIST | | | |
| | F1 score | | AUROC | | F1 score | | AUROC | |
Method	S_c	S_o	S_{d1}	S_{d2}	S_c	S_o	S_{d1}	S_{d2}
Informer	96.9 ± 0.3	78.4 ± 0.6	95.8 ± 1.0	95.7 ± 1.1	99.0 ± 0.1	87.9 ± 2.4	99.5 ± 0.2	93.9 ± 0.8
DUQ	96.8 ± 0.3	72.4 ± 3.2	91.3 ± 2.3	90.9 ± 1.6	99.0 ± 0.1	91.4 ± 0.2	92.6 ± 1.1	91.2 ± 0.1
E-MLP	96.7 ± 0.2	52.1 ± 1.7	77.9 ± 1.8	76.7 ± 2.2	98.8 ± 0.1	85.1 ± 3.3	83.6 ± 4.9	82.2 ± 2.8
M-MLP	96.7 ± 0.2	52.6 ± 1.8	77.6 ± 1.8	76.4 ± 2.2	98.8 ± 0.1	85.1 ± 3.3	83.7 ± 4.9	82.2 ± 2.8
E-MIMO	95.6 ± 0.2	73.5 ± 1.4	95.7 ± 1.2	93.7 ± 1.1	96.7 ± 0.3	85.5 ± 1.4	92.1 ± 1.7	86.1 ± 2.3
M-MIMO	95.6 ± 0.2	73.2 ± 1.2	95.2 ± 1.1	93.4 ± 1.0	96.7 ± 0.3	85.6 ± 1.5	92.2 ± 1.6	86.1 ± 2.3
E-DE	96.9 ± 0.2	55.8 ± 1.4	91.2 ± 1.3	88.0 ± 2.1	99.1 ± 0.1	89.7 ± 1.6	86.9 ± 2.9	88.7 ± 1.1
M-DE	96.9 ± 0.2	55.9 ± 1.6	91.0 ± 1.2	87.8 ± 2.0	99.1 ± 0.1	89.7 ± 1.6	86.9 ± 2.8	88.6 ± 1.1

Table 3. Results on text datasets with the same score highlighting as in Table 2: Similar to the results on image datasets, informer provides competitive classification without the robustness deficiencies of the other baselines.

| | Reuters | | | | Newsgroups | | | |
| | F1 Score | | AUROC | | F1 Score | | AUROC | |
Method	S_c	S_o	S_{d1}	S_{d2}	S_c	S_o	S_{d1}	S_{d2}
Informer	90.0 ± 1.6	83.7 ± 2.2	93.7 ± 0.9	91.0 ± 2.0	91.9 ± 0.7	78.8 ± 1.2	88.1 ± 4.7	87.0 ± 5.9
DUQ	89.2 ± 2.5	80.8 ± 5.3	88.2 ± 3.2	95.1 ± 1.0	86.7 ± 5.6	73.6 ± 4.5	70.6 ± 8.0	68.8 ± 8.0
E-MLP	89.5 ± 1.6	63.0 ± 8.3	62.6 ± 8.5	83.2 ± 4.5	91.6 ± 0.8	82.1 ± 1.2	53.7 ± 8.2	68.2 ± 3.1
M-MLP	89.5 ± 1.6	62.4 ± 8.3	62.2 ± 8.4	82.4 ± 4.6	91.6 ± 0.8	81.9 ± 1.2	54.4 ± 8.2	68.9 ± 3.4
E-MIMO	89.0 ± 1.3	87.7 ± 2.8	92.5 ± 1.6	97.3 ± 1.1	89.3 ± 0.9	80.1 ± 1.2	76.4 ± 4.0	77.9 ± 3.7
M-MIMO	89.0 ± 1.3	87.0 ± 2.9	91.8 ± 1.7	96.2 ± 1.4	89.3 ± 0.9	80.2 ± 1.2	78.0 ± 3.8	79.2 ± 3.9
E-DE	90.1 ± 2.0	80.1 ± 6.1	86.6 ± 3.4	96.2 ± 0.3	91.7 ± 1.0	82.6 ± 0.7	74.7 ± 1.9	75.4 ± 2.5
M-DE	90.1 ± 2.0	79.3 ± 5.9	86.0 ± 3.4	95.1 ± 0.4	91.7 ± 1.0	82.2 ± 0.7	75.6 ± 1.9	76.1 ± 2.6

and DE is fixed to 5, matching the number of ICs. All models are optimized with Adam. The informer decision boundary σ is optimized at a higher learning rate via SGD due to the low optimization complexity. All methods are optimized w.r.t. *learning rate* and *weight decay*. Additionally, DUQ is optimized w.r.t. *gradient penalty* and *length scale*. Regarding informer, we perform a sweep over the loss scaling factors α_i.

The best informer model is selected in two steps: 1) The model configurations whose decision boundary has converged to a static value are selected. 2) The final model is chosen by the highest macro F1 score. While there are many possible decision boundaries in reconstruction error space that accurately split the classes, we argue that the smallest decision boundary leads to the tightest hull around the inlier classes and the best generalization towards outlier robustness. We select the best DUQ model by the multi-step approach proposed by its authors. The best model of the remaining baselines is chosen by macro F1 score.

5   Results

Having applied the aforementioned experiment setup, the results in Table 2 and Table 3 show that each method expresses similar performance on the classification split S_c. When exposed to contextual outliers and dataset shift, the MLP baseline expresses major robustness deficiencies with a weak performance in 20/24 cases on S_o, S_{d1} and S_{d2}. While MIMO, DE, and DUQ improve the model robustness, the informer robustness scores significantly exceed the performance of all baselines. Not only does informer achieve the most top robustness scores but also in contrast to all baselines never yields any weak robustness scores. Therefore, the subjective uncertainty scores of informer are more sensitive to outliers, making it the most robust method.

Table 4. Representative samples and their reconstructions from each split expressing either min U_t, max U_e or max U_a. The samples clearly show that different uncertainty types can be captured by the informer architecture.

	S_c samples						S_o rest samples						S_{d1} rest samples					
	min U_t		max U_e		max U_a		min U_t		max U_e		max U_a		min U_t		max U_e		max U_a	
Label	t-shirt	pull.	t-shirt	pull.	t-shirt	pull.	shirt	shirt	aboot	sandal	shirt	shirt	1	0	6	3	7	0
Orig.																		
$IC_{t\text{-shirt}}$																		
$IC_{pullover}$																		
$p(\text{t-shirt}|\mathbf{x})$	100.0	0.0	0.0	0.0	95.8	96.1	99.9	0.7	0.0	0.0	99.4	98.3	92.8	0.0	0.0	0.0	65.7	67.6
$p(\text{pullover}|\mathbf{x})$	0.0	99.9	0.0	0.0	96.4	95.5	0.0	99.9	0.0	0.0	98.9	99.0	0.0	71.9	0.0	0.0	51.8	49.1
U_t	0.0	0.0	1.0	1.0	0.99	0.99	0.0	0.01	1.0	1.0	1.0	0.99	0.07	0.28	1.0	1.0	0.86	0.82
U_a	–	0.0	0.0	0.0	0.96	0.96	0.0	0.08	0.0	0.0	0.99	0.99	0.0	0.0	0.0	0.0	0.56	0.54
U_e	–	1.0	1.0	1.0	0.04	0.04	1.0	0.92	1.0	1.0	0.01	0.01	1.0	1.0	1.0	1.0	0.44	0.46

We further explored the robustness of each IC by comparing the histograms for the inlier classes and the rest classes from the different splits. As shown in Fig. 3a, each IC learns the OVR relationship, explaining the competitive classification results. As shown in Fig. 3b, the inlier class is less separated from the S_o rest classes than the S_d rest classes. This suggests that contextual outliers are reconstructed more accurately than dataset shift samples, possibly allowing to capture aleatoric and epistemic uncertainty separately.

This finding is supported by Fig. 4a, which visualizes samples of high aleatoric uncertainty in the top right corner and samples of high epistemic uncertainty in the bottom left corner, per Eq. (9). Some of the S_c and S_o samples express high aleatoric uncertainty, whereas S_d samples are predicted with high epistemic uncertainty and never yield high aleatoric uncertainty. The predicted epistemic and aleatoric uncertainty is well-aligned with human perception, as shown in Table 4. The two S_c samples with max U_a have middle-sized sleeves adding significant classification ambiguity even for the human eye. Interestingly, the S_c samples with $\max U_e$ cannot be assigned to any of the two classes as they are mislabeled dresses and thus correctly rejected by the model. Similar conclusions can be drawn from the selected S_o samples. S_{d1} samples with $\max U_a$ have comparably low aleatoric uncertainty and high U_t, further showcasing the method's effectiveness of rejecting OOD samples.

In contrast to informer, DUQ can only capture U_t while unable to differentiate between different uncertainty types, as shown in Fig. 4b, with samples of all splits indistinctly spread over the bottom left triangle. We presume that DUQ does not separate aleatoric and epistemic uncertainty since the transformation from input to embedding space can produce artifacts that map OOD data to areas of higher aleatoric uncertainty in embeddings space. This deficiency is prevented within informer by learning a tight hull around the inlier class within each IC, as shown by [11,14] for DAE. If these hulls overlap, this is a strong indicator of true aleatoric uncertainty within the data, as seen in the examples in Table 4.

In conclusion, the informer architecture yields competitive classification results over the full range of experiments while being highly robust to outliers and dataset shift. This level of robustness is not observed for any of the strong baselines. Furthermore, informer can distinguish between aleatoric and epistemic uncertainty, which is impossible for the baselines. The subjective uncertainty predictions also match humans' perceptions of ambiguity and unknownness. All these insights make this method compelling in open-world deployment scenarios.

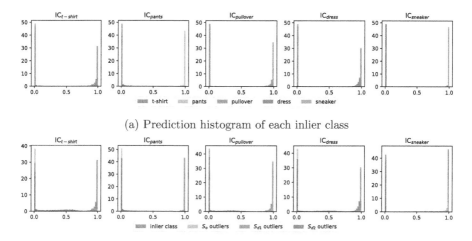

(a) Prediction histogram of each inlier class

(b) Histogram of inlier predictions and outliers predictions of split S_o, S_{d1} and S_{d2}.

Fig. 3. Histogram of IC predictions $\varphi_i(\mathbf{x}) = p(c_i|\mathbf{x})$: While the inlier class is well-separated from observed rest classes, there are few outlier samples primarily from split S_o that are falsely predicted as inliers with high confidence.

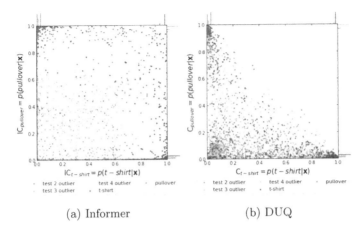

(a) Informer   (b) DUQ

Fig. 4. Comparing the prediction scatter of informer ($IC_{pullover}$ and $IC_{t-shirt}$) to DUQ's centroids ($C_{pullover}$ and $C_{t-shirt}$) w.r.t. inlier classes pullover/t-shirt and S_o/S_{di} rest classes. Due to the majority of samples overlapping in the dense corners, we added histogram bars on the top and right edge for visual support.

6 Conclusion

Deploying models in the open world poses various challenges to traditional DNN methods. Generally, the empirical risk minimization is solely focused on inlier separation and does not consider dataset shift and outlier exposure prevalent in open-world scenarios, potentially leading to uncontrollable and harmful behavior in the open-world setting. To this end, we proposed the informer architecture as an ensemble of autoencoder-based OVR classifiers that is highly robust to such corruptions. Furthermore, informer can estimate the overall uncertainty within a prediction and subdivide the uncertainty into epistemic and aleatoric uncertainty in a principled way. We demonstrated its robustness superiority over two ensemble methods [6,9], uncertainty quantization method DUQ [21] and traditional MLPs throughout various experiment settings and datasets. Finally, we empirically verified informer's capability of differentiating between aleatoric and epistemic uncertainty that is well-aligned with human perception. For future work, we are considering applying informer to real-world scenarios, such as medical diagnosis which requires robustness and accurate uncertainty estimation.

Acknowledgement. In parts, the authors of this work were supported by the Competence Center for Machine Learning Rhine Ruhr (ML2R) which is funded by the Federal Ministry of Education and Research of Germany (grant no. 01|S18038B).

References

1. Amodei, D., Olah, C., Steinhardt, J., Christiano, P., Schulman, J., Mané, D.: Concrete Problems in AI Safety. arXiv preprint (2016)
2. Bendale, A., Boult, T.E.: Towards Open Set Deep Networks. In: Proceedings of the IEEE Conference on Computer Vision and Pattern Recognition (2016)
3. Boult, T.E., Cruz, S., Dhamija, A.R., Gunther, M., Henrydoss, J., Scheirer, W.J.: Learning and the Unknown: surveying steps toward open world recognition. In Proceedings of the AAAI Conference on Artificial Intelligence (2019)
4. Depeweg, S., Hernandez-Lobato, J.-M., Doshi-Velez, F., Udluft, S.: Decomposition of uncertainty in Bayesian deep learning for efficient and risk-sensitive learning. In: International Conference on Machine Learning (2018)
5. Gal, Y.: Uncertainty in Deep Learning. PhD thesis, University of Cambridge (2016)
6. Havasim M., et al.: Training Independent Subnetworks for Robust Prediction. arXiv preprint (2020)
7. Hendrycks, D., Gimpel, K.: A baseline for detecting misclassified and out-of-distribution examples in neural networks. In: Proceedings of the International Conference on Learning Representations (2017)
8. Hüllermeier, E., Waegeman, W.: Aleatoric and epistemic uncertainty in machine learning: an introduction to concepts and methods. In: Machine Learning (2021)
9. Lakshminarayanan, B., Pritzel, A., Blundell, C.: Simple and Scalable Predictive Uncertainty Estimation Using Deep Ensembles (2017)
10. Liu, J., Lin, Z., Padhy, S., Tran, D., Weiss, T.B., Lakshminarayanan, B.: Simple and principled uncertainty estimation with deterministic deep learning via distance awareness. Adv. Neural Inf. Process. Syst. **33** (2020)
11. Lübbering, M., Gebauer, M., Ramamurthy, R., Bauckhage, C., Sifa, R.: Decoupling autoencoders for robust one-vs-rest classification. In: IEEE 8th International Conference on Data Science and Advanced Analytics. IEEE (2021)
12. Lübbering, M., Pielka, M., Henk, I., Sifa, R.: Datastack: unification of heterogeneous machine learning dataset interfaces. In: 2022 IEEE 38th International Conference on Data Engineering Workshops (ICDEW), pp. 66–69. IEEE (2022)
13. Lübbering, M., Ramamurthy, R., Gebauer, M., Bell, T., Sifa, R., Bauckhage, C.: From imbalanced classification to supervised outlier detection problems: adversarially trained auto encoders. In: Farkaš, I., Masulli, P., Wermter, S. (eds.) ICANN 2020. LNCS, vol. 12396, pp. 27–38. Springer, Cham (2020). https://doi.org/10.1007/978-3-030-61609-0_3
14. Lübbering, M., Gebauer, M., Ramamurthy, R., Bauckhage, C., Sifa, R.: Bounding open space risk with decoupling autoencoders in open set recognition. Int. J. Data Sci. Analyt. (2022)
15. Lübbering, M., Gebauer, M., Ramamurthy, R., Pielka, M., Bauckhage, C., Sifa, R.: Utilizing representation learning for robust text classification under datasetshift. In: Proceedings of the Conference "Lernen, Wissen, Daten, Analysen" (2021)
16. MacKay, D.J.C.: A practical Bayesian framework for backpropagation networks. Neural Comput. **4** (1992)
17. McGregor, S.: Preventing Repeated Real World AI Failures by Cataloging Incidents: The AI Incident Database. arXiv preprint (2020)
18. Pennington, J., Socher, R., Manning, C.D.: Glove: global vectors for word representation. In: Proceedings of Conference on Empirical Methods in Natural Language Processing (EMNLP) (2014)

19. Scheirer, W.J., de Rezende Rocha, A., Sapkota, A., Boult, T.E.: Toward open set recognition. IEEE Trans. Pattern Anal. Mach. Intell. **35** (2013)
20. van Amersfoort, J., Smith, L., Jesson, A., Key, O., Gal, Y.: On feature collapse and deep kernel learning for single forward pass uncertainty. arXiv preprint (2021)
21. Van Amersfoort, J., Smith, L., Teh, Y.W., Gal, Y.: Uncertainty estimation using a single deep deterministic neural network. In: International Conference on Machine Learning, PMLR (2020)

Gait Adaptation After Leg Amputation of Hexapod Walking Robot Without Sensory Feedback

Jan Feber[(✉)] [iD], Rudolf Szadkowski[iD], and Jan Faigl[iD]

Department of Computer Science, Faculty of Electrical Engineering, Czech Technical University in Prague, Technická 2, 166 27, Prague 6, Czech Republic
{feberja1,szadkrud,faiglj}@fel.cvut.cz
https://comrob.fel.cvut.cz/

Abstract. In this paper, we address the adaptation of the locomotion controller to change of the multi-legged walking robot morphology, such as leg amputation. In nature, the animal compensates for the amputation using its neural locomotion controller that we aim to reproduce with the Central Pattern Generator (CPG). The CPG is a rhythm-generating recurrent neural network used in gait controllers for the rhythmical locomotion of walking robots. The locomotion corresponds to the robot's morphology, and therefore, the locomotion rhythm must adapt if the robot's morphology is changed. The leg amputation can be handled by sensory feedback to compensate for the load distribution imbalances. However, the sensory feedback can be disrupted due to unexpected external events causing the leg to be damaged, thus leading to unexpected motion states. Therefore, we propose dynamic rules for learning a new gait rhythm without the sensory feedback input. The method has been experimentally validated on a real hexapod walking robot to demonstrate its usability for gait adaptation after amputation of one or two legs.

Keywords: Gait adaptation · Robot locomotion · Leg amputation · Hexapod walking robot · Damage compensation · Emergent system · Dynamic system · CPG-RBF

1 Introduction

Dealing with damaged limbs is desirable to keep the walking robot operable in a long-term mission. During the mission, various leg malfunctions can occur, such as a leg can get stuck, be crashed by a fall of a heavy object or stop working correctly due to component wear. It might be preferable to amputate (lose) the leg instead of keep using the damaged limb. Hence, we need a mechanism to deal with the locomotion change after the leg amputation.

Supplementary Information The online version contains supplementary material available at https://doi.org/10.1007/978-3-031-15934-3_54.

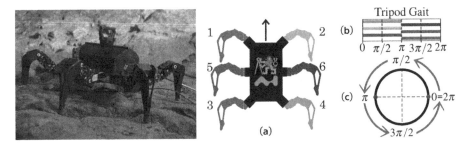

Fig. 1. On the left, a photo of the hexapod walking robot used in experiments is shown. The (a) presents the schema and labeling of the robot's legs. The arrow points in the walking direction. (b) and (c) are different ways of describing the tripod gait pattern, which is used in our experiments as a starting point before the amputation. The colorful bars in (b) correspond to the swing duration within the movement phase ($[0, 2\pi)$ on the horizontal axis). The colors correspond to color labeling from (a). (c) presents the phase as a cycle, as it repeats periodically. The colorful dots represent the start of the corresponding leg's swing (i.e., the value ϕ_i^s). The dots are overlapping because the start of the swing is the same for the legs within the triplets $(1, 3, 6)$ and $(2, 4, 5)$. (Color figure online)

Adjusting to morphological changes like amputation is essential for living organisms to survive. Existing organisms have voluntary leg amputation included as their defense mechanism called autotomy, and some species are even able to regenerate the lost limb after a certain time [5]. Nevertheless, both types of species (with and without the ability to regrow the lost limb) adapt to the morphological change after the amputation. The adaptation mechanisms observed on legged animals are imitated by researchers in developed biomimetic models.

A frequently used biomimetic mechanism is the concept of the *Central Pattern Generator* (CPG), a recurrent neural network producing rhythm underlying the locomotion [8]. The CPG's resistance to perturbations is utilized in CPG-based locomotion controllers [17]. The periodic movement induced by CPGs is called a gait pattern. It is a repetitive motion pattern described by the mapping between the phase of the gait and limb movement timing. The movement of each leg consists of swing (the leg's forward movement) and stance, the backward movement of the leg pushing against the ground, and moving the body forward. The swing and stance repeat periodically, altering each other.

Damage-compensation approaches for hexapod control can be based on sensory feedback such as the WALKNET architecture [2,12,13] or [9,10]. However, the sensory feedback, especially in the case of leg malfunction, may not be reliable. Moreover, the feedback is strongly influenced by the terrain changes, such as feedback on an uneven vs. plane surface or feedback on sand or mud differs from feedback on a pavement. Hence, it is desirable to have an adaptation method that does not rely on explicit sensory feedback.

In this work, we propose dynamic rules to adjust the legs' movement rhythm producing a stable gait pattern with one amputated leg or one amputated leg on each side of the robot's body. The proposed approach is based on the CPG-RBF architecture [11] connecting the CPG with the *Radial Basis Function* (RBF) neurons that encode the mapping between the CPG's phase and the robot's motion. As the centers of RBF neurons are placed along the CPG's cyclic attractor, the RBF neurons are activated periodically producing the rhythm for locomotion. In the previous work, we proposed a method for mapping the RBF neurons on the limit cycle ordered correctly to produce a rhythm for a given gait pattern [4]. In the present work, we extend the method to enable gait adaptation to the amputation of one or two legs. We propose self-organizing dynamics that adapt to changed morphology caused by an amputation with respect to *Inter-Leg Coordination Rules* (ICRs) [2], where the RBF centers are shifted around the limit cycle to avoid the ICR violation. We demonstrate the usability of the proposed method by its deployment on a real hexapod walking robot and experimental validation in four different scenarios with one and two amputated legs.

2 Related Work

Various architectures used in CPG-based controllers can be found in the literature. Architectures with one or more uncoupled CPGs for each leg have been proposed [9,10]. On the contrary, architectures with inter-coupled CPGs and synchronized by sensory input can be found [7,14,16]. Besides, the controllers can consist of two sub-modules: amplitude control, providing the magnitude of actuation, and phase control, providing the actuation in which the CPG is involved. Hence, we can further distinguish approaches based on the phase control mapping between the movement and the CPG's phase.

The mapping can be a continuous, binary-phase switch or the generalization of the latter, a multi-phase switch. Continuous mapping transforms the CPG signal directly into the motion commands by reshaping the waveform with different continuous functions [15,16]. As the motion commands are tightly coupled to the waveform, any change of the CPG-generated waveform requires finding a new continuous function providing the appropriate commands, which is generally a complex problem. On the other hand, the dependency between the waveform and commands is relaxed in the binary-switch mapping that uses the CPG as a timing switch between the stance and swing phases, with each of the phases having its control rules [6].

In this paper, we follow the multi-phase switch represented by the CPG-RBF architecture [11,14]. We propose to take advantage of the multi-phase methods compared to the continuous mapping, which is the independence of the CPG model. In contrast to the binary-switch, the multi-phase model enables more control over the motion because we gain more information about the ongoing gait phase than switching only between swing and stance modes.

Existing architectures dealing with leg malfunctions include WALKNET [2] further developed in [12,13]. There are methods relying on the sensory feedback as a coupling mechanism for the CPGs that are not interconnected directly but interact indirectly through the sensory feedback from the environment [9]. A principle of tegotae incorporating the sensory feedback to influence the CPGs phase by detecting unwanted gait behavior is introduced in [10]. However, we assume the sensory feedback might be unreliable after body and leg damage in the proposed approach. Therefore, we propose an adaptation of the locomotion to the morphology change only with respect to (w.r.t) the coordination rules. The proposed method is an extension of the parametrizable gait generator based on the CPG-RBF architecture [4] that reacts to the leg amputation by adjusting the RBF neurons w.r.t. the inter-leg coordination rules.

3   Problem Specification

The gait phase controller drives the leg movement rhythm that controls the swing and stance timing. The controller should follow the *Inter-leg Coordination Rules* (ICRs) observed from gaits of hexapod insects [2] to ensure stability. Three rules can be defined as follows.

1. While a leg is lifted-off, suppress the lift-off of the consecutive leg.
2. If the leg touches the ground, initiate the lift-off of the consecutive leg.
3. Do not lift off the contralateral legs at the same time.

Following the ICRs, the exact gait pattern is given by the phase offset $\Delta\phi$ of the consecutive legs motion phase (e.g., for the tripod gait $\Delta\phi = \pi$) that corresponds to the swing phase duration [1].

The ICRs, in combination with gait-determining $\Delta\phi$, work well for regular gait patterns; however, the conditions change with the leg amputation. For instance, the amputated leg behaves like in the swing phase, (i.e., being lifted-off of the ground) and its contralateral and consecutive leg can never undergo the swing movement, based on the ICRs. The relations between the legs have to be adjusted to keep the controller functional after the amputation.

With lowering the number of legs, we also need to consider the number of legs supporting the robot's body, i.e., the legs in the stance phase. An example is using the tripod gait (leg triplets $1, 3, 6$ and $2, 4, 5$ altering in the swing phase longing for half of the period, see Fig. 1) with no adjustment after the amputation of the leg 6. It results in both remaining legs from the right side of the robot's body being lifted simultaneously; therefore, the robot has no support on the right side and falls. The original gait patterns have to be modified in the case of the amputation to prevent the robot's body from falling to the ground.

The swing duration $\Delta\phi$, corresponding to the phase offset of consecutive legs' movement, can also conflict with the ICRs after the amputation. Let us consider the tripod gait with the amputation of the leg 6. The legs 2 and 4 have to alter each other to keep at least one leg from the body's right side on the ground to support the robot's body and keep the swing phase length equal to $\Delta\phi = \pi$. It means that their respective contralateral legs can not undergo the swing simultaneously, according to the third ICR. Hence, one of the legs 1 or 3 has to undergo the swing simultaneously with the leg 5, which is, however, in contradiction with the first ICR. The swing duration $\Delta\phi$, corresponding to the minimal phase offset of consecutive legs, has to be modified in some cases to maintain the gait stable according to ICRs.

The gait rhythm is given by the phases in which the legs undergo swing and stance movement. The beginning and end of the swing (the swing end is the start of the stance) are given by the activation phase $\phi_i^s \in [0, 2\pi)$ and $\phi_i^e \in [0, 2\pi)$, respectively.

In our previous work [4], we introduced a mechanism for mapping the RBF centers positions within the CPG's phase space based on the phase activation values. Hence, the problem of moving the RBF centers within the CPG's phase space simplifies to shifting the activation phases ϕ_i^s and ϕ_i^e within the interval $[0, 2\pi)$. In this paper, we propose dynamic rules depending on the ICRs, swing duration $\Delta\phi$ and knowledge about limb amputation. The proposed dynamics update $\Delta\phi$ and the swing start and end phases ϕ_i^s and ϕ_i^e are shifted for each functioning leg i to achieve a stable gait pattern compliant with ICR.

4   Proposed Locomotion Adaptation to Leg Amputation

We propose update rules for swing duration $\Delta\phi$ and start phase ϕ_i^s that continually minimize the motion errors inferred from the: (i) detected ICRs violations; and (ii) over-safe states. At any time t, the ICRs determine whether the i-th leg should be in stance, $d_i(t) = 1$, w.r.t. other legs motion $s_j^{sw}(t)$ and damage $s_j^{dmg}(t)$ states; where $s_j^{sw} = 1$ denotes the j-th leg in the swing, while $s_j^{dmg} = 1$ denotes the j-th leg being amputated. The motion states $\mathbf{s}^{sw}$ determine whether the robot is in an over-safe state. The proposed system adjusts the swing duration, and minimizes the duration of the over-safe state and ICRs violation; thus, the swing phases ϕ_i^s converge to a gait configuration allowing the hexapod robot to walk again.

4.1   Morphology Information

The restrictions given by the ICRs based on the robot's morphology do not provide clear guides for the leg relations after a significant morphology change, like an amputation. In the original work [2], where the ICRs were proposed, are rules related to the load distribution among the legs. However, the rules require non-trivial sensory feedback, which does not have to be available nor undistorted. Hence, we propose to add the following four rules to the ICRs that complement the originally introduced ICRs [2], altering the consecutivity and contralaterality within the legs after the leg amputation. The proposed *Consecutivity and Contralaterality Adjustment Rules* (CCARs) are as follows.

1. The most-front left (right) functional leg is a contralateral leg for the most-front right (left) functional leg.
2. The most-hind left (right) functional leg is a contralateral leg for the most-hind right (left) functional leg.

3. If the leg i is contralateral leg of the leg j that becomes contralateral leg for the leg k due to the proposed rule 1. or 2., then the contralateral relation between the legs i and j is no longer active.
4. If the leg j: (i) has consecutive leg k, and (ii) is the i-th leg's consecutive leg, and (iii) is not functional, then the leg k becomes the consecutive leg of the leg i.

The application of the CCARs enables us to use the ICRs even for a robot with amputated legs. An example of the relations after the amputation is visualized in Fig. 2.

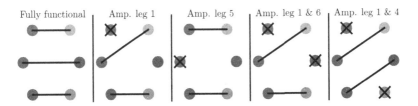

Fully functional   Amp. leg 1   Amp. leg 5   Amp. leg 1 & 6   Amp. leg 1 & 4

Fig. 2. The schema presents scenarios of the amputation in our experiments and the application of the CCARs 1., 2. and 3., where contralateral relation is depicted by the edge between respective legs' nodes. A cross over the node represents amputation. The colors of the legs' nodes correspond to the leg labeling in Fig. 1

4.2   Gait Swing Control

The gait is determined by the swing starts ϕ_i^s and the swing duration $\Delta\phi$ that parameterize the control signal generated by the employed CPG-RBF architecture

$$\dot{y} = \omega + \alpha(t)\sin(y), \tag{1}$$
$$\varphi(t; \phi) = \exp(-\lambda(y(t) - \phi)^2), \tag{2}$$

where ω is the CPG frequency and the hyperparameter λ determines the width of the bell-shaped RBF signal. The model (1) is a simplified CPG model, where the perturbation $\alpha(t)$ is considered to be zero during the locomotion learning. The i-th leg swing start is driven by the RBF signal $\varphi_i^s(t) = \varphi(t; \phi_i^s)$ and the end with $\varphi_i^e(t) = \varphi(t; \phi_i^s + \Delta\phi)$. The peaks of the signals $\varphi_i^s(t)$ and $\varphi_i^e(t)$ switch the motion state $s_i^{sw}(t)$ to one and zero, respectively.

4.3   ICRs Violation Detection

The swing control should be configured so that it minimizes the duration of the possible ICRs violations and over-safe state. The violation of the ICRs can be inferred from the motion $\mathbf{s}^{sw}(t)$ and amputation $\mathbf{s}^{dmg}(t)$ states using propositional logic as follows.

Let $f : (\mathbf{s}^{\mathrm{sw}}, \mathbf{s}^{\mathrm{dmg}}) \rightarrow \mathbf{d}$ represent the ICRs as a boolean function that maps the legs swing and damage to required stances $\mathbf{d} \in \{0,1\}^6$, where $d_i = 1$ represents the i-th leg is required to be in stance and thus not lose the balance. Therefore, if the leg is required to be in the stance but is in the swing, $d_i(t) \wedge s_i^{\mathrm{sw}}(t)$, we can detect the rule violation. We distinguish the rule violation at the start and end of the swing

$$a_i^{\mathrm{s}}(t) = d_i(t)s_i^{\mathrm{sw}}(t)[\![\varphi_i^{\mathrm{s}} > \delta]\!], \tag{3}$$
$$a_i^{\mathrm{e}}(t) = d_i(t)s_i^{\mathrm{sw}}(t)[\![\varphi_i^{\mathrm{e}} > \delta]\!], \tag{4}$$

respectively, where $\delta = 0.95$ is the hyperparameter thresholding the RBF neuron signal peak. The violation signals a_i^{s} and a_i^{e} are then smoothed by integration

$$\dot{v}_i^{\mathrm{s}/\mathrm{e}} = \begin{cases} 1 - v_i^{\mathrm{s}/\mathrm{e}} & \text{if } a_i^{\mathrm{s}/\mathrm{e}} = 1, \\ -v_i^{\mathrm{s}/\mathrm{e}} & \text{if } a_i^{\mathrm{s}/\mathrm{e}} = 0, \end{cases} \tag{5}$$

outputting the error signals for the start v_i^{s} and end v_i^{e} of the i-th leg swing.

4.4 Phase Action Values Ordering

The swing start ϕ_i^{s} minimizes the duration of ICRs violation by the following update rule w.r.t. the motion error signals

$$\dot{\phi}_i^{\mathrm{s}} = v_i^{\mathrm{s}} - v_i^{\mathrm{e}} + \mathrm{sgn}(\phi_i^{\mathrm{s}} - \phi_j^{\mathrm{s}} + \pi)(\phi_i^{\mathrm{s}} - \phi_j^{\mathrm{s}} + \pi)^2, \tag{6}$$

where the first two terms push the swing start outside the time interval during which the i-th leg should be in the stance, the third term is a regularization pushing the i-th leg into the antiphase to its contralateral j-th leg, and the function $\mathrm{sgn}(x)$ is the sign function.

4.5 Swing Duration Adjustment

The long-term ICRs violation $v(t) = \sum_i v_i^{\mathrm{s}}$ or over-safe state $o(t) = \prod_i (1 - s_i^{\mathrm{sw}}(t))$ (when all legs are in the stance at the same time) require a change in the swing duration. We propose to detect the long-term error states with two *Leaky-Integrate&Fire* (LIF) neurons $c_o(t)$ and $c_v(t)$. The LIFs $c_o(t)$ and $c_v(t)$ integrate their respective inputs $o(t)$ and $v(t)$ and it fires if the LIF state surpasses the threshold. The LIF firing indicates the long-term error state, which is then addressed by the swing duration update rule

$$\Delta\dot{\phi} = \begin{cases} \xi & \text{if } c_o \text{ fires,} \\ -\xi & \text{if } c_v \text{ fires,} \\ 0 & \text{otherwise} \end{cases} \tag{7}$$

where $\xi = 0.2$ is the speed of $\Delta\phi$ decrease and increase.

The update rules for the swing duration $\Delta\phi$ and swing phase ϕ_i^{s} minimize the motion error duration continually. The feasibility of the proposed approach has been experimentally verified on real hexapod walking robots; the results are reported in the following section.

5   Experimental Results

The feasibility of the proposed solution has been evaluated on four amputation scenarios deployed on a real hexapod walking robot. All the presented scenarios start with the robot walking using a pre-trained tripod gait, which is interrupted by amputation after five hundred iterations (approximately two complete gait cycles). The scenarios are depicted in Fig. 2, where two of them show the adapting process after the amputation of one leg (the legs 1 and 5), and the other two show the amputation of two legs denoted 1 & 6, and 1 & 4. Each of the four scenarios was run ten times, where the proposed algorithm converges to a stable solution as indicated in Fig. 3. Since the ICRs violation indicator v_i^s, inducing the rhythm change, approaches zero, the gait pattern is compliant to the ICRs adjusted by the proposed CCARs.

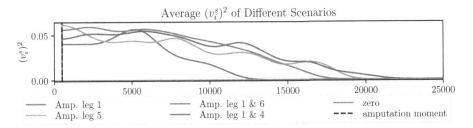

Fig. 3. The average of the value $(v_i^s)^2$ with increasing iteration number during the performed amputation scenarios depicted in Fig. 2 computed from ten experimental trials performed. Each color represents the average value of $(v_i^s)^2$ for each leg from all experiments of the particular scenario. Blue and orange curves show the one leg amputation scenarios for the leg 1 and 5, respectively. The two legs amputation scenarios for the pairs 1 & 6 and 1 & 4 are depicted in green and red, respectively. The dashed black line represents the moment of the amputation. The standard deviations in the last state are $5 \cdot 10^{-17}, 4 \cdot 10^{-6}, 4 \cdot 10^{-6}$ and $3 \cdot 10^{-6}$ for the scenarios represented by blue, orange, green, and red lines, respectively. (Color figure online)

Examples of the resulting gait patterns are visualized in Fig. 4, where the upper plots show the gait schema right after the amputation and the lower plots present the adjusted gait rhythm. Note the adjustment of the swing length and the difference in the amount of conflicting areas between one and two amputated legs scenarios.

The update rule for the swing duration $\Delta\phi$ and the activity of the LIF neurons is demonstrated in Fig. 5.

The four experiments were realized with deployment on the real hexapod walking robot [3] depicted in Fig. 1. The robot has six legs, each with three joints made of the Dynamixel AX-12 servomotors. The body motion is achieved by the open-loop controller setting the joint angles resulting in a swing and stance motion. The swing of each i-th leg is parameterized by the swing start ϕ_i^s

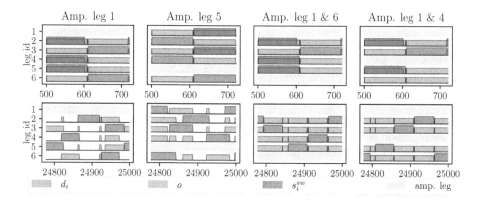

Fig. 4. Visualization of approximately one gait period of the leg rhythm for performed amputation scenarios introduced in Fig. 2. The upper plots show the state right after the amputation, which occurred in the 500-th iteration. The lower plots show adjusted rhythm after the converged learning. Each row of the sub-figure represents one leg (given by the leg's number on the vertical axis). The yellow bar indicates the amputated leg; the grey bar represents the swing phase of the motion; the red bar represents the state when $d_i = 1$ for the i-th leg; and the green bar represents the over-safe state $o = 1$. (Color figure online)

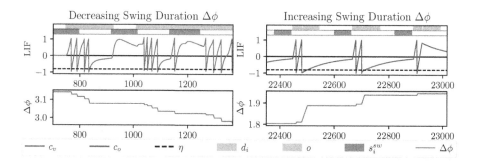

Fig. 5. Visualization of the LIF mechanism (red and green curves in the upper plots) and its influence on the swing duration $\Delta\phi$ (blue curve in the lower plots). The left LIF is inhibited by the violation of the ICRs and CCARs indicated by bars above the plot, where the grey bar represents the swing phase, and the red bar represents the area in which the performance of the swing action would violate the rules. Note, that the LIF (red line) is dependent on v_i of all legs while the shown grey and red bars represents only one leg's swing and rules violation indicator. Once the LIF integrates into one, it fires and decreases its value below the threshold indicated by the dashed black line. The value below the threshold induces lowering $\Delta\phi$ in the lower plot. The same mechanism is applied in the right plot, where the inhibition is provided by the over-safe state o (shown by the green bar in the schema above the plot) if no violation is detected. However, here hitting the threshold implies the growth of $\Delta\phi$. (Color figure online)

and end ϕ_i^e phases, given by the proposed phase controller, and by two additional phases ϕ_i^m and ϕ_i^{cm} placed in phase between ϕ_i^s and ϕ_i^e (i.e., middle of the swing) and between ϕ_i^e and ϕ_i^s (i.e., middle of the stance), respectively.

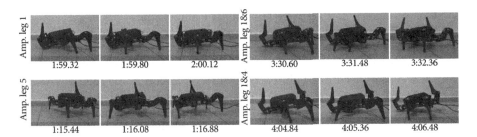

Fig. 6. Snapshots of the resulting gaits for all four performed experimental scenarios. The amputation was simulated by lifting the amputated leg above the robot's body so as not to touch the ground. The robot walks from right to left. The numbers below the photos represent the experiment time in the format *minutes: seconds*. The length of the learning process is influenced by the impact of the amputated leg absence on the gait stability. In general, the loss of the most-front (most-hind) leg is worse for the stability than the loss of the middle leg, because the most-front (most-hind) leg prevents the body from falling forward (backward), while the middle leg *"only"* improves the overall balance. Hence, the new gait rhythm learning process was longer for experiments with amputated front or hind legs (i.e., scenarios Amp. leg 1 and Amp. leg 1 & 4) than for experiments with the middle leg amputated (i.e., Amp. leg 5 and Amp. leg 1 & 6).

In the experimental setup, the robot walked forward for two gait cycles of the tripod gait on an office floor. Then, the amputation was simulated by permanently lifting the corresponding legs so they do not touch the ground in any gait phase. The robot reacts to the amputation by organizing the gait pattern into a pattern compliant with the ICRs and producing a new gait that enables the robot to continue its forward motion. The experimental performance is captured in Fig. 6 and video supplementary materials.

We can conclude that the proposed method converges to a stable solution in all reported experimental scenarios. The stable solution is a new gait pattern adjusted to the morphological changes caused by leg amputation.

6   Conclusion

We proposed and experimentally verified self-organizing dynamics for changing the gait rhythm after leg amputation on a hexapod walking robot. The method builds on the CPG-RBF-based controllers, and we propose an alternative and complementary solution for damage-control for architectures based purely on sensory feedback. The proposed method detects the violation of the *Inter-leg Coordination Rules* extended by the proposed *Consecutivity and Contralaterality*

Adjustment Rules. The detections is then used to adjust the rhythm to avoid the violation in the following gait cycles. The rhythm change itself is not always enough to avoid the rules violation. Hence, the proposed mechanism introduces the dynamic change of the swing phase duration to support resolving the conflict. In combination, the swing phase duration change and the shift of the swing in the phase produce a new gait rhythm after the amputation.

The feasibility of the method is demonstrated by its deployment on the real hexapod walking robot in four various amputation scenarios. However, it is intended to be used with sensory-based amputation compensation methods. In the case of sensory-feedback failure, the proposed method would compensate for the gait control. Two shortcomings can be addressed in future work. The method needs further adjustments to be applicable for robots with different morphology than hexapods. Besides, the proposed method does not resolve the loss of two or more limbs on the same side of the robot's body by using the introduced rules.

Acknowledgment. This work has been supported by the Czech Science Foundation (GAČR) under research project No. 21-33041J.

References

1. Chen, W., Ren, G., Zhang, J., Wang, J.: Smooth transition between different gaits of a hexapod robot via a central pattern generators algorithm. J. Intell. Robot. Syst. **67**(3), 255–270 (2012)
2. Dürr, V., Schmitz, J., Cruse, H.: Behaviour-based modelling of hexapod locomotion: linking biology and technical application. Arthropod Struct. Dev. **33**(3), 237–250 (2004). Arthropod Locomotion Systems: from Biological Materials and Systems to Robotics
3. Faigl, J., Čížek, P.: Adaptive locomotion control of hexapod walking robot for traversing rough terrains with position feedback only. Robot. Auton. Syst. **116**, 136–147 (2019)
4. Feber, J., Szadkowski, R., Faigl, J.: Gait genesis through emergent ordering of RBF neurons on central pattern generator for hexapod walking robot. In: Conference Information Technologies - Applications and Theory (ITAT), pp. 114–122 (2021)
5. Fleming, P.A., Muller, D., Bateman, P.W.: Leave it all behind: a taxonomic perspective of autotomy in invertebrates. Biol. Rev. **82**(3), 481–510 (2007)
6. Fukuoka, Y., Kimura, H., Hada, Y., Takase, K.: Adaptive dynamic walking of a quadruped robot 'Tekken' on irregular terrain using a neural system model. In: 2003 IEEE International Conference on Robotics and Automation (Cat. No. 03CH37422), vol. 2, pp. 2037–2042 (2003). https://doi.org/10.1109/ROBOT.2003.1241893
7. Gay, S., Santos-Victor, J., Ijspeert, A.: Learning robot gait stability using neural networks as sensory feedback function for central pattern generators. In: 2013 IEEE/RSJ International Conference on Intelligent Robots and Systems, pp. 194–201 (2013). https://doi.org/10.1109/IROS.2013.6696353
8. Mantziaris, C., Bockemühl, T., Büschges, A.: Central pattern generating networks in insect locomotion. Dev. Neurobiol. **80**(1–2), 16–30 (2020)

9. Miguel-Blanco, A., Manoonpong, P.: General distributed neural control and sensory adaptation for self-organized locomotion and fast adaptation to damage of walking robots. Front. Neural Circ. **14**, 46 (2020). https://doi.org/10.3389/fncir.2020.00046

10. Owaki, D., Goda, M., Miyazawa, S., Ishiguro, A.: A minimal model describing hexapedal interlimb coordination: the Tegotae-based approach. Front. Neurorobot. **11** (2017). https://doi.org/10.3389/fnbot.2017.00029

11. Pitchai, M., et al.: CPG driven RBF network control with reinforcement learning for gait optimization of a dung beetle-like robot. In: Tetko, I.V., Kurková, V., Karpov, P., Theis, F. (eds.) ICANN 2019. LNCS, vol. 11727, pp. 698–710. Springer, Cham (2019). https://doi.org/10.1007/978-3-030-30487-4_53

12. Schilling, M., Cruse, H., Arena, P.: Hexapod walking: an expansion to Walknet dealing with leg amputations and force oscillations. Biol. Cybern. **96**(3), 323–340 (2007)

13. Schneider, A., Paskarbeit, J., Schaeffersmann, M., Schmitz, J.: Hector, a new hexapod robot platform with increased mobility - control approach, design and communication. In: Rückert, U., Joaquin, S., Felix, W. (eds.) Advances in Autonomous Mini Robots, pp. 249–264. Springer, Heidelberg (2012). https://doi.org/10.1007/978-3-642-27482-4_24

14. Szadkowski, R., Faigl, J.: Neurodynamic sensory-motor phase binding for multi-legged walking robots. In: International Joint Conference on Neural Networks (IJCNN), pp. 1–8 (2020)

15. Thor, M., Manoonpong, P.: A fast online frequency adaptation mechanism for CPG-based robot motion control. IEEE Robot. Autom. Lett. **4**(4), 3324–3331 (2019). https://doi.org/10.1109/LRA.2019.2926660

16. Yu, H., Gao, H., Ding, L., Li, M., Deng, Z., Liu, G.: Gait generation with smooth transition using CPG-based locomotion control for hexapod walking robot. IEEE Trans. Industr. Electron. **63**(9), 5488–5500 (2016). https://doi.org/10.1109/TIE.2016.2569489

17. Yu, J., Tan, M., Chen, J., Zhang, J.: A survey on CPG-inspired control models and system implementation. IEEE Trans. Neural Netw. Learn. Syst. **25**(3), 441–456 (2014)

Hierarchical Dynamics in Deep Echo State Networks

Domenico Tortorella(✉) , Claudio Gallicchio , and Alessio Micheli

Department of Computer Science, University of Pisa,
Largo B. Pontecorvo, 3, 56127 Pisa, Italy
domenico.tortorella@phd.unipi.it, {gallicch,micheli}@di.unipi.it

Abstract. Reservoir computing (RC) is a popular approach to the efficient design of recurrent neural networks (RNNs), where the dynamical part of the model is initialized and left untrained. Deep echo state networks (ESNs) combined the deep learning approach with RC, by structuring the reservoir in multiple layers, thus offering the striking advantage of encoding the input sequence on different time-scales. A key factor for the effectiveness of ESNs is the echo state property (ESP), which ensures the asymptotic stability of the reservoir dynamics. In this paper, we perform an in-depth theoretical analysis of asymptotic dynamics in Deep ESNs with different contractivity hierarchies, offering a more accurate sufficient condition of the ESP. We investigate how different hierarchies of contractivity affect memory capacity and predictive performance in regression tasks, concluding that structuring reservoir layers in decreasing contractivity is the best design choice. The results of this paper can potentially be applied also to the design of fully-trained RNNs.

Keywords: Deep echo state networks · Deep reservoir computing · Recurrent neural networks

1 Introduction

Reservoir computing (RC) [18,20,21] is a design paradigm for efficiently trained recurrent neural networks (RNNs), whose core idea is to separate the dynamical part of the network, i.e. the reservoir, from the feed-forward readout. Echo state networks (ESNs) are a particular class of RC recurrent neural networks in which weights are randomly initialized and kept fixed, while only a linear readout layer is trained [15]. The effectiveness of ESNs is enabled by the echo state property (ESP) [13,24], which ensures that the state embedding is asymptotically stable with respect to perturbations of the initial conditions. A sufficient condition for the ESP is the contractivity of the state transition function, which additionally ensures that the embedding space of input sequences is intrinsically organized in a suffix-based structure [3,12].

Deep ESNs [7] extended the RC approach to deep learning [16] by arranging multiple reservoirs in layers. Previous results [8,9] suggest that a proper architectural design of deep reservoirs can have a tremendous impact in applications,

© The Author(s), under exclusive license to Springer Nature Switzerland AG 2022
E. Pimenidis et al. (Eds.): ICANN 2022, LNCS 13531, pp. 668–679, 2022.
https://doi.org/10.1007/978-3-031-15934-3_55

outperforming shallow ESNs thanks to the ability to represent the input sequence on different time-scales [7,10]. However, current theoretical results provide only loose bounds for state embedding stability [4,11], and as a consequence over-constrain reservoir layers to possess increasing levels of contractivity in order to ensure the ESP. In this work, we deepen the theoretical analysis of Deep ESNs dynamics, and provide a weaker ESP sufficient condition that enables different hierarchies of contractivity. In doing so, we provide a theoretical insight into how varying contractivity in layers can affect asymptotic stability behavior under initial state and input perturbation. We also analyze experimentally the impact of different contractivity hierarchies in solving tasks.

The rest of this paper is structured as follows. In Sect. 2 we introduce the Deep ESN model. A theoretical analysis of reservoir dynamics is presented in Sect. 3, while in Sect. 4 we perform experiments to analyze how different hierarchies of dynamics affect memory capacity and predictive performance. Finally, in Sect. 5 we draw our conclusions, and delineate future research directions and applications.

2 Deep Echo State Networks

A Deep ESN is an RC model in which the reservoir part is structured in a stacking of untrained recurrent layers [7]. In other words, a Deep ESN is a multi-layered RNN architecture in which the recurrent hidden layers are left fixed after initialization, and only an output readout layer is adapted on a training set. The input sequence is fed only to the first reservoir layer, while each successive level in the deep architecture receives the output of the previous one, as illustrated by Fig. 1.

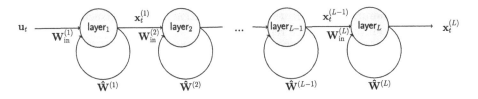

Fig. 1. Hierarchical reservoir architecture in a Deep ESN.

We denote by L the number of reservoir layers, while N_U and N_Y are respectively the dimensions of input and output spaces. For simplicity, we assume that all reservoir layers have the same number of units N_R. We denote by $\boldsymbol{u}_{1...T}$ an input sequence $\langle \boldsymbol{u}_1 \cdots \boldsymbol{u}_T \rangle$ of T time-steps, and by $\boldsymbol{u}_t$ its values at time-steps $1 \leq t \leq T$; $\mathbf{x}_t^{(\ell)}$ will analogously denote the state value of layer ℓ at time-step t. We assume that the inputs $\boldsymbol{u}_t$ and states $\mathbf{x}_t^{(1)}, ..., \mathbf{x}_t^{(L)}$ belong to the compact sub-spaces $\mathcal{U} \subset \mathbb{R}^{N_U}$ and $\mathcal{X} = [-1, 1]^{N_R}$, respectively. The operation of each reservoir layer is described in terms of discrete-time non-linear dynamical systems, whose state update equations are given in the form of iterated mappings $F^{(1)}, ..., F^{(L)}$. At each time step $t > 0$, the state of the first layer $\mathbf{x}_t^{(1)} \in \mathcal{X}$ is computed as

$$\mathbf{x}_t^{(1)} = F^{(1)}(\mathbf{u}_t, \mathbf{x}_{t-1}^{(1)}) = \tanh\left(\mathbf{W}_{\text{in}}^{(1)} \mathbf{u}_t + \hat{\mathbf{W}}^{(1)} \mathbf{x}_{t-1}^{(1)}\right), \tag{1}$$

while the state of each successive layer $\ell > 1$, i.e. $\mathbf{x}_t^{(\ell)} \in \mathcal{X}$, is computed by taking as input the previous layer state $\mathbf{x}_t^{(\ell-1)} \in \mathcal{X}$:

$$\mathbf{x}_t^{(\ell)} = F^{(\ell)}(\mathbf{x}_t^{(\ell-1)}, \mathbf{x}_{t-1}^{(\ell)}) = \tanh\left(\mathbf{W}_{\text{in}}^{(\ell)} \mathbf{x}_t^{(\ell-1)} + \hat{\mathbf{W}}^{(\ell)} \mathbf{x}_{t-1}^{(\ell)}\right). \tag{2}$$

In Eq. (1) and (2), $\mathbf{u}_t \in \mathcal{U}$ represents the input at time step t, $\mathbf{W}_{\text{in}}^{(1)} \in \mathbb{R}^{N_R \times N_U}$ and $\mathbf{W}_{\text{in}}^{(\ell)} \in \mathbb{R}^{N_R \times N_R}$ (for $\ell > 1$) are the input weights and the inter-layer connections, and finally $\hat{\mathbf{W}}^{(\ell)} \in \mathbb{R}^{N_R \times N_R}$ is the recurrent weights matrix. The parameters are randomly initialized and re-scaled in order to satisfy stability constraints. We have omitted bias terms for ease of notation. Further notice that the mathematical description reported above generalizes the case of standard (shallow) ESN, which is achieved whenever a single reservoir layer is considered in the recurrent architecture (i.e., $L = 1$), following the dynamics described in Eq. (1).

In a sequence-to-sequence setting, target predictions $\mathbf{y}_t \in \mathbb{R}^{N_Y}$ for each timestep are made by a simple readout layer exploiting the state in each reservoir layer:

$$\mathbf{y}_t = \mathbf{W}_{\text{out}} \begin{bmatrix} \mathbf{x}_t^{(1)} \\ \vdots \\ \mathbf{x}_t^{(L)} \end{bmatrix} + \mathbf{b}. \tag{3}$$

The weights $\mathbf{W}_{\text{out}} \in \mathbb{R}^{N_Y \times L N_R}$ and $\mathbf{b} \in \mathbb{R}^{N_Y}$ are the only model parameters obtained by training, usually learnt by non-iterative algorithms such as Moore–Penrose pseudo-inverse or ridge regression [18].

The effectiveness of Deep ESNs is ensured by the echo state property (ESP), which guarantees that the state is asymptotically stable with respect to perturbations in initial conditions [13,24]. To state it in formal terms, let us define the global state transition function $\bar{F} : \mathcal{U} \times \mathcal{X}^L \to \mathcal{X}^L$, acting on global states $\bar{\mathbf{x}}_t = [\mathbf{x}_t^{(1)} ... \mathbf{x}_t^{(L)}]$ computed for each t by Eq. (1) and (2). An input sequence $\mathbf{u} = \langle \mathbf{u}_1 ... \mathbf{u}_T \rangle$ is encoded by applying iteratively $\bar{F}$ from $t = 1$ to the end, according to the following definition:

$$\hat{F}(\mathbf{u}, \bar{\mathbf{x}}_0) = \begin{cases} \bar{F}\left(\mathbf{u}_T, \hat{F}(\mathbf{u}_{1...T-1}, \bar{\mathbf{x}}_0)\right) & \text{if } \mathbf{u} = \langle \mathbf{u}_1 ... \mathbf{u}_T \rangle \\ \bar{\mathbf{x}}_0 & \text{if } \mathbf{u} = \langle \rangle \end{cases} \tag{4}$$

with $\bar{\mathbf{x}}_0 = [\mathbf{x}_0^{(1)} ... \mathbf{x}_0^{(L)}]$ as initial state for $t = 0$. For a Deep ESN, we say that the ESP holds[1] if for any input sequence $\mathbf{u}$ and any pair of global initial states $\bar{\mathbf{x}}_0, \bar{\mathbf{x}}_0' \in \mathcal{X}^L$:

---

[1] More details on uniform convergence requirements can be found in [24].

$$\|\hat{F}(\boldsymbol{u}_{1...T}, \bar{\mathbf{x}}_0) - \hat{F}(\boldsymbol{u}_{1...T}, \bar{\mathbf{x}}_0')\| \to 0 \quad \text{uniformly for } T \to \infty. \tag{5}$$

A necessary condition [4] for the ESP in Eq. (5) can be derived by analyzing the stability of the reservoir system with respect to perturbation of the null state $\bar{\mathbf{x}}_0 = \mathbf{0}$ under null input $\mathbf{u}_t = \mathbf{0}$, which is satisfied by imposing

$$\rho(\hat{\mathbf{W}}^{(\ell)}) < 1 \quad \text{for all layers } 1 \le \ell \le L, \tag{6}$$

where $\rho(\hat{\mathbf{W}}^{(\ell)})$ denotes the spectral radius (i.e. the largest absolute eigenvalue) of the matrix $\hat{\mathbf{W}}^{(\ell)}$. However, condition (6) does not ensure that the ESP holds for all non-null inputs, nor gives any information regarding the system's dynamical behavior under initial state perturbation in this latter case.

3   Hierarchical Dynamics and Asymptotic Stability

A sufficient condition for the ESP relies on the contractivity of the state transition function [4], namely that the distance between two states evolving from different initial conditions under same input sequence is exponentially vanishing,

$$\|\hat{F}(\boldsymbol{u}_{1...T}, \bar{\mathbf{x}}_0) - \hat{F}(\boldsymbol{u}_{1...T}, \bar{\mathbf{x}}_0')\| \le C^T \|\bar{\mathbf{x}}_0 - \bar{\mathbf{x}}_0'\| \quad \text{with } C < 1. \tag{7}$$

The value of coefficient C quantifies the contractivity of $\hat{F}$: the smaller it is, the more $\hat{F}$ is contractive. However, even assuming the contractivity condition (7), in a Deep ESN the initial state perturbation in layer $\ell = 1$ produces an exponentially vanishing perturbation in the input of all subsequent layers $\ell > 1$. Therefore, in the following Proposition 1 we characterize the dynamical behavior of a generic reservoir layer F in this circumstance.

Proposition 1. *Let $F : \mathcal{U}_F \times \mathcal{X}_F \to \mathcal{X}_F$ be a layer state transition function with compact input space $\mathcal{U}_F$ and compact state space $\mathcal{X}_F$.[2] Assume that F is Lipschitz continuous and contractive, i.e. for all $\mathbf{u}, \mathbf{u}' \in \mathcal{U}_F$ and $\mathbf{x}, \mathbf{x}' \in \mathcal{X}_F$*

$$\|F(\mathbf{u}, \mathbf{x}) - F(\mathbf{u}', \mathbf{x}')\| \le B \|\mathbf{u} - \mathbf{u}'\| + C \|\mathbf{x} - \mathbf{x}'\|, \quad B > 0, \quad 0 < C < 1. \tag{8}$$

Let $\mathbf{u}_t'$ be an exponentially vanishing perturbation of the input $\mathbf{u}_t$, i.e. satisfying

$$\|\mathbf{u}_t - \mathbf{u}_t'\| \le D_0 \, t^k \, D^t \quad \forall t > 0, \quad \text{for some } D_0 \ge 0, \, 0 < D < 1, \, k \ge 0, \tag{9}$$

and let $\mathbf{x}_0'$ be the perturbation of initial state $\mathbf{x}_0$.
The dynamical state perturbation is then uniformly upper bounded by

$$\|\mathbf{x}_t - \mathbf{x}_t'\| \le E_0 \, t^{k+1} \, E^t \quad \forall t > 0, \quad \text{for some } E_0 \ge 0, \, 0 < E < 1, \tag{10}$$

and thus it is exponentially vanishing too.

---

[2] The reservoir layers $F^{(\ell)}$ defined in Sect. 2 have state space $\mathcal{X}_F = \mathcal{X} = [-1, 1]^{N_R}$, and input space either $\mathcal{U}_F = \mathcal{U} \subset \mathbb{R}^{N_U}$ if $\ell = 1$ or $\mathcal{U}_F = \mathcal{X}$ if $\ell > 1$.

Proof. By the Lipschitz continuity hypothesis (8), at time step $t > 0$:

$$\|\mathbf{x}_t - \mathbf{x}'_t\| = \|F(\mathbf{u}_t, \mathbf{x}_{t-1}) - F(\mathbf{u}'_t, \mathbf{x}'_{t-1})\|$$
$$\leq B \|\mathbf{u}_t - \mathbf{u}'_t\| + C \|\mathbf{x}_{t-1} - \mathbf{x}'_{t-1}\|$$
$$= B \|\mathbf{u}_t - \mathbf{u}'_t\| + C \|F(\mathbf{u}_{t-1}, \mathbf{x}_{t-2}) - F(\mathbf{u}'_{t-1}, \mathbf{x}'_{t-2})\|$$
$$\leq \dots$$
$$\leq B \|\mathbf{u}_t - \mathbf{u}'_t\| + BC \|\mathbf{u}_{t-1} - \mathbf{u}'_{t-1}\| + BC^2 \|\mathbf{u}_{t-2} - \mathbf{u}'_{t-2}\| +$$
$$\cdots + BC^{t-2} \|\mathbf{u}_2 - \mathbf{u}'_2\| + BC^{t-1} \|\mathbf{u}_1 - \mathbf{u}'_1\| + C^t \|\mathbf{x}_0 - \mathbf{x}'_0\|$$
$$= B \sum_{\tau=1}^{t} C^{t-\tau} \|\mathbf{u}_\tau - \mathbf{u}'_\tau\| + C^t \|\mathbf{x}_0 - \mathbf{x}'_0\|$$
$$= C^t \left(\|\mathbf{x}_0 - \mathbf{x}'_0\| + B \sum_{\tau=1}^{t} \frac{\|\mathbf{u}_\tau - \mathbf{u}'_\tau\|}{C^\tau} \right)$$

Taking into account the bound (9) on input perturbation:

$$\|\mathbf{x}_t - \mathbf{x}'_t\| \leq C^t \left(\|\mathbf{x}_0 - \mathbf{x}'_0\| + BD_0 \sum_{\tau=1}^{t} \tau^k \left(\frac{D}{C} \right)^\tau \right)$$

We now distinguish three cases:

– if $D < C$, then

$$\|\mathbf{x}_t - \mathbf{x}'_t\| \leq C^t \left(\|\mathbf{x}_0 - \mathbf{x}'_0\| + BD_0 t^k \sum_{\tau=1}^{\infty} \left(\frac{D}{C} \right)^\tau \right) = \|\mathbf{x}_0 - \mathbf{x}'_0\| C^t + \frac{BD_0}{1 - D/C} t^k C^t;$$

– if $D = C$, then

$$\|\mathbf{x}_t - \mathbf{x}'_t\| \leq C^t \left(\|\mathbf{x}_0 - \mathbf{x}'_0\| + BD_0 \sum_{\tau=1}^{t} \tau^k \right) \leq \|\mathbf{x}_0 - \mathbf{x}'_0\| C^t + BD_0 t^{k+1} C^t;$$

– finally, if $D > C$, then

$$\|\mathbf{x}_t - \mathbf{x}'_t\| \leq C^t \left(\|\mathbf{x}_0 - \mathbf{x}'_0\| + BD_0 t^k \sum_{\tau=1}^{t} \left(\frac{D}{C} \right)^\tau \right)$$
$$\leq C^t \left(\|\mathbf{x}_0 - \mathbf{x}'_0\| + BD_0 t^k \frac{1 - (D/C)^{t+1}}{1 - D/C} \right)$$
$$\leq \|\mathbf{x}_0 - \mathbf{x}'_0\| C^t + \frac{BD_0 D/C}{D/C - 1} t^k D^t.$$

Taking into account the compactness of $\mathcal{X}_F$, we have $\|\mathbf{x}_0 - \mathbf{x}'_0\| \leq \operatorname{diam}(\mathcal{X}_F)$, where $\operatorname{diam}(\mathcal{X}_F)$ is the diameter of $\mathcal{X}_F$. Thus, in all three cases the thesis is satisfied by the uniform bound

$$\|\mathbf{x}_t - \mathbf{x}'_t\| \leq \underbrace{2 \max \left\{ \operatorname{diam}(\mathcal{X}_F), \frac{BD_0}{1 - D/C}, BD_0, \frac{BD_0 D/C}{D/C - 1} \right\} t^{k+1}}_{E_0} \underbrace{\max\{C, D\}^t}_{E}.$$

$\square$

Since the state transition functions $F^{(\ell)}$ defined in (1)–(2) are Lipschitz continuous with constants $B_\ell = \|\mathbf{W}_{in}^{(\ell)}\|$ and $C_\ell = \|\hat{\mathbf{W}}^{(\ell)}\|$ (where $\|\cdot\|$ denotes the spectral norm), we are now ready to state a sufficient condition for the ESP in a Deep ESN.

Proposition 2. *Let $F^{(\ell)}$, $1 \leq \ell \leq L$, be the state transition functions in a Deep ESN with L reservoir layers as defined in Eqs. (1) and (2). If these are all Lipschitz continuous and contractive, i.e.*

$$C_\ell = \|\hat{\mathbf{W}}^{(\ell)}\| < 1 \quad \text{for all layers } \ell, \tag{11}$$

then the ESP holds.

Proof. Let $\mathbf{x}_0^{\prime(1)} \in \mathcal{X}$ be the perturbation of the initial state $\mathbf{x}_0^{(1)} \in \mathcal{X}$ in the first layer $\ell = 1$. Then, by Lipschitz continuity, at each time step $t > 0$ the magnitude of state perturbation is uniformly upper bounded by

$$\|\mathbf{x}_t^{(1)} - \mathbf{x}_t^{\prime(1)}\| \leq C_1^t \|\mathbf{x}_0^{(1)} - \mathbf{x}_0^{\prime(1)}\| \leq C_1^t \operatorname{diam}(\mathcal{X}) \to 0 \quad \text{as } t \to \infty.$$

Since the input of subsequent layers is the output of previous ones, we can apply Proposition 1 to obtain uniform upper bounds in layers $\ell > 1$ that satisfy

$$\|\mathbf{x}_t^{(\ell)} - \mathbf{x}_t^{\prime(\ell)}\| \leq E_0^{(\ell)} t^{\ell-1} E_\ell^t \to 0 \quad \text{as } t \to \infty.$$

Having demonstrated uniform bounds of state perturbation magnitudes by null sequences in all reservoir layers, the proof is concluded. □

The crucial insight that has allowed us to improve upon the previous theoretical analysis of [4] is to consider contractivity and dynamics layer by layer, instead of dealing with the global state transition function $\bar{F}$ as a monolithic block. Indeed, in our analysis we are able to separate the contributions to state perturbation coming from input perturbation from those accounted for by initial state perturbation, while the conflation of both in the analysis of [4] led to an over-estimation of the state transition function's contractivity coefficient due to the inclusion of a contribution weighted by $B_\ell = \|\mathbf{W}_{in}^{(\ell)}\|$ cumulated over layers. As a consequence, the sufficient ESP condition of [4] constrained reservoir layer to have increasing contractivity (i.e. decreasing values of coefficients C_ℓ), while Proposition 2 enables different hierarchies of dynamics along the reservoir layers:

- 'expanding' dynamics, with decreasing contractivity, i.e. increasing values of contractivity coefficients $C_1 < C_2 < ... < C_L$;
- 'fixed' dynamics, with constant contractivity $C_1 = C_2 = ... = C_L$;
- 'contracting' dynamics, with increasing contractivity, i.e. $C_1 > C_2 > ... > C_L$ as required by theory in [4].

Figure 2 shows the upper bounds on state perturbation derived in Proposition 1 for the three hierarchies with contractivity coefficient reported in each plot, assuming $B = 1$ and $\|\mathbf{x}_0 - \mathbf{x}_0'\| = 1$. In the contracting hierarchy, the

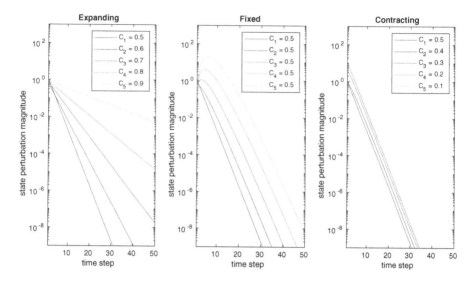

Fig. 2. Hierarchical dynamics in a Deep ESN according to Proposition 1.

dynamics are regulated by the largest constant C_1, thus all have the same upper bound. In the fixed hierarchy, the state perturbation can be amplified in deeper layers by a polynomial factor (coming from case $D = C$ in Proposition 1's proof), while vanishing with roughly the same asymptotic behavior, albeit with varying delays. Finally, in the expanding hierarchy we observe how the dynamics can be greatly differentiated according to each layer's C_ℓ, with deeper layers allowing the effects of initial state perturbation to carry on in the long term.

Since the state transition function in a Deep ESN defines a time-invariant dynamical system, the effect on states $\mathbf{x}_t$ for $t > T$ of a time-limited perturbation of the input sequence $\mathbf{u}_t$ for $t \leq T$ are equivalent to an instantaneous state perturbation in $t = T$ with the original unperturbed input sequence. Therefore, understanding the dynamics under initial state perturbation as we have done in this section gives important insights regarding how much information on input sequence prefixes is kept in the state $\mathbf{x}_t$. This can be also theoretically interpreted as a result of the equivalence between *state contracting* and *input forgetting* properties in ESNs [13, 24].

The theory developed in this section enables the design of asymptotically stable deep reservoirs that can offer a larger memory capacity. By adopting an expansive hierarchy of contractivity, the deep reservoir state can represent longer input suffixes, thus allowing improvements in tasks that require a longer input history. Since the results of this section are based exclusively on the Lipschitz constants of each layer's transition function, they also apply to fully-trained RNNs. In this case, an expansive hierarchy can be introduced e.g. via constraints on weights regularization during training.

4   Experiments

In this section we examine how the theoretical results developed in Sect. 3 regarding Deep ESN dynamics can be applied to the design of deep reservoirs, by evaluating how different hierarchies impact the performances in memory capacity (Sect. 4.1) and regression tasks (Sect. 4.2).

In all experiments, input weights $\mathbf{W}_{in}^{(\ell)}$ are sampled from a uniform ensemble in $[-\omega_\ell, \omega_\ell]$, where the scaling parameter ω_ℓ is assumed to be equal to 1 in all layers if not otherwise specified. Recurrent weights $\hat{\mathbf{W}}^{(\ell)}$ are sampled from a uniform ensemble in $[-1, 1]$ and re-scaled in order to satisfy $\|\hat{\mathbf{W}}^{(\ell)}\| = C_\ell$. The latter are chosen to obtain different contractive hierarchies according to the following relation:

$$C_\ell = r^{\ell-1} C_1, \tag{12}$$

where the parameter r controls whether the hierarchical dynamics are expanding ($r > 1$), fixed ($r = 1$), or contracting ($r < 1$). We consider different values of C_1 in the experiments. Furthermore, we follow standard practice in exploring also values of C_ℓ that can violate the sufficient ESP condition [17].

4.1   Memory Capacity

In this experiment we measure the short-term memory capacity [2,14] of Deep ESN, by evaluating how well it is capable to recall delayed versions of the input based on current reservoir states. While factors such as reservoir size and type of recurrent matrix also impact memory capacity [23], previous analyses have shown that contractivity is related to memory length in ESNs and RNNs [3,12].

In the Memory Capacity (MC) task [7], the input sequence is made of 6000 scalar values sampled i.i.d. from the uniform distribution in the range $[-0.8, 0.8]$. A linear readout is trained to reconstruct inputs $u_{t-\tau}$ from reservoir states $\mathbf{x}_t$ as $y_t^{(\tau)}$ for each delay $\tau > 0$.

The memory capacity score is defined [7,14] as

$$MC = \sum_{\tau=1}^{\infty} \text{corr}^2 \left(u_{t-\tau}, y_t^{(\tau)} \right), \tag{13}$$

where the squared correlation is computed over all time-steps of the sequence. In the MC task this value is approximated by considering delays up to $\tau = 200$.

As in [7], we use a Deep ESN with $L = 10$ layers of $N_R = 10$ units each, and an input scaling factor $\omega_1 = 0.1$. We use the first 5000 time-steps for training, with a washout interval of 1000 steps, and we reserve the remaining 1000 time-steps for testing, again following the experimental setting of [7]. In our experiment, we evaluate different values of the first layer's contractivity coefficient C_1, namely 0.1, 0.5 and 0.9, for the three hierarchies of contractivity.

Table 1 reports the results averaged over 10 different reservoir initializations. We first notice that an expanding hierarchy of contractivity ($r = 1.1$) offers much higher memory capacity MC than the other two hierarchies for all three values

Table 1. MC task, average memory capacity scores with standard deviation. (Higher score is better.)

Dynamics	$C_1 = 0.1$	$C_1 = 0.5$	$C_1 = 0.9$
Expanding ($r = 1.1$)	8.292 (0.211)	23.318 (1.130)	28.743 (4.084)
Fixed ($r = 1$)	7.824 (0.222)	14.463 (0.277)	23.340 (0.706)
Contracting ($r = 0.9$)	7.235 (0.067)	12.262 (0.382)	16.905 (0.452)

of C_1. Notice also that fixed contractivity ($r = 1$) offers a more limited but consistent improvement over contracting dynamics ($r = 0.9$): this is explained by the polynomial factor in the former's dynamics bounds that amplifies short-term input variations. In general, this experiment confirms the inverse relation between contractivity and memory capacity [3,14]. In particular, notice that contracting dynamics ruled by a larger C_1 offer better memory capacity than fixed dynamics ruled by smaller C_1. Overall, all these results are in agreement with the theoretical expectations of Sect. 3 concerning asymptotic behavior and preservation of input history.

4.2 Regression Tasks

We now evaluate how different hierarchies impact the predictive performance in four regression tasks on univariate time series (i.e., $N_U = N_Y = 1$).

The first three benchmarks are next-step prediction task, i.e. $y_t = u_{t+1}$. In the Laser task [22] the input values u_t are sampled intensities from a far-infrared laser in chaotic regime, re-scaled by a factor of 0.01. The datasets MG17 and MG30 are instances of the Mackey–Glass time series [1,19], obtained by discretizing the non-linear differential equation

$$\frac{\mathrm{d}}{\mathrm{d}t} u(t) = \frac{0.2\, u(t - \tau)}{1 + u(t - \tau)^{10}} - 0.1\, u(t) \tag{14}$$

for two values of the τ parameter that controls the chaotic regime (respectively, $\tau = 17$ and $\tau = 30$). The values are then shifted and squashed as in [13,15]. Finally, the last dataset NARMA10 [5,6] is generated from a non-linear auto-regressive moving average system of order 10. At each time-step, the input u_t is sampled from a uniform distribution in $[0.0, 0.5]$, while the target output y_t is given by the following relation

$$y_t = 0.3\, y_{t-1} + 0.05\, y_{t-1} \sum_{i=1}^{10} y_{t-i} + 1.5\, u_{t-10}\, u_{t-1} + 0.1. \tag{15}$$

In all four tasks we use the first 5000 time-steps for training, with a washout interval of 100 steps, and we reserve the remaining 5000 time-steps for testing. We fix the reservoir architecture at $L = 5$ layers of $N_R = 100$ units each, according to the model selection results in [5], and use an inter-layer scaling

Table 2. Laser task, average MSE with standard deviation.

Dynamics	$C_1 = 0.2$	$C_1 = 0.5$	$C_1 = 0.9$
Expanding ($r = 1.2$)	<u>3.609</u> (0.977) $\cdot 10^{-3}$	<u>1.178</u> (0.353) $\cdot 10^{-3}$	<u>0.802</u> (0.239) $\cdot 10^{-3}$
Fixed ($r = 1$)	7.676 (2.204) $\cdot 10^{-3}$	1.827 (0.652) $\cdot 10^{-3}$	1.347 (0.459) $\cdot 10^{-3}$
Contracting ($r = 0.8$)	8.057 (2.271) $\cdot 10^{-3}$	3.186 (0.797) $\cdot 10^{-3}$	1.461 (0.448) $\cdot 10^{-3}$

Table 3. MG17 task, average MSE with standard deviation.

Dynamics	$C_1 = 0.2$	$C_1 = 0.5$	$C_1 = 0.9$
Expanding ($r = 1.2$)	<u>0.781</u> (0.082) $\cdot 10^{-9}$	<u>0.180</u> (0.029) $\cdot 10^{-10}$	<u>0.146</u> (0.049) $\cdot 10^{-11}$
Fixed ($r = 1$)	2.137 (0.238) $\cdot 10^{-9}$	0.929 (0.136) $\cdot 10^{-10}$	0.521 (0.092) $\cdot 10^{-11}$
Contracting ($r = 0.8$)	2.609 (0.229) $\cdot 10^{-9}$	2.508 (0.368) $\cdot 10^{-10}$	2.481 (0.454) $\cdot 10^{-11}$

Table 4. MG30 task, average MSE with standard deviation.

Dynamics	$C_1 = 0.2$	$C_1 = 0.5$	$C_1 = 0.9$
Expanding ($r = 1.2$)	<u>0.760</u> (0.060) $\cdot 10^{-8}$	<u>2.449</u> (0.080) $\cdot 10^{-9}$	<u>1.908</u> (0.237) $\cdot 10^{-9}$
Fixed ($r = 1$)	1.102 (0.057) $\cdot 10^{-8}$	3.664 (0.184) $\cdot 10^{-9}$	2.426 (0.126) $\cdot 10^{-9}$
Contracting ($r = 0.8$)	1.385 (0.067) $\cdot 10^{-8}$	5.050 (0.327) $\cdot 10^{-9}$	3.225 (0.120) $\cdot 10^{-9}$

Table 5. NARMA10 task, average MSE with standard deviation.

Dynamics	$C_1 = 0.2$	$C_1 = 0.5$	$C_1 = 0.9$
Expanding ($r = 1.2$)	<u>2.500</u> (0.084) $\cdot 10^{-3}$	<u>0.636</u> (0.035) $\cdot 10^{-3}$	<u>0.256</u> (0.069) $\cdot 10^{-3}$
Fixed ($r = 1$)	4.406 (0.218) $\cdot 10^{-3}$	1.637 (0.103) $\cdot 10^{-3}$	0.629 (0.037) $\cdot 10^{-3}$
Contracting ($r = 0.8$)	7.970 (0.073) $\cdot 10^{-3}$	2.855 (0.143) $\cdot 10^{-3}$	1.275 (0.138) $\cdot 10^{-3}$

factor $\omega_\ell = 0.1$ for layers $\ell > 1$. We evaluate different values of the first layer's contractivity coefficient C_1, namely 0.2, 0.5 and 0.9, for the three hierarchies of contractivity. We use values of r different from the MC task to compensate for the smaller reservoir depth.

Mean squared errors (MSE) averaged over 10 reservoir initializations are reported in Tables 2, 3, 4 and 5. The results confirm our observations in the memory capacity task. For all values of C_1, an expanding hierarchy ($r = 1.2$) offers significantly lower error than fixed contractivity ($r = 1$), which in turn offers lower error than contracting dynamics ($r = 0.8$). We also again notice that contractivity in general plays a significant role in task predictive performance, with dynamics ruled by larger constants offering lower regression errors; observe that in particular contracting dynamics ruled by a larger C_1 offer better regression errors than fixed dynamics ruled by smaller C_1. This consistent behavior in all four regression tasks highlights the advantage of preserving information regarding the input history in reservoir states, and can be attributed to the Markovian nature of the tasks [3].

Even though our objective was not to improve upon previous results of the regression tasks, the predictive performance reached by the expanding hierarchy with $C_1 = 0.9$ provides better or on par predictive performance with respect to the results of [5]. This begs for the exploration of the combined effects of reservoir topology with contractivity hierarchy in future works.

5   Conclusions

In this paper, we have investigated the hierarchy of dynamics in Deep ESNs. We have performed a detailed theoretical analysis of the asymptotic behavior in each reservoir layer, which allowed us to prove a weaker sufficient condition for the ESP, improving upon the results of [4]. Through experiments, we have examined how the different contractivity hierarchies allowed by our theory impact memory capacity and predictive performance in four regression tasks. We have found that organizing the reservoir layers in decreasing contractivity, i.e. by rescaling reservoir weights to have increasing spectral norms in deeper layers, offers a great improvement in both metrics. Beyond a direct application in the design of Deep ESNs, the results of this paper can also potentially be applied to fully-trained RNNs, e.g. as an initialization condition or as a constraint on weight regularization.

Acknowledgements. This work was partially funded by the project BrAID under the Bando Ricerca Salute 2018 - Regional public call for research and development projects aimed at supporting clinical and organizational innovation processes of the Regional Health Service - Regione Toscana.

References

1. Doyne Farmer, J.: Chaotic attractors of an infinite-dimensional dynamical system. Physica D Nonlinear Phenom. **4**(3), 366–393 (1982). https://doi.org/10.1016/0167-2789(82)90042-2
2. Gallicchio, C.: Short-term memory of deep RNN. In: Proceedings of the 26th European Symposium on Artificial Neural Networks, Computational Intelligence and Machine Learning, ESANN 2018, pp. 633–638 (2018)
3. Gallicchio, C., Micheli, A.: Architectural and Markovian factors of echo state networks. Neural Netw. **24**(5), 440–456 (2011)
4. Gallicchio, C., Micheli, A.: Echo state property of deep reservoir computing networks. Cogn. Comput. **9**(3), 337–350 (2017). https://doi.org/10.1007/s12559-017-9461-9
5. Gallicchio, C., Micheli, A.: Reservoir topology in deep echo state networks. In: Tetko, I.V., Kůrková, V., Karpov, P., Theis, F. (eds.) ICANN 2019. LNCS, vol. 11731, pp. 62–75. Springer, Cham (2019). https://doi.org/10.1007/978-3-030-30493-5_6
6. Gallicchio, C., Micheli, A.: Richness of deep echo state network dynamics. In: Rojas, I., Joya, G., Catala, A. (eds.) IWANN 2019. LNCS, vol. 11506, pp. 480–491. Springer, Cham (2019). https://doi.org/10.1007/978-3-030-20521-8_40

7. Gallicchio, C., Micheli, A., Pedrelli, L.: Deep reservoir computing: a critical experimental analysis. Neurocomputing **268**, 87–99 (2017)
8. Gallicchio, C., Micheli, A., Pedrelli, L.: Design of deep echo state networks. Neural Netw. **108**, 33–47 (2018). https://doi.org/10.1016/j.neunet.2018.08.002
9. Gallicchio, C., Micheli, A., Pedrelli, L.: Comparison between DeepESNs and gated RNNs on multivariate time-series prediction. In: Proceedings of the 27th European Symposium on Artificial Neural Networks, Computational Intelligence and Machine Learning, ESANN 2019, pp. 619–624 (2019)
10. Gallicchio, C., Micheli, A., Pedrelli, L.: Hierarchical temporal representation in linear reservoir computing. Smart Innov. Syst. Technol. **102**, 119–129 (2019). https://doi.org/10.1007/978-3-319-95098-3_11
11. Gallicchio, C., Micheli, A., Silvestri, L.: Local Lyapunov exponents of deep echo state networks. Neurocomputing **298**, 34–45 (2018). https://doi.org/10.1016/j.neucom.2017.11.073
12. Hammer, B., Tiňo, P.: Recurrent neural networks with small weights implement definite memory machines. Neural Comput. **15**(8), 1897–1929 (2003). https://doi.org/10.1162/08997660360675080
13. Jaeger, H.: The "echo state" approach to analysing and training recurrent neural networks-with an erratum note. Technical report 148, German National Research Institute for Computer Science (2001)
14. Jaeger, H.: Short term memory in echo state networks. Technical report 152, German National Research Institute for Computer Science (2002)
15. Jaeger, H., Haas, H.: Harnessing nonlinearity: predicting chaotic systems and saving energy in wireless communication. Science **304**(5667), 78–80 (2004). https://doi.org/10.1126/science.1091277
16. LeCun, Y., Bengio, Y., Hinton, G.: Deep learning. Nature **521**(7553), 436–444 (2015). https://doi.org/10.1038/nature14539
17. Lukoševičius, M.: A practical guide to applying echo state networks. In: Montavon, G., Orr, G.B., Müller, K.-R. (eds.) Neural Networks: Tricks of the Trade. LNCS, vol. 7700, pp. 659–686. Springer, Heidelberg (2012). https://doi.org/10.1007/978-3-642-35289-8_36
18. Lukoševičius, M., Jaeger, H.: Reservoir computing approaches to recurrent neural network training. Comput. Sci. Rev. **3**(3), 127–149 (2009). https://doi.org/10.1016/j.cosrev.2009.03.005
19. Mackey, M.C., Glass, L.: Oscillation and chaos in physiological control systems. Science **197**(4300), 287–289 (1977). https://doi.org/10.1126/science.267326
20. Tanaka, G., et al.: Recent advances in physical reservoir computing: a review. Neural Netw. **115**, 100–123 (2019)
21. Verstraeten, D., Schrauwen, B., d'Haene, M., Stroobandt, D.: An experimental unification of reservoir computing methods. Neural Netw. **20**(3), 391–403 (2007)
22. Weigend, A.S.: Time Series Prediction: Forecasting The Future And Understanding The Past. Routledge, May 2018. https://doi.org/10.4324/9780429492648
23. White, O.L., Lee, D.D., Sompolinsky, H.: Short-term memory in orthogonal neural networks. Phys. Rev. Lett. **92**(14), 148102 (2004). https://doi.org/10.1103/physrevlett.92.148102
24. Yildiz, I.B., Jaeger, H., Kiebel, S.J.: Re-visiting the echo state property. Neural Netw. **35**, 1–9 (2012)

Jacobian Ensembles Improve Robustness Trade-Offs to Adversarial Attacks

Kenneth T. Co[1,2](✉) [iD], David Martinez-Rego[2] [iD], Zhongyuan Hau[1],
and Emil C. Lupu[1] [iD]

[1] Imperial College London, London SW7 2AZ, UK
{k.co,zy.hau17,e.c.lupu}@imperial.ac.uk
[2] DataSpartan, London EC2Y 9ST, UK
david@dataspartan.com

Abstract. Deep neural networks have become an integral part of our
software infrastructure and are being deployed in many widely-used and
safety-critical applications. However, their integration into many systems
also brings with it the vulnerability to test time attacks in the form of
Universal Adversarial Perturbations (UAPs). UAPs are a class of perturbations that when applied to *any input* causes model misclassification.
Although there is an ongoing effort to defend models against these adversarial attacks, it is often difficult to reconcile the trade-offs in model accuracy and robustness to adversarial attacks. Jacobian regularization has
been shown to improve the robustness of models against UAPs, whilst
model ensembles have been widely adopted to improve both predictive
performance and model robustness. In this work, we propose a novel
approach, Jacobian Ensembles – a combination of Jacobian regularization and model ensembles to significantly increase the robustness against
UAPs whilst maintaining or improving model accuracy. Our results show
that Jacobian Ensembles achieves previously unseen levels of accuracy
and robustness, greatly improving over previous methods that tend to
skew towards only either accuracy or robustness.

Keywords: Adversarial machine learning · Computer vision ·
Jacobian regularization · Ensemble methods

1 Introduction

Deep neural networks (DNNs) have achieved widespread use in many applications including image classification [15], real-time object detection [20], and
speech recognition [12]. Despite these advances, there is an increasing recognition that DNNs are exposed to systemic vulnerabilities in the form of Universal Adversarial Perturbations (UAPs): where a single adversarial perturbation
causes a model to misclassify a large set of inputs [19]. Thus, it is important to

K.T. Co—Supported in part by the DataSpartan research grant DSRD201801.

E. Pimenidis et al. (Eds.): ICANN 2022, LNCS 13531, pp. 680–691, 2022.
https://doi.org/10.1007/978-3-031-15934-3_56

ensure that neural networks are robust to such devastating attacks whilst still maintaining their state-of-art accuracy on benign datasets.

UAP present a systemic risk, as they enable practical and physically realizable adversarial attacks. They have been demonstrated in many widely-used and safety-critical applications such as camera-based computer vision [2,7,8,18] and LiDAR-based object detection [10,11]. UAPs have also been shown to facilitate realistic attacks in both the physical [23] and digital [24] domains. In some cases, UAPs also enable very resource-efficient black-box attacks on DNNs [3,5].

An insufficiently studied aspect of existing defenses against UAPs is the trade-off between clean accuracy, or the model's performance on a benign dataset, and its robustness to adversarial attacks. Indeed, a model with increased robustness to UAPs is desirable, but reduced clean accuracy could translate to reduced utility and additional financial or security costs depending on the application. Existing defenses primarily consider robustness to adversarial attacks, but neglect the cost it incurs on the model's performance for the original task. For example, defenses like adversarial training or too much regularization improve robustness but greatly reduce clean accuracy [6,13,21].

Jacobian regularization (JR) has previously been shown to improve robustness against UAPs. However, JR can damage clean accuracy for large amounts of regularization [6,13,21]. *Model ensembles* on the other hand has widely been shown to achieve better classification performance and stability than a single (best) classifier [16,26]. Ensembles are created by combining the outputs of multiple base learners to generate an improved prediction.

In this work, we propose combining JR and model ensembles during training to create *Jacobian Ensembles*. JR is used to drastically improve the model's robustness to UAPs while the ensemble methods stabilize the model's predictions and improve its clean accuracy. JR and model ensembles individually each have been shown to improve UAP robustness but at some cost to clean accuracy [4,6]. We show that Jacobian Ensembles greatly improve on the accuracy-robustness trade-off when compared to either JR or model ensembles individually. First, we theoretically show that increasing the number of base learners in a model ensemble improves the expected robustness of classifiers. Then, we empirically verify our theoretical findings by applying JR with popular ensemble methods bagging [1], snapshot ensembles [14], soft voting [26] to DNNs trained on the popular benchmark datasets: MNIST [17], Fashion-MNIST [25] and then evaluating their robustness against UAPs.

To summarize, we make the following contributions:

- We derive theoretical formulations for robustness of ensemble methods and show that the robustness to UAPs increases monotonically with the number of base learners.
- We empirically verify our theoretical results and show that Jacobian Ensembles, a combination of Jacobian regularization and ensembles, achieves the best accuracy-robustness trade-off as measured by a combined weighted accuracy metric.

2   Background

2.1   Universal Adversarial Perturbations

Let $f : \mathcal{X} \subset \mathbb{R}^D \to \mathbb{R}^C$ be logits of a piece-wise linear classifier with input $\mathbf{x} \in \mathcal{X}$. We, define $F(\mathbf{x}) = \arg\max(f(\mathbf{x}))$ to be the output of this classifier and write $\tau(\mathbf{x})$ as the true class label of an input $\mathbf{x}$. **Universal Adversarial Perturbations (UAP)** are perturbations $\delta \in \mathbb{R}^n$ to the data that satisfy $F(\mathbf{x} + \delta) \neq \tau(\mathbf{x})$ for sufficiently many $\mathbf{x} \in \mathcal{X}$ where $\|\delta\|_p < \varepsilon$. The latter condition $\|\delta\|_p < \varepsilon$ constrains the magnitude of the perturbation and is often some ℓ_p-norm and small $\varepsilon > 0$ [19]. Given a classifier f, UAPs are generated by maximizing the loss $\sum_i \mathcal{L}_f(\mathbf{x}_i + \delta)$ with an iterative stochastic gradient descent algorithm [4,22] where $\mathcal{L}$ is the model's training loss, $\{\mathbf{x}_i\}$ are batches of inputs, and δ are small perturbations that satisfy $\|\delta\|_p < \varepsilon$.

2.2   Model Ensembles

An ensemble consists of combining multiple classifiers (base learners) to obtain a resulting ensemble that has better accuracy or predictive performance on aggregate than any individual base learner. In practice, it is widely accepted that combining multiple classifiers can achieve better classification performance than a single "best" classifier [16,26]. Ensembles are typically generated in two ways: sequentially and in parallel. After generating the base learners the combination of their outputs is taken rather than choosing a single "best" learner [26].

In this work, we will analyze ensemble methods that aggregate their base learners in a convex combination. Formally, we define an ensemble $\mathcal{F}$ as a convex combination of M base learners f_i: $\mathcal{F}(x) = \sum_{i=1}^{M} c_i f_i(x)$ where $\sum_{i=1}^{M} c_i = 1$ and $0 < c_i < 1$, $\forall i$. This is typical as many ensemble methods aggregate their methods via averaging or a similar form of weighted sum [26]. Note however that this will exclude some boosting algorithms such as AdaBoost that are typically not convex combinations [9].

Popular algorithms like *Bagging* [1] and newer methods like *Snapshot Ensembles* [14] take the average of their base learners. Other methods like *Soft Voting* [26] use a convex combination of their model outputs to vote. We refer the reader to each ensemble methods' corresponding paper for further details on how the base learners are generated. For this work, we will consider Bagging, Snapshot Ensembles, and Soft Voting.

2.3   Jacobian Regularization

Let $f(\mathbf{x})$ be the logit output of the classifier for input $\mathbf{x}$, we write $\mathbf{J}_f(\mathbf{x})$ to denote the input-output Jacobian of f at $\mathbf{x}$. To train models with Jacobian regularization (JR) [6,13], the following joint loss is optimized:

$$\mathcal{L}_{\mathrm{joint}}(\theta) = \mathcal{L}_{\mathrm{train}}(\{\mathbf{x}_i, \mathbf{y}_i\}_i, \theta) + \frac{\lambda_{\mathrm{JR}}}{2}\left(\frac{1}{B}\sum_i \|\mathbf{J}(\mathbf{x}_i)\|_F^2\right) \tag{1}$$

where θ represent the parameters of the model, $\mathcal{L}_{\text{train}}$ is the standard cross-entropy training loss, $\{\mathbf{x}_i, \mathbf{y}_i\}$ are input-output pairs from the mini-batch, and B is the mini-batch size. This optimization uses a regularization parameter λ_{JR}, which allows the adjustment between regularization and classification loss.

The primary idea is to reduce the Frobenius norm of the input-output Jacobian $\|\mathbf{J}(\mathbf{x}_i)\|_F$ to decrease the model's sensitivity to small perturbations such as UAPs. JR shows some promise in improving robustness to UAPs. However, it can often simultaneously decrease the model's clean accuracy [6] especially for large values of λ_{JR}.

3   Bounds on UAP Effectiveness for Model Ensembles

In this section, we derive theoretical bounds for the expectation and variance of the Frobenius norm of the Jacobian of model ensembles. Note that we only consider ensembles that take a convex combination of their base learners. Similar to [6], we restrict the Frobenius norm of the Jacobian of a model to improve robustness against UAPs.

We show that using model ensembles result in tighter bounds on the Frobenius norm of the Jacobian, suggesting improved robustness and stability versus a single classifier. Our main result in **Theorem** 1 shows that increasing the number of base learners decreases both the upper and lower bounds of the expectation and variance for the Frobenius norm of the ensemble's Jacobian.

Proposition 1. *Let x_i be independent random variables drawn from a Normal distribution $x_i \sim \mathcal{N}(\mu, \sigma^2)$ for a fixed mean μ and variance σ^2. Define $\overline{x} = \sum_{i=1}^{M} c_i x_i$ where $\sum_{i=1}^{M} c_i = 1$ and $0 < c_i < 1$, $\forall i$. We then have the following:*

$$\frac{\sigma^2}{M} \le \sum_{i=1}^{M} c_i^2 \sigma^2 < \sigma^2 \tag{2}$$

Proof. By linearity of Normal distributions: $\overline{x} \sim \mathcal{N}(\mu, \sum_{i=1}^{M} c_i^2 \sigma^2)$. We then derive bounds for $\sum_{i=1}^{M} c_i^2$ when $M \ge 2$:

$$\sum_{i=1}^{M} c_i^2 = \sum_{i=1}^{M} c_i^2 + 2\sum_{i=1}^{M}\sum_{j \neq i} c_i c_j - 2\sum_{i=1}^{M}\sum_{j \neq i} c_i c_j$$

$$= \left(\sum_{i=1}^{M} c_i\right)^2 - 2\sum_{i=1}^{M}\sum_{j \neq i} c_i c_j$$

$$= 1 - 2\sum_{i=1}^{M}\sum_{j \neq i} c_i c_j$$

Since $c_i c_j > 0$ for all pairs i, j, then it follows that we have the upper bound $\sum_{i=1}^{M} c_i^2 < 1$. Note that equality: $\sum_{i=1}^{M} c_i^2 = 1$ is only possible in the degenerate case (when $c_i = 1$ for exactly one i and $c_j = 0$ for $i \neq j$).

For the lower bound, we use Cauchy-Schwarz inequality to get:

$$\left(\sum_{i=1}^{M}(c_i \cdot 1)\right)^2 \le \left(\sum_{i=1}^{M}c_i^2\right)\left(\sum_{i=1}^{M}1^2\right) = \left(\sum_{i=1}^{M}c_i^2\right)\cdot M$$

The left hand side reduces to 1, so it follows that $\sum_{i=1}^{M}c_i^2 \ge \frac{1}{M}$ with equality when $c_i = \frac{1}{M}$ for all i. Multiplying all sides with σ^2 gives the desired bounds. $\square$

Let $\mathcal{F}$ be an ensemble of M base learners f_i: $\mathcal{F}(x) = \sum_{i=1}^{M}c_i f_i(x)$ where $\sum_{i=1}^{M}c_i = 1$ and $0 < c_i < 1$, $\forall i$. Let $\mathbf{J}_{\mathcal{F}}$ denote the Jacobian of $\mathcal{F}$ and $\mathbf{J}_i$ the Jacobian of f_i for all i. It follows that $\mathbf{J}_{\mathcal{F}} = \sum_{i=1}^{M}c_i\mathbf{J}_i$.

Theorem 1. *Let each matrix $\mathbf{J}_i \in \mathbb{R}^{C \times D}$ be comprised of the independent random variables $_i a_{pq} \sim \mathcal{N}(\mu, \sigma^2)$, where $_i a_{pq}$ is the element on the p-th row and q-th column of matrix $\mathbf{J}_i$. It follows that their convex combination $\mathbf{J}_{\mathcal{F}}$ satisfies:*

$$CD\left(\frac{\sigma^2}{M} + \mu^2\right) \le \mathrm{E}(\|\mathbf{J}_{\mathcal{F}}\|_F^2) < \mathrm{E}(\|\mathbf{J}_i\|_F^2) \tag{3}$$

$$CD\left(\frac{4\mu^2\sigma^2}{M} + \frac{2\sigma^4}{M^2}\right) \le \mathrm{Var}(\|\mathbf{J}_{\mathcal{F}}\|_F^2) < \mathrm{Var}(\|\mathbf{J}_i\|_F^2) \tag{4}$$

Proof. Taking the square of Frobenius norm, we have the following for the Jacobian of a single model:

$$\|\mathbf{J}_i\|_F^2 = \sum_{p=1}^{C}\sum_{q=1}^{D}|_i a_{pq}|^2$$

The moments of $\|\mathbf{J}_i\|_F$ are proportional to the moments of the random variables $_i a_{pq}^2$. These follow a chi-squared distribution with 1 degree of freedom, and have the expectation and variance:

$$\mathrm{E}(_i a_{pq}^2) = \mathrm{Var}(_i a_{pq}) + [\mathrm{E}(_i a_{pq})]^2$$
$$= \sigma^2 + \mu^2$$
$$\mathrm{Var}(_i a_{pq}^2) = \mathrm{E}(_i a_{pq}^4) - [\mathrm{E}(_i a_{pq}^2)]^2$$
$$= \mu^4 + 6\mu^2\sigma^2 + 3\sigma^4 - \mu^4 - 2\mu^2\sigma^2 - \sigma^4$$
$$= 4\mu^2\sigma^2 + 2\sigma^4$$

Define $\bar{a}_{pq} = \sum_{i=1}^{M}c_i \, _i a_{pq}$, the elements of $\mathbf{J}_{\mathcal{F}}$. Note that $\bar{a}_{pq} \sim \mathcal{N}(\mu, \sum_{i=1}^{M}c_i^2\sigma^2)$. Thus for the ensemble model's Jacobian, we have:

$$\|\mathbf{J}_{\mathcal{F}}\|_F^2 = \sum_{p=1}^{C}\sum_{q=1}^{D}|\bar{a}_{pq}|^2$$

It is clear that the moments of $\|\mathbf{J}_{\mathcal{F}}\|_F$ are proportional to that of $\bar{a}_{pq}^2$. These random variables follow a chi-squared distribution with M degrees of freedom, and have the following expectation and variance:

$$\mathrm{E}(\bar{a}_{pq}^2) = \sum_{i=1}^{M} c_i^2 \sigma^2 + \mu^2$$

$$\mathrm{Var}(\bar{a}_{pq}^2) = 4\mu^2 \sum_{i=1}^{M} c_i^2 \sigma^2 + 2\left(\sum_{i=1}^{M} c_i^2 \sigma^2\right)^2$$

Applying **Proposition** 1, we then have the following bounds for the expectation and variance for these random variables:

$$\frac{\sigma^2}{M} + \mu^2 \leq \mathrm{E}(\bar{a}_{pq}^2) < \mathrm{E}(_i a_{pq}^2)$$

$$\frac{4\mu^2\sigma^2}{M} + \frac{2\sigma^4}{M^2} \leq \mathrm{Var}(\bar{a}_{pq}^2) < \mathrm{Var}(_i a_{pq}^2)$$

As the random variables are independently drawn, our desired result follows:

$$CD\left(\frac{\sigma^2}{M} + \mu^2\right) \leq \mathrm{E}(\|\mathbf{J}_{\mathcal{F}}\|_F^2) < \mathrm{E}(\|\mathbf{J}_i\|_F^2)$$

$$CD\left(\frac{4\mu^2\sigma^2}{M} + \frac{2\sigma^4}{M^2}\right) \leq \mathrm{Var}(\|\mathbf{J}_{\mathcal{F}}\|_F^2) < \mathrm{Var}(\|\mathbf{J}_i\|_F^2) \qquad \square$$

Conclusion. These are proportional to the expectation and variance of the Frobenius norms of our Jacobian matrices, so we can derive the following conclusions in this scenario. Ensembles decrease both the expected value and variance of the Jacobian's Frobenius norms when compared to that of a single model's. As M increases, the lower bounds of both the expectation and variance decreases.

Averaging is one of the most common methods for aggregating base learner outputs in an ensemble [16, 26], so it is important to consider this case. When the ensemble is done via averaging, i.e. $c_i = \frac{1}{M}$ for all i, this achieves the equality condition for the lower bounds of both $\mathrm{E}(\bar{a}_{pq}^2)$ and $\mathrm{Var}(\bar{a}_{pq}^2)$. Therefore, increasing the number of models in the ensemble *strictly decreases* the expectation and variance of the ensemble's Jacobian's norm $\|\mathbf{J}_{\mathcal{F}}\|_F$.

This theoretical result gives us the motivation on how model ensembles also improve the stability of models and thus their robustness to UAPs. We show this by deriving the above bounds on the Frobenius norm on their Jacobian. As model ensembles have also been shown to have improved performance over a single classifier, this makes it an ideal candidate for improving both model accuracy and robustness. In the next section, we explore the robustness of model ensembles and verify our theory with empirical results.

4   Experiments with Jacobian Ensembles

4.1   Experimental Setup

Jacobian Ensembles. To apply Jacobian Ensembles, we only need to include the Jacobian regularization as described in Eq. 1 to the joint loss of standard ensemble methods. The Jacobian regularization parameter λ_{JR} is tested for values between 0 and 2: where the resulting models manage to maintain good accuracy as informed by previous work [6].

We evaluate the following ensemble methods: *Bagging* [1], *Snapshot Ensembles* [14], and *Soft Voting* [26]. For these, we evaluate all experiments with ensembles trained on 1, 3, 6, and 9 base learners. Effectively, one base learner is similar to using no ensemble method at all.

Models and Datasets. We use the MNIST [17] and Fashion-MNIST [25] datasets. These are popular image classification benchmarks, each with 10 classes, and 28 by 28 pixel images whose their pixel values range from 0 to 1. For the DNN architecture, we use a version of LeNet-5 [13,17], which we refer to as LeNet.

UAP Attacks. We evaluate the robustness of these models to UAPs generated via iterative stochastic gradient descent with 100 iterations and a batch size of 200. Perturbations are applied under ℓ_∞-norm constraints. The ε we consider in our attacks for this norm are from 0.10 to 0.25, this perturbation magnitude is equivalent to 10%–25% of the maximum total possible change in pixel values. UAPs are generated over 50 different random seeds, and we report UAPs with the highest attack success rate, as this would represent the worst-case scenario.

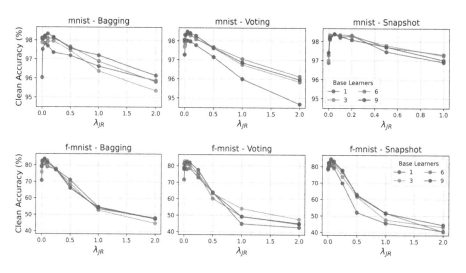

Fig. 1. Clean accuracy of LeNet on MNIST (top) and Fashion-MNIST (bottom) for various Jacobian regularization strengths λ_{JR} and with varying number of base learners per ensemble method.

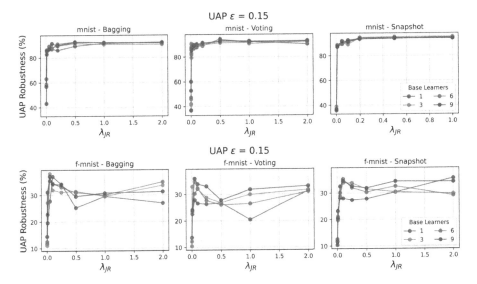

Fig. 2. Model robustness against UAP with $\varepsilon = 0.15$ of LeNet on MNIST (top) and Fashion-MNIST (bottom) for various Jacobian regularization strengths λ_{JR} and with varying number of base learners per ensemble method.

Metrics. The following metrics are evaluated on the entire 10,000 sample test sets for each dataset. *Clean Accuracy* is the accuracy of the model on the test set. *Model Robustness* measures the accuracy of the model on the test set when the corresponding worst-case UAP is applied or present. We then average this model robustness over all the UAP attack scenarios that we consider, ℓ_∞-norm of $\varepsilon = 0.10, 0.15, 0.2, 0.25$, to get an overall *mean UAP Accuracy*.

4.2 Improvements with Jacobian Ensembles

Clean Accuracy. In Fig. 1 there is a rapid degradation in clean accuracy when λ_{JR} is large. This is when JR is more heavily weighted, and this is consistent with previous work [6,13] as too much regularization damages accuracy on the test set. However, having a small amount of JR is still noticeably more beneficial than no JR as indicated by the clean accuracy when considering λ_{JR} in the range of 0 to 0.1 for both datasets across all settings.

We also see benefits of using ensembles: models with more than one base learner have noticeably better clean accuracy across all settings in Fig. 1. Overall, Jacobian Ensembles, which is a combination of ensemble methods and JR, achieves the best performance in our experiments.

Model Robustness. In the interest of space, we only present the robustness results for a particular UAP attack strength $\varepsilon = 0.15$ in Fig. 2. In terms of robustness, trends for both datasets are slightly different since Fashion-MNIST is a more difficult dataset than MNIST: a regularly trained LeNet on MNIST can

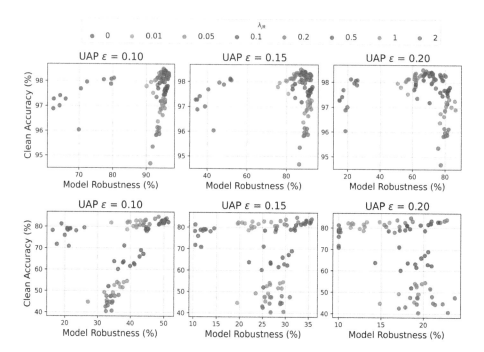

Fig. 3. Clean accuracy versus robustness trade-off of LeNet on MNIST (top) and Fashion-MNIST (bottom) labeled by λ_{JR} for various UAP attack strengths ε.

be expected to have 98–99% clean accuracy whereas it is 90–91% for the same model on Fashion-MNIST. Thus, it is expected that models on Fashion-MNIST are considerably less robust. For most settings, the general trends in Fig. 2 show that ensembles have a robustness benefit. JR monotonically increases robustness for MNIST and for Fashion-MNIST has a range between $0 < \lambda_{JR} < 0.5$ that achieves the best robustness.

In conclusion, ensemble methods with more than one base learner introduce measurable advantages in both accuracy and robustness. These advantages become even more pronounced when combined with JR. Next we analyze the general trade-off between accuracy and robustness.

4.3   Accuracy-Robustness Trade-Off

In Fig. 3, we plot the accuracy versus robustness of the various models we trained under the different configurations accounting for various ensemble methods, number of base learners, and λ_{JR} values. The best models achieve both high accuracy and robustness, so these will be on the top right side of the graph.

In a scenario when robustness is not accounted for (i.e. $\lambda_{JR} = 0$), models would appear in the top left. They are trained to have good accuracy, but remain extremely vulnerable to adversarial attacks like UAPs. On the other hand, models that overcompensate for robustness such as those with very high

Table 1. Weighted accuracy (in %) of LeNet for MNIST (top) and Fashion-MNIST (bottom). The first 3 rows show the models with highest weighted accuracy. The bottom 3 rows show the *best* weighted accuracy of models trained with only JR, only ensemble, and "standard training" (neither JR nor ensemble).

Model			MNIST accuracy (%)		
Ensemble	Learners	λ_{JR}	Clean	Avg. UAP	Weighted
Snapshot	3	0.50	97.8	82.8	**90.3**
Snapshot	9	0.50	97.7	82.3	90.0
Snapshot	3	0.20	98.3	81.5	89.9
JR Only	1	0.05	98.4	74.2	86.3
Bagging	6	0	98.1	42.8	70.4
Standard	1	0	99.1	31.9	65.5
Model			Fashion-MNIST accuracy (%)		
Ensemble	Learners	λ_{JR}	Clean	Avg. UAP	Weighted
Bagging	9	0.05	83.9	43.2	**63.5**
Bagging	6	0.05	83.4	43.0	63.2
Snapshot	9	0.10	83.2	42.4	62.8
JR Only	1	0.10	79.0	31.2	55.1
Bagging	9	0	91.2	12.7	51.2
Standard	1	0	90.8	12.1	50.9

regularization (e.g. $\lambda_{JR} = 2$), will appear on the bottom right. As these models sacrifice a significant amount of clean accuracy for improved robustness, especially against UAP attacks with larger strength ε. These delineations become clear when labeling the models according to their λ_{JR} value as in Fig. 3. Thus, the role of λ_{JR} is evident in improving overall robustness.

To better capture the model performance on both benign and adversarial inputs, we compute the *Weighted Accuracy* by averaging the clean accuracy and mean UAP accuracy. In practice, the defender can adjust the weighting of each accuracy metric in their final assessment to better match their application and risk profile. We choose the mean as the base setting.

Next, we perform an ablation study on the effect of only JR and only ensemble models compared against the top 3 Jacobian Ensembles with the best weighted accuracy in Table 1. We find that Jacobian Ensembles achieve the best weighted accuracy. To compare, we also show in the bottom 3 rows for each table the best models with only JR, only ensembles, and neither JR nor ensembles. The best Jacobian Ensembles have a clear advantage with average UAP accuracy over the non-Jacobian Ensembles whilst maintaining very close clean accuracy. This difference is even more pronounced on the Fashion-MNIST dataset.

Differences between the two datasets MNIST and Fashion-MNIST also show in Table 1. Since MNIST is an easier dataset, performance degradation by large $\lambda_{JR} = 0$ are not as prominent, so larger λ_{JR} are favored by the combined score.

For Fashion-MNIST, a large λ_{JR} is detrimental as the base model begin with a relatively low clean accuracy (<91%). In both cases, ensembles demonstrate a noticeably large boost in weighted accuracy, and further tuning is likely to improve their performance.

5   Conclusion

In this work, we propose Jacobian Ensembles to significantly increase model robustness against UAPs whilst maintaining the clean accuracy of models. Our results show that Jacobian Ensembles takes the advantages of both Jacobian regularization and model ensembles to achieve superior accuracy and robustness than each of these methods on their own, as measured by our weighted metric.

In addition, we derive theoretical upper and lower bounds on the robustness to UAPs for model ensembles, showing that increasing the number of base classifiers in the models' ensembles reduces the expected Frobenius norm of their Jacobian and thus improves stability. We then empirically verify our results and show that a combination of both JR and ensembles achieve the best performance.

These results give us confidence in recommending Jacobian Ensembles as a general methodology when training models as UAPs present a great threat to model adoption and safety. Our results show that it is indeed possible to maintain great test accuracy whilst achieving significant UAP robustness in previously unseen levels of accuracy-robustness trade-off. Thus, it is indeed possible to get the best of both worlds.

References

1. Breiman, L.: Bagging predictors. Mach. Learn. **24**(2), 123–140 (1996)
2. Brown, T.B., Mané, D.: Adversarial patch. arXiv preprint arXiv:1712.09665 (2017)
3. Co, K.T., Muñoz González, L., de Maupeou, S., Lupu, E.C.: Procedural noise adversarial examples for black-box attacks on deep convolutional networks. In: Proceedings of the 2019 ACM SIGSAC Conference on Computer and Communications Security, CCS 2019, pp. 275–289 (2019). https://doi.org/10.1145/3319535.3345660
4. Co, K.T., Muñoz-González, L., Kanthan, L., Glocker, B., Lupu, E.C.: Universal adversarial robustness of texture and shape-biased models. arXiv preprint arXiv:1911.10364 (2019)
5. Co, K.T., Muñoz-González, L., Lupu, E.C.: Sensitivity of deep convolutional networks to Gabor noise. arXiv preprint arXiv:1906.03455 (2019)
6. Co, K.T., Rego, D.M., Lupu, E.C.: Jacobian regularization for mitigating universal adversarial perturbations. In: Farkaš, I., Masulli, P., Otte, S., Wermter, S. (eds.) ICANN 2021. LNCS, vol. 12894, pp. 202–213. Springer, Cham (2021). https://doi.org/10.1007/978-3-030-86380-7_17
7. Eykholt, K., et al.: Physical adversarial examples for object detectors. In: 12th USENIX Workshop on Offensive Technologies, *WOOT* 2018 (2018)
8. Eykholt, K., et al.: Robust physical-world attacks on deep learning visual classification. In: Proceedings of the IEEE Conference on Computer Vision and Pattern Recognition (CVPR), pp. 1625–1634 (2018)

9. Freund, Y., Schapire, R., Abe, N.: A short introduction to boosting. J. Japan. Soc. Artif. Intell. **14**(771–780), 1612 (1999)

10. Hau, Z. Co, K.T., Demetriou, S., Lupu, E.C.: Object removal attacks on lidar-based 3d object detectors. arXiv preprint arXiv:2102.03722 (2021)

11. Hau, Z., Demetriou, S., Muñoz-González, L., Lupu, E.C.: Shadow-catcher: looking into shadows to detect ghost objects in autonomous vehicle 3d sensing. In: Bertino, E., Shulman, H., Waidner, M. (eds.) ESORICS 2021. LNCS, vol. 12972, pp. 691–711. Springer, Cham (2021). https://doi.org/10.1007/978-3-030-88418-5_33

12. Hinton, G., et al.: Deep neural networks for acoustic modeling in speech recognition: the shared views of four research groups. IEEE Sig. Process. Mag. **29**(6), 82–97 (2012)

13. Hoffman, J., Roberts, D.A., Yaida, S.: Robust learning with Jacobian regularization. arXiv preprint arXiv:1908.02729 (2019)

14. Huang, G., Li, Y., Pleiss, G., Liu, Z., Hopcroft, J.E., Weinberger, K.Q.: Snapshot ensembles: train 1, get m for free. In: International Conference on Learning Representations (2017)

15. Krizhevsky, A., Sutskever, I., Hinton, G.E.: ImageNet classification with deep convolutional neural networks. In: Advances in Neural Information Processing Systems (NeurIPS), pp. 1097–1105 (2012)

16. Kuncheva, L.I.: Combining Pattern Classifiers: Methods and Algorithms. Wiley (2014)

17. LeCun, Y., Bottou, L., Bengio, Y., Haffner, P.: Gradient-based learning applied to document recognition. Proc. IEEE **86**(11), 2278–2324 (1998)

18. Matachana, A.G., Co, K.T., Muñoz-González, L., Martinez, D., Lupu, E.C.: Robustness and transferability of universal attacks on compressed models. arXiv preprint arXiv:2012.06024 (2020)

19. Moosavi-Dezfooli, S.M., Fawzi, A., Fawzi, O., Frossard, P.: Universal adversarial perturbations. In: Proceedings of the IEEE Conference on Computer Vision and Pattern Recognition (CVPR), pp. 1765–1773 (2017)

20. Redmon, J., Divvala, S., Girshick, R., Farhadi, A.: You only look once: unified, real-time object detection. In: Proceedings of the IEEE Conference on Computer Vision and Pattern Recognition (CVPR), pp. 779–788 (2016)

21. Roth, K., Kilcher, Y., Hofmann, T.: Adversarial training is a form of data-dependent operator norm regularization. In: Advances in Neural Information Processing Systems (NeurIPS) (2020)

22. Shafahi, A., Najibi, M., Xu, Z., Dickerson, J., Davis, L.S., Goldstein, T.: Universal adversarial training. arXiv preprint arXiv:1811.11304 (2018)

23. Thys, S., Van Ranst, W., Goedemé, T.: Fooling automated surveillance cameras: adversarial patches to attack person detection. In: Workshop on The Bright and Dark Sides of Computer Vision: Challenges and Opportunities for Privacy and Security (CVPRW) (2019)

24. Tramèr, F., Dupré, P., Rusak, G., Pellegrino, G., Boneh, D.: Adversarial: perceptual ad blocking meets adversarial machine learning. In: Proceedings of the 2019 ACM SIGSAC Conference on Computer and Communications Security, CCS 2019, pp. 2005–2021 (2019). https://doi.org/10.1145/3319535.3354222

25. Xiao, H., Rasul, K., Vollgraf, R.: Fashion-MNIST: a novel image dataset for benchmarking machine learning algorithms. arXiv preprint arXiv:1708.07747 (2017)

26. Zhou, Z.H.: Ensemble Methods: Foundations and Algorithms. CRC Press (2012)

Liquid State Machine on Loihi: Memory Metric for Performance Prediction

Rajat Patel[ID], Vivek Saraswat[✉][ID], and Udayan Ganguly[ID]

Department of Electrical Engineering, Indian Institute of Technology Bombay, Mumbai, India
vsaraswat009@gmail.com, udayan@ee.iitb.ac.in

Abstract. Liquid State Machine (LSM) is a spiking variant of recurrent neural networks with promising results for speech, video and other temporal datasets classification. LSM employ a network of fixed and randomly connected neurons, called a reservoir. Parameter selection for building the best performing reservoir is a difficult task given the vast parameter space. A memory metric extracted from a state-space approximation of the LSM has been proposed in the past and empirically shown to be best-in-class for performance prediction. However, the working principle of this memory metric has not been studied. We first show equivalence of LSM simulated on MATLAB to those run on Intel's neuromorphic chip Loihi. This enables us to perform in-depth statistical analysis of the memory metric on Loihi: effect of weight scaling and effect of time averaging window. Analysis of state space matrices generated with a reasonably sized averaging window reveal that the diagonal elements are sufficient to capture network dynamics. This strengthens the relevance of the first order decay constant based memory metric which correlates well with the classification performance.

Keywords: Liquid State Machine · Loihi · Memory metric

1 Introduction

Liquid State Machines (LSM) are Spiking Neural Networks (SNNs), which come under the field of reservoir computing. It consists of a reservoir of neurons recurrently connected randomly with random non-plastic synapses followed by a discriminator layer (Fig. 1 (a)). The reservoir is able to project input times series data into a hyperdimensional space which can be clustered and classified by the discriminator layer more effectively [10]. A major advantage of LSMs is that the plastic synapses are limited to the discriminator layer while the reservoir consists of non-plastic synapses, reducing the total training burden [7]. LSM has shown state-of-the-art results for classification of various time series [1,3,13], speech [15,16], video [14] datasets, and reinforcement learning [12].

E. Pimenidis et al. (Eds.): ICANN 2022, LNCS 13531, pp. 692–703, 2022.
https://doi.org/10.1007/978-3-031-15934-3_57

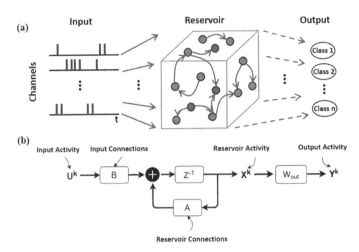

Fig. 1. (a) Liquid State Machine schematic, (b) Corresponding state-space approximation of LSM

One of the main challenges of using LSM for different tasks is tuning the reservoir such that it produces the best classification performance. Performance prediction metrics alleviate this problem as they can be derived from the reservoir dynamics alone without the need for elaborate training and testing. Kernel quality [8], class separation [11] and Lyapunov exponent [5] are some of such metrics. They are based on the separation property of the reservoir i.e. ability to separate two close inputs. Lyapunov exponent, a measure of chaotic behavior of a network, long outperformed other metrics mentioned by showing best correlation with performance and identifying edge of chaos operation [2]. In contrast, the memory metric (τ_M) proposed by Gorad et al. [6] is based on a linear state-space mapping of LSM (Fig. 1(b)) which estimates the extent that past excitation predicts the future linearly to embody the "memory" of the network. Memory metric has empirically outperformed Lyapunov exponent making a strong case of it being the preferred metric for performance prediction.

However, the working principle of the memory metric estimation requires further examination. In order to perform in-depth statistical analysis to answer these questions, we first demonstrate equivalence of networks run on Intel's neuromorphic chip Loihi to MATLAB simulations. Equipped with the power and time efficiency of Loihi, the following questions need to be addressed: (1) Why does a metric based purely on self-excitation (diagonal) terms [6] while ignoring the cross-excitation (non-diagonal) terms of the reservoir's state space matrix precisely predict the performance? (2) What is the role of the averaging time window size used to extract the state space matrices and subsequently the memory metric? A comparison and focus of our work with other relevant works is summarised in Table 1.

Table 1. Contribution of this work vis a vis state-of-the-art

Work	Platform	Considered metric	Connectivity experiment	Winner metric
2007 [8]	CPU	Lyapunov exponent, VC dimension	Scaling	Lyapunov exponent
2014 [2]	CPU	Lyapunov exponent, Kernel quality, Class separation, Spectral radius	Learning	Lyapunov exponent
2019 [6]	CPU	Lyapunov exponent, Memory metric	Scaling	Memory metric
This	Loihi, CPU	Lyapunov exponent, Memory metric	Scaling, Learning	Memory metric

2   Background on Performance Metrics

2.1   Lyapunov Exponent

Lyapunov exponent (μ) has long been used in characterizing the separation of two close trajectories in dynamical systems. For LSMs, the metric characterizes the rate of separation in activity of reservoir generated by two nearly identical inputs [5]. Edge-of-chaos state of reservoir associated with high performance [8] is based on Lyapunov exponent approaching unity. For inputs u_i and u_j and their reservoir responses x_i and x_j, $\mu(t)$ is defined as:

$$\mu(t) = ln\frac{||x_i(t) - x_j(t)||}{||u_i(t) - u_j(t)||} \tag{1}$$

2.2   Memory Metric

State-space representation is widely used for modeling linear systems. Interestingly, it is used to model non-linear dynamics of LSM in [6]. Spike rates obtained by averaging over moving time window are used to model the state-space approximation for the reservoir (Fig. 1(b)):

$$X^{k+1} = AX^k + BU^k \tag{2}$$

X^k and U^k are reservoir and input signal spike rates respectively at time instant k and A and B are constant matrices. Matrices A and B can be obtained using actual spike rate X and input U as follows:

$$X_{+1} = [A|B]_1[X|U]_0 \tag{3}$$

$$[A|B]_1 = X_{+1}pinv([X|U]_0) \tag{4}$$

X_{+1} is one time step shifted version of X. $pinv$ is the Moore-Penrose inverse and $[A|B]_i$ represents the concatenation of matrices A and B in dimension i. The memory of N dimensional state space (Eq. 5) with N time constants is defined using Eq. 6. $diag(a, b, c)$ indicates a diagonal matrix with a, b and c as diagonal elements.

$$\dot{X} = -diag(\frac{1}{\tau_1}, \frac{1}{\tau_2}, ..., \frac{1}{\tau_N})X \tag{5}$$

$$\tau_M = \frac{1}{N}\sum_{i=1}^{N}\tau_i \tag{6}$$

For matrix A, the above definition can be used by considering vector a of diagonal elements of A. For discrete system with h as time-step, memory metric τ_M is:

$$\tau_M = \frac{1}{N}\sum_{i=1}^{N}\frac{h}{1-|a_i|} \tag{7}$$

Time-step is fixed to 1 ms throughout this work. Thus, the metric provides insight into how the current activity of the reservoir will affect future activity. This has shown very good correlation with performance [6].

3   Loihi vs Matlab

3.1   Neuronal Model Used in Loihi

The basic neural model for Loihi [4] is a variation of the leaky-integrate-and-fire model. Spike train is represented by a sum of Dirac delta functions $\sigma(t) = \sum \delta_k(t-t_k)$, where t_k is the time of the k-th spike. The synaptic response current $u_i(t)$ is:

$$u_i(t) = \sum_{j\neq i}w_{ij}(\alpha_u * \sigma_j) + b_i, \quad \alpha_u(t) = \frac{1}{\tau_u}e^{(-t/\tau_u)}H(t) \tag{8}$$

where w_{ij} is the synaptic weight from neuron j to i, $\alpha_u(t)$ is the synaptic filter impulse response, τ_u is the time constant and $H(t)$ is a unit step function and b_i is a constant bias current. The membrane potential $v_i(t)$ integrates current, and the neuron sends out a spike when $v_i(t)$ passes its firing threshold θ_i. The neuron remains at resting potential for refractory period τ_r after it spikes. A discrete and quantized version of these equations is implemented on Loihi and hence need to be validated with ideal MATLAB simulations.

$$\dot{v}_i(t) = -\frac{1}{\tau_v}v_i(t) + u_i(t) - \theta_i\sigma_i(t) \tag{9}$$

3.2   Neuron Level

A periodic spike train with period of 5 ms is given as an input to a single neuron ($\tau_V = 4\,ms$, $\tau_U = 2\,ms$, $\tau_r = 2\,ms$ and $V_{th} = 5760\,mV$). The synapse through which spikes travel to the neuron has weight $w_{in} = 55$. Figure 2 shows the neuronal voltage, current, and spikes obtained on MATLAB and Loihi for the single neuron case. The mean difference in current was less than 2%. This difference affects neuronal voltage only when it is very close to the threshold.

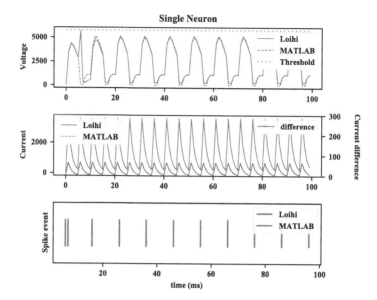

Fig. 2. Effects of reduced precision on single neuron are shown. One spike is shifted due to error in voltage computation near threshold.

Table 2. Parameters for 10 and 150 neurons reservoir

Parameter	Value	Parameter	Value
τ_v	4 ms	V_{th}	$100 \cdot 2^6 mV$
τ_u	3 ms	w_{in}	50
τ_r	2 ms	w_{ee}, w_{ei}	36
Excitatory : Total	0.8	w_{ie}, w_{ii}	-54
F_{res}	4	p_{in}	0.5

Table 3. Reservoir parameter for T1-46 task

Parameter	Value	Parameter	Value
τ_v	64 ms	V_{th}	$400 \cdot 2^6 mV$
τ_u	1 ms	w_{in}	160
τ_r	3 ms	w_{ee}, w_{ei}	60, 120
Excitatory : Total	0.8	w_{ie}, w_{ii}	-40
F_{in}	4	λ	3
K_{ee}, K_{ei}	0.3, 0.45	K_{ie}, K_{ii}	0.6, 0.15

3.3 Reservoir Level

We create a small reservoir (10 neurons) and a moderate size reservoir (150 neurons) for simulations. Input to reservoir connections are made using bernoulli random variable p_{in}. Intra-reservoir connections are chosen randomly with fan out F_{res} fixed. All parameter values are mentioned in Table 2.

As the neuron receives input from multiple neurons (Fig. 3(a) and (b)), the arithmetic operations increase, and along with it the error. The error in spike times propagates to other neurons and hence increases with time. This error increases for a reservoir size of 150 neurons (Fig. 3(c)). However, an idea of reservoir level effect is obtained by obtaining total neuronal spikes at each time instant (13.6% deviation) and total spikes for each neuron across simulation time (4.13% deviation). So, the reservoir level activity is not as badly affected as individual neuronal spike times (Fig. 3(d)).

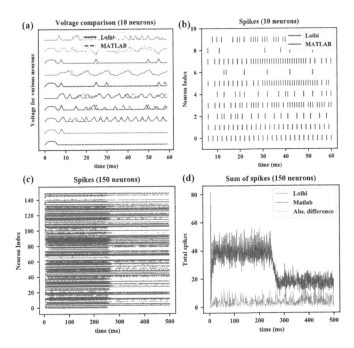

Fig. 3. Effects of reduced precision for 10 neuron reservoir. Intra-reservoir connections increase (a) voltage error and (b) spike mismatch. Effects of reduced precision for 150 neuron reservoir. (c) Spike event mismatch and (d) Population level mismatch.

3.4 TI-46 Spoken Digit Recognition

We use TI-46 spoken digits dataset for comparing the performance of Loihi and MATLAB. The dataset used contains 500 spoken digits (0–9) utterances from 5 speakers. The inputs are converted to spikes using Lyon auditory cochlear model [9]. Parameters are used from setup in [6]. The output of the pre-processing block is 77 spike trains per input. A reservoir of 125 neurons ($5 \times 5 \times 5$ grid) is used. The connection topology is based on lambda model where two neurons a and b are connected with probability:

$$P(a,b) = K \cdot e^{\frac{-d^2(a,b)}{\lambda^2}} \tag{10}$$

where λ is effective connectivity distance and $d(a,b)$ is the euclidean distance. Weights and the constant K depend on kind of pre-synaptic and postsynaptic neuron e.g. K_{EI} for excitatory to inhibitory connection [7]. Parameters for connections and neurons are described in Table 3.

The input spikes projected in the high dimensional space of reservoir have to be classified to one of the ten digits. We chose a simple linear classifier (Eq. 11) and minimize the least square loss. X_s contain features from reservoir for given input, W_{out} contains the weights of the classifier and Y is one-hot encoded output. We use total spikes per reservoir neuron across simulation time as our

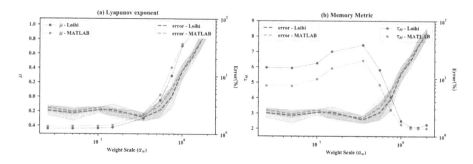

Fig. 4. (a) μ, error vs. α_w (b) τ_M, error vs. α_w. Error rate and behavior of both metrics is similar across platforms. τ_M peaks in minimum error region while μ increases monotonically.

Table 4. Performance on T1-46 digit recognition task

Implementation	Test Accuracy %
MATLAB (64-bit)	98.3
Loihi (8-bit)	98.5
Reservoir-less	93.8
Gorad et al. [14]	99.09
Verstraeten et al. [6]	99.5

Table 5. Correlation of metrics with performance

Error Region (%)	|PCC|			
	MATLAB		Loihi	
	μ	τ_M	μ	τ_M
≤ 70	**0.78**	0.71	**0.77**	0.70
≤ 10	0.88	**0.89**	0.77	**0.82**
≤ 5	0.05	**0.58**	0.41	**0.61**

X_s (125-dimensional vector). For training and testing, 5-fold cross-validation is used.

$$Y = X_s W_{out} \tag{11}$$

It has been shown that effective connectivity distance λ and reservoir weight scaling α_w are enough for exploring all major dynamics of a reservoir [7]. We cover the different activity states of a reservoir (no intra-reservoir spike propagation to chaotic). For calculating Lyapunov exponent, μ, we use 2 utterances per digit for a single speaker (20 in total). Time window for getting spike rates for state space approximation is kept at 50 ms. As τ_M is not based on separation, we use only one utterance per digit by a single speaker (10 in total). Hence, both the metrics require a small fraction of the dataset for predicting performance.

We were able to run 180 reservoirs in parallel on Loihi (utilizes 18% of neurons on one chip). The test accuracy obtained on both Loihi and MATLAB is close to state-of-the-art models for LSMs of similar reservoir size (Table 4). A slight decrease compared to other works is due to the use of a simpler linear classifier. Memory metric and Lyapunov exponent behavior with varying α_w and corresponding error rate for both platforms are shown in Fig. 4. With variation in α_w, a 'U' shaped curve for error is obtained. Loihi hardware runs give similar performance. τ_M peaks in the minimum error region while μ increases monotonically. This makes τ_M a better fit for performance prediction. Pearson correlation coefficient (PCC) for τ_M and error rate is better than the PCC for μ and error rate in low error regions (Table 5).

4   Analysis of Memory Metric

4.1   Effect of Weight Scaling (α_w)

Memory metric only makes use of diagonal elements of matrix A (Eq. 7) which should ideally capture the effect of neuron on itself. Figure 5(a)–(c) shows the reservoir spike rasters for three values of α_w (almost no intra-reservoir connections to highly chaotic and uncorrelated) indicating how recurrent connections within reservoir combine with input spikes to generate reservoir dynamics.

Figure 5(d)–(f) shows matrix A for above values of α_w along with extracted τ_M. There is an increase in no. of diagonal elements and memory when going from Fig. 5(d) to Fig. 5(e) followed by sharp decrease in Fig. 5(f). This is associated with increased spike propagation in intra-reservoir connections. One of the reasons that it is reflected in diagonal elements is due to the recurrent connections and averaging window based spike rates being used to model state space. An important aspect of the observed behavior of memory metric is that how well the state space has modeled the actual reservoir spike rate. PCC is calculated for estimated $\hat{X}$ (by using U, A and B) and actual spike rate X. The correlation is very strong in non-chaotic regions as shown in Fig. 5(g).

4.2   Effect of Averaging Window (win)

The length of the moving window used for getting the spike rate plays an important role for a linear state space approximation to non-linear dynamics. Figure 6(a)–(c) shows matrix A for various time windows. For an example spike train in Fig. 6 (d), the ability of different window sizes to capture the temporally varying spike rates is demonstrated. Figure 6 (e) shows PCC for estimated $\hat{X}$ and actual spike rate X along with τ_M and their variation with window size for the spoken digits reservoir. Hence, a more accurate state space representation (higher PCC) is again correlated with a higher observed memory metric. This behavior is maintained for a decent range of window size.

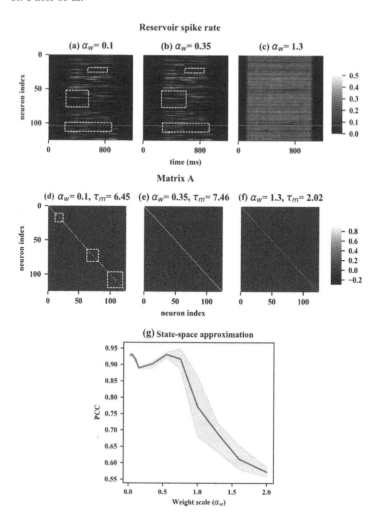

Fig. 5. Spike rate (window = 50) increases with weight scaling (α_w) as intra-reservoir connections increasingly contribute to spikes of connected neurons. Matrix A vs. α_w (d) Very low intra-reservoir spike propagation leads to quick decay of activity along with no activity for many neurons (highlighted in grey dashed boxes and contrasted with (e)). Hence, diagonal elements are on the weaker side. (e) Intra-reservoir connections increases causal activity leading to slower decay of activity and hence stronger diagonal elements. (f) High uncorrelated activity with strong intra-reservoir connections weakens diagonal elements and strengthens non-diagonal elements. (g) Effectiveness of state space model vs α_w. Strong dependence on input U gives high PCC for low α_w. For high performance regions, high PCC indicates effective modeling. For chaotic state, the state space approximation fails.

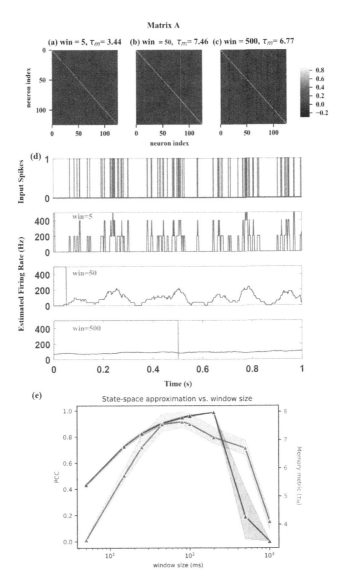

Fig. 6. Matrix A vs. window size for the same reservoir. (a) Spike rate changes very fast due to binary nature of spikes which leads to ineffective modeling and hence weak diagonal values. (b) Spike rate change is gradual and effects of gently decaying activity are captured making diagonal values strong. (c) Large window makes spike rate almost constant along with loss of information. (d) An example input spike train and estimated firing rate using windows of size 5, 50 and 500. Small window sizes lead to sharp changes whereas long window sizes lead to smearing out and nearly constant firing rates. An intermediate window size captures the temporally varying firing rate of input spikes. (e) τ_M and PCC vs. window size for same reservoir. Appropriately large window size is necessary for effective state space modelling and τ_M is strongly correlated with this effectiveness.

5   Conclusion

Memory Metric has been shown to be the best in-class for performance prediction of LSMs. We establish the equivalence of LSM on Loihi chip with MATLAB simulations. This expands the applicability and robustness of the performance prediction metrics for networks run on accelerated hardware. We show that slowly decaying causal reservoir activity generated through spike propagation from recurrent intra-reservoir connections is captured in the diagonal elements of reservoir state-space matrix. The reservoir is best modelled by state-space when it is around the edge of chaos and appropriate averaging window size is used for spike rates. The extracted memory metric is high both for a well-captured state space approximation and a high network performance. This analysis and generalization of memory metric deems it a very powerful tool for designing and tuning high performing LSMs for very large scale networks.

Acknowledgements. We thank Intel Neuromorphic Research Community (INRC) for providing us remote access to Loihi. We also thank Apoorv Kishore and Ajinkya Gorad for providing valuable insights and helping with the MATLAB simulations.

References

1. de Azambuja, R., Klein, F.B., Adams, S.V., Stoelen, M.F., Cangelosi, A.: Short-term plasticity in a liquid state machine biomimetic robot arm controller. In: 2017 International Joint Conference on Neural Networks (IJCNN), pp. 3399–3408. IEEE (2017)
2. Chrol-Cannon, J., Jin, Y.: On the correlation between reservoir metrics and performance for time series classification under the influence of synaptic plasticity. PLoS ONE **9**(7), e101792 (2014)
3. Das, A., et al.: Unsupervised heart-rate estimation in wearables with liquid states and a probabilistic readout. Neural Netw. **99**, 134–147 (2018)
4. Davies, M., et al.: Loihi: a neuromorphic manycore processor with on-chip learning. IEEE Micro **38**(1), 82–99 (2018)
5. Gibbons, T.E.: Unifying quality metrics for reservoir networks. In: The 2010 International Joint Conference on Neural Networks (IJCNN), pp. 1–7. IEEE (2010)
6. Gorad, A., Saraswat, V., Ganguly, U.: Predicting performance using approximate state space model for liquid state machines. In: 2019 International Joint Conference on Neural Networks (IJCNN), pp. 1–8. IEEE (2019)
7. Ju, H., Xu, J.X., Chong, E., VanDongen, A.M.: Effects of synaptic connectivity on liquid state machine performance. Neural Netw. **38**, 39–51 (2013)
8. Legenstein, R., Maass, W.: Edge of chaos and prediction of computational performance for neural circuit models. Neural Netw. **20**(3), 323–334 (2007)
9. Lyon, R.: A computational model of filtering, detection, and compression in the cochlea. In: IEEE International Conference on Acoustics, Speech, and Signal Processing, ICASSP 1982, vol. 7, pp. 1282–1285. IEEE (1982)
10. Maass, W., Natschläger, T., Markram, H.: Real-time computing without stable states: a new framework for neural computation based on perturbations. Neural Comput. **14**(11), 2531–2560 (2002)

11. Norton, D., Ventura, D.: Improving liquid state machines through iterative refinement of the reservoir. Neurocomputing **73**(16–18), 2893–2904 (2010)
12. Ponghiran, W., Srinivasan, G., Roy, K.: Reinforcement learning with low-complexity liquid state machines. Front. Neurosci. **13**, 883 (2019)
13. Rosselló, J.L., Alomar, M.L., Morro, A., Oliver, A., Canals, V.: High-density liquid-state machine circuitry for time-series forecasting. Int. J. Neural Syst. **26**(05), 1550036 (2016)
14. Soures, N., Kudithipudi, D.: Deep liquid state machines with neural plasticity for video activity recognition. Front. Neurosci. **13**, 686 (2019)
15. Verstraeten, D., Schrauwen, B., Stroobandt, D., Van Campenhout, J.: Isolated word recognition with the liquid state machine: a case study. Inf. Process. Lett. **95**(6), 521–528 (2005)
16. Zhang, Y., Li, P., Jin, Y., Choe, Y.: A digital liquid state machine with biologically inspired learning and its application to speech recognition. IEEE Trans. Neural Netw. Learn. Syst. **26**(11), 2635–2649 (2015)

LogBERT-BiLSTM: Detecting Malicious Web Requests

Levi S. Ramos Júnior[✉][ID], David Macêdo[ID], Adriano L. I. Oliveira[ID],
and Cleber Zanchettin[ID]

Centro de Informática, Universidade Federal de Pernambuco,
Recife, PE 50.740-560, Brazil
{lsrj,dlm,alio,cz}@cin.ufpe.br
http://www.cin.ufpe.br

Abstract. The digitalization of society potentialized services provided through the Internet, such as information sharing, entertainment, and education. With the rise of end-user services, we also verify the growth of attacks. Unfortunately, most defensive techniques of Web Intrusion Systems cannot deal with the complexity of cyber attacks on HTTP requests. Nevertheless, machine learning approaches are now a promising tool in different areas that can help to detect known and unknown attacks on day zero. We propose a new approach to detect possible attacks on HTTP requests based on machine learning. The new model LogBERT-BiLSTM uses BERT and Bidirectional LSTMs to detect anomalies in data. Experiments compared the proposed approach with literature models on CSIC 2010 and ECML/PKDD 2007 datasets. In addition, we created a new dataset of HTTP requests to evaluate the model performance. The proposed model obtained detection rates consistently above 95% of accuracy on the evaluated datasets.

Keywords: Web requests · LogBERT-BiLSTM · Attack detection

1 Introduction

Web servers are widely used and essential for many organizations, regardless of business area, and are constant targets of numerous attacks that cause enormous damage. Thus, developers and security experts must build secure systems to prevent these attacks. Among all network communication protocols among servers, the HTTP (Hypertext Transfer Protocol) is used by most web applications to communicate between web browsers and web servers. There are usually two types of HTTP messages: requests (*requests*) sent by the client to trigger an action on the server and the responses (*responses*), the replica of the server's requests. Among the numerous web security solutions, the web application firewall (WAF) is a component that explicitly applies to web services. Inspection of HTTP traffic can prevent attacks originating from the Internet using security vulnerabilities. However, current WAFs typically work on a rules-based model

© The Author(s), under exclusive license to Springer Nature Switzerland AG 2022
E. Pimenidis et al. (Eds.): ICANN 2022, LNCS 13531, pp. 704–715, 2022.
https://doi.org/10.1007/978-3-031-15934-3_58

and rely heavily on attack signatures to detect and prevent intrusions. In addition, they must have sufficient characterization and generalization capability to analyze normal or malicious behavior, which in practice is a time-consuming and laborious task [8]. In contrast to this approach, some anomaly detection approaches to study the user's behavior, whether client or server, and detect if the behavior is normal or anomalous using machine learning techniques.

Therefore, some intrusion detection techniques use machine learning for web servers based on HTTP requests. In [18] and [8] both use the request line. The request line comprises the HTTP method, the HTTP-URL, and the HTTP version. They assume that the vast majority of attacks on the web are implemented by manipulating the HTTP-URL, as the experiments considered only the CSIC 2010 dataset [15] which contains only HTTP-URL attacks. However, other attacks can also use other parts of the HTTP header, such as *Session Hijacking and Cross-Site Request Forgery (CSRF)* that utilize the user's session cookie on the page. Another approach is to extract resources from URLs as in [2,17] and [12], which consists of selecting the most relevant attributes extracted from the URLs contained in the requests. These approaches tend to have difficulty detecting attacks, as the complete request has more information than the URL alone can provide. Thus, most works in the literature use only the URL to extract information and try to predict possible attacks on HTTP requests.

Still, there are some efficient approaches based on deep learning, especially recurrent neural networks (RNNs), which are already used in the literature [4,9], and [5] to deal with this problem. Unfortunately, these models rely on log analysis to preprocess unstructured log data and, therefore, suffer from losing important information during interpretation. Log parsers remove the jagged part of the log messages and retain the constant part to get the meaning of the log. In this process, existing Log Parsers produce various parsing errors, which reduce detection performance [9]. Finally, it is worth mentioning that these models still impose some specific adjustments to the set of data used, and none of these deal with HTTP requests.

This paper proposes using the BERT model to learn sequential patterns of HTTP requests and represent the information. We use a BiLSTM layer from this representation to add bidirectional information in this context and allow the hidden state vector to capture past and future information in each connection. Therefore, the proposed LogBERT-BiLSTM approach removes the parser log phase of the process and uses all the requests' information to detect possible attacks. We evaluate the proposed approach on four datasets, three public datasets, ECML/PKDD 2007, CSIC 2010, BGL, and finally, one dataset generated in this paper from a security asset *F5 Big-IP*.

2   Related Work

HTTP requests are widely used in communication between clients and web servers. Given this scenario, several attempts were created to detect or prevent attacks based on HTTP requests. This section will show some works that have tried these goals with different architectures.

Yu et al. [18] its scope was only on HTTP requests from the CSIC 2010 [15] dataset. His project consisted of 3 steps: application of TextCNN [7] for feature extraction; creating URL-based statistical resource transfer; and building an SVM model on the last layer of TextCNN to perform classification based on the concatenated features. Its preprocessing consisted of removing duplicate requests, converting each character of the requests to lowercase, and decoding characters encoded by browsers or attackers. In the data processing step, they use TextCNN to extract features automatically, and later this information is fed into a CNN network with 2×64, 3×64, 4×64, and 5×64.

Lu et al. [10] built a log parser that structures the log lines and creates a unique key for each input. The less-used information is excluded from these keys [10]. This log parser applies a window-based partitioning, where padding or truncation is used to get consistent string lengths. Mainly, they first created a trainable matrix whose shape equals a single log $\times$ embedding size [3]. After that, the embedding is inserted into a CNN network: 3 CNN layers in parallel with sizes 3×128, 4×128, and 5×128.

Xiaohui et al. [8] created DeepWAF to detect malicious HTTP requests and, similar to Yu et al. [18] only worked with CSIC. First, the request to the web server is parsed from the HTTP headers and the message body. After preprocessing, a URL is generated to feed the detector. Next, this same URL is decoded as in [18], lowercase and finally, the URL is divided following the sequence of special characters. And in the classification step, several RNNs are combined with CNN, LSTM, CNN+LSTM, and LSTM+CNN.

Le et al. [9] proposed NeuralLog that consists of three steps: preprocessing, neural representation, and transformer-based classification. The first step is log preprocessing. After that, each log message is encoded into a semantic vector using BERT. Finally, it leverages the model used in [16] to detect anomalies [9].

The above works presented significant advances, but few have explored machine learning approaches in this context. Nevertheless, deep learning techniques are a promising approach to learning from legitimate or malicious sample data without the requirement for classical log parsing tasks and detecting web attacks.

3   LogBERT-BiLSTM

The purpose of LogBERT-BiLSTM is to predict attacks from HTTP requests. HTTP requests are messages sent by the client to initiate an action on the server. This detection work is based on the information in the *HTTP Request* fields. These fields contain several types of information that may be useful. Furthermore, LogBERT-BiLSTM is not restricted to HTTP requests only; it can detect anomalies in other types of logs, as will be shown later.

LogBERT-BiLSTM is an improved supervised algorithm based on *Bidirectional Encoder Representations from Transformer (BERT)* and *Bidirectional Long Short Term Memory (BiLSTM)*. It adopts BERT as the data entry part and BiLSTM as the classification part of the model.

Each log message is an HTTP Request. HTTP header fields are a list of strings sent and received by the client program and the server in each HTTP request. These headers are generally invisible to the end-user and are only processed or logged by the server and client applications. They define how the information sent over the connection is encoded (as in Content-Encoding), client session verification, and identification (as in browser cookies, IP address, and user-agent), among others.

LogBERT-BiLSTM uses all text and content to extract the semantics and meaning of the logs. Figure 1 shows the architecture of LogBERT-BiLSTM.

3.1 Preprocessing

Initially, as the logs were extracted in text format, it was necessary to create a Python script to convert them to CSV with the separation of data in columns from a Regex[1]. It is possible to search, validate, and change any character pattern in any text with regex. The next step with CSV was to make the data lowercase and remove all special characters. These removed special characters contain accents, punctuation, and math signs. Figure 2 shows a request and Fig. 3 shows how it looks after preprocessing.

3.2 Tokenization and Transformer-Based Classification

Tokenization aims to divide strings into subword token strings, convert token strings into ids, and reverse processes. In addition, in this step, token insertions such as *[CLS], [PAD], and [SEP]* serve, respectively, to indicate the beginning of the sentence, padding for sentences to reach the defined token size, and to indicate the end of the sentence. The tokenization process is shown in the sequence from Fig. 4, 5, 6 and Fig. 7.

BERT works with fixed-length strings. Therefore, we will use a simple strategy to choose the maximum length. Let us store the token length of each request and then perform the average and choose the best value to avoid making the embedding array sparse and not risk losing much information from larger requests. In the case of the Log-Security dataset, the maximum length was 400. It is worth mentioning that BERT can only receive a sequence of a maximum of 512 tokens.

4   Experiments

LogBERT-BiLSTM was evaluated on four datasets and used the AdamW optimizer with the learning rate at $2e-5$ and the batch size at 16 and 5 epochs. Table 2 showed the data after running the models on each dataset and was developed in Pytorch at GoogleColab, using Tesla T4 GPU with 16 GB. The models that served as baseline comparison are:

---

[1] Regex is the abbreviation of the English *Regular Expressions*, for regular expressions.

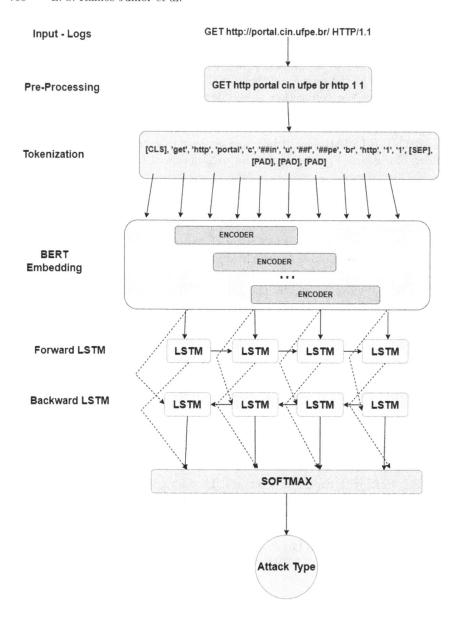

Fig. 1. Architecture of the LogBERT-BiLSTM proposal. The input in the model is the HTTP requests and then a treatment of the input data by making it lowercase and removing special characters. The *BertTokenizer* realizes the tokenization process separating the words into subwords. In this step, we add tokens as *[CLS]*, *[PAD]* and *[SEP]*, more details in the Sect. 3.2. In the BERT Embedding step, after receiving a sequence of 512 tokens, we generate the representation of the sequence. The next step adds a BiLSTM network consisting of two LSTMs: one receiving input in a forward direction and the other reverse. Finally, after processing the information and extracting the context, the model labels whether the HTTP request is an attack or not.

```
GET   /sell-media-search/?keyword=%22%3E%3Cscript%3Ealert
      %281337%29%3C%2Fscript%3E HTTP/1.1\r\n
Host: sismil.7rm.eb.mil.br\r\n
User-Agent: Mozilla/5.0 (Windows NT 10.0; Win64; x64)
...
```

Fig. 2. HTTP request for an XSS attack attempt on a provider's web server.

```
get sell media search keyword 22 3e 3cscript 3ealert 281337
    29 3c 2fscript 3e http 1 1 r n
host sismil 7rm eb mil br r n
user agent mozilla 5 0 windows nt 10 0 win64 x64 r n
...
```

Fig. 3. Request HTTP after initial handling of stripping special characters and making it lowercase.

```
['get', 'sell', 'media', 'search', 'key','##word', '22', '3',
    '##e', '3', '##cs', '##cript','3','##e', 'http', '1',
    '1', ...]
```

Fig. 4. BERT to avoid the cases of the unknown token [UNK], uses the algorithm *WordPiece* that splits a word into several subwords, in order to maintain the context.

```
[101, 1243, 4582, 2394, 3403, 2501, 12565, 1659, 124, 1162,
    124, 6063, 13590, 124, 13003, 7340, 25567, 23493,
    102,...]
```

Fig. 5. The unique IDs of the words or subwords corresponding to the request in Fig. 2. Where IDs 101 and 102 indicate [CLS] and [SEP] which serve, respectively, to indicate the beginning of the sentence and to indicate the end of the sentence.

```
[101,1243, 4582, 2394, 3403, 2501, 12565, 1659, 124, 1162,
    124, 6063, 13590, 124, 102, ...,0, 0, 0, 0, 0, 0, 0, 0,
    0, 0, 0]
```

Fig. 6. For the case of log entries smaller than the maximum size provided, it is necessary to add padding [PAD] to the sentences to compose the maximum length and normally the value 0 is used.

```
[1, 1, 1, 1, 1, 1, 1, 1, 1, 1, 1, 1, 1, 1, 1, 1, 1, 1, 1, 1,
    1, 1, 1, 1, 1, 1, 1, 0, 0, 0, 0, 0, 0, 0, 0, 0..., 0]
```

Fig. 7. *Attention Mask* is a binary tensor that indicates the position of filled indices. For *BertTokenizer*, 1 indicates a value that must be met, while 0 indicates a populated value.

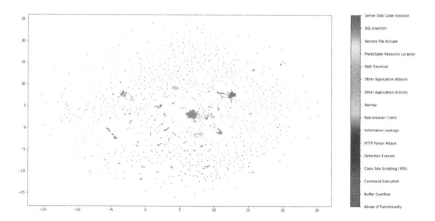

Fig. 8. Visualization of the representation space of the Log-Security dataset using *UMAP*. It is possible to verify some clusters in the center, such as *SQL_Injection, Command Execution and Buffer Overflow* attacks. For the three types of attacks, some characteristics can be highlighted: for SQL_Injection, there is a need for some keyword like *DDL/DML* in SQL request; for Command Execution, with specific commands like - *cat, run* etc. Finally, in cases of Buffer Overflow, the highlight is the size of its requests, so these types of attacks have well-defined patterns. It is also possible to notice small groups of Normal and *Other Application Attacks* classes, reflecting several requests with similar characteristics. However, it is normal that these two classes do not have any standardization.

- **Word2Vec**, which handles word embedding in the traditional way;
- **CNN** [10], without BERT and using *Fasttext*;
- **BERT**, using *BertForSequenceClassification* without another class for classification;
- **BERT-CNN**, using BERT and with a CNN class as [10]; and
- **NeuralLog** [9], model using BERT and without Log Parser approach.

4.1 Datasets

We used four datasets, three public datasets, ECML/PKDD 2007, CSIC 2010, BGL, and finally, one generated from a security asset *F5 Big-IP*. Table 1 shows the characteristics of each dataset.

ECML-PKDD 2007 was developed in a controlled competition environment, while CSIC 2010 contains data generated from traffic directed to an e-commerce Web server and BGL is from supercomputer logs, for more details of each dataset [14,15] and [13]. The choice for the BGL Dataset [13] was to show the versatility that LogBERT-BiLSTM has in being able to be used in any scenario that deals with anomalies in logs.

The dataset created in this work was extracted from security assets initially configured to filter only requests considered offensive; these requests would already be labeled based on the knowledge of equipment signatures. All Dataset

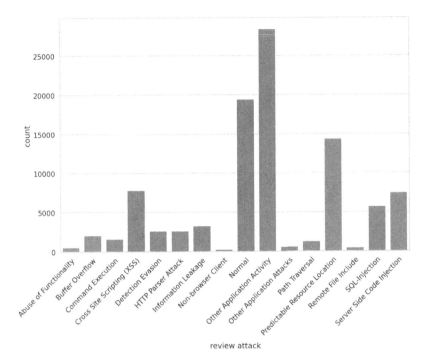

Fig. 9. Distribution of classes in the Log-Security Dataset. In terms of attack type the *Other Application Attacks* represents attacks that do not fall into the more explicit attack classifications. [1]

Table 1. Dataset characteristics

Dataset	Category	Size	Classes	Anomalies
BGL [13]	Supercomputer	4.7M	Binary	348.460
Log-Security	Request HTTP	98K	Multi	67.265
CSIC 2010 [15]	Request HTTP	97K	Binary	25.000
ECML/PKDD [14]	Request HTTP	50K	Multi	15.110

requests are destined for Internet sites hosted on a provider's internal infrastructure. Figure 9 and Fig. 8 show characteristics of the Log-Security dataset.

5 Discussion and Results

To assess the competitive performance of LogBERT-BiLSTM, we compared it with other approaches. In addition, we analyze the execution time in the inference and the performance of each model. We use the metrics: **Precision, Recall, F1-Score and Accuracy**.

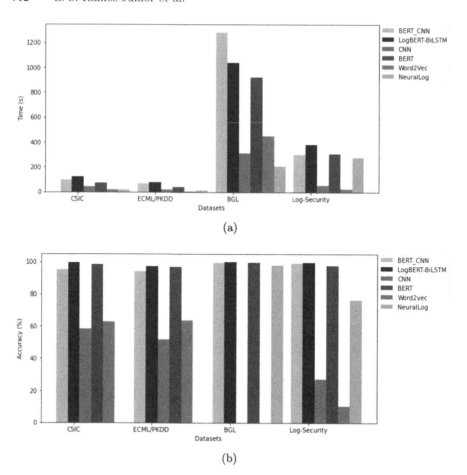

Fig. 10. (a) Shows the runtime in the prediction of each model. The LogBERT-BiLSTM was not the longest in execution time for the BGL dataset, in the others it had the longest run time. (b) Graph shows the performance of the models based on the accuracy metric. It is possible to visualize the efficiency of models that use BERT in their architecture, except for NeuralLog, which still showed difficulty.

In this section, we will discuss the results and the performances of the tried models compared to the one proposed in this article, LogBERT-BiLSTM.

5.1   Evaluating the Performance of Models

The shape of the embedding can explain the superiority that LogBERT-BiLSTM has over Word2Vec. Because the traditional method deals with word-based context forms, while LogBERT-BiLSTM uses BERT. As for the CNN model scenario, our approach is still ahead, as the embedding created by them *logkey2vec* was developed in Word2Vec. Moreover, they implemented a log parser to find the constant parts in the logs.

Table 2. Performance comparison between models and datasets

Dataset	Model	Recall (%)	Precision (%)	F1-score (%)	Accuracy (%)
CSIC 2010 [15]	Word2Vec	63	62	62	62.66
	BERT	98	97	98	98.4
	BERT-CNN	95	95	95	95.06
	Le et al. [9]	–	–	–	–
	Lu et al. [10]	58	58	58	58.34
	Ito et al. [6]	n/a	n/a	n/a	98.8
	Kuang et al. [8]	n/a	96.92	95.57	96.44
	LogBERT-BiLSTM (Ours)	**100**	**100**	**100**	**99.50**
ECML/PKDD 2007 [14]	Word2Vec	63	50	56	63.48
	BERT	96	96	96	96.83
	BERT-CNN	94	94	94	94.23
	Le et al. [9]	–	–	–	–
	Lu et al. [10]	52	52	52	51.64
	LogBERT-BiLSTM (Ours)	**96**	**97**	**97**	**97.26**
BGL [13]	Word2Vec	–	–	–	–
	BERT	100	99	99	99.61
	BERT-CNN	100	99	99	99.58
	Le et al. [9]	98	98	98	98.7
	Lu et al. [10]	–	–	–	–
	Meng et al. [11]	94	97	96	n/a
	Guo et al. [5]	92.32	89.40	90.83	n/a
	LogBERT-BiLSTM (Ours)	**100**	**100**	**100**	**99.98**
Log-Security	Word2Vec	10	18	10	10.18
	BERT	98	97	97	97.43
	BERT-CNN	99	99	99	99.23
	Le et al. [9]	76	76	76	76.24
	Lu et al. [10]	27	27	27	26.80
	LogBERT-BiLSTM (Ours)	**99**	**100**	**99**	**99.51**

"–" The model failed to reproduce results with the original project settings.
"n/a" There was no result in the original article.

In the case of NeuralLog, two factors affect its performance for the HTTP request scenario. The first is the action of excluding the numerical data from the requests and the other is that in its implementation there is the creation of a window composed of 20 log messages to build log sequences, similar to [11]. Another point that can be highlighted is the difficulty that NeuralLog had in the CSIC and ECML datasets. However, it achieved great results in a similar scenario of class imbalance in the BGL dataset.

BERT and BERT-CNN models use the same settings and hyperparameter values as LogBERT-BiLSTM. The difference is that BERT uses the standard BertForSequenceClassification class, which has only one dense layer with dropout in the output, and BERT-CNN uses a convolutional network configuration used in [10].

Regarding the objective of Fig. 10a, which shows the execution time in the prediction stage, the model with the longest time in most data sets was the LogBERT-BiLSTM. This delay occurs due to the use of the BiLSTM network, which, as it is a bidirectional structure, allows capturing past and future information, giving the network greater learning power. Despite this disadvantage in terms of time, Fig. 10b and Table 2 show that it was superior to all other models tested and in the literature. Another point of Fig. 10a is the extended time in the BGL dataset due to its 4.7 million logs.

6   Conclusion and Future Work

Log anomaly detection is essential to protect computer systems from malicious attacks. This paper proposes the LogBERT-BiLSTM, a new supervised model for detecting attacks on HTTP requests based on BERT and BiLSTM, which can detect log anomalies in different environments. For training, LogBERT-BiLSTM considers all HTTP request information as input without the need for *Log Parser* and with the exclusion of only special characters. After training, LogBERT-BiLSTM can detect attacks on HTTP requests efficiently. Moreover, based on experimental results on four log datasets and compared to other literature models, LogBERT-BiLSTM outperformed traditional and state-of-the-art approaches to detect HTTP request attacks and log anomalies.

Future works should consider evaluating the proposed method in other datasets and apply unsupervised machine learning techniques. Finally, there is the possibility of predicting zero-day attacks based on suspicious requests by combining the proposed approach, the number of requests in a short time, geographical IP location, and other contextual information.

References

1. Assigning attack signatures to security policies, February 2022. https://techdocs. f5.com/kb/en-us/products/big-ip_asm/manuals/product/asm-bot-and-attack-signatures-13-0-0/1.html
2. Althubiti, S., Yuan, X., Esterline, A.: Analyzing http requests for web intrusion detection, October 2017
3. Chen, Z., Liu, J., Gu, W., Su, Y., Lyu, M.R.: Experience report: deep learning-based system log analysis for anomaly detection. CoRR abs/2107.05908 (2021). https://arxiv.org/abs/2107.05908
4. Du, M., Li, F., Zheng, G., Srikumar, V.: DeepLog: anomaly detection and diagnosis from system logs through deep learning, pp. 1285–1298 (2017). https://doi.org/10. 1145/3133956.3134015
5. Guo, H., Yuan, S., Wu, X.: LogBERT: log anomaly detection via BERT. In: 2021 International Joint Conference on Neural Networks (IJCNN), pp. 1–8 (2021). https://doi.org/10.1109/IJCNN52387.2021.9534113
6. Ito, M., Iyatomi, H.: Web application firewall using character-level convolutional neural network, pp. 103–106 (2018). https://doi.org/10.1109/CSPA.2018.8368694
7. Kim, Y.: Convolutional neural networks for sentence classification. CoRR abs/1408.5882 (2014). http://arxiv.org/abs/1408.5882
8. Kuang, X., et al.: DeepWAF: detecting web attacks based on CNN and LSTM models (2019). https://doi.org/10.1007/978-3-030-37352-8_11

9. Le, V., Zhang, H.: Log-based anomaly detection without log parsing. CoRR abs/2108.01955 (2021). https://arxiv.org/abs/2108.01955

10. Lu, S., Wei, X., Li, Y., Wang, L.: Detecting anomaly in big data system logs using convolutional neural network (2018). https://doi.org/10.1109/DASC/PiCom/DataCom/CyberSciTec.2018.00037

11. Meng, W., et al.: LogAnomaly: unsupervised detection of sequential and quantitative anomalies in unstructured logs. In: IJCAI (2019)

12. Odumuyiwa, V., Chibueze, A.: Automatic detection of http injection attacks using convolutional neural network and deep neural network. J. Cyber Secur. Mobil. **9**, 489–514 (2020)

13. Oliner, A., Stearley, J.: What supercomputers say: a study of five system logs (2007). https://doi.org/10.1109/DSN.2007.103

14. Raïssi, C., Brissaud, J., Dray, G., Poncelet, P., Roche, M., Teisseire, M.: Web analyzing traffic challenge: description and results (2007)

15. Torrano-Gimenez, C., Perez-Villegas, A., Alvarez, G.: A self-learning anomaly-based web application firewall, vol. 63, pp. 85–92, January 2009. https://doi.org/10.1007/978-3-642-04091-7_11

16. Vaswani, A., et al.: Attention is all you need. CoRR abs/1706.03762 (2017). http://arxiv.org/abs/1706.03762

17. Xuan, C., Dinh, H., Victor, T.: Malicious url detection based on machine learning. Int. J. Adv. Comput. Sci. Appl. (2020). https://doi.org/10.14569/IJACSA.2020.0110119

18. Yu, L., et al.: Detecting malicious web requests using an enhanced textCNN (2020). https://doi.org/10.1109/COMPSAC48688.2020.0-167

ML-FORMER: Forecasting by Neighborhood and Long-Range Dependencies

Zengxiang Ke, Yangguang Cui, Liying Li, and Tongquan Wei[⊠]

School of Computer Science and Technology, East China Normal University,
Shanghai, China
tqwei@cs.ecnu.edu.cn

Abstract. As sensors are deployed widely, collected data present features of large quantity and high dimensionality, which pose enormous challenges to multivariate long sequence time-series forecasting (MLTF). Existing methods for MLTF tasks can not efficiently capture neighborhood and long-range dependencies, resulting in low prediction accuracy. In this paper, we propose a novel multivariate long sequence time-series method, called ML-Former, that captures both neighborhood and long-range dependencies to enhance the prediction capacity. Specifically, ML-Former first conducts a time-series embedding that integrates neighborhood dependencies, positions, and timestamps. Then, it captures neighborhood and long-range dependencies by using a time-series encoder-decoder. Furthermore, an innovative loss function is designed to improve the convergence of ML-Former. Experimental results on three real-world datasets show that ML-Former reduces forecasting error by up to 35.4% compared with benchmarking methods.

Keywords: Multivariate long sequence time-series forecasting · Hidden Markov model · Neural networks

1 Introduction

With the rapid development of Internet of things, a huge number of sensors has been deployed in various applications such as environment monitoring, traffic control, and manufacturing factories [2]. In general, sensor data have inherent characteristics of high-dimensionality, and exhibit dynamic dependencies among historical time series [1]. Thus, it is promising to mine valuable information from these time series. For instance, by mining relevant sensor time series, a power plant can prevent impending abnormalities of production machinery and eliminate faults in time [4]. In this paper, we focus on forecasting multivariate long sequence time series.

This paper was partially supported by Shanghai Municipal Science and Technology Major Project (2021SHZDZX), and Shanghai Trusted Industry Internet Software Collaborative Innovation Center.

E. Pimenidis et al. (Eds.): ICANN 2022, LNCS 13531, pp. 716–727, 2022.
https://doi.org/10.1007/978-3-031-15934-3_59

In the recent past, many works have focused on utilizing a substantial amount of historical multivariate time-series data to make long-term sequence predictions, that is, multivariate long sequence time-series forecasting (MLTF) [6,17]. An effective solution to the tricky MLTF tasks is capturing long-range dependencies from long sequence time series. For instance, Zhou et al. [17] first proposed a Transformer-based model, called Informer, that uses a ProbSparse self-attention mechanisms to capture long-range dependencies in long sequence time series. Based on Informer, Guo et al. [4] developed a stacked-Informer network and used it to predict electrical line trip faults. Jacek et al. [6] further designed an Informer-based model that adopts a sparse self-attention mechanisms to obtain dependencies information. However, all the above methods rely on self-attention mechanisms, resulting in a high GPU memory footprint and making these methods unaffordable in real-world applications. In addition, self-attention mechanisms-based methods fail to efficiently capture neighborhood dependencies from long sequence time series, they show excellent performance in capturing long-range dependencies, though.

We consider that it is beneficial to improve prediction accuracy by capturing neighborhood dependencies efficiently. HMM [3] is a statistical Markov model that generates random sequences by a Markov process following the state transition probability. MLTF tasks generates a random sequence and can essentially be regarded as the hidden Markov model (HMM) [3]. Based on the hidden Markov model (HMM), capturing neighborhood dependencies can improve prediction accuracy. For example, in the task of predicting the temperature of next week, the temperature of the current week has more impact than that of the previous week. Therefore, it is valuable to solve MLTF tasks by extracting neighborhood dependencies from long sequence time series.

To this end, we propose a novel model to accurately predict multivariate long sequence time-series via capturing neighborhood and long-range dependencies efficiently, called ML-Former. The remarkable contributions of this paper can be summarized as follows.

- We develop a time-series embedding to capture neighborhood dependencies and fuse neighborhood dependencies, positions, and timestamps.
- We design a time-series encoder-decoder of low GPU memory footprint to capture neighborhood and long-range dependencies from long sequence time series.
- We propose a long sequence time-series loss function with the decay mechanism, which can promote convergence during training of MLTF tasks.
- Experiments on three real-world datasets demonstrate that our proposed ML-Former achieves precision improvement by up to 35.4% compared with all benchmarking methods.

2   Problem Formulation and Overview of the Proposed Model

The focus of this paper is to improve prediction accuracy on MLTF tasks. In this section, we first formulate the studied problem and then present our model.

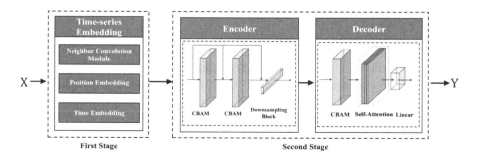

Fig. 1. The architecture of ML-Former. ML-Former is trained by our long sequence time series loss function. In the self-attention of the decoder, the orange layers are dot product operations. (Color figure online)

2.1   Problem Formulation

In this work, we aim at enhancing the prediction capacity on MLTF tasks. At time step t, a multivariate variable of dimension N is represented as $\mathbf{s}_t \in \mathbb{R}^N$ and $\mathbf{s}_t[i] \in R$ denotes the value of the i-th variable. Given a sequence of α-time-step on a multivariate variable, denoted as $\mathbf{X} = \{\mathbf{s}_{t_1}, \mathbf{s}_{t_2}, \ldots, \mathbf{s}_{t_\alpha}\}$. Our goal is to establish a mapping function $\mathbf{f}(\cdot)$ from $\mathbf{X}$ to $\mathbf{Y}$, where $\mathbf{Y} = \{\mathbf{s}_{t_{\alpha+1}}, \mathbf{s}_{t_{\alpha+2}}, \ldots, \mathbf{s}_{t_{\alpha+\beta}}\}$ is a β-time-step sequence of future predicted values.

2.2   Overview of the Proposed Method

The overview of our method is shown in Fig. 1. Our scheme takes a sequence of historical α time-step data X as inputs and outputs a sequence β-time-step of future values Y. There are two key components in our method that a time series embedding and a time series encoder-decoder. Specifically, ML-Former takes a two-stage workflow to solve MLTF tasks. In the first stage, we design a time-series embedding that contains the neighbor convolution module (NCM), the position embedding, and the time embedding. NCM is designed to capture neighborhood dependencies. Furthermore, we propose NCM, the position embedding, and the time embedding to solve the heterogeneities of timestamps, positions, and values.

In the second stage, we develop a time-series encoder-decoder to precisely capture neighborhood and long-range dependencies, which can be successfully addressed by Convolutional Block Attention Modules (CBAMs) and self-attention mechanisms. Besides, we reduce GPU memory footprint by employing CBAMs. Finally, we propose the long sequence time series loss function with the decay mechanism to help the convergence of ML-Former training.

3   Methodology

In this section, we first represent a time-series embedding, which captures neighborhood dependencies and fuses information of data. Then, we describe a time-series encoder-decoder to capture neighborhood and long-range dependencies. Finally, we show a long sequence time-series loss function to facilitate the convergence of ML-Former training.

3.1   Time-Series Embedding

The time-series embedding aims at capturing neighborhood dependencies from long sequence time series and fusing sensor data, sensor data generation timestamps, and sensors positions. The structure of time-series embedding is shown in Fig. 1. Specifically, the time-series embedding is composed of the neighbor convolution module (NCM), the position embedding, and the time embedding. The above three submodules are calculated in parallel, that is,

$$\mathbf{V} = Time(\mathbf{T}) + Position(\mathbf{X}) + NCM(\mathbf{X}), \tag{1}$$

where $\mathbf{X}$ denotes sensor data, $\mathbf{T}$ is the time of data generation, $Time(\mathbf{T})$ represents the time embedding, $Position(\mathbf{X})$ indicates the position embedding, and $NCM(\mathbf{X})$ means the neighbor convolution module. It is observed in [13] that there are local spatial-temporal correlations in multivariate time series. As a result, data generation timestamps and sensors positions play a key role in time series forecasting. In this context, the heterogeneity of time information, location information, and sensor data are a tricky challenge to discover valuable information [9]. To deal with these problems, we employ NCM, the position embedding, and the time embedding to solve the information heterogeneity. Specifically, the time embedding is utilized to covert time information into vectors. We decompose time into the vector form of $[year, month, day, hour, minute, second]$ and calculate the vector by adopting a one-dimensional convolutional network. In the position embedding, we adopt sine wave position encoding [15] to assign the position information for time series.

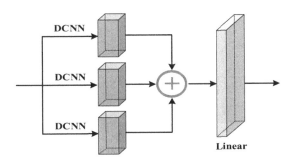

Fig. 2. Neighbor convolution module

It is noteworthy that the core of our proposed time-series embedding is NCM. In this work, we borrow the idea of inception [12,14] to design NCM. NCM provides a simple and effective tool to extract neighborhood dependencies within time series by using the excellent information extraction ability of convolutional neural networks (CNNs). Our proposed NCM consists of three one-dimensional convolutional layers and one linear layer, as shown in Fig. 2. NCM uses three one-dimensional dilated convolutional neural network (DCNN) with different convolutional kernel sizes to broaden the receptive field and reduce computational complexity. The results of the three DCNN are weighted average to facilitate the gradient decreases. Formally, the feature vectors from three DCNN are integrated using the fully connected layer, that is,

$$\mathbf{X}' = \frac{1}{3}(Conv^1(\mathbf{X}) + Conv^2(\mathbf{X}) + Conv^3(\mathbf{X})), \tag{2}$$

$$\mathbf{X}'' = Linear(\mathbf{X}'), \tag{3}$$

where $\mathbf{X}$ denotes sensor data.

3.2   Time-Series Encoder-Decoder

This subsection elaborates on the proposed time-series encoder-decoder. The input of the time-series encoder-decoder is the feature vector $\mathbf{V}$ obtained from the time series embedding. The time-series encoder-decoder extracts neighborhood and long-range dependencies. As shown in Fig. 1, the time-series encoder-decoder contains two parts: encoder and decoder. The encoder consists of Convolutional Block Attention Modules (CBAMs) and a downsampling block. The decoder is composed of a CBAM, a self-attention mechanism, and a linear layer.

Convolutional Block Attention Module: Existing methods [7] cannot capture neighborhood dependencies and long-range dependencies well. Therefore, existing methods are not well suited for MLTF tasks. Although self-attention mechanisms have a powerful ability of [15] extracting features, it shows weak performance in capturing neighborhood dependencies and taking up huge GPU memory. To solve the problem of huge GPU memory footprint [16] and capture neighborhood dependencies, we innovatively improve CBAMs. The architecture of CBAM is shown in Fig. 3.

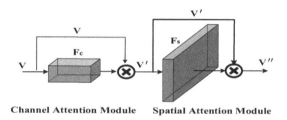

Channel Attention Module   Spatial Attention Module

Fig. 3. Convolutional block attention module

CBAM is an attention mechanism module that combines the channel attention module and the spatial attention module [16]. The input is a feature vector $V \in \mathbb{R}^{T \times D}$ where T represents the input length of time series and D denotes the dimension of time-series encoder-decoder. CBAM infers attention vectors along the channel attention module $\mathbf{G_c}$ and the spatial attention module $\mathbf{G_s}$ in turn. The process of CBAM can be given as

$$\mathbf{V'} = \mathbf{G_c}(\mathbf{V}) \otimes \mathbf{V}, \tag{4}$$

$$\mathbf{V_{CBAM}} = \mathbf{G_s}(\mathbf{V'}) \otimes \mathbf{V'}, \tag{5}$$

In the channel attention module, the input is the feature vector $\mathbf{V}$, and the output is the channel attention vector $\mathbf{G_c} \in \mathbb{R}^{1 \times D}$. First, the channel attention module applies global max pooling $\mathbf{G_{max}}$ and global average pooling $\mathbf{G_{avg}}$ to aggregate the information of feature vectors. Then, the feature vector is calculated and summed by the shared multilayer perceptron MLP. Finally, we employ the rectified linear unit [11] $ReLU$ instead of the sigmoid activation function to accelerate the convergence of the model. The channel attention module is defined as follows

$$\mathbf{G_c}(\mathbf{V}) = ReLU\left(MLP\left(\mathbf{G_{avg}}\left(\mathbf{V}\right)\right) + MLP\left(\mathbf{G_{max}}\left(\mathbf{V}\right)\right)\right). \tag{6}$$

In the spatial attention module, the input is the channel attention vector $\mathbf{V'}$ and the output is the spatial attention vector $\mathbf{G_s} \in \mathbb{R}^{T \times 1}$. First, we employ global max pooling $\mathbf{G_{max}}$ and global average pooling $\mathbf{G_{avg}}$ remove redundant information and concatenate them. To adapt MLTF tasks, we then design a one-dimensional convolutional layer to convert the feature vector into the spatial attention vector. The process of the spatial attention module can be summarized as

$$\mathbf{G_s}(\mathbf{V'}) = ReLU(\mathbf{G^k}([\mathbf{G_{avg}}(\mathbf{V'}) \; ; \; \mathbf{G_{max}}(\mathbf{V'})])), \tag{7}$$

where $\mathbf{G^k}$ denotes a one-dimensional convolutional layer with k kernel, and the symbol ";" means concatenation operation.

Downsampling Block: We design a downsampling block to extract features, remove redundant features and reduce memory footprint, as shown in Fig. 4. The downsampling block consists of a residual block [5], one batch normalization, and one max-pooling layer. First, we design a residual block to extract

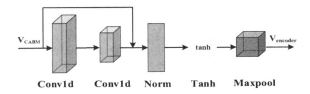

Fig. 4. Downsampling block

high-level features and achieve feature reuse. Second, we employ batch normalization $Norm$ to enhance the generalization ability of the model and apply the $Tanh$ activation function. Finally, the max-pooling layer is employed to remove redundant features and reduce the memory footprint. The computation process of the downsampling block can be given as

$$\mathbf{V_{down}} = Norm\left(\mathbf{V_{CBAM}} + Conv\left(Conv\left(\mathbf{V_{CBAM}}\right)\right)\right), \tag{8}$$

$$\mathbf{V_{encoder}} = MaxPool\left(Tanh(\mathbf{V_{down}})\right). \tag{9}$$

Decoder: The decoder aims to capture the long-range dependencies and generate a sequence of future predicted values. Given a feature vector $\mathbf{V_{encoder}}$ as the input, the decoder consists of a CBAM, a self-attention mechanism, and a linear layer. The architecture of the decoder is shown in Fig. 1. First, we adopt the CBAM to expand the receptive field and fuse features, as described in the previous Subsect. 3.2. Then, although adopting the time-series embedding module and CBAMs expands the receptive field [10], it still shows weak performance in capturing long-range dependencies. In this context, we design a self-attention mechanism to capture long-range dependencies [17]. Finally, the feature vector is mapped to the required dimension by the linear layer. In this way, we obtain the sequence of future predicted values.

3.3 Long Sequence Time-Series Loss Function

In this paper, we design an innovative and effective loss function to help the convergence of ML-Former training. Since MLTF tasks and HMM both can generate a random sequence of states following the state transition probability [3], we safely regard MLTF tasks as the hidden Markov model. According to HMM, it is more difficult to predict the later time series on MLTF tasks. Traditionally, the L1 loss function (L1) and MSE loss function (L2) are widely used in existing methods [4,17] to train models for MLTF tasks. However, in L1 and L2, the same weights are assigned to predicted time series of different sequences. Obviously, L1 and L2 do not follow the state transition probability and are not well suited for MLTF tasks.

Inspired by the focal loss [8], we utilize the characteristics of MLTF tasks and HMM to design a unique loss function, called long sequence time series loss function (LSTLF). Then, we introduce the core idea of our LSTLF. In MLTF tasks considered, the loss function is designed to characterize the difference between the sequence of future predicted values $\mathbf{Y}$ and the sequence of future values $\mathbf{Y}'$. First, we split $\mathbf{Y}$ and $\mathbf{Y}'$ into τ segments to characterize the order of the time series, namely $\mathbf{Y} = \{\mathbf{Y_1}, \mathbf{Y_2}, \ldots, \mathbf{Y_i}, \ldots, \mathbf{Y_\tau} \mid i \in [0, \tau]\}$ and $\mathbf{Y}' = \{\mathbf{Y'_1}, \mathbf{Y'_2}, \ldots, \mathbf{Y'_i}, \ldots \mathbf{Y'_\tau} \mid i \in [0, \tau]\}$. We calculate L1 and L2 for each segment in LSTLF. Furthermore, we add a weight coefficient η to avoid excessive smoothing problems and reduce the influence of extreme points with large slopes. In this context, we design a weighted factor η for L1 and a weighted factor $1 - \eta$ for L2, where hyperparameter $\eta \in [0, 1]$ holds. We design the decay mechanism that assigns weights $(\frac{\tau - i}{\tau})^2$ for each segment in the order i of each segment to focus on the former time series. In a nutshell, our designed LSTLF can be defined as

$$\mathcal{L} = \frac{3}{\tau} \sum_{i=0}^{\tau-1} \left(\frac{\tau - i}{\tau} \right)^2 \left[\eta |\mathbf{Y_i} - \mathbf{Y'_i}| + (1 - \eta) \left(\mathbf{Y_i} - \mathbf{Y'_i} \right)^2 \right]. \qquad (10)$$

4 Evaluation

We first describe experimental settings and then evaluate our ML-Former in terms of Mean Absolute Error (MAE), Mean Squared Error (MSE), and GPU memory footprint.

4.1 Experimental Settings

Datasets: We conduct experiments on three public benchmark datasets. The datasets can be outlined as follows.

- ETTm1 (Electricity Transformer Temperature) [17]: The ETTm1 dataset is a collection of data collected from 7 electricity transformers every 15 min.
- ECL (Electricity Consuming Load) [17]: This dataset is a collection of the hourly power consumption of 321 clients.
- Traffic [7]: The traffic dataset is a collection of hourly traffic flows at 862 locations on California roads.

Baselines: To evaluate the accuracy of our method, we compare ML-Former with four baseline methods. Informer [17] is a transformer-based method employs the ProbSparse Self-attention mechanism. Self-attention [15] is a transformer-based method utilizes self-attention mechanisms. Query-Selector [6] is an informer-based model adopts sparse attention mechanisms. LSTNet [7] is a deep neural network combines on CNNs and RNNs.

Table 1. Comparison of multivariate long sequence time-series forecasting results

Methods	Metrics	ETTm1					ECL					Traffic				
		24	48	168	336	720	24	48	168	336	720	24	48	168	336	720
ML-Former	MSE	**0.2438**	**0.3307**	**0.4273**	**0.5261**	**0.6153**	**0.2295**	**0.2306**	**0.2567**	**0.2829**	**0.2901**	**0.5973**	**0.6101**	**0.6597**	**0.6726**	**0.6647**
	MAE	**0.3190**	**0.3712**	**0.4372**	**0.5131**	**0.5490**	**0.3329**	**0.3339**	**0.3548**	**0.3675**	**0.3686**	**0.3164**	**0.3256**	**0.3513**	**0.3523**	**0.3489**
Informer	MSE	0.3912	0.4753	0.8431	0.9623	0.8809	0.2614	0.2929	0.3373	0.3307	0.5754	0.6240	0.6498	0.8407	1.1158	1.4616
	MAE	0.4053	0.4765	0.6926	0.7589	0.7072	0.3637	0.3805	0.4169	0.4103	0.5426	0.3490	0.3690	0.4512	0.5914	0.7823
Self-attention	MSE	0.4132	0.4442	0.7228	0.8356	0.8923	0.2387	0.2658	0.2812	0.2863	0.3079	0.6215	0.6301	0.6780	0.6999	0.7568
	MAE	0.4275	0.4370	0.6436	0.7048	0.7299	0.3485	0.3625	0.3769	0.3763	0.3877	0.3459	0.3491	0.3761	0.3780	0.4104
Query-Selector	MSE	0.3780	0.4932	0.7534	0.8145	1.0312	0.2616	0.2717	0.3799	0.3921	0.3117	0.6445	0.7702	0.7988	0.7122	0.7535
	MAE	0.3879	0.4809	0.6503	0.6691	0.8001	0.3621	0.3680	0.4535	0.4657	0.3952	0.3830	0.4769	0.4926	0.4198	0.4430
LSTNet	MSE	1.3572	1.4461	1.7308	3.5181	2.1708	0.3809	0.4050	0.4323	0.4500	0.4619	1.3343	2.4428	2.2968	2.6894	6.0485
	MAE	0.9133	0.9366	1.0494	1.2408	1.2339	0.4274	0.4408	0.4546	0.4648	0.4754	0.8463	0.9383	0.9780	1.0138	1.3037

Hyper-parameter Tuning: We set five different prediction lengths [17], that is, $24, 48, 168, 336, 720$ for the three datasets. We adopt the Adam optimizer to train ML-Former in 8 epochs. The learning rate starts from $1e^{-4}$, decaying five times smaller every two epochs. All experiments are repeated three times, and the random seed is fixed during the training process. All models are trained and tested on a single Nvidia RTX 2080Ti GPU.

Metrics: We apply two common performance metrics, that is, Mean Absolute Error (MAE) and Mean Squared Error (MSE). For MSE and MSE, lower values are better.

4.2 Main Results

Table 1 depicts the accuracy achieved by our proposed method and baseline methods on three datasets. We use bold text to highlight the best results. From Table 1, we summarize that:

First, compared with baseline methods, our proposed method ML-Former achieves the best accuracy on all prediction lengths. Furthermore, the result of ML-Former rises smoothly and slowly within the growing prediction length. This indicates that our ML-Former has the more outstanding prediction capacity on MLTF tasks.

Second, compared with self-attention mechanisms-based methods, namely Informer, Self-attention, and Query-Selector, our ML-Former model can achieve accuracy improvements of up to 45.12%, 37.03%, and 35.4% respectively. The reason why our model can obtain better accuracy than self-attention mechanisms-based methods is that ML-Former can capture neighborhood dependencies by the time series embedding and CBAMs. Furthermore, our long sequence time series lose function can improve the prediction accuracy.

Third, compared with the CNN-based model LSTNet, our proposed model ML-Former considerably improves the performance of prediction across all datasets. As the prediction length increases, the performance of ML-Former improves more significantly than LSTNet. That is because ML-Former can extract long-range dependencies by self-attention mechanisms.

Table 2. Comparison of different loss functions

Methods	Metrics	336			720		
		L1	L2	Our	L1	L2	Our
ML-Former	MSE	0.5632	0.6011	**0.5261**	0.8247	0.7629	**0.6153**
	MAE	0.5430	0.5854	**0.5131**	0.6701	0.6440	**0.5490**
Self-attention	MSE	0.8108	0.8356	**0.7230**	0.8294	0.8923	**0.8182**
	MAE	0.6888	0.7048	**0.6369**	0.7063	0.7299	**0.6979**
Informer	MSE	0.7896	0.9623	**0.6850**	0.9878	0.8809	**0.8344**
	MAE	0.6682	0.7589	**0.6046**	0.7758	0.7072	**0.6941**
Query-Selector	MSE	0.7765	0.8145	**0.7415**	0.9717	1.0312	**0.8737**
	MAE	0.6724	0.6691	**0.6539**	0.7810	0.8001	**0.7264**

4.3 Study of the Long Sequence Time-Series Loss Function

Taking the ETTm1 dataset (at 336 and 720) as an example, we compare our proposed long sequence time-series loss function (LSTLF) with the L1 loss function (L1) and the MSE loss function (L2) to verify the effectiveness and generalization of our LSTLF. To make a fair comparison, we keep all hyperparameters the same in each example. Table 2 describes the accuracy achieved by our proposed LSTLF and benchmarking loss functions on the ETTm1 dataset (at 336 and 720). Compared with L1 and L2, our proposed LSTLF can improve accuracy by 9.35% and 11.67% on average. The reason is that our designed decay mechanism for LSTLF is suitable for the characteristics of MLTF tasks.

4.4 Ablation Study

In ablation study, to verify the effectiveness of the essential components, we design three variants of ML-Former and compare three variants with ML-Former on the ETTm1 dataset. The three variants can be described as follows.

- w/o EMB: We replace the time-series embedding with a linear layer.
- w/o CBAM: We replace CBAMs with self-attention mechanisms.
- w/o LSTLF: We replace the long sequence time-series loss function (LSTLF) with the L1 loss function.

Figure 5 plots the accuracy achieved by our ML-Former and three variants. Compared with w/o EMB, our ML-Former can achieve accuracy improvements of up to 66.34%. That phenomenon proves that the time-series embedding is effective to improve prediction accuracy by capturing neighborhood dependencies. Furthermore, ML-Former can improve accuracy by using the fused data information obtained in the time-series embedding. Compared with w/o CBAM, our ML-Former can achieve accuracy improvements of up to 54.11%. The reason for better accuracy is ML-Former can capture neighborhood dependencies by using CBAMs. Compared with w/o LSTLF, our ML-Former can improve accuracy up to 25.39%. Since the decay mechanism of LSTLF is suited for MLTF tasks, our LSTLF performs well in improving the prediction accuracy.

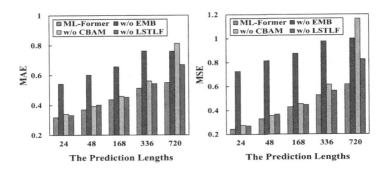

Fig. 5. Ablation study on three components

4.5 Study of GPU Memory Footprint

We conduct experiments to evaluate the GPU memory footprint during training. The training parameters are set as follows: the batch size is 16, the input length is 336, and the output length is 720. Table 3 compares the GPU memory footprint of our ML-Former and benchmarking methods on the ECL dataset (at 720). Clearly, the GPU memory footprint of our method is significantly lower than that of baselines methods. As observed, the GPU memory footprint of our ML-Former is 52.12%, 46.85%, 49.81%, and 33.16% less than that of Self-attention, Informer, Query-Selector, and LSTNet, respectively. In addition, ML-Former can obtain better accuracy compared to benchmarking methods. The reason is that ML-Former has few layers, and employs CBAMs with a low memory footprint. However, self-attention mechanisms-based methods have a high GPU memory footprint. Besides, since LSTNet has numerous layers, it demands a high GPU memory footprint.

Table 3. Comparison of GPU memory footprint

Methods	MSE	MAE	GPU memory
ML-Former	**0.2498**	**0.3681**	**4187** MB
Self-attention	0.3284	0.4021	8680 MB
Informer	0.5754	0.5426	7878 MB
Query-Selector	0.3265	0.4093	8343 MB
LSTNet	0.4619	0.4754	6265 MB

5 Conclusion

In this paper, we study the multivariate long sequence time-series forecasting problem and propose a novel ML-Former to efficiently capture neighborhood and long-range dependencies. Specifically, to capture the neighborhood and long-range dependencies, we first design a time-series embedding and a time-series encoder-decoder with a low GPU memory footprint. Then, we carefully design a long sequence time-series loss function to promote convergence during training of MLTF tasks. Our experiments demonstrate that our ML-Former can achieve accuracy improvements of up to 35.4% as compared to benchmarking methods.

References

1. Chicharro, D., Ledberg, A.: Framework to study dynamic dependencies in networks of interacting processes. Phys. Rev. E **86**(4), 041901 (2012)
2. Cui, Y., Cao, K., Cao, G., Qiu, M., Wei, T.: Client scheduling and resource management for efficient training in heterogeneous IoT-edge federated learning. IEEE Trans. Comput. Aided Des. Integr. Circ. Syst. **41**(8), 2407–2420 (2022)

3. Fine, S., Singer, Y., Tishby, N.: The hierarchical hidden Markov model: analysis and applications. Mach. Learn. **32**(1), 41–62 (1998)

4. Guo, L., Li, R., Jiang, B.: A data-driven long time-series electrical line trip fault prediction method using an improved stacked-informer network. Sensors **21**(13), 4466 (2021)

5. He, K., Zhang, X., Ren, S., Sun, J.: Deep residual learning for image recognition. In: Proceedings of the IEEE Conference on Computer Vision and Pattern Recognition, pp. 770–778 (2016)

6. Klimek, J., Klimek, J., Kraskiewicz, W., Topolewski, M.: Long-term series forecasting with query selector-efficient model of sparse attention. arXiv preprint arXiv:2107.08687 (2021)

7. Lai, G., Chang, W., Yang, Y., Liu, H.: Modeling long-and short-term temporal patterns with deep neural networks. In: Proceedings of the International ACM SIGIR Conference on Research Development in Information Retrieval, pp. 95–104 (2018)

8. Lin, T.Y., Goyal, P., Girshick, R., He, K., Dollar, P.: Focal loss for dense object detection. In: Proceedings of the IEEE International Conference on Computer Vision, pp. 2980–2988 (2017)

9. Lin, Z., Li, M., Zheng, Z., Cheng, Y., Yuan, C.: Self-attention ConvLSTM for spatiotemporal prediction. In: Proceedings of the AAAI Conference on Artificial Intelligence, pp. 11531–11538 (2020)

10. Luo, W., Li, Y., Urtasun, R., Zemel, R.: Understanding the effective receptive field in deep convolutional neural networks. In: Advances in Neural Information Processing Systems, pp. 4905–4913 (2016)

11. Nair, V., Hinton, E.: Rectified linear units improve restricted Boltzmann machines. In: Proceedings of the International Conference on Machine Learning (2010)

12. Oord, D., et al.: WaveNet: a generative model for raw audio. arXiv arXiv:1609.03499 (2016)

13. Song, C., Lin, Y., Guo, S., Wan, H.: Spatial-temporal synchronous graph convolutional networks: a new framework for spatial-temporal network data forecasting. In: Proceedings of the AAAI Conference on Artificial Intelligence, pp. 914–921 (2020)

14. Szegedy, C., Vanhoucke, V., Ioffe, S., Shlens, J., Wojna, Z.: Rethinking the inception architecture for computer vision. In: Proceedings of the IEEE Conference on Computer Vision and Pattern Recognition, pp. 2818–2826 (2016)

15. Vaswani, A., et al.: Attention is all you need. In: Advances in Neural Information Processing Systems, pp. 5998–6008 (2017)

16. Woo, S., Park, J., Lee, J., Kweon, S.: CBAM: convolutional block attention module. In: Proceedings of the European Conference on Computer Vision, pp. 3–19 (2018)

17. Zhou, H., et al.: Informer: beyond efficient transformer for long sequence time-series forecasting. In: Proceedings of the AAAI Conference on Artificial Intelligence, pp. 11106–11115 (2021)

Real-Time Display of Spiking Neural Activity of SIMD Hardware Using an HDMI Interface

Bernardo Vallejo-Mancero[1](✉) , Clément Nader[1], Jordi Madrenas[1] ,
and Mireya Zapata[2]

[1] Department of Electronic Engineering, Universitat Politècnica de Catalunya,
Barcelona, Spain
{bernardo.javier.vallejo,nader.clement,jordi.madrenas}@upc.edu
[2] Centro de Investigación en Mecatrónica y Sistemas Interactivos - MIST,
Universidad Tecnológica Indoamérica, Quito, Ecuador
mireyazapata@uti.edu.ec

Abstract. Spiking neural networks (SNN) are considered the third generation of artificial networks and are powerful computational models inspired by the function and structure of biological neural networks, to solve different types of problems such as pattern recognition, classification, signal processing, among others.

SNN have also aroused the interest of neuroscientists intending to obtain new knowledge about the functions of the neuronal system through the analysis of the patterns observed in spike trains. Therefore, in addition to the development of hardware solutions that allow the execution of the different neural models, it is important, to provide tools for the visualization and analysis of the spike trains and the evolution of the neural parameters of the affected neurons in real-time.

This work describes a new solution that takes the hardware emulator of evolved neural spiking system (HEENS) as the starting point, which is a bio-inspired architecture that emulates SNN using reconfigurable hardware implemented in field-programmable gate arrays (FPGAs). Reported development includes new dedicated hardware modules to interface HEENS with the high definition multimedia interface (HDMI) port, ensuring execution cycles within a time window of at least 1 ms, a period considered real-time in many neural applications.

Tests of the synthesized architecture including the new tool have been carried out, executing different types of applications. The result is a friendly and flexible tool that has successfully allowed the visualization of pulse trains and neural parameters and constitutes an alternative for the monitoring and supervision of the SNN in real-time.

Keywords: Spiking neural network · FPGA · Raster plot · Real-time HDMI display

Work supported in part under project RTI2018-099766-B-I00 by the Spanish Ministry of Science, Innovation and Universities, the State Research Agency (AEI), and the European Social Fund (ESF).

1   Introduction

In the brain, information is represented by means of spikes, which are binary space-time events represented on millisecond time scales. These spikes propagate through neural networks, forming neural representations of sensory information that are processed and involved in perception, movement, behavior, and cognition [1].

In SNNs, each neuron is a complex processing machine that deals with the reception, processing, and transmission of binary events similar to event potentials in the brain. Because of the large computational density, traditional architectures require too much power and resources. Being the most widespread solution the use of reconfigurable hardware with a high level of parallelism [2].

HEENS is a hardware architecture whose main features include scalability, programmability, quick start-up, and low latency ensuring the operation in the scale considered real-time [3,4]; however the latter suffers from a potential degradation risk due to the monitoring of spikes. In the initial version, a custom protocol developed on Ethernet is used [5], which is useful for debugging but bottlenecks are produced and may increase latency.

These problems raised the search for a suitable monitoring solution for neural architectures that work in real time, considering that data visualization and analysis are important to understand the principles of information processing in neural systems. One of the alternatives is to develop a hardware module that does not interfere with the real-time operation of the system, working in parallel with HEENS in the FPGA programmable logic and described in a hardware description language (VHDL), which helps to determine any pattern of spike activity that has been generated.

The graphical interface includes two areas, the first to view the spikes as a raster plot, and the second is dedicated to monitoring the neural parameters of four selected neurons. The raster plot is a graph traditionally used to visualize multiple spike trains [1], and is a two-dimensional representation where the horizontal axis represents time, the vertical axis corresponds to active neurons, and each individual spike is represented by a point in a coordinate plane (x, y).

In the following, Sect. 2 the HEENS architecture and its most important features are briefly described. In Sect. 3 the tool implementation is explained, including the resources used, the hardware blocks, and the developed interface. In Sect. 4 the tool usage in the execution of two examples using different neural models is introduced. Finally, in Sect. 5, the conclusions are presented.

2   HEENS Architecture

In the recent years, hardware designers started working on accelerators dedicated to the execution of spiking neural algorithms. Some of the most relevant Neuromorphic architectures are: BrainScale [6], Neurogrid [7], TrueNorth [8], SpiNNaker [9], and Loihi2 [10]. Each one differs from the others by the number of neurons or synapses they can implement, the flexibility of implementing neural models, real-time execution and the type of technology, among others.

Trying to contribute with another solution our research group developed HEENS architecture. The previous architectures are powerful but either lack flexibility or require too many resources. HEENS was developed to simplify SNN prototyping with a re-configurable architecture that is easily scalable, evolutionary, user-friendly, and with real-time operation and monitoring.

HEENS is an architecture aimed at emulating SNN in real-time. It allows the interconnection of several chips (nodes) through a ring topology (see Fig. 1). The system has been described in VHDL and it has been synthesized on several FPGAs of the Xilinx 7 and ZYNQ family.

The node architecture consists of two parts: the HEENS multiprocessor, which uses the single instruction, multiple data (SIMD) computational approach, and an address event representation - synchronous ring topology (AER-SRT) point-to-point communication module that allows multi-node communication [2]. In the ring, a master chip (MC) node controls the configuration and network execution by means of the AER bus, and communicates with a host computer by means of Ethernet. The other nodes are called neuromorphic chips (NCs). The MC can also contain a multiprocessor and operate standalone, without other NCs.

The multiprocessor consists of an array of processing elements (PE) emulating individual biological neurons. Each PE has the capability to emulate more than one neuron by means of time multiplexing without the need to consume extra computing resources, which is denoted as virtualization. This multiplexing strategy exchanges resources with an increase in execution time.

The control unit (Fig. 1) is in charge of managing the complete data flow and instructions of the PE array through a Sequencer. Instructions are read from a single instruction memory block. For its implementation, the MC is divided into two sections: the processing system (PS) and the programmable logic (PL). In the latter, the hardware architecture is implemented. The two sections are connected thanks to an advanced extensible interface (AXI4) buses.

The HEENS processing sequence to emulate the biological behavior of neurons is divided into five operation phases [12]:

- Initialization (Iph), for the identification and assignment of an identifier (chip ID) for each node that is part of the ring.
- Configuration (Cph), the configuration data is sent to each node of the ring, information that includes the neural algorithm, the synaptic and neural parameters, as well as the mapping of the synaptic connections.
- Execution (Eph), here the neural and synaptic algorithms are processed by calculating and updating the neural parameters.
- Distribution (Dph), is responsible for the transmission and propagation of the spikes through the ring, this stage is also used for network monitoring [11].
- Evolution (EvPh), phase that allows to modify the topology, allowing the creation or elimination of synaptic connections and/or full neurons.

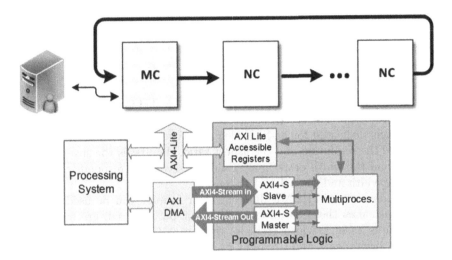

Fig. 1. HEENS architecture with one master chip (MC) and n neuromorphic chips (NCs) connected as a ring.

3   Real-Time Display Implementation

Several commercial and free to use applications for raster plot visualization are currently available, important to mention are Matlab [14] with its set of libraries for graphic work and analysis data and Neuroexplorer [15] with a monitoring and analysis interface that includes its own data acquisition system. These and other tools are popular but they require the development of an additional communication interface to communicate with HEENS.

Considering the need to create the interface, a solution was developed that allows direct visualization using the HDMI port and a monitor without the need to use any additional software tool. The HDMI Raster plot is a hardware block developed for the visualization of spikes and neural parameters without affecting the execution and distribution phases of the architecture, avoiding the introduction of unnecessary delays. The display was implemented in the PL area, taking advantage of the HDMI port that several ZYNQ family development boards include.

Different types of software and hardware tools are used to develop and implement the architecture. Python is used to develop the user interface and the generation of the configuration file, the Xilinx software development kit (SDK) is used in the programming of the PS on the MC, the MC processor is programmed in C++ language, and finally VHDL is used for the architecture description of the programmable logic.

The Hardware used for the implementation of the MC are FPGAS of the Xilinx Zynq family [16], which integrate software programmable ARM cores in Processor System (PS) together with the hardware Programmable Logic (PL).

The development boards used are the Zedboard and the ZC706. They differ mainly in the number of resources of the PL section.

3.1 Screen Display via HDMI

In the development boards used, the HDMI is provided for transmitting digital audio and video [13]. The HDMI cable carries four differential pairs for data and clock channels dedicated for audio, video and synchronization. Two important concepts are the resolution and the aspect ratio, the first is the size in pixels of the height and the width of an image, and the second corresponds to the ratio between the width and the height in pixels.

To communicate via HDMI, different color formats can be used. First one is RGB which uses the separation of the color between red, green, and blue. Another one is YCbCr, which uses also three signals: Y is the luminance component (the brightness), and Cb and Cr are the color difference signals for blue and red, respectively [17].

To work with screens that use FPGA, considerations must be taken regarding the frequency used. The refresh rate of the screen defines the pixel clock at which the FPGA has to work to communicate with the screen. The monitors commonly work with a refresh rate of 60 frames per second. To work with a screen resolution of 1920 × 1080, which is the default one, the pixel clock was fixed at 150 MHz.

3.2 Communication with HEENS

The display block is in charge of processing the information at the moment the HEENS system is on the spike distribution phase. Information is fed to a first in-first out (FIFO) block, adapting the data from HEENS to its own form of representation suitable to be displayed on the monitor through its own dedicated blocks (see Fig. 2).

The spike data flow is as follows: first, the PE array generates and encodes the spikes, which are written into the FIFO during the execution phase, and are read during the distribution phase. This FIFO contains all the neuron addresses that have produced a spike during the last execution phase. The neurons addresses are stored on 18 bits: 7 for the chip ID, 3 for the virtualization level, 4 for the row, and 4 for the column (see Table 1). In order to represent the neurons, their addresses have to be converted to an integer value. This value determines a position in a block RAM (BRAM) that is equivalent to the screen pixel to be activated.

Table 1. Spike address event format.

	Chip ID	Virt.	Row	Col
No. bits	7	3	4	4

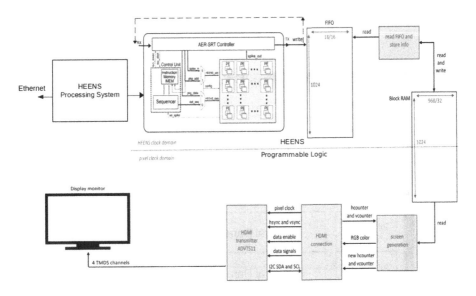

Fig. 2. Raster plot and plot of internal neural parameters. [19]

The screen generation block is in charge of reading the BRAM and to provide functions that allow position counter generation, to be able to scroll vertically and horizontally on the screen, as well as color generation for data in the visible area. The colors are generated in the RGB format, because of simplicity. Together with the control signals, they are connected to the HDMI connection block.

The used FPGA boards include an integrated HDMI transmitter, the ADV7511 circuit, that supports HDMI output. This chip has to be programmed via Inter-Integrated Circuit (I2C), and it is in charge of receiving the data, colors, enable and clock signals for synchronization. It produces the 3 data output channels and the clock channel, which will then be sent and carried by the HDMI connector.

For the implementation of the internal neural parameters display, a dedicated FIFO memory is used [11]. The whole communication system principle is similar to the one for the raster plot. However, the values inside the FIFO are now 16-bit signed values. One of the most important parameters that is interesting to observed in SNNs is the neural membrane potential. The new plot is meant to display the value of 4 chosen neurons as a function of the time. The selection of neurons can be easily changed by modifying a register in the FPGA PS.

Because the screen refresh rate is 60 frames per second, it takes $1/60$ s to display a full screen, which is equal to 16.67 ms. As this can cause the data not to remain stable during that period, producing alterations in the graph shown, a buffer is created in which the data is temporarily stored until a new frame can be written, directly interacting with the block RAM.

3.3   Raster Plot

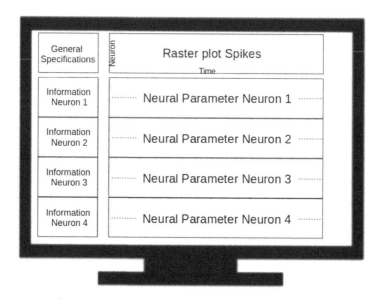

Fig. 3. Distribution of the display area.

The raster plot shows the spiking neurons with time. The spike dot size have been set a resolution of 1 screen pixel and the current time is defined as the number of emulation phases (execution plus spike distribution loop), since in real time one emulation phase has been set to 1 ms. Time starts at zero and increments at the end of every distribution phase. In addition, a delay hardware block adjusts the emulation cycle to 1ms in order to fulfill the real-time condition. On the screen, 1024 timestamps are displayed at a time (approximately one second). Then, the plot is shifted at the refresh rate by introducing the new values at the right.

The display HDMI is implemented in full high definition (FHD) 1080p, 1920×1080, with 16:9 aspect ratio. The screen is divided into 4 zones. The first one, at the left, shows the specific data of the network and algorithm being executed. The second one (top right) shows a raster plot of the neuron activity. The third zone (right) is dedicated to the display of neuronal parameters with information of the monitored neurons. Finally, at the left information of the selected parameter is shown (see Fig. 3).

The display block allows the display of ASCII characters. For this purpose, a public font defined in VHDL was adapted [18], and specific blocks were created for the definition and generation of the text and to determine its position and orientation. Among the messages that are shown there are the board name, the number of columns, rows and virtual levels, the number of chips on the ring, as well as the execution time.

4   Experimental Results

In this section the tool operation is demonstrated, as well as the execution of different examples using the HEENS architecture.

Several models of spiking neurons have been developed, some of them have more similar behavior to biological networks and others are more computationally driven.

For the examples, two different spiking neural models are tested: The Leaky Integrate and Fire (LIF) model, which is viewed as the best-known instance of the spiking neuron model because of its simplicity and low computational cost [19], and the Izhikevich model which is one of the most efficient and with a good biological approximation [20].

The operation flow starts with the definition of the neural model followed by the netlist where the neural circuit is specified. Next, the existing HEENS software development tools are executed to create the configuration file and to program the FPGA [4]. Once this step is done, the connected monitor should show the interface with the fixed panels waiting for the algorithm to run.

In the Fig. 4 we can see the percentage of resource utilization in the implementation of HEENS for an array of 4×8 PEs on the development board ZC706. The total number of BRAM blocks on this board is 545, comparing the version that includes the HDMI display and the version without implementing it, this is the most used resource, the percentage difference between the two versions is 8% and corresponds to 46 blocks dedicated to the HDMI display.

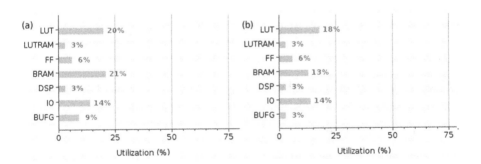

Fig. 4. (a) Percentage of resource utilization with HDMI display block (b) Percentage of resource utilization without HDMI display block.

4.1   Leaky Integrate and Fire Model

The first example corresponds to two delay lines in which the output neuron firing time depends on the synaptic weight of its connection. The graph shows the time difference of the membrane potential increase until the threshold value is exceeded.

In the foreground, the raster plot of the neurons can be seen. For some of them, due to the high density of spikes and the periodicity of their activation, it appears to be a single blue line.

This simple application is implemented with an array of 4×8 processing elements and 4 virtual layers. The total number of emulated neurons is 10 and the membrane potential monitoring is carried out on neurons 0, 35, 65 and 100 that correspond to the output neurons of each delay line (see Fig. 5).

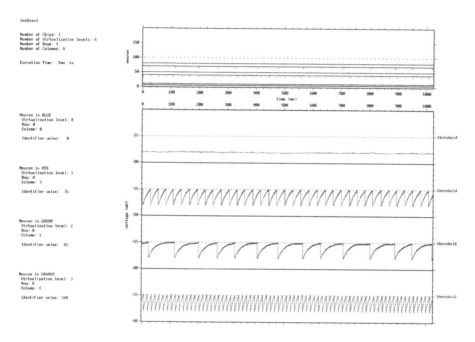

Fig. 5. Display example of Leaky Integrate and Fire model. (Color figure online)

4.2 Izhikevich Model

The second application example corresponds to the execution of the Izhikevich neural model with a topology in which all neurons are interconnected [22].

In the foreground, a greater number of spikes can be observed. The neuronal model corresponds to chattering type neurons that can fire high-frequency bursts of spikes, as can also be seen in the first two membrane potential monitoring graphs.

This application is implemented with an array of 4×8 processing elements and 0 virtual layers. The total number of emulated neurons is 16 and the monitoring is carried out on neurons 1, 3, but now two parameters of each one are monitored: the synaptic weight and the membrane recovery mechanism represented by the u parameter of the Izhikevich model (see Fig. 6).

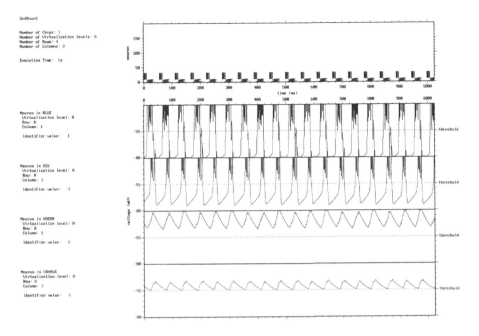

Fig. 6. Display example of Izhikevich model.

5   Conclusion

The HEENS architecture aims to contribute to the existing need for systems capable of emulating SNNs in real time with efficient hardware. The implemented functions of this work make the system more user-friendly and flexible.

The proposed display hardware blocks is an alternative to solve the problem of SNN monitoring in real-time, allowing the user to know the status of the network while it is running without delays due to possible bottlenecks that may arise when trying to send a large amount of generated data.

Although when implementing the tool there is a resource overhead that could affect the number of maximum neurons to be implemented, thanks to the optimization of the size of the memories (most used resources) the limits are maintained both in the version for Zedboard and in the version for the ZC706 card.

Working with reconfigurable hardware opens the possibility to introduce new functions in future versions, such as including options to maximize and minimize the plot area, setting the pause option without affecting the execution of the network, include more analog channels and zoom functions, among others.

References

1. Somerville, J., Stuart, L., Sernagor, E., Borisyuk, R.: IRaster: a novel information visualization tool to explore spatiotemporal patterns in multiple spike trains. J. Neurosci. Methods **194**(1), 158–171 (2010). https://doi.org/10.1016/j.jneumeth.2010.09.009
2. Guo, W., Fouda, M.E., Eltawil, A.M., Salama, K.N.: Neural coding in spiking neural networks: a comparative study for robust neuromorphic systems. Front. Neurosci. **15**(March), 1–21 (2021). https://doi.org/10.3389/fnins.2021.638474
3. Madrenas, J., et al.: Towards efficient and adaptive cyber physical spiking neural integrated systems. In: 2020 27th IEEE International Conference on Electronics, Circuits and Systems (ICECS), pp. 1–4 (2020). https://doi.org/10.1109/ICECS49266.2020.9294982
4. Zapata, M., Balaji, U.K., Madrenas, J.: PSoC-based real-time data acquisition for a scalable spiking neural network hardware architecture. In: IEEE Third Ecuador Technical Chapters Meeting (ETCM) 2018, pp. 1–6 (2018). https://doi.org/10.1109/ETCM.2018.8580286
5. Oltra, J.A., Madrenas, J., Zapata, M., et al.: Hardware-software co-design for efficient and scalable real-time emulation of SNNs on the edge. In: IEEE International Symposium on Circuits and Systems (ISCAS) 2021, pp. 1–5 (2021). https://doi.org/10.1109/ISCAS51556.2021.9401615
6. Spilger, P., et al.: hxtorch: PyTorch for BrainScaleS-2: perceptrons on analog neuromorphic hardware. Commun. Comput. Inf. Sci. **1325**, 189–200 (2020). https://doi.org/10.1007/978-3-030-66770-2_14
7. Benjamin, B.V., et al.: Neurogrid: a mixed-analog-digital multichip system for large-scale neural simulations. Proc. IEEE **102**(5), 699–716 (2014). https://doi.org/10.1109/JPROC.2014.2313565
8. Debole, M.V., et al.: TrueNorth: accelerating from zero to 64 million neurons in 10 years. Computer **52**(5), 20–29 (2019). https://doi.org/10.1109/MC.2019.2903009
9. Furber, S.B., Galluppi, F., Temple, S., Plana, L.A.: The SpiNNaker project. Proc. IEEE **102**(5), 652–665 (2014). https://doi.org/10.1109/JPROC.2014.2304638
10. Orchard, G., et al.: Efficient neuromorphic signal processing with Loihi 2. In: IEEE Workshop on Signal Processing Systems, SiPS: Design and Implementation, 2021-October(1), pp. 254–259 (2021). https://doi.org/10.1109/SiPS52927.2021.00053
11. Zapata, M., Vallejo-Mancero, B., Remache-Vinueza, B., Madrenas, J.: Monitoring implementation for spiking neural networks architecture on Zynq-7000 all programmable SoCs. In: Russo, D., Ahram, T., Karwowski, W., Di Bucchianico, G., Taiar, R. (eds.) IHSI 2021. AISC, vol. 1322, pp. 489–495. Springer, Cham (2021). https://doi.org/10.1007/978-3-030-68017-6_73
12. Zapata, M., Jadan, J., Madrenas, J.: Efficient configuration for a scalable spiking neural network platform by means of a synchronous address event representation bus. In: 2018 NASA/ESA Conference on Adaptive Hardware and Systems (AHS), 2018, pp. 241–248 (2018). https://doi.org/10.1109/AHS.2018.8541463
13. High-Definition Multimedia Interface. Version 1.3a. Hitachi, Matsushita, Philips, Silicon Image, Sony, Thomson, Toshiba, pp. 12–21 (2006)
14. MATLAB-Simulink. (n.d.). https://es.mathworks.com/products/matlab.html. Accessed 18 July 2022
15. NeuroExplorer—Plexon. https://plexon.com/products/neuroexplorer/. Accessed 18 July 2022

16. Zynq-7000. (n.d.). https://www.xilinx.com/products/silicon-devices/soc/zynq-7000.html. Accessed 18 July 2022

17. Campos, N.: RGB to YCbCr conversion. Playing with bits and pixels. sistenix.com, 21 August 2016. https://sistenix.com/rgb2ycbcr.html. Accessed 18 July 2022 (see pp. 16, 34)

18. Derek-X-Wang. VGA-Text-Generator. Github. 5 December 2015. https://github.com/Derek-X-Wang/VGA-Text-Generator. Accessed 18 July 2022. (see pp. 50, 51)

19. Kasabov, N.K.: Time-Space, Spiking Neural Networks and Brain-Inspired Artificial Intelligence. SSBN, vol. 7, pp. 138–139. Springer, Heidelberg (2019). https://doi.org/10.1007/978-3-662-57715-8

20. Izhikevich, E.: Simple model of spiking neurons. IEEE Trans. Neural Netw. **14**(2003), 1569–1572 (2003)

21. Nader, C.: Real-time display of a multiprocessor Spiking Neural Network. (Master Tesis). Universitat Politècnica de Catalunya (2022)

22. Caruso, A.: Izhikevich neural model and STDP learning algorithm mapping on spiking neural network hardware emulator. (Master Tesis). Politecnico di Torino - Universitat Politècnica de Catalunya (2020)

Sailfish: A Fast Bayesian Change Point Detection Framework with Gaussian Process for Time Series

Haizhou Du$^{(\boxtimes)}$ ⓘ and Yang Zheng

Shanghai University of Electric Power, Shanghai, China
`duhahaizhou@shiep.edu.cn`

Abstract. By detecting the changing trend, Change point detection (CPD) can describe the underlying behavior of the system with time series (e.g., equipment failure detection, auxiliary medical diagnosis, and climate change detection, etc.). However, in the current big data environment, how quickly obtaining time-series data dependencies and accurately detecting change points is still a challenge. We propose Sailfish, an unsupervised change point detection framework based on the Gaussian process for time series data. In comparison with existing CPD designs, Sailfish has two novel features: 1) using the deep Gaussian process as a hidden variable transformer and 2) integrating the Gaussian process into a bi-LSTM cell for capturing past and future embedded feature trends. Our extensive experiments show that the Sailfish significantly outperforms five state-of-the-art CPD methods with a faster speed and higher accuracy on three public real-time-series datasets. Especially on the large volume of datasets, Sailfish can achieve up to a 60% reduction in training time and 13% F1-score improvement with little overhead compared to the state-of-the-arts.

Keywords: Change point detection · Gaussian process · Bi-Long short term memory · Bayesian neural network

1 Introduction

Change point detection (CPD), an analytical method to identify the times associated with abrupt series transitions, usually be estimated by attributes such as the continuity, distribution, or shape of the time series data, can be used to extract meaning from non-annotated data. Specially, the detection of time-series changes can often bring more valuable or enlightening knowledge, such as financial data analysis [6,14], climate change detection [3,15], equipment operation monitoring [8,17] etc. Furthermore, CPD methods can be employed in related problems of temporal segmentation, event detection and temporal anomaly detection.

Currently, relevant scholars researched change-point detection for time-series from different fields and angles. According to whether the label of the change point is required, it can be divided into supervised method and unsupervised method. The basic idea of the supervised methods are to collect enough time

ⓒ The Author(s), under exclusive license to Springer Nature Switzerland AG 2022
E. Pimenidis et al. (Eds.): ICANN 2022, LNCS 13531, pp. 740–751, 2022.
https://doi.org/10.1007/978-3-031-15934-3_61

series of different state distributions, combine the category labels of these samples, and then train a classifier [5,10]. However, supervised methods often require high-quality labels, and it is challenging to train effective classifiers with extremely uneven samples. The unsupervised methods use the observed time series to establish a mathematical model to analyze the current data statistically and then implements the change point strategy to output the change time. However, the description of time series in mathematical models built by unsupervised learning often with solid assumptions, such as time distribution is independent and identically distributed [11,22]. Recently, some scholars used self-supervised and unsupervised deep learning to extract time features to detect change points [7,9,12], but it takes a long time to train a deep learning model on large datasets. Furthermore, for many applications in which data is continuously collected, time series with be characterised by slowly varying temporal shape and statistical properties. How to design a fast and unsupervised CPD framework for handling these change point associated with such time series data is still remain a challenge.

This paper proposes Sailfish, which is a fast Bayesian change point detection framework with Gaussian process for time series data. We try to use an unsupervised learning approach to find an efficient and general change points representation for efficient CPD tasks. The intuition is to maximize the availability of time series data by learning a representation to reflect the local correlations present in the time series by modeling the connection between time series prediction model and this representation. It is assumed that a change point is more likely to occur whenever the learned representation differs significantly in a time-series window.

The **main contributions** of this paper are as follows:

- We propose the Sailfish, which is a fast Bayesian change point detection framework with a deep Gaussian process for time series. To our best knowledge, this is the first time to solve the CPD issue by a deep Gaussian process.
- We introduce Gaussian processes as a hidden variable transformer for specialized LSTM cells to capture uncertainty in time-series data.
- We integrate the bi-LSTM structure into the Sailfish framework. This bidirectional structure can compare the positive and negative direction vectors in a time window to quickly determine the change point without additional complicated settings.
- In our extensive experiments, we tuned those hyperparameters well and achieved better performance. Finally, experimental results show that the Sailfish can achieve up to 60% reduction in training time and also improve the F1 performance by 13% compared to the state-of-the-arts with little overhead.

The rest of this paper is organized as follows. Section 2 describes the framework of Sailfish. Section 3 gives a comprehensive evaluation of our work and finally we draw the conclusion in Sect. 4.

2   The Design of Sailfish Framework

In this section, we show the design of the Sailfish framework. We first introduce the definition of the problem in Sect. 3.1. Second, we provide the overview of our framework in Sect. 3.2. Finally, we give the design details of Sailfish framework in the rest subsections.

2.1   Problem Definition

In a multivariate time sequence $\{X_1, X_2...X_t\}$ of the vector $X_i \in \mathbb{R}^d$, we try to estimate the time associated with a change like the time rows (t), and we define a *change point* as the point in time before which the future vector change. Thus, the differences between future and expected views can be used to measure the transition to the next paragraph.

$$\theta = \text{Sailfish}(X_i). \tag{1}$$

$$\theta = \begin{cases} 0, & \text{no change point,} \\ 1, & \text{exist change point,} \end{cases} \tag{2}$$

θ denotes the label obtained from the Sailfish framework. If θ is equal to 1, the current time point is a change point. If θ is equal to 0, there is no change point at all.

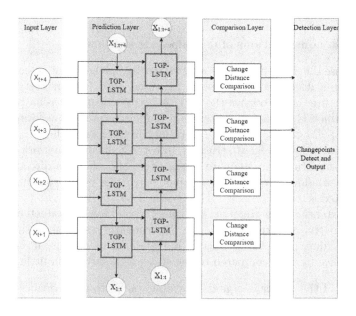

Fig. 1. The overview of Sailfish framework.

2.2   The Overview of Sailfish Framework

The architecture of Sailfish framework is shown in Fig. 1. The framework contains four layers: the input, prediction, comparison, and detection layers.

We adopt a sliding window approach [9] to learn continuous windows as the information representation of the input layer. The data passes through the prediction layer, which is a bidirectional recurrent neural network consisting of TGP-LSTM (temporal Gaussian process-long short term memory) cells, to obtain a pair of embedding representations $(X_h, \underline{X}_h)$ and computes the change distance (indicating the similarity of distributions) between the embedding representations in the contrast layer to estimate the point of change. Temporal data associated with smaller similarity values are less likely to be change points. Finally, the change point label θ is output by the detection layer. In the following subsections, we provide the details of each layer.

2.3   Input Layer

In the input layer, we apply a sliding window technique for obtaining data flexibility and providing sufficient time-series data support for the prediction layer. As shown in the Fig. 2, the responsibility of the input layer is to put the data into the recurrent neural network by a vector through the sliding window.

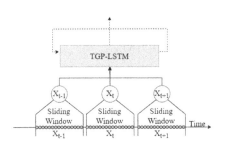

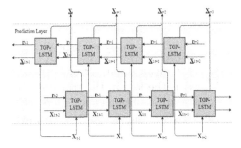

Fig. 2. Input layer with sliding window where the solid line represents the data and the dashed line represents the embedding vector.

Fig. 3. Prediction Layer. The bi-LSTM structure is used to input the data vector X_t. The output forward embedding vector and reverse embedding vector $(X_{1:t}, \underline{X}_{1:t})$ are used as the historical embedding representation of the data.

2.4   Prediction Layer

The details of the prediction layer are shown in the Fig. 3. Intuitively, the occurrence of the change point indicates that the past and future data distribution has changed. In order to obtain the change point detection basis in a one-time window without setting up a complex structure to compare multiple time windows before and after. We apply the bi-LSTM output past time embedding vector $X_{1:t}$ and the future time embedding vector $\underline{X}_{1:t}$ to form an embedded vector pair $(X_{1:t}, \underline{X}_{1:t})$ to get the change point by comparing the distance of these embedded vectors. We will explain how to obtain the embedding vector of the time series through the novel cell and the hidden state transformer.

TGP-LSTM. The TGP-LSTM cell is shown in Fig. 4., and the X_t is as the input from the input layer. The intermediate state $X_{1:t}$ and the predicted value X_{t+1} are as the output of the cell. RGP represents the Recurrent Gaussian process equation will show in Eq(15), and the operation process of LSTM is as follows:

$$\theta X_{1:t-1} = \phi_{\text{forget}}(W_f \circ r_{t-1}) \circ X_{1:t-1}, \tag{3}$$

$$X_{1:t} = \phi_f(W \circ X_t, U \circ \hat{X}_{1:t-1}) + \phi_r(W_r \circ r_{t-1}), \tag{4}$$

$$r_t = \text{RGP}(r_{t-1}, X_{1:t}), \tag{5}$$

$$\hat{X}_{t+1} = \text{DNN}(V \circ X_{1:t}, Q \circ r_t), \tag{6}$$

W, U, V, Q represents the weight of the TGP-LSTM and r_t is the deep learning extension of run-length defined in the flowwing definition1.

The output $\hat{X}_{t+1}$ can be compared with the actual data to train the recurrent neural network by back-propagation. The loss function of the neural network is as follows:

$$loss = loss_1 + loss_2, \tag{7}$$

$$loss_1 = \text{MSE}(X_{t+1}, \hat{X}_{t+1}), \tag{8}$$

$$loss_2 = \log p(X_{1:t}) - \text{KL}[q(R, f) \| p(R, f | X)], \tag{9}$$

$loss_1$ is the mean square error between the predicted value and the actual data, and $loss_2$ is the loss in the transformer part, representing the distance between the distribution obtained by inference and the actual distribution. The mathematical basis of our design is described as following.

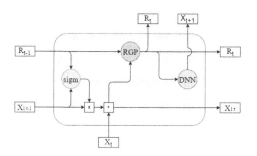

Fig. 4. TGP-LSTM Cell

Bayesian Change Point Detection

Definition 1. *(run length). Let the run-length r_t be a non-negative discrete variable denoting the number of time steps elapsed at time t since the last change point. It holds that $r_t = 0$ at a change point.*

The exact inference on the run-length distribution is made recursively using the following message-passing algorithm:

$$p(r_t, X_{1,t}) = \sum_{r_{t-1}} p(r_t, r_{t-1}, X_{1,t})$$

$$= \sum_{r_{t-1}} p(x_t|r_t, X^{r_t})p(r_t|r_{t-1})p(r_{t-1}, X_{1,t-1}). \tag{10}$$

Equation (10) gives the recursive formulas of r_t and r_{t-1}, and the relationship between them is shown in Eq. (11) in traditional Bayesian methods, which is a hazard function:

$$P(r_t|r_{t-1}) = \begin{cases} H(r_{t-1}+1) & if \quad r_t = 0, \\ 1 - H(r_{t-1}+1) & if \quad r_t = r_t + 1, \\ 0 \ otherwise, \end{cases} \tag{11}$$

the function $H(\tau)$ is the hazard function.

$$H(\tau) = \frac{P_{\text{gap}}(g = \tau)}{\sum_{t=\tau}^{\infty} P_{\text{gap}}(g = \tau)}, \tag{12}$$

in the special case is where $P_{\text{gap}}(g = \tau)$ is a discrete exponential (geometric) distribution with timescale λ, the process is memoryless and the hazard function is constant at $H(\tau) = \frac{1}{\lambda}$

Usually, the hazard function is a constant or time-related function [1,4], which makes the hazard function not flexible enough to deal with complex time series data. In the next subsection we will describe how to construct a feature transformer suitable for deep learning.

Gaussian Process. Gaussian processes can capture time series uncertainty [13]. In the Gaussian process, it is assumed that each data point is generated by the corresponding latent variable x_t, which can be represented as r_t here. These latent variables form a Markov chain, which denote that for any time step t, we can only generate r_{t+1} through the conditional action on r_t, which is described by the formula as $p(r_{t+1}|f, r_t)$ and $p(x_t|r_t)$. The following equations can express the entire Gaussian process model:

$$f \sim \text{GP}(\text{m}(\cdot), \text{k}(\cdot, \cdot)), \tag{13}$$

$$r_1 \sim N(\mu_{p_1}, \sigma_{p_1}), \tag{14}$$

$$r_{t+1}|f, r_t \sim N(f(r_t), \mathbf{Q}), \tag{15}$$

$$x_t|r_t \sim N(Cx_t + d, \mathbf{R}), \tag{16}$$

C is the linear mapping, we take the "process noise" covariance matrix $\mathbf{Q}$ and $\mathbf{R}$ to be diagonal, encouraging the transition function to account for all correlations between latent dimensions. $m(\cdot)$ and $k(\cdot, \cdot)$ denote the Gaussian process average function and covariance function, respectively. The following subsection will describe combining state-space models and bayesian methods through recurrent neural networks.

TGP-CPD. The series observation is $\{x_1, x_2 ... x_t\}$. The input is the observed data x_t, the historical data h_{t-1} and r_{t-1}. The output is the next time observation data x_{t+1} and the current time run-length r_t, which should be described by the equation:

$$p(x_{t+1}, r_t) = f(x_t, h_{t-1}, r_{t-1}), \tag{17}$$

$$p(x_{t+1}, r_t | x_t, h_{t-1}, r_{t-1}) = p(x_{t+1}|X_t, r_t)p(r_t|X_t, r_{t-1}). \tag{18}$$

The relationship between the recurrent neural network state h_t, the intermediate state r_t, and the observation sequence $\{x_1, x_2 ... x_t\}$ is shown in the Fig. 5.

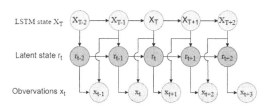

Fig. 5. Relationship between the cyclic neural network state X_T, the intermediate state r_t and the observation sequence $\{x_1, x_2 ... x_t\}$.

2.5   Comparison Layer and Detection Layer

The positive and negative embedding vectors of bi-LSTM will have different distributions when the change occurs. Therefore, in order to quickly determine the change points of the time series, we compare the change distance $\text{Dis}(X_{1:t}, X_{1:t})$ (This paper uses Euclidean distances to represent the change distance between embedded pairs) between the embedding pairs of the forward LSTM and the reverse LSTM and use the peak search algorithm [20] to find the local max value in the region and the time window associated with these local values are considered to have change points. In the next section, we will compare the performance of our method with five state-of-the-art methods.

3 Experiments and Evaluation

In this section, we evaluate the Sailfish with other baselines and present the analysis results on different datasets. Sailfish is implemented using Pytorch2.7 and Python3.7. We run all the experiments on the Intel Core i7 and Nvidia RTX 2060Ti with 16 GB memory.

3.1 Datasets

We demonstrate the effectiveness of our approach on a variety of applications, including web service traffic analysis Yahoo! Benchmark, human activity identification HASC, dam environmental data Fishkiller, and angle differences of bee movements Beedance. As shown in Table 1, T is length of time series, labels is average number of labeled change points.

Table 1. Datasets description.

Dataset	T	Sequences	Domain	#Labels
Fishkiller [21]	45175	1	$\mathbb{R}$	899
HASC [16]	39397	1	$\mathbb{R}^3$	65
Yahoo [19]	1432.13	15	$\mathbb{R}$	36
Beedance [18]	826.66	6	$\mathbb{R}^3$	19.5

3.2 Baseline

We compare Sailfish with the five state-of-the-art methods, two bayesian methods BOCPD [1], BOSD [2] and three deep learning methods CPMAN [12], KL-CPD [7], TS-CP2 [9]. In order to avoid inconsistencies and implementation errors, we use open-source code to evaluate the baselines.

3.3 Evaluation Metrics

Evaluation of the characteristics of the model based on the F1 score metric. In evaluating the effectiveness of each CPD method [7,9], error detection at change points is an essential factor.

$$F_1 = \frac{2 * precision * recall}{precision + recall}. \tag{19}$$

In addition to the F1-score, we also compared the training time t (the time required to complete an epoch of training) of deep learning on three datasets. T can reflect the speed of model training on the same dataset and the required computing resources.

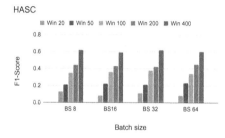

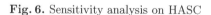

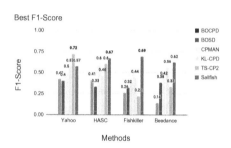

Fig. 6. Sensitivity analysis on HASC   **Fig. 7.** Best F1-Score

3.4   Sensitivity Analysis

In this subsection, we mainly analyze the influence of two key parameters, window size and batch size, on the results of the HASC dataset. The two most important parameters of Sailfish are window size and batch size. Through the sensitivity analysis of these two parameters, We can catch the insight of Sailfish.

As shown in Fig. 6, Sailfish is sensitive to the window size. When the BS is 8, the F1 of the window 400 is 0.62, and the F1 of the window 100 is 0.35. For batchsize, it can be seen that the difference between the highest and the lowest of the same window is only 0.03. The reason is that our Sailfish needs to use the time-series information in the time window. Increasing the time window can obtain more historical data information, enhancing the effect.

3.5   Best F1 Comparison

Fig. 7 shows the best F1-Score performance of Sailfish and five state-of-the-art methods. Although Sailfish does not perform as well as KL-CPD on the Yahoo dataset, it can also get the second best score, while Sailfish is 0.67 and 0.69 as the best performance on the HASC and Fishkiller datasets, respectively. After analysis, our method performs similarly to the baseline methods when the datasets are small in sizes, such as the Yahoo and Beedance datasets. However, Sailfish shows excellent performance when the data is large. We use a particular bidirectional LSTM structure to obtain the time information before and after. The LSTM model has an advantage in dealing with large amounts of data, so Sailfish performs better on datasets with large amounts of data.

3.6   Comparison Table

Table 2 shows the performance of the Sailfish and five state-of-the-art baseline methods on four real datasets. In this subsection, we mainly compare the impact of different time windows on the change point detection method, and we also give The amount of time a deep learning method trains for an epoch when it achieves the best result.

From the results in the Table 2, it is evident that our method is in the top two on all datasets, and the training time is shorter. In the Yahoo dataset, our method is only slightly inferior to TS-CP2 and better than other methods. However, in the Fish killer dataset, compared with the TS-CP2 method, our method improves the F1-Score by 0.4 , and at the same time, we shorten the training time by about half compared to TS-CP2.

Sailfish performs so well in training time because we incorporate change point detection into the LSTM model, so Sailfish is similar to traditional LSTM in training time. However, baseline methods such as TS-CP2 use a contrastive learning technique to detect change points and requires multiple positive and negative samples to be input into the TCN model, which becomes a computational burden.

Table 2. The performance of Sailfish compares with other baselines on the Yahoo, HASC, Fishkiller and Beedance datasets. The following time represents the time for the deep learning method to train an epoch when the best effect is achieved.

Dataset	Window size	50	100	200	400	Time epoch/s
	Methods	F1-score				
Yahoo	BOCPD	0.31	0.27	0.333	0.42	\
	BOSD	0.35	0.3	0.25	0.4	\
	CPMAN	0.22	0.25	0.33	0.32	**2**
	KL-CPD	0.54	0.57	0.54	0.53	20
	TS-CP2	**0.68**	0.58	**0.62**	**0.72**	4
	Sailfish	0.58	**0.6**	0.6	0.57	3.9
HASC	BOCPD	0.21	0.3	0.33	0.41	\
	BOSD	0.22	0.3	0.32	0.33	\
	CPMAN	0.31	0.33	0.3	0.4	68
	KL-CPD	**0.34**	**0.4**	0.4	0.46	60
	TS-CP2	0.32	0.32	0.4	0.6	107
	Sailfish	0.23	0.38	**0.45**	**0.62**	**50 (53%)**
Fishkiller	BOCPD	0.15	0.2	0.26	0.25	\
	BOSD	0.18	0.31	0.32	0.32	\
	CPMAN	0.23	0.2	0.35	0.4	40
	KL-CPD	**0.31**	0.33	**0.42**	0.5	70
	TS-CP2	0.24	0.18	0.2	0.22	115
	Sailfish	0.17	**0.35**	0.4	**0.69**	**30 (65%)**
Beedance	BOCPD	0.13	0.14	0.12	0.14	\
	BOSD	0.26	0.32	0.28	0.38	\
	CPMAN	0.32	0.28	0.35	0.42	16
	KL-CPD	0.56	0.53	0.48	0.54	22
	TS-CP2	0.27	0.29	0.23	0.33	31
	Sailfish	**0.62**	**0.59**	**0.55**	**0.57**	**14 (54%)**

4 Conclusion

We propose Sailfish, a fast and unsupervised change point detection framework for time series, which is the first time using the Gaussian process as a transformer to capture temporal relationships and adopting a bidirectional structure to obtain change point basis in a time window to avoid additional before-and-after comparisons. The experimental results show that our method can reduce the training time by up to 60% and improve the F1-Score by 13% with little overhead.

References

1. Adams, R.P., MacKay, D.J.: Bayesian online changepoint detection. arXiv preprint arXiv:0710.3742 (2007)
2. Agudelo-Espaa, D., Gomez-Gonzalez, S., Bauer, S., Schlkopf, B., Peters, J.: Bayesian online prediction of change points (2019)
3. Ahmadi, F., Nazeri Tahroudi, M., Mirabbasi, R., Khalili, K., Jhajharia, D.: Spatiotemporal trend and abrupt change analysis of temperature in Iran. Meteorol. Appl. **25**(2), 314–321 (2018)
4. Alami, R., Maillard, O., Féraud, R.: Restarted Bayesian online change-point detector achieves optimal detection delay. In: International Conference on Machine Learning, pp. 211–221. PMLR (2020)
5. Camci, F.: Change point detection in time series data using support vectors. Int. J. Pattern Recogn. Artif. Intell. **24**(01), 73–95 (2010)
6. Chahuán-Jiménez, K., Rubilar, R., De La Fuente-Mella, H., Leiva, V.: Breakpoint analysis for the Covid-19 pandemic and its effect on the stock markets. Entropy **23**(1), 100 (2021)
7. Chang, W.C., Li, C.L., Yang, Y., Póczos, B.: Kernel change-point detection with auxiliary deep generative models. arXiv preprint arXiv:1901.06077 (2019)
8. Dao, P., Weasenforth, K., Hollon, J., Payne, T., Kinateder, K., Kruchten, A.: Machine learning-based stability assessment and change detection for geosynchronous satellites. In: The Advanced Maui Optical and Space Surveillance Technologies Conference, p. 39 (2018)
9. Deldari, S., Smith, D.V., Xue, H., Salim, F.D.: Time series change point detection with self-supervised contrastive predictive coding. In: Proceedings of The Web Conference 2021. WWW 2021, Association for Computing Machinery (2021). https://doi.org/10.1145/3442381.3449903
10. Desobry, F., Davy, M., Doncarli, C.: An online kernel change detection algorithm. IEEE Trans. Signal Process. **53**(8), 2961–2974 (2005)
11. Dette, H., Gösmann, J.: A likelihood ratio approach to sequential change point detection for a general class of parameters. J. Am. Statist. Assoc. **115**(531), 1361–1377 (2020)
12. Duan, Z., Du, H., Zheng, Y.: Trident: change point detection for multivariate time series via dual-level attention learning. In: Nguyen, N.T., Chittayasothorn, S., Niyato, D., Trawiński, B. (eds.) ACIIDS 2021. LNCS (LNAI), vol. 12672, pp. 799–810. Springer, Cham (2021). https://doi.org/10.1007/978-3-030-73280-6_63
13. Ialongo, A.D., Van Der Wilk, M., Hensman, J., Rasmussen, C.E.: Overcoming mean-field approximations in recurrent gaussian process models. In: International Conference on Machine Learning, pp. 2931–2940. PMLR (2019)

14. Jeon, S.Y., Ryou, H.S., Kim, Y., Oh, K.J.: Using change-point detection to identify structural changes in stock market: application to Russell 2000. Quantit. Bio-Sci. **39**(1), 61–69 (2020)

15. Kale, S.: Climatic trends in the temperature of çanakkale city, Turkey. Nat. Eng. Sci. **2**(3), 14–27 (2017)

16. Kawaguchi, N., et al.: HASC challenge: gathering large scale human activity corpus for the real-world activity understandings. In: AH 2011 (2011)

17. Lu, G., Zhou, Y., Lu, C., Li, X.: A novel framework of change-point detection for machine monitoring. Mech. Syst. Signal Process. **83**, 533–548 (2017)

18. Oh, S.M., Rehg, J.M., Balch, T., Dellaert, F.: Learning and inferring motion patterns using parametric segmental switching linear dynamic systems. Int. J. Comput. Vis. **77**(1), 103–124 (2008)

19. Researchers, A., et al.: Yahoo ! research webscope data sets (2003)

20. Truong, C., Oudre, L., Vayatis, N.: Selective review of offline change point detection methods. Signal Process. **167**, 107299 (2020)

21. Zhang, M., Sawchuk, A.A.: USC-HAD: a daily activity dataset for ubiquitous activity recognition using wearable sensors. In: ACM Conference on Ubiquitous Computing (2012)

22. Zou, C., Yin, G., Feng, L., Wang, Z.: Nonparametric maximum likelihood approach to multiple change-point problems. Annals Statist. **42**(3), 970–1002 (2014)

SAM-kNN Regressor for Online Learning in Water Distribution Networks

Jonathan Jakob[1], André Artelt[1,3]($\boxtimes$), Martina Hasenjäger[2],
and Barbara Hammer[1]

[1] Bielefeld University, Bielefeld, Germany
aartelt@techfak.uni-bielefeld.de
[2] Honda Research Institute, Offenbach, Germany
[3] University of Cyprus, Nicosia, Cyprus

Abstract. Water distribution networks are a key component of modern infrastructure for housing and industry. They transport and distribute water via widely branched networks from sources to consumers. In order to guarantee a working network at all times, the water supply company continuously monitors the network and takes actions when necessary – e.g. reacting to leakages, sensor faults and drops in water quality. Since real world networks are too large and complex to be monitored by a human, algorithmic monitoring systems have been developed. A popular type of such systems are residual based anomaly detection systems that can detect events such as leakages and sensor faults. For a continuous high quality monitoring, it is necessary for these systems to adapt to changed demands and presence of various anomalies.

In this work, we propose an adaption of the incremental SAM-kNN classifier for regression to build a residual based anomaly detection system for water distribution networks that is able to adapt to any kind of change.

Keywords: SAM-kNN regressor · Incremental · Anomaly detection

1 Introduction

Water is the foundation of (our) life – we need water for drinking, cooking, hygiene and farming. Water distribution networks (WDNs), which distribute water from the supplier to the customers, are therefore considered as critical infrastructure. A major problem for water utility companies (and society in general) are anomalies that cause loss or contamination of water – e.g. leakages such as pipe bursts, sensor faults, pollution, cyber-physical attacks, etc. [1,3,15].

J. Jakob and A. Artelt—Contributed equally.

We gratefully acknowledge funding from the VW-Foundation for the project *IMPACT* funded in the frame of the funding line *AI and its Implications for Future Society*, and funding from the European Research Council (ERC) under the ERC Synergy Grant Water-Futures (Grant agreement No. 951424).

E. Pimenidis et al. (Eds.): ICANN 2022, LNCS 13531, pp. 752–762, 2022.
https://doi.org/10.1007/978-3-031-15934-3_62

Because of water shortages, among others caused by climate change, (drinking) water becomes an increasingly valuable resource that should not be wasted. However, it was estimated that leakages in WDNs lead to a loss of more than 45 million m^3 of drinking water in developing countries – even highly developed countries such as the island of Cyprus looses approx. up to 25% of their drinking water due to leaky pipes [11].

Because of the increasing availability of sensors (e.g. pressure sensors) in WDNs, water utility companies nowadays use computer systems for (autonomously) monitoring their networks [14]. These systems are realized using methods from engineering, statistics and machine learning (ML) [2]. While many different and successful methods for anomaly detection and localization have been proposed [17], these methods are usually not able to adapt to an occurring change or anomaly. These systems might be able to detect anomalies but once the anomaly is detected, they are "blind" for everything else that happens while the detected anomaly is present – the systems must be recalibrated or refitted which becomes challenging because a large amount of data (and therefore collection time) is needed. Adaptation to changes – in case of WDNs anomalies or simply changes in the water consumption behavior of the customers (i.e. changed demand) – can be natural handled by online learning methods.

Online learning [4] can be considered as a sub-field of machine learning which deals with models that are trained incrementally – i.e. they can learn from a data stream instead of a fixed training set only. For example, they can be used for electricity price prediction [20] or electric load forecasting [19].

In this work, we contribute to online learning for regression problems and water distribution networks as a particular field of application. More specifically, our contributions are:

- We propose SAM-kNN regression, a memory based online learner for regression problems.
- We evaluate our proposed SAM-kNN regression method in the context of anomaly detection in water distribution networks.

The remainder of this paper is structured as follows: After briefly reviewing related work in Sect. 2, we introduce the problem setting we are considering in this work (see Sect. 3). Next, in Sect. 4 we propose SAM-kNN regression for online learning, which we empirically evaluate in the context of anomaly detection in water distribution networks (see Sect. 5). Finally, this work closes with a summary and conclusion in Sect. 6.

2   Related Work

Incremental or online learning is a machine learning paradigm in which a model is updated after each data sample that is fed into it. This paradigm is especially suited for large data sets, that are too big to be processed in batch fashion, or in situations where data becomes available only sample after sample – e.g. in the form of a potentially infinite stream of data. Incremental learning has made great strides in recent years [5], with most applications set in a classification environment [7,9,10,12,18,21].

One particular system is the SAM-kNN classifier [13]. This incremental algorithm was created to perform on long data streams, using its internal memory structure to alleviate the problem of catastrophic forgetting when frequent concept changes are expected.

On the other hand, only a few approaches that utilize incremental learning for regression problems exist. In [19] the authors use an incremental variant of the support vector regressor (SVR) to build models for electricity price prediction. [20] uses a similar SVR, paired with phase space reconstruction for time series to facilitate electrical load forecasting. In [6] a wide range of incremental regression algorithms are compared for their use in exoskeleton control.

However, all of these publications utilize standard incremental algorithms and do not explicitly build a new model to work with. We, on the other hand, propose a reformulation of the SAM-kNN classifier for regression as a standalone algorithm.

3   Problem Setting

Incremental or online regression is the task of predicting a response variable $y \in \mathbb{R}$ from a stream $S = \{x_1, x_2, x_3, ...\}$ of variables $X \in \mathbb{R}^n$. Hereby, a new instance of the incremental model is learned for each incoming sample of the data stream.

We work on water distribution networks that have several internal nodes n. These nodes are equipped with sensors, that measure water pressure and flow rate. Each sensor provides read outs at specific time intervals t. For every node, this creates a potentially infinite data stream of sensors values $S = \{(s_1, y_1), (s_2, y_2), (s_3, y_3), ...\}$, where $s_i \in \mathbb{R}^{n-1}$ represents the sensor values of all but one node in the network and the predictor variable $y_i \in \mathbb{R}$ represents the sensor value at the remaining node.

This means, that we use the read outs of $n - 1$ nodes to predict the value of the nth node using an incremental regression algorithm. Said algorithm processes the stream S instance after instance by generating a sequence of models $H = \{h_1, h_2, h_3, ...\}$, where $h_{i-1}(s_i) = \hat{y}_i$. After each prediction the true value y_i is revealed and a new model h_i is learned.

We use the *Interleaved train test error (ITTE)* as a cost function to train the model:

$$E(S) = \sqrt{\frac{1}{t} \sum_{i=1}^{t} (h_{i-1}(s_i) - y_i)^2} \tag{1}$$

This ITTE measures the *Root Mean Squared Error (RMSE)* over every model h_i up to a given time point t.

Whenever the local error $h_{i-1}(s_i) - y_i$ exceeds a certain threshold, this means, that more water than predicted flows through the observed node. This is taken as an indication for a water leak and an alarm will be triggered. Being an incremental algorithm, our model will then automatically adjust to the new circumstances so that accurate prediction of the water flow will be maintained throughout the leak. Our model, which will be explained in detail in the next section, has the capability to remember long term concepts and therefore, as soon as the water leak is fixed, it will revert back to the normal circumstances.

4   Model

Our proposed model is an adaption of the Self Adjusting Memory (SAM) [13], an incremental classifier, to regression. This approach is based on two distinct internal memories, the Short-Term (STM) and the Long-Term memory (LTM). Hereby, the STM is a dynamic sliding window over the last m samples, that is supposed to only hold the most recent concept of the data stream:

$$M_{ST} = \{(x_i, y_i) \in \mathbb{R}^n \times \mathbb{R} \mid i = t - m + 1, ..., t\} \qquad (2)$$

The LTM, on the other hand, is a collection of p samples, which hold older concepts, that do not contradict the STM and might still be of use in the future:

$$M_{LT} = \{(x_i, y_i) \in \mathbb{R}^n \times \mathbb{R} \mid i = 1, ..., p\} \qquad (3)$$

Additionally, there is the combined memory (CM), which is a simple union of the STM and the LTM:

$$M_C = M_{ST} \cup M_{LT} \qquad (4)$$

Each memory induces a kNN regressor that can be used independently from the others. To determine which kNN is used for every new incoming data sample, the ITTE (see Sect. 3) is tracked for all sub-models and the one with the lowest current ITTE is chosen.

4.1   Model Parameters

The proposed model has three parameters that are continuously adapted during deployment:

1. The size m of the STM sliding window
2. The data samples in the LTM
3. The ITTEs of the three sub-models

Additionally, there are three hyperparameters that can be chosen robustly and are set before deployment:

1. The number of neighbours k
2. The minimum size L_{min} of the STM
3. The maximum size L_{max} of the LTM

4.2 Model Adaption

Whenever a new data sample arrives, it is added to the STM, which means that this memory grows continuously. However, since it is supposed to hold only the most recent concept, a reduction of the STM window size is performed on a regular basis. This is facilitated by testing smaller window sizes at every iteration and choosing the one that is optimizing the ITTE. Tested windows are:

$$M_l = \{(x_{t-l+1}, y_{t-l+1}), ..., (x_t, y_t)\} \tag{5}$$

where $l \in \{m, m/2, m/4...\}$ and $l \geq L_{min}$.

$$M_{ST_{t+1}} = \underset{S \in \{M_m, M_{m/2}, ...\}}{\arg\min} E(S) \tag{6}$$

Whenever the STM is shrunk in size, the data samples O_t that fall out of the sliding window are not discarded.

$$O_t = M_{ST_t} \setminus M_{ST_{t+1}} \tag{7}$$

Instead, they undergo a cleaning process, and those, that are still consistent with the new STM are added to the LTM. Afterwards, the whole of the LTM is cleaned as well, to ensure consistency with the STM at all times. When the LTM reaches its maximum size, samples get discarded in a way that ensures minimal information loss.

4.3 Cleaning Process

The process to clean a set of samples with respect to the STM is defined in the following way:
A set A is cleaned by another set B regarding an example $(x_i, y_i) \in B$

$$clean : (A, B, (x_i, y_i)) \mapsto \hat{A} \tag{8}$$

where $A, B, \hat{A} \subset \mathbb{R}^n \times \mathbb{R}$ and $(x_i, y_i) \in B$.

$\hat{A}$ is defined in five steps:

1. Determine the k nearest neighbours of x_i in $B \setminus (x_i, y_i)$ and find the maximum distance

$$\Delta_x^* = \max \left\{ d(x_i, x) \mid x \in N_k(x_i, B \setminus (x_i, y_i)) \right\} \tag{9}$$

2. Compute the maximum weighted difference of y_i and $y \in N_k(x_i, B \setminus (x_i, y_i))$

$$\Delta_y^* = \max \left\{ \left(\frac{y_i - y}{e^{\frac{x_i - x}{\Delta_x^*}}} \right) \mid y \in N_k(x_i, B \setminus (x_i, y_i)) \right\} \tag{10}$$

3. Determine all samples in A that are within Δ_x^* of x_i

$$C = \{(x, y) \in A \mid d(x_i, x) < \Delta_x^*\} \qquad (11)$$

4. Compute the weighted differences of y_i and $y \in C$

$$\Delta_y = \left\{ \left(\frac{y_i - y}{e^{\frac{x_i - x}{\Delta_x^*}}} \right) \mid y \in C \right\} \qquad (12)$$

5. Discard samples from C that have a larger weighted difference than Δ_y^*

$$\hat{A} = A \setminus \{(x, y) \in C \mid \Delta_y(x) > \Delta_y^*\} \qquad (13)$$

Furthermore, the cleaning operation for the full set B

$$clean : (A, B) \mapsto \hat{A}_{|B|} \qquad (14)$$

is defined by iteratively applying the former cleaning for all $(x_i, y_i) \in B$

$$\hat{A}_0 = A$$
$$\hat{A}_{t+1} = clean(\hat{A}_t, B, (x_{t+1}, y_{t+1}))$$

In summary, when the STM is shrunk in size, the process to clean the discarded set O_t is described by the operation:

$$clean(O_t, M_{ST_{t+1}}) \qquad (15)$$

After that, the LTM is cleaned as well:

$$clean(M_{LT_t}, M_{ST_{t+1}}) \qquad (16)$$

4.4   Compression of the LTM

When new samples are added to the LTM while it reaches maximum capacity, old samples need to be discarded. To avoid a significant information loss, samples are discarded in an iterative process one after another until $|M_{LT}| < L_{max}$ again. Hereby, the data sample with the lowest distance to any other two samples is chosen for every iteration of the discarding process.

4.5   Final Model

The complete pseudocode of our proposed model is given in Algorithm 1.

Algorithm 1. SAM-kNN Regression

Input: Data stream S, one s_i at a time
Output: $\hat{y}_i$ for every s_i

1:   $M_{ST}, M_{LT} = \{s_0, ..., s_{L_{min}}\}$ ▷ Initialize STM and LTM
2:   $E_{ST}, E_{LT}, E_C = 0$ ▷ Initialize tracked errors
3:   **for** $s_i \in S \setminus \{s_0, ..., s_{L_{min}}\}$ **do**   ▷ Loop over the remaining data stream
4:       $BM = argmin(E_{ST}, E_{LT}, E_C)$ ▷ Find best memory with lowest error
5:       $\hat{y}_i = kNN_{BM}(s_i)$ ▷ Predict with kNN of best memory
6:       Update E_{ST}, E_{LT}, E_C
7:       $M_{ST} = M_{ST} \cup \{s_i\}$ ▷ Add current sample to STM
8:       Evaluate smaller STM sizes
9:       **if** STM is reduced **then**
10:          $O_t = M_{ST_t} \setminus M_{ST_{t+1}}$ ▷ Take discarded samples from STM
11:          $clean(O_t, M_{ST_{t+1}})$ ▷ Clean discarded samples with respect to new STM
12:          $M_{LT} = M_{LT} \cup clean(O_t, M_{ST_{t+1}})$ ▷ Add cleaned samples to LTM
13:          $clean(M_{LT}, M_{ST_{t+1}})$ ▷ Clean new LTM with respect to new STM
14:       **end if**
15: **end for**

---

5 Experiments

We empirically evaluate our proposed method in an online scenario for detecting leakages and sensor faults in water distribution networks – all experiments are implemented in Python[1].

5.1 Data

We use a version of the L-Town water distribution network as used in [16], as a prominent realistic benchmark for anomaly detection – we only use Area A which consists of 661 nodes, 766 links, and 29 (optimally placed) pressure sensors. We build and simulate 10 scenarios where the first 5 scenarios each contain a single leakage – we vary position, time and size of the leakage – and the remaining 5 scenarios each contain a single different sensor fault (position is varied):

- Scenario 6: Sensor measurement is overflowing over time – i.e. it is going to infinity over time.
- Scenario 7: Gaussian noise is added to the sensor measurement.
- Scenario 8: A constant value is added to the sensor measurement.
- Scenario 9: Sensor measurement is set equal to zero.
- Scenario 10: Sensor measurement is shifted by a small amount.

Each scenario is simulated (using WNTR [8]) for 3 months and pressure sensors are sampled every 5 min.

---

[1] Implementation is available on GitHub: https://github.com/andreArtelt/SAM-kNN-Regressor_OnlineLearning_WDNs.

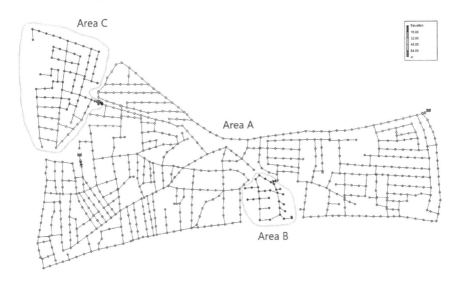

Fig. 1. L-Town network [16] – we only use "Area A" where we have 29 pressure sensors.

The data stream of sensor measurements is post processed by using a sliding window of size 4 – we average all samples dimensional wise in this time window, so that we end up with 29 dimensional samples.

5.2 Setup

We compare our proposed SAM-kNN regressor (see Sect. 4) to several other online learning regressors. In order to justify the introduced overhead of the SAM architecture, we compare its performance to vanilla regressors (kNN regression and linear regression) wrapped as online learners by using the river toolbox[2].

For each pressure sensor, we build a corresponding virtual sensor based on all other pressure sensors – i.e. we try to predict (using a regressor) the pressure based on the past pressure values of all other pressure sensors (see Sect. 3). These virtual sensors are then used for a residual based anomaly detection – i.e. an alarm (detected anomaly) is raised when the predicted pressure value deviates too much from the observed pressure measurement. For each scenario, the processed data stream is fed as batches of 200 samples to the regressors (realizing the virtual sensors).

For each regressor, we evaluate the performance of the resulting anomaly detector – since we are interested in the detection of a single anomaly (leakage and sensor fault), we report true positives (TP), false positives (FP) and false negatives (FN). Note that the true positives and false negatives are always either 0 or 1 because we only check whether an alarm was raised when the single anomaly was present or not – however, for the false positives, we count every single false alarm.

---

[2] https://github.com/online-ml/river.

5.3 Results

The results for leakage detection, for each regressor and each scenario, are shown in Table 1. Likewise, the results for sensor fault detection are shown in Table 2. We observe the same/similar effects for both types of anomalies (leakages and sensor faults): We observe that linear regression completely fails to detect the anomaly – this indicates that a linear model is not sufficient to model the hydraulic dynamics in the water distribution network and hence fails to detect any anomalies. There is only one exception: For scenario 6 the linear model is able to detect the sensor fault – recall that in this particular scenario the sensor fault is characterized by a slowly overflowing sensor measurements (i.e. the pressure value goes to infinity), which is expected to be easily detected because it is a very "loud" fault. The kNN model shows good performance in detecting the anomaly but has a huge number of false positives – i.e. it is too sensitive and raises lots of false alarms. Our proposed SAM-kNN shows the best performance – it is able to consistently detect the anomalies while having a small number of false positives only. The huge reduction of the false positives in comparison

Table 1. Leakages: evaluation of residual based anomaly detection in water distribution networks – note that each scenario consists of approx. 23000 samples.

Method	Metric	Scenario 1	Scenario 2	Scenario 3	Scenario 4	Scenario 5
SAM-kNN	TP	1	1	1	1	1
	FP	48	20	3	20	17
	FN	0	0	0	0	0
kNN	TP	1	1	1	1	1
	FP	17057	19216	11146	19082	18751
	FN	0	0	0	0	0
Linear regression	TP	0	0	0	0	0
	FP	0	0	0	0	0
	FN	1	1	1	1	1

Table 2. Sensor faults: Evaluation of residual based anomaly detection in water distribution networks – note that each scenario consists of approx. 23000 samples.

Method	Metric	Scenario 6	Scenario 7	Scenario 8	Scenario 9	Scenario 10
SAM-kNN	TP	1	1	1	1	1
	FP	155	20	157	96	156
	FN	0	0	0	0	0
kNN	TP	1	1	1	1	1
	FP	18596	18596	18596	18596	18596
	FN	0	0	0	0	0
Linear regression	TP	1	0	0	0	0
	FP	0	0	0	0	0
	FN	0	1	1	1	1

to vanilla kNN indicates that the overhead introduced by the SAM architecture actually pays off.

6   Summary and Conclusion

Inspired by the SAM-kNN classifier, we proposed SAM-kNN regressor as an online learner for regression. In contrast to other online learners, our proposed method comes with a memory component which allows it to remember past concepts quite easily. We empirically evaluated our proposed online learner in an anomaly detection scenario for a realistic water distribution network – our proposed online learner consistently outperforms other standard online learners.

Although our proposed method shows good performance for leakage and sensor fault detection (two very common anomalies), it is unclear, how well it performs for other (more complex) types of anomalies such as cyber-physical attacks, etc. Furthermore, another challenge is high-dimensional data – in this work our data had 29 dimensions which is already somewhat high but can still be managed by our kNN based method. However, in case of really high dimensional data, kNN will encounter performance problems – e.g. some kind of integrated dimensionality reduction might be required. We leave these aspects as future work.

Acknowledgment. We acknowledge the bachelor thesis by Augustin Harter (Bielefeld University) and Yannik Sander (Bielefeld University) which served as a mental starting point for this work.

References

1. Alexander, A., Julius, T., Andrew, T., Ezera, A., Christine, A.: Contamination potentials of household water handling and storage practices in Kirundo subcounty, Kisoro district, Uganda (2019)
2. Chan, T.K., Chin, C.S., Zhong, X.: Review of current technologies and proposed intelligent methodologies for water distributed network leakage detection. IEEE Access **6**, 78846–78867 (2018)
3. Farley, M., Trow, S.: Losses in Water Distribution Networks. IWA Publishing (2003)
4. Gama, J.: A survey on learning from data streams: current and future trends. Prog. Artif. Intell. **1**(1), 45–55 (2012)
5. Gomes, H.M., Read, J., Bifet, A., Barddal, J.P., Gama, J.: Machine learning for streaming data: state of the art, challenges, and opportunities. In: ACM SIGKDD Explorations Newsletter, pp. 6–22 (2019)
6. Jakob, J., Hasenjäger, M., Hammer, B.: On the suitability of incremental learning for regression tasks in exoskeleton control. In: IEEE Symposium on Computational Intelligence in Data Mining (CIDM). IEEE, December 2021
7. Jodelet, Q., Liu, X., Murata, T.: Balanced softmax cross-entropy for incremental learning. In: Farkaš, I., Masulli, P., Otte, S., Wermter, S. (eds.) ICANN 2021. LNCS, vol. 12892, pp. 385–396. Springer, Cham (2021). https://doi.org/10.1007/978-3-030-86340-1_31

8. Klise, K.A., Murray, R., Haxton, T.: An overview of the water network tool for resilience (WNTR) (2018)
9. Lei, C.-H., Chen, Y.-H., Peng, W.-H., Chiu, W.-C.: Class-incremental learning with rectified feature-graph preservation. In: Ishikawa, H., Liu, C.-L., Pajdla, T., Shi, J. (eds.) ACCV 2020. LNCS, vol. 12627, pp. 358–374. Springer, Cham (2021). https://doi.org/10.1007/978-3-030-69544-6_22
10. Li, H., Dong, W., Hu, B.G.: Incremental concept learning via online generative memory recall (2019). https://arxiv.org/abs/1907.02788
11. Liemberger, R., Marin, P., et al.: The challenge of reducing non-revenue water in developing countries-how the private sector can help: a look at performance-based service contracting (2006)
12. Liu, Y., Su, Y., Liu, A.A., Schiele, B., Sun, Q.: Mnemonics training: multi-class incremental learning without forgetting. In: 2020 IEEE/CVF Conference on Computer Vision and Pattern Recognition (CVPR). IEEE, June 2020. https://doi.org/10.1109/cvpr42600.2020.01226
13. Losing, V., Hammer, B., Wersing, H.: KNN classifier with self adjusting memory for heterogeneous concept drift. In: 2016 IEEE 16th International Conference on Data Mining (ICDM), pp. 291–300 (2016). https://doi.org/10.1109/ICDM.2016.0040
14. Makropoulos, C., Savić, D.: Urban hydroinformatics: past, present and future. Water **11**(10), 1959 (2019)
15. Nikolopoulos, D., Moraitis, G., Bouziotas, D., Lykou, A., Karavokiros, G., Makropoulos, C.: Cyber-physical stress-testing platform for water distribution networks. J. Environ. Eng. **146**(7), 04020061 (2020)
16. Vrachimis, S.G., et al.: BattLeDIM: battle of the leakage detection and isolation methods (2020)
17. Wu, Y., Liu, S.: A review of data-driven approaches for burst detection in water distribution systems. Urban Water J. **14**(9), 972–983 (2017)
18. Wu, Y., et al.: Incremental classifier learning with generative adversarial networks (2018). https://arxiv.org/abs/1802.00853
19. Yan, J., Tian, C., Wang, Y., Huang, J.: Online incremental regression for electricity price prediction. In: Proceedings of 2012 IEEE International Conference on Service Operations and Logistics, and Informatics, pp. 31–35. IEEE (2012). https://doi.org/10.1109/SOLI.2012.6273500
20. Yang, Y., Che, J., Li, Y., Zhao, Y., Zhu, S.: An incremental electric load forecasting model based on support vector regression. Energy **113**, 796–808 (2016). https://doi.org/10.1016/j.energy.2016.07.092
21. Zhu, Q., He, Z., Ye, X.: Incremental classifier learning based on PEDCC-loss and cosine distance (2019). https://arxiv.org/abs/1906.04734

Spatial-Temporal Semantic Generative Adversarial Networks for Flexible Multi-step Urban Flow Prediction

Lincan Li[1], Jichao Bi[1(✉)], Kaixiang Yang[1], and Fengji Luo[2]

[1] State Key Laboratory of Industrial Control Technology, Zhejiang University, Hangzhou 310012, China
{lilincan,jonny.bijichao,yangkaixiang}@zju.edu.cn
[2] The University of Sydney, Sydney, Australia
fengji.luo@sydney.edu.au

Abstract. Accurate multi-step citywide urban flow prediction plays a critical role in traffic management and future smart city. However, it is very challenging since urban flow is affected by complex semantic factors and has multi-scale dependencies on both spatial and temporal dimensional features. Moreover, it's difficult for most existing one-step urban flow prediction models to predict several future time steps in a short time accurately. Inspired by the success of Generative Adversarial Networks (GAN) in video prediction and image generation, in this paper we propose a Seq2Seq Spatial-Temporal Semantic Generative Adversarial Networks named STS-GAN for multi-step urban flow prediction. We regard citywide urban flow data in successive time steps as image frames of a video. Specifically, we first design a Spatial-Temporal Semantic Encoder (STSE) to capture relative semantic factors and spatial-temporal dependencies simultaneously at each time step, which consists of Residual Convolution units. Then a Seq2Seq GAN model is proposed to generate a sequence of future urban flow predictions based on historical data. Furthermore, by integrating GAN's adversarial loss with prediction error, our STS-GAN can effectively address the blurry prediction issue. Extensive experiments are conducted on two large-scale urban flow datasets in Beijing and Guangzhou, which demonstrate STS-GAN achieves state-of-the-art performance compared with existing methods.

Keywords: Spatial-temporal data mining · Urban flow prediction · Generative Adversarial Networks · Neural network models

1 Introduction

Spatial-temporal urban flow forecasting is a fundamental research problem for Intelligent Transportation System (ITS). Accurate citywide urban flow

---

J. Bi—This work is supported in part by National Natural Science Foundation of China under Grant No. 62106224, "Pioneer" and "Leading Goose" R&D Program of Zhejiang under Grant 2022C01178.

E. Pimenidis et al. (Eds.): ICANN 2022, LNCS 13531, pp. 763–775, 2022.
https://doi.org/10.1007/978-3-031-15934-3_63

prediction allows system manager to effectively control transportation networks and make better traffic planning [12].

In recent years, deep learning technology has been widely adopted in urban flow prediction and achieved superior results. Zhang et al. [18] proposed a CNN-based deep learning model named ST-ResNet for urban flow prediction. Yao et al. [15] proposed Spatial-Temporal Dynamic Network (STDN) for road-network traffic forecasting. More recently, some literature applied graph convolutional neural networks (GCN) to complete spatial-temporal forecasting tasks. Li et al. [6] proposed DCRNN, which adopted diffusion graph convolution and a Seq2Seq architecture to perform multi-step traffic prediction. STGATP [21] adopted attention-based spatial-temporal graph convolution to capture dynamic spatial-temporal features in traffic flows. STSGCN [10] introduced spatial-temporal synchronous modeling mechanism to capture the complex localized spatial-temporal correlations. However, we still identify some important issues that are worthy of investigation: (i) Most existing urban flow prediction models only focus on making predictions for the next one time step [3,11,16], there still lacks an effective and accurate multi-step prediction model. (ii) The patterns of urban flow are complex. In reality, lots of semantic factors such as weather, timestamp, POI, holiday and events can significantly affect the future citywide crowd flow [3,18]. How to take these semantic information into account is challenging. (iii) Deep learning models for urban flow prediction often suffer from the **blurry prediction issue**: learning to predict a successive sequence of future images is extremely challenging, which can cause a naive model to average together all possible futures into one single image [9,13].

To fill in the identified research gaps, we propose a Seq2Seq Spatial-Temporal Semantic Generative Adversarial Networks (STS-GAN) for accurate multi-step urban flow prediction. We consider urban flow at each time step as an image frame of a video to predict a sequence of future urban flow frames. The generator of STS-GAN is designed as an encoder-decoder structure. What's more, generator and discriminator both take CNNs, LSTM and Attention as main components. To capture semantic contexts, we elaborately design a Spatial-Temporal Semantic Encoder (STSE) to model semantic factors and spatial-temporal dependencies simultaneously. The main contributions of this work are as follows:

- We propose a novel STS-GAN framework for accurate multi-step urban flow prediction. STS-GAN integrates the merits of GAN's generate ability and Seq2Seq prediction ability by designing a weighted loss function consisting of adversarial loss and prediction error, which effectively address the blurry prediction issue.
- To capture the influence of complex semantic factors on citywide urban flow prediction. We first design a Spatial-Temporal Semantic Encoder (STSE) to capture relative semantic factors and spatial-temporal dependencies simultaneously at each time step, which consists of Residual Convolution units.
- Extensive experiments are conducted on two large-scale urban flow datasets in China, results demonstrate our model consistently outperforms other baseline methods.

2   Related Works

2.1   Spatial-Temporal Urban Flow Prediction

With the rapid development of smart city and deep learning technology, urban flow prediction has become a heat topic among researchers [11,16]. Traditional traffic prediction methods are mostly statistic-based such as ARIMA and SVR. These methods fail to capture the complex spatial-temporal dependencies of urban flow data. Recently, due to the powerful hierarchical feature learning ability of deep learning models in both spatial and temporal dimensions, a large number of deep learning models are proposed for urban flow prediction. Specifically, DeepST [19] firstly proposed to model urban flow data in three temporal scales: closeness, period and trend, then use CNN-based architecture to capture spatial-temporal dependencies. ST-ResNet [18] further proposed a CNN-based residual networks for urban flow prediction. DeepSTN+ [8] proposed ResPlus block to model the long-range spatial dependencies of urban flow in different regions, and SemanticPlus block to model the influences of external factors. However, the aforementioned models are originally designed for one-step prediction. In general, there still lacks an accurate and effective model which could perform multi-step urban flow prediction and at the same time address the blurry prediction issue.

2.2   Generative Adversarial Networks

Generative Adversarial Networks (GAN) [4] is a powerful generative deep learning model, which is capable of generating artificial samples as indistinguishable as possible. GAN consists of two components, a generator G and a discriminator D. GAN represents a probability distribution through the generator G that learns to directly produce samples from the desired distribution. The generator is trained adversarially by optimizing a minmax objective function together with the discriminator D [4,7,17].

When GAN is applied in traffic domain, generator G is usually employed to generate future traffic flow based on historical observations [14,17]. After the training procedure, G can accurately model the distribution of real traffic data and is able to predict future traffic states. Recently, GAN-based traffic forecasting has aroused the interest of many researchers, Yu et al. [17] proposed a graph convolution generative autoencoder for traffic speed estimation. Lin et al. [7] adopted a pattern sensitive adversarial learning framework to predict traffic flow. However, these methods still perform one-step prediction and have blurry prediction issue.

3   Preliminaries

Definition 1: Grid Region. A city is partitioned into $I \times J$ rectangular grids of the same size based on their longitudes and latitudes. Each grid represents a region of the city, and there are N ($N = I \times J$) regions in total.

Definition 2: Traffic InFlow/OutFlow. The traffic inflow/outflow for grid region (i, j) at t-th time interval is defined as follows:

$$x_t^{i,j,in} = \sum_{T_r \in P} |k > 1 | g_{k-1} \notin (i, j) \wedge g_k \in (i, j)|$$
$$x_t^{i,j,out} = \sum_{T_r \in P} |k \geq 1 | g_k \in (i, j) \wedge g_{k+1} \notin (i, j)| \tag{1}$$

where P is a collection of trajectories at t-th time interval. $T_r : g_1 \rightarrow g_2 \rightarrow ... \rightarrow g_{|T_r|}$ is a trajectory in P, and g_k is the geospatial coordinate; $g_k \in (i, j)$ means the point g_k lies within region (i, j), and vice versa. Citywide traffic inflow and outflow at t-th time interval can be denoted as a tensor $X_t \in R^{2 \times I \times J}$.

Problem Statement. Given historical urban flow matrix series $[X_{(t-T+1)}, ..., X_{(t-1)}]$, our goal is to predict citywide urban flow of the next k time slots, which can be formulated as:

$$[X_{(t-T+1)}, ..., X_{(t-1)}] \xrightarrow{f} [X_t, ..., X_{(t+k-1)}] \tag{2}$$

where T denotes the length of historical urban flow matrix series, f denotes the mapping function which maps the historical spatial-temporal network series into future predictions.

4   Methodology

This section introduces the proposed STS-GAN. It can be seen from Fig. 1 that STS-GAN has two main components: the generator G and discriminator D. G is formulated as an encoder-decoder framework to generate a sequence of k time steps future predictions. Following previous works [3,8,18], the input historical urban flow data consists of three temporal scales (i.e. trend, period and closeness). The historical urban flow data and corresponding semantic factors are first processed by Spatial-Temporal Semantic Encoder (STSE) block to integrate both spatial-temporal and semantic features with residual convolution units. After that, the latent flow tensors are processed by a CNN layer and an LSTM layer, and then an attention mechanism is applied to capture the weights of the flow tensors in different time slots for predicting the future tensors. The decoder consists of an LSTM layer and a deconvolution layer to transform a vector back to the same size as original urban flow tensor. The discriminator D takes both generated urban flow data and the real urban flow data to form a pair of inputs. D tries to distinguish whether a sequence is real or generated by G. The generator G and discriminator D are trained iteratively, and the training procedure is completed when D cannot distinguish between the generated urban flow sequence and real urban flow sequence.

4.1   Spatial-Temporal Semantic Encoder

To begin with, we give a brief definition of semantic information and explain how we process semantic information data. Urban flow is easily affected by semantic information such as weather conditions, special events, and refined timestamp

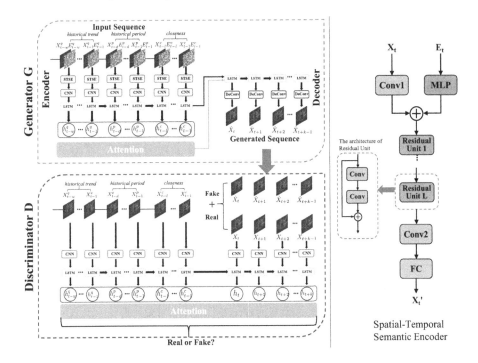

Fig. 1. The architecture of our proposed STS-GAN and STSE block.

information [3]. Specifically, we take day-of-week/is weekend/is holiday as the refined timestamp information. The temperature data is scaled into range $[0, 1]$ using Min-Max normalization method. For weather conditions, we consider six categories of weather including sunny/cloudy/rainy/thunderstorm/foggy/snowing, and use One-Hot Encoding to process weather conditions. Also, One-Hot Encoding is employed to process refined timestamp information. The semantic information tensor at time step t is denoted as E_t.

We design a Spatial-Temporal Semantic Encoder (STSE) to simultaneously capture spatial dependencies and the influence of semantic factors. The architecture of STSE is shown in the right part of Fig. 1. STSE consists of residual units and multi-layer perceptron (MLP). At time step t, the input historical urban flow tensor X_t and semantic factors E_t are first processed by a convolution layer and MLP respectively, then added together. The operation of Conv1 layer is formulated as:

$$X_t^{(1)} = f(W_{conv}^{(1)} * X_t + b_{conv}^{(1)}) \tag{3}$$

where $*$ denotes convolution operator, f denotes the activation function; $W_{conv}^{(1)}$ and $b_{conv}^{(1)}$ denote learnable parameters.

We extract the features of semantic information tensor E_t using MLP, which consists of two fully-connected-layers:

$$M_t = f(f(E_t \cdot W_1 + b_1) \cdot W_2 + b_2) \tag{4}$$

where W_1, W_2 and b_1, b_2 are weights and biases, f denotes activation function. The output of MLP is reshaped to $M_t \in R^{2 \times J \times K}$, the same shape as X_t.

Following that, X_t and M_t are concatenated together and input into residual units. The concatenated tensor is processed by L stacked residual units, and finally processed by another convolution layer (Conv2). The procedure is formulated as follows:

$$\begin{aligned}
S_t^{(1)} &= X_t^{(1)} + M_t, \\
S_t^{(l+1)} &= S_t^{(l)} + F(S_t^{(l)}; \theta_t^{(l)}) \quad l = 1, ..., L, \\
\tilde{S}_t &= f(W_{conv}^{(2)} * S_t^{(l+1)} + b_{conv}^{(2)}).
\end{aligned} \tag{5}$$

where F is the residual function, and $\theta^{(l)}$ includes all learnable parameters in l-th residual unit; $*$ denotes convolution operation; f denotes activation function; $W_{conv}^{(2)}$ and $b_{conv}^{(2)}$ are learnable parameters and $\tilde{S}_t \in R^{2 \times I \times J}$. The result $\tilde{S}_t$ is then fed into generator's following layers for processing.

4.2   Generator G

Seq2Seq model has advantages in handling sequential data. In our work, we aim to use a sequence of historical urban flow data $X = \{X_{t-T+1}, X_{t-T+2}, ..., X_{t-1}\}$ to predict a sequence of future urban flow data $\hat{X} = \{\hat{X}_t, \hat{X}_{t+1}, ..., \hat{X}_{t+k-1}\}$, whose scenario is highly suitable for Seq2Seq model. Therefore, we formulate G as an encoder-decoder structure to generate multi-step urban flow prediction.

As shown in the upper left part of Fig. 1, G contains an encoder and a decoder. In encoder part, the input urban flow data $\{X_t = X_{t-T+1}, X_{t-T+2}, ..., X_{t-1}\}$ is first fed into a CNN layer to capture the spatial dependencies, then send to an LSTM layer to capture the temporal dependencies among the urban flow in different time steps. The hidden states of historical urban flows at time step t is denoted as: $\mathbf{H} = [h_{t-T+1}, h_{t-T+2}, ..., h_{t-1}]$.

In reality, different historical urban flow data have different impacts on the target time interval, and the impacts vary a lot over time [21]. Inspired by this, we introduce the temporal attention mechanism to G. Given the previous output $\{z_1, ..., z_{n-1}\}$ of the LSTM layer in decoder part, the n-step LSTM prediction y_n can be calculated by $y_n = g(z_{n-1}, h_n, c_n)$. Where $g(\cdot)$ denotes the mapping function of generator G, h_n denotes the hidden state of the decoder part LSTM in time step n, c_n denotes the context vector calculated by temporal attention mechanism. The calculation procedure of temporal attention are formulated as follows:

$$\alpha = softmax(ReLU(HW_H + E_t W_z + b_\alpha)) \tag{6}$$

where W_H, W_z and b_α are learnable parameters. $\alpha = \{\alpha_1, ..., \alpha_n\}$ is a sequence of attention score vector. Finally we get the context vector of temporal attention mechanism as follows:

$$\hat{c}_n = \sum_{i=1}^{n} \alpha_i \cdot h_i \tag{7}$$

For decoder part of G, y_n is fed into the LSTM layer in the decoder and the output of LSTM layer is $\hat{Y}_{de} = \{y_t, ..., y_{t+k-1}\}$, and then processed by a deconvolution layer to generate final prediction sequence $\hat{X} = \{X_t, ..., X_{t+k-1}\}$.

4.3 Discriminator D

Given a pair of ground-truth urban flow data and generated urban flow data $\{X, \hat{X}\}$, the discriminator D tries to distinguish which is real and which is generated by G. The prediction error of D will guide G to generate more realistic data. The architecture of D is shown in the lower part of Fig. 1. Before entering the discriminator, historical urban flow data $\{X_{t-T+1}, X_{t-T+2}, ..., X_{t-1}\}$ are merged with the real future urban flow data $\{X_t, X_{t+1}, ..., X_{t+k-1}\}$ and the generated future urban flow data $\{\hat{X}_t, \hat{X}_{t+1}, ..., \hat{X}_{t+k-1}\}$ to form a pair of samples $\{X, \hat{X}\}$. The paired samples are input to a CNN layer and LSTM layer to learn spatial-temporal dependencies. Finally, the temporal attention mechanism (as aforementioned in Generator G) is applied on the output of LSTM.

4.4 The Objective Function of STS-GAN: A Weighted and Integrated Loss Function

In this work, we adopt Wasserstein GAN (WGAN) [1] as our adversarial learning framework. WGAN uses Wasserstein distance to measure the distance and divergence between the real data distribution and the generated data distribution from G. Thus, the objective function of WGAN is as follows:

$$\min \max E_{x \sim p_{data}}[f_w(X)] - E_{z \sim p(z)}[f_w(g_\theta(Z))] \tag{8}$$

where θ represents the parameters of generator, $f_w(\cdot)$ denotes a parameterized family of functions $\{f_w\}_{w \in W}$ that are all K-Lipschitz for K. Given n pairs of real and generated urban flow data $\{X_i, \hat{X}_i\}_{i=1}^n$, the objective function of our GAN model can be formulated as:

$$L_{GAN} = \min_\theta \max_w \sum_{i=1}^n (f_w(X_i)) - \sum_{i=1}^n (f_w(g_\theta(\hat{X}_i))) \tag{9}$$

Since GAN is originally designed for new data generation rather than prediction tasks, to make the generated future urban flow data more realistic and address the blurry prediction issue in multi-step prediction [9,13], we add Mean Squared Error (MSE) to the total objective function of the proposed STS-GAN. MSE is a commonly adopted loss function in prediction tasks, which is formulated as follows:

$$L_{MSE} = \sum_{i=1}^n (X_i - \hat{X}_i)^2 \tag{10}$$

Furthermore, to adaptively adjust the importance of GAN's adversarial loss and the prediction loss, we assign a hyper-parameter β to the total objective function of STS-GAN. Combining Eq. 9, Eq. 10 and β, the overall objective function of STS-GAN is:

$$Loss = \beta L_{GAN} + (1 - \beta)L_{MSE} \tag{11}$$

The integrated objective function has lots of advantages. Given a sequence of historical urban flow data, if there are several potential future predictions, the adversarial loss will help the model to select the most possible one, which address the blurry prediction issue.

5 Experiments

5.1 Datasets and Implementation Details

The statistics of the two citywide urban flow datasets are introduced as follows.

TaxiBJ. This dataset is generated with GPS trajectory data of more than 34,000 taxis in Beijing city from four different periods. The dataset contains a total of 22,459 available flow maps with size $2 \times 32 \times 32$ corresponding to the Inflow/OutFlow in each time step (i.e. 30 min). The semantic factors include weather conditions, temperature, and refined timestamp information (day-of-week/is weekend/is holiday).

GZ-mobility. GZ-mobility dataset is originally provided by our research partner–GeTui corporation. This dataset is collected from mobile phone Location Based Services (LBS), which records over 300,000 mobile phone users' real-time locations in Guangzhou city within three months in 2019. All data are collected with the permission and agreement of users, and their IDs are anonymized. Each record contains an anonymous user ID, timestamp, real-time latitude and longitude, as well as other external information. We process the dataset into $2 \times 32 \times 32$ flow maps with 15-minute time interval. The semantic factors include weather conditions, temperature, and refined timestamp information (day-of-week/is weekend/is holiday).

Parameters Setting. The proposed STS-GAN is implemented using PyTorch framework. Experiments are conducted under the environment with one Intel Xeon E5 CPU and one NVDIA TESLA V100 GPU for neural network computing acceleration. We use the Min-Max normalization method to scale the urban flow into $[-1, 1]$ and re-scale the predicted results back to the normal values in evaluation. The historical time slots length for closeness/period/trend is set to 8, 2, 2, respectively. In STSE block, the convolutions of Conv1 and Conv2 use 16 filters of size 3×3 and 2 filters of size 3×3, respectively. In residual units, all convolution using 15 filters of size 3×3. We set the number of residual units $L = 2$ for TaxiBJ and $L = 4$ for GZ-mobility. The CNNs in generator G and discriminator D contain 4 layers. We set the size of hidden state of LSTM as 200. The STS-GAN model is trained using RMSProp optimization with learning rate 0.001, the batch size is set as 32.

5.2 Evaluation Metrics and Baseline Methods

Mean Absolute Error (MAE) and Root Mean Square Error (RMSE) are adopted as evaluation metrics:

$$MAE = \frac{1}{N*k} \sum_{i=1}^{N} \sum_{t=t+1}^{t+k} |\hat{x}_t^i - x_t^i|$$

$$RMSE = \sqrt{\frac{1}{N*k} \sum_{i=1}^{N} \sum_{t=t+1}^{t+k} (\hat{x}_t^i - x_t^i)^2}$$

$$(12)$$

where N is the total number of testing samples, $\hat{x}_t^i$ is the prediction of sample i and x_t^i id the corresponding ground-truth.

We compare our model with the following baseline methods: (1)ARIMA, (2)GRU [2], (3)DCRNN [6], (4)ST-ResNet [18], (5)STSGCN [10], (6)STFGNN [5], (7)GCGAN [20] and (8)GE-GAN [14]. Among these methods, ARIMA and GRU are classical time series prediction models, DCRNN utilizes diffusion graph convolution and Seq2Seq architecture to capture spatial and temporal correlations, respectively. ST-ResNet is a CNN-based deep learning model for spatial-temporal urban flow prediction. STSGCN and STFGNN are recently proposed GCN models which shown superior performance in traffic prediction. GCGAN and GE-GAN are two advanced generative adversarial learning frameworks used for traffic forecasting.

5.3 Experiment Results and Sensitive Study

Results Analysis of One-Step Prediction. Table 1 shows a thorough performance comparison of different methods. Results demonstrate our STS-GAN consistently outperforms other baseline methods. ARIMA and GRU perform badly in all experiments, because they only capture temporal dependencies and cannot modeling spatial dependencies. STS-GAN has better performance than ARIMA and GRU, because it's capable of capturing spatial dependencies by Spatial-Temporal Semantic Encoder and CNN layers. ST-ResNet only utilizes residual CNNs to model spatial-temporal correlations, which fails to capture the temporal dynamics inside urban flow data and shows limited performance. Although DCRNN takes advantage of Seq2Seq architecture to perform multi-step prediction, the recurrent framework is quite redundant and still have blurry prediction issue. STSGCN and STFGNN show promising results in fixed sensor network with relatively small scale such as PeMS dataset, but lose their advantages in region-based urban flow prediction. For adversarial learning frameworks, GCGAN does not consider multi-scale temporal dependencies and semantic factors, which is inferior to ST-ResNet and other GCN-based methods. GE-GAN utilizes a very simple WGAN network to generate traffic speed predictions, which results in worse performance.

Table 1. Comparison on RMSE and MAE for one-step prediction.

Method	GZ-mobility		TaxiBJ	
	RMSE	MAE	RMSE	MAE
ARIMA	23.46	14.97	22.78	13.65
GRU	21.83	13.05	21.37	12.38
GE-GAN	19.22	12.66	20.63	11.84
GCGAN	17.49	10.84	19.26	11.13
DCRNN	15.63	9.36	18.36	10.57
ST-ResNet	14.61	8.72	16.69	9.45
STSGCN	13.35	7.83	16.17	9.14
STFGNN	11.94	6.58	15.58	8.63
STS-GAN	**8.75**	**4.92**	**13.87**	**7.25**

Comparison on Multi-step Prediction. In this part we evaluate the performance of several baseline methods on multi-step urban flow prediction. To study the influence of future step k on model performance, we select five representative methods (GRU, GCGAN, DCRNN, ST-ResNet, STS-GAN) for comparison under different prediction step k. Table 2 shows the results on TaxiBJ dataset with k set to 3, 4, 6, 8, 9, 12, 15 and 16. It can be seen from Table 2 that with the increase of future step k, the MAE and RMSE for all methods keep increasing. This is reasonable because predicting a larger future scale is always harder than predicting a smaller scale. Furthermore, STS-GAN consistently outperforms other compared methods in terms of both MAE and RMSE, which demonstrate the effectiveness of the proposed model. Finally, among these methods, GRU and ST-ResNet show severely worse performance with the increase of prediction step, whereas DCRNN and GCGAN have better performance. This is because DCRNN takes advantage of diffusion convolution layers and Seq2Seq architecture, while GCGAN integrates Seq2Seq model with adversarial learning.

Table 2. Performance comparison on TaxiBJ under different prediction step k.

Index	Method	$k = 1$	$k = 3$	$k = 4$	$k = 6$	$k = 8$	$k = 9$	$k = 12$	$k = 16$
RMSE	GRU	21.37	22.56	23.38	25.28	27.13	28.86	32.85	35.69
	GCGAN	17.26	17.57	18.61	19.43	20.45	20.96	21.38	23.49
	DCRNN	18.36	18.48	19.06	20.36	21.83	22.72	24.26	27.58
	ST-ResNet	16.69	18.35	20.27	22.14	24.63	26.25	27.79	29.61
	STS-GAN	**13.87**	**14.13**	**14.92**	**15.68**	**16.75**	**17.39**	**19.24**	**21.43**
MAE	GRU	12.38	13.52	14.59	15.37	17.86	18.27	21.46	24.94
	GCGAN	10.83	11.97	12.75	13.32	13.68	14.15	15.82	17.85
	DCRNN	10.57	11.25	12.13	14.08	15.95	16.31	18.17	21.63
	ST-ResNet	9.43	11.29	12.38	14.59	17.14	17.96	19.36	22.05
	STS-GAN	**7.25**	**7.86**	**8.47**	**9.19**	**10.03**	**10.88**	**12.25**	**13.72**

Sensitive Study on β. The hyper-parameter $\beta \in [0, 1]$ is used to balance the importance of GAN's adversarial loss and the prediction MSE loss for addressing the **blurry prediction issue**. A larger β means the adversarial loss is more important than the prediction error in total loss of Eq. eq:eq12. When β is too large, the effect of prediction MSE loss is neglected. In this case, STS-GAN cannot address the multi-step prediction blurry issue. On the other hand, when β becomes too small, STS-GAN will not consider the effect of adversarial loss and the model degenerates to most existing prediction models.

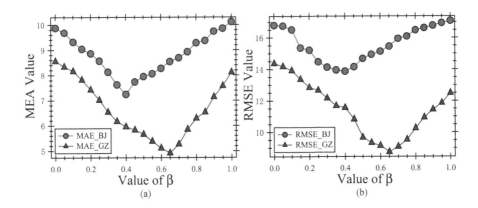

Fig. 2. The effect of hyper-parameter β on STS-GAN performance.

To investigate the influence of β on our model performance, we conduct experiments on $k = 4$ multi-step prediction and set the value of β ranging from 0 to 1 with a step of 0.05. Figure 2 (a) shows the MAE value change with different β and Fig. 2 (b) shows the RMSE value change with different β. It can be seen that MAE and RMSE values change remarkably with the increase of β on both TaxiBJ and GZ-Mobility datasets, which demonstrate that β has a significant impact on STS-GAN's performance. It can be seen that a too large or too small β will hurt the performance of STS-GAN and the best β for TaxiBJ dataset is 0.4, and 0.65 for GZ-Mobility dataset. When only MSE loss is considered with very small β(i.e. $\beta \rightarrow 0$), the performance of STS-GAN decreases significantly, which is caused by the blurry prediction issue. We introduce adversarial learning framework to successfully alleviate blurry prediction. The results also demonstrate that a suitable β can help improve the performance of STS-GAN.

6 Conclusion

In this paper, we present a novel urban flow prediction model called STS-GAN which integrates sequence-to-sequence model and adversarial learning architecture for accurate multi-step urban flow prediction. Specifically, STS-GAN employs the designed Spatial-Temporal Semantic Encoder (STSE) block to model the influence of semantic factors on urban flow. Moreover, STS-GAN explicitly considers multi-scale temporal dependencies to model the global historical temporal correlations. In addition, we propose a weighted and integrated loss function consisting of adversarial loss and prediction error to handle the blurry prediction issue. Extensive experiments are conducted on two large-scale urban flow datasets in Beijing and Guangzhou, demonstrating the superiority of our model over other advanced methods. In the future, STS-GAN is a general adversarial learning model and can be applied to solve other spatial-temporal tasks.

References

1. Arjovsky, M., Chintala, S., Bottou, L.: Wasserstein gan (2017)
2. Chung, J., Gulcehre, C., Cho, K., Bengio, Y.: Empirical evaluation of gated recurrent neural networks on sequence modeling. In: NIPS (2014)
3. Geng, X., et al.: Spatiotemporal multi-graph convolution network for ride-hailing demand forecasting. In: AAAI (2019)
4. Goodfellow, I., et al.: Generative adversarial nets. In: NIPS (2014)
5. Li, M., Zhu, Z.: Spatial-temporal fusion graph neural networks for traffic flow forecasting. **35**(5), 4189–4196 (2021)
6. Li, Y., Yu, R., Shahabi, C., Liu, Y.: Diffusion convolutional recurrent neural network: data-driven traffic forecasting. In: ICRL (2018)
7. Lin, Y., Dai, X., Li, L., Wang, F.Y.: Pattern sensitive prediction of traffic flow based on generative adversarial framework. IEEE Trans. Intell. Transp. Syst. **20**(6), 2395–2400 (2018)
8. Lin, Z., Feng, J., Lu, Z., Li, Y., Jin, D.: Deepstn+: context-aware spatial temporal neural network for crowd flow prediction in metropolis (2019)
9. Ma, D., Zhang, F., Bull, D.R.: Gan-based effective bit depth adaptation for perceptual video compression. In: ICME (2020)
10. Song, C., Lin, Y., Guo, S., Wan, H.: Spatial-temporal synchronous graph convolutional networks: a new framework for spatial-temporal network data forecasting. In: AAAI (2020)
11. Song, X., Wu, Y., Zhang, C.: TSTNet: a sequence to sequence transformer network for spatial-temporal traffic prediction. In: Farkaš, I., Masulli, P., Otte, S., Wermter, S. (eds.) ICANN 2021. LNCS, vol. 12891, pp. 343–354. Springer, Cham (2021). https://doi.org/10.1007/978-3-030-86362-3_28
12. Sundar, R., Hebbar, S., Golla, V.: Implementing intelligent traffic control system for congestion control, ambulance clearance, and stolen vehicle detection. IEEE Sens. J. 1109–1113 (2015)
13. Wang, S., Cao, J., Chen, H., Peng, H., Huang, Z.: Seqst-gan: Seq2seq generative adversarial nets for multi-step urban crowd flow prediction. **6**(4), 22–45 (2020)
14. Xu, D., Wei, C., Peng, P., Xuan, Q., Guo, H.: Ge-gan: a novel deep learning framework for road traffic state estimation. Transp. Res. C Emerg. Technol. (2020)
15. Yao, H., Tang, X., Wei, H., Zheng, G., Yu, Y., Li, Z.: Modeling spatial-temporal dynamics for traffic prediction. arXiv preprint arXiv:1803.01254, pp. 922–929 (2018)
16. Ye, J., Zhao, J., Ye, K., Xu, C.: How to build a graph-based deep learning architecture in traffic domain: a survey. IEEE Trans. Intell. Transp. Syst. 1–21 (2021)

17. Yu, J.J.Q., Gu, J.: Real-time traffic speed estimation with graph convolutional generative autoencoder. IEEE Trans. Intell. Transp. Syst. **20**(10), 3940–3951 (2019)
18. Zhang, J., Zheng, Y., Qi, D.: Deep spatio-temporal residual networks for citywide crowd flows prediction. In: AAAI (2017)
19. Zhang, J., Zheng, Y., Qi, D., Li, R., Yi, X.: DNN-based prediction model for spatio-temporal data (2016)
20. Zhang, Y., Wang, S., Chen, B., Cao, J.: GCGAN: generative adversarial nets with graph CNN for network-scale traffic prediction. In: IJCNN (2019)
21. Zhu, M., Zhu, X., Zhu, C.: STGATP: a spatio-temporal graph attention network for long-term traffic prediction. In: Farkaš, I., Masulli, P., Otte, S., Wermter, S. (eds.) ICANN 2021. LNCS, vol. 12893, pp. 255–266. Springer, Cham (2021). https://doi.org/10.1007/978-3-030-86365-4_21

Topic-Grained Text Representation-Based Model for Document Retrieval

Mengxue Du, Shasha Li, Jie Yu[✉], Jun Ma[✉], Bin Ji, Huijun Liu, Wuhang Lin, and Zibo Yi

College of Computer, National University of Defense Technology, Changsha, Hunan, China
{dumengxuenudt,shashali,yj,majun,jibin,liuhuijun, wuhanglin,yizibo14}@nudt.edu.cn

Abstract. Document retrieval enables users to find their required documents accurately and quickly. To satisfy the requirement of retrieval efficiency, prevalent deep neural methods adopt a representation-based matching paradigm, which saves online matching time by pre-storing document representations offline. However, the above paradigm consumes vast local storage space, especially when storing the document as word-grained representations. To tackle this, we present **TGTR**, a **T**opic-**G**rained **T**ext **R**epresentation-based **Model** for document retrieval. Following the representation-based matching paradigm, TGTR stores the document representations offline to ensure retrieval efficiency, whereas it significantly reduces the storage requirements by using novel topic-grained representations rather than traditional word-grained. Experimental results demonstrate that compared to word-grained baselines, TGTR is consistently competitive with them on TREC CAR and MS MARCO in terms of retrieval accuracy, but it requires less than 1/10 of the storage space required by them. Moreover, TGTR overwhelmingly surpasses global-grained baselines in terms of retrieval accuracy.

Keywords: Neural retrieval · Text representation · Topic granularity · Space compression

1 Introduction

Recently, deep learning based semantic representations have attracted much research attention and been widely used in the document retrieval field. Recent methods propose to fine-tune deep pre-trained language models (PLMs) such as BERT [3] to assess matching degrees of query-document pairs [3,10,25]. They achieve the state-of-the-art performance of the document retrieval task by concatenating query-document pair and feeding it into a PLM to calculate the

This work was supported by Hunan Provincial Natural Science Foundation Project (No. 2022JJ30668) and (No. 2022JJ30046).
M. Du and S. Li—Contributed equally to this work.

matching degree. Unfortunately, despite these methods achieve great success, they come at a steep increase in time cost, which is unacceptable in practical application scenarios.

In order to improve the retrieval speed, researchers propose a representation-based framework, where they encode query and document into word-grained representations [10], as shown in Fig. 1(a). And then they assess the matching degree of a query and a document pair by calculating the similarity of their representations. Benefit from the decoupling computation of queries and documents, the representation-based framework can pre-store document representations offline. Thus the online retrieval only needs to encode the query while it obtains the document representations from local storage directly. However, the representation-based framework come at a steep increase in space cost to store document representations. For example, when using ColBERT [10] to generate document representations, it requires 154 GiBs to store the TREC CAR corpus and 632 GiBs to store the MS MARCO corpus, where the document sizes of two corpora are only 2.9 GiBs and 15.6 GiBs, respectively. In this paper, we explore a novel method to compress document representations, with the goal of saving storage space and guaranteeing the retrieval accuracy as well.

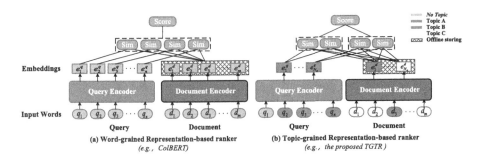

Fig. 1. The matching paradigms of word-grained retriever (a) and the proposed method (b). Given a query and a document, (a) and (b) encode them into word-level embeddings and topic-level embeddings, respectively. (b) reduce the length of document's representation from the word count level to the topic count level, which means it significantly compresses the space cost of offline storing documents' representations.

To address the above issues, we proposes TGTR, a topic-grained text representation-based document retrieval model, as shown in Fig. 1(b). To be specific, we first model the topics distribution of documents and queries to obtain every word's latent topics, and then use Attention network to obtain topic-level embeddings by fusing words' contextual embeddings with the same topic. The motivation is drawn from the fact that, in general, users are only interested in documents consisting of information closely related to their search topic. The information in a document may cover multiple topics, and users tend to pay more attention to those parts of the document which are closely related to the query topic and less attention to the remainder. Unfortunately, previous document retrieval models [7,9,10,12,19] ignore to take the topic information into account. In addition, the problem is particularly acute for long documents.

We see the following intuitive benefits when using topic-grained representations of queries and documents to retrieval documents.

1) Compresse the space cost of storing document representations. Compared to word-grained retrievers, the proposed topic-grained retriever can compress the size of the document representations by one order-of-magnitude, and the compression rate increases as the document length increases.
2) Keep a balance of the amount of information between each embedding in query and document's representations. We think it's the main reason why TGTR can achieve better retrieval accuray than the alternative methods described in Sect. 2.
3) Break the existing information fusion that follows the structure of the article. We fuse the contents sharing the same topic together across the whole article. It's a process of distilling the representive information of a document. Furthermore, we find that no-topic words are frequently filler words. Which indicates our model is effective at filtering out redundant information.

In summary, this work makes the following contributions:

1) We propose a novel document retrieval model that introduces topic-grained representation to the task for the first time;
2) Our model guarantees retrieval accuracy while significantly compressing the storage space of the document representations;
3) Our model obtains competitive performance compared to all baselines on two benchmark datasets in terms of retrieval accuracy, but it requires less than 1/10 of the space cost compared to them.

2   Related Work

Classical information retrieval (IR) systems rely on exact lexical match [21], we call them lexical retrievers. Lexical retrievers can process queries very quickly. Nowadays, they are still widely used in production systems [7]. Recently, researchers have utilized deep learning to improve traditional lexical retrievers, including document expansions [16,17], query expansions [13] and term weight estimation [2].

In the past few years, information retrieval researchers have introduced a range of neural models for semantic retrieval [6–10,12,19,25]. Due to the specific requirements of time efficiency, researchers proposed the representation-based retrieval framework. [3,6,7,9–11,19,23].

Khattab. Omar et al. [10] first proposed a word-grained representation-based retriever, we call this type of models word-grained retrievers. Word-grained retrievers provides state-of-the-art performance at that time while resulting in significant storage overhead. COIL [7] is another word-grained retriever which stores the token embedding in an inverted list. Representing queries and/or documents separately with a single embedding is an important method to compress document representations, which we call global-grained retrievers [6, 9, 19]

Global-grained retrievers also generate word-level embeddings firstly, but then they fuse the sequence of embeddings into one by various means. Sentence-BERT [20] explores the effect of using 1) [CLS] embedding; 2) average pooling; 3) max pooling to fuse the BERT embedding sequence, respectively. However, This type of models can seriously impair retrieval accuracy. we attribute it to that the amount of information between query and document in the real world is often asymmetric ($|query| \ll |document|$), which leads to an imbalance of the amount of information between each embedding in query and document's representations.

In summary, current representation-based retrievers face the tradeoff of the space cost (document representations) and retrieval accuracy. TGTR effectively reduces the cost of space by constructing the topic-grained representation, without compromising retrieval accuracy.

3   TGTR

In this section, we present our topic-grained text representation-based model for document retrieval. Before we present the framework, some preliminary about representation-based matching paradigm are introduced. Then the TGTR framework are described in detail.

3.1   Preliminary

In the field of document retrieving, specially for deep models, it's very common to assess the matching degree of a query-document pair by representing the query and/or document as a sequence of vectors which we called representation-based matching paradigm. Given a query sequence $Q = [q_1, q_2, ..., q_n]$ and a document sequence $D = [d_1, d_2, ..., d_m]$, both q_i and d_j represent a word. Firstly, encoding a query and document into representations E^q and E^d, then calculating the similarity between E^q and E^d [22]. As Fig. 1(a) shows, traditional word-grained retrievers encode every word into a fixed-length embedding $E^q = [e_1^q, e_2^q, ..., e_n^q]$ and $E^d = [e_1^d, e_2^d, ..., e_m^d]$.

By design, the representation-based matching paradigm isolates almost all of the computations between queries and documents to enable pre-computing document representations offline [10]. It proceeds over the documents in the collection in batches, once the documents' representations are produced, they are saved to disk using 32-bit or 16-bit values to represent each dimension. In Fig. 1, we use the rectangular box with decorative pattern to identify the part of offline storing.

Generally, per embedding in representation is about hundreds of dimensions and storing a dimension needs at least 16-bit. The number of a document's embeddings stored by word-grained retrievers is approximately equal to the document length, making huge space cost. As Fig. 1(b) shows, we propose to encode the document with N_d representative topics into topic-grained representations $E^d = [e_1^d, e_2^d, ..., e_{N_d}^d]$ rather the traditional word-grained representations. The idea's purpose is to reduce the number of the document's embeddings to compress the space cost of storing documents' representations.

3.2   Model Architecture

Figure 2 depicts the architecture of TGTR, which comprises four components. We will cover these components in detail in this section.

Topic Recognizer. The topic recognizer uses traditional topic generation model to recognize latent topics of every word in documents and queries. As Fig. 2(A) shows, given a query sequence $Q = [q_1, q_2, ..., q_n]$ and a document

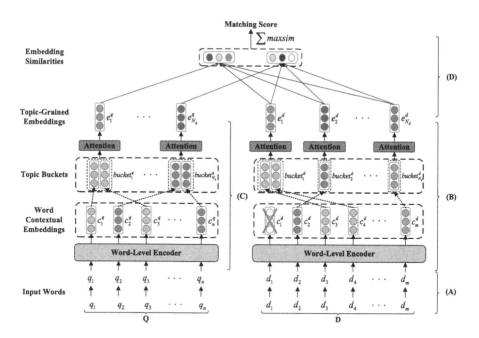

Fig. 2. The architecture of TGTR. (A) Topic recognizer; (B) Query encoder; (C) Document encoder; and (D) Matching Assessment Mechanism. Given an input query sentence Q and a document sentence D, (A) recognizes latent topics of every word in documents and queries, and then (B) and (C) encode the query and the document to sequences of topic-grained embeddings by three stages, separately. Finally, (D) uses maximum similarity operation to output final matching score between the query and the document.

sequence $D = [d_1, d_2, ..., d_m]$, topic recognizer gives their words different topic colors by analyzing their topics distributions.

To be specific, we use Latent Dirichlet Allocation (LDA) [1] to model documents and queries' latent topics. Algorithm 1 depicts the process of obtaining words' topics. Firstly, we obtain the text-topic distribution Array as well as the topic-word distribution Array (line 1–2). We then set threshold θ_t to extract the representative topics for each text (line 3–8). In the same manner, we set fixed threshold θ_{wf} and ratio threshold θ_{wr} to extract the representative words in a text under its representative topics (line 9–11). Finally, a two-dimensional table M is generated for each text (line 12). The dim of row in M represents a word, while the dim of column represents a potential topic. Note a word may have more than one or zero latent topics. The words without any latent topics are considered meaningless and discarded after helping other words to generate contextual embeddings (see the red cross symbol in Fig. 2).

Algorithm 1. Topic Recognizer of TGTR

Input:
    The text-words array, text2words;
    The number of texts, m;
    The number of topics, k;
    The trained topic model, LDA;
    The word frequency builder, Vectorizer;
    The threshold for extracting representative topics , θ_t;
    The fixed and ratio threshold for extracting representative words, θ_{wf}, θ_{wr};
Output:
    The list of potential topics of words in all texts, text2word2topics;
1: textVectorizer $\leftarrow$ Vectorizer.transform(text2words)
2: text2topics, topic2words $\leftarrow$ LDA.transform(textVectorizer)
3: **for** $d \in [1, 2, ..., m]$ **do**
4:     $M \leftarrow [\,]$, text2word2topics $\leftarrow [\,]$
5:     **for** $t \in [1, 2, ..., k]$ **do**
6:         **if** text2topics$[d, t] \geq \theta_t$ **then**
7:             Get the distribution of words in the d-th text
8:                 under the t-th topic dis$_{dt} \leftarrow$ topic2words
9:             $l \leftarrow |\text{dis}_{dt}|$
10:            **for** $w \in [1, 2, ..., l]$ **do**
11:                **if** dis$_{dt}[w] \geq \theta_{wf}$ **or** dis$_{dt}$.getorder$(w)/l \leq \theta_{wr}$ **then**
12:                    $M[w]$.append(t)
13:                **end if**
14:            **end for**
15:         **end if**
16:     **end for**
17:     text2word2topics.append(M)
18: **end for**
19: **return** text2word2topics

Document Encoder. We then encode the document to a sequence of fixed-length embeddings. This part comprises three stages.

Stage 1: Encode word-level contextual embeddings. Given a document D, TGTR first maps each word d_i into its contextual embedding c_i^d by using Word-Level Encoder (WLE). Though we can complete this part of work by using methods such as in [3,5], We focus on BERT [3] to keep consistent with the major baseline. Note BERT uses WordPiece embeddings with a 30,000 token vocabulary, thus a word can be tokenized to several tokens. Strictly speaking, the i-th word's contextual embedding c_i^d may comprises more than one token embedding, which we hope readers will notice. The process of this stage is summarized as Eq. 1.

$$[c_1^d, c_2^d, ..., c_m^d] := \text{WLE}(d_1, d_2, ..., d_m) \tag{1}$$

Stage 2: Word-topic mapping. As mentioned above, we obtain a two-dimensional word-topics table M for every document by modeling latent topics. The dim of row in M represents a word, while the dim of column represents a potential topic. Every word's contextual embedding obtained in Stage 1 is mapped to the buckets corresponding to topics they have. A word may be mapped into multiple buckets or filtered out (regarded as meaningless). The bucket corresponding to the i-th topic is marked as $bucket_i^d$. The process of this stage is summarized as Eq. 2, where N_d is the number of representative topics the document d has.

$$[bucket_1^d, bucket_2^d, ..., bucket_{N_d}^d] := \text{Mapping}(c_1^d, c_2^d, ..., c_m^d) \tag{2}$$

Stage 3: Generate topic-grained representation. The model TGTR uses **Attention** network to obtain topic-level embeddings, which we call topic-grained representation. Considering different words with the same topic have different amount of information, we assign different weights to different words. For the bucket corresponding to the t-th topic $bucket_t^d : [u_1, u_2, ..., u_{B_t}]$ outputed by stage 2, denote the attention weight of u_i as α_i:

$$\alpha_i = q_t{}^T \tanh(W \times u_i + b) \tag{3}$$

$$\alpha_i = \frac{\exp(\alpha_i)}{\sum_{j=1}^{B_t} \exp(\alpha_j)} \tag{4}$$

where W and b are parameters, q_t is the attention query vector, $tanh$ is the activation function and B_t is the size of the t-th topic bucket. The final embedding of t-th topic e_t^d is the summation of the word-level embeddings in $bucket_t^d$ weighted by their attentions.

$$e_t^d = \sum_{i=1}^{B_t} \alpha_i u_i \tag{5}$$

Query Encoder. Our query encoder has a very similar architecture with document encoder, they share model parameters but have a few difference in input processing. We prepend BERT's start token [CLS] followed by a special token [D] when input a document sequence. In the same manner, we prepend BERT's start token [CLS] followed by a special token [Q] when input a query sequence.

Matching Assessment Mechanism. Finally, we use a maximum similarity (MaxSim) operation to output our final matching score. Given the query's topic-grained representation $E^q : [e_1^q, e_2^q, ..., e_{N_q}^q]$ and the document's topic-grained representation $E^d : [e_1^d, e_2^d, ..., e_{N_d}^d]$, the matching score of query q and document d is assessed by MaxSim operation between E^q and E^d. To be specific, we applies MaxSim between one of the query embeddings and all of the document's embeddings, then we sum all items up as final score $S(Q, D)$. The process of this part is summarized as Eq. 6.

$$S(Q, D) = \sum_{i \in [|E^q|]} \max_{j \in [|E^d|]} e_i^q (e_j^d)^T \tag{6}$$

Notice our Matching Assessment Mechanism has no trainable parameters.

Training. The training objective is to learn representations of queries and documents so that query-positive document pairs have higher matching score than the query-negative documents pairs in training data. Given a query Q together with its positive documents D^+ and m negative documents. $\{D_i^-\}_{i=1}^m$, we minimize the loss function:

$$L(Q, D^+, \{D_i^-\}_{i=1}^m) = -\log \frac{\exp(S(Q, D^+))}{\exp(S(Q, D^+)) + \sum_{i=1}^m \exp(S(Q, D_i^-))} \tag{7}$$

4 Experiment Methodology

4.1 Datasets

Following previous work [10], our experiments use two datasets, which differ in data size, to evaluate our model in document retrieving tasks.

TREC CAR. TREC CAR is introduced by Dietz et al. [4] in 2017, is a composite data set based on Wikipedia containing approximately 29 million articles. Our assessment was performed on the test set used in TREC 2017 CAR, which contained 2,254 queries.

MS MARCO. MS MARCO [15] is a dataset introduced by Microso in 2016 for reading comprehension and adapted in 2018 for retrieval. It is a collection of 8.8M passages from Web pages, which were gathered from Bing's results to 1M real-world queries.

4.2 Baseline Methods

We adopt three types of baselines for comparison.

Lexical Retriever. Lexical Retriever retrieve document based on lexical matching rather than semantic matching. In this type, we choose three traditional methods [14,21,24] and three network methods [2,16,17] as our baselines.

Global-Grained Retriever. Global-grained retriever retrieve document with global-grained representations of queries and documents. In this type, we choose BERT [3] and DPR [9] as our baselines.

Word-Grained Retriever. Global-grained retriever retrieve document with word-grained representations of queries and documents. In this type, we choose ColBERT [10] and COIL [7] as our baselines.

5 Experiment Details

5.1 Implementation Details

The complete training details are given below:

- We fit LDA model by using Scikit-learn machine learning library [18]. We apply variational inference with expectation-maximization to learn model's parameters and get the distributions described in Sect. 3. The number of latent topics K is a hyper-parameters here, and we set other two hyper-parameters α and η to $1/K$ by default.
- We choose the max query length as 32 and the max doc length as 180 at dataset MS MARCO. Since TREC is much larger than MS MARCO, we set max query length 48 and max doc length 250 in TREC.
- We use BERT as pre-trained word-level embedding encoder to embed the query and document sentences with the embedding dimension of 768 and the vocab size of 30522.
- We then apply attention operation for every topic buckets by different query vectors. The parameters W and b are shared by all buckets.
- The dimension of final topic-level embedding dim is 768. We passes the embeddings through a linear layer with no activations to control their dimensions. As we discuss later in more detail, we typically fix dim range as (64, 128, 256, 512, 768). We set dim=256 by default.

5.2 Experiment Results

Table 1 shows the retrieving performance of TGTR and our baselines over two datasets.

Compared to Word-Grained Retrievers. The results show that TGTR performs almost 10 times better than the word-grained baselines in terms of space cost with no loss in terms of retrieval accuracy on MS MARCO. On TREC

CAR, TGTR performs almost 12 times better than the word-grained baselines in terms of space cost with 2.3% and 2.0% loss in terms of MRR@10 and MAP on MS MARCO.

Compared to Global-Grained Retrievers. The results show that TGTR overwhelmingly outperforms global-grained retrievers in terms of space cost and retrieval accuracy over both datasets. Note our model outperforms global-grained

Table 1. Retrieving performances of TGTR and baseline models. We report the performances of our model with the embedding dimension $dim = 256$. Improvement, degradation or equivalent with respect to TGTR in terms of MRR@10, Recall@1K and MAP is indicated $(+/-/-)$. The unit of 'Space' is (GiBs). Results not applicable are denoted 'n.a.'.

(a) Performance comparisons on MS MARCO.

Method	Space (GiBs)		MRR@10		Recall@1K	
Lexical retriever						
BM25	n.a.	n.a.	0.187	−48.2%	0.857	−11.5%
Doc2query	n.a	n.a	0.215	−40.4%	0.891	−8.0%
DeepCT	n.a.	n.a.	0.243	−32.7%	0.910	−6.0%
DocTTTTTquery	n.a	n.a	0.277	−23.3%	0.947	−2.2%
Global-grained retriever						
BERT	25.3	×1.6	0.310	−14.1%	0.929	−4.0%
DPR	n.a	n.a	0.311	−13.9%	0.952	−1.7%
Word-grained retriever						
COIL	n.a	n.a	0.355	−1.7%	0.963	−0.5%
ColBERT	154.0	×9.9	0.360	−0.3%	**0.968**	−
Topic-grained retriever						
TGTR	**15.6**	**×1**	**0.361**	−	**0.968**	-

(b) Performance comparisons on TREC CAR.

Method	Space (GiBs)		MRR@10		MAP	
Lexical retriever						
BM25	n.a.	n.a.	n.a.	n.a.	0.153	−50.2%
TextRank	n.a.	n.a.	0.160	−63.0%	0.120	−60.9%
Doc2query	n.a	n.a	n.a	n.a	0.181	−41.0%
DeepCT	n.a.	n.a.	0.332	−23.3%	0.246	−19.9%
Global-grained retriever						
BERT	83.2	×1.6	0.376	−13.2%	0.273	−11.1%
Word-grained retriever						
ColBERT	632.1	×12.3	**0.443**	**+2.3%**	**0.313**	**+2.0%**
Topic-grained retriever						
TGTR	**51.4**	**×1.0**	0.433	−	0.307	−

retrievers in terms of space cost because we reduce the embedding dimension by passing the original embeddings through a linear layer.

Compared to Lexical Retrievers. The results show that TGTR overwhelmingly outperforms lexical retrievers in terms of retrieval accuracy over both datasets. Note lexical retrievers don't need store documents' representations, so the compare between our model and them in terms of space cost is not available.

Summary. Compared to word-grained baselines, TGTR is consistently outperforming them on MS MARCO and be competitive with them on TREC CAR in terms of retrieval accuracy, but it performs almost 10 times better than them in terms of space cost. Moreover, TGTR overwhelmingly outperforms lexical and global-grained baselines in terms of retrieval accuracy.

6   Analysis

6.1   A Comparison of Trade-Off Quality

In this section, we assess the trade-off quality between space efficiency and retrieval accuracy of three types of representation-based retrievers. We use the quotient of MRR and Space as the trade-off score. We use BERT and ColBERT to represent the global-grained retriever and word-grained retriever, separately. Topic-grained Retriever is our model.

Table 2 shows the results. It seems that our model significantly outperforms other two types of retrievers in term of trade-off quality and the word-grained retriever performs the worst.

Table 2. Comparisons of trade-off quality among three types of retrievers.

Method	MRR/Space (1e−3)			
	MS MARCO		TREC CAR	
Global-grained retriever	12.3	−46.8%	4.5	−46.4%
Word-grained retriever	2.3	−90.0%	0.7	−91.7%
Topic-grained retriever	**23.1**	−	**8.4**	−

6.2   Embeddings Dimension and Bytes per Dimension

Two of the most attractive features in our model is the embeddings dimension and the bytes per dimension. Figure 3 shows the impact of above two features on the model performance. As Fig. 3(a) shows, retrieval accuracy increases sublinearly with the increase of above two features in our model. Figure 3(b) clearly shows that it might contribute to higher trade-off quality by reducing the above two features. As Fig. 3(c) shows, retrieval accuracy increases sublinearly with the increase of space cost in our model. It seems that when the embedding dimension is small enough, further compression can cause great accuracy damage.

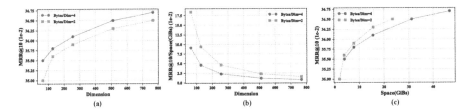

Fig. 3. (a) and (b) show the impact of embeddings dimension and the bytes per dimension on MRR@10 and trade-off quality (MRR/Space), separately. (c) shows MRR@10 vs Space(GiBs) as functions of the embeddings dimension and the bytes per dimension.

7   Conclusions

This paper presents TGTR, a novel retrieval model that employs topic-grained text representation for document retrieval. The key of our model is modeling the topics distribution of documents and queries to obtain every word's latent topics, and then using Attention network to obtain topic-level embeddings by fusing words' contextual embeddings with the same topic. Our experiments on MS MARCO and TREC benchmark datasets demonstrates the advantage of representing texts as topic-grained embeddings for document retrieval task. These results suggest that our model guarantees retrieval accuracy while significantly compressing the storage space of the document representations.

References

1. Blei, D.M., Ng, A.Y.: Latent dirichlet allocation. J. Mach. Learn. Res. **3**, 993–1022 (2003)
2. Dai, Z., Callan, J.: Context-aware term weighting for first stage passage retrieval. In: SIGIR, pp. 1533–1536 (2020)
3. Devlin, J., et al.: Bert: pre-training of deep bidirectional transformers for language understanding. arXiv:1810.04805 (2018)
4. Dietz, L., Verma, M.: TREC complex answer retrieval overview. In: TREC (2017)
5. Feng, Z., Tang, D., et al.: Pretraining without wordpieces: learning over a vocabulary of millions of words. arXiv:2202.12142 (2022)
6. Gao, L., Callan, J.: Condenser: a pre-training architecture for dense retrieval. arXiv:2104.08253 (2021)
7. Gao, L., Dai, Z.: Coil: Revisit exact lexical match in information retrieval with contextualized inverted list. arXiv:2104.07186 (2021)
8. Guo, J., Fan, Y.: A deep relevance matching model for ad-hoc retrieval. In: The 25th CIKM, pp. 55–64 (2016)
9. Karpukhin, V., Oğuz, B.: Dense passage retrieval for open-domain question answering. arXiv:2004.04906 (2020)
10. Khattab, O., Zaharia, M.: Colbert: Efficient and effective passage search via contextualized late interaction over bert. In: SIGIR, pp. 39–48 (2020)
11. Lu, S., He, D.: Less is more: pretrain a strong siamese encoder for dense text retrieval using a weak decoder. In: 2021 EMNLP, pp. 2780–2791 (2021)

12. Ma, X., Guo, J.: Prop: pre-training with representative words prediction for ad-hoc retrieval. In: The 14th WSDM, pp. 283–291 (2021)
13. Mao, Y., He, P.: Generation-augmented retrieval for open-domain question answering. arXiv:2009.08553 (2020)
14. Mihalcea, R., Tarau, P.: Textrank: bringing order into text. In: The 2004 EMNLP, pp. 404–411 (2004)
15. Nguyen, T., Rosenberg, M.: Ms marco: a human generated machine reading comprehension dataset. In: CoCo@ NIPS (2016)
16. Nogueira, R., Lin, J., Epistemic, A.: From doc2query to docttttquery. Online preprint 6 (2019)
17. Nogueira, R., Yang, W., Lin, J., Cho, K.: Document expansion by query prediction. arXiv:1904.08375 (2019)
18. Pedregosa, F., et al.: Scikit-learn: machine learning in python. J. Mach. Learn. Res. **12**, 2825–2830 (2011)
19. Qu, Y., Ding, Y.: Rocketqa: an optimized training approach to dense passage retrieval for open-domain question answering. arXiv:2010.08191 (2020)
20. Reimers, N., Gurevych, I.: Sentence-bert: sentence embeddings using siamese bert-networks. arXiv:1908.10084 (2019)
21. Robertson, S.E., et al.: Some simple effective approximations to the 2-poisson model for probabilistic weighted retrieval. In: SIGIR 1994, pp. 232–241. Springer, London (1994). https://doi.org/10.1007/978-1-4471-2099-5_24
22. Sun, Q., Wu, Y.: A multi-level attention model for text matching. In: Kůrková, V., Manolopoulos, Y., Hammer, B., Iliadis, L., Maglogiannis, I. (eds.) ICANN 2018. LNCS, vol. 11139, pp. 142–153. Springer, Cham (2018). https://doi.org/10.1007/978-3-030-01418-6_15
23. Zamani, H., et al.: From neural re-ranking to neural ranking: Learning a sparse representation for inverted indexing. In: The 27th CIKM, pp. 497–506 (2018)
24. Zhai, C., Lafferty, J.: A study of smoothing methods for language models applied to ad hoc information retrieval (2001)
25. Zheng, Z., Hui, K.: Bert-QE: contextualized query expansion for document re-ranking. arXiv:2009.07258 (2020)

Training 1-Bit Networks on a Sphere:
A Geometric Approach

Luis Guerra[1]([✉]), Ajanthan Thalaiyasingam[2], Gil Avraham[1], Yan Zou[1],
and Tom Drummond[1]

[1] Monash University, Melbourne, Australia
luis.guerrafernandez@monash.edu
[2] Australian National University, Canberra, Australia

Abstract. Weight binarization offers a promising alternative towards building highly efficient Deep Neural Networks (DNNs) that can be deployed in low-power, constrained devices. However, given their discrete nature, training 1-bit DNNs is not a straightforward or uniquely defined process and several strategies have been proposed to address this issue yielding every time closer performance to their full-precision counterparts. In this paper we analyze 1-bit DNNs from a differential geometry perspective. We part from noticing that for a given model with d binary weights, all possible weight configurations lie on a sphere of radius $\sqrt{d}$. Along with the traditional training procedure based on the Straight Through Estimator (STE), we leverage concepts from the fields of Riemannian optimization to constrain the search space to spherical manifolds, a subset of Riemannian manifolds. Our approach offers a principled solution; nevertheless, in practice we found that simply constraining the norm of the underlying auxiliary network works just as effectively. Additionally, we observe that by enforcing a unit norm on the network parameters, our network explores a space of well-conditioned matrices. Complementary to our approach, we additionally define an angle based regularization that guides the auxiliary space exploration. We binarize a ResNet architecture in order to demonstrate the effectiveness of our approach in the tasks of image classification on the CIFAR-100 and ImageNet datasets.

Keywords: 1-bit Neural Networks · Geometric optimization · Conditioning

1 Introduction

Ranging from low rank matrix decompositions [9,23,51], pruning [18,29,52] and sparsification [27,35], quantization [7,14,40], architecture search [31,41,53], efficient submodules [19,22,50], weight sharing [15] and more, methods for compressing DNNs have appeared in all forms in recent years due to the increasing demand of efficient models deployable in cellphones, embedded systems, wearable devices, *etc.*. Quantization, and in the extreme case, binarization, comprises an appealing choice due to the high compression rates and multiplication-free convolutions.

However, 1-bit DNNs come at an expense. Training them to perform a specific task poses untrivial challenges. Due to their discrete nature, optimizing them is equivalent

Supported by the Australian Centre for Robotic Vision.

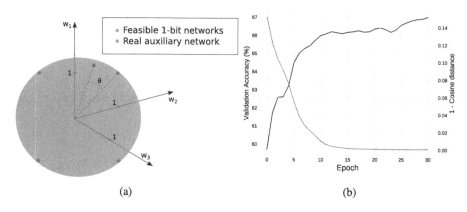

Fig. 1. a) All possible 1-bit neural networks lie on a $(d-1)$-dimensional hypersphere with radius $\sqrt{d}$. By leveraging Riemmanian optimization techniques, we restrict the exploration to points only on such hypersphere, although in practice simply normalizing works just as well. Additionally, angle penalization operates as regularization between the real auxiliary network and the quantized one. b) Cosine distance during fine-tuning along with Top-1 ImageNet validation accuracy using angle penalization. As the angle between the real and quantized vectors decreases, the validation accuracy increases.

to solving a combinatorial problem with d variables, where d, the number of weights in the network, is a value in the order of millions. Exploring the space of solutions results infeasible with traditional methods; thus, numerous approaches have been proposed in the context of DNNs including the widely accepted procedure based on the Straight Through Estimator [3] originally presented in [7], and later followed by works and variants such as [33,40], proximal methods [1,45] and relaxations [34,47].

In this paper with attack the problem from the perspective of geometric optimization, and refer the reader to [5] for further insights. Providing priors to the optimization framework, in the form of constraints, can considerably reduce the search space to only feasible solutions while preserving a smooth surface. This work parts from noticing that, given a static DNN with d binary weights, all the possible weight configurations lie on a $(d-1)$-dimensional hypersphere $\mathbb{S}^{d-1} = \{x \in \mathbb{R}^n : x^T x = 1\}$ residing inside a d-dimensional space. Spherical manifolds belong the class of Riemannian manifolds; therefore, as previously described, it is possible to leverage concepts of differential geometry in order to stick only to valid solutions at every step of the training process, this is, constraining the parameters of our network to a unit sphere. Additionally re-scaling the channel-wise latent weight vectors of the entire network, re-scales the magnitude of gradient vectors correspondingly.

In order to further comprehend the inner operation of our method, we provide an analysis of the conditioning number of the layers of our network during training [39]. We observe that constraining the magnitude of the weights leads to better convergence by improving the conditioning number of each layer. We draw a relation between the L_2, spectral and Lipschitz norms previously used to improve generalization and convergence [38,48]. Our method additionally acts as a direct replacement to techniques such as weight decay reducing the number of hyperparameter design choices.

Finally, we complement our approach with the scheme proposed by Liu *et al.* [32]. In a similar line to our work, Minimal Hyperspherical Energy (MHE) [32] aims at enforcing filters' diversity by projecting the filters of each layer on a hypersphere and evenly distributing them on it. This is popularly known as the Thompson/Thames problem.

2   Related Work

Geometric Deep Learning. Geometric optimization relies on the concepts of retraction and vector transport, which are relaxations of the classical geometric concepts of motion along geodesics and parallel transport, in order to solve constrained optimization problems where the solution lies on a manifold. The field of deep learning has experienced a growing interest in bridging these two fields [4,10,24,42,44]. Our work is not the first one to approach Binary Neural Networks (BNNs) from the geometric perspective. Anderson and Berg studied the high-dimensional properties of binarized weight vectors with respect to the full-precision auxiliary versions used in the STE procedure [2]. Their analysis showed that BNNs are able to learn due to small angle between those two vectors, which allows binary vectors to approximate the dot products. In an attempt to reduce this angular bias, [30] learns a pair of rotation matrices used to rotate the weight vectors at each training epoch. Several other works have resorted to filter-wise scalings to additionally reduce the norm gap [40].

Another relevant work is weight normalization [43], which can be seen as an extension of our work to real vectors, where the authors decouple the magnitude and direction of the weight vectors, leading to faster convergence.

Conditioning. In the context of DNNs, conditioning has been a major subject of study as it has been shown that ill-conditioned networks are very sensitive to input perturbations and led to shallow, unstable minima [48]. Initialization strategies [16,37] attack the problem from a statistical approach by aiming to restrain the mean and variance under some range, and consequently the internal activations and gradients, mitigating the issue of exploding gradients and achieving better convergence properties. Particularly [11] noted that DNNs training becomes unstable when the singular values of the Jacobian in each layer are larger than 1. Our approach indirectly constrains these values to be smaller than the unit.

3   Preliminaries: Optimization on Riemannian Manifolds

Consider the problem of optimizing a real-value DNN, but constraining the L_2 norm of the weights to a unit hypersphere $\mathbf{w} \subset \mathbb{S}^{d-1}$, or to the more general case of an arbitrary Riemannian manifold $\mathbf{w} \subset \mathcal{M}^{d-1}$. This is feasible due to the concepts of gradient projection and parameters retraction which will be explained bellow.

First order optimization methods such as vanilla Stochastic Gradient Descent (SGD) are based on the update formulation:

$$\mathbf{w}_{t+1} = \mathbf{w}_t - \alpha_t \mathbf{g}_t \tag{1}$$

where $\mathbf{g}_t \in \mathbb{R}^n$ is a vector in the loss surface pointing in the slope direction and along with $\alpha_t \in \mathbb{R}$ defines the step size. Analog theory has been developed for optimization on non-linear manifolds defined by constraints:

$$\min_{\mathbf{w} \subset \mathcal{M}^{d-1}} \mathcal{L}(\mathbf{w}). \tag{2}$$

In order to rely on conventional unconstrained DNN optimization techniques, we consider:

$$\min_{\mathbf{w} \in \mathbb{R}^d} \mathcal{L}(\mathbf{w}) \tag{3}$$

and restrict $\mathbf{w}$ to lie on the manifold M^{d-1} embedded in the Euclidean space $\mathbb{R}^n$. To do so, the generalization of Eq. 1 to a manifold $\mathcal{M}$ consists of a 2 step process. First the gradient $\mathbf{g}_t$ is projected to a tangent plane to $\mathcal{M}$ at $\mathbf{w}_t$ to obtain $\hat{\mathbf{g}}_t$. The update step is performed and $\mathbf{w}_{t+1/2}$ now lies on this tangent plane, however has escaped $\mathcal{M}$. Second, in order to bring back $\mathbf{w}_{t+1/2}$ to the curve, the operation of retraction is performed, which is only valid for elements lying on the mentioned tangent plane, resulting in $\mathbf{w}_{t+1}$.

Formally, the tangent space at $\mathbf{w}_t \in \mathcal{M}$, denoted $T_t^{\mathbf{w}}\mathcal{M}$ is the linear subspace of $\mathbb{R}^n$ defined by:

$$T_t^{\mathbf{w}}\mathcal{M} = \{v \in \mathbb{R}^n : v = f'(0) \text{ such that } f(0) = \mathbf{w}_t\}. \tag{4}$$

With the tangent plane defined, if f is a network on the Euclidean space, then $\hat{f}$, its restriction to $\mathcal{M}$, will have gradient:

$$\hat{\mathbf{g}}_t = \operatorname{grad}\hat{f}(\mathbf{w}_t) = \operatorname{Proj}_t^{\mathbf{w}}(\mathbf{g}_t) \tag{5}$$

that is, the classical gradient followed by a projection onto the tangent space. Subsequently an SGD step is taken followed by a retraction mapping, completing the sequence of steps:

$$\mathbf{w}_{t+1} = \operatorname{Ret}_{\mathbf{w}}(x_{t+1/2}), \qquad \mathbf{w}_{t+1/2} = x_t - \alpha_t \hat{\mathbf{g}}_t \tag{6}$$

4   Training 1-Bit DNNs on a Sphere

Given a training dataset $\mathcal{X}$, consisting typically of samples with their corresponding targets drawn in minibatches of n elements, the task of training a 1-bit DNN with binary weights $\mathbf{b} \in \{1, -1\}^d$, is defined as follows:

$$\min_{\mathbf{b} \in \{-1,1\}^d} \mathcal{L}(\mathcal{X}, \mathbf{b}). \tag{7}$$

Optimizing them corresponds to solving a outrageous combinatorial problem with millions of variables. However, it is easy to notice that all the possible weight configurations lie on a $(d-1)$-dimensional sphere. Thus, the obligued question is: *Is it possible to leverage this information to address the problem?* We find the answer in the field of Riemannian optimization, which subsumes hyperspheres optimization along with multiple other differentiable manifolds.

In Sect. 3, the concepts of gradient projection, retraction and steps for traversing Riemannian manifolds were explained. In this section we will extend them to the particular case of spheres starting with the tangent space.

The tangent space to S^{d-1} at $\mathbf{w}$ is the set of orthogonal vectors to this same point, $T_{\mathbf{w}}S^{d-1} = \{\gamma \in \mathbb{R}^d : \mathbf{w}^T\gamma = 0\}$. The orthogonal projection onto the tangent plane is defined as:

$$\text{Proj}_{\mathbf{w}}(\xi) = \xi - \mathbf{w}\mathbf{w}^T\xi, \qquad \xi \in \mathbb{R}^d \tag{8}$$

For the retraction there are two options which we compare in our experiments section. A simple choice is normalization to unit norm:

$$\text{Ret}_{\mathbf{w}}(\Delta) = \frac{\mathbf{w} + \Delta}{\|\mathbf{w} + \Delta\|}, \qquad \Delta \in \mathbb{R}^d \tag{9}$$

where $\|\cdot\|$ denotes the Euclidean norm in $\mathbb{R}^n$. A second possibility is

$$\text{Ret}_{\mathbf{w}}(\Delta) = \mathbf{w}\cos\|\Delta\| + \frac{\Delta}{\|\Delta\|}\sin\|\Delta\|, \qquad \Delta \in \mathbb{R}^d \tag{10}$$

which corresponds to the *exponential mapping*.

Nevertheless, so far we have ignored the second constraint, which is the discreteness of the solution space on the sphere, this is, $\mathbf{b}$ is only allowed to take values in $\{-1, 1\}^d$, making it incompatible with SGD given it relies on infinitesimal steps over smooth surfaces. In order to address this issue and simultaneously to evaluate only feasible network candidates, we can resort to a number of techniques like incremental quantization [12, 46], reformulating the problem as a hashing problem [20] or using proximal operators [45].

In this work we rely on the widely accepted Straight Through Estimator [3] originally employed by [7, 21, 40]. At each iteration the network is projected to its nearest valid neighbor by means of the $\text{sign}(\cdot)$ function. The loss is evaluated at this point and the gradient is computed. Subsequently the gradient vector is translated to the original location w and an angular update step is taken. The whole process, STE and angular step is depicted in Algorithm 1.

By re-scaling the auxiliary channel-wise weight vectors, the magnitudes of the channel-wise real and quantized vectors will match, and so the corresponding magnitudes of the gradients. Note that adjusting the learning rate does not fix the gradient magnitude mismatch given that the filters in the different layers have different number of parameters.

4.1 Projecting Filters, Layers and Entire Networks

We tested our approach on filter-wise, layer-wise and network-wise unit norm spheres. Given the large amount of parameters in the layer-wise and network-wise cases, the magnitudes of the auxiliary weights, particularly in the deeper layers, will be very small. However unlike techniques like weight-decay, they are bounded on how much they can shrink, and there is no need for manually tuned hyperparameters. In our experiments we observed that this constrain increased the generalization of the network in the filter-wise and layer-wise cases, but harmed it in the network-wise case. In order to shed light

---

Algorithm 1: One training epoch of 1-bit DNN on a sphere

Require: 1-bit DNN weights $\mathbf{w}$, loss function $\mathcal{L}$, epoch t and optimizer

Get epoch learning rate α_t;

for *number of mini-batches* **do**

    Get mini-batch data $\mathbf{x}$

    Get nearest valid network: $\hat{\mathbf{w}} = \text{sign}(\mathbf{w})$

    Forward pass and compute loss $\mathcal{L}(\mathbf{x}, \hat{\mathbf{w}})$

    Compute gradients $\mathbf{g}$ of $\mathcal{L}$ w.r.t. $\hat{\mathbf{w}}$

    Transport gradients from $\hat{\mathbf{w}}$ to $\mathbf{w}$

    Add momentum term to $\mathbf{g}$

    if *optimizer == Adam* **then**

        Update gradients moments

        Process gradients

    end

    Project gradients $\mathbf{g}$ onto tangent plane of $\mathbf{w}$ using $\text{Proj}_{\mathbf{w}}(\mathbf{g})$

    Update $\mathbf{w} = \mathbf{w} - \Delta\mathbf{w}$ with $\Delta\mathbf{w} = \alpha_t\mathbf{g}$

    Retract $\mathbf{w}$ back onto the sphere using $\text{Ret}_{\mathbf{w}}(\Delta\mathbf{w})$

end

---

on this behavior, we investigated the effect of normalizing on the conditioning of the network. In Sect. 6 we describe the procedure followed to analyze the conditioning and generalization of the network.

4.2   Implementation Remarks

Efficient Computation of Projection onto Tangent Hyperplane. Note that the projection onto the tangent plane can alternatively be computed as:

$$P_x\xi = (I - \mathbf{w}\mathbf{w}^T)\xi \tag{11}$$

however this method involves computing a restrictively large Gram matrix of x in terms of memory and computation, therefore should be avoided. In order to efficiently project we use the following matrix association:

$$P_\mathbf{w}\xi = \xi - \mathbf{w}(\mathbf{w}^T\xi) \tag{12}$$

4.3   Relation to Spectral and Lipschitz Normalizations

Our work saves a close relation to spectral normalization presented in [38,48]. Yoshida and Miyato [48] demonstrated that penalizing the spectral norm of weight matrices in networks reduces the sensitivity to perturbations and subsequently exhibit higher generalization. The spectral norm of a weight matrix $\sigma(\mathbf{M})$ is defined as:

$$\sigma(\mathbf{M}) = \max_{\mathbf{h}:\mathbf{h}\neq 0} \frac{\|\mathbf{M}\mathbf{h}\|}{\|\mathbf{h}\|} \tag{13}$$

which corresponds to the largest singular value of $\mathbf{M}$. For any matrix norm $\|\cdot\|$, the spectral norm or spectral radius $\sigma(\mathbf{M})$ of this matrix has as upper bound:

$$\sigma(\mathbf{M}) \leq \|\mathbf{M}\| . \tag{14}$$

Therefore, constraining the L_2 norm of $\mathbf{M}$ implicitly constrains the spectral norm. As an extension to [48], Miyato *et al.* [38] applied this technique to stabilize the training of the discriminator in Generative Adversarial Networks (GANS) [13]. This is accomplished by controlling the Lipschitz norm $\|\mathbf{L}\|_{Lip}$ of a each of the discriminator's layers $\mathbf{L}$. In order to control $\|\mathbf{L}\|_{Lip}$, it is sufficient to control the spectral norm of the weight matrix $\sigma(\mathbf{L})$. Thus, normalizing every layer $\mathbf{L}$ by its largest singular value $\mathbf{L}_{SN} = \mathbf{L}/\sigma(\mathbf{L})$ consequently constrains the entire Lipschitz norm of the model.

5 Angle Penalization

In this section we present a complimentary contribution consisting in formulating quantization as a regularization problem. This regularization, allows for accurate gradient propagations, stabilizing training while using the STE. In contrast to [8], in our proposed approach, angles, rather than distances, between pairs of corresponding real and quantized vectors are penalized. Given that quantized vectors are fixed, this regularization encourages the real vectors to lie near any scaled version of the quantization set, we denote it Angle Scaled Quantization (ASQ).

Formally, in order to optimize Eq. (7), we re-formulate DNN scaled quantization as a regularization term in the network's loss function:

$$\mathcal{L}(\mathcal{X}, \mathbf{b}, \mathbf{w}) = \mathcal{L}(\mathcal{X}, \mathbf{b}) + \beta R_{ASQ}(\mathbf{w}), \tag{15}$$

where $\mathbf{w} \in \mathbb{R}^d$ is the auxiliary network and $\beta > 0$ is a quantization enforcing hyperparameter.

We re-arrange the i-th filter of each convolutional layer into a 1-dimensional vector $\mathbf{v}$. In order to minimize the angle between this vector and its quantized version, we can equivalently maximize their cosine distance:

$$R_{ASQ}(\mathbf{v}) = \frac{1}{N} \sum^{N} \left[1 - \frac{\mathbf{v} \cdot \text{Quant}(\mathbf{v})}{\|\mathbf{v}\|_2 \cdot \|\text{Quant}(\mathbf{v})\|_2} \right], \tag{16}$$

where N is the number of filters across the whole network and $\| \cdot \|_p$ denotes the L_p norm. Note that $\text{Quant}(\mathbf{v})$ is a reference vector and should be not included into the optimization graph, therefore gradients should not be propagated through it.

For the particular binary weights case, it can be alternatively computed as:

$$R_{ASQ}(\mathbf{v}) = \frac{1}{N} \sum^{N} \left[1 - \frac{\|\mathbf{v}\|_1}{\|\mathbf{v}\|_2 \cdot \sqrt{n}} \right], \tag{17}$$

where n is the number of elements in $\mathbf{v}$.

The euclidean distance between a randomly initialized vector and its quantized representation will be larger than with a scaled version of the same; thus, adding channel-wise scalings potentially speeds-up the convergence. Additionally, angle penalization restricts the exploration region of the auxiliar real-value vectors to regions near the quantized vectors. The channel-wise scalings are obtained analytically as in [40].

Progressively increasing the parameter β encourages the network to slowly converge to a scaled quantized representation. In Fig. 1, we plot the cosine distance during training against validation accuracy using a pretrained model with channel-wise scalings. As the angle between the real and quantized vectors decreases, the validation accuracy increases which further validates the usefulness of angle penalization.

5.1   Compatible Approaches

Drawing inspiration from the Thomson or Tammes problems (depending on the restrictions), also known as spherical coding or packing, Liu *et al.* [32] investigated the formulation of this problem in the context of DNNs motivated by the task of increasing the discrimination capacity of the networks filters. The approach is formulated as a regularization, termed Minimum Hyperspherical Energy (MHE). Adding a MHE term on the loss encourages the projections onto the sphere of the channel-wise weight vectors to be as evenly spaced as possible. However, using the enterity of the sphere will cause half of the channels to have a negatively correlated or reflected counterpart. Therefore, the authors extended the formulation to operate uniquely on half of the sphere, termed Half-space MHE.

Particularly, in the context of the Thomson problem the MHE regularization is defined as:

$$R_{MHE} = \frac{1}{N(N-1)} \sum_{i=1}^{N} \sum_{j=1, j \neq i}^{N} \frac{1}{\left\| \arccos\left(\hat{\mathbf{F}}_i^T \hat{\mathbf{F}}_j\right) \right\|} \tag{18}$$

where $\hat{\mathbf{F}} = \frac{\mathbf{F}}{\|\mathbf{F}\|}$. Note that the MHE loss term does not push the network filters to lie on the sphere. In fact, it only penalizes the angular distance of their projections in order to encourage diversity, which supports our rationale on angular learning encoding semantic information.

This formulation is naturally complementary to our approach; thus, in order to explicitly prevent filter redundancy we extend our scheme based on this principle. We modify our task loss function to encourage the channels to be evenly spaced, while strictly constraining each vector to lie on the unit sphere, unlike [32]. Formally, we redefine the loss in Eq. 3 to include this component with weighting η:

$$\mathcal{L}(\mathcal{X}, \mathbf{b}, \mathbf{w}) = \mathcal{L}(\mathcal{X}, \mathbf{b}) + \eta R_{MHE}(\mathbf{w}) \tag{19}$$

6   Conditioning Analysis

The condition number provides a good estimate for the density of pathological curvatures which exist in the loss surface. These can also have the interpretation of erratic

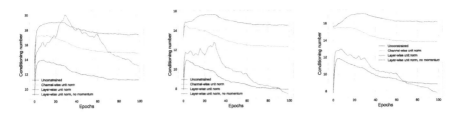

Fig. 2. Conditioning number for layers 3, 8 and 13 across training epochs on a Resnet-18 network trained on Tiny-Imagenet.

local minimas which cause effects such as vanishing gradients. Therefore, imposing a well-conditioned Hessian matrix on the loss surface behaves as a smoothing process which eliminates local minima and mitigates common optimisation issues that arise when optimising deep neural networks. In Fig. 2, we show the conditioning numbers across training for layers 3, 8 and 13 of a ResNet-18 network trained on Tiny-ImageNet. All the methods start from randomly sampled weights using standard initialization schemes. During the initial iterations they all bounce and subsequently stabilize. Layer-wise unit spheres appear to be very sensitive to momentum as can be appreciated. Both modes of our spherical constraints, channel-wise and layer-wise, improve the conditioning of the layers significantly. Notably layer-wise with no momentum provided the lowest and most stable curves, particularly in the early layers.

7 Experiments

In this section, we tested our approach on a Resnet-18 [17] architectures in the task of image classification on the CIFAR dataset and the large-scale dataset, ImageNet (ILSVRC-2012) [26]. Unless specified otherwise, we projected the auxiliary weights onto channel-wise spheres, and for binarization we used the procedure in BinaryConnect (BC) [7] as the base algorithm.

We implemented our training scheme using the Pytorch framework. For the ImageNet experiments, a pretrained model taken from the official Pytorch Zoo was used as initialization for the full-precision weights in all the cases. As common convention, the first and last layers were not quantized.

7.1 Evaluation on CIFAR

We tested on the CIFAR-10 and CIFAR-100 image classification datasets using a ResNet-18 adapted for CIFAR as detailed in [17]. All our networks were trained from scratch using ADAM for the cases where ASQ was used, and SGD otherwise. Our results, depicted in Table 1, indicate that our method exhibits high generalization on small models and works well in combination with MHE. We tested projecting both channel-wise and entire layers, with channel-wise providing the best results. We compared against our implementation of Binary Connect.

Table 1. Top-1 Validation accuracy (%) for a Resnet-18 on the CIFAR dataset.

Dataset	Method	Top-1
CIFAR-100	Full precision	66.9
	BC [7]	53.9
	BC + MHE [7]	53.6
	Spherical Projection (channel-wise)	56.7
	Spherical Projection (channel-wise) + MHE	**57.3**
	Spherical Projection (layer-wise)	54.3

7.2   Evaluation on ImageNet

The ImageNet 2012 dataset contains 1.2M training and 50k validation labeled images spread across 1000 categories. Top-1 and Top-5 single crop, predicted classes are provided. Only the Top-1 is used to compute the loss.

We used different training regimes depending whether ASQ was used or not. For the networks trained with ASQ, we used SGD with initial learning rate of $1e^{-3}$ with angle penalization hyperparameter $\beta = 5$, and multiplied by a factor of 1.3 at every epoch. The learning rate is updated by a factor of 0.1 at epochs 20, 25 and 30. For networks without ASQ we used ADAM [25] with an initial learning rate of $1e^{-5}$.

Table 2. Top-1 validation accuracy (%) for ResNet-18 on ImageNet. LS = Learnable Scalings

Method	Bitwidth(W/A)	Top1	Top 5	Width(x)	Top1	Top5
BWN [40]	1/32	60.8	83.0	–	–	–
HWGQ-BWN [6]	1/32	61.3	83.9	–	–	–
TWN [28]	2/32	61.8	84.2	–	–	–
BC [7] + LS	1/32	61.4	83.7	–	–	–
BC [7] + LS + L_2	1/32	61.8	84.2	–	–	–
BC [7] + LS + angle (ours)	1/32	60.5	83.1	–	–	–
1-bit-per-weight [36]	1/32	–	–	2.5	68.97	88.49
Spherical projection (ours)	1/32	61.2	83.9	2.5	–	–
ASQ (ours)	1/32	62.7	84.8	2.5	70.37	88.75
ASQ + MHE (ours)	1/32	60.2	82.6	2.5	69.98	88.35
Spherical projection + ASQ (ours)	1/32	62.7	84.8	2.5	**70.51**	**88.85**
Spherical projection + MHE (ours)	1/32	61.5	83.8	2.5	–	–
Spherical projection + ASQ + MHE (ours)	1/32	**62.9**	**84.9**	2.5	70.25	88.55

In Table 2 we report our ImageNet results for 1-bit weights and full-precision activations on Resnet-18. We tested using channel-wise learnable scalings and replacing our angle penalization with a L_2 distance penalization on BC. Our approach outperformed BC and Binary Weight Networks (BWN). Additionally we performed ablations for the spherical normalization, angle penalization with analytic scalings (ASQ), and Minimum Hyperspherical Energy (MHE).

Our results indicate that our method outperforms vanilla BC, BC using learnable scalings, and BC with learnable scalings and L_2 penalization. In order to compare against [36], we performed tests in a WideResnet with 2.5x multiplier [49].

8   Ablation Studies

Normalizing vs Exponential Mapping Retraction. In Table 3 we present results for the two types of retractions used, namely simple normalization and exponential mapping, described in Sect. 4. As can be observed, normalization performed better but not by a significant margin.

Table 3. Left: Different retractions onto the hypersphere (tested on ImageNet on a ResNet-18 network) **Right:** Angle penalization on a ResNet-50 trained on ImageNet. LS = Learnable Scalings.

Retraction	Top-1 Acc	Top-5 Acc
Normalization	**61.2**	**83.9**
Exponential Mapping	61.0	83.7

Method	Top-1 Acc	Top-5 Acc
BWN [40]	70.4	89.7
BC [7] + LS	69.2	88.8
ASQ (ours)	**70.7**	**89.0**

Angle Penalization. In this section we investigate the effect of the angle penalization described in Sect. 5. In Table 3 we performed ablations isolating our angle penalization from the spherical projection on a ResNet-50 network trained on ImageNet demonstrating the efficiency and scalability of out method. We compared against analytical scalings with no penalization (BWN) and learnable scalings.

9   Conclusion

A novel geometric perspective on 1-bit DNNs optimization was presented. By projecting the auxiliary weights onto channel-wise spheres and formulating the problem of quantization as an angle based regularization, we were able to improve the performance of these networks by adding priors into the exploration space. We drew a relationship between our normalization and Lipschitz normalization previously used to stabilize networks during training. Finally, we delved into the operation of the network, particularly observing a superior conditioning number of the weight matrices attained by our method, leading to improved training. We validate our results on the large-scale dataset ImageNet obtaining 62.9% top-1 accuracy on our best performing 1-bit DNN.

References

1. Ajanthan, T., Dokania, P.K., Hartley, R., Torr, P.H.: Proximal mean-field for neural network quantization. In: Proceedings of the IEEE International Conference on Computer Vision, pp. 4871–4880 (2019)
2. Anderson, A.G., Berg, C.P.: The high-dimensional geometry of binary neural networks. arXiv preprint arXiv:1705.07199 (2017)
3. Bengio, Y., Léonard, N., Courville, A.: Estimating or propagating gradients through stochastic neurons for conditional computation. arXiv preprint arXiv:1308.3432 (2013)
4. Bonnabel, S.: Stochastic gradient descent on Riemannian manifolds. IEEE Trans. Autom. Control **58**(9), 2217–2229 (2013)
5. Boumal, N., Mishra, B., Absil, P.A., Sepulchre, R.: Manopt, a Matlab toolbox for optimization on manifolds. J. Mach. Learn. Res. **15**(42), 1455–1459 (2014). https://www.manopt.org
6. Cai, Z., He, X., Sun, J., Vasconcelos, N.: Deep learning with low precision by half-wave gaussian quantization. In: Proceedings of the IEEE Conference on Computer Vision and Pattern Recognition, pp. 5918–5926 (2017)
7. Courbariaux, M., Bengio, Y., David, J.P.: BinaryConnect: training deep neural networks with binary weights during propagations. In: Proceedings of the Advances in Neural Information Processing Systems, pp. 3123–3131 (2015)
8. Darabi, S., Belbahri, M., Courbariaux, M., Nia, V.P.: BNN+: improved binary network training. arXiv preprint arXiv:1812.11800 (2018)
9. Denton, E.L., Zaremba, W., Bruna, J., LeCun, Y., Fergus, R.: Exploiting linear structure within convolutional networks for efficient evaluation. In: Proceedings of the Advances in Neural Information Processing Systems, pp. 1269–1277 (2014)
10. Gao, Z., Wu, Y., Jia, Y., Harandi, M.: Learning to optimize on SPD manifolds. In: Proceedings of the IEEE/CVF Conference on Computer Vision and Pattern Recognition, pp. 7700–7709 (2020)
11. Glorot, X., Bengio, Y.: Understanding the difficulty of training deep feedforward neural networks. In: Proceedings of the 13th International Conference on Artificial Intelligence and Statistics, pp. 249–256 (2010)
12. Gong, R., et al.: Differentiable soft quantization: bridging full-precision and low-bit neural networks. In: Proceedings of the IEEE International Conference on Computer Vision, pp. 4852–4861 (2019)
13. Goodfellow, I., et al.: Generative adversarial nets. In: Advances in Neural Information Processing Systems, pp. 2672–2680 (2014)
14. Guerra, L., Zhuang, B., Reid, I., Drummond, T.: Switchable precision neural networks. arXiv preprint arXiv:2002.02815 (2020)
15. Han, S., Mao, H., Dally, W.J.: Deep compression: compressing deep neural networks with pruning, trained quantization and Huffman coding. In: Proceedings of the International Conference on Learning Representations (2016)
16. He, K., Zhang, X., Ren, S., Sun, J.: Delving deep into rectifiers: Surpassing human-level performance on ImageNet classification. In: Proceedings of the IEEE International Conference on Computer Vision, pp. 1026–1034 (2015)
17. He, K., Zhang, X., Ren, S., Sun, J.: Deep residual learning for image recognition. In: Proceedings of the IEEE Conference on Computer Vision and Pattern Recognition, pp. 770–778 (2016)
18. He, Y., Liu, P., Wang, Z., Yang, Y.: Pruning filter via geometric median for deep convolutional neural networks acceleration. In: Proceedings of the IEEE Conference on Computer Vision and Pattern Recognition (2019)

19. Howard, A.G., et al.: MobileNets: efficient convolutional neural networks for mobile vision applications. arXiv preprint arXiv:1704.04861 (2017)
20. Hu, Q., Wang, P., Cheng, J.: From hashing to CNNs: training binary weight networks via hashing. In: Proceedings of the AAAI Conference on Artificial Intelligence, vol. 32 (2018)
21. Hubara, I., Courbariaux, M., Soudry, D., El-Yaniv, R., Bengio, Y.: Binarized neural networks. In: Proceedings of the Advances in Neural Information Processing Systems, pp. 4107–4115 (2016)
22. Iandola, F.N., Han, S., Moskewicz, M.W., Ashraf, K., Dally, W.J., Keutzer, K.: SqueezeNet: AlexNet-level accuracy with 50x fewer parameters and <0.5 mb model size. arXiv preprint arXiv:1602.07360 (2016)
23. Jaderberg, M., Vedaldi, A., Zisserman, A.: Speeding up convolutional neural networks with low rank expansions. arXiv preprint arXiv:1405.3866 (2014)
24. Kasai, H., Sato, H., Mishra, B.: Riemannian stochastic recursive gradient algorithm. In: International Conference on Machine Learning, pp. 2516–2524. PMLR (2018)
25. Kingma, D.P., Ba, J.: Adam: a method for stochastic optimization. In: Proceedings of the International Conference on Learning Representations (2015)
26. Krizhevsky, A., Sutskever, I., Hinton, G.E.: ImageNet classification with deep convolutional neural networks. In: Proceedings of the Advances in Neural Information Processing Systems, pp. 1097–1105 (2012)
27. LeCun, Y., Denker, J.S., Solla, S.A.: Optimal brain damage. In: Advances in Neural Information Processing Systems, pp. 598–605 (1990)
28. Li, F., Zhang, B., Liu, B.: Ternary weight networks. arXiv preprint arXiv:1605.04711 (2016)
29. Li, H., Kadav, A., Durdanovic, I., Samet, H., Graf, H.P.: Pruning filters for efficient convnets. In: Proceedings of the International Conference on Learning Representations (2017)
30. Lin, M., et al.: Rotated binary neural network. arXiv preprint arXiv:2009.13055 (2020)
31. Liu, H., Simonyan, K., Yang, Y.: DARTS: differentiable architecture search. In: Proceedings of the International Conference on Learning Representations (2019)
32. Liu, W., et al.: Learning towards minimum hyperspherical energy. In: Advances in Neural Information Processing Systems, pp. 6222–6233 (2018)
33. Liu, Z., Wu, B., Luo, W., Yang, X., Liu, W., Cheng, K.T.: Bi-Real Net: enhancing the performance of 1-bit CNNs with improved representational capability and advanced training algorithm. In: Proceedings of the European Conference on Computer Vision (2018)
34. Louizos, C., Reisser, M., Blankevoort, T., Gavves, E., Welling, M.: Relaxed quantization for discretized neural networks. In: Proceedings of the International Conference on Learning Representations (2019)
35. Louizos, C., Welling, M., Kingma, D.P.: Learning sparse neural networks through l_0 regularization. In: Proceedings of the International Conference on Learning Representations (2018)
36. McDonnell, M.D.: Training wide residual networks for deployment using a single bit for each weight. arXiv preprint arXiv:1802.08530 (2018)
37. Mishkin, D., Matas, J.: All you need is a good init. arXiv preprint arXiv:1511.06422 (2015)
38. Miyato, T., Kataoka, T., Koyama, M., Yoshida, Y.: Spectral normalization for generative adversarial networks. arXiv preprint arXiv:1802.05957 (2018)
39. Pennington, J., Worah, P.: The spectrum of the fisher information matrix of a single-hidden-layer neural network. In: Advances in Neural Information Processing Systems, pp. 5410–5419 (2018)
40. Rastegari, M., Ordonez, V., Redmon, J., Farhadi, A.: XNOR-Net: ImageNet classification using binary convolutional neural networks. In: Leibe, B., Matas, J., Sebe, N., Welling, M. (eds.) ECCV 2016. LNCS, vol. 9908, pp. 525–542. Springer, Cham (2016). https://doi.org/10.1007/978-3-319-46493-0_32

41. Real, E., Aggarwal, A., Huang, Y., Le, Q.V.: Regularized evolution for image classifier architecture search. arXiv preprint arXiv:1802.01548 (2018)
42. Roy, S.K., Mhammedi, Z., Harandi, M.: Geometry aware constrained optimization techniques for deep learning. In: Proceedings of the IEEE Conference on Computer Vision and Pattern Recognition, pp. 4460–4469 (2018)
43. Salimans, T., Kingma, D.P.: Weight normalization: a simple reparameterization to accelerate training of deep neural networks. In: Advances in Neural Information Processing Systems, pp. 901–909 (2016)
44. Sato, H., Kasai, H., Mishra, B.: Riemannian stochastic variance reduced gradient algorithm with retraction and vector transport. SIAM J. Optim. **29**(2), 1444–1472 (2019)
45. Schulman, J., Wolski, F., Dhariwal, P., Radford, A., Klimov, O.: Proximal policy optimization algorithms. arXiv preprint arXiv:1707.06347 (2017)
46. Yang, J., et al.: Quantization networks. In: Proceedings of the IEEE/CVF Conference on Computer Vision and Pattern Recognition, pp. 7308–7316 (2019)
47. Yin, P., Zhang, S., Lyu, J., Osher, S., Qi, Y., Xin, J.: BinaryRelax: a relaxation approach for training deep neural networks with quantized weights. SIAM J. Imaging Sci. **11**(4), 2205–2223 (2018)
48. Yoshida, Y., Miyato, T.: Spectral norm regularization for improving the generalizability of deep learning. arXiv preprint arXiv:1705.10941 (2017)
49. Zagoruyko, S., Komodakis, N.: Wide residual networks (2016)
50. Zhang, X., Zhou, X., Lin, M., Sun, J.: ShuffleNet: an extremely efficient convolutional neural network for mobile devices. arXiv preprint arXiv:1707.01083 (2017)
51. Zhang, X., Zou, J., He, K., Sun, J.: Accelerating very deep convolutional networks for classification and detection. IEEE Trans. Pattern Anal. Mach. Intell. **38**(10), 1943–1955 (2016)
52. Zhuang, Z., et al.: Discrimination-aware channel pruning for deep neural networks. In: Proceedings of the Advances in Neural Information Processing Systems (2018)
53. Zoph, B., Le, Q.V.: Neural architecture search with reinforcement learning. In: Proceedings of the International Conference on Learning Representations (2017)

A Neural Network Approach to Estimating Color Reflectance with Product Independent Models

Asei Akanuma[✉] and Daniel Stamate

Data Science and Soft Computing Lab, Department of Computing, Goldsmiths, University of London, London, UK
{ma905aa,d.stamate}@gold.ac.uk

Abstract. In the paint and coatings industry, traditionally color reflectance modelling is performed individually for each coating product. This is because a coating product contains color samples that are mixed from several colorants and a binder which have a unique chemical property that requires modelling to be carried out individually when done analytically. This work proposes a superior approach for color reflectance modelling based on Neural Networks, which is capable of modelling multiple coating products concurrently using a single model, allowing for a modelling approach that is generic and independent of the coating products. In this study we demonstrate that our Neural Network model optimized to predict color reflectance for multiple coating products using a dataset with 4150 color samples containing 18 distinct coating products, is able to perform better (RMSE 3.73) than an widely employed analytical model, Kubelka-Munk (RMSE 8.24), which is conventionally used for the same task.

Keywords: Prediction modelling · Neural Networks · Color · Paints · Reflectance

1 Introduction

1.1 Color Matching and Color Prediction Models

Color matching is an essential task in the paints and coatings industry, which involves mixing colorants and binders in specific quantities which are called recipes, to create a specific color, and is usually performed by specialized technicians. To assist their work and to speed up the process of discovering new recipes, Computer Colorant Formulations (CCF) are often used, which utilize various color prediction software. Implementations of CCF are often based on an analytical model which is derived from radiation transfer theory, for example the Kubelka-Munk analytical model (K-M) [1] which is preferred for its simplicity and ease of use. Previous works have explored the use of Artificial Neural Network (ANN) models, as color prediction models which provide alternatives to the analytical models. In the works by Bishop et al. [2, 3], ANNs were used to predict recipes of dye concentrations from CIELab coordinates. Bezerra and Hawkayard [4] used ANNs to predict concentrations of florescent dyes from spectral reflectance values. Westland et al. [5] used ANNs to predict spectral reflectance for mixtures of inks printed on cards. Furferi and Governi [6] applied ANNs to correct spectral reflectances from an analytical model, and to estimate spectrophotometer readings for carded fiber. Hung et al. [7] used ANNs to predict color properties of cotton fabrics. Jawahar et al. [8] employed ANNs to predict tri-stimulus values for leather dyeing. Hemingray and Westland [9] devised a system which uses several ANN models to predict spectral reflectance for fiber blends. Pan et al. used an ANN based approach similar to [10], to learn mappings between different color spaces [11].

In this study, we propose a color prediction approach based on ANNs that can successfully model color reflectance for a broad range of coating products. We distinguish our approach from traditional color modelling which is limited to modelling a single coating product by using a dataset of color recipes with one kind of binder, for a coating product. Our approach is different by having the ability to model multiple coating products using a single model, thus learning to predict multiple coating products concurrently, and leading to a color reflectance prediction model which is generic and independent of the coating products. As such, we refer to our approach as a product independent model approach. In the sequel, we discuss our ANN modelling approach in which we successfully model a dataset with 18 different coating products, and provide prediction performance comparisons with conventional K-M based analytical models.

2   Methodology, Analyses and Results

2.1   Dataset and Metrics

The data used in this study originates from a database of paint color recipes used for coatings. The database includes recipes for 4150 colors which belong to 18 distinct coating products, where each product contains between 170 and 220 recipes. They are produced by mixing no more than 4 out of 55 kinds of colorants/binders (37 are colorants and 18 are binders). The recipes have overlapping use of colorants between products, but each product uses a unique binder. The spectral reflectance curves for the color recipes are measured by a spectrophotometer which is a device that precisely measures electromagnetic energy at specific wavelengths of light, which allows us to accurately identify the colors. The measurements of the reflectance spectra include the visual spectrum (in the range of 400 to 700 nm at 10 nm step intervals, which are 31 in total) using a D/8 type of spectrophotometer. All variables in the data are numerical and continuous, and thus this work is a regression task of predicting 31 target variables.

The purpose of this study is to propose a prediction modelling approach that is able to predict color reflectance for the recipe samples, to be optimally close to the spectrophotometer's measured color reflectance. We evaluate our model using the dE_{CMC} color difference equation [11] which provides an approximate distance of perceived color difference between the measured and predicted colors. The performance results are calculated by finding the average dE_{CMC} for the test set predictions for a reference illuminant. We also evaluate the RMSE performance.

2.2   Descriptions of the Variables

The following gives a description of all the variables used in this work.

Input Variables

- The recipe comprising the concentrations of the colorants/binders in percentages: a sparse vector of length 55.
- The measured spectral reflectance curve of the undercoat (background) color on which the recipe color coating is applied: a vector of length 31.
- A product ID which acts as an identifier of the coating product from which the sample originated: a one-hot vector of length 18.
- A layer thickness which describes the thickness of the coating applied: a scalar.

The Target Variables

- The measured spectral reflectance curve of the resulting color from the recipe mix: a vector of length 31.

2.3   ANN Product Independent Model: Implementation and Results

A Feed-Forward ANN product independent model was tuned using the Adam optimizer to minimize the Huber loss which we opted for to prevent the impact of outliers in our dataset. The ANN was trained to minimize the loss up to a maximum of 2000 epochs. To control overfitting the network was regularized with L1 and L2 penalties, and with early stopping criteria to find the appropriate training length by observing if a validation loss did not improve after 200 epochs based on a validation set randomly selected, and representing 10% of the training set. The ANN was trained on a 90% and 10% split for train and test set respectively, the split being based on a stratified sampling with respect to the products.

Table 1. Prediction Performance Comparisons of Product independent models

Model	RMSE	Mean dECMC
K-M single model for 18 products	4.19	0.80
K-M product independent model	8.24	2.00
ANN product independent model	3.73	1.33

Table 1 summarizes our results and provides a comparison of performances for our ANN product independent model (bottom row) with the traditional single product K-M analytical models built individually and separately for each single product for 18 products (top row), and with a product independent K-M analytical model (middle row).

While the performance of the traditional single K-M model is stable (dE_{CMC} is 0.8), the performance of K-M product independent model presents significant challenges in modelling this dataset with 18 products which contain several binders, which analytical models are inept at modelling concurrently, resulting in an average dE_{CMC} performance of 2. By comparison our method provides an average dE_{CMC} of 1.33 and demonstrates that our ANN approach has superior capability for learning a product independent model. Our ANN model performs best when comparing RMSE performances, however we find that the single product K-M models yields better performance for average dE_{CMC}.

3 Conclusion and Future Work

This study proposed a color modelling approach that is product independent, and is the first of this type in literature, to our knowledge. We demonstrated that our ANN product independent color prediction model performs better than a K-M product independent model, in terms of both RMSE and $\mathbf{dE_{CMC}}$, and achieves a better RMSE performance than a K-M single product model. Our future work includes improving our $\mathbf{dE_{CMC}}$ performance and enhancing our product independent approach by expanding the number of products in our dataset. Our expectation is that through a larger scale implementation of our ANN product independent model approach, we can achieve substantially better color prediction over traditional analytical models.

References

1. Nobbs, J.H.: Kubelka-Munk theory and the prediction of reflectance. Rev. Prog. Color. (SDC) **15**, 66–75 (1985)
2. Bishop, J.M., Bushnell, M.J., Westland, S.: The application of neural networks to computer recipe prediction. Color **16**(1), 3–9 (1991)
3. Bishop, J.M., Bushnell, M.J., Usher, A., Westland, S.: Neural networks in the colour industry. In: Proceedings of AIENG 1991, Oxford, UK, pp. 423–434 (1991)
4. Bezerra, C.deM., Hawkyard, C.J.: Computer match prediction for fluorescent dyes by neural networks. Color. Technol. **116**(5–6), 163–169 (2000)
5. Westland, S., Iovine, L., Bishop, J.M.: Kubelka-Munk or neural networks for computer colorant formulation? In: Proceedings of the SPIE, vol. 4421, pp. 745–748 (2002)
6. Furferi, R., Governi, L.: Prediction of the spectrophotometric response of a carded fibre composed by different kinds of coloured raw materials: an artificial neural network-based approach. Color. Res. Appl. **36**, 179–191 (2011)
7. Hung, O.N., et al.: Using artificial neural network to predict colour properties of laser-treated 100 percent cotton fabric. Fibers Polym. **12**(8), 1069–1076 (2011)
8. Jawahar, M., Kannan, N., Babu, C., Manobhai, M.K.: Artificial neural networks for colour prediction in leather dyeing on the basis of a tristimulus system. Color. Technol. **131**(1), 48–57 (2015)
9. Hemingray, C., Westland, S.: A novel approach to using neural networks to predict the colour of fibre blends. Color. Technol. **132**(4), 297–303 (2016)
10. Pan, Q., Katemake, P., Westland, S.: Neural networks for transformation to spectral spaces. In: ACA 2016 China, Color Driving Power, Proceedings. ACA, CFCA, CAC (2016)
11. CMC: Calculation of small color differences for acceptability. Text. Chem. Color. **21**(11), 18–21 (1989)

Linear Self-attention Approximation via Trainable Feedforward Kernel

Uladzislau Yorsh and Alexander Kovalenko[(✉)] [iD]

Faculty of Information Technology, Czech Technical University in Prague,
Prague, Czech Republic
{yorshula,kovalale}@fit.cvut.cz

Restrictive limitation of Transformers [18] due to the quadratic complexity of self-attention mechanism motivated a new research field of *efficient Transformers* [17], which approximate the original architecture with asymptotically faster models.

Despite the fact that Transformers are pervasive, unbiased and able to virtually handle arbitrarily long dependencies, the quadratic space and time complexity limit Transformer applications on long sequences. In this connection, various findings on approximating the attention with asymptotically faster modules have been made in order to tackle longer sequences. However, given the absence of a unified and systematic benchmark, overall evaluating remained uncertain until Tay et al. [16] published the benchmark for efficient Transformer models called "Long Range Arena", that consists of task of various data types.

In pursue of the faster computation, Efficient Transformers demonstrate an impressive variety of approaches—models attaining sub-quadratic attention complexity can utilize a notion of sparsity [2,3,15] or a low-rank approximation of inputs [19,20] to reduce an amount of attended keys; another ways to reduce complexity include locality-sensitive hashing [12], key pooling [21], additional memory to store information in compacted form [7,14] or hybridization with another architectures, such as CNNs [1,8].

Often based on strong mathematical basis, kernelized approaches allow to approximate an attention with linear complexity while retaining high accuracy. The work by Katharopoulos et al. [11] describes an approximation consisting of computing an attention by a dot product of projected queries and keys. Consequently, the work by Choromanskik et al. [4] demonstrated that such an approximation can be arbitrarily precise and mathematically robust, while the work by Chowdhury et al. [5] reported that the projection can be learned. Therefore, in the present paper we aim to expand the idea of trainable kernel methods to approximate self-attention mechanism of the Transformer architecture.

Our Contribution: given that feedforward neural network with at least one hidden layer [6], arbitrary non-linearity, and arbitrary number of neurons is able to approximate any well-behaved function to any accuracy that gives feedforward neural network the potential of being universal approximator [9]. Therefore, we propose that trainable kernel function $\phi(\cdot)$ can approximate traditional softmax attention efficiently. Therefore, we study the possibility of using the feedforward neural network to represent $\phi(\cdot)$. We experiment with the architecture of $\phi(\cdot)$ and

E. Pimenidis et al. (Eds.): ICANN 2022, LNCS 13531, pp. 807–810, 2022.
https://doi.org/10.1007/978-3-031-15934-3_67

test its performance on the three Long Range Arena tasks—text classification, document matching and ListOps, following the instruction on limitation [16] the number of trainable parameters in the model to provide comparable metrics.

Kernelized Model. Kernelized models are based on the following factorization of an attention operation:

$$\text{Att}(q_i, K, V) = \sum_{j=1}^{L} \frac{\kappa(q_i, k_j)}{\sum_{j'=1}^{L} \kappa(q_i, k_{j'})} v_j \approx \frac{\phi(q_i)^T \sum_{j=1}^{L} \phi(k_j) v_j^T}{\phi(q_i)^T \sum_{j=1}^{L} \phi(k_j)}$$

where q_i is a query token, K and V are key and value matrices, $\kappa(q, k)$ is a kernel function to model ($\exp(q^T k)$ for a base Transformer) and $\phi(\cdot)$ is a projection function we approximate. The $\phi(\cdot)$ is required to be positive to maintain numeric stability, and can vary from simple functions like ELU + 1 to stochastic softmax kernel approximations. In our work, instead of approximation strategies with strong priors we employ a general function such as feedforward NN.

Feedforward Kernel. We start with a single-layer FFN, defined as:

$$\phi(\mathbf{X}) = Softplus(\mathbf{XW})$$

where $W \in R^{n \times n}$ is the layer weight matrix. Surprisingly, this model already shows the notable performance gain over the Performer and comes close to the leader of the original LRA paper. Following the [10], we can boost performance by forcing the orthogonality via orthogonal initialization and regularization.

We also tried to stack more layers, but observed no performance gain – with or without normalization layers in between. We tried the GELU and logistic sigmoid non-linearities.

GLU Kernel. Gated Linear Units are defined as:

$$GLU(\mathbf{X}) = \mathbf{XW}_f \odot \sigma(\mathbf{XW}_g)$$

where $\sigma(\cdot)$ is a logistic sigmoid and W_f, W_g are weight matrices. This layer provides and element-wise nonlinearity and may represent more complex functions, but requires a doubled parametrization compared to a linear one.

For the purposes of our model, we need to modify the last GLU to force the positive output:

$$GLU_{output}(\mathbf{X}) = Softplus(\mathbf{XW}_f) \odot \sigma(\mathbf{XW}_g)$$

We also force the orthogonality of W_f in these units in the same way as in the previous subsection. We refer this regularized units as O(rthogonal)GLU.

To mitigate the parametrization growth we apply transforms head-wise, and suggest that gating does not require that amount of information as the input transform. Thus, we can approximate the W_g with, say, two low-rank matrices of sizes $n \times r$ resp. $r \times n$ where $r < \frac{n}{2}$ is the W_g approximation rank. We refer this unit as A(pproximated)OGLU.

Gating. Compared to the orthogonal single-layer FFN, a single-layer OGLU model converges even faster and shows significantly less score variance between runs. These units can also be sequentially stacked with a benefit, up to some extent. On the other hand, the doubled parametrization will not allow stacking more than two units without going beyond the 10% of additional parameters.

By approximating the gating weight matrix, we are able to stack more units – but according to the Table 1, this brings no advantage with the higher computational costs. We used the matrices of rank $r = n/4$ to approximate the gate, reducing the layer parametrization by 25%.

Experiments. Following the recommendations from [16], we replicate the learning schedule and all the hyperparameters that relate to our model, while keeping additional parametrization below 10% Due to the limitation in computational power, we restrict ourselves only to the three LRA tasks—BPE text classification, BPE text matching and ListOps, with input lengths $4K/4K/2K$ respectively. To provide comparable and reproducible and results, we used the gradient accumulation in order to simulate larger batch sizes. Each model was trained five times to observe model behavior and to avoid so-called *black swans*—random seeds that give radically different results [13]. Mean and best results are reported in Table 1.

Table 1. Results of our models on the chosen LRA tasks, mean results for five runs. We denote by † models that show significant variance in results.

Model	Complexity	Classif.	Matching	ListOps
Transformer	$\mathcal{O}(L^2)$	64.27	57.46	36.37
Linear kernel†	$\mathcal{O}(CL)$	65.77	73.51	18.54
1× GLU	$\mathcal{O}(CL)$	65.82	72.17	18.67
2× GLU	$\mathcal{O}(CL)$	65.99	73.36	18.42
3× GLU	$\mathcal{O}(CL)$	65.87	72.60	18.68
Orth. linear kernel	$\mathcal{O}(CL)$	65.86	72.63	18.19
1× OGLU	$\mathcal{O}(CL)$	65.95	72.50	18.45
2× OGLU	$\mathcal{O}(CL)$	66.02	72.96	18.32
3× AOGLU	$\mathcal{O}(CL)$	66.06	72.57	18.45

Acknowledgement. This research is supported by the Czech Ministry of Education, Youth and Sports from the Czech Operational Programme Research, Development, and Education, under grant agreement No. CZ.02.1.01/0.0/0.0/15003/0000421.

References

1. Bello, I., Zoph, B., Vaswani, A., Shlens, J., Le, Q.V.: Attention augmented convolutional networks (2020)
2. Beltagy, I., Peters, M.E., Cohan, A.: Longformer: the long-document transformer (2020)
3. Child, R., Gray, S., Radford, A., Sutskever, I.: Generating long sequences with sparse transformers (2019)
4. Choromanski, K., et al.: Rethinking attention with performers (2021)
5. Chowdhury, S.P., Solomou, A., Dubey, A., Sachan, M.: On learning the transformer kernel (2021)
6. Cybenko, G.: Approximation by superpositions of a sigmoidal function. Math. Control Signals Syst. **2**(4), 303–314 (1989)
7. Dai, Z., Yang, Z., Yang, Y., Carbonell, J.G., Le, Q.V., Salakhutdinov, R.: Transformer-xl: Attentive language models beyond a fixed-length context. arXiv preprint arXiv:1901.02860 (2019)
8. Gulati, A., et al.: Conformer: convolution-augmented transformer for speech recognition (2020)
9. Hornik, K.: Approximation capabilities of multilayer feedforward networks. Neural Netw. **4**(2), 251–257 (1991)
10. Jia, K., Li, S., Wen, Y., Liu, T., Tao, D.: Orthogonal deep neural networks (2019)
11. Katharopoulos, A., Vyas, A., Pappas, N., Fleuret, F.: Transformers are RNNs: fast autoregressive transformers with linear attention (2020)
12. Kitaev, N., Kaiser, Ł., Levskaya, A.: Reformer: the efficient transformer (2020)
13. Picard, D.: Torch.manual_seed(3407) is all you need: on the influence of random seeds in deep learning architectures for computer vision (2021)
14. Rae, J.W., Potapenko, A., Jayakumar, S.M., Lillicrap, T.P.: Compressive transformers for long-range sequence modelling (2019)
15. Roy, A., Saffar, M., Vaswani, A., Grangier, D.: Efficient content-based sparse attention with routing transformers (2020)
16. Tay, Y., et al.: Long range arena: a benchmark for efficient transformers (2020)
17. Tay, Y., Dehghani, M., Bahri, D., Metzler, D.: Efficient transformers: a survey (2020)
18. Vaswani, A., et al.: Attention is all you need (2017)
19. Wang, S., Li, B.Z., Khabsa, M., Fang, H., Ma, H.: Linformer: self-attention with linear complexity. arXiv preprint arXiv:2006.04768 (2020)
20. Xiong, Y., et al.: Nyströmformer: a nyström-based algorithm for approximating self-attention. arXiv preprint arXiv:2102.03902 (2021)
21. Zhang, H., et al.: Poolingformer: long document modeling with pooling attention. arXiv preprint arXiv:2105.04371 (2021)

Author Index

Printed in the United States
by Baker & Taylor Publisher Services

Printed in the United States
by Baker & Taylor Publisher Services